The New Illustrated EVERYMAN'S ENCYCLOPAEDIA

Consultant Editor: John Paxton
Editor of *Everyman's Dictionary of Abbreviations* and *The Statesman's Year-Book*

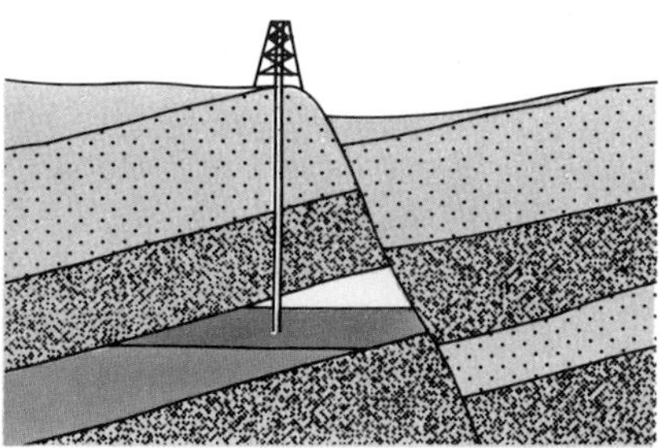

VOLUME FIVE

Acknowledgements

The publishers would like to thank the following individuals and organisations for their kind permission to reproduce the photographs in this book.

The J. Allan Cash Photolibrary 1153, 1279; **Bettmann Archive/ BBC Hulton Picture Library** 1171, 1178, 1317, 1375, 1389, 1426, (Evening Standard Collection) 1433; **The Bridgeman Art Library** (Roy Miles Gallery, London) 1213, (Narodni Gallery, Prague) 1418, (Private Collection) 1339, (Victoria & Albert Museum) 1218, 1243; **Cleveland Museum of Art, Ohio** 1379; **Bruce Coleman Ltd.** 1164, 1175, 1409, (G. Ahrens) 1405, (M. Berge) 1285, (R. Burton) 1354, (E. Crichton) 1179, 1381, (A.J. Deane) 1209, (N. Devore) 1284, 1403 below, (J. Ehlers) 1399, (J. Foott) 1201, (K. Gunnar) 1336, (C. Henneghien) 1403 above, (N.R. Lightfoot) 1187, (L.C. Marigo) 1373, (N.O. Tomalin) 1200, (WWF/H. Ungius) 1185 below; **Colorsport** 1185 above; **Douglas Dickins** 1323, 1326; **E.T. Archive** (Dagli Orti/ Louvre, Paris) 1255, (Dagli Orti/National Palace of Mexico) 1363, (Tate Gallery) 1287, (Usher Gallery, Lincoln) 1265; **Mary Evans Picture Library** 1223; **Sonia Halliday Photographs** 1229, 1410, (F.H.C. Birch) 1246 above, 1261; **Robert Harding Picture Library** 1242, 1266, 1315, 1316, 1366, 1368, (A. Faulkner/ Taylor) 1424, (Gascoigne) 1357, (B. Hawkes) 1342, (Magdalene College, Cambridge) 1238 above, (W. Rawlings) 1313, 1380, 1383, (Staatsbibliothek, Berlin) 1420, (T. Wood) 1198; **David Hardy** 1422; **Michael Holford** 1253, 1305, 1349, 1372, (American Museum, Bath) 1404, (Collection Countess Bobrinskoy) 1246 below, (British Museum) 1335, (E. Hurwicz) 1204, (National Gallery, London) 1337, (Collection Sir Roland Penrose) 1260; **Alan Hutchison Library** 1211, (B. Gerard) 1321, (R.N. Giudicelli) 1207; **The Kobal Collection** 1280; **Chris Linton** 1370; **Mansell Collection** 1154, 1157, 1226, 1277; **Courtesy of National Film Archive/Stills Library** 1365 below; **National Gallery, London** 1244, 1262, 1294, 1348; **National Portrait Gallery, London** 1216, 1268, 1334, 1358, 1359, 1386, 1401, 1427; **Picturepoint** 1234, 1295, 1325, (Carnavalet Museum, Paris) 1365 above, (Chicago Art Institute) 1350, (Metropolitan Museum of Art) 1392; **Max Planck Institute/Spacecharts** 1331; **Ronald Sheridan's Photo Library** 1196, 1338; **The Sutcliffe Gallery** 1257; **Tate Gallery** 1188, 1267, 1377, 1428; **Topham Picture Library** 1159, 1230, 1232, 1397, 1413, (C. Lim) 1221; **ZEFA** (R. Bond) 1245, (Boutin) 1215, (Colin Caket) 1193, (R. Everts) 1318, (R. Kayaert) 1194, (Orion Press) 1195, (Photri) 1238 below, (G. Ricatto) 1290, 1436, (K. Scholz) 1362, 1387, (H. Schumacher) 1416, (Starfoto) 1254.

ILLUSTRATIONS BY
Clyde Surveys Ltd
Hayward & Martin
Ian Stephen
Linden Artists
Oxford Illustrators Ltd
Wayne Ford

This edition published 1984 by
Octopus Books Limited
59 Grosvenor Street, London W.1.

under licence from
J.M. Dent & Sons Limited
Aldine House, 33 Welbeck Street, London W.1.

ISBN 0 86273 156 9

Printed and bound by
Graficromo S.A.,
Cordoba, Spain.

The New Illustrated EVERYMAN'S ENCYCLOPAEDIA

VOLUME FIVE

Nicholas of Cusa (1401–64), German cardinal and theologian. He became doctor of canon law at Cologne University and received his holy orders in 1430. He became archdeacon of Liège and attended the Council of Basel (1432). He was a skilled diplomat. He was also ahead of his contemporaries in positing the rotation of the Earth about the Sun and in advocating reform of the Julian Calendar. He wrote several works on civil and ecclesiastical polity; more important, however, are his numerous philosophico-theological writings, most of which are concerned with the problem of man's knowledge of God. Of these the most fundamental is *De Docta Ignorantia*, 1440.

Nicholson, Ben (1894–1982), British painter, son of Sir William Nicholson. Not formally trained, he began as a realistic still-life painter but in the early 1930s began making abstract paintings and compositions carved in low relief using geometrical forms with studied refinements. He worked for a period at St Ives in Cornwall, with his second wife, the abstract sculptress Barbara Hepworth, and from 1958 he worked in Switzerland.

Nicholson, Jack (1937–), US film actor, whose first success was as the drunken Southern lawyer in *Easy Rider*, 1969. Known as a versatile star with a preference for unusual or difficult subjects, his subsequent films have included *Chinatown*, 1974; *The Passenger*, 1974; *One Flew Over the Cuckoo's Nest*, 1976; and *The Shining*, 1980.

Nicholson, Sir William Newzam Prior (1872–1949), British painter and designer. He collaborated with James Pryde in producing the 'Beggarstaff' posters, which owed their inspiration to Whistler and Toulouse-Lautrec and were noted for their effective simplicity. Nicholson next produced woodcuts in colour, which were published in collections under the titles *London Types*, *Characters of Romance*, *Twelve Portraits*, etc. His first appearance as a painter in oils was in exhibitions of the International Society. The Tate Gallery, London, has two of his best portraits: *W. E. Henley* and *Miss Jekyll*. He also designed costumes and settings for the stage.

Nickel, metallic chemical element, symbol Ni, atomic number 28, atomic weight 58·71. It was first isolated by Cronstadt in 1751 from nickel arsenide. The two most important sources are the ores garnierite, from New Caledonia in the South Pacific, and pentlandite, from Sudbury, Ontario. With the exception of meteoric nickel, the metal is nearly always found in association with cobalt. The method of extraction depends on the ore; the Sudbury ore is associated with copper, the New Caledonian ore with iron. After these metals have been removed, the crude nickel can be refined either by electrolysis or the Mond process (by reduction with water gas and carbon monoxide).

Pure nickel is a silvery-white metal; its corrosion resistance makes it useful for laboratory tools. So-called 'nickel-silver' contains no silver at all and is technically a brass; the alloy is used for a wide range of utensils and cutlery, and is frequently used in electro-plating (EPNS). Two important alloys of the metal with iron are permalloy and mu-metal; these make use of nickel's noticeable magnetic qualities, and are used in certain types of magnets. A third alloy with iron, invar, contains 36 per cent nickel; it has virtually no thermal coefficient of expansion, making it useful for such things as the pendulums of clocks, and scientific instruments.

Nickel, when used with chromium, is an important additive in steel, producing a range of properties such as hardness, durability, resistance to fatigue, and high temperature operation. Stainless steel contains 18 per cent nickel and 8 per cent chromium.

Nickel Silver, see GERMAN SILVER.

Nicklaus, Jack (1940–), US golf champion, acknowledged as the world's greatest golfer. He surpassed Bobby Jones's record of 13 major championships when he won the USPGA title for the third time (1973). He turned professional after winning two US Amateur championships, and in 1962 became the youngest winner of the US Open. He was the first golf player to exceed two million dollars in official earnings. By 1980 he had won 19 major championships.

Nicobar Islands, see ANDAMAN AND NICOBAR ISLANDS.

Nicodemus, Pharisee and member of the Sanhedrin. Jesus early won his secret allegiance and gave him the memorable discourse on the new birth. Nicodemus sought Jesus by night to avoid critical eyes, yet in the Sanhedrin, when his colleagues proposed to condemn Jesus unheard, he had the courage to risk suspicion by contending for a fair and legal procedure. He joined Joseph of Arimathaea in providing honourable burial for Jesus.

Nicol Prism, of calcium carbonate or Iceland spar; superseded by polaroid.
See also POLARISATION OF LIGHT.

Nicolai, Otto (1810–49), German composer. He lived in Italy, 1838–41; he then became conductor of the Court Opera at Vienna, and founded the Philharmonic concerts. In 1848 he was appointed conductor of the cathedral choir and the opera in Berlin, where his comic opera *The Merry Wives of Windsor* was produced.

Nicolle, Charles Jules Henri (1866–1936), French bacteriologist. He was director of the Pasteur Institute at Tunis, and studied North African infectious diseases, discovering the transmission of typhus by lice and of leishmaniasis by the dog flea. In 1928 he received the Nobel Prize for medicine.

Nicolson, Sir Harold George (1886–1968), British diplomat, historian and biographer. He married in 1913 Victoria Sackville-West. In 1929 he retired from the diplomatic service to devote himself to writing and politics. He was one of the early members of Sir Oswald Mosley's new party in 1931, but left when its fascist tendencies became more overt. At the general election of 1935 he was returned as National Labour member for West Leicester, a seat he held until 1945. He was always a powerful critic of the policy of appeasement towards Germany. He joined the Labour party in 1947.

Nicolson published a large number of historical works, biographies and novels as well as contributing regularly to the *Spectator* and *The Observer*. He was also a well-known broadcaster.

Nicopolis (Greek, city of victory), ancient city of Epirus, Greece. It was situated on the Gulf of Arta, and was founded by Octavian to commemorate his victory at Actium in 31 BC. Many Roman antiquities are to be seen on the site.

Nicosia (Greek *Levkosia*), capital of Cyprus, on the plain of Mesaoria, on the right bank of the River Pedias, 60 km from Famagusta. Between 1192 and 1489 Cyprus was ruled by the French Lusignans, and during this period the fine Gothic cathedral was built. The present walls, exactly circular in plan, were laid out by the Venetians for artillery defence in 1567. In 1570 a siege of Nicosia by the Turks began, and after two months the Venetians had been driven out. The 300 years of Turkish occupation were, in general, uneventful, although the town was constrained within its walls for defence purposes. In 1878 British Vice-Admiral Lord Hay took over Cyprus and raised the British flag over Nicosia.

In recent years Nicosia has spread beyond its city walls, and has developed industries. Factories have been built with government funds, and there is a free zone/industrial estate, close to Nicosia International Airport. Population (1978) 121,500.

Nicotiana, a genus of 66 plants in the Solanaceae, a number of which are grown in gardens. *N. alba*, the sweet-scented tobacco plant, bears panicles of white funnel- and star-shaped flowers. *N. tabacum* is the tobacco plant of commerce although *N. rustica* (the original tobacco plant) and others are also used.

Nicotine, a liquid alkaloid obtained from the dried leaves of the tobacco plant (*Nicotiana tabacum*), first synthesised in 1904. Nicotine is exceedingly poisonous, a few drops in the stomach being sufficient to cause death due to respiratory paralysis. It is readily absorbed through the skin and nicotine poisoning is generally due to careless handling when used as an insecticide.

Pharmacologically, nicotine first stimulates, and then paralyses all ganglia of the autonomic nervous system and has a similar effect on skeletal muscle. It is the main pharmacologically active compound in tobacco, and smoking one cigarette causes nicotine to be absorbed into the bloodstream. Dependence on nicotine develops and is characterised by a strong desire to continue to take the drug and to increase the dose; physical dependence may also be present. Manufacturers are attempting to reduce the nicotine, as well as the tar, content of cigarettes, while still retaining the psychic dependence that cigarettes cause.
See also SMOKING.

Nicotinic Acid (nicotinamide), an oxidation product of nicotine. It is one of the vitamins of the B_2 complex. It occurs in liver, yeast, wheat and rice, and is said to be so stable that it has been detected in barley taken from the tomb of Tutankh-Amen (1350 BC). Shortage of nicotinic acid in the diet is responsible for the skin disease pellagra, which is common in peoples living chiefly on maize.

Niebuhr, Barthold Georg (1776–1831), German statesman and historian. In 1816 he went to Rome as Prussian ambassador, and during his residence there discovered and published fragments of Cicero and Livy. He resigned the embassy in 1823 and settled at Bonn. Here he rewrote and published the first two volumes of his *Roman History* (first published 1811–12).

Nielsen, Carl (1865–1931), Danish composer. He studied at the Copenhagen Conservatoire under Gade. He was conductor of the royal orchestra in 1908–14 and became conductor of the Musical Society and director of the Conservatoire. With an independent style and a strong sense of counterpoint and melody, Nielsen is one of the 20th century's great symphonists. Works include two operas; incidental music for Oehlenschläger's *Aladdin*; six symphonies; *Saga-Dream* for orchestra; concertos for violin, flute and clarinet; chamber and piano music; *Commotio* for organ; the cantata *Springtime on Fyn*; and songs.

Niemeyer, Oscar (1907–82), Brazilian architect. He has designed numerous buildings in Rio, also most of the public buildings for the new capital, Brasilia, since 1958 in an expressive style in the Baroque tradition.

Niemöller, Martin (1892–), German pastor of the Protestant Evangelical Church and anti-Nazi theologian. He served in the First World War as a U-boat commander. Ordained in 1924, Niemöller became pastor of the wealthy Berlin-Dahlem parish (1931–37). A strong supporter of nationalism, he welcomed National Socialism and joined the Nazi party; but in 1933 he led a campaign against totalitarian control of the Lutheran Church and became an opponent of the Nazi regime. He founded the Pastor's Emergency League (Pfarrenotbund) to defend the Lutheran faith. At first the League had 7000 members, but Nazi persecution resulted in only 1000 parsons left to reject the oath of allegiance to Hitler in 1938. Arrested in March 1938, he was put into Sachsenhausen concentration camp, but refused to recant or accept release on condition that he would not preach. Later he was sent to Dachau. In 1947 he was elected first bishop of the reformed Evangelical Church of Hesse-Nassau. A determined pacifist from the Second World War, Niemöller was elected one of six presidents to the World Council of Churches, 1961.

Niepce, Joseph Nicéphore (1765–1833). French physicist and an inventor of photography. He joined Daguerre in 1829. Their collaboration led to the introduction, after Niepce's death, of the daguerreotype process.

See also PHOTOGRAPHY.

Nietzsche, Friedrich Wilhelm (1844–1900), German philosopher and poet. Nietzsche became professor of philology at Basel University (1869). In 1879 ill-health forced him to retire and he led a wandering life in Italy, Switzerland and Germany until 1889, when he went insane. Previously little read, he was world-famous by the time of his death, though for many years the suppressions, distortions and forgeries of his sister, Elizabeth Förster-Nietzsche, confused the history of his life and exaggerated those elements in his philosophy that might be labelled 'proto-Nazi'.

The early influences on Nietzsche were the philosophy of Schopenhauer and Wagner's music. Wagner was a close friend from 1869 until their estrangement c.1874, and it was partly to defend his music that Nietzsche wrote *Die Geburt der Tragödie*, 1872 (The Birth of Tragedy), with its celebrated distinction between the 'Apollonian' and 'Dionysian' spirits. There followed a series of books which constitute a critique of 19th-century thought, and point out the radical consequences for morality of the fact that 'God is dead'. The famous *Also Sprach Zarathustra*, 1883–85 (Thus Spoke Zarathustra) is a poetic-allegorical exposition of Nietzsche's theories of the Will to Power, Eternal Recurrence and the Superman. *Jenseits von Gut und Böse* 1886 (Beyond Good and Evil), *Götzen-Dammerung*, 1889 (Twilight of the Idols) and other works extended the Nietzschean critique. The thought of Nietzsche exercised an immense influence on writers and thinkers throughout Europe.

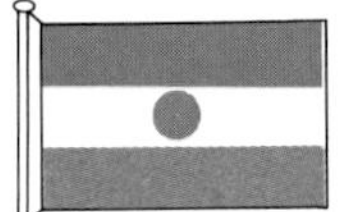

Niger
Area: 1,186,500 km²
Population: 5,300,000
Capital: Niamey

Niger, landlocked republic in West Africa, between Nigeria to the south and Algeria and Libya to the north. Area 1,186,500 km^2.

The land lies mainly between 300 and 500 m, but rises above 1400 m in the Aïr mountains in the centre of the country, and falls below 200 m in the Niger river valley in the extreme south-west. The dominant element in the environment is climate, for most of Niger lies within the Sahara. The people are chiefly Hausa; the other major group are the Songhay, indigenous to Mali. There are minorities of Tuareg and Fulani. The population totalled 5,300,000 in 1979, and the main towns are Niamey (the capital) and Zinder.

Niger's economy is predominantly agricultural. The Sahel drought has severely affected food supplies. Livestock is the main source of wealth but its quality is poor. Major crops include millet, groundnuts, cassava, and sorghum.

The discovery of uranium in Niger, and its exploitation by France, provided a great opportunity for the economic development of the country; since 1974 the government has taken a firmer hold over its production. Cassiterite and gold are also mined and oil exploration is under way. Uranium is the most important export.

In 1974 the constitution was suspended following a military coup. Executive power now rests with the 12-member Supreme Military Council, composed entirely of army officers, with Lieutenant-Colonel Seyni Kountché as head of state.

The official language is French.

History. As the population of the area consists of a mix of nomadic and sedentary peoples, no great kingdoms or states were established, in the past. Even so the Muslim leaders in Niger did manage to effect fierce resistance to the French military conquest, which was completed around 1906. In the 1950s political opposition in Niger against French rule was organised by the Swaba party but in the 1958 referendum it failed to mobilise support from the electorate and was officially banned in 1959. Niger gained independence in 1960 under President Diori. In 1974 the army carried out a coup and set up the Supreme Military Council, headed by Lieut.-Col. Kountché.

Niger, largest river system in West Africa with a total catchment area of 1·5 million km^2; the Niger river itself having a total length of 4200 km. The headwaters of the Niger rise in the Guinea Highlands, along the northern borders of Sierra Leone and Liberia, and flow some 1500 km north-east through the Republic of Guinea into the Republic of Mali, where at the town of Bourem it swings south-east for 1400 km, to its confluence with the Benue at Lokoja in Nigeria. The combined river then flows 450 km due south to reach the sea via numerous distributaries of the vast Niger Delta that covers 36,000 km^2.

The upper Niger once formed a large inland lake in the area of southern Mali, and has, in geological terms, only recently become joined with the lower Niger. The inland basin still remains as an area through which the river meanders via many channels and lakes between Ke-Macina and Tombouctou.

The upper basin is well watered, but the rainfall declines from 2000 mm in the headwaters to 1040 mm near Bamako and to less than 250 mm at Tombouctou on the edge of the Sahara Desert; the great floods of the river thus supply a lifeline to the peoples of south-east Mali, and the river flows southwards again into the humid tropics below Lokoja. The river is not navigable throughout, and the rapids near Bussa have been harnessed by the building of the Niger Dam at Kainji, impounding a large lake, thus supplying large amounts of cheap hydroelectric power, sufficient for nearly half Nigeria's current requirements.

The Niger Delta represents a vast accumulation of riverine sediment over 10,000 m deep. Within these sediments petroleum has formed and been trapped, and the area has recently become one of the world's major oil-fields.

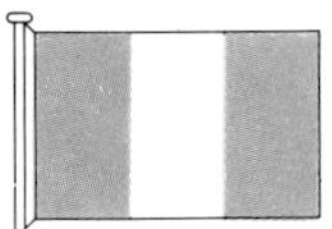

Nigeria
Area: 923,773 km²
Population: 81,000,000
Capital: Lagos

Nigeria, federal republic of West Africa, bounded on the north by Niger, on the north-east by Chad, on the east and south-east by Cameroon, on the west by Benin (formerly Dahomey), and on the south by the Bight of Benin. The federation comprises at present 19 states. Area 923,773 km^2.

Vast plains and low plateaus along the southern coastal zone lead into the delta of the River Niger, tropical Africa's greatest oil producing area. North from the delta between the Benue and Niger rivers is a domed area, culminating in the Jos (or Bauchi) plateau (1200–1300 m). North-eastwards granitic rocks dip gently below the sands and clays of the Chad basin, and in the north-west a series of low escarpments mark a similar transition towards Sokoto and the interior basin of the Niger. The eastern border of Nigeria contains broken and rugged country, along the Cameroon border.

Nigeria contains a great diversity of peoples and cultures. The larger groups are the Hausa and Fulani in the north, the Ibo in the east, and the Yoruba in the south-west. Lagos, the capital, is the only conurbation in the country, but other major cities are Ibadan, Ilorin, Kano, Ogbomosho, and Port Harcourt. The total population was estimated at 81 million in 1978.

The staple crops in the south include yams, coco-yams, cassava, plantains, maize, and oil-palms, and those of the drier north are millet, sorghum, and upland rice. The tsetse fly hinders cattle rearing in the south, but large numbers are kept by the Fulani in the north and some are driven south to provide meat there. The chief cash crops are cocoa, grown on most farms in Western State, and groundnuts grown in many parts of the north, but especially around Kano. Others are rubber, particularly in Mid-West State, and cotton, particularly in North-Central state. Mining of coal around Enugu and tin around Jos was established early in this century, but these are now entirely overshadowed by the oil industry. Some industries are heavily concentrated in Lagos, but others such as textile and cement manufacture are quite widely distributed, and craft industries are important in many towns. The currency unit is the *naira*.

Under the 1978 constitution Nigeria is a sovereign federal republic. The head of state is the President, directly elected, in whom all executive power is vested. The National Assembly consists of a Senate and a House of Representatives. Although English is the official language, Hausa in the north, Yoruba in the west, and Ibo in the south-east, are all important and current languages.

History. The early inhabitants, trade, culture, and the Muslim religion found their way from Egypt and the Arab countries into northern Nigeria. The Hausa states in the west and the Yoruba kingdoms in the south were also of ancient origin. Benin, an offshoot of the Yoruba kingdom, was visited by the Portuguese in 1486 and by the English in 1553, who found there a prosperous, well-organised society. The 17th and 18th centuries were periods of decline brought about by wars, political dissensions, famines, and the slave trade. British interest in the area increased and exploration began as a preliminary to the development of commerce. In 1861 the British purchased Lagos from a chief. In 1885 a British claim to a protectorate over Nigeria was recognised by the Berlin Conference and the southern part of the country, apart from the Lagos territories, was named the 'Oil Rivers Protectorate'. The northern part of the country was brought under government control in 1900. In 1914 the North and South were united to form the colony and Protectorate of Nigeria. A federal structure was first introduced in 1946 and full independence was granted to the federation in 1960. Nigeria became a republic in 1963.

In 1966 Nigeria, which had been considered to be the most politically stable of the new African nations, was the subject of a coup, and a military government, under Ironsi, was set up. In 1966 a further coup, again led by sections of the army, overthrew the Ironsi regime and brought to power Gen. Gowon. While discussions on a future federal government were taking place in Lagos, rioting broke out in Northern Nigeria, the principal victims being Ibo civilians. The military governor of the Eastern Region recalled all Ibo people to their homeland, and the Ibo people decided to secede from Nigeria and establish the independent state of Biafra. This led to full-scale civil war that lasted until 1970 when Biafra surrendered. Although the government was anxious that there should be no recrimination after the war, ethnic loyalties have consistently inhibited national development plans. In 1975 Gowon was overthrown and Brig. Murtala Ramat Mohammed became head of state, only to be killed in a coup in 1976. In 1977–78 a new constitution was drafted and Nigeria returned to civilian rule in 1979, led by President Shehu Shagari. Widespread corruption and the imminent collapse of Nigeria's economy, however, resulted in another military coup in December 1983. Shagari was overthrown, the 1978 constitution suspended and a military council set up, led by Major-General Mohammed Buhari.

Nigeria. *An annual fishing festival, held on the River Sokoto at Argungu.*

Night Heron. *The species* Nycticorax nycticorax.

Night Heron, *Nycticorax*, genus of birds of the family Ardeidae, order Ciconiiformes, of very wide distribution. They are most active at night. The black-crowned night heron, *N. nycticorax*, breeds in southern Europe and North America. The bird is 60 cm long. The top of its head and its back are black, its wings are black and grey and its breast is pale grey or white.

Nighthawk, American name for several members of the nightjar family Caprimulgidae, order Caprimulgiformes. Nighthawk most commonly refers to the *Chordeiles* species of North America, including *C. minor* which breeds widely as far north as southern Alaska, and migrates south to Argentina.

Nightingale, Florence (1820–1910), British reformer of hospital nursing. Her self-sacrificing services to the wounded during the Crimean War made her name famous throughout Europe. She wrote several pamphlets on nursing and hospitals, and a fund was raised in 1857 for training nurses, now carried out at St Thomas's and King's College Hospitals in London.

Nightingale, *Luscinia megarhynchos*, a member of the family Muscicapidae, containing well over a thousand species including the thrushes and warblers. The male bird arrives in Europe from central Africa in the middle of April, a few days before the female, going almost invariably to the woods and copses which have always been the haunts of its species. The nightingale's song is unique in its variety and sustained melody. It can be heard by day as well as by night. The nest is often made on the ground, of dry grass and leaves, and four to six olive-green eggs are laid. The male's song continues until the young are hatched. The female is slightly smaller than the male, but exhibits no definite distinction of plumage. The upperparts are chestnut-brown; the long rounded tail is reddish-brown, and the breast is dull greyish-white, tinting to brown. The diet consists mainly of insects and small worms. The winter migration begins as early as July, and is completed before the end of August. *L. luscinia*, the thrush nightingale of eastern Europe, is a louder but not such a sweet songster. Both species also sing in their winter ranges in Africa.

Nightjar, *Caprimulgus europaeus*, of the family Caprimulgidae, order Caprimulgiformes, is a bird with a breeding range extending over most of western Eurasia. It is 26 cm long and characterised by brown plumage, intricately speckled and barred in buff and grey, giving perfect daytime concealment. It is nocturnal but may be seen at dusk flying silently after insects which it catches on the wing. Dusk is also the best time to hear its song, a sustained, churring trill which alternates occasionally between two pitches. If the female appears, the song may be followed by a wing-clapping display flight.

Nightshade, common name for several plants, all belonging to the Solanaceae except enchanter's nightshade which is an unrelated plant belonging to the Onagraceae. All the solanaceous nightshades are reputed to be poisonous; by far the most dangerous is the deadly nightshade or dwale (*Atropa belladonna*), a herbaceous plant about 1 m tall, with oval leaves, bell-shaped purplish flowers and glossy black berries, like small cherries. All parts of the plant are very poisonous to humans, containing the alkaloids atropine and hyoscyamine. Woody nightshade or bittersweet, *Solanum dulcamara*, is a climbing plant with a slightly woody stem, common on waste ground and in marshy habitats. Black nightshade (*S. nigrum*) is a herbaceous plant with white flowers and globular black berries.

Nihilism (Latin *nihil*, nothing), as a philosophic term dates from the 12th century, and may be said to signify the sceptical attitude of mind which denies everything, even existence. In more modern times, however, nihilism came to stand for an amorphous body of social and political discontent which manifested itself among the Russian educated classes. Its currency in Russian intellectual circles owed much to Turgenev's famous novel, *Fathers and Sons*, where the chief protagonist of the creed recognises no authority, doubts every general principle and value, and accepts only scientifically demonstrable facts and utilitarian criteria.

Nihon, see JAPAN.

Niigata, seaport city of Nigata-ken, Japan, 255 km north-west of Tokyo, an important centre of rice production and general commerce, and leading port on the Sea of Japan coast. It has oil refining, petrochemical and machine-tool industries. Population (1979) 439,000.

Nijinska, Bronislava (1891–1972), Russian choreographer. Sister of Vaslav Nijinsky, Bronia was one of the greatest choreographers of this century. First encouraged by Diaghilev, she later worked for many companies in Europe and America. During his time as director of the Royal Ballet, Frederick Ashton invited her to restage the witty *Les Biches* (1924) and her enduring masterpiece *Les Noces* (1923).

***Nijinsky** as the Golden Slave in Rimsky-Korsakov's* Schéhérazade. *The costume was designed by Bakst.*

Nijinsky, Vaslav (1890–1950), Russian ballet dancer and choreographer. At the age of ten he entered the Imperial School of Ballet as a student under Nicolai Legat. His extraordinary talent soon became evident, and in 1908 he graduated as a member of the Imperial Ballet, making his début in the ballet of Mozart's *Don Giovanni*. In 1910 he resigned because, it is believed, the propriety of his costume in *Giselle* was questioned. However, he had already won a European reputation, particularly with his creation of the parts of the Egyptian slave in Bakst's *Schéhérazade* and Harlequin in Fokine's *Carnaval*, during the seasons of Russian ballet organised in Paris by Diaghilev in 1909 and 1910. In 1911 he left Russia with the company which Diaghilev formed with headquarters in Monte Carlo. Nijinsky added to his triumphs—particularly in Fokine's ballets, *Le Spectre de la Rose* and *Petrouchka*. In 1913 he succeeded Fokine as *maître de ballet*, and in *L'Après-midi d'un Faune*, *Jeux* and *Le Sacre du printemps* he created a new non-classical style of dancing, violently controversial at the time. In August 1913 he went to South America with the Ballets-Russes and married Romola de Pulszky, a member of the company. The marriage caused a break with Diaghilev. Nijinsky endeavoured to maintain a London season with his own company, but was unsuited to the administrative work involved and his health broke down. On the outbreak of the First World War he and his family were interned in Hungary, but in 1915 he was allowed to go to the USA, where he again joined the Ballets-Russes. His new ballet, *Till Eulenspiegel*, produced in New York in 1916, was ineffectual. There followed a short season in Spain at the invitation of Diaghilev. A South American tour by Nijinsky in 1917 proved a failure and he retired to St Moritz. His mental instability, noticeable even in the earlier years when he was devoted to his art almost to the exclusion of normal adult responsibility, now became more evident, and from 1918 he was able to take no further active part in ballet. He was the greatest of male dancers, the rôle of whom he revolutionised. His technique, interpretation and characterisation amounted to genius, and were combined with wonderful lightness of movement.

See also BALLET.

Nijmegen, town in Gelderland province, Netherlands, on the River Waal. It was formerly a residence of the Carolingian emperors, and the beautiful park, the Valkhof, occupies the site of the old palace. The town manufactures beer, prussian blue, leather, pottery, cigars, and gold and silver work. Population (1980) 147,614.

Nikisch, Arthur (1855–1922), Hungarian conductor, initially a violinist in the Vienna court orchestra (1874–77). He conducted the Leipzig Opera (1879–87), the Boston Symphony Orchestra (1889–93), the Leipzig Gewandhaus Orchestra (1895–1922), and also the Berlin Philharmonic, from 1897. He was noted for his performances of Wagner.

Nikolayev, capital city, economic and cultural centre of Nikolayev *oblast*, Ukraine USSR, on the Southern Bug estuary north-east of Odessa. It is an industrial centre with large shipyards, agricultural engineering, food and light industries, and one of the chief Black Sea ports. It was founded in 1784, with a shipyard built in 1788; it has been a commercial port since 1862, and has had large-scale industry since 1895. Population (1980) 449,000.

Nikon (1605–81), Patriarch of Moscow, 1652–58, a Mordvin by origin. He introduced several reforms (e.g. unification of the ritual) which were rejected by part of the clergy and of the laity (the Old Ritualists or Old Believers), thus causing the schism in the Russian Church. Nikon's attempt to put the authority of the Church above that of the State led to conflict with the tsar Alexis Mikhailovich. Defeated in this struggle, Nikon was condemned by the Church council, 1666–67, and confined to a monastery.

Nikopol, town in the Dnepropetrovsk *oblast* of the Ukrainian SSR, USSR, on the Dnieper 90 km south-east of Krivoi Rog. It is a centre of metallurgy and engineering, the focus of a rich manganese mining area, and a river port. It was founded in the 18th century, becoming a town in 1782. Population (1977) 146,000.

Nile (Semitic *nihal*, river), longest and most important river of Africa; its source is in the vast lake of Victoria Nyanza, which stands at an altitude of 1190 m above sea-level. The Nile leaves the Victoria Nyanza at its northern extremity, and flows in a north-westerly direction, passing through the Ibrahim and Kioga lakes. It leaves the central African highlands at Fauvera and turns westward, being now known as the Somerset Nile. Between Fauvera and the Albert Nyanza the river falls at least 300 m, with many cataracts, such as the Murchison Falls (36 m). After leaving this lake, and receiving as a tributary the Semlike Nile from Albert Nyanza, the river begins its northerly course and flows through the plains of the eastern Sudan. It is now navigable and has a sinuous course. The main river is split up into several channels. From Fashoda to Khartoum the river is known as the White Nile (Bahr-al-Abiad), and the name 'Nile' is simply given to it only after the junction with the Blue Nile (Bahr-al-Azrek), which joins it at Khartoum. Between 16° and 24°N latitude there are six groups of cataracts, the largest being at Wadi Haifa. The lower basin is very small in area, varying in width from 2 km in Nubia to 20 km in Upper Egypt, that is to say, the region over which the annual inundations of the river extend. It is the extent of the inundation which determines the prosperity of the country during the ensuing season. North of Cairo the delta of the Nile, which has a width of 200 km and an area of 22,000 km^2, commences, with many canals, lakes, etc. The most important branches are the Damietta and the Rosetta, each 235 km long.

Irrigation was begun by Mohammed Ali; in 1842 he called in Mougel Bey, a Frenchman, who built the Cairo barrage, Water was conducted to the land by irrigation canals, but the control of the water robbed the land of silt, and its productivity decreased. Bey's barrage was used until 1883, when British engineers rebuilt it, increasing the depth of water so that it travelled down the irrigation canals with increased velocity and carried the silt with it. The Aswan (Assaun) dam, begun in 1895 and finished in 1902, was heightened in 1912.

The Nile has the longest basin of any river although the area of that basin (2,867,704 km^2), is surpassed by those of the Amazon and Mississippi; the length from the outlet at the Victoria Nyanza is 5589 km.

Nile, Battle of the. On 28 July 1798 a British fleet under Nelson surprised a French fleet at anchor in Abukir Bay. All but two of the French ships were destroyed. This was the first fleet action in which Nelson was in command. The battle destroyed French naval power in the Mediterranean and Napoleon's earliest ambitions.

Nile, Blue (Arabic *Bahr-al-Azrek*), African river rising in Lake Tana (or Tsana) in Ethiopia, at an elevation of 2150 m. It unites with the White Nile (Bahr-al-Abiad) at Khartoum. Its length is about 1450 km, 800 km of which are navigable at high water. In Ethiopia it is called Abai.

Nile, White (Arabic *Bahr-al-Abiad*), African river rising in Lake Victoria, one of the chief branches of the main Nile river. It flows through about 3700 km of flat marshy country, and is fed by the Sobat on the east and the Bahr-al-Ghazal on the west. Egypt's ability to maintain the mass of her people largely depends on the uninterrupted flow of the White Nile.

Nilo-Hamites, name referring to groups of peoples living in Kenya, Uganda, Tanzania and the southern Sudan, speaking Nilo-Hamitic languages. They include the Karamojong, Turkana, Nandi, Kipsikis and Masai. See also HAMITES.

Nilotes, name referring to peoples speaking Nilotic languages. They live in the Sudan (Shilluk, Nuer, Dinka, Burun and Anuak), parts of Uganda (Lango, Acholi and Alur), and western Kenya (Luo). The Shilluk and Anuak have a divine kingship; most of the other peoples have a clan-based organisation without kings or powerful chiefs. Most are savannah pastoralists, owning cattle which are of great social and ritual importance.

Nilsson, Birgit (1918–), Swedish soprano, educated at the Royal Academy of Music, Stockholm, where she made her début in 1946. She has sung at Bayreuth, Covent Garden, the Metropolitan and at La Scala, Milan. Well known for her Wagnerian rôles, she was also notable in the title rôle of Verdi's *Aida*, in Puccini's *Tosca* and *Turandot*, and in Strauss's *Elektra* and *Salome*.

Nimbus, see CLOUD.

Nîmes (formerly *Nismes*), French town, capital of the *département* of Gard, 100 km north-west of Marseilles. It is celebrated for its Roman remains, including the amphitheatre (converted into a fortress in the Middle Ages); a temple in the style of the Parthenon; the temple of Diana; an ancient tower, 28 m high; two Roman gates, and the aqueduct of the Pont du Gard. Silks, carpets, footwear, brandy and machinery are manufactured, and there is a trade in wines, grain and other foodstuffs. Population (1975) 133,942.

Nimrud, ancient Assyrian military capital of Kalkhu. The citadel by the River Tigris, 39 km south of Mosul, was excavated after 1847. Among the principal discoveries were the sculptured reliefs of human-headed winged bulls now in the British Museum. The city was founded on an earlier village site by Shalmaneser I c.1200 BC; rebuilt by Ashurnasirpal II in 879 BC; flourished until c.640 BC, and was destroyed by the Medes in 612 BC. Between 1949 and 1963 further palaces, inscriptions and ivories were found. See also ASSYRIA.

Nineveh, a capital of ancient Assyria, on the east bank of the Tigris, opposite the modern city of Mosul. By c.2300 BC Nineveh was probably a garrisoned outpost of the Agade. The earliest Assyrian ruler to have built a palace at Nineveh seems to have been Shalmaneser I (c.1260 BC). At present the evidence shows that at least a further 12 kings built palaces there. The most important building in Nineveh was done by Sennacherib (705–681 BC). He planned the fortifications, restored temples, built the most magnificent palaces and conducted water from the hills by canals. Ashurbanipal's reign (669–c.633 BC) was the 'golden age' of Assyria and of Nineveh. He established the great royal library at Nineveh. He sent to all the temples of Babylonia and had clay-tablet copies made of their epics, hymns and incantations. The Assyrian kingdom and Nineveh continued for c.20 years after his death.

Nineveh fell in 612 BC, the 14th year of the Babylonian king, Nabopolassar (625–605 BC), who joined Cyaxares and the Medes in their attack and siege of the city.

The excavations begun by Layard in 1845 at Nimrud and Kuyunjik constituted a landmark in archaeology. In 1847 he discovered the palace of Sennacherib, which was largely unearthed, 1849–51. From 1852 Hormuzd Rassam continued the excavation and found Ashurbanipal's palace and library.

Ningbo (Ning-po, city of calm waves), a former treaty port and an important trading city of Zhejiang province in China, on the Yongjiang (river) 25 km from its mouth, and 155 km east of Hangzhou. Manufactures include silks and other fabrics, gold, silver, and lacquered wares, carved wood, furniture, and carpets. Tea, raw cotton, and straw goods are among the exports. The city serves as a distributing station for Shanghai and has been developed into an important fishing port. It was linked by rail with Hangzhou in 1955. New industries include textiles, engineering, and diesel engines. Population (1970) 350,000.

Ningxia Hui Zizhiqu (Ningsia Hui Autonomous Region), autonomous region and province of China which was separated from Gansu province in 1958. The Huanghe crosses the central part of the province in a south-west to north-east direction, across a broad alluvial plain. The climate is generally very dry and irrigation is essential for agriculture on this plain. Rice, spring wheat, millet, and kaoliang are the main crops. Soya beans, tobacco, and cotton are also produced. Coal-mining takes place at Shizuishan. The capital of the province is Yinchuan. Area 77,000 km^2; population (1972) 2,500,000.

Ninian, Saint (c.360–c.432), Christian missionary preacher, probably born in Strathclyde, Scotland. He was consecrated bishop of the southern Picts by Pope Siricius, in Rome, in 394. He founded the church of Candida Casa (White House), at Whithorn, in Wigtownshire. According to Bede, Ninian preached to the Picts of all southern Scotland as far north as the Grampians. His feast is on 16 September. Ninian's career is chronicled by Bede in the *Historia Ecclesiastica*; and by Ailred of Rievaulx in the *Life of St Ninian*.

Niobium, or columbium, metallic chemical element, symbol Nb, atomic number 41, atomic weight 92·9064. It is usually associated with tantalum, and occurs in the minerals tantalite, columbite and fergusonite. The metal is obtained by reducing the chloride with hydrogen in a red-hot tube, or by reducing the oxide with carbon in an electric furnace. It is a steel-grey metal of relative density 8·56, which burns on heating in air, and is soluble in warm concentrated sulphuric acid. Its resistance to corrosion makes it suitable for the manufacture of chemical apparatus.

Nippon, or Nihon, native name for the whole of Japan.

Nippur, modern Niffer or Nuffar, ancient city of Sumer and Babylonia, c.161 km south-east of Baghdad. It was continuously occupied from Neolithic to Parthian times. As the seat of Enlil, chief god of the Sumerian pantheon, it occupied a position of religious and political importance.

Nirvāna (Sanskrit; Pāli *Nibbana*, literally blowing out, extinction), Enlightenment, the final goal of Buddhist endeavour. Nirvāna is often misunderstood as meaning self-annihilation; but what is annihilated is the 'delusion of self' which is inherent in suffering.

Nirvāna has been described as the extinction of the Three Fires of Desire, Hatred and Delusion (or Acquisitiveness, Aversion and Confusion). The Buddha referred to it as 'not-born, not-become, not-made, not-compounded' in contrast to the 'born, become, made, compounded' existence as we know it. Since it is beyond duality, relativity, time and space, it is often expressed in negative terms. Perhaps the most that can be said about it is that as Absolute Truth or Ultimate Reality, it simply is, and can never be analysed, only experienced. Furthermore, it can be realised in this life. A being who realises Nirvāna is known as an *Arahat* (Pāli; Sanskrit *Arhat*), for whom there will be no more rebirth.

Niš, town in Serbia, Yugoslavia, on the River Nišava. It was the birthplace and the summer residence of Constantine I the Great. Niš is an important road and rail junction and has chemical and agricultural foodstuff industries. Population (1971) 98,000.

Nishinomiya, city in Hyōgo-ken, Japan, between Ōsaka and Kōbe; an important city of the Hanshin Industrial Zone. A centre of the chemical and heavy industries, it is traditionally known for the manufacture of '*sake*'—Japanese rice wine. Population (1979) 394,000.

Nisi, Decree, see DIVORCE.

Niterói, city in the state of Rio de Janeiro, south-east Brazil, standing on the opposite shore of the harbour to Rio, with which it is connected by ferries. It is mainly a residential area. Population (1980) 386,185.

Nitric Acid, see NITROGEN.

Nitrogen, non-metallic chemical element, symbol N, atomic number 7, atomic weight 14·0067, formerly called 'azote.' It is found in nature as an unreactive gas, the chief constituent of the atmosphere (78 per cent by volume). It is also found in animal and vegetable matter and in various minerals either as ammonium compounds or as nitrates such as saltpetre. Nitrogen is colourless, tasteless, odourless, slightly less soluble than oxygen in water, and slightly lighter than air, in which it was discovered by Rutherford in 1722. At ordinary temperatures nitrogen is inert, but it combines with several metals to form nitrides on heating. A curiosity is the highly unstable form of 'active' nitrogen obtained on passing an electrical discharge through the gas. Small amounts of nitrogen are essential to plant life, which take in nitrogen either as salts or through bacterial activity.

Nitrogen forms five oxides: nitrous oxide ('laughing gas'), N_2O, used as an aerosol propellant (e.g. in whipped cream dispensers); nitric oxide, NO; nitrogen trioxide, N_2O_3; nitrogen dioxide, NO_2; and nitrogen pentoxide, N_2O_5. The latter dissolves readily in water to form nitric acid, one of nitrogen's most important commercial compounds. The acid readily chars dry organic matter, and attacks metals, forming nitrates or oxides. All nitrates are soluble in water and decompose at high temperatures. The other important commercial compound of nitrogen is ammonia, NH_3. With hydrogen, nitrogen forms the important 'metallic' radical ammonium.

Nitrogen Cycle. The nitrogen cycle is a process by which plants obtain their nitrogen from nitrates in the soil, animals obtain their nitrogen from plant proteins, and complex dead residues are changed by micro-organisms to available forms of plant food. The whole cycle takes place in stages: protein breakdown, by which the proteins of dead plants and animals are broken down by putrefactive bacteria; ammonification, where the products of protein breakdown are converted by fungi and bacteria to ammonia; and nitrification of the ammonia to nitrate, which takes place in two stages. First, one type of bacteria oxidises the ammonia to nitrite, then the oxidation is completed by a second type. The nitrates are then utilised by plants.

Nitrogen, Fixation of, any process in which elementary nitrogen is converted into useful nitrogen-containing compounds, particularly connected with artificial manures, explosives, nitric acid and ammonia.

Nitrogen Narcosis, intoxication produced by breathing the gas nitrogen under increased pressure. It is a particular danger for underwater divers using compressed air. Narcosis usually beings at a depth of about 30 m and can lead to convulsions and unconsciousness.

Nitroglycerine, $C_3H_5(ONO_2)_3$, glyceryl trinitrate, or propane-1,2,3-triyl trinitrate, colourless odourless liquid crystallising in two forms at 13·5 and 2·2°C. It was first produced by Sobrero in 1846 by the action of nitric acid on glycerine. It is prepared by adding glycerine to a mixture of sulphuric and nitric acids containing 0·5 per cent or less water at a temperature less than 18°C. The product, above its melting-point, is an oily liquid. Nobel first successfully manufactured this 'explosive oil' in 1862. Nitroglycerine is very sensitive to shock and friction. The solid (melting-point 13·2°C) is very sensitive, and therefore care has to be taken with explosives containing nitroglycerine to prevent them freezing. Mixing with ethylene glycol dinitrate (a nitro-glycol) reduces the freezing point. Storage temperatures must also be kept below 50°C as the stability is greatly reduced at higher temperatures. Nobel developed a range of explosives based on nitroglycerine which have been used extensively ever since; these include ballistite, dynamite and blasting gelatine (a jelly formed by solution of nitrocellulose in nitroglycerine). Nitroglycerine and some of its derivatives have been used medicinally to reduce blood pressure.

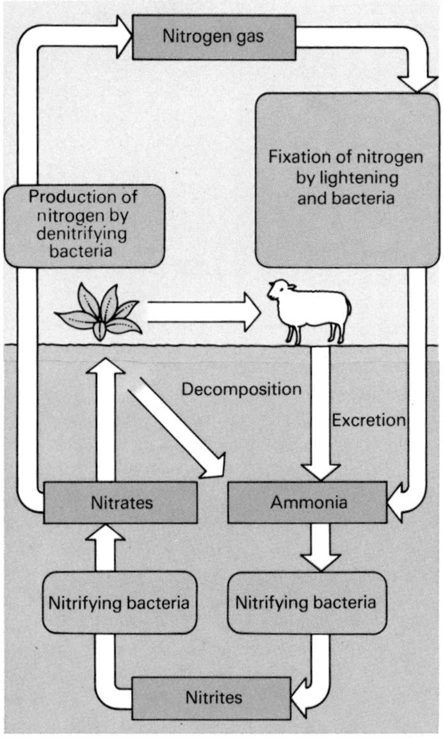

Nitrogen Cycle. *Nitrogen is constantly recycled through the environment from living to dead tissue and back again by the action of bacteria and plants.*

Nitrotoluenes. The nitration of toluene leads to the formation of a mixture of *ortho* (1:2) and *para* (1:4) nitrotoluenes, $CH_3C_6H_4(NO_2)$, which can be separated by fractional distillation. They are both employed in the colour industry. *Meta*-nitrotoluene is obtained from *para*-toluidine by converting it first into its acetyl derivative and then nitrating the latter. The resulting *meta*-nitro-*para*-acetotoluide on hydrolysis and diazotisation in alcohol yields *meta*-nitrotoluene. There are a number of dinitrotoluenes, $CH_3C_6H_3(NO_2)_2$, the most important being the (1:2:4) compound obtained by the further nitration of toluene. Trinitrotoluene, or TNT, is used as a powerful explosive and is obtained by the nitration of toluene.

Nits, see ANOPLURA; MALLOPHAGA.

Niue, coral island in the South Pacific Ocean, in latitude 19° 2′ S and longitude 160° 52′ W, with an area of 25,931 ha. Formerly part of the Cook Islands, annexed with them to New Zealand in 1901, but administered separately after 1903. In October 1974 Niue gained self-government in free association with New Zealand. Straw-plaiting is one of the chief occupations, and hats, bananas, copra, baskets and kumaras are exported. Population (1980) 3288.

Niven, David (1909–83), British film actor. He usually played military roles (*Carrington V.C.*, *The Guns of Navarone*), light comedy heroes (*My Man Godfrey*, *Around the World in 80 Days*), or a combination of the two (*The Best of Enemies*); but he won an Academy Award for his performance as a seedy military fraud in *Separate Tables* (1958). He wrote a best-selling autobiography, *The Moon's a Balloon*, 1973, and its sequel, *Bring on the Empty Horses*, 1975.

Nivki (Gilyaks), a 4400-strong group of Paleo-Asiatic-speaking fishermen and sea-mammal hunters of Eastern Siberia. They use dogs as draught animals, as food, as symbols of wealth and as a medium of exchange. Today, with collectivisation, they have added agriculture to their activities.

Nixon, Richard Milhous (1913–), 37th President of the USA. Elected vice-president in 1952, he served until 1960, playing a more extensive rôle in government than previous vice-presidents, in part because of the poor health of President Eisenhower. In 1960 he was the Republican presidential candidate, but was narrowly defeated by John F. Kennedy. In 1968 he regained the Republican nomination, and defeated Hubert Humphrey for the presidency.

Despite his modest achievements he won re-election in 1972 by a landslide, but immediately faced allegations of irregularities and illegalities conducted on his behalf in his re-election campaign and within the White House. Despite his success in extricating the US from Vietnam, congressional and judicial investigations, along with press exposures of the so-called Watergate affair, undermined public support. He also exacerbated congressional opposition by excessive use of the veto power and extensive impoundments of funds appropriated by Congress. In February 1974 Congress began enquiries to determine if grounds existed to impeach the president. Nixon denied any direct involvement in the alleged illegalities, but in the face of a unanimous decision of the Supreme Court ordering the release of certain evidence, transcripts of conversations between the president and his staff were made public. They revealed that the president had sought to cover up the Watergate incident. President Nixon resigned on 9 August 1974, in the face of impending impeachment.

Nizhni Novgorod, see GORKI.

Nizhni Tagil, city in Sverdlovsk *oblast* of the RSFSR, USSR, on the eastern slopes of the central Urals. It has a vast iron and steel works, the largest railway-car plant in the USSR, and coking and chemical plants. Iron and copper ores and gold are mined nearby. It was founded in 1725 as an ironworks; the first experimental railway in Russia was built here in 1834. Population (1980) 400,000.

Nkomo, Joshua (1917–), Zimbabwe politician. He became president of the African National General Congress, and went abroad when it was banned. On his return to Rhodesia he became president of the Zimbabwe African Peoples' Union (ZAPU) in 1961. Nkomo was imprisoned by the Rhodesian government from 1963 to 1964, and was confined to a restricted area until December 1974 when he was released to participate in new talks on Rhodesia's future. He was elected leader of the 'moderate' wing of the African National Council (ANC) inside Rhodesia in September 1975 and pledged himself to achieve immediate majority rule in Rhodesia. His efforts to achieve this through peaceful negotiation with Smith ended with the collapse of the talks in March 1976, after which he committed himself to the military struggle, joining forces with Robert Mugabe and the campaign waged by the guerrillas of the Patriotic Front. He attended the Lancaster House Conference in 1979 and contested the 1980 elections as leader of the Patriotic Front. He was appointed minister of Home Affairs in Mugabe's government, but dismissed in 1982, he left Zimbabwe in 1983, returning later that year.

Nkrumah, Kwame (1909–72), Ghanaian politician. In 1949 he founded the Convention People's party (CPP), which agitated for immediate self-government for the Gold Coast. In 1950 the British imprisoned him for inciting illegal strikes, but in 1951 he was released to become leader of government business in the Gold Coast Assembly. Nkrumah was prime minister of the Gold Coast from 1952 to 1957; of Ghana from 1957 to 1960; and was president of Ghana from 1960, wielding increasingly authoritarian powers. In February 1966 his government was overthrown while Nkrumah was abroad, in a coup organised by part of the army. He subsequently went to Guinea, where, six years later, he died. Under Nkrumah's leadership Ghana had acquired an impatience and intransigence, which resulted in the severing of aid links from Western countries, and an ideological commitment to the USSR and Eastern Europe.

Nō, a form of Japanese drama largely created by Zeami Motokiyo (1363–1443) and his father Kanami Kiyotsugu (1333–84), who between them wrote the majority of the 250 *nō* plays which are still performed virtually unchanged. They are short, highly stylised plays, based on Buddhist ritual and traditional themes, set to music, and involving both mime and speech. Comic interludes called *kyogen* were included in the programme. Kanami was originally a priest and developed the plays under shogun patronage; thus *nō* drama became a largely aristocratic art-form.

Noah, or Noe, son of Lamech, the biblical flood hero, builder of the ark in which he and his family survived the deluge, patriarch of mankind, and inventor of wine and viticulture.

Alfred Nobel. *The inventor in later life.*

Nobel, Alfred Bernhard (1833–96), Swedish engineer and chemist. He discovered and patented the explosive mixture known as dynamite, and later also ballistite or smokeless powder. He bequeathed a trust for five annual prizes, to be awarded, without distinction of nationality or sex, for eminence in physics, chemistry, physiology or medicine, literature, and the furtherance of international peace.

Nobel Prizes, prizes awarded, by the Swedish Academy of Science, for physics and chemistry; by the Stockholm Faculty of Medicine, for physiology or medicine; by the Swedish Academy, for literature; and by a committee elected by the Norwegian Parliament, for peace. The prizes, which amount to about £35,000 each, are awarded from the income of a capital sum of £1,750,000 left on trust by the Swedish scientist Alfred Nobel. A prize for economics funded by the Swedish National Bank has been awarded since 1969.

Nobelium, metallic chemical element, atomic number 102, symbol No; a member of the group of actinides. It was discovered in 1958 by Dr Albert Chiorso, as a result of the bombardment of curium. Isotopes of mass 251 to 257 have been made, and have half-lives varying from 1 second to 3 minutes.

Nobile, Umberto (1885–1978), Italian aviator and aeronautical engineer. He designed the dirigible *Norge* which made the successful Rome-Alaska trans-Polar flight in the Amundsen-Ellsworth-Nobile expedition of 1926. He led the *Italia* airship expedition which flew to the North Pole but was wrecked off North East Land. He was rescued by a Russian ice-breaker after 40 days.

Nobility is a term which has at different times denoted biological or even racial superiority, a desirable political arrangement, or an honour bestowen as a reward for services rendered. The English nobility of the Conquest and Middle Ages was essentially feudal and military and based upon a solid foundation of landed property. The modern nobility of England resembles the old feudal nobility in no other respect than in the fact that it may possess landed estates; for the rest it consists of a heterogeneous body of peers, some with patents entitling them to sit in the Upper House and some without, and baronets, and knights, the great majority of whom possess titles of recent creation, awarded for political or other public services. The English system has been to maintain the peers and their immediate children as a high nobility and to allow their junior descendants to merge into the middle class. In contrast the European nobility has always tried to maintain itself as a privileged caste, a fact that has brought it into direct conflict with the bourgeoisie and proletariat.

Noble, English coin, first minted by Edward III in 1344. On one side was stamped a ship to commemorate the victory of Sluys. It disappeared from circulation by the early 17th century.

Noctilucent Clouds (luminous night clouds), very rare clouds which are only recognised at dusk or dawn at exceptionally great height (about 80 km). Usually observed near sunrise or sunset in northern Europe in summer, they resemble cirrus and have a bluish-white to yellowish colour. It is probable that they are partly composed of meteoric or volcanic dust.

Nocturne, 'night piece' or instrumental serenade, generally of a quiet, lyrical character, but sometimes (as in Chopin) with a more agitated middle section. The typical style has an ornate, expressive melody over a 'rocking' accompaniment. As a piano piece it originated with John Field.

Noguchi, Hideyo (1876–1928), Japanese bacteriologist and pathologist. He made researches into immunity against snake poisons and in 1904 published *The Action of Snake Venom upon Cold-blooded Animals.* At the Rockefeller Institute, which he joined in 1904, he did valuable work on the aetiology of syphilis and the cultivation of spirochaetes; he also studied the aetiology of trachoma and yellow fever, of which latter disease he died when conducting investigations in West Africa.

Noise has become a problem of importance to society as a result of the extensive use of machinery. Modern industrialised countries use machines, vehicles and processes which consume large amounts of energy, and it is inevitable that some of this energy will be converted into noise, which does not merely constitute an annoyance, but in some extreme cases, e.g. players in pop groups, can be a

danger to health. There are more than 40 noise measures, all in some way based on the decibel, which attempt to quantify noise according to human response to frequencies, sound tonal values, duration or number of events, and many other variables.
See also ACOUSTICS; DECIBEL; SOUND.

Nolan, Sidney (1917–), Australian painter, a leading figure of the modern Australian School. Wartime travel about the Australian continent made him aware of its unique landscape which he vividly interpreted. Incidents and legends of colonial days provided him with subjects. A *Leda and the Swan* series, 1960, extended his rendering of legend. He has designed settings for Stravinsky's *Sacre du Printemps*. Works by him are in the principal Australian galleries, the Tate Gallery, London, and Museum of Modern Art, New York.

Nolde, Emile (1867–1956), German painter. One of the leaders of the Expressionist movement in Germany, he was much influenced by Gauguin and primitive art. From 1905 to 1907 he was associated with the Die Brücke group. He painted biblical subjects marked by a barbaric intensity of colour, still-life, and the landscape of his native region on the Danube-German border.

Nolle Prosequi, an entry in the record of an English court which indicates that the Crown, in a criminal prosecution, desires to proceed no further with the case.

Nollekens, Joseph (1737–1823), British sculptor. In 1760 he went to study in Rome, where Garrick met him and commissioned him to execute a bust. This was so successful that Sterne also sat for him. He increased his income by trading antiques and by stock exchange speculation, and was so successful that at his death he had made £200,000. He returned to England in 1770, and was soon the fashionable sculptor of the day, eccentric in character but very able in portraiture.

Nom-de-plume, see PSEUDONYM.

Nomad (Greek *nomas*, roaming), member of a tribe or community roaming from place to place. Nomads fall into two major categories: *pastoralists*, such as the Bedouin Arabs of the Arabian Peninsula, and the Turkic and Mongol peoples of Central Asia, who depend on domesticated livestock and shift their location according to the state of pasturage; *nomadic hunters and gatherers* such as the Kung of the Kalahari who change their location with the seasons according to the availability of wild plants and animal food as well as water. Travelling tinkers and traders such as the gypsies can also be termed nomads.

Nome, town south of the Seward Peninsula, north-western Alaska, on the northern shore of Norton Sound, 21 km west of Cape Nome. It is the centre of a gold-mining district and the commercial and supply centre for North-West Alaska. Nome is a seaport (open May–November). Fur farming, trapping and fishing are important activities. Population (1970) 2488.

Nomenclature, see NAMES.

Nominalism, as opposed to Realism, was one of the two philosophic doctrines of the Middle Ages which arose from a consideration of the nature of species, and genera. Nominalism implies a belief that 'universals', i.e. genera and species, are mere names. The Nominalists deny that the concept, or class, has an existence of its own beyond the individuals which make up the class. A narrower form of Nominalism held that even concepts or ideas are not really general.
See also SCHOLASTICISM.

Nonconformity, or Dissent, in religion, in 17th-century England signified remaining within the Anglican Church, yet refusing to conform to certain ceremonial practices such as the sign of the cross in baptism, and the ring in marriage.
The modern meaning of Nonconformity, or Dissent, describing Protestants outside the Anglican Church, derives from legislation passed after the restoration of Charles II which penalised the dissenting churches.

Nones, in the Roman calendar, the ninth day before the Ides, i.e. the fifth of all months except March, May, July and October, when it is the seventh.

Non-Euclidean Geometry. In the *Elements* by Euclid, the fifth postulate (or axiom) states that if two lines AA' and BB' are cut by a transversal AB, and if the sum of angles ABB' and BAA' $<\pi$ (180°), then AA' and BB' will meet. Many commentators took the view that this statement was not sufficiently obvious to qualify as an axiom which was supposed to be a self-evident truth. Commentators attempted to prove the fifth postulate as a theorem derived from the other axioms.
In the 19th century several mathematicians, including Bolyai, Gauss, Lobachevski and Riemann, recognised that the failure to produce a logical contradiction showed that the fifth postulate is independent of the other axioms: it cannot be proved as a theorem from them, and Euclidean geometry is simply a system that includes the fifth postulate while other systems could be constructed in which the fifth postulate is not true. These other systems are called non-Euclidean geometries. It has been demonstrated that non-Euclidean geometries do not describe the 'Euclidean' space of everyday experience, but it is possible to think of physical systems that they do describe. The process of investigating different versions of axiomatic systems has become one of the most fruitful methods of discovery in modern mathematics, especially in algebra and topology.

Non-Jurors, those clergy of the Church of England and schoolmasters who after the revolution of 1688 refused to take the oath of allegiance to William and Mary. They were headed by William Sancroft, Archbishop of Canterbury, and included seven other bishops: Ken of Bath and Wells, White of Peterborough, Lake of Chichester, Turner of Ely, Frampton of Gloucester, Thomas of Worcester, and Lloyd of Norwich. About 400 of the lower clergy refused to take the oath, and their secession gravely weakened the High Church party. Non-Jurors continued to exist, in diminishing numbers, into the 19th century, preserving the apostolic succession by ordaining their own bishops, and producing a revision of the Anglican liturgy. In Scotland the Episcopalians ceased to be Non-Jurors after the death of the Young Pretender in 1788.

Non-metals, one of the two classes into which chemical elements are divided. They may be gases, liquids or solids at ordinary temperatures, and most of the liquid and solid non-metals are easily converted into the gaseous state at comparatively low temperatures. They are brittle, if solid, generally have a low relative density, and are bad conductors of heat and electricity. The non-metals form acidic oxides, they are not acted upon by dilute mineral acids, and generally form stable compounds with hydrogen. The distinction between non-metals and metals is, however, by no means always well defined, and several elements, such as arsenic and antimony, possess characteristics of both classes. Examples of non-metals are oxygen, nitrogen, chlorine, helium, carbon, sulphur, boron, phosphorus and silicon.
See also METALS.

Nono, Luigi (1924–), Italian composer, a serialist (and Schoenberg's son-in-law), notable for his clarity of procedure and socio-political concerns. He studied with Bruno Maderna and Hermann Scherchen. The main trend in Nono's compositions is the dissemination of anti-fascist and pro-communist propaganda, through the texts of such vocal works as *Epitaffio per Garcìa Lorca*, *Ricorda quello che ti hanno fatto in Auschwitz*, the opera *Intolleranza 1960* (revised 1970), and *The Illuminated Factory*. Up to 1964 Nono wrote numerous orchestral works, but subsequently concentrated mainly on the electronic-vocal medium.

Non-woven Fabrics, see FABRICS, NON-WOVEN.

Nootka, North American Indian peoples belonging to the Wakashan linguistic group. They live on the west coast of Vancouver Island, near Nootka Sound. They number about 2000, and were famed as whale catchers.

Nordenskiöld, Adolf Erik, Baron (1832–1901), Swedish geographer and explorer. After several scientific expeditions to Svalbard and Greenland, and two voyages north of Siberia, he became the first to navigate the north-east passage in 1878–79. He contributed to the science of geographic research, particularly in his work *Periplus*, 1897.

Nordic denotes the tall, blond, dolichocephalic (long-headed) race found mainly in Scandinavia and, to a lesser extent, in Germany, Denmark and other countries.

Nordic Council, an assembly of elected representatives from the Scandinavian parliaments, established in 1952. Denmark, Norway, Sweden and Finland each send 18 delegates, and Iceland six. A Nordic Council of Ministers was formed in 1971. The aim of the Council is a state of affairs whereby the Scandinavian countries can constitute an integrated area within which the citizens may move, live and work, enjoying equal treatment regardless of nationality. Good results have been achieved, especially in legislation and social welfare. A joint labour market has been established which allows a Scandinavian to apply, without formalities, for work in any country. In 1952 passport regulations were abolished between the Scandinavian countries. In the legal field each country now recognises the criminal and civil verdicts pronounced in the other countries.

Nore, The, sand-bank at the mouth of the River Thames. The Nore mutiny took place in the vicinity in 1797.

Norfolk, maritime county of Eastern England, bounded to the north and north-east by the North Sea, to the north-west by Lincolnshire and the Wash, to the west by Cambridgeshire, and to the south by Suffolk. Area 956,974 ha.

The coastline is mainly flat and low, and has suffered much from erosion, though thousands of hectares have been reclaimed from the Wash around King's Lynn. There are few inlets, and numerous sandbanks make the coast dangerous. Inland the surface is mostly level, and includes in the west a part of the Fens known as the Bedford Level. The main rivers are the Yare and the Great Ouse. A feature of the county is the Broads, a series of beautiful lakes famous for fishing, water fowl and boating. The many windmills in this area are now largely derelict. The soil is varied, with chalk, sand and loam prevalent in different districts. Agriculture flourishes, wheat and barley being grown in great quantities. Large numbers of turkeys are reared. The principal manufactured products are boots and shoes, and there are flour mills and mustard works; there are fisheries at Yarmouth. Norwich is the county town; Yarmouth and King's Lynn are the principal ports. The healthy climate and long stretches of sand have made Yarmouth, Cromer, Hunstanton and other coastal towns favourite resorts. Sandringham is a royal country residence. Population (1981) 693,490.

Norfolk, port of Virginia, USA, part of the metropolitan area of Norfolk-Portsmouth (population in 1980, 800,000) and of the larger urban cluster sometimes referred to as the cities of Hampton Roads. Norfolk lies on the south side of the Roads, which is the estuary of the James river; it forms one of the finest natural harbours in the world. The city was first laid out in 1682, and grew on the 18th-century trade with the West Indies. Its growth to its modern dimensions was the result of two developments: the choice of Norfolk as the home dockyard and the base of the US Atlantic Fleet, and the shipment of coal by rail from the Appalachian coalfield to the Atlantic. Population (1980) 266,979.

Norfolk Island, in the Pacific Ocean and under Australian administration. It was discovered by Captain Cook in 1774, and shortly afterwards made a penal settlement. In 1856 it became the home of the descendants of the Bounty mutineers who were moved from Pitcairn Island. It is 8 km long and 4 km wide, with an area of nearly 35 km². Population (1980) about 1700.

Norman, name given to the people of Normandy and their descendants in the European countries conquered by them. The word is identical with Northman or Norseman, but is mostly restricted to the mixed race which came into existence after the conversion of the heathen Norse settlers and their adoption of French culture. Besides invading and conquering England in the 11th century the Normans conquered and settled in southern Italy and Sicily.

See also VIKINGS.

Norman Architecture, see ENGLISH ARCHITECTURE.

Norman Conquest, name given to the conquest of England by William of Normandy, made possible by his victory at the battle of Hastings on 14 October 1066, and to the government subsequently imposed upon the country by him and his successors. Domesday Book shows the extent to which Normans had become owners of land within 20 years of the battle of Hastings. The affairs of Church and state were completely in Norman hands; yet the break with the past was far from complete, for William continued, or adopted, many established Anglo-Saxon institutions for the greater stability of his own system. One basic difference was the introduction of feudal land tenure, for the Saxon system was not built on the feudal essential, namely the granting of a definite piece of land in return for definite services.

Norman-French, the dialect of Normandy, differing in some respects from Parisian French. Norman-French was of considerable literary importance in the Old French period. The French spoken in the Channel Islands is a Norman dialect.

Normandy (French *Normandie*, formerly a province in northern France bordering on the English Channel, now divided into the *départements* of Seine-Maritime, Eure, Orne, Calvados and Manche. It is in general a very fertile, richly cultivated land. Its chief agricultural products are corn, flax, hemp, colza and apples (from which cider is made); its fisheries and manufactures are of great importance and its horses the best in the country; sheep and dairy-farming are important industries. There are iron-ore mines near Caen. The principal towns are Rouen, Dieppe, Le Havre and Cherbourg.

The province was first called Normandy after Charles the Simple, in 912, had given it to Rolf or Rollo, the leader of a band of Norse rovers, to be held by him and his heirs as a fief of the French crown. His descendant, William II, son of Robert II, became Duke of Normandy in 1036, and in 1066 established a Norman dynasty on the throne of England. Normandy was conquered by Philip Augustus (1203–04). It remained a part of the French monarchy except for 34 years after the Battle of Agincourt.

Norn, now extinct Norse speech of Caithness, Orkney and Shetland; the origin of the name is the Norse *norroenà* (Norwegian). The Norse speech was introduced into Shetland and Orkney about the 9th century by the Vikings and also into the Faeroes where, in a form closely akin to Icelandic, it still remains. Elsewhere it survived longest in the remote island of Foula where in 1773 the Rev. George Low discovered that 'there are some who know a few words of it' and was able to collect a few remnants of songs.

Norns, female spirits in Scandinavian mythology. Good or evil Norns fixed the fate of every child at birth, but in a special sense there are three Norns, personifying past, present and future, dwelling at Urd's Well at one of the roots of Yggdrasill.

Norrköping, town and port of Sweden in Östergötland, 180 km from Stockholm, on both banks of the River Motala. There are paper, textile, engineering, and timber mills as well as shipbuilding yards. Population (1978) 120,250.

Norrland, traditional term describing the northernmost region of Sweden.

Norroy King of Arms, see HERALD'S COLLEGE.

Norse Languages, term which may be used of the Scandinavian languages from the earliest times up to the end of the medieval

Normandy. *Fruit orchards in the rich agricultural region of the Pays d'Auge, east of Caen.*

period. They are a sub-branch of the Germanic main branch of the Indo-European family of languages. Norse may be chronologically subdivided into three periods. Primitive, or Old, Norse was spoken up to about AD 700 in Scandinavia, parts of Finland, north Slesvig, and the south shore of the Baltic. It was similar to Primitive Germanic, although from the earliest times there are dialectal differences. Viking Norse (800–1100) spread geographically with the Viking expansion: to Russia, to the Orkneys and Shetland Islands, where it was spoken as late as the 18th century, to the Hebrides, Isle of Man, and parts of Ireland and England, to Normandy and to the Faeroes, Iceland and Greenland. (Apart from the Faeroes and Iceland, Norse subsequently died out in all these places.) By the end of this period, a dialectal split had established itself between the West Norse languages (spoken in Norway and its dependencies, including Iceland) and the East Norse languages (those of Sweden, Denmark and their colonies).

By 1100, the formal conversion to Christianity of the Scandinavian countries was complete and the Latin alphabet began to be used for writing the Norse languages. The period up to 1500 is known as the Literary Norse period. See also DENMARK, *Language*; ICELAND,

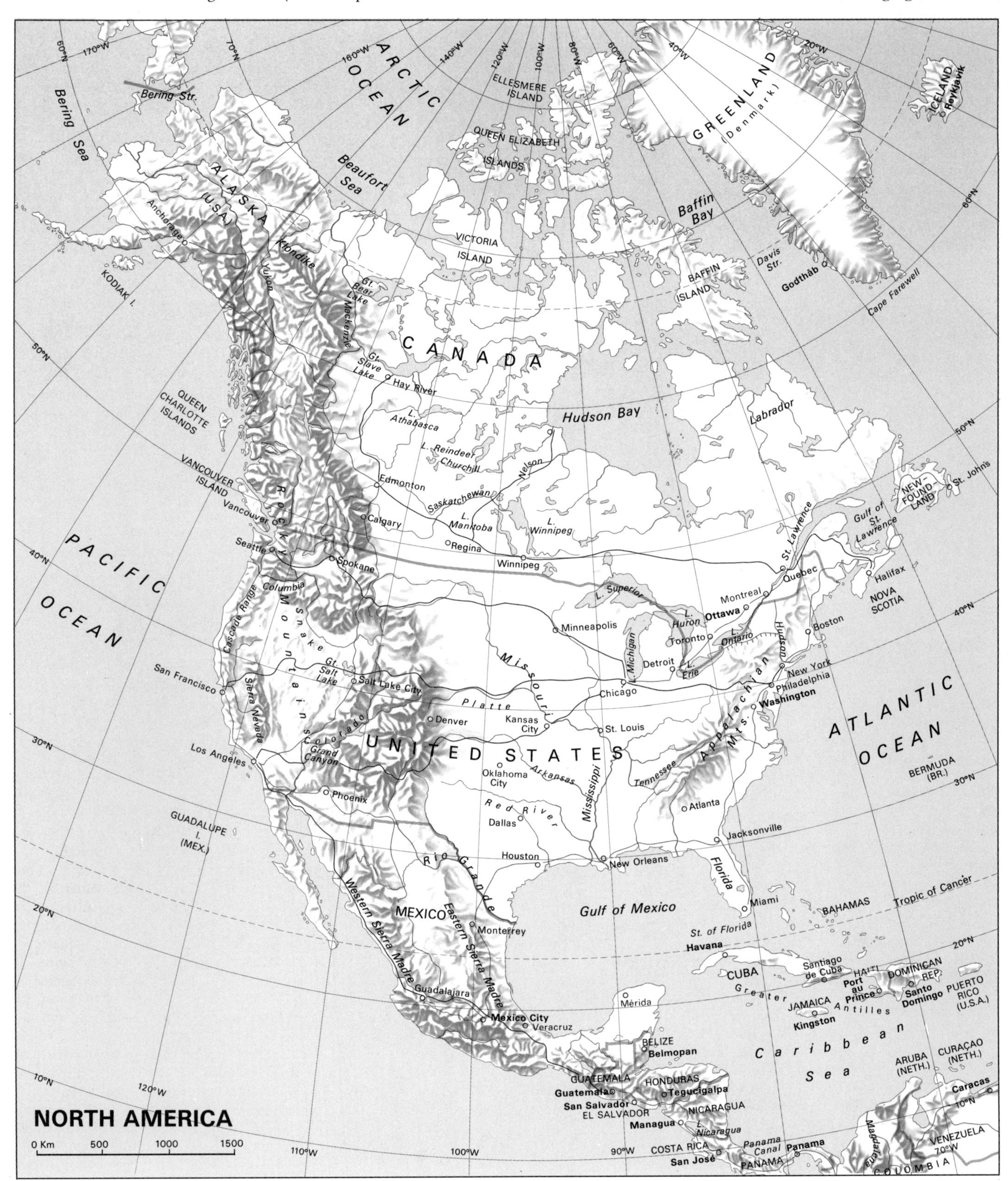

Language; NORWAY, *Language*; SCANDINAVIAN LANGUAGES; SWEDEN, *Language*.

Norsemen, see VIKINGS.

North, Frederick, 2nd Earl of Guilford, better known as Lord North (1732–92), British statesman. In 1767 he became chancellor of the Exchequer and leader of the House of Commons in the Grafton administration, and in 1770 prime minister. He acted as the mouthpiece of the king. North was personally opposed to the American war, but allowed the king to influence him against his better judgment. He resigned in March 1782, but with Charles James Fox formed a government which lasted from April to December 1783, after which he did not again hold office.

North, Sir Thomas (c.1535–1601), English translator, best known for his classic translation of Plutarch's *Lives of the Noble Grecians and Romans*, from the French translation, 1559, by Jacques Amyot. North's translation, in vivid, idiomatic English, is the source of Shakespeare's knowledge of ancient history; in *Antony and Cleopatra* and *Coriolanus* North's language is often followed.

North America, the third largest of the continents, shaped like an inverted triangle, with an area of 24,400,000 km^2. It is one of the most developed regions of the world yet only contains about 8 per cent of the world's population. The name America is derived from Amerigo Vespucci, the supposed discoverer of the mainland in 1497. A definition of North America is difficult because Mexico belongs culturally and linguistically to Latin America. Geographically, the term includes the Central American republics as well. Danish-speaking Greenland is also connected physically to the continent, but otherwise is quite distinct. It is separated from Asia by the Bering Strait and from South America by the Isthmus of Panama.

See also entries for individual countries.

North American Native Languages. Among the better known larger groups of languages spoken in North America are Eskimo, now regarded by some scholars as a branch of the Ural-Altaic linguistic family, Athabascan, Shoshonean, Algonkian, Caddoan, Iroquois, Muskhogean and Siouan, all of which are considered American Indian or Amerind, or 'Red Indian languages'.

The Eskimo, or Innuit, occupy the seaboard, from north-east Greenland to the mouth of the Copper River in West Alaska and have numerous, widely differing dialects. Navaho is one of the main Athabascan languages; it is spoken by some 25,000 people living in North Arizona. The Shoshoneans were mainly centred in the region of the Rocky Mountains. The Algonkians are much better known: their main linguistic branches include Blackfoot or Siksika, Micmac, Cheyenne, Arapohoe, and Cree, which was reduced to writing about 300 years ago. The Caddoans live mainly on the Red River in Louisiana, along the rivers of north-east Texas, in Kansas and in Nebraska. Cherokee is now the main Iroquoian language; the Cherokees employed their own script, a syllabary which was the most developed writing ever created by an American native. Muskhogean territory extends along the rivers flowing into the Gulf of Mexico parallel to the Mississippi. The ethnical history of the native peoples of the 'Pacific slope' is entirely different from those of the rest of North America, which is reflected in their numerous languages.

See also MEXICAN AND CENTRAL AMERICAN NATIVE LANGUAGES; SOUTH AMERICAN NATIVE LANGUAGES.

North Atlantic Treaty, signed on 4 April 1949 at Washington by the USA, Great Britain, Canada, France, Belgium, the Netherlands, Luxembourg, Norway, Denmark, Iceland, Italy and Portugal, by which the USA associated itself with the Western European countries in security arrangements for their common or mutual defence against possible aggression. The pact had its origins in the history of the years 1947–48, during which failure to come to terms with the Soviet Union and its satellites forced the Western countries to seek economic and security arrangements among themselves.

North Borneo, see SABAH; SARAWAK.

North Cape, headland on the island of Magerøy, Norway, the most northerly point of Europe, being in latitude 71°10′21″ N. A road to the North Cape was opened in 1956. The midnight sun is seen from 14 May to 30 July.

North Carolina (Tar Heel State), a state of the USA, on the southern Atlantic coast, bordered on the north by Virginia, on the west by Tennessee, and on the south by South Carolina and Georgia. It stretches from the coastal sandbars, which front it on the Atlantic seaboard and enclose behind them the sounds, or coastal lagoons, across an intermediate area of swamps (the northernmost of which is known as Dismal Swamp), to the coastal plain and thence to the Appalachian Piedmont and the Appalachian Mountains. The latter culminate in the Great Smoky Mountains (which are enclosed in a national park) and the Unaka range, where Mount Mitchell reaches 2037 m above sea-level.

Many small farms, often operated by black tenant farmers, have been either abandoned or consolidated into larger units. On the fully commercial farms remaining, tobacco is the chief source of income. Cotton, although still occupying 60–70,000 ha, has greatly diminished in importance, and on the lands thus freed, a range of other cash crops is now raised, e.g. soybeans and peanuts, and the worn-out lands lend themselves well to use for producing broiler fowls. There are over 8 million ha of forest. Industrialisation began in the reconstruction period after the American Civil War with cotton textiles and tobacco, and these industries have gained rather than lost ground. To these have been added chemicals, electronics, food-processing, furniture and brick-making.

The 1980 population was 5,737,140. The capital is Raleigh. The state area is 136,197 km^2.

The North Carolina coast was first explored in 1584. The territory was granted to various 'proprietors' by Charles I and Charles II of England, but in 1728 the Crown resumed control.

North Dakota (Flickertail State), north-central state of the USA, bounded on the north by Canada. The state is composed almost entirely of plains. There are coal (little worked) and oil deposits (the Williston basin). The east forms part of the central lowlands, with an altitude of some 300 m and ample rainfall for cultivation. To the west rises the tilted surface of the Great Plains, reaching 1000 m and with so low a rainfall that crops give way to stock-rearing. North Dakota is a wheat state (3·6 million ha), one of the main wheat producers of the USA. There are significant areas of barley, potatoes, sugar beet and flax. The ranches in the western part accommodate over two million head of cattle.

North Dakota shares with its neighbour, South Dakota, the distinction of having the lowest urban proportion of its population. The largest city, Fargo, has a population of only 61,280, and is, in any case, on the extreme eastern edge. North Dakota was admitted as a state of the Union in 1889. The capital is Bismarck. Population (1980) 652,437.

North Downs, see DOWNS, NORTH AND SOUTH.

North-East Passage, route, first navigated in full by A. E. Nordenskiöld in 1878–79, from European waters to the Pacific Ocean by way of the north coast of the USSR. Now commonly known as the Northern Sea Route and heavily used by Soviet merchant shipping.

North German Confederation, league of German states established in 1867, linking, under Prussian leadership, the 22 states north of the River Main. The king of Prussia was president and commander-in-chief of the army of the Confederation.

See also GERMAN HISTORY.

North Island, see NEW ZEALAND.

North Korea
Area: 125,500 km^2
Population: 15,852,000
Capital: P'yŏngyang

North Korea, officially the Democratic People's Republic of Korea, came into being in 1948 when a Communist republic was declared north of the 38th parallel. It is bounded by China to the north, the USSR to the north-east, the Sea of Japan to the east, the Yellow Sea to the west, and South Korea to the south. It occupies only one-quarter of the actual Korean peninsula. Area 125,500 km^2. The estimated population in 1975 was 15,852,000. P'yŏngyang is the capital.

Only 16 per cent of North Korea is arable. Farming is carried out by work teams as in the Chinese communes and agricultural co-operatives are responsible for a range of local-government functions. About one-quarter of the arable area is used for rice growing. In addition cotton forms an important industrial crop. Prominence in economic planning has been given to the growth of heavy industry. Considerable attention has been paid to expanding the production of coal, iron-ore and steel. The machine, fertiliser, cement and chemical industries are also growing.

The 'highest organ of power' is the Supreme People's Assembly, which elects the President of the republic, the Central People's Committee, the president of the Central Court, and others. The President 'directly guides' the

Central People's Committee, whose members all belong to the Central Committee of the party.

The official language is Korean.

History. The Democratic People's Republic of Korea was created in 1948. In 1950 the North Koreans launched a successful attack on the non-Communist Republic of Korea in the south. By the time a truce was signed in 1953 North Korea was ruined. Economically it claimed to have recovered from the worst effects of the war by the early 1960s, concentrating national efforts on collective farms and obtaining industrial aid from the USSR and Eastern Europe. From 1961 there was clearly some disagreement with these allies and since 1971 North Korea has been actively seeking financial and technical assistance from Japan and the West.

See also KOREA, *History*; SOUTH KOREA, *History*.

North Ossetian Autonomous Soviet Socialist Republic, in the south-east RSFSR of the USSR, on the northern slopes of the central part of the main Caucasus range, and the adjacent lowland crossed by the River Terek. There are lead, zinc, silver and other mineral deposits. Maize, sunflowers and wheat are grown, and horticulture and sheep raising are carried on. Industries include non-ferrous metallurgy and food. The area was formed as the North Ossetian Autonomous Oblast in 1924, and became a republic in 1936. The capital is Ordzhonikidze. Area 8000 km^2. Population (1980) 602,000, mostly Ossetians and Russians.

North Pole, see ARCTIC OCEAN; ARCTIC CIRCLE.

North Rhine-Westphalia (German *Nordrhein-Westfalen), Land* of West Germany, in the Federal Republic, bounded on the west by Belgium and the Netherlands. It comprises the former Prussian province of Westphalia, the governmental districts of Cologne, Aachen, Düsseldorf (once parts of the Rhine Province), and Lippe. It contains the important coalfields of the Ruhr and Aachen, and the large brown coalfield of the Ville to the west of Cologne. It is the industrial heart of Germany particularly within the triangle extending from Bonn in the south to Hamm in the north-east and Wesel in the north-west. Population (1979) 17 million; capital, Düsseldorf.

North Sea, occupies the continental shelf region between the British Isles, Scandinavia and the west coast of Europe, north of the Straits of Dover. Area 575,000 km^2; average depth about 100 m. In the centre the Dogger Bank extends east to west forming a barrier that shallows to 13 m. A channel, with depths ranging from 300 to 600 m, follows the coast of Scandinavia reaching as far south-east as the Skagerrak. The surface water temperature has ranges of 2–16 °C off the Danish coast to 7–13 °C in the north-west where it is influenced by the west wind drift current. The eastern part is generally ice-covered in winter due to the fresh water coming from the Baltic Sea. The major rivers entering the North Sea are the Rhine, Meuse, Elbe, Forth, Humber, and the Thames. The tidal range varies from about 6 m along the English coast to about 1 m along the Scandinavian coast, and the height of the frequent storm surges, caused by atmospheric depressions, can be up to 2 m. The relatively shallow North Sea is an excellent area for fish and is a major fishing ground for species of flat, bottom-living fish. During the 1970s the North Sea became a very important area as a source of oil.

North Sea Canal (Dutch *Noord Zee Kanaal*), Netherlands, completed in 1876, links Amsterdam with the North Sea. It is one of the largest artificial inland waterways in the world, 24 km long, 100 m wide and 12 m deep, lying at 10 m above sea-level.

North Sea Oil and Gas. The discoveries of natural gas and then oil in the North Sea since the mid 1960s have made the United Kingdom and some other European countries almost self-sufficient in their energy needs. The discovery in 1959 of the Slochteren gas-fields in the Netherlands established the probability of similar deposits under the North Sea. British Petroleum discovered the first offshore gas-field, West Sole, in 1965, but the oil companies had to wait until 1969 for the discovery by Phillips of the first major oil-field, the Ekofisk, in Norwegian waters.

North Sea gas was first brought ashore (from West Sole to the Easington terminal in North Humberside) in 1967. The first commercial quantities of North Sea oil were landed by tanker in 1972 from the Dan field in Danish water. Oil flowed from the UK sector in 1975. By 1982 there were approximately 900 oil-wells in the 20 fields of the UK sector with recoverable reserves estimated at 12 billion barrels. They employed roughly 58,000 people and produced 13,772,800 barrels of crude (1 barrel = 7·2 metric tonnes). This represents an income to the UK Government of £6·4 billion. Of the remaining fields in the UK sector, six were producing gas and seven were still under development. The UK became a net exporter of crude oil in 1981. Denmark produced 12·3 million barrels from three fields in 1982; their first gas field is to come on stream in 1984. Germany relaunched its offshore exploration programme, though reserves of gas and oil are likely to be low. The Netherlands, whose reserves are mostly gas, pumped their first crude ashore in 1982. Norway, which has three gas-fields, produced 200 million barrels from its 10 oil-fields and may have reserves of 2 billion barrels.

North-West Frontier, area of the Indian subcontinent, one of the great frontiers of the former British Empire. It is nearly 3200 km long, stretching from Karakoram Mountains in the north of Kashmir to the Arabian Sea. In the far north it is bordered by China. Further west it adjoins Turkestan along the Pamirs and then turns south through the

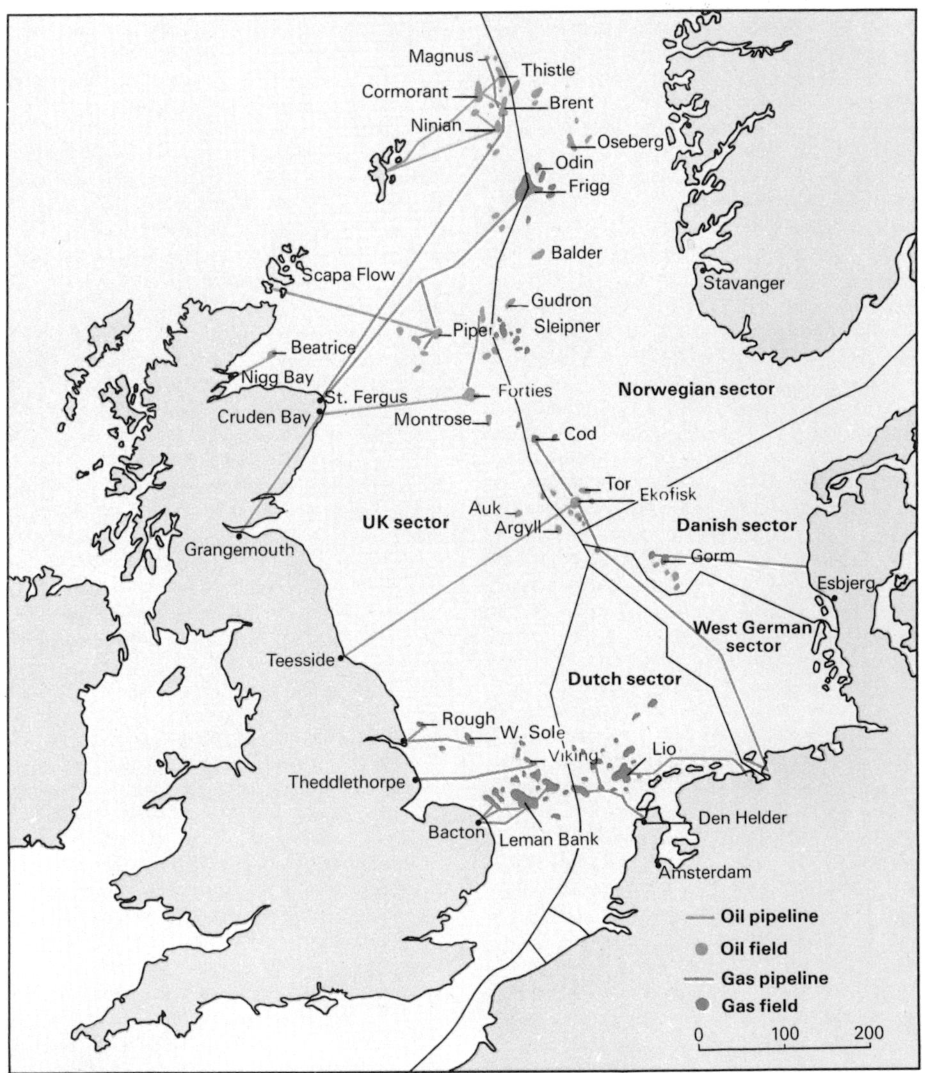

North Sea Oil and Gas. *The sea-bed is divided into national territories, with Britain and Norway controlling most of the fields. Oil was first produced in commercial quantities in 1972.*

mountain hinterland of the Afghan border tribes. From Chitral to Baluchistan, the boundary follows the 'Durand Line', as agreed with the Afghan government in 1894. Throughout its length the frontier traverses Muslim territory, much of which is still occupied by warlike tribesmen.

In 1849 the North-West Frontier areas were annexed by the British, and formed part of the Punjab until the North-West Frontier Province, administered from Peshawar, was created in 1901. The greater part of the British army in India was concentrated on the frontier or in cantonments in the Punjab. In 1947, on partition, the province became part of Pakistan.

See also AFGHANISTAN, *History*; INDIAN HISTORY; PAKISTAN, *History*.

North West Mounted Police, see ROYAL CANADIAN MOUNTED POLICE.

North-West Territories, territory of Canada, comprising the mainland north of 60°N, bounded by Yukon Territory in the west and Hudson Bayin the east, and the islands between the Canadian mainland and the North Pole, including those in Hudson Bay, James Bay and Hudson Strait. Area 3,379,683 km².

In the western part is the great river system of the Mackenzie and Great Bear Lake and Great Slave Lake. Geologically the territory is dominated by the Laurentian Shield which occupies all but the western districts where the sedimentary rocks of the continental interior reach north to the Arctic Ocean. Only between June and September do temperatures rise above freezing, and throughout the year the soil is permanently frozen to great depths. The northernmost part of the mainland and the islands are devoid of trees, being covered by grass and scrub (tundra) on which vast herds of caribou graze. Agriculture is limited to a few places near settlements where market gardening, root crops, cattle and dairy cows are kept. Most foodstuffs have to be imported.

The fur trade and mining are the chief industries. The most valuable fur is white fox; others trapped are beaver, mink, lynx and red fox. Gold and silver are among the minerals mined on the northern shore of Great Slave Lake and another rich gold-bearing area has been found near Contwoyto Lake. Uranium concentrates and radium are produced from pitchblende ore at the Eldorado mine on Great Bear Lake. To encourage the development of the North-West Territories, the Mackenzie Highway was built between Grimshaw, Alberta, and Hay River on Great Slave Lake, with an extension to Yellowknife. The main settlements are Fort Laird, Yellowknife, Norman Wells, Port Radium and Fort McPherson. The total population in 1980 was 46,386, of whom about two-thirds are Indians and Eskimos.

North Yorkshire, see YORKSHIRE, NORTH.

Northallerton, market town in North Yorkshire, England, the administrative centre for North Yorkshire county, and the site of a Brigantian and Roman fort. Leather goods and engineering products are made. Population (1981) 9622.

Northampton, county and market town in Northamptonshire, England, on rising ground on the left bank of the River Nene, 108 km north-west of London. The 12th-century church of the Holy Sepulchre incorporates one of the very few round churches in the country. Boot- and shoe-making is the staple industry; other industries include leather-trimming and the manufacture of leather goods, shoe machinery, ladies' clothing, electric lifts, fire grates, motor-car accessories and models; also motor-body building, engineering, printing and brewing. Northampton was designated a New Town and has undergone much expansion. Population (1981) 145,421.

Northamptonshire, midland county of England, originally included in the Mercian kingdom, and part of Tostig's earldom in the 11th century.

The surface is mainly level or broken with low hills, and the scenery is beautiful and well wooded. The principal rivers are the Avon, Nene, Welland, Cherwell, Leam and Ouse. The Grand Union Canal crosses the county. Ironstone in large quantities, limestone and clay are worked, and a particular kind of building stone known as Weldon stone. The mild climate, level surface and rich soil are admirable for agriculture. Farming of all kinds flourishes, wheat and barley being the principal crops, while cattle and sheep are reared extensively. Apart from agriculture the main industries are ironstone quarrying, light engineering, and the manufacture of footwear, Northampton being the centre of the English leather trade. Area 2370 km²; population (1981) 527,532.

Northcliffe of St Peter in Thanet, Alfred Charles William Harmsworth, 1st Viscount (1865–1922), British newspaper proprietor. After founding a successful weekly in 1888, with the aid of his brother Harold Sidney, later Lord Rothermere, Harmsworth bought the London *Evening News* in 1894 and in 1896 began the *Daily Mail*, a revolution in journalism from its inception, with ideas of make-up and presentation of news items which were widely copied by its rivals. In 1908 he became proprietor of *The Times*, retaining the controlling interest until his death. Northcliffe was made a viscount in 1917 and during the First World War he was made director of propaganda to enemy countries. He was a great journalist whose prime aim was to humanise and extend the scope of the daily newspaper; he was the first to see that women could be interested in a newspaper.

See also JOURNALISM; NEWSPAPERS.

Northern Ireland, see IRELAND, NORTHERN; ULSTER.

Northern Lights, see AURORA.

Northern Rhodesia, see ZAMBIA.

Northern Sea Route, system of shipping lanes traversing the coastal waters north of Siberia from the Bering Strait in the east to the straits between the Barents Sea and the Kara Sea in the west. Because of ice, the route is navigable for only two-four months during July–October.

Northern Territory, a territory of the Commonwealth of Australia, lying north-west of Western Australia, north of South Australia, and west of Queensland. It is not a state and is administered by the Commonwealth government. Its total area is 1,346,200 km². The chief islands off the coast are Melville, Bathurst, Croker, Groote Eylandt and Wessel.

The low, flat coastline of 1675 km seldom reaches a height of 30 m and has sandy beaches and mud flats, thickly fringed with mangroves. Inland there is a general rise southwards to the 18th parallel of latitude, where higher land forms the watershed between the rivers flowing northwards to the sea, and those forming the interior systems. Towards the centre of the continent the land is higher and there are several mountain ranges, generally with an east-west trend. The main one is the Macdonnell Range, which reaches 1525 m.

The area is sparsely populated. In 1979 the total population was 108,700, of whom 50,612 lived in Darwin, the capital, and 16,500 in Alice Springs. The Aborigine population was about 86,000.

Transport difficulties and the great distance from markets have prevented economic development. Much of the interior is desert and the rigorous climate has hindered agricultural development. Sorghum is the main crop but peanuts, pineapples and bananas are also grown. Stock-raising has long been the mainstay of the economy. Main beef cattle areas are the Alice Springs, Barkly Tablelands, and the Victoria river districts.

The Northern Territory is rich in mineral resources and mining is the second most important industry. The biggest export-earner is bauxite from Gove. Uranium is also important, and there are significant deposits at Rum Jungle, Jim Jim, and Nabarlek. Gold and copper are mined at Tennant Creek and Warrego; silver, lead and zinc at McArthur river; and manganese on Groote Eylandt. There are considerable deposits of oil and natural gas at Palm Valley and Meerenie.

An administrator, appointed by the governor-general, with nine appointed and eight elected members, constitute the Legislative Assembly.

History. The coast was surveyed in 1818 and in 1838 and 1839. Port Darwin was charted in the latter year. Early settlements at Port Essington, Fort Dumas and Raffles Bay came to nothing, but Darwin's future was assured when it was selected as the terminal for the submarine cable from Java.

The South Australian government, yielding to popular sentiment, abandoned the project of developing the Territory by non-Europeans. This restrictive policy foreshadowed the so-called White Australia policy.

Northmen, see VIKINGS.

Northrop, John Howard (1891–), US biochemist and biologist; he worked at the Rockefeller Institute for Medical Research, Princeton, New Jersey. Northrop shared the Nobel prize in 1946 for his work on enzymes, having been the first biochemist to crystallise an enzyme (urease).

Northstead, Manor of, see CHILTERN HUNDREDS.

Northumberland, Dukes and Earls of. Since the time of the Norman Conquest there has been an earl of Northumberland, but the title did not become hereditary until 1377, when Henry, Baron Percy, became earl. Except for a period of forfeiture, the title of earl remained in the Percy family until the death of the 11th Earl in 1670; his daughter married Charles Seymour, Duke of Somerset, and their son Algernon, 7th Duke of Somerset, became earl of Northumberland in 1749. He died without male issue and his son-in-law, Sir Hugh Smithson, became earl and took the name of Percy: in 1766 he was created duke of Northumberland.

Northumberland, John Dudley, Duke of (c.1502–53), English politician and soldier. He was already powerful when Henry VIII died and soon became the real power behind Edward VI. In 1551 he was created duke of Northumberland, and in 1553 he married his son to Lady Jane Grey, hoping thereby to retain his authority after Edward's death. He was primarily responsible for the attempt to make Jane queen of England, and after Mary's accession was executed for treason.

Northumberland, English county, covering an area of 5034 km^2, extending from Tyneside to the Scottish border. The greater part is rural and thinly populated. The Cheviot Hills, along the Anglo-Scottish border, rise to 810 m. They are succeeded to the south and east by the dales of the Till, upper Aln, upper Coquet, Rede and Tyne rivers. Further east lie uplands at a height of 250–450 m above sea-level. There are extensive forests in the west and much upland is used by the army. The remainder provides pasture for sheep and cattle supported by winter fodder from the valleys. The coastal plateau north of the Coquet is characterised by arable agriculture and large farms. South of the Coquet, coal measures underlie the coastal plateau. Coal once supported numerous mining villages but the 180,000 people living in these districts now depend on a variety of manufacturing industries and on employment on Tyneside. Tourist attractions include the remains of Hadrian's Wall, numerous medieval and restored castles, Hexham Abbey, Lindisfarne priory, and the walls of Berwick-upon-Tweed. The Northumberland National Park occupies 1490 km^2 in the west of Northumberland. The Farne Isles, 8 km east of Bamburgh, maintain large seal and bird colonies. Population (1981) 299,905.

Northumberland Strait, in Canada, separates Prince Edward Island from Nova Scotia and New Brunswick. Length 210 km, width 15–50 km.

Northumbria, one of the greatest Anglo-Saxon kingdoms of England, situated between the Humber and the Forth, originally consisted of two independent kingdoms, Bernicia and Deira. In 827 Eanred, king of Northumbria, formally acknowledged the supremacy of Egbert of Wessex. From 876 to 954 Northumbria was largely controlled by the Danes, and subject to increasing Scandinavian immigration. After the battle of Stainmore (954) the permanent separation of Northumbria from the rest of the English kingdom ended.

Northumbria was for a considerable period the chief seat in England of literary and missionary activity, and of Christian art. In the Golden Age of the Conversion, Cuthbert flourished in his monastery at Lindisfarne, Bede at Wearmouth and Jarrow, and St Wilfrid at Hexham and Ripon. In 731 Bede at Jarrow wrote his famous *Ecclesiastical History*.

Northwich, one of the Cheshire salt towns, on the River Weaver, 30 km south-west of Manchester, England. There is a fine 16th-century church, but the town has suffered severely from subsidence caused by brine pumping. This is now controlled and the chemical industry is prominent in the town, with also some engineering works. The 1981 population was 17,126.

Norway
Area: 323,895 km^2
Population: 4,078,900
Capital: Oslo

Norway (Norwegian *Norge*), Scandinavian kingdom occupying the western and northern part of the Scandinavian peninsula. It is surrounded on three sides by the sea, on the south by the Skagerrak, on the west by the North Sea and Atlantic Ocean, and on the north by the Barents Sea. By the treaty of 1920 Norway was given sovereignty over Spitsbergen archipelago; including the outlying islands, Norway's area is 323,895 km^2. Norway has a frontier with Sweden of 1650 km, with Finland of 725 km, and with the USSR of 196 km.

The country is a high plateau, intersected in the south-east by great valleys and in the west by deep fjords and bays. More than half its surface is over 600 m high. The *skjaergård* is the island zone of striated rock with little vegetation. The outer islands are low-lying, but towards the mainland they are higher. The fjords have all the characteristics of glaciated valleys, being long, narrow, and straight, with uneven floors. Gorges extend inland above the level of the fjords, with torrents flowing down from the high uplands. The plateaus are the upland surface above the gorges and rise steeply from the west coast towards the main watershed of Norway; they are more extensive in the south. Heavy snowfall produces ice caps and glaciers. The Jostedalsbreen is the largest permanent snowfield in continental Europe.

The estimated population in 1980 was 4,078,900. The interior is generally so mountainous that the population is settled almost entirely along the coast. With the exception of some 20,000 Lapps, living in the most remote northern regions, the inhabitants of Norway are generally a Scandinavian race, akin to the Germanic nations. The chief towns are Oslo (the capital), Bergen, Trondheim and Stavanger.

Encouraged by the harshness of the land and the enormous length of the coastline, fishing remains an important occupation, still mainly pursued from small boats. Cod, herring, mackerel and salmon are caught. Less than 3 per cent of the land surface is cultivated, and farming is supported by government subsidies. The majority of farms are so small that a second income is necessary, usually forestry. Mineral resources, forests, and water power have provided the basis of a strong economy, notable for pulp and paper and other wood products, food processing, and aluminium and other metal products. Shipbuilding and electro-technical engineering are also important. Engineering is the largest single industrial employer. Because of the abundant hydro-electric power available, many electrometallurgical plants have been set up. A new

Norway. *The steep mountain sides and deep water of Geiranger Fjord, near Ålesund.*

growth industry is the building of oil rigs and oil supply industry equipment for the North Sea.

In Norwegian currency 100 *øre* = 1 *krone.*

The constitution of Norway is dated 17 May 1814, but has been modified since that date. It vests the legislative power in the *Storting* (Parliament), which is divided into an upper and lower house. The royal veto in regard to Acts may be exercised twice, but a Bill which passes three separate *Stortings* becomes law without royal assent. A system of proportional representation is used, with multi-member constituencies.

The national language is Norwegian.

History. The Viking period ended in the 11th century with the conversion of Norway to Christianity. Olaf II (c.1015–30) came to be regarded as Norway's first great national champion, establishing both the royal power and the Christian Church on a national basis in opposition to the claims of the local chieftains. Magnus Eriksson, hereditary king of Norway, was elected king of Sweden in 1319 so that the two kingdoms became nominally united. From that time until the 20th century the history of Norway is dependent on that of other parts of Scandinavia. In 1397, by the Union of Kalmar, all Scandinavia was declared to be 'eternally united under one sovereign'. The Danish hegemony in this union led to frequent conflicts between the Swedish and Danish nobility, while Norwegian interests were largely neglected. In the Napoleonic wars, Norway suffered from Denmark's support of Napoleon and the consequent British blockade of the country. In 1814 the two thrones of Norway and Sweden were united with Bernadotte as king. The union was never successful and in 1905 was dissolved. Norway voted for a monarchy rather than a republic and chose Prince Charles, second son of the Crown Prince of Denmark, as king. He was crowned King Haakon VII in 1906. In 1942, despite Norway's neutrality, the Germans invaded and appointed Quisling as 'minister president' of a puppet government. After the liberation in 1945 Quisling and his colleagues were executed. King Olaf V succeeded Haakon VII in 1957. Norway is a member of the North Atlantic Treaty Organisation and in 1959 joined the European Free Trade Association. In 1972 a referendum decided that Norway should not join the European Economic Community.

Language. From the late Middle Ages until the early 19th century, Danish was the official written language of Norway. In Norway today there are two official language variants, *landsmål* or *nynorsk* (New Norwegian), and *bokmål. Bokmål* is a development of the Dano-Norwegian spoken in Norway under Danish rule. *Nynorsk* owes its formation primarily to the work of the poet and linguist Ivar Aasen, whose *Det norske Folkesprogs Grammatik*, 1848, collated the various Norwegian dialects in an attempt to create a language with its roots in the native tradition. The two languages share many of the same forms, although there are differences of both grammar and vocabulary. There is a flourishing literature in both languages, and both are taught in schools and used in the civil service.

Literature. The literature of Norway cannot be considered in isolation from that of other Scandinavian countries, particularly Iceland and Denmark. Specifically Norwegian literature has its earliest origins in medieval oral tradition. It was not until the 17th century that a creative writer of any stature emerged, in the poet Petter Dass, followed in the 18th century by the dramatist Ludvig Holberg, and before the achievement of Norwegian independence from Denmark in 1814, Norwegian culture was largely overshadowed by Danish. The most important event in 19th-century literature was the national revival. Perhaps the most significant work was completed by the linguist and vernacular poet Ivar Aasen, founder of the *landsmål* movement. Of the next period the great names are Henrik Ibsen and Bjørnstjerne Bjørnson, whose reputation and influence were worldwide. Less internationally known, but of central importance in the development of the Norwegian novel, are Alexander Kielland and Jonas Lie. The age of 'the four greats', Ibsen, Bjørnson, Kielland, and Lie, was perhaps the 'Golden Age' of Norwegian literature, though the 1890s saw the flowering of a different kind of genius; a neo-romantic decade of poetic imagination and self-confessed subjectivity. From this period rose the most dominating modern figure in Norwegian literature, Knut Hamsun.

In the 20th century, the novel has been the dominant literary form. In recent years, there has been a trend towards the documentary novel in the works of experimental writers such as Jens Bjørneboe (1920–76) and Dag Solstad (1941–). In modern Norwegian poetry, an outstanding figure is Arnulf Øverland, whose fastidious sense of words is complemented by a strong passion for social justice; he was one of the earliest opponents of nazism. The most conspicuous of modern Norwegian dramatists was the aristocratic individualist Gunnar Heiberg (1857–1929), whose *Balkonen*, 1894 (*The Balcony*, 1922), and *Kjærlighetens Tragedie*, 1904 (*The Tragedy of Love*, 1921), are considered Norwegian classics.

See also SCANDINAVIAN ARCHITECTURE; SCANDINAVIAN LANGUAGE; SCANDINAVIAN MUSIC.

Norwich, city and county town of Norfolk, England, 32 km from the coast, in the valley of the Wensum, about 185 km north-east of London. The Norman castle is attributed to William Fitz-Osbern (c.1120). Norwich Cathedral dates from the 11th century. There are over 30 city churches, mostly built of flint in late Decorated or Perpendicular style. The art galleries contain the finest collection in the country of the works of John Crome, John Sell Cotman, and other artists of the Norwich School of landscape painting.

The traditional industry of Norwich is shoe manufacturing, specialising in good-quality shoes for women and children. Other large industries include those of mustard, starch, cereals, confectionery, electrical and structural engineering, printing, insurance, brewing, silk and silk dyeing. For centuries Norwich has been the leading market town in East Anglia, with large cattle, provision and fish markets. Population (1981) 122,270.

Norwich School, painters belonging to the Norwich Society of Artists founded in 1803 by John Crome and Robert Ladbrooke. It included professional painters, drawing masters and amateurs, and was unique in being the only regional school of painting in England with an autonomy comparable to that of the great Italian local schools. It was partly inspired by Crome and partly by J. S. Cotman who joined in 1807. Their followers included John Berney Crome, George Vincent, James Stark, Joseph and Alfred Stannard, John Thirtle, Thomas Lound, Henry Ninham and S. D. Colkett. The East Anglian heath and woodland, the river Yare, and Norfolk coast provided many of their subjects and their style owes much to the Dutch 17th-century painters such as Cuyp, Ruisdael and Hobbema. The school flourished in the first half of the 19th century.

Nose, the organ of smell, which also warms and moistens the air we breathe. The supporting framework of the external nose consists of a bony part and five main cartilages. The bridge of the nose is formed by the nasal bone and the frontal processes of the maxilla (upper jaw). The orifices or nostrils are guarded by small hairs which protect the nasal cavities from particles of dust or small insects. Above the aperture in each nostril is a slightly expanded cavity, the vestibule. Above the vestibule the nasal passage is divided into two parts, the upper or olfactory, and the lower or respiratory portion.

The olfactory region is lined with mucous membrane, yellowish in colour, with olfactory glands embedded in it. The stimulation of our sense of smell is not well understood. To have an odour a substance must be volatile, that is, it must release molecules into the air that we breathe. Furthermore these molecules must be soluble in the mucus covering the olfactory area, in order to excite the olfactory cells. The perception of odour is not so delicately differentiated in man as in some of the lower animals.

The commonest nasal disorder is rhinitis, involving inflammation of the mucous membrane; its acute form is coryza or a cold in the head. Rhinitis is an allergic manifestation in some cases, the allergens being certain dusts or pollens, as in hay fever.

See also NOSEBLEED.

Nosebleed. The causes may be local or general. A blow is the commonest local cause, while internal damage may occur from the introduction of a foreign body. Congestion of the very vascular nasal mucous membrane, as in a cold, is a frequent cause of minor nosebleeds. Among general causes, hypertension in the elderly is the most usual. Repeated attacks may be a sign of serious blood disorder or of any condition in which the normal blood clotting mechanism is interfered with. As a first-aid measure it may be stopped by placing steady pressure on the affected side of the nose for about 15 minutes. Any clot formation should not be disturbed by blowing or sniffing.

Nossi-Bé, volcanic island 13 km from the north coast of Madagascar, 22 km long by 16 km broad. There are numerous craters and crater lakes, and forests. Its chief products are sugar, oils for perfume, rum, vanilla, black pepper and bitter oranges. Area 300 km^2; population 26,000.

Nostradamus, or Michel de (Nostredame) Notredame (1503–66), famous French astrologer and physician. For many years he practised as a physician, and gained a high reputation for his skill in stemming the tide of the great plagues. Catherine de Médicis brought him to her court, and he was consulted by Henry II and Charles IX. His *Centuries*, prophecies in rhymed quatrains, was published in 1555 and received great acclaim. Written in symbolical language, it can be interpreted as having foretold with uncanny precision a number of historic events up to the present time, including the French Revolution and the rise and fall of Napoleon and Hitler.

Not Proven, in Scots criminal law is the third verdict, apart from guilty and not guilty, which the jury may return. It enables the trial to be re-opened in certain circumstances.

Notables, The, advisory assemblies of notable personages summoned by the kings of France in times of stress. These assemblies had no constitutional authority and their transactions were of a purely private and confidential nature. The best known was that convoked by Louis XVI in 1787 in order that the privileged classes might be consulted on a more equitable system of tax collecting.

Notary Public. The English notary's chief duties are to note bills of exchange, to authenticate copies of private documents and deeds, to attest instruments such as powers of attorney about to be sent abroad, to receive affidavits of mariners, and administer oaths. The powers of a notary public in the USA are wider; he may take depositions relating to the recording of testimony, and take proofs of debts in bankruptcy.

Notation, in music, the art of representing musical sounds and their modifications by notes, signs, etc. Between 990 and 1050 notation was much improved by Guido d'Arezzo. Pitch is expressed by the positions of notes and the presence of clefs on sets of five lines, called 'staves'. Duration is defined by variously shaped notes. Key and metre are indicated by signatures. In recent years composers have experimented with new forms of notation.

Nothofagus, a genus of about 35 species of deciduous and evergreen trees of the same family (Fagaceae) as beech. They are native to the Antipodes and South America. *N. obliqua*, Roblé beech, *N. procera* and *N. cunninghamii* are valuable timber trees.

Notochord, the supporting rod of closely packed cells characteristic of those animals that comprise the phylum Chordata. The notochord runs lengthwise from the anterior to the posterior end, and is situated immediately ventral to the spinal cord. See also CHORDATA.

Nôtre, André Le, see LE NÔTRE, ANDRÉ.

Notre-Dame de Paris. The first stone of the cathedral was laid in 1163, on the site of an ancient Merovingian cathedral. The general structure was completed in 1245. After undergoing many depredations in the 18th century, Notre-Dame was restored by Viollet-le-Duc in 1845–64. It is a magnificent example of the first two periods of Gothic, the west front and the transepts all having great rose windows.

Nottingham, city and county town of Nottinghamshire, England, on the River Trent, 200 km north-west of London, an important rail centre. The River Trent is navigable to the sea, and gives access to Newark, Gainsborough and the Humber ports. Nottingham Castle, originally built on Castle Rock by William the Conqueror, was dismantled during the Protectorate and restored in 1878.

The principal industries include the manufacture of lace, hosiery, chemicals, mechanical products, tobacco and cycles, as well as general engineering works. Other important industries are bleaching, dyeing, spinning, tanning, brewing, coal-mining, and furniture. Population (1981) 271,080.

Nottinghamshire, midland county of England bounded on the west by Derbyshire, the south by Leicestershire, the east and north-east by Lincolnshire, and the north by Humberside and South Yorkshire. The county forms part of the extensive lowland to the east of the southern Pennines, the greater part being between 30 and 120 m above sea-level. Only in the west, around Mansfield, is there hilly country reaching an elevation of 180 m. Sherwood Forest, famous for its connection with Robin Hood, is now included in the parks that form what is known as the Dukeries. The principal river is the Trent. On the west there are extensive coal-mines. Gravel and gypsum are extracted, and sandstone, limestone and clay are worked. The principal manufactures are lace, hosiery and other textiles, pharmaceutical products, tobacco, telecommunication equipment, and cycles; and there are iron foundries and engineering works. The greater part of the county is under cultivation, the east being predominantly agricultural. Arable farming is the principal activity, the main crops being barley, wheat, sugar beet and potatoes. Area 218,533 ha; population (1981) 982,631.

Nouakchott, capital of Mauritania in West Africa. It is a new settlement, as the country was administered before independence from St Louis in Senegal. Lying within an arid environment, near the coast, it has only a small economic base, but its population had reached an estimated 134,986 by 1976.

Nouméa, or Numea, also called Port-de-France, capital of the French overseas territory of New Caledonia, exports nickel, chrome and copra. Population (1976) 74,335.

Noun, part of speech which includes all words used as names. It covers common nouns (names of concrete objects), proper nouns (specific names of people, places, etc.), and abstract nouns (names of abstract qualities such as truth, beauty, misery, etc.).

Nouvelle Vague, or 'new wave', term used to describe the work of Chabrol, Godard, Truffaut, Resnais, and other French directors, prominent since the late 1950s, who rejected the 'literary' style of the classic French film. They admired the classic Hollywood cinema, particularly 'B' movies of the gangster genre, but disdained their coherent narrative flow, seeking instead a vital spontaneity, which brought rich aesthetic rewards.

See also CINEMA.

Nova Lisboa, see HUAMBO.

Nova Scotia, province of Canada, consisting of Nova Scotia proper (a peninsula extending east from New Brunswick) and Cape Breton Island at its north-eastern end. The two parts are linked by a causeway across Canso Strait. The peninsula is 450 km long; its combined length with Cape Breton Island is 560 km. Area (province) 55,000 km², of which 52,840 km² are water surface. The south-west to north-east trend of the peninsula follows the prevailing direction of the northern Appalachian Mountain system. The Nova Scotia highlands rise from around 300 m in the south to 400 m in the north.

The population was 853,100 in 1980. The capital is Halifax; other main towns are Dartmouth, Sydney, Glace Bay and Truro.

Fishing has always been of great importance in the economy of Nova Scotia. Fish processing plants, over 100, have been established around the coast. Cod has traditionally been the main catch and makes up the bulk of the fish which goes to the Canadian and United States markets. The herring fishery has expanded rapidly since 1963.

Forests cover 72 per cent of the land area and pulp and paper production is now the main industry, with six mills at Pictou, Lunenburg, Port Hawkesbury and Liverpool.

About 14 per cent of the province is farmland. The main areas are around the Bay of Fundy. Fruit and vegetables have increased in importance with the advent of modern food-processing techniques. Grass thrives in the cool damp climate, which accounts for the importance of dairy and beef cattle.

The provincial output of coal is around 2,400,000 t. Other minerals include the world's largest single deposit of barite at Windsor; gypsum is also mined at Windsor; salt in Cumberland county at Port Hawkesbury; and lead and zinc in the valley of the Salmon river and at Meat Cove. Most industrial development is concentrated in the urban complexes of Halifax/Dartmouth—shipbuilding, oil refining, transport, cars, electronics, clothing, engineering and plastics; and Sydney/Glace Bay—coal-mining, iron and steel, metal fabricating, machinery, and a car tyre plant.

The legislature consists of a lieutenant-governor and a House of Assembly of 46 members, elected by popular vote for five-year terms.

In 1605 French colonists settled at Port Royal. The old name of the colony, Acadia, was changed in 1621 to Nova Scotia by Sir William Alexander. In 1867 the province entered the dominion of Canada.

Novae, stars which appear suddenly, remain bright for a few days, and then fade away. Such stars are not new but faint stars suffering an outburst of radiation which for a short while makes them shine with an absolute magnitude in the range -6 to -10, that is at least 100,000 times more brightly than the Sun.

Such stars are not uncommon; but it is only about once in ten years that one is sufficiently close to us to become a conspicuous naked-eye object. The star blows off its outer shell with velocities of ejection of the order of 1000 km/s. The growing shell initially behaves like the photosphere of a super-giant star, and pours out rapidly increasing amounts of white light. As the expansion continues it grows more diffuse; the continuous spectrum fades, leaving mainly monochromatic radiations which decay slowly.

It has been hypothesized that the stars subject to a nova outburst are close binaries that have evolved so far that the initially larger member has become a white dwarf while the other is in its red giant phase. As the outer layers of this latter swell out beyond the Lagrangian surface some of the material is attracted to the white dwarf where the surface gravity is so high that the extra matter produces proton-proton reactions in the hydrogen. The energy thus suddenly released ejects the surface layer into space so that the remainder can relapse to its former white-dwarf state. Similar phenomena, *supernovae*, may be as much as 10,000 times brighter than ordinary novae. Their light may equal or exceed the total light of all other stars in a galaxy. They are thought to be massive stars in the last stages of evolution.

See also ASTRONOMY; PULSARS; RADIO ASTRONOMY; STAR.

Novalis, pseudonym of Friedrich von Hardenberg (1772–1801), German poet and philosopher. He fell in love with Sophie von Kühn who was then 15. The death of Sophie, and of his brother Erasmus, both in 1797, was a severe shock. The tragedy aroused in Novalis a poetic and mystic strength. Feeling himself ecstatically united with his dead beloved, he tried to free the spirit from material things, and many of his poems contain a note of mysticism. Novalis is now considered one of the most important of the early Romantics.

Novara (ancient *Novaria*), Italian city, capital of Novara province in Lombardy, situated some 45 km west of Milan. Buildings of note include the ruined Sforza castle. Novara lies between the Piedmont and Lombardy plains. It processes rice from the surrounding plain, and flour and cheese, and has textile, precision engineering and chemical plants. Population (1979) 101,947.

Novaya Zemlya, or New Land, archipelago in the Arctic Ocean between the Barents and Kara Seas; administratively in the Arkhangelsk *oblast* of the USSR. It is a continuation northwards of the Urals and is divided into two large and numerous small islands by the narrow strait of Matochkin Shar. The islands extend 925 km from north to south and have a total area of over 83,000 km².

Novel, a literary form, which may be said to consist typically of a long prose story—though it is best to differentiate it from prose fiction as a whole by criteria involving complexity of art. The novel, as it is now known, is only about 200 years old. Fiction in prose goes back about 2000 years. The term 'novel' was originally used to mean a fresh, new story, but later it was applied more loosely to denote any story in prose (as opposed to a story in verse).

The novel's first major period of development came during the late Italian Renaissance, when the stimulus of foreign travel, increased wealth, and changing social patterns produced a greater interest in the events of everyday life, as opposed to religious teaching, legends of the past, or fictional fantasy. With the growth of literacy, the novel rapidly developed from the 18th century to become, in the 20th century, the major literary form.

Novella, an Italian word used in English for a short novel, probably less than 20,000 words, which exhibits most of the characteristics of the novel. A novella is a work of fiction more complex than a long short-story, but not of novel stature. The form originated in Italian Renaissance fiction (for example, Boccaccio's *Decameron* is a collection of *novella*) and it came to stand for one characteristic in particular, that of roundedness of plot, whereby the reader feels satisfaction in the conclusion of the story.

Novello, Clara, see NOVELLO, VINCENT.

Novello, Ivor (David Ivor Davies, 1893–1951), British songwriter, son of the music teacher Clara Novello Davies (1861–1943). His song *Keep the Home Fires Burning* was very popular during the First World War. He composed for musical plays and revues, wrote plays, and had a long run of successes with his musical comedies *Glamorous Night*, *Careless Rapture*, *Crest of the Wave*, *The Dancing Years*, *Perchance to Dream* and *King's Rhapsody*.

Novello, Vincent (1781–1861), English composer, organist and publisher. Besides composing church music, he edited many collections, including Purcell's sacred music. These he published, laying the foundations for the publishing firm of Novello, properly started by his son, Joseph Alfred (1810–96). His daughter Clara Novello (1818–1908) was regarded as the greatest English soprano of her day.

November, the 11th month of the modern

calendar year. The name reflects its former position of ninth month in the ancient Roman calendar.

Novgorod, capital of Novgorod *oblast*, USSR, one of the oldest Russian cities and an ancient centre of Russian culture. It is situated on the River Volkhov, 6 km from Lake Ilmen on the main Moscow–Leningrad highway, and has electrical engineering, chemical and food industries. It is a treasury of Russian architecture of the 11th–19th centuries, including many fine churches of the Novgorod School (12th–16th centuries) with a number of well-preserved frescoes and icons. The city has been known since the 9th century. The main centre of foreign trade, it obtained self-government from Yaroslav the Wise in 997, and achieved independence in 1136. Captured and annexed by Ivan III of Muscovy in 1478, it retained its commercial position until the construction of St Petersburg. Population (1980) 192,000.

Novi Sad (German *Neusatz*), town in Serbia, Yugoslavia, capital of the autonomous province of Vojvodina, situated on the left bank of the River Danube. It has long been a centre of Serbian culture, but is today a busy river port and an industrial and commercial centre. Population (1971) 213,861.

Novice, person who, after a period of probation as a postulant, is admitted to a religious order to be trained, usually for one year, in the religious life, with a view to becoming a professed member of the order.

Novokuznetsk, or Kuznetsk Sibirski (formerly Stalinsk), city in the Kemerovo *oblast* of the RSFSR, USSR, in South Siberia on the South Siberian railway, chief industrial centre of the Kuznetsk Basin. There is an iron and steel plant, the Kuznetsk Metallurgical Complex (first production in 1932), one of the largest in the USSR, based on iron ore from nearby Shoria and from Magnitogorsk in the Urals, and on local coking coal; there are also ferro-alloy and aluminium plants, chemical, light and food industries, and a big hydroelectric power station. Population (1980) 545,000.

Novosibirsk (formerly *Novonikolayevsk*), capital city, economic and cultural centre of Novosibirsk *oblast*, RSFSR, USSR, on the River Ob and the Trans-Siberian Railway, the largest city in Siberia. It has large engineering and varied light and food industries, and is a transport centre. A branch of the USSR Academy of Sciences was set up in 1933; in 1956 it became the Siberian division of the Academy and all branches in Siberia and the Far East are subordinated to it. Novosibirsk was founded in 1833 when a railway bridge was constructed there over the Ob. Population (1980) 1,328,000.

Novotný, Antonin (1904–75), Czech president, a founder member of the Czech Communist party in 1921. He worked in the underground movement during the German occupation of Czechoslovakia, and was imprisoned in concentration camps from 1941 to 1945. Novotný became president of Czechoslovakia in 1957: in 1967 his resistance to reform resulted in his resignation.

Noyes, Alfred (1880–1958), English poet. Encouraged by George Meredith, he devoted himself to poetry. His first volume, *The Loom of Years*, 1902, was followed by his popular sea epic, *Drake*, 1906–08. In 1913 he delivered the Lowell lectures in the United States on 'The Sea in English Poetry', and was professor of modern English literature at Princeton, 1914–23. Later he settled in the Isle of Wight, and in 1930 he became a Roman Catholic. He is best known for his sea verse and fairy stories.

Nozzle, a shaped exit to a duct or volume through which a fluid flows under pressure and emerges as a high-velocity jet. Nozzles are used in many applications for producing high-speed jets including steam turbines, rocket motors and the ordinary garden hose. The entry to the nozzle is usually convergent, which accelerates subsonic flow. The velocity may reach the speed of sound at the section of minimum area. A divergent portion downstream then accelerates the flow.

Nu, U (1907–), Burmese politician. Nu became the first prime minister of the Burmese Republic, 1948–56, and served further periods as prime minister, 1957–58, and 1960–62. After the coming to power of the Ne Win government U Nu spent some years in custody (1962–66) and then went to live in exile.
See also BURMA, *History*.

Nuba, Negro agriculturalists of the Sudanese Nuba Hills living in culturally and linguistically heterogeneous, autonomous groups. Noted for their body painting, they have resisted the often violent attempts of their surrounding Arab neighbours to impose control, but now Islam is penetrating and today many Nuba speak Arabic.

Nubia, tract of country, with no precise limit, in north-east Africa, anciently known as Ethiopia to the Greeks and as Kush to the Pharaohs and, broadly, lying between Egypt and the Gezira area. The principal tribes are the Djowabere and El Gharbye, who extend from Aswān to the Wadi Halfa.
The part of Nubia between Aswān and Wadi Halfa is called Lower Nubia and is under Egyptian jurisdiction; Upper Nubia belongs to the Republic of the Sudan. There are numerous temples and other ancient remains of the Egyptians. The creation of Lake Nasser has drowned some of these, others have been dismantled and rebuilt elsewhere.
See also ETHIOPIA.

Nuclear Fallout, precipitation of the products of an atomic bomb or hydrogen bomb. These products are nearly all radioactive. Most fallout is complete in several hours. Once the short-lived products have decayed (after a few days) the chief problem is inhalation and ingestion. The isotope Sr^{90} accumulates in bone. Its radiation may lead to cancer, including leukaemia. The effects of Sr^{90} (half-life 28 years) are long lasting. Radioactive caesium (Cs^{137}) with a half-life of 27 years is another hazard. Relatively little is known of the consequences to subsequent generations of the mutation of genes.

Nuclear Medicine, see IRRADIATION; RADIOTHERAPY.

Nuclear Power, power produced from reactions involving the nuclei of atoms. Two reactions which release energy are fission of the nuclei of some heavy elements, and fusion of the nuclei of certain light elements. The former is employed in power stations and for marine propulsion.
Importance. It is estimated that economic fossil fuel reserves (coal, oil, etc.) will be exhausted in 20–50 years (oil) or 200–400 years (coal). The ecological consequences of burning up valuable resources at such a rate is a matter for great concern. However, it is estimated that the resources of nuclear power derivable from fission are many times as large as the energy available from fossil fuel reserves. Moreover it is thought that the controlled fusion process utilising light elements will make available energy equivalent to 100 million times the present economic fossil fuel reserves and could provide power reserves lasting many millennia.
The development of the advanced gas-cooled reactor in the UK and the pressurised-water reactor in the USA makes nuclear power competitive with other sources. Its further application is, however, held back by questions of safety and concern about environmental pollution.
Power Production from Fission. Most nuclear reactors rely on the fission of uranium 235 (U^{235}). Natural uranium contains two predominant isotopes, chemically identical types of uranium, but differing in atomic mass: 0·7 per cent is U^{235}, 99·3 per cent is U^{238}. A nucleus of U^{235} may undergo fission on being struck by a neutron. When this occurs the nucleus is split and emits a large quantity of energy and also, on the average, about 2·5 new neutrons, travelling with high velocity. It can be arranged that one of these newly emitted neutrons strikes another U^{235} nucleus, and causes that to fission and produce still more neutrons, which cause further fission, and so on. It is thus possible to achieve a *chain reaction* whereby the fission reaction becomes self-propagating. The heat emitted is utilised to raise steam which is passed through conventional turbines driving alternators which produce electricity. The energy available in a given weight of U^{235} equals that produced by about 3 million times the weight of coal.
Moderators and Uranium Enrichment. When U^{238} absorbs high velocity (fast) neutrons, many are absorbed without producing fission. It is consequently not possible to sustain a chain reaction. In *thermal* reactors, the fission neutrons are slowed down by passing them through a *moderator* such as graphite or heavy water (D_2O), with which they collide and lose speed without being absorbed. As 'slow' neutrons, the fissionable collisions with the 0·7 per cent U^{235} occur so readily that a chain reaction is possible. Alternatively, increasing the concentration of U^{235} makes possible a chain reaction with either slow or fast neutrons. The fuel is then referred to as *enriched* uranium. Using it, a thermal reactor may use ordinary water as a moderator.
Enriched uranium is produced by making uranium hexafluoride gas (UF_6) diffuse through porous materials. Enrichment occurs through the faster diffusion rate of U^{235}. Enrichment leads to a small reactor core and savings in cost. Over the life of the fuel, the build-up of fission products means the accumulation in the fuel rods of unwanted elements, some of which are neutron absorbers which poison the fuel. Enrichment allows a higher proportion of the fuel to be 'burnt up' usefully. At this stage it is only the

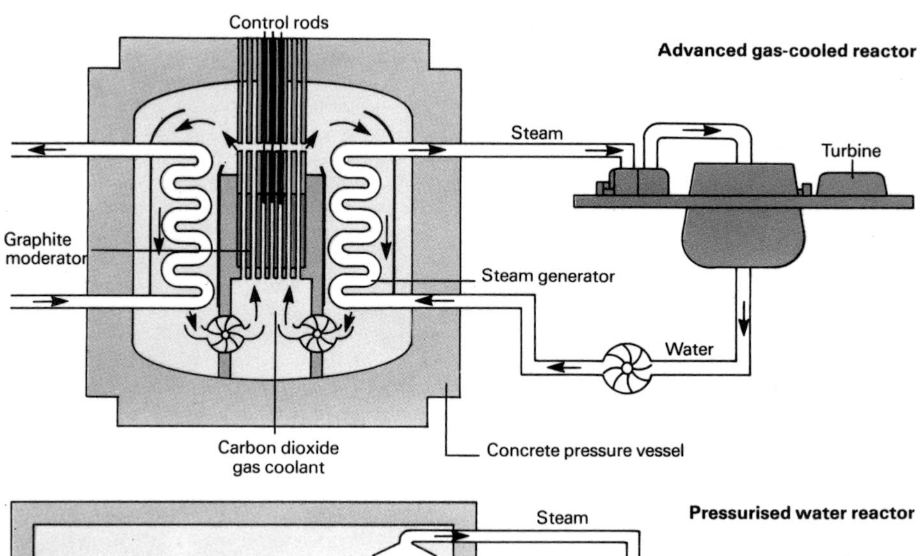

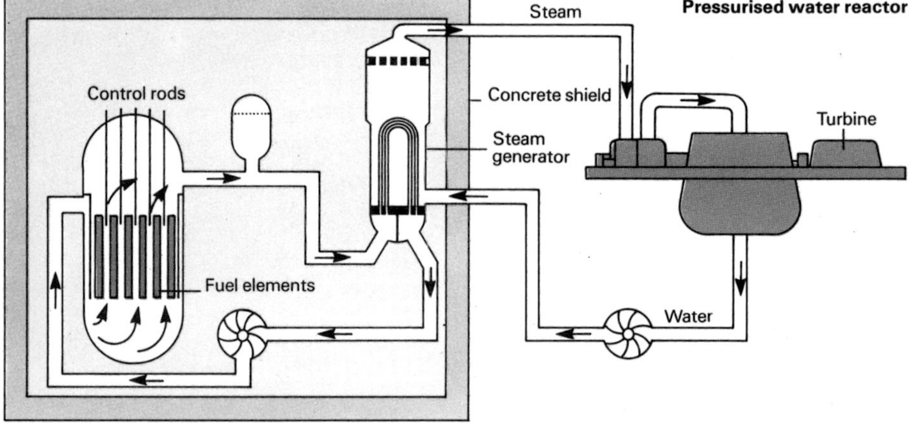

Nuclear Power. *The principal nuclear methods of electricity generation in the UK and USA.*

thermal reactor which has produced power on a commercial scale, fast reactors still being in the experimental stage except in France and the Soviet Union.

Control of reactors is achieved by varying the number of neutrons in the core. In the thermal reactor this is done by control rods made from non-fissile materials having good neutron-absorbing properties, such as boron or cadmium. Any reactor control system is designed so that it will 'fail safe'.

Breeder Reactors. When neutrons are absorbed by U^{238}, some is converted to plutonium. Plutonium is called a 'fertile' material, since it may be converted into the fissionable fuel Pu^{239}. It is possible for a reactor to breed more fissionable fuel (Pu^{239}), by conversion of the fertile U^{238}, than the amount of fissionable fuel (U^{235}) consumed in the process. Since U^{235} is only present as 0·7 per cent of natural uranium, this can increase the utilisation of the limited known reserves of uranium by up to a factor of 50.

Reactor Types. The first reactor to demonstrate a chain reaction was a thermal reactor built by Fermi and others in 1942, at the University of Chicago, using natural uranium and a graphite moderator. The first UK reactor at Windscale was designed to produce plutonium. Commercial electricity was first generated in the UK at Calder Hall in 1956. British reactors use gas cooling. Later designs have used enriched uranium to allow higher-temperature operation to make electrical generation more efficient.

American reactors use liquid coolants: H_2O, D_2O, or liquid sodium. The *pressurised light-water* reactor uses H_2O as both coolant and moderator. Enriched uranium is essential, because H_2O is a neutron absorber.The water circulates at high temperature and pressure, passing through a heat exchanger to generate steam.

See also ATOM; FUSION REACTOR.

Nuclear Weapons, see ATOMIC BOMB.

Nucleic Acids, compounds formed by the linking of smaller compounds called nucleotides. They undertake protein synthesis and the storage and transmission of genetic information.

Mononucleotides contain three components: phosphoric acid, a pentose (a 5-carbon sugar), and a nitrogenous base. Ribonucleotides contain the sugar ribose, while deoxyribonucleotides contain 2-deoxyribose. There are two types of nitrogenous base: purines, such as adenine and guanine; and pyrimidines, such as uracil, thymine and cytosine. Nucleotides perform many functions in the body: for example, ATP (adenosine triphosphate) is the body's energy factor and UDP (uracil diphosphate) is a sugar-carrying coenzyme, but their most prominent rôle is to act as building-blocks for the nucleic acids.

Deoxyribonucleic Acid (*DNA*) consists of a combination of four deoxyribonucleotides. DNA molecules are paired in the cell and two long chains are wound around each other in a regular double helix. The bases on one chain line up against specific bases on the other. Adenine (A) always pairs with, or lines up against, thymine (T), while guanosine (G) pairs with cytosine (C). The molecule reproduces itself by uncoiling, each chain then acting as a blue-print for new chain formation. DNA is the carrier of genetic information, and is also the blueprint for protein synthesis.

Ribonucleic Acids (*RNA*) consist basically of ribonucleotides. They contain uracil instead of the nucleotide thymine. RNAs are not paired like DNAs. mRNA, or messenger RNA, is the essential connection between the genetic information stored in DNA and protein synthesis. It is a long, single chain molecule, constructed according to the pattern of the DNA base sequence. It then uses its base sequence as a blueprint for the assembly of amino-acids. The compounds which actually attach to amino-acids are the transfer RNAs (tRNA). There is one tRNA for every amino-acid. Protein synthesis is carried out by a third type of RNA, ribosomal RNA.

See also CHROMOSOME.

Nucleophiles, in chemistry, reagents which take part in chemical reactions by donating their electrons, or a share in their electrons, to an electron-deficient substrate. Many are reducing agents or bases. Some examples are: Na, SO_2, CN^-, OH^-, NH_3.

Nucleus, in biology, the largest single inclusion within the cytoplasm of most cells. It is bounded by a double membrane with numerous pores which provide contact between the nucleus and the rest of the cell. Inside the nucleus are the nucleic acids DNA and RNA which carry and transmit the genetic code.

See also CELL; GENETICS.

Nudibranchia, or sea slugs, an order of invertebrate animals in class Opisthobranchia of phylum Mollusca that have no shell. The animals are slug-like in appearance and respire via the body surface, which may have specialised cerata (finger-like extensions) to increase the surface area. In dorids, e.g. the sea-lemon, secondary gills are developed around the anus in place of the cerata. They are mainly carnivorous although a variety of feeding habits are found.

Nuevo Laredo, town in Tamaulipas state, Mexico. Situated on the right bank of the Río Bravo which separates Mexico from the USA, the town is one of the most important points of entry into Mexico. Important as a frontier town, it is also the commercial centre of a productive cotton-growing and cattle-raising area. Population (1977) 214,028.

Nuffield, William Richard Morris, 1st Viscount Morris of Nuffield (1877–1963), British industrialist and philanthropist. One of the most important men in the development of the British car industry, William Morris started at 15 with a bicycle-repair business and extended his activities to selling and maintaining motor cycles and then cars. He set up works at Cowley near Oxford and brought out his first car in 1913. Morris achieved great business success in the 1920s and 1930s by concentrating on producing cars as cheaply as possible to capture large markets. He adopted the mass-production techniques pioneered by Henry Ford in the USA. He supplemented the range of popular family cars with a range of sports cars under the brand name MG (Morris Garages). In 1927 Morris took over Wolseley Motors Limited, and in 1936 Riley (Coventry) Limited. He was made a baron in 1934, and created Viscount Nuffield in 1938. He devoted much of his personal wealth to charity, including endowing the Nuffield Foundation.

Nuits St Georges, see FRENCH WINES.

Nukus, town and capital, economic and cultural centre of the Karakalpak ASSR, USSR, in the Khorezm oasis on the right bank of the Amu Darya at the beginning of its delta. It was founded in 1932 and has metalworking, food and furniture industries. Population (1975) 90,000.

Nullarbor Plain, an enormous plateau of some 260,000 km^2, extending westward from Ooldea, South Australia, into Western Australia and northwards from the coast of the Great Australian Bight to the Great Victorian Desert. The plain is a former seabed, underlain by large cave systems. Its vegetation is mainly saltbush and blue bush (the plain's name means 'treeless'); there are some sheep-stations. It was discovered by the explorer Eyre in 1841; the coastal side is crossed by the Eyre Highway.

Nullity of Marriage, see DIVORCE.

Number, in grammar, expresses the singular, dual or plural state of a noun, pronoun or verb, as it refers to one, two or more things.

Numbers are used to count and measure, and to distinguish things according to their size or position. The positive integers (the natural or whole numbers) are used for counting and for describing position (or order). Fractions (or rational numbers) are used for measurement when something is measured in terms of a fixed unit and a number of equal parts of that unit. Negative numbers are used in measurement to indicate the direction of measurement with respect to a fixed datum (for example, in measuring temperatures).

Numbers that cannot be described in terms of fractions are called irrational. Examples are $\sqrt{2}$, π and e. Every rational number can also be represented as a decimal, that either terminates or is periodic (recurring). An irrational number has only a decimal representation, that neither terminates nor is periodic.

The set consisting of all rational and irrational numbers is called the set of real numbers and is denoted by **R**. The set of positive real numbers (that is, real numbers greater than zero) is denoted by $\mathbf{R}^+$. Real numbers can be defined in terms of their algebraic and analytical properties. The real numbers with the operations of addition and multiplication form a field and it is an ordered field in the sense that the relationship $<$ ('is less than') satisfies the following rules: (1) for any pair of elements a and b, one and only one of the following statements is true—$a < b$, $a = b$, $b < a$; (2) for any c, $a < b$ implies $a + c < b + c$; (3) for any $c > 0$, $a < b$ implies $ac < bc$ and for any $c < 0$, $a < b$ implies $bc < ac$.

See also COMPLEX NUMBERS; NUMERALS.

Numbers, Book of (so-called from the census figures included), the fourth book of the Pentateuch, deals with the travels of the Israelites from the second to the fortieth year of the Exodus. It also contains collections of laws and narrates the institution of the Levites and priestly duties.

Numbers, Theory of, the branch of mathematics concerned with solving problems about positive integers. Many of these problems are concerned with the properties of prime numbers. One of the most famous is Goldbach's conjecture (made in 1742) that any even number greater than 4 can be expressed as the sum of two odd prime numbers (for example, $6 = 3 + 3$, $8 = 5 + 3$, $48 = 29 + 19$, etc.). Although there is every reason to believe that this conjecture is true it has never been proved, and it is a good example of the way that a problem in the theory of numbers can be stated very simply yet be very difficult to solve. Perhaps the most famous unsolved problem is the 'last theorem' of Pierre de Fermat, who was the first mathematician to study the theory of numbers.

Despite the difficulties of some problems, much of the theory of numbers can be understood without a knowledge of higher mathematics and has always fascinated amateur mathematicians.

Numeiry, Jaafar Mohammed (1930–), Sudanese soldier and president. He served in the Sudanese armed forces, took part in the campaigns against the south, and was arrested in 1966 for plotting against the government. In May 1969 he led a coup which overthrew the government of civilian politicians. He became head of the revolutionary command council and prime minister. After thwarting a Communist-led coup in July 1971 he was elected president and became head of the Sudan Socialist Union. Initially he led the Sudan towards the Eastern bloc and into closer co-operation with Egypt and Libya, but he reversed this after 1971.

His major achievement was the conclusion, in 1972, of an agreement ending the 17-year civil war with southern Sudan by granting the area autonomy within a united Sudan. He was re-elected, in 1977, to a second term as president.

Numerals. A numeral is a sign employed to express a number. 'Arabic numerals' are the symbols 0, 1, 2, 3, 4, 5, 6, 7, 8, 9, though the adjective 'arabic' is slightly misleading as they actually derive from Indian numerals. 'Roman numerals' are the symbols I (=1), V (=5), X (=10), L (=50), C (=100), D (=500) and M (=1000). The arabic numerals now in common use have proved particularly efficient as an international system for writing down numbers, especially as the use of a 'place-value' notation system means that calculations can be performed with great ease.

Place-value Notation and Number Bases. The most important feature of arabic numerals is the use of place-value notation. Perhaps the best way to see how this works is to imagine that counting is carried out by threading beads onto a row of wires. As each object is counted it is represented by a single bead threaded on the right-hand end wire. The wire has only enough room for nine beads. To count the tenth object, one bead is put on the next wire and all beads are taken off the end wire. Then the beads are used to fill up the end wire again and so on. Thus each bead on the second wire represents ten; on the third wire one hundred; on the fourth wire one thousand and so on. To write this down, all that is needed is nine symbols to represent from one to nine beads (the arabic numerals 1 to 9), and one symbol for zero (0) to represent an empty wire, without which place-value notation would be impossible. The symbols are written out in the same places as the wires: the value of a numeral depends on the place that it is in. Ten is called the base, or radix, of this denary system. Any other number could be used as a base. In electronic computers, numbers are usually represented to base two, the binary system, in which only two symbols (0 and 1) are needed.

See also NUMBERS.

Numerology, the science of numbers. The idea that the universe is interconnected in a grand design has always been part of the occult tradition, and from very early times, numbers have held a mystical and symbolical significance in respect of this belief.

2nd century, Indian
10th century, Arabic
Middle Ages, Western Arabic
Middle Ages, Eastern Arabic
11th, 12th century, Roman origin
12th, 15th century Byzantine
12th century, French
14th century, Italian
15th century, Italian
16th century, Italian

Numerals. The development of numerals from the 2nd century AD *to the 16th century.*

Pythagoras evolved the theory that the ultimate significance of all things was their numerical value, and that universal order was based on numerical relationships. In biblical literature, certain numbers have mystical importance, particularly the number 40. Each letter of the Hebrew alphabet has a numerical value, and by the system *Gematria*, Kabbalists converted Hebrew words into numbers and then into other words sharing the same numbers in order to discover mystical relationships between words. Numerology has always had a prominent place in magical rites and processes. It is also used as a method of prognostication and character analysis, based on substituting numbers for the letters composing an individual's name, or finding the numerical value of birth dates, etc.

Numidia, Roman name for a district of northern Africa, consisting of all territory eastward from the River Mulucha (now Moluya) to the Carthaginian frontier on the River Tusca (Wadi-el-Berger). In the 3rd century BC Numidia was inhabited by two great kindred tribes, the Massyli and the Massaesyli, dwelling east and west respectively of the River Ampsaga. On Jugurtha's defeat Numidia became virtually subject to Rome. Diocletian made it one of the seven provinces of the diocese of Africa.

Numismatics (from Greek *nomisma*, a coin with customary value, currency), study of coins and currency both as objects themselves and as a means of obtaining information in the fields of history, economics, sociology, archaeology, art, etc.

See also COINS.

Nun (Latin *nonna*), called in the Roman canon law *monialis*, strictly speaking a woman under solemn vows.

See also CONVENT.

Nunatak, an isolated mountain peak projecting above the level of a continental ice-sheet. Nunataks were first recognised in Greenland and have subsequently been noted extensively in Antarctica.

Nunc Dimittis, or The Song of Simeon, from Luke's gospel, canticle, so called from its opening words, *Nunc dimittis servum tuum, domine* (Lord, now lettest thou thy servant depart). It forms part of the Roman Catholic office of compline and the Anglican office of Evening Prayer.

Nuneaton, market town in Warwickshire, England, on the River Anker, 15 km north-east of Coventry. Nuneaton has quarries, brick works, and manufactures of woven or worsted articles, elastic, ribbon, etc., and of tiles, sanitary pipes and glazed bricks. A nunnery, founded in 1150, gave the town its name. Population (1981) 71,530.

Nuremberg (German Nürnberg), city in Bavaria, Federal Republic of Germany, on the Pegnitz, 149 km north-west of Munich. The earliest settlement grew up around a royal fortress. It rose rapidly to importance owing to its position at a junction of two great trade routes. In 1219 it was declared an imperial city and it became the finest city in Germany; the Golden Bull ordained that every German emperor should convoke his first diet there. It was the first of the imperial cities to embrace Protestantism (1525). After the Thirty Years' War its prosperity declined. In 1806 it was incorporated into the kingdom of Bavaria. The 14th-century Frauenkirche contains work by Adam Kraft, and has a 16th-century clock with moving figures of the seven Electors paying homage to Charles IV. There is a Dürer museum in this his native city. Among its diversified industries are electrical engineering, lorries, cameras and optical goods, clocks, fertilisers and toys. There is an annual toy fair. Population (1979) 484,184.

Nuremberg Trial, international trial of major German war criminals following the Second World War, between November 1945 and October 1946. It ended in the conviction and sentence of most of the surviving leaders of the Third Reich for their part in crimes against humanity. The charter of the court was agreed upon by the USA, Britain, the USSR and France. It was the creation of the court, not the enunciation of the law, that was the novelty.

The trial was under the presidency of Lord Justice Lawrence (later Lord Oaksey). The tribunal consisted of four members. The accused included Hermann Goering; Rudolf Hess; Joachim von Ribbentrop, Reich foreign minister; Julius Streicher, governor of Franconia; Erich Raeder, naval commander-in-chief from 1935 to 1943; Adm. Karl Doenitz; Albert Speer, Reich minister of armaments and war production; and Martin Bormann, chief of Hitler's chancellery, who was tried in absentia.

The indictment charged the defendants with crimes against peace by the planning, preparation, initiation, and waging of wars of aggression, which were also wars in violation of international treaties and agreements, with war crimes and with crimes against humanity. All the defendants were represented by counsel. Of the 22 prisoners present at the trial, only three were acquitted. The tribunal sentenced 12 to death, three to imprisonment for life, and four to lesser terms. The Soviet judge dissented from the acquittals. The Allied Control Council rejected all appeals for clemency by the prisoners and also rejected the plea by Goering, Jodl and Keitel to be shot instead of hanged. Shortly before he was to have been hanged, Goering committed suicide. The remaining Nazis sentenced to death were hanged at Nuremberg on 16 October.

Nureyev, Rudolf (1939–), Soviet dancer of Tatar origin. He joined the corps de ballet at Ufa at 15, and a year later was accepted at the Kirov Ballet school, Leningrad. In 1961, after appearing with the Kirov Ballet in Paris, he caused a sensation by breaking his connection with that company. After dancing with the Cuevas Ballet he joined the Royal Ballet as guest artist, forming a great partnership with Fonteyn and being acclaimed as the most exciting male dancer since Nijinsky. He has produced many variants of the classical repertory for numerous companies and danced all over the world in modern dance works as well as classical ballet.

Nurmi, Paavo (1897–1973), Finnish athlete; his name appears 19 times in the official world records lists, more than that of any other athlete. In the 1920 Olympics he won the 10,000 m and the cross country, and came second in the 5000 m. In the 1924 Games (his most spectacular), he won the 1500 m, 5000 m (within just over an hour of each other), the cross country and 3000 m team events. In 1928 he won the 10,000 m, and was second in the 5000 m and the steeplechase.

Nursery Rhymes, jingling rhymes invented to amuse children, or in some cases survivals of ancient folklore, invocations, or incantations preserved from remote antiquity. The jingling metre and doggerel rhymes, in which the sense is often sacrificed to the attempted rhyme, have been handed down orally from one generation to another. The verses generally consist of a rhyming couplet or a quatrain in which the second and fourth lines rhyme, and there is frequently a refrain accompanying the traditional musical settings which have also been handed down.

Nursery School, in Britain is intended to

Nuremberg Trial. *The Nazi leaders of the Third Reich on trial in 1946. From the left are Goering, Hess, Doenitz, Ribbentrop, Raeder, Keitel, Shirach, Kaltenbrunner and Sauchel.*

provide for the healthy physical and mental development of children between 2 and 5 years of age. Its purpose is twofold: nurture and education. In recent years, the provision of nursery schools by local authorities has not developed very greatly, despite powerful pleas and pressures that they should do so. However, there has been a remarkable development in play-groups for children of this age group, organised voluntarily and co-operatively in various local buildings by parents and others. Only about 2 per cent of all pre-school children in England and Wales are able to attend official, maintained nursery schools or classes.

The nursery school movement in the USA dates from the 1920s when Child Development Institutes came into being, and there has since been a rapid spread of nursery schools. Emphasis is laid on the relation between school and home, and between learning and play, and these trends are influencing education as a whole.

See also EDUCATION; INFANT SCHOOLS; KINDERGARTEN.

Nursing. Sick nursing has evolved into a highly skilled profession since the work of Florence Nightingale in the Crimean War. In ancient times there were hospitals, or at least some kind of dispensary system, for the sick poor, in Egypt, India, Greece and Rome, but organised nursing as a branch of medical treatment may be said to have begun amongst the deacons of the early Christian Church. After the 4th century the care of the sick was the responsibility of the monastic orders. The Reformation caused a secular system to be introduced. However, until the middle of the 19th century all the skill that nurses possessed was acquired in the course of their work on the wards. Germany saw the birth of a new system of organised training at the foundation of the institute of Pastor Fliedner in 1836 at Kaiserworth; and it was here that Florence Nightingale trained.

Nursing is no longer the female-dominated profession it once was; indeed a large proportion of nurses are now men. Many men work in psychiatric hospitals, but their numbers have increased rapidly in general hospitals as well.

Training includes experience of general and psychiatric nursing in both a hospital and community setting. Great emphasis has recently been laid on the need for preventive medicine; consequently there are increased opportunities for health visitors, school nurses and occupational health nurses in industry. Others prefer nursing privately either as agency nurses or in private hospitals or nursing homes. Work is also available with the armed services and overseas in hospitals and in medical missions.

Nut, see FRUIT.

Nutation, (Latin *nutare*, to nod), in astronomy, the small oscillatory motion of the Earth's axis which is superimposed on its steady precession.

The term is also used in botany for the spiral growth movements of a stem, most clearly seen in climbing plants, e.g. bindweed.

Nutcracker, *Nucifraga*, genus of birds of the crow family, Corvidae, order Passeriformes. *N. caryocatactes*, the Eurasian species, is about the size of a jackdaw, having a brown back, with a long white spot on each feather, dark brown head, white tipped outer tail-feathers, black feet and a black bill. In flight and habits it resembles the jay. It feeds usually on pine-cones in its normal habitat, the pine woods extending right across eastern Europe and Asia to Japan. The nest is a big, clumsy structure, and about three eggs are laid, which are very light green, spotted with pale brown. The North American species, *N. columbianus*, has similar habits.

Nuthatch, *Sitta europaea*, bird of family Sittidae, order Passeriformes, fairly common in Europe. Its plumage is bluish-grey above, and the undersurface is light reddish-brown or buff; the throat is white, and the tail-feathers have white tips. The bill is powerful and wedge-shaped, and is used to force away the bark in the search for insects, and to break nuts; but the tail, unlike that of a woodpecker, is not used as a prop against the tree trunk. The bird is a skilful climber, able to descend a tree head downwards. The nest is made commonly in a hole in a tree, and the mouth of it is plastered up with mud, except for a hole just big enough to give the bird admittance. In it are laid about seven white eggs, spotted with reddish-brown.

Nutmeg, kernel of the fruit of several species of *Myristica*, of the family Myristicaceae, tropical trees or shrubs, natives of Asia, Madagascar and America. The fleshy part of the fruit is eaten as a sweetmeat, resembling candied fruit; the seed is enveloped in a yellowish-red aril, the mace. Nutmegs yield a yellow fat, called oil of mace, and by distillation an almost colourless essential oil. The grated or powdered seed is used in cooking.

Nutrition, the study of the food we eat and how our bodies use it. There are six classes of nutrients: water, carbohydrates, proteins and fats, which are dealt with here, plus vitamins and trace quantities of minerals, which are usually available in adequate quantities in a balanced diet.

Water is the most important nutrient, and it is usually readily available. Humans and animals die from water deprivation sooner than from starvation.

Carbohydrates are compounds of carbon, hydrogen and oxygen. The major groups are starches, sugars, and cellulose and related materials. Their main function is to provide energy. They are efficient sources of glucose, which the body requires for brain functioning, utilisation of foods, maintenance of body temperature, and to provide energy for body movements. They are not necessarily essential in adults: meat-eating tribes consume very little carbohydrate. When carbohydrate intake exceeds the body's needs, it can be changed into fat and stored in the body. Familiar good sources of starch are cereals and cereal products such as pastas and bread, legumes, and potatoes. In the past 150 years sugar has tended to replace starch in the diet of Western countries. This has been shown to raise blood lipid (fat) levels in some individuals.

Cellulose and related materials, also called 'unavailable carbohydrate', 'roughage', or 'dietary fibre', form the stiff, structural materials of vegetables, fruits and cereals. Cellulose cannot be digested, so it has no direct nutritive value. However, it provides bulk to the diet and influences the absorption of nutrients. Lack of fibre in the diet is thought to be related to diseases such as those of the large intestine, obesity, coronary heart disease, and diabetes mellitus.

Proteins are more complicated compounds of carbon, hydrogen and oxygen. They consist of smaller units, amino-acids, and their main dietary function is to provide the amino-acids the body needs for growth and maintenance of tissue. The body needs more protein in conditions of growth and repair – for example for pregnant mothers, growing children, and people suffering from burns, disease or stress. A complete protein contains all the amino-acids essential for health; animal foods (except gelatin) are complete proteins. Plant proteins are incomplete, but eating several different kinds of vegetables makes up the deficiencies.

Fats, or lipids, are also composed of carbon, hydrogen and oxygen. They are concentrated sources of energy, and contain vitamins A, D, E, and K. They slow the emptying time of the stomach, and thus make meals more satisfying, and add taste and variety of texture to the diet. Butter, margarine and cooking oils are major sources of fat; others are meat, milk, cheese, eggs, and biscuits and cake made with fats. Fats are classed as saturated or unsaturated according to their chemical structure; in general saturated fats are hard at room temperature, unsaturated fats are not. Statistics have indicated that saturated fats (generally animal fats) are connected with the incidence of heart disease, and that a diet containing unsaturated fats (the vegetable oils) is to be preferred.

See also MINERALS IN FOOD; VITAMINS.

Nutritional Deficiency Diseases are of two kinds: primary deficiency diseases, which are caused by an inadequate supply of an essential nutrient, and secondary deficiency diseases, which result from the body's inability to absorb or metabolise a nutrient.

Ariboflavinosis is due to a deficiency of riboflavin (vitamin B_2). It is common in parts of Africa, India, Indonesia, the Caribbean, and Newfoundland, but is not fatal. *Beri-beri*, resulting from a lack of thiamine (vitamin B_1), occurs with general malnutrition and alcoholism; it is probably still common in remote areas. It is treated by doses of thiamine. Iodine deficiency can cause *goitre*, an enlargement of the thyroid gland which shows as a large swelling in the neck. Severe iodine deficiency can cause *cretinism*, characterised by stunted growth and mental retardation. Both diseases can be prevented or alleviated by iodine in the diet.

Anaemia can be caused by iron deficiency; in the Middle East, Africa and Asia as much as 20 per cent of the population is affected in this way. *Megaloblastic anaemia* is due to a deficiency of folic acid, and commonly goes with general malnutrition. *Pernicious anaemia* is a deficiency of vitamin B_{12}, and is often an inherited disease due to a natural inability to absorb the vitamin; it is treated by injection of the vitamin. It is sometimes found in vegans.

Rickets is caused by a deficiency of vitamin D,

resulting in a failure to absorb calcium. In the adult form, *osteomalacia*, calcium is lost from the bones. *Scurvy* is caused by a dificiency of ascorbic acid (vitamin C). In all three diseases doses of the appropriate vitamin are the remedy.
The gravest nutritional problem is *protein energy malnutrition* (PEM), due to inadequate diet; it is prevalent in India, South-East Asia, Africa, the Middle East, the Caribbean, and South and Central America.

Nuts, see SCREWS, BOLTS AND NUTS.

Nuvolari, Tazio (1892–1953), Italian racing driver. Nicknamed the Flying Mantuan, he is considered one of the greatest drivers of all time. His career began with motor-cycles in 1923. From 1929 to 1933 he drove Alfa Romeos for Scuderia Ferrari and between 1935 and 1938 he joined the Auto Union Team. After the war he raced mainly Maseratis, although his health was failing. He won many European Grand Prix, as well as the Le Mans (1933) and the US Vanderbilt Cup (1936), among others.

Nyakyusa, Bantu people of Tukuyu district, southern Tanzania, numbering about 300,000. They are cultivators; the staple crop is plantains. They have a peculiar village organisation. The men of each village are all of the same age and have been brought up together in one neighbourhood. The young men found new villages and then marry at more or less the same time.

Nyamwezi, one of the largest groups of Bantu people in Tanzania, living on the plains surrounding the town of Tabora. Although they suffered greatly from Arab slavers from Zanzibar in the 19th century, they became involved in the trade themselves, one of their chiefs, Mirambo, becoming overlord of much of central Tanzania with the assistance of the Arab trader Tippu Tip. Most of the Nyamwezi are farmers.

Nyanda (Fort Victoria), oldest town in Zimbabwe, established by the Pioneer Column on its march to Mashonaland in 1890, 303 km south of Harare. The ancient Zimbabwe ruins are 27 km south-east of Nyanda, which is also close to national parks at Kyle and Mushandike. Population (1979) 24,000, of whom 2300 are whites.

Nyasa, Lake, see MALAWI, LAKE.

Nyasaland, see MALAWI.

Nyerere, Julius Kambarage (1921–), Tanzanian politician. In 1954 he founded the Tanganyika African National Union (TANU) and by 1958 was a member of the Legislative Council. From 1958 to 1960 he was leader of the Elected Members Organisation, chief minister from 1960 to 1961, and eventually prime minister from May 1961 to January 1962. Nyerere became Tanganyika's first executive president in December 1962 and played the leading rôle in the incorporation of Zanzibar into the new republic of Tanzania in 1964. His economic and political philosophy of Ujamaa, the co-operative socialist community, evolved from a perception of meaningful human life being always within a community and from a realisation that economic development in Tanzania would be successful only if the participation of the peasantry, the farmers, could be guaranteed. In the notable Arusha Declaration of 1967 and in a series of pamphlets, Nyerere stressed that Tanzania would become the egalitarian and self-reliant nation he envisaged only through the process of first villagisation, and *then* the move to the real socialist community.
Nyerere has a keen interest in African political developments, and was in the forefront of Tanzanian support for liberation movements in Mozambique and Angola. He played a leading rôle in efforts to break the Rhodesian regime, and declared publicly his disapproval of Amin's government of Uganda.

Nyköping, seaport and capital of Södermanland county, Sweden, at the head of the Byfjord, on the Baltic coast, 160 km south-east of Stockholm. Fifteen national diets were held at Nyköping between the 13th and 15th centuries. It has a good harbour, vehicle assembly plants, metal industries and textile manufactures. Population (1978) 64,099.

Nylon, the first truly synthetic fibre, discovered by W. H. Carothers, and commercially produced in 1938. The polymer is formed by condensing a diamine with a dibasic acid to form a polyamide. The original type is formed from hexamethylene diamine and adipic acid, each containing six carbon atoms, hence the name nylon 6:6.
Nylon fibres are used for ladies' stockings and tights, lingerie, for hard-wearing applications such as hose, carpets, and industrial uses, in blends with many other fibres and as a stretch yarn in foundation garments, ski pants and knitwear. They are also used to make small engineering components such as gear-wheels and bearings. In 1974 production of nylon fibre was 2,594,000 t or 7·6 per cent of world fibre production.
See also FIBRES AND FIBROUS SUBSTANCES; PLASTICS; SPINNING.

Nymphaea, water-lily, a genus of about 50 species of aquatic plants with heart-shaped floating leaves, chiefly of the northern hemisphere, in the family Nymphaeaceae. *N. alba* is the common white water-lily of Europe. Cultivated varieties and hybrids are grown in garden pools. A species of *Nymphaea* is thought to have been the sacred lotus of ancient Egypt.

Nymphaeaceae, the water-lily family, a family of dicotyledons consisting of three genera including about 60 species of aquatic or marsh plants, found in all parts of the world. There is usually a thick stem or rhizome creeping in the mud and bearing large leaves, usually more or less round in shape and generally floating on the water, but sometimes submerged or standing clear of the surface. The flowers are usually large and showy; their parts are numerous, with sepals grading into petals, and petals into stamens.

Nymphomania, insatiable sexual needs in a woman which may be linked with other forms of greed, and may operate as a defence against feelings of sexual inadequacy.
See also SEXUALITY, HUMAN.

Nymphs, female demi-gods with whom the ancients peopled many parts of nature e.g.: *Oceanids*, nymphs of the open sea; *Nereids*, nymphs of the Aegean; *Nyads*, nymphs of fresh water—rivers, lakes, streams; *Dryads*, nymphs of trees (also *Hamadryads*). Alternatively the maiden companions of certain goddesses, e.g. Artemis.

Nyren, John (1764–1837), English cricketer and writer on cricket. He was a moderate batsman and a good fielder at point and middle wicket, but his fame rests on his account of the Hambledon players, *The Cricketers of My Time*, contained in *The Young Cricketer's Tutor*, edited by Charles Cowden Clarke (1833). This book, which is generally regarded as the classic of cricket literature, led Andrew Lang to describe Nyren as the Herodotus of cricket.

Nysa (German *Neisse*), river of Central Europe, which rises in northern Bohemia, Czechoslovakia, and then forms the boundary between Poland and the districts of Dresden and Kottbus, German Democratic Republic, joining the Oder south of Fürstenberg. With the Oder it has formed the boundary between East Germany and Poland since 1946. Length 225 km.

O

O, fifteenth letter of the English alphabet, the only vowel in the language which more or less corresponds in sound with the *o* of German, French and other European languages. Besides the name-sound as in *cone* it has the short sound as in *lot* and a third sound as in *monk*, identical with that of *u* in *cut*. Other values of *o* are exemplified in *lemon*, *woman*, *women*. The North Semitic alphabet had no vowel *o*; it was a purely consonantal alphabet. The Greeks therefore adopted a Semitic letter which had no Greek counterpart to represent *o*. Later this became *omicron* (short *o*) and *omega* was added to represent long *o*.
See also ALPHABET.

Oahu, an island in Honolulu County, Hawaii. It is the third largest and most populated of the Hawaiian group. Two parallel mountain ranges, the Koolau and Waianae, are connected by a central plateau. The most important towns are Honolulu (the state capital), Pearl Harbor and Waikiki. Area 1575 km^2. Population (1980) 761,964.

Oak. There are about 450 species of oak, genus *Quercus*, in the Fagaceae, widely distributed throughout the world. The best known and most important commercially are European oaks, including English oaks, *Q. robur*, pedunculate oak, and *Q. petraea*, durmast oak; American oaks, *Q. rubra*, *Q. virginiana*, *Q. alba* and other species; and Japanese oak, *Q. mongolica*. *Q. ilex*, of the

Mediterranean region, is the evergreen holm oak.

The leaves of most deciduous oaks are oval, with deep rounded lobes, and in autumn the tint changes to bronze and pale brown. The flowers are borne in small groups on stalks which later bear acorns. Cork is the bark of *Q. suber*, the cork oak.

See also FORESTRY; TIMBER.

Oak-apple Day (29 May), day of the restoration of Charles II to the English throne in 1660, specially celebrated at the Royal Hospital when oak-leaves or oak-apples are worn in memory of the king, who took refuge in an oak-tree while fleeing from his pursuers (6 September 1651).

Oak-gall, and oak-apple, galls that occur on oak trees. The abnormal production of plant tissue takes many forms. The gall-wasp, *Cynips kollari*, for instance, causes the familiar marble galls on young oaks by laying its eggs, which hatch into the fat grubs found inside the galls.

Oak Ridge, town and district in Tennessee, USA, given over to a section of the atomic bomb project, and officially known as the Clinton National Laboratory until 1948 when its name was changed to Oak Ridge National Laboratory. It is still important as a major research centre of atomic energy.

Oakham, county town of Rutland (formerly England's smallest county), absorbed into Leicestershire in 1974. It lies in the Vale of Catmose, 17 km south-east of Melton Mowbray. Oakham Castle (12th century) has a good Norman hall. The town is a centre for hunting. There are manufactures of shoes and knitted garments. Population (1981) 7996.

Oakland, city in central California, USA, and a part of the San Francisco-Oakland metropolitan area. It lies on the eastern, or inland, side of San Francisco Bay, at the point where the first transcontinental railway from the east terminated. It has extensive port facilities and a naval yard and naval air station. Population (1980) 339,288.

See also SAN FRANCISCO.

Oaks, The, one of the five classic races of the English turf. It was named after the 12th Earl of Derby's hunting lodge in the Epsom area and instituted in 1779, a year before the Derby. The Oaks is contested by three-year-old fillies over a distance of 2·40 km, each carrying 57 kg.

Oakum, fibrous matter obtained from old ropes. It was used for caulking boats.

Oarfish, a species of large teleost fish, *Regalecus glesne*, in family Trachypteridae (the ribbon-fishes) of order Lampridiformes, remarkable for its shape and internal organisation. They are among the longest fishes known, most specimens observed measuring over 3 m in length, while some are recorded to have exceeded 6 m. The long slender ventral fins, by which the oarfish is distinguished from the other ribbon-fishes, become long paddle-tipped filaments. The oarfish is found in all seas from the Mediterranean and northern seas to the southern Atlantic, and from the Indian Ocean to the coast of New Zealand.

OAS, see ORGANISATION OF AMERICAN STATES.

OAS, see ORGANISATION DE L'ARMÉE SECRÈTE.

Oasis, a fertile area in the desert where springs support vegetation, varying from a few palm trees and scrub to hundreds of square kilometres supporting extensive cultivation.

Oast-house, a building containing kilns for drying hops. The hops are placed on horse-hair covered floors, which are heated from below, and the oast-house is so constructed as to allow a constant draught of warm air to pass through and out at the top.

Oastler, Richard (1789–1861), British social reformer, famous as the protagonist of the Ten Hours Bill in the campaign for factory reform. In 1830 children were employed in the worsted-mills for 13 hours a day with an interval of half an hour, and in the woollen-mills 15 hours with an interval of 2 hours. His was one of the chief names associated with this reform, others being John Fielden, Michael Sadler and Lord Shaftesbury.

Oates, Lawrence Edward Grace (1880–1912), British explorer. He was a member of the party which reached the South Pole in 1912 in Captain Scott's last Antarctic expedition. On the return march Oates, who had severe frostbite and feared that he would be a hindrance to his companions, deliberately left his tent to die.

Oates, Titus (c.1649–1705), English anti-Catholic conspirator. In 1678 he concocted the 'Popish Plot'. This imaginary plot was supposed to involve the murder of the king, the placing on the throne of the Catholic Duke of York, the burning of London, and slaughter of Protestants. In the period 1678–79 London was seized by panic. Many innocent Catholics were executed and Oates himself became a popular hero. After the accession of James II, Oates was found guilty of perjury and condemned to be pilloried, brutally flogged, and imprisoned for life. He regained his liberty on the accession of William and Mary in 1688.

Oath. An oath may be defined as a solemn declaration to a superior or divine being, or in the name of something held sacred, by which the declarant either undertakes to speak the truth or promises to do something in the future, on pain of calling down divine or preternatural wrath. Oaths of the former, or assertory, kind may be exemplified by the affidavit, the statutory declaration and the oath of a witness in a court of law; the latter, or promissory, kind by the oath of allegiance.

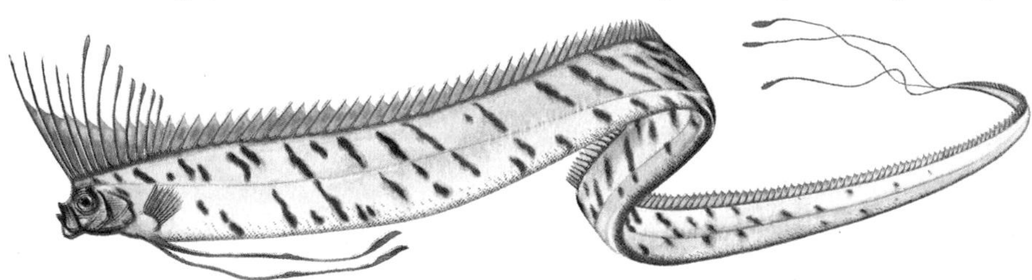

Oarfish. Regalecus glesne *has a flat body, about 30 cm broad, and grows up to 3 m.*

Oats, the seeds of the genus *Avena*, in the grass family Gramineae. The origin of the cultivated species is unknown, none of them occurring in a truly wild state. Two main races are recognised, common oats (*Avena sativa*), with open spreading panicles, and Tartarian oats (*A. orientalis*), with contracted one-sided panicles. The wild oat, *A. fatua*, is a serious weed of other cereals, especially in eastern England.

Oats are used mostly to feed animals, especially horses. They are prepared for human consumption as oatmeal or as porridge.

Oaxaca, capital of Oaxaca state in Mexico, its full name being Oaxaca de Juárez. Situated at the foot of the mountain San Felipe de Agua and near the Río Atoyac, it is the commercial and distribution centre of an agricultural and cattle-raising district, but apart from food processing it has little industry. More important are its handicraft industries associated with the indigenous Indians, and the tourist industry. Population (1978) 131,193.

Ob, one of the largest rivers in the USSR, in Western Siberia; it rises in the Altai Mountains in two headstreams (Katun and Biya), and flows northwards into the Gulf of Ob in the Kara Sea (an inlet of the Arctic Ocean) via a delta of over 4000 km^2. Its length from the confluence of its two headstreams to its outlet is 3650 km; from the source of the Irtysh, its chief tributary, some 5410 km; drainage basin 2,990,000 km^2. The river is very wide and sluggish for most of its course; the middle reaches flow through extensive swamps, frozen for much of the year. The river is navigable for the major part of its course during the summer months, and is chiefly used for transporting timber, grain, peat and coal. The chief ports along its banks are Novosibirsk and Barnaul.

Obadiah (Hebrew, servant or worshipper of Yahweh), one of the 12 minor prophets. Nothing is known of him, and his book, the shortest of the prophetic writings, is at the same time one of the most difficult and interesting.

Oban, port of Argyll and Bute District, Strathclyde Region, Scotland. An important service, tourist and communications centre in the western Highlands. The unfinished McCaig's Tower is a conspicuous landmark. The main manufactures are whisky and tweed, and fishing is also carried on. Population (1981) 8134.

Obasanjo, Olusegun (1937–), Nigerian army officer and politician. After completing his training in Britain he returned to Nigeria. During the Nigerian Civil War he became commander of the Third Marine Commando Division.

Following Gen. Gowon's overthrow in July 1975, he became chief-of-staff, Supreme Headquarters, and was appointed head of state following Gen. Mohammed's assassination in February 1976.

Obbligato (Italian, obligatory), instrumental part in a musical composition, performing an important soloistic function, usually in an accompaniment to a vocal solo but vying in virtuosity with the voice. Handel included horn obbligati in his opera *Giulio Cesare* and Schubert used the clarinet in the song *Der Hirt auf dem Felsen*.

Obeah, a magical cult practised on certain Caribbean islands, especially Jamaica. It originated in the worship of the snake-god, Obi—the spirit of evil, and includes animal sacrifice (formerly human as well). Voodoo, practised in Haiti, is a form of Obeah.

Obeche, *Triplochiton scleroxylon*, a large tree of tropical western Africa in the family Sterculiaceae. It produces a rather soft, light timber, also called African whitewood because of its white colour, which is used for plywood, blockboard and shelving.

Obeid El, see EL OBEID.

Obelisk, four-sided monumental pillar with a pyramidal top. Associated in Egypt with sun worship, the earliest obelisk still in position at Heliopolis dates from the 12th dynasty.

Oberammergau, Alpine village in Bavaria, Federal Republic of Germany, on the Ammer, 70 km south-west of Munich. It is famous for its Passion Play, performed every ten years in fulfilment of a vow made by the villagers in 1633 when they were saved from the plague. Population (1970) 4900.

Oberhausen, city in North Rhine-Westphalia, Federal Republic of Germany, on the Rhine–Hern Canal, 29 km north-east of Düsseldorf. It has heavy industries including the manufacture of iron, steel, machinery, chemicals and glass. Its outskirts are now a continuation of those of Duisburg and Essen. Population (1980) 229,300.

Obesity, an abnormal excess of body fat. Obesity usually results from a consumption of food, particularly fat and carbohydrates, which exceeds the normal requirements (which vary from individual to individual). In other cases the amount of obesity seems to bear no direct relation to the food intake. The endocrine glands play a part in the control of body weight. Thus there is a tendency to obesity after middle-age when endocrine function becomes less active. Inactivity of the thyroid and pituitary glands causes obesity.

Obey, André (1892–1975), French writer. A playwright and actor-manager, his plays include *Viol de Lucrèce*, 1931; *Noë*, 1931; *La Bataille de la Marne*, 1932; and (with Denys Amiel) *La Souriante Madame Beudet*, 1922. He has also written novels, among them *L'Enfant inquiet*, *Le Gardien de la ville*, and *Le Joueur de triangle*. In 1946 he was appointed administrator of the Comédie Française.

Obiter Dictum, a judicial utterance made in the course of a judgment, but not in itself strictly necessary for the decision upon the matters at issue.

Oblast, territorial administrative unit in the USSR, corresponding to a province.

Obligation, Days of, also Holidays of, in the Roman Catholic Church, days on which abstinence from servile (i.e. manual or gainful) labour and attendance at mass are commanded.

Oboe, woodwind instrument with a double-reed mouthpiece and a conical bore. The normal compass is from B flat below the treble stave to about F above the stave. The oboe has rich, penetrating and varied tones. It derives from the medieval shawm and was first developed during the 17th century. Larger members of the oboe family are the oboe d'amore (a minor third lower), the cor anglais, and the heckelphone or baritone oboe (an octave lower).

Obote, Milton (1924–), Ugandan politician. He joined the National Congress party when it was founded in 1952, and became a member of the Uganda National Congress in 1958. He led a political faction of his own after the split in the Congress party, and eventually this faction joined with the Uganda People's Union (UPI) to form the Uganda People's Congress (UPC), led by Obote. Its main platform was to reduce the power of Buganda within Uganda, but in 1961 he became prime minister in a national coalition government of UPC and the Buganda royalist party (KY). In 1966 Obote led the 'nationalist' opposition to the Kabaka Mutesa II of Buganda. Obote sought to broaden his popular appeal by economic and constitutional reforms, but was overthrown by a military coup, led by Maj.-Gen. Amin, January 1971. From 1971 to 1980 Obote was in exile in Tanzania but, after the overthrow of Amin's regime, returned to become president of Uganda.

Obrenovich, Serbian dynasty founded by Milos Obrenovich which held power in Serbia from 1815 to 1903, except the years 1842 to 1858.

O'Brien, Conor Cruise (1917–), Irish politician, journalist and author. From 1962 to 1964 O'Brien was vice-chancellor of Ghana University, and from 1965 to 1969 Schweitzer professor of the humanities at New York University. Between 1978 and 1981 he was editor-in-chief of *The Observer*. His publications include: *Camus*, 1969; *A Concise History of Ireland*, 1972.

O'Brien, Edna (1932–), Irish novelist, who later moved to England. Edna O'Brien is best known for her stories of Irish girls who attempt to break with native parochialism and come to terms with city culture. Her novels include *The Country Girls*, 1960; *The Lonely Girl* (later called *The Girl With Green Eyes*), 1962; *Girls in their Married Bliss*, 1964; *Casualties of Peace*, 1966; *A Pagan Place*, 1970, dramatised in 1972; and *Night*, 1972. Her collection of stories, *A Scandalous Woman*, appeared in 1974, and the autobiographical *Mother Ireland* in 1976. She also writes film scripts and poetry.

O'Brien, Flann, pseudonym of Brian O'Nolan (1911–66), Irish writer. His exuberant style, in which seriousness, surrealism and farce are blended, has given novels like *At Swim-Two-Birds*, 1939, *The Hard Life*, 1961, and *The Dalkey Archive*, 1964, a high critical reputation. *At Swim-Two-Birds* is considered his masterpiece, a mixture of humour, violence, fantasy and satire, owing a good deal to Gaelic comic tradition. His fantasy, *The Third Policeman*, 1967, has a more sombre colouring.

O'Brien, Kate (1897–1974), Irish novelist and playwright. Her first novel, *Without My Cloak*, 1931, was awarded the Hawthornden and the Tait Black Memorial prizes. *The Ante-Room*, 1934, and *The Last of Summer*, 1943, contain shrewd pictures of the Irish temperament, with a background in County Clare. Other novels are *Mary Lavelle*, 1936; *Pray for the Wanderer*, 1938; and *That Lady*, 1946. Among her plays are *The Bridge*, 1927, and *The Schoolroom Window*, 1937. *Farewell Spain*, 1937, is a travel book. Her later works include *The Flower of May*, 1953; *My Ireland*, 1962; and *Presentation Parlour*, 1963.

O'Brien, William (1852–1928), Irish journalist and patriot. In 1880 he established *United Ireland*, in order to popularise the aims of Parnell and the Land League. After sitting on the Land Commission of 1903 he threw his influence into the conciliation policy which looked for the union of Irishmen of all creeds and classes. He represented several constituencies until 1918, when he and his friends stood aside in favour of the Sinn Fein party.

O'Brien, William Smith (1803–64), Irish patriot. He sat in Parliament and, although a Protestant, favoured Catholic emancipation. He joined the Repeal Association of Daniel O'Connell, but in 1846 seceded to the Young Ireland party. In 1848 he led an abortive rising in Tipperary.

Obscene Publications. Under English law the test of what is obscene depends to a large extent upon whether it would tend to corrupt or deprave those to whom it is likely to be published or to whom it may reasonably be inferred from the circumstances that the defendant contemplated publication, or into whose hands he could reasonably expect it to come after he had published it.

The opinions of experts as to the literary, artistic, scientific, or other merits of the article may be heard, in order to show that publication of the article is or is not justified as being for the public good, on the grounds that it is in the interests of science, literature, art or learning, or any other subject of public concern.

In addition to these provisions, the Department of Customs and Excise may confiscate obscene matter entering the country and the Post Office may seize obscene articles which are being distributed through the post.

Observants, see FRANCISCANS.

Observatory. *The McMath solar telescope at Kitt Peak National Observatory, Arizona.*

Observatory, a location or institution devoted to the observation of natural phenomena outside the control of the observer, e.g. astronomical, magnetic, meteorological, seismological, tidal and vulcanological phenomena. Astronomical observatories date back to very early times if we include obelisks, pyramids, temples and stone circles, all of which undoubtedly had astronomical uses. Public observatories like those in Paris (founded 1667) and Greenwich (founded 1675) grew out of the economic need to provide a reliable method of oceanic navigation, and also to provide a sound basis for large-scale surveying. Astronomical research tended to be left to the universities or, even more frequently, to privately supported individuals. By the middle of the 19th century many universities supported at least a small observatory. Inevitably significant progress tended to be confined to those institutions which had the largest and best equipped telescopes, especially if these were located in a good climate. The outstanding success of the Lick Observatory and Hale Observatories in California fully impressed astronomers with the need for locating their instruments on good mountain sites.

In the United States, the National Science Foundation provides the funds for the National Radio Observatory at Green Bank, West Virginia; for the Kitt Peak National Observatory, Arizona; and the Cerro Tololo Inter-American Observatory in Chile. The University of California operates the Lick Observatory and the California Institute of Technology is very closely associated with the Hale Observatories.

To supplement their national organisations Belgium, Denmark, France, the Federal Republic of Germany, the Netherlands and Sweden agreed in the mid- 1950s to co-operate in setting up a southern station. This European Southern Observatory is at La Silla in the Chilean Andes not far from La Serena. In Britain support of all forms of astronomy is one of the functions of the Science and Engineering Research Council (SERC) established in 1965. It administers the Rutherford Appleton Laboratory at Chilton, the Royal Greenwich Observatory at Herstmonceux, and the Royal Observatory in Edinburgh.

'Observer, The', oldest surviving English Sunday newspaper, founded in 1791 on a capital of £100 by a young Irishman, W. S. Bourne, whose elder brother, W. H. Bourne, managed the new paper's finances. By 1799 they had established *The Observer* with a circulation in London and the provinces. Early in the 19th century *The Observer* was acquired by W. L. Clement, a pioneer in the field of pictorial journalism and the first man to establish a newspaper syndicate. In 1870 it was bought by Julius Beer, and with his son he conducted the paper with such distinction that it achieved much of the status and quality for which it is known today. In 1905 *The Observer* was bought by Lord Northcliffe, who appointed J. L. Garvin as editor. The first Lord Astor acquired *The Observer* in 1911 and in 1945 the second Lord Astor, and his son the Hon. David Astor, vested the ownership of the paper in a trust. In 1976 the American-owned Atlantic Richfield company acquired a 90 per cent stake in the newspaper, but in the early 1980s the publication was purchased by the UK-based Lonrho company.

Obsidian, an igneous effusive rock formed by the rapid chilling of molten lava, resulting in the formation of a natural glass. When massive, obsidian shows the conchoidal fracture and razor-sharp edges characteristic of glassy materials. Volcanic glass may also occur as a froth (pumice) or strands (Pelées Hair). Crystalline inclusions may be present, as may crystalline aggregates of incipient crystallisation (snowflake obsidian).

Obstetrics (Latin *obstetrix*, midwife; from *obstare*, to stand before), that part of medicine which deals with pregnancy, childbirth and the puerperium (the period immediately after childbirth).

Modern Developments. The relief of pain has travelled a long way since the early days of the science, and all midwives are now trained in the use of analgesics. 'Trilene', which is efficient and safe, is now the standard analgesic. 'Twilight sleep' is attained with such drugs as pethidene, and by epidural anaesthesia.

Antenatal care and the early detection of abnormalities, together with an ever improving standard of health and physique in young women, have led to a marked reduction in the number of cases of childbirth needing operative interference in delivery. A much improved technique in caesarean section and safe anaesthesia has made this operation one of choice in all cases in which there might be undue hazard to mother and child if delivery were left to follow its natural course. The special complication of toxaemia in pregnancy is becoming better understood and can usually be controlled. Haemorrhage is a complication which, thanks to modern methods of blood transfusion, has to a large extent lost its terrors.

The discovery by Landsteiner and Wiener in 1940 of the rhesus factor in the blood increased our knowledge of an important condition known as haemolytic disease of the newborn. About 5 babies in every 1000 births suffer from it, and of these there is a risk that between 10 per cent and 80 per cent will be still-born.

See also CAESAREAN SECTION.

Ocarina, musical wind instrument of metal or terracotta, in shape resembling an egg. The sound is very sweet. There are ten finger-holes, a whistle-like mouthpiece, and a large internal cavity. The Chinese hsüan (c.1300 BC) was its prototype.

O'Casey, Sean (1884–1964), Irish dramatist. Reared in the Dublin tenements, which often serve as a setting for his plays, O'Casey exploited the sheer comedy, coupled with intense tragedy, to be found by discerning eyes in grim slum dwellings. His Abbey Theatre career began in 1923. His *Juno and the Paycock*, produced in 1925, was a great success in London. It was followed by *The Plough and the Stars* in 1926. These plays established him as a master of comedy and pathos on the grand scale, native in idiom and convincingly true. He forsook the purely realistic theatre for fantasy, as in *The Silver Tassie*, 1928, and *Within the Gates*, 1933, both expressionist plays. When Yeats refused to stage the former there was a rupture, lasting many years, between O'Casey and the Abbey Theatre. O'Casey wrote an artistically unsuccessful play, *The Star Turns Red*, 1940, to propagandise his socialist views. *Purple Dust*, 1940, a farce, and *Red Roses for Me*, 1943, an emotional symbolic piece about the political condition of Ireland, were more successful. *Oak Leaves and Lavender*, 1946, *Cock-a-Doodle Dandy*, 1949, and *The Drums of Father Ned*, 1956, all exhibit O'Casey's characteristic qualities of vigorous comedy, lyrical feeling for Ireland, and compassion for the suffering, though not always with complete artistic control.

O'Casey lived in England from 1928. He wrote a lengthy autobiography of which the separate parts are *I Knock at the Door*, 1939; *Pictures in the Hallway*, 1942; *Drums under the Window*, 1945; *Inishfallen Fare Thee Well*, 1949; *Rose and Crown*, 1952; and *Sunset and Evening Star*, 1954.

Occam, William of, see OCKHAM, WILLIAM OF.

Occitan, see PROVENÇAL.

Occleve, Thomas, see HOCCLEVE, THOMAS.

Occultation, the cutting off from view of one body by another passing in front of it. In astronomy the most frequent occulting body is the Moon. The practically instantaneous disappearance (or reappearance) of a star at the Moon's limb is a striking phenomenon which clearly demonstrates the absence of any significant lunar atmosphere. In a similar way the position and structure of a radio source can be determined if it is occulted by the Moon. Occultations of stars by planets are rare and of short duration, but they are carefully observed for the information they can give about the planet's atmosphere and diameter.

Occultism, umbrella term for subjects generally considered beyond the range of normal knowledge, and often classified as supernatural, esoteric, magical, mystical, etc.

Occupational Diseases. There are few occupations entirely free from risk of disease. Even agricultural and other outdoor workers are liable, in consequence of exposure to the weather and the sun's rays, to contract cancer of the skin (epithelioma) and to come into contact with poisonous agricultural chemicals. Writers, telegraphists and typists are all liable to cramp of the hand, musicians may acquire callosities and emphysema, whilst clergymen tend to suffer from laryngitis, a disease which they share with teachers, singers and public speakers. Medical men, in addition to the obvious hazards of infection, are reputedly prone to peptic ulcers and coronary artery disease.

Industrial diseases include anthrax, or woolsorters' disease, which affects chiefly the lungs and spleen, and is often fatal. Workers in mines, tunnels and sewers are sometimes attacked by spirochaetal jaundice (Weil's disease) and by hookworm (ancylostomiasis). Poisons which may affect workers include metals such as lead, arsenic, antimony, mercury and nickel; non-metallic substances, as for instance phosphorus, carbon disulphide, and a large number of coal-tar products (benzene, aniline, trinitrotoluene, pictric acid, etc.) used in dyeing and as explosives; gaseous poisons, e.g. chlorine, arsine and the gases of coal-mines. Other very important occupational diseases are pulmonary tuberculosis and asbestosis, caused by the inhalation of foreign particles; also dermatitis, ulceration and cancer of the skin induced by irritating chemicals, such as alkalis, paraffin, chromium salts, tars, oils and the like. Finally mention should be made of the risks to operatives using radioactive substances.

Occupational Health and Safety Legislation. In Great Britain the Health and Safety at Work, etc. Act 1974 (which came into force on 1 April 1975) marked the beginning of a new era in the history of legislation on occupational health and safety. The 1974 Act for the first time recognised that it is people at work—any kind of work—who need protection. Previously, legislation had been passed piecemeal to deal with dangers affecting specific groups of workers.

Early 19th-century legislation only affected the textile and allied industries. From 1860 to 1864 Acts were passed to include in the existing factory legislation a number of non-textile industries. The Acts from 1878 to 1895 were concerned mainly with factory hygiene, safety, control of overtime and reduction of hours of labour for children.

It became increasingly clear that very detailed rules were required for specific processes. Putting these rules in an Act of Parliament was too cumbersome a procedure and so the 1891 and 1895 Acts empowered ministers to make detailed regulations. This system was continued and extended in subsequent Acts so that by 1975 about 400 separate sets of regulations were in force.

Health and Safety at Work Act 1974. A committee was appointed in 1970 to consider the workings of occupational health and safety legislation. It reported in 1972 that the legislation followed 'a style and pattern developed in an earlier and different social and technological context'. It criticised the multiplicity of regulating Acts and inspectorates, the fact that the patchwork of legislation still left some employees unprotected, and the lack of encouragement of safety-consciousness by management and workers. The Health and Safety at Work etc. Act 1974, implemented many of the committee's proposals.

Occupational Psychology, see INDUSTRIAL PSYCHOLOGY.

Occupational Therapy. The value of treatment by occupation has been recognised from the earliest days of medicine and that is basically what occupational therapy is. Activities are specifically chosen for individual patients to aid recovery and resettlement, or to minimise the effects of a permanent disability.

Occupational therapists work with both the physically and psychiatrically disabled. Domiciliary work now plays a very important rôle and an increasing number of patients are being treated in their own homes. Occupational therapy must be prescribed by a doctor, who will refer the patient and indicate the diagnosis and aims of treatment. After assessments to ascertain the patient's ability and limitations, the therapist is responsible for planning specific treatment and explaining it to the patient. Occupational therapy departments are designed to provide assessment and treatment.

Ocean, the vast area of water that covers about 71 per cent of the Earth's surface. The proportion of land to water in the northern hemisphere is 2:3 while in the southern hemisphere it is 1:4·7.

The floor of the ocean has a number of distinctive physical features. At the edge is the continental shelf, which is, geologically, part of the continent and usually lies at a depth of less than 200 metres. From the edge of the shelf the continental slope descends at a gradient of 60 metres/km. At its foot is a gentler slope, the continental rise formed largely from sediment washed down the continental slope. The abyssal plain is the feature that can be considered as the bottom of the ocean. It lies at a depth of about 5 km and accounts for about 40 per cent of the Earth's surface area. It is relatively smooth and flat, its major topographic feature being the ocean ridges that rise to within 2 km of the ocean surface and mark the region of formation of new ocean crust. The deepest points are the ocean trenches where old ocean crust is being absorbed back into the mantle. The deepest of these is the Mindanao Trench off the Philippines which is 11,524 metres deep.

The 1,349,929 million cubic km of water that constitutes the oceans was mostly derived from outgassing of water vapour from cooling rocks as the Earth consolidated. Its saltiness is due to the mineral matter—mostly sodium chloride but with some magnesium and calcium carbonates as well—dissolved in it. The saltiness, or salinity, may be as high as 41 parts per thousand in semi-landlocked areas such as the Red Sea but is usually around 35 parts per thousand. The water is constantly in circulation with warm surface currents moving from the Equator to the poles and cold currents returning. Light can penetrate only a short distance into the ocean water, the blue wavelengths travelling furthest and fading out at a depth of about 100 metres. Sound waves travel at about 1500 metres per second through ocean water but this varies with the salinity and temperature. The principal oceans of the world are: Pacific, 166 million km^2; Atlantic, 82 million km^2; Indian, 73·6 million km^2; Antarctic, 35 million km^2; Arctic, 12·2 million km^2.

Ocean Island, or Banaba, situated in the Pacific Ocean, 0°52′S, 169°35′E. In 1900 the island was taken under British rule, and in 1916 was formally annexed to the Gilbert and Ellice Island colony (see Kiribati). It is very rich in high-grade phosphate, formerly extracted by the British Phosphate Commission. Area 6·5 km^2; population (1980) 300. During the Second World War, the island was occupied by the Japanese.

Oceania, see AUSTRALASIA and OCEANIA.

Oceania, Languages of. Four different groups of languages are included under the term Oceanic: Tasmanian, which ceased to be spoken in the 19th century; Australian, many of which are now also extinct; Papuan; Austronesian. Although estimates vary, it is likely that between 1000 and 1500 languages are spoken in Oceania, the great majority only by a few hundred or a few thousand people. This has always caused social and educational problems. In certain places a mission language is understood over a fairly wide area. Several varieties of pidgin are used over the whole region of eastern New Guinea and neighbouring island groups. The best known is *Tok pisin* (Neo-Melanesian).

Oceanic Ridge. An oceanic ridge extends continuously for more than 60,000 km under the world's oceans. Various names have been allocated to different sections of the ridge (Mid-Atlantic Ridge, East Pacific Rise, etc), but the system is essentially a unified one of broad uplift along the centre line of the oceans. Whereas the profiles in the East Pacific Rise are fairly smooth, the crest of the North Atlantic Ridge is characterised by a rift valley with block-faulted flanks. Parts of the crest lie above sea-level, thus producing the Azores and Iceland, but generally the crest lies 2000–3000 m below the ocean's surface. The crest is also characterised by perpendicular fracture zones and the centres of shallow earthquakes.

See also GEOTECTONICS; RIFT VALLEY.

Oceanography, the study of the oceans. Modern oceanography involves the study of the topography and composition of the ocean bed by means of sonar imaging and long-distance sampling equipment; the composition and physical properties of the water by instruments and samplers that can be deployed at varying depths; the movements of the seawater by tracking devices and satellite surveillance; and the animal and plant life by direct observation. Sophisticated sensing equipment and computers, mounted on research ships, aircraft and satellites, are the tools of the modern oceanographer.

The beginning of modern oceanography came with the voyage of HMS *Challenger* between 1872 and 1876 sponsored by the British Government in which a team of naval and civilian scientists explored the Atlantic, Pacific and Indian oceans using equipment that was being developed to assist in the laying of undersea telegraph cables. The first oceanographic institutes were established in the early 1900s by Prince Albert of Monaco and Paris.

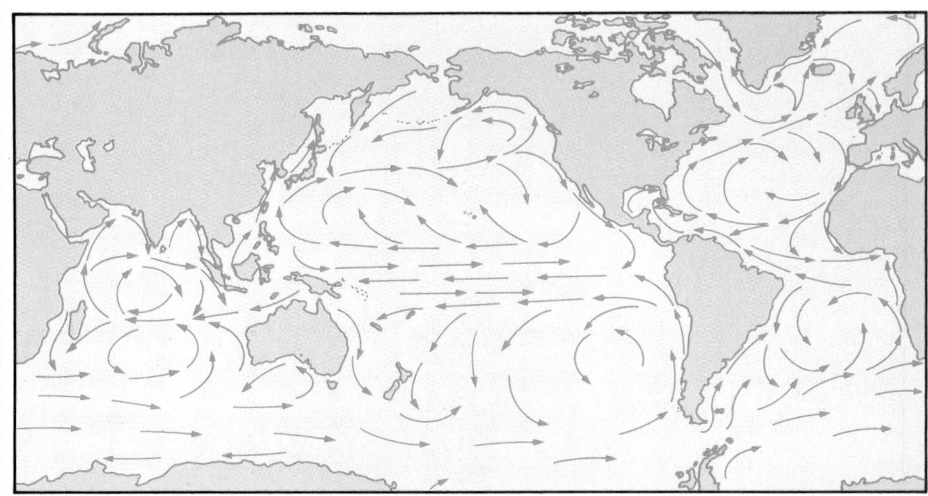

Ocean. *The surface currents of the world's oceans are organised into five great gyres. They are wind driven and reflect the pattern of atmospheric circulation above.*

Since the end of the Second World War the oceans have been explored for mineral and fuel reserves, and as a source of food. Oceanographic studies have made possible the extraction of continental-shelf oil and also the establishment of tidal power stations. The management of fish stocks and other food supplies relies on oceanographic work. Oceanography can also be used to predict the effects of coastal erosion and the movement and effect of polluted waters.

Oceanus, in Greek mythology, god of the river which was believed to encircle the Earth.

Ocelot, and tiger-cat are popular names applied to *Felis pardalis*, a species of family Felidae, order Carnivora, found in tropical America. It is a beautiful animal, 70–100 cm long, and has a tail about 30 cm long; the colour is usually tawny, with dark spots or bars. The ocelot is a good climber, and feeds for the most part on birds and small animals caught in its native forests.

Ochil Hills, range of hills in Scotland, in Central and Tayside Regions, extending for about 40 km from the Firth of Tay to Bridge of Allan. The highest summit is Ben Cleuch (721 m). In the past, coal, iron, copper and lead were extensively mined but today it is mainly rich pasture for sheep and cattle.

Ochre, name given to several varieties of native earths, which consist of a mixture of hydrated oxide of iron with silica and alumina. They range in colour from light yellow to brown. The incrustations of oxides of other metals, e.g. antimony, bismuth and nickel, are also called ochres though they are not so important. Red and yellow ochres are prepared by grinding and washing, and are extensively used as pigments.
See also PIGMENT.

Ocimum, a genus of annuals and shrubs in the family Labiatae, bearing whorls of white flowers. *O. basilicum* is the sweet or common basil, which is grown in kitchen gardens.

Ockham, William of, also Occam (1290–1349), called 'Doctor Singularis et Invincibilis', Franciscan Nominalist philosopher. In philosophy he revived the tenets of Nominalism in a modified form. 'Ockham's Razor' is a dictum which states *Entia non sunt multiplicanda praeter necessitatem* (Entities are not to be multiplied without necessity). In the struggle between church and state, Ockham took the view that in secular matters it was the secular ruler who was supreme, and that civil government was not subject to the pope.

O'Connell, Daniel (1775–1847), Irish patriot and orator, known as 'The Liberator'. In 1823 he formed the Catholic Association, to campaign for Catholic emancipation and the repeal of the Act of Union. His great organising ability and powerful oratory were fundamental in securing the former in 1829; O'Connell then entered Parliament and began his second great campaign. He organised mass meetings all over Ireland, but in 1843 was imprisoned for sedition. When he was released, after a few months, the Irish famine had pushed repeal of the Union into the background.

O'Connor, Feargus Edward (1794–1855), Irish agitator and Chartist. He was an active supporter of the Reform Bill of 1832, and was returned to Parliament for County Cork.

October Revolution. *A political demonstration by soldiers in 1917.*

He allied himself with the 'physical force' Chartists, and in 1840 was imprisoned for seditious libel. From 1847 he sat in the House of Commons for Nottingham, and led the great Chartist demonstration at Kennington in 1848. He was declared insane in 1852.

O'Connor, Frank, pseudonym of Michael O'Donovan (1903–66), Irish novelist and playwright. O'Connor's short stories have been compared with those of Chekhov. Their material is basically provincial life in Cork, but he brings to his theme a wide human sympathy and careful elegance owing much to his reading in other literatures, especially Russian and French.
O'Connor is also the author of the novels *The Saint and Mary Kate*, 1932, and *Dutch Interior*, 1940, as well as an excellent history of Irish literature, *The Backward Look*, 1967.

Ocotea, a genus of tropical trees in the family Lauraceae, bearing tough alternate leaves and bunches of small green flowers. *O. bullata* yields a timber known as stinkwood. *O. opifera* exudes a volatile oil.

Octane, C_8H_{18}, hydrocarbon of the alkane series. Normal octane has a boiling point of 125·6°C and may be obtained in the pure state by heating octyl iodide with zinc and dilute hydrochloric acid. It may also be synthesised by heating *n*-butyl iodide with sodium. *Iso*-octane has a boiling point of 116°C and may be synthesised by the action of sodium on a mixture of propyl and isoamyl iodides, and fractionally distilling the product. Octanes are found in petroleum and used in motor fuel, the performance of one octane isomer (2,2,4-trimethylpentane) being used as the standard for petroleum performance.
See also OCTANE NUMBER.

Octane Number, measure of the anti-knock value of gasoline. The fuel under test is put into a Co-operative Fuel Research (CFR) engine, a single-cylinder variable-compression engine developed by the CFR Committee in the USA. It is matched at the critical compression ratio (i.e. the compression ratio at which knock is first apparent) with a blend of two reference fuels, one of high anti-knock value, *iso*-octane, and one of low anti-knock value, normal heptane. The result is expressed as an octane number, which is the percentage of *iso*-octane, arbitrarily given an octane number of 100, in a blend with normal heptane (octane number 0) which matches the fuel under examination, e.g. a fuel matched by a blend of 80 per cent of *iso*-octane and 20 per cent of heptane would have an octane number of 80. The scale is extended beyond 100 by using reference fuels containing additions of tetraethyl lead.
See also KNOCKING.

Octave, interval in music comprising the eight notes of the diatonic scale, called the tonic, supertonic, mediant, subdominant, dominant, submediant, leading-note and octave. It has five intervals of a whole tone and two of a semitone in its diatonic form. The octave of any note has double the number of vibrations per second of that note, giving an effect of unison.

Octavia, sister of the Roman Emperor Augustus. She was married first to Marcellus, consul in 50 BC, and on his death (40) to Mark Antony, who quickly abandoned her for Cleopatra.

Octavia (b.c.AD 40), daughter of the Emperor Claudius and Messalina, and wife of Nero, who in AD 62 divorced her in order to marry Poppaea Sabina and had her put to death.

Octavo (8vo), term used in bookbinding for a book or sheet of printed paper which has been folded three times to one-eighth of its original size, so forming 8 leaves or a section of 16 pages.

Octet, chamber composition for eight mixed instruments, usually in several movements, and in some kind of sonata or suite form.

An example is Schubert's Octet, for clarinet, horn, bassoon, string quartet and double bass. The Mendelssohn Octet is unusual in its choice of two string quartets instead of the more normal mixture of wind and strings.

October, the 10th month of the modern calendar year. The name reflects its former position of eighth month in the ancient Roman calendar.

October Revolution, seizure of power by the Bolsheviks in Russia on 7 November (25 October Old Style) 1917. The Military Revolutionary Committee of the St Petersburg Soviet, composed of Bolsheviks, Left Socialist Revolutionaries and Anarchists, overthrew Kerenski's provisional government with the help of the Red Guards, whereupon a new 'Provisional Workers' and Peasants' government' was set up—the Council of People's Commissars.

Octobrists, Russian political party, so called after the Imperial Manifesto of 17 October 1905 which introduced the constitution. Octobrists were right-wing liberals and drew their support from the right wing of the Zemstvo movement, business men, and liberal civil servants. Their leader was A. I. Guchkov. They were the majority party in the 3rd and 4th Dumas, and participated in the 'progressive bloc' during the First World War, and the 1917 provisional government.

Octopus, a genus of molluscs (class Cephalopoda, subclass Dibranchia) with eight arms and without the internal shell or 'bone' which is found in the mantle of many cephalopods. The body is oval or rounded, and the tentacles have suckers. Octopuses are widely distributed on the shores of almost all temperate and tropical seas, and do not attain the great size of some of the squids, although the giant octopus of the Pacific may have a span of 10 m. Octopuses spend the daytime hidden in the shadow of rocks, but are more active at night. Recent studies have led to the conclusion that the octopus is a highly intelligent animal, comparing favourably with higher vertebrates in this respect.

Ode (Greek *ōdē*, a song), rhymed or (rarely) unrhymed lyric poem, frequently in the form of an address, usually exalted and stately in style, and often in varied or irregular metres, the length being commonly between 50 and 200 lines. Among the best known in English poetry are Milton's 'On the Morning of Christ's Nativity', Shelley's 'Ode to a Skylark', Keats's 'Ode to a Nightingale', all of the so-called lyric type; and Dryden's 'Alexander's Feast' and Wordsworth's 'Ode on the Intimations of Immortality', both of the so-called false Pindaric type.
See also LYRIC.

Odense, capital and important port of Fyn island and country, Denmark, on the Odense river, 140 km south-west of Copenhagen. Its main industries are textiles, electrical equipment, foundries, sugar refineries and shipbuilding yards. Odense exports agricultural and dairy produce. King Canute II and other Danish kings are buried in the Gothic cathedral, and the town was the birthplace of Hans Christian Andersen, whose home now contains a museum. Population (1980) 168,528.

Oder (Czech and Polish, *Odra*), river of Eastern Europe, which rises in Moravia, flows north through the Moravian Gate in the Sudeten Mountains, and enters the Baltic Sea through the Zalew Szczeciński. Its principal tributaries are the Warta and Nysa rivers; with the Nysa it has formed since 1946 the boundary between the German Democratic Republic and Poland. It has extensive canal systems connecting it with the Spree, Havel and Vistula, and the rich industrial area of Silesia. Length 866 km.

Odessa, capital city of Odessa *oblast* of the Ukrainian SSR and a major industrial, cultural and resort centre of the USSR, on the north-west coast of the Black Sea. It has large engineering, food, textile and chemical industries. It is a very important transport centre with a seaport (the second largest in the country after Leningrad), three railway lines, and an airport. It is an Antarctic whaling fleet base and one of the most attractive and best planned cities in the USSR.
Known since 1415, it first belonged to Lithuania, then to the Crimean Tatars, and became Turkish in 1764; the Turkish fortress was stormed by the Russians in 1789 and the region annexed in 1791. It became a centre of the Ukrainian cultural and national movement, of Jewish culture, of the labour movement, and of social democracy. Population (1980) 1,057,000.

Odontoglossum. *These epiphytic orchids are found naturally at high altitude.*

Odets, Clifford (1906–63), US playwright. After an early career as an actor, he became associated with the Guild Theatre in New York in 1928, and his first play *Awake and Sing* was produced by the group in 1935. In the same year he made his name with a one-act play, *Waiting for Lefty*, written for the New Theatre League. The play, based on the New York cab strike of 1934, was sensational for its social implications. Other plays include *Till the Day I Die*, 1935; *Paradise Lost*, 1935; *Golden Boy*, 1937; *The Big Knife*, 1949; *Winter Journey*, 1952; and *The Flowering Peach*, 1955. His work shows the influence of Sean O'Casey.

Odilo, Saint (c.962–1049). In 994 he became abbot of Cluny, and under his rule the Cluniac house increased from 37 to 65. Known throughout Christendom for his liberality to the poor, he was a friend of popes and princes.

Odin (English Woden, German Wotan), the 'raging one', major Germanic god, identified by the Romans with Mercury, hence Woden's day (Wednesday) for *Mercurii dies*, French *mercredi*. Odin appears as the source of wisdom. As war-god he gives gifts such as swords and determines the course of battles. Although he may give victory, Odin's most characteristic rôle is as a giver of death, using his valkyries to choose the slain warriors who will be conveyed to Valhalla.
See also AESIR; MYTHOLOGY; NIBELUNGS.

Odinga, (Ajuma) Oginga (1912–), Kenyan politician. In 1959 he became president of the Kenyan Independence Movement, and in 1960 he became vice-president of the Kenya African National Union (KANU). Odinga became eventually minister for Home Affairs, then vice-president and, finally, minister without portfolio, in the government of the independent Kenya after 1964. But in 1965 and 1966 he became involved in an ideological debate with Mboya and was identified as a radical. In 1969 Odinga was imprisoned.
On his release in 1972 Odinga rejoined KANU, but his attempt to seek election in the 1974 general election under a KANU ticket was thwarted when KANU rejected his nomination.

Odo (c.1036–97), Bishop of Bayeux, half-brother to William the Conqueror and co-regent of England with William Fitz-Osbern in 1067.

Odo of Cluny, Saint (c.879–942), French abbot. In 909 he became a Benedictine at Baume, and in 927 abbot of Cluny. Under his government the monastery began to exert its influence throughout France and in Italy, and greatly enhanced the prestige of the Benedictine order.

Odoacer, or Odovacar (c.435–93), German soldier. He became a captain in the imperial bodyguard at Rome, and, by leading a revolt and dethroning Romulus Augustulus, he established in 476 on Italian soil, in place of the imperial government, a German kingdom. He took the title of king of Italy, and reigned until his power was overthrown, in 493, by Theodoric the Great, king of the Goths. Odoacer was then put to death.

Odontoglossum, a genus of 200 orchids, most of which are natives of South America. Usually from 5 to 40 flowers are borne on a long spike but, in a few species, these spikes are branched and bear a hundred or more blooms. The colours are chiefly brown, yellow or white, often with spots.

Odysseus (son of wrath), Latin Ulysses (from a western Greek form *Olysseus*, wolf), in Greek legend, son of Laertes, ruler of Ithaca; his wife was Penelope. He sailed with the Greeks to Troy, and was renowned for his courage, cunning and eloquence. The most famous part of his story is that of his ten years' wandering by sea after the fall of Troy, as told in Homer's *Odyssey*.

Odyssey, see HOMER.

Oedema (Greek *oidema*, swelling), localised or generalised swelling, owing to an excessive collection of fluid in the tissues. Under normal circumstances, the cells of the body receive their nutrition and oxygen from the lymph or plasma, as it leaves the capillary vessels and bathes the tissues. This fluid then returns to the circulation either through the capillaries again or via the lymphatic vessels. Any condition that affects the permeability (the ability of the wall to let fluids pass in and out) of the capillaries or blocks the return of the fluid to them or to the lymphatic vessels will result in oedema. Oedema itself is not a disease but is a sign of disease in one of the body systems. Treatment is usually directed towards eliminating the disease that has caused the swelling.

Oedipus, see THEBAN LEGEND.

Oedipus Complex, term used in psychoanalysis for a child's unconscious or subconscious sexual feelings for the parent of the opposite sex, often accompanied by hostility or aggression towards the parent of the same sex. According to Sigmund Freud, who developed the concept in *The Interpretation of Dreams*, 1899, and named it after the legendary Greek hero who unknowingly killed his father and married his mother, this is a normal development between the ages of three and five, and is succeeded by identification with the parent of the same sex. The concept is no longer accepted as wholly valid.

Oehlenschläger, Adam Gottlob (1779–1850), Danish poet and playwright. Decisive in his literary development was an encounter with Henrik Steffens, who converted him to Romanticism. His *Digte*, 1803, established him as the leading Romantic poet of Denmark and marked the beginning of a new era in Danish literature.

Oenothera, a genus of hardy annuals, biennials and perennials of the Onagraceae, natives of America. *O. biennis* is the fragrant, yellow-flowered evening primrose. The flower with its long tube is suited to pollination by long-tongued moths.

Oersted, Hans Christian (1777–1851), Danish physicist. During a lecture in 1819 he brought a magnetic compass near a wire carrying electric current and noticed that its needle was deflected. Oersted himself played little part in the further development of electromagnetic theory. He published *Naturlaerens mechaniske Deel* (The mechanical part of physics), 1844, and wrote numerous studies in chemistry, popular science, metaphysics, etc. His name was formerly used for a unit of magnetic field strength equal to $10^3/4\pi$ A/m.

Oesophagus, see GULLET.

Oestridae, a family of the order Diptera, class Insecta. These are the botflies and warble flies. The larvae cause myiasis (invasion of the tissues by fly larvae) in animals. The adults are rather large, brownish, hairy flies, with mouthparts that are reduced or vestigial. The larva is a large maggot covered with spines. All botflies and warble flies are important for the damage they cause to livestock, where their presence can retard growth, reduce milk and meat yield, and render hides worthless.

Oestrogen, one of two female hormones secreted by the ovaries. The hormone is responsible for the development of secondary sex characteristics and the reproductive organs: uterus, Fallopian tubes and vagina. Extra oestrogen is produced during menstruation, ovulation and pregnancy. Synthetic preparations of oestrogen are used in treating certain disorders, such as the relief of symptoms during menopause.

Oestrous Cycle, the reproductive cycle of female animals, especially mammals. On one or more occasions during the breeding season the female is receptive to the male and is said to be 'in heat'; this is the period of *oestrus* and is accompanied by ovulation, i.e. the discharge of an egg from the ovary. Oestrus is preceded by a period known as *pro-oestrus*, when the vagina swells and becomes increasingly vascular, in preparation for coitus, and it is followed by the period of *post-oestrus*, when the uterus hypertrophies ready to receive the egg if fertilisation has occurred, so that *post-oestrus* then merges into pregnancy. The menstrual cycle of women corresponds to the oestrous cycle of other mammals, but it is distinguished particularly by the bleeding of menstruation, which is absent or inconspicuous in other species.

The changes occurring in the oestrous cycle are brought about by the hormone *oestrogen* produced in the ovary, and responsible also for the development of the secondary sexual characters (as for instance the breasts) at puberty.

See also BIRTH CONTROL; MENSTRUATION.

O'Faoláin, Seán (1900–), Irish novelist, short-story writer and biographer. His first book, *Midsummer Night's Madness*, a collection of short stories, appeared in 1932.

O'Faoláin's novels include *A Nest of Simple Folk*, 1933; *Bird Alone*, 1936; *Come Back to Erin*, 1940; and *Teresa*, 1946. Of his biographies, the best is *King of Beggars: a Life of Daniel O'Connell*, 1938. He edited the works of Thomas Moore, 1929, and the autobiography of Wolfe Tone, 1937. *She Had To Do Something*, 1938, is a play; *A Summer in Italy*, 1950, and *South Sicily*, 1953, are travel books. In 1962 he published *I Remember, I Remember*, and in 1965 *Vive Moi!*, an autobiography.

Offa (fl.757–96), King of Mercia. He succeeded Ethelbald, and by the time he died had re-established Mercian supremacy in southern England, the King of Wessex being his dependant, and his influence extending into Northumbria.

See also OFFA'S DYKE.

Offaly, inland county in the province of Leinster, Republic of Ireland; bounded on the west by the River Shannon. The surface is flat, the northern part being occupied by the Bog of Allen, but the Slieve Bloom Mountains lie along the border between Offaly and Laois, the greatest altitude being 528 m. There are some rich pastures and grazing districts. Oats, barley, wheat and potatoes are grown and cattle, sheep, pigs and poultry bred. The chief towns are Tullamore, Birr and Edenderry. Area 1997 km²; population (1979) 57,342.

Offa's Dyke, great earthwork made about AD 785 by Offa of Mercia as a boundary between the English and Welsh.

See also DYKE.

Offenbach, Jacques (1819–80), German-French composer. His only large-scale opera, *Les Contes d'Hoffmann*, occupied him for many years, but he left it unfinished; it nevertheless achieved wide popularity. He wrote 89 operettas including *Orphée aux enfers*, *La Belle Hélène*, *La Vie Parisienne*, *La Grande Duchesse de Gérolstein*, *La Périchole*, and *Dick Whittington and his Cat*.

Offenbach, city in Hessen, Federal Republic of Germany, on the Main, 10 km east of Frankfurt. Its commercial prosperity dates from the settlement of Huguenots in the 17th century. There are leather, chemical (artificial fibre) and engineering industries. Population (1980) 111,200.

Offertory (Latin *offertorium*, oblation), the presentation of the unconsecrated bread and wine at the altar during the Eucharist or mass.

Official Receiver, or Liquidator. See BANKRUPTCY; COMPANY; RECEIVER, OFFICIAL.

Official Secrets. The Official Secrets Acts make it an offence in Britain, to approach or enter any 'prohibited place' for any purpose prejudicial to the safety or interests of the state; to make any sketch, plan, model or note calculated to be useful to an enemy; or to obtain or communicate to any other person any information which might be or which is intended to be useful to an enemy. The law further makes it an offence to do certain things. These include the unauthorised use of a naval, military, air force or police uniform, forging or tampering with passports or military or naval passes or permits; retaining an official document without authority to retain it; or allowing any other person to have possession of an official document issued for the use of the accused alone; or communicating a secret official code word or password; or being in unlawful possession of any such code or password.

Offset Printing, see LITHOGRAPHY.

O'Flaherty, Liam (1897–), Irish novelist. His first novel, *Thy Neighbour's Wife*, appeared in 1923, and was followed in 1925 by *The Informer*, which won the Tait Black Memorial Prize, and was also successfully filmed. A master of the short story, he published many collections. *Darkness*, 1926, is a tragedy and *Two Years*, 1930, *I Went to Russia*, 1931, and *Shame the Devil*, 1934, are autobiographical.

Ogaden, an area of eastern Ethiopia which is bounded north, east and south by Somalia. Semi-desert, it supports a nomadic population who are mainly Somali Muslims. Somalia has a long-standing dispute with Ethiopia over possession of the Ogaden; recurrent clashes and guerilla actions developed into a war in 1977–78.

Ogam, or Ogham (spelt in Old Irish *Ogom* or *Ogum*), word of uncertain origin and meaning applied to a form of cryptic script used by some Celtic peoples in the British Isles. The use of the Ogam scripts continued until the Middle Ages.

Ogbomosho, city in Western State, Nigeria, 50 km south-west of Ilorin. It is situated on the plateau of Yorubaland, in the savanna zone at the intersection of roads from Ilorin, Oyo, Oshogbo and Ikoyi. The town was founded in the mid-17th century as an outpost of the Oyo empire, and did not grow significantly until settled by Oyo refugees from the Fulani *jihad* (holy war). Today it is the third largest urban centre in Nigeria after Lagos and Ibadan. It is a focus of commerce and trade for the Yoruba farmers of the surrounding region (dealing in cattle, staple crops, cotton and palm oil). Population (1975) 432,000.

Ogden, Charles Kay (1889–1957), British

linguist. From 1925 he developed Basic English, a simplified form of English with a limited vocabulary of 850 words chosen for their ability, through paraphrase, to do the work of the entire vocabulary of English. Ogden's hopes that it would supersede artificially created languages like Esperanto have not come to fruition.

Ogdon, John (1937–), British pianist. He won the 1962 Tchaikovsky Competition in Moscow, and has since appeared all over the world in a wide repertory of classical and modern works. He is also a composer.

Ogee, moulding formed by two curves, the upper concave and the lower convex; the adjective ogee is frequently applied to a type of pointed arch.

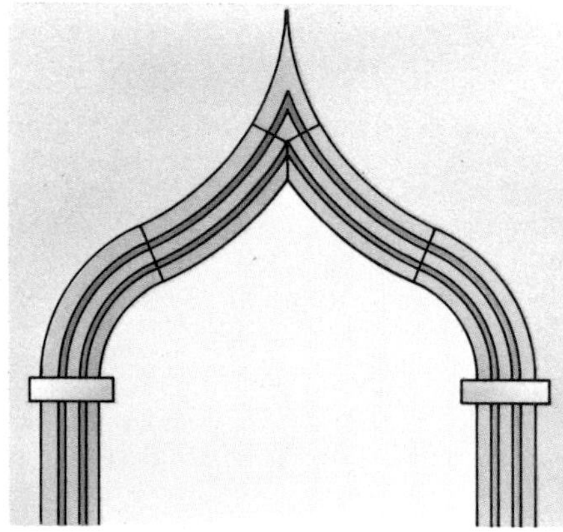

Ogee, a convex-concave arch style often found in later forms of Gothic architecture.

Oglethorpe, James Edward (1696–1785), British general and philanthropist, founder of the state of Georgia. In 1722 he became MP for Haslemere, and in 1729 was chairman of the parliamentary committee on debtors' prisons. In 1732 he obtained a charter for settling the colony of Georgia in America as a refuge for paupers and a barrier for British colonies against Spanish aggression and in 1733 accompanied the first settlers to the colony and founded Savannah. He successfully defended Georgia after the outbreak of war with Spain in 1739 and ensured that the new colony grew and prospered. Returning to England in 1743, he fought against the Jacobite insurrection of 1745 but was accused of failing in his military duties and, although acquitted, he resigned his commission.

O'Hara, John Henry (1905–70), US novelist. His novels, which are of the terse, hard-boiled school, include *Appointment in Samarra*, 1934; *Butterfield 8*, 1935; *A Rage to Live*, 1949; *The Farmer's Hotel*, 1951; *From the Terrace*, 1959; and *The Lockwood Concern*, 1965. He also wrote many short stories.

O'Higgins, Bernardo (1778–1842), Chilean patriot, soldier and statesman, generally known as the Liberator of Chile. He led the Chilean patriot forces against the Spanish royalists in 1810. O'Higgins defeated the Spaniards at Chacabuco in 1817, and became governor of Chile. O'Higgins's progressive administration was ended by a revolt led by the landed aristocracy in 1823.

Ohio (Buckeye State), state of the USA, lying between Lake Erie and the Ohio river, which forms its southern boundary for over 700 km. The south-eastern section of Ohio belongs physically to the Appalachian plateau province and is hilly and deeply dissected; westwards and northwards relief becomes gentler and the north-western corner of the state comprises the Maumee river plains, which are flat and fertile. Drainage is either south to the Ohio (by the Miami, Scioto and Muskingum rivers) or north by Lake Erie (Maumee, Sandusky and Cuyahoga rivers). Coal deposits are widespread in the Appalachian section of Ohio. Limestone is also commercially important. Forests of hardwoods originally covered almost the whole state; today, they occupy about one-fifth of the surface. Agriculture generally ranges in profitability from poor in the Appalachian sections of the state to excellent on the Maumee plains. In terms of farmers' receipts, the principal farm commodities are dairy products, cattle, soybeans and corn. Ohio is the second largest producer of tomatoes in the USA after California. It lies on the coal and iron route between Appalachian coal and Great Lakes iron ore, and so possesses a number of steel centres, e.g. Cleveland and Youngstown. It also benefits industrially from the heavy waterborne traffic along the Ohio river and from the overspill of the automobile industry and its components from neighbouring Michigan. The state has an area of 106,764 km^2 and a 1980 population of 10,797,419. The state was admitted to the Union in 1803 and since 1816 the capital has been at Columbus.

Ohio, river of the USA, second largest affluent of the Mississippi, formed by the union of the Allegheny and Monongahela at Pittsburgh, Pennsylvania. It flows south-westwards for 1580 km, with a width of between 365 and 1220 m, and with its tributaries drains an area of 528,100 km^2. The principal towns upon its banks are Pittsburgh, Cincinnati and Louisville (where there are falls). It is navigable from Pittsburgh.

Ohm, Georg Simon (1787–1854), German physicist. In 1825 he started his study of electricity and, in that year, produced Ohm's Law. In 1827 he published *Die galvanische Kette, mathematische bearbeitet* ('The Galvanic circuit treated mathematically') which was a complete exposition of the theory of electricity. The SI unit of electric resistance (1 VA^{-1}) is called the ohm.

Ohm, see OHM'S LAW; UNITS, ELECTRICAL.

Ohmmeter, instrument for measuring electrical resistance.
See also ELECTRIC METERS.

Ohm's Law states that for a given electrical conductor at constant temperature and carrying steady direct current, the ratio between the voltage across the ends and the current is constant. The ratio is called the resistance.
See also CURRENT ELECTRICITY; UNITS, ELECTRICAL.

Oidium, a genus that includes the asexual forms of various fungi (Erysiphaceae) of subdivision Ascomycotina, the mildews and moulds. In this stage the white cobweb-like mycelium produces simple conidiophores, from which the conidia (asexual spores) quickly germinate and grow in chains, covering the host plant with a mealy powder.

Oil, see OIL WELLS; OILS AND FATS; PETROLEUM.

Oil-colour, the most flexible and variable painter's medium, developed in the early 15th century by the Van Eycks. The material consists of pastes of pigments, ground in fatty vegetable oils (linseed, poppy, nut) often with a little wax, resin or varnish, and diluted with a small amount of turpentine. Linseed oil may be made more viscous by exposure to sunlight, or by boiling in an enclosed flask to make 'stand oil'. The surface to which it is applied is usually canvas or panel, which may be prepared with an oil-bound or size-bound chalk, gesso or white lead ground, sometimes tinted. Paint is applied with brushes of pig's bristle or sable, or with a palette-knife. Paints dry by absorbing oxygen from the air. To avoid cracking, each layer of paint must be allowed time to dry. A vital part of the painter's equipment is a palette, usually made of varnished wood, and shaped to be comfortably held in the hand. The colours are squeezed from tubes or bladders to form a range around the edge of the palette.
See also PAINTING; PAINTING TECHNIQUES.

Oil of Vitriol, see SULPHURIC ACID.

Oil-painting, see OIL-COLOUR; PAINTING.

Oil Palm, see PALM OIL; PALMAE.

Oil Shale, a fine-grained shale containing solid organic material known as kerogen, which yields oil on distillation.

Oil Wells. Natural (crude oil) most commonly occupies the pore spaces between the grains of sedimentary rocks. Two factors are essential to hold the petroleum in its reservoir. Firstly a suitable impervious 'cap' rock or seal to prevent its escape into higher layers, and, secondly, a 'structural' or 'stratigraphical' closure to trap the oil and prevent its further movement within the layer. The deposits are usually associated with water and gas—the water, being the heavier, occupying the lower part of the structure. The method used in the recovering of petroleum from these natural reservoirs is by the sinking of wells.
Investigations by geologists in a given area determine whether conditions in geological time have favoured the formation of oil. If so the terrain is studied for evidence of the types of structure in which oil is known to occur. Air surveying is widely used. Gravimeters are employed to measure differences in gravitational force resulting from variations in the densities of the rock layers beneath the surface. Rock layers can also be mapped by seismic methods. In modern drilling the first structure of the drilling rig to be built is the derrick, this being, in the case of permanent wells, a structural steel tower usually about 15 m high. The 9-metre square derrick floor, which is surfaced with boards and stands 2–4 m off the ground, is the working platform for the crews. The hoisting winch or 'draw-works' by which the drill pipe, casing and tubing are handled is driven by three or four engines installed behind it.
The hoisting equipment consists of the crown block (pulley) on top of the derrick, a travelling block which moves up and down the derrick by means of the hoist, and a multiple cable arrangement. The drill proper consists of a steel drill-pipe with a cutting tool, known as a bit, at its lower end. The drill-pipe is rotated by a turntable mounted in the derrick floor. At first the oil rises to the surface under natural pressure, but later it may be necessary to lift it by mechanical

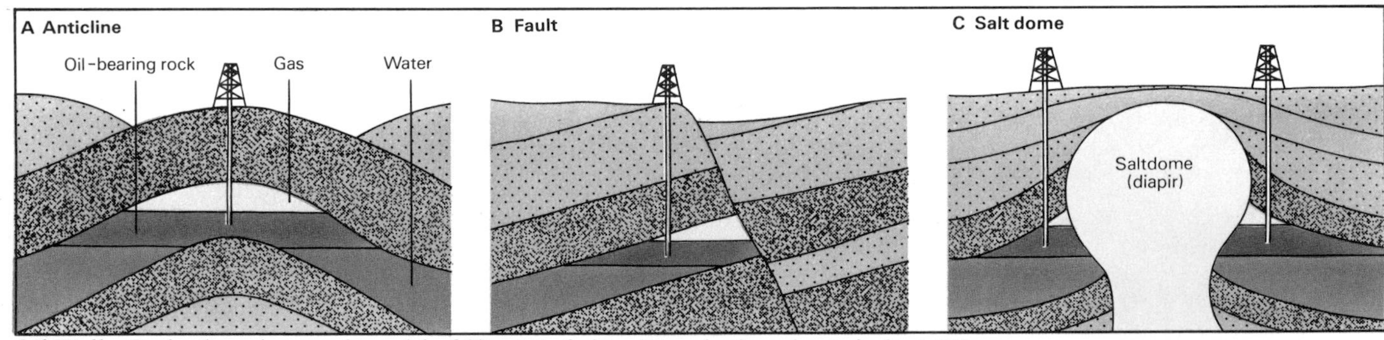

Oil Wells. *Crude oil may be trapped in rock by folding (A), faulting (B), or by the upthrust of a diapir (C).*

pumping or by creating artificial pressures in the oil-bearing formation. Oil is produced from depths of over 5·5 km, and exploratory boring has reached over 6·0 km. The presence of oil deposits beneath the sea-bed has led to the development of drilling from rigs on platforms or barges which form artificial islands. In recent years, more and more wells have been and are being drilled into formations under the sea. Consideration is being given to still greater depths where drilling may be carried out on the ocean bed within submersible chambers. The internal structure would be pressurised with a mixture of helium-oxygen if human drillers were to be used, but the possibility of using robot drillers is not ruled out.
See also North Sea Oil and Gas; Petroleum.

Oilcake, the richest and most concentrated of cattle foods, manufactured from oil-bearing seeds after they have been crushed to extract some of the oil.

Oils, Essential, see Essential Oils.

Oils and Fats are divided into three classes: (1) glyceryl esters of fatty acids (the lipids), which occur in plants and animals; (2) hydrocarbon or mineral oils, which are obtained largely from petroleum; and (3) essential oils. Class (1) is divided into those substances which are liquid at room temperature (oils) and those which are solid at room temperature (fats), there being no chemical difference between them. They are isolated from plant and animal tissues by pressure or by solvent extraction. One of their most important properties is the number of double bonds present in the fatty acid component (the degree of unsaturation). The more double bonds there are present, i.e. the greater the degree of unsaturation, the higher the iodine value (the ability to react with iodine at the double bonds). Oils with high ($\geqslant 150$) iodine values (drying oils) harden in air and are used in paint, e.g. linseed oil (iodine value ~ 200). Oils with iodine values in the range 100 to 150 (semi-drying oils) are used in paints, e.g. safflower oil (iodine value ~ 140), or for cooking purposes, e.g. cottonseed oil (iodine value ~ 110). Oils with low (< 100) iodine values (non-drying oils) are used in soap, e.g. olive oil (iodine value ~ 85). They are soluble in non-polar solvents (ether, benzene, etc.), insoluble in water (on which they float), and react with hot aqueous sodium hydroxide (saponification).
Class (2) consists of compounds of carbon and hydrogen containing between 4 and 10 carbon atoms, obtained by the distillation of crude petroleum, which occurs naturally in the Americas, the Middle East and USSR, and has recently been obtained in commercial quantities from the offshore areas of the UK. It is used mainly for lubrication purposes.
See also Essential Oils; Iodine Value.

Ointment, a fatty semi-solid preparation, generally containing some medicinal agent, and intended to be applied to the skin or mucous membrane for curative purposes. The fatty base may be any substance that does not have an injurious action on the tissues and is not liable to putrefaction.

Oireachtas, name of the Parliament of the Republic of Ireland. It consists of the president of the Republic, a Lower House, called Dáil Éireann, and a Senate, called Seanad Éireann.

Oise, river of France, a tributary of the Seine, rises in the north of the *département* of Ardennes, and flows south-west, joining the Seine at Conflans-Sainte-Honorine after a course of 302 km, for the last 150 km of which it is navigable.

Oistrakh, David Fyodorovich (1908–74), Russian violinist. One of the great violinists of the century, he became internationally famous when he won the Brussels Competition in 1937. He taught at the Moscow Conservatory from 1934. His son Igor Davidovich (1931–), is also a world-famous violinist.

Ōita, city and seaport of Ōita-ken, north-eastern Kyūshū, Japan, 170 km east of Nagasaki. It is the centre of a rapidly growing zone of heavy industry, including oil refining and the manufacture of iron and steel. Population (1980) 341,000.

Okapi, the native name of the species of family Giraffidae, in suborder Ruminantia of order Artiodactyla, that was discovered by Sir Harry Johnston in 1901 in the Semliki forest, Zaire; it is known scientifically as *Okapia johnstoni*. This giraffe-like animal differs from its relatives in having a rather short tail, a short, thick neck and no external horns. The coloration is curious: the limbs bear long, dark stripes, the back and sides are reddish-brown, while the limbs and part of the head are of a creamy colour. Very little is known of the habits of the okapi beyond that they live in pairs in dense forests.

Okavango, river of south-western Africa, about 1100 km long, rising near the Cuanza's sources, east of Benguela, and forming part of the boundary between South-West Africa (Namibia) and Angola for nearly 800 km. It finally flows into an immense inland swamp. Excluding this delta region, the catchment area is 200,000 km^2.

Okayama, city in Okayama-ken, Japan, 120 km west of Kōbe. It is a centre of education and commerce for south-western Japan. The city is famous for its traditional Japanese garden, the Korakuen. Main industries are cotton spinning and the manufacture of matting. Population (1980) 537,000.

O'Keeffe, Georgia (1887–), US painter. Her paintings are of landscape and still-life treated in a somewhat surrealist manner and she ranks among the pioneers of modern art in the USA.

Okeghem, Johannes (c.1425–c.1495), Flemish composer. He became *maître de chapelle* at the French court, where he served for nearly 40 years. One of the foremost exponents of a truly contrapuntal style in church music, Okeghem was influential as composer and teacher. His pupils included Josquin des Prés.

O'Kelly, Sean Thomas (1882–1966), Irish journalist and political leader; one of the original members of the Sinn Fein movement, he was Speaker of the first Dáil Eireann. He represented Dublin North in the Dáil and held several ministerial posts. He was proprietor and editor of the *Nation*, general secretary of the Gaelic League, and vice-president of the Fianna Fáil party. In 1945 he succeeded Douglas Hyde as president of Ireland.

Okhotsk, Sea of, inlet of the North Pacific in East Siberia, USSR, divided from the ocean by the Kamchatka Peninsula and the Kuril Islands, and from the Sea of Japan by Sakhalin and Hokkaido. Its main feeder is the River Amur. It is ice-covered from October to June. The inlet is a rich fishing ground and attempts to keep it as a Soviet preserve in recent years have led to quarrels with Japan. Chief ports: Magadan and Korsakov. Average depth 777 m; maximum depth 3372 m; area 1583 km^2.

Okinawa, Pacific island of the Ryukyu Islands group, 520 km from the Japanese mainland, and the largest island in Okinawa-ken. The island is 106 km long from north to south, 20 km wide, has an irregular coastline, and covers 1220 km^2. After 1945 the island was occupied by the United States, but in 1972 it reverted to Japanese control. Sugar cane and pineapples are the main crops, and some income is derived from the large American base on the island.

Oklahoma (Sooner State), south-central state of the USA, with an area of 181,090 km^2, lying between Texas on the south, Arkansas and Missouri on the east, and Kansas to the north. Westwards, the so-called 'panhandle' of the state extends as a narrow strip, 250 km long and 60 km wide, to touch the state of

Colorado. The eastern end of the state belongs geographically to the upland province of the Ozark plateau and the Ouachita Mountains; elevations reach 700 m and over. The hill country is dissected by the valleys of the Arkansas, Canadian and Red rivers and their tributaries. West of the hills, most of the state is occupied by the generally level surface of the southern Great Plains. The eastern hills are extensively forested; the state possesses nearly 2 million ha of commercial forest land. The plains are grassland, cultivated in the east, and given over to ranching in the west.

Oklahoma's farm income derives first and foremost from the 5 million or more cattle the state raises each year. Among the crops raised, wheat is the most valuable; other crops of value are peanuts, sorghum and cotton. Of more significance to the state is its mineral wealth. It is a large producer of natural gas and petroleum.

Oklahoma was established first by the US government as Indian Territory. As the demand for land among white Americans continued, however, the government in 1889 made available a million hectares of Indian Territory for white settlement (followed later by other areas) and a series of spectacular 'runs' by white settlers occurred. Those who settled land without awaiting government sanction were known as 'sooners'. In 1907 the territory was admitted as a state of the Union, and the Indian tribes were given reservations within it.

The 1980 population of the state was 3,025,266. There are only two cities of any size in the state—Oklahoma City (the capital) and Tulsa.

Oklahoma City, capital of Oklahoma, USA, on a fork of the Canadian river. It was settled in 1889, but has grown enormously under the influence of oil discoveries. It is an important commercial, industrial and distribution centre for a rich oil-producing and agricultural area. Population (1980) 403,213.

Okra, see HIBISCUS.

Okrug, territorial administrative unit in the USSR, corresponding to a district, and forming part of an *oblast* or *krai*.

Olaf I, known as Olaf Tryggvesson (969–1000), King of Norway. On being proclaimed king in 995 he began the conversion of the country to Christianity and built the first churches. He fought with both Sweden and Denmark, and finally met his death when he was waylaid and defeated by the combined Swedish and Danish fleets.

Olaf II, known as Saint Olaf (995–1030), King and patron saint of Norway. He tried to suppress paganism with severity. Olaf was dethroned by Canute in 1028, but in 1030 he returned to Norway with an army. In a battle with Canute's forces at Stiklestand Olaf was defeated and killed. He was canonised in 1164 and recognised as patron saint of Norway.

Olaf V (Alexander Eduard Christian Frederik) (1903–), King of Norway. He succeeded his father, Haakon VII, in 1957. He married (1929) Princess Märtha of Sweden (d. 1954), and their only son, Prince Harald (1937–), is heir presumptive to the Norwegian throne.

Öland, long and narrow Swedish island in the Baltic, separated from Sweden by Kalmar Sound (now bridged). It is 136 km long and 16 km at its broadest, and covers an area of 1344 km². It is wooded in parts, and has good pasture for cattle. There are good fisheries all round the coast. Borgholm, on the west coast, is the capital and only town. Population (1970) 20,000.

Olax, a typical genus of the family Olacaceae, consisting of shrubs and trees inhabiting tropical regions of Asia, Africa and Australia. The species are smooth evergreens and have a disagreeable odour.

Olbers, Heinrich Wilhelm Matthäus (1758–1840), German physician and astronomer. His new method of calculating the orbit of a comet won him fame. He discovered the asteroids Pallas (1802) and Vesta (1807), and the Olbers comet of 1815. He is chiefly remembered in connection with the paradox associated with his name which occurs in cosmology.

Old Bailey, a street in the City of London, between Newgate Street and Ludgate Hill, its name is commonly applied to the Central Criminal Court.

Old Catholics, see CATHOLICS, OLD.

Old English Sheepdog ('Bobtail'), formerly much used by shepherds and drovers in the southern counties of England and Wales, but now kept mainly as a companion and show dog. The hard, shaggy coat should be free from curl, and have a dense waterproof undercoat. Its colour may be any shade of grey, grizzle, blue, or blue merle, with or without white markings.

'Old Glory', flag of the UNITED STATES OF AMERICA.

Old Man's Beard, see CLEMATIS.

'Old Pretender', see STUART, JAMES FRANCIS EDWARD.

Old Red Sandstone, see DEVONIAN SYSTEM.

Old Sarum, see SARUM, OLD.

Old Testament, see BIBLE.

Old Vic Theatre, Waterloo Road, London. It opened on 11 May 1818 as the Royal Coburg; in 1833 the name was changed to the Royal Victoria Theatre in honour of the young princess. It had become a home of sensational melodrama when in 1880 Emma Cons, a social worker, reopened it as the Royal Victoria Coffee Music Hall, offering 'a purified entertainment and no intoxicating drinks'. In 1898 Lilian Baylis, niece of Emma Cons, joined her as manager of the theatre. The first complete season of Shakespeare's plays was presented in 1914, and by 1923 the Old Vic had become the first theatre in the world to present the complete cycle. In 1929 Ninette de Valois joined the theatre and laid the foundations of the Sadler's Wells Ballet; the new theatre at Sadler's Wells was opened in 1931.

During the Second World War the Old Vic was damaged by enemy action on 19 May 1941, and did not open again until 1950. On 15 June 1963 the Old Vic closed after a performance of *Measure for Measure*, and reopened on 22 October as the temporary home of the National Theatre company. In October 1976 the new National Theatre complex was opened by the queen, since when the Old Vic has been used by the Young Vic and other companies.

Old World, a term used to describe Europe, Africa and Asia as being distinct from the New World of the Americas. The term was widely used by European emigrants to Canada and the United States; it is also used by naturalists in describing the geographical distribution of species.

Oldcastle, Sir John, also known as Lord Cobham (d. 1417), English Lollard and rebel. He is said to have been a friend of Prince Henry, later Henry V. In 1413 Archbishop Arundel found him guilty of heresy, but Oldcastle escaped from the Tower. He was declared outlawed in 1414 and seemed to have plotted various rebellions. He was later captured and executed. Oldcastle has been thought by some to be the original of Shakespeare's Falstaff.

Oldenburg, Claes, or Thure (1929–), Swedish-born artist, who has spent much of his life in the US. A precursor of Pop Art, Oldenburg was the inventor of 'happenings'—experimental works based on everyday objects, sometimes involving people. Particularly known are his soft-sculptures: renderings of modern commodities and consumables in incongruous soft materials.

Oldenburg, former grand duchy of north Germany (after 1918 a republic), comprising the province around the town of Oldenburg, the principality of Lübeck (north of the state of that name), and the principality of Birkenfeld. The total area was 6425 km²; total population 500,000. Oldenburg was a constitutional ducal monarchy, hereditary in the male line. In 1180 the counts of Oldenburg and Delmenhorst succeeded in establishing the independence of their territories after the downfall of Henry the Lion. This family continued to rule until 1918, giving, moreover, new dynasties to Denmark, Russia and Sweden.

Oldenburg, city in Lower Saxony, Federal Republic of Germany, on the Hunte, 132 km north-west of Hanover. It was once the capital of the duchy of Oldenburg. It has the former ducal palace (now a museum), and is the centre of an agricultural region. It also has electrical industries and food processing plants. Population (1980) 136,400.

Oldfield, Anne (1683–1730), commonly known as 'Nance', English actress, made her début in 1700, and in 1703 played the part of Lady Betty Modish in Cibber's *Careless Husband*. She soon came to be recognised as one of the most accomplished actresses of the day.

Oldham, town in the new Greater Manchester Metropolitan County, England. Situated 10 km north-east of Manchester, it lies on the lower slopes of the Pennine upland. Though traditionally a cotton town, it has industries including aircraft and electrical engineering as well as the long-established mechanical engineering works, originally for textile machinery. Population (1981) 95,467.

Olduvai Gorge, situated on the Serengeti Plain in Tanzania, is the site of important archaeological excavations carried out under the direction of Dr L. S. B. Leakey. The geological sequence at Olduvai Gorge is almost complete, running back from the present day to nearly two million years ago. For much of this time a lake was present in the region which acted as a focal point for many animals including hominids. This site has produced finds such as *Australopithecus* *boisei*, *Homo habilis*, and early forms of *Homo erectus*.

See also ANTHROPOLOGY; MAN.

Oleaceae, the privet family of dicotyledonous trees and shrubs. The leaves are borne in opposite pairs, and the flowers, which usually have four joined petals, are characterised by having only two stamens. The genera include: *Chionanthus*, *Forsythia*, *Fraxinus* (ash), *Jasminum* (jasmine), *Ligustrum* (privet), *Olea* (olive), and *Syringa* (lilac).

Oleander, or rose bay, *Nerium oleander*, a handsome evergreen shrub belonging to the Apocynaceae, with fragrant flowers, rather like carnations, of various shades of pink, red and white. A native of the Mediterranean region, its large, willow-like leaves when bruised have a powerful and disagreeable odour, and are poisonous to human beings and animals.

Olearia, a genus of Australasian evergreen flowering shrubs of the Compositae, bearing in summer a profusion of daisy-like flowers as well as ornamental foliage. Some are grown in gardens as daisy bushes.

Oleaster, see ELAEAGNUS.

Olefins, or alkenes, in chemistry, hydrocarbons of the ethylene series, with one carbon-carbon double bond, having the general formula C_nH_{2n}. The simplest olefin is ethylene itself, C_2H_4.

Oleic Acid, or *cis*-octadec-9-enoic acid, $CH_3{\cdot}(CH_2)_7{\cdot}CH{:}CH(CH_2)_7{\cdot}(COOH)$, unsaturated fatty acid with one double bond, occurs in combination with glycerol as olein in virtually all fats and glyceride oils. It is a major component in most liquid vegetable oils and the principal acid in palm oil, groundnut oil, olive oil, sesame oil and sunflower oil. Chemically pure oleic acid is a tasteless, odourless liquid at ordinary temperatures and does not absorb oxygen when exposed to the air.

See also FATTY ACIDS.

Oleograph, name given to a picture done in oil colours by a chromo-lithographic process, the print being mounted on canvas and varnished to imitate an original oil painting.

Olfactory Nerve, see CRANIAL NERVES; NOSE.

Olibanum, see FRANKINCENSE.

Oligarchy (Greek *oligarchia*, the government of the few), the constitution amongst the ancient Greeks where a portion of the community was in possession of power, for example the governments of Thebes, Megara and Corinth. At this time, although it was acknowledged that an 'aristocracy' often developed into an 'oligarchy', the two were distinguished, 'oligarchy' signifying the government of the wealthy, who were looked upon as directing their efforts towards their own aggrandisement and the maintenance of their own power and privileges, while 'aristocracy' meant the rule of the best people for the public good.

Oligocene, see TERTIARY SYSTEM.

Oligochaete, see EARTHWORMS.

Oligopoly, in economics, a situation where the market for a commodity is dominated by a small number of relatively large firms. In such a market each firm has to take account of the effects of its own decisions on the behaviour of the others. For instance, if it cuts its prices there is very likely to be retaliation.

Olivares, Gaspar de Guzmán, Count-Duke of (1587–1645), Spanish statesman. He became grand chamberlain to Philip IV, and from 1621 to 1642 was the real ruler of Spain. His foreign policy involved Spain in a series of disastrous wars, while at home his fiscal policy resulted in crushing taxation. Olivares was overthrown and exiled in 1642.

Olive, *Olea europaea*, a slow-growing tree of the Oleaceae, with undivided leaves and axillary clusters of green flowers followed by pendulous, lustrous, blue-black oily fruits. While green and unripe, the fruits are bottled or pickled in brine. Olive oil is extracted by pressure from the ripe fruit. The tree has been cultivated since ancient times, especially on the borders of the Mediterranean Sea. The wood is soft, but takes a high polish, and is used for making small articles.

Olive Branch Petition, final effort made by the American colonists in 1775 to conciliate the British government, after the outbreak of hostilities in the War of American Independence. The only answer given to the appeal was a declaration in Parliament to take stern measures against the 'conspirators and insurgents' in America.

Olive Oil, the fixed oil pressed from the fruit of the olive tree, *Olea europaea*. The olive tree has been cultivated from the earliest times in Greece, Italy, southern Spain, Asia Minor and other Mediterranean countries, and has been introduced elsewhere. The fruit is pressed to a pasty consistency, enclosed in woollen bags and subjected to considerable pressure. Olive oil is considered to be the finest of the edible oils and, in contrast to other vegetable oils, it is generally consumed as a food without refining or further processing.

Oliver, Isaac (1565–1617), miniature-painter of Huguenot extraction. Brought to England in 1568, he was a pupil of Nicholas Hilliard, but unlike him introduced light and shade into miniatures, and was his rival from c.1600, popular at the court of James I. His son Peter (1594–1648) was also 'limner' to the Stuart court, working in his father's style. He copied Italian paintings from Charles I's collection, in miniature.

Olives, Mount of, situated east of Jerusalem, is connected intimately with the life of Jesus, for on the western slope lay the Garden of Gethsemane. The Mount of Olives is 992 m above sea level, and on its summit are many churches and convents, the most ancient being the small octagonal church of the Ascension (5th century).

Olivier, Laurence Kerr, Baron (1907–), British actor-manager and producer. He first appeared on the stage as Katharine in a schoolboys' performance of *The Taming of the Shrew* at Stratford-on-Avon. From 1926 to 1928 he was at the Birmingham Repertory Theatre, and later with Gielgud at the New Theatre, London, alternating with him in the parts of Romeo and Mercutio. In 1935 he joined the Old Vic company, where his reputation was chiefly made. He was outstanding as Hamlet, Romeo, Richard III, Macbeth and Titus Andronicus. His second wife, Vivien Leigh, appeared with him as Ophelia and Lavinia. He also appeared in many modern parts, including the Duke in *Venus Observed*, Archie Rice in *The Entertainer*, Bérenger in *Rhinoceros* and both Becket and Henry II in Anouilh's *Becket*. He directed and starred in the films of *Henry V*, *Hamlet* and *Richard III*, and has appeared in a wide variety of other films.

In 1961 Olivier was appointed head of the National Theatre, and in 1963, in which year he married the actress Joan Plowright, he opened the Old Vic as the company's temporary home. He appeared there in many leading parts which have further enhanced his reputation, among them Uncle Vanya, Edgar in *The Dance of Death*, Chebutikin in *The Three Sisters*, and Tyrone in *Long Day's Journey Into Night*. He was also director of the Chichester Festival Theatre from its inception in 1961 until 1965. In 1970 he was created a life peer. The Olivier theatre, part of the National Theatre's new premises, was named in his honour.

Olivine, the name given to a series of ferromagnesian silicate minerals, ranging from a magnesium-rich form (forsterite) to an iron-rich form (fayalite). Olivine rarely occurs as crystals, but is found as rounded grains or granular masses; it has a hardness of 6, specific gravity 3·22–4·39 (dependent on composition), and has a conchoidal fracture. Forsterite is almost pure Mg_2SiO_4 and fayalite is Fe_2SiO_4. Olivine is typically a mineral of basic and ultrabasic rocks, sometimes forming large rock masses, when it is termed dunnite (from the New Zealand locality, Mount Dun). The olivine used as a gem stone is called peridot.

Ollenhauer, Erich (1901–63), German politician. He was deprived of German citizenship in 1935. He took refuge in France (1938–41) and Britain (1941–46). After the Second World War he returned to the Federal Republic of Germany, and succeeded Schumacher as chairman of the Social Democrats in 1952, guiding the party towards a more moderate and popular stance in the country.

Olm, see AMPHIBIA.

Olomouc (German *Olmütz*), town of Czechoslovakia, in northern Moravia, 65 km north-east of Brno and on the River Morava. Until 1640 it was the capital of Moravia. It is a picturesque town and is the seat of an archbishop. It has a university (1576) with a notable library. There are iron, steel, engineering and textile industries. Population (1979) 101,000.

Olympia, plain in Elis, bounded on the south and west by the Rivers Alpheus and Cladeus respectively; scene of the Olympic Games. The most important site was the *Altis*, a grove sacred to Zeus. The Olympicium, or temple of Zeus Olympius, was a magnificent building, containing the 'Callistephanus', or wild olive tree, which furnished the garlands of the Olympic victors.

Olympia, town, seaport and capital of the state of Washington, USA, on Budds Inlet about 80 km from Seattle. The chief industry is lumbering, but fishing and mining are also carried on, and the manufacture of metal products, farm machinery and canning equipment are also important. Population (1980) 27,447.

Olympiad, period of four years between each celebration of the Olympic Games; 776 BC was reputed to be the first year of the first olympiad.

Olympic Games. The opening ceremony of the 1980 Olympics in Moscow.

Olympic Games. This article is concerned with the modern Olympic Games; for the original Greek Games, see CLASSICAL GAMES. The first modern Olympic Games, the inspiration of Baron Pierre de Coubertin, were held in Athens in April 1896. About 300 competitors (men only) from 13 countries took part in a total of 42 events from 10 different sports. From this primitive beginning the Games have grown and the standards have improved out of all recognition.

The Games occur every four years, following the ancient Greek Olympiad pattern, although the two world wars prevented those of 1916, 1940 and 1944 being held. A cycle for winter sporting events was established in 1924. The Olympic Movement is directed by the International Olympic Committee (IOC). At least 15 sports from a list of over 20 events must be included in the Games. Originally the amateur rules were very strict, but over the years, particularly since the Second World War, the growing popularity of the Games has led to sporting success resulting in great financial benefits to gold medallists, who thus turn to professionalism. Many people advocate that the distinction between amateurs and professionals should be abolished, but the IOC have tried to follow a middle course. Moreover, although the IOC has laid down that the Games are contests between individuals and not countries, and there are no official tables of medals winners, obviously national prestige is at stake and many competitors are in fact, if not in name, professionals.

See also CLASSICAL GAMES; COUBERTIN, BARON PIERRE DE; WINTER OLYMPICS.

Olympus, name of several mountains in Greece. The most famous is the high range on the borders of Thessaly and Macedonia, separated from Mount Ossa by the vale of Tempe. Its highest point is 2917 m. It was supposed by the ancient Greeks to be the home of their gods.

See also MYTHOLOGY.

Omagh, market and county town of County Tyrone, Northern Ireland, on the Strule, among the foothills of the Sperrin Hills. Population (1981) 41,137.

Omaha, chief commercial city of the state of Nebraska, USA, it lies on the right bank of the Missouri river, 32 km north of the mouth of the Nebraska river. The city is an important shipping, transport and industrial centre; it was the eastern terminus of the first transcontinental railway, the Union Pacific. It is one of the major centres of the meat-packing industry. Population (1980) 311,681.

Omahas, North American Indian people, most of whom now live in eastern Nebraska. They belong to the Siouan linguistic group and number about 1200.

Oman, Sir Charles William Chadwick (1860–1946), British historian. He was Chichele professor of modern history at Oxford, retiring from the latter post in 1946, and Conservative MP for Oxford University, 1919–35. He wrote on a wide range of subjects but came to specialise in military history. Among his works are *A History of England before the Norman Conquest*, 1910; and *A History of the Art of War in the Sixteenth Century*, 1937.

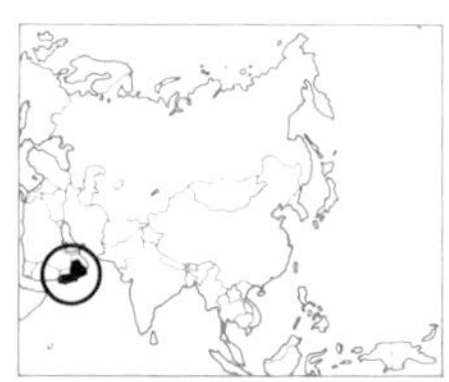

Oman
Area: 212,400 km²
Population: 820,000
Capital: Muscat

Oman (formerly Muscat and Oman), an independent sultanate in the south-east corner of the Arabian Peninsula, bounded on the north by the Gulf of Oman, on the west by the United Arab Emirates and the Rub 'al Khali desert in Saudi Arabia, on the south and east by the Arabian Sea, and in the south-west by the People's Democratic Republic of the Yemen. The landward boundaries, however, remain largely undefined and have been disputed. A small enclave at the tip of the Musandam Peninsula also belongs to Oman. The total area is approximately 212,400 km^2. Oman has a fjord type of coastline, with long deep inlets shut in by deep-walled cliffs. The interior a plateau lies at about 200 m.

The population of Muscat and Oman is estimated at about 820,000. There is a considerable proportion of Iranians, Baluchis, Indians and Pakistanis in the sultanate's population. The principal centres of population are Muscat (the capital), Sur and Nizwa. Most of Oman consists of desert, mountain ranges and scrub land. As a consequence only 40,000 ha are cultivated in the whole country,

Oman. *Wadi Fida in northern Oman has a regular flow of water allowing the growth of palms.*

mainly on the north-east coastal plain (the Batinah), and in some oasis settlements behind the Hajar Mountains. The main crops include dates, limes, onions, tobacco, mango and some bananas, all of which are grown for local consumption. Lucerne is also grown for animal fodder. The main beef-producing region is Dhofar, in the south-west of the country.

Oil production is the country''s most important economic activity. The original four fields in the Fahud region are declining, however, although this has been offset by rising production from the Saih Rawl fields further south. Copper deposits have been discovered in the Hajar Mountains west of Sohar. Asbestos, phosphates, manganese and chrome also exist.

Oman is a sultanate ruled directly by Sultan Qaboos bin Said. Constitutionally, Oman is a monarchy; the Sultan rules by decree with the advice of a council of ministers.

Arabic is the official language, but English is also spoken for business purposes.

History. Western Oman was the source of the great frankincense trade in southern Arabia and fell to the Islamic empire in the 7th century AD, but soon asserted its independence through the schism of Ibadhism, which held the religious leader, or imam, as the political ruler. In 1507 the Portuguese took the ports and were soon joined by the Dutch and British trading posts. Oman benefited from its increased wealth and was able to expel the Portuguese in 1650, and by 1730 had taken its possessions in East Africa. Civil war broke out early in the 18th century as a result of the shift of power from the interior. The Al Bu Said dynasty of Muscat (which still rules) were the victors in 1749. They allowed a division of authority within the country: the imam would remain in the interior but political power would rest on the coast. Oman's government and economy remained medieval until the mid-20th century. In 1970 Shaikh Said was deposed by his son, Qabous, with British approval. Qabous promised reforms, and has developed housing, education, communications and health services. In 1981 a state advisory council of 45 members was established.

Omar I, or Umar ibn al-Khattab (d.644), Muslim caliph from 634 to 644. He subdued Egypt, Palestine and Syria, defeated the Persians, and was the first to have the title of Commander of the Faithful (Amir al-Mu'minīn). He introduced the new Arabian calendar.

Omar Khayyám (c.1034–c.1130), Persian poet, mathematician and astronomer. Omar Khayyám revised the calendar at the invitation of the Seljuk Sultan, Malik Shah, and became famous throughout the East as a mathematician; one of his works on algebra was known in Europe. His name is inseparably connected with Edward FitzGerald who translated his *Rubáiyát* (or quatrains) into English in 1859. The authenticity of many of the quatrains has been questioned.

Ombudsman, Scandinavian term for an official appointed to investigate complaints against the actions of government departments. Sir Edmund Compton was appointed the first British ombudsman in August 1966.

Omdurman, town in the Sudan, on the west bank of the Nile, facing Khartoum. It is a trading centre and a pilgrim's resting place, and was the chief town during the regime of the Mahdi (1884–98). On 2 September 1898 British forces under Kitchener, advancing up the Nile after the victory of Atbara, defeated the forces of the Khalifa. The battle, in which Winston Churchill took part, is noted for the last full-scale cavalry charge of modern history. The city trades in hides, textiles and livestock. Population (1973) 305,308.

Omelette, eggs beaten lightly, with the addition of milk or water, herbs, cheese, mushrooms, ham, bacon, fish or game, and salt and pepper for seasoning, according to the requirements, and cooked in a buttered pan. For sweet omelettes sugar is used instead of seasonings, and fruit may be added.

Omen, name applied by the ancients to signs which were supposed to indicate good or bad fortune, for example the appearance of snakes or the flight of birds.

Omnibus (Latin, for all), name of a public conveyance which has undergone considerable modifications from its early form. Originating in Paris, it was introduced to London in 1829 by George Shillibeer. Its characteristic was that it plied for hire throughout its route instead of being available, like the stage-coach, only to those who pre-booked at offices. The characteristic double-decked British vehicle originated with the Great Exhibition of 1851, and the 26-seat London garden seat horse-bus in 1881. Motor buses were the subject of experiment from 1897 onwards and became established in 1903. The first electric trolley-buses were operated in 1911; they often replaced trams and they in turn have been largely replaced by the diesel (or oil-engined) bus.

See also ELECTRIC TRACTION.

Omphalea, a genus of tropical climbing shrubs, of the Euphorbiaceae. *O. megacarpa*, hunter's nut, yields large nutritious nuts and is cultivated in the West Indies.

Omphalodes, a genus of annuals and perennials of the Boraginaceae, bearing sprays of white or blue flowers. *O. linifolia* (Venus's navelwort), a white-flowered annual, *O. luciliae* (rock navelwort), a blue-flowered perennial, and *O. verna*, blue-eyed Mary, are grown in gardens.

Omsk, capital city, economic and cultural centre of Omsk *oblast* of the RSFSR, USSR, on the Irtysh and the Trans-Siberian Railway. It has engineering, oil refining, wood-processing, and varied light and food industries. It was founded in 1716 as a Russian fortress in the southern defence line of West Siberia. After the Trans-Siberian railway reached the city it became the commercial centre of West Siberia. The Bolsheviks were overthrown in Omsk in 1918, and for over a year it was the centre of anti-Bolshevik struggles in Siberia and the seat of Kolchak's government. There has been rapid industrial development since the Second World War. Population (1980) 1,028,000.

Onagraceae, a dicotyledonous family of herbs and shrubs, generally with opposite pairs of simple leaves. The colour and position of the flowers varies, but the sepals and petals are generally in fours, and all are joined together with the stamens, to form a tube above the ovary. Genera include *Clarkia*, *Epilobium* (willowherb), *Fuchsia*, *Godetia*, *Oenothera* (evening primrose), and *Zauschneria*.

Onassis, Aristotle Socrates (1906–75), Turkish-born Greek shipping magnate. When the family business was ruined by fighting between Turks and Greeks, Aristotle was sent to Buenos Aires to rebuild the family fortunes. By the age of 25 he was a millionaire. In the Depression year of 1932 he moved into ship-owning by buying six freighters from a Montreal company for $120,000 (about 1 per cent of their cost when new). The Second World War considerably increased Onassis's fortune: his ships were badly needed by the Allies and market rates for carrying freight were high. Onassis's first marriage ended in divorce in 1960. In 1968 he married Jacqueline Kennedy, widow of John Kennedy, the US President. At his death, Onassis was estimated to have a personal fortune of $500 million.

Onchocerciasis, an infection of humans caused by *Onchocerca volvulus*, a nematode worm and a close relation of the parasites causing filariasis and dracontiasis. Onchocerciasis is of major public health importance in parts of Africa and South America.

Oncidium, a very large genus of epiphytic orchids, in the family Orchidaceae, chiefly found in Peru, Ecuador, Mexico and the West Indies.

Ondes Musicales, or Ondes Martenot, electrophonic instrument invented by Maurice Martenot in 1928. Messiaen and other French composers have written for the instrument.

Onega, lake in north-west European USSR; the second largest in Europe. Area 9700 km^2 (without islands). It is connected by the River Svir with Lake Ladoga and the Baltic, and by artificial waterways with the White Sea and the Volga.

Oneida, North American Indian people, who belonged to the Iroquois Confederacy. They now number about 2500.

O'Neill, Eugene Gladstone (1888–1953), US dramatist. Stricken with tuberculosis, while in a sanatorium he wrote some realistic one-act plays which were published at his father's expense. Upon restoration to health he went to Harvard University and took a course in dramatic writing. *The Moon of the Caribees and Six Other Plays* was published in 1919. In the same year appeared *Beyond the Horizon*, his first full-length play. This won the Pulitzer prize in 1920, an honour later gained by three more of his plays. *Emperor Jones*, 1921, was an experiment in expressionism. Out of O'Neill's knowledge of the docks and the sea grew *Anna Christie*, 1922, another study in realism. *Desire Under the Elms*, 1924, reverts to realism, being a tragedy of passion on a New England farm. *The Great God Brown*, 1925, has been acclaimed as one of the finest imaginative productions in American literature. Here O'Neill showed his growing distaste for mere naturalism and his increasing employment of symbolism. *Strange Interlude*, 1928, is one of the strangest of all his dramas; here he adapts interior monologue to the stage. O'Neill deals largely with the depressed classes, and especially with the colour problem, though his *Mourning Becomes Electra*, produced in London in 1938, was a powerful

Ontario. *The picturesque Artist's Lake in the Killarney Provincial Park, north of Georgian Bay.*

and sombre modern psychological study of the Electra complex. His *Days Without End*, 1934, is a modern miracle drama. In 1936 he was awarded the Nobel prize. Later works include *The Iceman Cometh*, 1946, and *A Moon for the Misbegotten*, 1947. He left an autobiographical drama, *Long Day's Journey into Night*, which was produced after his death and won the Pulitzer prize, his fourth award.

O'Neill, Jonjo (John Joe) (1952–), British national hunt jockey. At the start of the 1977–78 season he left Gordon Richards' stables to go freelance and became champion jockey with a record 149 winners. He won his second championship in the 1979–80 season. O'Neill is noted for his prodigious strength and unquenchable will to win.

O'Neill, Shane, 2nd Earl of Tyrone (c. 1530–67), Irish chief and rebel, made a treaty with the English at Drumcree (1563); captured the chief of the MacDonnells (1565); invaded the Pale (1566); burned Armagh (1566); was defeated by the O'Donnells at Letterkenny in 1567, and murdered by the MacDonnells at Cushendun.

Onion, the bulb of *Allium cepa* in the Alliaceae, which is probably a native of central or western Asia, and cultivated from a remote period.

Onions, C(harles) T(albut) (1873–1965), British philologist. In 1896 he joined the staff of the *Oxford English Dictionary*, and became joint editor, 1914–33. He was also editor of the *Shorter Oxford English Dictionary*, 1944, and the *Oxford Dictionary of English Etymology*, 1966.

Onions, George Oliver (1873–1961), English novelist. He changed his name in later life to George Oliver, but wrote as Oliver Onions. His first book was *The Compleat Bachelor*, 1901, but his first real success was with the trilogy of novels *In Accordance with the Evidence*, 1912; *The Debit Account*, 1913; and *The Story of Louie*, 1913. *Poor Man's Tapestry*, 1946, was awarded the Tait Black Prize. His highly effective ghost stories were collected in *Widdershins*, 1911; *Ghosts in Daylight*, 1924; and *The Painted Face*, 1929. He married Berta Ruck, the novelist.

Onitsha, town in East-Central State, Nigeria, on the east bank of the Niger river, north of its delta. Onitsha grew up as a market town where the ferry connecting east and west Nigeria met the river trade from the coast. It developed during the 19th and 20th centuries to become the biggest market in West Africa. Population (1975) 220,000.

Onobrychis, a genus of leguminous herbs or shrubs with pinnate leaves and axillary spikes of purple, red or white flowers. *O. viciifolia* is the fodder plant sainfoin.

Onomatopoeia (Greek *onoma*, word; *poiein*, to make), figure of speech in which the sound of words corresponds with the sense they convey. Many single-syllable words are onomatopoeic, such as 'bang', 'clink', 'splash'. See also FIGURE OF SPEECH.

Onopordum, see THISTLE.

Ontario, south-east province of Canada, separated from the USA by the Great Lakes and the St Lawrence. It is bounded in the north-east by Hudson Bay, in the east by Quebec, and in the west by Manitoba. Area 1,068,630 km^2, of which 127,686 km^2 is water surface. The north makes up by far the greatest division of the province and exhibits a rolling surface smoothed out by ice action, pitted with innumerable lakes. The vegetation cover in this area is a mixture of coniferous forest, bog and marsh areas, with extensive areas of bare rock and open water, particularly in the north.

The inhospitable nature of the northern area has limited settlement to isolated communities which have grown up around pulp, paper and sawmilling centres, mineral deposits and a few localities where agriculture can be practised. The Great Lakes peninsula on the other hand is the most densely populated region of Canada.

Climatically this is undoubtedly the most favoured part of Canada, with a long growing season and ample rainfall.

Livestock farming of one form or another is by far the most important—cattle, hogs and sheep form 41 per cent of all units and dairy 30 per cent—but these farms will also have a proportion of their land under field crops such as maize, wheat, other grain, and vegetables. The Niagara escarpment is famous for its peach and cherry orchards; the sandy deltaic deposits of Elgin and Norfolk counties have important tobacco crops; the clay deposits have sugar beet.

The mineral resources of the Great Lakes peninsula are limited to the small oil-field at Sarnia, limestone quarrying, and sand and gravel workings. The minerals of the north are to be found in several very rich metal-bearing belts. The Temiskaming belt in northern Ontario produces cobalt, silver and gold; Sudbury has the world's largest deposit of nickel as well as copper, lead and zinc, gold, silver, platinum and copper; Trimmins is a major producer of gold; and Nipigon of iron ore and gold.

Apart from ore smelting and pulp and paper making, the main industry development within the province is concentrated into the small peninsula area. The iron and steel industry in and around Hamilton provides the raw materials for the heavy engineering of the area, light engineering, the automobile industry, agricultural machinery, and a full range of durable goods plants. Oil refining and associated petrochemical plants cluster around Sarnia making use of oil piped in from Alberta. Flour milling and food processing are other major industries. Over 50 per cent of the labour force are employed in administration, finance, retailing and wholesaling.

The provincial government is headed by a lieutenant-governor and comprises a legislative assembly elected for five years. The capital is Toronto and Ottawa is the seat of the dominion government. Other important cities are Hamilton, Windsor, London, Kitchener and Sudbury.

Before the American War of Independence the country was sparsely populated by Indian tribes, but on the close of the war in 1783 thousands of British Empire Loyalists crossed into Canada and settled in the Ontario region. The region was called Upper Canada until 1867, when it received provincial status. Population (1976) 8,264,465.

Ontario, Lake, lake of North America, the smallest of the Great Lakes, forming part of the boundary between Canada and the USA. Its length is 310 km and its mean width is about 80 km; its mean depth is 86 m. The St Lawrence river forms its outlet on the north-east, while in the south-east it receives the waters of Lake Erie, by means of the Niagara river. It is connected to Lake Erie, by means of the Welland Ship Canal, improved as part of the St Lawrence Seaway project. Its area is 19,555 km^2, and it contains several islands at its eastern end. The chief Canadian ports on its shores are Toronto, Hamilton, Kingston, Port Hope and Coburg, while Oswego, Sackett's Harbor and Charlotte are on the American side.

Ontology (Greek *ontos*, present participle of the verb *einai*, to be; *logos*, theory), the name given to that branch of philosophy which deals with the concepts of essence, existence, etc., investigating the nature of existence, what kinds of things can be said to exist, and the various senses of the verb 'exist'.

Onyx, see SILICA.

Oolite, a limestone composed of rounded grains (ooliths) which are made up of concentric layers of radiating fibres of carbonate. They are formed by the accretion and growth of carbonate fibres on a nucleus such as a grain of sand or a shell fragment, occurring as a result of the constant movement of sand and shell debris in an environment where carbonate is being deposited; this accounts for the even, concentric coating of carbonate material. Pisolite or peastone is the name given to a coarse oolitic limestone, where the ooliths are 3–6 mm in diameter. These rocks often contain algal remains, thought to play a part in building the large ooliths.

Oort, Jan Hendrik (1900–), Dutch astronomer, born at Franeker, Friesland, is best known for his work on the structure of the Galaxy, particularly for his demonstration in 1927 of its rotation and his exploitation of the 21-centimetre hydrogen radiation to outline its spiral structure.

Op Art, term that gained currency in the 1960s, used to describe abstract art in which optical effects give the spectator the sensation that part or all of the work is moving. Bridget Riley and Victor de Vasarely are the best known Op artists, and the style has had considerable influence on contemporary design.

Op Art. *Fragments, 1965, by the British artist Bridget Riley.*

Opah, or moonfish, a member of the order Lampridiformes, family Lamprididae. This family consists of only one genus, *Lampris*. These fishes may be up to 2 m long and weigh approximately 200 kg. They are widely distributed in warm seas. The flesh is edible, and well flavoured.

Opal, see SILICA.

OPEC, see ORGANISATION OF PETROLEUM EXPORTING COUNTRIES.

Open Field Farming, a system of cultivation which has been carried on in many periods and places; the characteristic agricultural system in Anglo-Saxon and medieval England. The arable land of a village was divided into two or three great open fields. One field was left fallow each year so that it could recover from previous sowings; if there were three fields the other two were planted with autumn and spring sown crops. Each field consisted of hundreds of strips, and the strips farmed by each family were scattered over the fields. By the end of the 18th century the open field system had almost disappeared from England, the fields being enclosed and made into consolidated holdings.

Open Golf Championship. Many countries have their own Open Golf Championship, but there is only one 'Open'—the British Open (though the word 'British' is never used). Traditionally played on seaside links courses in England and Scotland, the Open was first contested at Prestwick in Scotland in 1860 and won by Willie Park snr. Prestwick remained the Open venue until 1873 when it moved to St Andrews. Since then, a different course hosts the Open each year. Over the ensuing years, the Open title has become very much an American preserve, with British wins a rarity. The last British winner was Tony Jacklin at Royal Lytham in 1969. This century, only one golfer has won three successive Opens—Peter Thomson of Australia. He was also runner-up on two occasions, a record of consistency unmatched by any golfer before or since.
See also GOLF.

Open Hearth Process, see IRON AND STEEL, *Production of Steel from Iron*.

Open University, The, a nation-wide organisation in Britain, founded 1969, by which people can study at home for degrees. In the 1980 academic year there were 60,000 undergraduates and 8000 associate students. No qualifications are required for entry and the intention is to provide for adults aged over 21 years.

Opencast Mining, see MINING.

Opera, drama in which the text is wholly or partly sung and accompanied by an orchestra. Late in the 16th century an aristocratic Florentine circle of musicians and literary men, reacting against the polyphonic style and attempting to revive the principles of Greek drama, began to write dramatic works in a new declamatory style—recitative. The leaders were Peri and Caccini and the poet Rinuccini. The first great master of opera was Monteverdi.

The Italian Lully incorporated the ballet, and established the tradition of French grand opera, under the patronage of the court. In England the foundations of a native opera, based on the masque, were consolidated by Purcell, whose *Dido and Aeneas* (1689) was a solitary pointer to the English opera that might have been. By the end of the century the leading influence was the Neapolitan school under Alessandro Scarlatti, and the form became rigidly standardised. In the early 18th century the greatest exponent of Italian opera was Handel in England. The reforms of Gluck were in essence a return to the principles of Monteverdi. He opposed the supremacy of the singer, and concentrated on dramatic expression and characterisation. French comic opera flourished in Paris from the middle of the century; ballad opera became popular in England and the *Singspiel* in Germany. The German romantic opera of Weber stems partly from Mozart and the *Singspiel*, partly from French grand opera under Cherubini and Spontini. Paris became an important centre dominated by Meyerbeer and Auber from about the 1830s, presently joined by Offenbach. In Italy the singer still reigned supreme in the operas of Rossini, Donizetti and Bellini. German dramatic music was dominated by Wagner after the production of his *Rienzi* (1842) and *Der Fliegende Holländer* (1843). Influenced by Weber and others, he evolved a new form, with the stage action and the musical thought closely interrelated. In Italy, Verdi, in his last operas *Otello* and *Falstaff*, reached a musico-dramatic balance on the highest level. Mascagni and Leoncavallo sacrificed musical values to dramatic sensationalism; a criticism that may also be levelled against Puccini. In France, Berlioz attempted an alternative kind of epic opera in *Les Troyens* and Gounod attempted to bridge the gap between the outworn conventions of French grand opera and *opéra-comique*. Debussy's *Pelléas et Mélisande* is a work of impressionistic suggestion that has found no true successor. Russian opera began with Glinka and Dargomizhsky and reached its height in Mussorgsky's *Boris Godunov* (1874). The operas of Richard Strauss rank among the most imposing achievements of 20th-century European opera; but the most remarkable examples are perhaps Schoenberg's *Erwartung* and *Moses und Aron*; Busoni's *Doktor Faust*; Berg's *Wozzeck*; and Hindemith's *Mathis der Maler*. In Britain opera gained ground with the success of Britten's *Peter Grimes* (1945). Tippett treated contemporary psychological themes in *The Midsummer Marriage* and *The Knot Garden*.

The form has developed towards oratorio (Stravinsky's *Oedipus Rex*), towards cabaret and music-theatre (in the work of Kurt Weill), and towards vaudeville and mixed media.
See also MASQUE.

Operetta, originally applied to a short opera, the term is now generally used of light, or comic, operas or musical comedies characterised by songs and spoken dialogue. One of the earliest and most successful exponents of operetta was Jacques Offenbach (1819–80), who, in *Orphée aux enfers*, 1858, and *La belle Hélène*, 1864, used classical subjects to satirise contemporary French society. These were followed in England by the Savoy Operas of W. S. Gilbert and Arthur Sullivan, written between 1870 and 1896, the best known of which are *HMS Pinafore*, 1878, and *The Mikado*, 1885. In Vienna at the same time Johann Strauss the younger (1825–99) was writing more-straightforwardly romantic and melodic operettas such as *Die Fledermaus*, 1874, and *The Gipsy Baron*, 1885. In the 20th century operetta received fresh impetus in the USA, where its cross-fertilisation with musical comedy produced such successful hybrids as George Gershwin's *Porgy and Bess*, 1935, and Leonard Bernstein's *Candide*, 1956, and *West Side Story*, 1957.

Ophelia, see CHIRATA.

Ophicleide (Greek *ophis*, a serpent; *kleis*, a key), brass instrument, the bass of the obsolete key bugle, patented in 1821. Parts for it occur in Mendelssohn's *Elijah* and Verdi's *Requiem*, but these are now played by the tuba.

Ophidia, see SNAKE.

Ophiopogon, see SNAKESBREAD.

Ophiuchus, 'the Serpent-Bearer', a large equatorial constellation containing part of the ecliptic. It was in the south-east corner of this constellation that Kepler's star, the most recent supernova in our galaxy, appeared in 1604.
See also NOVAE.

Ophrys, a genus of hardy terrestrial orchids with beautiful flowers, many of which bear a remarkable resemblance to insects. *O. apifera*, the bee orchid, is about 20–30 cm tall, and has three to nine bee-like flowers in a loose spike.

Ophthalmology (Greek *ophthalmos*, eye; *logos*, discourse), the science of the eye, its anatomy, physiology, visual functions and diseases.

Ophthalmoscope, an optical instrument designed for examining the surface of the retina of the human eye, invented by Helmholtz (1851). With the modern instruments the structure and health of the cornea, aqueous humour, crystalline lens, vitreous humour and retina may be investigated. An estimate of the refractive error of the eye may also be made.

Ophthalmoscopy enables the practitioner to observe the only visible part of the functioning vascular system, hence it is important in the diagnosis of the health of the eyes and of the whole body.

Ophuls, Max, real name Max Oppenheimer (1902–57), German film director; Ophuls was a theatre director in Germany, made his first film in 1930, and worked in various parts of Europe and the USA before settling in France from 1950. His most famous films, *Leibelei*, 1932, and *La Ronde*, 1950, are adaptations from Schnitzler suffused with a sad *fin-de-siècle* sexuality. Others are *Le Plaisir*, 1951, and the self-indulgent *Lola Montès*, 1955.

Opie, John (1761–1807), British painter. In 1782 he received a commission from the king, and soon became a fashionable portrait painter, among his subjects being Johnson, Burke and Fox. He was also an historical painter.

Opitz, Martin (1597–1639), German poet. In 1625 he was crowned poet laureate at Vienna by the Emperor Ferdinand II. He was given the title of von Boberfeld in 1629 and became historiographer to Ladislaus IV of Poland in 1638. His poems (*Teutsche Poemata, Weltliche Poemata, Geistliche Poemata*) tend to be didactic, cold and formal. In his *Buch von der deutschen Poeterey*, 1624, he stresses the importance of clarity and adherence to rules.

Opium, the juice of the oriental poppy *Papaver somniferum*, obtained by cutting the unripe seed capsule and leaving it overnight before collecting the exuded juice. Opium grows well in Turkey, Greece, Yugoslavia, Bulgaria and parts of India. It has a bitter, nauseous taste and a heavy narcotic odour. Its pharmacological properties are due to the many alkaloids—principally morphine, codeine, thebaine, papaverine, noscapine and narceine—which it contains.

The use of opium is usually begun to relieve pain or insomnia, and after a month's use the individual becomes dependent on the drug. If taken in excess opium is poisonous. For smoking opium a special pipe is required, and effects are much the same as when it is swallowed. Opium can be given in the form of laudanum, a tincture prepared by dissolving opium in dilute alcohol.

See also Drug Dependence.

Opium War, name given to hostilities between Britain and China in 1840, following the destruction of British ships taking opium to China. The war resulted in the cession of Hong Kong and the treaty ports.

See also China, *History*.

Opole (German *Oppeln*), town of Poland, capital of Opole province, on the River Oder, 273 km south-east of Warsaw. It was the capital of a duchy, 1163–1532, and then passed into the hands of the Hapsburg family. There are flour, machinery and cement industries. Population (1974) 96,820.

Oporto (Portuguese *Pôrto*), city of Portugal, capital of Pôrto district, on the River Douro, 5 km from its mouth on the Atlantic coast 280 km north of Lisbon. It is the second city of the country, and has been an important town since the time of the Moorish supremacy. An outer harbour to take large vessels was constructed at Leixões in 1890. Oporto is famous for the wine which it exports. In addition the port has a trade in fruit, olive oil and salt. There are foundries, textile, sugar, pottery, glass, tobacco, paper, and foodstuff industries. Population (1974) 311,800.

Opossum, American Indian name applied to various members of the family Didelphidae, in the order Marsupialia. The opossum is the only native North American marsupial. All are arboreal, except *Chironectes minimus*, an aquatic species, and nocturnal; they are carnivorous or insectivorous. The chief genus is *Didelphis* and consists of 23 species, varying in size from that of a cat to a rat. The commonest of these is *D. virginiana*, which occurs in the USA. The young are carried by the mother in her pouch.

Opossum, Didelphis *sp.*

Oppeln, see Opole.

Oppenheim, Edward Phillips (1866–1946), English novelist. His departure from school for the family leather business is amusingly told in his autobiography, *The Pool of Memory*, 1941. Altogether Oppenheim wrote some 150 books and was among the best contemporary writers of 'thrillers'.

Oppenheimer, Sir Ernest (1880–1957), chairman of De Beers Consolidated Mines Limited, and many other South African and Rhodesian mining companies, and one of the world's leading industrialists. In 1902 he was sent to South Africa in connection with the firm's interests in Kimberley. In 1908 he was elected a member of the city council and became mayor in 1912, which office he held till 1915. Oppenheimer was an extremely generous philanthropist.

Oppenheimer, J. Robert (1904–67), US physicist. From 1928 he taught at California Institute of Technology and the University of California, developing at that university an outstanding school of theoretical physics. In March 1943 he was chosen by the US Army to head a scientific laboratory from which emerged the atomic bomb. He became chief executive of a $60,000,000 project with 4500 workers, including such eminent physicists as Enrico Fermi and Niels Bohr. Subsequently he was appointed to a board of seven members to suggest US policy on atomic energy. He was president of the American Physical Society, and, from 1947 until 1966, director of the Institute for Advanced Study, Princeton. He pressed hard for international control of the atomic bomb, and tried to prevent the USA from building a hydrogen bomb. In 1954, the Atomic Energy Commission found Oppenheimer a security risk; this unwarranted slur on his character was eventually disbelieved.

Opposition. A celestial body is said to be 'in opposition' when its celestial longitude differs from that of the Sun by 180°. An exterior planet is then most favourably placed for observation, being closest to the Earth and on the meridian at midnight.

Opsonins (Greek *opsónein*, to obtain food). The capacity of the white blood corpuscles to absorb and digest invading bacteria by phagocytosis depends on the presence of opsonins in the blood serum: white corpuscles washed free from serum are unable to carry out phagocytosis. In addition to normal opsonin, which has a generalised action on all bacteria, special opsonins or bacteriotropins are formed against specific bacteria as a result of immunisation.

See also Immune Response; Immunology.

Optic Nerve, see Cranial Nerves; Eye.

Optical Brighteners, compounds incorporated into detergent formulations which fluoresce with a blue colour when absorbed onto fabrics and give them a brighter appearance. They are usually dyes which absorb radiation in the ultraviolet region of the spectrum at about 360 nm and fluoresce by emitting light in the blue region at 430 to 444 nm.

Optical Illusions may involve mistakes of visual perception of form, distance, size or movement. Pictorial optical illusions are often obtained by deliberate or unintentional use of false perspective, sometimes by effects of contrast or irradiation, sometimes by unaccustomed use of the visual sense, e.g. by staring at the same point in a picture for a long time.

Optician. An 'ophthalmic optician' is a person having the prescribed qualifications in optics, including the measurement of errors of refraction, in orthoptics, and in the fitting and supply of optical appliances. A 'dispensing optician' is a person having the prescribed qualifications for the fitting and supply of spectacles.

Optics, science of light and vision, usually divided into: (1) physical optics; (2) physiological optics; and (3) geometrical optics. The basic postulates of geometrical optics are: (1) straight line propagation in uniform media; (2) reflection and refraction of rays at a smooth boundary between media according to simple laws; (3) the inverse square law of light intensity; (4) reversibility of ray paths; and (5) non-interference of rays which cross each other.

Geometrical optics shows how optical images are formed by mirrors and lenses: light rays from a single point can reunite at a second point after reflection at a concave mirror or refraction through a convex lens; these points are known as object and image respectively. On closer analysis the rays are found to pass near but not exactly through the image point, due to aberrations in the lens or mirror. Optical design is concerned with calculating combinations of lenses and mirrors to reduce

aberrations to an acceptable minimum. An alternative formulation of geometrical optics is based on Fermat's principle; this states roughly that when light passes from A to B through an optical system (A and B not being in general object and image) the path it takes is such that the time of travel is less than for any other nearby path.
See also ABERRATIONS OF LENSES; REFLECTION AND REFRACTION OF LIGHT.

Optimism (Latin *optimus*, best), word having both a strictly philosophic and a popular sense. The well known doctrine of Leibniz, in his *Essais de Theodicée*, 1710, that 'everything is for the best in this best of all possible worlds', may be taken as the extreme of the optimistic philosophic doctrines. Leibniz did not mean that everything in the world was perfect but that of all the infinite number of possible worlds which presented themselves to the mind of the Creator, the existing one was the best possible. The milder form of optimism, which holds that on the whole the universe is advancing towards a better state of things, is more properly called meliorism or evolutionism. In the popular sense of the word optimism means the belief that 'there is a soul of goodness in things evil', and that whatever exists is right in some inscrutable fashion, or can be made the means of good. Alternatively optimism may simply mean the habit of 'looking on the bright side of things', which naturally springs from a belief in the ultimate triumph of good. The opposite of optimism is pessimism.

Opuntia, see PRICKLY PEAR.

Opus (Latin, work). Its abbreviation 'op.' is generally used as a prefix to enumerations of a composer's works. Its Italian equivalent, *opera*, at first had the same meaning, but is now used almost exclusively in its later specific sense.

Opus Dei (Societas Sacerdotalis Sanctae Crucis et Opus Dei), international Roman Catholic association whose members are dedicated to fulfilling Christian ideals within their personal lives and to spreading Christian doctrine.

Opus Signinum, common form of Roman walling and pavement made of cement in which crushed brick or tile is incorporated.

Oracle (Latin *oraculum*), place at which a deity answers the questions of his votaries through the mouth of his inspired minister, and hence the answer itself. The practice is common among most ancient peoples, but Greek oracles are the best attested, the most celebrated being that of Apollo at Delphi.

Oracle, see TELETEXT.

Oradea (formerly German *Grosswardein*), town of Romania on the River Criş, 130 km west of Cluj. Reputedly founded in 1080 by St Ladislaus, it was the seat of Greek Orthodox, Roman Catholic and Uniate bishops. Its industries are various, including machine tools, chemicals and mining equipment manufacture, and food processing. Population (1979) 178,407.

Oral Contraception, see BIRTH CONTROL.

Oran, capital of Oran department in Algeria, a fortified seaport standing at the mouth of a small stream, at the foot of the Sainte Croix, 115 km north-east of Tlemçen. It was a French naval station before Algerian independence and has a moderately good harbour, but there is an excellent one at Mers-el-Kebir, 5 km distant. It is a centre of the wine industry, and has a large export trade in grain, wine and spirits, livestock, hides and wool, and esparto grass. Population (1973) 325,000.

Orang-utan, *Pongo pygmaeus*, a member of the primate family Pongidae, which is found solely in Borneo and Sumatra. The flat, almost dished condition of the face is very marked and the forelimbs touch the ankles when the animal is erect. The orang-utan is arboreal, and sleeps in a nest which it builds in the trees. In habit it is solitary except during the mating season, and it mainly eats fruit. The species is now in danger of extinction; the adults are killed and the young stolen by poachers and sold, mostly through Indonesia.

Orange, House of, ruling family of a once independent principality now included in the *département* of Vaucluse, France, and today occupying the throne of the Netherlands. The male line of Gerald Adhemar (fl.1086) ended in 1174 when the heiress married Bertrand de Baux. Nine princes of his line followed one another until another heiress, Marie de Baux, married Jean de Châlons in 1393. His descendant, Philibert (1502–30), was an able soldier and for his part in the campaign of Charles V was rewarded by the emperor with extensive possessions in the Netherlands. Philibert was succeeded by his nephew, René of Nassau-Châlons. René on his death in 1544 devised his titles and estates to his first cousin, William of Orange-Nassau, William the Silent. His great-grandson became William III of Great Britain; but on his death in 1702 the succession was disputed by the King of Prussia and John of Nassau-Dietz. The Peace of Utrecht (1713) effected a compromise. The Prussian claim was abandoned, the territory of Orange was incorporated in France, and John was given the title of Prince of Orange. In 1815 his descendant, William VI, became King of the Netherlands as William I.
See also NETHERLANDS, *History*.

Orange, river in southern Africa, which rises in the Maluti Mountains of Lesotho. For almost its entire length of 2300 km the river has cut a deep channel; only in the Boegoeberg–Augrabies Falls section does the valley open out, and here almost all the irrigable alluvial land is concentrated. The watershed cannot be determined accurately in the Kalahari, but the drainage basin is about 850,000 km^2. Tributaries include the Vaal and Caledon. In its lower course the Orange forms the boundary between South Africa and South-West Africa (Namibia).

Orange, town of western New South Wales, Australia, and the centre of an agricultural and pastoral district. It is a growing manufacturing centre with woollen mills, electrical engineering, sawmilling and meat processing industries. Population (1980) 31,050.

Orange, French town in the *département* of Vaucluse, 21 km north of Avignon. Orange was the capital of the county, later the principality, of Orange from the 11th to the 16th centuries; in 1544 it passed to William the Silent, and hence gives its name to the ruling family of Holland. It was taken in 1672 by the French. Population (1975) 26,468.

Orange, see CITRUS FRUITS.

Orange Free State, province of South Africa, once a Boer republic, bounded on the west and south by Cape Province, the Orange river forming the southern boundary; on the north by the Vaal river; and the east by Lesotho and Natal. Area 129,150 km^2.
The Highveld of the Orange Free State, with the Transvaal, lies across the westward-sloping surface of the plateau of Southern Africa, the Vaal and Orange river system carrying the waters to the east through the Kalahari to the Atlantic. Its surface consists mainly of undulating, grassy plains and plateaus. The population of the Orange Free State in 1970 was 1,649,306, including 295,903 whites, 1,317,308 Africans, and 36,090 coloureds. The main towns are Bloemfontein (the capital), Kroonstad, Bethlehem and Welkom.
Cereals, tobacco and fruit are grown, and the province supports about one-quarter of all white-owned cattle and sheep in South Africa, on 11 per cent of the grazing land. The Orange Free State's goldfields produce 28 per cent of all gold outside the Communist bloc. Two of the 11 Orange Free State goldmines also produce uranium. The Vereeniging-Clydesdale coalfield, with reserves of about 3000 million t, supplies one-fifth of South Africa's coal production.

Orange Society, an Irish political society with the professed objects of the defence of the Protestant faith and succession. In 1795, when the Protestant party was in the ascendant, the Orange Society was formed (taking its name from William of Orange), and it worked to secure Protestant dominance. It was organised as a secret society, arranged in lodges. During the 19th century it spread widely, having lodges not only in Ireland but also in England (especially Liverpool), Scotland and Canada. The society keeps as its high festival the annual (12 July) commemoration of the battle of the Boyne.

Orangemen, see ORANGE SOCIETY.

Orangery, building having large windows on its south side, used for growing oranges. There are examples at the palaces of Hampton Court, Kensington Palace and Versailles (all built between c.1680 and c.1710).

Oratorio, religious music for concert performance, consisting of solos and choruses, with instrumental accompaniment. The term has been variously defined at different periods, and in the early 17th century, oratorios had action, scenery and costumes. The origin is usually traced to the oratory of St Philip Neri in the 16th century. Carissimi was important as a developer of the Italian oratorio, set to Latin words. Under his successors, the oratorio was normally in Italian and virtually indistinguishable in style from opera. In France, Charpentier (1634–1704) developed Carissimi's ideas in his *Histoires sacrées*. English oratorio was created by Handel. Early 18th-century German oratorios were normally on the Italian model, but later composers in Germany and elsewhere were influenced by Handel. Among the best-known oratorios are Handel's *Messiah*, Haydn's *Creation*, Mendelssohn's *Elijah*, Berlioz's *Childhood of Christ* and Elgar's *Dream of Gerontius*.

Orbit, the path in which a body moves under the action of external forces. In astronomy these forces are usually gravitational, and the orbits of interest closed curves which are essentially Keplerian ellipses slightly perturbed by the disturbing action of other relatively remote bodies.

Orcades, Latin for ORKNEY ISLANDS.

Orcagna (L'Arcagnuolo), nickname (the archangel) of Andrea di Cione (c.1308–c.1368), Florentine painter, sculptor and architect. His only certain surviving painting is an altarpiece in the Strozzi Chapel, Santa Maria Novella, Florence. As an architect he was responsible for the church and tabernacle of Or San Michele, Florence. He left several unfinished works, completed by his brothers Nardo and Jacopo.

Orchard (Old English *ortzeard*, which probably originated from the Latin *hortus*, garden; and the Old English *geard*, fence). Formerly, it included both herbs and fruit trees, but now is used specifically for a large or small plantation of fruit trees.

Orchestra, body of instrumental players. The term originally meant the semi-circular space in front of the stage in the ancient Greek theatre where the chorus danced and sang. The modern orchestra arose about 1600 from the practice of using more than one player to a part in a string ensemble. It was mainly the opera house and the church that helped to establish the orchestra as an organisation in its own right. About the middle of the 18th century, wind instruments, formerly used when special effects were required, provided background harmony and occasionally emerged as soloists. The wind instruments normally found in an early 18th-century orchestra (e.g. Stamitz's orchestra at Mannheim) were flutes or recorders, oboes, bassoons and horns. Clarinets also appeared (consistently in Mannheim) but did not become standard until the end of the century. Trumpets, horns and timpani were ordinarily used in military or festive music. The 19th century saw the steady expansion of the wind section; Beethoven introduced trombones in his 'Pastoral' symphony. The dominating rôle of the strings was reduced, and the harp, previously used almost exclusively in the theatre, was introduced. Mechanical improvements made to all wind instruments enabled a wider range of notes to be written into their parts. Percussion instruments such as the bass drum, cymbals and triangle were now to be found in symphonic music, and to these were added the glockenspiel, xylophone and celesta. Wagner contributed to the expansion and emancipation of the wind group, and Berlioz and later Mahler made use of vast orchestral resources.

See also BAND; OPERA; PERCUSSION INSTRUMENTS; WIND INSTRUMENTS.

Orchidaceae, the family to which orchids belong, consisting of about 20,000 species in 800 or more genera. All Orchidaceae are herbaceous plants, with a worldwide distribution, although they are most diverse and abundant in humid tropical forests, where most orchids are epiphytes, being attached by specialised roots to the trunks of trees and also having hanging roots with an outer spongy water-storage layer or *velamen*. Most orchids of temperate regions are ground-rooted.

All Orchidaceae depend for successful growth on an association or mycorrhiza formed between their roots and the filamentous hyphae of certain fungi. Orchid flowers are extraordinary, both in botanical features and in diversity of colour and form. The fruit of *Vanilla fragrans* is the vanilla pod of commerce. This and the flowers of genera such as *Cattleya*, *Cymbidium*, *Dendrobium*, *Epidendrum*, *Odontoglossum* and *Paphiopedilum* are the main economically valuable products of the family.

Orczy, Emmuska, Baroness (1865–1947), Hungarian-born English novelist. In 1895 she published her famous novel, *The Scarlet Pimpernel.* Then followed more than 40 novels of a similarly romantic character, chiefly of the period of the French Revolution, including many 'Pimpernel' sequels, such as *The Elusive Pimpernel*, 1908, most of which were very popular. Her writings included essays, historical novels and detective stories. *Links in the Chain of Life*, 1947, is an autobiography.

Ordeal Bean, see CALABAR BEAN.

Order of Merit, see MERIT, ORDER OF.

Order of the Golden Dawn, The, an organisation of magic in Britain which existed from the end of the last century to the beginning of the Second World War. Among its members were such prominent figures as the poet, W. B. Yeats; the author, A. E. Waite; the actress, Florence Farr; and the magician, Aleister Crowley.

Orders, Holy, the ministry of the Roman Catholic, Orthodox, Anglican and other episcopal churches, and the sacrament by which it is handed on and perpetuated. In the Roman Catholic Church there have been four major orders (bishops, priests, deacons and subdeacons), and four minor (acolytes, exorcists, readers and doorkeepers). Subdeacons, exorcists and doorkeepers were suppressed by Paul VI, readers also being enabled to discharge the functions of subdeacons. Of the major orders, the first three are the holy orders *par excellence*. Holy orders are conferred sacramentally by the laying-on of hands by a bishop. The bishop conferring them must himself have been validly consecrated by another bishop in the apostolic succession.

The Church of England abandoned the minor orders and subdiaconate at the Reformation, but retained the three principal major orders (which most of the Protestant bodies rejected, setting up ministries of their own on what they considered to be the New Testament model).

The Presbyterian Church accepted only one order of the ministry, that of presbyters (priests), rejecting the need of a bishop for ordination.

Orders, Monastic, see MONASTICISM.

Orders of Architecture, the conventional systems of columns in classical architecture: Doric, Ionic, Corinthian, Tuscan and Composite. The main elements of all orders are the *stylobate* on which the columns stand, the *column* with its *capital* forming a transition from support to load; and the *entablature*, consisting of the *architrave* bridging the gap from column to column, the *frieze*, more or less decorative, and the *cornice*, which projects to throw off rain.

Greek Doric columns stand directly on the stylobate; in later Doric and all other orders they stand on a profiled *base*. Below the base may be a square *plinth*. The column shaft is frequently channelled into concave *fluting*.

The Doric order was composed in the 7th century BC, probably in the area near Corinth. Ionic was composed in Ionia (south of modern Izmir) 50 to 100 years later. In 5th-century Athens the Corinthian capital was invented as a variant form in the Ionic order. The Romans treated Corinthian as a separate order, their favourite, and gave it a special

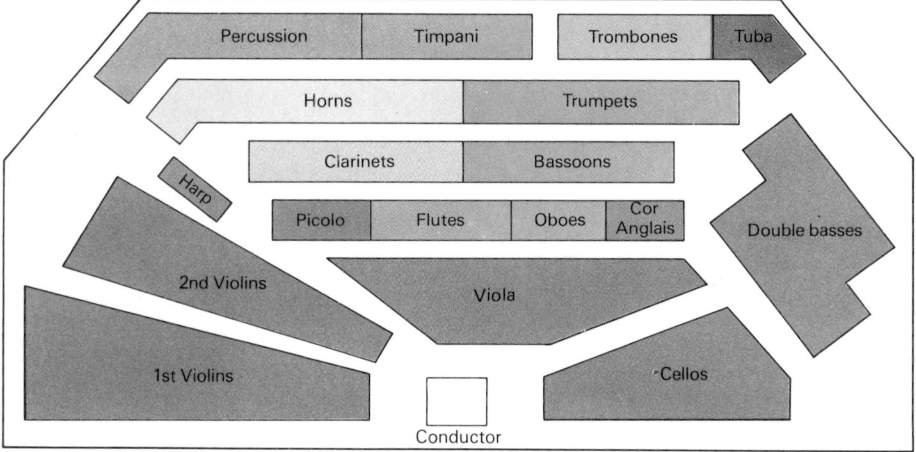

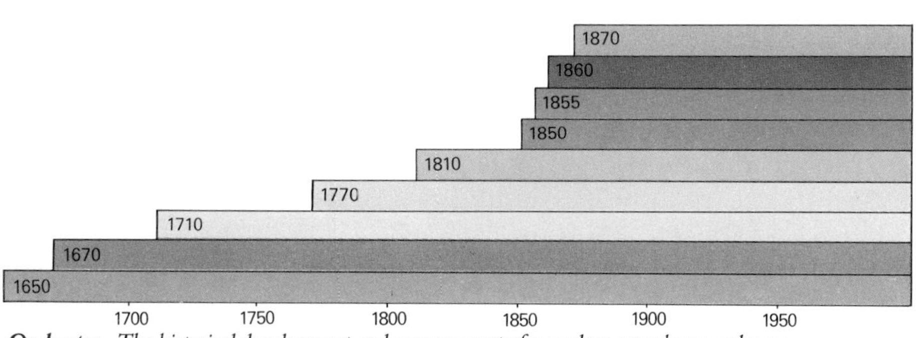

Orchestra. *The historical development and arrangement of a modern symphony orchestra.*

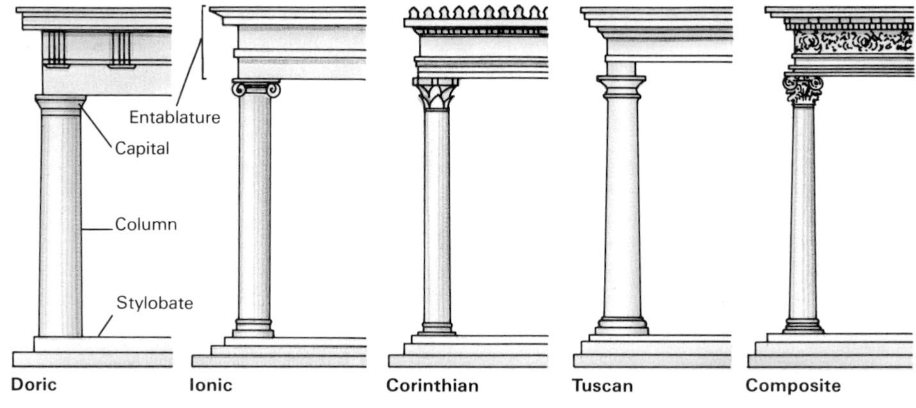

Orders of Architecture. *The three classical orders, Doric, Ionic, and Corinthian were supplemented by Tuscan and Composite in the Renaissance.*

cornice, while Renaissance architects added two more orders: Tuscan (based on Roman Doric and Vitruvius' description of the Etruscan temple) and Composite (used in Rome from the late 5th century BC). A conventional series of decreasing ruggedness and increasing grace was established: Tuscan, Doric, Ionic, Corinthian, Composite.
From the first, rules of proportion were probably used in designing the orders, but the only surviving set are those given by Vitruvius. They were regarded as fundamental by Renaissance architects, several of whom tried to establish ideal versions of the five orders.

Orders of Knighthood in the United Kingdom. The following are the principal orders within which honours are currently granted.
The Most Noble Order of the Garter, the oldest European order of chivalry, was founded according to tradition in 1348. One of its several legends of origin describes how the Countess of Salisbury's garter was dropped at a court festival and picked up by King Edward III who, observing the significant smiles of the onlookers, tied it round his own knee and uttered the celebrated words *'Honi soit qui mal y pense'*, 'Shame on him who thinks evil of it'. The order has undergone many changes and now consists of the sovereign and 24 knight companions, plus royal princes and foreign royalty.
The Most Ancient and Most Noble Order of the Thistle was founded in 1687 and revived in 1703 by Queen Anne. The order's motto is 'Nemo me impune lacessit' (No one provokes me with impunity', the motto of all the Scottish regiments, generally rendered in the vernacular as 'Wha daur meddle wi' me?'). By a statute of 1827 the order is to consist of the sovereign and 16 knights.
The Most Honourable Order of the Bath was founded traditionally in 1399 by Henry IV and revived by George I in 1725. Its motto is *'Ich dien'*, 'I serve', the motto of the Prince of Wales. The order has been revised and enlarged on several occasions, and now contains civil and military divisions, and three classes: Knights or Dames Grand Cross (GCB); Knights or Dames Commander (KCB, DCB); and companions (CB).
Order of Merit, see MERIT, ORDER OF.
The Most Distinguished Order of St Michael and St George was founded in 1818, after the cession of Malta to Britain and the submission of the Ionian Islands to a British protectorate, for the purpose of honouring distinguished Maltese and Ionians. The order has been revised and enlarged 15 times. There are three classes: Knights or Dames Grand Cross (GCMG); Knights or Dames Commander (KCMG, DCMG), and companions (CMG).
The Royal Victorian Order, founded by Queen Victoria in 1896 'as a reward for personal services to the queen and her successors'. Motto: 'Victoria'.
The Most Excellent Order of the British Empire, instituted in 1917, having both civil and military divisions, awarded to both men and women for services rendered to the British Empire. It has five classes: Knights or Dames Grand Cross (GBE); Knights or Dames Commanders (KBE or DBE); Commanders (CBE); Officers (OBE); Members (MBE). Motto: 'For God and Empire'.
Companions of Honour, see COMPANIONS OF HONOUR, ORDER OF THE.

Ordinaries, the term given to certain basic heraldic charges of a geometrical nature. An *ordinary of arms* is an heraldic dictionary in which arms are arranged alphabetically according to the principal ordinaries they contain.

Ordinary, in canon law, an ecclesiastic of superior standing who exercises his jurisdiction according to the normal discipline of the Church. In the Anglican Church it usually means the bishop or his chancellor.

Ordination, sacrament by which holy orders are conferred in the Christian Church. In the Roman Catholic, Orthodox and Anglican churches ordination can be conferred only by a bishop. Among Presbyterians, ordination is performed by the body of presbyters, acting by one of their number previously appointed. Here also the imposition of hands is used. The act by which a bishop is made is called consecration. Some Protestant churches limit ordination to the recognition of a call to preach the gospel.

Ordovician System, geological system occurring above the Cambrian and below the Silurian Systems. It began about 510 million years ago and ended between 435 and 460 million years ago. Ordovician rocks in Britain outcrop over much of Wales and part of the Welsh Borders, also in the Lake District, the Southern Uplands of Scotland, the north-west Highlands of Scotland, and in the west and east of Ireland.
The Ordovician is divided into a number of smaller units: at the base is the Arenig series, followed by the Llanvirn, Llandeilo, Caradoc and Ashgill series. The rocks are divided into zones on the basis of the graptolite faunas found within them.

Ordzhonikidze (formerly *Vladikavkaz*; 1944–54, *Dzaudzhikau*), capital city and economic centre of the North Ossetian ASSR, USSR, in the North Caucasus on the Terek river. It is an important industrial and cultural centre (machine-building, electric engineering, glass, food, and light industries). It was founded as a Russian fortress in 1784. Population (1980) 283,000.

Ore and Ore Dressing. An ore generally consists of metal-bearing minerals, together with an earthy material or 'gangue'. Before the metals can be extracted from the minerals as much as possible of the earthy material must be removed from the ore, the process being known as ore dressing. In ore dressing rock ores are first broken down in jaw-, gyratory- or roll-crushers, or in stamp mills, then in some cases finely ground in ball mills. 'Concentration' follows: magnetic material can be separated from non-magnetic in the magnetic separator. Jigs and concentrating tables and the old goldminer's pan all depend upon separation of the less dense 'tailings' and denser 'concentrates' into two layers, when the ore is treated with a stream of water. After concentration the mineral must be filtered and dried ready for the extraction processes.
See also METALLURGY.

Örebro, capital of Örebro county in Sweden, near the western end of Lake Hjälmaren, 85 km south-west of Västerås. It was formerly a place of assembly of the diet which, in 1529, here decreed the establishment of Lutheranism in Sweden. Manufactures include machinery, chemicals, footwear and matches, and the chief state railway workshop is here. Örebro is an inland port and a railway junction. Population (1978) 116,969.

Oregano, see ORIGANUM.

Oregon (Beaver State), one of the United States of America, bounded on the north by Washington, and west by the Pacific Ocean. Area 251,177 km², including 1632 km² of water. The principal rivers are the Columbia and its branches, the Willamette, Snake and Owyhee. The Columbia, which is 22 km wide at its mouth, is navigable, via the Snake, from the Pacific to the Idaho state line. Large ocean-going vessels can reach Portland, 173 km inland. The Cascade Range mountains, which have extinct volcanic peaks 1200 to 3350 m high, run north-south, dividing the state into two unequal regions. The western third of the state, bordering the Pacific, has a mild, equable and moist climate, with very fertile valleys. East of the Cascades is dry plateau country, with some productive irrigated valleys, rising to the folded lava-flows of the Blue Mountains. Agriculture is the main occupation, and a part of the land on the majority of farms is irrigated. Farming is of four main types: (1) commercial wheat farming; (2) ranching and beef cattle raising in the higher and drier areas; (3) dairy farming, particularly in the Willamette valley; and (4) the production of field crop specialities. Oregon shares with Washington the forests of the Pacific North-West, the main US supplier of softwoods to the nation. Its main asset is the great stands of Douglas fir to be found on the coastal mountains and the western slopes of the Cascades. There are few mineral resources, but the state shares in the great water power resources of the Columbia and the Snake rivers.

In 1980 the population was 2,632,663.

Oregon was the name formerly given to the whole territory west of the Rocky Mountains, claimed by the USA as far as 54°40′N. This claim was resisted by the British government, which asserted a right to the entire territory. The boundary dispute was, however, settled on the 49th parallel. The northern portion is now Washington. The territorial government was organised in 1848, and in 1859 it was admitted as a state.

Oregon Pine, see Douglas Fir.

Orel, capital city, economic and cultural centre of Orel *oblast*, USSR, on the River Oka south of Moscow. It is an important industrial centre with engineering (agricultural and textile machinery), light and food industries, and also a railway junction. It was founded in 1566 as a fortress town, becoming a provincial capital in 1778. Population (1980) 309,000.

Orenburg, capital city, economic and cultural centre of Orenburg *oblast*, USSR, on the River Ural. It has extensive engineering, flour, meat, leather and clothing industries, and is an important transport centre. Since 1744 it has been the administrative centre of the southern Urals and the adjoining steppe areas, the main point of trade with Kazakh SSR and Central Asia, and the base for the Russian advance into Central Asia. The discovery of natural gas nearby in the late 1960s has stimulated the recent growth of the city. Population (1980) 471,000.

Orense, capital of the province of Orense, Spain, on the left bank of the River Minho. An important town under the Suevi, it was sacked by the Moors in the 8th century. It has a remarkable seven-arched bridge, begun in the 13th century, of which the central arch is 38 m high. Textiles, ironware, leather and chocolate are produced. Population (1981) 96,085.

Orestes, legendary son of Agamemnon and Clytaemnestra. When Agamemnon was murdered at the instigation of Clytaemnestra, Orestes escaped and killed Clytaemnestra. For the crime of matricide, he was driven mad, and pursued by the Erinyes.

Øresund, or the Sound, strait leading from the Kattegat to the Baltic Sea, between Sweden on the east and the Danish island of Sjaelland on the west. Its length is 128 km and its narrowest breadth between Helsingør and Hälsingborg is 5 km; the deepest part is about 25 m.

Orff, Carl (1895–1982), German composer He had his first success with a setting from *Carmina Burana*, 1937. His opera *Antigonae* was chosen for the Salzburg Festival of 1949. Orff wrote music of popular appeal whilst breaking away from the use of romantic harmony by concentrating on rhythm as the source of melody.

Orford, Robert Walpole, 1st Earl of, see Walpole, Robert, 1st Earl of Orford.

Organ, musical instrument in which compressed air is released through a set of pipes tuned to produce notes of different pitch. The organ was invented by Ktesibos of Alexandria in the 3rd century BC.

During medieval times the organ became more elaborate. The compass increased, and a complex though sensitive key action developed connected to a keyboard. The three or four ranks of pipes known as a *Blockwerk* were increased in number. By the 15th century a wind chest had been developed making it possible for the player to select ranks from the *Blockwerk* by using 'stops' to prevent the other pipes from sounding. The number of keyboards (manuals) increased to two, three, or four, each connected to a separate organ or 'division' with the facility of playing on two (or more) at once by means of manual 'couplers'. A separate 'pedal organ' was also developed, played with the feet. The culmination of this development was during the late Baroque (c.1650–1750). Later, with the introduction of pneumatic and electro-pneumatic action to the keyboards, the player lost the sensitive touch of the earlier instrument. Organs were much larger and were voiced 'romantically' with 'string-tones'. Several divisions were enclosed in 'swell' boxes to achieve diminuendo and crescendo, the whole aimed at simulating orchestral sounds. Electro-pneumatic action made possible such gigantic instruments as that in the Convention Hall, Atlantic City, USA, which has seven manuals and over 33,000 pipes. In the second half of the 20th century there has been a gradual return to the classical principles of organ building as perfected in the 1700s. The electronic or electrophonic organ (invented by Hammond in 1934) has enjoyed some popularity.

See also Regal.

Organic Chemistry, study of the compounds of carbon. The term was originally applied to the study of the behaviour and reactions of compounds obtained directly or indirectly from living organisms. The majority of carbon compounds are formed between carbon and the non-metallic elements hydrogen, nitrogen, oxygen, sulphur, fluorine, chlorine, bromine, iodine and phosphorus. Organic compounds are extremely numerous and diverse. There are also many organo-metallic compounds. The reason for this great variety is that carbon-carbon bonds are very strong. Whereas chains of atoms of all other elements are characteristically short and unstable, chains of carbon atoms, even very long and complex chains, are highly stable. Its linkages with the other non-metals listed above are also very stable. Carbon uniformly has a valency of 4, and carbon atoms have the remarkable and almost unique power of linking up together to form chains, rings, etc., which constitute the framework of the compound molecules. Thus butane, $CH_3{\cdot}CH_2{\cdot}CH_2{\cdot}CH_3$, has a straight chain of 4 carbon atoms; C–C–C–C–; isobutane, $(CH_3)_2CH{\cdot}CH_3$, a branched chain:

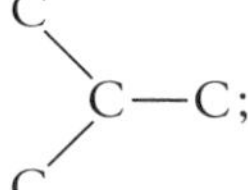

and benzene C_6H_6, and cyclohexane a chain or ring of six carbon atoms:

```
   C—C
  /   \
 C     C.
  \   /
   C—C
```

A common feature of organic compounds is the occurrence of double carbon-to-carbon bonds, as in 1-butene, which has a straight chain of four carbon atoms, one pair of which is doubly bonded (C═C—C—C—). Triple carbon-to-carbon bonds also occur, but to a much lesser extent.

Organic compounds are classed in several divisions, of which the two principal are the aliphatic compounds and the aromatic compounds. Aliphatic compounds may theoretically be regarded as ultimately derived from methane, CH_4, while benzene and its derivatives are classed as aromatic. The main distinction in structure between the two groups is that the aromatic substances contain a closed nucleus of apparently unsaturated carbon atoms, e.g. benzene,

Oregon. *Crater Lake in the Cascade Range is formed in the caldera of an extinct volcano.*

```
       H   H
       C—C
     //     \\
  HC           CH
     \       /
       C=C
       H   H
```

while the aliphatic compounds have open chains of carbon atoms, e.g. pentane, $CH_3{\cdot}CH_2{\cdot}CH_2{\cdot}CH_2{\cdot}CH_3$. Heterocyclic compounds contain a closed ring consisting partly of carbon atoms and partly of other multivalent atoms, e.g. pyridine,

```
       H   H
       C=C
     /     \
   N         CH
     \\     //
       C—C
       H   H
```

Another important distinction between aromatic and aliphatic compounds is that the benzene-ring 'double bonds' of aromatic compounds are unreactive in contrast to the double bonds of unsaturated aliphatic compounds.

Reactions in organic chemistry are mainly those in which one functional group is substituted for another in a molecule, or those where a new functional group is added onto the molecule.

See also ALIPHATIC COMPOUNDS; AROMATIC COMPOUNDS.

Organic Husbandry, the practice of agriculture and horticulture in all their phases based upon the use of organic materials and natural methods, to the exclusion of chemical fertilisers, dusts and sprays, and artificial forcing of stock for their produce. The essential feature is the return of the residues of organic life, such as plant remains, and animal and human excreta to the earth. This restores and builds soil fertility. A naturally fertile soil means vigorous plants; better plant food means healthy animals and humans. The cycle is thereby complete.

Organisation de l'Armée Secrète (OAS), clandestine ultra-right-wing organisation founded by Gen. Raoul Salan in Madrid, in May 1961. Its prime object was to keep Algeria French. It was responsible for bomb outrages in both Algeria and France. After Algeria became independent, in July 1962, the OAS concentrated all its activities in France, hoping to destroy the Gaullist regime, and made several attempts on de Gaulle's life. Salan was captured in 1962 and sentenced to life imprisonment, and Bidault, the movement's political leader, settled in exile in Brazil in 1963.

Organisation for Economic Co-operation and Development (OECD), an organisation which in 1961 superseded the Organisation for European Economic Co-operation (OEEC). The member countries of the OECD are: Australia, Austria, Belgium, Canada, Denmark, Eire, Finland, France, German Federal Republic, Greece, Iceland, Italy, Japan, Luxembourg, the Netherlands, New Zealand, Norway, Portugal, Spain, Sweden, Switzerland, Turkey, the UK and the USA.

The aims of the OECD are to promote economic growth and employment and a rising standard of living for its members; to contribute to the sound economic growth of developing countries; and to further the expansion of world trade. Members' economic policies are regularly reviewed.

Organisation for European Economic Co-operation (OEEC), formed after the Marshall Plan for European Recovery was inaugurated by the USA in 1948; the 16 European nations which had accepted the Marshall offer met in Paris to set up the OEEC, and outlined a plan for the restoration of the European economy by the end of 1951. The OEEC was superseded by the Organisation for Economic Co-operation and Development in 1961.

Organisation of African Unity (OAU), was founded on 25 May 1963 as an intergovernmental body, representative of all independent African states, but excluding the white regimes of Rhodesia, as it was then, and South Africa. As well as setting out to protect the independence of African states, it aims for harmony among member states.

Organisation of American States (OAS), had its basis in a meeting in Washington in April 1890 of representatives of the American republics, called to foster mutual understanding and co-operation. In 1948 the charter of the OAS was adopted; the Alliance for Progress was established in 1961. The OAS has generally taken a rigidly anti-Communist view and in 1962 Cuba was expelled because of its Soviet alliances.

Organisation of Arab Petroleum Exporting Countries (OAPEC), formed in 1967–68; its current members are the United Arab Emirates, Algeria, Bahrein, Egypt, Iraq, Kuwait, Libya, Qatar, Saudi Arabia and Syria. Its importance derives from its use of oil as a political weapon. The first attempt in this direction was made in 1967, when the Arab oil exporting countries decided to cut off supplies to Britain, the USA and the German Federal Republic in retaliation for their aid to Israel in the Middle East war of that year.

Oriental Dance. *Classical and folk dances in India express a rich cultural heritage.*

Organisation of Petroleum Exporting Countries (OPEC), set up in 1960 to represent the major oil exporting countries (apart from Canada and the USSR) in their dealings with the oil producing companies. Its members are Abu Dhabi, Algeria, Indonesia, Iran, Iraq, Kuwait, Libya, Nigeria, Qatar, Saudi Arabia and Venezuela. After the dollar devaluation of February 1973, OPEC negotiated a new oil-pricing agreement with the major Western oil companies to compensate for losses in the purchasing power of oil revenues, and to modify the formula for future price calculations in the light of currency fluctuations.

See also ORGANISATION OF ARAB PETROLEUM EXPORTING COUNTRIES.

Organistrum, see HURDY-GURDY.

Organum, see POLYPHONY.

Orgasm, see SEXUALITY, HUMAN.

Oriel Window, window projecting from an upper storey and supported by a bracket or corbelling. Oriel windows were commonly used in late Gothic domestic architecture.

Oriental Dance. The dances of the East may be divided broadly into two types: the folk or community dances and the classical. The folk-dances fall under various headings; there are, for example, sacrificial, propitiatory, talismanic, seasonal, marital, courtship, fertility, instructional and celebratory forms still existing in the different regions of Asia. The classical or artistic forms of dance are, by and large, closely connected with religion. Indeed, in India and South-East Asia dance has played a principal rôle in Hindu worship. It is only comparatively recently that sacred classical dance has become available to secular audiences in theatres, but even here it leans heavily upon its religious themes and atmosphere.

Much of China's classical dance has existed within the framework of her opera. It was only in this century that Mei Lan Fang redefined and reinforced the art of dance.

Japan's forte has always been the dance-theatre. *Bugaku* dates from the 7th century and was performed exclusively for the royal family. It was only after the Second World War that *Bugaku* was seen by the public. The aristocracy patronised the Noh theatre which encompassed symbolic, emotional, heroic and humorous situations. The commoners, however, had to wait till the end of the 16th century for a dance-theatre of their own. This was *Kabuki*, the innovation of O Kuni. All rôles are played by men.

Oriental Drama. The Eastern drama originated in religious celebration. In China, the first manifestations were probably associated with ancestor worship, and the formation of a regular drama (achieved by the end of the 8th century BC) was nourished by folk-song and folk-dance. The basic features of Chinese drama consist of highly stylised movement and gesture, with dialogue intoned to musical accompaniment from a traditional repertory. Scenery is minimal, but costumes are elaborate and richly coloured, and designed to be emblematic of the character of the wearer. Plots are traditional and stock characters recur.

Oriental Drama. *Kabuki plays, based on Japanese legends, use male actors exclusively.*

In both the aristocratic *Noh* and the popular *Kabuki* plays of Japan, stylised movement and gesture are also of great importance and scenery is again very spare. *Noh* plays originated in the 14th century AD, when they were performed by Shinto priests before aristocratic audiences, and the origin of *Kabuki* was from Chinese forms in the 16th century AD. *Kabuki* follows certain Chinese conventions; since the plots are well known the main interest for the spectators is the virtuosity of the actors. In the *Noh* play dance and chanting by a chorus are major features; as in Greek drama, the chorus comments upon the action.

In India, a classical Hindu (Sanskrit) drama was developed by 100 AD, and had probably been in the process of formation for several centuries preceding the Christian era. By the 5th century AD this drama, which shared the stylised acting, spare use of scenery and elaborate costume of Chinese drama, was fully mature and at its artistic peak. As in Europe, the 15th and 16th centuries saw a literary and dramatic renaissance, and spectacular play-cycles depicting the legends of Rama and Krishna were first performed in the temples, later moving into the streets. These cycles made much use of song and dance as well as of a chorus, narrator and stock characters, and their loosely constructed plots allowed improvisation.

In modern times, there has been experiment with, and imitation of, Western dramatic styles throughout the East. Puppet-drama too has enjoyed centuries of popularity and retains much of its vitality and appeal.

See also PUPPETS; ORIENTAL DANCE.

Orientation (Latin *oriens, orientis*, the rising sun), of buildings may be either: (1) the position or 'aspect' of a building in relation to the cardinal points; or (2) the siting of a church with its main axis east-west, the chancel being at the east end. Early Christian churches, however, were oriented towards the west (e.g. St Peter's, Rome). Mosques and synagogues in any part of the world are invariably oriented towards Mecca and Jerusalem, respectively.

Orienteering, a form of cross-country running in which competitors navigate round a course from point to point using specially drawn maps and a compass. The sport originated in Scandinavia. It arrived in Britain with the formation of the Scottish Orienteering Association in 1962 and the British Orienteering Federation in 1967. The sport caters for a wide range of age and ability. Competitors compete in age-group classes from 'under 12' to 'over 50', and are given courses from 1·5 km to about 20 km in length.

Competitions usually take place in forested or partly forested terrain. Control cards are punched to show that the competitors have visited each point and on crossing the finish line their time is calculated.

Origami, the Japanese art of paper folding. It is a traditional craft with an extensive literature and is divided into ceremonial origami, used, for instance, for decorating gifts, and the more widely known and practised art of model-making in which paper is folded to represent birds, animals, flowers, etc.

Origanum, a genus of aromatic herbs and sub-shrubs of the Labiatae. *O. marjorana* is the sweet marjoram, of Europe and Asia. *O. vulgare,* the common marjoram, with purple or white flowers, is also aromatic. *O. onites* is the pot marjoram.

Origin of Life. Life was most probably created from the reducing (hydrogen-rich) gases of the atmosphere that were dissolved in the oceans. Under the action of lightning and ultra-violet light simple molecules were transformed into the fundamental organic molecules of living matter. The primeval oceans, rich in non-biologically produced organic material, have been described as 'organic soup', a concept developed by J. B. S. Haldane and A. I. Oparin.

It is also possible that life may have been created during an ice-age. With the idea that material is concentrated by freezing and that the crystalline nature of ice might assist molecular alignment, Leslie Orgel took a dilute solution of some of the basic constituents of the primeval atmosphere and froze it over several days. Organic molecules were formed, including adenine, one of the four bases of the DNA molecule.

Whether a self-copying molecule was made many times or on one isolated occasion is not known, but from the ubiquitous nature of nucleic acids (DNA and RNA molecules) it could be inferred that these substances constitute the only molecular system possible that can carry and transmit genetic information from one generation to the next.

Original Sin, sinfulness inherent in human nature since the Fall, in contrast to actual sin which is the conscious breaking of God's law. The doctrine is based on the story of Adam and Eve (Genesis ii and iii) as elaborated by St Paul, especially in Romans v.

Orinoco, third largest river of South America, being next in importance to the Amazon and Plata (River Plate). Its source is in the Sierra Parima, Venezuela, near the Brazilian border. The entire course is about 2400 km, of which 1440 km below the Atures cararacts and 960 km above them to the Maipures cataracts are navigable. The head of uninterrupted navigation is at the confluence of the Orinoco with the Apure, 1243 km from the mouth of the river. In the flood season (April–September), following the rains, the lower course becomes an immense lake, covering the plains for some miles to the east of the Apure. The lower half of the Orinoco is navigable by river steamers and provides essential transport to the iron and steel industry centres around Ciudad Bolivar and also to the oil-fields in the north-east plains. The area of the basin is about 962,000 km^2.

Orioles, in family Oriolidae, order Passeriformes, are birds found only in the Old World; the American oriole, or Baltimore bird, belongs to a separate family, the Icteridae. The birds eat insects, seeds and fruit. The plumage is generally very brilliant, and the male bird utters a flute-like note. *Oriolus oriolus*, the golden oriole of Europe, is orange-yellow in colour with black wings.

Orion, a bright equatorial constellation which is a conspicuous feature of the evening sky from December to March. The four bright stars, Alpha (Betelgeuse), Gamma (Bellatrix), Beta (Rigel), and Kappa mark the shoulders and legs of Orion, while between them 'the Belt' is formed by Delta, Epsilon and Zeta, three almost equally bright second magnitude stars equally spaced in a straight line. Southwards from the Belt is a line of fainter stars marking 'the Sword'. One of these, Theta, is not really a star but the brightest part of 'the Great Nebula in Orion'. Both Betelgeuse and Rigel are first magnitude stars and are supergiants but while

Orkney Islands. *The Ring of Brodgar, north of Stromness dates from the Bronze Age.*

Betelgeuse is red, Rigel, like most of the bright stars in the Orion area, is steely-blue.

Orissa, state of India occupying part of the coastal plains of the Bay of Bengal and extending inland to include part of the Eastern Ghats and covering 155,842 km². On the plains, which include the valley and great delta of the Mahanadi river, live most of the state's 26 million people. They are principally rice growers. Near the sea, swampy lowland prevails; Chilka Lake is in this region. Inland, the hill tracts of the Ghats and part of the Chota Nagpur plateau contain considerable mineral wealth, particularly iron ore. Manganese ore, chromite, coal, bauxite and limestone are also mined. Steel, paper and chemicals form the heavy manufacturing base of the economy. Urban centres are few, the largest being Cuttack. The state is a linguistic and cultural unit: Oriya is the language of the vast majority and 97 per cent of the population is Hindu. State government based at Bhubaneswar is through a single chamber.

The Oriyas trace their history back to the kingdom of Utkal. Their country was divided during the period of Muslim domination, but a nationalist revival developed under the British. Their demand for a separate province was conceded in 1936. After independence the rulers of 48 princely states merged their lands into the single state of Orissa.

Orizaba, city of Mexico, in the state of Veracruz, 370 km south-east of Mexico city, at an altitude of 1260 m. There is a considerable trade in sugar and tobacco; it is the chief textile manufacturing town in Mexico and there are railway workshops. Nearby is the dormant volcano of Orizaba or Citlaltépetl, at 5658 m the highest in Mexico. Population (1978) 118,354.

Orkney Islands, separated from Caithness District, Highland Region, by the Pentland Firth. They lie between 58°41′14″ and 59°23′2″N latitude and between 2°22′2″ and 3°25′10″W longitude; and are 73 in number at low water, of which 28, besides Mainland, or Pomona, are inhabited.

Many brochs, chambered cairns and burial mounds remain as evidence of prehistoric and Norse settlements. During the greater part of the 10th century they were ruled by independent Scandinavian *jarls* (earls), but in 1098 they became subject to the Norwegian crown and remained Scandinavian till 1468, when they were given to James III of Scotland. There was a big influx of farmers from north-east Scotland in the mid-19th century and two world wars have also brought many others to reside permanently in Orkney.

The surface is irregular, and the land is indented by numerous arms of the sea. Next to Mainland, the most important of the islands are North and South Ronaldsay, Hoy, Rousay, Stronsay, Flotta, Shapinsay, Eday, Sanday and Westray. The climate of the Orkney Islands is comparatively mild, considering their northerly latitude. The exports are chiefly agricultural produce and cattle. The chief towns are Kirkwall, the capital, and Stromness. The area of the Orkney Islands is 963 km². Population (1981) 18,906.

Orlando, Vittorio Emanuele (1860–1952), Italian jurist and statesman. He succeeded Boselli as premier in 1917. In the Inter-Allied Peace Conference in Paris, 1919, he was one of the 'Big Four'. Retiring from politics after Mussolini came to power, he returned to the Constituent Assembly to fight unsuccessfully against the peace treaty after the Second World War.

Orlando, city in Florida, USA, in the heart of a citrus-growing area, for which it acts as a processing and shipping centre. The city's population in 1980 was 127,811.

Orléans, Dukes of. The title 'Duke of Orléans' was created by Philip VI, and conferred on his son, Philip. When the 3rd Duke ascended the throne of France as Louis XII in 1498, the Duchy lapsed. Louis XIII in 1626 bestowed the title of Duke of Orléans on Jean Baptiste Gaston, a son of Henry IV, but the title was not revived after his death until, in 1660, Louis XIV revived it in favour of his brother, Philip. Descendants of this line are living at the present time; a brief account of the principal persons who have held the title follows:

Louis (1372–1407), younger son of Charles V, was created Duke of Orléans in 1392. He married Valentina, daughter of the Duke of Milan. His quarrel with Philip II, Duke of Burgundy, on the question of his wife's claims to Milan culminated, after the death of Philip, in his being murdered by one of the partisans of John, Philip's successor.

Charles (1391–1465), commonly called Charles d'Orléans, eldest son of the above duke. He married Isabella, the widow of Richard II of England, in 1406; in 1415 he was captured at Agincourt, and kept a prisoner in England until November 1440. He spent most of the rest of his life at Blois. He was one of the finest of the late medieval French poets.

Philippe I (1640–1701), son of Louis XIII of France, was created Duke of Orléans in 1660, and married Henrietta, sister of Charles II of England, the same year. After her death (rumoured to have been by poison at the Duke's instigation) he married Charlotte Elizabeth, daughter of Charles Louis, Elector-Palatine of the Rhine.

Philippe II (1674–1723), Regent of France, son of the above. On the death of Louis XIV he became sole regent, and on Louis XV attaining his majority in 1723 Philippe continued in power as his prime minister. A notorious libertine, Philippe was also a patron of the arts and philosophy.

Louis Philippe Joseph (*Egalité*) (1747–93), born at St Cloud, was principally notable for his democratic views during the Revolution, when he took the name of Philippe Egalité, and voted for the death of Louis XVI, his cousin. He was, however, subsequently guillotined. His son later became king as Louis Philippe.

Orleans, Maid of, see JOAN OF ARC, SAINT.

Orléans, French town, capital of the *département* of Loiret, on the right bank of the River Loire. Caesar called Orléans *Cenabum*; in imperial times it was known as *Civitas Aureliani*, and it was later the capital of the province of Orléanais. Orléans is a road, rail and canal junction. There is an extensive trade in agricultural produce and wine, and machinery, electrical goods, confectionery and textiles are manufactured. Population (1975) 109,956; conurbation 209,234.

Orme's Head. The Great Orme's Head is a conspicuous limestone promontory, west of

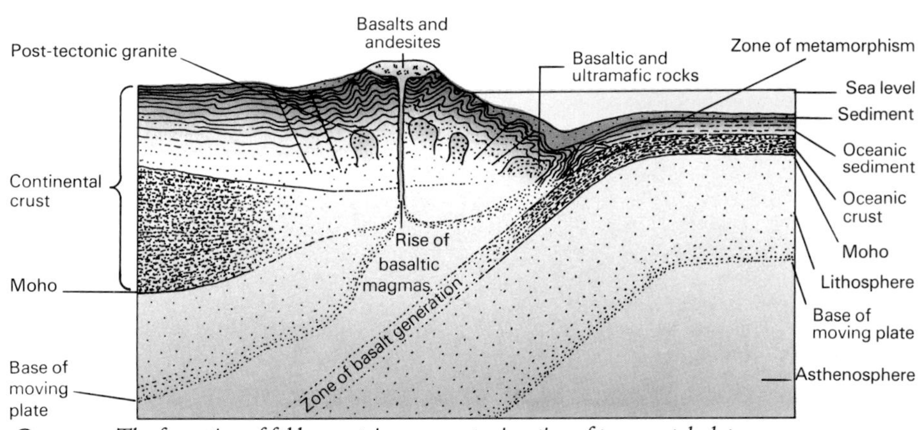

Orogeny. *The formation of fold mountains occurs at a junction of two crustal plates.*

Llandudno, North Wales, rising to 207 m above the Irish Sea. The lighthouse is visible at a distance of 40 km. The Little Orme's Head, 141 m, lies to the east.

Ormolu (French or *moulu*, ground gold), brass containing copper with about 40 per cent of zinc and of a golden-yellow colour. The principal use of ormolu is for the mountings of furniture. Small articles are made from ormolu, and it is also a basis for cloisonné work, long produced in China.

Ormonde, James Butler, 1st Duke of (1610–88), Anglo-Irish Royalist soldier. He acted for Charles I against the Irish rebels in 1643, and in the following year was appointed lord-lieutenant of Ireland. In 1648 he was Royalist commander in Ireland, where, after the execution of the king, he proclaimed Charles II. He was defeated by Cromwell in 1649, and fled abroad to join the king. On the Restoration he was made lord high steward of the household and was again lord-lieutenant of Ireland in 1661–69 and 1677–82, and once more in 1684.

Ornaments, in music (e.g. appoggiatura trill, mordent), embellish a vocal or instrumental melody, and are usually indicated by appropriate signs. From the 16th to the 18th centuries ornaments were added by performers where they were not indicated by the composer.
See also NOTATION.

Ornithogalum, the star of Bethlehem, a genus of bulbous plants of the family Liliaceae, bearing white, greenish-white or yellow flowers. *O. nutans* and *O. umbellatum* are grown in gardens. *O. thyrsoides* is the chincherinchee of South Africa.

Ornithology, the branch of zoology covering all aspects of birds.
See also BIRD.

Orobanchaceae, a family with 14 genera and about 200 species of scaly, succulent plants that do not possess green leaves and are parasitic on the roots of other plants. Among the genera are *Orobanche* (broomrape) and *Lathraea* (toothwort). In flower structure they resemble the Scrophulariaceae (foxglove family).

Orogeny, a period of mountain building, involving intense deformation and the subsequent uplift of the rocks involved in an orogenic belt to form a fold mountain chain. Regional metamorphism takes place at depth in the orogenic belt together with the emplacement of granite batholiths. Orogeny occurs in the crust when a plate of lithosphere containing continental crust collides with another plate. At the present time most active mountain chains (those around the Pacific) lie on continental plates which are in collision with the ocean crust, but it is known that collisions of two continental plates have occurred in the past; the Himalayas resulted from the collision of the Indian and Asian continental plates.
As the new fold mountain range is uplifted, two very distinct facies of sediment are deposited; these sediments were first recognised in the Alps, but have been found to characterise many older orogenic belts. Flysch is the term used to describe a sequence of marine sediments laid down in long troughs associated with the submarine ridges of the rising mountain belt. Molasse is the term used to describe largely continental deposits derived from the rapid erosion of the newly uplifted mountains.

Orontes, or Nahr-al-Asi (the rebellious), river of northern Syria and Turkey, which rises in the Lebanon, and flows first north through Homs to Antioch, and then turns south-west and enters the Mediterranean Sea 65 km north of Latakia. Length 400 km.

Orozco, José Clemente (1883–1949), Mexican painter and graphic artist. First studying architecture, he turned to painting in 1909 and became one of the most eminent mural painters. His principal achievements have as their theme the martyrdom and endurance of man, intensely conveyed in murals at the orphanage, Guadalajara, and the Church of Jesus Nazareno, Mexico City.

Orpheus, legendary Greek poet and musician; husband of Eurydice. Presented with a lyre by Apollo, and instructed by the Muses in its use, Orpheus enchanted not only men and beasts, but also trees and rocks. Having lost Eurydice, Orpheus retired to the mountain caves and scorned the advances of the Thracian women, who, in revenge, tore him limb from limb in frenzy.

Orr, John Boyd, see BOYD ORR, JOHN, 1ST BARON.

Orrery, a mechanical model of the solar system showing the motions of the planets round the Sun and of the Moon round the Earth. The first one seems to have been constructed about 1700 by the famous clockmakers Thomas Tompion and George Graham. It was originally called a planetarium but the name was changed when Rowley constructed an improved version in 1715 for Charles Boyle, Earl of Orrery.

Orris Root, the rhizome (underground stem) of *Iris florentina*, a violet-scented iris occurring in southern Europe. A starch or flour is prepared from the rhizome for use in the manufacture of scented powders and dentifrices. The plant is cultivated for this purpose in Italy.

Orsk, town in Orenburg *oblast* of the RSFSR, USSR, on the River Ural in the southern Urals. It is the centre for the Orsk-Khalilovo metallurgical complex (iron and steel, non-ferrous metallurgy) at the nearby town of Novotroitsk. Orsk itself has nickel-smelting, heavy engineering, oil-cracking and meat-packing plants. It was founded in 1735 as a Russian fortress. Population (1980) 252,000.

Ortega y Gasset, José (1883–1955), Spanish philosopher and essayist. Ortega's early works, such as *La Rebelión de las masas*, 1930 (*The Revolt of the Masses*, 1932), and *España invertebrada*, 1921 (*Invertebrate Spain*, 1937), ascribe contemporary problems to the triumph of mass tastes in modern democratic societies. His study of modern art and literature, *La Deshumanización del arte*, 1925 (*The Dehumanization of Art*), welcomes the complexity of the modern arts as an antidote to popular taste. His anti-democratic views were somewhat modified by events in Nazi Germany, and his later works emphasise human freedom. Although deeply distrustful of socialism and democratic politics, he was not a fascist, and was in fact viewed with suspicion by the Franco regime in Spain.

Ortelius, Wortels Abraham (1527–98), Flemish geographer and mathematician, born at Antwerp, of German parents. His *Theatrum orbis Terrarum*, 1570, was the first atlas, and he also wrote *Synonomia Geographica*, 1578.

Orthodontics, see DENTISTRY.

Orthodox Church, see EASTERN ORTHODOX CHURCH.

Orthography (Greek *orthos*, correct; *graphein*, to write), art of setting down words correctly as regards their component letters according to accepted usage; in other words, the art of accurate spelling. Accurate spelling should properly be a reliable guide to the pronunciation of the word spelt, but since —in Western European languages at least— the number of symbols used for the representation of speech seems always to have been less than the number of sounds used, it is probable that orthography has never perfectly served its purpose. The spelling of Italian and Spanish is fairly consistent, that of German less so, while in French and English there are extensive inconsistencies and arbitrary oddities.
See also PHONETICS.

Orthopaedic Surgery (Greek *orthos*, straight; *pais*, child), the branch of surgery concerned with bones, joints, muscles, nerves and any tissues so injured or diseased that deformity or impairment of function may result; its applications are by no means confined to children. Physiotherapy is one of the main aids to orthopaedic surgery.

Orthophosphoric Acid, see PHOSPHORUS.

Orthoptera, an order of the class Insecta, subclass Pterygota. These are the grasshoppers, locusts, and crickets. They are medium-sized to large (10 mm–100 mm) insects which may be winged, with reduced wings, or without wings. The mouthparts are mandibulate (chewing); the prothorax is large; the hindlegs are usually large and modified for jumping; auditory and stridulating organs are usually present; and metamorphosis is slight. Several species include pests of agricultural importance.
See LOCUSTS.

Orthoptics, see REFRACTION, ERRORS OF; SQUINTING.

Orton, Joe (1933–67), English playwright. His first staged play, *Entertaining Mr Sloane*, 1964, and the later *Loot*, 1966, were notable for their black humour, farcical situations and homosexual eroticism, which Orton used to show what he believed to be the viciousness and hypocrisy of contemporary British society. Orton was murdered by his flatmate, Kenneth Halliwell.

Oruro, city of Bolivia, and capital of the department of the same name. It is the centre of Bolivia's great tin-mining area. Silver, copper and wolfram are also worked in the district. The city stands at an altitude of 3630 m. It is an important railway centre, lying on the Antofagasta–La Paz line. Population (1976) 124,414.

Orvieto, Italian town in Umbria, 45 km north-west of Terni. The beautiful Italian Gothic cathedral (13th–16th centuries) has a magnificent façade with mosaics, bas-reliefs and bronze sculptures. The white wine of the district is famous. Population (1974) 8800.

Orwell, George, pseudonym of Eric Arthur Blair (1903–50), English novelist and essayist.

From 1922 to 1927 he served in Burma with the Indian Imperial Police, recording this experience in *Burmese Days*, 1934. In horrified retreat from imperialism, he moved towards socialism and even anarchism. A period of poverty during which he was successively tutor, teacher, dishwasher, tramp and bookshop assistant, is described in *Down and Out in Paris and London*, 1933.

In 1936 he fought on the Republican side in the Spanish Civil War, and was wounded. He wrote about the war in *Homage to Catalonia*, 1938. During the Second World War Orwell worked for the BBC, writing and monitoring propaganda. In 1945 he published *Animal Farm*, a satiric parable attacking the Soviet Union (and Stalin). Orwell was distrustful of all political parties and ideologies, and the fruit of this distrust was his finest novel, *Nineteen Eighty-Four*, 1949, set in a future world divided between warring super-powers but which had as its real target contemporary Cold War politics.

Oryx, genus of antelopes, of the subfamily Hippotraginae, found in Africa, Arabia and Syria. Both sexes have long, annulated horns. *O. leucoryx* (the Arabian oryx), *O. gazella* (the gemsbok or beisa) and *O. tao* (the scimitar-horned oryx) are the three species now recognised.

Oryza, a genus of tall marsh grasses of the family Gramineae, of which *O. sativa*, rice, is the most important species.

Osage, war-like North American Indians of the Siouan linguistic group. The 3500 survivors live in Oklahoma.

Ōsaka, second largest city of Japan, 24 km from its seaport of Kōbe, situated on the Pacific coast of Honshū, in the most densely populated part of the country. As early as the 17th century, Ōsaka had emerged as the leading centre of commercial activity in Japan. During the latter part of the 19th century, Ōsaka was noted particularly for its flourishing cotton textiles industry. Ōsaka is the administrative and cultural capital of western Honshū. Industries include shipbuilding, machine tools, textiles, rubber, celluloid and cement. The population in 1979 amounted to 2,600,000.

Osborne, John (James) (1929–), British actor and dramatist. His first play, *Epitaph for George Dillon*, was written in collaboration with Anthony Creighton. *Look Back in Anger* was produced with great success by the English Stage Company in 1956, and initiated a revival of British drama. It was followed in 1957 by *The Entertainer*, in which Sir Laurence (later Lord) Olivier played the leading part. Subsequent work includes *Luther*, 1960; *Inadmissible Evidence*, 1964; *A Patriot for Me*, 1964; *Hotel in Amsterdam*, 1967; *West of Suez*, 1971; and *Sense of Detachment*, 1972. He has written television plays and the Oscar-winning screenplay of the film *Tom Jones*, 1964, and has acted in films and on television.

Osborne House, in the Isle of Wight. It was designed by Prince Albert and Thomas Cubitt in the Italianate style. Queen Victoria died there in 1901. Edward VII, in 1902, made a gift of the building and grounds to the nation, to be used as a convalescent home for officers.

Osborne Judgment, British trade union action brought in the King's Bench Division, taken to the Court of Appeal and, finally, to the House of Lords (1909). The decision declared null and void a trade union rule which provided for an enforced levy on members towards the payment of the salaries of MPs, and thereby checked the growing political power of the unions. The judgment was largely nullified in the Trades Union Act of 1913.

Osbourne, Lloyd (1868–1947), US novelist and collaborator with Robert Louis Stevenson, his stepfather. He collaborated with Stevenson in writing *The Wrong Box*, 1889; *The Wrecker*, 1892; and *The Ebb-Tide*, 1894.

Oscar II (1829–1907), King of Sweden and Norway (of the latter until 1905). In 1872 he succeeded his brother, Charles XV, as king of the two nations. When Norway separated from Sweden (1905) it is attributed to Oscar's broadmindedness and insight that there were no serious popular uprisings. During his reign great strides were made in national development and geographical discovery.

***Osborne House** was built for Queen Victoria in the 1840s to Prince Albert's specifications.*

Oscillation, swinging or vibration. The motion of a simple pendulum is typical. Suppose the bob is displaced and then released. It swings along an arc and then back, and so on. It oscillates about the equilibrium position, the distance between limits of travel being the amplitude. The time taken between successive passages through any point in the same direction is called the period. For any given pendulum of constant length this period is always the same if the pendulum is not restrained and the amplitude is small. See also RESONANCE; SIMPLE HARMONIC MOTION.

Oscillators, electronic devices for producing sustained voltage oscillations, usually of sinusoidal waveform. Its frequency may be fixed or varied. It consists basically of an amplifier with positive feedback from the output, through a frequency-defining network, back to the input. Oscillation will be maintained when the gain of the amplifier is just sufficient to compensate for the loss in the network: the 'loop gain' is then said to be unity. The frequency of oscillation is such that the phase shift around the loop is zero. For operation at frequencies of up to about 100 kHz, the network usually consists of resistors and capacitors; the 'Wien Bridge' is typical of such 'R-C' (resistance-capacitance) oscillators.

Oscillatory Circuit, electric circuit with capacitance and inductance, in which energy surges between the electrostatic and electromagnetic forms, as the energy of a swinging pendulum surges between potential at the top of the swing and kinetic at the bottom. The energy stored in a capacitor of capacitance C charged to e volt is $\frac{1}{2}Ce^2$, and when the capacitor discharges through an inductance L, the current i builds up electromagnetic energy $\frac{1}{2}Li^2$. As in the swinging pendulum, the energy flows back, charging the capacitor again, and the process continues with decreasing amplitude until the energy is dissipated as heat or electromagnetic radiation.

See also RESONANCE, ELECTRIC.

Oscilloscope, an instrument for the display of electrical waveforms (or of any phenomenon that can be translated into these), generally on a screen.

See also CATHODE-RAY TUBE.

Oshawa, city of Ontario, Canada, on Lake Ontario, 48 km east of Toronto. It has a good harbour, and is the centre of a rich agricultural district. The most important industry is motor-car and truck manufacturing; other industries include motor accessories, castings, brass and copper fittings, plastics, pharmaceuticals, builders' supplies, sheet-metal materials, woollens, pottery and glass bottles. Population (1976) 107,023.

Oshogbo, town of Western State, Nigeria, on the Oshun river, 293 km north-east of Lagos. After the construction of a rail link with Lagos in 1906, Oshogbo developed as a trading and commercial centre, particularly for cocoa and palm oil. Local cotton is woven and dyed, and there is tobacco processing. Population (1975) 282,000.

Osier, a tree or shrub of the willow genus, *Salix*, grown for the long pliant shoots for such uses as basket-making. They are grown in plantations known as holts, in rich, deep alluvial soil, subject to flooding.

Osijek, town in Croatia, Yugoslavia, on the River Drava. Its site has been occupied since Neolithic times. It is the cultural and economic centre of Slavonia, manufactures textiles and furniture, and is an agricultural market. Population (1971) 84,000.

Osipenko, see BERDYANSK.

Osiris, an Egyptian god established in the Nile delta about the 5th Dynasty, always represented as a dead king with crown, shroud, and holding crook and flail. His cult may be Syrian, a form of the god of vegetation who dies annually and comes to life again. The Egyptian version mainly concerns his death at the hands of Set and resurrection as ruler of the dead.

By the Middle Kingdom, the identification of the dead king with Osiris had been extended to commoners, so that every dead man was known as Osiris So-and-so. This Osiris cult spread rapidly and in the Late Period, Osiris became the chief god, even superseding Ra as ruler of the world.

Osler, Sir William (1849–1919), Canadian physician and humanist scholar. A versatile man, Osler influenced pathology, clinical and scientific medicine, and epidemiology. His famous *Principles and Practice of Medicine*, 1892, was the most popular text-book in the English language with several generations of medical students and practitioners. Among Osler's contributions to scientific medicine must be included his investigations of the blood-platelets, his researches on the malarial parasite, his studies in malignant endocarditis, and his writings on angina pectoris and allied disorders. Tuberculosis was also one of his special subjects. Osler was also a humanist and classical scholar, bequeathing his magnificent library of over 7500 items to McGill University.

Oslo (formerly *Christiania*), capital city and county of Norway, situated in the south-east at the head of the Oslo Fjord.

Founded in 1024, in 1624 it was completely burnt down and replanned by Christian IV (hence the name Christiania). He was a Danish king and, following Norway's separation from Denmark (1814) and from Sweden (1905), the city reverted in 1925 to its original Norwegian name, Oslo.

Formerly timber was the city's main industry. Now, however, the economy is much more varied, with a very considerable manufacture of both consumer and capital goods. Oslo is Norway's biggest port both in volume of trade and also as port of registration for merchant shipping. Population (1980) 454,872.

Osman I, or Othman, or Othoman (1259–1326), surnamed al-Ghazi (the conqueror), Turkish ruler, the founder of the Ottoman dynasty. Osman succeeded his father as chieftain in 1288, and in 1299 conquered part of Bithynia. This new accession of territory rendered him sufficiently powerful to attack the Byzantines with success. In 1301 he defeated Emperor Andronicus II at Baphaeon, and he continued his career of conquest until his death.

Osmium, metallic chemical element, symbol Os, atomic number 76, atomic weight 190·2. Its chemical and physical properties are very similar to those of iridium and platinum. It occurs associated with iridium in the alloy osmiridium, which is found in platinum ores. The platinum ore is first treated with aqua regia, the osmiridium being left as an insoluble residue. This alloy is then fused with common salt in a current of chlorine, the iridium being converted into Na_2IrCl_6, and the osmium being converted into OsO_4, osmium tetroxide. Metallic osmium is obtained by the addition of an alkaline formate. It forms well-defined alkaline salts called osmates and osmiamates, red or green in colour. Osmium is used as a catalyst, and the tetroxide is largely used in the preparation of specimens for microscopic examination.

Osmosis, intermixture of fluids separated by a porous membrane, first studied by the Abbé Nollett, 1748. He found that if a solution of cane-sugar was contained in a vessel, the bottom end of which was closed with an animal membrane (e.g. parchment) and placed in pure water, the latter entered into the cane-sugar solution, thus raising the level in the inside vessel until the hydrostatic pressure resulting was equal to the force tending to make the water enter. This force is known as osmotic pressure. A membrane which allows water molecules to pass but not solute molecules is called semi-permeable. It was shown by Van't Hoff that the laws of osmotic pressure are similar to those relating to gas pressure. The pressure varies directly with the concentration, temperature being constant, and for a definite concentration is nearly proportional to the absolute temperature. The intake of water by root hairs and its passage from cell to cell in animal and plant bodies are osmotic processes.

Osmunda, or royal fern, a genus of very handsome ferns. The brown sporangia (reproductive organs) are borne in branched masses at the tips of the fronds, replacing the upper leaflets. The fronds are twice or thrice divided into pinnae, and sometimes attain a length of 2 m or more. There are a number of species; *O. regalis*, the royal fern, is one of the most handsome, and is also known as the flowering fern.

Osnabrück, city in Lower Saxony, Federal Republic of Germany, on the Hase, 125 km south-west of Hanover. It was made a bishopric by Charlemagne and belonged to the Hanseatic League. There is a fine Gothic cathedral (11th–13th centuries). There are important iron, steel, car, and paper industries. Population (1980) 157,800.

Osprey, *Pandion haliaetus*, order Falconiformes, a cosmopolitan bird of prey which feeds on fish. Its length is about 60 cm and its wing expanse nearly 2 m. The plumage is dark brown on the upper surface and white on the underparts. The head and throat are white with streaks of light and dark brown. The nest is often made in trees near the seashore or lakeside.

Ossa, mountain in northern Thessaly, Greece, east of the River Piniós. Olympus is opposite, and between them is the vale of Tempe. Ossa is 1952 m high.

Ossian (Fawn), latinised form of the Gaelic Oisin, a semi-mythical Gaelic bard who is claimed by both Scotland and Ireland, and the presumed author of a number of narrative poems dealing with the deeds of Finn MacCumhal and Cu Chulainn.

Ostade, Adriaen van (1610–84), Dutch painter and etcher, a pupil of Frans Hals. He was very versatile, painting everything except marine pieces, but he is best known for scenes of peasants carousing or brawling, painted in a manner similar to Brouwer. He was Jan Steen's master.

Ostade, Isaack van (1621–49), Dutch painter, the brother and pupil of Adriaen Ostade. His subjects were also mainly drawn from peasant life, notably games on ice and village scenes.

Osteichthyes, the class containing the bony fishes. The head covering and the scales are based on bone. They have a swim bladder, which may be modified into lungs. The gills are covered by an operculum. In some classification schemes this class is not used and the two subclasses, Actinopterygii, the ray-finned fishes, and Sarcopterygii, the fleshy-finned fishes, are raised to class status. Subclass Sarcopterygii, which includes the fleshy-finned fishes, has two orders: order Crossopterygii is represented today by the coelacanth, and order Dipnoi by the lungfishes. Subclass Actinopterygii, which includes all those fishes whose fins are supported by bony rays, may be divided into three infraclasses: Chondrostei includes the sturgeons, birchirs and reedfishes; Holostei includes the garpikes and bowfins; and Teleostei includes about 20,000 species of bony fishes.

Osteitis, inflammation of the bone. *Osteitis deformans* (Paget's disease), is a chronic disease of uncertain cause in which bone tissue is absorbed and later replaced by excessive deposits of bone tissue under the periosteum (covering membrane) and within the marrow cavity.

Ostend (Flemish *Oostende*; French *Ostende*), port in the province of West Flanders, Belgium, a seaside resort on the North Sea, 120 km west of Brussels. With Antwerp and Ghent it is a major port of Belgium. There is a school of navigation, an important fish market and the summer palace of King Leopold I. Population (1980) 70,125.

Osteoarthritis, see ARTHRITIS.

Osteology, that part of anatomy which deals with bones and their uses.

See also BONE.

Osteomyelitis, inflammation of the medullary cavity, or 'marrow', of a bone. The bone marrow, being highly vascular, is prone to infection by blood-borne organisms. Injury often appears to be a predisposing factor. Osteomyelitis is more common in children and young people whose bones are not yet fully grown. Pus must be surgically drained, but antibiotics now hasten the cure of what used to be a lengthy and grave illness.

Osteopathy, a system of therapeutics based on the normalising of the body and its functions on the assumption that a structural derangement of skeletal parts (the 'osteopathic lesion') is a significant factor in all disease. By manipulation it endeavours to remove such abnormalities and thus re-establish the integrity of the body in functional activities. The theory of osteopathy was formulated by an American doctor, Andrew Taylor Still, in 1874. Osteopathy must be distinguished from manipulative surgery as practised by orthopaedic surgeons. According to Still, all diseases are caused by obstruction of arteries or nerves because of the pressure of maladjusted bones, especially of the vertebrae of the spinal column.

Osterley Park, West London. An Elizabethan house, it was extensively remodelled by Robert Adam c.1760–80, in particular by the insertion of an Ionic portico to the entrance façade.

Österreich, see AUSTRIA.

Ostia, ancient port of Rome, situated on the southern mouth of the Tiber, 22 km south-west of the city. Claudius I built an improved harbour 3 km to the north-west (*Portus Ostiensis* or *Portus Augusti*), and another (*Portus Trajani*) was built by Trajan in AD 103. The town's prosperity derived from its salt works.

Ostracism (Greek *ostrakon*, tile, potsherd), form of banishment practised at Athens, Argos, Megara and Miletus. It was used for the first time in 487 and for the last in 417 BC. An annual vote of the ecclesia was taken to decide whether or not ostracism should be applied that year; if it was in favour, each citizen might inscribe on a potsherd the name of the citizen he wished to be banished. The ballot was secret, and a quorum of 6000 votes was needed to impose the penalty—ten years' exile, but without loss of property or civil rights. Only ten persons are known to have been ostracised.

Ostracoda (Greek *ostrakon*, shell), a subclass of crustacea in phylum Arthropoda. They are an aquatic group, largely marine, with about 2000 species, which, apart from one exception, are all very small and all enclosed in a bivalve shell. The egg hatches as a nauplius larva, which undergoes metamorphosis before becoming the adult. Ostracods are of great significance in micro-palaeontology as indices in the correlation of strata, and therefore of considerable importance in, for example, oilfield exploration work.

Ostracoderms (shell-skinned), a primitive order of the class Agnatha. They lived from the Late Silurian to the close of the Devonian era, and were heavily armoured vertebrates with bony plates and scales, no paired fins, and tending to be bottom dwellers.

Ostrava (German *Ostrau*), town of Czechoslovakia, capital of the region of North Moravia, on the River Ostravice near its confluence with the Odra. It stands in the Moravian Gap, between the Sudeten Mountains and the Carpathians, the traditional military gateway from Vienna to Poland. It has coal, iron, steel, engineering, oil refining and chemical industries. Population (1979) 322,000.

Ostrich, the largest living bird, the male standing about 2·5 m high. The single species, *Struthio camelus*, forms the order Struthioniformes and is found in most parts of Africa south of the Sahara. The bill is wide and flat, the small head has large eyes, while the long neck has a sparse covering of down feathers. The legs are long, with naked lower 'thighs' and the feet have two large toes bearing broad claws. The male is polygamous and incubates the eggs at night, but the female may sit on them during the day.

The ostrich tends to occur in deserts and open plains, where it is found in small flocks. It runs at a high speed, with head outstretched and wings spread. Its food is mainly vegetable and it can go for a long time without water.

Ostrich, South American, see RHEA.

Ostrogoths, see GOTHS.

Ostrovsky, Aleksandr Nikolayevich (1823–86), Russian playwright who belonged to the Gogol school of Critical Realism. Most of his plays are about contemporary Russian society, particularly the merchant class. Ostrovsky exercised a dominating influence on playwriting in Russia in the second half of the 19th century and is considered the real founder of Russian national dramaturgy. Among his best-known plays are *Easy Money*, 1856, and *The Storm*, 1859.

Ostwald, Friedrich Wilhelm (1853–1932), German chemist. His process of forming nitrogen oxides by the oxidation of ammonia enabled German manufacture of explosives in the First World War to be maintained despite the loss of Chilean nitrate imports. His numerous works embrace general chemistry, principles of natural science, energy, and electrochemistry; and works on Comte and Schopenhauer.

Oswald, Saint (c.605–42), King of Northumbria, 634–42. Oswald spent some years on Iona where he was converted to Christianity. In 633 he became king of Northumbria. Oswald established Christianity throughout his kingdom with the help of St Aidan whom he summoned from Iona. He was defeated in battle and killed by Penda at Maserfield in 642.

Oswald, Saint (c.992), English monk and archbishop of York, said to be of Danish descent. He was associated with St Dunstan and St Ethelwold in the revival of ecclesiastical discipline and monastic life in England, himself founding the abbey of Ramsey and the monastery at Worcester, which later became the cathedral priory. He was made bishop of Worcester in 961 and archbishop of York in 972.

Oswald, Lee Harvey (1939–63), the presumed assassin of US president John F. Kennedy in Dallas, Texas on 22 November 1963. Oswald had lived in the USSR and was an admirer of Fidel Castro. Two days after his arrest for the killing he was himself shot dead in the Dallas police headquarters by Jack Ruby, a nightclub owner. Although the Warren Commission which investigated the president's assassination concluded that there was no evidence of a conspiracy, some doubt still exists about the exact circumstances of the killing.

Oświęcim (German *Auschwitz*), town of Poland, in Katowice province, near the mouth of the Sola river, 32 km south of Katowice. Chemicals are manufactured, and there are coal-mines in the district. Population (1972) 41,000.

See also AUSCHWITZ; CONCENTRATION CAMP.

***Ottawa.** Parliament buildings in the federal capital of Canada.*

Oswy (612–70), King of Northumbria. He succeeded to Bernicia on the death of his brother, St Oswald. In 654 Penda, King of Mercia, was killed in battle against Oswy. Oswy was temporarily overlord of Mercia and southern England, but in 657 Mercia threw off his rule. For the rest of his reign he was simply King of Northumbria. Oswy was a champion of Christianity and a patron of learning and the Church.

Othman, or Uthman (c.574–656), the third caliph of the Muslims. One of the early converts to Islam, he ranked among its most zealous supporters and linked himself still more closely to Mohammed by becoming his son-in-law and private secretary. He was elected to succeed Omar as caliph in 644 and was responsible for the final definitive recension of the text of the Koran. Othman was a pious, well-meaning old man, but a weak ruler. He became widely unpopular because of accusations of nepotism and was murdered by Mohammed, a son of Abu Bakr, in 656 during a rising of the partisans of Ali.

Otoliths, or ear stones, are concretions, usually calcareous, that occur in the ears of fishes and are in contact with the sensory cushions supplied by the acoustic nerves. Their function is as an organ of balance, and they vary greatly in size, but are commonly minute. Corresponding concretions occur in many other animals.

Otranto (ancient *Hydruntum*), Italian seaport in Apulia, on the Strait of Otranto (connecting the Adriatic Sea with the Ionian Sea), 35 km south-east of Lecce. In later Roman times it succeeded Brundisium as the chief Italian port for Greece. It has a ruined castle from which Horace Walpole took the title of his romance, *The Castle of Otranto*. Population (1974) 3700.

Ottawa, capital of the dominion of Canada, in Ontario, on the Ottawa river at its confluence with the Rideau. Ottawa lies 335 km north-east of Toronto and 177 km west of Montreal on the Trans-Canada Highway. A handsome city, picturesquely situated on a cluster of hills overlooking the Ottawa river, it is regularly laid out in rectangular blocks between the Chaudière and Rideau Falls, and is divided into two parts by the Rideau Canal. The city's origins date back to 1826 when a town grew up around the headquarters of the British Army engineers who were building the Rideau Canal. In 1858 Queen Victoria chose it to be the capital of Canada, at that time comprising only what are now the provinces of Quebec and Ontario. In 1867, on confederation, it was made the capital of the dominion. In addition to pulp and paper, other industries include metal working, machine-tool engineering, printing and publishing, as well as food processing and textile and leather products. Only a small proportion of the city's labour force work in manufacturing. Population (1976) (city) 304,462; (metropolitan area) 521,341.

Ottawa, major river of Canada, rises on a watershed on the opposite side of which rise the St Maurice and Saguenay. After a course of over 1125 km it falls into the St Lawrence by two mouths, which form the island of Montreal, and its drainage area measures about 207,200 km². The Ottawa is connected with Lake Ontario at Kingston by the Rideau Canal.

Ottawa, North American Indian people, belonging to the Algonquian linguistic family, whose original home was on the upper Ottawa River. They fought many wars with British and American colonists during the 18th and 19th centuries. One of their most famous chiefs was Pontiac. Today they number under 2500 and most of them live in Michigan.

Ottawa Agreements, concluded between Britain and the self-governing dominions at the Ottawa Economic Conference in 1932, were part of the growth of protectionism in response to the economic depression of the 1920s and 1930s and effectively marked the end of Britain's long-standing free trade policy. The agreements have been superseded by other arrangements, notably the General Agreement on Tariffs and Trade (1947), and by Britain's membership of the European Community.
See also TARIFFS.

Otter, the most adaptable member of the weasel tribe in family Mustelidae of order Carnivora, subfamily Lutrinae. The European otter is *Lutra lutra.* They are able to climb, swim and run for a short distance as fast as a fox. European otters vary in size and weight; the average adult's head and body are about 76 cm and the tail 46 cm long. The skull, with its small facial space, bears a considerable resemblance to that of a seal, and the neck is large, so that the head appears to be directly attached to the body. The tail is long, tapering and flattened, the limbs are short and the toes webbed. The fur consists of long, close, glistening hairs, with a short, fine underfur.
European otters appear to breed only once a year. The female makes a nest in a hollow in a river bank, and the cubs remain with her for the greater part of their first year. The dog otter is polygamous, and wanders great distances. Some otters descend to estuaries and the sea coast, where they live on rock fish, molluscs and crustaceans. In fresh water, eels and frogs, as well as a few birds and mammals, form the principal food.

Otter-shrew, a mammal of the order Insectivora that looks like an otter. It lives in West African streams and rivers, has thick fur, brown on the back and sides and white on the belly, and a long, laterally-flattened tail for swimming. It eats fish and crustaceans. The largest species, *Potamogale velox*, the giant water-shrew, is about 62 cm long, almost half of which is tail.

Otterhound, descendant, like other hounds, of the old sleuth hound, and long bred in a few districts for otter hunting. It has many of the fine qualities and powers of the bloodhound and foxhound; it is essentially a water dog, capable of great endurance. The colour may be grey, buff, yellowish, black, or rufous-red mixed with black or grey. The average height is about 58 cm and the weight 36 kg.

Otto I, or Otto the Great (912–73), German Emperor. He succeeded his father, Henry I, the Fowler, as the elected king of the Germans in 936, and throughout his reign was, as Henry had been, engaged in a constant struggle against the dukes whose sovereign powers he gradually reduced, without, however, managing to deprive them of their decisive rôle in the election of the king.
In 962 he was crowned emperor by Pope John XII, whom, in the following year, he deposed for treachery, thus establishing that hold over the papacy which served to disguise the fundamental weakness of his and his successors' position as kings of Germany.

Otto IV (c.1174–1218), Holy Roman Emperor. In 1197, on the death of the Emperor Henry VI, Otto became the Guelph candidate for the throne in opposition to Philip of Swabia, who was supported by the Ghibellines. After a long struggle Philip was victorious, but he was assassinated in 1208 and Otto was crowned emperor in 1209. He at once became involved in a conflict with Pope Innocent III, and was excommunicated and deposed in 1212.

Otto, Nicholas August (1832–91), German engineer. He became interested in engines, subsequently building up a successful business in manufacturing gas engines. His four-stroke cycle engine, designed in collaboration with E. Langen, was originally known as the Otto silent gas engine and is described in a British Patent of 1876; it was the first successful internal combustion engine.

Otter. *A sea otter,* Enhydra lutris, *lies on its back, cracking open a clam with a stone.*

Ottoman Empire, see TURKEY, *History*.

Otway, Thomas (1652–85), English dramatist. His tragedy, *Alcibiades*, was produced in 1675 and *Don Carlos* followed in 1676. *Titus and Berenice,* a tragedy adapted from Racine, and *The Cheats of Scapin*, a farce from Molière, were acted on the same night in 1677, and *Friendship in Fashion* appeared in 1678. But Otway is best remembered for *The Orphan*, 1680, and *Venice Preserved*, 1682, domestic tragedies which preserve some of the power of the Elizabethan dramatists, and which have been successfully revived in modern times.

Ouagadougou, capital of Upper Volta in West Africa. The town incorporates several old Mossi settlements, but urban growth dates mainly from the establishment of a French administrative post and a mission station in 1904. The town has become a route focus, notably since the railway from Abidjan, Ivory Coast, reached it in 1954, but its pre-eminence as a commercial centre is challenged by Bobo-Dioulasso. Its population was estimated at 172,660 in 1979.

Ouessant, see USHANT.

Ouida, pseudonym of Marie Louise de la Ramée (1839–1908), English novelist. Her first novel was *Granville de Vigne*, 1861–63, subsequently known as *Held in Bondage*. *Strathmore*, 1865, had the distinction of being parodied by Burnand in *Punch*. She published more than 60 books, among the best being *Under Two Flags*, 1867; *Puck*, 1870; *Folle Farine*, 1871; and *Moths*, 1880.

Ouija Board, a method of obtaining spirit messages, usually associated with spiritualism. It consists of a small wooden board with a pointer, placed on a smooth surface and surrounded by letters of the alphabet. The medium, or particular person wishing to communicate with the spirits, places his or her hand lightly on the board, which is then said to move of its own accord, spelling out answers to questions asked. Sometimes an up-ended glass is used instead of a board.

Oujda, city of eastern Morocco, near the Algerian border. It was founded in 944 by the Berbers but was destroyed and rebuilt so many times that it became known as the 'city of fear'. The Moroccan and Algerian railway systems meet here and it is also a modern tourist centre. Population (1971) 175,532.

Oulachan, see CANDLE-FISH.

Ould Daddah, Moktar (1924–), Mauritanian politician. He was appointed prime minister on 28 June 1959 and, on 20 August 1961, the first president of the Islamic Republic of Mauritania. He was re-elected for further five-year terms on 7 August 1966, 8 August 1971, and 8 August 1976.

Oulu, or Uleåborg, chief town of Oulu province, Finland, a seaport at the mouth of the River Oulu in the Gulf of Bothnia. Oulu is a major service centre for the north, and the seat of a university and diocese. Its industries include wood-pulp, chemicals, fertilisers and engineering. Population (1979) 93,420.

Ounce, see METROLOGY.

Ounce, see SNOW LEOPARD.

Our Father, see LORD'S PRAYER.

Ouro Prêto (Portuguese, black gold), town and former capital of the state of Minas Gerais, Brazil, 525 km by rail from Rio de Janeiro. Gold (at Passagem), manganese and iron ore are mined in the district, which is also an agricultural and fruit-growing area. There are also textile mills and shoe factories. The town, built on rocky ground 4200 m above sea-level, is a remarkable storehouse of colonial and Baroque architecture and in 1933 was made a national monument. There is a museum of mineralogy and precious stones and a mining school. Population (1970) 24,000.

Ouse, river of Yorkshire, England, formed by the junction of the Swale and Ure near Boroughbridge, and flowing south-east to unite with the Trent, 13 km south of Goole. The two rivers then form the Humber. The Ouse is 97 km long. It is navigable for vessels drawing up to 6·4 m to York, a distance of 68 km, and for large ships to Goole.

Ouse, river of Sussex, England, rising in the Weald 8 km south-east of Horsham, and flowing southwards through the South Downs to the English Channel at Newhaven. Uckfield and Lewes are major towns on its banks. Length 48 km.

Ouse, or Great Ouse, river of England, rising near Brackley in Northamptonshire, and flowing throuth Buckinghamshire, Bedfordshire, Cambridgeshire and Norfolk. It enters the Wash at King's Lynn. Its course is very tortuous, but generally in a north-easterly direction. Length about 250 km; navigable as far as Little Barford.

Ouspensky, Peter D. (1878–1947), Russian mystic and author. He became a disciple of Gurdjieff, but eventually left his movement, although they kept in contact. His philosophy, principally influenced by Gurdjieff's teaching, deals largely with the fourth and higher dimensions, as set out in his various books, for instance, *Tertium Organum*.

Outcrop, in geology, the total area over which any unit of rock occurs at the surface of the Earth. The term may also be used to describe the exposed part or parts of a rock unit.

Outer Mongolia, see MONGOLIAN PEOPLE'S REPUBLIC.

Outlawry. Article 39 of Magna Carta laid it down as a cardinal principle of English liberty that no freeman should be outlawed (*sittagetur*), except by the lawful judgment of his equals or by the law of the land. The consequences of outlawing were that he might be slain by the first person who chanced to meet him, and that he suffered forfeiture of both lands and goods. This was changed in the reign of Edward III, when it was provided that none but the sheriff should be empowered to put an outlaw to death. Outlawing was abolished in 1938.

Outram, Sir James (1803–63), British soldier. He rendered valuable service in the first Sikh war, from 1847 to 1851 was resident at Baroda, and from 1855 in Oudh. He went with Havelock to the relief of Lucknow, and commanded the garrison there during the second siege.

Outwash Plain, or *sandur* (Icelandic), is a deposit laid down by meltwater near the margins of the ice-sheet. As the meltwater escapes from the ice via a series of braided streams the terminal moraine is breached and the sediment redistributed downstream as a series of stratified fluvio-glacial deposits known as outwash plains, valley trains or sandurs. Outwash plains tend to have very gentle slopes, although some are terraced as a result of changing levels of stream activity.

Ouwater, Albert van (active c.1450–80), Netherlandish painter, known for his landscape backgrounds. *The Raising of Lazarus* (Berlin) is his only surviving undisputed work. His style shows connections with the Van Eycks and also Dieric Bouts, while he was probably the master of Geertgen tot Sint Jans.

Ouzel, see DIPPER; RING OUZEL.

Ovary, one of the two female reproductive organs in which the ova, the human eggs and the female sex hormones are produced. There is one on each side of the uterus, which is placed in the centre of the pelvic cavity. Each is in close proximity to the uterus and the Fallopian tubes. Each ovary contains groups of germinal cells, known as Graafian follicles, and in the centre of each of these is a primitive ovum. It has been estimated that there are 30,000 such ova in the ovary at birth. The ovary is oval and is about 3·5 cm long and 1·5 cm thick. Ovulation, or rupture of the wall of the Graafian follicle, occurs in the majority of women midway between two menstrual periods. An ovum is liberated and passes by way of the Fallopian tubes into the uterus. If it has been fertilised it develops, but if not it is washed out in the menstrual period. The ovary also produces the female sex hormones oestrogen and progesterone.

Ovary, in plants, that part of the carpel that contains the ovule, and from which the fruit will later be formed.

See also BOTANY; FERTILISATION; FLOWER; FRUIT; OVULE; SEED.

Oven, the oldest types of oven are arched in shape, and built of stone or brick, and heated by burning a wood fire within them. Coke or anthracite is often used as fuel. Ovens for more general use are best made of iron, and are usually heated externally by flues, regulated by dampers, which convey the heat from a fire. Most commercial ovens are now heated electrically and even heat distribution is ensured by the use of an internal fan.

Oven-birds, popular name for a family, Furnariidae, of South American passerine birds. This is a large family which includes the miners, earthcreepers, cinclodes, spinetails, and canasteros. The true oven-birds are members of one genus of the family including *Furnarius rufus*, the rufous oven-bird. It is so called on account of its oven-like nest, which is a massive structure, weighing often about 3½ kg and placed on the bough of a tree. It is composed of mud and pieces of sticks and straw and animal hairs. The white eggs are laid upon a bed of soft dry grass in a large chamber which is reached through an antechamber. The birds are monogamous, and share the duties of incubation.

Overbeck, Johann Friedrich (1789–1869), German painter. In Rome, 1810, he was instrumental in forming the group of artists, the Nazarenes. He was the leader of the revival of Roman Catholic art, intensely idealistic but not a great painter.

Overhead Charges, also described as 'indirect expenses', 'establishment charges', oncost', 'burden', are those business expenses, such as rent, management salaries, bookkeeping, accountancy and interest on loans, which cannot be directly attributed to a particular piece of work.

Overijssel, province in the north-east of the Netherlands, extending from the IJsselmeer to the West German frontier. The land consists largely of sandy flats, covered with waste stretches of heath and fen, but there is some fertile pasture land along the shores of the IJsselmeer, where cattle-rearing and cheese- and butter-making are the chief industries. Reclamation in the east has added to the fertile soil. Cotton-spinning is carried on in the district of Twente, and fishing from the ports of the IJsselmeer. The principal towns of the province are Zwolle (capital), Enschede and Hengelo. Area 3927 km²; population (1981) 1,027,836.

Overseer, parochial official who was charged with the supervision of the poor in England and Wales. The office was established in 1601 and abolished in 1927. The overseer formulated and levied poor-rates, and prepared valuation, jury and voters' lists.

Overture, a musical work intended to serve as an introductory piece to a larger composition, usually an opera, but often an independent composition for concert use. It can nowadays be a piece of programme music. Overtures were first introduced in Rome c.1630. The Italian dramatic overture was in three sections —fast, slow, fast, with obvious bearing on the form of the classical concerto. The French overture, as used by Lully, was in two or three parts: a slow introduction, a lively *allegro* in fugue form, and occasionally a closing section contrasted with the middle section. This type became popular in England, and was used by Purcell and Handel.

In the 19th century an interest arose in the concert overture as an independent entity, for example Tchaikovsky's *Romeo and Juliet*, Mendelssohn's *Fingal's Cave* and Elgar's *Cockaigne*, all of which resemble the symphonic poem. Another type of overture is a pot-pourri of themes from the opera.

Ovett, Stephen Michael (1955–). British middle-distance runner who has twice broken the one mile world record and in 1980 set a new 1500 m world record of 3 min 31·36 sec at Koblenz.

Ovid, Publius Ovidius Naso (43 BC–AD 17), Latin poet. He held legal appointments at Rome, but devoted most of his time to poetry and pleasure. In AD 9, having long enjoyed the favour of the Emperor Augustus, he was suddenly banished to Tomis on the Black Sea, where he died. The pretext was his licentious poem *Ars Amatoria*, which had been published ten years earlier. The real cause remains uncertain.

The *Metamorphoses*, his greatest poem, is an epic collection of stories whose common theme is transformation. This work was very popular and influential in medieval Europe when its stories inspired many other writers and artists.

Oviedo, capital of the province of Oviedo, Spain. In the 9th century it was the capital of the kingdom of the Asturias and, later, a centre of resistance to the Moors. Oviedo has ironworks, and makes munitions, textiles, cement, glass, pottery, chemicals, and leather goods. Population (1981) 190,123.

Oviparous, refers to animals whose young develop in eggs outside the mother's body. This occurs in birds, some fishes, reptiles and insects.

Some animals are *ovoviviparous*; the eggs are retained within the mother's body until the young animal is ready to hatch. All the food needed for development is in the egg, as it is in birds' eggs, but the young benefit from the protection of the mother's body. They hatch within her body, as in salamanders, or just after the eggs are laid, as in some snakes.

The next step in nourishing the developing embryo is when it feeds on fluids within the mother's reproductive organs. This is a transition phase towards the *viviparous* state, in which the embryo is directly nourished by its mother's blood through the wall of the uterus (womb).

See also DEVELOPMENTAL BIOLOGY; EGG; EMBRYOLOGY.

Ovulation, see OVARY.

Ovule, a minute body of a circular or ovoid shape which occurs in the ovary of a flowering plant. Ovules may be solitary or numerous. After fertilisation by the action of pollen they become seeds. An ovule consists principally of the nucellus, a central mass of tissue in which the embryo sac is embedded. The latter contains an abundance of protoplasm and a number of small cells including the egg cell which forms the embryo after fertilisation. The nucellus is covered by one or more coats or integuments, and in most cases it is attached by a short stalk or funicle to the placenta, a ridge of tissue in the ovary. At the anterior end, the micropyle, a narrow canal or opening, leads to the nucellus. Down this the pollen tube passes in fertilisation. See also PLACENTATION.

Ovum, see EGG; EMBRYOLOGY.

Owain ap Gruffydd, see GLENDOWER, OWEN.

Owen, Robert (1771–1858), British industrialist and philanthropist. He was the co-owner of successful mills at Lanark, where, eventually, he instituted a system of co-partnership and also started schools for infants. His scheme, then an entire novelty, attracted much attention. He wished to improve the conditions of labour, and especially of child labour, and was the prime mover of the Factory Act in 1819. His communistic settlements in England and America proved to be failures, and he suffered financial loss.

Owen, Wilfred (1893–1918), English poet. In the First World War he enlisted in the Artists' Rifles, but was invalided home in 1917 and sent to Craiglockhart War Hospital, where Siegfried Sassoon, his fellow patient, encouraged him in writing verse. Sent back to France as a company commander, he won the MC, but was killed a week before the armistice in the crossing of the Sambre Canal. His *Poems*, 1920, edited by Sassoon, shatter the illusion of the glory of war, revealing its hollowness, wreckage, and the beauty it ruins. His verse is among the most moving of all First World War poetry.

Owen Falls, rapids of the Victoria Nile in Uganda, situated 5 km below the outlet from Lake Victoria. The hydroelectric and flood control scheme was opened in 1954 and supplies power not only in Uganda but also to Kenya.

Owens, Jesse (1913–1980), US athlete, famous for two immortal double-feats: in 1935, within an hour, he first equalled the world record (9·4 seconds) for the 100 yards (91·44 m), then cleared a long jump distance of 8·13 m (the first time 8 m had been exceeded—a record which stood for a quarter of a century). Then, 20 minutes later, he ran 220 yards (200 m) in 20·3 seconds, creating another world record, and finally he hurdled 220 yards in 22·6 seconds, a further world record. At the 1936 Olympics at Berlin he won four gold medals—for the 100 and 200 m, the long jump and for his part in the 4 × 100 m relay.

Owl, bird of the order Strigiformes, distinguished from all other birds of prey, except the osprey, by the tarsus (of the leg bones) being half the length of the tibia, while the outer toe can be turned backwards or forwards at will. Owls are mostly nocturnal in habit, but some hunt for food in full daylight. The head is always large, the neck short and contracted, the eyes are directed forwards and are surrounded by a characteristic ruff of feathers. The short beak is hooked. Owls have long been the subject of much superstition, being universally regarded as birds of ill omen. This has undoubtedly had much to do with their ruthless persecution, and only in recent years has it been realised that they are the most important check upon the excessive multiplication of rodents. In addition to these, reptiles, fish and insects are eaten, and some species have been observed to feed on carrion. Indigestible remains of the food are cast up in the form of pellets. There are two owl families: Tytonidae includes ten species of barn owls; and Strigidae includes about 120 species of typical owls.

Ox, see CATTLE.

Ox-bow Lake, a lake located in an abandoned meander channel, formed either by a flood causing a straightening of a meandering channel, or by the downstream migration of a loop. Overbank flooding causes clay and silt to be deposited in such lakes which are therefore frequently reduced to marshes and ultimately clay plugs.

Ox-eye Daisy, dog daisy or horse daisy, *Leucanthemum vulgare* (*Chrysanthemum leucanthemum*), a perennial herb of the Compositae. It has daisy-like flower-heads with white rays and yellow disc florets.

Ox-pecker, a starling-like bird of the subfamily Buphagidae, order Passeriformes, of which there are two species, found in Africa, one with a red bill, the other with a red and yellow one. They are strong fliers, of great swiftness, and insectivorous in habit. Their various names, of which rhinoceros bird is one, are derived from their method of seeking food on the backs of large animals, such as rhinoceroses and oxen.

Oxalic Acid, or ethanedioic acid, $(COOH)_2$, the first and most important member of the homologous series of dibasic acids of the general formula $HOOC(CH_2)_nCOOH$. It occurs as its acid potassium salt in many plants, especially in the wood-sorrel (*Oxalis acetosella*), and rhubarb leaves. In small quantities it is made in the laboratory by combining sodium and carbon dioxide at 360°C, or by quickly heating sodium formate to a high temperature. On the commercial scale it is prepared from cellulose in the form of sawdust. The sawdust is fused with a mixture of potassium and sodium hydroxides in iron pans. Potassium and sodium oxalates are formed, extracted with water, and treated with the requisite amount of sulphuric acid, when oxalic acid crystallises out in large, transparent, rhombic prisms. The acid is poisonous, but the calcium salt passes through the system unchanged. Thus, in case of poisoning, lime water or chalk is administered. Oxalic acid is used as a metal cleaner and a bleach for textiles and leather.

Owl. *Examples from the two families of the order Strigiformes, which contains 130 species.*

Oxalidaceae, wood-sorrel family, a dicotyledonous family of about 875 species in three genera. They are chiefly tropical, but a few grow in temperate zones. They generally have compound leaves, and coloured flowers with five petals and ten stamens. The fruits are capsules or berries. The genera are *Eichleria*, *Biophytum* and *Oxalis*.

Oxalis, a genus of annuals, perennials and evergreens, usually with trifoliate leaves. The seeds are shot out with some force from the capsule when ripe. *O. acetosella* is the common wood-sorrel, *O. corniculata* the procumbent yellow sorrel, and *O. stricta* the upright yellow sorrel. *O. deppei* has edible and radish-like roots, for which the plant is grown in France. *O. pes-caprae* can become a serious weed in mild areas.

Oxburgh Hall, Norfolk, England, was built about 1482, and has been the home of the Bedingfeld family for nearly 500 years. It was substantially restored in the 18th and 19th centuries, although its outward appearance is much the same as in Tudor times. The 24-metre gate tower is virtually unaltered.

Oxenstierna, Axel Gustafsson, Count (1583–1654), Swedish statesman. He became chancellor to Gustavus II (1611). During the king's absence (1614–16) Oxenstierna looked after affairs at home. After Gustavus's death at Lützen (1632) he took over the government of Sweden, and it was his courage and resourcefulness which kept the Protestant League together. In the Danish war of 1643–45 his tactical skill again proved invaluable. During the brief rule of Queen Christina, Oxenstierna was handicapped by the jealousy of his young mistress.

Oxfam. Started in Britain in 1942 with the concern of a group in Oxford for the starving of war-torn Greece, Oxfam has tried since to respond in a practical way to human need throughout the world.

Oxford, Edward de Vere, 17th Earl of (1550–1604), English courtier and poet. He went to Cambridge University at the age of 8 and succeeded to the earldom and the hereditary office of Lord Great Chamberlain in 1562, when he was 12. Of unruly temperament, he lost friends through his insolence and pride, and his fortune by extravagance. He had some reputation as a writer of short poems, and is said to have written plays, one of which has survived. Oxford is one of several unlikely claimants put forward as the writer of Shakespeare's plays.

Oxford, city, episcopal see and county town of Oxfordshire, England, situated at the confluence of the Thames and the Cherwell, 84 km north-west of London (102 km by rail). Its importance in early times is shown by the first mention of it in history, which occurs in the *Anglo-Saxon Chronicle* for 912. Here we read that in this year Edward, son of Ethelred, took possession 'of London and Oxford and all the lands obedient to those cities'.

Oxford. *The roof tops of Exeter College, founded in 1314 by the Bishop of Exeter.*

Teaching is known to have been carried on at Oxford since the early years of the 12th century. The fame of the university grew steadily, until by the 14th century it was the equal of any in Europe. In the present age its reputation remains high.

Before 1914 Oxford was regarded solely as a university city and market town, printing being then its only considerable industry. Between the two wars the Oxford motor industry expanded rapidly, and the success of the motor industry at Cowley must be attributed to the initiative and ability of its founder, Lord Nuffield. Population (1981) 98,521.

Oxford and Asquith, Countess of, see ASQUITH, EMMA ALICE MARGARET.

Oxford and Asquith, 1st Earl of, see ASQUITH, HERBERT HENRY.

Oxford and Mortimer, Robert Harley, Earl of (1661–1724), English statesman. He was Speaker of the House of Commons in 1701, and chief secretary of state in 1704, which post he resigned four years later. In 1710 he was nominated chancellor of the Exchequer. He took part in the secret negotiations with France which resulted in the Treaty of Utrecht in 1713. Harley was an inveterate political intriguer, corresponding simultaneously with both Jacobites and Hanoverians.

Harley amassed a great collection of books. His son Edward, 2nd Earl of Oxford (1689–1741), increased his father's collections. After his death the books, prints and pamphlets were sold to Thomas Osborne, in 1742, and the manuscripts were bought by the British Museum.

See also HARLEIAN COLLECTION.

Oxford Clay, see JURASSIC SYSTEM.

Oxford Group, name given in 1928 to the movement initiated in Oxford in 1921 by Dr Frank N. D. Buchman, who defined it as 'a Christian revolution, whose aim is a new social order under the dictatorship of the Spirit of God, making for better human relationships, for unselfish co-operation, cleaner business, cleaner politics, for the elimination of political, industrial and racial antagonisms'. Since 1938 its work has usually been known by the name of Moral Rearmament.

Oxford Movement, known also as the Tractarian Movement, and by its supporters as the Catholic Revival. It attempted to make the Church of England realise the primitive and Catholic principles on which the Movement believed the Church of England depended. Its immediate cause was the government's abolition of ten Irish bishoprics in 1833, which led many to ask on what the Church could rest if attacked by the government. The reply came from Oxford in the insistence on the divine mission of the Church as the extension of the Incarnation. The movement was led by Keble, Pusey, Newman and Froude.

See also ANGLO-CATHOLICS.

Oxford University Press, department of, and wholly owned by, the University of Oxford, by far the largest institution of its kind in the world. Its principal departments include the three publishing divisions at Oxford: the academic division, which publishes learned works under the imprint 'Clarendon Press'; the general division, which publishes books of more general interest including such series as the Oxford Books of Verse, the Oxford Standard Authors and the World's Classics, as well as Bibles and prayer books, reference books, notably the great *Oxford English Dictionary*, music books and sheet music, and children's books; and the educational division. There is also the printing works, a large distribution centre and many foreign branches.

Oxfordshire, Midland county of England, bounded to the south by Berkshire, to the east by Buckinghamshire, to the north-east and north-west by Northamptonshire and Warwickshire, to the west by Gloucestershire, and to the south-west by Wiltshire, covering an area of 261,352 ha. It occupies much of the Thames basin above Goring Gap. In the north lies part of the Cotswold Hills, while in the south and south-east are the White Horse Hills and the Chiltern Hills. The main river is the Thames, with its tributaries the Windrush, Evenlode, Cherwell, Ock and Thame. The scenery in the Thames valley is extremely beautiful, and includes many favourite river resorts, such as Abingdon, Goring, Henley-on-Thames and Wallingford. The soil is good and agriculture flourishes. Some iron ore is mined in the north and there are aluminium works at Banbury. The chief manufactures are motor vehicles at Cowley (Oxford), blankets at Witney, gloves at Woodstock, agricultural implements and engines at Banbury, tweed, lace and paper mills. At Woodstock is Blenheim Palace. Of the monastic buildings few remain, the abbey church at Dorchester-on-Thames being the most important. There are a number of beautiful churches besides those in Oxford itself, including those of Iffley, Adderbury and Minster Lovell. Population (1981) 515,079.

Oxidation, chemical process whereby substances take up or combine with oxygen, as, for example, when magnesium burns in air, $2Mg + O_2 = 2MgO$. A substance containing hydrogen can sometimes lose some or all of it in the form of water when oxidised. Thus ethanol, CH_3CH_2OH, is oxidised to acetaldehyde, CH_3CHO, by potassium dichromate and sulphuric acid. Further oxidation, by the addition of oxygen, produces acetic acid, CH_3COOH. Thus the result of oxidation may be either an increase of oxygen or a decrease of hydrogen. Oxidation has come to mean an increase in the electronegative content of a molecule, or even more simply, electron loss. Reduction is the reverse process, and always accompanies oxidation.

Oxide Paint, paint in which the colour of the pigment is due entirely to inorganic iron compounds. The pigments mix well, are inert and permanent, and vary in colour from dark red to black through purple.

Oxides, binary compounds formed by the union of elements with oxygen. They may be divided into seven classes: (1) basic oxides; (2) acidic oxides; (3) neutral oxides; (4) amphoteric oxides; (5) suboxides; (6) higher oxides; (7) composite oxides. Basic oxides are the oxides of metallic elements which react with acids to form salts and water, e.g. $CaO + 2HCl = CaCl_2 + H_2O$. Acidic oxides are the oxides of non-metallic elements which react with bases to form salts and water, e.g. $SO_3 + 2NaOH = Na_2SO_4 + H_2O$. Some, but not all, of the acidic oxides dissolve in water to form acids. Neutral oxides are oxides which are neither acidic nor basic, e.g. nitrous oxide (N_2O), carbon monoxide (CO). Amphoteric oxides are oxides of elements which are neither truly metallic nor truly non-metallic and which behave either as a basic oxide or as an acidic oxide under appropriate conditions, e.g. $ZnO + H_2SO_4 = ZnSO_4 + H_2O$; $ZnO + 2NaOH = Na_2ZnO_2 + H_2O$. According to the modern theory of acids and bases, water is an amphoteric oxide since it gives hydrogen ions (acidic) and hydroxyl ions (basic), $H_2O \rightleftarrows H^+ + OH^-$. Suboxides are oxides of metals or non-metals which contain less oxygen than the normal oxides in which the element shows its normal valency, e.g. lead suboxide, Pb_2O. Higher oxides are oxides which possess more oxygen than the normal oxides. They include the peroxides, which liberate hydrogen peroxide on treatment with a dilute acid, e.g. BaO_2, and dioxides, which do not liberate hydrogen peroxide in this way, e.g. MnO_2. Composite oxides are oxides of metals that react chemically as though they were mixtures of two oxides of the same metal. These oxides are not, however, mechanical mixtures of the two oxides, e.g. red lead, Pb_3O_4, behaves as $2PbO{\cdot}PbO_2$ and on treatment with nitric acid forms lead nitrate from the PbO part and leaves PbO_2 as a brown residue. Oxides in which the proportion of element to oxygen is two or three are sometimes called sesquioxides, e.g. chromium sesquioxide, Cr_2O_3.

Oxlip, *Primula elatior*, a handsome plant with a very limited distribution in woodlands in the eastern part of England, also in Europe and western Asia. It is intermediate in character between the primrose and the cowslip, but may be distinguished from the rather common hybrid between these two plants by the absence of folds in the throat of the tubular flower.

Oxus, see Amu Darya.

Oxy-acetylene Welding, see Welding.

Oxychlorides, compounds which may be looked on as being intermediate between oxides and normal chlorides. Their formation is generally brought about by the addition of excess water to the chlorides, but only a few metals form oxychlorides, and the compounds are not easily prepared pure or of definite chemical composition. The oxychlorides may be regarded as basic chlorides, or rather as the anhydrides of such, e.g. bismuth oxychloride (BiOCl) may be regarded as the anhydride of the basic bismuth chloride. Non-metals such as phosphorus form oxychlorides, e.g. $POCl_3$.

Oxygen, chemical element, symbol O, atomic number 8, atomic weight 15·9994. It is the most abundant and important element. It forms 23 per cent by weight of air, 89 per cent of water and about a half of all the rocks which comprise the crust of the Earth. It was discovered by Scheele (1771), but the discovery was not published until after Priestley (1774) had described its preparation from mercuric oxide. The gas is produced on the small scale by the decomposition of potassium chlorate. On a commercial scale, it is now obtained by the distillation of liquid air and as a by-product in some electrolytic operations.

Oxygen is a colourless gas, tasteless, odourless, and slightly heavier than air. Liquid oxygen is a pale steel-blue liquid which boils at −182·5°C, at which temperature its relative density is 1·1315. The liquid is strongly magnetic. The gas has very powerful chemical affinities, combining directly with most other elements, particularly at high temperatures. It will react with iron, phosphorus, sodium and potassium at ordinary temperatures (i.e. the metals are oxidised). The process of oxidation may proceed so rapidly as to cause the metal or body to burn. Such oxidation accompanied by light and heat is known as combustion. Oxygen is the only gas capable of supporting respiration, and bodily heat is maintained by the slow combustion of digested foodstuffs by the oxygen taken in by respiration. Commercially the gas is used for producing very high temperatures, as in the oxy-hydrogen blowpipe flame used for welding. The element oxygen exhibits allotropy, in that it exists both as the diatomic oxygen molecule, O_2, and ozone, O_3.

Oxymoron (Greek *oxus*, sharp; *moros*, dull), figure of speech (meaning literally 'pointedly foolish') in which contradictory words are used together, as in Tennyson's:

> His honour rooted in dishonour stood,
> And faith unfaithful kept him falsely true.

See also Figure of Speech.

Oxypetalum, a genus of evergreen twining plants of the Asclepiadaceae, bearing fragrant blue, rose, orange and purple flowers; natives of South America. Plants formerly classified in the genus *Tweedia* are now placed in *Oxypetalum*.

Oxytropis, a genus of perennial plants of the Leguminosae, bearing decorative pinnate leaves and sprays of white, yellow, blue or purple flowers. They are occasionally grown in gardens.

Oyo, town in Western State, Nigeria, about 200 km north of Lagos, on the border of the forest and savanna zones. The present site of Oyo was settled in the early 19th century by refugees from the wars and disturbances in Yorubaland. The modern town is a centre of craft industry, local trade and commerce. Population (1975) 140,000.

Oyster, *Ostrea*, large genus of class Bivalvia in phylum Mollusca, represented on nearly every shore. The bivalve shell is unequal, the upper valve being flat and thin, the lower one, by which the shell adheres to a rock or other submarine body, being concave and larger. They are hinged together by an elastic, toothless ligament. The oyster gets its food, which consists of very minute organisms, by lying with the valves open, four flat labial palps or lips assisting movement of the food collected by the ciliated gills to the large dilatable mouth. On each side are a pair of simple gills placed between the folds of the mantle. All produce vast numbers of eggs; the common oyster is reputed to produce more than 1,000,000 during the summer.

The number of localities suitable for oyster culture is limited, as oysters cannot breed where the water is cold in summer, and cannot exist where there is sand; the latter works its way into the hinge of the shell and prevents it from opening and closing, and soon kills the animal. One family of oysters is important in the pearl industry, especially in the Far East where young oysters are seeded to induce the production of a pearl around the irritant.

Oyster-catcher, mussel-picker or sea pie, *Haematopus ostralegus*, order Charadriiformes, a common bird on shores around the world, though it often goes up rivers many miles inland to breed. It may nest at a height of over 500 m. The long, red bill is perfectly adapted for forcing open the shells of molluscs, but both marine and terrestrial worms and insects are also consumed. The birds are about 40 cm long; the head, neck and upper parts are black, and the underparts white; pure white specimens occasionally occur.

Oyster Plant, see Salsify.

Ozark Mountains, an upland area in the south central USA, comprising the Ozark plateau (to which the name is most properly attached), the Springfield plateau, the Boston Mountains, and the Salem upland. The general elevation ranges from 300 to 400 m, but crests in the Boston Mountains rise to 800 m. The Ozarks are a wooded area of poor farming in Missouri and Arkansas and have a distinctive hillbilly culture comparable with that of the Appalachian Mountains, but increasing recreational use of the area is breaking down its former isolation.

Ozone, allotropic form of oxygen found in very small quantities in the lower atmosphere but in considerable quantities at a height of 50 km above sea level. Ozone is formed out of the oxygen of the air by an electrical machine (one producing sparks) in operation, and when lightning discharges occur; it is also found in the oxygen prepared from the electrolysis of water. The gas is best obtained by exposing pure dry oxygen to the influence of a silent electric discharge. The gas is slightly soluble in water, 4·5 cm^3 dissolving in 1 l of water. It condenses to an intensely deep blue liquid which boils at −112°C, and is a very explosive substance. Ozone is a powerful oxidiser. It decolorises vegetable colours, and acts at once upon most metals, silver and mercury being converted into oxides. Sulphides are converted into sulphates; unlike oxygen, ozone liberates iodine from potassium iodide. This latter constitutes a rough test for the presence of the gas. Ozone has formula O_3, i.e. it contains three atoms to the molecule, whereas the oxygen molecule contains two atoms.

P

P, sixteenth letter of the English and other Western European alphabets, descended, through the Greek, Etruscan and Latin alphabets, from the North Semitic *pe*. P in Sanskrit, Greek and Latin is replaced by *f* in the Germanic tongues (see F). Words beginning with *p* in English and its kindred Germanic tongues are almost all of foreign origin, as *pain* (French *peine*, Latin *poena*), *plough* (Polish *plug*), *pit* (Latin *puteus*, a well).

See also Alphabet.

Paarl, town of Cape Province, South Africa, situated 58 km by rail from Cape Town. Some of South Africa's best wines are produced here. It derives its name from three gigantic boulders which dominate the town and were thought to resemble a pearl. There are large jam and canning factories, flour mills and light industries, including plastics, textile mills and tobacco factories. Population (1970) 48,597, of whom 14,370 are whites.

Pabst, George Wilhelm (1885–1967), German film director. After working in the theatre and writing scenarios, Pabst directed *The Joyless Street*, 1925, with Garbo. His most famous films are *Westfront 1918*, 1930, and *Kameradschaft*, 1931, pacifist stories of the First World War which provoked Nazi demonstrations, and *The Threepenny Opera*, 1931, after Brecht and Weill. During the 1930s he worked in France and Hollywood, returning to Germany for the duration of the war. Later films include *The Trial*, 1948, *The Last Act*, 1954, and *Jackboot Mutiny*, 1955.

Paca, South American rodent mammals in the family Dasyproctidae, to which the agoutis belong. There are only two species; these differ from the agoutis in having five digits on all the limbs instead of three. *Cuniculus paca*, the spotted cavy, is one of the largest of rodents, measuring about 60 cm long and 35 cm high. The body is covered with short, stiff, wiry hairs and the tail is greatly reduced. It is nocturnal, vegetarian, and lives in a superficial burrow in forests near water; the female produces a single young at a birth. The flesh is edible.

Pacaraima, Sierra, range of mountains in the Guiana Highlands, and extending from west to east for over 800 km. They form a watershed between the basins of the Orinoco and Río Branco rivers. Highest peak, Mount Roraima (2810 m).

Pace, measure of length, derived from the Latin *passus*. The latter, however, was measured from the heel-mark of one foot to the mark where it next touched the ground, thus equalling, in the modern sense of the word, two paces. The Latin *passus* was a little less than 5 ft (1·5 m); a thousand of them went to a Roman mile.

Pacemaker, Artificial, a mechanical device designed to stimulate the heart by producing regular electrical stimuli, and used mostly in the treatment of heart block, when the heart rate is usually too slow for the maintenance of an adequate blood supply to the body, particularly to the brain. In such cases, an artificial pacemaker can either be implanted in the body or worn outside, with a wire threaded through a vein into the heart. The former type is called a permanent artificial pacemaker, while the latter is a temporary artificial pacemaker.

Pacemaker, Cardiac, a small area in the wall of the right atrium of the heart, that spontaneously generates regular electrical stimuli which spread through the heart and make it contract.

Pacheco, Francisco (1564–1654), Spanish painter, scholar and writer. In 1611 he visited Madrid and eventually opened a school of painting in Seville. Among his pupils here was Velázquez (who married his daughter), Cano, and perhaps Zurbarán. He belongs to the transition period between Mannerism and a more natural Baroque style, and he held that art should have a spiritual purpose and not just imitate nature. He was a censor of paintings for the Inquisition, but is most important for his treatise *El Arte de la Pintura* which took 30 years to write and was finished 1637/8, and published in 1648.

Pachydermata, a classification of mammals proposed by Cuvier for a number of thick-skinned, non-ruminant, hoofed animals. It has now been superseded.

Pacific Islands, Trust Territory of, groups of 2141 small islands which are administered as a UN Trust by the United States. The territory extends from 1° to 22°N and from 142° to 172°E; it is ethnically and geographically Micronesian, and includes the Marshall and Caroline islands. The Northern Mariana Islands were also included until 1978. The Marshalls and eastern Carolines are mainly coral, seldom rising to more than 10 m above sea level; the western Carolines are volcanic and mountainous. The most important industry is tourism; the main products are fish, coconuts, taro and breadfruit. Population (1980) 116,974.

The islands were taken from the Germans by the Japanese in 1914, taken again by the United States in 1944 and have been administered as a Trust Territory since 1947.

Pacific Ocean, largest division of the hydrosphere, extending from the Southern Ocean (latitude 40°S) to the Bering Strait, i.e. practically to the Arctic Ocean; it is, however, coextensive with the Southern Ocean to latitude 80°S; it divides the Old and New Worlds, and is roughly bisected by the 170°W longitude meridian; greatest breadth, 16,000 km; length, 11,000 km. In shape it is very roughly pentagonal, very broken to the west and south-west, where it communicates with the Indian Ocean; it has an area of 163,000,000 km^2, or nearly 40 per cent of the whole water extent of the world.

The average depth of the Pacific Ocean is 4200 m, and exceeds that of the other oceans; the western half is deeper than the eastern, and the north as opposed to the shallower south. The greatest known depths are 11,524 m in the Mindanao Trench, east of the Philippines, and 11,022 m in the Marianas Trench.

The Pacific is noted for its large number of oceanic islands grouped in the central and western regions; they are all volcanic or coral, many being atolls, and number over 2500, with an area of 180,000 km^2. The Pacific is also unique in its complete girdle of volcanoes on the continental coast and islands, with their accompanying manifestations of earthquakes.

Pacifist, one who believes that all war is wrong and that international affairs could and must be settled without it. The term is often restricted to those who refuse to fight in time of war.

Padang, city in West Sumatra province, Indonesia. Its nearby port of Emmahaven exports coffee, rubber, spices, copra and timber. Padang has one of Indonesia's major cement works and is linked by rail to the Ombilin coalmine. Population (1975) 225,000.

Paddington, district of north-west London, situated north of the borough of Kensington. Until c.1820 it was still a village, but its choice as terminus for the Great Western Railway in 1832–38 brought rapid development. The Paddington Canal to Uxbridge was originally built between 1795 and 1801, then in 1805 linked with the Grand Union Canal. The famous Shillibeer omnibus service from Paddington Green was opened in 1829.

Paddle-steamer, forerunner of screw-driven steamships, boat propelled by paddle-wheels, which are driven by steam. The use of boats with paddle-wheels dates from very ancient times, both the Romans and Egyptians being acquainted with some form of them. In 1803 Robert Fulton made his first trip, and in 1807 Stevens built a paddle-steamer, the *Phoenix*, which plied for six years on the Delaware, whilst in the same year the *Clermont* of Fulton reached a speed of 8 km/h on a trial trip. During the next decade the number of steamers on the Mississippi increased, and from 1835 the speed attained was greater. The *Comet* of Henry Bell, first built in 1804 and wrecked in 1820, was the first paddle-steamer employed regularly and successfully in Great Britain. The paddle-steamer is now obsolete, although some have been preserved.

Paddle-wheel, wheel used for propelling a boat or ship. As originally tried, it consisted essentially of a series of paddles or paddle-like spokes inserted in an axle drum or wheel. In its eventual development flat boards were fitted more or less radially round the circumference, so as to press backward like a succession of paddles against the water. Two wheels were generally used, one on each side of the vessel, a little aft of midships, so as to catch the top of waves; in river steamers, where there is no great depth of water, one wheel only, placed at the stern, was sometimes used.

See also PADDLE-STEAMER.

Paddy, see RICE.

Paderborn, city in North Rhine-Westphalia, Federal Republic of Germany, 24 km south of Bielefeld. Charlemagne held the first Saxon parliament here in 777 and the city was the scene of a meeting between Charlemagne and Pope Leo III in 799. In the Middle Ages the city was a member of the Hanseatic League. Metal working, agricultural machinery, calculators, computers, textiles and furniture are the main industries. Population (1970) 68,700.

Paderewski, Ignacy Jan (1860–1941), Polish pianist, composer and statesman. He studied at Warsaw and Berlin. Remarkable for strong personal views as an artist, he developed his talent in his own way. In 1884 he went to Vienna to study under Leschetizky. Between 1887 and 1891 he played in Vienna, in Germany, and in Paris, London and America. He also composed piano works, including a concerto and the *Polish Fantasia* with orchestra; the opera *Manru*, and a symphony. His idol was Chopin, in the interpretation of whose music he was supreme. He was the first prime minister and minister of Foreign Affairs of the Polish Republic, 1919–20.

Padua (Italian *Padova*; ancient *Patavium*), Italian city and capital of Padua province, situated on the canalised part of the Bacchiglione, 35 km west of Venice. In 1318 it came under the rule of the Carraresi, and in 1405 was taken by Venice. It was occupied by the French in 1797, was ceded to Austria in 1814, and became part of united Italy in 1866. The great Romanesque Gothic Basilica of St Anthony, the six Byzantine domes of which tower above the city, contains the tomb of the saint; the high altar of the Basilica has bronzes by Donatello. In the Scrovegni Chapel are frescoes by Giotto, and in the church of the Eremitani frescoes by Mantegna. The city is now more of an industrial than an agricultural centre, with engineering, clothing and man-made fibre industries. Population (1979) 242,216.

Padus, see PO.

Paean, originally, in Greek mythology, physician of the gods, but later a title of Apollo as deliverer from evil and hence songs in his honour, and ultimately battle, victory or festive songs.

Paediatrics, the branch of medicine concerned with the health of young children. It has developed largely in the 20th century, as physicians became aware of the special problems involved. It is now recognised that there are fundamental differences in physiology and anatomy between children and adults, which may make adult-style treatment inappropriate.

Paestum (Greek *Poseidōnia*, modern *Pesto*), ancient Greek colony in Lucania, southern Italy, situated near the Gulf of Salerno; founded from Sybaris c.600 BC. Later subject to the Lucanians, it eventually (273 BC) came under Roman rule, when its name was altered to Paestum. Under the Empire it was famous for its roses. The ruins of three Doric temples (6th–5th centuries BC) are among the most remarkable remains of antiquity.

Pagan, ancient city with ruins of several thousand Buddhist temples, and situated on the east bank of the Irrawaddy. Said to have been founded c.850, it probably represents one of the earliest purely Burmese centres in upper Burma. Pagan dominated the whole country until its own decline in the late 13th century, when it was captured by the Mongols. Its temples date from the late 11th to the 13th centuries. Pagan has continued to have great religious importance.

Paganini, Niccolò (1784–1840), Italian violin virtuoso. He began his career at the age of 15 and for nearly 40 years he toured Europe with sensational success. He was renowned chiefly for his technique, his double-stopping and harmonics being unsurpassed, as were his roundness and beauty of tone in soft passages. As a composer for string instruments (including the guitar) he produced work of distinctive character.

Page, Sir Earle Christmas Grafton (1880–1961), Australian statesman. He entered parliament as a member of the newly-formed Country party in 1919 and was leader of the party, 1920–39. He was prime minister of Australia for a short period in 1939. Page was the Australian representative in the British war Cabinet, 1941–42.

Page, Sir Frederick Handley (1885–1962), British aeronautical pioneer and inventor of the slotted wing for aircraft. He was one of the early pioneers of flying and founded Handley Page Limited in 1909. In the First World War Page designed and built the heavy bomber, the world's first multi-engined aircraft, and in 1919 he was running a civil aircraft service to the Continent. Under his direction Handley Page Limited became one of the leading aircraft manufacturers and when in 1924 it merged with Imperial Airways, forerunner of BOAC, later to become British Airways, Handley Page Limited provided nine of the fleet of 14 planes. Page's Heracles airliner was an outstanding machine in the 1930s. During the Second World War Handley Page Limited produced the Harrow, Hampden and Halifax bombers and the Hastings military transport. Among Page's other designs were the W8, Hannibal, Hermes, and the giant Victor jet bomber.

Page, youth of noble or gentle birth who waits on royal and noble personages. In the Middle Ages a boy who wanted to become an esquire and afterwards a knight served an apprenticeship as a page at court or in the castle of some nobleman.

Paget, Sir James (1814–99), British surgeon; he discovered *Trichina spiralis*, the worm contained in uncooked pork, which causes trichinosis. Two diseases are named after him —Paget's disease of the nipple (eczema with subsequent cancer) which he described in 1874, and osteitis deformans (a disease of bone) described in 1876.

Pagnol, Marcel (1895–1974), French playwright and film director. He became a teacher of English but later took up writing for the stage. After his first success *Topaze*, 1928, a satire, he produced a trilogy of plays on Marseilles characters, *Marius*, *Fanny* and *César*, 1929–36, which were made into films. Pagnol then founded a film company and started editing a review, *Les Cahiers du film*, for the advocacy of his ideas on the art of the cinema. He stressed the importance of dialogue and simplicity in films. His films include *Merlusse*, 1935; *La Femme du Boulanger*, 1938; *La Belle Meunière*, 1947; *Manon des Sources*, 1952; *Judas*, 1953; and *Lettres de mon Moulin*, 1954. Pagnol was the first film producer elected to the Académie Française, 1946.

***Pagoda** of the Summer Palace, Peking.*

Pagoda, originally a temple where a relic of the Buddha is enshrined. At Tanjore, India, the upper portion is an elongated and elaborately sculptured pyramid 30·5 metres high. The most famous Burmese pagoda is the Shwe Dagôn at Rangoon, which is bell-shaped and plated with gold. Chinese and Japanese pagodas are influenced by the shape of the old Chinese watch-tower. They are polygonal towers with ornamental roofs projecting on many storeys. The 7th-century pagoda of Hōryūji near Nara, Japan, has only five storeys; others have as many as thirteen. See also STUPA.

Pago-Pago, harbour of the island of Tutuila, American Samoa, which nearly bisects the island. It is one of the best harbours in the South Seas, and until 1951 was a US naval station.

Pahlavi, Mohammed Riza Shah, see MOHAMMED RIZA SHAH PAHLAVI.

Paignton, popular seaside resort in Devon, England, on Torbay, 4 km south-west of Torquay. Among places of interest are the remains of the bishop's palace, once the residence of Miles Coverdale, translator of the Bible into English.

Pain, term derived from the Old French *peine* meaning a penalty—an etymology which reflects the ancient association of bodily suffering with guilt. A more scientific interpretation of the significance of pain is a sensation warning the organism of impending physical harm and demanding an avoidance response.

The physiological basis of pain is not completely understood, but as with all the other *sensory modalities* (touch, vision, hearing, taste) the nervous system is responsible for receiving and integrating the signal and the conscious awareness of pain. Unlike other sensory modalities, pain does not seem to have specially adapted receptors, but is mediated by naked nerve endings in almost every tissue of the body. These nerve fibres travel from the periphery to the spinal cord where they enter the lateral spinothalamic tracts and ascend to the thalamus of the brain, which is a vital centre in the perception of pain. Although pain only results from the stimulation of specific pain receptors, they respond to electrical, mechanical, thermal and, especially, chemical stimuli of adequate intensity.

In addition to the anatomical and physiological considerations, there are psychological aspects of pain. Firstly the distress caused by pain is not simply determined by the intensity of the stimulus causing the pain, but is influenced by many psychological variables.

The first line of treatment for pain is with *analgesic* (pain-relieving) *drugs*, which range in efficacy from aspirin to morphine. Intractable pain can be attacked with a variety of surgical procedures.

Paine, Thomas (1737–1809), English author and politician. In 1774 he went to America with a note of introduction from Benjamin Franklin. Here he helped edit the *Pennsylvania Magazine* and, supporting the cause of independence, wrote pamphlets, among them *Common Sense*, 1776, in which he discussed the causes of the dispute with England and which influenced the Declaration of Independence, 1776.

In 1787 he returned to England and in 1791, in reply to Edmund Burke's critical *Reflections on the French Revolution*, he published the first part of *The Rights of Man*, his most famous work. Beginning as a defence of the French

Revolution, it develops to advocate an end to poverty, illiteracy, unemployment and war. A year later he issued the second part and fled to France to escape prosecution. He was at once elected a member of the Convention, in which he opposed the execution of Louis XVI, and was imprisoned until the death of Robespierre. He published *The Age of Reason*, in support of deism and opposing organised religion, in 1794 and in 1802 returned to America where he died seven years later in New York.

Paint consists of finely powdered, insoluble materials, principally pigments suspended in liquid binding media, and possesses the property of drying to adherent films on exposure to the atmosphere or the application of heat. Paints are used for the decoration and protection of all types of articles and buildings, and for artistic purposes. The principal function of pigments is to impart colour and opacity, although there is a further group of materials, known as extenders, which also act as pigments. The most common extenders are ground barytes, blanc fixe (precipitated barium sulphate), china clay, and whiting (calcium carbonate).

Binding media consist of drying or semi-drying oils and/or resins and are thinned, if necessary, with suitable solvents such as turpentine, white spirit, the coal-tar hydrocarbons or, in the case of special paints, with certain alcohols, esters, ketones and chlorinated hydrocarbons. Linseed oil is still the main drying oil used in paints, although large quantities of tung oil (Chinese wood oil) and dehydroxylated castor oil are also used. It is nearly always necessary to process such drying oils by refining or by heat treatment in order to improve their performance.

Resins used in paints can be classified as either natural resins or synthetic resins, although the former have to a very large extent been replaced by the latter. The commonest natural resin is rosin (colophony), which is the residue remaining after the distillation of turpentine from the exudation of the pine-tree. The most important class of synthetic resins is the alkyds. These give paints of the highest durability, of excellent gloss retention, and good drying properties. Polyurethane polymers are now extensively added to paints to give better drying and additional toughness and flexibility.

Driers must be added to paints containing drying oils in order to accelerate the drying process. These are catalysts which increase the rate of oxidation or polymerisation of the oils such as the resinates, linoleates, naphthenates, or octoates of lead, cobalt and manganese.

Water paints basically follow the above pattern, except that water is used in place of organic solvents, and additions of water-soluble or water-dispersable substances may be made. Plastic emulsion paints are water paints based on emulsions of polymers such as polyvinyl acetate or polystyrene, and are characterised by excellent washability and resistance to lime. Thixotropic paints, thick paints which become liquid on shaking and which have excellent non-drip properties, have become popular in recent years.

See also LUMINOUS PAINT.

Painted Lady, *Vanessa cardui*, butterfly of the family Nymphalidae, which migrates to Europe from North Africa. The caterpillar feeds on thistles and other plants. In North America it is known as the thistle butterfly.

Painter's Colic, see POISONOUS ELEMENTS.

Painting. The decoration of surfaces with pigments is known in some form or other all round the world. It has, however, a place of special importance in the West where it has been elevated to the dominant visual art.

The tradition began in Ancient Greece. Although all Greek paintings have perished, we can reconstruct the Greek achievement from written accounts, decorated ceramics and Roman copies. Great emphasis was placed on the human figure, usually in the form of deities or the heroes and heroines of mythology but portrayed with accurate proportions and in convincing illusory space. The Romans continued the Greek style of painting but at the end of the Empire it all but vanished. A more stylised and decorative art continued in the Byzantine Empire in the Eastern Mediterranean and this helped inspire the revival of painting in the West that took place in the Middle Ages. From the 12th century, a different type of painting appeared in France and spread through Europe. This Gothic style established a newly lyrical approach, with elongated figures outlined as gracefully curving shapes. Some of the finest examples date from the 14th century in Italy, particularly by Sienese artists such as Simone Martini.

In nearby Florence, a return to the more solemn and three-dimensional painting of the Ancient world began at about the same time with Giotto. Further developments had to wait until the early 15th century with Masaccio and Fra Angelico beginning the movement known to us as the Renaissance, self-consciously returning to models surviving from Greece and Rome in sculpture or scenes carved on sarcophagi. By the end of the century, full understanding of the human body and the depiction of illusory space had again been mastered, reaching a high point with Leonardo, Raphael, Michelangelo and Titian in the first half of the 16th century. However, by the end of the century an exaggerated and courtly style known as Mannerism had taken hold. The Renaissance had meanwhile spread to Northern Europe. In the 15th century, a naturalistic art had grown up in Flanders with painters such as Rogier van der Weyden and Jan van Eyck. This current merged with the ideals of the Italian Renaissance in the work of Dürer in Germany in the decades around 1500.

The 17th century was an outstanding period for Western painting. In Italy, Flanders, the Netherlands, France and Spain, great artists worked on a wide variety of subject matter and in differing styles. The essential division was between the exuberant and powerfully flamboyant Baroque of Rubens and the controlled Classicism of Poussin which harked back more rigorously to the art of the Ancients. Other great painters introduced their own individual types of sombre naturalism: Caravaggio in Italy, Velasquez in Spain and Rembrandt in the Netherlands. The latter country also saw a flowering of naturalistic landscape and realistic still-life.

In the 18th century, the aristocratic Rococo style came to the fore, developing out of the wistful nostalgia of Watteau in the early years of the century towards a pleasure-loving lightness with Boucher and Fragonard. In England, a unique type of bourgeois realism triumphed with Hogarth, and later in the century Reynolds established the Royal Academy to promote a high-minded approach to art. A lighter naturalism prospered at the same time with Gainsborough. In France, the reaction to the Rococo was drastic and after the Revolution of 1789 a severe Neo-Classicism was adopted as the official style, led by J. L. David and taken into the 19th century by Ingres. In England and Germany, a poetic Romanticism emerged with Blake and Friedrich, and also an incomparable naturalism in landscape painting with Constable and Turner. French Romanticism had its high priest in Delacroix, concentrating on the freedom and inner emotional life of the artist and painting in an impassioned and colourful style. By mid-century, the Realism of the great novelists of the period found a counterpart in Courbet.

From the 1870s, the exaggerated naturalism of Impressionism reasserted the artist's personal vision of nature in opposing the dead hand of official academic art. Monet, Renoir and others attempted to show the world as they saw it—as light. From these beginnings began a sequence of minor artistic revolutions that has continued into the 20th century. The Post-Impressionists such as Van Gogh and Cézanne began the process by which the appearance of the real world became reinterpreted by painters, at first distorted or simplified for expressive ends but then denied altogether. Picasso and Braque achieved the reconstruction of representational art with Cubism in the years around the First World War. During the 1930s, complete abstraction emerged with painters such as Mondrian. It should be noted, however, that the dominant current, represented by artists such as Picasso, almost always preserved some recognisable subject. The years since the Second World War have seen an increasingly confused art world. At first Abstract Expressionism in the United States seemed to triumph; more recently, minutely representational styles have come to the fore.

See also LANDSCAPE PAINTING; PORTRAITURE.

Painting and Decorating, term denoting the process of applying paint and other materials for protective and decorative purposes. The dual term derives from the fact that the most important function of paint is to preserve a surface (e.g. wood from decay, metal from corrosion), but its use can be extended to enhance the appearance of the surface and make it aesthetically pleasing. Decorating also includes the use of wall-hangings.

A good painting system must consist of several coats—a primer appropriate to the particular type of surface, undercoats to give thickness and opacity, and a finishing coat to provide a surface resistant to local conditions of exposure. A wide range of paints is available to suit special purposes; heat-resistant paints, for example, are used for boilers and radiators. Thixotropic paints are of special value to amateur decorators; they are so thick as to be virtually unspillable but thin under the shearing action of the brush when applied.

Wall-hangings include paper, the main choice, and also a wide range of fabrics, veneers, and plastic and metallicised panels. Wallpapers are made in a variety of weights and printed in many ways; some are embossed, others imitate satin or leather. Many modern papers are coated after printing with a film of vinyl resin which makes them extremely tough and washable.

Painting Techniques usually entail the grinding of pigments with a 'medium' to make a paint which is then rendered manageable by a 'diluent', and perhaps subsequently protected by a wax or 'varnish' applied when the paint is thoroughly dry. Diluents are 'essential' oils, the most generally used being turpentine. Venice turpentine is a more viscous preparation which enriches the substance of paint, as do varnishes such as mastic, dammar, copal and amber. Mastic or wax can be used for final varnishing.

Oil-colours use fatty vegetable oils, preferably cold-pressed, which 'dry' by the absorption of oxygen.

Tempera colours are mixed with egg-yolk, perhaps emulsified with oil. Casein, prepared from cream cheese, is another form of tempera. Parchment glue is the medium of distemper. These last three techniques use water as the diluent. Water-colour, used also for miniature painting, is made with gum and glycerine. Encaustic painting uses beeswax. See also ACRYLIC; FRESCO.

Paisley, Ian Richard Kyle (1926–), Ulster politician and clergyman. He became leader, or moderator, of the Free Presbyterian Church of Ulster in 1951. Paisley is a prominent member of the Protestant community in Northern Ireland, strongly opposed to union with the Republic of Ireland and in favour of Ulster continuing to be part of the United Kingdom. In 1970 he was elected as Protestant Unionist MP at Westminster for North Antrim and was leader of the Protestant Unionist party. He is also a European member of Parliament.

Paisley (Roman *Vanduara*), town in Renfrew District, Strathclyde Region, Scotland, on both sides of the White Cart river, 5 km above its confluence with the Clyde, and 11 km south-west of Glasgow. In the early 18th century the town was already noted for its manufacture of shawls, silk-gauze, muslin and linen; but the staple industry today is the making of thread. Other industries are varied and include dyeing, bleaching, distilling, engineering, shipbuilding, and the manufacture of chemicals, carpets, etc. Population (1981) 84,789.

Pakistan
Area: 803,943 km²
Population: 80,000,000
Capital: Islamabad

Pakistan, republic of South Asia. It is bounded on the west by Iran, north by Afghanistan and the USSR, north-east by China, east and south-east by India, and south by the Arabian Sea. In the east lies the territory of Jammu and Kashmir, hotly disputed by both India and Pakistan ever since 1947, of which Pakistan controls the north-western part. Pakistan consists of four provinces: Baluchistan, North-West Frontier, Punjab and Sind. Area 803,943 km².

Pakistan. *Harvesting in the Hunza Valley, a disputed area also claimed by India.*

The country lies at the western edge of the Indo-Ganges Plain. The Himalaya Mountains and the foothills occupy the whole of the northern half; their average height is over 6000 m and the group includes Nanga Parbat (8126 m) and K2 (8611 m). A ring of mountains formed by the Himalayas, Hindu Kush, and Pamirs cuts off northern Pakistan from Central Asia to the north. Between the mountains and the Indus Plain is a series of plateau regions at descending altitudes. The Indus Plain covers an area of 51,800 km² and stretches south to the Arabian Sea for over 1000 km. The rest of Pakistan is mostly arid or semi-arid desert lands including the Baluchistan plateau in the south-west, the Sind between the Indus and Chenab, and the northern extension of the Thar desert.

The total population of the country (excluding Jammu and Kashmir) was estimated in 1980 at over 80 million. The two cities of Karachi and Lahore are by far the most important. The capital is Islamabad. The total cultivated area in 1975 was 19·2 million ha. Cereal crops predominate, with wheat, the most important, covering 7 million ha. Rice (which is partly a cash crop and thus for export) and millets are also important food crops. The most significant cash crops are cotton and sugar cane. Cotton is vital not only for export but also as the main resource for the local textile industries. Agriculture is entirely dependent on irrigation from the Indus system.

Raw material based industries, particularly cotton, dominate the industrial sector. A wide range of other industries have also developed —steel rolling, refining, and consumer goods manufacture around Karachi, and traditional craft based industries around Lahore and in the Punjab. Although deposits of coal and salt have been exploited for many years, Pakistan's most important mineral resources are the natural gas fields in Baluchistan.

The present constitution was promulgated in 1972–73 and provides for a bicameral legislature of a National Assembly and Senate. The prime minister and his Cabinet are normally answerable to the legislature, but martial law was imposed in 1977 and the constitution has since been held in abeyance. The country is officially a Federal Democratic Islamic Republic. Urdu is the national language.

History. The Islamic state of Pakistan was created, on Indian independence in 1947, out of the North-West Frontier Region, the north-western region of Punjab, Baluchistan and Sind, and the eastern region of East Bengal. The creation of Pakistan was the occasion for massacres of both Muslims and Hindus as they fled to the appropriate states. Mohammed Ali Jinnah became the first governor-general of Pakistan. In 1956 a new constitution declared Pakistan an Islamic republic. In 1958 the President abolished all political parties and declared martial law; Ayub Khan was first the martial law administrator and then assumed the presidency. In 1969 he resigned and was succeeded by the army commander-in-chief, Yahya Khan. In the 1970 general election Shaikh Mujibur Rahman's Awami League won the majority of the East Pakistan seats in the National Assembly; Zulfikar Ali Bhutto's Pakistan People's party won a clear majority in the West. Mujib's demand for total autonomy for the East led Yahya to suspend the constitution in 1971. West Pakistan troops invaded the East and Mujib was arrested. The subsequent defeat of Pakistan by Indian forces led to the creation of Bangladesh in 1972. The precedent set by Bangladesh led to a new danger of breakaway movements from other states. In 1973 a guerrilla war began in Baluchistan, and there was unrest in the North-West Frontier Province. By 1975 guerrilla activities had spread to Sind and the Punjab. In 1977 after a general election and civil disorder the army seized power, with General Zia ul Haq in control. Martial law was imposed and political and trade union activity banned. Ex-prime minister Bhutto was hanged. In 1981 the President created an advisory Federal Council to assist his Cabinet.

Paladin, name given to the 12 peers of Charlemagne, such as Roland, and also to knights-errant generally. The word 'paladin' is derived from the Latin *palatinus*, and literally denotes a courtier, member of a royal household, or a person connected with a palace.

Palaeobotany, the study of fossil plants and trees.

Palaeocene, see TERTIARY SYSTEM.

Palaeoclimate, or the climate of the geological past. Climatic factors such as wind direction, rainfall, atmospheric and sea-water temperatures may be deduced from a careful examination of certain sedimentary rocks and the fossils contained within them.

Palaeoecology, the study of the ecology of fossil forms of life. Fossils were once animals and plants and their distribution and development in past times were governed by the same environmental factors, for example, temperature, humidity, climate, soil type, intensity of solar radiation, food variety and availability, salinity and depth of water, and interaction with other individuals of the same species and with other plants and animals, which control the ecology of present-day living organisms.

Palaeogeography, the reconstruction of the geographical distribution of land and sea at some time in the geological past. The reconstruction is based on evidence seen in sedimentary rocks.

Palaeography (Greek *palaios*, old; *graphe*, writing), the study of old modes of writing. When dealing with any piece of writing, the palaeographer has two main tasks; firstly to decipher and read it, and secondly to date and place it by comparing its script with other examples. The palaeographical study of its external features is essential for the elucidation of its internal contents. Palaeography is therefore an indispensable aid to all historical and literary disciplines based on written records.

In the widest sense of the word, palaeography deals with all written documents or engraved monuments, in any language, on any writing material, from any period. However, it is more usually concerned with the narrower field of manuscripts, that is, writings on flexible materials such as papyrus, parchment or paper.

The subject of palaeography divides naturally according to the various alphabets and languages; Greek, Latin (also employed for the Western vernacular languages), Hebrew, Arabic, and so on. Two classes of writing can generally be distinguished; 'cursive' or 'current' scripts, basically the fast, ordinary handwriting employed for everyday purposes and for documents; and 'book' scripts, the slow, careful hands in which works of literature were usually written before the invention of printing. But this distinction of the two classes by the intended purpose does not always hold good. There are any number of gradations between cursive and formal scripts, in hands which show characteristics of both groups.

Palaeolithic, see STONE AGE.

Palaeomagnetism is the magnetism preserved in rocks containing iron minerals such as magnetite and haematite. When sedimentary rocks containing these minerals are deposited, or iron-bearing igneous rocks crystallise, the iron minerals orientate themselves parallel to the Earth's magnetic field at that time. By measuring this original (or residual) magnetism it is possible to determine the palaeolatitude at which the rock formed and the position of the Earth's magnetic poles at that time. Determinations carried out at successive horizons in a sequence of rocks show that the apparent position of the poles has varied considerably in the geological past, and this is one of the major pieces of evidence supporting plate tectonics. Reversals of the Earth's magnetic field have occurred many times and at irregular intervals in the past. Radiometric dating combined with palaeomagnetic measurement of lava flows had established a world-wide sequence of reversals for the last four million years. This palaeomagnetic reversal sequence is also seen in the basalts of the ocean floors, and was the key to the theory of sea-floor spreading.

Palaeontology is concerned with the study of the past life of the Earth, how it lived and died, how it evolved through geological time, the environments in which it lived, and the interaction between life and the environment. The materials available for study are fossils, the preserved remains of organisms or traces of their activities. There are, however, limitations imposed by preservation on how much information can be retrieved about past life because, except in exceptional circumstances, only the parts of organisms which are most resistant to decomposition are likely to be preserved as fossils. In practice this usually means a mineralised shell or skeleton, and by far the great majority of fossils are of such 'hard parts'. A consequence of this is that fossils are extremely rare in Pre-Cambrian rocks, because these were deposited before organisms began to develop mineralised shells or skeletons some 600 million years ago.

Since palaeontology deals with once-living organisms it is closely related to biology, and there are many problems and methods in common. For example the same system of classification, employing Linnaean nomenclature, is used. Similarly it is possible to divide palaeontology into palaeozoology (concerned with past animal life) and palaeobotany (concerned with past plant life), and to distinguish micropalaeontology (which deals with microscopic fossils, both plants and animals) from macropalaeontology (vertebrate and invertebrate).

There are also important differences between palaeontology and biology. Not least is the kind of information available. Palaeontologists have available for study only some of the morphological features of an organism, and from this have to attempt reconstruction of the complete organism—what it looked like and how it functioned and the kind of environment it lived in (palaeoecology). These are usually directly observable in living organisms, but must be among the main aims of palaeontology. Palaeontology also has to deal with the evolution of organisms through a long span of geological time, unlike biology which is concerned with only the present and comparatively recent past.

There are also some strictly non-biological aspects of palaeontology, for example in establishing age relations and correlation of rocks (biostratigraphy). Finally, study of the distribution of fossils (palaeobiogeography) may give information about the geography of the past—the relative positions of the continents, and of climatic belts.

See also FOSSIL.

Palaeozoic, subdivision of geological time between the Pre-Cambrian and the Mesozoic eras, from 597 to 235 million years ago. It includes the Cambrian, Ordovician and Silurian Systems, forming the Lower Palaeozoic, and the Devonian, Carboniferous and Permian Systems which form the Upper Palaeozoic. The Palaeozoic era is marked by the first appearance of fossils in any profusion, and the Lower Palaeozoic is characterised by invertebrate faunas of trilobites, graptolites and brachiopods. The graptolites and trilobites die out in the Upper Palaeozoic, while corals and crinoids become more abundant. Fish first appear in the Ordovician, and become abundant in the Devonian. The first land plants also appeared in Devonian times. Amphibia and reptiles developed in the Carboniferous.

There were two major orogenic periods in the Palaeozoic: the Caledonian orogeny occurred in the Lower Palaeozoic and the Hercynean or Variscan orogeny in the late Upper Palaeozoic.

Palaiopaphos, see PAPHOS.

Palamas, Kostes (1859–1943), Greek author. From 1886 he published many volumes of poetry, notably *Life Immovable*, 1904, *The Twelve Lays of the Gipsy*, 1907, and *The King's Flute*, 1910, as well as criticism and short stories.

A master of prose and verse, he opposed the prevailing Romanticism and assimilated the influence of the Parnassians and Symbolists. Fiercely opposed to what he saw as the stifling effects of the 19th-century archaistic outlook, he became recognised as the leader in Athens of the 'demotic movement'.

Palanquin, type of litter used in the East for carrying one person; the most common form was a closed box. Poles were passed through rings, and the palanquin was carried by two or four men.

Palate, the roof of the mouth. It is composed of the *hard* palate, a bony structure covered with mucous membrane, and the *soft* palate, a muscular flap attached to the posterior edge of the hard palate. A soft projection, the *uvula*, hangs downwards at the rear of the oral cavity. The nasal and oral parts of the pharynx communicate behind the soft palate.

See also CLEFT LIP AND PALATE; TONSIL.

Palatinate, former territory of Germany, originally consisting of a district on the Rhine around Heidelberg. This district was united, in 1329, with a portion of Upper Bavaria later known as the Upper Palatinate. In the 16th century Heidelberg, the capital of the electors palatine, became a great centre of Calvinism. But Frederick V, having failed in his attempt to become king of Bohemia, lost his lands and the electoral title passed to his Bavarian cousins. In 1648 the Lower Palatinate was given back to his son, Charles Louis, and a new, or eighth, electorate was created in his favour. During the War of the Spanish Succession John William, the Elector of the Lower Palatinate, received the Upper Palatinate also, but the latter was restored to the Elector of Bavaria at the end of the war. On the death of the Elector Maximilian Joseph, the last of the Bavarian male line, in 1777, the two Palatinates were reunited. In 1801 the portions of the Rhine Palatinate on the left bank of the river were taken by France, Baden received Heidelberg and Mannheim, and the rest fell to Hesse-Darmstadt. Later the diminished Lower Palatinate formed a district of Bavaria, with Speyer as the capital. The Upper Palatinate formed a district of Bavaria under the title of Upper Palatinate and Regensburg, with Regensburg as the capital. Lower Palatinate is now part of the *Land* of Rhineland-Palatinate and Upper Palatinate of the *Land of* Bavaria.

Palatine (Latin *palatium*, a palace). A count palatine was, under the Merovingian kings of France, a high judicial officer. After the time of Charlemagne a similar title was given to any powerful feudal lord to whom a province was made over with judicial powers, and the district so governed was called a palatinate or county palatine.

Palau Islands, or Belau Islands, group of the west Caroline Islands, in the West Pacific Ocean. Latitude 2°–9° N; longitude 130°–135° E. There are 26 islands, of which six are inhabited. The total area is about 429 km². The group is surrounded by a coral reef. The islands are mountainous, well watered and fertile. In 1919 the Treaty of Versailles placed them under Japanese mandate. After forming a major Japanese base during the Second World War, the Palau Islands became part of the US Trust Territory of the Pacific in 1947. Population (1980) 12,177.

Palawan, most south-westerly island province of the Philippines. It has a mountainous backbone with peaks rising to 2085 m and a narrow coastal plain. It has the lowest population density of all the provinces as most of the island is forested, and it is also the most remote. Rice, corn, beans and sweet potatoes are grown, and commercial fishing is important. Minerals include manganese, guano, chromite and mercury. Area: island 11,785 km²; province 14,895 km². Population (1970) for the province was 232,322.

Pale, The, or The English Pale, name applied to that part of Ireland in which English law was acknowledged. The dominion of England was for some centuries after the conquest of Ireland by Henry II restricted to the Pale, the boundaries of which varied, but which included Kildare, Louth, Meath and Dublin. The Pale as an entity disappeared when Ireland was completely occupied in Elizabethan times.

See also Ireland, *History*.

Palembang, city in south-east Sumatra, Indonesia, 72 km from the mouth of the Musi river. With an oil-rich hinterland, Palembang is one of Indonesia's major oil ports and the site of its biggest refinery and petrochemical complex (at Plaju) and fertiliser plant (Pusri). Although mainly oil-based, Palembang's manufacturing includes rubber factories, iron foundries and shipyards. Population (1975) 699,000.

Palencia, capital of the province of Palencia, Spain, on the River Carrión. The first university in Spain was founded here in 1208, but was transferred to Salamanca in the same century. Rolling-stock, agricultural machinery, textiles, pottery, and soap are manufactured, and there is a bell-foundry. Population (1981) 74,080.

Palermo (ancient *Panormus*), Italian seaport and capital of Palermo province and Sicily itself. It is on the northern coastal plain of the Conca d'Oro, on a bay of the Tyrrhenian Sea. Of Phoenician origin, Palermo became the chief town of Sicily under the Arabs (831–1072) and has continued ever since then in that position. The Norman-Byzantine legacy (11th–13th centuries) includes numerous churches; the magnificent Gothic cathedral containing the tomb of Frederick II; and the Palazzo dei Normanni including the Palatine Chapel with its mosaics. Population (1979) 693,949.

History of Palestine. *A propaganda poster showing the Dome of the Rock mosque in Jerusalem, Islam's third most holy place, in Palestinian guise.*

Palestine, History of. Palestine is an historic region of the Middle East, now partially bounded by Syria and Lebanon to the north, Jordan to the east, Sinai to the south, and the Mediterranean to the west. Under Arab rule Palestine was counted part of Syria. One of the Caliphs, Abdul Malik (685–705), tried to make Jerusalem a Holy City to rival Mecca and Medina, and built for it the Dome of the Rock. Jerusalem was captured by the Crusaders in 1099 but when the last Crusaders left Palestine, late in the 13th century, it fell under the sovereignty of the Mameluke Sultans of Egypt. This lasted until the Ottoman Conquest of 1517.

From the time of the Crusades the Jews had been persecuted by successive regimes and had fallen into a minority. By the mid-19th century the thoughts of Jews had been turning increasingly to Palestine, prompted by pogroms in Russia and Romania. Early immigrants settled in self-governing agricultural colonies and Tel Aviv was founded in 1909 as the first all-Jewish city of modern times. By 1914 Jews in Palestine numbered 100,000 but they suffered greatly during the First World War, being sympathetic to the Allied cause. In 1918 Palestine was captured by a British force assisted by a Jewish Brigade. Meanwhile the Zionist movement had been pressing the claims of Jewry to a national home in Palestine. To this the British government had given its blessing in the Balfour Declaration of 1917. The Amir Feisal agreed to Zionist claims, provided his own demands elsewhere were met. They were not, and any hope of peaceful agreement between Arab and Zionist concerning the future of Palestine disappeared. After the Second World War Britain's proposal of partition was rejected by both Jews and Arabs and the question was referred to the United Nations, who voted for partition. Britain refused to implement the resolution, which it believed was doomed to failure and withdrew its mandate on 15 May 1948, the day following the proclamation of the state of Israel. The status of many Palestinian Arabs has changed from that of being indigenous inhabitants to that of refugees, living in camps which provide a breeding ground for the Palestine Liberation Organisation. Since the Arab-Israeli wars the Palestinians' rôle has become increasingly a key political factor in a settlement.

See also Israel, State of.

Palestine Liberation Organisation (PLO), the umbrella organisation for political and military groups of Palestinians. It contains organisations which range from the large and comparatively moderate el-Fatah to the leftist Popular Front for the Liberation of Palestine. The PLO was formed in 1964 and Yasser Arafat became chairman in 1969.

Palestrina, Giovanni Pierluigi da (1525–1594), Italian composer. In 1551 he became *maestro di cappella* of the Julian Choir at St Peter's, Rome and in 1555 held a similar post at S. Giovanni in Laterano. He had by this time established himself as a composer and dedicated the *Missa Papae Marcelli* to Pope Marcellus II. He became *maestro* at S. Maria Maggiore in 1561 and director of the Roman Seminary in 1565. Palestrina composed nearly 100 masses and about 300 motets, other church music and madrigals. Palestrina's sacred polyphonic music represents the finest achievements of the period.

Palette, see Oil-Colour.

Palgrave, Francis Turner (1824–97), English poet and anthologist. He was the author of several volumes of poetry and essays, but is best remembered for his anthology, *The Golden Treasury of Songs and Lyrics*, 1861.

Pāli, the traditional and scriptural language of Theravāda Buddhism; also used in reference to the canonical literature itself—hence the *Theravāda Canon* is alternatively known as the Pāli Canon.

Pāli is specifically a Buddhist language. Apart from a few grammatical works, practically everything written in Pāli relates to Buddhism. It continues to be preserved in the *Theravāda* Buddhist countries (Sri Lanka and parts of South-East Asia).

Palimpsest (Greek *palimpsēstos*, scraped again), a piece of parchment or other material from which, as an economy measure, the first text has been scraped or washed away to be replaced by a second. There are references to palimpsests in ancient literature (in Plutarch, *Moralia*) and palimpsest papyri have survived. The recycling process was

used throughout the period of the manuscript book (until the end of the 15th century) but especially in the 7th to 9th centuries.
See also BOOK; MANUSCRIPTS.

Palindrome (Greek, running backwards), sentence, phrase or word reading the same from either end, for example *Roma tibi subito motibus ibit amor*; Napoleon's alleged reply when asked if he could have invaded England, 'Able was I ere I saw Elba'; and 'Dog a devil deified, deified lived a god'.

Palissy, Bernard (c.1510–c.1590), French potter and enameller. In 1548 the Constable de Montmorency ordered several works from Palissy. During the next 15 years Palissy succeeded in producing that distinctive ware called by his name, earthenware moulded in high relief with life-like water creatures, shells, fishes, lizards, leaves and other natural objects, and covered with coloured lead-glazes of wonderful harmonies. Although saved from the Massacre of St Bartholomew's Day by Catherine de Médicis, with the renewed persecution in 1586, Palissy was imprisoned in the Bastille, where he died about four years later. Anatole France published his *Oeuvres complètes*, 1880.

Palk's Strait, gulf and channel of the Indian Ocean, between India and Sri Lanka, north of the shoals called Adam's Bridge. The Dutch named it after Governor Palk. At the narrowest part it measures 64 km across.

Pall, stiffened square of linen used to cover the Eucharistic chalice. The name also refers to the rich cloth used to cover a coffin while it stands in the church.

Palladio, Andrea (1508–80). He was one of the greatest Italian architects of the late Renaissance, and the style which he used has received the name Palladian. It was an attempt to revive the severity and dignity of Roman architecture, and was derived from Vitruvius and from a study of the Roman monuments that remained. Its earliest exponent in England was Inigo Jones. Palladio greatly influenced the architecture of his day by his work, *I quattro libri dell' Architettura*, 1570, which was immediately translated into most European languages. His chief buildings were the Palazzo della Ragione, Vicenza (commissioned 1545); numerous private palaces at Vicenza; many villas in the neighbourhood; and the churches of S. Giorgio (begun 1566) and Il Redentore (begun 1576) at Venice.
See also ITALIAN ARCHITECTURE; VILLA.

Palladium, metallic chemical element, symbol Pd, atomic number 46, atomic weight 106·4; one of the 'platinum metals' found in the platinum ore which occurs in small grains and rare nuggets in alluvial deposits and river and sand principally in Brazil, California, and the Urals. It is a lustrous white metal (melting point 1549°C and relative density 11·8) which is not acted on by air at ordinary temperatures. Palladium forms the exception in the platinum group of metals by dissolving in hot nitric acid. Palladium shows oxidation states 0, 1, 2, 3 and 4 in its compounds. The metal has the special property of absorbing large volumes of hydrogen to form an interstitial hydride. Palladium is used in dentistry, jewellery and scientific instruments.

Palladium, image of Pallas Athena, particularly the legendary image preserved at Troy and upon whose safety depended the city's survival. It was said to have fallen from heaven as a gift from Zeus to the founder of Ilion, and to have been stolen by Odysseus and Diomedes, the second of whom carried it to Greece. According to another account Troy had two palladia, one brought by Aeneas to Italy.

Pallas, in astronomy, the second minor planet to be discovered. It was found by Olbers in 1802. The orbital period is 4·61 years and its mean distance from the Sun 2·77 astronomical units.

Pallas, appellation of the Greek goddess Athena, possibly meaning virgin.

Pallium, narrow circular strip of cloth, with two pendants which hang down, one over the breast, the other at the back, worn by the pope and by archbishops. The pallium symbolises the supreme pastoral power.

Palm (tree), see PALMAE.

Palm Beach, town in Florida, USA. The original Palm Beach was an island section of the sand bars which line the east coast of Florida. With the growth of tourism along this coast, resort development has occurred almost continuously along the shore from Palm Beach to Miami, 100 km to the south.

Palm Fruit, the fruit of numerous varieties of the oil palm *Elaeis guineensis*, native to the tropical regions of West Africa, but also cultivated in plantations on a wide scale in Indonesia and Malaysia.
Palm fruit produces two different varieties of oil, palm oil from the mesocarp and palm-kernel oil from the seed kernel. The mesocarp and palm kernel each contain up to 50 per cent of oil. After the oil has been expressed the oilcake is used to feed cattle.

Palm-kernel Oil, obtained from the hard kernel of the oil-palm fruit, is similar in almost every respect to palm oil. Refined palm-kernel oil, which sets to a white fat when cooled below 26°C, is used in margarine manufacture or is 'hardened' by hydrogenation for use in confectionery, chocolate, synthetic cream and ice cream. The expelled cake and solvent-extracted meal are used in animal compound feeding stuffs.
See also PALM FRUIT.

Palm Oil, obtained largely from west and central Africa, and from Malaysia, is also produced in North and South America. The oil is prepared from the fruits of such trees as *Elaeis guineensis*. Palm oil is used in the manufacture of soaps, candles, lubricants, and in the iron- and tin-plate industries.

Palm Sunday, last Sunday in Lent, the Sunday before Easter, obtains its name from the palm branches spread on the road before Jesus' entry into Jerusalem (Matt. xxi).

Palma, capital of the Balearic Islands, Spain, standing on a wide bay of the south-west coast of Majorca. It has a very fine Gothic cathedral, begun in 1230, and near to it the *Almudaina*, a former royal palace, which dates from the 14th century. Palma has a busy harbour, a trade in grain, wine, silk and fruits, and manufactures of glass, textiles, shoes and liqueurs. It is a popular tourist resort. Population (1981) 304,422.

Palma Giovane, 'The Younger', Jacopo, or Giacomo (c.1544–1628), Italian painter. He was the grand-nephew of Palma Vecchio. He emulated the style of Titian, Tintoretto and Paolo Veronese, and studied the Antique at Rome (1559–67). He completed Titian's *Entombment* after his death. The architect A. Vittorio became his patron and he worked on the redecoration of the Doge's Palace after the fires of 1574 and 1577.

Palma Vecchio, 'The Elder', Jacopo, or Giacomo d'Antonio de Negreti (c.1480–1528), Italian painter of the Venetian school. He studied under Bellini and came under the lasting influence of Giorgione and Titian. Among his best works are *Santa Barbara* (Venice); *A Holy Conversation* (Naples and Leningrad); *St Jerome, The Virgin Enthroned* (Vicenza); *Adoration of the Magi* and various portraits, including the *Portrait of a Poet*, and *Flora* (National Gallery, London).

Palmae, a family of about 200 genera and 1500 species of woody monocotyledonous plants, most being called palms, some rattans. They are mainly tropical and subtropical. Except in the doum palm, *Hyphaene*, of North Africa, the stem is unbranched. In some palms, such as *Nipa*, the stem is very short and all leaves arise from ground level; in others there is a strong trunk which may grow as tall as 50 m, the leaves being usually confined to a crown at the top of the trunk.
The individual flowers are generally relatively small, but are often borne in huge sprays or catkin-like groups. The fruits range from small berries and nuts to the gigantic coco de mer, *Lodoicea*, which weighs several kilograms.
Palmae is a family of great economic importance. Fibres from the coconut palm, *Cocos nucifera*, have world-wide use for ropes and matting; and the epidermis peeled from the leaflets of *Raphia pedunculata* yields raffia. Sugar is obtained from the wounded stems of *Arenga*, and the stems of other genera give sago. The date is from *Phoenix dactylifera*, and the seed of the coconut yields coconut oil. The betel nut is obtained from *Areca catechu*. Palm oil comes from the fruit of *Elaeis*.

Palmas, Las, see LAS PALMAS.

Palmer, Arnold (1929–), US golf champion, and one of the world's best-known and most popular players, he was the first to become a millionaire through his overall success at the game. Turning professional in 1955, his immediate winning of the Canadian Open was the first of an extraordinary list of victories which included four US Masters titles as well as the Open championships of the US and Britain.

Palmer, Samuel (1805–51), British landscape painter and etcher. As early as 1819 he showed three pictures at the Royal Academy, a remarkable record for a boy of 14. He and other worshippers of Blake formed a group at Shoreham, Kent, called 'the Ancients', between 1826 and 1835, and in this period Palmer excelled, mainly in sepia and water-colour, at landscapes charged with symbolism, e.g. *The Bright Cloud*, 1829 (Tate Gallery).

Palmerston, Henry John Temple, 3rd Viscount (1784–1865), British statesman. He succeeded in 1802 to the Irish peerage, and five years later entered the House of Commons. Within 12 months he became lord of the Admiralty under the Duke of Portland, and in 1809 accepted the secretaryship of war, which, under various prime ministers, he held until 1828. He became foreign minister under Grey in 1830, and remained in that office (except during Peel's brief administration) until 1841. In Opposition until 1846, in that year he became foreign secretary under Lord John Russell. When in 1851 he expressed his approval of Napoleon III's coup d'état, without having consulted the queen or his colleagues, he was dismissed from office.

Palmerston became home secretary under Aberdeen in 1852, and strongly advocated a firm attitude against Russia. The Crimean War broke out in 1854, mismanagement was rampant, and Aberdeen resigned in the following year. By general consent Palmerston became prime minister, and his vigorous action soon brought about a more satisfactory condition of affairs. He was defeated in 1857 on the China War question, whereupon he dissolved Parliament and appealed to the nation, and was promptly returned to power. He was defeated again the following year on the Conspiracy to Murder Bill. In the meantime, however, he had suppressed the Indian Mutiny, 1857–58. In 1859 he again formed a government, and so strongly was he supported that it was said that he was 'prime minister for life', his following being almost entirely personal.

Palmerston was to many of his contemporaries the ideal British minister, firm, tactful, humorous, and blessed with great common sense that enabled him to extricate the country and himself from awkward situations. He was the most popular prime minister of the day. Home affairs, however, never really interested him, and for the last 30 years of his life his views on most domestic subjects were far more conservative than those of the majority of his party.

Palmerston North, town of North Island, New Zealand, 140 km north of Wellington. The centre of a thriving dairy and sheep-raising country, it was proclaimed a city in 1930. Massey University is situated here. Population (1980) 90,400.

Palmetto Leaves, leaves of *Sabal palmetta*, a fan-palm, native of Central America, which are used in making hats and mats.

Palmistry, or cheiromancy (Greek *cheir*, a hand; *mantikē*, divination or prophecy), the art of reading a person's character and potential destiny from the general contours of his or her hand, and, in particular, from the lines upon the palm.

The chief lines are those of heart, head and life, but all small markings, crosses, etc. must be taken into account, the rules upon which an adequate judgment is based being extremely complex.

Palmitic Acid, or hexadecanoic acid, $C_{15}H_{31}COOH$, most important and most abundant of the saturated fatty acids, found widely distributed as mixed glycerides in animal, vegetable and marine fats and oils. It is a major constituent of lard, tallow, palm oil and cocoa butter, and is a tasteless, odourless and hard crystalline substance, melting to a colourless liquid at 63°C.

Palmyra, Roman name for an ancient city called Tadmor which existed at least as early as the 2nd millennium BC. It stood in an oasis of the Syrian desert, 240 km north-east of Damascus; its position on important trade-routes brought it great wealth. Palmyra recognised the suzerainty of Rome not later than AD 15, but remained self-governing. The years 130–270 were those of its greatest prosperity. Remains include a huge temple of Bel, walls, a theatre, and a colonnaded street with triumphal arch.

Palolo Worm, certain polychaete worms that show swarming epitokous behaviour. This is a reproductive phenomenon which has evolved to ensure the fertilisation of eggs by sperm when they are released externally. The normal worm, at a certain time, converts into the sexual form, or epitoke, by transformation or budding. Gametes (sex cells) form and at specific periods in the lunar cycle these epitokes swarm on the surface, releasing eggs and sperm simultaneously.

Samuel Palmer. The Bellman, *painted between 1863 and 1866, portrays a timeless rural setting.*

Palomar, Mount, Observatory, see HALE OBSERVATORIES.

Palpitations, abnormal awareness of rapid or irregular beating of the heart. The condition may be caused by anxiety, overexertion, excitement, or excessive use of alcohol, tobacco or stimulants such as coffee and tea. Rarely, it may be due to heart disease. Except in the latter case, it is not serious and no treatment is required other than moderation in the use of alcohol and tobacco, and reassurance.

Palsy, see PARALYSIS.

Paludan-Müller, Frederik (1809–76), Danish poet. His successful *Dandserinden*, which shows traces of Byron's influence, appeared in 1833. The 'lyrical drama' *Amor and Psyche* was published in 1834.

During 1841 to 1848 he was busy with his greatest work, *Adam Homo*, which has become a Danish classic. This satirical look at his own society was followed by several graceful idylls, including *Tithon*, 1844, and *The Death of Abel*, 1845, and finally the beautiful poem *Adonis*, 1874.

Palynology, the science of pollen analysis. Besides its use in honey and hay fever investigations, the analysis of fossil spores and pollen is important in palaeobotany. Pollen grains extracted from Quaternary peats, Tertiary brown coals, and other deposits can not only be used as index fossils enabling regional correlations to be made, but also allow the composition and migration of ancient forests, and fluctuations in past climates, to be worked out.

Pamirs, mountainous region forming the nucleus of the central Asiatic highland system located chiefly in the Gorno–Badakhshan Autonomous Oblast of the Tadzhik SSR, USSR, but also extending into Afghanistan and China (Sinkiang-Uighur province). It connects the highlands of the Hindu Kush and Karakoram with those of the Tien Shan and Kunlun, and is often termed the 'Roof of the World'. On three sides the plateau is bordered by high mountains. The length of the Pamirs proper (within the USSR) is about 275 km, and about 250 km wide.

The chief peaks in the north are Communism Peak and Lenin Peak, and in the east Kongur (7579 m) and Muztagh Ata (7555 m).

Pampas (Spanish *pampa*, Quechua *bamba*, plain), wide treeless plains found in Argentina, stretching from the Río Colorado north to the Gran Chaco, and from the foothills of the Andes east to the Paraná and the Atlantic coast. They rise gradually from the coast, and the eastern portion is covered with grasslands and supports large herds of cattle, sheep and horses, whilst the west is more sterile. The characteristic vegetation is the 'pampas' grass which grows to a height of 2–3 m. Area about 650,000 km². The name pampas is also applied to other similar plains on the Atlantic coast.

Pampas Grass, a genus of beautiful South American perennial grasses. *Cortaderia selloana* is the best known in gardens. The large, upright, plume-like white or silvery panicles of flowers appear in September and October.

Pampero, see WIND.

Pamphlet, in a general sense, signifies a

small treatise occupying fewer pages than a book, on some subject of current or temporary importance. The question may be of a social, personal, political or ecclesiastical nature, controversial or otherwise, in which the writer tries to appeal to the public.

An immense impetus was given to pamphlet-writing by the Marprelate controversy in 1589, as instanced by the writings of Nashe, Thomas Cooper, the Harveys, and others. Robert Greene likewise caused diversion by his social pamphlets exposing the roguery of Elizabethan London, the most famous being *A Notable Discovery of Coosnage*, 1591, and *A Defence of Coney-Catching*, 1592.

Political pamphlets were to multiply quickly during the Caroline reigns, particularly during the Civil War period when leading Puritans, including Milton, contended in argument. It was at this time that the pamphlet established itself as an organ of radical debate. The proliferation culminated in Queen Anne's time in what Dr Johnson designated the age of pamphlets, enlisting such able writers as Addison, Steele and Swift. The pamphlet was also a powerful weapon and influence later in the 18th century, in the revolutionary movements of France and America. Thomas Paine was one of the most successful of pamphlet writers, and his *Rights of Man* is perhaps most famous.

Pamplona (Basque *Iruna*), capital of the province of Navarra, Spain, on a hill by the Arga. It was formerly capital of the kingdom of Navarre. There is a beautiful Gothic cathedral with an 18th-century façade, other old churches, fine old houses, and remains of the medieval walls, as well as a modern university. It is famous for its annual eight-day St Fermin festival when bulls are run through the streets with men and boys skilfully dodging them in front. Population (1981) 183,126.

Pan, Greek divinity, guardian of flocks and herds; usually called a son of Hermes, he was supposed to wander through the mountains and valleys of Arcadia either in the chase or leading a dance of nymphs to the accompaniment of the *syrinx* (pipes of Pan), which he invented. His sudden appearance was dreaded by travellers, whence 'panic'. The Greek word *pan* means 'all', and Pan also came to be regarded as the personification of Nature, the existing order of things.

Pan-American Highway, planned in 1924 to connect North America with the Central and South American republics and when complete will run for about 16,150 miles (25,000 km). Funds are being supplemented by US and World Bank assistance.

Pan-American Union. In 1890 an International Union of American Republics was convened to organise the publication of comprehensive commercial data in the four languages of Britain, Spain, Portugal and France. From this beginning there grew the Pan-American Union in 1911 at a congress in Buenos Aires. The stated objects of the union are to develop inter-republic commercial and diplomatic relations and to organise co-operation in such matters as communications and customs.

The ninth international conference of American states, held in 1948, adopted a charter for the setting up of the Organisation of American States. Membership comprises the 21 American republics on a basis of equality. The permanent and central organ of the Organisation, housed in Washington, is the Pan-American Union, which acts as a permanent secretariat and clearing-house.

Pan-Americanism, movement intended to bring the American republics into closer association for the promotion of trade, cultural interests, peace and security.

Pan-Arab Movement, the movement for an Arab union or federation. Because of geographical, historical, ethnic and cultural differences, this has remained more of an aspiration than a fact. The closest the Arab world has come to union has tended to be under the force of arms.

There have been a number of unsuccessful attempts at political union, notably the United Arab Republic (1958–61), comprising Egypt, Syria and Yemen; between Jordan and Iraq in 1958; and Libya with Egypt in the year after 1971, and with Tunisia in 1974. Since 1971 a loose grouping, the Federation of Arab Republics of Egypt, Syria and Libya, has been in existence.

Pan-Slavism, movement for the union in policy and culture of all the Slav races, in which Russia has taken the lead as the great political representative of these races. The movement began about 1830, and the spread of the national spirit in Europe considerably strengthened it. A congress was held at Prague in 1848, to which most of the Slav races sent representatives. In the 1860s Russia used Pan-Slavism as an instrument of tsarist imperialism, for strengthening the Russian hold on Poland and the Ukraine, and for furthering Russian aspirations in the Balkans in the Austrian Empire.

Following the Second World War Russian foreign policy was concentrated on a deepening *cordon sanitaire* of sovietised states on its western border as a counterpoise to the 'Western democratic bloc'. This was Pan-Slavism used as an instrument of Soviet imperialism.

Panama
Area: 77,082 km²
Population: 1,890,000
Capital: Panama

Panama, country of Central America and co-extensive with the isthmus of Panama running east to west in the shape of an elongated letter S. To the north is the Atlantic (Caribbean Sea) on which Panama has a 752-kilometre coastline, and to the south the Pacific and a 1216-kilometre coastline. Bordered by Colombia in the east and Costa Rica in the west, the country is 772 km long and varies in width from 60 to 170 km, with a total area of 77,082 km^2 excluding the Canal Area of 1453 km^2. The Panama Canal bisecting the country on a north-west to south-east axis dominates the life of the republic.

Panama is a mountainous country with fertile plains and valleys, heavily forested hills and, in parts, dense jungle. Two main mountain ranges form the backbone of the country; in the west the ranges of Chiriquí and Veracruz which enter Panama from Costa Rica and have typical heights of about 1200 m. In the east the San Blas Mountains run along the Atlantic coast to Colombia. The country falls roughly into five main regions: the 8 km wide strip of land on each side of the canal; the sparsely populated Caribbean lowlands; the dense jungle area of Darién in the south-east; the central provinces reaching down to the Pacific; and the highlands in the west.

The population was estimated to be 1·89 million in 1980. The population is very unevenly distributed geographically, with 85 per cent living on the Pacific side of the country and 15 per cent living in the cities of Panama (the capital) and Colón and in the Canal Area.

Panama's economy is unlike most others in Latin America. The country survives by importing several times as many goods as it exports and paying the difference through selling services to the Canal Area. Rice is grown on 80 per cent of the farms and is the staple food of the country. Maize, cocoa, and coffee are also grown for local consumption. The main export crop is bananas. Fishing is quite important to the economy and shrimp and fishmeal are both exported. Forest resources are large and mahogany is especially valuable. The nation is now self-sufficent in beef production. Manufacturing is mainly oriented towards home consumption with the exception of petroleum refining. Panama has no mineral resources to speak of. The unit of currency is the *balboa*.

Government. The present constitution was introduced in 1972. Legislative power is vested in the single-chambered National Assembly, consisting of deputies elected on a community basis. There is a Legislative Council of 54 members. Executive power was vested in the President elected by popular vote for a six-year term. There is a vice-president and a cabinet of ministers. The official language is Spanish.

History. Intervention by the USA helped to secure Panama's independence from Colombia in 1903, and shortly afterwards recognition came from the remaining powers. But it was not until 1914 that Colombia agreed to recognise the independent status of Panama. In 1936 a new treaty permitted the USA, in the event of war, to defend the canal in any way necessary. The US government paid Panama $10 million for the Canal Zone rights, and, from 1913, $250,000 yearly. This was increased by later treaties to $1·9 million. Although in 1965 the US announced that they had agreed to annul the 1903 treaty, movement towards greater Panamanian control of the canal was thwarted by a new phase of political instability after a coup by the National Guard in 1968. At last, in 1979, Panama assumed sovereignty over the Canal Area.

Panama Canal Area, formerly Canal Zone, strip of land some 8 km wide, on both sides of the centre line of the Panama Canal. The area was granted to the USA as the Canal Zone by the treaty of 18 November 1903 with Panama. In the treaty Panama granted to

Panama Canal. *A freighter negotiates a lock on the canal, linking the Atlantic to the Pacific.*

the USA the use in perpetuity of the zone and, within its ambit, the exclusive control for police, judicial, and sanitary purposes. A new treaty, ratified by Panama and the USA in 1978, altered arrangements made under previous treaties. The Area is 1453 km² and of this 426 km² are occupied by Gatun Lake. The USA maintains control over all lands, waters and installations, including military bases, necessary to manage, operate and defend the canal. Panama has general territorial jurisdiction, and uses all other areas in the former Zone. Panamanian law applies, and Panama is responsible for some former duties of the old Canal Company and Canal Zone Government. The population of the Canal Area is about 34,700.

Panama, Gulf of, inlet of the Pacific Ocean, formed by a curve of the isthmus, contains the Pearl Islands with their fisheries. Width 192 km, from Point Caracoles on the east to Point Mala on the west.

Panama, Isthmus of, joins North and South America. Latitude 9°N, longitude 79°30′W; length 768 km, breadth 59–176 km. Its eastern end separates the Gulfs of Panama (Pacific) and Darién (Atlantic).

Panama Canal, designed in 1879 by Ferdinand de Lesseps as a tide-level canal. The estimate of cost was about £24 million, and the work was to be completed in 1888. With less than one-quarter of the work done and £74 million estimated debt, the Panama Canal company was forced into liquidation in 1889. Up to 1902 £60 million had been spent, only £12 million effectively. Work on the canal was finally started by the Americans in 1905, and in 1920 President Wilson declared it formally completed, but traffic had passed through since 1914. The canal cost $366,650,000, exclusive of appropriations for its defence.

It lies between the 8th and 10th northern parallels of latitude and the 79th and 80th western meridians of longitude. It connects the Caribbean Sea with the Pacific Ocean. It runs from north-west to south-east almost at right angles to the axis of the isthmus. In passing through the canal from the Atlantic to the Pacific a vessel goes through a dredged channel at least 90 m wide, 12 m deep at mean low water, and 9·5 km long, leading to the Gatun locks, which raise the vessel from sea-level to Gatun Lake, a rise of 25·5 m. After the lake comes Culebra Cut (now Gaillard Cut), 90 m wide, 13·5 m deep, and 11·2 km long. At the Pacific end of this cut are Pedro Miguel locks, 1·2 km long with a drop of 9·3 m to the level of Miraflores Lake. The ship then enters Miraflores locks, and thus reaches the level of the Pacific Ocean. The average time of passage is 8 hours. The total length of the canal from entrance to entrance is 43·85 nautical miles. The ports of entry for the Canal are Cristóbal on the Atlantic side and Balboa on the Pacific. The maximum traffic capacity of the canal is about 12,000 ships in a year. All ships passing through the canal have to pay tolls except the government ships of the republics of USA, Panama and Colombia. The canal is operated by a US agency, the Panama Canal Commission.

Panama City, capital of the republic of Panama, situated near the Pacific entrance to the Canal, and the country's leading city commercially, politically and culturally. Panama City was founded in 1673 after the old city had been destroyed by the buccaneer Henry Morgan. Much of Panama's industry is in and around the city, and the city is the chief distribution centre handling 75 per cent of all imported goods, nearly half the cattle trade, and nearly all the trade in fruit and vegetables. Population (1980) 467,000.

Panathenaea, annual festival in honour of Athena, held in late summer. Every fourth year it was celebrated with particular splendour and called the greater Panathenaea; the intervening celebrations were known as the lesser Panathenaea.

Panax, a genus of shrubs and trees in family Araliaceae that has ornamental pinnate or digitate leaves, and umbels of cream, green or white flowers. Some species yield the ginseng root.

Panay, island of the Philippines, mountainous in the west and hilly in the east, with a densely populated, intensively farmed central plain region supporting coconuts, citrus fruits, rice, sugar and tobacco. Fish farming is important, coal and copper are mined, and horses raised. It is divided into four administrative provinces. Area 11,515 km². Population (1970) 2,144,544.

Pancreas, a long, narrow, racemose gland composed of two kinds of tissue. In humans the pancreas lies behind the stomach, the larger end lying within the bend of the duodenum, and the narrow end in contact with the spleen. The cells of one kind of tissue are similar to those of the parotid gland and secrete the pancreatic juice containing trypsin, which converts proteins into amino acids such as leucine and tyrosine; amylase, similar to ptyalin, which converts starch into sugar, chiefly maltose, but partly dextrose (glucose); and lipase, which digests fats into fatty acids and glycerol. These digestive juices are poured into the duodenum at the middle bend, entering via a common duct together with the bile for the gall bladder; they are viscid and alkaline, due to the presence of sodium carbonate.

The cells of the second kind of tissue form the islets of Langerhans, and their secretion contains insulin (Latin *insula*, an island), which is important in carbohydrate metabolism. If the pancreas is removed, the amount of sugar in the blood increases, and some is excreted in the urine, as in diabetes mellitus, a disease in which the carbohydrate metabolism is disturbed.

Panda, mammals of two genera of the family Procyonidae, order Carnivora. The cot-bear, red or lesser panda (*Ailurus fulgens*) is a raccoon-like mammal and almost exclusively vegetarian. It is found only at a height of about 3000 m in the Himalayas. Its total length is about 100 cm. The thick fur is rich chestnut or rusty red on the upper part and black on the limbs and under part. The face has white markings, and the long, bushy tail bears a series of indistinct reddish-brown rings. The feet have large semi-retractile claws, and the animal applies nearly the whole of the sole of the foot to the ground when walking.

The giant panda, the familiar black and white zoo animal (*Ailuropoda melanoleuca*), is also allied to the raccoons, but does not resemble them. It is a rare animal principally found in the Szechuan province of China. Little is known about the giant panda in its natural state, beyond the fact that bamboo leaves are its natural food; it is solitary and arboreal.

Pandanus, or screw pine, of the family Pandanaceae. These are tropical plants with long, often spiny, strap-shaped leaves, and prop roots that emerge from the stem above the ground. Some are trees with branched trunks. Flowers occur in separate male and female heads, and the fruits (globular or oblong, up to 30 cm across) are sometimes eaten after cooking. *P. tectorius* is cultivated in South-East Asia for its leaf-fibres. *Pandanus* is a genus of Monocotyledons, not a true pine.

Pandemic, see EPIDEMIC.

Pandora (all gifts), mythological Greek version of Eve. When Prometheus stole fire from heaven, the gods created a woman who should bring misery to men. Epimetheus made her his wife, forgetting the counsel of his brother Prometheus to accept no gift from

Pangolin. *The Chinese pangolin,* Manis pentadactyla.

the gods. Pandora had brought with her a box containing every human woe. Epimetheus opened it and they all escaped, hope alone remaining. A later version makes the box contain every blessing which would have accrued had not Pandora raised the lid.

Panegyric (Greek *pan*, all; *agora*, assembly) originally meant a 'festival speech', such as that in which Isocrates urged the Greeks to unite against Persia. The term then came to mean a public eulogy, such as the earlier funeral oration of Pericles over the Athenians who fell in the first year of the Peloponnesian War. In modern times the term is used for a formal or elaborate eulogy in a public speech or public writing.

Panel Beating, process used in sheet-metal work, to shape the metal for duct work and trunking. Machine fabrication is rapidly taking the place of hand-work, but panel beating by hand is still used to repair the bodywork of motor cars.

Panel Walls fill the spaces between the vertical and horizontal framing members of a structure. They need to possess all the qualities of other types of external walls except that they do not have to carry imposed vertical loads. They may therefore be light in weight, and are generally of sandwich or cavity construction. They must usually also provide a degree of fire, sound and thermal insulation.

Panelling, covering of a surface in a building, such as a door, ceiling or wall, with panels, i.e. sunken or raised compartments, usually framed at the edges. They may be of wood, stone, plaster or man-made materials, e.g. polystyrene. Ceiling plaster panels, often most ornately moulded, were a common form of interior decoration from the 16th to the 19th centuries, while Wren popularised for a time the use of stone and marble panelling, much favoured by Italian Renaissance craftsmen. Wood, too, has been a favourite material for panelling since the late Middle Ages. In modern times, the development of plywood has led to entirely new methods of construction.

Pangaea, continent which existed around 200 million years ago and comprised Gondwanaland and Laurasia.

Pangolin, or scaly ant-eater, seven species of mammal that are placed in their own order, Pholidota. They are found in Africa, India, Sri Lanka, Indonesia, Borneo, China and Taiwan. The body is covered with large, overlapping horny plates except on the muzzle, sides of the head, throat, chest and belly, and varies in length, according to the species, from 30 to 100 cm, exclusive of the prehensile tail, which is about twice as long as the body. The single family, Manidae, may be divided into two groups, distinguished by geographical distribution. In the Asiatic group are three species: *Manis javanica*, *M. pentadactyla* and *M. crassicaudata*. In the African group are the long-tailed pangolin (*M. longicaudata*), the white-bellied pangolin (*M. tricuspis*), the short-tailed pangolin (*M. temminckii*) and the giant pangolin (*M. gigantea*). The two West African species *M. longicaudata* and *M. tricuspis* are arboreal. With its bony overlapping scales, which protect it against carnivorous animals, the pangolin is probably quite safe when it rolls up into a ball. Its natural food consists of ants and termites. The young pangolins are carried about on the mother's tail.

Panicum, a large genus of grasses, the most important of which is *P. miliaceum*, millet.

Panini, Giovanni Paolo, also Pannini (c.1692–1765), Italian painter, noted for architectural paintings of Rome and 'caprices' in which its ancient monuments are freely combined. These were very popular and started a vogue. He was a member of the Academy of St Luke (president 1754–55), and of the French Academy at Rome. His example encouraged Canaletto to make his views of Venice.

Pankhurst, Dame Christabel (1880–1958), British worker for women's suffrage and the daughter of Emmeline Pankhurst.

Emmeline Pankhurst, *a 1927 portrait by Georgina Brackenbury.*

Pankhurst, Emmeline (1858–1928), British feminist leader. In 1879 she married Richard Marsden Pankhurst, a lawyer, and they served together on the committee that promoted the Married Women's Property Act. Widowed in 1898, she formed the Women's Social and Political Union in 1903. From 1906, as a 'militant', she was frequently arrested and in 1913 sentenced to three years' penal servitude in connection with the blowing up of Lloyd George's house at Walton. When the First World War broke out Mrs Pankhurst called off the suffrage campaign and went recruiting in the USA. In 1926 Mrs Pankhurst was adopted as Conservative MP for an East London Constituency but died in 1928, only a month before Stanley Baldwin's Representation of the People Act gave women full equality in the franchise.

Pankhurst, Sylvia Estelle (1882–1960), British suffragette, daughter of Emmeline Pankhurst. She became a pacifist in 1914 and in 1921 was imprisoned for six months for seditious publications.

Panorama, term for a wide view, but having particular reference to long paintings usually on canvas stretched round the inside walls of circular buildings, intended to create the illusion of real scenery seen from a central vantage point (sometimes called a cyclorama). A journey through scenery could be simulated by revolving a canvas round stationary spectators. The first completely circular panorama was shown by Robert Barker (1739–1806) at Leicester Square, London, in 1792. An instant success, it featured 'The English Fleet anchored between Portsmouth and the Isle of Wight' (the rotunda had a height of 5 m and diameter 14 m). Among the painters of later, larger panoramas were Pierre Prevost, Charles M. Bouton and Louis J. M. Daguerre, who later collaborated with Bouton on the diorama. The panorama and the diorama, together with the Eidophusikon of De Loutherbourg, are considered today as the forerunners of motion pictures.

Panpipes, early form of musical instrument, consisting of a series of reeds or pipes of graduated length fastened together, which when blown across produce the notes of the scale. It survives as a folk instrument. One of its rare appearances in classical music is in Mozart's *The Magic Flute*.

Pansy, common name of plants of the subgenus *Melanium*, a part of the botanical genus *Viola*. Pansies are distinguished from violets by having their standard petals directed upwards and leaf-like outgrowths (stipules) at the base of the true leaf stalk. Garden pansies have been selected for bloom size and pattern since the 19th century, and are hybrids, *V.* × *wittrockiana*, probably between *V. tricolor*, heartsease, and a form of *V. lutea*.

Pantagruel, see RABELAIS, FRANÇOIS.

Pantheism (Greek *pan*, all; *theos*, God), a speculative system which identifies the universe with God (and therefore may be called *akosmism*), or, with a less 'religious' emphasis, God with the universe. The latter form of pantheism is open to the accusation of atheism; the former has often been the expression of a profound and mystic religion, e.g. among the Hindus. The antiquity of pantheism is undoubtedly great, but it is a later development of thought than polytheism; it most probably originated in the attempt to divest the popular system of its grosser features, and to give it a form that would satisfy the requirements of philosophical speculation. Greek pantheism doubtless originated in the same way as that of India. The theory of Anaximander may be described as a system of atheistic physics or of materialistic pantheism. Xenophanes was the first classical thinker to formulate a religious pantheism. But the most decided and the most profoundly religious representatives of this philosophy were the 'Alexandrian' Neoplatonists, in whom we see clearly, for the first time, the influence of the East upon

Greek thought. Modern pantheism appears first in Giordano Bruno, burned at Rome for his opinions in 1600. According to him the universe is, properly speaking, not a creation, but only an emanation of the infinite mind. Spinoza's system is based on certain definitions and axioms. After a long, firm-linked chain of reasoning, he concludes that there is but one substance, infinite, self-existent, eternal, necessary, simple and indivisible, of which all elements are but modes. This substance is the self-existent God. In Germany, Fichte, Schelling and Hegel all promulgated systems of a thoroughly pantheistic and ideal character.

Pantheon, temple in the Campus Martius at Rome, now the church of S. Maria della Rotunda. It was built, and most probably designed, by the emperor Hadrian (AD 117–138) on the site of an earlier temple. The name derives from a much later tradition that it was a temple 'of all the gods' (Greek *pantōn tōn theōn*). The Pantheon is a circular building, the largest of its kind in antiquity. The name is also applied to a famous church in Paris designed by Soufflot in 1755.

Panther, see LEOPARD; PUMA.

Panticapaeum, see KERCH.

Pantomime, among the ancient Romans, denoted not a spectacle but a person. The pantomimes (*pantomimi*) were a class of actors who acted their parts only in dumb show. Modern pantomime denotes not the performer but the piece performed, the character of which is, strictly speaking, that of a harlequinade. The Christmas pantomime or harlequinade, now an essentially British entertainment, derives from the performances of the commedia dell'arte. It is a swift-moving entertainment, part revue and part music-hall or variety performance.

Paolo di Dono, see UCCELLO, PAOLO.

Paolo Veronese, see VERONESE, PAUL.

Paotow, see BAOTOU.

Papacy, the office of Pope. In Roman Catholic theology the pope (Latin *papa*, in origin a term of affectionate respect) succeeds St Peter not only as Bishop of Rome, where he ministered and died, but in the commission to rule and guide the Church committed to Peter by Jesus (Matt. xvi. 18–19; John xxi. 17).

Since Vatican II it has been emphasised that the Pope should exercise his power in conjunction with the collegiate authority of the episcopate, and in an ecumenical spirit befitting his title.

Papadiamandopulos, Ioannis, see MOREÁS, JEAN.

Papadopoulos, George (1919–), head of the Greek government from 1967 to 1973. In 1967 Papadopoulos, then a colonel in the Greek army, with two other officers, seized control of the government. Although King Constantine remained titular head of state, his power was greatly reduced and he later fled the country. With Papadopoulos as prime minister, elections to parliament and the freedom of the press were both suspended. In 1973 he abolished the monarchy, declared Greece a republic and himself the first president. However, he was overthrown in another military coup and in 1974 was charged with treason. A sentence of death was commuted to one of life imprisonment.

Papagayos, see WIND.

Papal States, or States of the Church, were those portions of Italy formerly under the dominion of the Pope. The temporal rule of the papacy was finally suppressed in 1870 when Rome was invaded by the Italian army. The total area of the states in 1859 was 41,440 km², and the population was over 3 million. In 1929, after 59 years of disagreement, the 'Roman Question' was settled in a Concordat between the Italian government and the papacy, which granted the Pope independence and the control of a small area known as the Vatican State.

Papandreou, George (1888–1968), Greek politician. Papandreou was imprisoned by the Italians in 1942, but escaped to Cairo in 1944, and was appointed premier. He returned to Athens in October 1944 as head of a government of national unity, but was soon replaced by Plastiras. In November 1963 he became premier of Greece, retaining this position until dismissed by King Constantine in July 1965. Following the Colonels' coup of April 1967 Papandreou was placed under house arrest.

Papaver, see POPPY.

Papaveraceae, a flowering plant family of about 25 genera and 120 species, mostly north temperate and subtropical. They are mostly herbaceous. Their white or yellow sap contains poisonous alkaloids. The leaves are usually lobed or compound. The flowers have two sepals, four petals, many stamens and a central superior ovary; they are often large and brightly coloured. The family includes *Papaver*, *Eschscholzia*, *Glaucium*, *Meconopsis*, *Macleaya* and *Chelidonium*.

Papaya, see PAWPAW.

Papeete, capital of the island of Tahiti, on the north-west coast. Chief port and trading centre of the island, and administrative centre for the whole of French Polynesia. Population (1977) 62,735. Exports are copra, phosphates and vanilla.

See also SOCIETY ISLANDS.

Papen, Franz von (1879–1969), German politician. He organised an aristocratic group, known as the *Herrenklub*, in Berlin, which in 1932 prevailed on Hindenburg to appoint an authoritarian government of noblemen under Papen as chancellor of the Reich. Papen helped Hitler to power and by 1933 he was vice-chancellor under Hitler. As minister to Austria he prepared the *Anschluss*. During the Second World War he was minister to Turkey. Indicted as a war criminal at the Nuremberg trial in 1946, he was one of three to be acquitted, but was arrested by a German court and sentenced under the denazification laws to eight years' detention in a labour camp.

Paper, substance made of vegetable material, and used for writing or printing upon, or for packaging. The principal raw materials are wood, esparto grass, and rag. The cheaper form of paper, made from wood, is produced by pulping whole logs, bark and all, with grindstones in water; this pulp contains many impurities and is used mainly to make newsprint. Better quality paper is produced from pulp made from logs with the bark removed: the wood is broken up into chips and then boiled under pressure with chemicals to leave just pure cellulose. Esparto grass is treated similarly, and a high-quality paper is made from it. Rag is used for the very top-quality papers, including those used for banknotes.

Various other substances are added to the pulp, such as size, sulphate of ammonia, colouring matter, and china clay, the latter being used to provide a better printing surface. The pulp is fed in a thin state to the wet end of the paper machine, and onto a continuous belt of finely woven wire cloth, supported on rollers. The water is drawn out, leaving the fibre of the original material. The paper is finally dried by passing it between heated cylinders. Glazed paper is further passed through highly polished rollers, a process known as calendering. The finished paper is either reeled or cut into sheets.

Thin cardboard can be made in a similar way; for greater thickness a number of sheets are laminated together.

The earliest form of paper was papyrus, made from the grass of that name by the Egyptians from about 3500 BC. It was made by flattening the thin layers forming the stem of the reed and drying them in the sun. This method was superseded in AD 105 by that of Tsai-Lun, a Chinese, who broke plants down into their original fibres by beating them, and then formed the fine fibres into a web or sheet of paper. In the 8th century the Arabs learned from Chinese prisoners how to make paper; from the Arabs the art of paper-making spread to the Moors of Morocco, who introduced it into Europe during their occupation of Spain. By the 11th century paper was being made in Spain and Italy, and from there it spread north to France, Germany and England. Paper was being made in England by 1490. The first machine for making a continuous web of paper, as distinct from individual sheets, was set up at Frogmore, Hertfordshire, in 1799.

Paper Money. The paper bank-note is now the principal currency in the UK and elsewhere. The gold sovereign disappeared from circulation during the First World War, and although the gold standard was restored in 1925, there was no restoration of the gold coinage, or of the right to exchange the individual note for gold at the Bank of England. By 1932 Great Britain had abandoned the gold standard, and the gold from the Issue Department of the Bank of England had been transferred to the Exchange Equalisation Account. Thus the pound note, although legal tender, no longer enjoys a gold backing and has become inconvertible currency. Although the Bank of England note is not subject to the limitation in number which gold imposes, the importance of limitation is now fully appreciated, and the issue of notes is placed strictly under the control of Parliament.

See also BANKS AND BANKING; CURRENCY; MONEY.

Paphos, name of three towns of south-west Cyprus. The oldest (also called *Palaiopaphos* or *Kouklia*), 2 km inland, was in antiquity the centre of the cult of Aphrodite, a place of pilgrimage, with a very ancient temple, ruins of which remain. The present-day population is 9000. The second town (*Neapaphos*) is situated 16 km to the north-west, and originated as the port of the first town. Under the Romans it grew to be the capital and chief port of Cyprus. It declined in the 4th century, and under the Turkish regime it was almost deserted. The third, modern, town (also called *Ktima*) was built on a bluff overlooking the harbour.

Papier-mâché, rigid material produced either by pasting together many sheets of thin paper, or by mixing glue with paper pulp. The practice of making papier-mâché is of Eastern origin. Boxes, trays, bowls and many other articles were at one time made in this way in great variety, and finished by lacquering and gilding and painting.

Papilionoideae, or Papilionatae, one of the three subfamilies of Leguminosae. The flowers are bilaterally symmetrical and papilionaceous or butterfly shaped, as for instance in the sweet pea. The group is sometimes raised to family status, and is then called Papilionaceae.

Papillon, or butterfly dog, derives its name from the large, erect, spreading ears of the prick-eared variety. It is a smart breed, with small, arched skull, pointed muzzle, and dark eyes. The ears are erect or drooping, according to the variety. The drop-eared variety is called Phalene. The chest is deep, and the back rather long. The coat is long and silky, usually white with black, black and tan, on red markings; a white blaze is desirable. The tail is long and carried over the back. The ideal height is 20–30 cm at the shoulder, and the maximum weight is 5 kg. It has become very popular.

Papio, see BABOON.

Paprika, see CAPSICUM.

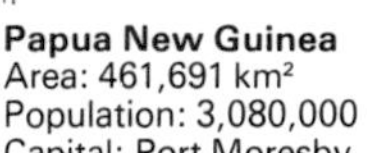

Papua New Guinea
Area: 461,691 km²
Population: 3,080,000
Capital: Port Moresby

Papua New Guinea, state lying to the east of Indonesia and to the north of Australia. It consists of the eastern section of the island of New Guinea and a number of smaller islands, including the Bismarck archipelago (New Britain, New Ireland) and the northern part of the Solomon Islands. Area (mainland) 394,766 km^2; (islands) 66,925 km^2. The capital is Port Moresby. Population (1979 estimate) 3,080,000.

The country lies wholly within the tropics and has a very irregular and indented coastline. The terrain on the mainland varies from the swampy lowland of the Fly, Turama and Kikori rivers to the high central mountains which rise to 4036 m (Mount Victoria). The islands are a mixture of high volcanic and low-lying coral formations.

Over 90 per cent of the population is engaged in subsistence agriculture, growing roots or tubers, or small-scale cash crop farming. The chief agricultural exports are coconuts, copra, cocoa, coffee, rubber, palm oil, and tea. Forestry is a sizeable activity and exports of sawn timber are growing steadily. Fishing is also a developing sector.

A comparatively recent development is the exploitation of the country's extensive mineral wealth, chiefly copper, gold, silver and oil. The main source of copper is the island of Bougainville.

Papier-mâché. *A mid-Victorian English chair. The manufacture of papier-mâché furniture in England dates from the late 18th century.*

Executive power is exercised by the governor-general, acting on the advice of the Cabinet. Legislative power is vested in a unicameral house of assembly containing 109 members elected by universal adult suffrage for a term of five years.

Altogether there are some 700 different languages, but pidgin and, to a lesser extent, standard English are also spoken.

History. In 1526–27 the Portuguese navigator Don Jorge de Meneses sailed along the coast of New Guinea and gave it the name Papua, meaning 'woolly-haired'. In 1884 a British protectorate was proclaimed over the south portion of the eastern half of New Guinea. In 1888 the territory was annexed to the Crown. The federal government of Australia assumed control in 1901; in 1906 a proclamation declared that New Guinea would be known as the territory of Papua. In 1972 the territory was renamed Papua New Guinea and the country became independent in 1975.

Papule (Latin *papula*, pimple), a small, round, solid elevation of the skin.

See also RASH.

Papyrus (Greek *papuros*, paper; also *bublos*, *biblos*, hence Bible). The term papyrus is of Egyptian origin, meaning 'the growth of the River (Nile)'. It is a straight stout, tall, reed-like aquatic plant, *Papyrus antiquorum* or *Cyperus papyrus*, which in ancient times grew profusely in Egypt on the River Nile. The ancient Egyptians used the stems of this plant to make ropes, mats, sandals, framework of light rowing boats, and for other purposes, but the principal importance, at least to modern eyes, was the use of papyrus as writing material. A detailed account of the way in which the papyrus was treated in Egyptian 'paper factories' is given by Pliny the Elder (*Naturalis historia*, xiii. 74 ff.). A section from the lowest part of the stem, the pith, was cut vertically into thin strips; these were laid, some vertically and others transversely, pressed together, and dried in the sun. Uneven patches were smoothed or pressed away, and the surface was polished more or less carefully according to the quality to be produced. The sheets were then glued together into a roll. The lengths of the rolls varied; some were 9 to 12 m long, but we are told of some that were 45 m long, and would contain the whole *Iliad* or *Odyssey*. The oldest books known are written on rolls of papyrus, and the earliest preserved written papyri go back to the first half of the 3rd millennium BC. Papyrus was not employed for literary purposes only. In Egypt, Greece, Rome, Syria, etc., it was for many centuries the chief material used for writing for all ordinary purposes, such as legal documents, receipts, petitions, notices of birth, and official and private letters. Its employment for these purposes continued until the middle of the 11th century, while as writing material for books it was gradually displaced by parchment or vellum, which had superseded it in the 4th century AD. Greek was the administrative language of Egypt from the conquest by Alexander, 333–32 BC, through the Ptolemaic, Roman and Byzantine periods until a century or so after the Arabic conquest, 639–41 AD. The great majority of surviving papyri are in Greek and were found during the 19th and 20th centuries in Middle and Upper Egypt, where they have been preserved through the dry climate and the encroachment of the desert on previously inhabited areas.

See also BOOK; MANUSCRIPTS; PAPER; PARCHMENT; VELLUM.

Parable (by derivation: 'putting things side by side'), originally the name given by the Greek rhetoricians to an illustration avowedly introduced as such. In Hellenistic and New Testament Greek it came to signify an independent fictitious narrative, employed for the illustration of a moral rule or principle. This kind of illustration is found in the Old Testament and New Testament, particularly in the discourses of Jesus Christ. The parable differs from the fable in the probability or verisimilitude of the story itself, and agrees with it in the essential requisites of simplicity and brevity.

Parabola, locus of a point P whose distance from a fixed point (the *focus*) is equal to its distance from a fixed line (the *directrix*). The parabola is a conic section made by a plane cutting a conic surface in a direction parallel to a tangent plane and is a special case of the conics governed by the relations $SP = ePM$, e being called the *eccentricity* of the curve. For the parabola, $e = 1$. The path of a projectile when not truly vertical is practically a parabola except for interference of air and other irregularities. In analytical geometry the equation for a parabola in the simplest form, taking the origin at the vertex, is $y^2 = 4px$, where the focus is the point $(p, 0)$. All curves of the form $y^n = px^m$ are classed as parabolas; $y = px^3$ is the cubical parabola, $y^2 = px^3$ is the semi-cubical parabola.

Paracelsus, or Theophrastus Bombastus von

Hohenheim (1492–1541), Swiss physician. He was an alchemist, and the founder of medical chemistry. In two separate ways he had a powerful influence on the thought of his time. Firstly, he redirected alchemy from the fruitless attempt to transmit base metals into gold to the useful channel of preparing medicinal products. Secondly, his interest in using pure compounds, rather than indeterminate mixtures, paved the way to an understanding that chemical compounds are distinguished by their elemental composition.

Paracetamol, an aniline derivative with analgesic (pain-relieving) and antipyretic (fever-reducing) actions, used for headache, toothache and, to a lesser extent, for rheumatism; it is useful for people who are sensitive to aspirin and, since it does not damage the stomach, it can be given to patients with gastric ulcers.

Parachute, device for allowing people or goods to descend safely from a height. Small parachutes were in use during the early years of ballooning (1783 onwards). The first human parachute drop (from a balloon) was by the Frenchman A. J. Garnerin in Paris in 1797. The first lives to be saved by jumps from aeroplanes were those of two German aviators in 1918. Parachutes today are used not only for dropping from aircraft, but also for sending down supplies, and for acting as auxiliary brakes for high-speed aircraft when landing. The conventional aircrew parachute of today is fully automatic.

Parachuting for sport, sometimes known as sky-diving, has become increasingly popular since the early 1950s, and displays and international events are held in many parts of the world. Free-fall parachuting includes delayed drops, aerial acrobatics, and precision landings.

Parachute and Airborne Troops. The first expression is sometimes loosely used to cover the meaning of the second. Airborne troops may be transported in gliders or powered aircraft which land and disembark small units complete in the assembly area, or, as parachute troops proper, they may drop by parachute from aircraft, together with the greater part of their weapons and equipment. All the infantry and a proportion of other arms of a modern airborne division are trained as parachute troops.

Parachuting was originally developed for military purposes, but is now a thriving sport. The sport is divided into two categories: accuracy and free-fall. In accuracy competitions, participants jump from a height of between 600 m and 2000 m and aim to land as closely as possible to a 3 m-wide bulls-eye at the centre of a 35 m-wide target. In free-fall parachuting, competitors jump from a height of between 1800 m and 2000 m and must complete a series of prescribed manoeuvres in 30 seconds (25 if jumping from 1800 m) before opening their parachutes. Points are awarded for the accuracy and style with which these manoeuvres are carried out.

Paraclete (Greek *paraklētos*, one called alongside, i.e. to help), name given to the Holy Spirit by Christ, who promised his disciples the paraclete would take his place as their teacher and guide after he left them (John xiv–xvi).

Paradise (from Greek *paradeisos*, a park or enclosure), word first used in Greek by Xenophon for a Persian enclosed park or pleasure ground. It occurs several times in the Old Testament, notably in Neh. ii. 8, where it is translated as 'forest'. In Christian literature it is used sometimes for the earthly paradise, the garden of Eden, and sometimes as equivalent to heaven. Sometimes the word means an intermediate state lower than that of heaven, as in Luke xxiii. 43 and in Dante's *Purgatorio*.

Paradise Fish, *Macropodus opercularis*, a species of spiny-finned fishes of the family Anabantidae, order Perciformes, found in Asia. As in the related fighting-fishes (*Betta*), the males, when in breeding colours, are very pugnacious.

Paradox (Greek *para*, against; *doxa*, opinion), figure of speech which may be described as an epigram containing an apparent contradiction which, on closer examination, reveals a substratum of truth, as in Shakespeare's 'Cowards die many times before their deaths', or Wordsworth's 'The child is father of the man'.

See also FIGURE OF SPEECH.

Rip cord pulled
Pilot-chute released
Sleeved canopy
Sleeve
Rigging lines
Pilot-chute pulls sleeve from canopy which inflates from apex downwards
Canopy fully deployed

***Parachute.** Parachute deployment in a free-fall jump. The parachutist's posture aids stability.*

Paraffin, see KEROSINE.

Paraffin Wax (Latin *parum affinis*, small affinity), solid, waxy substance obtained when crude oils are distilled. It consists of higher members of the group of alkanes, which are also termed paraffins. For very many years paraffin wax was used almost entirely for the manufacture of candles, but the treatment of paper and board for packaging purposes has superseded candle-making as the major application for these waxes. Paraffin wax is also used to make textiles water-repellent, for the preservation of foodstuffs, and for various polishes.

See also WAX.

Paraguay
Area: 406,752 km²
Population: 3,000,000
Capital: Asunción

Paraguay lies in the centre of South America bordered by Bolivia in the north-west and north, Brazil in the north-east and east, and by Argentina in the south-east, south, and south-west. Having an area of 406,752 km² it is the third smallest South American country and shares with Bolivia the peculiarity of being landlocked. The climate is subtropical.

The Río Paraguay, flowing north to south, divides the country into two distinct regions: the Gran Chaco to the west of the river and the Eastern Region on the other side. The Chaco, making up two-thirds of the total area of the republic, consists of a flat featureless plain made up from great thicknesses of silt brought down from the Andes by innumerable streams. For the most part it is covered by scrub forest. The eastern region forms two distinct areas—the highlands in the east and the lowlands in the west—the line of demarcation being a great scarp or line of cliffs running roughly parallel to the Río Paraguay. The highlands, ranging in elevation between 300 and 600 m, are densely forested. The Lowlands, economically the most important of the regions, form the floodplains of the Paraná and Paraguay but also comprise stretches of undulating land with rolling hills either wooded or covered with savanna. Paraguay's three main rivers, the Paraguay, the Paraná and the Pilcomaya (running west to east across the Chaco), all join to form part of the La Plata river system. There are two important lakes, the Ypoá flowing out to the Río Tebicury and the Ypacarai leading to Río Salado.

In 1980 the population was estimated at 3,000,000. Asunción, the capital, has a population of 462,800. No other town approaches the size of the capital, the next largest being Caaguazú and Coronel Oviedo. Ethnically the vast majority of the people are mestizo, a mixture of Spanish and Indian stock. There are around 50,000 pure-bred indians.

The country remains largely undeveloped for

the cultivated area covers only 3 per cent of land area. Similarly, the enormous hardwood and cedar forests remain largely untouched. Some efforts have been made towards the reform of the agrarian sector.

The major crops are maize, beans, rice, sugar, fruit, cotton and tobacco. The main agricultural exports are timber and cattle. Most industry is concerned with local consumption or with the processing of agricultural products. There is a small oil refinery but no truly mechanical industries. There are also few exploitable minerals and only limestone is important.

The unit of currency is the *guaraní*.

The present constitution was introduced in 1967 and provides for a highly centralised administration. Executive power rests in the President, who is elected by popular vote for a term of five years and he can seek immediate re-election. There is a senate composed of at least 30 members, and a chamber of deputies. In addition there is a council of state whose members are appointed by the President; during parliamentary recess he can govern through this council by decree.

The official language is Spanish, but Guaraní is widely spoken by the indigenous population.

History. The first colony was settled in Paraguay in 1537 and the country became a viceroyalty of Peru. In 1811 Paraguay was the first of the Spanish American colonies to obtain its independence. Between 1865 and 1870 it was involved in the War of the Triple Alliance against Brazil, Argentina and Uruguay, and emerged, severely defeated, from Latin America's most bloody war of the 19th century. A totally dislocated economy and an inadequate male labour force did not prevent Paraguay engaging, from 1927, in a series of armed clashes with Bolivia over the Chaco territory that comprised a third of Paraguay and which at the time was thought to contain fabulous unexploited resources. These reached a head in the Chaco War (1932–35). The human and material costs of this war, in which Paraguay gained most of the disputed territory, were responsible for a period of political unrest, terminated in 1954 by the seizure of power by Gen. Alfredo Stroessner. His government has been characterised by some material progress at the cost of severe authoritarian government. He was re-elected in 1978 and 1983.

Paraguay, important river of South America. Rising in the Brazilian state of Mato Grosso, it flows south-west and then south for nearly 2560 km through the centre of Paraguay, forming the country's main means of transport and communication. It is navigable for steamers to the mouth of the Cuiabá, 160 km above the town of Corumbá, in Brazil.

Paraguay Tea, see MATÉ.

Parakeet, small, long-tailed parrots, of order Psittaciformes, with a moderate beak. Among the best known are the ring-necked parakeets, genus *Psittacula*, which are very common in India and Africa, and in some districts are serious pests of agriculture. Their gay plumage and hardiness make them a popular pet and large numbers are exported. The crested ground parakeet, or cockatiel, is another hardy bird, and breeds rapidly in captivity. It and the undulated grass parakeet or budgerigar are natives of Australia; both are popular as pets.

Paraldehyde $(C_2H_4O)_2$, a colourless liquid (boiling point 124°C), obtained by adding a drop of concentrated sulphuric acid to acetaldehyde. It is used as a hypnotic (the so-called 'knock-out drops' of the crime novels) but it has a very unpleasant taste and makes the breath smell. It may be given by injection to a very agitated person and is a safe drug in fairly large doses although dependence will develop if use is prolonged.

Parallax is the change in the direction of an object caused by a change in the position of the observer. When the two positions of the observer are the ends of a base line of known length, measurement of the parallactic angle enables the distance to the object to be calculated trigonometrically. This is the principle of the rangefinder and of the triangulation method in surveying. The method is particularly important in astronomy for measuring the distance to members of the solar system and to the nearer stars. See also ABSOLUTE MAGNITUDE; STAR.

Parallel Lines are straight lines which lie in the same plane but have no points in common.

Paralysis, the loss of the ability to contract the muscles voluntarily following an interruption of their motor drive supply. The nervous pathway to skeletal muscle consists essentially of two nerve cells, the upper and lower motor neurons. The *upper motor neuron* originates in the motor cortex of the brain and sends its long fibre across the mid-line of the body to end at a certain level in the spinal cord. There it connects with the *lower motor neuron* which runs to supply a group of muscle fibres. Upper motor neuron paralysis may result from damage to the nerve anywhere between the cerebral cortex of the brain and the spinal cord. If the lesion is the result of a vascular accident (haemorrhage or thrombosis) in the brain, *hemiplegia* (paralysis of a group of muscles on the opposite side of the body) will occur. Destruction of a lower motor neuron leads to profound atrophy of the individual muscle concerned. The muscle is flaccid (decreased tone) and tendon reflexes are lost. Poliomyelitis is a disease which selectively destroys the lower motor nerve cell in the spinal cord, producing such a paralysis. If the lower motor neuron is damaged more peripherally by trauma, accompanying sensory fibres are also likely to be involved.

Paramagnetism, see INDUCTION, MAGNETIC.

Paramaribo, capital and chief port of Surinam (formerly Netherlands Guiana), on the Surinam river, 24 km from the sea and 344 km from Georgetown (Guyana). It is the centre of the colony, and is on air routes between the USA, Brazil and the Netherlands. There is a deep-water frontage of 2 km. Population (1980), urban district, 67,718.

Paraná, capital of the province of Entre Rios, Argentina. Situated on the left bank of the River Paraná, it is 584 km by rail and 640 km by river from Buenos Aires to the south. It is the export point for the great cattle, sheep and grain country which makes up the province. Once the capital of Argentina (1853–62). Population (1975) 127,635.

Paraná, one of the most important rivers of South America, formed by the confluence of the Rio Grande and the Paranaíba. Both rise in the state of Minas Gerais, Brazil, and flow north-west and west to the point of confluence. As the Paraná the two rivers first flow in a south-west direction through Brazil, then south, forming the boundary between Brazil and Paraguay. Thence it sweeps west between Paraguay and Argentina to receive its main tributary, the Paraguay. It then flows south-west to Rosario and south-east to unite with the Uruguay in the Plata estuary. Cataracts and rapids render it unfit for navigation over much of its course, but for the last 1600 km it is always navigable even by large steamers. Its total length is about 4000 km, and the area of the basin has been estimated at nearly 2600 km^2.

Parapet, low wall which acts as a protection on bridges, terraces, flat roofs, etc. In Renaissance architecture parapets are generally balustrades. In Gothic architecture the parapet is merely a continuation of the wall carried up above the edge of the roof and often machicolated.

Paraphrase (from Greek *para*, beside, *phrazein*, to tell), name given to a restatement of a passage in prose or verse which brings out its meaning with greater lucidity, without altering the sense of the original by change, addition or subtraction. In music a paraphrase is a free adaptation of a piece of music so as to suit it to other instruments.

Paraplegia, paralysis caused by injury to the spinal cord. All parts of the body below the site of the injury are affected, typically the legs and lower portion of the trunk.

See also PARALYSIS.

Parapsychology, science of the study of psychic phenomena not conforming to natural laws as currently understood.

Paraquat, see HERBICIDES.

Parasites (Greek *parasitos*, one who eats beside, or at the table of, another, or at another's expense), living organisms which pass the whole or a part of their existence on or in other living organisms (hosts) without conferring any benefit. They do this essentially for the purpose of obtaining nourishment from their hosts, not merely for shelter. Often one creature lives in intimate association with another purely as a commensal. For instance, small sea-anemones are transported in the claws of two species of crabs, which take any food the anemones cannot completely swallow. The anemones probably gain from the transportation more opportunities of catching prey. Some small fishes shelter beneath the 'umbrella' of large jellyfishes, others in the gullet of large sea-anemones, and one in the hind gut of a sea-cucumber. But in none of these and other similar cases does one of the commensals live or rear its young at the expense of the other. In other cases two organisms become mutually dependent and cannot live without each other's contribution. Lichens, which are algae and fungi growing together, are an example of this co-operation, which is called symbiosis or mutualism.

Parasitism occurs in many different phyla of the animal kingdom. The parasites of importance highest in the animal kingdom are the ticks, mites and fleas. Among insects parasites are numerous, including aphids, or plant-lice, the gall-wasps and gall midges, and many others parasitic on plants. Among flatworms, the Platyhelminthes, and roundworms, the Nematoda, parasitism is very frequent and gives rise to a number of serious diseases. The Protozoa, the unicellular animals, include a large variety of parasitic organisms, such as those that cause malaria, sleeping sickness (trypanosomiasis) and amoebic dysentery.

Parasitic Plants and Fungi, those plants that rely entirely on other organisms for their food supply. They cause serious losses of cultivated plants, the dodders (*Cuscuta*) often doing considerable damage to crops of clover and lucerne. The broomrapes (*Orobanche*) are so dependent on their hosts that unless they are in immediate contact with them, their seeds cannot germinate. Toothwort (*Lathraea squamaria*) also has no chlorophyll. Mistletoe, eyebright, yellow rattle and cow-wheat are partial parasites, for all these plants contain chlorophyll and can assimilate carbon dioxide, although they are dependent upon their hosts for water and salts. Among the fungi, the most important group of parasitic plants, the rusts and smuts do considerable damage to cereal crops; the mildews to hops, grape vines, gooseberry plants and various fruit trees. *Phytophthora infestans* is the cause of potato blight, which led to the Irish potato famines in 1846–48. Ringworm and other skin diseases of man are caused by parasitic fungi. Most extraordinary of the numerous parasitic plants of the tropics is the huge-flowered *Rafflesia* which grows in the Malayan forests.

Parasitology, the scientific study of parasites and their effects.

Parathyroid Glands, a group of small, paired endocrine glands associated with the thyroid gland in the neck. In man there are two pairs of parathyroids, usually embedded in the substance of the thyroid. In spite of their small size—their combined weight in man is only about 10 mg—they are essential to life. Their removal results in a fall in the concentration of calcium in the blood, a condition known as 'tetany' (not to be confused with 'tetanus', which is an infection). Calcium plays an essential rôle in the workings of most tissues in the body, but the most striking effect seen in tetany is muscular paralysis. Since the act of breathing requires muscular activity, untreated tetany ultimately results in death by suffocation. The fall in the blood calcium is the consequence of the sudden removal from the blood of parathyroid hormone (PTH). PTH is normally released into the bloodstream from the parathyroid glands, and raises the blood calcium concentration by extracting calcium from the bones, which are the body's largest store of calcium. PTH is thus part of a negative feedback system: when blood calcium levels fall, PTH is released, calcium levels in the blood rise, and PTH is no longer produced.

Paratyphoid Fever, an acute infectious disease very similar to typhoid fever, but often less severe. It is caused by *Salmonella paratyphi* A, B or C. The carrier state is also a problem. Vaccines for this disease are less effective than those for typhoid fever.

Parchment, skin of the sheep, lamb, goat, pig or calf, prepared for writing upon.

Pardon. In Britain the royal prerogative of pardon is exercisable only on the advice of the home secretary. In practice it is used only after conviction and sentence.

In the USA the Constitution gives the president the power to pardon offences against the US government except in the case of the impeachment of public officers.

Pardubice (German *Pardubitz*), town of central Czechoslovakia, in East Bohemia on the River Elbe. It has oil and sugar refineries, chemical and brewing industries, and a trade in grain and timber. Population (1979) 92,000.

Parenchyma, a plant tissue formed of living cells of varying size, shape and structure. It forms the cortex or the pith of a stem and is very porous, with large spaces between the cells.

Pareto, Vilfredo (1848–1923), Italian sociologist and economist. In *Cours d'économie politique*, 1897, and other writings, he applied his mathematical gifts to problems of neoclassical economic theory, then turned to sociology. *Trattato di Sociologia generale*, 1916, translated into English in 1935 as *Mind and Society*, was his major contribution to the science, marked in particular by his view of social leadership as cyclic in nature.

Parinirvāna (Sanskrit; Pāli *Parinibbana*), term used by Buddhists when referring to the physical death of the Buddha or of a being who has realised Nirvāna and will not be reborn.

Paris, capital city and *département* of France, built on both banks of the River Seine about 175 km from its mouth, with the Île de la Cité at the centre. The height of the city above sea-level varies from 26 to 125 m; the highest point is the hill of Montmartre. Geographically, Paris occupies an important position, being situated on a fertile plain, on ground of recent alluvial formation, between the confluences of the Oise and the Marne with the Seine, and at the point where the Rhône-Seine route linking the Mediterranean and the English Channel is joined by the route from south-west France and Spain. The *ville de Paris* has a population of over 2 million, but 8 million live in metropolitan Paris.

Paris is the seat of the president of the republic, who resides at the Palais de l'Elysée. The National Assembly is housed at the Palais Bourbon, and the Senate at the Palais de Luxembourg. Paris is the core of a highly centralised national administration, the focus of the French road and rail networks, the most important city for higher education, research, finance, and tourism in France and also the country's leading industrial area.

The Île de la Cité, the largest of the Seine islands, is the nucleus of modern Paris. The earliest known settlers were a small tribe of Gauls, the Parisii, who were followed by the Romans. In the Frankish invasion Paris was captured by the Merovingian king Clovis, who made Paris his capital in 508. Charlemagne (768–814) made Paris a country and it became a duchy under Charles the Bald. The Capetians, the line which ruled France from 987 until the Revolution, made Paris the permanent capital of France. The University of Paris dates from the early 13th century and Paris soon became the intellectual centre of Europe. Much of medieval Paris was, however, demolished during the long reign of Louis XIV, in order to accommodate such

Paris. *The Parc du Champ de Mars seen from the top of the Eiffel Tower.*

magnificent schemes as the Place de la Concorde and the Panthéon. Napoleon, too, undertook to modernise Paris and his planners drove 60 new streets through the city. The impetus was carried on even after the restoration of the monarchy and between 1815 and 1848 many new bridges and 55 new streets were made. The great changes which have made modern Paris were effected during the Second Empire under Baron Haussmann; many remnants of medieval Paris were swept away and 22 new boulevards and avenues were laid out. The centre of present-day Paris is still confined to a roughly oval shape by a ring of former fortifications. The River Seine flows between broad stone embankments, spanned by more than 40 bridges in its course. The Île de la Cité, the Île de St Louis, and the busiest part of Paris across the river are to be found within the circuits of the boulevards which have replaced the ramparts of Louis XIII on the north and of Philip Augustus on the south.

Paris, in Greek legend, second son of Priam, king of Troy. When born he was exposed on Mount Ida, but was brought up by a shepherd and married Oenone, deserting her for Helen. He was called upon by Zeus to decide as to which was the fairest, Hera, Athena or Aphrodite. Hera offered him the sovereignty of Asia, Athena renown in war, and Aphrodite the fairest woman, Helen, for his wife. He decided in favour of Aphrodite and she helped him to carry off Helen, wife of Menelaus. From this arose the Trojan War. In the war Paris killed Achilles, but was wounded. He returned to his wife, Oenone, but she refused to heal him and he died. Oenone, remorseful, killed herself.

Paris, name of two famous *pantomimi* (ballet dancers) in imperial Rome. One, a favourite of Nero, was put to death by him as a rival (AD 67). The other, a favourite of Domitian, was put to death in AD 87 for alleged intrigue with the empress.

Paris, a genus of herbaceous perennials in the family Liliaceae, with a stout rhizome and erect stem, bearing four whorled net-veined leaves, and a solitary green flower followed by a berry-like fruit. *P. quadrifolia* is herb paris of Europe and Asia; *P. polyphylla*, a Himalayan species, is grown in gardens.

Paris Opera Ballet. Since 1871 the name of the national ballet of France has been the *Théâtre National de l'Opéra* but it can trace its origins back to 1669 when it was called the *Académie Royale de Musique*. The present ornate building dates from 1875 and was designed by Garnier, hence its nickname *Palais Garnier*. The ballet company knew greatness in the 18th century and blossomed again during the Romantic era. Serge Lifar gave it new life in 1930s and until the 1960s it still had a considerable reputation.

Paris, Treaties of, name given to various international peace treaties signed in Paris: the treaty signed on 10 February 1763, by Britain, France and Spain at the end of the Seven Years War; the treaty signed on 3 September 1783, between Britain and the American commissioners, recognising American independence; the treaty of 30 May 1814, between the Allies and France after the abdication of Napoleon; the treaty concluded on 20 November 1815 between the same signatories after the final overthrow of Napoleon; and the treaty of 30 March 1856, signed by Great Britain, France, Turkey, Sardinia and Russia at the close of the Crimean War. The peace conference after the First World War, which drew up the Versailles peace treaty, was held in Paris in 1919–20; and the peace conference held in Paris after the Second World War in 1946 drew up the peace treaties between the Allies and Italy, Hungary, Bulgaria, Romania and Finland.

Parish, the smallest unit of organisation in the Church of England, which, from the middle of the 16th century began to acquire secular functions, beginning with highways in 1555 and poor relief in 1601. Parishes or groups of parishes continued to be used as administrative units for various functions until the reform of local government in the 19th century, when they became the smallest unit of local government in rural areas in England and Wales. This continued to be the case following the reorganisation of local government in 1974.

Park, Mungo (1771–1806), Scottish explorer. In 1795 the African Association sent him to explore the course of the River Niger. The journey was full of difficulties and setbacks. At last, in July 1796, he found the much sought after Niger, and followed the river downstream from Ségou. But he had to turn back, finally collapsing with fever after having traced the course of the river for almost 500 km. On his return in 1799 he published his *Travels*. He then established himself as a surgeon but in 1805 he returned to the Niger. This expedition was a much more ambitious one and consisted of some 70 Europeans, as well as native guides and carriers. By the time they had reached the Niger only 11 Europeans were left alive. With the help of the one soldier still capable of work, Park built, out of two canoes, a serviceable boat, giving letters to a native guide to take back to Gambia for transmission to England. Mungo Park perished in the rapids at Bussa; but not before he and his companions had navigated 1600 km of the river.

Park, either ground, attached to a country house, often designed by famous landscape architects such as Capability Brown, or an enclosure in a town ornamentally laid out for public recreation. The word is also used for a large tract of land kept in its natural state for the public benefit. Among the most famous parks, public or natural, may be mentioned Hyde Park and Regent's Park in London, the Bois de Boulogne in Paris, and the Tiergarten in Berlin.
See also COMMONS AND COMMON FIELDS.

Park Chung Hee (1917–79), Korean statesman. He was selected by the young officers who planned the coup of May 1961 to head the Supreme Council for National Reconstruction and was elected president of the Republic in October 1963 and re-elected in 1967 and 1971. He was assassinated in 1979.
See also SOUTH KOREA, *History*.

Parker, Charlie (1920–55), US jazz alto saxophonist who, with Dizzie Gillespie, founded a new-style 'bop'. With Louis Armstrong, he was the outstanding stylistic innovator in jazz. He extended the harmonic, rhythmic and melodic horizons and increased the technical aspects of jazz musicianship.
See also JAZZ.

Parker, Dorothy Rothschild (1893–1967), US satirist and humorist, She became a journalist, and was for a time book-reviewer on the *New Yorker*. Though satirical, and famous for her wit, she could also command pathos, as in her short story 'Big Blonde', which won the O. Henry Prize in 1929.

Parker, Matthew (1504–75), English archbishop of Canterbury. In 1544 he was elected master of Corpus Christi College, Cambridge, and in 1545 vice-chancellor of the university, in which capacity he manfully opposed the spoliation with which the colleges generally were threatened. In 1552 he was installed as dean of Lincoln, but lived in retirement during Mary's reign, to be promoted, on the accession of Elizabeth, to the archbishopric of Canterbury. He sought to establish in England a *via media* between Roman Catholicism and Puritanism. An eminent scholar and antiquarian, he did much to establish that appeal to history and sound learning which became a feature of traditional Anglicanism.

Parker of Waddington, Hubert Lister Parker, Baron (1900–72), English judge. He became a judge of the King's Bench in 1950; lord justice of appeal, 1954; and lord chief justice of England, 1958–71.

Parkinson's Disease, paralysis agitans, first described by James Parkinson in 1817, is a disease of middle or late life, and is due to pathological changes in the basal ganglia (a collection of nerve cells deep in the cerebral hemispheres of the brain). True Parkinson's disease has an unknown cause, although very similar conditions have been produced by hardening of the cerebral arteries, encephalitis, and by large amounts of phenothiazine tranquillisers. The hallmarks of Parkinson's disease are a stooped posture, a fast shuffling gait, hypokinesia (poverty of movement), increased muscle tone, and a tremor which is present at rest and disappears with activity. Although there is no treatment which reverses the underlying neural pathology, the introduction of the drug L-dopa has proved a great relief even to those in the advanced stages of the disease.

Parkman, Francis (1823–93), US historian. He devoted his life to historical writing. His books are still standard authorities on the history of colonial North America. His principal works are: *The Conspiracy of Pontiac*, 1851; *The Jesuits in North America*, 1867; and *Montcalm and Wolfe*, 1884.

Parlement, the French tribunals which before 1789 were invested with sovereign judicial authority, and political and magisterial powers which eventually made them instruments of monarchical tyranny. This supreme power was soon turned against the monarchy. Under Louis XIII the pretensions of the parlement increased. On the death of Louis XIV the parlement attempted to recover its old authority, and formally took the name 'sovereign court'. Finally, in 1792 the parlement was abolished on the ground that the nation had never concurred in the election of its members.

Parliament, the supreme legislative authority in the United Kingdom. Constitu-

Houses of Parliament. *An engraving made around 1870. The present buildings were completed in 1860. Sir Charles Barry was the principal architect.*

tionally it consists of the sovereign, the House of Lords and the House of Commons. A parliament is the period between the proclamation authorising new elections to the House of Commons and the summoning of a new parliament.

The term 'parliament' was probably first used in England by Matthew Paris in 1246, and introduced through the Normans or through intercourse with the French kingdom. Until 1295, with the summoning of the 'Model Parliament' by Edward I, there appears to have been for the most part but one legislative chamber. The struggle between the king and the greater feudal barons was probably the predisposing cause of popular liberties; for the kings generally found themselves forced to secure the support of the people at large. The Commons were from time to time drawn into alliance with baronial factions, but attempts to introduce continuous control of the Crown broke down in the face of the barons' reluctance to undertake such an onerous task. Finance and judicial business were the chief concerns of the representatives, and the king's court established a superiority in these matters over local feudal courts. Parliament was (and is) a 'high court'. 'No taxation without representation' has been the peculiar genius of English government at almost all times.

Towards the close of the Middle Ages, the influence of Parliament declined, more and more of the general petitions which were a chief function being referred to the executive branch of the government. This process, analogous to the decline of parliaments in France, Spain and Germany, was halted only when the Tudors recognised the importance of attaching mass opinion to their benevolent dictatorship. In Henry VIII's reign Parliament was establishing a continuity important for the future. The breach with Rome was effected through Parliament and with parliamentary approval, since a façade of popular action was thus built up. Yet the fact that Henry used and consulted Parliament gave the institution an ever-increasing importance. The Commons came into collision with Elizabeth on several occasions, e.g. on the question of the queen's marriage and the settlement of the succession, 1566; on ecclesiastical matters, 1571 and 1593; and on monopolies, 1601. The control which the council had exercised over parliamentary deliberations began to give way to a new group of Commons leaders. With James I and Charles I this process developed with growing speed to the inevitable outcome in civil war.

During the Interregnum a period in which Parliament undertook executive authority was followed by one in which it lost all authority to Cromwell, whose rule convinced the nation that arbitrary government was not to be tolerated. The folly of James II reinforced the lesson, and the peaceful revolution of 1688 marked the beginning of parliamentary dominance over the Crown, and of the responsibility of the executive to Parliament.

The clause in Magna Carta against the imposition of arbitrary aids found renewed expression in the Bill of Rights, 1689, which made illegal the levying of money for the Crown by pretence of prerogative, without leave of Parliament. The Bill of Rights gave the deathblow to prerogative for all time, and made it clear that the king was a monarch with powers limited by Parliament. Henceforth the history of Parliament is that of party government: the wielding of the prerogative power by the party in the majority in the House of Commons, or rather by the Cabinet.

But the victory over prerogative achieved by the revolution of 1688 was a far cry from the ideals of a democratic Parliament; for there followed the tremendous struggle for electoral reform and the defranchisement of the 'rotten boroughs', that culminated in the Reform Act of 1832.

The House of Lords has undergone no essential change in its composition ever since that composition was stereotyped in the Middle Ages, though life peers sit in the House. Since the decision of the Committee of Privileges in the Wensleydale case (1856) no life peer was allowed to sit in the House of Lords until 1958, when the Life Peerages Act authorised the creation of life peers. The power of the House of Lords has, however, declined considerably. It never enjoyed greater formal powers than the Commons, but exercised power through the influence and patronage of its members. This influence and patronage declined steadily in the 19th century, and the powers of the Lords were formally curbed by the Parliament Acts of 1911 and 1949.

See also CABINET; EXECUTIVE; HOUSE OF COMMONS; HOUSE OF LORDS.

Parliament, Houses of, officially known as the Palace of Westminster, being originally a royal residence from the time of Edward the Confessor (who built the original palace) until Henry VIII. In 1547 Edward VI granted the use of its chapel of St Stephen to the Commons and there they remained until a fire in 1834 destroyed all the palace except Westminster Hall, the crypt of St Stephen's Chapel and the cloisters. A new Palace of Westminster was begun in 1840 in a rich adaptation of Gothic designed by Sir Charles Barry, assisted by A. W. Pugin. After Barry's death in 1860 the completion was carried out by his son, E. M. Barry. The House of Commons was destroyed by bombs in 1941. A new chamber designed by Sir Giles Gilbert Scott, substantially on the lines of the former building, was begun in 1948 and formally opened in 1950. The exterior features of the Houses of Parliament include the Clock Tower, 96 m high, containing the hour-bell known as 'Big Ben' after Sir Benjamin Hall, who was the first commissioner of works when it was installed, and the Victoria Tower, 98 m high, at the southern end.

Parliamentary Commissions for Administration, see OMBUDSMAN.

Parma, Italian city and capital of Parma province, situated on the River Parma, 85 km north-west of Bologna. It was probably Etruscan in origin, and was colonised by the Romans in 183 BC; it is crossed east–west by the Aemilian Way. In the 16th century it was the seat of the Farnese family. From 1749 the Bourbons ruled Parma, including Marie Louise of Bourbon-Parma, wife of Napoleon. Parma still retains the atmosphere of a small capital. Its main rôle is as the centre of its agricultural district. Population (1979) 176,945.

Parmenides (b.c.515 BC), Greek philosopher, born at Elea in southern Italy. He wrote a poem, *On Nature*, of which fragments survive. In opposition to the earlier monists, Thales, Anaximander and Anaximenes, who maintained that the world had developed from a single element, Parmenides held that there is no change or multiplicity.

Parmentiera, a genus of eight fruit-bearing trees of the family Bignoniaceae, which flourishes in tropical countries. *P. cerifera*, known as the candle tree, is a fodder plant.

Parmigianino, Girolamo Francesco Maria Mazzola, also Parmigiano (1503–40), Italian painter. He followed the style of Correggio, combining it with the influence of Raphael and Michelangelo, and exaggerating the height and slenderness of his figures to Manneristic proportions. In 1524 he went to Rome and was soon employed by Clement VII. He was in that city when it was stormed by the imperialists under Bourbon in 1527, and was working on his picture of *The Vision of St Jerome* (now in the National Gallery, London) when soldiers burst into his studio. Having agreed to execute several frescoes in the church of S. Maria della Steccata, Parma, after repeated delays he was thrown into prison for breach of contract. He died soon afterwards at Casalmaggiore.

Parnassia, a genus of perennial herbs in family Saxifragaceae native to northern temperate regions; *P. palustris*, grass of Parnassus, is found in marshy places in Europe and Asia.

Parnassians, The, a 19th-century school of French poets. The name derives from *Le Parnasse contemporain*, a periodical devoted to poetry, three series of which appeared, in 1866, 1871 and 1876, and in which some of their poems were first published. The movement, deriving in part from the 'art for art's sake' school of Gautier and de Banville, represented a reaction against Romanticism. The Parnassians were much influenced by the scientific and philosophical climate of the age, in particular by scientific positivism. Their aim was to create poetry that was impersonal and intellectual, not subjective and sentimental, in tone, and impeccable in form. The leading members of the school were Leconte de Lisle and Heredia, others being Sully Prudhomme, Coppée, Dierx, Ménard and Mérat.

Parnassós, mountain of central Greece, rising to 2460 m, overlooking Delphi. It has two main peaks, called in classical times Tithorea and Lycorea. It was regarded as one of the most holy mountains of Greece, and was sacred to Dionysus, Apollo and the Muses.

Parnell, Charles Stewart (1846–91), Irish politician. He was in 1879 elected president of the National Land league, formed with the object of securing the ownership of land in Ireland for the occupiers. In 1880 Parnell was unanimously elected to the leadership of the Home Rule party at Westminster.

In 1886, the Conservatives and Liberals being nearly equal in numerical strength, he threw in his lot with Gladstone and turned out the Conservative government. His price was the introduction of a Home Rule Bill, which was brought in and rejected. In 1890 Parnell was cited as co-respondent in a divorce action brought by Capt. O'Shea, a member of the Irish party, against his wife. As a result Gladstone publicly stated that it was impossible for Parnell to remain leader of the Irish party. The majority of the party deserted him, and his refusal to resign the leadership even at this point caused a rift from which the party never fully recovered. In June 1891 he married Mrs O'Shea and died in the following October.

Parody (Greek *parōdia*, from *para*, beside, and *ōdē*, a song), writing, either in prose or verse, in which an author's style is copied and his sentiment mimicked in order to ridicule the original; or in which what is written on one subject is altered and applied to another by way of burlesque. The *Batrachomyomachia* (Battle of Frogs and Mice), which was ascribed to Homer, is among one of the earliest known surviving parodies.

Parole. To the lawyer parole evidence is the spoken word as opposed to written evidence; in military parlance parole is a system whereby an officer prisoner of war is released, either completely or from close confinement, on giving promises binding him in honour to conform to the agreed conditions. But the most common use of the word today is to refer to systems of conditional release from prison before the expiry of sentence.

Parole is to be distinguished from remission, which indicates release before the end of sentence as a reward for good conduct, without supervision, or the possibility of recall. A parolee is on licence for part or all of the unexpired term; his licence entitles him to be at large provided that he submits to supervision and maintains good behaviour.

Paros (Greek *Páros*), second largest island of the Cyclades group, Greece, in the Aegean Sea, 7 km west of Naxos. The island has a central mountain (771 m) which contains marble; this was famous in ancient times for use in sculpture and there are still quarries 6 km east of the capital, Paros. Other products of the island are wine, fruit and potatoes. Paros was first colonised by Ionian Greeks. Area 194 km^2.

Parotid Gland, the largest of the salivary glands. It is situated below the external ear; its duct (Stensen's duct) is 5 cm long and opens on the buccal surface of the cheek opposite the second upper molar tooth. The gland secretes saliva containing ptyalin, potassium, traces of urea and mineral salts.

Parr, Catherine (1512–48), Queen of England, sixth wife of Henry VIII. She had already been widowed twice before she married Henry in 1543. After the death of Henry she contracted a marriage with Thomas Seymour, Lord-Admiral of England, who neglected and ill-treated her. She died after giving birth to his daughter.

Parrot. *The ground-dwelling kakapo,* Strigops habroptilus, *of New Zealand.*

Parrot, any species of Psittacidae, sole family of the order Psittaciformes, most abundant in the warmer parts of Australia and South America, though numerous in other tropical regions. The plumage is often gorgeously coloured, but a few are soberly tinted. Most of them are arboreal in habit, but the owl parrot or kakapo of New Zealand is flightless and usually lives on the ground, though it can still climb trees. Another New Zealand parrot differs from the rest of the group in having developed carnivorous habits. The characteristic large, powerful and much-arched bill, with its elongated tip, is well adapted in most parrots for tearing up fruit and cracking nuts. Many species are favourite cage-birds. The best talker is the African grey parrot, *Psittacus erithacus*. The sexes are hard to distinguish, and as males are rarely imported, it is almost unknown for parrots to breed in captivity.

Parrot Fishes, or parrot wrasses, fishes of the family Scaridae in order Perciformes. The teeth of this group have coalesced to form extremely hard beaks which are able to bite off pieces of coral; these, with seaweed and molluscs, form the principal food. The fish are all brilliantly coloured, and some attain a length of 1 m.

Parry, Sir (Charles) Hubert Hastings (1848–1918), British composer. One of the chief architects of the development of modern British music, he fostered the progress of many younger composers. His achievements were misunderstood by his contemporaries and he is now virtually unknown save for his settings of Milton's *Blest Pair of Sirens* and Blake's *Jerusalem*. His orchestral works include five symphonies, symphonic variations and the *Elegy for Brahms*. His choral music includes a setting of Dunbar's *Ode on the Nativity*.

Parry, Sir William Edward (1790–1855), British rear-admiral and explorer. Parry commanded expeditions to the Arctic; the first three voyages were attempts to discover the North-West Passage, and the fourth, from Spitsbergen, to reach the North Pole, in which he reached 82° 45′ N latitude. He explored Lancaster Sound, Barrow Strait and Melville Sound, and sailed nearly halfway through the North-West Passage. In 1825 he was made hydrographer to the Admiralty, and later rear-admiral.

Parry Islands, group in the Arctic Ocean belonging to Canada, west of Baffin Bay and north of Lancaster Sound, Melville Sound and Barrow Strait. The Parry Islands include Bathurst, Melville, Cornwallis and Prince Patrick Island, are covered with tundra and are uninhabited. Sir W. E. Parry, after whom they are named, visited them in 1819.

Parsec, a unit of astronomical distance measurement equal to 3·26 light-years. It is the distance at which the radius of the Earth's orbit subtends an angle of one second.

Parsees, or Parsis, the last surviving ethnic group of the pre-Arabic Persians. When the Arabs conquered Persia in the 7th century the Parsees fled to India rather than give up their ancient Zoroastrian religion which, unlike Hinduism, does not call for asceticism, but diligence and purity. Most of the Parsees live in Bombay, and number barely 100,000. For over 1300 years they have kept intact their individuality and independence of habit and customs, and a mode of living which enabled them easily to adopt Western culture. They are enterprising, foremost in the trade, science, politics and arts of India.

Parsley, *Petroselinum crispum*, a biennial flavouring and garnishing herb with much-divided leaves. Parsley belongs to the Umbelliferae and is native to southern Europe.

Parsnip, *Pastinaca sativa*, a biennial in family

Umbelliferae from Europe, much cultivated for its edible tap-roots.

Parson (Latin *persona*, person), the priest of a parish or ecclesiastical corporation, so called because 'by his *person* the Church, which is an invisible body, is represented'. A parson has the freehold of the parsonage house, tithes and other dues. Strictly speaking, the rector in holy orders is a parson while the vicar is not. In common usage any ordained clergyman is known as a parson.

Parsons, Sir Charles Algernon (1854–1931), British inventor and engineer. He is best known for the steam turbine which bears his name, and which he rendered suitable for the generation of electricity and propulsion of ships. The first turbine was produced in 1884; the torpedo boat *Turbinia* was the first to be fitted with turbine engines. Other inventions of his are an improved variety of gramophone and non-skid motor tyre chains.

Parthenocissus, a genus in the Vitidaceae, deciduous climbers with twining or adhesively tipped tendrils, closely akin to *Ampelopsis* and *Vitis*. *P. quinquefolia*, of eastern North America, is the true Virginia creeper, though the term is also applied to *P. inserta*. *P. henryana*, *P. himalayana* and *P. tricuspidata* are Asiatic species, beautiful in autumn colour.

Parthenogenesis, see ASEXUAL REPRODUCTION.

Parthenon (from Greek *parthenos*, a virgin), the most celebrated temple of ancient Greece, and one of the finest pieces of architecture in the world; it receives its name from its dedication to the virgin goddess Athena. It was commenced in 447 BC and finished in 432 BC. Its architects were Ictinus and Callicrates, but the whole of the work was carried out under the supervision of the sculptor Phidias, by whom the gold and ivory statue of Athena Parthenos was executed. The temple is situated on the south side of the Acropolis at Athens. In 1801–04 much of the sculpture was removed by Lord Elgin and eventually sold to the British Museum.

Parthia, situated to the south-east of the Caspian Sea, and corresponding to the northern portion of the Persian province of Khorassan; originally subject to Persia, and later to the Seleucidae. The Parthian empire grew in importance, until at the time of its greatest power, under Mithridates I and II, it extended to the Euphrates, Caspian Sea, Indus and Indian Ocean. From the 1st century BC onwards Parthia was often at war with Rome. The Parthian mounted archers were famous, and from their method of shooting as they appeared to retreat comes the expression a 'Parthian shot'. In AD 226 the country was annexed to the newly established Persian empire of the Sassanidae.

Particle, in grammar, part of speech, usually a small word such as an article, conjunction, preposition or interjection, which acts in a sentence to indicate general meaning or relationship, or function.

Partisans, see GUERRILLAS.

Partnership. In English law a partnership is the relationship which exists between two or more persons carrying on a business in common with a view to profit. Voluntary associations include unincorporated clubs and societies and also corporations, but partnerships are distinguishable from the first by being necessarily for business and for profit, and are different from the corporations in that they have no personality in law which is separate from that of their members.
See also COMPANY.

Partridge, Eric Honeywood (1894–1979), New Zealand-born British lexicographer. His most important work was his *Dictionary of Slang and Unconventional English* (revised edition), 1970. Another was his *Usage and Abusage* (revised edition), 1954, a guide to good English.

Partridge, game birds of the family Phasianidae, order Galliformes. It is usually the grey partridge, *Perdix perdix*, that is associated with the name. Also common in Europe is the red-legged partridge, *Alectoris rufa*. Partridges pair very early in the year, the males, like the males of most gallinaceous species, being very pugnacious. The nest is made with a minimum of trouble on the ground in fields or hedgerows, and contains from 10 to 20 olive brown eggs. The hen hatches them, but the male is attentive to her during incubation. The young remain with their parents for some months, forming coveys of about 20 birds.

Parts of Speech, in grammar, divisions into which words can be grouped according to their function or form. For English they are generally taken to be: noun, adjective, verb, participle, article, pronoun, preposition, adverb and conjunction.
See also GRAMMAR.

Pasadena, city of southern California, USA, and part of the Los Angeles conurbation. It lies in the foothills of the San Gabriel Mountains, 16 km north-east of the centre of Los Angeles, and developed originally as a health resort, with a fine mountain-slope climate and subtropical vegetation. Today it is the seat of California Institute of Technology and the Huntington Library and Art Gallery. Population (1980) 119,374.

Pasargadae, ancient city of Persia. Cyrus II the Great made it his capital and built a number of palaces and temples there. Pasargadae was situated near the River Polvar, about 88 km north-east of Shiraz. The principal ruins include the tomb of Cyrus.
See also PERSIAN ART AND ARCHITECTURE.

Pascal, Blaise (1623–62), French mathematician and devotional author. In his teens he discovered an alternative basis for a theory of conic sections to the analytical theory constructed by Descartes. Towards the end of 1642 Pascal began to devise a mechanical adding machine, and in 1645 became the first person to manufacture and sell a mechanical device for computing. In 1654 he corresponded with Fermat about problems of chance and formulated the elementary laws of probability. This led to the study of the binomial coefficients which are represented by 'Pascal's triangle'. In 1655 he retired to the Jansenist monastery of Port-Royal, where he wrote *Lettres provinciales* (1656–57), defending Jansenism against the Jesuits, and *Pensées sur la religion* (1669), a metaphysical work.
See also BINOMIAL THEOREM.

Pascal, see COMPUTER.

Pascal, SI unit of pressure, 1 newton per square metre.
See also METROLOGY.

Pasha, title derived from the Persian, and applied to commanders of high rank, naval, military or civil, in the Turkish Empire. At one time it was limited to princes of the blood. Every general or governor of a province was *ex officio* a pasha.

Pashto, an East Iranian language which is an official language of Afghanistan alongside Dari (Afghan Persian, spoken mainly in the west). Pashto is spoken by the Pashtuns of East Afghanistan and in adjoining areas of Pakistan.

Pasmore, Victor (1908–), British painter and designer. He was one of the founders of the Euston Road School, 1937–39, and first became of note for pictures in the late-Impressionist tradition. About 1947 he abandoned representation and began to work as an abstract painter, progressing to three-dimensional reliefs in modern materials. From 1954 to 1961 he was master of painting, Durham University, and was consulting designer for Peterlee New Town from 1955.

Pasolini, Pier Paolo (1922–75), Italian film director and writer. Pasolini's poetry (*La Meglio gioventù*, 1954; *L'Usignuolo della Chiesa Cattolica*, 1959) and novels (*Ragazzi di vita*, 1955; *Una Vita violenta*, 1959; *Il Sogno d'una cosa*, 1962) reflect his commitment to the common people and their language. He edited the magazine *Officina*, 1955–59, and various collections of popular poetry. Since his first feature film, *Accatone*, 1961, dealing with the brutalised life of the poor in a manner reminiscent of the novels, Pasolini's Marxism has been expressed in the brilliant, highly complex and sometimes obscure treatment of such films as *The Gospel According to St Matthew*, 1967; *Oedipus Rex*, 1968; *Theorem*, 1968; *Porcile*, 1969; *Medea*, 1970; *Ostia*, 1970; *Arabian Nights*, 1974; and *Salò*, 1975.

Pasque Flower, *Pulsatilla*, a genus of Ranunculaceae so called because of its purple flowers which appear about Easter time.

Passacaglia, originally a Spanish dance, but now an instrumental composition based on a ground. One of the best-known examples is Bach's Passacaglia for organ.

Passage, Court of, formerly a civil court of record in the borough of Liverpool.

Passant, in heraldry, an animal seen in profile walking forwards with the dexter forepaw raised, e.g. the lions passant guardant in the English royal arms.

Passau, city in Bavaria, Federal Republic of Germany, 148 km north-east of Munich. It is on the Austrian border, at the confluence of the Danube, the Inn and the Ilz. In 739 St Boniface made it a bishopric; the bishop became a prince of the empire in the 13th century, and it developed into a river port of great importance. On the suppression of the bishopric in 1803 the town became a Bavarian possession. Passau is dominated by its massive Baroque and Gothic cathedral (14th–17th centuries) and by a great fortress, begun in the 13th century. It has machinery, textile and pharmaceutical industries. Population (1970) 31,600.

Passchendaele, see WORLD WAR, FIRST.

Passenger Pigeon, *Ectopistes* (or *Columba*) *migratoria*, North American bird whose sudden and complete disappearance is the most remarkable in zoological history. It was probably the most gregarious bird in existence, and migrating flocks filled the sky for days. The birds were slaughtered for food, and in one year 15,000,000 dead birds were dispatched from Michigan and Pennsylvania. In 1888 it failed to take up its usual breeding quarters, and then disappeared without trace, the last known specimen dying in 1914 at Cincinnati Zoological Gardens. Its main features were its long wings and longer narrow tail.

Passeriformes, the order of perching or passerine birds, characterised especially by the four-toed foot, three toes directed forwards and one, the hallux, backwards. The hallux is not reversible. This is by far the largest order of birds, consisting of 5000 to 6000 species in 56 families, over half the number of known birds.

Passfield, Lady, see WEBB, BEATRICE.

Passfield, Sidney James Webb, Baron (1859–1947), British Socialist, historian and statesman. His greatest achievement is the placing of the British Socialist movement in its historical setting by the books he wrote in collaboration with his wife, Beatrice Webb. Although he held Cabinet rank in two Labour governments, he was never a prominent figure in public life. Yet in practical achievement he accomplished more than most politicians of his day in the development of social and political reform. Through the Fabian Society, of which he was one of the pioneers, he played the most conspicuous part in converting British socialism from a propaganda of social revolution to a programme for the working-class movement, and more than any other led the Labour party to accept the Fabian interpretation of socialism. But his greatest interest was education; and the subsequent revolution in educational administration, the transfer of control to local authorities, the development of secondary education, and the enlargement of the university system were all for the most part due to his efforts. The Fabian programme, much of which the Education Act of 1902 embodied, was also his work.

Passion Flower, *Passiflora*, in family Passifloraceae, a genus of 400 climbing herbs and shrubs many of which bear flowers of a form that led devout settlers in South America to give the plants their name. The three stigmas were held to symbolise the crosses of Christ and the thieves; the anthers, the Virgin Mary, Mary Magdalene, Mary the mother of James, St John and Joseph of Arimathaea. The filaments inside the petals were the multitude who mocked Christ; the ten parts of the perianth, the ten faithful apostles; and the digitate leaves and tendrils, the hands and scourges of those who scourged him. *P. caerulea* is best known in cooler gardens. *P. quadrangularis* is the granadilla, grown for its fruit.

Passion Music. From the earliest days of the Christian Church the history of the Passion of Christ was read during Holy Week; by the 8th century it was being solemnly chanted. In the Roman Church the Passion gospels are sung in plainchant by priests, one taking the words of Christ, another the words of the evangelist and a third those of other characters. The people (*turba*) are, when possible, represented by the choir, for whom music was written by Palestrina and Victoria. The same elements are retained in the German Passion, from Schütz (four settings) to Bach, St Matthew and St John settings.

Passion Play, drama which treats of the events surrounding the Crucifixion and Resurrection of Christ. This type of play was common throughout Western Europe in the late Middle Ages. The best known modern example is the Oberammergau Passion Play, first mentioned in 1633 in connection with a vow made by peasants after a severe occurrence of the plague, that they would perform a passion drama once in every ten years.
See also MIRACLE PLAY.

Passion-tide, the last two weeks before Easter in the Christian year.
See also EASTER.

Passive Immunisation, a technique used to give immediate protection to an individual who is thought to have contracted a disease caused by bacterial toxins, notably diphtheria, tetanus and gas gangrene. An injection of serum containing preformed antitoxin (antibody against the toxin) is given to the patient, which immediately provides effective immunity that lasts for several weeks. The injection of preformed antitoxin bestows immediate immunity upon the recipient passively, whereas active immunisation stimulates the recipient's immune system to provide self-protection. Passive immunisation also occurs in mammals from the mother's blood across the placenta, while the foetus is in the womb, or through the mother's milk. This provides the newborn baby or animal with initial protection against infection until its body can manufacture sufficient antibodies to defend itself.

Passos, John Roderigo Dos, see DOS PASSOS, JOHN RODERIGO.

Passover (Hebrew *pesach*), first of the three great festivals ordained by the Pentateuchal codes. According to Exodus xii., it was instituted to commemorate the *exodus* from Egypt, in particular the 'passing over' of the houses of the Israelites (distinguished by the sprinkled blood on the door-posts) by the angel of the Lord when the first-born of the Egyptians were slain. The order of its celebration was to be thus: a lamb or kid, a male of the first year, without blemish, was to be killed, roasted and eaten with unleavened bread and bitter herb '... for thou camest forth out of the land of Egypt in haste ...' (Deut. xvi. 3.) They were, therefore, to eat in haste, standing, with their loins girded, their shoes on their feet and their staves in their hands. During the seven days of the feast only unleavened bread, called *matzah*, was to be eaten. (Passover is still celebrated with a ceremonial meal on the first two nights, known as the Seder (order), accompanied by the recital of the Hagadah (story of the Exodus).

Passport, document of identity and nationality for overseas travel. In Britain passports may be obtained from Passport Offices in London, Liverpool, Glasgow, Newport and Peterborough, according to the area in which a person lives, although a British Visitor's Passport is obtainable from a Crown Post Office.

Pasta, the generic term for a dough made from ground wheat and water. There are a great number of pasta products on sale, which include macaroni, spaghetti, ravioli, vermicelli and lasagne. They are all made from semolina, particles of ground wheat, coarser than flour, which is obtained from a very hard type of wheat with a high gluten content, usually grown in Italy.

Pastel, or crayon drawing, art-medium developed in the 17th and 18th centuries from the use of white chalk to add highlights to black or red chalk. A full range of colours in soft chalk was used by such French masters as Quentin de La Tour, Chardin, J. B. Perronneau (1715–83) and the Swiss J. E. Liotard (1702–90). In England, pastel was used by Francis Cotes and John Russell in the 18th century. In the 19th century, pastel was used by Toulouse-Lautrec, Millet, Whistler and, above all, Degas.
See also DRAWING; PAINTING; PAINTING TECHNIQUES.

Pasternak, Boris Leonidovich (1890–1960), Soviet writer, one of the most outstanding modern Russian poets. As a young man he joined the Futurist literary movement. After 1934 Pasternak led the life of an 'internal emigré' in the Soviet Union, considering that the Stalinist 'cultural revolution' had resulted in cultural reaction. Unable to publish original works, he often turned to translating. During the 'thaw' after Stalin's death in 1953, he completed *Dr Zhivago*, about the fate of an intellectual in Soviet Russia, but was only able to have it published abroad, where it was enthusiastically received. For his total output Pasternak was awarded the Nobel Prize for literature in 1958, but was compelled to decline the award.

***Louis Pasteur,** best remembered for his pioneer work on pasteurisation and inoculation.*

Pasteur, Louis (1822–95), French chemist and bacteriologist. He studied chemistry and physics, and worked especially on isomeric compounds. In 1852 he was appointed professor of chemistry at Strasbourg. For his work on tartaric acid crystals he was awarded the Rumford Medal of the Royal Society (1856). He was appointed professor of chemistry at Lille in 1854. In the breweries of this town he examined the 'diseases' of beer, wine and vinegar, and discovered that fermentation is caused by micro-organisms. He also disproved the old theory of 'spontaneous generation' by showing that bacteria are present in the atmosphere and that injured living tissue does not become infected if it is protected from them. These researches, having proved the germ theory of disease, led directly to Lister's epochal work on antisepsis. His recommendation of heat treatment for beer led to pasteurisation. In 1865 he carried out a masterly and classical research on the disease attacking the silkworm, but in the midst of this work he suffered a cerebral haemorrhage and never entirely recovered from the consequent paralysis. He next turned to the study of chicken cholera and, by investigating the causal virus, demonstrated the principle of preventive inoculation; by attenuating (weakening) the virus and then inoculating it, a mild attack of the disease was produced in the subject, thus conferring immunity. A similar result followed his work on anthrax (1881), the bacillus of which had already been discovered. In 1880 Pasteur began experiments on rabies (hydrophobia) which were to lead to the most startling discovery of his career. Although he did not succeed in isolating the virus, he located it in the central nervous system and was able to produce a vaccine of attenuated virus. On 16 July 1885 he inoculated Joseph Meister, an Alsatian boy who had been bitten by a rabid dog; the child did not develop rabies. A great wave of enthusiasm and generosity following this discovery led to the foundation of the Pasteur Institute in Paris, where Pasteur was able to carry on his work and train others.

Pasteurisation, method of food preservation, named after its inventor, Louis Pasteur. The process is used for milk, and sometimes for beer, wine, cheese as well as other foodstuffs. It destroys harmful bacteria by heating the food to a temperature less than boiling point (generally 63°C–72°C) and then cooling it quickly.

Pastiche, or pasticcio, in literature or art, either a patchwork of borrowings, or work in imitation of another's style. In music it can also mean a stage entertainment for which the music was not written by a single composer, but put together from various earlier works by any number of composers. The words were therefore written to the music, not the reverse. In 18th-century Italy, however, words as well as music, especially from Metastasio's works, were often used for a pastiche. The form was especially fashionable in the 18th century, although the ballad opera and vaudeville were both kinds of pastiche.

Pasto, city of south-west Colombia, capital of Nariño department, on a slope of the Pasto volcano (4200 m). It is the centre of an agricultural and cattle-raising area but production is mainly consumed locally. There are some gold mines in the vicinity. Population (1978) 140,700.

Paston Letters, correspondence of a Norfolk family of that name, together with state papers and other documents, covering the period from 1422 to 1509. They form an invaluable source of information on 15th-century life and manners, and on conditions during the Wars of the Roses, as well as giving vivid portraits of some of the Paston family.

Pastoral Letter, letter addressed by the bishop of a diocese to the whole body of clergy and the people under his jurisdiction. Such letters are usually read out from the pulpit of each parish church.

Pastoral Poetry describes country life, and includes pastoral drama, in which the characters represent shepherds or other country people. Except in such cases as the Dorset poems of Barnes, it is a perfectly artificial genre, and the rural setting does little more than mask the thoughts and emotions of the country and era in which the pastorals are produced.

Pastoral Staff, see CROSIER.

Pastoral Theology, branch of theology which deals with the duties of the clergy as shepherds of souls.

Pastoralism, a mode of subsistence achieved by tending and herding domesticated animals which provide their owners with food (milk, blood, meat) and their material culture (leather and skins for clothing, tents, bones and horns for other implements). In addition, pastoralists trade animal products for cereals, salt, tea, sugar and clothes.

Pastoralists view their nomadic animal-centred life as the ideal but many produce a major portion of their food by agriculture. Frequently proud and independent, pastoralists are often noted raiders and fighters.

The overgrazing of pastoralists is thought to be one of the causes of the steppe and desert conditions of the Sahara, the Mediterranean shores and the Middle East.

Pasture, term loosely applied to all grassland which is grazed at any time. It may refer to permanent pasture, temporary pasture or ley, or even to rough grazing on hills.

Patagonia, a geographically homogeneous region of southern South America. The vast majority of the region lies within Argentina, comprising the provinces of Neuquén, Río Negro, Chubut, Santa Cruz, and the territory of Tierra del Fuego, with the remainder in the extreme south belonging to Chile. Patagonia stretches from the River Colorado to the Beagle Channel, 1600 km to the south. Essentially it consists of a plateau sloping eastwards from the Andes Mountains to the cliff coastline on the Atlantic Ocean. Most of the plateau is over 600 m high with a number of outcrops of higher hills. It is crossed from west to east by a number of rivers flowing through deep canyons. In the west are a series of lakes, the most famous being Lake Nahuel Huapí. For the latitude the climate is mild though towards the south it becomes progressively colder and the prevailing winds fiercer. The whole area suffers from lack of rainfall, particularly in the east. Sheep raising on a large scale (about 20 million head), both for meat and wool, is the main economic activity. There are oil-fields in Neuquén, Chubut and Tierra del Fuego, and the Río Turbio coalfields are in Santa Cruz. The region is sparsely populated, particularly in the south, and the only towns of importance are Punta Arenas (population (1970) 70,000) and Comodoro Rivadavia (75,000).

Patching, see NEEDLEWORK.

Patchwork, see EMBROIDERY.

Patel, Vallabhbhai Jhaverbhai (1875–1950), Indian Nationalist leader. His association with Gandhi and the Indian National Congress began in 1916, and lasted till his death. He soon showed a remarkable flair for organisation, and was largely responsible for the striking success of many of the mass demonstrations and civil disobedience campaigns stimulated by the Congress.

In the interim government of India, formed in 1946, he became home minister and minister in charge of information and broadcasting. After independence and partition in 1947 he remained in these posts and also became *de facto* deputy prime minister under Jawaharlal Nehru.

His death deprived India of the most clear-headed and experienced of its leaders.

Patella, see KNEE.

Paten, a shallow, circular dish used in the celebration of mass. In the Roman rite it is made of gold or silver gilt and solemnly consecrated. The corresponding vessel in the Eastern liturgy is the discus. A paten is also used in the Anglican and Lutheran communion services.

Patenier, Joachim (c.1480–1524), Dutch painter. A pupil of Quentin Matsys, he worked at Antwerp and is noted as one of the earliest painters to make landscape a main element in pictorial composition. In 1521 he met Dürer, who mentions him as a landscape painter.

Patents, in the UK, or more correctly letters patent, are documents in which the Crown vests a subject with special rights or privileges; e.g. the sole right to make, use, and vend an invention for a limited period. Such a grant creates a monopoly in favour of the patentee.

Pater, Walter Horatio (1839–94), English critic. Through Ruskin's influence he became interested in art, and built a reputation as the leading authority on aesthetics.

He first made a name in 1873 with his *Studies in the History of the Renaissance*, and in 1885 he published his greatest work, *Marius the Epicurean*, a kind of historical novel of the time of Marcus Aurelius, which preached the pursuit of beauty. A master of polished and cultured prose, he taught the doctrine of 'art for art's sake', and represents the most earnest side of the Aesthetic Movement.

Paterson, 'Banjo', pseudonym of Andrew Barton Paterson (1864–1941), Australian balladist. Writing under the name 'The Banjo', he belonged to the 'Bulletin School', a group of balladists in the 1890s who found inspiration and publication in the intensely nationalist weekly, *The Bulletin*. His first collection, *The Man from Snowy River and Other Verses*, 1895, brought him immediate fame and sold over 100,000 copies. The title poem has been known by heart all over Australia since its first publication.

The Australian balladists of the 1890s made articulate a unique 19th-century folklore which had grown up around the camp-fires in the lonely outback, and Paterson collected *Old Bush Songs Composed and Sung in the Bushranging, Digging and Overland Days*, 1905, and used some of them in his ballads. It is believed that he based Australia's unofficial national anthem, 'Waltzing Matilda', on an earlier bush song.

Paterson, William (1658–1719), Scottish financier. He was a wealthy and influential merchant. He was one of the founders of the Bank of England in 1694 and he became a director. In 1695, owing to a disagreement with his colleagues, he withdrew from the board and devoted himself to the ill-fated New World colony at Darien, founded in 1698.

Paterson, city of New Jersey, USA, and part of an industrial and residential conurbation in the valley of the Passaic river. Paterson was selected as the site of an industrial settlement in 1791, on the basis of the water power available from the Passaic Falls. It grew, as did neighbouring Passaic, with the textile industry; Paterson specialised in silks, and Passaic in handkerchiefs. In time these trades declined, and the two cities switched to the manufacture of mill machinery and to associated industries. Population (1980) 137,970.

Pathans, 14 million Pashto-speaking peoples of north-west Pakistan and eastern Afghanistan who claim descent from a follower of the Prophet Mohammed, Abdur Rashid. In high river valleys, e.g. the Swat Valley, they are sedentary agriculturalists with 'saintly' lineages mediating between their fellow landowning lineages. In higher areas Pathans are nomadic pastoralists or traders.

All Pathans are Muslims; they have a strict sense of honour and feuds are common.

Pathé, Charles (1863–1957), French pioneer film producer, who with his brothers in 1911 founded Pathé Frères Ltd, a subsidiary of the company which produced Britain's first newsreel (issued twice weekly under the title of *Pathé News*) and the weekly screen magazine, *Pathé Pictorial*.

See also CINEMA.

Pathet Lao, name of the Communist party in Laos, although the meaning of the phrase is simply 'Lao country'. The movement was founded in 1949 by a small group of Lao dissidents led by Prince Souphannouvong, who emerged in 1975 as the president of the Laos Republic, but from the beginning had support and probably some measure of direction from the Vietminh. It took the Pathet Lao until 1975 to take over the country, and this was hastened by the fall of nearby countries also to the Communists.

Pathetic Fallacy, phrase coined by John Ruskin to describe the type of personification which depicts nature or objects as sympathising with human feelings. An example is taken from Tennyson's *Maud*:

> The red rose cries, 'She is near, she is near';
> And the white rose weeps, 'She is late'.

See also FIGURE OF SPEECH.

Pathology, the science of disease, including structural abnormalities not usually regarded as diseases. Until Virchow published his *Cellular Pathology* in 1850, the science was hardly in existence, for not until the microscope revealed the fact that man was a community of living cells was it recognised that their vicissitudes were the true basis of the study of human disease. Pasteur's work showed how science could wage war on germs inimical to cells. Koch's discovery of the anthrax bacillus in 1876 and the tubercle bacillus in 1882, by his culture method of isolating bacteria, led to the discovery of the organisms responsible for many infectious diseases. Lister's work in antiseptic treatment of wounds was of equal importance, and Jenner's in smallpox. In 1893 Theobald Smith, in the case of bovine malaria or Texas fever, showed for the first time that external parasites, such as ticks, could act as intermediary hosts and transfer disease from animal to animal. Ehrlich's researches in chemotherapy, Metchnikoff's study of immunity, and the discovery of antitoxin by von Behring were also landmarks in the general advance.

This century has seen the birth of the clinical pathologist. The science now includes bacteriology immunology, histology, morbid anatomy, haematology and chemical pathology. Bacteriology and immunology were the first laboratory sciences to intrude into bedside medicine. The natural consequence was the development of measures for immunisation and the prevention of epidemics.

Chemical pathology is now largely the science of blood chemistry, a science brought into importance by the discovery of insulin in 1922 by Banting, Best and Macleod, and the consequent need to estimate the sugar content of blood in diabetics being treated with insulin. Since chemical change is the basis of all physiological function, the importance of the biochemist will continue to increase in the future in the diagnosis, control and cure of disease. The ability to grow tissue cells in culture, the invention of the electron microscope and the development of new biochemical analytical techniques have opened up the new science of microbiology, in which much progress is being made in the elucidation of cellular structure and function. Tissue typing, the classification of tissues in much the same way as blood is identified into blood groups, is an essential preliminary to organ transplant operations and is now part of pathology.

See also BACTERIA; CANCER; PARASITES.

Patience, generic name for card games for one player. There are over 500 patience games, some requiring skill and luck, some merely luck. Until the end of the 19th century rules were passed down orally, and there may still be games unrecorded. Many patiences, however, differ little from their fellows except in the nature of their lay-out. Most are based on the principle of building the whole pack in ascending or descending sequence on specified 'foundation cards': if the player succeeds in this he 'wins'.

Patio (Spanish), in a Spanish or Spanish-American house, an inner courtyard, corresponding to the Italian *cortile*. It is now used in English for an external terrace (which can also be raised or sunken) leading onto a garden.

Patmore, Coventry Kersey Dighton (1823–96), English poet. In 1849 he contributed to the journal of the Pre-Raphaelites, the *Germ*. While not identified with the intellectual movement of the mid-19th century or with the Pre-Raphaelites, his homely themes are written in a simple, dignified manner. *The Angel in the House*, 1863, is really a novel in verse, presenting domestic virtues and the wife as spotless fount of all goodness. The poem's more philosophical parts reveal the mysticism which is developed further in *The Unknown Eros*, a series of odes notable for the poet's power of expressing intricate thought in verse.

Patmos (Greek *Pátmos*), volcanic, rocky and barren Greek island in the Dodecanese Islands in the eastern Aegean. Here St John the Evangelist is believed to have written his Revelation after his banishment by Domitian in the year 95. The monastery of St John was founded in 1088 by St Christodulus. Area 57 km².

Patna, capital of Bihar state, India, on the Ganges river, 450 km north-west of Calcutta. It was founded in the 5th century BC and under the name of Pataliputra was the capital of several kingdoms during the ensuing centuries. Its modern growth dates from the British period when it became an administrative and transport centre 7 km upstream from the old city. Population (1981) 811,249.

Paton, Alan Stewart (1903–), South African writer. His famous novel, *Cry, the Beloved Country*, 1948, revealed to the world the situation of the blacks in South Africa, and Paton was one of the founders of the Liberal Association, which developed into the Liberal Party. He was its president until it was declared illegal in 1968.

Patras (Greek *Pátrai*), port of Greece, capital of Achaea department, situated on a narrow, fertile coastal plain on the Gulf of Patras. It was an important city under the Roman emperor Augustus and was made capital of Achaea under the Eastern Empire. Its port is the third largest in Greece. It is more concerned with passenger traffic than cargo, but it imports coal and foodstuffs, and exports agricultural products. Population (1981) 140,878.

Patras, Gulf of, inlet of the Ionian Sea, opening out of the Gulf of Corinth, between Aetolia to the north and Achaea to the south, on the west coast of Greece. Length 48 km.

Patriarch (Greek *patriarchēs*, head of a family), name given to the scriptural fathers of the human race, e.g. Noah, and also to the great progenitors of the Hebrew race, Abraham, Isaac, Jacob and Jacob's 12 sons.

Patriarch, in the Christian Church, the bishop of certain metropolitan sees, especially in the East. The title is also used by the heads of several national Orthodox churches: Russia (since 1589), Georgia, Bulgaria, Serbia and Romania.

Patriarchy, term used to mean rule by the father or senior men of the community. Since the term can be applied to a number of phenomena (e.g. modes of descent, rules of inheritance, etc.) which seldom all occur together, anthropologists tend to avoid it as imprecise.

Patricians and Plebeians. In Roman history the distinction between patricians and plebeians is first noted in the period following the expulsion of the kings (i.e. the 5th century BC). The word patrician comes from *pater*, father, the Roman Senate being known as *patres*. The patricians therefore were the clan which monopolised membership of the Senate whilst the plebeians formed the rest of the citizen body of Rome.

The struggle of the *plebs* to gain political equality is known as the 'Struggle of the Orders'. The chief landmarks in this conflict were: the creation of the office of Tribune and the popular assembly in 493 BC; the publication of the law (Twelve Tables) in 451 BC; concession of the right of intermarriage between patricians and plebeians, in 445 BC; admission of plebeians to the quaestorship (421 BC), consulship (366 BC), dictatorship (356 BC), censorship (351 BC) and praetorship (337 BC). Finally in 287 BC it was recognised that formal decisions of the *plebs* were legally binding on the whole body of the citizens, including patricians. In theory the popular assembly became the sovereign body in Rome; in practice the Senate, now open to plebeians, retained control of affairs.

During the 3rd century, the distinction between plebeians and patricians became less important, though patricians continued to take pride in their distinguished ancestry. Plebeians could assume the traditionally patrician magistracies, but patricians were not allowed to become tribunes, unless they were adopted into a plebeian family.

Patrick, Saint (c.389–c.460), patron saint of Ireland, son of a Roman official. Having studied for the priesthood (probably in Britain, not in Gaul), he was ordained, and soon afterwards sent by the pope to Ireland as a missionary. In a little more than ten years he had the whole country studded with churches, staffed by a zealous native clergy, to whom a tide of conversions was steadily flowing, and he established the seat of the primacy at Armagh.

St Patrick left two documents of great value and unquestioned authenticity: his *Confession* and his *Epistle to Coroticus*, which present a remarkable self-portrait.

Patrol (ultimately from French *patrouiller* = *patouiller*, to flounder in mud), detachment of troops sent out in advance of the main body to reconnoitre the country and gain information as to the position and movements of the enemy. The same duties are now often carried out by armoured cars or tanks, and of course by reconnoitring aircraft. The chief non-military use of the term is in connection with motorised police detachments and the fire-fighting sections of forestry services.

See also SCOUTS.

Pattern-making, see CASTING.

Patterson, Floyd (1935–), US boxer; outstanding as an amateur, he won the middleweight class at the 1952 Olympics; became the youngest winner of the world heavyweight championship, 1956, defeating Archie Moore in five rounds. He defended the title successfully four times before being beaten by Ingemar Johansson when he was floored seven times, but regained his title (the first man to win it twice) by knocking out Johansson in five rounds. He finally lost the championship to Sonny Liston in a one-round fight; he was too light (at 82 kg) to match the heavy fighters. His autobiography, *Victory Over Myself*, appeared in 1969.

Patti, Adelina (1843–1919), Italian soprano. In 1859 she made her stage début in New York. In 1861 she first sang at Covent Garden as Amina in Bellini's *La Sonnambula*, creating a sensation with the purity, flexibility and evenness of her voice. She later sang throughout Europe, in Russia, and in North and South America. After 25 seasons at Covent Garden she returned there in 1895 for six performances.

Patton, George Smith (1885–1945), US general. He commanded the Seventh Army in the invasion of Sicily. In April 1944 he was transferred to the Western Front, taking command of the Third Army. He cut off the peninsula of Brittany and then swept on to Paris, the German frontier and the Siegfried line. In the advance to the Rhine, he played a leading part. Crossing the Rhine at Frankfurt, he maintained the impetus of his advance through central Germany and into Bohemia. In April 1945 he was nominated a full general and his army occupied Bavaria. Owing to his scepticism over the necessity for the 'de-Nazification' programme, he was removed from the command of the Third Army and transferred to the command of a skeleton force, the Fifteenth Army.

Pau, French town, capital of the *département* of Pyrénées-Atlantiques, on the River Gave de Pau. It was the capital of Béarn and of French Navarre. The castle was the birthplace of Henry IV of France. Pau trades in horses, wine, leather and rugs. It is a holiday resort. Population (1975) 85,860.

St Paul. A 15th-century mural from the church at Kyperounda, Cyprus.

Paul, Saint (c.AD 3–c.67), born at Tarsus in Cilicia. Though a Jew of the tribe of Benjamin, a Hebrew born of Hebrews, he was by birth also a Roman citizen. He is first mentioned in connection with the martyrdom of St Stephen (Acts vii). His Jewish name was Saul, the form Paul being used in the Greek and Roman world. He was educated in the learning of the times, and later went to Jerusalem to study the laws and traditions of his people under Gamaliel, a distinguished rabbi. Being a man of great talent, ardent mind and inflexible resolution, and devotedly attached to the institutions of his country, he contemplated with alarm and anxiety the progress of the new religion. Accordingly he took an active and prominent part against the Christians, pursuing them with zeal and unrelenting fury. He obtained letters from the Sanhedrin to the synagogue of the Jews at Damascus, and also to the governor, authorising him to arrest and bring to Jerusalem any disciples he found there. While on this journey his miraculous conversion took place (Acts ix). The journeys and events of his laborious life up to his captivity in Rome are described in Acts xiii–xxviii. He may subsequently have revisited the East and Spain. Paul was martyred at Rome.

The letters and speeches of Paul were all directed to one purpose, the proof of Christ's claims to be the Messiah promised in the Old Testament and the exposition of what those claims meant, with exhortations to the fulfilment of moral duties and advice as to the management of ecclesiastical affairs.

Paul I (1754–1801), Russian Emperor, son of Peter III and Catherine II, succeeded his mother in 1796. He re-established primogeniture as the basis for succession to the throne. He was strangled during a palace revolution in favour of his son Alexander I. Russian foreign policy under Paul I sought to resist the domination of Europe by either France or Britain.

Paul I (1901–64), King of the Hellenes, brother of George II, whom he succeeded in 1947. In 1938 he married Princess Frederika of Brunswick. Paul and his wife made determined attempts to popularise the Greek monarchy, identifying it closely with Greek aspirations in Cyprus.

Paul III, Alessandro Farnese (b.1468), Pope, 1534–49. Easy-going, luxurious, worldly minded, and a shameless nepotist, he was nevertheless a powerful instrument of the counter-Reformation, approving the Society of Jesus, 1540, introducing the Inquisition into Italy, 1542, establishing the Index, 1543, and summoning the Council of Trent. A patron of the arts, he began the Palazzo Farnese, built the Sala Regia in the Vatican, commissioned Michelangelo's 'Last Judgment' in the Sistine Chapel, and invited him to resume work on St Peter's.

Paul VI, Giovanni Battista Montini (1879–1979), Pope, 1963–79. After serving as attaché in the apostolic nunciature at Warsaw, 1923–24, he joined the secretariat of state in Rome; substitute secretary of state to Cardinal Pacelli (later Pius XII), 1937–39; to Pius XII, 1939–52; pro-secretary of state, 1952–54; archbishop of Milan, 1954–63, cardinal, 1958; succeeded John XXIII, 1963, and reconvoked the Second Vatican Council.

Paul, Jean, see RICHTER, JEAN PAUL FRIEDRICH.

Paul, Vincent de, see VINCENT DE PAUL, ST.

Paulhan, Jean (1884–1968), French essayist and critic. He was editor of the *Nouvelle revue française* from 1925 to 1940 and his writings include *La Guérison sévère*, 1925; *Le Guerrier appliqué*, 1930; *Les Fleurs de Tarbes*, 1941; *Clef de la poésie*, 1944; *Entretien sur des faits divers*, 1945; *De la paille et du grain*, 1948; *Les Causes célèbres*, 1949; and *L'Aveuglette*, 1953.

Pauli, Wolfgang (1900–58), Swiss-US physicist. He worked on Niels Bohr's interpretation of atomic spectra in terms of quantum theory, and made discoveries which served Bohr as the main factor in his explanation of the periodic system of the elements. In 1925 he announced the 'exclusion principle' that, in an atom, there can be only two electrons at each energy level—one with a positive spin, the other with a negative spin. He became a professor at the Zürich Institute of Technology in 1928. In 1931 Pauli postulated the existence of an uncharged elementary particle (which Fermi called a 'neutrino') produced when beta particles are emitted. He moved to Princeton in 1940, was awarded the Nobel Prize for physics in 1945, and became a naturalised US citizen, 1946.

Pauling, Linus Carl (1901–), US chemist. His main work was on the nature of the chemical bond and the structure of crystals and molecules, including proteins, and he was awarded the 1954 Nobel Prize for chemistry. He campaigned for a nuclear test ban treaty, and was awarded the 1962 Nobel Peace Prize, thus becoming the first man to receive two Nobel prizes.

Paulinus, Gaius Suetonius, Roman governor of Britain, AD 59–62. He subdued the rebellious Iceni and defeated Boadicea in 61. Consul in 66, he was one of Otho's generals in the unsuccessful campaign against Vitellius, 69.

Paulinus, Saint, full name Pontius Meropius Paulinus (c.353–431), early Christian priest and poet. Prefect of Rome for a time, he went to Spain, became a Christian (c.390) and later bishop of Nola in 409. Some of his letters, and most of his poems, are extant. With Prudentius he is regarded as the foremost Christian Latin poet of the patristic period.

Paulownia, a genus of trees from Asia in the family Scrophulariaceae. *P. tomentosa*, the foxglove tree, produces upright sprays of lilac flowers before the leaves open.

Paulus, Friedrich von (1890–1957), German field marshal who commanded German forces at Stalingrad in one of the bloodiest actions of the Second World War. Ordered by Hitler to hold out at all costs, the Germans, hopelessly encircled, were besieged by the Russians from November 1942 to 31 January 1943 when they capitulated. Paulus, interned, founded the pro-Soviet union of German Officers. Repatriated by the Russians in 1953, he settled in the German Democratic Republic.

Paupers, see MENDICANCY; POOR LAW, HISTORY OF; VAGRANTS.

Paustovski, Konstantin Georgievich (1892–1968), Soviet author, one of the most popular and widely respected modern Russian writers. He travelled widely and wrote in a lyrical vein about some of the more remote parts of his country. Although he began to publish before the October Revolution and became a full-time writer in 1927, he did not come to the notice of general readers abroad until much later. He played a leading part in the 'thaw' following Stalin's death, and published a long autobiographical work, *Story of a Life*, in which his phenomenal memory, lucid prose style and gentle humour are displayed to the full. He also wrote historical and nautical stories and plays.

Pavane, or pavan, couple dance popular in the 16th century and probably Italian in origin. The French pavane was assimilated into English court circles and became known as the English pavane. This version was slow, stately and simple in arrangement, and some of the finest Tudor music was written for its accompaniment. The music was usually in 2-4 to 4-4 time, but dances of Spanish origin were generally in triple time.

Pavarotti, Luciano (1935–), Italian tenor. In 1961 he won the international competition at the Teatro Reggio Emilio, and in the same year made his début there as Rodolfo in Puccini's *La Bohème*. He subsequently appeared at Covent Garden (1963) and Glyndebourne (1964). In 1965 he toured Australia with the Sutherland-Williamson company and made his début at La Scala, Milan. He first sang in the USA in 1968. His other roles include Alfredo, Manrico and Riccardo in operas by Verdi, Arturo in Bellini's *I puritani* and Edgardo in Donizetti's *Lucia di Lammermoor*.

Pavese, Cesare (1908–50), Italian novelist. He wrote some poetry (*Lavorare stanca*, 1936, and *Verrà la morte*, 1951), but his primary importance is as a writer of novels and long short stories. Pavese, a realistic writer, is at his best in his treatment of the myth of youth and innocence, and his greatest work, *La luna e i falò*, 1950, was translated into many languages. Other novels include *La Spiaggia*, 1942; *Feria d'agosto*, 1946; *Il compagno*, 1947; and *La bella estate*, 1949. He committed suicide at the age of 42.

Pavia (ancient *Ticinum*), Italian city and capital of Pavia province, situated on the Ticino, 30 km south of Milan. It was founded by the Ligurii, and became the capital of the Longobards until it was taken from them by Charlemagne in 774. In 1359 it was taken by the Visconti. It was annexed by Austria in 1714, was pillaged by Napoleon in 1796, and became part of united Italy in 1859. The basilica of San Michele is of Longobard foundation and there the kings of Italy (6th to 11th centuries) and various emperors were crowned. Pavia is a university town that is also an agricultural and industrial (sewing machines especially) centre. Population (1974) 90,600.

Pavilion, either (1) a lightly constructed building for recreation or display; or (2) a decorative projecting section of a larger building, usually square and often domed.

Pavlodar, town and capital of Pavlodar *oblast*, USSR, north-west of Semipalatinsk. It has an important manufacturing industry (tractors, aluminium, shipbuilding, ferro-concrete products). Population (1980) 281,000.

Pavlov, Ivan Petrovich (1849–1936), Russian physiologist remembered chiefly for work on the conditioned reflex and the physiology of digestion. He discovered the nerve fibres affecting the action of the heart and the secretory nerves of the pancreas. He worked on the physiology of circulation and digestion, especially the secretion of the digestive glands; his discoveries reformed all ideas of the processes of digestion and were the foundation of modern knowledge on the subject. Using live dogs, he made a study of conditioned or acquired reflexes associated with definite areas of brain cortex. Subsequently he began to study the higher nervous activity of man, using individuals with functionally and anatomically diseased brains. He was a complete mechanist, believing that all action depends upon conditioned reflex. On his 85th birthday the Soviet government, which he was always criticising, provided him with an extensive new laboratory in Leningrad and a pension. He won the Nobel Prize for medicine, 1904. See also BEHAVIOURISM.

Pavlova, Anna (1881–1931), Russian ballerina. She entered the state-endowed Imperial Ballet School in St Petersburg, where in 1906, having passed rapidly through all its grades, she became prima ballerina. She first danced outside Russia in 1907. In 1909 she and Nijinsky appeared in Paris with the Diaghilev Ballet, but thereafter she danced with her own company. Although not an innovator, by her own transcendent genius as a dancer she spread the popularity of ballet much wider than did the Diaghilev Ballet, laying the foundation for the world-wide interest in ballet today. Her most famous dance was *Le Cygne*, which Michel Fokine arranged for her to music by Saint-Saëns. From 1912 her home was at Ivy House, Hampstead, London, and this now contains a museum dedicated to her memory.

Anna Pavlova, as portrayed in Penrose's Pictorial Annual, *1912–13.*

Pawnbroker. The Pawnbrokers Act of 1960 defines a pawnbroker as one who keeps a shop and purchases or takes in goods, paying or lending on these any sum not exceeding £50 under an agreement, expressly or reasonably to be implied, that the goods may be afterwards repurchased or redeemed. A pawnbroker may not act without a licence from the Inland Revenue Commissioners.

Pledges must be redeemed within six calendar months from (and exclusive of) the day of pawning (with an additional seven days' grace). Pledges for £2 or under if not redeemed become the pawnbroker's absolute property. Pledges for more than £2 must be sold by auction, and any pawnbroker may purchase at the sale.

Pawnee, North American Indian people,

the plants growing on them or by chemical reaction. Land uses vary from pasture and horticultural crops, to forestry; peats have been cut traditionally for domestic fuel whilst the USSR and the Irish Republic have peat-fired power stations. Sphagnum peat is also extensively used as a soil conditioner in horticulture, and has been used in compressed form as an insulating material in Norway and the USSR.

Peat Moss, see SPHAGNALES.

Pecan, see CARYA.

Peccary, two species of tropical American pigs, which differ from old-world swine by the presence of a strong-smelling gland in the middle of the back, secreting a musky substance, and by the upper tusks being directed downwards instead of upwards. They have no tail and the hind feet have only three digits. Adult animals are about 40 cm in height and weigh about 23 kg. The collared peccary (*Tayassu tajacu*) extends from Patagonia to the southern border of the USA. The white-lipped peccary (*T. albirostris*) ranges between Mexico and Paraguay, where it associates in large herds which often seriously damage cultivated crops. Both peccaries are pugnacious and dangerous, capable of inflicting severe bites. They are often hunted with dogs and guns. They belong to family Tayassuidae of suborder Suiformes (peccaries, pigs and hippopotamuses) of the order Artiodactyla.

Peccary. *The collared peccary,* Tayassu tajacu, *is found from Mexico to South America.*

Pechora, navigable river in north-east European USSR. It rises in the Ural Mountains and flows northwards into the Barents Sea. Length 1809 km; drainage basin 322,000 km². The chief ports are Pechora and Naryan-Mar. The basin is the coldest region of Europe and has the thickest snow cover; there are large coal deposits.

Pechstein, Max Hermann (1881–1955), German painter. Pechstein became a member of the famous Expressionist group Die Brücke in 1906, but his works contained more sensual decorative elements than those of, for example, Kirchner; they were also clearly influenced by primitive art. *Under the Trees* (Detroit) is probably his best known work.

Peckinpah, Sam (1926–), US film director. He became writer and director for a number of television Westerns, including the *Gunsmoke* and *The Westerner* series. His first feature film was *The Deadly Companions*, 1961, followed the same year by *Ride the High Country* (UK title: *Guns in the Afternoon*). Producer conflicts marred *Major Dundee*, 1964, and he spent a few jobless years until *The Wild Bunch*, 1969, restored his reputation. His films have an elegiac note that counterbalances their harsh violence, the most lyrical being *The Ballad of Cable Hogue*, 1970. *Straw Dogs*, 1971, made in England, took him out of his milieu, but *Junior Bonner*, 1971 and *Pat Garrett and Billy the Kid*, 1973, continue his exploration of the dying West.

Pecos, river of the USA, rising in north-east New Mexico, and flowing south-east, through Texas, to join the Rio Grande, 55 km north-west of Del Rio. Its principal importance is as a source of irrigation. Important dams on the river are Alamogordo, Avalon, McMillan and Red Bluff. Length 1490 km.

Pécs (German *Fünfkirchen*), town of south-west Hungary, capital of the county of Baranya, at the foot of the Mecsek Mountains, 170 km south of Budapest. It dates from Roman times, and its bishopric was founded by St Stephen in 1009. The first Hungarian university was established here in 1367. The principal industries are the manufacture of pottery and agricultural machinery, tanning, distilling and meat-packing. Coal is mined nearby, and there is an airport. Population (1980) 170,000.

Pedal (from Latin *pes*, foot), name given to a lever worked by the foot in various musical instruments, also on a bicycle, etc.

Pedigree, tabular view of the members of a family, with the relations in which they stand to each other, together, usually, with some slight notice of the principal events of the life of each, such as the time and place of birth, marriage, death and burial. Elaborate pedigrees are also compiled for thoroughbred dogs, horses, etc.
See also GENEALOGY.

Pediment, see TEMPLE, CLASSICAL.

Pediment (topography), a desert surface cut across bedrock or alluvium, with a straight or slightly upward long profile and usually covered with a thin veneer of alluvium.

Pedlars, see HAWKERS AND PEDLARS.

Pedometer, instrument which indicates the distance walked. Shaped like a watch and carried in the pocket, it is so constructed that when the body is raised by the spring of the foot a lever acts upon the wheels and an index-hand indicates on a dial plate the number of paces (usually) or the number of kilometres (more rarely and less accurately) travelled.

Pedro I, Dom Pedro de Alcántara (1798–1834), Emperor of Brazil, 1822–31. Son of John VI of Portugal. In 1807, when Napoleon's troops invaded Portugal, the royal family went to Brazil. On his father's return to Portugal in 1821 he became regent of Brazil, and, declaring for Brazilian independence, was crowned emperor in 1822. As a monarch he was not a success and was forced to abdicate in 1831.

Pedro II, Dom Pedro de Alcántara (1825–91), Emperor of Brazil. His father, Pedro I, abdicated in 1831, and, after several regencies, he was crowned in 1840. He was an able and enlightened ruler who was hostile to slavery and contributed much to the political, economic and social development of Brazil. He was forced to abdicate in 1889 when Brazil was declared a republic.

Pedro the Cruel (1334–69), King of Castile and León, succeeded in 1350. He became suspicious of everyone and the rest of his reign was occupied in reinforcing his own authority as a feudal tyrant and in wars against Aragon and Granada. The epithet 'Cruel' derives from the murder of his brother Don Fadrique in 1358. Oppressive taxes destroyed the popularity he had earned for even-handed justice. His other brother Henry returned from France at the head of other exiles, and supported Du Guesclin with forces from Aragon and France and with aid from the pope. Pedro was routed at Montiel and slain.

Peebles, royal burgh (since 1367) and former county town of Peebleshire, now in Borders Region, Scotland, situated at the confluence of the Eddleston with the Tweed, 37 km south of Edinburgh. Industries include woollen mills. Population (1981) 6705.

Peel, John (1776–1854), Cumberland yeoman, who for some fifty years maintained a pack of hounds at Caldbeck. He is known chiefly as the hero of the song *D'ye ken John Peel*, said to have been written impromptu by his friend, John Woodcock Graves, about 1829.

Peel, Robert Peel, 2nd Baronet (1788–1850), British statesman. In 1812 he became chief secretary for Ireland for six years, during which period he opposed Catholic emancipation and established the Royal Irish Constabulary. Four years later he entered Liverpool's Cabinet as home secretary, which office he retained until the premier's death in 1827. His reforms included the reduction in the number of capital crimes, prison amelioration, and the foundation of the Metropolitan Police (hence nicknamed 'Peelers' or 'Bobbies'). In the following year he was, under Wellington, home secretary and leader of the House of Commons, and in 1829, being convinced of its necessity for the peace of Ireland, supported Wellington's measure for Catholic emancipation. In 1834 he became prime minister and chancellor of the Exchequer, but he held office only for a few months. In Opposition he set himself the task of organising the Conservative party, and in 1839, when Melbourne resigned, he was invited to form his second government, but abandoned the task in consequence of the 'bedchamber question'. He became prime minister again in 1841. He held no office save that of the first lord of the Treasury, but he was for all effective purposes chancellor of the Exchequer. As a financier he proved himself extremely capable, and introduced many reforms.
He was at first opposed to the repeal of the Corn Laws, but after the failure of the harvest in 1845 he became convinced of its necessity. Peel carried his Corn Law Bill, and he was bitterly attacked for his change of face on this question. A few days after this measure became law he was defeated on an Irish Bill, and retired from office. He was thrown from his horse on Constitution Hill on 29 June 1850, and died from his injuries three days later. Peel was distinguished for the intellectual honesty which led him to sacrifice his own interests and those of his party for the sake of measures he considered necessary for the general welfare.

Peel, town on the west coast of the Isle of Man, 18 km from Douglas at the western end of the one valley crossing the central mountain range. It was formerly a major fishing port, but it is now mainly a holiday and residential centre with a population in 1971 of 3081.

Peele, George (1556–96), English dramatist and poet. At Oxford he had a reputation as a poet and wrote his *Tale of Troy*, 1589. His first play was *The Arraignment of Paris*, 1584, and this was followed by many others, including *The Battle of Alcazar*, printed 1594, *The Old Wives' Tale*, printed 1585, and *David and Bethsabe*, printed 1599, most of which were successful. He wrote many miscellaneous verses, the best perhaps being the 'gratulatory poem' *The Honour of the Garter*, 1593.

Peerage, see NOBILITY.

Peewit, see PLOVER.

Pegasus, in Greek myth, winged horse which sprang from the blood of Medusa when her head was struck off by Perseus.

Pegasus, in astronomy, a large constellation named after the mystical winged horse. To the naked eye its most conspicuous feature is 'the Great Square' formed by the four stars Alpha, Beta and Gamma Pegasi, and Alpha Andromedae.

Pegmatite, a very course-grained rock of varied mineralogy. Pegmatites occur as irregular dykes, sills and segregations in the margins of granites and the surrounding country rock; they originate from the elements which are unable to incorporate themselves in the silicate lattices of the granitic minerals, and are consequently squeezed out of the granite as it cools. Pegmatites usually contain quartz, feldspar, white mica (muscovite), tourmaline and beryl. Other minerals of uncommon occurrence are also often present. 'Specimen' and gem quality minerals are often found in pegmatites.

Pegu, town and township of Burma, capital of Pegu division, it stands on the river of the same name, 72 km north-east of Rangoon. The town was founded in the latter half of the 6th century and rose to a position of great importance in the 16th and 17th centuries as capital of the Mon empire which was overthrown by Burma in 1757. Township: area 2871 km²; population (1973) 254,761.

Péguy, Charles Pierre (1873–1914), French writer. In 1900 he founded a publication which was destined to become famous, the *Cahiers de la quinzaine*. These were complete books, often written by Péguy himself, on some burning topic of the day.

Influenced by Bergson, he proved himself a passionate seeker of the truth. The anticlerical socialists and many Catholics were puzzled by Péguy, who was at the same time an ardent Catholic and an ardent socialist. In the Dreyfus Affair he became a zealous Dreyfusard. As a lover of French history and a devout Catholic at heart, he dedicated much of his poetry to a celebration of Joan of Arc.

Peine Forte et Dure, form of torture once applied by the law of England to those who, on being arraigned for felony, refused to plead and stood mute, or who peremptorily challenged more than 20 jurors, which was considered a contumacy equivalent to standing mute. In the early 13th century this penalty seems to have consisted merely of strict imprisonment with low diet, but by the reign of Henry IV it had become the practice to load the offender with weights and thus press him to death; and till nearly the middle of the 18th century pressing to death was the lawful mode of punishing persons who stood mute on their arraignment for felony.

Peipus, Lake, or Lake Chudskoye (Russian, Chudskoye Lake), situated between the Estonian SSR and the Pskov *oblast* in north-west RSFSR, USSR. Area 3550 km² (liable to sudden fluctuations), average depth 7 m, maximum depth 15 m. Its southern arm forms Lake Pskov and is connected with the Gulf of Finland via the River Narva. It was here that Alexander Nevski defeated the Teutonic Knights in 1242.

Peirce, Charles Santiago Sanders (1839–1914), US physicist and logician. Peirce was the first philosopher to use the term 'pragmatism' in connection with philosophy to connote a common-sense system in which belief is identified with action. When William James, professing to follow Peirce, substituted Truth for Belief in this formula (thus producing a pragmatism the opposite of Peirce's), Peirce renamed his own principle pragmaticism.

Pekan, see MARTEN.

Peking (Chinese *Beijing*), the capital of China, it lies in the alluvial plain between the Pai Ho and the Yungting Ho rivers and is partly encircled, at distances of 16 to 30 km, by mountains which are crowned with the eastern section of the Great Wall; it faces the Gulf of Chihli to the south-east. The name Peking signifies 'the Northern Capital', to distinguish it from Nanjing, 'the Southern Capital'. It was made the capital successively by the Khitan (Liao), the Nüchen (Qin), and the Mongolian (Yuan) invaders from the 10th to the 14th centuries. In the Yuan dynasty it was called Tatu, 'the Great Capital'. Yung-lo, the third emperor of the Ming dynasty, removed his capital fron Nanjing to Peking in 1421, and most of its present palaces, temples, and city walls have been built since his time. The Manchus captured the city in 1644, and it remained the capital of China until 1928, when Chiang Kai-shek moved his government to Nanjing and renamed Peking, Peiping, meaning 'Northern Peace'. In 1949, Peking was re-established as the capital of China.

Peking now consists of three parts; with the two old cities as its centre, it is flanked by two newly-added suburbs in the north-west and east. The former, stretching 12 km to the Summer Palace, is the cultural city, occupied by the science institutes of the Academia Sinica, the National Peking University, the Tsinghua University, and more than 20 other universities and colleges. The eastern suburb is being developed into an industrial zone with textile mills and machinery factories. Metal fabricating, electronics, and the chemical industries are significant new developments.

Old Peking is composed of two cities. The square Inner City (known in Europe as the Tatar City) is surrounded by a massive stone wall 15 m high and 18 m thick, each side measuring 7 km. The Outer City, adjoining the southern wall of the Inner City, is oblong in shape, with its longer sides running east–west for 8 km. In the western part of the Inner City there is a chain of artificial lakes, the excavated earth forming hills which are covered with the rock-gardens, apartments, and temples of the erstwhile Imperial Winter Palace, now open to the public. The square Palace City (perimeter 10 km) is in the centre

***Peking.** The 15th-century Temple of Heaven in the outer city of the old town.*

of the Inner City. In recent years the municipal area of Peking, which is under central government jurisdiction, has been repeatedly expanded, and its area is now some 8400 km². Similarly its population has grown from a little more than a million before the war to about 8·7 million in 1980.

Peking Man, representatives of the species *Homo erectus*, whose skeletal remains were found in caves at Zhou Koutian, China.

Pekingese, or Pekinese, breed of lap-dog. It is of Chinese origin, and differs from the English toy spaniel in having a flat skull and tail curved over the loins. It is heavy in front, with a short, broad muzzle, but is somewhat lighter behind. Long-haired, with a thick undercoat, it is red, fawn, cream, white, brindle, black and tan, black or parti-colour. The weight is up to 5 kg.

Pelagic Fauna. The ocean can be divided into two main parts, benthic and pelagic. The former includes all of the sea bottom, while the latter concerns the whole mass of water. Pelagic animals are those that move freely in the sea between the surface and the sea floor. Some have limited powers of movement and are generally small (plankton), while others are larger and more active and are not at the mercy of the currents. The most numerous of the non-microscopic plankton animals are the crustaceans, especially the copepods.

Pelagius (?360–?420), British monk and theologian, leader of a 5th-century heresy in the Christian Church, author or systematiser of the doctrine called after him Pelagianism. According to this doctrine there is no original sin, and man does not need grace in order to avoid actual sin and to attain salvation; his free will is sufficient for this purpose, though grace makes the attainment of salvation easier.

Pelargonium, commonly but incorrectly called geranium, a genus of 250 perennial plants in the family Geraniaceae which, since their introduction from southern Africa at the beginning of the 18th century, have been valued as greenhouse and border plants.

Pelasgi, name used by classical writers to describe the pre-Hellenic population of Greece. The term 'Pelasgic' was applied to any survival from prehistoric times. Thus the earliest fortification on the Acropolis was called the 'Pelasgian Walk'.

Pelé, full name Edson Arantes do Nascimento (1940–), Brazilian footballer. He is arguably the greatest player of all time, scorer of more than 1000 goals in competitive matches; a fast, strong, skilful forward, without a weakness.

Pelée, Mount, see St Pierre.

Pelham, Henry (c.1695–1754), English statesman. He entered Parliament in 1717, and seven years later became secretary for war. He was paymaster of the forces in 1730, and in 1743 first lord of the Treasury and chancellor of the Exchequer. His influence in the House of Commons was based upon systematic corruption.

Pelican, *Pelecanus*, a genus of birds in order Pelecaniformes characterised by the four toes being united by a web. They have a huge extensile or dilatable pouch, and the legs are short and the feet large, the tail short and rounded, the neck long and the body large and ponderous. The wings are long and expansive, and the birds are capable of rapid flight, and also of soaring without perceptible movement of the wings. The species are widely distributed, frequenting the seashore and margins of lakes, and feeding almost exclusively on fish, which are deposited in the pouch for subsequent digestion. The white pelican, *P. onocrotalus*, is now found around the Mediterranean. Its plumage is white, tinged with red. *P. erythrorhynchus*, the rough-billed pelican, occurs in North America, where the only diving pelican, the brown, *P. occidentalis*, is also found. Species also occur in Australia and Asia.

Pella, ancient town of Macedonia, between Salonica and Edessa. The birthplace of Philip II and Alexander the Great, it was the ancient capital of Macedonia. The site was unearthed in 1957.

Pellagra, one of the nutritional deficiency diseases. It is due to lack of the pellagra-preventing vitamin nicotinamide.

Pellegrini, Carlo (1839–89), Italian caricaturist. His work in *Vanity Fair* from 1869, over the signature 'Ape', consisting of a series of portraits of public men, is one of the best examples of personal caricature.

Pellitory of the Wall, *Parietaria diffusa*, in the family Urticaceae, a perennial herb, with reddish brittle stems, hairy leaves and clusters of small flowers. It usually grows on walls.

Pelmanism, a name of several types of memory and card games based on a system of mind and memory training, known by the same name, and devised in the late 19th century by W. J. Ennever.

Peloponnesian War, conflict between Athens and Sparta, with their respective allies, 431–404 BC. The real cause was the hatred inspired among the mainland, Dorian and oligarchical states (of which Sparta was the chief) by the commercial prosperity of Athens, which rested on her control of an empire composed principally of maritime, Ionian and democratic states.

The Peloponnesian War falls into three periods. From 431 to 421 the belligerents ravaged one another's territory without any decisive result. This first period closes with the Peace of Nicias. The second period ends with the annihilation of the Athenian armament at Syracuse, 413. In the third period, 412–404, the Spartans inflicted an overwhelming defeat on the last Athenian naval squadron at Aegospotami (405), and in the following year installed at Athens the violent and reactionary government of the Thirty Tyrants.

Peloponnesus (Greek *Pelopónnesos*), the peninsula forming the southern part of Greece, connected with central Greece by the isthmus of Corinth, on either side of which lie the Gulfs of Lepanto and Patras. It is an administrative division of Greece. Patras is the chief port. Area 21,636 km²; population 986,900.

Pelops, in Greek legend, son of Tantalus. Pelops travelled to Elis, where King Oenomaus of Pisa was offering the hand of his daughter Hippodamia to anyone who could beat him in a chariot race. Pelops bribed Myrtilus, the king's charioteer, to remove the linchpin from his master's car in return for half the kingdom. In consequence, during the race, Oenomaus was hurled from his chariot and killed. Pelops succeeded to the throne and married Hippodamia, but would not keep faith with Myrtilus. One day, as they were driving along a cliff-top, he flung him into the sea, and Myrtilus, as he sank, cursed the whole race of Pelops, a curse which took effect upon the Atreids.

Pelota, a generic name for a range of court games played variously with a ball and glove, bat, basket, racket, or sometimes barehanded. There are 13 basic forms falling into two categories: *jeux direct*, in which the players face each other, sometimes across a net, and play the ball as in tennis; *jeux indirect*, in which the ball is played off a wall. Eleven forms of the game fall into the latter category, and rules and scoring vary greatly.

Pelotas, second city of the state of Rio Grande do Sul, Brazil. Situated on the left bank of the São Goucala river, it is a commercial and industrial centre for a rich agricultural region whose main products are cattle, sheep, rice and wheat. The town has tanneries, flour mills, a refrigeration plant, and plants for the processing of several agricultural products. Population (1975) 231,900.

Pelts, see Fur.

Pelvis, the bony basin which supports the abdominal viscera and distributes the weight of the trunk to the two legs. It is formed by the sacrum, the coccyx and the hip bones; each of the hip bones consists of three originally separate bones, grown together in the adult: the ilium, ischium and pubis. At the junction of these a socket is formed which takes the ball-end of the femur, or thigh-bone. The female pelvis is broader but shallower, while having a greater capacity; the bones are more slender, the inlet more circular; it is in general modified for child-bearing.

Pemba, island off the east coast of Africa, 48 km north of Zanzibar and part of the Republic of Tanzania. A fertile and beautiful island, its Arabic name was al-Huthera, or the Green Island, its green hills rising abruptly from the sea. The whole of the south-west is devoted to clove-growing. Besides the trade in cloves there is a trade in copra. Area 984 km²; population (1978) 205,850.

Pembroke, market town of Dyfed, south-west Wales. Its castle (c.1207) was the birthplace of Henry VII. Pembroke Dock was created in 1814 in conjunction with the Royal Navy dockyard. It is now a general industrial town on the River Cleddau, an arm of Milford Haven. Population (Pembroke and Pembroke Dock) (1981) 15,618.

Pembroke Corgi, see Welsh Corgi.

Pen (Latin *penna*, feather). The modern pen had its origin in the reed or calamus, which is still used for writing in the East. The ancient Egyptians, like the Chinese and Japanese of the present day, used a brush for writing, while the Romans and Greeks used the sharp point of a stylus to scratch their characters on waxen tablets. It is impossible to say when the quill feather superseded the reed; but because of its suitability for writing on vellum, the quill feather was the main pen of the Middle Ages, and indeed even of modern times down to the 19th century. The steel nib, first introduced in London in

1803 by Wise, came into general use about 1830, when James Perry and Joseph Gillott of Birmingham began to make them by machinery.

In fountain pens, the penholder takes the form of a hollow shaft containing a reservoir of ink which is released so as to maintain a steady flow during writing. The first effective fountain pens appeared soon after 1860; in their earliest form most needed to be charged with ink by means of an independent filler. Ultimately a feed was evolved which is controlled by sub-reservoirs beneath the nib.

P.E.N. International, founded in London in 1921. The first president was John Galsworthy. P.E.N.'s aims are to promote friendship among writers everywhere and to oppose any interference with freedom of communication. Through its Writers in Prison Committee it does what it can to aid writers persecuted for expressing their views.

Penal Servitude, see PRISONS.

Penal Statute, one which imposes a pecuniary penalty or some other form of punishment for the breach of its provisions.

Penance (Latin *paenitentia*), in ecclesiastical reference (1) a virtue, of which the chief acts or manifestations are contrition or sorrow for sin, and satisfaction or self-inflicted punishment in atonement for sin; (2) a censure, i.e. a punishment imposed by ecclesiastical law, and involving deprivation of spiritual goods; (3) the sacrament of confession; (4) the satisfaction imposed by the priest in this sacrament.

Penates, see LARES.

Pencil, as an art-medium, the most convenient instrument for drawing. It consists of a stick of graphite of various degrees of hardness, encased in wood. It came into general use in the 19th century. Coloured pencils, or crayons, are made with chalks and wax preparations.

Pencil, in optics, a narrow beam which converges to or from a given point.

Penda (c.577–654), King of Mercia, c.632–654, was the first to make his kingdom powerful and independent of Northumberland. With Cadwallon, he defeated and killed Edwin of Northumbria at Hatfield (632). Penda also conquered and killed Oswald of Northumbria at Maserfield (641). This victory made Penda the most powerful king in England. Oswy, King of Northumbria, killed Penda in battle at Winwaed (unidentified) in 654.

Pendant. In late Gothic or Tudor architecture, a boss projecting downwards, like a stalactite, from a vault or ceiling. The most celebrated pendant vault is that of Henry VII's Chapel, Westminster Abbey.

Pendant, long narrow flag.

See also FLAG; PENNANT.

Penderecki, Krzysztof (1933–), Polish composer, noted for his modern compositional techniques and original system of notation. His *Threnody for the Victims of Hiroshima*, 1960, for string orchestra, established his reputation. His other well-known work is the *Passion According to St Luke*, 1963–66, which is traditional in form but experimental in technique.

Pendulum, a heavy particle suspended from a fixed point by a fine, inextensible, light, rigid thread so that it is free to oscillate in a vertical plane. For a simple pendulum the oscillations are isochronous, i.e. the time for each complete oscillation is always $t = 2\pi\sqrt{(l/g)}$ where t is time, l the length of the pendulum, and g the local acceleration due to gravity. Thus the period is independent of the mass of the bob. This formula is true only for a small arc of swing. If ϕ is the half-angle of swing in radians, a good approximation to $t = (1 + \phi^2/16)2\pi\sqrt{(l/g)}$.

The density of the Earth was found by means of a pendulum by Maskelyne in 1774; in 1832 at Arthur's Seat, Edinburgh, by determining the attraction from the vertical due to the mass of a mountain; and by comparing oscillations at the surface and bottom of a mine by Airy in 1856. Foucault, in 1851, by means of a pendulum, rendered the rotation of the Earth visible.

Pendulum, see RADIESTHESIA.

Penelope, in Greek legend, wife of Odysseus. In his long absence during the Trojan War, Penelope was wooed by persistent suitors, but put them off saying she had to finish a robe, while she undid by night her work of the day. Odysseus returned to claim her and killed the suitors. Penelope represents wifely faithfulness.

***Penguin.** Both these species are gregarious, breeding in large colonies.*

Penguin, common name of the six genera and about 17 species of family Spheniscidae, the only family of the order Sphenisciformes, found only in the southern hemisphere, and characterised by the modification of the wings into paddles and flippers. The wing is long and always remains open. The feathers are tiny. The legs of the birds are placed far back, and in the water the feet are stretched out straight behind and held motionless, the wings working rapidly as if being used in flight. The position of the legs causes the gait of the birds on land to be very awkward, but on snow slopes they are able to toboggan at a rapid pace, propelling themselves with the powerful legs assisted by the wings. They are essentially aquatic birds, and they come inshore chiefly for the breeding season, when it is estimated that they assemble in rookeries by the thousands.

The nest is often no more than a slight hollow in the ground. Two eggs are laid, and both birds, but chiefly the male, attend to their incubation. Both parents are very devoted to the young, one always staying to guard them, the other bringing them sea crustaceans and other small animals, which the young take by pushing their beaks far down the parent's throat. The emperor and king penguins possess a pouch, in the form of a feathered fold of skin near to the feet on the central surface, used to shelter the eggs and young.

With the exception of a single tropical species which inhabits the Galapagos Islands, and a few others, penguins are almost confined to the colder regions. The largest species is the emperor penguin, which breeds far south during the winter darkness. It is nearly 1·2 m tall, and the plumage is dark slate on the back and white on the underparts, with yellow spots on the head.

Penguin Books, publishing enterprise founded in 1935 by Allen Lane and his two brothers. Its original aim was to provide low-priced reprints of good fiction in large popular editions. It was so successful that in 1937 a complementary series, Pelican Books, was begun in order to develop 'the diffusion of knowledge' through cultural and scientific books. Subsequent series include Penguin Classics (in new translations), Puffin Books for children, Penguin Modern Classics, etc.

Penicillin, an antibiotic produced from the fungus *Penicillium notatum*. The name penicillin is derived from the green mould or fungus *Penicillium* (Latin, a brush, referring to the appearance of the spore-bearing branches under the microscope); various species of *Penicillium* are common on decaying and damaged fruit such as oranges and on cheese. In 1928, Sir Alexander Fleming observed that a culture of *Staphylococcus* bacteria growing in his laboratory was contaminated with a colony of *Penicillium*, later identified as *P. notatum*. Fleming noted that the growth of bacteria was retarded close to the mould, and subsequent experiments showed that the inhibitory action was also exerted on other bacteria, such as the haemolytic *Streptococcus* and the organisms of pneumonia, gonorrhoea and diphtheria.

Penicillins interfere with the synthesis of the bacterial cell wall and are therefore bactericidal. Penicillin is particularly useful as an antibacterial agent, since it is non-poisonous to most people even in large doses. A few people, however, have a sensitivity to penicillin and its derivatives and others develop sensitivity. More recently, it has been found that bacteria, particularly staphylococci, originally killed by penicillin, produce an enzyme, penicillinase, which breaks down penicillin and thus become resistant to it and breed resistant strains. These drawbacks led to a more cautious and selective therapeutic use of penicillin, to a search for other and more effective antibiotics, and also for other types of penicillin against which staphylococci would be unable to develop resistance.

Penicillium, a genus of fungi with about 250 species, in subdivision Ascomycotina. They are greenish or bluish moulds, cosmopolitan in origin.

See also PENICILLIN.

Peninsular Malaysia, that part of the Federation of Malaysia comprising the Malay

Peninsula. Known as the Federation of Malaya until the formation of Malaysia in 1963, the region has subsequently been called West Malaysia. The term Peninsular Malaysia is now used officially, and 'Sabah and Sarawak' are used in place of East Malaysia.

Peninsular War (1808–14). In October 1807 Napoleon concluded the secret treaty of Fontainebleau with the king of Spain, with the intention of conquering and partitioning Portugal. In November the French army under Junot seized Lisbon. By early 1808 Napoleon had sent 100,000 more troops into Spain, ostensibly to reinforce Junot. In May Charles IV surrendered the Spanish crown by the Treaty of Bayonne to Napoleon, who bestowed it on his brother, Joseph. In June Portugal appealed for aid from the British, who landed an expedition at Coruña and compelled Junot to sign the Convention of Cintra at Torres Vedras, by which he evacuated Portugal and retired to France.

Napoleon led the grand army in person into Madrid on 4 December. The British, under Sir John Moore, conducted a well-planned diversionary movement, ending in the retreat to Coruña. Napoleon returned to France, and in the battle of Coruña on 16 January 1809 the British army was victorious.

For the next four years the war was inconclusive, until in 1813 the withdrawal of French troops, necessitated by the disaster in Russia, swung the advantage in favour of the British army under Wellington. Joseph was beaten at Vitoria on 21 June and fled to France. Soult immediately returned from France to take command, but could not prevent Wellington from taking San Sebastian, crossing the Bidassoa into France, and taking Pamplona. From this time the history of the war is the gradual weakening and continued defeats of Soult, who, in April 1814, signed a convention for the suspension of hostilities.

Penis, the phallus of male animals, especially mammals, by means of which sperm, which later fertilise the ovum, are transferred to the vagina of the female during mating (coitus or copulation). In man, a mammal, the penis is a cylindrical erectile organ which terminates in the glans, the latter covered by the prepuce or foreskin. It is the foreskin that is removed by the operation of circumcision. Internally the mammalian penis contains three spongy areas: the two corpora cavernosa dorsally and the single corpus spongiosum ventrally. As a result of nervous stimuli, the corpora become engorged with blood and cause the erection of the penis for copulation. The corpus spongiosum is traversed by the urethra, the passage for the urine.

See also REPRODUCTION.

Penitentiary, general term for places of detention for long-term prisoners. In the USA both federal and state prison systems use the term 'penitentiary', and it was also used in 19th-century England.

Pen-Ki, see BENXI.

Penn, William (1644–1718), English Quaker, founder of Pennsylvania. He became a Quaker about 1667, and in the following year was imprisoned for publishing his *Sandy Foundation Shaken*. Released from the Tower in 1669 by his father's influence, he was perpetually persecuted for expressing his religious views. His father's death brought him a fortune and a claim against the Crown which he commuted for a grant of land in North America, where he founded, in 1681, the colony of Pennsylvania for his persecuted co-religionists. He was in England from 1684 for 15 years and took an active part in religious controversy. His friendship with James II brought some advantages to the Quakers. The closing years of his life were clouded by financial difficulties and mental illness.

Pennant (a compromise between 'pendant' and 'pennon'), general name for most pointed flags which are long in the *fly* as compared with the *hoist*.

Pennatula, the sea pen, is a genus of coral (Anthozoa) of the subclass Alcyonaria. A fairly common British species is *P. phosphorea*, so called because of its phosphorescent character.

Pennell, Joseph (1857–1926), US artist and author. In 1884 he married Elizabeth Robins, with whom he collaborated in producing numerous books of travel and description, amongst which are *Our Sentimental Journey through France and Italy*, *A Canterbury Pilgrimage* and *Our Journey to the Hebrides*. They were close friends of the artist Whistler, whose biography Pennell published in 1908.

Pennine Alps, see ALPS.

Pennines, mountain group of England, beginning to the south of the lower Tyne valley and extending to the middle of Derbyshire and the north of Staffordshire. It is sometimes called the 'backbone of England', but is more in the nature of a series of uplands than a chain of mountains. The chief summits are Cross Fell (893 m), Whernside (736 m), Ingleborough (723 m), Pen-y-ghent (693 m), and Kinder Scout (636 m).

Pennsylvania (Keystone State), one of the 13 original states of the USA; bounded on the north by New York state and Lake Erie, on the east by New York state and New Jersey, on the south by Delaware, Maryland and West Virginia, and on the west by West Virginia and Ohio. Its total area is 117,412 km^2, of which 950 km^2 is water surface (excluding Lake Erie). It comprises within its borders the low-lying Atlantic coastal plain in the east, along the Delaware valley, and the rolling hills of the Appalachian Piedmont. Some five-sixths of the state are occupied by the Appalachian Mountains and by the Allegheny plateau, a deeply dissected wilderness of forested uplands which are remote, infertile and for the most part inaccessible.

The Delaware river drains the whole of the eastern part of the state, and runs into Delaware Bay, a 48 km long inlet of the Atlantic Ocean, thus forming an immense estuary. Other rivers are the Susquehanna, with its tributaries, West Branch and Juniata, and in the west the Allegheny river and the Monogahela unite, forming the Ohio.

There are immense bituminous coalfields and also large fields of anthracite coal, though both (especially anthracite) are suffering serious decline. During much of the 19th century, Pennsylvania was the centre of American oil production. Supplies are now almost exhausted. The state produces over 20 per cent of the USA's steel, and large quantities of coke, pig-iron and ferro-alloys, Pittsburgh being the traditional centre of the smelting industry. The Philadelphia region forms a port area rivalling New York in terms of cargo tonnage handled.

There are 7,082,005 ha of forest land, and lumbering is a source of wealth in the north. In the south and south-west there are forests of hemlock and virgin beech. Of the commercially significant farms in the state, about one half are dairy farms. Tobacco, mushrooms and apples are important.

Slate, limestone and marble quarries abound, especially in the district round Philadelphia.

Charles II gave to William Penn in 1681 large grants of land in this state, but the first settlers were Swedes, and it was once called New Sweden. In many farming areas the larger part of the population is still derived from the early German settlers, such as the Pennsylvania 'Dutch' who represent one of a number of religious groups, known as the 'plain-folk', who were attracted to Pennsylvania in colonial days by its founder's policy of religious toleration.

The population of Pennsylvania in 1980 was 11,824,560. Its capital is Harrisburg, but its largest cities are Philadelphia and Pittsburgh.

Penny, most ancient of English coins. First mentioned in the laws of Ine, King of the West Saxons, it weighed then about $\frac{1}{240}$ of the Saxon pound weight.

Pennyroyal, *Mentha pulegium*, a fragrant prostrate mint (family Labiatae) which grows in damp places in Europe. It bears ovate, nearly smooth leaves with clusters of small mauve flowers in the axils of the upper leaves.

Pennywort, the common name for certain plants whose round leaves have the stalk attached at the centre. *Umbilicus rupestris*, in family Crassulaceae, is wall pennywort, or navelwort, a native perennial of rocks and walls, and *Hydrocotyle vulgaris*, in the family Hydrocotylaceae, is a creeping semi-aquatic perennial, also known as white-rot.

Penny Banks were first established in Britain about 1850, and rising from 200 in 1860, became very numerous. Their object was to furnish easy means for the thrifty, and especially children in schools, to accumulate savings from slender resources.

See also SAVINGS BANKS.

Penology, the study of legal punishment as distinct from the study of the criminal, though the two subjects cannot be wholly separated, since punishment must have some relevance to the persons punished and no penal system can be effective that ignores the character of the criminal and the problem of the causation of crime. The impulse to punish wrongdoing is so deep-rooted that many people accept the imposition on the law-breaker of penalties which involve varying degrees of unpleasantness without giving thought to the underlying purpose of state punishment.

Penry, John (1559–93), Welsh Puritan. He was the printer of the 'Martin Marprelate' tracts, which attacked the episcopal structure of the Church of England. He was forced to flee to Scotland in 1590, and on returning to England was condemned to death and hanged.

Pensacola, city of Florida, USA. It lies on Pensacola Bay, a fine anchorage used by the Spaniards, who founded the city and protected it by a fort, now Fort Pickens, on the harbour bar. Today it is a naval base and fishing port, with industries based on such regional commodities as forest products and nylon yarn. Population (1980) 57,619.

Penstemon, a genus of perennial plants in the family Scrophulariaceae. They are natives of North America, bearing blue, purple, lilac, scarlet, rose or yellow flowers, and are of great value in the garden.

Pentagon, home of the United States Defense Department and the world's largest office building, on the Virginia side of the Potomac river, Washington DC, USA. It was built (1941–43) to accommodate the increase in the personnel of the US Defense Forces Staff, and cost about $64,000,000. There are 27 km of corridors, and it possesses the largest private telephone exchange in the world.

Pentagram, pentacle, pentangle or pentalpha, symbol of the microcosm, a figure of five straight lines forming a five-pointed star. Found frequently in early ornamental art, it was used as a mystic symbol by the Pythagoreans, by astrologers and necromancers in the Middle Ages, and it still continues to be employed by occult and secret societies. Together with the sign of the cross, it came to be used on doorways and thresholds as a charm to keep away witches and evil spirits.

Pentateuch (i.e. 'The Five Rolls', though the Greek *teuchos* originally meant 'roll-case'). The name for the five Books of Moses, the first five in the Bible (Genesis, Exodus, Leviticus, Numbers, Deuteronomy).
See also TORAH.

Pentecost, or Shavuot (Feast of Weeks), Jewish Old Testament festival observed on 6 and 7 Sivan, celebrating the end of the grain harvest 50 days after Passover, but also associated by the rabbis with the giving of the Ten Commandments on Mount Sinai.

Pentecostal Churches, a group of Christian churches which first emerged in the USA in the late 19th and early 20th centuries. Their uniting theme is the idea of spiritual renewal through baptism by the Holy Spirit, as at the original feast of Pentecost. The baptised believer may then receive one of the miraculous gifts linked with Pentecost – 'speaking in tongues', or the ability to prophesy or heal. The Pentecostals are fundamentalist in character, modelling their practices on those found in the *Acts of the Apostles*. The movement has now spread to most parts of the world.

Pentland Firth, channel separating the Orkney Islands from Caithness District, northern Scotland. It is 20 km long and 8–13 km wide. There is a ferry, but strong tidal currents and whirlpools render navigation dangerous. The Pentland Skerries, 8 km north-east of Duncansby Head, include two islets, one of which has a lighthouse, and some rocks.

Pentland Hills, a ridge of hills in Lowland Scotland within the regions of Lothian and Borders. The ridge runs north-east from Carnwath to within 20 km of the centre of the city of Edinburgh. The mean height is upwards of 300 m, the breadth 6–10 km. The highest points are Scald Law (579 m) and Carnethy (576 m).

Penza, capital city, economic and cultural centre of Penza *oblast*, USSR, west of Kuibyshev. There are large precision and other engineering industries, also food and light industries. It is an important railway junction (four lines). It was founded in 1663 as a military and administrative centre. The old cultural centre of the black earth belt, it was the capital of the Penza province from 1719. Population (1980) 490,000.

Penzance, seaport and holiday resort in Cornwall, England, and centre of an important market-gardening and agricultural area, situated at the head of Mount's Bay, 12 km north-east of Land's End, and 32 km south-west of Truro. There is a good harbour and docks, and the climate is very mild. Penzance is the only port of departure for the Scilly Isles, which are some 64 km to the south-west. With Newlyn, now incorporated in the borough, it is a principal fishing centre. St Michael's Mount is nearby. Population (1981) 19,521.

Peony, a group of perennial herbs and shrubs in the family Paeoniaceae from Europe, Asia and North America, which includes some magnificent garden flowers. They have white, pink, red or yellow blooms.

'People's Daily' (*Jen-min Jih-pao*), Chinese newspaper published every morning in Peking. The organ of the Chinese Communist party, it is more a government bulletin board than the usual concept of a newspaper. It was in Hopei province towards the end of the civil war in 1948 that the *People's Daily* was established as the main party paper, moving to Peking in 1949.

Pentagon. *The building covers 13.8 hectares and consists of five concentric rings.*

Samuel Pepys. *A portrait, now in his old college of Magdalene, Cambridge. Pepys's diary was written between 1660 and 1669.*

Peoria, city and capital of Peoria county, Illinois, USA, on the Illinois river, an air, rail and highway centre near a bituminous coalfield and in an extensive agricultural area. Peoria is a grain and livestock market and distilling centre, and manufactures tractors and earth-moving equipment. Population (1980) 124,160.

Peperomia, a genus in the family Piperaceae, of about 1000 annual or perennial herbs of tropical or subtropical regions. *P. marmorata, P. metallica, P. sandersii* of South America and others are grown as ornamental foliage pot plants.

Pepin le Bref (c.714–68), King of the Franks, was the younger son of Charles Martel and father of Charlemagne. In 751 Pepin was crowned first Carolingian king of the Franks. In 754 he aided the pope against Aistulf, king of the Lombards; he forced Aistulf to give up Ravenna to the pope, and by this act, which is known as the 'donation of Pepin', laid the foundation of the temporal power of the papacy. The rest of his life was spent in wars against the heathen Saxons, the Duke of Aquitaine, Bavaria and the Saracens.

Pepper, one of the most important spices. It is derived from the climbing, *Piper nigrum*, which is native to Sri Lanka and southern India and has also been introduced into Malaysia, Thailand, Indonesia and Borneo. Both 'black' and 'white' pepper are obtained from the same plant.
See also CAPSICUM.

Peppercorn Rent, nominal rent, in theory involving the annual payment from lessee to lessor of one peppercorn; it was used in connection with long leases as a device for giving a leasehold the practical effect of a freehold.
See also LAND TENURE.

Peppermint, see MINT.

Pepperwort, species of *Lepidium*, a genus in the Cruciferae.

Pepsin, an enzyme elaborated in the body by the gastric mucosa. It has the property of causing chemical changes by which the proteins of food material are converted into peptones. Pepsin is also produced commercially by drying the mucous lining of the stomach of a pig or calf.

Peptic Ulcer, an ulcer occurring in the stomach or duodenum. The main symptom of such ulcers is pain in the upper abdomen. In gastric ulcers (i.e. those occurring in the stomach) the pain commonly occurs after a meal and is usually relieved by acid-neutralising tablets (antacids). In the case of duodenal ulcers the pain often occurs when the stomach is empty and is relieved by food or antacids. Gastric ulcers on occasion become malignant (cancerous), whereas duodenal ulcers almost never undergo malignant change.

Pepys, Samuel (1633–1703), English administrator and diarist. In 1660 he became a clerk of the Privy Seal and clerk of the 'Acts of the Navy'. He managed to make a fortune out of the perquisites of his office; at the same time he was a zealous reformer of abuses. A popular but false estimate of Pepys is as 'a painstaking departmental official', but at the Admiralty, Pepys carried out, in the teeth of opposition, drastic and far-reaching reforms.

Pepys's library was left to Magdalene College, Cambridge, where his *Diary* remained neglected until 1819, when the Rev. J. Smith began to decipher it. This *Diary* remains one of the most vivid and minute authorities for the events of the Restoration period, of the manners and scandals of the court, and of Pepys's own interests and weaknesses.

Perambulator, see PEDOMETER.

Perception, the reception and interpretation of external stimuli which impinge on sense organs, and the awareness and interpretation of impulses, feelings and emotional states of mind.

Perceval, Spencer (1762–1812), British politician. He was solicitor-general in Addington's administration, and chancellor of the Exchequer under Portland in 1807. He became prime minister in 1809, and was assassinated on 11 May 1812 in the lobby of the House of Commons.

Perch, *Perca fluviatilis* order Perciformes, a common large family of spiny-finned fishes. It will only spawn in still waters, which are its preferred habitat. The greatest weight of *P. fluviatilis* on reliable record is 4·5 kg. It is greenish, with vertical, dark bars extending from the back down the sides. The flesh, firm and white, is appreciated in Russia and elsewhere.

Percussion, one method used in diagnosis in medicine, which, as its name implies, involves tapping and the eliciting of sounds. The affected part is tapped with the first three fingers, with a small rubber-tipped hammer, or, more usually, the fingers of one hand are laid flat on the body surface and are tapped by the second finger of the other hand. Hollow organs give a resonant note and solid organs a dull note.

Percussion Instruments are musical instruments made from vibrating solids or from stretched membranes, which are sounded by beating or shaking. Most percussion instruments produce sounds of indefinite pitch, the exceptions being bells, the xylophone family, timpani and the celeste, a keyboard instrument whose hammers strike metal bars. See also BELL; CYMBALS; DRUM; GONG.

Percy, noble Anglo-Norman family. Its founder, William de Percy, accompanied the Conqueror to England. One of the family assisted in obtaining Magna Carta. His great-grandson became marshal of England and was made earl of Northumberland (1377). When Bolingbroke assumed the crown, with the title Henry IV, he created Percy the earl constable of England. In the fourth year of that reign, the earl and his son, Sir Henry Percy, nicknamed Hotspur, rebelled against the king, but Hotspur was slain at the battle of Shrewsbury in 1403. Henry V restored the title to a son of Hotspur.

The Percy family is now represented only in the female line.

Peregrine Falcon, see FALCON.

Pereira, Aristides Mana (1924–), President of the Cape Verde Islands. His political career began when he was a co-founder (along with Amilcar Cabral) of the African Party for the Independence of Guinea and Cape Verde (PAIGC) in 1956. He held a number of offices within the PAIGC hierarchy. In 1972 he became secretary-general, and in 1975 he was elected the first president of the independent Cape Verde Islands.

Pereira, town of western Colombia, in the department of Caldas, 64 km by rail from Manizales. It is a modern city overlooking the Cauca valley. It is a centre of the coffee and livestock industries. Its industries include coffee milling, clothing, confectionery, brewing and mineral waters. Population (1975) 210,000.

Pérez Galdós, Benito (1843–1920), Spanish novelist. His novels are divided into two groups. The 34 *Episodes nacionales* (started in 1873) tell the history of Spain between the Battle of Trafalgar, 1805, and the restoration of the monarchy in 1874, attempting to retrace the birth of the modern Spanish nation in the 19th century. The other novels deal mainly with aspects of Madrid life and include his most famous works, such as *La desheredada*, 1881, the tragic story of a young girl's delusions of grandeur; *La de Bringas*, 1884, an effective picture of the pretensions of court life; *Miau*, 1888, the story of the madness and suicide of an idealistic civil servant; *Fortunata y Jacinta*, 1886–87, a magnificent study of class relations in Madrid as reflected in the marriage and affairs of a bourgeois youth; *Angel Guerra*, 1891, a study of religious fanaticism and misplaced idealism; and the *Torquemada* series, 1889–95, which traces the rise and fall of a self-made materialist in a society still ridden with aristocratic pretensions.

Performance Tests, see MENTAL TESTS.

Perfumery. Perfumes obtained from plants are the essences to which the flowers and leaves owe their fragrant odours; the art of perfumery deals with the extraction and properties of those essences and their blending for toilet purposes or industrial use. The true perfumes are essential or volatile oils (French *otto*), contained in minute sacs in leaves, as in mint; in wood, as in sandalwood; in bark, as in cinnamon; in seeds, as in nutmeg; in the rind of fruit, as in lemon; in petals of flowers, as in rose and lavender; or, as in the case of orris, in the rhizome.

Of animal perfumes there are only four in use: musk, civet, ambergris, and castor (castoreum). All are extremely powerful and are used as fixatives to make perfume blends last longer.

Synthetic chemistry has been successful in the preparation of substitutes for the natural products; in other cases synthetic chemists have made products with similar perfumes although they are in other respects different. Terpineol, one of the commonest aromatic synthetics used in perfumery, is the basis for lilac, lily, and many other compounds. Oil of cassia is mainly cinnamic aldehyde, $C_6H_5CH{:}CH.CHO$. Vanillin, from the pod of the vanilla bean, can now be synthesised in the laboratory. Coumarin, the perfume of tonka beans, is prepared from *o*-cresol through salicylaldehyde; bromostyrolene is a substitute for hyacinth oil and jasmine oil is substituted by benzyl acetate.

See also ATTAR OF ROSES; EAU DE COLOGNE.

Perga, ancient city, the ruins of which are situated in the province of Konya, Asiatic Turkey, 20 km north-east of Antalya. An important city of Pamphylia, it was famous for the worship of a local nature-goddess identified by the Greeks with Artemis, but is now more famous as the starting point of St Paul's first missionary journey.

Pergamum, ancient city of Mysia in Asia Minor, capital of the kingdom of Pergamum and afterwards of the Roman province of Asia. It was a place of some importance as early as 420 BC. After the death of Alexander the Great (323 BC), Lysimachus obtained possession of the city, but was ousted in 283 by Philetaerus, governor of the fortress. The latter died in 263, bequeathing Pergamum to his nephew Eumenes I, who died in 241 and was succeeded by his cousin Attalus I. Attalus and his son Eumenes II allied themselves closely with Rome, as a result of which their territory was progressively enlarged until it included almost the whole of western Asia Minor. Attalus III died in 133 BC and left his dominions to Rome.

Pergola, an arbour or walk covered with creepers and constructed of trelliswork or wooden joists above.

Pergolesi, Giovanni Battista (1710–36), Italian composer. Although throughout his short life he suffered from ill health, he composed several masses, the famous *Stabat Mater* and other church music, secular cantatas, oratorios, some instrumental works and nine operas.

Pericarditis, inflammation of the pericardium. This can be due to infection by bacteria (such as tuberculosis), viruses, fungi, injury, bleeding, kidney infection, or sometimes follows coronary thrombosis. The patient may have pain in the chest and a fever with breathlessness and palpitations. General treatment includes absolute rest with a light diet and the use of analgesics for pain. More specific treatment is directed to the cause of pericarditis.

Pericardium, the thin double membrane covering the outside of the heart and the roots of the major blood vessels leaving the heart. There is a fine space between the two layers of the pericardium called the pericardial cavity. Usually, a small amount of fluid is present which acts as a lubricant, reducing friction between the two layers of the pericardium as they rub against each other when the heart beats.

Pericarp, see FRUIT.

Pericles (c. 490–429 BC), Athenian statesman. By 469 Pericles was regarded as leader of the democratic party as opposed to Cimon. In 461, he supported Ephialtes, who carried a measure to restrict the powers of the Areopagus, and secured the ostracism of Cimon. Pericles likewise enjoyed the confidence of his fellow citizens as a military commander, and his most outstanding successes in this field were the recovery (446) of Euboea, which had revolted from Athens, and the reduction of Samos (440). After the death of Cimon (449) the conservative, land-owning party was led by Thucydides, son of Melesias; but on the ostracism of Thucydides in 443 Pericles was left without a rival.

He spent the years 440–432 beautifying Athens with public buildings. Meanwhile his enemies did their best to destroy his reputation; but failing in this, they attacked him through his friends.

On the outbreak of the Peloponnesian war (431), which Pericles had long foreseen, he urged the Athenians to rely wholly upon their seapower; and their neglect of that advice led to ultimate disaster. At the end of the first year's campaign Pericles delivered the celebrated funeral oration which forms perhaps the most memorable statement of Athenian values and aspirations.

Renowned for his dignified bearing and splendid eloquence, he was also a man of unimpeachable honour and courage. Under his leadership Athens attained the zenith of her artistic glory, her imperial greatness, and her commercial prosperity.

Perigee, point on orbit closest to the Earth.

Periglacial Processes, see GLACIATION.

Périgueux, French town, capital of the *département* of Dordogne, on the River Isle. It is the seat of a bishopric, and has Roman remains and many old buildings, including a Romano-Byzantine cathedral. There are railway workshops, tanneries, food-canning factories and a trade in truffles, grain and wine. Population (1975) 37,670.

Perihelion, point on orbit nearest to the Sun. Earth is at its perihelion on 4 January.

Perim, island in the strait of Bab-el-Mander, 2·5 km from the coast of Arabia and 155 km west of Aden, People's Democratic Republic of Yemen. The British occupied it in 1857 because of its proximity to the Suez Canal and it remained a coaling station until 1936. There is no fresh water available and little vegetation. Area 13 km^2; population c. 300.

See also ADEN.

Perineum, that part of the external floor of the pelvis which lies between the anus and the vulva in the female and between the anus and scrotum in the male. It is a tough sheet of ligaments and muscles.

Period and Periodicity. Scientifically the word period is often used to denote the time-spacing of a continuous cycle of events which continually repeat themselves in a definite order. Thus the succession of days, the beating of the heart, and the revolution of the astronomical bodies is periodic. The idea underlies the theories of wave motion in sound, light and electricity.

Periodic Law. Newlands (1864), in formulating his 'law of octaves', pointed out that if the chemical elements are arranged in order of their atomic weights, every eighth element shows strong resemblances. Lothar Meyer stated that 'the properties of the chemical elements are periodic functions of their atomic weights', having been led to this conclusion by a study of atomic volumes and chemical properties of elements. Mendeléev enunciated the periodic law to cover the observed data. The so-called law was extremely useful in the correction of inaccurate atomic weights (e.g. beryllium) and as a stimulus towards the discovery of new elements.

See also CHEMISTRY.

Periodic System, see CHEMISTRY.

Periodicals, see MAGAZINES; NEWSPAPERS.

Periostitis, inflammation of the periosteum or fibrous membrane investing the greater part of the surface of the bones. It may be due to injury or infection. In acute infective cases swelling and suppuration occur with considerable constitutional disturbance, and septicaemia may follow. Chronic periostitis may be due to infection from syphilis, tuberculosis, actinomycosis, or may be arthritic in origin. Osteitis and osteomyelitis, affecting respectively the bone substance and the bone marrow, are conditions which may be associated with periostitis. Any abscess formation must be drained surgically and, fortunately, antibiotic therapy has assisted considerably in reducing the severity of this disease.

Peripatetics (Greek *peripatētikos*, walking about), name given to the philosophical school deriving from Aristotle.

Periscope, instrument that came into prominence during the First World War, when it was necessary for trench observers to see without being seen. The submarine periscope can be rotated about the axis of the tube to enable the observer to see objects in any horizontal direction from the submarine. Periscopes have been manufactured which, with a tube of only a few centimetres in diameter, give a field of view with clear vision; binocular as well as monocular types have also been produced. They are fitted with high- and low-power magnification, range-finders, sky-searchers, and special filters for varying conditions of light.

Perissodactyla, hoofed quadrupeds characterised by the possession of an odd number of toes on the hind foot, and by the presence of a third trochanter (projection) on the femur or thigh bone. There are three living families of Perissodactyla: (1) Equidae or horses; (2) Tapiridae or tapirs; and (3) Rhinocerotidae or rhinoceroses. In addition, there are a number of extinct forms.

Peristalsis, rhythmical wave-like muscular contractions which occur in certain hollow organs under the control of the involuntary nervous system and propel the contents along, e.g. in the alimentary canal during digestion.

Peristyle, in classical architecture, a range of columns around a building or courtyard.

Peritoneum, the largest serous (i.e. serum-moistened) membrane in the body, forming a double-walled sac. The parietal layer lines the inner walls of the abdomen, and the visceral layer clothes the abdominal organs, the space between the layers being filled with a film of fluid. The various organs are attached to some part of the abdominal wall or adjacent organs by *ligaments*. Peritoneal ligaments attached to the intestines are called *mesenteries* while those of the stomach are the *omenta* (greater and lesser). Blood and lymph vessels are carried in the connective tissue of the mesenteries.

See also PERITONITIS.

Peritonitis, inflammation of the peritoneum. It occurs in the acute and chronic form, and may be local or general. The onset is sometimes difficult to distinguish from colic. Commencing with a local pain, it spreads all over the abdomen and becomes intense; the breathing is shallow and rapid, the pulse rapid, the temperature raised, and vomiting is an early symptom. The abdomen is rigid, and the face pinched, drawn and anxious; cold sweats and thirst are other symptoms after the abdomen becomes swollen with fluid. Common causes are infection from appendicitis or from the perforation of any part of the alimentary canal. Treatment consists in removing the cause of the infection, relieving pain, giving antibiotics, sucking out the stomach contents through a tube, and providing intravenous fluids.

Periwig, see WIG.

Periwinkle, or winkle, common name applied to the genus *Littorina*, a mollusc which occurs very commonly on shores. There are four common species. *L. littorea*, the common or edible winkle, occurs at mid-shore levels and can be recognised by the dark concentric rings on its grey shell. It grows up to 2·5 cm in height. The rough periwinkle (*L. saxatilis*), which is now believed to consist of several subspecies, has a rough feel to its shell. It occurs higher up the shore than *L. littorea*. The flat periwinkle (*L. littoralis*) has a flat-topped rounded shell and is commonly found on the seaweed *Fucus* (wrack) at mid-shore levels. *L. neritoides*, the small periwinkle, only grows to about 0·5 cm high and occurs in crevices on the upper shore.

Periwinkle, *Vinca*, a genus of hardy perennial herbs or sub-shrubs in the family Apocynaceae. The greater periwinkle, *V. major*, and the lesser periwinkle, *V. minor*, are handsome blue-flowered plants used in gardens for shady positions.

Perjury, crime of wilfully making a false statement on oath as a witness (or interpreter) in a law court, such a statement being material to the question in issue and made deliberately or without belief in its truth.

The term 'false swearing' applies to false oaths not taken in the course of judicial proceedings, e.g. false declarations with reference to marriages, births or deaths, in bankruptcy matters, or by a voter.

'Subornation of perjury' is procuring another to commit perjury. It is punishable as perjury itself.

Perkin, Sir William Henry (1838–1907), British chemist. He is best known for his researches on dyes and coal-tar colourings, and several processes were invented by him. He may be said to have founded the coal-tar colour industry.

Perm, capital city, economic and cultural centre of Perm *oblast*, USSR, on the River Kama. It is one of the main commercial and transport centres, especially after the first Trans-Ural railway was built from Perm to Yekaterinburg (now Sverdlovsk) in 1874. It is an important industrial centre (machine-building, chemical plants, oil-processing, timber), and has a musical and theatrical tradition. It was founded in 1723 as a settlement next to a copper-works. Population (1980) 1,008,000.

Permafrost, a condition of perennially frozen ground which results from a negative heat balance at the Earth's surface. It is underlain by unfrozen ground and shows its best expression in an arc around the Arctic Ocean approximately north of the Arctic Circle. Permafrost can be either continuous, discontinuous or sporadic. In northern Canada, continuous permafrost extends to over 390 m in depth, thinning southwards to about 30 m in thickness at the southern limit of continuous permafrost, but permafrost has been proved to a depth of over 600 m in northern Siberia. The southern limit of discontinuous permafrost approximates roughly to the −2°C mean annual isotherm, but in East Asia it extends far south of this as a result of relict conditions from the Pleistocene ice ages. The permanently frozen ground is overlain by a zone of annual thaw, or active layer, which thaws in the summer and re-freezes in the autumn giving a moisture-holding zone trapped between two frozen layers. This 'sandwich' zone is subjected to great pressures as a result of the downfreezing from the surface and pressures are released at weak points in the freezing surface layer, producing severe engineering problems for constructors of buildings, roads, railways, pipelines and airstrips.

Permalloy, see NICKEL.

Permanent Court of International Justice, see INTERNATIONAL COURT OF JUSTICE.

Permeke, Constant (1856–1952), Belgian painter, the most powerful representative of Expressionism in Belgium. He studied art in Bruges and Ghent and produced his first important works in England where he stayed during the First World War. His *Les Fiancés* is one of his principal works (Brussels Museum). He is celebrated for scenes of peasant life.

Permian System, geological division occurring above the Carboniferous and below the Triassic Systems. The Permian System began about 280 million years ago and ended about 235 million years ago. Permian rocks are relatively poorly developed in Britain, reaching a maximum thickness, where exposed, of only 270 m in Durham. They occur in North-East and North-West England, on either side of the Pennines, the English Midlands, Devon, and the Midland Valley and Southern Uplands of Scotland. The Permian is often classed together with the overlying Triassic as the New Red Sandstone or Permo-Triassic System.

Permutations and Combinations are the technical terms used in mathematics for various kinds of rearrangements and selections of a definite number of objects from a given set of objects. To illustrate the definitions take a set of three objects (a, b, c). The permutations of all the objects from the set are: $a, b, c; a, c, b; b, a, c; b, c, a; c, a, b; c, b, a$. The permutations are different arrangements of the three items. The number of possible permutations of all the elements of a set with n elements is $n(n-1)...2.1$, which is usually denoted by $n!$ This formula is derived by observing that the first item in any permutation can be chosen in n ways; for each of these ways the second item can be chosen in $n-1$ ways, and so on. The permutations of two elements chosen from the three in the example are: $a, b; b, a; a, c; c, a; c, b; b, c$.

The number of permutations of r items chosen from n items is denoted by ${}_nP_r$ and is

$$n(n-1) \ldots (n-r-1) = n!/(n-r)!$$

Combinations are simply subsets of a set and no attention is paid to arrangement or order of the items. Thus the combinations of two items from the three in the example are: $a, b; a, c; b, c$. The number of combinations of r items chosen from n items is denoted by $\binom{n}{r}$ and is equal to the number of permutations of r items chosen from n divided by the number of possible permutations of those r items; that is

$$\binom{n}{r} = \frac{n!}{(n-r)!\,r!}$$

$\binom{n}{r}$ is also the coefficient of x^r in the expansion of $(1+x)^n$ according to the binomial theorem and is therefore called a 'binomial coefficient'.

Pernettya, a genus of small evergreen shrubs, in the family Ericaceae, native to South America and Australasia. *P. mucronata* and its varieties are esteemed for their profuse pink berries in autumn gardens.

Pernik, town of western Bulgaria, capital of the province of Pernik, 25 km south-west of Sofia. Its chief activities are coal-mining and steel production. Population (1979) 91,428.

Perón, Juan Domingo (1895–1974), former President of Argentina. He was one of the chief leaders in the military coup of 4 June 1943 which overthrew President Castillo. From that time he was the power behind the president. In 1943–44 he was president of the National Department of Labour, and in 1944–45 was both minister of War and vice-president of the Republic simultaneously. In 1946 he was elected president. With the help of his extremely able wife Eva (d.1952), Perón had soon established himself as a demagogic, nationalist dictator. The living standards of the working class were raised by Perón, but the economic basis of his policy was unsound, and resulted in crisis and inflation. Perón was overthrown in September 1955 by a military coup and left the country. He made an unsuccessful attempt to return in 1964.

From 1964 to 1973 he lived in Spain where he maintained close links with Argentina. In 1973 Perón was elected president for a second term; his performance was unspectacular. He died in 1974 and was succeeded in office by his second wife, Isabel.

Perpetual Motion has been sought by many earnest experimenters in the past, despite its scientific impossibility. A perpetual motion machine would be one that moved and continued to move for ever without receiving any supply of energy from an external source. The requirements of such a machine are either that it shall be perfectly frictionless, or if friction is present, that the machine shall create energy in order to overcome the friction. The first requirement, complete absence of friction in a real machine, is impossible, and the second violates the law of conservation of energy.

See also THERMODYNAMICS.

Perpignan, French town, capital of the *département* of Pyrénées-Orientales, on the River Têt. It was the old capital of Roussillon, built on the site of the Roman *Ruscino*, where the eastern route to Spain crosses the Têt. There is a vast citadel enclosing the castle of the kings of Majorca. The fine Gothic cathedral was begun in 1324. Perpignan is an important commercial centre for wine, fruit and vegetables, and manufactures textiles and paper. Population (1975) 107,971.

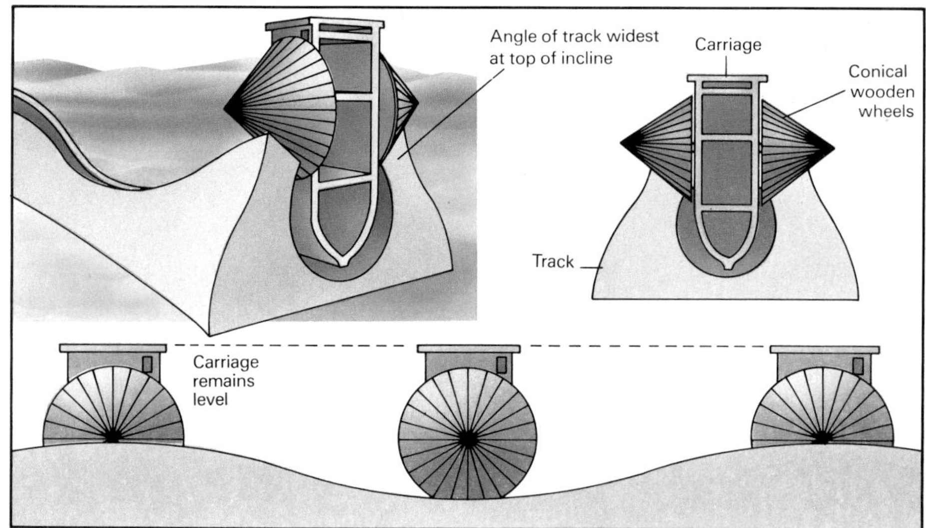

***Perpetual Motion.** An early 19th-century design for a self-moving carriage. As the vehicle slid down the incline, the track narrowed and the carriage rose, keeping the passenger compartment level. Once set in motion it was supposed to go on for ever – completely impossible of course.*

Perrault, Charles (1628–1703), French writer. He contributed to the famous quarrel of the ancients and moderns in the poem *Le Siècle de Louis le Grand*, 1687, which was intended to prove that modern authors were superior to the ancients.
However, the work that more than any other has preserved his name is the collection of fairy tales *Contes de ma mère l'Oye*, 1697, which includes *Sleeping Beauty, Red Riding Hood, Bluebeard, Puss-in-Boots* and *Cinderella.*
Perrault, Claude (1613–88), French architect. He was by profession a physician, but became the architect of the Louvre, his east front colonnade (1665) ranking among the finest buildings of the 17th century. He also designed the Observatory at Paris, c.1667, and translated Vitruvius's *De Architectura*, 1673.
Perrin, Jean Baptiste (1870–1942), French physicist, professor of physical chemistry at the University of Paris. In 1895 he showed that cathode rays consist of negatively charged particles, and are not waves. Perrin then used Einstein's work on Brownian motion to give a measurement of the size of molecules. He published this work in 1913.
Perron, a platform outside the entrance door to a building, with steps leading up to it, often in a double flight.
Perry, Fred (1909–), the most successful British tennis player since 1906, winning the Wimbledon singles in 1934, 1935 and 1936 —the first such sequence since 1912. He was also holder of the World Table Tennis Championship.
Perry, Matthew Calbraith (1794–1858), US naval officer. In 1853 he led an expedition to Japan and negotiated a treaty which in effect reopened communication between that country and the rest of the world after 250 years of isolation.
Perry, alcoholic liquor which is manufactured from certain varieties of pears as cider is from apples. It is sweet and pale, and contains about 3 to 8 per cent alcohol. It is made chiefly in England in the counties of Gloucestershire, Hereford and Worcester, Somerset and Devon.
Persephone, in Greek myth, daughter of Zeus and Demeter, called in Latin Proserpina.
Persepolis, Greek name for the official capital of the Persian Empire, 65 km east of Shiraz. It superseded Pasargadae in the reign of Darius I. The huge palace, with its treasury and splendid works of art, was built on an artificial terrace. It was partly destroyed in 331 BC during Alexander's occupation but there are considerable remains.
See also PERSIAN ART AND ARCHITECTURE.
Perseus, legendary Greek hero. Acrisius, king of Argos, was warned by an oracle that his daughter Danäe would bear a son who would kill him. He kept Danäe prisoner, but Zeus transformed himself into a shower of gold, penetrated Danaë's prison and became by her the father of Perseus. Acrisius set Danäe and Perseus adrift in the Aegean but by the intervention of Zeus they were saved by King Polydectes of Seriphos. After Perseus had reached manhood, Polydectes fell in love with Danaë and, wishing to get rid of Perseus, sent him to fetch the head of Medusa. Guided by Athena and Hermes, Perseus acquired the winged sandals, the magic wallet, and the helmet of Pluto which made its wearer invisible. With these, a sickle from Hermes and a mirror from Athena, Perseus flew on Pegasus to the abode of the Gorgons. Finding them asleep, he cut off Medusa's head with the sickle—watching her in the mirror, because direct sight of the monster would have turned him to stone—and put it into the wallet on his back. On the way home Perseus rescued and married Andromeda, and (according to some versions) used the Gorgon's head to turn Atlas to stone. When he arrived at Seriphos, he rescued Danaë from Polydectes and then presented the Gorgon's head to Athena. On returning to Argos he fulfilled the original prophecy by accidentally killing his grandfather.
Perseus, in astronomy, a bright northern constellation in the Milky Way containing many interesting objects. Its second brightest star, Beta Persei, is Algol, the best known of the eclipsing binary stars. The double cluster *h* and Chi Persei is just visible to the naked eye as two hazy patches of light close to one another. The Perseid meteors, which appear regularly during the last week of July and the first two weeks of August, are remnants of Comet 1862 III.
Pershing, John Joseph (1860–1948), US soldier; commander-in-chief of American Forces in France in the First World War. When the USA broke off diplomatic relations with Germany early in 1917, Pershing was given command of the US forces. In 1921 he became chief of staff of the army, and retired in 1924, Pershing's greatest quality was resolution; as a strategist he had little subtlety. His story is told in *My Experiences in the World War*, 1931.
Persia, see IRAN.
Persian Art and Architecture. The art of the Achaemenid empire, heir to that of the Assyrians and Babylonians, is known to us mostly from the imposing ruins of the successive capitals of Pasargadae, Persepolis and Susa. The palaces, constructed on a monumental scale, owe much to the forms of Egypt and Greece. A striking feature is their sculptural decoration, memorialising the person and majesty of the Great King, who is portrayed in the company of his counsellors, armies and subject peoples.
The conquest of the Persian empire by Alexander the Great intensified a process of the Hellenisation of art. Under the rule of the Sassanid dynasty, Persian art again asserted its independence. Such architectural innovations as the dome and the vault were introduced; while the great reliefs carved in rock faces are worthy successors of the Achaemenid sculptures.

***Persepolis.** Huge sculptural reliefs on the remains of the ancient imperial palace of Persia.*

With the coming of the Arabs, Persian art had to be adapted to the needs of the religion of Islam. Yet it succeeded in retaining its distinctive character, and even exercised a considerable influence on other countries of the Muslim world. Designs were abstract and geometric or composed of floral ornament in which the arabesque plays a prominent rôle. Arabic script is often introduced into the design. A feature of Persian buildings, both secular and religious, is the application of polychrome decoration on interior and exterior surfaces.
The combination of line and colour in a harmonious composition is seen at its best in the carpet, probably Persia's greatest artistic achievement. The earliest surviving carpets date from the 16th century. The carpets of this and the following century are among the finest ever produced. Some, especially those made in factories under royal patronage, depict hunting scenes; others were decorated with flowers, while a group from southern Persia has boldly drawn arabesques, and another from the Caucasus region is decorated with highly stylised floral and animal ornament. Rug weaving survives to this day among the nomad peoples of Iran.
The Persian potters of the 12th and 13th centuries were producing glazed wares second only to China and the Islamic countries of the Near East. Persian pottery combines brilliance of colour with decoration perfectly adapted to the form of the vessel. There was a remarkable revival of pottery beginning at the end of the 16th century.
Miniature painting thrived from c.1300 and reached maturity in the 15th century. At its best, the Persian miniature is executed in a firm yet delicate line and with a wonderful understanding of colour harmony. This innate decorative sense of colour and intricate design appears in illuminations illustrating the sagas and court life in palace and garden. The greatest master was Bihzad, born in 1450.
Persian Cat, see CAT.
Persian Gulf, an almost land-locked body of water lying between the Arabian Peninsula and Iran, with Iraq at its head, and which has access to the Gulf of Oman and the Indian Ocean through the narrow Straits of Hormuz. It covers an area of 239,000 km² and has an average depth of 26 m. The water temperature is high, being from 24°C to 36°C at the Straits of Hormuz and from 18°C to 36°C at its head, where the rivers Tigris, Euphrates and Karun flow into the Gulf. Apart from a few small rivers on the Iranian shore, these are the only sources of fresh water in the Persian Gulf as the annual rainfall is very small. With the high air temperatures found in this region, evaporation is large and consequently the salinity of the water is high. The tides in the gulf are quite large, especially at its head and in the Straits of Hormuz where the tidal range can be about 3–4 m.
Vast oil and gas fields lie under the gulf and its coastal region, especially to the south.

Persian Art. *A 17th-century panel of glazed tiles from a garden pavilion at Isfahan.*

Persian History. *Pre-Islamic History.* The earliest identifiable prehistoric settlements of ancient Persia (modern Iran) date from 7000–6000 BC. The Iranians appear to have entered Persia by two routes, the Caucasus and Transoxiana, around the beginning of the first millennium BC. The Assyrians knew of the Persians in 844 BC and of the Medes in 836. In 533 Cyrus II the Great, founder of the Achaemenid Empire, defeated the Median king and joined Median Persia. He then conquered Lydia, the Greek cities on the coast of Asia Minor, and Babylon (539) and its dependencies, including Syria. In the east he sought to establish a stable frontier against the nomads of Central Asia, but was killed in battle against them in 530.

Under Darius (522–486 BC), who succeeded Cyrus's son, the empire was divided into 20 satrapies, the administration reorganised, and a network of roads created. Darius then enlarged the boundaries of Persia as far eastward as the Indus, and invaded, unsuccessfully, both Russia and Greece. Xerxes succeeded on the death of Darius, his father, and continued the war with Greece, only to be defeated at Salamis, Plataea and Mycale. Subsequently a number of Greek cities in Asia Minor were liberated from Persia. After the death of Darius III (336–330) Persia became part of the Macedonian Empire, which itself broke up after the death of Alexander the Great in 323 BC. Seleucus seized Babylon, subdued the whole of Persia as far as the Indus, and won Syria and the eastern portion of Asia Minor. Most of these areas were, however, lost under Antiochus I (280–261) and, under Antiochus IV (175–164), the Seleucidae lost Mesopotamia to the Parthians. Parthian rule was in its turn brought to an end in AD 227 and two years later Ardashir was crowned the first king of the Sassanid dynasty. Wars with Rome raged intermittently throughout the next three centuries until at the accession of Yazdegerd III (632–651) peace was concluded. Then the Arabs swept out of Arabia, and the Sassanid Empire, exhausted by war and taxation, was in no position to resist their advance.

Islamic History. Persia became incorporated in the dominions of the caliphs and the population was converted to Islam. In the 8th century Persian influence increased and Persians played an important part in the country's administration. After the Buyids entered Baghdad in 945, until the overthrow of the caliphate by the Mongols in 1258, the caliph ceased to exercise effective sovereignty, and merely acted as titular head of Sunni Islam. The domains of the Buyids eventually fell to the Ghaznavids, Seljuqs and others.

The Ghaznavid dynasty was defeated in 1055 by the Seljuqs, under whose rule the main lines of the administrative and economic structure which lasted down to the 20th century, were laid. The Great Seljuqs were followed in Persia by a number of succession states until the Mongols entered Baghdad in 1258 and brought the Abbasside caliphate to an end. The dynasties that succeeded were extinguished between 1381 and 1387 by Tamerlane, whose empire, fell by 1447. For history from the 15th century to modern times, see IRAN, *History*.

Persian Language. A sub-branch of the Indo-Iranian or 'Aryan' main branch, belonging to the Indo-European languages. The other sub-branch is Sanskrit. Persian may be distinguished as Old Persian, used on the monuments of the Achaemenidae dynasty (middle 6th century to the second half of the 4th century BC); Middle Persian of the Parthian or Arsacidae period (250 BC–AD 225), and of the Sassanidae period (AD 225–651), terminated by the Arab conquest; with the growth of semi-independent dynasties in Persia in the 9th century AD, Modern Persian began to flourish.

Modern Persian is a direct descendant of the south-central Middle Persian dialect, and is written in the Arabic script, though with some additional letters. A knowledge of Arabic was indispensable to the converts of Islam, for religious worship and the correct reading of the Koran, and Arabic speech and writing largely influenced modern Persian. Persian writers made significant contributions to the development of medieval Arabic literature and culture. Numerous Persian dialects exist, for example Kurdish is spoken in Kurdistan, and Luri by the Lurs and Bakhtiaris.

See also ARABIC LANGUAGE; ARABIC LITERATURE.

Persian Literature. Modern Persian begins as a literary language in the early 9th century AD. The first great classical poet was Rudaki (d.c.954). With him began the court poetry of modern Persia. He was followed during the period 10th to 16th centuries by, among others, Firdausi, who wrote the *Shahnama*, the national epic of Persia, which incorporates the heroic legends of early Iran; Omar Khayyam; and the three great lyric poets Saadi of Shiraz, Jalal-ud-din Rumi and Hafiz. A later poet, of epic fame, is Hatif of Isfahan (d.1784). Important poets of the 19th century are Qa'ani (d.1853), Yaghma and Surush, whose elegant work almost equals that of the classical poets.

The verse forms are restricted with few exceptions to the *ruba'i* or quatrain; the *ghazal*, a poem in couplets, interlocked with a single rhyme at the end of each couplet; the *qasida*, a dedicatory poem, similar in form to the *ghazal* but longer; and the *mathnavi*, an epic or narrative poem in rhymed couplets.

One of the earliest Persian prose works is the abridged translation of the *Universal History of Tabari* by Bal'ami (d.996), while one of the most celebrated is the *Gulistan* of Saadi. The 13th and 14th centuries are also notable for the historical works of Juwayni and Rashid al-Din (c.1250–1318). There is also an abundant Persian literature belonging to Islamic India.

Persian drama was in the past confined mainly to religious passion plays and translations from European works. New developments began in the second half of the 19th century when writers such as Malkam Khan (d.1908) and Zayn al-'Abidin Maragha'i began to discuss social and political themes. This modernist movement was reflected in the work of novelists Bozorg Alavi, Gholamhossein Sa'edi, and Simin Danishvar. Modern Persian literature has also produced a body of original poetry of which Nima Youshij is the greatest exponent.

See also ARABIC LITERATURE; INDIA, *Literature*.

Persian Wars, intermittent conflict between the Achaemenid empire of Persia and the Greek city-states, 490–449 BC. The initial attack by Darius I in 490 ended with the Greek victory at Marathon in the same year. The second Persian War began in 480 BC, when Xerxes invaded Greece and burned Athens. His forces, however, were defeated at the naval battle of Salamis, and again at Plataea and Mycale in 479. In 468 the Greeks counter-attacked and won a victory on the Eurymedon. The struggle was renewed in 450; but in the following year the Persians agreed to the Peace of Callias, whereby their fleets were banned from Greek waters.

Persimmon, several species of *Diospyros* in the Ebenaceae. D. lotus is the common persimmon or date plum of Asia.

Personal Property, or personalty, in English law, comprises all chattels or moveables such as jewels, money, as well as choses in action, as opposed to real estate or interest in land. Leasehold or chattels-real are ranked as personalty and always devolve on intestacy as such. In Scots law classification into heritable and moveable property is almost parallel to the English division into real and personal property.

See also REAL PROPERTY.

Personality, see PSYCHOLOGY.

Personification, figure of speech in which human attributes are given to abstract qualities, to objects or to animals. An example from Milton is:

> Sport that wrinkled Care derides,
> And Laughter holding both his sides.

A common and ancient form in European poetry, it has a particularly important relationship with allegory, as many allegorical

works, for example, Bunyan's *Pilgrim's Progress*, include characters, such as Despair, which are personifications of abstract qualities.
See also FIGURE OF SPEECH.

Personnel Management, the function of management concerned with making the best use of the human resources of an organisation. This function is, in all but the smallest organisation, the job of a specialist manager who acts as an adviser to the other managers in the organisation. The job of personnel management may be divided into the following major categories: (1) selection; (2) wage and salary payment systems; (3) training and development; (4) industrial relations; (5) manpower planning.

Perspective, in the visual arts, means both *recession* and *simulation* of it in a picture. In ancient Rome, extensive landscapes and complicated architecture were frescoed on walls to give spaciousness to interiors, but the simulation was done by guesswork. The accurate rendering of how objects appear to diminish with distance, and how intervals close up, became possible when the architect Brunelleschi invented a geometrical construction.
The basis of perspective is that parallel lines running into the distance appear to converge in a 'vanishing point' on the horizon opposite an observer's eye. This convergence of 'orthogonals' becomes a chequerboard diminishing in correct perspective if *horizontals* are drawn through all the points where the *orthogonals* are cut by a *diagonal*, drawn from a 'distance point'.

Perspiration, see DIAPHORETICS; SKIN.

Perth, city and royal burgh in Tayside Region, Scotland, formerly called St Johnstoun, 70 km north-west of Edinburgh, on the banks of the River Tay. Perth is a renowned tourist centre, with iron foundries, dye-works, whisky-blending and whisky-bottling plants, and light engineering industries. It is also an important centre for agricultural products and noted for the sale of pedigree livestock, particularly young beef bulls. Population (1981) 41,998.

Perth, capital of Western Australia, on the Swan river near its mouth, 19 km north-east of Fremantle. It was founded in 1829 and created a municipality in 1856. Its growth and prosperity resulted from the discovery of gold in 1893 at Kalgoorlie, but its development in the last few decades has been based on the export of primary products (wool, wheat, fruit, timber and dairy produce) and manufactures (machinery and electronics). Population (1979) 883,600

Peru
Area: 1,285,216 km²
Population: 17,293,100
Capital: Lima

Peru, Republic of, situated on the north-western side of South America. It comprises an area of 1,285,216 km^2, and is bordered by Ecuador and Colombia in the north, by Brazil in the east, and by Bolivia and Chile in the south-east and south. In the west it faces the Pacific Ocean and has a coastline of over 2000 km. Peru is the fourth largest Latin American country (by area).
The dominant geographical feature is the mountain system of the Andes which run through the centre of Peru from north-west to south-east and occupy about one-third of the whole country. This causes the country to fall into three major natural divisions: the coastal area, the sierra, and the selva (jungle).
The coastal area runs the length of the coastline between the Pacific and the Andes, varying in width between 20 and 200 km. The area is almost rainless and apart from the 90 rivers flowing from east to west it is desert. The area contains most of Peru's largest cities: Lima, Callao, Chiclayo, Trujillo, and Chimbole, all with over 200,000 inhabitants, and is in fact the economic heart of Peru.
The sierra region covers the mountain system of the Andes comprising high-level plateaus at an average altitude of 3000–4000 m, and 20 main mountain ranges or *cordilleras*, rising to many peaks of more than 6000 m. The highest mountain in Peru is Huascarán, in the department of Ancash, at 6768 m.
The selva (or montaña) is the third and largest natural region, occupying more than half of Peru but having only 10 per cent of its population. In fact it consists of two distinct regions: the eastern slopes of the Andes (the montaña or Ceja de Selva), forested and cut by valleys, and the Amazonian plains further east covered with tropical forest and jungle. Much of it is unexplored and rivers form the main means of communication. The two main rivers are the Ucayali and Marañón, both great tributaries of the Amazon.
The 1979 census reported a total population of 17,293,100. The majority of the population is of mixed race mestizo, though the rural population is predominantly Indian. The capital Lima is the commercial and political centre of Peru. Its port Callao is only 12 km away. Arequipa is the commercial centre of southern Peru.
The commercial sector of agriculture has generated many of Peru's exports since the 19th century. The sugar and cotton estates of the north have been especially important in terms of exports. The agrarian reform has expropriated land from a limited number of very large landowners. The main commercial estates were not divided up but turned into cooperatives.
The fishing industry is important because of the huge numbers of anchovy and other species brought by the Humboldt (or Peruvian) Current. Considerable efforts are being made to industrialise, and resources are being transferred from agriculture into this sector. Manufacturing is heavily concentrated in the coastal area and around two-thirds of the workers are employed in the Lima–Callao agglomeration.
Mining produces some of the main exports: iron ore, copper, zinc, lead and silver. Petroleum is produced in considerable quantities.
The unit of currency is the *sol*.
The present constitution was introduced in 1980. The legislative body is a bicameral Congress of a senate (60 members) and a chamber of deputies (180 members), who are elected concurrently with the President and for the same term of office. The executive consists of the President and a Council of Ministers appointed by him.
The official languages are Spanish and Quechua.
History. The Inca Empire flourished from about AD 1000 until Pizarro's arrival and the defeat and death of Atahualpa in 1532. It extended over Peru, Bolivia and Ecuador, and its influence extended even to the Gran Chaco. Peru remained under Spanish rule until 1821 and its mineral wealth meant that the viceroyalty enjoyed a prosperous history. After the end of Spanish rule, however, economic stagnation was accompanied by civil unrest until the guano boom, which

Perspective. *The vanishing point of a picture can be located by drawing a series of lines (orthogonals) linking features at the same level. When these are intersected by lines drawn parallel and at right angles to the horizon, a chequer-board pattern is created, diminishing in correct perspective.*

***Peru.** A river valley in southern Peru, near Cuzco, the ancient capital of the Incas.*

lasted from the 1840s until the late-1870s, raised the revenues of central government. Prosperity was shattered by a disastrous war with Chile (1879–83) and the replacement of guano by nitrates on the world market. Since the Second World War the USA has supplied military and economic aid to Peru. US interests in Peruvian mineral wealth and industry are substantial, and this fact has helped to inflame the latent anti-Americanism of left-wing groups in the country. In 1962 the army, fearing left-wing action, established a military junta, although constitutional elections were held again in 1963. Political stalemate and inflation prompted another military coup in 1968 and brought to power reformist officers, who demanded agrarian reform and an extensive programme of nationalisation of foreign-owned property and banking. In 1975 the reformist wing in the armed forces was displaced by conservative officers, and in 1980 civilian rule was reintroduced.

Peru Balsam, see BALSAM.

Perugia (ancient *Perusia*), Italian city and capital of Perugia province and the region of Umbria. It is built on a hill commanding the Tiber valley, 135 km north-west of Rome. Originally an Etruscan city, it was taken by Octavian in 40 BC and by Totila in the 6th century. There are Etruscan walls and a gateway. Textiles, chemicals, lace and machinery are manufactured, and there is a large trade in agricultural produce. Population (1979) 139,871.

Perugino, Pietro, properly Pietro Vanucci (1446–1523), Italian painter, one of the masters of the Umbrian school. He is said to have been a pupil of Piero della Francesca and probably an assistant to Verrocchio. His first public work was the execution of the frescoes in the Palazzo Communale in Perugia (1475). In 1480 he was one of the group of artists chosen by Sixtus IV to embellish his newly finished Sistine chapel, and painted the *Delivery of the Keys to St Peter*, a work which particularly shows his method of painting distance by rendering the effects of space and atmosphere, a method which his pupil Raphael carried to perfection. Perugino led a wandering life: in 1489 he painted the noble frescoes in the Collegio del Cambio of Perugia, but after 1502 he worked mostly at Florence. His *Virgin and Child, with SS Michael and Raphael* and four other works are in the National Gallery, London.

Peruvian Bark, or Jesuit's bark, bark of various trees of the genus *Cinchona*.
See also CINCHONA.

Perversion, in psychology, any form of adult sexual behaviour where heterosexual intercourse is not the preferred goal. It is regarded as a distortion of normal psychosexual development, and can be seen as representing a return to forms of infantile sexuality. Common forms of perversion in this strict sense include: exhibitionism; voyeurism; sadism and masochism; fetishism. Perverse qualities may enter into other aspects of behaviour to create a situation in which the normal give and take in a satisfying personal relationship is obstructed. Sexual perversions are better called sexual deviations.
See also HOMOSEXUALITY; SEXUALITY, HUMAN.

Pesaro (ancient *Pisaurum*), Italian town and seaside resort, capital of the province of Pesaro e Urbino, 60 km north-west of Ancona. It is on the Adriatic coast, at the mouth of the River Foglia, and has a 15th-century ducal palace, a cathedral, and a music school founded by Rossini, who was born here. There are furniture, motorcycle and fishing industries. Population (1974) 72,100.

Pescadores (Chinese *P'enghu*), group of about 64 basaltic islands off the west coast of Taiwan in the China Sea. Since 1949 they have been occupied by the Chinese Nationalist refugee government in Taiwan. Millet and rice are grown and there are good fisheries offshore. Area 130 km². Population (1972 estimate) 120,000.

Pescara (ancient *Aternum*), Italian city and seaport, capital of Pescara province, situated on the Adriatic 160 km north-east of Rome. It is the chief town of Abruzzo region and has a wide variety of small factories (clothing, foodstuffs, building materials, etc.) spreading up the Pescara river valley, beside its major industries of shipbuilding, tourism and fishing. Population (1979) 137,059.

Peseta, the standard unit of currency in Spain, containing 100 centesimos. The peseta was first issued in 1868.

Peshawar, city of Pakistan, metropolis of the Pathans, and capital of the North-West Frontier province on the Bara river. It stands close to the foot of the Khyber Pass into Afghanistan and has for centuries been a centre of the transit trade between the Indian subcontinent, Afghanistan and Central Asia. Having been in Muslim occupation since about AD 1000, it was taken by the Sikhs in 1833, and by the British in 1849. Population (1972) 366,000.

Peso, name of the monetary unit of several Latin American countries, Paraguay, Colombia, Mexico, the Argentine, etc. It is usually divided into 100 centavos.

Pessimism, an attitude of mind that sees things from the worst angle (Latin *pessimus*, worst). As such it is the opposite of optimism, the view that everything will come out for the best in the end. Pessimism regards life as devoid of hope, and true happiness, dignity, purpose and beauty as unobtainable in this world. Sometimes this is compensated for by seeking some other world in which hopes may be realised. In modern philosophy, pessimism runs strong, especially in the works of Schopenhauer, whose notion of the will as the cause of all pain and evil is strongly reminiscent of Buddhist thought. A more recent philosophy strongly tinged with pessimism is Existentialism in its atheistic versions. These are much concerned with the futility of all human activity, and with the cosmic fears that beset us, especially the fear of nothingness.

Pest, see BUDAPEST.

Pestalozzi, Johann Heinrich (1746–1827), Swiss educational reformer. When he adapted his theories to educate 'according to nature' to the institute which he founded at Yverdon (Neuchâtel), his ideas were spread through the various foreign teachers who came to him and influenced the whole course of modern education. He wrote *Abendstunde eines Einsiedlers*, 1780; *Lienhardt und Gertrud*, 1781; and *Wie Gertrud ihre Kinder lehrt*, 1801.
See also EDUCATION.

Pesticide, see HERBICIDES; INSECTICIDES.

Pestilence, see BLACK DEATH; CHOLERA; EPIDEMIC; PLAGUE; SMALLPOX; TYPHUS FEVER.

Pétain, Henri Philippe Benoni Omer Joseph (1856–1951), French soldier and statesman. He was made colonel in the French army in 1912, when he was placed at the head of the 33rd Infantry at Arras. After being in the retreat from Belgium, 1914, Pétain was placed in command of the 6th Division, which fought at the Marne, and was soon afterwards in command of the 33rd Army Corps, which covered Arras.

In 1916 Joffre placed him in command of the army formed to relieve Verdun. Pétain soon fulfilled the promise with which his name was to be associated for the next quarter of a century: 'Ils ne passeront pas!'. In July 1918, Pétain was entrusted with the general attack by all French forces. He was made a marshal in November 1918.

In May 1940 Reynaud called him into his Cabinet as vice-premier, but by this time Pétain had become convinced that German victory was inevitable, and was soon urging an immediate French capitulation. On 16 June he formed a Cabinet and asked Hitler for an armistice. After this he became 'chief of the French state', abolished the republican constitution, and substituted an authoritarian form of government for that part of France which remained unoccupied until the Allied landings in North Africa in late 1942.

His real authority, however, was never complete. After 1942 Pétain's position as head of the state was more uncertain than ever, all effective authority having passed to Laval and the Germans. He had retired from the active political scene by the end of 1943. When the Allied invasion of Europe began he left Vichy and was taken to Belfort and later to Sigmaringen. In April 1945 he voluntarily returned to France, where he was arrested and interned. On a charge of treason he was tried and sentenced to death, this being commuted to life imprisonment.

Petasites, a genus of perennial rhizomatous herbs in family Compositae, closely related to coltsfoot, found in Europe, Asia and North America. It includes *P. fragrans*, winter heliotrope, and *P. hybridus*, butterbur.

Peter, Saint, leader of the 12 apostles, born at Bethsaida, on the western side of the sea of Galilee; during the period of Christ's ministry his residence was at Capernaum. He was married, but we are not told whether or not he had children. His name was at first Simon (or Symeon, Acts xv. 14), which was changed by Jesus into Cephas, an Aramaic word signifying a stone or rock, in Greek, *petra*, whence Peter. With Andrew, his brother, he followed the occupation of a fisherman. Both were disciples of John the Baptist (John i. 40 ff.), by whom they were taught that Jesus was the Messiah. While following their occupation on the sea of Galilee, Jesus called them to be his disciples, promising that he would make them 'fishers of men'. Peter was the first to acknowledge Jesus as the Christ and son of God, and in response Jesus told him that 'on this rock' he would build his church (Matt. xvi. 18). With James and John, Peter witnessed the Transfiguration (Matt. xvii). During the trial of Jesus Peter denied his master three times (Luke xxii. 54–62), but was restored after the Resurrection (John xxi).

***St Peter.** Statue outside St Peter's, Rome.*

Following the gift of the Holy Spirit on the Day of Pentecost, Peter's sermon converted 3000 Jews (Acts ii). Later he preached to Cornelius, the first gentile to become a Christian (Acts x). Two epistles in the New Testament bear Peter's name.

The tradition that Peter reached Rome is now generally accepted as genuine, but the Roman Catholic claim of a 25-year episcopate there lacks evidence other than a tradition noted by Jerome (c.AD 400). Peter is believed to have been executed c.67 by being crucified upside down.

Peter I, the Great (1672–1725), first Emperor of Russia. When Peter's half-brother Fëdor III died in 1682 without issue, the Patriarch of Moscow and the leading boyars decided that Peter should be the tsar rather than his older, but incompetent, half-brother Ivan. The latter's older sister Sophia, however, organised a coup by the palace guards which resulted in the coronation of Ivan and Peter as joint tsars, with the appointment of Sophia as regent. The next seven years Peter spent in a village near Moscow with his mother. Physically and mentally far in advance of his years, and receiving no systematic education, Peter picked up a mass of knowledge and technical skills. In 1689, having received information of a plot by Sophia against him, Peter forced her to resign and sent her to a convent. Peter left nominal precedence to Ivan, but in fact ruled the country himself.

Peter's first care on assuming the government was to form an army disciplined according to European tactics. He also strove to create a navy and a merchant fleet. Eager for knowledge, he left Russia in April 1697, in the guise of an inferior embassy official; he visited the three Baltic provinces, Prussia and Hanover, reaching Amsterdam, where he worked for some time as a shipwright. To his other studies he added the study of astronomy, natural philosophy, geography, and even anatomy and surgery. In the following year he visited England, leaving with 500 English engineers, artificers, surgeons, artisans and artillerymen.

In 1700 Peter entered into an alliance with the kings of Poland and Denmark to make a combined attack on Sweden. He appropriated a portion of Ingria, in which he laid the foundation of the new capital, St Petersburg, 1703, which in a few years became the Russian commercial depot for the Baltic. In the long contest with Sweden the Russians suffered a series of defeats, until Peter totally routed the Swedish king at Poltava, 8 July 1709. He next prepared for war with the Turks, who at the instigation of Sweden had declared war against him. In this contest Peter lost a previous conquest, the port of Azov and the territory belonging to it. In 1721 peace was made with Sweden. In 1722 Peter commenced a war with Persia and compelled the shah to hand over the three Caspian provinces along with the towns of Derbent and Baku.

Peter introduced many reforms, the most important of which were the abolition of the Moscow Patriarchy and its replacement by a synod subordinated to the tsar; the reform of the central government, with the setting up of specialised government departments; the reform of provincial administration, with the appointment of provincial governors; the introduction of a properly organised military and civil service open to any suitable person irrespective of origin; and financial reforms, including the introduction of a poll tax. After the end of the Northern War in 1721 Peter was proclaimed emperor, and in 1722 promulgated a new law of succession, which enjoined that each monarch should nominate his own successor.

***Peter I, the Great.** In his twenties he worked abroad as a shipwright, as portrayed here.*

Peter I, Karageorgevich (1884–1921), King of Serbia. He was the grandson of Karageorge, who had headed the Serbian insurrection of 1804 against the Turks. He was proclaimed king of Serbia in 1903. In the First World War he shared in the Serbian retreat across Albania and only returned to the capital in November 1918, being invited, shortly afterwards, to accept the crown of Yugoslavia, the triune kingdom of Croats, Serbs and Slovenes.

See also SERBIA.

Peter II (1923–), King of Yugoslavia, 1934–45. In March 1941 Peter was proclaimed king. The German invasion compelled him to seek refuge in England. Conflict with other Allied governments was caused by Peter's support of Draža Mihajlović and his hostility to Tito. In 1945 the new Yugoslav regime abolished the monarchy, and Peter has since lived in exile abroad.

Peter, First and Second Epistles of. These two epistles must be considered separately. 1 Pet. was written to gentile Christians of Asia Minor from Rome.

With 2 Pet. there is a difference in style from 1 Pet.; but if, as is most probable, 1 Pet. owes its style to an amanuensis, 2 Pet. may owe its to another. Similarities with the Epistle of Jude may be due to both authors using a common source. There is a close connection in thought between 1 and 2 Pet., both of which draw upon a common stock of ideas. There is, however, no attempt in one epistle to imitate the other, such as might be expected of a forger; and 2 Pet. explicitly claims to be the writer of 1 Pet., and refers to 'our most dear brother Paul'.

Peter I Øy, ice-covered island in Antarctica, about 24 km long and 8 km wide, lying in 68°50′S, 90°35′W. Lars Christensen Peak (1210 m) is the highest point. The island was discovered by a Russian naval expedition led by Bellingshausen in 1821. The first landing took place in 1929 by the second *Norvegia* expedition. Norway claimed sovereignty by royal proclamation in 1931.

Peter the Cruel, see PEDRO THE CRUEL.

Peter the Hermit (c.1050–1115), itinerant French monk, lived for some time as a hermit in Palestine. Returning to the West, he preached the first crusade, in which he fought. Afterwards he founded the Augustinian monastery of Neumoutier in Flanders.

Peterborough, city and designated 'new town' in Cambridgeshire, England, on the River Nene, 64 km north-east of Northampton. It is a bishop's see and has a fine cathedral, begun in 1117, formerly the church of a Benedictine monastery. The Peterborough Chronicle, or later Anglo-Saxon Chronicle, was composed by monks here.

Peterborough grew up as, and remains, the marketing centre for an important agricultural area. It has also become an industrial centre, the chief trades being engineering, brick-making, canning and textiles. Population (1981) 115,410.

Peterborough, town of Ontario, Canada, on the Otonabee river, 113 km north-east of Toronto and 45 km north of Lake Ontario. It is an important manufacturing centre and has a large cereal mill and electrical goods plant. The largest deposit of nepheline in the world, used in the manufacture of glass, is being mined north of the city. The town serves a beautiful lake district which annually attracts visitors from the USA and Canada for summer recreation. Population (1971) 58,110.

Peterhead, fishing port, important harbour and centre for the oil industry of the North Sea, in north-east Grampian Region, Scotland. Keith Inch, linked by a bridge across the harbour to the town proper, has fish-curing, shipbuilding, fuel oil, and grain-drying establishments. The main industries now are those related to the oil industry of the North Sea. Other industries include shipbuilding, ship-repairing, granite quarrying, polishing, textile manufactures, precision engineering, fish and food canning. Population (1981) 17,015.

Peterhof, see PETRODVORETS.

Peterlee, new town in County Durham, England, midway between Sunderland and Hartlepool. Peterlee, named after the miner's union leader, was established in 1948 to replace some of the 19th-century housing in the mining villages of the district, to provide alternative industrial employment, and to act as a service centre. Population (1981) 22,756.

Peterloo Massacre, name given to the happenings of 16 August 1819 in St Peter's Fields, Manchester. On that date a large body of people held a peaceful meeting in favour of parliamentary reform. The magistrates became nervous and ordered the arrest of the principal speaker. As the yeomanry attempted to obey them, they were pressed by the mob, the hussars were sent in to help, and, in the general panic which followed, 11 people were killed and about 500 injured. The 'massacre' aroused great public indignation but the government stood by the magistrates and passed the Six Acts, to control future agitation.

Peter's Pence, also Romescot, Romfeoh, a tax or tribute, imposed by the pope on the English at the beginning of the 10th century, of a penny for every hearth or house, payable at Lammas Day (1 August). From England the practice spread to other European countries. In England the payment of Peter's Pence and other papal exactions was finally forbidden in an Act passed in 1534 as part of the English Reformation legislation.

Pethidine, a synthetic drug, which is used as an analgesic and as a substitute for morphine, though it is less powerful than the latter. It is given by mouth or by intramuscular injection. It is used in childbirth to reduce labour pains; it has little effect on uterine contractions but may prolong the birth time. Pethidine is generally preferred to morphine in the relief of pain after surgery because it is less likely to cause constipation and has less depressant action on respiration and coughing. Pethidine has only weak hypnotic (sleep-producing) activity.

Petiole, the stalk of a leaf. It is usually cylindrical and narrow, but occasionally is elaborated into very remarkable forms, such as the pitchers of pitcher plants and the cladodes of butchers' broom.

Petipa, Marius (1818–1910), French dancer and choreographer who became the chief architect of the Imperial Russian Ballet. In St Petersburg from 1862 until his retirement in 1903 he created a magnificent repertory of lavish stagings that showed the brilliance of the Russian dancers. His greatest achievements came when working with composers like Glazounov, in *Raymonda*, 1898, and above all Tchaikovsky, in *Swan Lake* (with Ivanov, 1895) and *The Sleeping Beauty*, 1890.

Petit, Roland (1924–), French dancer and choreographer, husband of the dancer Renée (Zizi) Jeanmaire. He trained at the Paris Opera Ballet School, and was first dancer at the Opera, 1940–44. He co-founded the Ballets des Champs-Élysées and formed several other French companies; since 1972 he has directed the Ballet de Marseille. He has had an international success with updated versions of the classics, strikingly modern ballets and full-length spectacles. Among his most notable works are: *Le Jeune homme et la mort* (with Cocteau), *Carmen*, *Le Loup*, *Cyrano de Bergerac*, *Notre Dame de Paris*, *Coppélia* and *Casse Noisette*.

Petit Mal Epilepsy, an unusual form of epilepsy affecting children almost exclusively. It is characterised by brief periods of loss of awareness, during which the child does not fall down or apparently lose consciousness, but becomes inaccessible to verbal communication. These periods last for only a few seconds, but if very frequent may make it difficult for the child to follow a lesson or conversation, and so his education may suffer. The cause of this form of epilepsy is unknown, but it is not due to brain damage. Drugs are available which will control the symptoms, and the disorder usually resolves as the child grows up.

Petition of Right (1628), document embodying parliamentary demands presented to Charles I by his third Parliament. The Commons resolved themselves into a Committee of Grievances to consider 'the liberty of the subject in person and estate', especially in matters of taxation. The Petition, the principal authors of which were Thomas Wentworth and John Pym, forbade arbitrary imprisonment, compulsory billeting, the issue of commissions of martial law, and the levying of gifts, loans and benevolences without the consent of Parliament. The Petition gained the consent of both Houses of Parliament and was given the royal assent.

Petition of Right, constitutional means by which alone, until 1947, the subject could obtain legal relief against the Crown. A petition of right was presented to the Crown through the Home Office, which transmitted it to the attorney-general. By the Crown Proceedings Act 1947, government departments can be sued on their contracts and for the torts of their servants. The petition of right is thus obsolete except for proceedings against the Crown in its private capacity.

See also OMBUDSMAN.

Petits Chevaux, see ROULETTE.

Petőfi, Sándor (1823–49), Hungarian poet. The greatest and best-known Hungarian lyrical poet, Petőfi had a short, hard and tempestuous life. He wrote mainly brief lyrics, often based on folk themes and peasant life, or about his love of women and his homeland—this last leading him to take an important part in the 1848 Revolution. He walks the tightrope between epigrammatic simplicity and romantic banality with inimitable and untranslatable brilliance.

Petra, famous ruined city of Jordan, situated in the bed of Wadi Musa, on an ancient caravan route some 185 km south-west of Amman. Petra was the capital of the Nabataeans. It lies in a steep-sided basin, and contains over 750 tombs and tomb-temples, their façades cut in the living rock, constructed chiefly between 100 BC and AD 100.

Petrarch, in full, Francesco Petrarca (1304–74), Italian poet and leader of the revival of learning. He began to study law at Montpellier, and subsequently at Bologna, but found the profession repugnant to his poetic

temperament, and to his passionate admiration for classical literature, in which Cicero and Virgil were his chief models. According to his own report, in 1327 for the first time he saw Laura, who was the ideal love of his life. She died in 1348 and is known only through Petrarch's references to her, being the chief inspiration of his sonnets. Petrarch's contributions to Italian literature moulded the lyric poetry of the Renaissance.
In 1340 he received invitations from the University of Paris and from the senate of Rome to accept the laurel crown of the poet. He was the first to receive the honour of this revived ceremony on the Capitol when his coronation took place there on 8 April 1341. Petrarch knew no Greek, his Latin was stiff and showed little true scholarship, but he inspired the new feeling in Italy and Europe towards study of the classics and more than anyone else determined the intelligence of young scholars towards ancient learning.

Petrassi, Goffredo (1904–), Italian composer. He won early success with his *Partita* for orchestra (1932) and continued as a brilliant orchestral composer (writing seven concertos for orchestra). In the late 1950s he renewed his prominence with a succession of smaller instrumental works in an avant-garde idiom. Though mainly an instrumentalist, his big choral works, *Psalm IX*, *Coro di morti* and *Noche oscura*, were of prime importance.

Petrel, general name covering the order of oceanic birds Procellariiformes, including the albatrosses, fulmars, shearwaters, storm petrels and diving petrels, all of which have a hooked bill, rudimentary hind toes and tubular nostrils. The stormy-petrels, or 'Mother Carey's chickens', are put into the family Hydrobatidae or typical petrels. The plumage of the stormy-petrel, *Hydrobates pelagicus*, is smoky brown with a broad band of white above the tail. Marine crustaceans constitute the natural food, but the bird has acquired the habit of following ships to collect scraps that fall overboard. It is able to run lightly over the surface of the water with the aid of its wings.

Petrie, Sir William Matthew Flinders (1853–1942), distinguished British archaeologist and egyptologist. He began work in Egypt in 1880, and produced the first systematic archaeological record of the area. He excavated at Tunis, Naucratis, Abydos and Memphis, among other places. Petrie established new and improved methods of excavating and recording. He emphasised the importance of everyday objects, cross-dated Egyptian and Greek finds to establish a comparative chronology, studied the stratigraphy of occupation sites; and was the first to use a method of sequence-dating by which an object could be placed in its correct chronological sequence irrespective of its date.

Petrifaction, the process by which the fossilised remains of animals or plants are replaced by minerals such as calcite, silica, iron pyrites or calcium phosphate. If the mineral-bearing waters infiltrate slowly into the minute cellular cavities, the finest structural details of an organism may be perfectly preserved. But frequently it is only the gross external shape of the original fossil which remains after petrifaction.
See also FOSSIL.

Petrochemicals, see PETROLEUM REFINING.

Petrodvorets (formerly *Peterhof*), town in Leningrad *oblast* of the RSFSR, USSR, on the southern shore of the Gulf of Finland, 29 km from Leningrad. It is famous for its 18th- to 19th-century imperial palaces and parks with majestic fountains and cascades begun by Peter the Great in 1714. Population (1974) 63,000.

Petrography, see PETROLOGY.

Petrol, the term used in the UK for gasoline or motor spirit and often including aviation spirit. These fuels are blended mainly from petroleum products with a boiling point range of 40–175°C, and are used in spark-ignition engines for road transport, motor boats and piston-engined aircraft. All commercial petrols contain many additives that are intended to improve combustion, control corrosion and prolong engine life.
See also KNOCKING; TETRAETHYL LEAD.

Petroleum, a naturally occurring mixture of organic compounds, mainly hydrocarbons, but also including many other elements (small amounts, up to several per cent, of sulphur, oxygen, and nitrogen; traces of vanadium and nickel; and minute amounts of chlorine, arsenic, lead, etc.) usually combined in complex organic structures. The term petroleum is usually used to include natural gas but it is not customary to include under this heading shale oil and certain very heavy and highly viscous semi-solid oils, e.g. tar sands. Another name, crude oil, is normally used to describe liquid petroleum oils capable of being pumped from the well-head.
Petroleum was formed from the remains of marine plant and animal life which existed many millions of years ago. Some of the remains of this organic matter were deposited along with rock-forming sediments under the sea where they were decomposed by bacteria which changed the fats of the sediments into fatty acids which were then changed into an asphaltic material called kerogen. This was then converted over millions of years into petroleum by the combined action of heat and pressure.
The modern oil industry originates in the discovery of oil in western Ontario in 1857 followed by Edwin Drake's discovery in Pennsylvania in 1859. Rapid development followed in other parts of the USA, Canada, Mexico, and then Venezuela. By 1900 an area of only 10 square kilometres near Baku (then in Russia) was producing over half the world output.
The original percussion method of drilling has been superseded by rotary drilling. Oil once discovered will usually flow to the surface during the early production life of the well because of pressure in the reservoir. Eventually it is usually necessary to pump the oil.
Crude petroleum colour ranges from green or yellow to brown or black, while it may have an acrid, unpleasant smell or be practically odourless. Crudes usually contain hydrocarbons of three main types, namely paraffins, naphthenes, and aromatics.
Paraffins are straight or branched carbon chains with the general formula C_nH_{2n+2}, naphthenes are cyclo-paraffins usually containing five or six carbon atoms joined in a ring (formula C_nH_{2n}), and aromatic compounds are unsaturated ring compounds based on the simplest member of the group, benzene, C_6H_6.
Rises in crude prices imposed by the Organisation of Petroleum Exporting Countries in 1973–74 have made difficult oil fields now economic to explore. As all energy resources become scarcer, petroleum may be partially conserved for uses for which there are few alternatives (e.g. for aircraft propulsion and petrochemical manufacture).
See also BENZINE; BENZOLE; DIESEL FUELS; GASOLINE; KEROSINE; KNOCKING; OCTANE NUMBER; PETROL; SHALE OIL; TETRAETHYL LEAD.

Petroleum Refining. Crude petroleum is seldom suitable for immediate use, and must be separated into a number of fractions and often modified chemically before use. The initial separation of petroleum constituents is effected by fractional distillation which separates the compounds according to their boiling-points. The resulting compounds span the volatility range from the gases methane, ethane and propane at one end to waxes, heavy oils and bitumens at the other.
Gases such as methane, ethane, propane and butanes are used in the refinery as fuels and to produce 'synthesis gas' (carbon monoxide and hydrogen) which is the starting point for the manufacture of methanol, ammonia, and chemicals based on these compounds. Ethylene and propylene are used as raw materials for the manufacture of petrochemicals. Propane, butanes and butenes may be liquified and used as liquefied petroleum gas (LPG). Gasolines, (petrol), kerosines and diesel fuels are used to power the internal combustion engine. Lubricating oils are sophisticated blends of oils and additives. Waxes end up as candles, polishes, insulators, waterproofers and waxed paper.
Bitumen, the residue from the distillates, is used in road making and for building purposes. A wide range of solvents are marketed, for the manufacture of paints, printing inks, insecticides, adhesives, etc. Other products (e.g. benzene, toluene and xylenes) are used as intermediates in the manufacture of polymers (e.g. nylon and terylene) and synthetic rubbers.
Distillation. The first stage of all refining processes is an initial fractional distillation which splits the crude oil into a number of parts according to their boiling-points using a fractionating column (or bubble tower). Crude oil is heated to about 300°C, and is pumped into the tower at an intermediate point mostly in the vapour form. As the mixture of vapours rises through the tower it passes through compartments gradually decreasing in temperature. As they reach temperatures slightly below their own boiling-points the various vaporised fractions condense into the trays and leave the column. In this way the least volatile (heavy) vaporised fractions leave the column in the form of gas oil or diesel oil only a little above the vapour intake. Kerosine and white spirit condense higher up the column, and the lightest fractions, including gasoline, propane and butane, together with the small amounts of natural gas found in crude petroleum, leave the top of the column still in gaseous form.

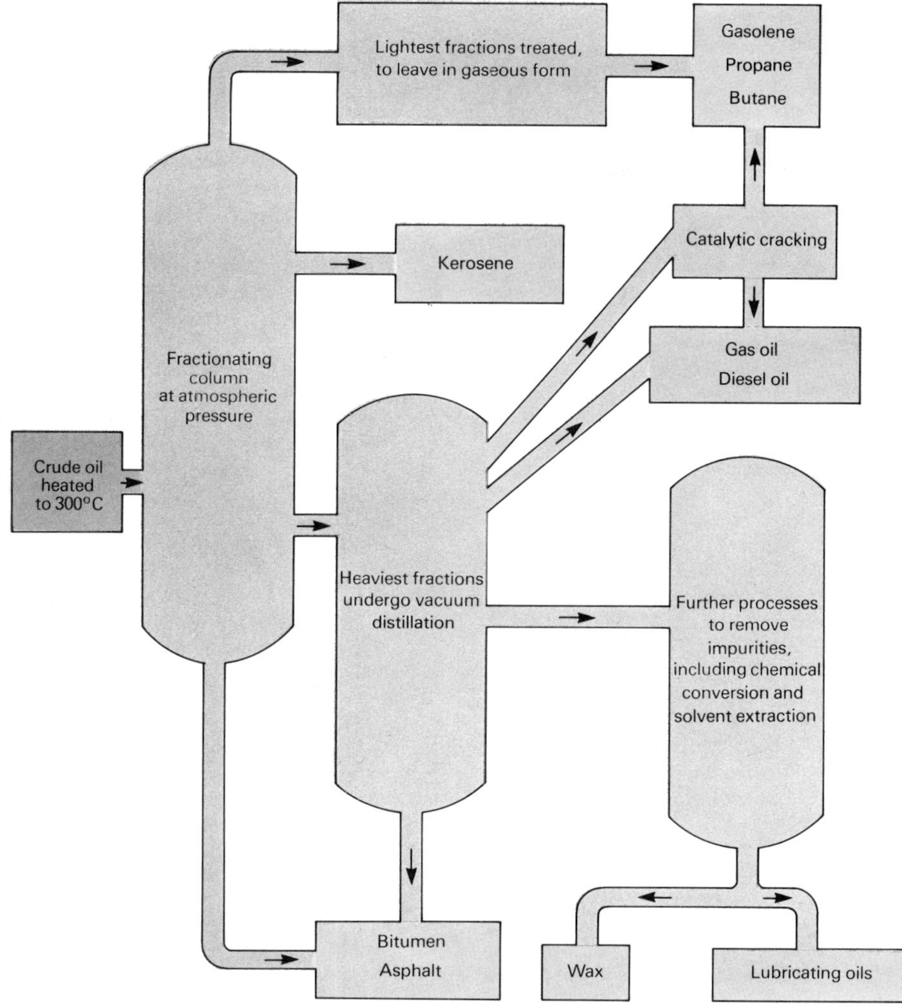

Petroleum Refining. *A flow chart showing the processes and products of crude-oil refining.*

Cracking and Reforming. Several cracking processes have been used, the earliest being the thermal cracking of oils to improve the octane number of gasoline. The heat caused the larger molecules to break down (crack) into smaller ones, particularly olefines which increase the octane number of the fuel.

Catalytic cracking ('catcracking'), first used in 1936, uses a catalyst to assist the cracking which, as a result, becomes a more selective process producing good yields of high octane gasoline.

Isomerisation, Polymerisation and Alkylation. Straight-chain C_5 and C_6 hydrocarbons may be catalytically converted with platinum at about 150°C into branched-chain compounds which have a higher octane number. This is known as isomerisation.

Polymerisation is a process used to join together two or more small molecules to form a larger one. In petroleum processes large amounts of C_3 and C_4 hydrocarbons are formed as by-products and they may be catalytically polymerised, e.g. $C_3H_6 + C_4H_8 \rightarrow C_7H_{14}$.

A similar process, known as alkylation, involves the combination of *iso*-butane and *iso*-butene to form *iso*-octane, a very valuable gasoline component.

Petrology, or petrography, is the study of rocks with regard to their chemistry, mineral content, texture and mode of formation.

Techniques of petrology include visual inspection with the aid of a hand lens: an experienced geologist can determine much of the composition and origin of a rock in this way. For more detailed study, a thin section of the rock is cut 30 μm in thickness and studied using a petrological microscope. The petrological microscope, invented in the 19th century, uses polarised light which, when transmitted through a thin section, suffers characteristic changes dependent upon the minerals present in the thin section. These changes manifest themselves as colours dependent upon the mineral species and its orientation. Thus an experienced petrographer will be able to identify the minerals present in the rock. Various textural features of the rock such as cleavage, schistosity and crystal shape will give clues to the history of the rock under investigation. After optical examination sophisticated analytical chemical techniques are used to determine the exact bulk chemical composition of the rock and the minerals of which it is formed. The mode of formation of the rock and its subsequent history can be deduced.

Petropavlovsk, capital city of the North Kazakhstan *oblast* of the Kazakh SSR, USSR, in the south-west Siberian Plain, on the River Ishim. Engineering and metal-working are important, and there is a large meat-packing factory. The town was founded as a fortress in 1752, and became a town in 1807. The Trans-Siberian railway was laid through it in 1896. Population (1980) 209,000.

Petropavlovsk-Kamchatski (formerly Petropavlovsk), seaport town on the eastern shore of the Kamchatka Peninsula in the Soviet Far East, and capital, economic and cultural centre of Kamchatka *oblast*, USSR. It is an important naval base and fishing port and was founded in 1740 by Bering as an administrative, naval and trading base. Population (1980) 219,000.

Petrópolis, town in the state of Rio de Janeiro, Brazil. Situated in the hills at an altitude of 840 m above sea-level, about 50 km inland from the city of Rio de Janeiro, it has an excellent climate and good scenery and is much used as a summer resort by residents of Rio. There is some manufacturing, mainly cotton, silk and tobacco. Population (1975) 216,582.

Petrosian, Tigran Vartanovich (1929–), Soviet chess master, born at Tbilisi. A grandmaster from 1952, he was twice champion of the USSR before defeating Botvinnik to gain the world championship in 1963. He won a match against Spassky in 1966 but lost the title to him in 1969. His attempt to become challenger was checked in 1971 by the American Bobby Fischer.

Petrozavodsk, capital city of Karelian ASSR, USSR, on the shores of Lake Onega, north-east of Leningrad. It has engineering and metal-working industries (tractors for the timber industry). It was founded in 1703 as a cannon foundry under the name Petrovskaya Sloboda. Population (1980) 238,000.

Petticoat Lane, former name for Middlesex Street, which runs north from Aldgate High Street, in the Borough of Tower Hamlets, London. Since the late-19th and early-20th centuries Jewish immigration and the post-war Asian immigration into Whitechapel, it has been noted for the Sunday-morning clothes and general market.

Petty Officer, rating in the Royal Navy analogous to the non-commissioned officer in the army, a chief petty officer ranking with a sergeant-major and a petty officer with a sergeant.

Petunia, a genus of annual or perennial herbs in the family Solanaceae, with attractive funnel-shaped flowers of various colours. They are much cultivated.

Petworth House, West Sussex, England. The house was rebuilt c.1688–96 by the 6th Duke of Somerset, designed by an unknown but probably French architect. The contents include many paintings by J. M. W. Turner, who often stayed at Petworth. There is a room carved by Grinling Gibbons.

Peucedanum, a genus of herbaceous plants in the family Umbelliferae. *P. ostruthium*, masterwort, and *P. officinale*, sulphur root, have been used as veterinary medicines.

Pevensey, village in East Sussex, England, the site of a massacre of the British by Saxons in AD 491. William I landed at Pevensey Bay in 1066. Pevensey has a notable castle. Population (1971) 2675.

Pevsner, Antoine (1886–1962), Russian artist. He studied in Kiev and St Petersburg before going to Paris (1911), where he lived mainly as a Cubist painter before returning to Russia after the 1917 revolution.

There he and his brother, the artist Naum Gabo, took part in the development of Constructivism. In 1921 he left Russia, settling in France. He and Gabo designed the ballet *La Chatte* for Diaghilev, 1927.

Pevsner, Sir Nikolaus (1902–83), scholar of art and architecture; emeritus professor of the history of art at Birkbeck College, London. His many publications include *Pioneers of the Modern Movement*, 1936; *An Outline of European Architecture*, 1942; *Sources of Modern Art*, 1962. He made a major contribution to English scholarship by undertaking and editing the monumental series *The Buildings of England*.

Pews, enclosed seats in churches. Early churches had no seats, except perhaps for stone benches round the walls. The growing popularity of preaching during the later Middle Ages led to the provision of seats for the important and infirm, though most of the people still stood. After the Reformation a desire for warmth and comfort during the lengthy sermons led to the development of enclosed 'box-pews', the possession of which became a coveted status-symbol. Some were furnished with desks and cushions, and even fireplaces. The 19th century saw in these an undesirable mark of class distinction; and in most churches they were replaced by uniform benches or chairs, which now for the first time filled most of the available space in the church.

Pewter, a grey alloy in which tin is always the main constituent. The other ingredients are included to harden the alloy: in the Middle Ages they were copper or brass for the highest quality pewter, and lead for the less good. Lead is no longer used because of its toxicity, and antimony is now the most common admixture. Pewter was used for making drinking vessels, plates, candlesticks, etc., where silver was too expensive. The finest pewter items to be made were either German or French.
See also METALWORK.

Peziza, a genus of cup fungi in subdivision Ascomycotina. They are usually found in clusters on decaying wood or organic matter.

Pfennig, German coin, representing a hundredth part of a mark, since 1871.

Pforzheim, city in Baden-Württemberg, Federal Republic of Germany, on the Enz, 35 km north-west of Stuttgart. It lies on the northern border of the Black Forest. The city has important jewellery and watch-making industries employing 30,000 people, and has a goldsmiths' training school. Electrical industries are of increasing importance. Population (1980) 106,700.

pH is a measure of hydrogen ion concentration (H^+) of a solution and is therefore an indication of acidity. Hydrogen ion concentration (H^+) is expressed in terms of quantities of hydrogen ions present in grams per litre. Pure water, which self-ionises to a certain extent, contains 0.0000001 g of hydrogen ions per litre. Therefore $(H^+) = 10^{-7}$ for pure water. As pH value is given by $-\log_{10}(H^+)$, for pure water $pH = -\log_{10}(10^{-7}) = 7$. An acidic solution has a greater concentration of hydrogen ions than pure water, and hence has a pH value less than 7. Similarly, an alkaline solution has a pH value greater than 7. The pH is often of the greatest importance in biological and chemical reactions.
See also ACID; INDICATOR; NEUTRALITY.

Phaëthon (shining one), used by the Greeks as an epithet or surname of Helios (the Sun), but more commonly of the son of Helios and Clymene, who asked his father to let him drive the chariot of the Sun across the heavens for one day. Phaeton could not control the horses and came too near the Earth, nearly setting it on fire.

Phaeton, an open four-wheeled carriage (most commonly) drawn by one or two horses; there are varieties known as pony, mail and spider phaetons.

Phalanx, name given to the formation of the heavy infantry of the ancient Greek armies. It consisted of a series of parallel columns of men standing close one behind the other. The Spartan phalanx was the original of this formation, and consisted of soldiers standing from four to eight men deep. The Macedonian phalanx, the last of this formation, was 16 men deep. The soldiers were armed with swords and 4-metre pikes. They were flanked by light infantry and cavalry. The Romans defeated the phalanx by a combination of missile attacks and harassing tactics.

Phalaris, tyrant of Acragas (Agrigentum) in Sicily (c.570–554 BC). He perished in an outbreak of popular fury roused by his monstrous cruelty. He is celebrated for the brazen bull in which he is said to have burned his victims alive.

Phalarope, birds of the family Phalaropodidae which includes three species: the red-necked phalarope, *Phalaropus lobatus*, breeds mostly in polar regions; the grey phalarope, *Phalaropus fulicarius*, has similar breeding areas; Wilson's phalarope, *Phalaropus tricolor*, is confined in summer to Canada and the USA. They are small birds, resembling sandpipers, with a characteristic way of swimming whilst feeding, giving them the appearance of pirouetting.

Phallus, representation of the male generative organ, used at certain Dionysiac festivals in ancient Greece, as a symbol of the powers of procreation, and an object of common worship in the nature-religion of the east. It had many names, for example (Hindu) lingam.

Phanerogamia, a synonym of Spermatophyta, the seed-bearing plants, which include the Gymnosperms, evergreens, and the Angiosperms, flowering plants.

Phantasy, in everyday use, means day dreaming and imagining, and is usually spelled fantasy. In psychoanalytic terms it refers to the creative imaginative activities that underlie all thought and feeling. In the young infant, phantasy of which he is unaware accompanies all basic biological functions. The content and meaning of these phantasies can become very important to the infant, affecting his subjective experience and understanding of these basic biological functions.
Although adult phantasy retains its infantile quality, it undergoes more abstract elaboration which includes greater regard for external events. It is still marked by wishful thinking and gratification of basic sexual and aggressive feelings, which may not be admissible to the more conscious aspects of the personality.

Pharaoh, Anglicised Hebrew form of the title, meaning Great House, of Egyptian kings from the New Kingdom onwards.

Pharisees (Aramic *Perīshīn*, separated), religious sect among the Jews, first heard of in the latter half of the 2nd century BC, but probably descended from the Chasidim or 'Pious' (Hassidaeans), who passively resisted Antiochus Epiphanes at the beginning of the Maccabean revolt.
The Pharisaic scribes developed a minute casuistry to apply the Law to every detail of life (the 'tradition of the elders'), but in doing so found ways of evading many grave moral obligations, for which Christ stigmatised them as hypocrites. At their best, however, they were inspired by a genuine spiritual ideal, though an impossible one for fallen man, to achieve perfection in God's service by obedience to a formal code. The Pharisees, who numbered c.7000, did much service to their people by their uncompromising patriotism and by their opposition to the liberal opinions of the worldly Sadducees; but they rapidly became the slaves of formalism, and their very servitude rendered them overweening in their pride as the only observers of the Law.

Pharmacology (Greek *pharmakon*, a drug), the scientific study of drugs and their mode of action. In its widest aspect, it is the science concerned with change effected in the function of living material, either by the direct action of chemical compounds or by their effect on its environment. The first treatise known on pharmacology was that of Dioscorides (c.AD 60), and on it all subsequent pharmacopoeias have been founded. Since rational treatment of disease must depend on knowledge both of the disease and of the drug and its action, pharmacology is dependent on pathology, chemistry and physiology. Investigation of the action of drugs is made difficult by the fact that drugs acting in very different ways may apparently produce the same effect. Difficulties arise also in connection with the classification of drugs. The method of administration of the drug and the size of the dose are also studied.
See also MEDICINE.

Pharmacopoeia (Greek *pharmakon*, a drug; *poiia*, making), a book containing lists of drugs, including the chemical, approved and proprietary names, with details of standard preparations for comparison. The clinical uses, toxic effects, administration and fate in the body of the drugs are described. National pharmacopoeias are published in many countries, of which the *United States Pharmacopoeia*, revised every ten years, the French *Codex* and the *European Pharmacopoeia* are most widely used.

Pharmacy (Greek *pharmakon*, a drug), deals with the sources, preparation and dispensing of medicines.

Pharos, a lighthouse, a meaning derived from the lofty tower erected by Ptolemy II on the island of Pharos, one of the seven wonders of the ancient world.

Pharsalus (modern Phersala), town of ancient Thessaly, Greece, 38 km south-west of Larissa. It was near Pharsalus that Caesar defeated Pompey the Great in 48 BC.

Pharynx, a cone-shaped fibromuscular tube which extends from the base of the skull to the level of the sixth cervical vertebra, where it becomes continuous with the oesophagus (gullet). It is the common portal to the alimentary and respiratory tracts, and is made up of three portions: the nasopharynx, the oropharynx and the laryngopharynx. The nasopharynx lies above the soft palate and behind the nasal cavities. The soft palate is elevated during swallowing and prevents food from being forced up into the nasopharynx. On each lateral wall of the nasopharynx is the narrow orifice of the Eustachian or auditory tube. This tube, which equalises the pressure in the ear with the air pressure outside, often allows infection to spread from the nose to the middle ear. The oropharynx lies below the soft palate and extends down to the inlet of the larynx. It lies behind the mouth and its most important contents are the tonsils. The laryngopharynx lies behind the larynx and is in free communication with the oropharynx above and the oesophagus below.

Phase, in astronomy, denotes a particular state singled out from a regular series of recurring states. Probably its most frequent use is in connection with the appearance of the Moon as it waxes from new through the crescent phase to first quarter (half illumination), through the gibbous phase to full, back through the gibbous and crescent phases as it wanes from full to third quarter, and from third quarter to new.
See also MOON.

Phaseolus, a genus of twining annual or perennial tropical or subtropical herbs in family Leguminosae. *P. coccineus* is the parent species of the scarlet runner bean, *P. vulgaris* of the french beans; *P. lunatus*, the lima or duffin bean, is widely grown in tropical climates.

Phases of Matter. All matter exists either in a fluid or in a solid phase (or state). A higher temperature involves a higher kinetic energy of the particles so that solids are converted into fluids by increasing their temperature. Matter consists of particles (molecules, atoms or ions) which in general have a diameter of the order of 10^{-10} m. According to the kinetic theory of matter, the particles are all in a state of constant movement except at absolute zero. Various forces of attraction operate between particles, viz. electrostatic, gravitational and van der Waals', though these become less significant as the distance between the particles increases.
See also FLUID; GAS; SOLID; SURFACE TENSION.

Pheasant, substantive name of many species and genera of the bird family Phasianidae, in the order Galliformes. The typical pheasants are in the genus *Phasianus*, which has two species: the Japanese pheasant, *P. versicolor*, found in Japan, and the common pheasant, *P. colchicus*. The genus is distinguished by the very long wedge-shaped tail and the absence of a crest. *P. colchicus* was introduced from Russia and Asia Minor into Europe by the Romans; at least 30 local races are known, including the Mongolian pheasant and the ring-necked pheasant. Reeves's pheasant, *Symaticus reevesii*, a native of China, is over 2 m in length, and has yellow and brown spangled plumage. Other members of the family Phasianidae include the francolin, junglefowl, partridge and quail.
See also SHOOTING.

Pheidippides, or Phidippides, Athenian courier, sent to Sparta in 490 BC to announce the Persian invasion and demand help. He reached his destination on the second day after leaving Athens, having covered a distance of about 240 km. After the battle of Marathon he set out for Athens with news of the Greek victory, but collapsed and died on arrival.

Phellem, the outer corky protective layer of bark consisting of dead thickened spongy cells.

Phellogen, in plants, a cambium layer of cells, dividing in or just below the epidermis of dicotyledons to form phellem or cork. Phellogen and its derivatives are termed the periderm.

Phenolphthalein, $C_{20}H_{14}O_4$, is a white crystalline substance, slightly soluble in water, but dissolves readily in alcohol. It is used in volumetric analysis as an indicator for weak acids. With alkalis it gives a pink coloration, but the presence of acids destroys this coloration. Phenolphthalein is also used in medicine as a mild purgative.

Phenols, alcohols in which the functional hydroxy group is attached to an aromatic ring. In general, they are more polar, and hence more acidic, than similar saturated alcohols, but react as polar alcohols, in that the aromatic carbon-oxygen bond is hardly ever broken in reactions. They are prepared by isolation from coal-tar, or synthetically by the action of chlorine and alkali on benzene or toluene. A number of commercially important compounds are phenols with more than one hydroxy group, such as resorcinol or hydroquinone.
See also CARBOLIC ACID.

Phenomenalism, in philosophy, is the doctrine that we can know only how things appear to us, not things as they actually are, if indeed the second alternative is a meaningful one. Thus Hume holds that we know only our own impressions and ideas, and that nothing at all can be said of what lies beyond them. There are also phenomenalist theories of perception in which the existence of things is said to be no more that the sum of its appearances actual and possible, a theory found both in J. S. Mill and Bertrand Russell. A linguistic variant of this view holds that any statement in terms of material objects can be reduced to statements about sense data.

Phenomenology is the science of phenomena in philosophy, involving a contention that the existence of 'substance' is an illusion, that matter is no more than an indeterminate and unknown something underlying phenomena. It is the descriptive study of phenomena as they are immediately presented to experience. But phenomenology may also be described as a philosophic method which makes use of descriptions which are phenomenological in the usual sense of the word, yet which regards them only as a means of seeking something that lies beyond the phenomena. The chief exponent of the phenomenological movement in this later sense of the word was the German philosopher Edmund Husserl (d.1938), who taught at Freiburg University. The phenomenology of Husserl is indeed a description of the immediate data of consciousness; but whereas ordinary academic psychology allows itself to be monopolised by the object, Husserl considers the thinking subject; his psychology is a reflexive psychology.

Phenomenon (from Greek *phainomai*, I appear), that which appears, as distinguished from that which exists. The term was once used to denote the world of sense as opposed to the world of reason, but Kant has given it a more extended connotation. In the *Critique of Pure Reason* he says 'The undetermined object of an empirical intuition is called a phenomenon. The empirical intuition is a mere phenomenon in which nothing that can appertain to a thing in itself can be found. In the whole range of the sensuous world, investigate as we may, we have to do with nothing but phenomena'.
See also EMPIRICISM.

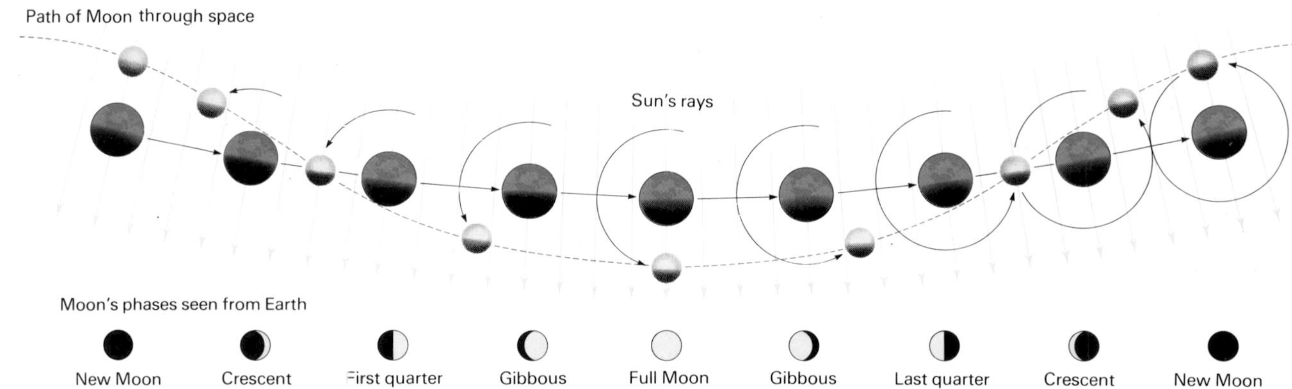

***Phase.** The visibility of the Moon from the Earth is dependent on its position relative to the Earth and the rays of the Sun.*

Phenylbutazone, $C_{19}H_{20}N_2O_2$, a derivative of pyrazolone with analgesic (pain-relieving) and antipyretic (fever-reducing) properties, but it is especially useful as an anti-inflammatory agent in rheumatoid arthritis when aspirin is no longer effective. Prolonged use leads to blood disorders and the blood cells must be counted regularly. It promotes excretion of uric acid and is therefore effective in gout.

Phenytoin (diphenylhydantoin), an anti-convulsant drug with slight hypnotic action, used in the treatment of epilepsy. However, it often causes damage to the gums, especially in children, and may also cause headaches, tremors, rashes and blood disorders.

Pheromone, a chemical substance produced by animals which acts as a 'chemical messenger' between one animal and another. Pheromones are detected by chemoreceptors, which may be defined as the organs of the sense of smell. Pheromones are used as sex attractants (moths and butterflies), for laying trails (ants), marking territory (dogs, deer, foxes). Queen bees produce a pheromone which inhibits the development of new queens in the hive. Many animals produce an alarm pheromone when danger threatens.

Phidias, or Pheidias (c.500–after 432 BC), sculptor of ancient Greece. Works which have been attributed to him are a colossal figure of Athena Promachos in bronze, the Lemnian Athena, a gilt Athena at Plataea and the Zeus at Olympia. He had the opportunity of proving his genius when Pericles appointed him to superintend the adornment of Athens. Phidias planned the erection of temples and public buildings and, chief of all, the Propylaea and the Parthenon. Phidias executed for the Parthenon the statue of Athena in ivory and gold c.438 BC, and six years later was accused of impiety in having introduced his own and Pericles's likeness on the shield of the goddess and of stealing the gold entrusted to him. He died either in prison or in exile. Phidias was regarded by ancient critics as the greatest of sculptors.

Philadelphia, the largest city of Pennsylvania and the fourth in terms of population in the USA. It lies 209 km north of Washington DC, and 129 km south-west of New York city, and is situated 160 km up the Delaware river at the junction with its tributary the Schuylkill. Philadelphia was founded by William Penn, the Quaker, in 1682 as a city in which men of all races might live, each following, unpersecuted, his own religion. It has the appearance of a European rather than an American city throughout much of its central area, and its historic quarters have been restored to something of their original appearance.

Important industries of Philadelphia and its environs are oil refining, iron and steel, printing and publishing, shipbuilding, and the manufacture of buses, textiles, clothing, alcohol, leather products, paper, tobacco products, electrical supplies, machinery, rugs, glass, medicines and processed foodstuffs.

The Philadelphia port district is one of the busiest in the USA. It has a total water frontage of 60 km, along two rivers. There is a large government navy yard at League Island, just upstream of the city.

In Independence Hall (completed in 1735) the constitution of the USA was framed and independence proclaimed, as its name indicates. In this building, too, is housed the famous Liberty Bell, rung to announce to the citizens that the declaration of independence from Great Britain had been adopted. Philadelphia was the capital of the federal states from the revolution until 1800, and the capital of Pennsylvania from 1683 until 1799 (Harrisburg is now the capital). The US mint was founded here in 1792.

Population (1980) (city) 1,688,210, (metropolitan area) 3,682,709.

Philadelphus, a genus of deciduous shrubs, in family Saxifragaceae, with about 70 species found in Europe, Asia or North America; *P. coronarius*, the mock orange or syringa, and *P. microphyllus* are parents of many beautiful garden hybrids esteemed for their summer flowering. (The botanical genus *Syringa* is the lilac.)

Philae, islet in the Nile, 8 km south of Aswān, in Nubia. It is the original site of temples built by Nectanebo I, the Ptolemies and Roman emperors. The Aswān Dam would have eventually caused permanent submersion. In 1975 work was begun on dismantling the temples prior to re-erection in an identical location on the neighbouring island of Agilkia.

Philately, term covering both the collecting of postage stamps and, more particularly, the study of their production and usage. The first adhesive postage stamps were issued in Britain in May 1840. However, it was not until the 1850s when most of the world's postal administrations began to issue their own postage stamps that philately became a recognised form of collecting.

The early collections covered the world, or large political groupings such as the British Empire. In the 1980s, with the total number of stamps issued by all countries since the 1840s exceeding 2,000,000, this is no longer feasible and collectors now tend to specialise either politically or thematically, or confine their attentions to stamps that illustrate some aspect of postal history. The demand for special-issue and commemorative stamps is such that many countries produce such issues with the philatelic market mainly in view.

Philby, Harry St John Bridger (1885–1960), British explorer and orientalist, born in Ceylon (Sri Lanka). He led the British political mission to central Arabia in 1917–18. Philby crossed the Arabian Peninsula and explored the southern provinces in 1920. He was British representative in Transjordan, 1921–24. He became a Muslim in 1930 and lived chiefly in Arabia as the friend and adviser of Ibn Saud. He crossed the Rub al Khali (Empty Quarter) desert in 1932.

Philby, Kim, see BURGESS AND MACLEAN CASE.

Philemon, Epistle to, the shortest of St Paul's epistles, written during his imprisonment; addressed to Philemon, an hospitable Christian of Colossae, asking him to take back his former slave, Onesimus, who, having first robbed his master, had run away, probably to Rome, where he had been converted to Christianity by Paul.

Philip, Saint, one of the first disciples of Jesus Christ and one of the apostles. He was a native of Bethsaida, a town near the sea of Tiberias. He has been confused with Philip the Deacon. Philip is said to have died naturally at Hierapolis, but in what year is not known; by another tradition he was crucified.

Philip II (382–336 BC), King of Macedonia, father of Alexander the Great. In the space of twenty years Philip succeeded first in establishing Macedonia as a great power, and finally in subduing and uniting the greater part of Greece under him.

Philip's unification of Macedonia involved reducing a number of semi-autonomous barons. In these wars Philip trained and perfected the army which was so successful both against the Greeks and later against Persia. The acquisition of Thrace (including the gold-mines of Pangaeus), Chalcidice and Thessaly, increased the economic strength of Macedonia and enabled Philip to maintain a large and powerful standing army.

Philip was able to seize Thermopylae with Theban consent in 346, and take the place of Phocis in the Amphictyonic League. This gave him a legal right to intervene in the affairs of southern Greece, and he retained control of the pass of Thermopylae.

Philip was assassinated in 336 BC. He bequeathed to Alexander a united Macedonia, dominant in Greece, and a highly skilled professional army, based on the novel use of the phalanx.

Philip II (1165–1223), King of France, commonly known as Philip Augustus. He succeeded in 1180. His reign was devoted to his attempt to consolidate the territory and power of the French Crown. He succeeded in subduing the Count of Flanders and the Duke of Burgundy.

Philip invaded Normandy. The fall of Château-Gaillard resulted in the practical conquest of Normandy, and virtually put an end to the Angevin empire. He gained influence in southern France by intervening against the Albigenses. The height of his success, however, was the battle of Bouvines in 1214, where he succeeded in defeating the combined forces of England and the Empire. The rest of his reign was occupied in administrative reforms.

Philip IV (1268–1314), commonly called 'Le Bel', King of France, succeeded in 1285. His attempt to levy taxation upon the clergy led to Pope Boniface VIII issuing the famous Bull, *Unam sanctam*, to which Philip replied by a wholesale confiscation of clerical property. The pope retaliated by an excommunication and a threat of interdict. Philip had the pope arrested and so maltreated that he died shortly afterwards. After the brief pontificate of Boniface's successor, Benedict XI, a French pope, Clement V, was elected and, under the influence of Philip, moved the papal court to Avignon, where it remained for 70 years.

Philip VI (1293–1350), King of France, first of the Valois kings. He succeeded in 1328. Edward III of England used his claim as a pretext for invading France in 1337. In a battle with the English off Sluis (1340) the French fleet was entirely destroyed. In 1346, Edward decisively defeated Philip at Crécy. See also CRÉCY, BATTLE OF.

Philip I (1478–1506), King of Castile, surnamed the Handsome. In 1496 he married Joanna, daughter of Ferdinand and Isabella, sovereigns of Castile and Aragon. In 1504, on the death of Isabella, who bequeathed the kingdom of Castile to her daughter, Philip, as well as his consort, assumed the regal title. He was crowned at Burgos with her, and, because of her insanity, governed on her behalf until his death.

Philip II, King of Spain 1556–98.

Philip II (1527–98), King of Spain, only son of the Emperor Charles V. Before the death of his father he married Maria of Portugal, who died in 1545, then in 1554, Mary I of England. In 1556 his father abdicated and Philip became the most powerful monarch in Europe. He left England after 14 months, disappointed that Mary had failed to bear him a son. After her death he was married for a third time, to Elizabeth of France.

He succeeded in breaking up the formidable league raised against him by the papacy and the French, and set himself up in Europe as the champion of the counter-reformation. He crushed heresy in Spain by means of an energetic use of the Inquisition, but failed in the Netherlands, where his oppressive measures and his heavy taxation led to revolt, civil war, and finally to the breaking away of the United Provinces (Holland). In 1570 he married Anne of Austria, who became the mother of Philip III. He annexed Portugal to Spain in 1580, claiming the throne on the extinction of the male in line. This was his most complete success. After the execution of Mary Queen of Scots, and goaded by the frequent raids of the English privateers on Spanish treasure-ships and settlements, he sent his Armada to England in 1588, but it was virtually destroyed.

His home policy had led to the practical bankruptcy of Spain, and his long war against the Moors led to the extinction of much of the trade of the country. Philip had great ability, but this was overshadowed by stubborn fanaticism, and by his usual unwillingness to listen to expert advice, or to delegate authority. He raised Spain to a dominant position in Europe, but left it with a governmental system which undermined its prosperity.

Philip III (1578–1621), King of Spain, son of Philip II, succeeded to the throne of Spain in 1598. He left the government of the country almost entirely in the hands of his incompetent minister, Lerma. Under Philip, the whole Moorish population, excepting Christians and young children, was expelled from Spain.

Philip IV (1605–65), King of Spain. He succeeded in 1621, and during the early part of his reign the country was governed by Olivares, whose foreign policy was largely disastrous. The Dutch captured many of the Spanish colonial possessions; Portugal recovered its independence in 1641, and two years later, by the defeat at Rocroi, the prestige of the Spanish army was badly shaken. After the Peace of Westphalia was signed in 1648 (under which Spain formally recognised the independence of the United Provinces), the Spaniards and French continued fighting until by the Treaty of the Pyrenees (1659) Spain ceded much territory to France. Philip is chiefly remembered as a patron of arts and letters, Velázquez being his court painter.

Philip V (1683–1746), King of Spain, the first of the Bourbon kings of Spain. He succeeded Charles II in 1700, entered Madrid in 1701, and at the end of the War of the Spanish Succession was by the Treaty of Utrecht guaranteed the throne of Spain, certain stipulations being made to prevent his obtaining the throne of France as well. Philip abdicated for a short time in 1724, but on the death of his son again ascended the throne.

Philip, Prince of the Realm and Duke of Edinburgh (1921–), husband of Elizabeth II, Queen of Great Britain and Northern Ireland, whom he married on 20 November 1947. Born in Corfu, the son of Prince Andrew of Greece, at 18 he entered the Royal Navy, serving throughout the Second World War in the Mediterranean and Far East. He renounced his rights of succession to the Greek and Danish thrones in 1947, and became a naturalised British subject, adopting the surname Mountbatten. Before his marriage he was created Baron Greenwich, Earl of Merioneth, and Duke of Edinburgh, and made KG; in 1957 he was granted the style and title of a Prince of the Realm. Since his wife's accession to the throne Prince Philip has accompanied her on all the principal state occasions and has undertaken a considerable number of independent public engagements. He has shown an especial interest in young people and in scientific matters, and his friendliness and informality have made him generally popular.

Philip the Bold (1342–1404). He was made Duke of Burgundy in 1363. His brother, Charles V, succeeded to the French throne. In 1382 he suppressed the Flemish rebellion with extreme ferocity. During the minority and subsequent imbecility of his nephew, Charles VI of France, he became regent of the country. Utterly ruthless, he governed his lands with vigour and efficiency, and was regarded as one of the best French generals of the period.

Philip the Deacon, one of the seven deacons chosen to relieve the 12 apostles of the burden of attending to charitable distribution (Acts vi. 5). He was driven from Jerusalem by the persecutions and went to Samaria to preach, where he had great success. Thence he was sent to baptise the eunuch of the Ethiopian queen Candace (Acts vi. 8). Philip then went on a preaching tour to Caesarea, and later he entertained Saint Paul and his company (Acts xxi. 8). Tradition says that eventually he settled in Asia Minor, but he has been confused with Saint Philip the apostle.

Philip the Good (1396–1467), Duke of Burgundy. He allied with Henry V of England in 1419, and captured Joan of Arc at Compiègne. But in 1435 he again made terms with Charles, and helped to expel the English from their French possessions. He was the founder of the Order of the Golden Fleece and a patron of the arts.

Philippeville, see SKIKDA.

Philippi, ancient city of Macedonia, on the Gangites. Philippi is chiefly famous as the scene of Octavian's victory over Brutus and Cassius (42 BC), and as the place where St Paul first preached the Gospel in Europe.

Philippians, Epistle to the, one of St Paul's so-called 'captivity epistles', written during his two-year imprisonment at Rome (Acts xxviii. 30), though some scholars claim Caesarea or Ephesus as the place of origin. The Church in Philippi had been established some ten years previously on the second missionary journey (Acts xvi, etc.), and was composed chiefly of pious gentiles. The epistle contains perhaps St Paul's most striking passage on the divinity of Christ and the Incarnation (ii. 5-11).

Philippines
Area: 300,000 km²
Population: 47,910,000
Capital: Manila

Philippines, Republic of the, archipelago situated over 800 km off the south-east coast of Asia between 4°40′ and 21°N. The islands are bounded on the west by the China Sea, on the east by the Pacific Ocean, and on the south by the Celebes Sea and the coastal waters of Borneo. The total land area of the Philippines is about 300,000 km^2, and includes the island of Luzon in the north, Mindanao in the south, large islands like Samar, Negros, Palawan, Panay, Mindoro, Leyte, Cebu, Bohol and Masbate, and over 7000 other smaller islands. The islands are mostly of volcanic origin, and the larger ones have long mountain ranges. Mount Mayon (2416 m), an active volcano, lies at the south-eastern extremity of Luzon, and Mount Apo (2593 m), also an active volcano on Mindanao, is the highest elevation in the archipelago.

Twenty-six eruptions of Mayon occurred

Phillipines. *200-year-old rice terraces on the hillsides near Banaue, northern Luzon.*

in the 19th century, the most destructive of which was in June 1897, when the town of San Fernando and many villages were destroyed. The most recent eruption of Mayon was in 1968.

The Filipinos, in the widest sense of the word, are a mingling of many races, speaking perhaps a hundred differing languages or dialects, professing different religions and living in various grades of civilisation. There are over 80 ethnic groups.

Manila the capital and main port, has the finest harbour in the Far East. The main cities, apart from Manila, are Quezon City, Cebu City, Davao City, Iloilo, Zamboanga, Caloocan and Bacolod. The total population of the Philippines in 1980 was estimated to be 47,910,000.

Despite recent efforts at industrialisation, the bulk of the Filipino workforce (48 per cent) is engaged in agriculture. Rice is the staple crop. Sugar is the leading export crop, followed by copra and coconut oil. The other crops grown include maize, hemp, tobacco, sweet potatoes and fruits.

With 40 per cent of the land area covered by forests it is natural that the timber industry should be an important part of the economy. Commercial fishing is also important. The country's pearl fisheries are in the Sulu Archipelago to the south.

The country is quite rich in mineral resources with copper deposits being the most valuable, but there is significant production of nickel, gold, silver, iron ore, manganese and chrome. The main industries are food processing, mineral processing, chemicals, petroleum refining and textiles.

The constitution of 1973 confirmed Ferdinand Marcos in power as President and Prime Minister with no fixed term of office. He is assisted by a cabinet of ministers. There is a legislative Assembly, but the President may legislate by decree.

In 1937 Tagalog, one of 87 native dialects in the Philippines, was designated as the official language. Tagalog, also known as Filipino, is spoken by 15 million Filipinos. English is a widely-spoken second language and is the medium of instruction in higher levels of education.

History. Spain took possession of the islands in 1565, named the colony after King Philip and introduced Catholicism to counteract the strong influence of Islam. The Philippines served Spain economically, and it was not until the latter half of the 19th century that Philippine products such as sugar, coffee, tobacco and hemp began to enter world trade to any significant degree. In 1898, when the Filipinos were on the verge of securing Philippine independence, US forces entered the Philippines as a consequence of the Spanish–American War and demanded, and obtained, the cession of the Philippines from Spain. The Filipinos did not finally achieve independence until 1946 and were forced to grant a number of important economic concessions to the US. The onerous nature of these concessions coupled with the sharp divisions between the landlord and an increasingly improverished and dispossessed peasantry gave rise to the Communist-led Huk rebellion (1946–54) which was eventually crushed by the combined US and Philippine armed forces. Martial law, declared in 1972, was ended in 1981 although President Marcos retained wide powers under new legislation for public safety and national security.

Philistine, term of contempt or reproach used in England at the beginning of the 17th century. Later it was applied to those whom the more enlightened or cultured considered lacking in taste and intellect, and it is still used to denote someone of vulgar or uncultured taste.

Philistines, race often mentioned in the Bible (*Pelishtim*), where they are said to be of Hamitic stock (Gen. x. 14). They originated from Caphtor (Amos ix. 7), commonly supposed to denote Crete, but Caphtor (Egyptian *Keftiu*) included the former Cretan dependencies in the Aegean and Ionia. They settled, perhaps before the Israelite invasion, on the south-west maritime plain of Canaan, the Plain of Philistia (Joel iii. 4, etc.). They gave their name to the whole country of Palestine. Their chief god, Dagon, was a corn-deity well known in Syria and Palestine. He is not, as was once thought, a fish god.

Their power was broken by David who formed them into his *élite* guards, the Cherethites and Pelethites (2 Sam. viii. 18). Very little is known of Philistine culture. Their political system was apparently a federation of city states, of which there were five, the Pentapolis.

Phillip, Arthur (1738–1814), British vice-admiral and first governor of New South Wales, his name being perpetuated in Port Phillip Bay, Victoria. As Capt. Phillip, in 1786, he took out from England a small fleet carrying about 705 convicts for Botany Bay, which he reached in January 1787. But he considered the spot ill-suited for a settlement and selected a place to the north of it which seemed to him to have the necessary qualifications, and, on 27 January 1788, the British flag was hoisted at Port Jackson, which he renamed Sydney, thus marking the beginning of the British occupation of Australia. He returned to England in 1792.

Phillips, John (1800–74), one of the most distinguished of early British geologists. He wrote numerous works on geology, including *Illustrations of the Geology of Yorkshire*, 1835; *Geology of Oxford and the Thames Valley*, 1871; besides *A Geological Map of the British Isles*, 1842, and *Memoirs of William Smith, the Father of English Geology*, 1844.

Phillpotts, Eden (1862–1960), English novelist and playwright. His books, which number over 150, include *Lying Prophets*, 1896; *My Devon Year*, 1903; *The American Prisoner*, 1904; *The Secret Woman*, 1905, perhaps his finest work; *Portreeve*, 1906; *Redcliff*, 1924; and *From the Angle of 88*, 1954. Phillpotts's novels are mostly of Devonian life and character. His most successful play was *The Farmer's Wife*, 1916.

Philo Judaeus, or Philo (Philon) the Jew (b.c.20–10 BC), Graeco-Jewish philosopher, exegete and apologist; a native of Alexandria. Though a Jew by birth, his studies were mainly in Greek philosophy. He was especially familiar with the writings of Plato, upon whose language his own is closely modelled; and it is for his attempts to reconcile Platonic philosophy with the Mosaic revelation that he is most famed.

Philodendron, a genus of ornamental climbing shrubs in the Araceae, natives of tropical America. Several are grown as house plants.

Philology, is used either (and particularly in Europe) to include both literary scholarship and the linguistic study of literary languages, both text-oriented; or purely to mean linguistics, particularly historical or diachronic linguistics (terms to which it is losing ground).

See also ETYMOLOGY; LANGUAGE; LINGUISTICS.

Philosopher's Stone, see ALCHEMY.

Philosophy, term of which the meaning has in the course of centuries undergone considerable modifications. Pythagoras is reputed to have been the first to use it, saying he was a 'philosopher', that is, a lover of wisdom (*philos* and *sophia*). No kind of knowledge was in those early days outside the scope of philosophy, which comprehended the whole range of human interests. With the growth of specialised knowledge philosophy could no longer include, though it still claimed to transcend in importance, all knowledge. In this sense the scholastics and neo-scholastics define philosophy as 'the knowledge of things through their highest (i.e. most universal and independent) causes'.

From the time of Aristophanes onwards the philosopher has been represented as unpractical, immersed in useless and chimerical speculations. But as Aristotle remarked, in order to prove that philosophy is vain and illusory we are compelled to philosophise. The sceptic is as much a philosopher as the idealist. There are experts in the special sciences who sometimes decry philosophy, yet tread upon philosophical ground while pursuing their most abstruse inquiries. Mathematics is ultimately concerned with questions of time and space, physics with matter and energy, art with beauty, ethics with virtue, and so on. Philosophy is thus seen to be a necessity of human activity; the pursuit of speculative truth has always engaged men's minds, although there have ever been those to say that the end was unattainable.

An understanding of what is meant by the term philosophy in present-day usage is necessary but by no means easy to acquire. Hardly any two writers are agreed as to the definition and boundaries of philosophy, and the word has different connotations in different countries. Kant has defined philosophical knowledge as knowledge through conceptions, as such; Herbart defined philosophy as the working out of concepts, and divided it into three departments, logic, metaphysics and aesthetics (including ethics). Comte and Spencer regarded philosophy as the unification and classification of the various sciences with a view to merely material ends. In the English language, until fairly recently, philosophy meant almost anything, as evidenced by the term 'natural philosophy', used by physicists.

Almost all 20th-century English-speaking philosophers regard philosophy as concerned with conceptual issues, investigating the concepts underlying our thinking on 'fundamental' questions (*which* questions are fundamental is often a major topic of controversy). The basic studies in philosophy are now usually taken to include metaphysics, epistemology, ethics, aesthetics and logic; second-order studies are the *philosophies* of science, history, mind (psychology), law, economics and other social sciences.

See also COSMOLOGY; EXISTENTIALISM; IDEALISM; MATERIALISM; POSITIVISM; POSITIVISM, LOGICAL.

Philosophy, Social, see SOCIAL PHILOSOPHY.

Phiz, see BROWNE, HABLOT KNIGHT.

Phlebitis, inflammation associated with thrombus or clot formation in a vein. This clotting is attended with particular danger, as if the clot becomes detached for any reason, emboli are carried away in the bloodstream and may lodge in an important organ and obstruct its circulation. Thus an embolus may lodge in the lung and cause a pulmonary embolism. The symptoms of phlebitis are pain, tenderness, swelling and oedema of the affected part and a cordy appearance of the vein itself. It is often associated with varicose veins of the leg, in which case it is superficial venous phlebitis, and the chance of subsequent embolus formation is less than when one of the deep veins is affected.

Phlebotomy, see VENESECTION.

Phlegm, the mucous secretion, with impurities such as dust and bacteria, expelled by coughing from the lower air passages.

Phlogiston Theory, an erroneous theory of combustion, elaborated by J. J. Becher and G. E. Stahl, and overthrown in the 18th century by the work of Lavoisier. Phlogiston was believed to be a substance which was given up by substances to the atmosphere when they burned.

Phlox, a genus of herbs in family Polemoniaceae. They are chiefly American; *P. drummondii* and varieties are grown as half-hardy annuals; *P. paniculata* and hybrids as border plants; and *P. subulata* among dwarf species in rock gardens.

Phnom Penh, capital city of Kampuchea (Cambodia), situated on the River Mekong, where a channel connects it with Tonle Sap 200 km north-west of Saigon. It is the site of the royal palace of Cambodia, having replaced Oudong as capital in the mid-19th century. In the French period it became a fine Western-style city, with tree-lined boulevards, and until 1970 it had escaped the ravages of war. In 1962 its population was 394,000, but during the war (1970–75) this was swelled by refugees from the heavily bombarded countryside—probably to over 2·5 million by 1975. After the Communist victory a large part of the population was forcibly moved back to the countryside. In early 1976, official sources put the population then at close on a mere 100,000. Since the Vietnamese take over in 1979 the city has recovered somewhat and in 1981 the population was estimated to be 400,000.

Phobia, inappropriate or extreme anxiety in a particular situation, or over a particular thing, the fear of which is so intense that the person cannot face it, even though he knows rationally that there is no real danger. For example, some people fear open spaces and can only feel safe enclosed in a building (agoraphobia). Conversely, others are handicapped by a terror of enclosed spaces and have to avoid such situations (claustrophobia). In other instances, the person may suffer a paralysing terror of a particular object such as a spider, mouse, moth or bee.

In general there are two approaches to the treatment of phobic states. Conditioning or behaviour therapy is directed towards the relief of the symptoms. Alternatively, the psychotherapeutic approach is directed towards uncovering the intense anxiety that underlies the phobic symptom so that, with the therapist's support, the person can face and resolve his unconscious fears.

Phocaena, see PORPOISE.

Phocidae, see SEAL.

Phocis (modern Fokîs), country of ancient Greece, north of the gulf of Corinth. Delphi, though within its borders, was controlled by the Amphictyonic League. The Phocian War (355–346 BC) ended in the conquest of Phocis by Philip of Macedon, who razed all its towns excepting Abae.

Phoenicia, in ancient times, did not signify a unified country or state, but rather a number of city states situated along the east coast of the Mediterranean from the Amanus mountains to Mount Carmel, all sharing a similar culture and language. The geographical boundaries of the area fluctuated; no two Greek or Roman writers agree on the limits to Phoenicia. Among the chief towns were Acco, Tyre, Sidon and Berytus (modern Beirut). The Phoenicians were probably the first navigators who ever sailed out of sight of land. They brought gold, silver and tin from Spain, copper from Cyprus and, perhaps, played a part in the Cornish tin trade. They established numerous trading posts along the shores of the Mediterranean.

Archaeological evidence shows that in the 18th century BC Phoenicia was under Egyptian control but then became independent and her cities were free to develop economic and military strength without outside interference. Briefly again an Egyptian province in the 15th century BC, Phoenicia's real glory began with the recovery of its independence in the 14th century BC. After the beginning of the 1st millennium BC large independent colonies were founded in Cyprus, North Africa, Malta, Sicily, Sardinia, Marseilles and Spain. Trading colonies were established in Greece, Egypt and other countries. Tyre enjoyed its golden age in the reign of Hiram (970–936 BC) but after about 800 BC Phoenicia was mostly under Assyrian, Babylonian or Persian domination. In 332 BC it was merged into the empire of Alexander the Great. From 197 it belonged to the Seleucidae until it was included in the Roman province of Syria (64 BC).

***Phoenicia.** A gold dish of the 14th century BC.*

Phoenix, capital city of Arizona, USA. It is situated on the Salt river, in the midst of the irrigated land in the valley of that river. Industry has overspilled from southern California, bringing Phoenix into the business of aeronautical manufacturing. Twenty per cent of the work-force of the area is employed in manufacturing, and there are over 1000 industrial establishments. Population (1980) 789,704.

Phoenix, in Egyptian and Oriental mythology, a sacred bird born from the sun. It was said to resemble an eagle in size and shape, but had red and gold plumage. According to one story, the bird placed itself on the burning altar at Heliopolis, and from the ashes there flew a young phoenix, freshly feathered. Another version is that it built for itself a nest in which to die, and that a new bird sprang from the corpse. There was never more than one phoenix at a time. For the Chinese the phoenix signified good; its appearance was a sign of prosperity, its departure calamity.

Phoenix Islands, group of eight small islands in the West Pacific Ocean between 2°30′ and 4°30′S latitude, and 171° and 174°30′W longitude. They became part of the Gilbert and Ellice Island Colony in 1937 and are now part of Kiribati. Enderbury and Canton Islands are under joint Anglo-American administration. Canton is an international airport. Area 41 km^2; population 1019.

Phon, unit of loudness used in acoustics. The loudness of a sound is the ratio of its pressure (p) to the standard sound pressure $p_0 = 2 \times 10^{-4}$ microbars which corresponds to auditory threshold at 1 kHz. Loudness in phons is defined by $20 \log_{10}(p/p_0)$.
See also DECIBEL.

Phonetics, the branch of linguistic science that deals with spoken language.
Articulatory Phonetics investigates and analyses the movements of the organs of speech used in producing the sounds and sequences of sounds occurring in spoken utterance. Elementary phonetic theory classifies the basic movements, or articulations, according to the state and direction of the air stream, and the degree of stricture of the air passage. A system of notation is essential for such definition: the best and most widely known is the International Phonetic Alphabet (IPA). This is based on the ordinary roman letters, supplemented by modified forms of these and of other alphabets.
Acoustic Phonetics. A normal speech-situation presupposes a receiver as well as a transmitter of the message; acoustic phonetics handles the receiving end.
Much instrumental work falls under the heading of acoustic phonetics. With the help of apparatus very accurate analyses can be made of the complex sounds that reach our ears. These are each composed of a combination or series of tones which we are, as a rule, unable to perceive separately but which affect our estimation of 'quality'; for example, the character of different musical instruments, of different voices, of different vowels, and so on. It is only by instrumental techniques that the component parts of a complex sound can be revealed and measured, and in this respect apparatus can convey more information about sounds than can the ear.

Phonology, term used in English to mean the study of the phonemes of a language (the term phonemics is also widely used). Whereas the precise definition of a phoneme has given rise to much difficulty and discussion, a working definition is that phonemes are the distinctive or significant phonic elements of a language.
See also LINGUISTICS; PHONETICS.

Phoronida, a phylum of about 16 species of marine worms that grow up to 20 cm long and live in tubes buried in the sand or attached to shells or rocks in shallow water. The body, which is a soft cylinder bulging at the bottom to accommodate the stomach, stays inside the tube, and only the front end, made up of spiral ridges covered with tentacles, projects. The spiral ridges form the lophophore, an organ found in two other invertebrate phyla. It has cilia which beat to guide a current of water containing microscopic food particles into the animal's mouth. From here the food passes down the body to the stomach, then through a U-turn up the intestine, and wastes emerge from the anus at the top of the animal near the lophophore. The circulatory, nervous and excretory systems are present but not highly developed. Reproduction is both sexual and asexual and some species have a free-swimming larva.

Phosgene, or carbonyl chloride, $COCl_2$, chloride of carbonic acid. When a mixture of equal volumes of carbon monoxide and chlorine is exposed to bright sunlight or passed over heated animal charcoal, direct combination occurs with the formation of phosgene. This compound, discovered by John Davy in 1811, is a colourless heavy gas, nearly 3·5 times as heavy as air, with a penetrating and suffocating odour which impairs the sense of taste, and is very poisonous, far more so than carbon monoxide. Phosgene has been used in chemical warfare. A practical application of the gas in industry is made in the preparation of polyurethane plastics and some insecticides.

Phosphates, salts of orthophosphoric acid, H_3PO_4. By the action of sodium hydroxide on this acid in calculated quantities, the following phosphates can be obtained: NaH_2PO_4, sodium dihydrogen phosphate, which is acid to litmus; Na_2HPO_4, disodium hydrogen phosphate; and Na_3PO_4, normal sodium phosphate, which is slightly alkaline and is used as a water softener. All the above are soluble phosphates. Silver phosphate is insoluble. Phosphates are important fertilisers. There are also pyrophosphates and metaphosphates, salts of pyrophosphoric acid and metaphosphoric acid respectively.
Soluble phosphates give precipitates with ferric chloride (yellow-white); with silver nitrate (yellow); and with warm ammonium molybdate (yellow).

Phosphatic Rocks, formed on the sea bed by the accumulation of organic remains—bone, scales and faecal material—in areas of deposition where other sedimentary material is absent.

Phosphor Bronze, copper-tin alloy to which phosphorus has been added; it is capable of being made tough and malleable. It is used chiefly for springs and for bearings: for springs the alloys contain about 5 per cent of tin; for bearings 10–15 per cent.

Phosphorescence. When an electron absorbs electromagnetic radiation, it can be promoted to a higher energy level: the electron is said to be excited. Often the energy is very quickly lost; the resulting emission of energy being known as fluorescence. However, if the radiation is emitted at times longer than 10^{-5} s the process is called phosphorescence. Phosphorescence may last minutes or hours. The term was first applied to describe that state of luminescence which certain substances show in the dark after exposure to light. In minerals phosphorescence may be shown by: (1) heating to a temperature below red heat (fluorspar); (2) friction (phosphorus and fused calcium chloride); (3) cleavage (mica, the two split portions exhibiting positive and negative electricity); (4) crystallisation (boracic acid after fusion).
See also BACTERIA.

Phosphorus, non-metallic chemical element, symbol P, atomic number 15, atomic weight 30·9738; discovered by Brand in 1674. It exists in two allotropic forms: (1) ordinary white phosphorus; (2) red phosphorus. It does not occur in nature in the free state, but usually in the form of phosphates, the most important of these being the two salts of calcium, phosphorite, $Ca_3(PO_4)_2$, and apatite, $CaF_2 \cdot 3Ca_3(PO_4)_2$. Calcium phosphate is present in all fertile soils and is a source of phosphate for plants; it also forms the mineral part of bones (60 per cent), and various compounds of phosphorus are found in the animal body, such as the brain and nerves.
White phosphorus is a waxy, transparent substance that becomes yellow or reddish from the action of light. It has a relative density of 1·83, melts at 44°C, and boils at 287°C. On account of its ready inflammability, white phosphorus is always kept under water, in which it is practically insoluble. It is, however, soluble in carbon disulphide, forming a solution which on evaporation leaves so fine a residue of phosphorus that it at once takes fire in the air. On exposure to moist air, white phosphorus glows and gives off garlic fumes and finally ignites. White phosphorus is very poisonous, and in large doses causes death in a few hours. Inhalation of the vapours of phosphorus sets up caries of the teeth and jaw, causing what is known as 'phossy jaw'.
Red phosphorus is formed when ordinary phosphorus is heated for some time to 250°C in an atmosphere free from oxygen. It is purified by boiling with caustic soda, and is obtained as a red powder made up of small crystals. It has a relative density of 2·05–2·34, does not take fire on exposure to air or chlorine, is insoluble in carbon disulphide and in caustic soda, and is not poisonous.

Photius (c. 820–91), Patriarch of Constantinople, in whose time there first occurred the dispute concerning the Filioque that still helps to divide the Eastern from the Western church. In 858 he was elected patriarch in place of Ignatius, who was deposed for political reasons. Pope Nicholas I, however, supported Ignatius and refused to recognise Photius, who in return excommunicated the pope. In 867 Photius convened a council at Constantinople to which the papal legates were not admitted, and denounced Latin errors, including the Filioque addition to the creed. He was treated as a saint by the Greek Church, and as an arch-enemy and cause of schism by the Roman Church. The cause of the schism undoubtedly lay deeper, in the age-long inability of the Eastern and Western empires to trust one another.

Photochemistry, branch of chemistry which deals with chemical reactions initiated, assisted or accelerated by exposure to light. Typical examples are the formation of carbohydrates from carbon dioxide, CO_2, absorbed from the air, and water from the soil,

in the presence of sunlight by green plants containing chlorophyll; the combination of hydrogen and chlorine, which is explosively rapid on exposure to sunlight but only very slow in the dark; the sensitivity of silver salts to light, which is made use of in photography; and the formation of vitamin D by humans and animals from sterols in the skin in the presence of sunlight.
See also FLUORESCENCE; PHOSPHORESCENCE.

Photocomposing, see PHOTOSETTING.

Photocopying, see COPYING.

Photoelectricity. The photoelectric effect is the emission of electrons from a metallic surface when light of an appropriate colour or wavelength falls on it. The effect was first observed in 1887 by Hertz who showed that electric sparks occur easily when the electrodes are illuminated with ultraviolet light.

Photoengraving, the photomechanical method of reproducing illustrations on a relief printing plate, or block. Such plates can be mounted and used for printing with ordinary type. *Line engraving* is used when the original is made up of lines, with no continuous tones. In *half-tone* engraving graduations of continuous tone can be reproduced by photographing the original through a screen, which breaks the picture up into dots of varying size. The coarsest screens are used for rough, absorbent paper such as newsprint, while fine screens are used for printing on high-gloss paper. In making the plates, the image is formed on a metal plate covered with light-sensitive emulsion, which is then etched to leave the black lines or dots raised.
See also PHOTOGRAPHY; PRINTING.

Photo-finish Camera, device used in racing events for accurately timing the winning order. Used extensively in horse-racing, it was first used for athletics in the 1948 Olympic Games. The ordinary camera makes one exposure, photographing the position of competitors at a particular moment. The photo-finish camera records on a moving film everything which happens on the finish line as it happens. It records to $\frac{1}{100}$ second, which in sprinting represents a difference of about 10 cm, though even this is too slow in some races.

Photofit, see IDENTIKIT AND PHOTOFIT.

Photogrammetry, the technique of making accurate measurements from photographs. Although photogrammetry is used in astronomy, engineering and medicine, its widest application is in the field of topographic mapping, where it is the principal survey method employed in all forms of basic mapping.
A photograph is a perspective projection of its subject and shows the correct planimetric relationships of features in planes parallel to the plane of projection. In mapping, where photographs taken vertically from aircraft are almost always used, the photographs are made parallel to the ground surface, optically, in a photogrammetric plotting machine to remove the effects of the tip and tilt of the aircraft. All remaining planimetric distortion in the photograph is then due to variation in altitude of the ground. This is removed by viewing two photographs of the same piece of land simultaneously, taken from different positions in the air (stereographic pairs). A three-dimensional optical model is then seen which can be plotted to give the correct positions of all features on the intended map regardless of their altitude.

Photography, literally 'drawing with light', usually refers to the recording of light images by means of light sensitive substances. Not only visible light, but infra-red, ultraviolet and X-rays may be recorded.
The two necessary requirements for photography are an image forming system and a suitable light sensitive material. The former was derived from the camera obscura which by 1800 was in widespread use as an artist's aid. The latter was found in the salts of silver. Thomas Wedgwood made the first recorded images on paper and leather treated with silver nitrate. He found no way to fix his images, which were thus not permanent. In 1829 Joseph Niepce entered into a partnership with Louis Jacques Mande Daguerre, a French artist, and after Niepce's death in 1833 Daguerre succeeded in improving the process to a practical form. The process, named Daguerreotype after its inventor, was announced in 1839.
William Henry Fox Talbot made paper sensitive to light by impregnating it with silver chloride, and was able to stabilise images with a solution of salt. In 1835 he took a photograph of a window at Lacock Abbey, his ancestral home. Sir John Herschel in 1839 suggested the use of hyposulphite of soda as a fixing agent.
Negatives on glass became possible in 1851 as a result of Frederick Scott Archer's discovery that collodion could provide a suitable coating to carry the light sensitive salts. The glass plate was heavy and fragile, and in 1885 George Eastman, an American, introduced a flexible roll of paper coated with a gelatin emulsion. In 1888 Eastman marketed the Kodak camera, and provided a developing and printing service. In the following year he produced the first celluloid roll-film.
With improvements in emulsion-making, enhanced quality and definition of negative materials have made possible greatly reduced negative sizes. Negatives 25 cm by 20 cm or larger were not uncommon; now, the largest in general use is 6 by 6 cm. The most popular sizes are 2·4 by 3·6 cm on 35 mm film, and 2·8 by 2·8 cm or 1·7 by 1·3 cm in cartridge cameras. In 1948 E. S. Land introduced a process which yields a finished print only a few seconds after exposure.
The camera. The earliest photographic cameras were generally two wooden boxes, one sliding within the other. One carried the lens, the other the plateholder and provision for focusing. Eastman's Kodak of 1888 was influential, and his simple Brownie box camera of 1900 popularised photography. The simple rollfilm camera has now largely been replaced by the cartridge loading cameras.
The introduction of the Leica camera in 1924 had a major influence on camera design. Based upon a prototype by the designer Oscar Barnack, this small camera using 35 mm cine film started the trend toward small format cameras. A coupled rangefinder system to assist focusing was first used on the Autographic Kodak Special of 1916. This has now been largely superseded by the single lens reflex. Large format single lens reflex plate cameras were popular from 1900 to the 1930s. From about the mid-1960s European markets became dominated by Japanese single lens reflex cameras such as Canon, Nikon, Minolta, Pentax, etc.

Photogravure, an intaglio printing process, i.e. one in which the ink forming the printed image is retained in cells (hollows) below the surface of a copper plate. The process is extensively used for printing magazines and food wrappings. The original (text and pictures) is photographed through a screen which breaks it up into dots on a gelatine sheet, which is laid on the plate. Different gradations of tone are represented by cells of varying depth in the gelatine. In etching, an acid eats through the gelatine and into the plate, producing cells of varying depth in the copper. In printing, the plate is inked, and then wiped clean with a *doctor blade*, leaving ink trapped in the cells. When paper is pressed on the plate the image is transferred. In *rotogravure* the plate is in the form of a cylinder for rotary printing.

Photometry, the science of measurement of light. Visual photometry is concerned with light as it affects the human eye. The eye is sensitive to only a small range of wavelengths and is not equally sensitive to all wavelengths within that range. Thus it is necessary to use

Photography. *Whitby Harbour, photographed by F. M. Sutcliffe in the 1870s.*

a detector filtered to ensure a sensitivity similar to that of the eye. General photometry is concerned with the measurement of any part of the spectrum from ultraviolet to infrared.

In general photometry intensity is expressed as power in watts or as the number of photons per second. If a surface is illuminated we can measure the number of watts per square metre falling on it. If we have a self-luminous body we measure the number of watts of light per square metre, and per unit solid angle of the source. In each case it may also be necessary to state the wavelength or frequency range to which the measurement refers. In visual photometry we have to start with a different unit; corresponding to the watt we have the lumen of light flux, lm, which is defined by the statement that an area of 100 mm^2 of platinum at its melting-point (1773°C) emits 60 lumens per unit solid angle. Visual photometry is complicated by the difficulties of comparing light of different colours. Averaged measurements have resulted in the definition of a 'standard observer' whose response to equal light powers of different wavelengths is given by a standard table. However, it is a somewhat arbitrary judgment and this problem is not completely solved.

Photon. Light, or more generally electromagnetic radiation, is emitted by atoms in discrete, indivisible bundles of energy or *quanta* called photons, the energy E of an individual quantum or photon being $E = hc/\lambda = hf$, where h is Planck's constant ($h = 6{\cdot}63 \times 10^{-34}$ J s or $4{\cdot}14 \times 10^{-5}$ eV s), c the velocity of light, λ the wavelength (colour) of the light, and f its frequency of vibration.
See also LIGHT.

Photosetting, or film setting, various methods of assembling type on photographic paper or film, without the use of metal. It is rapidly displacing hot-metal composition for books, magazines and newspapers. Most photosetting machines are in two parts: a keyboard, similar to a Linotype or typewriter keyboard, is used to punch a tape or produce a magnetic tape: a photographic unit then produces either a negative or a positive, at a speed of up to 30,000 characters an hour. Systems vary: some use a beam of light shining through an *image master*, consisting of a set of characters on a sheet of film; others use a cathode-ray tube to project the image, the tube being brought into action by computer. Copies for proofreading are produced by the dyeline process (for film) or by xerography (for paper positives).
See also COMPUTER COMPOSITION; TYPESETTING.

Photosphere, the surface layer of the Sun or a star from which most of the light by which we see it originates.
See also SUN.

Photostat, see COPYING.

Photosynthesis (Greek *phōs*, light; *synthesis*, a building up), the process whereby green plants make carbohydrates from carbon dioxide and water, using energy from sunlight. About 5×10^{16} g (50 billion tonnes) of carbon are fixed into organic compounds by photosynthetic organisms every year, much of this by phytoplankton living near the surface of the sea. Ultimately all forms of life depend on photosynthesis, and it is the only way in which extra energy (in the form of light) can be introduced into the Earth. Most of the carbon used is drawn from the air (which contains 0·03 per cent of CO_2, carbon dioxide); the plant also emits pure oxygen, which is essential for animal life.

Photosynthesis is not a single reaction, but a series of rapid, linked steps. It takes place in a chloroplast, the part of a cell which contains the green pigment chlorophyll. The first step involves the trapping of light energy; electrons are removed from the chlorophyll and water molecules are dissociated into hydrogen ions and oxygen, which is liberated into the atmosphere. In the next process the free electrons are 'transported' to an acceptor molecule known as NADP, giving it a negative charge. The NADP then combines with the hydrogen to become $NADPH_2$. At the same time other electrons combine with a substance, ATP, to form the high-energy molecule ADP, which is used to power the next process. In the third stage hydrogen from the $NADPH_2$ combines with carbon dioxide from the atmosphere to produce carbohydrates, the building material of starch and cellulose molecules. The first two steps occur only in light (the light reaction), while the third takes place in the dark (the dark reaction). ATP provides a store of power which can be drawn on by enzyme action for a variety of cell activities, such as chemical synthesis.

Phototaxis, see TROPISM.

Phototropism, the bending of a plant organ (e.g. a stem) in a growth response to the stimulus of light. Stems and flower stalks bend towards the light, and are said to be positively phototropic; most roots are negatively phototropic, growing away from the light, whilst leaf blades usually turn at right angles to the light. The positive phototropism of a stem or other organ is caused by the side towards the light growing at a slower rate than the side away from the light, so that a curve results. Phototropism is of obvious value in enabling the organs of plants to carry out their functions efficiently.
See also TROPISM.

Phototypesetting, see PHOTOSETTING.

Phrenology, pseudo-science based on the assumption that mental 'faculties' are localised in the brain, and that these areas are identifiable from peculiarities of bone formation on the skull. Phrenologists profess to discover an individual's talents by locating these 'bumps' or areas. The bones of the cranium have thicknesses and air spaces producing exterior unevenness but these bear no relation to the underlying cortex. Localisation of function does exist, but has no connection with external variations in the shape of the head.

Phrygia, ancient district of Asia Minor. Phrygia was subject in turn to the Lydian empire of Croesus, to the Persians, to Alexander the Great, and to the Seleucids; but under the last the north-eastern territory, adjacent to Paphlagonia and the River Halys, was conquered by Gauls and formed the western part of Galatia. The Romans gave Phrygia to Eumenes II of Pergamum. In 133 it became part of the Roman province of Asia.

Phryne (fl.c.340 BC), celebrated courtesan of ancient Athens. She served as model for the 'Aphrodite Anadyomene' of Apelles, and the 'Cnidian Aphrodite' of Praxiteles.

Phylacteries (called by the Jews *tephilin*), small cubical leather cases, two in number, one of which is worn on the forehead, the other on the inside of the left arm above the elbow. Each contains a strip of parchment or vellum inscribed with certain texts, viz. Exodus xiii. 1–10 and 11–16; Deuteronomy vi. 4–9 and xi. 13–21. The practice of wearing phylacteries, is still continued by orthodox Jews at weekday morning prayers.

Phyllite, foliated metamorphic rock in which the lustre of the disseminated mica is very prominent.

Phyllocladus, a genus of pines in the Phyllocladaceae family (Podocarpaceae), evergreen trees from the southern hemisphere. Botanically they are of special interest in that at an early stage of growth the leaves become reduced to scales and the branchlets become flattened into leaf-like structures.

Phyllotaxis, term used for the arrangement of leaves on a stem. It may be *spiral*, if the leaves are one at each node and alternating. If two or more leaves form a whorl at each node the phyllotaxis is *opposite*, if more, *verticillate*.

Phylloxera, a genus of plant lice related to aphids and belonging to the family Phylloxeridae in order Hemiptera (suborder Homoptera). The best known and most destructive species is *P. vitifoliae*, the grape phylloxera. This species is native to the middle and eastern USA, where it feeds on various varieties of grapes. To a certain extent the grapevines in these regions are immune to their attacks. About 1860 this species was accidentally introduced into France, and before adequate control measures were found, more than a third of the vineyards were destroyed. European vines are now grafted on resistant root stock.

Phylogeny, see CLASSIFICATION OF ANIMALS; CLASSIFICATION OF PLANTS; TAXONOMY.

Physalia, see PORTUGUESE MAN-OF-WAR.

Physalis, a genus of Mexican and American annual or perennial herbs, in family Solanaceae. *P. peruviana*, the Cape gooseberry, and *P. ixocarpa*, the jamberberry or tomatillo, are often grown for their fruit; *P. alkekengi*, the bladder cherry or Chinese lantern, for its ornamental lantern-like fruits.

Physical Education, method of acquiring and maintaining bodily fitness. It was not until after the publication of Rousseau's *Émile* in 1762 that the value of physical education as part of normal education began to be recognised. This conception was developed by the German pioneers, while Friedrich Froebel influenced physical education by his insistence on the importance of play in the growth of the child. In Denmark physical education became part of the normal school curriculum as early as 1814. A system of gymnastics, known as Swedish drill, with the German systems, was the basis of most physical education. Some modifications have been introduced, particularly in the direction of relating physical education more to the natural and rhythmical movements of the human body. From Germany and Scandinavia the cult of physical education spread to most European countries and to the USA.

It was at first linked mainly to military training or to remedial treatment for physical defects. Gradually, however, it came to be included in the normal school curriculum.

Physical Units. Measurements in scientific work are referred to by a basic system of units. Past systems include the cgs (centimetre-gram-second), MKS (metre-kilogram-second), and fps (foot-pound-second) systems. But in 1960, the SI (*Système Internationale*) was adopted by scientists and is becoming established throughout the world. See also METROLOGY.

Physicalism, in philosophy, the doctrine that all events can be reduced to statements expressed in the language of physical science and concerned with processes in the spatio-temporal framework of physics. Laplace's theory, that if we knew the positions and velocities of all the particles in the universe, then the laws of mechanics alone would enable us to predict the future course of the world, is one kind of physicalist theory. More recently, some have held that 'experience' can be reduced to statements in terms of physics. On this view, psychology is a branch of physical science.

Physics may be defined as investigation of the properties of matter and energy, except for those laws influenced by the presence of life (biophysics) and those which take into consideration interatomic changes (chemistry). The subject is subdivided into atom and atomic theory, current electricity, electrostatics, heat, light, magnetism, mechanics, quantum theory, relativity and sound.

Modern progress can be said to have begun about the time of Galileo (1564–1642) and Newton (1642–1727). Galileo's work on mechanics was continued by Newton, who stated certain generalisations which, until recently, appeared to epitomise the fundamentals of the whole subject; he also made important contributions to optics.

Faraday (1791–1867) and others showed that magnetism and electricity were related, that currents were surrounded by magnetic fields, and that changing magnetic fields could generate currents. This was developed by Maxwell (1831–79) into the electromagnetic theory of light.

During the 19th century it was established largely by Joule (1818–89) that heat was merely the kinetic energy of atoms and molecules. Gradually there emerged the idea of the conservation of energy: that there is, in any system isolated from all other bodies, an amount of energy that, although it may change from one form to another, always remains constant in amount.

According to classical theories, the Earth moved through a stationary aether, and it would be possible to measure its speed relative to the aether. The Michelson-Morley experiment revealed no trace of such movement, and led in 1905 to Einstein's theory of relativity. Among other consequences of this theory, Newton's laws of motion were shown not to be fundamental, but to be merely instances of more general laws. Moreover, the theory showed that the law of conservation of energy requires modification in that mass must also be regarded as energy; if mass disappears energy must be released in enormous amounts. The second big change of view resulted from the discovery by J. J. Thomson in 1895 of the electron, whose mass was shown to be only a small fraction of that of the lightest atom. This led to the electrical theory of the atom and opened the way for the practical use of the electron in radio and many other fields. A third fundamental change was due to the quantum theory. Propounded by Planck in 1900, this theory has proved the key to the understanding of a great number of atomic phenomena.

The discovery in 1932 of the neutron and the positron was followed by a rapid development of the understanding of nuclear phenomena. Nuclear physicists are trying to find an overall pattern in the properties of the many elementary particles.

Solid state physics is applied to electric, dielectric, magnetic, and other physical properties of solids in terms of their fundamental atomic structure, leading to electronics.

Other important branches of physics in which research is concentrated include low-temperature physics and plasma physics (the behaviour of materials at very low and very high temperatures respectively), and the nature of gravitation.

Physics, Modern. This term is used rather loosely to describe those branches of physics in which explanations of physical behaviour are given in terms of the electronic, atomic, and subatomic structure of matter, and the theories that have developed since c.1920 to account for the laws that matter obeys at these levels. One can approximately indicate the scope of the topic by describing it as containing all those aspects that require quantum theory and its developments to provide explanations. (In quantum theory there are limits to the energy that may be possessed by a particle in an atomic system.)

Elementary Particle Physics attempts to rationalise in terms of satisfactory schemes the various particles which are found when nuclear particles collide at very high energies (several thousand million electron volts). Various classifications of the particles can be made in terms of their masses and their types of interaction.

The interactions (other than the electromagnetic interactions) between elementary particles are of very short range and fall into two distinct classes—strong interactions a hundred times more powerful than the electromagnetic interactions, and weak interactions much less than a millionth of the strength of the electromagnetic interactions.

Nuclear Physics accepts neutrons and protons (generally, nucleons) as the basic constituents of nuclei (they are present in roughly equal numbers in many nuclei). It seeks to understand the structure of nuclei and their properties (e.g. spin, angular momentum and quadrupole moments) in both their normal and their excited states, and nuclear reactions at energies up to several million electron volts.

Atomic Physics is essentially based upon spectroscopic techniques for exploring the configurations (occupation of allowed electronic energy levels) and angular momentum states of atoms in their ground and excited states, and the interactions with the radiation field by which changes of state occur.

Molecular Physics extends a concern with allowed electronic energy levels and their occupation, to systems where electrons are shared between pairs or larger groups of atoms in molecules; it seeks explanations of the stabilities, structures and properties of molecules.

The Physics of Condensed Matter is concerned with a whole system of atoms or molecules constituting a crystal, an amorphous solid, or a glass, and with the resultant electrical, magnetic, optical and mechanical properties. This is easily the largest branch of modern physics.

Modern Optics is the term normally applied to the developments that have taken place in producing and operating with coherent radiation, that is radiation in which phase coherence of the waves is preserved over long distances. With ultra-short and very high pulses of radiation one enters the regime that is described as nonlinear optics.

Plasma Physics is the study of highly ionised matter. This can be produced by dissipating a very large amount of energy in a small volume of material.

Astro- and Space Physics is a very broad field involving radiation over a wide spectral range, the evolution of stars, and interstellar and interplanetary magnetic fields.

Mathematical Physics can be regarded as containing such topics as relativity, quantum field theory, quantum statistical mechanics, and the theory of phase transitions.

Physiocratic School (Greek *phusis*, nature, and *kratein*, to rule), name given to a group of French economists and philosophers of the 18th century. Their main doctrine was the superiority of nature to all man's work; thus they held all commerce was sterile, and the only fruitful labour was agriculture. Their head was François Quesnay and their chief practical exponent was Turgot.

Physiognomy, external appearance of the body and particularly the face, its features and expression, from which character can supposedly be divined. As a theory, physiognomy is ancient and many attempts have been made to place it on a scientific basis and render it useful as an art. Scientific interest in it was first aroused by the work of the 19th-century Swiss mystic, Johann Lavater. Charles Darwin posited a connection between the evolution of body structures in accordance with a predominant emotion in animals in *Expressions of the Emotions in Man and Animals*, 1873.

Physiology, that branch of the science of biology that is concerned with the functioning, as opposed to the structure, of living beings. For a sketch of its history, development and scope, see BIOLOGY. For special branches see CIRCULATION OF THE BLOOD; DIGESTION; HORMONE; RESPIRATION, EXTERNAL; and for plant physiology, see PHOTOSYNTHESIS.

Physiotherapy, the treatment of injury and disease by physical means, used to restore or improve function and to help patients achieve maximum efficiency in the activities of daily life, at home, at work or at leisure. It may also be employed as a prophylactic measure, to teach good posture, methods of relaxation, and correct ways of lifting and handling heavy and difficult objects.

The patient is treated mainly by movement, manipulative procedures, electrotherapy, and also by the application of heat and ultraviolet light. Exercises in water (hydrotherapy) can be given, using buoyancy to assist or resist movement. Sport, especially swimming, riding, archery and table tennis, is also employed as a remedial treatment. Physiotherapy is used to help patients with acute or chronic chest conditions to clear their lungs, to breathe correctly and to learn good postural habits.

Physostigma, see CALABAR BEAN.

Phytophthora infestans, a fungus of the Phycomycotina, responsible for potato blight. It attacks the leaves and stems of the plant, but passes the winter in a dormant state in the tubers. It caused the Irish potato famine of the mid-19th century.
See also PLANT DISEASES.

Phytoplankton, see PLANKTON.

Pi, Greek letter π, used as a symbol to denote the ratio of the circumference of a circle to its diameter, which is approximately 3·14159. π is an irrational number; it cannot be expressed as the ratio of two integers, and its expression as a decimal never terminates and never starts recurring. This was proved in 1761 by Johann Lambert. However, π can be calculated to any desired degree of accuracy. The most commonly used approximation is $^{22}/_{7}$, which is accurate to two decimal places, and was established by Archimedes. In 1973 a group of French mathematicians used a CDC 7600 computer to find an approximate value extending to 1,000,000 decimal places.

Piacenza (ancient *Placentia*), Italian city and capital of Piacenza province, on the right bank of the Po some 65 km south-west of Milan. In 219 BC Piacenza is mentioned as a Roman colony. In 1545 it was united with Parma. The 12th-century cathedral, in Lombard-Romanesque style, has curious and grotesque internal decorations. Its town hall 'Il Gotico' (1280) is one of Italy's most famous. The city is still basically an agricultural centre, trading and processing the district's produce; it is also a garrison town. Population (1979) 108,900.

Piaf, Edith Giovanna (Edith Gassion) (1915–63), French singer. At an early age she supported herself by singing in the streets. Later, in cabaret and music-hall, she rapidly made a name for herself singing wistful love songs or harsh songs of poverty and despair. Among the best known were *Mon Légionnaire* and her own *La vie en rose*.

Piaget, Jean (1896–1979), Swiss psychologist. His experimental psychology explored the stages in cognitive development, and the growth of judgment, reasoning and logical thought in the child, which have important implications for education.

Pianoforte, keyboard instrument known in the 18th century also as fortepiano, invented by Cristofori at Florence in 1709. Its main difference from the harpsichord was that its strings were struck by hammers, with variations in the force and touch applied by the performer making possible pronounced graduations of dynamics. By 1726 Cristofori had completed a pianoforte with a wide dynamic range, a strengthened frame, double action (in which when the key is depressed an intermediate lever conveys an impulse to the hammer, which hits the string), and a soft-pedal mechanism. A check device prevented the hammer from rebounding after striking the string. This action formed the basis of all subsequent pianoforte building. Developments in the 19th century included the introduction of metal bracings to reinforce the older wooden frames as the thickness of the strings and their tension was increased, and the introduction of the all-iron frame in 1825. A consideration of the normal action today shows that the key is simply a lever for raising the hammer, which is lifted to the string by a jointed piece of wood called the hopper. When the key is released the hammer falls back ready for the next stroke. The finger action in moving the keys also lifts the damper, a small felt-covered piece of wood which rests on the string. The depression of the right pedal (the sustaining pedal) has the effect of raising all the dampers so that other strings can vibrate in sympathy with those actually sounded. On the modern upright piano the left pedal ('soft' pedal) causes the hammers to move nearer the strings, weakening the force of the impact, and on the modern grand a slight horizontal movement prevents them from hitting all the strings in each case, three strings for top notes, two for low notes, and one only for very low (hence the indication *una corda* for the depression of the left pedal and *tre corde* for its release). The use of these two pedals gives the piano one of its special features. The piano's compass extends to over seven octaves.
See also KEYBOARD INSTRUMENTS.

Pianola, see PLAYER-PIANO.

Piastre (Latin *emplastron*, a plaster, hence anything flattened; Italian *piastra*, a coin), old Spanish silver coin called a piece of eight, being divided into eight silver reals. The Italian piastre or scudo was worth a little less. The piastre was also the name of the standard monetary unit of the Ottoman Empire. It is still in use in Egypt.

Piave, Italian river of Veneto. It rises in the Carnic Alps close to the Austrian border and flows south-west through the Cadore district and past Belluno, turning south-east where it flows out onto the northern plain and to the Adriatic 35 km north-east of Venice. Length 220 km.

Piazza, a formal space which is surrounded by buildings.

Piazzi, Giuseppe (1746–1826), Italian astronomer. On 1 January 1801 he discovered Ceres, the first known of the asteroids or minor planets.

Pica, a craving for unnatural food, such as chalk, especially in pregnancy. It is a symptom found in some forms of psychosis and emotional disturbances.

Picardy, province of France, composed of the modern *département* of Somme, and parts of the *départements* of Pas-de-Calais, Aisne and Oise. It came finally under the French crown in 1477. The capital was Amiens.

Picaresque Novel, or *novela picaresca*, name of popular origin given to a type of novel which describes the adventures of a *picaro* (rogue, in Spanish).
The popularity of novels describing low life and centring on a rascally hero began in Spain with the publication in 1554 of Hurtado's *Vida de Lazarillo de Tormes*. Hurtado's example was followed by Mateo Aleman, who wrote *Atalaya de la vida humana*, a title which was changed to *El picaro Guzman de Alfarache* by the public with whom it was so popular.
The Spanish novel had a direct influence on the French writer Lesage, who in his *Le Diable boiteux*, 1707, imitated Guevara's *El Diablo cojuelo*, 1641.
In England there existed a 16-century translation of Hurtado's *Lazarillo de Tormes*, which went through several editions, and in 1594 Thomas Nash's *Unfortunate Traveller* introduced the picaresque novel into English literature. In the 18th century low life and the manners of rogues provided many of the characters, settings and events for English novels in the hands of Defoe (*Moll Flanders*, *Colonel Jack*), Fielding (*Tom Jones*, *Jonathan Wild*), and above all Smollett (*Roderick Random*, *Peregrine Pickle*, *Humphry Clinker*).

Picasso. Weeping Woman, *painted in 1937.*

Picasso, Pablo Ruiz (1881–1973), Spanish painter. He began to paint very early (at La Ceruna) and fraternised with the artists of Barcelona Academy. He first arrived in Paris in 1900, and took up permanent residence there in 1903. At the beginning his work was influenced by the traditions of Degas and Toulouse Lautrec, but between 1901 and 1904 he turned to austere figure studies, blue being the dominant colour. Circus pictures followed, delicate and more varied in colour. After the 'blue' and 'rose' periods, 1907–09, Picasso and a fellow artist Georges Braque developed Cubism from the study of Cézanne combined with that of primitive art. After the First World War he reverted to more classical painting, and designed the décor of a number of ballets, but shortly before and after the Second World War his painting became violent, causing vehement criticism. The most notable example of this phase is Picasso's *Guernica*, painted in 1937 during the Spanish civil war. His later work has its Surrealistic aspect, but Picasso went freely from one style to another, and used various media. He practised sculpture, illustrated books (e.g. *Buffon*, 1942), in 1946 began to design pottery at Vallausis, near Antibes; from November 1953 to February 1954 he produced 180 drawings on the theme of artist and model. His paintings are in leading European galleries and at the Museum of Modern Art, New York; he is also represented in many private collections.

Piccard, Auguste (1884–1962), Swiss physicist. He was famous for his stratosphere flights with a free balloon and air-tight gondola in order to observe cosmic rays and other upper-atmosphere phenomena. In 1931, from Augsburg, he reached a height (with his assistant Kipfer) of 15,781 m and in 1932, from Zürich, 16,940 m. In 1947 he designed a 10-tonne diving bell or 'bathyscaphe' for deep-sea exploration on similar principles, and descended 3150 m in 1953. His publications include *Between Earth and Sky* (trans. C. Apcher), 1950, and *In Balloon and Bathyscaphe* (trans. C. Stead), 1956.

Piccard, Jacques Ernest Jean (1922–), Swiss scientist, the son of Auguste Piccard. Piccard collaborated with his father in creating the first bathyscaphes, making the world's deepest-ever dive (10,917 m) on 23 January 1960 in the *Trieste*; his account of the dive, written with R. Dietz, has been translated as *Seven Miles Down*, 1961. He went on to manufacture mesoscaphes (tourist submarines), and was chief scientist in the research submarine *Ben Franklin* which in 1969 made a 30-day, 2400-kilometre drift dive in the Gulf Stream. His publications include *The Sun Beneath the Sea*, 1971.

Piccolo (Italian abbreviation for *flauto piccolo*, meaning little flute), a woodwind instrument, similar in shape and technique to the flute, but smaller in size and an octave higher in pitch. It transposes up an octave.
See also WOODWIND INSTRUMENTS.

Pickering, Edward Charles (1846–1919), US astronomer. He became director of Harvard College Observatory in 1876, where he developed a visual photometer for measuring accurately the brightness of stars, and with it made 1·5 million measurements. In addition to cataloguing stellar magnitudes, he developed the use of photography in astronomy, and initiated the Harvard spectral classification of over 350,000 stars.

Picket, military term used in non-operational areas to denote a body of troops who patrol or remain ready for an emergency to enforce discipline, uphold law and order, deal with fires, etc. On operations a picket signifies a body of troops used for protective purposes. The word is also used in connection with industrial disputes.

Picketing. During a strike, the strikers may place people known as 'pickets' outside the entrance of the factory or workplace in order to dissuade other workers from replacing them and suppliers and customers from dealing with their employer. This is the activity called 'picketing'.

Pickford, Mary (1893–1979), American film actress, born Gladys Mary Smith, in Canada. She became known as 'America's sweetheart' of silent films with her portrayal of the innocent heroine in such films as *Poor Little Rich Girl*, 1917, *Pollyanna*, 1920, and *Little Lord Fauntleroy*, 1921. She was also a shrewd businesswoman and was instrumental in forming the United Artists Corporation in 1919 with Charlie Chaplin, D. W. Griffith and her second husband, Douglas Fairbanks. She retired from acting in the early 1930s.

Pickling, in metallurgy, the removal of scale, oxide or rust from metals by an acid, to restore their chemically clean surfaces. The pickling action in some cases is purely chemical dissolution of an oxide or carbonate in the acid of the pickle; in others it may be a mechanical removal of the scale by virtue of action between base metal and acid.

Pickling of Food, see FOOD PRESERVATION.

Picotee, used of flowers, especially when the plain coloured petals are edged with a second colour.

Picquet, see PIQUET.

Picric Acid, 2, 4, 6-trinitrophenol, lyddite, melinite or shinosite, a high explosive which has also been used as a dye. It is one of the trinitrophenols, $C_6H_2(NO_2)_3OH$, and is a yellow crystalline solid soluble in hot water (melting-point 122·5°C). It is prepared by adding sulphonated phenol to nitric and sulphuric acids. Many of the salts, particularly the lead salt, are very sensitive and explode on light impact detonating the whole charge. For this reason lead-free conditions are prescribed for its manufacture.
See also EXPLOSIVES.

Pictography, the most primitive stage of true writing, also known as picture-writing. A picture or sketch, termed 'pictograph', represents the object. A sketch of a man would indicate 'man'; the pictograph of an animal would represent that animal; a circle might represent the sun. Straight narrative can be thus recorded in a sequence of pictographs, but such pictures could not say enough. Therefore the pictographs also became ideographs: the pictures not only represent the things they show, but also the underlying ideas associated with those things; a circle for instance, might represent the 'day'. Pictography is found everywhere, among the ancient peoples of Egypt, Mesopotamia, Crete, Central America and China, as well as among some indigenous peoples of present-day North America, Africa and Asia.

***Picts.** An 8th-century Pictish cross-slab.*

Picts, an early people inhabiting Scotland and part of the north of Ireland from early times. *Picti*, meaning in Latin 'painted' or 'tattooed' people, were first mentioned by Eumenius in 297. By the end of the 3rd century the term had replaced *Caledonians* to describe the inhabitants of central and northern Scotland and *Picti* were frequently referred to as raiders of the frontiers of Roman Britain. By the end of the 7th century the Picts had created in Scotland a united kingdom, which extended from the Forth to the Pentland Firth. In 885 they defeated their major threat, the Northumbrians, at the battle of Nechtansmere, thus settling their southern boundary. They were involved in constant warfare with the Scots of Dalriada until, in the mid-9th century, Kenneth McAlpine, king of Dalriada, successfully laid claim to the Pictish throne and thus united the two kingdoms. The Picts have no surviving literature, but have left many fine carved monuments, memorial stones and crosses, some bearing the so-called 'Pictish Ogam'.

Picts' Wall, an old-fashioned name for Hadrian's Wall.

Picture Restoring, see RESTORATION.

Pidgin, or Pigeon (Chinese corruption of the English word 'business'), jargon developed from communications between European traders and native peoples in various parts of the world. Its basis is a European language (English, Dutch or French, etc.), but other words of wide currency are incorporated; its grammar is minimal. When developed and adopted as the national language of a people it is known as creole.
See also CREOLE.

Pieces of Eight, popular name given to old Spanish silver coins worth eight silver reals, hence the term piece of eight. Other names for it were piastre or dollar.
See also CAROLUS.

Piecework, system of payment of wages by results as opposed to payment by time-earnings. The simplest and oldest form of payment by results is individual piecework; group piecework is an extension of this; gang piecework prevails in jobs which need the close co-operation of several individuals; overhead piecework, based frequently on the normal output of the work as a whole, provides that, in whatever proportion it may be exceeded, in the same proportion the aggregate wages of the workers will be increased.
See also WAGES.

Pieck, Wilhelm (1876–1960), German politician. He left the Social Democratic party in 1918 to become a Communist, and was a member of the Reichstag, 1928–33. Subsequently he lived in the USSR. In 1935 he succeeded Thälmann as German Communist leader in exile, and from 1938–43 acted as general secretary to the Comintern. After the Second World War he helped the Russians to establish a communist regime in the Soviet zone of Germany, and was first president of the German Democratic Republic from 1949 until his death.

Piedmont (Italian *Piemonte*), region of north-west Italy, comprising the provinces of Alessandria, Asti, Cuneo, Novara, Turin and Vercelli. It contains part of the Alps including some of its largest massifs: Monte Viso (3841 m). Monte Rosa (4633 m) and Gran Paradiso (4061 m). The chief rivers are the Po and its tributaries the Tanaro, Dora Riparia, Dora Baltea and Sesia. Piedmont includes the western shore of Lake Maggiore. Agriculture and industry are fairly equally balanced in the region. The irrigated plains are dominated by rice growing (Vercelli, Novara) and dairying.

The hilly districts are famous for their wines (Asti, Casale Monferrato). Industry is well dispersed and prosperous: engineering and steel mainly in Turin province, textiles (Vercelli, Novara), and elsewhere clothes, glass, rubber, etc. The regional capital is Turin. Since the 18th century Piedmont belonged to the House of Savoy until it became the nucleus of a united Italy in the mid-19th century. Area 25,400 km². Population (1980) 4,531,141.

Pie-poudre, Court of, in England, was formerly held at fairs or markets to administer ready justice to buyers and sellers. It was so called from Old French *pied pouldre*, 'dusty foot'; justice was administered 'while the dust fell from the feet'. In most seaport towns there was a similar court dealing with cases arising out of ships.

Pier, in architecture a support or pillar, essentially a structural member as distinct from a 'pilaster', which is often merely of decorative value. It is also a breakwater or jetty built out into the sea.

Pierce, Franklin (1804–69), 14th President of the USA. He was a loyal Jacksonian Democrat, and was elected president in 1852, being largely a compromise candidate. His administration reflected his respect for state rights, economy, and a vigorous foreign policy. He was refused renomination in 1856.

Pieris, in botany, a genus of evergreen shrubs or trees in the Ericaceae; *P. floribunda*, *P. formosa* and *P. japonica* are popular garden shrubs with lily-of-the-valley-like flowers; *P. formosa* has bright red young leaves.

Pieris, in zoology, is the type genus of the family Pieridae, the white, sulphur and orange-tip butterflies, of order Lepidoptera. *Pieris* comprises the cabbage whites. The small white, *P. rapae*, is among the most destructive of all butterflies, destroying cabbage and other crucifer crops in both the Old and the New Worlds. The large white, *P. brassicae*, is equally destructive, but is not established in the New World. The green-veined white, *P. napi*, chiefly occurs on weed crucifers rather than crops.

Piero della Francesca, also called Pietro Borghese (c.1416–92), Italian painter. Piero was the pupil of Domenico Veneziano and is famous for geometric orderliness and the sympathetic harmony of his figures and settings. He visited Rome, where he painted frescoes in the Vatican for Nicholas V. These were immense works in the Vatican library, in poor condition as early as the 16th century, when Raphael was commissioned to replace them with his masterpieces. His most famous fresco works are those in S. Francesco of Arezzo, *The Story of the True Cross* at Borgo San Sepolcro, and the *Flagellation of Christ* in the Ducal Palace, Urbino. Piero was for a long time forgotten, but modern appreciation has steadily grown for the artist's consummate science in pictorial construction and power as a colourist.

Pierre de la Ramée, see RAMUS, PETER.

Pietermaritzburg, capital of Natal province, South Africa, 88 km north-west of Durban; founded by the Boers in 1839, and called after two of their leaders, Piet Retief and Gert Maritz.

Pietermaritzburg is the seat of an Anglican bishop and houses one campus of the University of Natal. The city has a large tannin extract factory, a furniture factory, footwear, blankets, aluminium ware, canvas goods, fencing and cables. Population (1980) 178,972, including 53,780 whites, 62,330 Africans, 51,438 Asians and 11,424 Coloureds.

Pietro in Vaticano, San, see ST PETER'S.

Piezoelectric Effect, see OSCILLATORS.

Piero della Francesca. The Baptism of Christ, *painted about 1442.*

Pig, any of several mammals in the family Suidae of the order Artiodactyla, the even-toed hoofed mammals. Pigs have four toes, but only two bear the weight of the animals. They are omnivorous, with a simple stomach, and do not chew the cud. A male pig is called a boar, and the female a sow or, when young, a gilt. Another name for pigs is swine.

Wild swine include the babirusa, bushpig, warthog and wild pig. Domestic pigs were first kept about 8000 years ago. They are used for pork and bacon, and for such byproducts as leather, lard, bristles and fertiliser.

Careful breeding over many years has produced breeds with long backs, giving more bacon, and stout hind limbs, making better hams. Of the many breeds several have attained international popularity. The *Large White* or *Yorkshire* is a good bacon pig, and its cross with the Danish *Landrace* now largely dominates the European market. The *Middle White* is an excellent pork pig, as is the *Berkshire*, a type evolved in England, 1850. The *Tamworth*, first bred in Staffordshire, has abundant, golden-red hair, and produces a very high proportion of very lean meat.

Pigs are naturally clean animals, and respond to good housing. Feed accounts for 75 per cent of production costs in pig rearing. If properly kept, pigs should give comparatively little trouble, but they are liable to some diseases, including *swine erysipelas*, caused by a bacterium, and which sometimes leads to death; *nutritional diseases*, especially shortages of vitamins A, D and E; and some parasitic infestations.

Pig Iron, see IRON AND STEEL.

Pig-sticking, a blood sport in which wild boar are pursued by mounted sportsmen armed with spears. It was a common sport in pre-Christian times and in modern times is particularly associated with the British Army in India in the 19th century.

Pigeon, or dove, any member of the family Columbidae, order Columbiformes. This order also includes the extinct dodo, solitaire and passenger pigeons, the tooth-billed pigeon, *Didunculus strigirostris*, of the Samoan Islands, and the beautiful crested crowned pigeons of New Guinea. Common species include the large wood pigeon, or ring-dove, *Columba palumbus*, which often does serious damage to crops; the stock-dove, *C. oenas*; the turtle-dove, *Streptopelia turtur*; and the rock-dove, *Columba livia*, from which many domesticated breeds of pigeons are derived.

Domestic pigeons exist in great variety, all parts of the body having been developed to give the marked characteristics of the different breeds, from the dainty fantail to the pouters and croppers which can distend the crop or pout; from the tiny tumblers to the huge runts. The scandaroon has a long curved beak, the owl a very short and stout one; in the carrier, which is not used like the homer for carrying messages, the beak and eye wattles are enormously developed. The pigeon following is now very large, and a great number of shows are held annually.

Pigeon Pea, see CHICK-PEA.

Pigeon Racing, timed races over various distances by specially trained homing birds derived from the common rock dove. All competing birds are banded and liberated together by a starter who records the time of release. When the birds enter their home lofts the band is removed and placed in a clock which records the time of arrival. The fastest bird wins. The sport originated in Belgium in the early 19th century.

Piggott, Lester Keith (1935–), British jockey; champion flat-racing jockey in 1960 and from 1964 to 1971. He has been successful in many classic races, and in 1977, with his eighth victory, achieved a record number of Derby wins. He often rides in France, where he has won the Prix de l'Arc de Triomphe, and has also won the Washington DC International in America.

Pigment, an insoluble substance which, in a divided form, imparts colour and opacity to other substances such as paints, plastics and rubber. The most important naturally occurring pigments are the earth colours; umbers and siennas (oxides of iron and magnesium) and the ochres (clay with iron oxide). Of the inorganic (manufactured) pigments, the whites are pigments of such metals as lead, zinc and titanium; blacks are basically carbon; yellows may be oxides of iron (the ferrite yellows), lead or zinc salts of chromium, or the cadmium salts of sulphur and selenium. Blues are few in number: Prussian blue is sodium ferrocyanide; aquamarine is manufactured from clays, soda ash, silica and sulphur. Greens are produced by mixing blue and yellow pigments. The Indian and Turkish reds are manufactured oxides of iron. Reds are also prepared from lead chromate and lead molybdate, and from cadmium salts of sulphur and selenium.

Organic pigments can be divided into the toners, or pure dyestuffs, and the lakes, in which the dyestuff is precipitated onto a transparent base such as aluminium hydroxide. The dyestuffs are many and varied and capable of producing an almost infinite variety of colours. Of particular note are the azo-pigments, derivatives of azo-benzene.

Pika, mouse-hare, calling-hare or piping-hare, a tailless mammal in the family Ochotonidae of order Lagomorpha, which also includes the hares and rabbits (family Leporidae). They have short ears, and there are no scent glands in the groin. Pikas are gregarious animals living in burrows and rock crevices in the mountainous regions of central Asia and North America. They lay up stores of food for the winter, but do not hibernate.

Pike, military weapon, consisting of a long shaft or handle with an iron head. As a weapon it has been in use from very ancient times, but the word itself dates from the 15th century.

Pike, members of the genus *Esox*, of the family Esocidae, order Salmoniformes; they are freshwater fishes and occur in the temperate parts of Europe, Asia and America. They are carnivorous, and prey on almost any animal they can obtain, from frogs and fishes to ducklings, rats, voles and newts; their voracity is notorious. The common pike, *E. lucius*, is olive-grey above, silvery below, and has pale spots. It is usually 0·5–1 m long, and weighs about 15 kg. The pike is characterised by the absence of scales on the head, by a long narrow body terminating in a forked caudal fin, and by a long broad, depressed snout. Other names of this species are jack, hake, luce and pickerel. *E. nobilior*, the maskinongy of North America, may grow to a length of 2 m.

Pike-perch, *Lucioperca lucioperca*, a species of fish common in the rivers and lakes of Europe and western Asia, and also found in North America. It may reach as much as 1 m in length. In North America fishes of the genus *Stizostedion* are also known as pike-perches. Both *Lucioperca* and *Stizostedion* are carnivorous, feeding on other fish.

Pilate, Pontius, see PONTIUS PILATE.

Pilatus, mountain of Switzerland, overlooking the southern shore of Lake Lucerne, between the cantons of Lucerne and Unterwalden. The Tomlishorn, its highest point, is 2133 m, and its ascent can be made by means of a railway. Its name is from 'pileatus', meaning capped.

Pilchard, *Sardina pilchardus*, a fish of the family Clupeidae, order Clupeiformes, related to both the herring and the sprat. It grows from 25 to 35 cm; it is bluish-green above, whitish underneath and on its sides. It is entirely marine in habit, and its eggs float near the surface of the sea, unlike those of the herring, which are attached to objects at the bottom. The young pilchard, before it has attained maturity, is known as the sardine, and as such forms a valuable fishery; the full-grown pilchard is used as an article of diet as well as for bait. The method of capture is usually by drift-net. *S. pilchardus* is most abundant off the coasts of Portugal and Morocco, and the English Channel and the Mediterranean.

In Canada, Africa, Australia and New Zealand the name pilchard refers to the genus *Sardinops*, which is closely related to *Sardina*.

Pilcomayo, river of South America. Rising in Bolivia, in the Eastern Cordillera about 96 km north-west of Potosí, it flows south-east through the Sierra region through the Chaco and joins the Río Paraguay a little south of Asunción. Its length is 1280 km.

Pile-driving, see PILING.

Pile Dwellings, see LAKE DWELLINGS.

Pilea, genus in the family Urticaceae. They are dwarf foliage plants with small green leaves. *P. muscosa*, artillery plant, a branching herb of tropical America, is grown as a house plant and has the habit of releasing pollen in a cloud when the stamens spring away from the sepals.

Piles, or haemorrhoids, are varicose conditions of the veins of the lower end of the rectum. They are known as internal or external, according to whether they are situated within or without the sphincter ani, the muscular ring that closes the anal orifice. In the former case they are covered with mucous membrane, and may be so protruded as to escape through the anal orifice; in the latter case they are covered with skin, and may either form hard tumours or discharge as bleeding piles. Piles are a symptom of any condition by which the veins of the lower bowel become congested; habitual constipation, pregnancy, growths in the rectum, and local inflammation. They may appear after a strong effort at defaecation.

Pilgrim, a person who travels to visit holy shrines, tombs or places of religious interest. The practice is found in most religions.

Pilgrim Fathers, a party of 102 Puritans, 74 men and 28 women, members of John Robinson's church at Leyden, who, on 6 September 1620, sailed from Plymouth, England, in the *Mayflower* to seek freedom of worship for their faith in New England. They landed on Plymouth Rock on 16 December 1620, and their settlement later formed part of Massachusetts, USA.

Pilgrimage of Grace, uprising which took place in 1536, in protest against the dissolution of the monasteries, but also against agrarian injustices resulting from the enclosure movement. Its leader was Robert Aske, and it affected all the northern counties, but especially Yorkshire and Lincolnshire. The insurgents, some 30,000 strong, took possession of York and then moved on to Doncaster. Aske persuaded his followers to disperse on promise of a pardon from the king and an investigation of their grievances. Henry lured him to London, and he was tried for high treason and eventually hanged at York (1573). The rising, however, had collapsed the preceding year.

Pilgrims' Way, prehistoric trackway linking East Kent with the Winchester district. It is of early Iron Age date at least and was used extensively in Roman times.

Piling is one of the most important processes in modern engineering, being used as a means of providing foundations for many larger projects. The purpose of piling is to transfer the load from a structure to lower levels in the ground when the upper levels are incapable of sustaining the load.

Piles can be made of timber, but because of rising costs, concrete (generally pre-stressed or precast concrete) is more widely used.

Pill, a small round mass containing one or more medicinal ingredients intended for absorption into the system from the stomach or intestines. It is a form especially applicable to those drugs that are taken in small doses, and recommends itself to most people on account of the ease in swallowing and the comparative absence of disagreeable taste. Any tablet taken for contraceptive purposes is often called 'the Pill'.

See also BIRTH CONTROL.

Pillar, in architecture, signifies any detached vertical mass, whereas a column is, strictly speaking, a pillar of fixed proportions.

See also ORDERS OF ARCHITECTURE.

Pillars of Hercules, see HERCULES, PILLARS OF.

Pillory, instrument for the public punishment of malefactors. It consisted of a wooden frame (with circular holes for the head and arms), in which the prisoner stood. It was abolished in England in 1837.

See also STOCKS.

Pillow Lava, the characteristic form of a submarine lava flow. As lava issues from a submarine vent the outer part of the flow cools and solidifies. Internal pressure from the still molten central portion cracks the outer skin and molten lava flows out of the cracks; the process is then repeated, giving rise to a flow shaped like a pile of globular masses.

Pilot, in shipping, person not belonging to any particular ship, who is authorised to conduct ships through certain rivers, roadsteads or channels, or into certain ports, and who is usually taken on board at a particular place for that purpose only.

Pilot Fish, *Naucrates ductor*, a small sub-tropical fish of the horse-mackerel family in order Perciformes, about 30 cm long, spindle-shaped, steel blue in colour and marked with five to seven dark vertical bars. It owes its name to its habit of accompanying ships and large fish, generally sharks, doubtless for the sake of food, for the pilot fish obtains much of its food from the parasitic crustaceans with which large fish are infested and also from the small pieces of food unregarded by the shark when it rends its prey. There is no truth in the old idea that pilot fish guide ships towards land.

Pilot Weed, see SILPHIUM.

Pilotis (French *pilotis*, stilts), pillars supporting modern reinforced-concrete buildings, and standing free in an open storey at ground-level, often utilised for car-parking.

Pilsen, see PLZEŇ.

Pilsudski, Józef (1863–1935), Polish statesman and soldier. After the armistice in 1918, Pilsudski became chief-of-state of the new Polish republic. In 1920 Pilsudski advanced against the Bolsheviks, but was eventually driven back on Warsaw where he finally defeated the Red Army (August 1920). He retired in 1923. In 1926 he overthrew the government in a military coup. From 1926 until his death he was minister of war, and during this period the Polish constitution was ignored until, in effect, a dictatorship was established.

Piltdown Man, or *Eoanthropus dawsoni*, name given to a series of bones found in Sussex gravel beds between 1908 and 1912 and originally thought to belong to the Early Pleistocene period. Piltdown man played an

important part in theories of human evolution until the 1950s when these fossils were exposed as fakes by newly developed dating methods. The fossils consisted of a jawbone from a young orang-utan, with the teeth filed flat, and portions of a skull. The skull bones were *Homo sapiens* (modern man), but from an ancient deposit; both had been stained to match the Piltdown gravel deposits.
See also MAN.

Pimenta, a genus of highly fragrant trees or shrubs in family Myrtaceae. *P. officinalis*, a shrub, is the pimento-bush or allspice of Jamaica; *P. acris*, a tree, the wild clove or bayberry of the West Indies.

Pimpernel, *Anagallis*, a genus of annual, biennial and perennial plants of trailing habit in family Primulaceae, bearing small, often numerous, flowers. Scarlet pimpernel, or poor man's weatherglass, *A. arvensis*, occurs in cornfields; bog pimpernel, *A. tenella*, is a tiny but beautiful bog plant, while the yellow pimpernel is *Lysimachia nemorum*.

Pimpinella, is a genus of annual and perennial plants in family Umbelliferae, including *P. saxifraga*, burnet saxifrage, and *P. major*. The fruit of *P. anisum* is the aniseed of commerce, and is grown in Mediterranean countries.

Pimple, see PAPULE; RASH.

Pin. The earliest pins were made of thorn, bone or ivory and can be traced back to 30,000 BC. The old form of pin was completed in 18 distinct operations, the head being made separately from the shank. Now the whole process is carried out by automatic machines.

Pinaceae, a family of coniferous trees, containing ten genera and 200 species, chiefly native to temperate regions. Important genera include *Abies*, *Cedrus*, *Larix*, *Picea*, *Pinus* and *Tsuga*.

Pinchbeck, reddish-yellow alloy of approximately 90 per cent copper and 10 per cent zinc. It was used formerly in the manufacture of cheap jewellery and watch-cases and is said to have been invented by Christopher Pinchbeck, an 18th-century London watchmaker.

Pincher, (Henry) Chapman (1914–), British journalist. He joined the *Daily Express* in 1945, being appointed defence, science and medical editor in 1946. He became one of the most famous investigative reporters in British journalism, especially in the defence field, and was given many awards.

Pincherle, Alberto, see MORAVIA, ALBERTO.

Pindar (518–438 BC), Greek choral lyric poet. His works were collected in 17 books, and included hymns, paeans, dithyrambs, processional songs, maiden-songs, hyporchemata, encomia, dirges and epinicians (odes for victors in the Games). These last, in four books, have survived complete. They celebrate victories gained in the Olympian, Pythian, Nemean and Isthmian games. Of his other poetry we have only fragments. Pindar's power lies not in his ideas, which are often naïve and muddled, but in an amazing splendour of language, rhythm and imagery, which has made his poetry impossible to translate, and fatal to imitate.

Pindus, range of mountains in Greece, forming the boundary between Thessaly and Epirus. Maximum height 2336 m.

Pine, *Pinus*, the large and important genus of coniferous tree species in family Pinaceae. Many pines are grown for their timber including the Scots pine (*P. sylvestris*), Corsican pine (*P. nigra* var. *maritima*), Weymouth pine (*P. strobus*), and Monterey pine, (*P. radiata*). The pitch pine (*P. ponderosa*), a native of North America, is perhaps the most valuable of all pines, and besides its valuable timber, it yields turpentine, pitch, tar and resin. The stone pine (*P. pinea*) is cultivated in Italy for its large edible seeds, and the maritime pine (*P. pinaster*) is extensively planted on sand dunes, which it binds together with its roots.

Pine Marten, *Martes martes*, a member of the weasel and badger family, Mustelidae, order Carnivora. It is distributed over the Old World. The body is long and lithe, about 45 cm long, with a tail of about 30 cm. The legs are short; the paws have five digits armed with claws. The fur is dark brown, lighter on the cheeks and on the sharp snout; the throat and under side of the neck are yellow. It is arboreal and frequents coniferous woods, whence its popular name.

Pineal Organ, pineal body or pineal gland, a dorsal outgrowth from the brain, variously called the pineal organ or pineal eye, found only in vertebrates. It has long been suspected of being an endocrine gland and it has now been demonstrated that in at least a few vertebrates its secretions can affect both the reproductive system and the pigment cells in skin. In larval amphibians, such as tadpoles, a known pineal hormone (melatonin) causes the skin pigment cells (melanophores) to contract and lighten the tadpole's colour. Through the pineal organ, the tadpole can perceive how much light is falling on its skin and so alter its colour suitably. In addition, most recent evidence suggests that diurnal rhythms are triggered by the amount of light received by this median 'eye'. In fishes and lizards also, it provides the mechanism by which the animal changes its colour to suit its background, again via melatonin. In reptiles it possibly influences temperature-regulatory behaviour, such as moving from sunlight to shade, and is well developed in the most primitive lizard, the tuatara (*Sphenodon*). In this animal it really resembles a third eye.
In mammals the functions of the pineal are obscure. There is some evidence that in man and rats pineal activity affects gonad growth.

Pineapple, *Ananas comosus*, in the family Bromeliaceae, a tropical and subtropical American fruit-bearing plant. The plant has a rosette of stiff, thick succulent leaves on a short, thick stem. The flowers grow in the centre of the rosette and fuse to form the compound pineapple fruit which is grown in plantations throughout the tropics.

Pinero, Sir Arthur Wing (1855–1934), English playwright. He went on the stage in 1874 and acted with Sir Henry Irving and others until 1881, when he retired and devoted himself exclusively to play-writing. His earlier plays were farces and comedies. *The Profligate*, 1889, was the first of his more serious dramas, and was followed in 1893 by *The Second Mrs Tanqueray*, an intelligent though melodramatic treatment of the 'woman with a past' theme. Encouraged by the success of this 'problem play', Pinero frequently took subjects of considerable importance for his themes, and produced *The Notorious Mrs Ebbsmith*, 1895, *Iris*, 1901, and *Letty*, 1903. *Trelawny of the Wells*, 1898, *The Gay Lord Quex*, 1899, and *Mid-Channel*, 1909, followed, all of them successful and still mildly interesting comedies.

Pink, see CARNATION; DIANTHUS.

Pink Eye, see CONJUNCTIVA AND CONJUNCTIVITIS.

Pink-root, or Indian pink, the common name for certain American species of the genus *Spigelia* in the Loganiaceae, also known as worm grass. Their roots are used in prevention and treatment of intestinal worm infestations.

Pinkerton, Allan (1819–84), US detective. He established the agency in Chicago which bears his name. He was appointed to the US secret service in 1861, and was prominent in many celebrated cases, assisting in breaking up the Molly Maguires.

Pinking, see KNOCKING.

Pinna, a genus of bivalve molluscs; the species are popularly termed wing-shells. Some species attain a length of about 60 cm and the long, delicate byssus (mass of threads by which they attach to rocks) is sometimes woven into cloth or made into gloves and bracelets.

Pinnace, formerly a small two-masted vessel, fully rigged and employed as tender to large ships. Also the name given to an eight-oared, double-banked, pulling and sailing boat formerly carried in capital ships in the Royal Navy. Today the larger warships carry one or more motor pinnaces.

Pinnacle, a pyramidal feature, often ornamented, and commonly crowning a buttress; there it serves a structural purpose because its weight helps to counteract the outward thrust of a vault or roof-truss.

Pinnipedia, see FUR SEAL; SEA-LION; SEAL.

Pinsk, town in Brest *oblast* of the Belorussian SSR, USSR, at the confluence of the Pina and Pripet rivers. It has light and woodworking industries, and is the land reclamation and irrigation centre of Belorussia. Known since 1097, in the 13th century it was the capital of Pinsk principality, then during the 14th century it became Lithuanian, 1569–1793, Polish 1920–39, and Russian 1793–1920. Population (1974) 77,100.

Pint, see METROLOGY.

Pintail Duck, *Anas acuta*, a handsome wild duck in the order Anseriformes. It has a long tail, the two middle feathers of which in the male taper to a sharp point, projecting some 13 cm beyond the others. The head is brown, the upper parts dark grey, with narrow black stripes, and the underparts white. It breeds throughout the northern hemisphere, in Asia, northern Europe and Canada.

Pinter, Harold (1930–), English dramatist, director and actor. His first full-length play, *The Birthday Party*, was badly received by the critics when first performed in London in 1958. It was successfully restaged in 1964, by which time *The Caretaker*, 1959, had been acclaimed as the work of a major talent. His third full-length play, *The Homecoming*, was performed by the Royal Shakespeare Company in 1965, and was followed in 1971 by *Old Times*, in 1975 by *No Man's Land* and in 1979 by *Betrayal*, staged by the National

Theatre. Pinter has written many short plays, some of which were first broadcast on radio or television and later staged: they include *The Room*, 1957; *The Dumb Waiter*, 1960; *A Slight Ache* (staged 1961); *The Collection*, 1961; *Landscape* (first staged 1969); and *Silence*, 1969.

Pinter's plays have been accurately described as 'comedy of menace'. They characteristically feature—at least in his earlier work—the disruption of the banal routine of nondescript characters by mysterious and hostile external forces. His thought and techniques have been influenced by Absurdist drama and particularly by Samuel Beckett.

Pinter has scripted several films, including *The Servant*, *Accident*, *The Go-Between* and *The French Lieutenant's Woman*; and his *The Caretaker* was successfully filmed.

Pintoricchio, Bernardino (Bernardino di Betto), also Pinturicchio (1454–1513), Italian painter. He assisted Perugino with his frescoes in the Sistine Chapel, and was engaged by various members of the Roman nobility to decorate their palaces. He also decorated a whole series of chapels in the church of S. Maria del Popolo in Rome. The most striking of his frescoes are those in the cathedral library at Siena, representing the history of Pope Pius II, and those in the Vatican Borgia Apartments.

Piombo, see SEBASTIANO DEL PIOMBO.

Pion, or pi-meson, see ELEMENTARY PARTICLES.

Piozzi, Hester Lynch (1741–1821), Welsh author. She married in 1763 Henry Thrale, and soon after became a close friend of Dr Johnson, who frequently stayed at the Thrales' house at Streatham, and travelled with them. Thrale died in 1771, and three years later she married Gabriel Piozzi, a musician.

She wrote in 1786 *Anecdotes of the late Samuel Johnson, LL.D.*, and two years later published her correspondence with the great man. She also wrote *The Three Warnings*, 1766, a poem which is said to have been partly Dr Johnson's work. *Thraliana*, 1942, contains her diaries and notebooks from 1766 to 1809.

Pipe (music), general term for any tubular wind instrument, particularly flutes, instruments with reeds and for the pipes of the organ, whose sounds are generated in the same way. Specifically, pipe is the name for the narrow-bored three-holed duct flute used with the tabor. Pipe and tabor was the normal accompaniment to the Morris and other folk dances.

See also FOLK-DANCE; MORRIS DANCE.

Pipe (tobacco). Tubes and primitive pipes for smoking tobacco, as distinct from other plants, were invented in the Americas before the time of Columbus, specimens having been found in ancient Indian mounds. Pipes and tobacco were brought to England by sea captains and colonists in the time of Hawkins and Drake, and the practice of smoking established itself between 1565 and 1590. Sir Walter Raleigh, who perfected a method of curing the leaf, helped to popularise smoking among the courtiers of his day.

See also TOBACCO.

Pipe Roll. Great Roll of the Exchequer, now kept in the Public Record Office, London. The accounts of the revenue collected by the sheriffs are contained in it; these were known as pipes.

Pipefish, the name for several elongated fish of the family Syngnathidae, order Gasterosteiformes, with a small gill opening and a single dorsal but no pelvic fins. The snout is prolonged into a tube, and the mouth is toothless. They are small marine fish, poor swimmers, and live near the coast in temperate and tropical regions. The eggs of some species are carried by the male in a brood pouch on the abdomen or the tail; in others they are embedded in the soft skin of the abdomen. Some species (e.g. *Microphis boaja*) have invaded freshwater rivers.

Pipeline, line or conduit of pipe sometimes many hundreds of kilometres long, by which oil is conveyed from an oil region to a market, or to reservoirs for refining; also a line for carrying compressed air, water (for domestic, industrial, or fire-fighting purposes), town gas, natural gas, sewage, or a line for conveying coal to power stations. There are several hundred large scale mineral pipelines throughout the world carrying coal, limestone, metal concentrates, etc. Water supplies have been piped over long distances since earliest times. Bamboo pipelines were built by the early Chinese, and clay or stone pipelines were widely used in Assyrian, Egyptian, Greek and Roman civilisations.

John Piper. *Impression of Lincoln Cathedral.*

Piper, John (1903–), British painter and writer. His water-colours and striking aquatints of architectural subjects made him famous. He made an important contribution to Festival of Britain designs, 1951, and designed stained glass for Llandaff and Coventry Cathedrals. Piper has also designed décors, including those for Britten's opera *Death in Venice*, and a number of illustrated books.

Piper, a genus in family Piperaceae of tropical shrubs, of which *P. betel*, betel pepper, the source of the betel leaf chewed in Asia, and *P. nigrum*, black or common pepper, are important. *P. cubeba* is the cubeb.

Piperaceae, the pepper family of over 2000 shrubs or herbs with small flowers in spikes, which are followed by somewhat fleshy fruits. The chief genera are *Peperomia* and *Piper*.

Pipette, glass tube drawn to a point at one end and usually provided with a bulb. It is graduated to deliver a specified volume of liquid. In order to fill a pipette the liquid is sucked up until it reaches above the graduation mark on the stem, and the finger is then placed on the upper end. By gradually releasing the pressure the level of the liquid is allowed to fall until coincident with the graduation mark.

Pipistrelle, any member of the bat family Vespertilionidae, genus *Pipistrellus*. There are about 40 species. The common pipistrelle, *P. pipistrellus*, ranges from western Europe to Japan and North Africa. Its body measures only 5 cm in length and its wingspan is 20 to 25 cm. The two most common American pipistrelles, *P. hesperus* and *P. subflavus*, are slightly larger. Female pipistrelles are smaller than the males. Pipistrelles live either singly or in colonies and hibernate for short periods in winter in the extreme north of their range. There is usually only one litter a year of between one and three young. Pipistrelles eat mainly insects.

Pipit, *Anthus*, genus of birds in order Passeriformes characterised by a slender, soberly coloured body and a notched and fairly long beak. The meadow pipit or titlark, *A. pratensis*, is the commonest European species. It is the chief victim of the cuckoo's habit of finding a foster-mother for its eggs. The tree pipit, *A. trivialis*, extends from Europe across central Asia, and the rock pipit, *A. spinoletta*, is found in Europe, Asia and North America.

Piqué, a ribbed cotton fabric, usually white, used for sportswear, dress shirts, shirt fronts, white waistcoats and dress goods.

Piquet, long-established card game, regarded by some as the most skilful of the two-handers. It is played with a pack of 32 cards, all below the sevens being removed. The cards used rank in the whist order. The players cut for deal. The non-dealer is 'Elder Hand'. 'Younger Hand' must deal the cards out either by twos or threes until each has 12. The remaining eight are called the stock. The object of the game formerly was to score 100 points before one's adversary, or nowadays the players may play six deals or a 'partie'. The scoring is by certain combinations, there being three possible scoring combinations, viz. (1) the *point*, i.e. the most of one suit; (2) the *sequence*, i.e. the greatest number of consecutives, not less than three of the same suit; (3) the *quatorze* or *trio*, i.e. four aces, four kings, four queens, or four tens, or three of each. Each player after the deal has a right to reject some of his cards and take others from the 'talon' stock. The actual play follows the ordinary rules of whist, i.e. the scoring is by tricks. Elder Hand begins the play, the dealer, prior to putting his card down, declaring his scoring combination. Much of the character of the game lies in the distinctively complicated method of scoring the combinations and the play.

Piracy. The essence of piracy is 'the pursuit of private as contrasted with public ends', and a pirate or sea-rover is primarily 'a man who satisfies his personal greed or his personal vengeance by robbery or murder in places beyond the jurisdiction of a state'.

In line with international law, English law provides that the courts have jurisdiction over all acts of piracy no matter if the act is committed on the seas or whether the victim of

the act is a British subject or the subject of a friendly foreign state, always provided that the offence is committed within Admiralty jurisdiction. By the Tokyo Convention Act 1967 jurisdiction is extended to give courts jurisdiction for acts of piracy committed anywhere by or against an aircraft.
See also BUCCANEERS; CORSAIRS; PRIVATEERS.

Piraeus (Greek *Piraiéus*), port of Attica, Greece, the seaport of Athens since about 485 BC, important in both ancient and modern times. Themistocles recognised its superiority to Phalerum and persuaded his countrymen to fortify it after the Persian wars, and connect it with Athens (about 8 km north-west) by the famous 'Long Walls'. Sulla destroyed the fortifications (86 BC), and from that time the town sank into obscurity until 1834. It was then rebuilt with arsenal depots, and a naval and military school. It is the largest port in Greece and was until the Second World War the second largest city; its boundaries were then merged with those of Athens and it is officially part of the Athens metropolitan area. It handles 70 per cent of Greece's imports, 40 per cent of its exports, and 90 per cent of passenger traffic. Its industries include chemicals, shipbuilding, engineering, milling, oil refining and distilling. Population (1971) 187,400.

Pirandello, Luigi (1867–1936), Italian novelist and playwright. His first book, *Mal Gioconda* (poems), appeared in 1889, and during the next 30 years he produced novels and short stories, numbering some four hundred. In 1910 Pirandello began writing for the stage, turning many of his short stories into plays. It is as a dramatist that he earned a European reputation, both for the technical brilliance and originality of his method and for his metaphysical choice of subject. His recurrent preoccupation was the impossibility of any absolute objective reality, and the relative nature of personality. His best-known plays are *Sei Personaggi in Cerca d'Autore*, 1921 (*Six Characters in Search of an Author*, 1929); *Enrico Quarto*, 1922; and *Ciascuno a Suo Modo*, 1924. Besides plays and stories he wrote *L'Umorismo*, 1908, a study in humour. Pirandello was awarded the Nobel Prize for literature in 1934.

Piranesi, Giovanni Battista (1720–78), Italian engraver, architect and archaeologist. He published numerous books of engravings on the antiquities of Rome which stress the awe-inspiring qualities of Roman architecture, which he loved and studied profoundly, and championed against Winckelmann. His prints won great popularity and helped shape the Romantic attitude towards Rome. Today he is perhaps even more esteemed for his *Carceri d'Invenzione* (*Imaginary Prisons*) etchings. Although trained as an architect, he designed only one building, S. Maria del Priorato in Rome.

Piranha, South American fish, genus Serrasalmus, which is in the carp order, Cypriniformes, of the bony fishes. Most are shorter than 60 cm, silvery to black, with sharp teeth. They swim in groups and attack and eat other fish. When an animal, or person, falls into the water the piranhas attack it, biting off pieces until only the skeleton is left.

Pirquet von Cesenatico, Clemens Peter, Freiherr (1874–1929), Austrian physician. In 1907 he introduced the *Pirquet test*, a skin reaction for the diagnosis of tuberculosis. He published work of fundamental importance on allergy, a term which he himself suggested; his writings on this subject include *Die Serumkrankheit* (with B. Schick), 1905; *Klinische Studien über Vakzination und Allergie*, 1907. He also published *Allergie des Lebensalters, die Bösartigen Geschwülste*, 1930, a study of the age and sex incidence of cancer.

Pisa. The Leaning Tower, 54 m high, leans a little more each year because of poor foundations.

Pisa (ancient *Pisae*), Italian city and capital of Pisa province, situated on both banks of the Arno, 70 km south-west of Florence. Once subject to Rome, it was a powerful and independent republic by the 11th century, and included Corsica, Sardinia and the Balearic Islands in its dominions. The crushing defeat of the Pisan fleet by the Genoese fleet off Meloria in 1284 robbed the city of its power. In 1399 it came into the hands of the Visconti, who sold it to Florence in 1405. The most famous of the magnificent buildings of Pisa are grouped together on the Piazza del Duomo in the north of the city: the marble archiepiscopal cathedral (begun 1063), the Campanile, or 'Leaning Tower', begun in 1173, the baptistry (begun 1153) and the Campo Santo. Pisa depends on the glass, textile and engineering industries, and tourism. Galileo was born here. Population (1979) 103,772.

Pisanello, Antonio (c.1395–1456), Italian painter and greatest of Italian medallists. His delightful and popular *Vision of St Eustace* (National Gallery, London) shows his exceptional sympathy for birds and animals, and his animal drawings are masterpieces of their kind. He worked on medals for Ferrara and other courts, and executed portraits of many of the princes of his time.

Pisano Andrea (c.1270–1348), Italian sculptor, real name A. de Pontedera, a pupil of, but not related to, Giovanni Pisano (see below). He settled in Florence and became famous as a worker in bronze and marble. Pisano executed the door of the baptistery in Florence and the bas-reliefs designed by Giotto for the lower storey of the campanile. His two sons, Nino and Tommaso, were also sculptors of ability. He became *capomaestro* (architect) of Florence Cathedral in 1336, and of Orvieto Cathedral in 1347.

Pisano, Giovanni, also Pisani (c.1245–1314), Italian sculptor and architect. He assisted his father Nicolò Pisano (see below) and was *capomaestro* (architect) of Pisa Cathedral. He designed the façade of Siena Cathedral (from 1284), introducing Gothic elements from France, was responsible for some of the carvings on Pisa baptistery and the great pulpits at Pistoia and Pisa Cathedral, and executed numerous statues.

Pisano, Nicolò, also Pisani, Nicola (c.1215–1278), Italian sculptor and architect. He carved the pulpit of the baptistery at Pisa and that of the cathedral at Siena. He and his son Giovanni (see above) were largely responsible for initiating the great revival and development of sculpture in Italy.

Pisces, 'the Fishes', an inconspicuous equatorial constellation and 12th sign of the zodiac which is usually represented as two fishes linked by a cord joining their tails.

Piscina (Latin, fish-pond, swimming-tank), originally a pond, tank or cistern of any kind; in ecclesiastical usage a small sink or perforated stone basin (French *cuvette*) in a niche south of the altar, at which the water used for the ablution of the chalice is poured away. They were rare in England till the 13th century.

Pisistratus (d.527 BC), tyrant of Athens. In 561 BC, he made himself tyrant, but he was expelled. Pisistratus retired to Macedonia, where he owned silver mines, and accumulated a fortune sufficient for him to return to Athens in 546 with the help of foreign mercenaries. He remained in power until his death in 527.
In the reign of Pisistratus and his sons, Athens was better governed than at any other time in her history. He had the support of all classes of society. Trade flourished in his reign, transforming Athens from a largely agricultural community to one based on trade and commerce. In this way he laid the foundations of the prosperity of Athens in the 5th century.
Pisistratus was a notable patron of the arts and of literature, and was believed in antiquity to have been responsible for the first written text of Homer.

Pisolite, see OOLITE.

Pissarro, Camille (1830–1903), French painter. He was influenced by Corot and Millet, becoming a notable member of the Impressionist school. In 1870 he went to England with Monet and painted a number of pictures of Sydenham and Upper Norwood; from 1874 he exhibited regularly with the Impressionist group. In 1885–88 he adopted the *pointilliste* technique, influenced by Seurat's optical theories. His most typical pictures are of the French countryside and peasant life, though he painted some brilliant impressions of the Paris boulevards.
See also IMPRESSIONISM.

Pissarro, Lucien (1863–1944), French artist, painter and wood-engraver. At 20 he left France and settled in London, where he set up the Eragny Press and produced finely printed volumes illustrated with his own woodcuts or engravings. His paintings, impressionist in manner, showed a feeling for the English countryside.

Pistacia, a genus of small trees of the Anacardiaceae from western Asia. *P. vera*, the pistachio-nut tree, bears small oval nuts containing an edible green kernel. *P. lentiscus* is the mastic tree, yielding the mastic of commerce. *P. terebinthus*, the turpentine tree, yields Chian or Cyprus turpentine, which exudes from incisions made in the trunk.

Pistil, see FLOWER.

Pistoia (ancient *Pistoria*), Italian town and capital of Pistoia province, some 28 km north-west of Florence. The older walled part of the town stands on a ridge of the Apennines. During the Middle Ages it was an important town (especially for banking), and it became part of the domain of the Medici in 1530. The cathedral (partly 12th century) contains a famous altar of silver. Pistoia has a wide range of industries including railway engineering, weaving, leather, cement and bedding. Population (1974) 55,400; municipality (1971) 94,000.

Pistol, any small firearm which can be held and fired with one hand and use for target shooting or close-range combat. It is widely accepted that the pistol took its name from the Italian city of Pistoia where it first became popular. Pistols were introduced in the early 16th century shortly after the invention of an effective wheel lock.

The automatic pistol was developed at the end of the 19th century, and owing to its higher rate of fire and greater accuracy it has replaced the revolver as a standard military weapon. Well-known military makes of pistol are the Mauser, Colt, Browning, Luger, Walther and Beretta.

See also FIREARMS.

Pistol Shooting is divided into two categories—rapid fire and free. In rapid fire, competitors fire 60 shots in groups of five at a target approximately representing the human form, measuring 160 cm by 45 cm and placed at a distance of 25 m. The target is divided into ten different scoring zones, with point values of between 1 and 10. The targets are presented face-on to the competitor for periods of either 8, 6, or 4 seconds, during which a group of five shots must be fired. The targets are then turned side-on, before again coming face-on for a further group of shots. Free pistol shooting is over a 50 m distance at a target 50 cm wide. Sixty shots, in groups of 10, are fired at this target, which unlike the one used in rapid fire shooting, does not move. Targets are graded in concentric circles, scoring 1 to 10. In each event, 5·6 mm calibre pistols are used; the competitor with the highest points total wins.

See also RIFLE SHOOTING.

Piston, Walter (1894–1976), US composer. His music is clear and finely disciplined, having some affinities with Stravinsky. Among his works are eight symphonies, concertos and other orchestral pieces, the ballet *The Incredible Flutist*, and a body of chamber music.

Piston, see INTERNAL COMBUSTION ENGINE; STEAM ENGINE.

Pit Vipers, see RATTLESNAKES.

Pitcairn Island, island in the Pacific Ocean, nearly equidistant from Australia and America, 25° 3′S latitude, 130° 8′W longitude. It is a British colony and, actually, the first British-acquired land in the South Seas. It has an area of 5 km². Its length is about 4 km, its width 1·6 km, and the coast is very rocky and inaccessible in most parts. Pitcairn Island has a fine climate; the soil is generally fertile, producing coconuts, bananas, breadfruit, yams, pineapples, tomatoes, etc. Oranges and pineapples are exported. It was discovered by Captain Carteret in his sloop *Swallow* (1767), who named it Pitcairn after the midshipman who sighted it. After his return to England Carteret published an account of the *Swallow*'s voyage: and there was a copy of the book in His Majesty's Armed Vessel *Bounty* when she sailed from Spithead in 1787. The island remained unoccupied until 1790, when it was occupied by the mutineers of the *Bounty*, under Fletcher Christian, first officer and leader of the mutineers, with some women from Otaheite. Pitcairn Island was brought within the jurisdiction of the high commissioner for the West Pacific in 1898, and in 1902 there were annexed to it the unhabited islands of Henderson, Ducie and Oneo, occasionally visited by the Pitcairners for the collection of wood and other purposes. The group is administered by the Governor in consultation with an Island Council. The Pitcairners elect their Island Council annually by popular vote of all the islanders over 18. The chief magistrate who presides over the Council is elected triennially. From 1952–70 the Governor of Fiji acted as Governor of Pitcairn. When Fiji became independent in 1970 the British High Commissioner in New Zealand became Governor of Pitcairn.

See also 'BOUNTY', MUTINY OF THE.

Camille Pissarro. A Corner of the Meadow at Eragny, *painted in 1902.*

Pitcairnia, a genus of perennial herbs in family Bromeliaceae, most from tropical America. Some species bear flowers in racemes of great beauty, and narrow or sword-shaped spiny leaves. Several species, including *P. corallina*, are grown.

Pitch, or inclination of a sloping roof, is reckoned as an angle with the horizontal, either in degrees, e.g. '30 degrees pitch', or as a ratio of rise to span, e.g. 'a pitch of 1:4'.

Pitch, the black residue obtained on the distillation of coal tar. The term is sometimes also used for the residue left on the distillation of petroleum, and for the naturally occurring petroleum residue found in Trinidad and elsewhere. The former is correctly termed 'bitumen' and the latter 'asphalt'; the term pitch should be confined to the residue from tar.

Pitch, exact height (or depth) of any musical sound according to the number of vibrations that produce it; also the standard by which notes are to be tuned. Pitch varied at different times and in different countries until the establishment in the first half of the 20th century of the internationally agreed standard of a frequency of 440 cycles per second for the A in the treble clef.

Pitchblende, or uraninite, the name given to the massive form of the uranium dioxide mineral, uraninite (UO_2).

Pitcher Plant, name given to plants having more or less cylindrical modified leaves which trap insects and similar small animals, digesting the bodies and absorbing nourishment from them. Insects are attracted by the plant's sweet secretions and red and green patterns. Having entered the 'pitcher', they are prevented from escaping by a toothed, overhanging rim, downward-pointing hairs and a smooth, waxy interior surface. The victims ultimately fall into the digestive fluid secreted by glands at the base of the trap. Botanically, the pitcher plants are placed in several genera, not all closely related to each other, including *Cephalotus*.

See also CEPHALOTACEAE; DARLINGTONIA CALIFORNICA.

Pitchstone, an acid igneous intrusive rock forming small dykes and sills.

Pithecanthropus erectus, name given to a group of *Homo erectus* found in Java by Eugène Dubois.

See also ANTHROPOLOGY; HOMO ERECTUS; MAN.

Pitlochry, town and health resort in Perth and Kinross District, Tayside Region, Scotland, on the River Tummel. Pitlochry is the centre of the Tummel-Garry hydroelectric scheme, and has distilling and tweed-making industries. Population (1981) 2610.

Pitt the Elder, William, 1st Earl of Chatham (1708–78), English statesman. In 1735 he entered Parliament as member for the family borough of Old Sarum. Pitt soon took an active part in the debates of the House of Commons, and his great powers of oratory quickly earned him a high reputation. He had, however, to struggle against the king's dislike, which blocked his political progress for a long time. Under Pelham he was appointed early in 1746 joint vice-treasurer of Ireland, but in May of the same year he was promoted to the position of paymaster-general of the forces.

On Pelham's death, Pitt had hoped to lead the House of Commons, and, disappointed in his ambition, he attacked the new leader, Sir Thomas Robinson, and the new prime minister, the Duke of Newcastle. He was dismissed late in 1755, but a year later he was invited to form an administration. In April 1757, dismissed by the king, he was, after a few weeks, recalled to power, and held office until October 1761. It was during this period that he was able to give the fullest proofs of his ability as a war minister, for he had returned with full powers to direct the Seven Years' War and to take charge of foreign affairs. His efforts were to secure Britain its North American empire, and to raise British prestige to a level unknown for a hundred years. In July 1766, Pitt was invited to form another administration, but was not well enough to do more than take the sinecure office of lord privy seal in his own ministry. This necessitated his accepting a peerage—a step that made him for a time very unpopular.

Pitt the Younger, William (1759–1806), British statesman, the younger son of William Pitt, 1st Earl of Chatham. He entered Parliament in 1781. His maiden speech, in favour of Burke's bill for economical reform, on 26 February, drew extravagant praise from Burke, Fox and North. He became chancellor of the Exchequer under Shelburne in 1782. When Shelburne resigned the next year, the king offered Pitt the Treasury, but Pitt declined as he could not then command the necessary support. A coalition ministry formed by North and Fox was defeated in December on the India Bill, and then Pitt, being still under 25 years of age, became first lord of the Treasury and chancellor of the Exchequer. His youth was against him, and he was in a minority in the House of Commons. He held to office until he felt he had the country with him, and then, in 1784, called a general election, which gave him a large majority.

He now devoted his attention to the finances of the nation. Among the measures he introduced was the institution of a sinking fund for the reduction of the national debt. He maintained a neutral attitude towards the French Revolution, but in 1793 France declared war on Britain, and then Pitt entered into alliances with many great European powers, and aided the coalition with large grants for the hiring of troops. The British navy was successful in its battles, but the coalition suffered severely on land, and there was much dissatisfaction at home, where the mob clamoured for Pitt's resignation. He effected the union of Great Britain and Ireland in 1800, but in the following year resigned office owing to the opposition of the king to a measure of Catholic emancipation. When war broke out again in May 1803, it was evident that the Addington ministry could not prosecute it effectively and a year later Pitt was again called to lead the country. He formed a third coalition, but Spain joined France, and the allied forces could not make headway against the combination. The capitulation of Ulm broke up the coalition, and it is said that the battle of Austerlitz was his death-blow.

Pitt the Younger, painted by Hoppner, 1805.

It was the ambition of Pitt to be a peace minister, and to devote himself to progressive domestic legislation, but it was his destiny from 1793 to be a war minister, and a war minister during a period of terrific conflict; as a result he felt forced to pursue a policy of domestic repression which has been much criticised.

Pitt-Rivers, Augustus Henry (1827–1900), British soldier and archaeologist. On succeeding to the Rivers estates at Rushworth in 1880 he instituted numerous scientifically conducted excavations, which he described in *Excavations in Cranborne Chase* (4 vols), 1887–98. Pitt-Rivers laid the foundations of modern excavation technique with its emphasis on accurate plans and relic-tables, the significance of stratification, the use of percussion to determine silted pits and ditches, and the great importance of common everyday objects.

Pittosporaceae, a dicotyledonous family of 200 shrubs and trees, chiefly Australian, with leathery, evergreen leaves, five-petalled flowers and capsular or berry fruits. *Billardiera*, *Pittosporum* and *Sollya* are typical genera, with species in cultivation.

Pittsburgh, second city of Pennsylvania, USA, situated near the western border of the state, at the confluence of the Monongahela and Allegheny rivers, which here join to form the Ohio. Both rivers are entrenched in deep valleys in the Allegheny plateau, and the suburbs of the city rise onto the heights above the rivers, leaving the valley bottoms in the occupation of industries and railway yards. The French built Fort Duquesne here in 1754. In 1758, when the elder William Pitt was prime minister of Britain, the British under General Forbes advanced on the fort, and the French destroyed it in the face of his advance. It was promptly renamed Fort Pitt, and the site of the fort is preserved today. Pittsburg became a synonym for iron and steel, particularly after the arrival in the 1860s of Andrew Carnegie. The industry drew to the city a large immigrant population which supplied its manpower, often working under very poor conditions; bitter industrial strife marred its record-breaking achievements in the manufacture of steel.

Pittsburgh remains a communication centre of great importance for road, rail, air and water, and is one of the largest inland ports in the world, with a busy trade. Population (1980) 423,938.

Pituitary Gland, an endocrine gland situated at the base of the brain responsible for the production of at least eight hormones: (1) growth hormone, (2) adrenocorticotrophic hormone (ACTH), (3) thyroid-stimulating hormone (TSH), (4) luteinising hormone (LH), (5) follicle stimulating hormone (FSH), (6) prolactin, (7) oxytocin, and (8) antidiuretic hormone (ADH). The first six hormones are made by the anterior pituitary (adenohypophysis), the last two by the posterior pituitary (neurohypophysis).

See also Hypothalamus.

Pius XI, Achille Ratti (b.1857), Pope, 1922–39. In 1921 he was created archbishop of Milan and a cardinal. His most outstanding achievement was the solution of the 'Roman Question' in 1929 by the Lateran treaty which restored the temporal power of the papacy and established a concordat between the Church and the Italian government. He protested against the pagan worship of the state in Fascist Italy, and the violation of natural law and justice in Nazi Germany. He also spoke out against atheistic communism which he condemned as 'a gospel full of errors and illusions'.

Pius XII, Eugenio Pacelli (b.1876), Pope, 1939–58. He was Pius XI's chief adviser in the latter's anti-Nazi policy. He made many vain efforts to prevent the Second World War by offers of mediation, though some now doubt his neutrality. He attempted to prevent Mussolini from taking Italy into the war, and after the close of fighting made efforts to aid the re-establishment of religion in Germany. He continually and strenuously opposed the ecclesiastical policy of Communist countries in Eastern Europe.

Pixy, or pixie, name given to one kind of fairy in Devon and Cornish folklore. Pixies were believed to kidnap children and to lead travellers astray.

Pizarro, Francisco (1478–1541), Spanish discoverer and conqueror of Peru. In early life he became a soldier and went to America. Among other expeditions, he took part in those of Vasco Nuñez de Balboa. When he had already served for 14 years he joined in a project for extending Spanish conquests along the south coast. In 1524 he sailed from Panama with a single ship and about 100 men. The expedition was not successful, and Pizarro returned in 1528 to Panama, and then to Spain. It was agreed that he could appoint himself governor over all the land he discovered, with supreme authority in all matters. The new expedition started in 1531, and Pizarro was now successful, completing the conquest of Peru between 1531 and 1541.

Pizzicato, term used in music for bowed string instruments, to denote that the strings are to be plucked with the fingers instead of sounded with the bow.

Place, Francis (1771–1854), British reformer. He was a friend of Robert Owen, Mill, Bentham and Hume. It was largely Place's agitation that brought about the repeal of the Combination Acts in 1824; but after the passing of the Reform Bill in 1832 his political influence declined.

Place-names, see NAME.

Placebo, a pharmacologically inactive substance administered either in the treatment of psychological illness or in the course of drug trials, depending for its effect on the power of suggestion rather than any inherent pharmacological property. Placebos are used in research and in double-blind clinical trials of new drugs, in which neither the patient nor the physician knows which is the drug and which the placebo. Chalk and lactose are often used as placebos.

Placenta, or after-birth, the structure which unites the foetal mammal to the womb of the mother until birth. Both foetal and maternal blood circulate in the placenta, establishing a nutritive connection. The connection is, however, merely by diffusion; as a rule there is no actual intermingling of foetal and maternal blood. It occurs as a double vascular sponge, which enables the foetus to obtain nourishment and oxygen from the blood of the mother, and to remove its waste (excretory) products. The foetus is connected to the placenta by the umbilical cord which has two arteries and one vein. The placenta is shed at birth.

Placenta, in botany, the swollen part of the carpel that bears the ovules.
See also FLOWER.

Placentation, the arrangement of the ovules in the ovary. Placentation is parietal when ovules are borne on the outer walls of the ovary, axile when in the angles formed by the meeting of the septa (dividing walls) in the middle of the ovary, basal when at the base of the ovary, apical when at the apex, and free central when on a column arising from the base.
See also FLOWER.

Placodermi, one of the five classes of fish. It is entirely extinct, having been most common during the Devonian period. Placoderms slightly resembled sharks or rays, but the head and the fore-part of the trunk were covered by bony protective plates. Most were small, 10 to 40 cm long, but a few reached several metres. There are six orders, classified mainly on the characteristics of the bony shielding plates.

Plague, a term often applied to any highly infectious disease of man occurring in epidemic or pandemic form, but properly restricted to that disease caused by the bacterium *Yersinia pestis* (formerly *Pasteurella pestis*) first discovered by Yersin and Kitasato in 1894. The plague bacillus exists among wild rodents, and becomes transmitted to man by the vector *Xenopsylla cheopis*, a rat-flea, which when infective may bite the skin, simultaneously injecting the microbes, and resulting in the formation of painfully swollen lymph nodes in the groin or armpit, which are called *buboes*. Bloodborne spread of the organism is usual, with fever, debilitating headache, often signs of delirium, disorientation, haemorrhages into the skin, signs of shock, and sometimes rigors (shivering). A form of meningitis may occur, and a terminal pneumonia is frequent. This bubonic form of the disease may be acquired also through contact with infected material from animals or man.
The *pneumonic* type of disease has a fatal outcome within 5 days if untreated, and is transmitted by inhalation of droplets carrying the bacteria that are coughed or sneezed out by the patient. Overcrowding and poor nutrition lead to a more rapid spread than would otherwise be the case, especially where pneumonic disease is found.

Plaice, *Pleuronectes platessa*, a flat-fish of order Pleuronectiformes, which occurs in the northern North Atlantic. The mouth is small, the scales smooth and minute; it varies from brown to black with bright red or orange spots above, and is white beneath. The eyes are on the right side. The average weight is about 1 kg, and though 37 cm is about the average length, specimens twice as large are sometimes caught. The female spawns early in the year, producing an enormous number of buoyant eggs.

Plaid, see HIGHLAND DRESS; TARTAN.

Plaid Cymru (Welsh, Party of Wales), Welsh political movement dedicated to separation from and independence of the United Kingdom in order to safeguard the culture, language and economic life of Wales.

Plain. The term is used in two contexts depending upon the scale of the landform. The small-scale, and strict, usage denotes a tract of land with only very minor variations in relief, e.g. floodplain, peneplain and pediplain. At the global scale a plain denotes a flat land which may be composed of numerous smaller plains of diverse origin. Plains occupy about 55 per cent of the Earth's land surface. Their origin is very complex: peneplains are formed by extensive weathering and erosion by rivers, and pediplains by the coalescing of numerous pediments in semi-arid areas. The largest plains currently being formed include those associated with some of the world's major rivers i.e. the Ganges, the Mississippi, the Volga and the Murray.
See also TOPOGRAPHY.

Plainsong, or plainchant, music used chiefly in the churches of the Roman Catholic communion for the greater part of the liturgy. In the early Church there were several forms of plainsong, but the Roman form gradually supplanted the others, and acquired the name of Gregorian Chant on account of the tradition that it was systematised and perfected by St Gregory the Great (590–604). During the period of polyphonic church music, from the 12th to the 16th centuries, plainsong melodies were used as a cantus firmus.

Plaintiff. In English law the plaintiff is the party who sues in a civil action, the party who is sued being the defendant. In Scotland, the parties are styled 'pursuer' and 'defender' respectively.

Planarian, non-parasitic flatworms of the class Turbellaria which, with Monogenea, Digenea and Cestoda, comprise the phylum Platyhelminthes. They are usually small, flat, soft creatures, common both in fresh water and in the sea, where they may be found under rocks and stones in pools. Some of them are brilliantly coloured. A common freshwater planarian is black, and may often be seen like a drop of black sealing-wax on the leaves of aquatic plants. It feeds on insects, small molluscs and worms. The mouth is on the underside of the body, the digestive system varies from a simple bulb-like pharynx to a many-branched intestine, and the skin is furnished with the protective vibrating hairs or cilia whence the name Turbellaria is derived. Planarians multiply sexually and also by division. The parasitic flukes appear to be derived from this group.

Planchon, Roger (1931–), French director and dramatist. Planchon is currently director of the Théâtre National Populaire. His avowed aim is to win a mass audience for the theatre by producing classic plays in ways which are comprehensible to, and entertaining for, the theatrically unsophisticated. To do so he has made much use of the theories and practice of Antonin Artaud and Bertold Brecht. Among his most notable productions have been those of *Henry IV*, Marlowe's *Edward II* and Dumas' *The Three Musketeers*.

Planck, Max Karl Ernst Ludwig (1858–1947), German physicist. In 1889 he was appointed professor of experimental physics at Berlin, and from 1913 to 1914 he was rector of Berlin University. Planck received the Nobel Prize for physics in 1918. Kirchhoff, under whom Planck had studied, had shown that, in an enclosure where all the objects were at the same temperature, the heat radiation was divided between different parts of the spectrum in a way that was independent of their nature. Planck set himself to discover the formula relating the energy of particular wavelengths with the wavelengths and temperature, using as a guide the accurate measurements made by Lummer and Pringsheim. Thus in 1900 Planck initiated the quantum theory, now one of the foundations of physics, with applications in nearly every branch of the subject.

Planck's Constant, a universal constant, $h = 6{\cdot}63 \times 10^{-34}$ J s, recurring throughout the quantum theory of matter. In many situations (e.g. for electrons in atoms) certain physical quantities (e.g. energy and angular momentum) are restricted to taking only certain, discrete values and not a continuous range of possible values. The values involve h, which thus places a size on the minimum values or smallness of these quantities. For instance, atoms radiate light in quanta or photons of energy hc/λ, where c is the velocity of light and λ the wavelength (or colour) of the light. For sodium street lamps, $\lambda = 5{\cdot}4 \times 10^{-7}$ m and the energy hc/λ of an individual photon is $3{\cdot}7 \times 10^{-19}$J so that a 100-watt

sodium lamp is emitting $100/(3{\cdot}7 \times 10^{-19}) = 2{\cdot}7 \times 10^{20}$ photons per second. Owing to the smallness of h, the light thus seems to be emitted as a continuous flow of energy, and we do not notice the discreteness of the individual photons.
See also QUANTUM THEORY; UNCERTAINTY PRINCIPLE.

Plane, name used in England for trees of the genus *Platanus*; in Scotland the name is sometimes used for *Acer pseudoplatanus*, the English sycamore. *Platanus*, the main genus of the family Platanaceae, typically has a thick waxy cuticle and bark which flakes off annually in patches from the trunk and larger branches. The London plane is well-suited to urban areas, being resistant to smoke and other air pollution; it is a hybrid (*P. × hispanica*) between *P. orientalis* from the Middle East and the North American *P. occidentalis*. Americans call the latter tree buttonwood or, confusingly, sycamore. The timber of *Platanus* is a valuable hardwood, tough, with a fine, straight grain.

Plane, in carpentry, a cutting and surface-smoothing tool, of which there are many varieties according to the nature of the surface they are required to produce: (1) planes for producing smooth surfaces of indefinite width; (2) planes used to form plane surfaces of definite and usually narrow width; and (3) planes designed to produce curved or moulded surfaces. Electric portable planes are now available.

Planetarium, originally a mechanical model of the planetary system; nowadays a building in which an elaborate optical projector forms images of the heavenly bodies on a hemispherical ceiling, demonstrating their apparent motions. The Zeiss planetarium was developed about 1924, and planetaria are now found in many cities, including over 60 in the USA alone.

Planets, the collective name given to nine of the larger members of the solar system that move round the Sun in almost circular orbits that are nearly coplanar. Originally the name, which is derived from the Greek and signifies 'wanderers', was applied to the seven bright heavenly bodies which were the only ones that could be seen to change their positions on the stellar background. Two of these seven, the Sun and the Moon, are no longer regarded as planets, but to the other five (Mercury, Venus, Mars, Jupiter and Saturn) have now been added the Earth, Uranus, Neptune and Pluto.
The planets are usually divided into two groups: Mercury, Venus, Earth and Mars, being comparable in size and density, are known as the 'terrestrial' planets; while Jupiter, Saturn, Uranus and Neptune, which are much greater in size, but of considerably lower density, are referred to as the 'major' planets. Pluto stands alone; by position it should be a major planet, by size a terrestrial one. It has been suggested that Pluto is not really a foundation member of the planetary system, but as its orbit indicates, a satellite of Neptune that has broken free. Nor does it obey Bode's law, that unexplained empirical relation that exists between the size of a planet's orbit and its position in the sequence of the planets outwards from the Sun, viz., the approximate distance of a planet from the Sun is given in astronomical units by $0{\cdot}4 + 0{\cdot}3 \times 2^n$, where $n = -\infty$ for Mercury, 0 for Venus, 1 for the Earth, 2 for Mars, 3 for the minor planets, 4 for Jupiter, 5 for Saturn, and 6 for Uranus. Neptune is somewhat closer than this 'law' would suggest, while Pluto is very much closer. All the planets have to obey Kepler's laws as these are a direct consequence of Newton's law of universal gravitation.
See also ASTRONOMY; CONJUNCTION; OPPOSITION.

Plankton (Greek *planktos*, wandering), name given to plants and animals found floating or drifting in water. Many plankton are colourless or faintly bluish, inconspicuous, gelatinous and transparent. Marine plankton are much richer than freshwater plankton in both kind and number of species. The number increases in fairly still water, and consequently lakes and ponds have more plankton than rivers. The plankton plants (phytoplankton) are small and many are unicellular. Some float passively, some can swim by means of flagella or cilia. Most of the algal groups are represented in the phytoplankton, but among the commonest are the diatoms, which are of many diverse forms, and the desmids (microscopic freshwater algae). The phytoplankton constitutes the ultimate food source of all aquatic animals, so the types and number of aquatic fauna depend on the phytoplankton. The animals (zooplankton) consist chiefly of Protozoa, Crustacea, Mollusca, Echinodermata, eggs of fish and other animals, larvae, and a few pelagic worms, e.g. *Sagitta*, the arrow worm. Great numbers of the phosphorescent protozoan, *Noctiluca*, form luminous areas in the sea. The plankton varies not only seasonally, but also in adjacent small areas and at different depths of water. Economically and ecologically, the importance of plankton cannot be overemphasised. It comprises the bulk of all aquatic living matter and directly or indirectly all animal life in the oceans is dependent on phytoplankton productivity. Thus, fishery success depends upon a healthy plankton population, and pollution, which affects the plankton, poses a threat to the whole sea.

Plant Classification, see CLASSIFICATION OF PLANTS.

Plant Diseases are of enormous economic importance, because the effects of epidemics on the yields of food crops can be catastrophic —for example the great Irish potato famine of the 1840s, caused by the potato blight fungus *Phytophthora infestans*. The main diseases are caused by groups of specialised living plant *pathogens*, including viruses, bacteria and fungi.
Viruses are often transmitted by insects or other plant pests acting as vectors. They cause a number of important diseases including tobacco mosaic, several potato diseases, sugar beet yellows, swollen shoot of cacao, and peanut rosette disease. Bacteria are relatively unimportant, but cause such diseases as black-arm in cotton, fire blight in pears, and crown

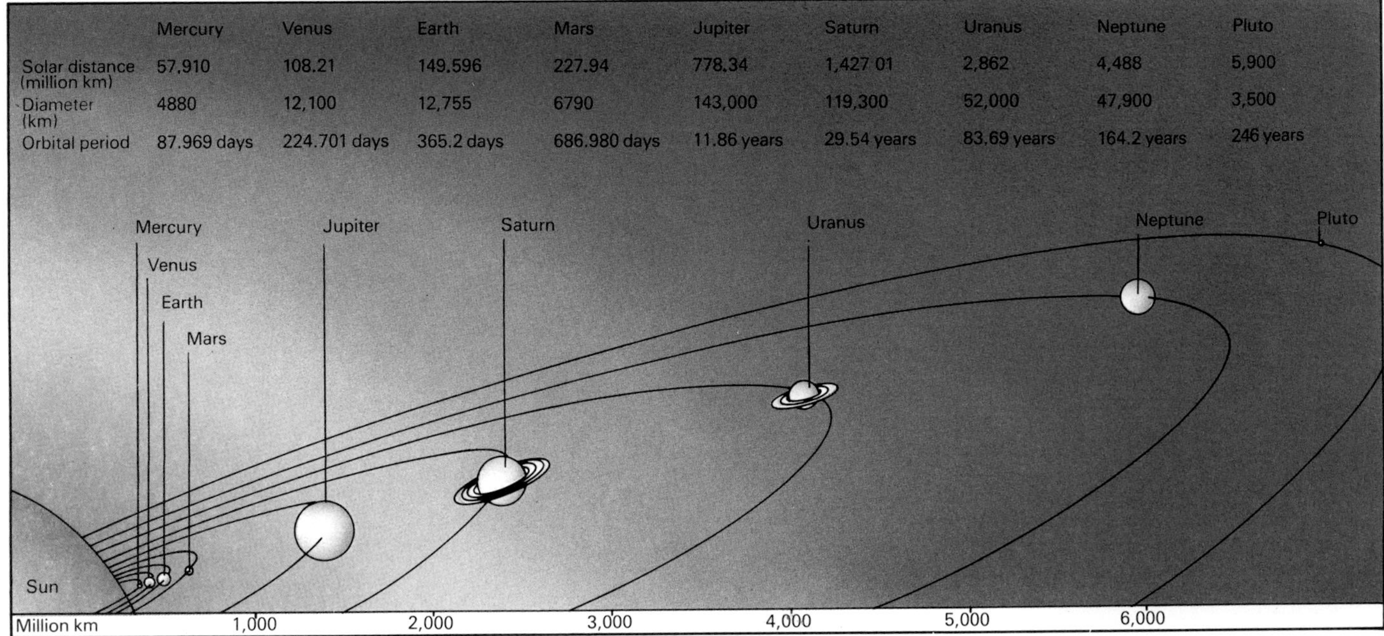

	Mercury	Venus	Earth	Mars	Jupiter	Saturn	Uranus	Neptune	Pluto
Solar distance (million km)	57.910	108.21	149.596	227.94	778.34	1,427 01	2,862	4,488	5,900
Diameter (km)	4880	12,100	12,755	6790	143,000	119,300	52,000	47,900	3,500
Orbital period	87.969 days	224.701 days	365.2 days	686.980 days	11.86 years	29.54 years	83.69 years	164.2 years	246 years

Planets. *The nine planets of the solar system reach out nearly 6000 million km from the Sun. (The Sun and planets are not drawn to scale.)*

gall. The largest number of plant pathogens are fungi. Diseases caused by fungi include the smuts and rust of grasses and cereals; silver leaf in plum; root rot; club-root in cabbage; potato blight; apple scab; brown rot; powdery mildew; and the damping-off disease of seedlings. Chemical sprays against pathogens and disease-carrying insects are very effective, but the best defence has proved to be the breeding of disease-resistant strains.

Plant Propagation. The controlled reproduction of plants to produce individuals with particular desirable characteristics. There are two main types of propagation: seed and vegetative. Seed propagation involves a sexual process and may result in progeny showing considerable variation from the original two parents. Vegetative propagation is an asexual process in which a single piece of one plant may be used to produce another part with identical characteristics.

See also BUDDING; GRAFTING; VEGETATIVE PROPAGATION.

Plantagenet, surname used of the Angevin house, which succeeded to the throne of England in 1154 in the person of Henry II, and ruled until the deposition of Richard II in 1399. The houses of York and Lancaster, which succeeded, being descended from Edward III, are generally included in the Plantagenet line. The name is said to have been derived from the custom of Geoffrey of Anjou, father of Henry II, of wearing a spring of broom (*Planta genista*) in his cap.

Plantaginaceae, a family of plants with ribbed or fleshy leaves usually in a rosette at the base of the plant, and flowers mostly borne in spikes. There are three genera, *Plantago* (plantain), *Littorella* and *Bougueria*.

Plantain, *Plantago*, a genus of herbaceous plants in family Plantaginaceae. The greater plantain, *P. major*, and *P. lanceolata*, are widespread weeds. Several Indian species have medicinal value. Water plantain is *Alisma*.

Plantain Eaters, genus of birds of the order Cuculiformes, which includes the cuckoos and touracos. There are two species, the violet plantain eater, *Musophaga violacea*, and Ross' plantain eater, *M. rossae*. They both occur in West African forests. They are quite large birds, about 76 cm long with beautiful plumage. *M. rossae* has violet black feathers with a red crest and much crimson under the wings. They feed on berries and other fruit.

Plantation, a man-made forest, created either by sowing seeds or by planting young trees; also an estate on which crops such as oil palm, rubber, sugar cane, sisal or cotton are cultivated. The term was originally applied specifically to the British settlements in America, and then to any large estate in North America or the West or East Indies, which was cultivated chiefly by Negro or other slave labour, living in distinct communities on the estate under the control of the proprietor or manager. In this sense the term plantation was synonymous with 'colony'.

In forestry, plantations are generally of one or just a few species of tree which are all of the same age, whereas 'natural' forests, especially those of hardwoods, contain numbers of different species, at all stages of development.

See also AFFORESTATION; FOREST; FORESTRY.

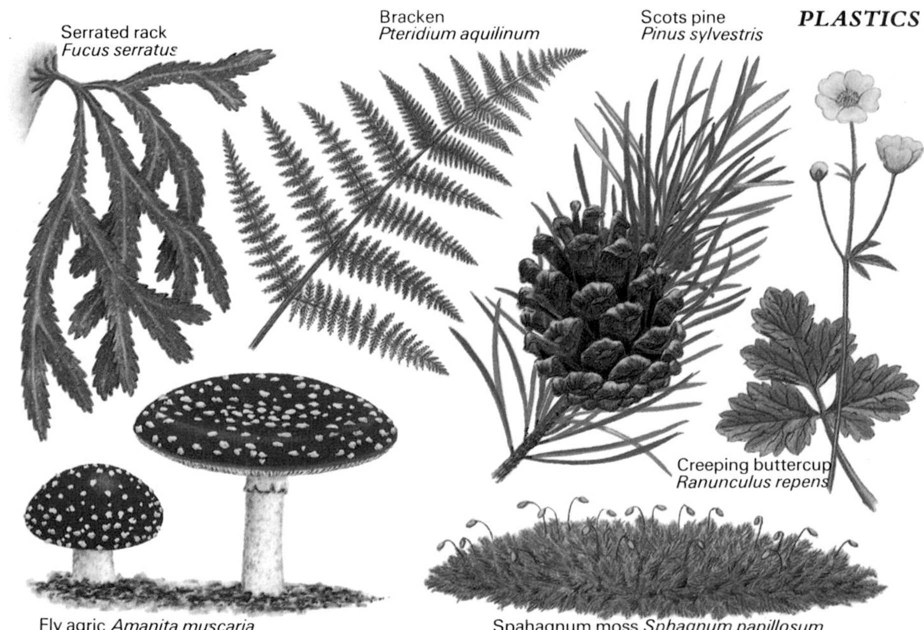

***Plants** exist in many forms. All of the above except the fungi can photosynthesise.*

Plants. Although there are obvious differences between the higher plants and the higher animals, it is not so easy to decide whether some of the lower organisms are plants or animals. The fundamental characteristic common to all green plants that distinguishes them from animals is the capacity to carry out photosynthesis, but the bacteria and fungi and some higher plants cannot photosynthesise, as they lack chlorophyll completely. These forms are either parasitic, obtaining their food from living plant or animal hosts, or saprophytic, obtaining their supplies from non-living organic material.

Three methods of reproduction are found in plants. Vegetative reproduction is very common in the lower plants, as is asexual reproduction. Sexual reproduction is found in all groups. Essentially, this implies that two gametes fuse to form a cell (zygote or fertilised egg) which will develop into a new individual. In many of the algae and fungi there is no apparent difference between the two gametes, but in the higher types they can be distinguished as male and female. In the angiosperms the gametes are extremely reduced and are represented by single cells. The male gamete is the pollen grain and the female gamete is the ovum in the ovary.

In ecological terms, plants represent the first link of the global food chain, without which there would be no higher forms of life. All carbohydrates and some vitamins are made by plants, using the Sun's energy, by photosynthesis. In this process, they convert carbon dioxide and water into the food and oxygen upon which all other organisms depend.

Plants, Classification of, see CLASSIFICATION OF PLANTS.

Plants, Distribution of, see ECOLOGY.

Plants, Flowering, see ANGIOSPERMS.

Plants, Parasitic, see PARASITIC PLANTS AND FUNGI.

Plasma, the straw-coloured liquid remaining after all cells have been removed from blood, for example by centrifugation. It contains all the soluble substances of the blood and is especially rich in proteins, which make up approximately 7 per cent of its total weight. These proteins include the antibodies crucial to the body's defence against infection, and the range of factors involved in blood clotting. More than half the protein concentration in plasma, however, is due to the small but numerous albumin molecules which are principally responsible for maintaining the osmotic pressure of the blood. Other constituents of the plasma are lipids, carbohydrates and a number of inorganic salts.

Plasma see SILICA.

Plasmodium (*plasma* and Greek *eidos*, form), the plant body or vegetative growth of a slime-mould or *Myxomycota*, consisting of a multinucleate, motile mass of protoplasm, generally reticulate and having no firm wall. It lives on decaying organic matter often in soil, producing minute spores. Some are parasitic, e.g. *Plasmodiophora brassicae*, the cause of clubroot in brassicas.

Plasmodium, the genus of Protozoans in the class Sporozoa that cause malaria.

Plaster, in building, is used to provide a uniform finish to walls and celings. For *lime plastering* quicklime (CaO) is obtained from lime ($CaCO_3$), by the process of calcination. *Gypsum plaster*, finely crushed gypsum ($CaSO_4.2H_2O$), is partially dehydrated by heating, producing *plaster of Paris* ($CaSO_4\frac{1}{2}H_2O$), technically known as hemihydrate gypsum plaster.

Plaster of Paris, see GYPSUM; PLASTER.

Plastic Surgery, see SURGERY.

Plastics. Plastics and rubbers are the two principal polymers. The most striking feature of polymers is their gigantic molecular size, running commonly into thousands of units and occasionally as high as millions. These giant molecules are composed of a large number of repeating units (monomers) forming a chain, and it is the nature of the chain links (their size and shape), together with the ways in which the links are arranged to form the chain, the length of the chain, and the disposition of the chains in space, that determine the nature of the material.

Natural polymers—cellulose, starch, resins, lignin, proteins and others—are the basis from which such materials as wool, cotton, flax, silk, leather, fur, wood, rubber and oils are derived. The first commercial exploitation of plastics came more than a hundred years ago with cellulose nitrate (celluloid), followed by many others including phenol formaldehyde (Bakelite) and synthetic rubbers.

The flexibility of the polymer material can be increased by the addition of plasticisers which, in simple terms, are liquids which fill up some of the spaces between the chains and so make it easier for them to move relative to one another.

Flexibility can be decreased by introducing a series of knobs or lumps in the chains, thus restricting their movement by making it difficult for the links to rotate. The substitution of the bulky chlorine atoms and the even larger benzene rings for some of the hydrogen atoms in the simple polyethylene chain produces, respectively, rigid PVC and polystyrene. Both these materials are stiffer than polyethylene but are also brittle, since the lumps prevent the dissipation of stresses by chain movements.

The ordering of the chains can also be increased by stretching. By stretching in one direction (monoaxial orientation) we can obtain the strong fibres used in textiles, and by stretching in two directions at right angles (biaxial orientation) we can increase the strengths of films, which not only allows the use of thinner films but which has led to the production of shrink-wrap packaging; the extended chains revert to their 'kinked' state on heating.

Polyolefins. Olefins are hydrocarbons which have one or more double bonds: ethylene ($CH_2 = CH_2$) is the simplest. Polyethylene and polypropylene are used to make, among other things, pipes, sheets, films, bottles and other containers.

Polystyrene. The polymerisation of styrene monomer (made from ethylene and benzene—both petroleum products). Toughened polystyrene was produced by the incorporation of synthetic rubbers. Expanded polystyrene foams are used for insulation and packaging.

Polyvinyl Chloride (PVC). The raw materials for PVC are ethylene and chlorine; incorporation of impact modifiers and plasticisers made it possible to use PVC for pipes, guttering and flexible sheets.

Acrylic Polymers. Polymethyl methacrylate is hard and strong and characterised by its high degree of clarity. It is accordingly extensively used for display signs, lighting fittings and aircraft windows.

Polytetrafluoroethylene (PTFE) is used to provide non-stick coatings on cooking utensils.

Polyamides. Nylon, the first polyamide, was developed in 1934 in the laboratories of E. I. du Pont de Nemours. Although used for the production of film, sheet and injection moulded articles, nylon is principally known for its applications in the textile field. Nylon yarn, once it has been stretched during the filament-forming process, is twice as strong as the same size of aluminium wire. Fabrics made from it can be set to any desired permanent shape by heat. These heat-set fabrics show little or no shrinking or stretching.

Other plastics include polyesters, silicones, epoxy resins, polyurethanes and a wide range of fibres.

Plastids, subcellular membrane-bound organelles found in all plant cells. Chlorophyll-containing plastids are known as chloroplasts. In flowers and fruits plastids containing various pigments are known as *chromoplasts,* while others may be colourless and concerned with the storage of carbohydrates; these are known as *leucoplasts.*

Plata, Río de la, or River Plate, has two meanings: in the precise sense it is an estuary with its outlet on the South Atlantic and forming the border between Uruguay and Argentina for about 272 km; in its more general meaning it is the mouth of a vast river complex which includes the Paraná, Paraguay and Uruguay rivers, and many other smaller ones. Its total length is estimated at nearly 3680 km. The area of its drainage basin is estimated at about 3,900,000 km^2.

Plataea, ancient Greek city of Boeotia. In 519 BC Athens secured the independence of Plataea in face of encroachment by Thebes. When the Persians invaded Attica in 490 BC Plataea sent her entire levy of 1000 men to support the Athenians at Marathon. Again in 480 the Plataeans took an active part in resisting the armies of Xerxes. In the following year they helped to defeat Mardonius. Plataea was razed to the ground (427), and then rebuilt (386) by the Spartans. Plataea was again destroyed, this time by Thebes, in 373. It was finally restored by Philip II of Macedon and Alexander the Great.

Plate, River, see PLATA, RÍO DE LA.

Plate Tectonics, see GEOTECTONICS.

Plateau, level elevated tract of land created by regional uplift without major deformation. Some geologists restrict the usage to high plains of flat-lying rocks. Others have observed that a plateau may be flat or extensively dissected by deep valleys. Amongst composite landforms incorporating the term plateau are intermontane plateau (e.g. the Colorado and Tibetan plateaus), lava plateau—e.g. the Deccan plateau in India and the Ethiopian plateau in East Africa), and submarine plateau (an elevated tract of the seabed, flat-topped but with steep sides).

See also LANDFORMS, STRUCTURAL.

Platen, see PRINTING.

Plath, Sylvia (1932–62), US poet. Her poetry reveals an obsession with illness, pain and mental suffering, increasingly taking the form of identification with the murdered and politically oppressed; she herself committed suicide. Her works include *The Colossus,* 1960; *Ariel,* 1965; *Crossing the Water,* 1971; *Winter Trees,* 1971; and a novel, *The Bell Jar,* 1963, originally written under the pseudonym Victoria Lucas.

Platinum, metallic chemical element, symbol Pt, atomic number 78, atomic weight 195·09. It occurs, only native, in grey granules containing gold, copper or iron, and some of the similar metals such as iridium, rhodium, osmium, etc. Platinum has a blue or greyish-white metallic lustre, is very ductile and malleable, with great tenacity; it is very heavy, with a relative density of 21·4, and its melting point is 1755°C; it welds at a red heat, its coefficient of expansion is low and allows sealing into glass vessels. This, and the fact that it is unaffected by the atmosphere and resists any single acid, cause it to be largely used in laboratories, and for electrical appliances. It forms alloys with most of the metals: lead and bismuth alloy very readily, while iridium and rhodium alloys are more highly resistant to heat, for which reason they are used in pyrometers. Spongy platinum is prepared by heating various of the compounds of platinum and is used commercially in the manufacture of sulphuric acid, causing heated oxygen and sulphur dioxide to combine on contact. It is also a catalyst in the manufacture of nitric acid by the oxidation of ammonia. If a solution of platinum tetrachloride is treated with a reducing agent, platinum is precipitated in the form of a fine powder called platinum black which is capable of absorbing large quantities of gases (for example, about 100 times its own volume of oxygen). Platinum forms many compounds and complexes in which it has a valency of 2 or 4.

Plato (427–347 BC), Greek philosopher. After the death of Socrates (399), he is said to have resided for a time with Euclid of Megara, and then to have travelled in Greece, Egypt and Italy. About 387 BC he returned to Athens and founded the Academy, over which he presided for the remainder of his life, except for two visits to Sicily. The first of these was in 367 when, following the death of Dionysius the Elder of Syracuse, he was invited by the tyrant's brother-in-law Dion to educate the new ruler, Dionysius the Younger. The scheme failed, but Plato was called upon once more (361–360), this time, and again unsuccessfully, to compose the differences between Dionysius and Dion. He then resumed his work at the Academy.

It is impossible here to provide even an adequate summary of the content and richness of Plato's thought, which has had—and still has—untold influence. It traverses the fields of metaphysics, epistemology, ethics and politics, and is written in a style unsurpassed for purity and elegance in all Greek prose. His central contribution to philosophy is the theory of 'Forms' or 'Ideas', according to which reality, the object of knowledge, consists not in particular and transient phenomena, but in the Forms or Ideas which are the pure types of each class of things, with the Form of the Good at their summit. Closely bound up with this theory are two others, namely that the soul is immortal and that knowledge is recollection.

Platte, river of the USA, formed at North Platte, Nebraska, USA, by the confluence of the North Platte and South Platte rivers, and flowing 500 km, mainly east, to the Missouri river 25 km south of Omaha. The three Platte rivers are unnavigable, but the western trails to Oregon and California followed them in the mid-19th century.

Plattensee, see BALATON, LAKE.

Platyhelminthes, or flatworms, the simplest phylum of the worm-like animals. They are practically all hermaphrodite, and include some of the most important internal parasites, such as tapeworms and the liver fluke. They are divided into four classes, of which one, Turbellaria, is non-parasitic. The others are Cestoda, the tapeworms, and the Monogenea and the Digenea, which were previously called trematodes. The tapeworms have long, flattened, ribbon-like segmented bodies, and a 'head', or scolex, usually provided with hooks and suckers. They have no mouth and no digestive canal, absorbing nourishment over the whole surface of the body. Besides numerous cestode parasites of mammals and birds, some are parasites of fishes. The trematodes are flukes, flat leaf-shaped worms with oval or lanceolate bodies, with a mouth and digestive canal. The most harmful parasite of this class is the liver fluke.

Platypus, see DUCK-BILLED PLATYPUS.

Plauen, town of the German Democratic Republic, on the Weisse Elster, at the foot of the Erzgebirge, 68 km south-west of Karl-Marx-Stadt. Its textile industry dates from the 15th century, and it has also steel and engineering industries. Population (1974) 82,000.

Plautus, Titus Maccius (c.254–184 BC), Roman comic poet. In c.224 BC he took to writing plays. Of these we have 20; 35 other titles are known. Plautus had a perfect command of language and metre. Taking as plots the conventional intrigues of Greek New Comedy, Plautus added his own brand of native wit and sharp character-drawing. Since the Renaissance he has been acknowledged as one of the greatest of ancient playwrights.

Playa (Spanish, shore or beach), a flat-floored bottom of an interior desert basin. Formerly a lake, its sun-baked floor indicates a previous base level of erosion. The term playa is also loosely used to denote a lake periodically filled with water. Generally the playa surface is encrusted with salts caused by precipitation from the highly saline water carried into the basin by internal drainage.
See also LAKE.

Player, Gary (1935–), South African golf champion, he was one of the 'Big Three' of world golf during the 1960s (with the Americans Arnold Palmer and Jack Nicklaus), winning championships all over the world. He is one of only four men to have won the four major titles (British and US Opens, USPGA and US Masters).

Player-piano, mechanical instrument. The basic player action consists of a system of valves and pneumatics, a vacuum chest, and exhausters and reserve. A music roll passes over a cylinder, which is perforated by openings connected by pipes to a piano-type action. There are also openings in the music roll, designed to reproduce the composition to be 'played'. Many piano rolls were made by composers such as Rachmaninov. Hindemith wrote pieces especially for instruments of the player-piano type.

Playfair, John (1748–1819), British geologist and mathematician. He wrote *Elements of Geometry*, 1812–14; *Outlines of Natural Philosophy*, 1812–16; and *Illustrations of the Huttonian Theory of the Earth*, 1802.

Playfair, Sir Nigel (1874–1934), British actor-manager. In 1918 Playfair assumed the management of the Lyric Theatre, Hammersmith, and soon became well known for his productions, among them *The Way of the World* and *The Beaux' Stratagem*, in which Dame Edith Evans first made a success, and Drinkwater's *Abraham Lincoln*.

Playing-cards, see CARDS, PLAYING.

Plays, see ACTING; DRAMA; THEATRE.

Plea, in English law, a term used to denote that which is pleaded, or alleged, by a party to an action, or by a defendant in criminal proceedings, in answer to the allegation of the other party or of the prosecution.

Pleadings, written documents of the parties to an action which do not set out the evidence in support of their cases, but merely the point or points in issue between them. All points must be raised in pleadings since, at the trial, a party will not be allowed to raise any matter not pleaded, but pleadings may be amended, with the leave of the court where necessary, at any stage. Pleadings in actions usually consist of (1) statement of claim, (2) defence, (3) counterclaim, (4) defence to counterclaim and reply.

Pleasence, Donald (1919–), British actor. Pleasence made his first London appearance in 1942, shortly before joining the RAF. From 1946 he gradually built up a reputation at Birmingham Repertory Company, the Bristol Old Vic and the Edinburgh Festival, as well as making numerous London appearances, including leading roles in *The Caretaker*, 1960, and *The Man in the Glass Booth*, 1967, for which he was named stage actor of the year. He has made many television and film appearances, notably in *The Caretaker*; *Doctor Crippen*; Polanski's *Cul-de-Sac*; and *The Barchester Chronicles*.

Pleasure, see EMOTION; ETHICS; HEDONISM.

Plebeians (also Plebes, Plebs), see PATRICIANS AND PLEBEIANS.

Plebiscite (*plebiscitium*, ordinance, decree), in Roman history, a law enacted by the plebs in their *comitia tributa* or *concilia plebis* on the rogation of a tribune. Originally these resolutions needed confirmation by the Senate, but later they came to be binding on the whole people. In modern politics a plebiscite is an expression of popular opinion obtained by vote from all the electors of the state.
See also REFERENDUM.

Plecoptera, an order of the class Insecta, subclass Pterygota. These are the stone flies. They are winged insects with mouthparts of the mandibulate (chewing) type, although the mouthparts may be vestigial. There are two pairs of membranous wings, the hind pair usually larger than the forewings, held flat along the back at rest. The abdomen usually ends in a pair of long cerci (appendages). Most species lay eggs in batches of 100 or more at a time. There are about 1300 species. Like the mayflies, they are used by anglers for bait.

Pledge, see PAWNBROKER.

Pléiade, group of seven French poets of the 16th century, the chief among them being Ronsard and Du Bellay.
The aim of the Pléiade was to break away from the medieval poetic tradition by going to classical Greek and Latin models, and to make the French language an instrument fit for all literary purposes. Their views were first set out in Du Bellay's *Défense et illustration de la langue française*, 1549.

Pleiades, the best known and most studied of the open star clusters. Situated in Taurus, the cluster which contains about a dozen blue stars of naked-eye brightness spread over an area little more than twice that of the full moon attracts the attention of even the most casual observer. A pair of field glasses will show at least fifty stars and a telescope several hundred more.
The estimated distance to the Pleiades is 400 light years. It is a comparatively young cluster and still contains a great deal of interstellar dust which forms faint reflection nebulae round the brighter stars.

Plekhanov, Georgi Valentinovich (1857–1918), Russian Marxist, 'the father of Russian Social Democracy'. In 1880 he emigrated to Western Europe, where he became converted to Marxism and in 1883 formed the Liberation of Labour Group, which played a most important part in propagating Marxism in Russia and in fighting the rival populist ideology. When the Russian Social Democratic Workers' Party was formed in 1898 Plekhanov decisively supported its more orthodox Marxist and politically minded wing, collaborating with Lenin. After the February Revolution in 1917 Plekhanov returned to Russia, where he formed a sharply anti-Bolshevik right-wing Social Democratic organisation 'Unity'. He died soon after the Bolshevik seizure of power.

Plenipotentiary, or Envoy Extraordinary, person accredited to some foreign sovereign and invested with unlimited power to negotiate a treaty or transact any other diplomatic business.

Plesiosaurs, a group of Jurassic and Cretaceous reptiles highly adapted for aquatic life. They had broad, flat bodies, long, flexible necks, and four large, well-developed, paddle-shaped limbs with extra finger-joints. The head was short and bore numerous pointed teeth. There are two groups, one with short heads and elongate necks (e.g. *Plesiosaurus* and *Elasmosaurus*), and the other with short necks and longer heads (e.g. *Pliosaurus*).
See also DINOSAURS.

Pleuracanths, freshwater, shark-like fishes with a symmetrical tail and a long fin down the back. They existed from Devonian to Triassic times, and were abundant in the Carboniferous period. Little is known of their ancestry.

Pleurisy, inflammation of the *pleura*, the serous membrane enveloping the lung. Each of the pleurae has a visceral and a parietal layer, between which is a closed space known as the pleural cavity. Normally the two layers are in fairly close contact, sliding over each other on a thin film of lubricating fluid during the movements of respiration. When the pleura is inflamed and roughened through invasion by micro-organisms, but no fluid is formed, in the condition known as dry pleurisy, the surfaces of the membranes pass over each other with a certain amount of friction which can be detected by the ear. In wet pleurisy, the effusion of fluid into the cavity may continue until as much as 4·5 l of fluid are included between the layers. The pleural sac is therefore distended, pressing on and collapsing the lung and interfering with breathing and other functions, in which case aspiration of the fluid may be necessary. The symptoms of pleurisy include fever and shivering, and pain in the side in the early stage; in diaphragmatic pleurisy the pain may be referred to the shoulder or to the abdomen.

Pleurisy Root, see BUTTERFLY WEED.

Pleven, town of northern Bulgaria, capital of the province of Pleven, 129 km north-east of Sofia. After a notable defence of the town, the Turkish leader, Osman Pasha, was forced to surrender to the Russians and Romanians here in 1877 during the Russo-Turkish wars. It is an agricultural centre and has textile, machinery, cement and ceramics industries. Population (1979) 122,916.

Pleyel, Ignaz Joseph (1757–1831), Austrian composer and piano manufacturer. He was musical director of Strasbourg cathedral (1789), conducted concerts in London (1792), and eventually settled in Paris, founding the piano factory there (1807). His compositions are largely forgotten.

Plimsoll, Samuel (1824–98), British politician. One of his objects was to protect the lives of sailors by enforcing a compulsory load line, which came to be generally known as the Plimsoll line.

Plinth, the base of a column, wall or pedestal. See also ORDERS OF ARCHITECTURE.

Pliny, Gaius Plinius Secundus, known as 'the Elder' (AD 23–79), Roman writer on many subjects. His scientific studies, pursued throughout his life, and especially between 55 and 68, won him fame as the most learned man of his age. His zeal for research led to his death by suffocation in the eruption of Vesuvius in 79.

Of all his writings (histories of the Germanic wars, of his own time, works on tactics, rhetoric and grammar) only the *Historia naturalis* remains. Containing 37 books, the *Historia naturalis* is a not always accurate encyclopaedic work on the universe, geography, man and other animals, plants and their use in healing, metals, precious stones, art and architecture, with digressions on human inventions and institutions.

Pliny, Gaius Plinius Caecilus Secundus, known as 'the Younger' (c.AD 61–c.112), Roman orator and author. He became an advocate (80), senator (c.81), military tribune in Syria (c.82), and after holding other high offices was finally consul under Trajan (100), and governor of Bithynia (111). Pliny was an intimate friend of Trajan and Tacitus, and studied rhetoric under Quintilian. His remaining works include the nine books of *Letters*, with a tenth containing his correspondence with Trajan.

Pliocene, see TERTIARY SYSTEM.

PLO, see PALESTINE LIBERATION ORGANISATION.

Plock (Russian *Plotsk*), town of Poland, in Warsaw province, 96 km west of Warsaw, on the River Vistula. It has a 12-century cathedral containing the tombs of Polish kings. There is a major oil refinery supplied by pipeline from the USSR. Population (1974) 84,663.

Ploeşti, capital of Prahova province, Romania, 56 km north of Bucharest. There are oil wells and refineries in the vicinity, it has a pipeline to Constanta, manufactures machinery for the oil industry, and is a road and rail junction. Population (1979) 207,000.

Plomer, William Charles Franklyn (1903–73), South African poet and novelist. In 1926, together with Roy Campbell, he founded *Voorslag* (Whiplash), the first South African literary magazine in English.

Plomer is generally acknowledged to be the first South African fiction writer in English who tried to portray Black people from their own point of view. His first novel, *Turbott Wolfe*, 1925, although immature in some respects, was very courageous in its time for suggesting that the human answer to South Africa's problem lay in miscegenation. Plomer was awarded the Queen's Gold Medal for Poetry in 1963. His *Collected Poems* were published in 1960.

Plotinus (AD 205–270), Greek philosopher, founder of Neoplatonism. Plotinus is an Idealist pure and simple. God is spirit, and all that can be attributed to him is goodness and unity. From him emanates intellect (*nous*), from which comes the world-soul, from which again emanate various forces (including the human soul), whence finally comes matter. Man's work is to return to union with God by eliminating from his life the unreal and material, and the final step in this union is that of ecstasy.

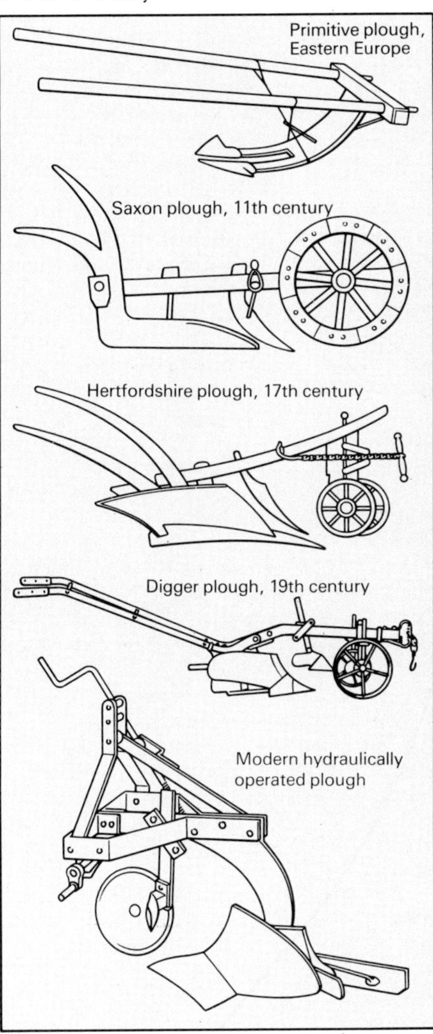

***Ploughs and Ploughing.** The development of the plough from Saxon times to the present day. The earliest ploughs made no more than a crude furrow. Not until later did they turn the earth over on one side of the plough share.*

Plough Agriculture. The use of the plough, usually drawn by a traction animal (ox, buffalo, horse), for agricultural production was confined until recently to Eurasia; swidden agriculture, which uses the hoe, was more widespread throughout the world. The plough probably originated in Asia, from where it spread to Europe, India and ancient Egypt.

Ploughs, whether made of wood or iron, are sufficiently heavy to restrict the mobility of the cultivators; the latter are generally sedentary. Special forms of property and land-tenure may be found in societies with this mode of subsistence, and, since it allows for higher yields than swiddening, one frequently finds that the surpluses are used to feed a significant non-productive population (bureaucrats, traders, craftsmen and soldiers), as in ancient Egypt, medieval Europe and the West today.

Plough Monday, or Rock Monday, first Monday after Epiphany (Twelfth Day), termination of the Christmas holidays, and herald of the ploughing season. The ancient custom of celebrating it by a procession and drawing a plough from door to door in the parish and begging 'plough-money' for rustic festivities still survives in parts of England.

Ploughs and Ploughing. From a remote period the plough has been the most important implement of husbandry. The first ploughs were little more than digging sticks to stir the soil; in some parts of the world these are still in use. Disc ploughs, which have the share and breast of the ordinary form displaced by a large steel concave cutting disc, are sometimes used for work in very hard or heavy soil. Turn wrest ploughs are used horizontally on hillsides. Double and multiple ploughs can be used on light land. Among special-purpose ploughs are the double-breasted or ridging plough and the subsoil plough.

The object of ploughing is to invert the top surface of the soil so as to pulverise it and turn under the surface plant growth and rubbish to be decomposed. The depth of ploughing depends on the condition of the soil and subsoil, and whether the crop that is next to occupy the land is deep or shallow rooting.

Plovdiv, city of central Bulgaria, capital of the province of Plovdiv, on the River Maritsa, 88 km south-east of Sofia. It was founded by Philip of Macedon as *Philippopolis*, and under the Roman Empire it was the capital of Thracia. It has textile, leather, engineering and tobacco industries, and is situated in a fertile fruit- and wine-producing district. Population (1979) 342,000.

Plover, name for various birds of the family Charadriidae, in the order Charadriiformes (the order containing waders, gulls and auks), characterised by a short bill, weak at the base and strong at the tip, the nostrils in deep longitudinal grooves. A typical species is the golden plover, *Pluvialis apricaria*, which is plentiful on moors and sea-coasts of most temperate parts of Europe in winter. It is about 26 cm long, and in winter the upper parts are a sooty black with large yellow spots, and white throat and underparts, changing to black in the spring. It nests on the ground. The ringed plover, *Charadrius hiaticula*, is a small bird with a black band on the throat. It is a common breeder around most European and North African coasts, nesting in a scrape on a beach or amongst shingle. The grey plover, *Pluvialis squatarola*, breeds in the Arctic and is similar in build to the golden plover but stouter and a mottled grey above in winter. Underparts also become black during the breeding season.

Plowright, Joan Ann (1929–), British actress, since 1961 wife of Lord Olivier. Her national reputation began in 1956 with her performances at the Royal Court Theatre, London, notably in Osborne's *The Entertainer*, Wesker's *Roots*, and Ionesco's *Rhinoceros*. Later successes include an award-winning St Joan, and parts at the National Theatre in Shakespeare, Molière and Chekhov.

Plücker, Julius (1801–68), German mathematician and physicist. He discovered that analytical geometry could be based on lines rather than points, utilising the principle of duality known in projective geometry. He studied the magnetic properties of crystals, and discovered that cathode rays are deflected by a magnetic field; and he recognised earlier than Bunsen that lines in the spectrum were characteristic of the substance emitting them.

Plum, *Prunus domestica*, in family Rosaceae; one of the most important hardy fruit-bearing trees. There are many varieties in cultivation including bullace, damson and greengage.

Plumage, see BIRD; FEATHERS.

Plumbaginaceae, a plant family of 10 genera and about 280 species. They are shrubs or herbaceous plants. The flowers have five sepals and the five petals are joined at the base into a tube, and are generally pink, mauve or blue. Members of the family include thrift (*Armeria*), *Ceratostigma*, *Plumbago* and sea lavender (*Limonium*).

Plumbago, a genus in the family Plumbaginaceae. *P. capensis*, a native of southern Africa, bearing pale-blue flowers, is cultivated.

Plumbing (Latin *plumbum*, lead), craft of working in lead and other metals or plastics, especially in building. The principal function of a plumber today is the running of pipes in buildings to provide water, central heating, and to conduct wastes out of the building. The appliances which require water, e.g. basins, baths and sinks, are also fixed by plumbers.

Plumer, Herbert Charles Onslow Plumer, 1st Viscount Plumer (1857–1932), British soldier. In the First World War he commanded, in turn, the 5th Army Corps (1915), the 2nd Army British Expeditionary Force (1915–17), the Italian Expeditionary Force (November 1917 to March 1918), and from 1918 the 2nd Army of the British Expeditionary Force in France and Flanders. His outstanding achievement on the Western Front was the victory of Messines Ridge in June 1917. In 1919 he was made governor of Malta, and in 1925 high commissioner of Palestine and Transjordan.

Plumeria, a genus of tropical American trees in family Apocynaceae, of which *P. rubra*, frangipani or Indian jasmine, is widely grown in warm countries for its highly scented blooms.

Plunket, St Oliver (1629–81), Roman Catholic primate of all Ireland and martyr, canonised in 1976. Plunket, Archbishop of Armagh, was falsely implicated in 1678 by Titus Oates in the Popish Plot against Charles II and was executed. He was the last man to suffer martyrdom in England for the Roman Catholic faith.

Pluralism, in philosophy (metaphysics), theory that all existence is ultimately reducible to a multiplicity of distinct and independent beings or elements. As such, pluralism is directly opposed to monism and is distinguished from dualism in that it postulates many realities and allows greater qualitative diversity.

Pluralism, in ecclesiastical parlance, the holding of more than one living or benefice at the same time. Despite attempts at reform, this abuse tended to recur throughout the history of the Christian Church. Pluralities were regulated by the act of 1838, which declared pluralities illegal except where the livings were of small value, close to each other, and situated in districts of a small population. The Pastoral Reorganization Measure, 1949, allowing the union of small parishes and the arrangement of team ministries, has made the older measures obsolete.

Plush (contraction from *peluche*, hairy fabric), kind of cloth or silk, nylon or other man-made fibres, cotton or wool, or a mixture of these woven like velvet but having a longer and softer nap. It is used chiefly for rich garments, upholstery and interior decoration.

Plutarch (c. AD 46–after 120), Greek writer, philosopher, moralist and biographer. Plutarch's *Parallel Lives* of Greeks and Romans, on which his fame chiefly rests, consists of 46 lives arranged in pairs for comparison (e.g. Theseus and Romulus; Alexander and Caesar), and four separate lives. Their interest is ethical rather than historical, and their influence has been vast. Plutarch's other writings, of which there are more than 60, are collected under the title *Moralia*. Their appeal lies in the common-sense quality of his views on ordinary human events.

Pluto, see HADES.

Pluto, in astronomy, the outermost of the planets, was discovered on 21 January 1930 by Clyde W. Tombaugh. Pluto moves in a very eccentric orbit, eccentricity 0·246, which is inclined at 17° 9′ to the ecliptic. It takes about 246 years to complete a revolution round the Sun and its distance from it varies from 30 to 50 astronomical units. Thus for some years before and after perihelion, which next occurs in 1989, Pluto is nearer the Sun than is Neptune. Pluto's mean distance from the Sun is 39·3 astronomical units. Its mass is 0·08 that of the Earth and its radius 0·47 of the Earth's. The rotation period found from periodic variations in its light is 6·390 days. Thus Pluto appears to be about the same size as Mars, with a similar albedo and density.

Pluton, a major igneous intrusion which has no obvious floor. In the Rockies of North America and in the Alps plutonic masses are seen to extend with uniform rock character over vertical distances of 3000–5000 m. Geophysical investigations indicate that the granites of south-west England extend downward for at least 15 km.

Plutons are usually composed of coarse-grained acid igneous rocks of granitic type. Stocks are plutons of small dimensions, only a few square kilometres in extent, while bosses are stocks which show a circular cross-section.

Plutonic, see IGNEOUS ROCKS.

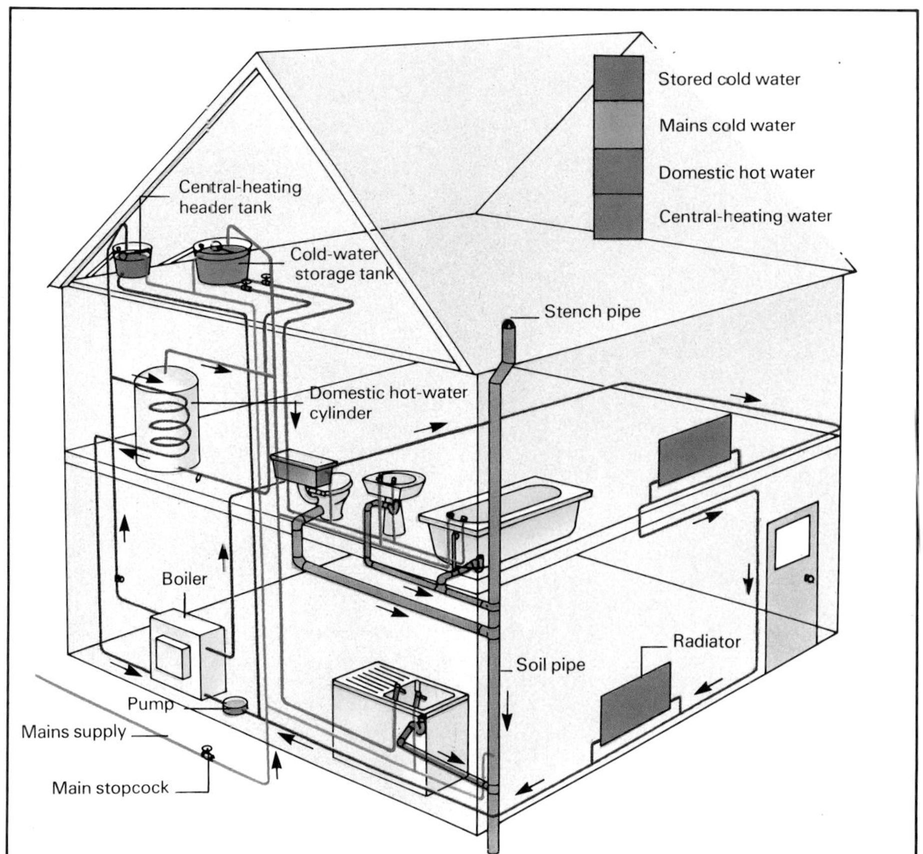

Plumbing. *The plumbing system of a typical centrally heated house. Apart from the kitchen cold-water tap, the installations are supplied via the cold-water-storage and central-heating header tanks.*

Plutonium, chemical element, symbol Pu, atomic number 94, atomic weight 242, one of the actinides; discovered in 1940. Plutonium is produced by the collision of a neutron with uranium, and so it is formed in uranium fuel rods in nuclear reactors. Since plutonium is itself an extremely efficient source of nuclear energy, it is extracted from used fuel rods for use in a different type of nuclear reactor. This process, whereby more nuclear fuel is produced than is used, is called 'breeding', and the reactors used are known as 'fast breeder reactors'.

Plymouth, pottery from the factory which made the first hard-paste porcelain in England, in Plymouth, Devon, founded by William Cookworthy in 1768. In 1770 the factory transferred to Bristol.

Plymouth, an important naval and commercial seaport in Devon, England, situated between the estuaries of the Tamar and Plym rivers, on the boundary of Devon and Cornwall, nearly 400 km south-west of London. Originally three separate towns—Devonport, East Stonehouse and Plymouth—an amalgamation took place in 1914 under the inclusive name of Plymouth. There are three harbours, Sutton Pool, Catwater (Cattewater) and the Hamoaze, which unite in Plymouth Sound. The chief government establishments, viz. the naval dockyard, barracks, gun wharves, etc., are at Devonport. At Stonehouse are the naval hospital, Royal Marine barracks, victualling yards, etc. Plymouth is the centre of trade.

It was from Plymouth that Drake, Hawkins and Grenville sailed on many of their great voyages; the *Mayflower* set forth from Plymouth with the Pilgrim Fathers to America; Capt. Cook led his first voyage of circumnavigation, and his last and fatal voyage of 1776, from this same port. Industries include the manufacturing of clothing, radio equipment, lubrication products and processed foods. Population (1981) 243,895.

Plymouth, town of Plymouth county, Massachusetts, USA, situated about 55 km south-east of Boston. It is the oldest town in New England, founded by the Pilgrim Fathers, who left Plymouth in England and settled here in December 1620. Population (1980) 35,913.

Plymouth Brethren, or Darbyites, religious movement which started in Dublin about 1827 and spread from there to Plymouth, Bristol, London and other towns. Originally a reaction against formalism and clericalism, it gained numerous converts, many of them of high social position, through the work of John Nelson Darby (1800–82). Divisions in the Plymouth meeting led, after much controversy, to a separation of the 'Open' from the 'Exclusive' Brethren. There have been many other internal disputes, but the movement continues strongly in several countries. Plymouth Brethren stand for a simple world-renouncing piety, regard the Bible as infallible, look for the speedy Second Coming of Christ, reject a professional ordained ministry, and 'break bread' together weekly in memory of the death of Christ.

Plymouth Sound, arm of the English Channel between Devon and Cornwall, covering an area of 2226 ha, affording good anchorage, and including the following inlets: the Catwater, Sutton Pool, Mill Bay, Stonehouse Pool and the Hamoaze, the latter being used as a naval harbour, and Cawsand Bay on the west.

Plynlimon, or more correctly Pumlumon, mountain of central Wales on the borders of Dyfed and Powys; its heights form a commanding viewpoint. It is chiefly formed of clay-slate with veins of lead. The Wye, Severn, Lynfant, Rheidol and Ystwyth rivers rise on its slopes. Height 753 m.

Plywood, thin layers of wood, with the grain running at right angles to one another, glued together under pressure. Plywood is extensively used in much joinery which was formerly worked in solid wood, e.g. panelling. Although the modern form of plywood has only been produced in recent years, certain forms of lamination have been used by woodworkers from very early times.

See also VENEERING.

Plzeň (German *Pilsen*), town of Czechoslovakia, formerly the capital of western Bohemia, 80 km south-west of Prague on the River Berounka. It is famous for its beer (Pilsener lager), and has coal, steel, chemical and engineering industries (Škoda works; founded 1869). Population (1979) 167,000.

Pneumatic Tools, appliances using compressed air as motive power. Rock drills are machines using compressed air for the perforation of rock by combined percussive and rotary action. Percussive pneumatic tools are used for concrete breaking, clay digging, chipping, caulking, riveting, etc. The action is similar to the rock drill, but the shank does not rotate. Rotary pneumatic tools are used for drilling, grinding, tapping, reamering, etc., and transmit rotary action to a twist drill or other attachment.

Pneumatic Trough, vessel used for collecting gases over a liquid (generally water). The trough is filled with water, and jars to contain the gas are filled with water and inverted on a 'beehive' shelf. The gas passes up through the perforated shelf and fills the jars by displacement. For the collection of gases soluble in water, the latter may be replaced by mercury.

Pneumatolysis, the process whereby chemical changes are induced in rocks at depth by the influence of gaseous material.

Pneumoconioses, a group of diseases caused by the continual inhalation of dust particles. The tissue of the lungs becomes fibrous through the continual small lesions and their repair, and so less capable of aerating the blood and less resistant to disease. Symptoms are shortness of breath and coughing. Pneumoconioses are even more severe if tubercular infection has also damaged the lung.

Anthracosis is caused by the inhalation of carbon particles and is found to a certain extent in the lungs of all town dwellers. Miner's lung is an extensive form of anthracosis due to the inhalation of large amounts of coal dust. Silicosis affects workers who inhale flint particles, silica or other mineral dusts. Workers at high risk are miners, stone masons, potters and quarry workers. Asbestosis is probably the most significant other form of pneumoconiosis. It is caused by prolonged exposure to asbestos dust at concentrations greater than 5×10^7 particles per square metre, and it is associated with an increased incidence of lung cancer.

The risk of all these diseases has been greatly reduced with the introduction of better working conditions, suitable ventilation, the use of exhaust fans, and the spraying of the air to make the dust particles stick together and drop from the atmosphere. Regular X-ray also helps the conditions to be recognised at an early stage so that treatment and, if necessary, a change of job can be arranged.

Pneumonia, inflammation within the lungs causing fever, difficulty in breathing, and impaired oxygenation of the blood in severe cases. Lobar pneumonia is a severe form due to infection by pneumococci which affects large segments of the lung. Smaller areas of pneumonia occur beyond obstruction of large air passages by foreign bodies or growths. Bronchopneumonia, which complicates virus infections, such as measles or influenza, any severe illness, or inhalation of material into the lungs, affects many small areas simultaneously. Bacteria may travel in the bloodstream to lodge in the lungs and cause widespread patchy pneumonia, an example being tuberculosis. Non-bacterial pneumonia generally causes less dramatic illness: it is usually caused by mycoplasmas or chlamydia (organisms intermediate between bacteria and viruses) or viruses.

Pnyx (Greek *Pnux*, from *Puknos*, crowded), original meeting place for the ecclesia at Athens, on a slope about 457 m east of the Acropolis.

Po (Greek *Eridanos*; Latin *Padus*), largest river of Italy, crossing the plains of Piedmont, Lombardy, Veneto and Emilia-Romagna. It rises at over 1830 m in the Cottian Alps, on the French border, 25 km west of Saluzzo, and flows past Saluzzo, north-east to Turin and Chivasso, and then in a tortuous course east past Casale, Piacenza and Cremona to the Adriatic, which it enters by a delta (55 km long). Among its chief tributaries are the Ticino (draining Lake Maggiore), Adda (draining Lake Como), Oglio (draining Lake Oseo) and Mincio (draining Lake Garda). The total length is 650 km, and the drainage area 70,000 km^2. The Po is navigable beyond Turin, and its valley is a highly productive agricultural area with maize, hay, grapes and rice being important crops.

Pocahontas (c.1595–1617), North American Indian princess. She is famous through John Smith's story in his *True Relation*, 1607, and *General History of Virginia*, 1624. Smith states that he was captured by the Indians and condemned to death, but was saved by the intervention of Pocahontas, then a little girl. When she grew up she married John Rolfe (c.1614), one of the Jamestown settlers, and went with him to England (1616). She died and was buried at Gravesend, Kent, after giving birth to a son, who subsequently returned to Virginia and is claimed as an ancestor by many prominent families there.

Pochard, any member of the duck family Anatidae. The most important species is the canvasback, *Aythea valiseneria*, which breeds in western North America. It is light grey with a black breast and russet head and neck. The European red-headed pochard, *A. farina*, breeds mainly in northern Scandinavia. The male's head and neck are chestnut-red; the breast, quill feathers and rump are black; the sides, upper parts and underparts are greyish-white. Pochards feed largely on water plants, for which they dive.

Pod, see FRUIT.

Podgorny, Nikolai Viktorovich (1903–83), Soviet statesman, president of the USSR from 1965 to 1977 and a member of the Politburo from 1960 to 1977. He was effectively removed from the presidency and replaced by Brezhnev.

Podium (Latin), in classical architecture, the high platform on which a building stands; also the wall round the arena of an amphitheatre.

Podolsk, town in Moscow *oblast* of the RSFSR, USSR, 40 km south of Moscow. It has engineering, electrical engineering and cement industries; its industrial development dates from the late 19th century. Population (1980) 203,000.

Podostemaceae, a family of mainly tropical plants growing attached to rocks in fast-flowing streams. The structure of the flowers suggests the family is related to the Saxifragaceae: the rest of the plant is so modified that it appears seaweed- or lichen-like, with no distinction between leaf, stem and root.

Podsol Soils develop in a distinctive zone in the cool climates of mid-latitudes, being best developed under coniferous forest or heathland vegetation which grow on freely drained sands and gravels deposited as glacial outwash material from which the fine particles have been removed by ice meltwater. They extend from approximately 66°N to 50°N and to a limited extent in the southern hemisphere. The soils are acidic in character and the lack of plant foods resulting from slow release weathering conditions and the excess of silica in the parent materials means that only the plants tolerant of acid conditions thrive. As the acidic soil environment reduces the number of micro-organisms which can thrive under these conditions, organic breakdown is slow and the transitional fermentation stage from litter to humus can be observed in the organic layers. The absence of soil fauna such as earthworms which turn over the upper soil layers means that a mat of organic matter builds up on the soil surface. Beneath the organic surface a bleached sandy layer exists, a white, ash-coloured horizon. Downward percolating rainwater, charged with organic acids, removes readily soluble plant foods. Aluminium, iron and organic compounds are also removed along with the finer clay particles, leaving a coarse textured and infertile upper mineral layer. These podsols may then progress to gleyed podsols as waterlogging occurs and may finally lead to conditions where air is excluded from the soil, leaving vegetation to accumulate on the surface. In this instance the soil is a peaty gleyed podsol which may, in extreme cases, lead to the formation of peats.

Poe, Edgar Allan (1809–49), US poet, story writer and critic. Unable to endure business life, Poe tried to support himself by literature in Boston. He published *Tamerlane and other Poems* under a pseudonym in 1827. Becoming destitute, he enlisted in the army under an assumed name, but was later appointed to a cadetship at the United States Military Academy. After six months he was court-martialled and dismissed for neglect of duty. From this time onwards he made a scanty living by contributing to American journals. His verse, though small in bulk, exhibits extraordinary powers of technique and knowledge of the subtleties of rhythm and syllabic change. Perhaps even more surprising was his ability to weave into his tales and poems such an atmosphere of wonder and terror. He was the first to give a definition of a short story and one of the first to practise the art. In *The Mystery of the Rue Morgue*, 1841, and other tales he was the originator of the modern detective story. He was no less notable as a critic.

Poema de mio Cid, Spanish epic poem of some 4000 lines, written about 1140. Its subject is an episode in the life of a Castilian soldier and condottiere, Rodrigo Diaz de Vivar, known as the Cid, telling in sober and realistic language of the Cid's victories over the Moors, and his capture of the great city and plain of Valencia. The Cid combines in his person the highest concept of valour and courtesy; and this, together with his skill as general and guerrilla warrior, has made him a Spanish national hero.

***Pocahontas.** An engraving from John Smith's* General History of Virginia, *1624.*

Poet Laureate (Latin *laureatus*, from *laurea*, the laurel-tree), title conferred by letters-patent to the royal household. Its origin is obscure. In ancient Greece the laurel wreath was the crown of honour of poets and heroes, and thus in English the word laureate came to mean eminent, generally, though not always, in a literary sense. John Dryden was the first English poet to receive the title by letters-patent in 1670.

Poetry, form of literary expression, distinguished from prose by a characteristic use of metre and line. However, its form and use are flexible and the difference between prose and poetry may not always be easy to define. W. J. Courthope, in his *History of English Poetry*, 1910, summed up poetry in the definition: 'The art of Poetry is a mirror for the imagination of men living in a society at once historic and free. Its time-honoured forms, epic, dramatic, didactic and lyric, are so many vehicles for the expression of ideas not merely existing in the mind of the individual poet, but representative of the action and character of those who live in his age and speak his language'.

See also ANTHOLOGY; BALLAD; FREE VERSE; HEROIC VERSE; LYRIC; METRE; ODE; SONNET.

Pogonophora, deep-water, bottom-living, elongated, tube-dwelling invertebrate animals found in the oceans near the continental slopes of the Pacific. They bear a crown of tentacles below which there is a short anterior section followed by a long trunk. The overall length varies from 10 to 85 cm. There is no mouth or anus. Presumably the food is collected by the tentacles and absorbed through the body covering.

Pogrom, (Russian, devastation, or riot), a mob attack approved or condoned or clandestinely organised by the authorities on the property and life of a religious, racial or national group. The term is generally used of such attacks on Jews. The term arose in connection with the widespread and recurrent attacks on Jewish property and persons in Russia in 1881 and in the years up to the First World War. Pogroms were introduced in Germany by Hitler.

Poher, Alain (1909–), French politician, President of the Senate since October 1968. By the terms of the constitution of the Fifth Republic he became interim president on the resignation of Gen. de Gaulle in 1969. He was an unsuccessful candidate in presidential elections, but became interim president again on the death of Pompidou in April 1974.

Pohutukawa, *Metrosideros tomentosa*, an evergreen tree in family Myrtaceae, with rich crimson, many-stamened flowers. It is native to the coasts of New Zealand, where it is known as the New Zealand Christmas tree.

Poikilothermy, coldbloodedness, the opposite of homoiothermy. Poikilothermic animals, invertebrates, fish, amphibians and reptiles, cannot regulate their blood temperature, which remains at the temperature of the environment. This explains why many reptiles are sluggish first thing in the morning, and only become fully active when they have sunned themselves and warmed up. Some mammals, such as the woodchuck, become poikilothermic when they hibernate.

Poincaré, Jules Henri (1854–1912), French mathematician and physicist. He did important work in analysis; in particular in the theory of differential equations. In 1895 he produced perhaps the first book on topology, then called 'analysis situs'. He contributed to celestial mechanics.

Poincaré, Raymond Nicolas Landry (1860–1934), French statesman. In January 1912 he succeeded Caillaux as prime minister, becoming also foreign minister. In 1913 he was elected President of the Republic. Amid the reverses of the war at the end of 1917 Poincaré accepted as premier his old opponent Clemenceau. Poincaré's term as president ended in 1920; he then re-entered the Senate. In January 1922 he again became prime minister and foreign minister. In 1924 he had to impose fresh taxation; the elections went against him, and he resigned. An acute financial crisis resulted in his recall to power in July 1926, and his government endured until July 1929, when he resigned on grounds of health.

Poinsettia, see EUPHORBIA.

Point, type height, see TYPE AND TYPE-FOUNDING.

Point-to-point Steeplechases. Steeplechases were so called in the first instance because they were races run from one point to another, the finish being near some prominent landmark such as a steeple or church spire. The modern 'point-to-point' chases are confined to amateur riders, male and female, and are held by the various hunts at the end of the hunting season. They are restricted to horses who have been regularly hunted. Nearly all point-to-point steeplechases are now run over made-up fences on a set course. See also HORSE RACING.

Pointe-à-Pitre, largest city and major port on the French island of Guadeloupe in the West Indies. It is the chief commercial town of the island with a picturesque old town centre. It has a good harbour and is also a route focus. Population (1974) 30,000.

Pointe-Noire, major port of the Congo People's Republic, situated on the Atlantic coast and the terminus of the railway from Brazzaville. Its port facilities were only completed in 1939 and its primary function is as an entrepôt. A new oil refinery handles the offshore oil deposits. Population (1978) 146,700.

Pointer, popular sporting dog, descended from Spanish dogs. The pointer is easily trained to point (i.e. to stop dead and remain rigid when it finds game at close quarters), and in America has been taught to retrieve. It usually stands about 63 cm at the shoulder and weighs 27 kg. The colour of the coat may be black, black and white, orange and white, lemon and white, or liver and white or tricolour.

Pointillism, see IMPRESSIONISM.

Pointing, finish of joint of brickwork. Pointing can be carried out as the brickwork proceeds or later. The main types of pointing are as follows: flush pointing; recessed pointing; keyed joints; struck weathered joint; bucket handle joint; and tuck pointing.

Poiret, Paul (1879–1944), French dress designer whose revolutionary styling was responsible for changing the shape of women's clothes in the early part of this century. He introduced a straight silhouette, soft classic shapes and soft fabrics.

He also designed furniture and other household items and substituted brilliant pinks and purples for the pastels previously fashionable.

Poison Gas, see CHEMICAL WARFARE; PHOSGENE.

Poisoning, Food, see FOOD-POISONING.

Poisonous Elements are used for many industrial purposes.

Mercury (Hg) compounds are used in making thermometers and batteries, in dentistry, in medicine (for ringworm and previously for syphilis, and as a purgative, although less toxic compounds are preferable), as fungicides and to stiffen felt hats (Lewis Carroll's 'Mad Hatter' was suffering from mercury poisoning). Some organic salts of mercury, e.g. phenyl mercury, are biodegradable, but methyl mercury is very toxic because it passes from the blood into the brain. It accumulates in the cerebellum, leading to muscular incoordination, and in the visual cortex, leading to blindness, and it destroys brain cells which cannot be replaced. Mercury also enters the kidney and liver cells and may cross the placental barrier, thus damaging the brain of the developing foetus. For the treatment of mercury poisoning the antidote dimercaprol is given by intramuscular injection. The stomach should be washed out and large quantities of egg albumin in milk or water should be given.

Arsenic (As) is used in ant poisons, insecticides, weed-killers, sheep dip, wallpapers, pottery, glass and some medicines. White arsenic is taken by mountaineers of Syria to add to endurance and has been used by some women to improve the complexion. Organic arsenic-containing compounds only release arsenic slowly and are therefore less likely to be as dangerous as the inorganic compounds. The digestive system is severely affected if arsenic is ingested and gastroenteritis, vomiting and diarrhoea may result. If inhaled, arsenic-containing dusts cause oedema of the lungs, shallow breathing, foamy coughing and restlessness. In chronic poisoning, after prolonged contact with arsenic, anaemia and liver damage result. Arsenic can be detected in the hair, nails, urine and faeces. Dimercaprol is a specific antidote for arsenic and the stomach should be washed out and milk, eggs, olive oil, barley water and ice (for thirst) may be given. Morphine will reduce the abdominal pain.

Antimony (Sb) is used in metal alloys, safety matches, medicines (tartar emetic), etc., and, like arsenic, combines with proteins to inhibit the normal metabolism of cells. Poisoning can be by ingestion (leading to severe gastro-intestinal disturbances), or by inhalation of the colourless gas stibine (SbH_3) (leading to headache, nausea, vomiting, jaundice, anaemia and weakness). Treatment is as for arsenic poisoning.

Lead (Pb) is used in type metal, batteries, paints, petrol, pottery glazes, rubber, brass alloys, and toys and jewellery coated with lead. Lead poisoning or plumbism is an occupational disease and affects workers in the pottery, painting and plumbing industries, and others who may absorb lead over long periods, especially in volatile form (e.g. tetraethyl lead used as an anti-knocking agent in petrol). The symptoms are mainly associated with the gastrointestinal system and the nervous system (both central and peripheral). Persons suffering from lead poisoning are restless, irritable, easily excitable and uncooperative. Recently studies have shown that children living in areas of high environmental lead content (e.g. near motorways) are often hyperkinetic (overactive and excitable).

For the emergency treatment of ingested lead compounds, magnesium or sodium sulphate, or emetic solutions should be given to wash out the stomach, followed by an antidote such as sodium calciumedetate or *penicillamine* (intramuscularly or intravenously) which combine with free (but not bound) lead and expedite its removal. However, these compounds only slowly remove lead from the brain. Lead compounds cause anaemia which may be treated with iron or a blood transfusion; morphine or other analgesics may be given as pain-killer for abdominal cramp. Other metals, e.g. copper, cadmium and silver, are also toxic.

Phosphorus (P) exists in two forms, the red (used in safety matches) is not toxic but the yellow, waxy fat-soluble form, which burns on contact with air, is very poisonous. Yellow phosphorus is used in rodent and insect poisons, in fireworks and in the manufacture of fertilisers. Phosphorus causes jaundice, fatty degeneration of the liver and kidneys, and gastrointestinal disturbances, and it interferes with fat, protein and carbohydrate metabolism and bone formation. The stomach should be washed with water or 0·1 per cent copper sulphate, and alkaline drinks (containing, e.g. sodium bicarbonate) should be administered. Morphine or pethidine will reduce the pain.

Poisons. There is no satisfactory definition of poison that will embrace all the examples, but substances which on entering the body and being in any degree absorbed produce death or injure health, though not by mere mechanical derangement, are poisonous. Introduction to the body may be by the mouth, by inhalation, by injection, or by absorption through the skin.

Classification may be according to source: vegetable, animal or mineral; or to chemical nature: organic, inorganic, acid, alkaloid. Modern classification divides poisons into *agricultural, industrial, medicinal* and *natural.* Agricultural poisons or pesticides include the fungicides, herbicides and insecticides. Industrial poisons include a wide range of chemicals such as hydrocarbons, nitrogen-containing compounds, corrosives, irritants, poisonous elements and poisonous gases. Medicinal poisons are dangerous drugs, and natural poisons include food poisoning; insect bites and stings; poisonous plants and fungi; and snake-bite.

Poitiers (Latin *Limonum*), French town, capital of the *département* of Vienne, at the confluence of the rivers Clain and Boivre, south-west of Tours. It was formerly the capital of Poitou. It dates from Roman times, and was later an important town of the Visigoths. The baptistry of St-Jean dates from the 4th century. Other notable buildings are the *hôtel de ville*, the *palais de justice* and the university (1432). The chief industries are the manufacture of textiles, electrical and metal goods, and brewing. Population (1975) 85,466.

Poiters, Diana of, see DIANE DE POITIERS.

Poitiers, Guillaume de, see GUILLAUME DE POITIERS.

Poker. A card game of essentially American origin. 'Draw' poker is the most popular form, and is practically synonymous with poker. A single pack of cards is used and five cards are dealt to each of generally half a dozen players, with the right to 'draw' five more. The object of the game is to make the best 'hand' according to certain combinations of cards. These combinations in order of value are: *a straight flush, fours, a full house, a flush, a straight, threes, two pairs, a pair, highest card,* where no hand has any one of the previously enumerated combinations.

A certain amount of money is fixed upon as the limit to the initial stake. One player starts the pool with a preliminary stake called the 'ante', which must not exceed half the limit

and which is made without looking at the hand. When the last round of betting is over the players turn up their cards; the best hand wins and takes the pool.
See also CARDS, PLAYING.

Poland
Area: 312,683 km²
Population: 35,382,000
Capital: Warsaw

Poland (Polish *Polska*), republic of eastern Central Europe (Polish People's Republic), lying between the Carpathians and the Baltic Sea. It is bounded on the east by the USSR, on the south by Czechoslovakia, and on the west by East Germany. After the Second World War Poland lost about 45 per cent of its territory to the Soviet Union, including Vilna, Polesye, Nowogródek, Wolyń, Tarnopol, Stanislawów, and parts of Lvóv and Białystok. To the west Poland gained some 104,635 km² from Prussia, which brought the frontier to the line of the Oder and Nysa rivers. The eastern boundary is the Curzon Line. Area 312,683 km².
Poland lies mostly on the great North European plain, bordered on the south by the Carpathians and the Sudeten Mountains. The average height of the country is only 173 m, with only 3 per cent of the area rising above 500 m. The plain is drained by the rivers Vistula, Oder, Bug and San, and there are many big lakes, which cover a total of 3200 km². The 480-kilometre Baltic coastline is flat and sandy, and the only natural harbours of significance are on the estuaries of the Vistula and Oder rivers.
The population was 35,382,000 in 1980. Almost all goods and services, except in agriculture, are produced in state-owned enterprises which employ nearly two-thirds of the labour force. Poland largely abandoned the system of collective farms in 1956. Instead farming circles have been organised on a co-operative basis to which about half the farmers belong, and this proportion is increasing. The chief crops are rye, potatoes, wheat and oats, but many specialist crops such as tobacco and fruits are grown in favourable areas and flax is widely grown. Cereal yields are highest in the western half of the country. Most farms keep some cattle and poultry but the density of cattle is highest in the south of Poland. Over one-quarter of Poland is forested.
The chief mineral resource is coal in Upper Silesia but brown coal, lead, iron, zinc, sulphur, oil and natural gas are exploited. Industry has been expanded and has spread more widely since 1950 so that almost all large and medium-sized towns contain large factories. The chief groupings of industry are on and around the coalfield of Upper Silesia, in the textile towns of the Łódź area, and in the Warsaw conurbation. New industrial areas have been developed since 1950 on the brown coal deposits at Konin, on the non-ferrous ore-fields near Legnica, and at Nowa Huta. The most important industrial employers are the engineering, foodstuffs, textiles and mining concerns.
The unit of currency is the *zloty*, which equals 100 groszy.
According to the constitution of 1952, authority in the state is vested in the *Sejm*, elected for four-year terms by all citizens over 18 years. This assembly elects a Council of State, composed of a chairman, a secretary, and 14 members. It also elects a Council of Ministers, which is the supreme executive and administrative organ. Members of the councils are carefully selected, and effective power lies in the politburo of the Communist United Workers' Party (UWP). Civilian government was replaced by martial law in December 1981.
Some 93 per cent of the population are Roman Catholics; this is the highest proportion of adherence to one church in Eastern Europe and is an unusual characteristic for a Communist country. The Catholic Church is thus a significant force, socially as well as politically, in the nations life.
The official language is Polish.
History. The first historical ruler, Prince Mieszko I (c.963/4–92), of the Piast dynasty, converted to Roman Christianity in 966, conquered Silesia and Cracow, and maintained his independence of the German Emperor. Succeeding reigns were marked by fluctuating territorial gains and losses and by uneasy relations with the Emperor, which sometimes deteriorated into total submission, or open warfare. The 16th century saw great cultural and political achievements, economic prosperity based on grain exports, as well as the growth of serfdom. Under Sigismund II Augustus, Lithuania was constitutionally joined to Poland by the Union of Lublin (1569) and a single Diet was created for the United Realm. Protestantism flourished and religious toleration was officially guaranteed (1573). Succeeding monarchs supported the Jesuits and the Counter-Reformation. After 1572 the monarchy became elective. In 1733–34 Russian and Saxon forces secured Poland for Augustus III of Saxony (1733–63). On the death of Augustus, Catherine II of Russia engineered the election of Stanisław Poniatowski as king. Certain reforms were initiated, but Russian interference and support of non-Catholic dissidents led to widespread conservative, Catholic and patriotic resistance. The resulting chaos encouraged Frederick II of Prussia to propose a partition of Poland, effected together with Austria and Russia in 1772. Poland lost a third of its territory and population and, in all but name, became a Russian protectorate. Poland was again partitioned by Russia and Prussia in 1793.
At the Congress of Vienna (1815) Poland was left partitioned. There was dissatisfaction with the new frontiers and nationalistic ferment continued throughout the 19th century. During the First World War all Poland was occupied by the Central Powers. The successive collapse of Russia, Austria and

Poland. *Strip farming in the Tatra Mountains on the Polish-Czech border. Amalgamation of farms has led to a decline in the rural population.*

Germany made Polish independence possible, and a republic was proclaimed on 11 November 1918. Repeated financial crises and political instability weakened the democratic constitution (adopted in 1921) and in 1926 Józef Piłsudski was brought to power by a military coup, ruling Poland until his death in 1935. In 1938–39 relations with Germany worsened. On 1 September 1939 German forces invaded Poland on three fronts. Warsaw capitulated to the Germans on 28 September and on 29 September Germany and the USSR agreed to divide Poland between them. A reign of terror and economic exploitation then began with the aim of turning the population into a slave labour force. In April 1945 the Oder and the Western Neisse became the new western border, leaving nearly all Silesia and Pomerania, and half of East Prussia in Poland. The Western powers recognised the new government in Warsaw. The key positions in the administration belonged to the Communist Polish Workers' party. A new constitution in 1952 followed the Soviet model. An unexpected rise in food prices in 1970 precipitated strikes and riots and savage government reprisals. In 1980 meat prices were raised and a wave of strikes followed, broadening into general political action. A strike committee led by Lech Wałęsa began negotiations with the government for the right to form independent trade unions and for political concessions; the former was achieved on 31 August 1980. In September Edward Gierek, the Communist Party secretary, suffered a heart attack and was replaced by Stanisław Kania. Various trade unions formed themselves into a national body, Solidarity, to press for further reforms. Conflicts between Solidarity and the government continued, to the extent that martial law was introduced on 13 December 1981. This was lifted on 22 July 1983 in an attempt to persuade the West to raise its economic sanctions, but the security powers given to the civil regime indicated that the changes were purely cosmetic.

Language. Polish, with Czech and Slovak, belongs to the Western group of the Slavonic languages. It has preserved many archaic Slavonic features, which contrast with a series of purely Polish characteristics. It uses the Latin alphabet, modified by diacritical marks.

Among the features of Polish are a fixed stress (on the penultimate syllable of a word), the presence of nasal vowels *ą* and *ę* (similar to French *on* and *in*), and the use of the third person singular for the polite form of address. An inflected language, the word order is very mobile, and it is rich in verbal meanings.

Literature. Poland's earliest literature was written only in Latin, and the development of vernacular writing in the 14th and 15th centuries is later than in the West. The golden age of Polish literature in the 16th century is marked by the work of Rej, a medieval moralist in a humanist era, Copernicus's *De revolutionibus* and J. Kochanowski, the most important early Polish writer.

In the 17th century the baroque, as in Spain, was to become a national style. In literature it is represented by the ornate verse of the elegant courtier J. A. Morsztyn and the historical epics of Twardowski and Wacław Potocki. The second half of the 18th century saw a vigorous revival of cultural and intellectual life.

Polish Romanticism combined the characteristic features of its European models (particularly German and English) with an intense commitment to the quest for national identity. Exiled by decree or conscience, the three great Romantic poets, Mickiewicz, Slowacki and Krasiński came to symbolise the spirit of the martyred nation. Romanticism was replaced by the sombre principles of realism or 'positivism' with its belief in practical endeavour based on *scientific* understanding. The three great novelists of the period are Orzeszkowa, Prus and Sienkiewicz.

The literature of the newly independent Poland of the inter-war period was rich and versatile. The most important writers before the Second World War include Andrzejewski, Choromański, Goetel, Bruno Schultz and Gombrowicz, while the period of development and experiment following the political changes around 1956 produced new names and new subjects.

Music. Polish church music was particularly fine during the 14th and 15th centuries. In the 16th century Cracow was a centre of music in central Europe. When the nationalist movement began in the 18th century, Polish composers began to incorporate the national songs and dances in their compositions. Chopin perfected the blending of national music and that which had international traditions. Moniuszko established a national opera and Karol Szymanowski was a crucial figure, absorbing the most advanced central European trends and drawing inspiration both from the Orient and the less familiar areas of Polish folk-music. The relaxation of cultural direction by the Communist party in the 1950s heralded a new age of experiment which, with such internationally-acclaimed composers as Penderecki (1933–), made Poland one of the centres of the avant-garde. The most considerable living Polish composer is probably Lutosławski (1913–).

***Roman Polanski** directing* Macbeth.

Polanski, Roman (1933–), Polish film director. After acting on both stage and screen, Polanski spent five years at the Lódź film school, during which time he made several short films including the surrealist *Two Men and A Wardrobe*, 1958, and assisted Andrej Munk on *Bad Luck*, 1960. His first feature, *Knife in the Water*, 1962, gained him critical notice and he came to England to make his next three films: *Repulsion*, 1965, *Cul-de-sac*, 1966, perhaps his finest film to date, and *The Dance of the Vampires*, 1967, all of which display his fascination with the grotesque and the perverse, though his ironic sense of humour allows him a certain critical distance from these fantasies. Both his most commercially successful films have been made in the USA: *Rosemary's Baby*, 1968, and *Chinatown*, 1973, in between which he completed a version of *Macbeth*, 1971, and *What?*, 1972. In 1980 he filmed Thomas Hardy's *Tess of the D'Urbervilles*.

Polar Bear, see BEAR.

Polar Front, see FRONTS.

Polar Light, see AURORA.

Polar Regions, see ANTARCTICA.

Polaris, in astronomy, 'the Pole Star', the name given to Alpha Ursae Minoris, a second magnitude star close to the north celestial pole. Due to precession this pole moves slowly relative to the stellar background. Polaris is a small-range Cepheid variable and its magnitude varies between 2·1 and 2·2 in a period of 3·97 days.

Polaris, the name given by the US navy to an intermediate range ballistic missile developed for launching from submerged submarines.

Polarisation of Light. Light, like other electromagnetic waves, is a transverse disturbance, i.e. both the electric and magnetic fields are perpendicular to the direction of travel. In light, only the electric field is usually significant. If the plane of the field were constant in relation to the direction of propagation, as it usually is in radio waves, the light would be polarised, and it would have different properties in different directions. The polarisation changes so rapidly that we cannot detect it and the light is said to be unpolarised. There are many ways of producing polarised light; the simplest is to pass ordinary light through a piece of polaroid. The directional property can then be seen by passing this polarised light through a second piece of polaroid and rotating it; the emergent beam will be bright or dark depending on the orientation of the second polaroid relative to the first. If light is polarised in a certain plane a polariser set at right angles will transmit no light.

Some crystals, in particular Iceland spar (calcium carbonate), can split light into two beams which are polarised at right angles to each other. This fact is the basis of the Nicol prism.

Polarising Microscope, instrument in which objects are viewed microscopically by polarised light. It assists in the identification of minute particles of crystals, minerals and biological tissues.

See also MICROSCOPE AND MICROSCOPY, OPTICAL; POLARISATION OF LIGHT.

Polarity of a body is the tendency which some bodies possess to set in a definite direction when acted upon by an external force. It may be natural or induced by external agencies. An example is a magnet; other instances may be found in electrostatics, current electricity and in molecules, which tend to have an uneven distribution of electrons.

Polaroid, trade name of sheet materials which polarise light. The commonest is based on a film of polyvinyl alcohol, with absorbed

iodine; the sheet is stretched to orient the polymer molecules after dipping in iodine solution and it is cemented between plastic protective sheets. The original (different) form was invented by E. H. Land in 1928.
See also Polarisation of Light.

Polder, name given in the Netherlands to the low-lying, marshy coastal regions, which from the 17th century onwards have slowly been reclaimed from the sea and converted into arable or pasture land.
See also Zuider Zee; IJsselmeer.

Pole, Reginald (1500–58), English cardinal and archbishop of Canterbury. He was given the deanery of Exeter, and might have secured high preferment if he had approved Henry VIII's divorce. Instead, he retired abroad. In 1536 he wrote *Pro Ecclesiasticae Unitatis Defensione*, in which he formulated his views on ecclesiastical affairs, with special reference to Henry VIII's conduct: and in the same year the pope made him a cardinal. In 1540 he was one of the three legates appointed to open the Council of Trent. Pole was one of a number of prominent churchmen who worked hard to effect a reconciliation with the Protestant theologians, and was at one time suspected of heresy. He came again to England in 1554 as papal legate, and two years later was appointed archbishop of Canterbury. It was his life's object to counteract the Reformation in England, and although he was not directly responsible for the deaths of Protestants in Mary's reign, he did not use his influence to stop them.

Pole, measure of length, equal to 5·5 yards (5·03 m). This unit is now little used in linear measurements, but has special interest on account of its seeming antiquity, for it can be equated to 10 Sumerian cubits.
See also Metrology.

Pole Star, see Polaris.

Pole Vault, see Jumping.

Polecat, *Mustela putorius*, a mammal belonging to the weasel family, Mustelidae, order Carnivora. The species name refers to the animal's fetid smell, which probably accounts for its never being tamed. The common European variety is 45 cm long, 12 cm being tail. White markings occur on the face, with its short ears and pointed nose, but otherwise its fur is dark brown above and black below. Its skin is called 'fitch' and makes excellent artists' brushes, but poor fur. The ferret is an albino domesticated variety of the polecat.
See also Marten.

Polemoniaceae, a plant family of 12 genera and about 300 species, mainly herbaceous with leaves in opposite pairs. The petals and sepals are both five in number and tubular in form; there are usually only three stigmas, a distinguishing feature of the family. *Phlox*, *Cobaea*, *Gilia* and *Polemonium* are members.

Poles, points where the Earth's rotational axis cuts the surface.
See also Antarctica; Magnet.

Poliakoff, Stephen (1952–), English playwright. After an award-winning seven-year period of work in the 'fringe', he became resident playwright to the National Theatre in 1976. His plays explore the moral vacuum of life in Britain today; its victims and manipulators. His plays include: *City Sugar*, 1975; *Strawberry Fields*, 1976; and the film *Runners*, 1983.

Police. Some kind of compulsion has always been necessary in the most primitive communities for securing effective observance of law and order. Sir Robert Peel provided the means for London's new police force with the Metropolitan Police Act of 1829, and by appointing two exceptional men as the first commissioners, but it was they, a veteran soldier, Col. Charles Rowan and a young barrister, Richard Mayne, who conceived and planned the structure and detail of the organisation. The first thousand of Peel's police in blue tailcoats and top hats, began their patrol on 29 September 1829. The New, or Metropolitan Police, became the model for the creation later of provincial forces: first in the boroughs following the Municipal Corporation Act 1835, and later in the counties after the passing of the County Police Act 1839. By the middle of the 19th century most boroughs had a paid police force, based as nearly as possible on the pattern of the Metropolitan Police.
A police strike in 1918 led to the setting up of the Desborough Committee of Inquiry. In consequence of its report the Police Act of 1919 was passed. Under this act the home secretary made regulations which standardised police pay and conditions of service throughout the country, and established the Police Federation, a representative organisation for officers below the rank of superintendent. The 1919 Police Act was followed by the Police Pensions Act 1921.
Between 1928 and 1933 the Commissioner, Lord Byng, and his successor, Lord Trenchard, reorganised the Metropolitan Police. New duties, such as traffic patrol, were provided for without any addition to the strength.
Throughout the post-war years the police work-load increased and a number of unrelated incidents in various parts of Britain, cumulative in their effect, gave rise to misgivings about the state of the police. A royal commission was appointed to review the constitutional position and the arrangements for control and administration of the police throughout Britain, including the functions of local police authorities and the accountability of the police, as well as their relationship with the public and the effectiveness of means of dealing with complaints by the public against the police. One of the greatest constitutional changes resulting from the commission was the section of the Police Act of 1964 which made the secretary of state answerable to Parliament for the general efficiency of the police.
Provincial police forces in England and Wales are maintained, equipped and housed by a police authority; two-thirds of the members of this body are appointed from the county council or councils concerned and one-third by the local bench of magistrates. The home secretary is the police authority for the Metropolitan Police.
Certain services, which it would be impracticable for each police force to provide on its own, are organised by the Home Office and police authorities, partly on a regional basis. These common police services include training facilities, forensic science laboratories, wireless and police promotion examinations.

Polidoro da Caravaggio, see Caravaggio, Polidoro Caldara da.

Poliomyelitis, an inflammation of the motor nerve cells of the brain and spinal cord, sometimes leading to paralysis. It was formerly called infantile paralysis, because children are particularly susceptible to it, and is commonly known as polio. It is caused by a virus, which enters the body by the mouth with contaminated food or drink. Infected people excrete the virus in their faeces, and imperfect hygiene is the principal way contamination and infection are spread.
The first symptoms are sore throat, muscular pains, headache and mild fever. Most cases recover quickly from this stage. In the second phase the virus attacks the central nervous system, and the patient may suffer paralysis: in the worst cases the breathing and swallowing muscles are paralysed, and victims can survive only by living in an iron lung.
Prevention is the main weapon in combating polio: strict attention to personal cleanliness is essential, especially as some people may carry the disease without knowing it. Preventative vaccines have been available since the 1950s, and in the developed countries the disease has been almost eliminated. It is still common in poorer countries. There is no specific treatment, but since exercise seems to hasten the onset of paralysis, early rest is advised.

Polish Corridor, German name, coined by Frederick the Great, to describe eastern Pomerania along the lower reaches of the Vistula and known also, officially, as 'Royal Prussia' when it was in Poland (1466–1772), and as 'West Prussia' after 1772. It was returned to Poland by the Treaty of Versailles in 1919, to give Poland access to the Baltic. Its existence was a factor in the events leading to the outbreak of war in Europe in 1939.

Politburo (abbreviation of Russian *Politicheskoe Byuro*, Political Bureau of the Central Committee of the Communist Party), main policy-making organ of the Communist Party of the Soviet Union. The first Politburo was formed on the eve of the October Revolution and was set up as a permanent institution in 1919. It was abolished in 1952, and replaced by a praesidium of the party's Central Committee. It was, however, restored at the 23rd Party Congress in 1966, and now has 15 members and seven candidate members. It is usually referred to as the 'collective leadership' of the party and country, and its power has tended to be more of this type since the dual form of leadership beginning in 1964. Leonid Brezhnev shared state and economic functions with other leaders while holding the title of General Secretary of the Communist Party from 1966.

Political Economy, the older name for economics, generally used in the early and mid-19th century.

Political Offences. Under English law there is no such thing as a political offence and a person is tried for his acts regardless of whether he acted out of any political motives. However, the political nature of an offence becomes relevant where a diplomatic representative of a foreign state makes a requisition for the apprehension of a fugitive offender to the home secretary who may, if the offence is political, refuse to order the issue of a warrant for arrest. He may at any time order a fugitive offender, accused or convicted of a political offence, to be discharged from custody.

Polk, James Knox (1795–1849), 11th President of the USA. From 1835 to 1839 he was Speaker of the US House of Representatives. In 1839 he was nominated by the Democrats of Tennessee as governor of the state and was elected. In 1844 he was nominated by the Democrats for the presidency and was elected. Polk, as president, said the country must settle the Oregon boundary and acquire California. Oregon, as then thought of, was a remote unsettled region between 42° and 54° 40′ N latitude. Britain proposed that 49° be the boundary line, and this was accepted. The Californian question was settled by the war with Mexico.

Polka, folk-dance performed in 2-4 time, said to have originated in Bohemia in the early 19th century. It is usually danced by couples and has many variations, particularly in Czechoslovakia. Many composers have written music for this dance, but the most famous have been the Czechs Dvořák, Smetana and Janáček.

Poll Tax, or capitation tax, tax levied on the individual. It was employed in ancient Athens, and several famous levies have been made in England. The first was in 1377, and that of 1380 led to Wat Tyler's rebellion. It was a favourite means of raising money under the Stuarts. Many US states have in the past employed a poll-tax to prevent blacks and 'poor whites' from voting, payment being made a prerequisite of the right to vote.

Pollack, *Gadus pollachius*, a fish closely related to the coal-fish; it belongs to the cod-fish family, Gadidae, order Gadiformes. It has no barbel hanging from its chin, and its lower jaw projects beyond the upper. Like others of its genus, it is carnivorous.

Pollaiuolo, Simone del, also 'Il Cronaca' (1454–1509), Florentine architect. He studied in Rome, and on returning to Florence was employed by Strozzi to complete the palace begun for him by Benedetto Maiano in 1489. He also designed the council hall of the Signoria and the Sacristy of San Spirito.

Pollarding, cutting back of the crown of a tree so that it shoots again at a height beyond the reach of browsing animals. It has been used for instance in willows, for the production of small-sized material for basket-making. Successive pollarding may produce contorted grain in the wood which is highly prized for the making of decorative veneers.

Pollen, the powder-like contents of the anthers of flowering plants. Each grain is a single cell enclosed in a thin inner coat, or *intine*, and a thicker outer coat, or *exine*. Pollen grains are of various forms, but characteristic of their species.

An analysis of pollen deposits can provide valuable information about the vegetation of a region in past ages. The air always contains a suspension of pollen grains from the plants currently in flower and some of these land in muddy areas or peat bogs where they become buried. The exine of pollen grains is very resistant to decay and their structure shows such a range of variation that it is often possible to identify the species or at least the genus of pollen grains that may be as much as a million years old.

Pollination, the transfer of pollen from an anther to a stigma, usually by the agency of insects or by the wind.

Self-pollination refers to deposition of pollen on the stigma of the flower in which it was formed. *Cross-pollination* is the term used if pollen is deposited on the stigma of another flower of the same species.

Pollock, Jackson (1912–56), US abstract painter. Influenced at first by Picasso and Surrealism, he became noted after 1946 for the energy with which he applied paint to a large-scale canvas or board to build up a complex network of dribbles and splashes. Described as 'action painting' or 'abstract expressionism', this form of painting had a wide influence in the post-war period.

Pollution, see AIR POLLUTION; ENVIRONMENTAL POLLUTION; WATER SUPPLY.

Pollux, Beta Geminorum, a first magnitude star in Gemini which with the second magnitude Castor, Alpha Geminorum, marks the heads of the Twins. It is thought that these two stars may have changed their relative brightness since Bayer's time for it would have been natural for him to have assigned Alpha to the brighter star.

Polo, Marco (1254–1324), Venetian traveller. At the time of his birth his father and uncle were absent on a commercial expedition to China, and they were asked to return by Kublai Khan. This they did in 1271, taking Marco with them, reaching the khan's court in 1275. The khan sent Marco as an envoy to Yunnan, Burma, Karakorum, Cochin and India, and for three years he acted as governor of Yangchow. The Polos finally left China in the entourage of a Mongolian princess, and returned by way of Sumatra, India and Persia (Iran) to Venice, which they reached in 1295. In 1298 Marco received the command of a vessel in the fleet fitted out against Genoa, and was made prisoner after the Venetian defeat at Curzola. While in captivity he dictated an account of his travels which has been translated into many languages.

Polo (Tibetan *pulu*, ball), a ball game played on horseback. One of the most ancient of games, it probably originated in Persia where it was certainly played before 500 BC. The beginning of the modern game in England dates from the 19th century. It was played by Englishmen in India from 1862 and in England from 1871. It is now very popular in Argentina.

A polo ground is 274 m long and 146 m wide if boarded, 182 m wide if unboarded. The goal posts are 7·3 m apart, and the winner of a match is the team scoring the most goals. There are four players in each team and a match is divided into seven-minute periods called chukkas. A match comprises from four to six chukkas. The stick consists of a cane handle set into a head which can take various forms. The ball, usually made from willow tree root, is 8·25 cm in diameter and weighs about 140 g.

Ponies are changed between chukkas and no pony is expected to play more than two chukkas during a day.

The governing body of British polo is the Hurlingham Polo Association.

Polo Pony, see HORSE; POLO.

Polo, Water, see WATER POLO.

Polonaise, or polonez, dance from Poland associated with court circles and performed as the opening ceremony before a ball. It is danced by couples, one behind the other in procession. Chopin wrote 13 polonaises, the most famous being that in A Major.

Polonium, chemical element, symbol Po, atomic number 84, approximate atomic weight 210; it occurs in uranium and thorium ores as a product of their radioactive decay. It was the first radioactive element to be

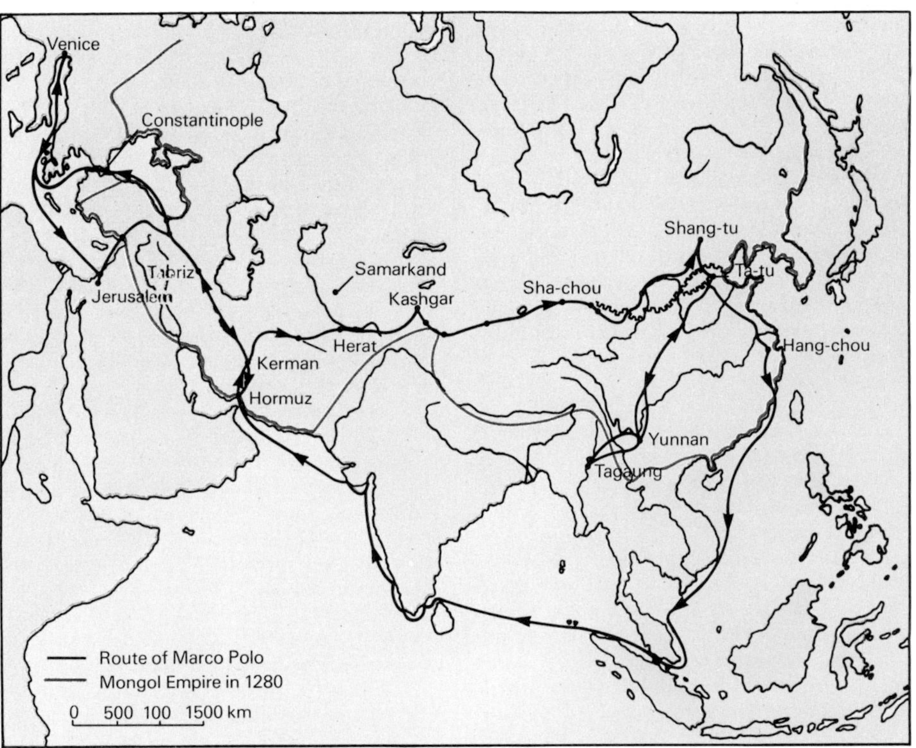

Marco Polo. *The route travelled on his journeys between 1271 and 1295. The account of his travels remained almost the only information available in Europe about the Far East for several centuries.*

isolated in a fairly pure state (by the Curies in 1898, in the course of investigations of the radioactive uranium ore, pitchblende), and is named after Poland, Madame Curie's native land. Polonium emits intense α-radiation, which evolves much heat, damages solutions and solids, and necessitates special handling precautions.

Poltava, or Pultowa, capital city, economic and cultural centre of Poltava *oblast*, USSR, on the River Vorskla south-west of Kharkov. There are food, textile and engineering industries, and the city is also a railway junction. Poltava has interesting 17th-19th century buildings. Known since 1174, it was a centre of the Ukrainian Cossacks in the 17th century and became provincial capital in 1862. In the 18th-19th centuries it was a lively commercial centre and in the 19th century it was one of the main centres of the Ukrainian literary and national movement. Population (1980) 284,000.

Poltergeist (German, noisy ghost), name given to an alleged ghost, agency or spirit manifesting unpleasantly in a house. Poltergeist disturbances include noises of every description, especially bell-ringing; movement, appearance and disappearance of objects; articles thrown about, strange smells and fire-raising. Serious physical injury is rare, although on occasions great force is displayed. All types of house, new or old, are apparently liable to infestation, which may cease as suddenly as it began, and for no apparent reason. Only rarely are poltergeist phenomena accompanied by an apparition.

Polyandry, marriage between one woman and several men. Frequently the co-husbands are brothers, the form known as 'adelphic polyandry'. Polyandry is found mainly in parts of Tibet, Assam and India, e.g. among the Nayar. It is usually associated with matrilineal descent.
See also POLYGYNY.

Polyanthus, a spring flower in family Primulaceae, of which many varieties, gold-laced, double and self-coloured, have been raised. The polyanthus originated as a cross between a coloured primrose and the cowslip.

Polybius (c.205–125 BC), Greek historian of Rome. After the Roman conquest of Macedonia (168 BC) he was taken with other hostages to Italy. Polybius was allowed to settle in Rome, where he was given access to the public records.
The *History of Polybius*, one of the most valuable records of antiquity, covered the period 221–146 BC. The first five books are extant; of the rest only fragments and abstracts have survived.

Polycarp, Saint (c.69–c.156), Bishop of Smyrna and one of the Apostolic Fathers of the early Christian Church. He is said to have been converted by St John the Apostle in 80. Polycarp was the author of an epistle to the Philippians. Shortly before the end of his life, he visited Rome to confer with Pope Anicetus as to the date for the celebration of Easter, and on his return to Smyrna was martyred.

Polychaete. The marine bristle-worms form class Polychaeta in phylum Annelida. They are secretive in habit, living in burrows in sand and mud or in rock crevices and under stones. They possess the basic annelid features but also have a pair of paddles or 'parapodia', one on each side of every segment, together with prominent bristles or 'setae', and a well-developed head with a pair each of eyes, antennae and palps. The group can be conveniently divided into two loosely defined groups: the Errantia (such as *Nereis*, the ragworm) which are free-living, i.e. swimming or crawling, and the Sedentaria (such as *Arenicola*, the lug-worm) which live permanently within a tube.

Polyclitus of Argos (fl.440 BC), Greek sculptor, pupil of the Argive sculptor Ageladas, and probably a late contemporary of Phidias and Myron. The various copies of his figures of male athletes, the *Doryphoros* or *Youth with Javelin* (Naples, Museo Nazionale, Florence, Uffizi, and the Vatican Museum), the *Diadoumenos* or *Youth Tying his Headband* (Athens, National Museum), and the *Diskophoros* or *Youth with a Discus* (Paris, Louvre) show Polyclitus's preoccupation with contrasting movements in the different parts of the body, and with proportion, a subject to which he devoted a theoretical work, the *Canon*. Other works by Polyclitus were a *Hercules* and a *Wounded Amazon*.

Polycotyledonous Plants, those which have more than two cotyledons, an uncommon condition almost confined to the Gymnosperms.

Polycrates, Greek tyrant of Samos, 535–522 BC. He established the naval supremacy of Samos in Aegean waters, and amassed a large fortune by piracy. A story is told (Herodotus, iii. 39 ff.) that in order to avoid the jealousy of the gods he threw into the sea his most valuable possession, a ring of exceptional beauty. This ring, however, was discovered inside a fish intended for his table.

Polyester, a synthetic fibre discovered in the UK in 1941 by J. R. Whinfield and J. T. Dickson. The polymer is formed by condensing an ester of terephthalic acid with ethylene glycol at temperatures above 200°C. The spinning of the fibre is by the melt-spun route and delustrants are usually added.
Chemical variants are made to obtain different dyeing properties or to provide higher melting points or other physical properties. The original fibre melts at about 250°C, is very strong, but does not absorb much water. It is resistant to most chemicals likely to be encountered during domestic use. The fibre is used by itself or in blends with wool, cotton and other fibres in many types of clothing and domestic textiles. The fibre is also used for ropes and many industrial uses.

Polygala, see MILKWORT.

Polygamy, marriage with more than one spouse simultaneously. There are two varieties; polygyny, one husband with several wives; and polyandry, one wife with several husbands.

Polyglot (Greek *polus*, many; *glōtta*, tongue), book which contains several versions of the same text in different languages, arranged side by side in parallel columns for ease of comparison. By far the greater number of such works have been editions of the whole or part of the Bible. Several polyglot dictionaries have also been issued. The word is also used to describe a person who speaks several languages.

Polygon, plane figure bounded by straight lines. The simplest polygon is the triangle. Polygons with more than three sides are named quadrilateral (4 sides), pentagon (5), hexagon (6), heptagon (7), octagon (8), nonagon (9), decagon (10), dodecagon (12), *n*-gon (*n*). In elementary geometry, it is usual to specify that the sides of a polygon can meet only at the vertices. A polygon is said to be 'regular' if all its sides are equal and all its interior angles (between adjacent sides) are equal. The sum of the interior angles of a convex *n*-gon is $(n-2)\pi$. Each interior angle of a regular *n*-gon is $(n-2)\pi/n$.

Polygonaceae, a family of about 40 genera and about 750 species of flowering plants. They are mainly herbaceous, having a brown membranous sheath or ochrea at the junction of stem and leaf-stalk. Flowers are usually small and green, white or pink, and are often conspicuous because of being grouped together in large numbers. A few, such as buckwheat (*Fagopyrum*) and rhubarb (*Rheum*) are used for food; some species of *Polygonum* are grown in gardens.

Polygonum, genus of flowering plants in the family Polygonaceae, which has a wide variety of habitat and growth-form. Species include knotgrass, *P. aviculare*, a small creeping weed now cosmopolitan; persicaria, *P. persicaria*; water bistort, *P. amphibium*; and black bindweed, *P. convolvulus*. *P. baldschuanicum*, a fast-growing woody climber, and *P. cuspidatum*, from temperate eastern Asia, are grown in gardens.

Polygyny, concurrent marriage between one man and more than one woman. It is practised in Africa, China and India, and permitted by Islam which allows a man to marry up to four wives. American Mormons were polygynous until legislation prohibited it in 1890.
See also MARRIAGE.

Polyhedron (Greek *polus*, many; *hedra*, a base), in solid geometry, a solid figure bounded by plane faces. Polyhedra are said to be regular when the faces are all congruent regular polygons; there are five such convex forms, often known as Platonic solids because Plato described them. They are: (1) The regular *tetrahedron*, of which each solid angle is formed by 3 equilateral triangles; it has 4 faces, 4 vertices and 6 edges. (2) The regular *octahedron*, of which each solid angle is formed by 4 equilateral triangles; it has 8 faces, 6 vertices and 12 edges. (3) The regular *icosahedron*, of which each solid angle is formed by 5 equilateral triangles; it has 20 faces, 12 vertices and 30 edges. (4) The cube, or regular *hexahedron*, of which each solid angle is formed by 3 squares; it has 6 faces, 8 vertices and 12 edges. (5) The regular *dodecahedron*, of which each solid angle is formed by 3 regular pentagons; it has 12 faces, 20 vertices, and 30 edges.

Polymerisation, see PLASTICS.

Polymers, chemical compounds built up of many small units. The polymer has the same empirical formula as each of its units but its molecular weight is a multiple of that of the unit. Thus paraldehyde, $C_6H_{12}O_3$, is a polymer of acetaldehyde, C_2H_4O, since it has the same atoms in the same ratio, and is directly obtainable from acetaldehyde. Some polymers with very large numbers of atoms in their molecules ('macro-molecules') are the basis of many modern synthetic fibres. Another, polyethylene, is an excellent electrical insulator. There are many naturally occurring polymers: starches; cellulose, the structural material of plants (cotton is pure cellulose); chitin, the material that makes the shells of crustacea and insects hard; proteins; and nucleic acids.

Inorganic natural polymers include silica, diamond and graphite.

See also PLASTICS.

Polynesia, islands between longitudes 170°E and 110°W in the east Pacific, the area included forming roughly a triangle, with Hawaii in the north, New Zealand in the south-west, and Easter Island in the south-east. Scattered widely over an ocean territory four times the size of Europe, these islands are inhabited by the Polynesians, a people of the Caucasoid race, who number 3·5 million (1970 estimate).

The islands themselves vary from high volcanic formations, such as Hawaii and Tahiti, to low coral atolls hardly above sea-level such as are found in the Tuamotu Archipelago, with many combinations of the two. The productivity of the islands varies accordingly, from the rich fertility of the high islands which bear all kinds of tropical fruits, to the barren atolls on which little but coconut trees can grow. Agriculture, fishing and copra are the main native industries.

Polynesians are tall, with light-brown skins and straight to wavy dark hair. The area was penetrated, beginning in the 1st millennium BC, from the west, with Fiji as the likely immediate homeland.

The most remarkable technological achievements of the Polynesians relate to their mastery of the sea. Without the aid of metals or mechanical devices, they constructed huge (up to 50 metres long), sail-rigged, double-hulled canoes capable of carrying 100 persons and food supplies for many weeks. Long ocean voyages were undertaken, navigated by means of a detailed knowledge of the heavens, winds, sea-currents and wave-patterns. The settlement of many of the Polynesian islands may be assumed to have been the result of deliberate voyages of emigration, undertaken by whole communities of refugees; though this is not to say that many landfalls were not also the result of accident, by vessels being swept off-course or by the blind search for new islands to colonise.

The paramount chieftaincies of the larger islands were politically unstable, and temporary hegemonies were forever dissolving in internecine war. Even during peaceful times, there was much cruelty and violence in Polynesian societies; punishments for infringement of chiefly prerogative were severe, many religious rituals demanded human sacrifices, and chiefly funerals involved orgiastic killings and mutilations. European contact exacerbated political turmoil (through the introduction of firearms and gratuitous military assistance given to rebellious chiefs), until colonial governments and protectorates were established in the 19th century.

Two centuries after the European invasion of the Pacific, Hawaii (the 50th state of the USA) can claim a Polynesian substratum only; central Polynesia remains French and Tahitians are becoming an urbanised proletariat, Easter Islanders are more Chilean than Polynesian, while the Maoris are a relatively deprived minority in New Zealand. Only Tonga has retained its traditional political system. However, many of the smaller island chains and isolated outliers preserve a characteristic Polynesian way of life.

***Polynesia.** The volcanic peaks of Raiatea, an island in the Tahitian archipelago.*

Polyp, a form of the animals in the phylum Coelenterata which is adapted for a sedentary mode of life. In general shape it is cylindrical and has a terminal 'mouth' surrounded by mobile tentacles. The animal involved in making coral is a well known example; the sea anemone is another. The other main form of coelenterate is the medusa, a free-living jellyfish organism adapted for a planktonic, free-drifting existence.

Polyphemus, in Greek legend, one of the Cyclops, dwelling on the west coast of Sicily. Odysseus with 12 companions entered the cave of Polyphemus, who devoured six of them for supper, keeping Odysseus and the rest for another meal. But Odysseus made him drunk, put out his one eye with a burning pole and escaped with his friends by hanging under the bellies of Polyphemus's sheep as they were let out of the cave next morning.

Polyphony is the interplay of two or more parallel melodic parts in instrumental or choral music, and implies the presence of counterpoint. It developed in the 16th century and early 17th century as a movement away from plainsong and harmonic blocks of sound, and culminated in the music of Palestrina, Lassus and Byrd. Although later music, such as that of Bach, is polyphonic, harmony has a more important rôle and the term is usually restricted to the earlier period. The development of polyphony went hand in hand with the appearance of families of instruments: strings, wind and keyboard instruments, e.g. violin family, recorders, etc. Its finest achievements can be seen in choral music, in the mass, motet and madrigal.

Polypodium, a genus of ferns in family Polypodiaceae, chiefly evergreen, and widely distributed throughout the world. *P. vulgare*, common polypody, is absent only from Australasia, and is the chief British species.

Polyporus, a genus of bracket or shelf fungi, family Polyporaceae, subdivision Basidiomycotina. They produce fruiting bodies on the outside of trees and cause heart rot within.

Polypropylene, compound formed by polymerisation of propylene. Polypropylene can be melt-spun into a fibre or formed into film and slit to form a tape. The fibre is one of the cheapest of all fibres and is used for ropes (which float on water), sacks, carpet pile and carpet backing. The fibre is marketed under many names such as Ulstron and Fibrite.

Polypus (plural, polypi), a tumour possessing a stem, or *pedicle*, by which it is attached to a tissue surface. Polypi are usually found on mucous membranes, as in the nose, bladder, uterus or rectum. The treatment in most cases is to remove them either by surgical excision or cauterisation (heat coagulation).

Polystichum, or shield fern, a genus in the family Aspidiaceae that is cosmopolitan in distribution and includes *P. aculeatum*, hard shield fern, *P. setiferum*, soft shield fern, and *P. lonchitis*, the holly fern.

Polytechnics, institutions in Britain covering a wide range of courses at further education level, ranging from university degree courses to diplomas of various kinds at a lower level. Admission is generally at 18 years and older.

Polytheism (Greek *polus*, many; *theos*, god), belief in many gods, as opposed to monotheism and atheism.

Polythene, see PLASTICS.

Pome, see FRUIT.

Pomegranate, *Punica granatum*, a handsome deciduous tree in the family Punicaceae. A native of south-west Asia, it is often grown for the beauty of its scarlet flowers. The fruit, slightly larger than an orange, is yellow to red, and is divided into several chambers containing seeds coated with a juicy, edible pulp.

Pomerania (German *Pommern*), former territory of Germany and maritime province of Prussia, lying on the southern shore of the Baltic. The Oder divided it into Hinterpommern (in the east) and Vorpommern (in the west). After the Second World War

Hinterpommern was incorporated in Poland, and Vorpommern became, for a time, part of the *Land* of Mecklenburg. Pomerania, which once included also West Prussia, was a sovereign duchy until 1637, when its dynasty became extinct.

Pomeranian, a popular toy dog which was developed in England by breeding from toy individuals which occurred in litters of the larger breed Pomeranian Spitz, or German Spitz, which is a national breed of Germany. Any whole-colour is permissible and so are parti-coloureds or white with evenly distributed patches. But these colours are becoming very rare and orange is now fashionable. The early variety weighed 10–15 kg but only the toy variety is now recognised, and it weighs up to 2·5 kg.

Pompadour, Jeanne Antoinette Poisson, Marquise de (1721–64), mistress of Louis XV. The king established her at Versailles in 1745 and bought her the estate of Pompadour, from which she took her title. Here she became the leader of a brilliant artistic and literary circle, amongst whom figured Voltaire. She soon turned her attention to state affairs as well, filling the most important offices with her favourites and making and unmaking, by turns, ministers, diplomatists and generals. No one obtained office except through her.

Pompano, fish of the genus *Trachinotus*, in order Perciformes of class Actinopterygii, the bony, ray-finned fishes. They are silver, warm-water, marine fish that grow to almost 50 cm in some species and almost 90 cm in others. They are a valuable edible fish.

Pompeii, ancient town of Campania in Italy, 3 km from the shore of the bay of Naples and situated at the foot of Mount Vesuvius. According to Strabo, it was first occupied by Oscans, afterwards by Etruscans, and then by Samnites; it was one of the last places in Campania to be reduced by the Romans. In AD 63 an earthquake destroyed a large part of the town, and the inhabitants were repairing and rebuilding when the city was overwhelmed by the eruption of Vesuvius, AD 79. In 1594, during the construction of an underground aqueduct, two inscriptions were found. In 1763 systematic excavations began and the greater part of the town has now been unearthed. The chief buildings are the great amphitheatre to seat 20,000 persons, one of the finest that has been discovered; the forum, with the public buildings on all sides of it; the paved way to the forum, which was for foot passengers only and adorned with many statues; the temples of Jupiter, Apollo, Isis and Zeus Meilichius, Vespasian and Fortuna Augusta, and the Doric temple which stands in another forum with a large and a small theatre adjoining, and three separate public bath-houses. Near the theatres were the barracks of the gladiators, where objects of personal use were discovered. The house of the Vettii has been restored as far as possible to show the actual conditions in which the wealthier classes of Pompeii lived at that time. Of the numerous objects of art found, many are very beautiful and some of the bronze statuettes are of exceptional workmanship. Many of the mural paintings, frescoes and mosaics are of high artistic merit.

Pompeius Magnus, Gnaeus, known as Pompey the Great (106–48 BC), son of Pompeius Strabo, and one of the great military leaders of the late Roman Republic.

In 67 BC Pompey was given a command to clear the Mediterranean of pirates. This command was unprecedented, in that it gave Pompey authority greater than that of the governors in every province with a Mediterranean coast. Pompey destroyed the pirates in six weeks. Opposition to Pompey in the Senate became strong. Pompey was therefore driven into alliance (later known as the first triumvirate) with Caesar and Crassus. To cement the alliance, Pompey married Caesar's daughter Julia.

Pompey is sometimes criticised (and pitied) for allowing Caesar to build up his power. When the first triumvirate began to look like breaking apart (following the deaths of Crassus and Julia), the Senate made him sole consul in 52 BC, and allowed him to hold his provincial command in Spain for a further five years *in absentia*. By contrast, the Senate insisted that Caesar should resign his command before returning to stand as consul. When Caesar refused to do this, it was to Pompey that the Senate looked to defend the republic.

Pompey lost the civil war, fled to Egypt, and was murdered on his arrival there.

Pompey, see POMPEIUS MAGNUS, GNAEUS.

Pompidou, Georges Jean Raymond (1911–74), French politician and administrator. He was head of the French Cabinet, 1958–59; a member of the Constitutional Council, 1959–62; and succeeded Debré as premier in 1962. Although inexperienced, he was successful as prime minister when de Gaulle was president, and as the effective leader of the Gaullists. After the 1968 student and worker revolt he led successful negotiations and organised the elections. He was then dismissed by de Gaulle, but was elected second president of the Fifth Republic, 1969. In the sphere of foreign policy he reversed many of his predecessor's policies, notably by welcoming British membership of the European Economic Community in 1971. After the death of de Gaulle he showed greater self-confidence, but met increasing left-wing opposition. From 1973 he showed signs of illness, and died suddenly in April 1974.

Ponce, a city of Puerto Rico. It is the major city in the south of the island, Playa de Ponce being the principal port of the island. Main industries include cement, paper, textile and iron production, canning, sugar refining and rum. Around 1670–80 the city was founded and named Nuestra Senora de Guadelupe de Ponce. The population was 188,219 in 1980.

Ponchielli, Amilcare (1834–86), Italian composer. In 1856 he produced his first opera, and after two ballets and three more operas came the opera *La Gioconda*, by which he is remembered.

Poncho, cloak having a hole for the head, worn by the Indians of South America and also by many of the Spanish inhabitants. It resembles a narrow blanket with a slit in the middle through which the head passes, so that it hangs down loosely before and behind, leaving the arms free.

Pond-skater, or water-strider, insects belonging to the family Gerridae in order Hemiptera (suborder Heteroptera). They usually live in large numbers on the surface waters of ponds, lakes or slow-flowing streams, and skate across the surface waters by means of rowing or jumping movements of the second and third pairs of legs. At the tips of their legs they have dense tufts of hairs that enable them to walk on the water surface. They are scavengers. *Gerris lacustris* is a commonly encountered species. It measures about 10 mm long.

Pondicherry, Union Territory of India, formerly a French possession. Its chief products are rice and millet, with increasing production of sugar-cane and groundnuts. Its major centre, also called Pondicherry, lies on the Coromandel coast, 196 km south of Madras. It was founded in 1674 and was later the capital of French India. Its main industry is textiles and coastal trading. The area was ceded to India in 1954. Area 479 km². Population (1981) 604,136.

Pondweed, *Potamogeton*, a cosmopolitan genus of floating or submerged plants in family Potamogetonaceae, with leathery leaves and spikes of small green flowers. *P.*

Pompeii. *The ruins and partly reconstructed remains of the once buried city.*

lucens, shining pondweed; *P. natans*, broad-leaved pondweed; *P. polygonifolius*, bog pondweed; *P. perfoliatus*, perfoliate pondweed; and *P. obtusifolius*, grassy pondweed, are common in the northern hemisphere.

Poniatowski, Prince Michel (1922–), French politician. He became an Independent Republican deputy in 1967. He was minister of the Interior under Giscard d'Estaing, 1974–77.

Ponta Delgada, city of the Azores, Portugal, capital of Ponta Delgada district, situated on the south shore of São Miguel island, 1450 km west of Lisbon. It has an excellent harbour, is a port of call for transatlantic ships, and is the commercial centre of the Azores, with a trade in fruit, wine, cereals, vegetables, sugar, tea, tobacco, sperm-whale oil and chicory. Population (town) 69,930; (district) 159,360.

Pontefract, or Pomfret, town of West Yorkshire, England. It is near the junction of the rivers Aire and Calder. There are ruins of the Norman castle (founded in 1069) where Richard II and Earl Rivers were put to death. Coal-mining is the principal industry; other industries include tanning, brewing, corn-milling, iron-founding, engineering, transport and furniture-making. Liquorice is used in large quantities for the famous 'Pontefract' or 'Pomfret' cakes. Population (1981) 31,971.

Pontevedra, capital of the province of Pontevedra, Spain, at the mouth of the Lérez. It has a 13th-century episcopal palace. Pontevedra has a naval radio station, and a trade in agricultural produce, wine, textiles and pottery. Population (1970) 52,452.

Ponti, Gio (1891–), Italian architect and designer. He is best known for the Pirelli Building in Milan (1958), on which he collaborated with Nervi. His earlier buildings in international modern style include the Institute of Mathematics, Rome University, 1934, and office buildings for the Montecatini Company, Milan, 1936 and 1951.

Pontiac (c.1712–69), chief of the Ottawa Indians, and reputed engineer of a conspiracy in 1763 against the British. With the help of other tribes he captured many forts and arranged successful ambuscades. In 1766 he yielded, and three years later he was assassinated in Illinois by one of his own people.

Pontianak, port of West Kalimantan province, Indonesia, on the River Kapuas. Its major exports are timber, rubber, palm oil and copra, and there is some rubber processing and a small timber-processing industry. The city has a significant Chinese minority, and its hinterland is exceptional in having Chinese rice cultivation. Population (1975) 247,000.

Pontifex, member of the official priesthood in ancient Rome, at whose head was the *pontifex maximus* (high priest). It supervised the state religion, and was the last court of appeal when any religious dispute arose. It further possessed considerable political influence through its control of the calendar and its power to intercalate days and regulate festivals. From Augustus onwards the Roman emperors assumed the functions and title of *pontifex maximus*. The title *pontifex pontificum* is now used by the popes.

Pontifical, liturgical book for the use of bishops in the Roman Catholic Church, containing prayers and rubrics for episcopal ceremonies other than the mass. Adjective from noun pontiff, describing things belonging to a bishop.

Pontine Marshes (Italian *Pontino Agro*; ancient *Pometinae Paludes*), stretch of territory in Lazio, Italy, extending for about 45 km along the coast of the Tyrrhenian Sea between Velletri and Terracina. They are crossed by the Appian Way, and were formerly notoriously unhealthy. Eventually, in 1926, the Italian government began extensive modern drainage schemes; the reclaimed land has been cultivated, and several new towns founded on it, including Latina.

Pontius Pilate, Roman *eques* appointed procurator of Judaea by Tiberius in AD 26. Under him in c.AD 30 Christ was crucified.

Pontoon, a floating dock or, more strictly, a floating bridge. The floating bridge has been used for military purposes from ancient times.

Pontus, in ancient geography, district in the extreme north-east of Asia Minor. About 301 BC a Persian satrap who had been left by Alexander to govern the region made himself independent and established a kingdom which was greatly enlarged by Mithridates. After the defeat of Mithridates by Pompey, in 64 BC, the western part of Pontus was joined to Bithynia to form a double province called Pontus and Bithynia. The remainder became a Roman province in AD 64.

Pontypool, industrial town in Gwent, South Wales, 13 km north of Newport, with manufactures of iron ware, nylon yarn, glass and soft toys. The first tinplate to be made in Britain was produced here in 1703. Population (1981) 36,761.

Pontypridd, town in Mid Glamorgan, South Wales, situated at the junction of the rivers Taff and Rhondda. There are chain and cable works and iron and brass foundries. Population 32,992.

Pony, see HORSE.

Poodle, breed of dogs of considerable antiquity. Poodles were formerly jet-black or pure white, but modern breeders have introduced many other shades. Their coat is a mass either of short curls or long ropy ringlets. Show poodles are trimmed in the 'lion-clip', with a huge mane and shorter coat on the hindquarters and bracelets on the legs. Pet poodles can be clipped in many different styles, the 'lamb clip' being one of the most popular.

Pool, see AMERICAN POOL; BILLIARDS.

Poole, seaport and resort, adjoining Bournemouth, in Dorset, England. There is trade in potter's clay, tiles, bricks, sanitary pottery, chemicals, caravans, food, confectionery, rope and sailcloth; there is also engineering and boatbuilding and repairing. Poole Harbour, a stretch of water 11 km long containing Brownsea Island, is a yachting centre. Population (1981) 118,922.

Pools, Football, see FOOTBALL POOLS.

Poon Wood, name given to the wood of *Calophyllum inophyllum* and other species. It is used for masts and spars.

Poona, city of Maharashtra state, India, 100 km south-east of Bombay on the Mutha and Mula rivers, 500 m above sea-level in the Western Ghats. It was the Maratha capital in the 18th century, a British hill resort in the 19th and 20th, and is now a commercial, manufacturing and military centre based on cotton textiles, rubber, paper, light engineering, pharmaceuticals and munitions. Population (1981) 1,685,266.

Poor Clares, see CLARE, SAINT.

Poor Law, History of. In England, until the dissolution of the monasteries, alms for the poor were dispensed by the Church. After the Reformation this unsystematic source of charity diminished and it was not until 1601 that the Poor Law Act for the first time regularised the English poor-law administration, financed by rates compulsorily levied on occupiers of property. By the 19th century widespread poverty among agricultural workers, inefficient and dishonest administration by overseers, and the heavy demands of 'outdoor' relief on the rates led to the appointment of a commission of inquiry in 1833. The resulting Poor Law Amendment Act of 1834 obliged all able-bodied paupers to go into a workhouse, which was supported by a group of parishes. Conditions in the workhouses were deliberately designed to deter the poor from 'going on the parish', and so keep down the rates.

The creation of new social services early in the 20th century removed many problems of economic hardship. The introduction in 1908 of the state 'means test' pensions for persons over 70 was the first major breach in the poor law. From 1911 the National Health Insurance scheme provided the incapacitated worker with medical treatment and cash benefits; from 1926 the field of the state pension scheme was extended. The Local Goverment Act 1929 abolished boards of guardians. Authority for administering the poor law, which itself remained unchanged, was transferred to counties and county boroughs. The Beveridge Report (1942) recommended the abolition of the poor law and this was accomplished in 1948.

Poor Man's Weatherglass, see PIMPERNEL.

Pop Art, movement in modern art, characterised by acceptance, and imitation or outright copying, of features taken from mass culture and commercialised media (television, films, newspapers and comics, advertising). Examples include Roy Lichtenstein's paintings derived from comics, Andy Warhol's silkscreens of Marilyn Monroe and silkscreened wooden Brillo boxes, and Claes Oldenburg's hamburgers and other objects rendered in unfamiliar sizes and materials. Adoption of mass-production techniques, particularly those of printmaking, marks a break with the tradition of the 'individual' work of art. Two tendencies in Pop Art are (1) to reproduce the pop image, as in Warhol's Campbell's Soup advertisement, and (2) to manipulate and distort it to obtain new effects, e.g. by making collages and 'environments'—a side of Pop Art related to Dada and Surrealism. Pop Art elements can be found in the work of US artists in the 1950s, e.g. Jasper Johns, Larry Rivers and Robert Rauschenberg. In the 1960s, as well as the artists mentioned earlier, Tom Wesselmann, Jim Dine, James Rosenquist and George Segal helped to establish Pop Art. British pop artists include Peter Blake, Allen Jones, Richard Hamilton, Richard Smith, Peter Phillips and Derek Boshier.

Pop Music in its present form originated in the mid-1950s with a fusion of rhythm and blues with romantic popular music. More uncompromising than that of the dance bands and ballad singers which preceded it, it was epitomised by the sounds of Elvis Presley, Little Richard, Chuck Berry and the Everly Brothers. Rock 'n' Roll was the expression of the newly affluent young. The end of the 1950s marked a new phenomenon: the emergence of the 'group' in place of the star name. In 1962, the Beatles emerged as leaders of the new beat groups, and for a while British groups, including the Rolling Stones, had virtually taken over the US charts. American influence was confined to the continuing success of Tamla, Burt Bacharach and Bob Dylan. The 'flower-power' cult, and the psychedelic movement, led to the development of a style known as 'acid-rock', the frenetic, improvisatory style being led by the British based Cream, and Jimi Hendrix. Widening experimentation led to 'pop' developing into a musical style that was certainly not 'popular music'.

During the 1970s, West Indian reggae music acquired a steady cult following. At the same time the 'disco' style emerged: bland, mid-Atlantic and ubiquitous. The violent backlash was the appearance of 'punk' rock, of British origins, with its calculated, if comic, nastiness. One of the outstanding contributions of the 1970s was the 'rock opera' *Tommy*, featuring The Who, while another group, Pink Floyd, carried the success of their multi-media event *The Wall* into the 1980s. The problem of 'pop' as well as 'popular' music is that both are by definition ephemeral, subject to the whims and fads of fashion.

Pope, Alexander (1688–1744), English poet. In 1715 the translation of the *Iliad* was begun, and published at intervals until 1720. It was enormously popular, and brought the poet £5000. The *Odyssey* followed (1725–1726), although with this he had the assistance of Broome and Penton. While translating these poems, Pope moved to Chiswick, where he lived from 1716 to 1718, and where he issued in 1717 a collected edition of his works, including the 'Elegy on the Death of an Unfortunate Lady' and the *Epistle of Eloisa to Abelard*.

In 1718, his father having died, he moved with his mother to his famous villa at Twickenham; the setting out of the grounds here became one of his chief interests and here also he received his friends, who included the most distinguished men of letters, wits, statesmen and beauties of the time.

Pope's position as a poet has been the subject of much contention among critics. There was a reaction against the neo-classicism of his poetry as Romantic tastes began to prevail later in the 18th century, and in the 19th century Pope was often inaccurately dismissed as bitter, malicious and 'unpoetic'. More recently the quality of his verse has again been recognised. He was the master of the heroic couplet, and in its polish and perfection he aimed to reflect the qualities of the true poet, a seer, a man of taste and dedication, committed to the preservation of human and social standards. These positive qualities lie behind the spleen and bitterness particularly of *The Dunciad* and *The Epistle to Arbuthnot* and they combine to give the mock-heroic vision a genuine touch of elegiac splendour and of tragedy. It is this sense of the poet's committed rôle which gives *The Rape of The Lock*, for all its surface delicacy and apparent triviality, a deep sense of human understanding and sympathy; it also prevents the *Essay on Man*, which is largely a reworking of received wisdom, from falling into complacency or conventionality.

Pope, see PAPACY.

Poplar, *Populus*, a genus of about 30 deciduous trees in family Salicaceae. The aspen (*P. tremula*); the white poplar or abele, *P. alba*; and the black poplar, *P. nigra*, are all from Europe and Asia. The columnar Lombardy poplar, a variety of *P. nigra*, and the balsam poplars or balm of Gilead, *P. gileadensis* and *P. trichocarpa*, are cultivated. Modern commercial poplars are hybrids with American species and called *P.x euramerica*. These are very fast-growing trees.

Poplin (French *popeline*), dress fabric, used also for upholstery, with a warp of silk and a weft of worsted which give a corded structure. It has been manufactured in Ireland (especially Dublin) from the early 18th century.

Popocatepetl (Aztec, smoking mountain), volcano, 72 km south-east of Mexico City, Mexico. The last serious eruption was in 1664, but minor ones have occurred since, the last few in the 1920s. Its crater rim lies above the snowline at 5340 m. With its twin Ixtacihuatl, it dominates Mexico City.

Popper, Sir Karl Raimund (1902–), Viennese-born British philosopher. He is best known for *The Open Society and Its Enemies*, 1945ff., in which he attacks the closed systems and 'ideal' societies of Plato, Hegel and Marx. However, his *Die Logik der Forschung*, 1934 (*The Logic of Scientific Enquiry*, 1960), proposing the criterion of falsifiability to distinguish scientific from pseudo-scientific theories, is Popper's most revolutionary contribution to scientific philosophy. His other publications include *Conjectures and Refutations: the Growth of Scientific Knowledge*, revised edition 1972.

Poppy, several herbaceous members of the family Papaveraceae. The red field poppies are *Papaver rhoeas* and related species; Shirley poppies are derived from *P. rhoeas*. The opium poppy, *P. somniferum*, yields opium from the milky juice of the unripe fruit, but the ripe seeds are harmless and may be used in cooking and for decorating bread. The showy perennial poppies of gardens are *P. orientale*. The yellow Welsh poppy is *Meconopsis cambrica*; the tall blue mountain poppy is *M. betonicifolia*, of the Himalayas. The yellow horned poppy of shingle banks is *Glaucium flavum*. The Californian poppy is *Eschscholzia californica*.

Popular Front, suggestion for political collaboration of Communists, Socialists and other left-wing parties against Fascism, advanced by the Communist International in 1935. The Popular Front platform provided for common resistance to Fascism. Popular Front governments were established in Spain and France. The Spanish Popular Front was overthrown by Franco during the Spanish Civil War, and the French one ended at the start of 1938.

Populares, originally the name given to those in republican Rome who challenged the claim of the senatorial oligarchy that noble birth necessarily produced great ability. The trouble arose because of the confused nature of the Roman constitution; theoretically the people were supreme, but in practice the conduct of affairs had traditionally been in the hands of the Senate. This traditional but unwritten right was challenged by the Populares, usually not from democratic motives but purely for their own ends.

Population. Knowledge of the total number of the world's inhabitants rested on very insecure foundations until relatively recent times. Even today there are areas in which no census has ever been taken, and much larger areas in which censuses are of doubtful validity. In 1960 it was suggested that current estimates of world population may be in an upward or downward error of over 50 million.

In Britain two aspects of population have become important at different times. In the 1930s anxiety was expressed concerning a possible decline in numbers, so great that the population would eventually not be replaced. Crude birth rates had fallen from the peak rates of the early 1920s, so that for the United Kingdom the figure was 15·8 compared to around 25 at the outbreak of the First World War.

After the Second World War there was a boom in 1946 and 1947 followed by another period of growth between 1956 and 1964. In the late 1970s the economic situation had a considerable negative effect on the birth rate which in 1977 fell to 11·6 in England and Wales but rose slightly towards 1979.

Pop Art. WHAAM! *by Roy Lichtenstein, 1963. The work is based on comic-strip art.*

The second feature of population change that has caused concern in Britain is the ageing of the population. The phenomenon applies to all highly developed countries and consists of an increase in the proportion of old people and a decline in the proportion of children.

Populism (Russian *Narodnichestvo*), Russian ideological and political trend, originating among the radical intelligentsia in the 1860s. Its precursors were Herzen and Chernyshevski, who thought that Russia, with its peasant communes, could reach socialism through a peasant revolution, avoiding the capitalist stage. Revolutionary populism was particularly strong in the 1870s, when more than a thousand students went to the countryside ('into the people'—hence the name 'populism') as propagandists.

Populus, see POPLAR.

Poquelin, Jean Baptiste, see MOLIÈRE.

Porbeagle, see SHARK.

Porcelain, name given to several groups of ceramic wares characterised by a white or near white body, a quality of translucency and a vitrified—and thus non-porous—body.

Hard-paste porcelain, or true porcelain in the European sense, was first made in China as early as the T'ang Dynasty (AD 618–907). It is made of kaolin and feldspathic petuntse. These two materials are mixed and fired to a temperature of 1300°C–1400°C when they fuse and form a white translucent cement around the opaque granules of kaolin. The body is so hard that it cannot be cut by ordinary steel. Potters of other Asiatic countries and then of Europe strove for centuries to imitate it. In Europe the secret of true porcelain was discovered in 1708 by Johann Friedrich Böttger (1682–1719), alchemist to the Elector of Saxony. In 1710 the Elector founded the Meissen factory under the direction of Böttger, who remained in charge until 1715. In France hard-paste porcelain was not made until 1769, at Sèvres. In England it was only made at Plymouth in 1768–70 by William Cookworthy, at Bristol by Champion from 1770, and later at New Hall, Staffordshire.

Soft-paste porcelain, or artificial porcelain, is the result of mixing of the clay with glass or the materials of glass, fused and powdered. It is fired at a lower temperature than hard-paste porcelain. During the 18th century it was made in France at Mennecy, Chantilly, Vincennes and Sèvres, and c.1745 it was first made in England at Chelsea and at Bow. Soon afterwards a porcelain factory started at Derby, and from 1750 to 1760 another factory operated at Longton Hall. The factory founded by Benjamin Lund in Bristol c.1750 was transferred two years later and became the famous Worcester factory producing a soapstone type of porcelain.

See also BISCUIT.

Porcupine (Latin *porcus*, pig; *spina* thorn), any species of the rodent family Hystricidae. All are characterised by the possession of spines and hollow quills, smooth-soled feet, non-prehensile tails, and the grinding teeth have external and internal folds. They are nocturnal and herbivorous. The best-known species is *Hystrix cristata*, the common porcupine, a native of southern Europe and North and West Africa. It is one of the largest of rodents, and its specific name is obtained from its crest of long hairs; the body spines are solid, and the tail bears hollow quills. There are eleven other species of *Hystrix*. The genus *Atherurus* contains four species, known as brush-tail porcupines. The remaining Old World porcupine is *Trichys lipura*. Tree porcupines belong to a different family (Erethizontidae) and are common to the New World.

Porcupine. *The white-tailed porcupine,* Hystrix leucura, *inhabits Asia and India.*

Porcupine Fish, see SEA PORCUPINE.

Pores, see SKIN.

Pori, or Björneborg, town of Finland, 95 km north-west of Turku, situated at the mouth of the River Kokemäki in the Gulf of Bothnia. Gradual uplifting of the land has necessitated the building of outports, and the present ones, Reposaari and Mäntyluoto, are the seventh seaward move. The chief industries are wood-processing, textiles, engineering, steel and chemicals. Population (1979) 79,430.

Porifera, see SPONGE.

Pork, the flesh of the pig. When cured it becomes bacon or ham. The quality of the meat varies with the age of the animal, its breeding and its diet.

Bacon pigs are usually older and fatter than those used for fresh pork. Chemical curing is done by soaking the meat in a solution of sodium and potassium salts or, in sweet cured bacon, brine solution with added sugar. Pickled bacon is known as plain or green to distinguish it from smoked bacon, which is first pickled, then smoked.

Ham is the top part of either a fore or hindleg, pickled and often smoked. Formerly most hams were dry-cured by being chilled, rubbed with and stacked in salt. The method of preservation varies with the country and district and imparts its own flavour to the ham, but in general, the joint is immersed in a salt solution for several days, then smoked over a wood fire. Salted hams must be soaked to remove the salt before being cooked.

Porosity. The porosity of a building material such as brick or stone is the ratio of pore space in the material to the total volume of the material. Porosity per cent is calculated from the apparent density d and the density of the powdered material s from the formula porosity per cent $= (s-d)/s \times 100$.

Porphyry, an ancient term denoting a decorative rock composed of large crystals, often feldspar or quartz, in a fine-grained matrix. Porphyry is not used as a geological term, but 'porphyritic' is used as a description of texture where appropriate.

Porpoise, any member of the cetacean family Phocaenidae. They have a triangular dorsal fin and spade-shaped teeth. The common porpoise (*Phocaena phocaena*) is mainly found in the coastal waters of the North Atlantic, where it feeds on fish such as herring and whiting.

Port, the left-hand side of a ship; originally called larboard.

See also STARBOARD.

Port Arthur, port of entry for the Sabine district of Texas, USA. It is on the western shore of Lake Sabine and communicates with the Gulf of Mexico by the Sabine-Neches waterway. It has important oil refineries, and exports petroleum, grain, cotton, rice and lumber. Population (1980) 61,106.

Port Arthur, see THUNDER BAY.

Port Arthur, see LÜDA.

Port-au-Prince, capital and chief port of the Republic of Haiti. The seat of Ouest *département*, it is situated on the west coast of Haiti in the Gulf of Gonave and has a fine natural harbour. The chief exports are coffee and sugar, and the city has sugar refineries. Population (1975) 458,675.

Port Augusta, seaport of South Australia, at the head of Spencer Gulf, 338 km from Adelaide. There is wool and wheat trade, and Port Augusta is a railway rolling-stock servicing centre. Population (1976) 13,092.

Port-de-France, see NOUMÉA.

Port Elizabeth, seaport and second city of Cape Province, South Africa, on the western shore of Algoa Bay. The town may be said to date from the arrival of the 1820 settlers, but as a military station it dates back to the end of the 18th century. Fort Frederick, which overlooks the city, was built by the British in 1799 and named after the Duke of York. The town was laid out in 1820 by order of the acting governor of the Cape, Sir Rufane Donkin, and named in memory of his deceased wife, Lady Elizabeth. The geographical position of Port Elizabeth makes it a most important export and import gateway of South Africa. Industries include motor assembly plants, shoes, foundries, sawmills, flour mills, canning factories, soap, tyres, furniture, chemicals, safety glass, electrical goods and cables. Population 386,577, including 119,694 whites, 167,241 Africans, 94,128 coloureds and 4914 Asians.

Port Glasgow, town (since 1668) of Inverclyde District, Strathclyde Region, Scotland, on the southern shore of the Firth of Clyde, 36 km north-west of Glasgow. It has a worldwide reputation for shipbuilding and ship-repairing and has one of the largest dry docks in Europe. Other industries include light engineering, clothing, textile, rope and needle manufacturing. Population (1981) 21,554.

Port Harcourt, port and capital of Rivers State, Nigeria. It grew up as a small port on the Bonny river, some 65 km from the coast. Between 1913 and 1926 a railway was built northwards via Enugu to link with the Lagos–Kano railway, and Port Harcourt became the outlet for coal from Enugu and tin from the Jos plateau, as well as the natural centre for the palm oil trade. Population (1975) 242,000.

Port Jackson, magnificent natural harbour on which is situated the city of Sydney,

New South Wales, Australia. It is an inlet about 29 km long and has an area of about 54 km². It was named by Captain Cook in 1770 in honour of Sir George Jackson, one of the secretaries of the Admiralty.

Port Kelang, port of Malaysia (formerly Port Swettenham, until 1971), 32 km south-west of the federal capital, Kuala Lumpur, to which it is linked by rail and the dual-carriageway Federal Highway. Port Kelang services Malaysia's major industrial area, the Kelang Valley, and a wide hinterland including Pahang.

Port Louis, town and capital of Mauritius, on the west coast. It stands in an excellent harbour, and is the main commercial port of the island, exporting sugar, coconut oil and aloe fibre. Population (1979) 146,101.

Port Moresby, port of entry and capital of Papua, New Guinea. There are copper deposits in the vicinity. It exports gold, rubber, timber and coffee. Population (1979) 122,000.

Port of Spain, maritime city of the West Indies, capital of Trinidad and Tobago, situated on the north-west coast of the island on the site of the old Indian village of Conquerabia, on the shores of the Gulf of Paria. It superseded San José d'Oruna (St Joseph) as the capital in 1783 during the Spanish tenure of Trinidad. The harbour of Port of Spain is safe but shallow. The port is, because of its geographical position, a hub of shipping routes in the Caribbean. Its population has been estimated (1972) at 65,400.

Port Pirie, seaport of South Australia, on Spencer Gulf, 219 km north-west of Adelaide. Mineral ores and wheat are exported, and there are smelting works for the Broken Hill silver and lead mines. Population (1976) 15,006.

Port-Royal des Champs, former Cistercian convent, 13 km south-west of Versailles, France. In the 17th century it became the centre of Jansenism. In 1709 the remaining members of Port-Royal were expelled and the buildings destroyed by order of Louis XIV.

Port Said, important town and port in Egypt, built on the west bank of the entrance to the Suez Canal, with a commodious harbour and discharging basin. Formerly the most important coaling station in the world, the town suffered from the Israeli occupation of the east bank of the canal 1967–73. Population (1970) 313,000.

Port Sudan, seaport of the Sudan, on the Red Sea, 65 km north of Suakin. It exports cotton, gum arabic, oil seeds and grain. Salt pans here supply the needs of the whole country. There is railway communication to Berber on the Nile. Population (1973) 123,000.

Port Sunlight, model village in Merseyside Metropolitan County, England, 5 km south-east of Birkenhead. It was founded in 1888 by W. H. Lever (Viscount Leverhulme) to house workers at his soap factory. Although some writers on 'model villages' speak of Port Sunlight as 'paternalistic', it is architecturally attractive and certainly far superior to the artisan environment of surrounding areas. Population (1971) 3142.

Port Swettenham, see PORT KELANG.

Port Talbot (Welsh *Aberavon*), port and industrial town in West Glamorgan, South Wales, 11 km east of Swansea, on the eastern tip of Swansea Bay, where the River Afan enters the Bristol Channel. The town is highly industrialised, and there are important manufactures of steel strip (British Steel Corporation) and chemicals. The port has been extensively modernised to take bulk carriers. Population (1981) 47,313.

Port Wine, fortified dessert wine, mainly deep red, though white when made from white grapes, exported over the bar of Oporto;. The port wine district in the Alto Douro some 80 km above Oporto slopes down precipitously to the river, and the cliffs of the valley are covered with terraces for the vines. Vintage port, the wines of a single good year, remain in wood in the lodges for two or occasionally three years before being shipped for bottling.
See PORTUGUESE WINES.

Portadown, town in County Armagh, Northern Ireland, on the River Bann, 40 km south-west of Belfast. It is now part of the new city of Craigavon. It grew up as a railway junction in the 19th century and has a variety of light manufacturing and food processing industries. Population (1971) 21,998.

Portal of Hungerford, Charles Frederick Algernon Portal, 1st Viscount (1893–1971), British air administrator, Marshal of the RAF. He served with great distinction in the First World War and between the wars received rapid promotion. From October 1940 to 1946 he was chief of the Air Staff, and thus bore much of the responsibility for shaping and directing RAF policy.

Porter, Cole (1893–1964), US composer. He was recognised on Broadway from the late 1920s. The most famous of his musicals is *Kiss Me Kate*; his songs include *Night and Day* and *Begin the Beguine*.

Porter, Katherine Anne (1890–1980), US short-story writer and novelist. Volumes of her stories are *Flowering Judas*, 1930; *Hacienda*, 1934; *Noon Wine*, 1937; *Pale Horse, Pale Rider*, 1939; and *No Safe Harbour*, 1949.

Porter, Peter (1929–), Australian poet. Porter's poetry, sardonic, observant, and occasionally stiff with anger and contempt, mostly written in England, marks him as belonging with English contemporaries rather than to Australia. His best work is in *Once Bitten, Twice Bitten*, 1961; *Poems Ancient and Modern*, 1964; *The Last of England*, 1970; and *Preaching to the Converted*, 1972.

Porter, W. S., see HENRY, O.

Porter, a beer of dark-brown colour and bitterish taste, brewed from malt partly roasted or browned by drying at high temperature. It was very popular in the 18th and 19th centuries in England, particularly in London.
See also BEER.

Portico, a roofed space, open on one side at least, and enclosed by a range of columns, which also support the roof. A portico usually forms the entrance to a building, but it may also stand free.

Porticus, a small chapel built on both north and south sides of some English pre-Conquest churches, and thus forming rudimentary transepts.

Portland, chief commercial city of Maine, USA, 240 km north-east of Boston, on Casco Bay. Portland is a rail centre, and also possesses an excellent harbour that handles as much as 25 million t of goods annually. Industries include paper, cellulose and clay products, and shoes. Printing and publishing, fishing, food packing, lumber, and petroleum distribution are also important. Portland was first settled in 1632, when it was known by the Indian name of Machigonne. It was the capital of Maine from 1820 to 1831. Population (1980) 61,572.

Portland, city of Oregon, USA, on the Willamette river, about 177 km (river distance) from the Pacific coast. Portland has an extensive harbour, and a large trade is carried on in lumber, grain, paper, wool, flour, livestock, meat, canned and frozen foods and other merchandise. Portland was founded in 1854, within a few years of the arrival in Oregon of the first party of overland migrants. It quickly became the chief commercial and regional centre of the new territory and its later growth was stimulated by the development of Alaska and the trade with Japan and the Pacific basin generally. Population (city, 1980) 364,246.

Portland Beds, see JURASSIC SYSTEM.

Portland, Isle of, peninsula of the coast of Dorset, England, 7 km in length, connected with the mainland by the Chesil Bank. It is known for its harbour of refuge with Royal Navy installations, and building stone. Population (1981) 10,915.

Portland Stone, a subdivision of the Portlandian series of rocks which forms part of the Upper Jurassic. The Portland stone in Dorset consists largely of a limestone packed with fossil shells. It is widely used an an ornamental stone.
See also BUILDING STONE.

Portland Vase, dark-blue glass ornamented with figures in relief in white opaque glass. It is 24·8 cm high and 18·4 cm in diameter. By tradition discovered in a sarcophagus at Monte del Grano, near Rome, in the 17th century, it was eventually sold to the British Museum in 1946. Josiah Wedgwood made a copy of it in a blue-black jasper stoneware in 1790. It is thought that 50 copies were made in his lifetime.

Portlaoise (formerly Maryborough), county town of Laois, Republic of Ireland, situated on a small tributary of the River Barrow, 80 km south-west of Dublin. There are flour mills and a factory making tennis balls. Population (1971) 6470.

Portmeirion, baroque seasonal holiday resort, designed by the architect Clough Williams-Ellis, on a private headland overlooking Tremadoc Bay, Gwynedd, North Wales.

Pôrto Alegre, capital of the state of Rio Grande do Sul, Brazil. It is built on the Guaiba where five rivers join and then flow into the Lagóa dos Patos. At the south end of the lake is the port and city of Rio Grande. Pôrto Alegre is the most important commercial centre of the far south. It is a port of call for ocean-going vessels which sail up the Lagóa dos Patos from Rio Grande. Chief exports are pinewood, rice, meat, hides, wheat and wool. The main industries include food processing, wool textiles, chemicals and tanneries. Population (1980) 1,108,883.

Porto Novo, capital of the People's Republic of Benin (formerly Dahomey), West Africa. Porto Novo, a port on a lagoon called Lake Nokoue, is linked by railway with other parts of Benin and with Lagos by internal waterway. It trades in palm oil, palm kernels and cotton. Population (1975) 104,000.

Portobelo, town on the north coast of the republic of Panama, 32 km north-east of Colón and on the Bay of Portobelo. Columbus used this port in 1502 and Drake died and was buried at sea in the bay. Today the population is less than 2000.

Portraiture, the art of rendering a person's likeness, real or imagined. Pictorial portraiture came into its own in the Byzantine era, when mural representations of saints were required by the Christian Church.

Though many art-forms ceased to be practised during the Dark Ages, portraiture continued in tomb-sculpture and brasses. The first medieval panel portrait of an individual is perhaps that painted in the mid-14th century by Girouard d'Orleans of King John the Good of France, while he was captive in England. This, and the 'cabinet' portraits of Van Eyck, Rogier Van Der Weyden, Memlinc, Van Der Goes and Holbein, adopted the format and technique developed for travelling altarpieces, and indeed were often in diptych form.

The portraitist's aim is to create a world peopled with his characterisations and part of his task is to establish a recognisable norm from which he can vary; for example, the iconic near-frontalism of El Greco, the 45° illumination of Rembrandt, or the characteristic mode of posing the sitter which reveals at a glance the authorship of Van Dyck, Gainsborough or Ingres. Painters such as Titian and Velazquez attained consistency by using their lifework to solve a technical problem. Not only individuality but also social background was represented, for example the merchant civilisation of 17th-century Holland, or the oligarchy of 17th- and 18th-century Britain.

Portsmouth, city, seaport and naval station covering the south-western part of Portsea Island and extending to the mainland of Hampshire, England, 118 km south-west of London. On the opposite side of the harbour is Gosport. The harbour is spacious enough to accommodate a large part of the Royal Navy and to float the heaviest ship in it. The dockyard covers an area of nearly 121 ha, has a school of naval architecture and many establishments connected with the requirements of the navy. The old *Victory*, Nelson's flagship, is now permanently berthed in the oldest dry dock in the world. The trade of Portsmouth is chiefly connected with the dockyard, the airport, and its factories, the building of ships and motor boats, and varied commercial undertakings. By the opening years of the 13th century Portsmouth had become a naval station of some importance, the docks enclosed by a strong wall, accommodating the royal galleys. Its importance as a naval dockyard began about 1545; in that year the English fleet assembled at Portsmouth prior to the naval engagement with the French off Spithead. Population (1981) 179,419.

Portsmouth, city in Virginia, USA, and part of the metropolitan area of Norfolk-Portsmouth. With Norfolk it shares the port functions of the south shore of Hampton Roads and like its English namesake it is essentially a naval town. Population (1980) 104,577.

Portugal
Area: 91,631 km²
Population: 9,862,700
Capital: Lisbon

Portugal (*República Portuguesa*), country of south-western Europe, occupying the western fifth of the Iberian Peninsula. It is bounded on the north and east by Spain, and on the west and south by the Atlantic Ocean. Its total area is 91,631 km² including the Atlantic Azores and Funchal islands, which are administratively part of metropolitan Portugal. Overseas Portugal in 1976 comprised the small island of Macao.

Portugal's mountains are continuations of the ranges in Spain; those of Galicia carry on into the Transmontane system (highest peak, Peneda, 1441 m). Between the Douro and the Tagus are two ranges, of which the southern is a continuation of the Sierra de Guadarrama. The rivers already mentioned have their sources in Spain. The Mondego, the longest wholly Portuguese river, rises in the Serra da Estrela and is 210 km long. The estimated population in 1979 was 9,862,700. The country's main cities are Lisbon (the capital) and Oporto.

Agriculture predominates over much of the country; large absentee estates in the south, worked by landless labourers and producing cereals and livestock, contrast with small family farms in the vine- and maize-growing north. Forests are important, producing cork, resins and turpentine. The textile industry employs about a third of the working population, and other important products are wine, fish, ceramics, footwear and cork. Shipbuilding and repair have become important activities with large yards at Lisbon and Setúbal.

The unit of currency is the *escudo*. All banks were nationalised in 1975.

In 1975 the constituent assembly, in which the socialists formed the largest group, drafted a new constitution. It provides for a President directly elected by all Portuguese over the age of 18, and for a legislative assembly of 263 members elected by universal suffrage under a system of proportional representation. The official language is Portuguese.

History. Ferdinand I of Castile and his son Alfonso VI won back from the Moors the land forming the country of Portugal. Alfonso III (1248–79) extended the kingdom of Algarve and strengthened it by marrying the daughter of Alfonso X of Castile. During the reign of John I (1385–1433) the period of expansion overseas and of geographical enterprise began. In the 15th and 16th centuries there was a period of discovery which made Portugal at one time the greatest maritime country in the world. In 1578 the country suffered an overwhelming disaster in the defeat and death of the young king Sebastian. Among the many claimants to the crown was Philip II of Spain, who marched into the country and had himself crowned king. From 1580 to 1640 Portugal remained under Spanish suzerainty. In 1640 Portugal regained its independence and John, Duke of Braganza, was crowned king. By 1703 Portugal had lost all its major colonies except Brazil, and was no longer one of the chief powers in Europe. In 1807 Portugal was occupied by the French and the crowning of Joseph Bonaparte, resulting in the Peninsular War, which continued until 1814. In 1816 John VI succeeded to the throne, but remained in Brazil and appointed a viceroy. This led to revolution in 1820 and the establishment of a more democratic form of government. Brazil obtained complete independence. A long period of misrule and confusion culminated in the proclamation of a republic in 1910. Portugal's internal situation remained unstable and government succeeded government, until Carmona became president in 1928. In 1932 Antonio de Oliveira Salazar became prime minister with dictatorial powers. Salazar's successor as premier, Marcelo Caetano, was neither politically able nor temperamentally much inclined to depart from Salazar's policies and in 1974 the Caetano regime was overthrown by the Armed Forces Movement under Gen. Spinola, a critic of the regime's African policies. For five months, with Spinola as president of the Junta of National Salvation, political parties grew; the African colonies of Angola, Guinea-Bissau, Mozambique and Rio Muni were granted their independence; ministers of the former regime were purged, the secret police abolished and business concerns nationalised. Spinola resigned in September 1974. National elections for the Constituent Assembly held in April 1975 gave the Socialist party of Mario Soares victory with 38 per cent of the vote.

Portugal. *The hill-side town of Castelo de Vide, near the border with Spain.*

Language. Portuguese is the language not only of the people of Portugal and the Azores, but also of those of Brazil, and of numerous African inhabitants of former Portuguese colonies in Africa. Brazilian Portuguese differs in details of pronunciation and vocabulary from European Portuguese, although the two languages remain quite mutually intelligible. Galician or Galego, spoken in northwestern Spain, is a dialect of Portuguese, strongly influenced by Spanish.

Phonetically, the most striking features of modern Portuguese are the frequent occurrence of nasal vowels, similar to French, a tendency to slur or omit unstressed vowels, and the pronunciation of final *s* and *z* like English *sh*. Grammatically, Portuguese retains many features which disappeared in Spanish in the medieval period, the verbal system having preserved numerous complex subjunctives simplified in later Castilian.

See also ROMANCE LANGUAGES; SPAIN, *Language*.

Portuguese Guinea, see GUINEA-BISSAU.

Portuguese India, formerly consisted of Goa, Daman and Diu. The territories were annexed by India in 1961.

Portuguese Man-of-War, common name for *Physalia*, a genus of the order Siphonophora in class Hydrozoa of phylum Coelenterata. It is remarkable for its brilliant blue colours, size, and the severity of the pain its tentacles are capable of inflicting on the human skin. This is a pelagic hydrozoan colony of feeding, reproductive and defensive individuals attached to the main individual, which has developed a float. The float catches the wind, and thus the animals are distributed over the sea. They inhabit the warmer parts of the ocean, but may occasionally be brought to temperate regions.

See also JELLYFISH.

Portuguese Man-of-War, Physalia physalis.

Portuguese Wines. Although best known for her fortified wines, madeira and port, Portugal is also a large producer of good table wine, the most famous of which is the slightly sparkling Mateus Rosé from the border of the Minho and Douro.

See also WINE.

Poseidon, Greek god, probably of pure Hellenic origin, consort of Earth and hence lord of earthquakes and of the freshwater streams that fertilise the soil. After his original worshippers entered Greece, his dominion was extended to the sea, with which he is principally associated in classical mythology. Here he is described as a brother of Zeus. Poseidon was also a god of horses, and may originally have been worshipped in horse form.

Posen, see POZNAŃ.

Positivism, philosophical system which confines itself to the data of experience, rejecting all *a priori* and metaphysical speculation. The founder of Positivism was Auguste Comte, who owed much to Saint-Simon. Positivism starts from the assumption that knowledge is based solely on the methods and discoveries of physical science, and attempts the revaluation of social and moral values in the light of the exact sciences. Comte adopted a 'religion of humanity', and proposed to dethrone the gods of existing religions and make the welfare of mankind the object of worship.

Positivism, Logical, school of philosophy arising out of the work of Comte and Wittgenstein, its main practitioners being the Vienna circle (Carnap, Schlick, etc.). The basis of their doctrines is the verification principle, viz. that the meaning of any statement is the method of its verification. There are two exhaustive categories of statement: analytic, *a priori*, necessary statements whose predicate holds true of the subject because it is included in the meaning of the subject-term; and synthetic, *a posteriori*, empirically verifiable statements. Any other sentence is a pseudo-statement, strictly 'meaningless' or 'nonsensical', e.g. theological or metaphysical statements, because these are *not* made about the world which is experienced by the senses. There can be no meaning in statements about the nature of God because His existence cannot be verified by sense experience. Again, propositions concerning aesthetics or ethics, e.g. that 'stealing is wrong' or that 'Keats's poetry is beautiful', contain only the expression of a subjective emotion and do not say anything about the objects they purport to discuss, since 'poetry', 'beauty', 'evil', etc., are not experienced by the senses. Logical Positivism was a movement of great influence in the 1930s and 1940s, especially in casting doubt on the value of speculative metaphysics. But by the mid-1950s very few philosophers accepted it except in radically modified form. The term Logical Positivism is often incorrectly used as an umbrella term to include various 'analytical' and 'linguistic' schools associated with Oxford and Cambridge.

Positron, or positive electron, one of the elementary particles having the same mass as the electron, and an electric charge of the same magnitude but opposite in sign. It is the antiparticle of the electron.

Possession. In English law corporeal possession, i.e. the possession of a material object, is the continuing exercise of a claim to the exclusive use of it.

Incorporeal possession, if it can be said to amount to possession at all, is the possession of any non-material object, e.g. a right to light or any other easement. Possession is evidence of ownership, and the possessor can put all other claimants to proof of their alleged titles (i.e. it is the proverbial nine points of the law).

Possum, any one of 50 species of Australasian marsupials in the suborder Diprotodontia and the family Phalangeridae. Some zoologists include koalas (family Phascolarctidae) with the possums.

Possums are found from Tasmania to New Guinea, and the largest members of the group, the cuscuses, are found in Sulawesi and the Solomon Islands. Several species of possums, the flying phalangers, glide, using folds of skin between front and hind limbs as wings.

Post-Impressionism, the phase of painting which followed Impressionism and is marked by reaction against fugitive, atmospheric effect, and a desire for firmer pictorial construction. Other points in Post-Impressionist technique are a perception of formal relations revealed in painting and the ability of the painter, if necessary, to dispense with representational details. It also began to stress the importance of subject matter, which was arbitrary for the Impressionists. Among the main representatives of Post-Impressionism are Seurat, Cézanne, Gauguin and Van Gogh. Post-Impressionism as a whole is not naturalistic painting. It is scarcely to be regarded as an organised movement and is much less specific than, for example, Cubism. Post-Impressionism did not reach England until 1911, when the first exhibition of works by modern French painters was held in London. Post-Impressionism in England was most strikingly represented by the Camden Town Group formed in 1911.

Post Mills, see WINDMILL.

Postal Services. During the Middle Ages private postal services were maintained by powerful institutions and heads of state. The emergence of European nation-states with strong central governments was reflected in the establishment of national systems of relay posts under state control. In France, for example, a Royal Postal Service was set up in 1477, and postal services were declared a state monopoly in 1672, while the first urban delivery, the Penny Post, was established in London in 1680. During the 18th and 19th centuries, as the stagecoach superseded mounted postboys on major routes, a fast and regular service was established in many European countries.

In 1837 major reforms were proposed by Rowland Hill, a British educator, including the adoption of a uniform rate of postage within Britain, regardless of distance, and prepayment by means of adhesive postage stamps. These were adopted in Britain in 1840, greatly simplifying and improving postal services, and by other countries worldwide more gradually, Brazil being one of the first in 1843. The advent of railway and steamship improved services further, enabling the sorting of mail to be carried out in transit. In 1875 the establishment of the General (later the Universal) Postal Union provided a framework for the exchange of international mail, which had previously been governed by a complex system of bilateral treaties.

The two main 20th-century developments

have been the introduction of airmail and of post office technology. Air deliveries were first used regularly on the London/Paris route in 1919, although a regular transatlantic service was only established in 1939. The labour intensive nature of sorting, transport and delivery process has led to the development of a variety of machinery, including facing and cancelling equipment and coding and sorting machines. Fully automated sorting involves a machine that reads certain elements (the postal code in the UK) in the address. A form of this (optical character recognition) has been in use in the USA since 1965; the American postal system is the largest and one of the most advanced in the world, with a high degree of automation and increasing use of air transport as against railway and highway post offices. The British system, on the other hand, is still based largely on a network of travelling railway post offices. A two-tier system of letter classification was introduced in the UK in 1968.
Modern postal systems are almost always state-controlled, and often provide a range of additional services, including a banking and money transfer system, the payment of some state benefits and the collection of certain taxes. In many countries telecommunications also come under post office management.

Posters. The printed notices and playbills of the 17th and 18th centuries are the true predecessors of the modern poster. The pictorial poster is essentially mid-19th century, Gavarni being one of the first artists to design successful advertisements of this kind. Jules Chéret is regarded as the father of pictorial posters, the idea of which was quickly adopted in Britain and America. The posters of Toulouse-Lautrec in the 1890s signalised, among other things, the power of colour and design to seize attention. Aubrey Beardsley introduced the flat poster, oriental in lack of perspective. Later came the Dudley Hardy school of designs, while among other later artists of note in poster painting are John Hassall and E. McKnight Kauffer, who produced striking landscapes in three or four boldly handled colours, and Ashley Havinden; in Germany, Ludwig Hohlwein; in France, Cassandre. Contemporary artists of particular note are Peter Max and Tomi Ungerer, both working in the USA.

Post-mortem Examination or autopsy, the examination of the body immediately after death.

Potash, or pot-ashes, common name for potassium carbonate, K_2CO_3.

Potassium, metallic chemical element, symbol K, atomic number 19, atomic weight 39·102; one of the alkali metals. It was first isolated by Davy in 1807 by the electrolysis of melted caustic potash, and occurs in the form of silicates in rocks such as feldspar, e.g., orthoclase ($KAlSi_3O_8$), and mica. Potassium is an essential constituent of plant food; when plants are burned the potassium is left in the form of carbonate, and this was formerly the chief commercial source of potassium compounds. The chief sources of potassium are carnallite ($KCl,MgCl_2,6H_2O$), sylvine (KCl), kainite ($MgSO_4,KCl,3H_2O$). Potassium is prepared by the electrolysis of fused potassium chloride.
Potassium is a soft, silvery-white metal, melts at 63·5°C, boils at 760°C, and has a relative density of 0·859. Potassium and its compounds give a lilac tint to the Bunsen flame. Potassium oxidises in moist air, and combines with the halogens more vigorously than sodium does. It reacts with water so vigorously that the evolved hydrogen catches fire and burns with a lilac flame. On account of its reaction on water and air, it must be kept in sealed tins or in naphtha.
In general, potassium compounds (especially the ionic salts) closely resemble the equivalent sodium salts. Potassium monoxide (K_2O), a yellow solid, is obtained by heating potassium nitrate with potassium. Potassium tetroxide (K_2O_4), formed when the metal burns in oxygen, is a yellow powder which is decomposed by water, forming potassium hydroxide, hydrogen peroxide and oxygen: $K_2O_4 + 2H_2O = 2KOH + H_2O_2 + O_2$. Potassium hydroxide is obtained: (1) by acting on water with potassium; (2) by boiling potassium carbonate with milk of lime; (3) by electrolysis of aqueous potassium chloride using special precautions. It is a white amorphous substance which melts at 360°C and absorbs moisture from the air. It is used to absorb gases, e.g. carbon dioxide. Potassium bromide and potassium iodide are useful in medicine and photography. Potassium chlorate is now largely obtained by electrolysis of a hot solution of potassium chloride. It is useful as an oxidising agent, e.g. in the preparation of the dye aniline black, in fireworks, in making matches, and in medicine. Potassium nitrate occurs naturally in rich soils. It is a white crystalline solid. It is used in the preparation of gunpowder and as a food preservative. Potassium cyanide crystallises in cubes and is extremely soluble in water. It is highly poisonous. It is a reducing agent, and is therefore useful in blowpipe analysis, e.g. $PbO + KCN = KCNO + Pb$. It is useful in electroplating. Large amounts of the cyanide are used in extracting gold from its ores, particularly in the Transvaal.

Potassium-Argon Dating, see DATING IN ARCHAEOLOGY (AND GEOLOGY).

Potassium Bitartrate, see CREAM OF TARTAR.

Potassium Bromide, KBr, colourless or white crystalline solid prepared by the action of bromine on potassium hydroxide solution. It was formerly used in medicine as a sedative in conditions such as epilepsy, delirium tremens, hysteria, sleeplessness and anxiety states. Its excessive use leads to a condition called bromism, or brominism, characterised by skin eruptions, growing muscular and sexual weakness, mental dullness and feebleness, leading to extreme depression and melancholia. In photography potassium bromide is used as a source of silver bromide for the sensitive film. It is transparent to low infrared radiation, and so is used in infrared spectroscopy as a support medium for the solid under study.

Potassium Permanganate, $KMnO_4$, compound prepared by warming an aqueous solution of potassium manganate. Potassium permanganate forms dark purple crystals which are sparingly soluble in water. It is a powerful oxidising agent, and is widely used as such in analytical chemistry, as the disappearance of its purple colour from solution signifies the completion of the reaction under study—hence no indicator need be added to the system.

Potato, several species of the genus *Solanum* in the family Solanaceae (the family that includes the tomato). The plant, native to the Andes, is herbaceous, with compound leaves, and underground stolons (stems) bearing several tubers, which are swollen parts of the stem. Commercial potatoes have whitish to purple skin, and white or yellowish flesh. The eyes are small buds occurring on the surface.
The potato was introduced to Europe in the 16th century.
The potato is subject to many diseases and pests. The fungus, *Phytophthora infestans*, which causes late blight, destroyed the Irish potato crop of 1845–47, causing severe famine and mass emigration. The diseases are controlled by the use of healthy seed, breeding new, resistant varieties, proper rotation of crops, and spraying the foliage with anti-fungal sprays.

Potato Beetle, see COLORADO BEETLE.

Potchefstroom, town in the south of Transvaal province, South Africa, on the Mooi River 151 km south-west of Pretoria. It is in the centre of an agricultural and gold-mining area and is a popular health resort. It is the oldest town in the Transvaal, and was founded by Voortrekkers crossing the Vaal in 1838, and named after their leader, Potgieter. Population (1970) 55,296, of which 23,581 are whites.

Potëmkin, Prince Grigori Aleksandrovich (1739–91), Russian statesman, favourite of Catherine II the Great. From 1774 Potëmkin was viceroy of New Russia, from 1784 field-marshal and president of the war department.

Potential, Magnetic, a mathematical concept used for calculating the distribution of magnetic flux in a region. The difference in magnetic potential between two points may be defined as the quantity of work required to carry a hypothetical unit positive pole from one point to the other. The potential at a point is the work required to bring a unit pole from infinity to that point.
See also MAGNETISM.

Potentilla, a genus of about 300 herbs and shrubs in the family Rosaceae, with pinnate or palmate leaves, and generally yellow or white flowers, followed by a group of small hard fruitlets, resembling a strawberry with no flesh. Several species are grown in gardens, especially varieties of the shrubby cinquefoil (*P. fruticosa*).

Potentiometer, instrument for comparing or measuring electric potential differences. It uses a 'zero' or 'null' method, in which zero deflection is observed; in measuring the electromotive force of batteries no current is taken and the true e.m.f. may be found. Its simplest form consists of a single wire of manganin or platino-iridium, usually 1 m in length. A standard cell is connected to one end; the negative terminal is connected through a switch and galvanometer to a sliding contact. The difference of potential produced by the battery tends to circulate a current through the circuit in one direction, while the e.m.f. of the standard cell tends to circulate current in the opposite direction. By adjusting the sliding contact the potential difference on one side can be made to equal the e.m.f. of the standard cell, and no current will flow in the cell circuit. The instrument can measure potential differences, resistances and currents.

Potholing, sport developed from speleology, the scientific study and exploration of underground 'caves', which has recently become popular in Britain and elsewhere in Europe. E. A. Martel was the great pioneer in this field in France, and Norbert Casteret did much to develop potholing, especially in the Pyrenees. An underground time record of 129 days was established at Cheddar in 1966 by David Lafferty, who remained there alone as part of an experiment to show the effects of isolation, with a view to their application to astronauts. Jean-Pierre Mairetet subsequently stayed down for 6 months in the French Alps in December 1966. In 1969–70 Milutin Veljković of Yugoslavia stayed down for 463 days in the Svrljig Mountains. The principal centres in Britain are the Craven area of Yorkshire, the Peak District of Derbyshire and the Mendip Hills in Somerset.

Potlatch, a competitive feast among the north-west-coast Indians of North America, especially the Kwakiutl tribe of British Columbia. It was given by individuals and clans to acquire high status and prestige. Blankets, plates of copper and slaves were given or destroyed. The custom was made illegal in Canada in 1884, but legalised again in 1951; modern potlaches are mild affairs.

Potomac, river of the eastern USA, rising in two branches in the Allegheny Mountains, and flowing as the boundary between Maryland, West Virginia and Virginia to empty into Chesapeake Bay. Its chief tributaries are the Shenandoah and the Monocacy. At Washington DC, 185 km from its mouth, it becomes tidal and navigable. Length 460 km.

Potometer, an apparatus for measuring the rate at which water is absorbed by a plant. Potometers are of different designs, but all consist of a graduated vessel into which the plant, or part of a plant, is sealed. The amount of water drawn into the plant from the vessel is recorded.

Potosí, capital of Potosí province in Bolivia, at an altitude of 3998 m. The silver mines, discovered in 1546, and now virtually abandoned, were the cause of its early prosperity. The main mining activities are now directed to tin, copper and zinc. Population (1974) 210,000.

Potsdam, city of the German Democratic Republic, capital of the district of Potsdam, and former capital of Brandenburg, on the River Havel, on the south-western outskirts of Berlin. The town was the second royal residence of Prussia, and has fine buildings of the 17th and 18th centuries; of these the most notable is *Sans Souci* (1745–47), the palace of Frederick II, whose tomb is in the garrison church. Population (1979) 126,933.

Potsdam Agreement, agreement arising out of the three-power conference held at Potsdam, 16 July–1 August 1945, between Churchill and Attlee for Britain, Truman for the USA, and Stalin for the USSR, to determine the future of Germany after the unconditional surrender of 7 May 1945. The Potsdam Agreement provided that: (1) a committee of foreign ministers of the USA, USSR, Britain, France and China should be established to frame peace treaties with Germany's allies, to be submitted to the UN. (2) The commanders-in-chief of France, Britain, the USA and the USSR should exercise supreme authority in their respective German zones. (3) The Allies should disarm and demilitarise Germany and Nazism should be entirely destroyed. (4) War criminals should be brought to trial.
See also GERMAN HISTORY.

Potter, (Helen) Beatrix (1866–1943), English writer. Her first illustrated stories were sent in letters to a child, and their popularity made her consider publishing them. *The Tale of Peter Rabbit*, 1902, *The Tailor of Gloucester*, 1903, *The Tale of Benjamin Bunny*, 1904, *The Tale of Mrs Tiggy-winkle*, 1905, stories about Jemima Puddle-Duck, Jeremy Fisher, Mrs Tittlemouse, Pigling Bland, and all her other animal characters, together with her excellent water-colour illustrations, proved lastingly popular. The stories are unsentimental, combining acute observation of nature with straightforward, economical prose, and convey truth through fantasy.

Potter, Paulus (1625–54), Dutch animal and landscape painter, born at Enkhuizen. He is famous for his life-size *Bull* in the Mauritshuis, The Hague. He was very precocious, but because of his early death his works are rare.

Potter, Stephen (1909–69), English writer. He is chiefly known for his humorous books, *The Theory and Practice of Gamesmanship, or the Art of Winning Games Wihtout Actually Cheating*, 1947; *Some Notes in Lifemanship*, 1950; and *One-Upmanship*, 1952.

Potteries, The, popular name for the six towns comprising the city of Stoke-on-Trent, England.

Pouched Mouse, or kangaroo-rat, any member of *Dipodomys*, a genus of rodents in the family Heteromyidae. There are 22 species of these jerboa-like creatures from North America. They are burrowing animals, with long hindlimbs and tails, and cheek-pouches. *D. heermanni* and *D. deserti* are well-known species.

Poulenc, Francis (1899–1963), French composer. He was a member of 'Les Six', and was influenced by Erik Satie and Jean Cocteau. In 1917 his work began to attract attention, and by 1924 Diaghilev had commissioned the ballet *Les Biches* from him. Other sizeable works are *Les Mamelles de Tirésias*; a Mass and *Stabat Mater*; the cantata *Figure humaine* to words by Éluard; *Concert champêtre* for harpsichord; concertos for two pianos and for organ; a sextet for wind and piano; a string quartet; and the opera *Dialogues des Carmélites*; he also wrote numerous piano pieces and songs, and music for plays and films.

Poultice (from the Latin *puls*, pottage), any substance applied to some part of the body with the object of promoting counter-irritation in the case of inflamed tissues or organs, of relieving pain, of accelerating suppuration, or of stimulating or soothing the skin.

Poultry, domesticated members of two orders of the bird class. Chickens and turkeys belong to different families of order Galliformes, and ducks and geese belong to order Anseriformes.

Over many thousands of years the great variety of colour and form that we can see today in chickens has evolved firstly by natural selection, and subsequently by man selecting and breeding from chance mutations. More than 100 breeds are recognised. Broadly speaking, there are two types of chickens kept for egg production, those of the White Leghorn type which produce white eggs and those of the Rhode Island Red, Light Sussex and Barred Rock types which produce brown or brownish eggs. Since the 1950s special strains have been produced for poultry meat. These usually have some Sussex or New Hampshire blood on the female side and are sired by males from rapidly-growing strains of Cornish and Rock crosses.

Modern methods of chicken raising include scientific feeding and keeping egg-layers in battery cages. Chickens are liable to a number of diseases, of which the worst are Newcastle disease, aspergillosis (a form of pneumonia) and salmonellosis, an intestinal disease.

Turkeys are bred for their meat, which is particularly popular at Christmas and (in the USA) at Thanksgiving. A small number of ducks are also kept for meat, and some duck eggs are eaten. Geese are raised in large numbers in some countries of continental Europe for their meat and for the production of *pâté de foie gras*, or for their feathers.

Pound, Ezra Loomis (1885–1972), US poet and scholar. One of the most important poets and critics of the 20th century, Pound had a

Ezra Pound. *The founder of the Vorticist movement, painted by Wyndham Lewis in 1939.*

great influence on the development of modern English and American poetry, and influenced many of the century's great writers, including W. B. Yeats, James Joyce, T. S. Eliot, Hemingway and D. H. Lawrence. He was one of the founders of the Imagist school of poetry. In 1915 he began writing his *Cantos*, adding to the sequence of this long and ambitious poem for the remainder of his life.

Pound broadcast from Italy during the Second World War, and was later accused of treason by the United States government. In 1946 he was declared mentally unsound and was confined in an asylum where he remained until 1958. In 1949 he was awarded the Bollingen prize for his *Pisan Cantos*, written while in confinement, where he also translated the odes of Confucius.

Pound, an enclosure in which cattle or other beasts are confined when taken trespassing or where lost dogs are kept.

Pound, weight, see METROLOGY.

Pourbus, Flemish family of painters which included Pieter Pourbus (1510–84), painter of religious and allegorical subjects who worked at Bruges; Frans Pourbus the Elder (1545–81), son of Pieter, who worked at Antwerp; Frans Pourbus the Younger (c.1569–1622) who painted portraits and was employed by Marie de Médicis in Paris.

Poussin, Nicolas (1594–1665), French painter. He went to Paris and in 1621 was working on the decorations in the Luxembourg Palace with Philippe de Champagne. In 1624 he went to Rome where he worked for some time with Domenichino and studied the art of Raphael and classical antiquity. Repeated official invitations drew him back to Paris in 1640 to work for Louis XIII and Cardinal Richelieu, but finding the artistic climate unfavourable he returned to Rome in 1642 and never left it again. Although his early paintings show a use of colour inspired by Titian, his work became increasingly cerebral and colour took on a secondary importance. His mythological, pagan works include the *Bacchanals* (National Gallery, London) which express a restrained sensuality in their formal harmony and rhythm. Religious subjects include the two sets of *Seven Sacraments*, 1642 and 1644–48. His history paintings established the standard from which the French Academy derived its doctrine of 'Great Art'. These include classical and biblical subjects such as the *Rape of the Sabines* (Louvre) and the *Triumph of David* (Dulwich). Poussin was a major influence upon the development of French art.

Powell, Anthony Dymoke (1905–), English novelist. His major work is a linked series of novels, with the general title 'A Dance to the Music of Time'. All twelve novels are narrated by a character named Nicholas Jenkins, and deal with his life and the life of the upper and upper middle classes in England from the 1920s onwards.

Powell, (John) Enoch (1912–), British politician. He became Conservative MP for Wolverhampton South-West in 1950 and was financial secretary to the Treasury, 1957–1958, and minister of health, 1960–63. His radical views on the social services and prices and incomes policy have often conflicted with those of the Conservatism of the day and since 1968 his attitude towards immigrants and his repatriation proposals have made him a national and bitterly controversial figure. In October 1974 he was elected as the United Ulster Unionist MP for South Down.

Power, of a number, the result of the number being multiplied by itself. The *m*th power of a number a is the result of multiplying a by itself $m - 1$ times. Formally, the *m*th power of a (where m is a positive integer) is the number a^m, where $a^1 = a$ and $a^m = a \times a^{m-1}$. More generally, a may be any element of a group. The process of computing a power is called involution.

Power, rate of doing work or expending energy. The SI unit is the watt, symbol W. Another unit gradually going out of use is horsepower, symbol h.p. The relation between the units of power is 1 h.p. = 33,000 lb ft/min = 550 lb ft/s. = 746 W. The usual way of expressing electrical energy is in kilowatt hours; 1 kWh is the energy spent in using a kilowatt of power for 1 hour. 1 kWh = 1000 × 3600 W s = $3{\cdot}6 \times 10^6$ J or, in stating annual consumption, in kW h = $3{\cdot}6 \times 10^{15}$ J.

See also METROLOGY.

Power Factor, of an electric circuit, the ratio of power given out to the power supplied i.e. average power/(r.m.s. voltage × r.m.s. current), where r.m.s. = root-mean-square. When the applied voltage is $\hat{V}\sin\omega t$ and the current is $\hat{I}\sin(\omega t - \phi)$, the average power is $VI\cos\phi$, where ϕ is the angle by which current lags voltage. Thus, for sinusoidal voltage and current having the same frequency, power factor = $VI\cos\phi/VI = \cos\phi$.

Power of Attorney, authority by one person, called the donor, to another, called the donee, under which the latter becomes authorised to act as the agent of the former. A power of attorney must be by deed.

Power Stations are buildings and sites where electric power is generated, using coal, oil, water power or nuclear energy to operate the prime mover.

Future demand for electricity is likely to be met from building new oil-fired, diesel, hydroelectric and nuclear power stations. There is still much development work going on to produce safe, efficient and reliable systems using nuclear energy. Although there is no danger of a nuclear explosion from such plants, there is always the danger of an inadvertent escape of radioactive material into the atmosphere, and it is advisable to build such power stations away from heavily populated areas.

See also HYDROELECTRIC POWER.

Powerboat Racing, the modern term for motorboat or speedboat racing, in inland or offshore waters. The sport began late in the 19th century and was launched by Alfred Harmsworth, the newspaper magnate. The first race was held in 1888. Races vary in length from 160 km to 4715 km (London to Monte Carlo).

Powis Castle, Powys, Wales. The late 13th-century walls and bastions remain, but the castle was adapted in Elizabethan times and again in the latter half of the 17th century. It became the home of Clive of India, created Earl of Powis, and contains many Clive relics.

Powys, John Cowper (1872–1963), English poet, essayist and novelist, brother of Llewelyn and Theodore Powys. Powys was a university extension lecturer for over 40 years, spending some 30 of them in the United States. Though he began his literary career as a poet, publishing several collections of verse, he is chiefly known for his long novels, the three best of which are *Wolf Solent*, 1929, *A Glastonbury Romance*, 1932, and *Owen Glendower*, 1940. He also published many volumes of criticism and social philosophy. His *Autobiography* appeared in 1934.

Powys, Llewelyn (1884–1939), English essayist and novelist, brother of John Cowper and Theodore Powys. His works include many sketches and stories from his years in Africa, including *Ebony and Ivory*, 1922, and *Black Laughter*, 1924. Volumes of essays are *Impassioned Clay*, 1931, and *Dorset Essays*, 1936. *Apples Be Ripe*, 1930, is a novel. *Confessions of Two Brothers*, 1916, was written in conjuction with J. C. Powys.

Powys, Theodore Francis (1875–1953), English novelist, brother of John Cowper and Llewelyn Powys. After 1905 he lived a secluded life in Dorset, and told of it in

Nicolas Poussin. Landscape with a Man Killed by a Snake *was probably painted in 1648.*

Soliloquies of a Hermit, 1916. His novels are usually set in Dorset, but use village life to describe the struggle between good and evil in allegorical terms. *Mr Weston's Good Wine*, 1927, is considered the best.

Powys, county of Wales, created in 1974 out of the former counties of Breconshire, Montgomeryshire and Radnorshire which now form districts within it. The new county has an area of 5077 km² and a population (1981) of 110,467.

The Brecknock District in the south is extremely mountainous with magnificent scenery, the highest ranges being the Brecon Beacons and the Black Mountains (Pen y Fan 885 m). The chief rivers are the Usk, Wye, Taff and Tawe, together with their many tributaries. More than half the county is included in a national park. The district is an important water-producing area, supplying Birmingham, Swansea, Cardiff and Newport. Agriculture is the district's chief occupation, the emphasis being on cattle and sheep rearing. Brecon is the major town in the district.

The Montgomery District is located in northern Powys. The surface is almost wholly mountainous (Plynlimon is 752 m), a large portion consisting of bleak elevated moorlands. The Severn, Lake Vyrnwy (Liverpool's main water supply) and the Dovey are the main watercourses. Cattle and sheep, and the pure breed of Welsh ponies are reared. At present administration is mainly concentrated in Welshpool.

The Radnor District is located in the centre of Powys between Brecknock and Montgomery. Over one-half of the district is 300 m or more above sea-level, the highest point being at 660 m in Radnor Forest. The main rivers are the Wye and its tributaries, and the Teme, which is excellent for trout. The only important industries are agriculture, forestry and quarrying; sheep-raising predominates. Llandrindod Wells, a noted spa and entirely modern, is the administrative centre.

Poynings, Sir Edward (1459–1521), English statesman. He became lord-deputy of Ireland (1494). In this capacity he convoked a parliament which passed what has come to be known as 'Poynings Law' (1494), enacting that no law could be valid in Ireland until it received the sanction of the English king and council. This law was not repealed until 1782.

Poznań, city of Poland, capital of Poznań province, on the River Warta, 282 km west of Warsaw. In 968 it became the first Polish bishopric, and it was the chief seat of the early Polish dukes. There are metallurgical, chemical, engineering and food industries, and there is trade in agricultural produce and timber. Population (1979) 544,000.

Pozsony, see BRATISLAVA.

Pozzuoli (ancient *Puteoli*), Italian seaport in Campania, on the Bay of Naples, 10 km south-west of Naples. It became a Roman colony in the 2nd century BC. There are Roman remains, including an amphitheatre and a half-submerged market place known as the Temple of Serapis. Population (1974) 63,500.

Praeneste (modern Palestrina), ancient hill city and villa resort of Latium, 37 km east of Rome by the Via Praenestina. Following a long, intermittent struggle with Rome, which ended in 338 BC, Praeneste was an allied city until after the Social War, when it received the Roman franchise. Praeneste was famous for its great sanctuary of Fortuna with an oracle called the 'Praenestine lots'.

Praetor, originally a title designating the Roman consul as leader of an army. After 366 BC it was applied to the annually elected curule magistrate who administered justice and was subordinate to the consuls. The office was open to the plebeians by 337. From 241 BC praetors were occasionally appointed to govern provinces; later they were regularly entrusted with this work immediately after their year of office, and were then called propraetors. They were attended by lictors. In later times the word came to mean mayor or chief magistrate.

***Prague.** The 15th-century Tyn (Hussite) church, in the old town.*

Praetorian Guard, imperial bodyguard in ancient Rome instituted by Augustus (2 BC), consisting of nine (later ten) cohorts of about 1000 men each, horse and foot, commanded by a prefect. They had higher rank and pay than the legions, and their term of service was 16 years instead of 20. They came to wield great power in choosing the new emperor. Constantine finally abolished them (AD 312). See also ROMAN ARMY.

Pragmatic Sanction (Greek *pragma*, business), solemn ordinance or Imperial rescript. The term *pragmatica sanctio* was used in late Roman law, and continued to be used in the legal phraseology of the Middle Ages and of modern Europe, particularly of a decree that defined the powers of a sovereign.

Pragmatism, a doctrine that is almost entirely a product of American thought. It was first clearly defined by Charles S. Peirce, but only during later years did it become recognised as a distinct system of philosophy, a development due mainly to professors William James (Harvard) and John Dewey (Columbia). Pragmatism may be defined as the philosophy of the expedient; it refuses to recognise as ultimate the speculative truths of metaphysics, and confines itself wholly to those truths which are definitely correlated to the actual facts of existence. Since the relation of such truths with facts is liable to constant growth and change, truth thus becomes an intellectual expedient just as right is a moral expedient.

Prague (Czech *Praha*; German *Prag*), capital of Czechoslovakia and of the Czech Socialist Republic, situated on both banks of the River Vltava. It lies almost in the geographical centre of the former province of Bohemia, of which it was formerly the capital. St Wenceslas built a church where the cathedral now stands, and in 973 Prague became a bishopric. Later there was an influx of German settlers, and the town grew steadily in importance. Prague is a beautiful city, known for the richness and variety of its Gothic and Baroque buildings. The mainly residential districts on the left bank are overlooked by the celebrated royal castle (16th–17th centuries) on the Hradčany hill. Near the castle is the Gothic cathedral of St Vitus (begun 1344 and completed 1929), in whose Wenceslas chapel the kings of Bohemia were crowned.

Important as a river port, Prague is also a centre of road and rail communications and has an international airport at nearby Ruzyně. It is an administrative, commercial and tourist centre and has numerous industries, including engineering, iron founding, brewing, and the manufacture of textiles, chemicals and foodstuffs. Population (1979) 1,189,000.

Prague Circle, a group of linguists, based on Prague since 1926, also known as the Prague School of Linguists. In its most famous period, up to 1939, its chief members were Vilém Mathesius, Nikolai Trubetskoi, Roman Jakobson, B. Trnka, V. Skalička, B. Havránek, S. Karcevski and J. Vachek, and its main impact was in the area of phonology.

Prairie (Latin *pratum*, meadow), a term with both generic and specific meaning. Generally, an expanse of natural grassland with few trees, found in many temperate regions of the world. Specifically, the name applies to the grasslands of North America.

Prairie-dog, or prairie marmot, any of the five species of rodents in the squirrel family, Sciuridae, and genus *Cynomys*. They are burrowing animals, averaging about 30 cm in length. All are found exclusively in North America. They live communally in burrows, known as towns.

Prairie-hen, *Tympanuchus americanus*, a bird of the family Tetraonidae, order Galliformes, which includes the grouse; the term is also applied to *Tetrao cupido*, a reddish-brown bird which is a near relative of *T. americanus*. Both species are natives of North America.

Prasad, Rajendra (1884–1963), first president of the Republic of India. Prasad became a member of the working committee of the All-India Congress in 1922, and president of the congress, 1934. When Rajagopalachari, India's last governor-general, declined to stand for election as president, Prasad was elected without opposition (January 1950). Re-elected in 1952 and 1957, he resigned in 1962. As president his constitutional powers were negligible; as the embodiment of the highest qualities in Indian character his influence was beyond measure.

Praseodymium, metallic chemical element, symbol Pr, atomic number 59, atomic weight 140·9077; discovered in 1885 by Auer von

Welsbach. It belongs to the group of lanthanides and occurs in monazite and similar minerals. Praseodymium is a scarce element, and its compounds are difficult to purify.

Pratella, Francesco (1880–1955), Italian composer. He led the Futurist movement, condemning Italian music as vulgar melodrama. His *Manifesto of Futurist Musicians* and *Technical Manifesto* caused considerable polemics and foresaw much that has since happened in music. But his own compositions are conventional and have remained in obscurity.

Prato, Italian town in Tuscany, on the Bisenzio river, 18 km north-west of Florence. It has a splendid 11th–15th-century cathedral which contains frescoes by Filippo Lippi and Agnolo Gaddi, and reliefs by Andrea della Robbia. The town is a very important producer of textiles, synthetic fibres, carpets and hosiery, but especially of woollen goods. Population (1979) 158,229.

'Pravda' (Truth), Soviet newspaper, organ of the Communist party, and the most influential and businesslike paper in the Soviet Union. Inspired by Lenin, it began in St Petersburg in 1912, but after the Revolution it moved to Moscow, 1918, and was proclaimed the principal party journal. It stands at the apex of the Soviet press system, disseminating official Party doctrine throughout the entire Soviet Union and giving priority to ideological articles.

Prawn, a group of Crustacea related to the shrimps, crabs and lobsters. Superficially prawns resemble the shrimps, but they differ in: (1) the length of the antennae; prawns' antennae are $1\frac{1}{2}$ times the length of the body whereas those of the shrimp are less than the body length; (2) the presence of a rostrum, the spike anterior to the eyes in the prawn; and (3) the second pair of legs in the prawn and the first pair in the shrimp, carries the largest pair of claws.

Leander serratus, the edible prawn, is 7 to 10 cm long, and is found among seaweed in rock pools and the lower intertidal zone, where it feeds largely as a scavenger.

Praxiteles (fl.c.364–330 BC), Athenian sculptor. His chief works have perished, including the *Aphrodite of Cnidus*. The first female nude since primitive times, this Venus ranked in antiquity next to the *Zeus* of Phidias at Olympia. It was destroyed by fire in AD 475, but a copy exists in the Vatican. Other works were a *Satyre*, *Eros of Thespiae* and *Apollo Sauroctonos*. His *Hermes*, a most important monument of 4th century art, was found in the Heraeum at Olympia (1877).

Prayer (Latin *precari*, to implore, entreat), in the deepest sense of the word, signifies the lifting up of the mind and heart to God. In a secondary sense it is also used of converse with, and petitions addressed to, lesser beings, such as the saints, the departed, and even the temporal sovereign. Prayer, however, is a term generally used in the specific sense of communion with God; as such it is essentially an act of religion and is found wherever there is a belief in a personal divinity or divinities.

Prayer, Book of Common, authorised service book of the Church of England. It is a book of *Common* Prayer in two senses: (1) it provides a uniform use for the whole Church of England; (2) the worship of the Church was to be 'common' in that it was to be made a corporate action in which priest and people joined together, rather than something done by the clergy in which the laity had no part but that of onlookers.

A litany in English to be added to the Latin service was first published in 1544, and in 1549 Edward VI's First Prayer Book contained the Order for Morning and Evening Prayer, Communion Service, and other rites in English. In the Second Prayer Book of 1552, the Communion Service was drastically revised in a Protestant direction.

On the accession of Mary I the Latin liturgy was restored. In 1559, the year after the accession of Elizabeth I, the Prayer Book of 1552 was restored, with some few but significant modifications in favour of a more traditional interpretation. This book was in all essentials the Prayer Book as it exists today. In 1645 the Book of Common Prayer was suppressed by Parliament, and its use was made a penal offence. It was brought back again at the Restoration.

By the beginning of the 20th century, it was generally recognised that the strict limits laid down by the Prayer Book had become too narrow for the needs of the time. A specially appointed commission deliberated between 1906 and 1920; and final proposals were submitted to Parliament in 1927. The proposed Book was bitterly opposed by Anglo-Catholics and Evangelicals. It was passed by the House of Lords, but rejected twice in the Commons. The Prayer Book of 1662 thus remained the only strictly legal standard of Anglican worship of the 20th century. In 1965 a measure permitting the experimental use of alternative forms of worship authorised by the Convocations received the royal assent; and the work of the liturgical commission has resulted in the publication in 1980 of the Alternative Services Book containing new forms of service to complement but not supplant those of the Book of Common Prayer. The Worship and Doctrine Measure, 1974, transferred liturgical authority from Parliament to the General Synod of the Church.

Praying Mantids, see MANTIDAE.

Pré, Jacqueline du (1945–), British cellist. She made her début in 1961 and was at once acknowledged as a remarkable talent with a vigorous technique. Although particularly associated with Elgar's cello concerto, she was also noted for her performances of Beethoven and Brahms. In 1967 she married the pianist and conductor Daniel Barenboim. In 1973 multiple sclerosis forced her to abandon her performing career; she continues to teach.

Preaching Friars, see DOMINICAN ORDER, THE.

Prebend, formerly the food, clothing, etc., of a secular priest or canon regular in the Christian Church, or the endowment from which this was provided, as distinct from the income of a benefice. Later it was applied to the endowment possessed by a cathedral or collegiate church for the support of a canon, who was in consequence known as a prebendary. Since the Victorian reforms the prebend (as distinct from residentiary canonry) is an honorary office, without a stipend.

Pre-Cambrian, the period of geological time from the initial cooling of the Earth some 4500–4700 million years ago until the start of the Cambrian, about 600 million years ago. It comprises the major part of geological time, and rocks of Pre-Cambrian age outcrop over vast areas of the continents, forming the so-called Pre-Cambrian shields. At least four major orogenic cycles occurred during Pre-Cambrian times, and so almost all the rocks are highly metamorphosed and folded. A simplified classification, based on world-wide correlation of dated orogenic periods, is as follows:

Early Pre-Cambrian, from about 4600 to 3500 million years ago. Very few rocks of this age are preserved. Those that are found are high-grade metamorphic rocks such as gneisses, basic and anorthositic igneous intrusions.

Middle Pre-Cambrian, from about 3500 to 2400 million years ago. During this period volcanic and sedimentary rocks accumulated in numerous linear sedimentary basins, and there was widespread intrusion of dyke swarms and anorthosites.

Late Pre-Cambrian, from about 2400 to 600 million years ago. New groups of sedimentary basins were initiated and further dyke swarms and anorthosites intruded. There was extensive crustal mobility between 1950–1550 million years ago, followed by a quiet interval and then further orogeny in the period 1150–850 million years ago.

Precedence is the order or rank in which persons should be placed on ceremonial occasions, and depends partly upon letters patent and partly upon ancient custom. In England and Wales questions of precedence are the responsibility of the Earl Marshal of England. In Scotland matters of precedence are regulated by the officers of the Lyon Court. The official table of precedence will be found in such reference books as *Burke's Peerage*. Precedence in the USA is always determined by the office a person holds and not by the rank he may hold.

Precentor, title of a canon or minor canon in an Anglican cathedral, originally the leader of a monastic or cathedral choir, but also in charge of vocal church music and superior to the organist. His seat is opposite that of the dean. In some churches in Scotland, where the organ or other musical instrument is not employed, the precentor is the leader of psalmody.

Precession is the slow conical motion of the Earth's axis and the analogous behaviour of tops, gyroscopes and other spinning bodies. The precession of the equinoxes was discovered by Hipparchus. The celestial longitudes appeared to be increasing steadily at a rate which he estimated as between 45 and 46″ of arc per year. (The currently accepted rate is 50·2″.) Newton explained this phenomenon in terms of the differential gravitational attractions of the Sun and Moon on the Earth's equatorial bulge, producing couples trying to turn the plane of the Earth's equator into the plane of the ecliptic. Since the Earth is spinning the effect of these disturbing couples is similar to that of gravity on a spinning top whose axis is inclined to the vertical. The top does not fall over but precesses steadily about the vertical to which it is inclined at a constant angle. Viewed on the celestial sphere, precession causes the Earth's orbital plane to precess in a period of 18·6 years and the mean pole of the equator to move steadily round a circle of radius 23° 27′ centred on the pole of the ecliptic in a period of 25,800 years. Nutation makes the actual pole move irregularly round this mean pole in a roughly circular path of radius 9″ of arc in a period of about 19 years. See also CELESTIAL SPHERE; DRACO; POLARIS; TIME; YEAR; ZODIAC.

Precious Stones, see GEM.

Precipitation, in meteorology, is defined as particles of liquid or solid water existing in a cloud, or which are falling or have fallen from it. The term covers rain, snow, hail, graupel, dew, hoar frost and rime. For any of these forms to exist atmospheric water vapour must condense to produce dew or hoar frost, fog or cloud. Precipitation which falls from clouds is of two broad types: uniform and steady, from widespread stratiform clouds; and showers, from relatively isolated cumuliform clouds. The first type tends to be continuous with fine particles, and the second starts and stops abruptly, with each shower being fairly violent but usually of less than one hour's duration. Not all precipitation from clouds reaches the ground; some may evaporate on the way down.

Clouds consist of water and ice particles and because they become heavier than the surrounding air the water falls as a result of gravity. It is unlikely that water particles will reach the ground very soon after they have formed; they are either carried into the higher parts of the cloud by upward currents or they evaporate on fallout from the cloud and pass into unsaturated air. The larger size raindrops in a cloud fall fastest and grow by collision with smaller ones and in deep clouds can reach a size which allows them to fall out and reach the ground. Two other methods of raindrop growth are known, each with distinctive precipitation: in aggregation ice crystals aggregate to produce snowflakes, in accretion water droplets freeze on to snowflakes as they go through the supercooled zone of a cloud, and by this process two other precipitation types are formed, rime (graupel) and hail.

Precipitation. If one of the products of the chemical reaction between substances in solution is insoluble, that product is thrown out of solution, i.e. it is precipitated. The substance thown out of solution is termed a precipitate and the action is termed precipitation.

Predestination, Christian concept in which belief in God's foreknowledge of the faith and merits of believers is combined with a belief in his predetermination of everything. The doctrine of predestination is contained in the Bible in such passages as Eph. i. 4–12, and especially in Rom. viii. 29–30.

Predestination became one of the distinguishing features of Calvinism. The doctrine has been variously interpreted in the Catholic and Protestant traditions. In favour of predestination, Aquinas is found against Duns Scotus, the Jansenists against the Jesuits, the Calvinists against the Arminians, Whitefield against Wesley.

Pre-existence, doctrine that man's soul had an existence apart before it became united to the body. It is Eastern in origin, and in the East it is generally associated with the doctrine of the transmigration of souls. Thus it is held by the Buddhists, and formed part of the Pythagorean system. The Pythagorean doctrine of reminiscence is based on it: genuine knowledge is gained by the soul in a prior disembodied state in which it is disencumbered of the senses. This view was also held by Socrates and portrayed in the dialogues of Plato.

Prefabrication, term apparently first used about 1943 to describe the manufacture of components of a building before its erection, so that only assembly is necessary on the site. It is facilitated by standardisation.

See also MODULAR CO-ORDINATION.

Pregnancy, the period of intrauterine development of the fertilised ovum. The time varies with the species of animal. In human beings the average duration is 280 days, plus or minus 14 days. Amenorrhoea (cessation of the menstrual periods) is the first symptom of pregnancy, but it is not diagnostic. Further symptoms which, taken in conjunction with amenorrhoea, are strongly presumptive of pregnancy are morning or evening nausea and vomiting, usually noticed from about the sixth week, a craving for certain foods and an aversion for others, low backache, frequency of micturition (urination), and often a feeling of depression and irritability. The breasts become enlarged and a small secretion of serum may be expressible from them.

From the third month onwards the pigment of the nipple and surrounding areola begins to get darker. The growing foetus starts to make movements at about the eighteenth week, and the feeling of these movements for the first time by the mother is referred to as 'quickening'. The gravid uterus begins to rise out of the pelvis after the third month, and from this time onwards may be felt through the abdominal wall as a gradually enlarging spherical tumour.

From six weeks onwards pregnancy can be positively diagnosed by tests that depend on the presence of human chorionic gonadotrophin hormone (HCG) in the urine of the pregnant woman. Pregnancy can also now be diagnosed by a blood test using radioimmune assay that gives an accurate result ten days after fertilisation of the egg.

Ectopic pregnancy occurs about once in every 300 pregnancies. It is a pregnancy anywhere other than within the uterine cavity. The commonest site is the Fallopian tube, but it can occur in the cervix, ovary and abdominal cavity. This type of pregnancy can rarely proceed normally and the foetus usually dies because of inadequate blood supply. The only treatment is surgical removal of the ectopic embryo and membranes.

In the absence of any contra-indication, modern practice is to allow the pregnant woman to lead as normal a life as possible within the natural limitations imposed by her physical condition. At the same time the antenatal period is now regarded by obstetricians as of great importance. By regular examination from when pregnancy is first suspected, it is possible to observe abnormalities in their earliest stage and take steps to correct them.

See also FOETUS.

Prehistory, the study of events and conditions before written or recorded history. Prehistory should not be confused with archaeology which is the study of material remains of all earlier periods; but prehistory is dependent on archaeology because of the shortage of all other sources of information. The boundary between prehistory and history varies widely and is often difficult to determine.

In his study of the remains of early man, the prehistorian considers and interprets age, material, function and social environment. The quest for food and dwelling, the conditions of commerce, trade, labour and communications, the way of worship, the presence of peace or war, and finally the burial and disposal of the dead, all come within his view. Discovery is the first concern, and then interpretation. The very great advance in our knowledge of prehistory made in recent years is largely the result of improved excavation and dating techniques.

The framework of prehistory continues to be provided by Thomsen's three age system—the successive technological ages of stone, bronze and iron. This chronology is relative, to the extent that it is based on stratigraphy: it does not determine the duration of the various periods, and it does not prove that a period in one area is contemporary with that in another.

Absolute chronology is provided by the measurement of the rate of decay of a variety of radioactive substances, of which C^{14} is the most useful in later prehistory, and by changes in climate which have taken place over a considerable part of the surface of the Earth. In the Pleistocene epoch a time-scale is provided by the Glacial Periods, the Interglacial Periods between them and by Pluvials, periods of heavy rain, which fell in some regions now dry, such as Zimbabwe and Iran. The question is complicated, and most recent studies of solar radiation, although most valuable, have not lessened the difficulties. Geochronology is still developing as a science. It remains to mention dendrochronology, the science of determination of date by observation of the annual growth-rings of trees. The possibilities of its use to the prehistorian in dating the timber-work of buildings are considerable.

See also ARCHAEOLOGY; BEAKER FOLK; BRONZE AGE; DATING IN ARCHAEOLOGY (AND GEOLOGY); IRON AGE; MEGALITHIC MONUMENTS; STONE AGE.

Premature Birth, see ABORTION; OBSTETRICS.

Premature Ejaculation, see SEXUALITY, HUMAN.

Prematurity, see BABY.

Premier, see CABINET; PRIME MINISTER.

Preminger, Otto Ludwig (1906–), Austrian film director, and associated with Max Reinhardt as actor and stage director. His films include *Angel Face*, 1952; *Carmen Jones*, 1954; *River of No Return*, 1954; *The Man with the Golden Arm*, 1955; *Anatomy of a Murder*, 1959; *Exodus*, 1960; *Advise and Consent*, 1962; *In Harm's Way*, 1964; *Tell Me That You Love Me, Junie Moon*, 1970; *The Human Factor*, 1979.

Premium, in insurance, the amount paid by the insured either as a single or a periodical payment to secure the protection of a policy which may provide for the payment of the insured or his representatives of a sum as indemnity for loss of or damage to goods; or

as compensation to employees or third parties; or a fixed sum at death, according to the type of policy.
See also INSURANCE.

Premium (in commerce). (1) In stock or share dealing, the premium is the excess in the value of any securities over the price of issue. (2) In finance, a premium is a bonus or sum given for the loan of money over and above the interest. (3) Any price paid in cash or kind by a buyer or seller in excess of the stated or agreed price, e.g. 'key money' paid for the lease of an apartment, is referred to as a premium; as are gifts offered in order to attract buyers for a product.

Preposition, part of speech, small word usually placed before a noun, or other equivalent word, to indicate a relationship. For example in 'he stood by the table', 'by' is the preposition.
See also PARTS OF SPEECH.

Pre-Raphaelite Brotherhood, a movement formed in 1848, primarily the creation of W. Holman Hunt, D. G. Rossetti and J. E. Millais, whose aim constituted a reaction against current art traditions and a 'return to nature', and the earnest spirit of art found in Raphael's precursors. Primarily 'literary' painters, they stressed the importance of serious moralising subjects using symbolism to underline the theme. They used bright colour, working on to a wet, white ground and produced paintings with an elaboration of carefully observed detail, due to working outdoors direct from nature. Strictly, the Pre-Raphaelite Brotherhood numbered seven members, though the movement was to acquire many adherents.

Prerogative, Royal, see CROWN.

Presbyopia, see REFRACTION, ERRORS OF.

Presbyterianism, form of church government in which the leading part is taken by presbyters or elders. It stands midway between the two systems of episcopacy and congregationalism. In Presbyterianism authority rests with a succession of councils, each consisting of ministers and elders. The present system owes its establishment to the French reformer Calvin and has taken firm root in such countries as Scotland, Northern Ireland, Switzerland and the USA. The Presbyterian Church has only one spiritual order, that of presbyters, divided into ministers and elders. The minister occupies the chief position in each congregation, dispenses the sacraments, and conducts the services of the church. The elders of the church are laymen, though ordained by the presbyters, and assist the ministers in matters of discipline.

Presbytery, in ecclesiastical architecture, the sanctuary, or that part of the choir of the church in which the high altar is placed. The name is sometimes extended to the whole choir. Also a modern Roman Catholic clergyhouse.

Prescription, in English law, broadly speaking, is that right given partly by common law and partly by the Prescription Act 1832, by which a person claims to be entitled, as owner, to easements or profits *à prendre* over or from the lands of another on the sole ground of long user.

President, one who 'presides' over or directs. In the final constitution of the USA the head of the Federal government was called 'president'. This is the most common meaning of the word, the head by election of a modern republic, such as the USA, France and Switzerland.

President of the Council, see PRIVY COUNCIL.

Presidium, see POLITBURO.

Presley, Elvis (1935–77), US pop singer. The most famous of the rock and roll singers of the mid-1950s, he starred in many films that showed off his personality and sultry good looks. Later, with age and the decline of rock and roll, he adopted a more conventional image and style.
See also POP MUSIC.

Press, The, see JOURNALISM; MAGAZINES; NEWSPAPERS.

Press Association, founded in 1868, the largest British home news agency and joint-owner, with London and Commonwealth newspapers, of Reuters, the British world news agency. The PA provides, by means of its own teleprinter plant over leased wires, a complete service of home news to British newspaper and television companies, and to Reuters and other news agencies for overseas distribution, and distributes to the British press, and the overseas news services of Reuters and Associated Press. It also provides news photographs and a high-speed sporting results service.

Press Council, an independent body founded by the British press in 1953 and financed by newspaper and journalistic organisations with the principal object of preserving the established freedom of the press. The Council aims to maintain the character of the British press in accordance with the highest professional standards and considers complaints about the conduct of the newspaper and periodical press from members of the public. The only redress it offers is the publication of its adjudications.

Press-gang, name given to the detachment of officers and men commissioned to execute warrants for the impressment of men to serve in the British navy. By an Act of 1835 the period of compulsory service for men impressed for the navy was limited to five years. Impressment, though in abeyance, is technically still legal.

Pressure, force per unit area, see COMPRESSION; GAS; HYDROSTATICS; METROLOGY.

Pressure Groups may be defined as agencies of political mobilisation which seek to influence the exercise of political power. They may be distinguished from political parties, which seek to exercise political power directly by assuming responsibility for government.

Pressure Welding, see WELDING.

Prestel, see VIEWDATA.

Prester John, probably a mythical character, ruler of a vast domain in the interior of Asia. A supposed letter from Prester John recounting the marvels of his realm to (in different versions) the Byzantine emperor, the pope, the Holy Roman emperor, or the king of France, was a popular text from the 12th century onwards, and efforts were made by the popes to communicate with him.

Preston, town in Lancashire, England, situated on the Ribble, in the middle of Central Lancashire New Town. Cotton was for many decades the mainstay of the industrial life of Preston, but in 1939 rayon manufacture

Pre-Raphaelite Brotherhood. Ophelia, *by Sir John Millais, 1852, was inspired by the tragic character in Shakespeare's* Hamlet.

began. Engineering, another traditional industry, has become gradually diversified, especially with the growth of motor and aircraft construction. Population (1981) 86,913.

Prestonpans, seaside town in Lothian Region, Scotland, 15 km east of Edinburgh, celebrated for the victory of Prince Charles Edward over the royal troops under Sir John Cope in 1745. Formerly noted as a centre of the salt and, until recently, the coal industries. Population (1981) 7620.

Prestwick, town, golfing centre and seaside resort in Strathclyde Region, on the Firth of Clyde, some 4 km from Ayr, and one of the most popular resorts in South-West Scotland. Nearby is Prestwick international airport. Population (1981) 13,532.

Pretoria, capital of the Transvaal, South Africa, and administrative capital of the republic (the legislature sits at Cape Town). It is situated at the foot of the Magaliesberg, 1370 m above sea-level. The city was founded in 1855 by Marthinius Pretorius, son of Andries Pretorius, the victor of the Blood river battle, after whom it was named. In 1860 it superseded Potchefstroom as the capital of the Transvaal. Pretoria is the headquarters of the South African Iron and Steel Corporation (ISCOR) which produces most of South Africa's steel and employs 37,000 people. Its other industries include engineering, diamonds and food processing. Population (1980) 528,407, including 351,590 whites.

Pretorius, Andries Wihelmus Jacobus (1799–1853), Dutch settler in South Africa, and soldier, leader of the great Boer trek in 1838, into what is now Natal. With a small force of farmers Pretorius won the famous battle of Blood River (16 December 1838). This led to the setting up of a republic of Natal, with Pretorius as first president.

Offers of farms were made to the Boers, but a considerable number of them recrossed the Drakensberg under the leadership of Pretorius and set up new republics between the Orange and Vaal rivers. Pretorius succeeded in subjecting all the districts in the Transvaal to one government without loss of life. The city of Pretoria, founded by his son, Marthinus Wessels Pretorius, was named in his honour.

Preventive Medicine, that aspect of medicine that aims at the prevention of disease. Personal hygiene promotes the health of the individual, so that he will be better fitted to withstand infection and less liable to acquire disease; it ranges from the prenatal care of the foetus and the mother to geriatrics, or the health-care of old age, which is now being increasingly studied. Personal hygiene includes the cleanliness of the body, care of the teeth and mouth, and, so far as possible, the commonsense rules of healthy living. Public hygiene, or environmental health, is concerned with such matters as the provision of adequate water supplies and the proper disposal of sewage, the safeguarding of food, and especially milk, superintendence of buildings, and so on. Many infectious diseases, as, for instance, measles, smallpox, scarlet fever, typhoid, puerperal fever and diphtheria, must by law be notified to the local community physician acting in his rôle of proper officer of the local authority, so that steps can be taken to prevent their spread. The advances made in the prevention of infectious diseases by immunisation may claim a large share of the credit due to preventive medicine. By this means smallpox has been eradicated from the world and diphtheria, poliomyelitis and, more recently, measles have been controlled.

Preventive medicine is of particular importance in tropical areas, where diseases such as malaria and yellow fever, with insect vectors, and others caused by intestinal parasites, may be controlled, or even prevented entirely, by the application of adequate preventive measures.

See also COMMUNITY HEALTH; ENVIRONMENTAL HEALTH; HYGIENE; NUTRITION; PUBLIC HEALTH; SEWAGE; VENEREAL DISEASE; WATER SUPPLY.

Prévert, Jacques (1900–77), French writer. He first made his name before the Second World War as a writer of film-scripts and during the war began writing poetry. His free verse, with a strong vein of humour and fantasy, was first collected in *Paroles*, 1946. Later volumes of verse are *Histoires*, 1946, *Spectacle*, 1951, *La Pluie et le beau temps*, 1955, and *Hebdomadaires*, 1972. Among the most famous films for which he provided scenarios are *Quai des brumes*, *Le Jour se lève*, *Les Enfants du paradis*, *Les Portes de la nuit* and *La Bergère et le ramoneur*.

Previn, André (1930–), US conductor and composer. Previn became known as a prolific composer of film scores before becoming music director of the Houston Symphony Orchestra, 1967–69; he was principal conductor of the London Symphony Orchestra, 1969–79, and of the Pittsburgh Symphony Orchestra from 1976. He has composed concertos for cello, violin and guitar, as well as orchestral pieces, and the musicals *Coco* and *The Good Companions*. He is also an accompanist of note.

Prévost d'Exiles, Antoine François (1697–1763), French writer, and generally known as the Abbé Prévost. He was brought up by the Jesuits, but abandoned monastic for military life, then re-entered a monastery, and finally left France for Holland and London. In 1734 he returned to Paris as chaplain to the prince de Conti.

He wrote many novels, mostly long and diffuse stories of love and adventure. He is famous chiefly as the author of *Manon Lescaut*, 1731, published as part of the *Mémoires d'un homme de qualité*. This story of a destructive passion is related with rare objectivity and psychological insight.

Priam (Greek *Priamos*), legendary king of Troy during the Trojan war, son of Laomedon. As an old man he took no active part in the fighting. He sought refuge at the altar of Zeus when Troy fell, but was killed by Neoptolemus, son of Achilles. By Hecuba he fathered Hector, Paris, Troilus and Cassandra.

Pribil of Islands, four volcanic islands in the Bering Sea, off Alaska, USA; an international seal reserve. The total area of the group is 440 km²; the largest islands are St Paul and St George. Their location is 57° N latitude, 170° W longitude.

Price, Harry (1881–1948), British psychic investigator. He founded and equipped (1925) the first laboratory in Britain for the scientific investigation of abnormal happenings, publishing the results of his researches in Britain and abroad in numerous books. He investigated the claims of the principal mediums and visited scores of haunted houses in Britain and several European countries. He formed a library of over 20,000 volumes on ghosts, magic and allied subjects, which he presented to the University of London.

Price, Leontyne (1927–), US soprano. Trained at the Juilliard school of music, she made a great impact in New York and Europe (1952–54), as Bess in Gershwin's *Porgy and Bess*. She subsequently appeared in opera on television, in San Francisco, Vienna, and at Covent Garden (1958–59), and then in Milan, at the Metropolitan Opera, New York, and in Paris, Rome and Buenos Aires. She is famous for her interpretation of Aida and other Verdi roles.

Price, a way of expressing how much a good or service is worth, as measured by the quantity of goods and services that one unit of the good (service) can be exchanged for.

The price of one good in terms of another is how many units of the second good are required in exchange for one unit of the first good. If all trading is done by the exchange of goods then this is known as a barter economy. Due to the inconvenience of barter the use of money developed, probably from the use of a small, light, easily divisible but high value good (e.g. gold) in barter, and now prices are expressed as the number of money units required in exchange for one unit of the good or service.

Prickly Heat, or *Miliaria populosa*, a skin disease common in tropical and subtropical lands. It is characterised by inflammation of the sweat-glands, leading to the formation of small red papules, and accompanied by a prickling or tingling sensation. Treatment is to cool the patient, increase his salt intake, treat any secondary infections with antibiotics and to use local soothing applications.

Prickly Pear, *Opuntia*, a genus in the family Cactaceae found in the Americas. They often make large shrubs and have spiny stems and short-tubed, yellow or red flowers. A few species are grown as ornamental plants indoors. The fruit of *O. ficus-indica* is the prickly pear and when ripe is edible.

Pride, Thomas (d.1658), English soldier and regicide: he entered the Parliamentary army in 1644 and distinguished himself at Naseby. In 1648, to prevent an agreement with King Charles I, Pride stopped nearly a hundred members from taking their seats in Parliament, an act which is known as 'Pride's Purge'. He was a commissioner at the trial of the king and signed the death warrant.

Priest, shortened form of presbyter (Greek *presbuteros*, an elder), minister of public worship, to whom it belongs especially to perform the sacrificial rites pertaining thereto. It seems evident that, in the primitive stages of society, these duties belonged to the head of the family. A later development made the head of the clan the natural representative in religious matters, and this stage can be seen in the biblical accounts of the patriarchal age. As the organisation of society became more defined, the priestly office was in many cases associated with the king. In other religions, such as those of Egypt and

India, the priests form a separate caste. The Jewish priesthood, inaugurated by the Mosaic law, was elaborately developed, and there is a parallel between the Jewish and Christian systems. The Christian hierarchy was not fully developed until post-apostolic times. In it the priesthood forms the second grade of the sacred ministry, exercising many, but not all, of the functions of the higher grade of the bishop. To the priests belong especially the functions of offering sacrifice, administering the sacraments, blessing and preaching.

Priestley, J(ohn) B(oynton) (1894-84), English novelist, dramatist and essayist. After publishing two novels, *Adam in Moonshine* and *Benighted*, he scored a noteworthy success with the long *Good Companions*, 1929, which was awarded the Tait Black Memorial Prize and was very popular. *Angel Pavement*, 1930, was also very successful.

In 1932 he began writing plays with *Dangerous Corner*, and followed it with many others, the chief of which are *Eden End*, 1935; *Time and the Conways*, 1937; *I Have Been Here Before*, 1938; *Johnson over Jordan*, 1939; *An Inspector Calls*, 1947; *The Linden Tree*, 1948; *The Glass Cage*, 1956; and the popular comedies *Laburnum Grove*, 1933; and *When We Are Married*, 1938. Many of his essays are collected in *Essays of Five Decades*, 1969; he has also written several non-fiction studies, including *English Journey*, 1935.

Priestley, Joseph (1733–1804), British chemist and clergyman. He met Franklin in London, and published *History and Present State of Electricity*, 1767. Priestley became a minister in Birmingham (1780–91); it was here a mob burnt his house, books, manuscripts and scientific instruments. He then settled in Pennsylvania (1794). His researches in chemistry were mainly with gases; in 1774 he discovered oxygen, which he obtained by heating mercuric oxide. He carried out further researches on nitric oxide, hydrochloric acid, sulphur dioxide, ammonia, air, carbon monoxide and silicon fluoride; examined the effect of different gases on the respiration of animals and plants, applied carbon dioxide to aerated water, and greatly improved the pneumatic trough.

Primaquine, a drug used in the short, intensive treatment of malaria, but too toxic for regular prophylactic administration, since it leads to disorders of the blood and gastro-intestinal system. It attacks the parasite in the liver stage of its life-cycle.

See also ANTIMALARIALS.

Primary Colours, or simple colours, are chosen so that any other colour can be produced by mixing them in proper proportions. For pigments they are usually taken to be red, yellow and blue.

See also COLOUR; SPECTRUM AND SPECTROSCOPE.

Primary Commodities, goods which depend on animal, vegetable and mineral resources and whose prices tend to fluctuate as a result of changes in demand and supply. The producers tend to be small and comparatively weak, while the buyers are powerful dealers and manufacturers.

Primary Education, the first stage of education in Britain under the 1944 Education Act. It includes nursery schooling and continues to the age of about 11.

See also EDUCATION; KINDERGARTEN; NURSERY SCHOOL.

Primary Schools, see INFANT SCHOOLS.

Primate, in the Roman Catholic Church, the bishop of certain major sees which once had jurisdiction over several provinces. There is now, however, no primatial jurisdiction. In the Anglican Church the Archbishop of York is styled Primate of England, and the Archbishop of Canterbury is Primate of All England. The title is also used in Ireland (for Dublin and Armagh), Canada and Australia.

Primates, Primata, the order of Mammals that includes all the apes, monkeys, marmosets and man in suborder Anthropoidea; and the lemurs and lorises in the suborder Prosimii. The order is characterised throughout by the development of the brain. As a rule, both forelimbs and hindlimbs bear five digits each, a thumb being usually, but not invariably, present; and except in man, the large toe is opposable to the other toes. With the same exception, Primata are mainly arboreal and are usually confined to warm climates.

Prime, formerly in the Roman Catholic church an office said in the first hour after sunrise, following matins and lauds. It was discontinued in the Roman Catholic Church following the reform of the Liturgy of the Hours, begun in 1963.

Prime Minister, or premier, the head of the government in the United Kingdom. He or she is appointed by the sovereign, but in asking someone to form a government the sovereign is constitutionally bound to invite the leader of the party with a majority of seats in the House of Commons, a situation which is normally determined by a general election. If the prime minister dies or resigns between elections the sovereign waits until the party concerned has elected a new leader. All governmental appointments are made by the sovereign on the advice of the prime minister.

Sir Robert Walpole is widely regarded as the first prime minister, but Walpole's career set a precedent for the post rather than established it firmly as part of the machinery of government. The first prime minister in the modern sense was probably William Pitt the Younger who clearly established the rôle of the prime minister as the dominant figure in the Cabinet.

Prime Number, a whole number which cannot be divided by any other number (except 1) without leaving a remainder.

See also NUMBERS, THEORY OF.

Primitive Methodism was founded around 1805 by William Clowes of Burslem and Hugh Bourne of Stoke-on-Trent. It was a revivalist splinter group from Wesleyan Methodism. The name Primitive Methodist was adopted in 1812, and by 1852 the sect was well organised, not only in Great Britain but as far afield as Australia, New Zealand, South Africa and the USA. In London, at the centre of Whitechapel, Thomas Jackson began a remarkable work of social service in the 1880s, particularly his 'Home for Friendless and Orphan Lads'. Primitive Methodists were reunited with the parent body in 1932 as part of the Methodist Church.

Primitive Painting. That art terminology is not subject to standard specifications is demonstrated by the flexible use of the word 'primitive'. It should not be applied to paintings merely because they are early—these should be called 'archaic'. Primitive is the highly creative phase which formulates concepts later to be developed in a classical phase. Former generations were right to regard Giotto as 'primitive' to Raphael and Michelangelo, for he first identified the principles they were to develop. Similarly the painters once called Flemish Primitives (and which included Van Eyck) laid the foundations for Titian, Rembrandt and Velázquez. The modern term Neo-Primitive, to describe the *Faux-naif*, should strictly speaking have been the less emotive 'Archaistic', a word wisely devised by classical scholars to describe a pseudo-archaic fashion in Roman sculpture of the time of the Emperor Domitian (examples in the Benevento Museo di Sannio).

Primo de Rivera y Orbaneja, Miguel, Marqués de Estella (1870–1930), Spanish politician. He became governor of Cádiz, 1915. In 1922 Primo was appointed military governor of Barcelona. During the summer of 1923, he organised a military revolution. The king, refusing to sign the premier's plan for suppressing the revolt, sent for Primo and made him president of a military directorate, suspending the constitution indefinitely. Primo formed the Unión Patriótica in imitation of Fascism. His greatest achievement was the solution of the Moroccan question. In 1925 he dissolved the directorate and became premier of a government into which he introduced a civilian element. This led to his unpopularity with the army, on whom his real power depended, and in 1930 he resigned and died in France.

Primo de Rivera y Sáenz de Heredia, José Antonio (1903–36), founder of the Spanish breed of Fascism, the Falange party in 1933. A distinctive blend of poetry and thuggery characterised his speeches. His party remained numerically insignificant in comparison with the major parties. José Antonio (as he was universally known) was shot at Alicante in November 1936, having been found guilty of complicity in the rising against the Republic five months earlier.

Primogeniture, state of being the first-born child of the same parents; in English law the term became more specialised and denoted the right (abrogated in 1925) by which, on the intestacy of the father, the eldest son or his issue succeeded to the real estate to the absolute exclusion of the younger sons and daughters.

See also HEIR; SUCCESSION.

Primordium, in botany an organ, cell or organised group of cells in the earliest stage of differentiation, before it has developed into its adult form.

Primrose, Archibald Philip, see ROSEBERY, ARCHIBALD PHILIP PRIMROSE, 5TH EARL OF.

Primrose, certain plants of the genus *Primula*, especially *P. vulgaris*, the common primrose of Europe and western Asia which produces pale yellow blooms in spring. The common primrose can hybridise with the cowslip; the hybrids are called false oxlips. The true oxlip is a distinct species, *P. elatior*. The garden polyanthus is derived from primrose-cowslip hybrids. The Cape primrose is *Streptocarpus*, and the evening primrose is *Oenothera*.

Primrose League, British organisation for spreading Conservative principles. It was instituted in 1833 by Lord Randolph Churchill and others, and is so called because the primrose was said, mistakenly, to be Disraeli's favourite flower.

Primula, a genus of family Primulaceae; familiar plants of the genus are auricula, cowslip, oxlip, polyanthus and primrose. A number of other species and hybrids are grown in gardens.

Primulaceae, a family of herbaceous plants with 25 genera and about 550 species. The flowers have five sepals and five petals united to form long or short tubes. The stamens are unusual in arising opposite to petals (in most flowers petals and stamens alternate with each other). The seeds are formed in a dry fruit which opens at the top, often by a lid. Many popular wild and cultivated flowers belong to this family, including *Anagallis* (pimpernel), *Androsace*, *Cyclamen*, *Dodecatheon*, *Hottonia* (water violet), *Lysimachia*, *Primula* and *Soldanella*.

Prince (Latin *princeps*, chief), epithet applied originally to the *princeps senatus* (first senator) at Rome, later adopted by the emperors from Augustus onwards. Hence it came to be used for one of the highest rank or holding the highest place and authority, and may mean the sovereign or ruler of the state. In modern English usage it usually describes the son of a king or emperor, the issue of a royal family, or the head of a principality or small state.

Prince Edward Island, smallest province of Canada, situated in the Gulf of St Lawrence, separated from Nova Scotia and New Brunswick by Northumberland Strait. The island is 225 km long and 6–55 km wide. Area 5656 km^2.

Deep bays divide the island into three peninsulas, almost corresponding to the three counties, Prince, Queens and Kings. The rocks are of soft red sandstone and nowhere does the land rise above 150 m.

Prince Edward Island is the most densely populated province in Canada. The total population numbered 122,500 in 1980 and the main town is Charlottetown (the capital).

The forest, which was mainly deciduous in type, is almost all felled. The island is famous for its potatoes which flourish in the deep sandy soils and mild climate. Oats and root crops are also grown. Bacon, poultry, butter and cheese are exported throughout the Maritime Provinces. Fishing is also important, especially lobster fishing.

Industries are small and are mainly agricultural: butter, cheese, fish curing and packing, slaughtering and meat packing, and canning of fruit and vegetables.

The earliest discovery of the island is not known. Jacques Cartier visited it in 1534 and named it Isle St-Jean, but it is also alleged that John Cabot sighted it in 1497. In 1603 Samuel de Champlain took possession of it for France. By the Treaty of Paris (1763), it became a British possession. In 1798 it received its present name in honour of Prince Edward, Duke of Kent, the father of Queen Victoria. The island did not join the dominion of Canada until 1873.

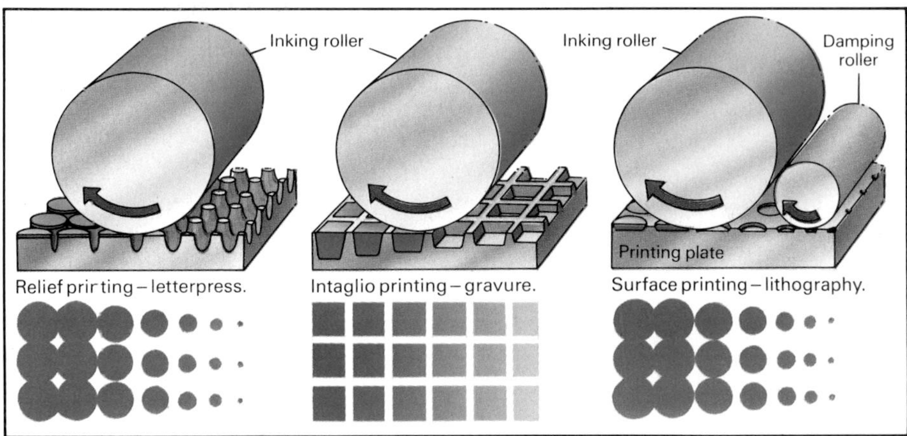

Printing. *The three principal techniques are distinguished by the character of the printing plate.*

Prince Edward Islands, two small islands in the southern Indian Ocean, 1930 km south-east of the Republic of South Africa, to which they belong. They were annexed by the South African government in December 1947, the chief purpose being the establishment of an air base.

Prince of Wales (title), see WALES, PRINCE OF.

Prince Rupert, seaport town at the western terminus of the Canadian National Railway, on Kaien Island, Port Essington estuary, British Columbia, Canada. Founded in 1909, it has since developed rapidly and has fisheries and fish canneries, and ships halibut, minerals, lumber and grain. Population (1976) 14,754.

Princess Royal, the eldest daughter of the sovereign in Great Britain, and formerly also in Prussia. The title is not always conferred; it was in use as early as the mid-17th century, and was most recently granted in 1952 to Princess Mary (1897–1965), daughter of George V.

Princeton, town of Mercer county, New Jersey, USA, 16 km north-east of Trenton. The university of Princeton owes its existence to a college founded at Elizabethtown in 1746, and moved to Princeton in 1756. It was then called the College of New Jersey. There are also a Presbyterian seminary, founded in 1812, the Rockefeller Institute for Scientific Research, and other educational institutions. Washington defeated the British here in 1777. Population (1980) 12,035.

Principe, see SÃO TOMÉ AND PRINCIPE.

Printed Circuit, a circuit or circuit component in electronics in which the wiring and some elements are photochemically produced on a flat board. The process began in the 1950s, and is now standard in the production of circuits for almost all electronic devices. The circuit is 'printed' using a baseboard of insulating material, which is coated with copper or other metal. The pattern of the circuit is transferred to the copper surface by a photographic process, and the unwanted metal is etched away. Integrated circuits and silicon chips are a development of the printed circuit system.

Printing, the process of reproducing an image from a master by means of ink and impression. There are three major printing processes: *relief printing*, or letterpress, in which the image is raised in relief, the ink is applied to the raised surface, and the image is taken off by pressing the paper against it; *intaglio printing*, in which the image is in the form of cells etched or engraved into the surface of a plate, the ink being trapped in the cells and wiped off the rest of the plate before the paper is applied; and *surface printing*, or lithography, in which the print is made from a plane surface which has been treated so that only the image areas will receive ink.

Letterpress printing is the oldest method, and it is still widely used. Printing from movable type was practised in China in the 13th century, and from wood blocks there and in Japan some centuries earlier. Printing as we know it today, however, began in Europe in the mid-15th century, first from wood blocks and then from movable type cast in an alloy of lead. The inventor of European printing methods was probably Johann Gutenberg of Mainz.

Composition, the setting of type, was done by hand until the invention of typesetting machinery in the 1800s. The individual letters are kept in partitioned trays, arranged in pairs, one above the other. Capital letters are in the upper case, small letters in the lower ones (hence the terms 'upper case' and 'lower case' for such letters). The typesetter, called a compositor, arranges the letters in a small tray, called a composing stick; from there the type is transferred to a long tray, a galley, from which a proof is taken so that the matter may be read and corrected. The corrected type is made up in page form in a large metal frame, called a chase. Mechanically composed type is made up in the same way. Hand-set type is now used only by a few 'jobbing' printers for display work such as posters.

A printing press basically consists of a flat bed on which the type rests, with facilities for inking it, applying paper to it, and taking the impression. In the simplest presses this is largely done by hand. More modern presses are of the platen type, in which the type is mounted vertically and the paper is carried to it by a steel plate, the platen. For long runs rotary machines are used: in these machines a web or continuous sheet of paper from a roll is fed through the machine. The type is converted into a curved plate by taking an impression from it on flong, a special form of cardboard, curving the flong, and casting a plate from it. Rotary machines are designed to cut and fold the printed paper, and wire stitch.

After 500 years, letterpress printing is gradually dying out and is being replaced by photogravure and offset lithography, and the use of type is giving way to cold composition, or photo-setting.

For other major printing methods see COLLOTYPE; LITHOGRAPHY; PHOTOGRAVURE; SCREEN PROCESS PRINTING.

Printmaking, the main form of reproducing pictures before the advent of photography. It survives now as an art form. All commercial forms of printing have been used, plus others carried out largely by hand, including such relief processes as woodcut, wood-engraving, and linocut; intaglio processes including aquatint, engraving, etching, mezzotint; planographic processes (lithography), and stencilling processes, (e.g. serigraphy and silk-screen).

The number of good impressions of a print that can be obtained varies with the technique and with the material from which the print is being taken, ranging from about 25 mezzotints to several thousand line engravings from steel plates. The value of a print depends on the engraver and the fineness of the impression, which decreases with the number taken. 'Artist's proofs' are valued because they bear the signature of the artist or engraver, or both.

See also BOOK ILLUSTRATION; PRINTING; and under individual printmaking processes.

Prior, James Michael Leathes (1927–), British Conservative politician; he was first elected MP in 1959. From 1970 to 1972 he held the post of minister of Agriculture, after which, from 1972 to 1974, he was deputy chairman of the Conservative Party. Between 1974 and 1979 he became a shadow spokesman, first for Home Affairs and later for Employment. After the return to power of the Conservatives in 1979 he became secretary for Employment, a post he held until 1981 when he was appointed secretary of state for Northern Ireland.

Prior, Matthew (1664–1721), English poet and diplomat. In 1690 he was appointed secretary to Lord Dursley (later Earl of Berkeley) who was English ambassador at The Hague. In 1700 he entered Parliament as a Whig, but joined the Tories in 1701. His poetry appears in *Poems on Several Occasions*, the chief collection being that of 1718. Prior is remembered for light occasional verse, epigrams and tales, in a graceful but colloquial manner, which link him with Swift and the wider Augustan achievement.

Priority, in its legal use, has several applications, e.g. as among creditors against a debtor or insolvent where the estate of the debtor is insufficient to meet all claims.

Priory, community of monks or nuns, governed by a prior or prioress. In most cases they are dependent upon abbeys, to which they are finally responsible.

Pripet (Russian *Pripyat*; Polish *Prypeć*), navigable river in south Belorussian and north-west Ukrainian SSRs, USSR, a tributary of the Dnieper. Length 775 km.

Priscian (fl.AD 500), Latin grammarian of Byzantium who was greatly influenced by the work of Apollonius Dyscolus. His *Institutiones Grammaticae*, in 18 books, mainly on the eight parts of speech and their morphology, sometimes analyses Latin as if it were Greek, but it remained popular throughout the Middle Ages (about a thousand manuscripts of the work are known) as a text book for the teaching of Latin.

Prism, a polyhedron which has two congruent and parallel faces called bases, and whose other faces (called lateral faces) are parallelograms formed by joining corresponding vertices of the bases. The altitude of a prism is the perpendicular distance between the bases. The volume is the product of the altitude and the area of a base. If the lateral faces are perpendicular to the bases the prism is called a right prism; otherwise it is an oblique prism.

Prism, Optical, a block of glass or other transparent material with plane faces, often of triangular cross-section, geometrical prism shape. Optical prisms are used mainly for changing the direction of a beam of light (turning prisms), for splitting white light into its component wave-lengths (dispersing prisms), and for producing polarised light.

See also NICOL PRISM; POLARISATION OF LIGHT; REFLECTION AND REFRACTION OF LIGHT.

Prisoners of War. A prisoner of war is any soldier, sailor or airman who has been captured by an opposing force either as a result of individual surrender or by unit capitulation. In ancient times prisoners of war could be and were killed or enslaved, unless the belligerents found it more profitable to exchange them or liberate them for ransom. For long, indeed, there were no generally accepted rules regulating the position and fate of prisoners of war, and it is only within comparatively recent years that definite regulations have been established. The existing law on the subject is based on Convention IV of The Hague Conference of 1907, which conference adopted, with certain changes, the rules made by The Hague Conference of 1899 and the articles relating to prisoners of war contained in the Geneva Convention of 1906. This was somewhat extended in the Geneva Convention of 1929, when delegates of 47 nations met at Geneva and ratified a further agreement on the treatment of prisoners of war. There was further revision in 1949.

See also RED CROSS, THE.

Prisons, places of detention. In Britain, until the early 19th century, the legal sentence for felonies was death, and for misdemeanours, fines, whipping, the pillory or stocks. Prisons were supposedly used for safe custody and for assisting the crown to exact its fines. In the 18th century, jails were generally run for private profit, and were the responsibility of the justices and the local authorities. The state was responsible for the convicts.

With the ending of transportation to Australasia in the middle of the 19th century the need for more convict prisons was intensified. Pentonville, the 'model prison', was built in 1842 based on the principle of solitary confinement. Many of the closed prisons in use today date from this period.

The modern view of prison sees it as an instrument of reform rather than punishment, but the old buildings still create an atmosphere of repression, and having been built for deterrence can only be partially adapted to a reformative process.

The 1930s saw the introduction of training for some prisoners, and of open prisons, but overcrowding was a growing problem. The Mountbatten Report of 1966 divided prisoners into four categories from the security viewpoint and the emphasis on increased security continued. There is also considerable emphasis on psychological approaches to the handling of prisoners, and the prison education service plays an important rôle.

In the Scandinavian countries, prisons, where they are still in use, have conditions which are by the standards of the UK very relaxed and pleasant. In France, where sentences are still much longer than in Britain, conditions are harsher than in the UK. The United States has prisons of all kinds, from advanced, electronically controlled, steel and concrete buildings to squalid, over-crowded, and ramshackle one-storey county jails. The conditions in which prisoners—especially political offenders—are kept under totalitarian regimes are generally appalling.

Pritchett, Sir V(ictor) S(awdon) (1900–), English novelist and critic. He spent much of his early life on the Continent, taught in many American universities, and became a director of the *New Statesman* and *Nation*. His novels and other works include *Clare Drummer*, 1929; *Shirley Sanz*, 1932; *Nothing Like Leather*, 1935; *Dead Man Leading*, 1937; *Mr Beluncle*, 1951; *When My Girl Comes Home*, 1961; *A Cab at the Door*, 1968; *The Camberwell Beauty*, 1974.

Private Press. A press whose productions reflect the owner's interests rather than commercial necessity.

Before the advent of printing there were a number of private presses, run either by royalty or by prelates, which were known as scriptoria. In more recent times Horace Walpole established the Strawberry Hill Press, at which, although he was no printer, a number of books and smaller pieces were produced by his craftsmen from 1757 to 1797. However, the outstanding figure, and the father, of the modern private-press movement was William Morris. He was not a printer, but his artistry is shown in the books which were printed at his Kelmscott Press (1890–98), the greatest of which was a Chaucer. His teaching and example influenced others. C. H. St John Hornby ran the Ashendene Press (1894–1935) and T. J. Cobden-Sanderson the Doves Press (1900–1917). These three presses are the most notable in Britain.

One of the most durable of private presses in the USA was founded by Mr and Mrs H. W. Trovillion at Hervin, Illinois, in 1908 and was run by them until their deaths in the 1960s. Other important American private presses include the Village Press, started in 1903 by F. W. Goudy and his wife Bertha at Park Ridge, Illinois, and that of Dard Hunter at Chillicothe, Ohio. There are at least 50 private presses operating in the USA.

In addition to the purely private press, others with similar ideals have set up as ordinary business concerns. Among the most noteworthy of these was the Shakespeare Head Press, founded by A. H. Bullen in 1904. Golden Cockerel Press, founded by H. M. Taylor in 1920, issued its first book a year later. Its private type face was designed by Eric Gill who in 1936, with his son-in-law, René Gill Hague, transformed the press into a limited company, Hague and Gill Ltd.

See also PRINTING; PUBLISHING.

Privateers, merchant adventurers granted a Letter of Marque by the Crown, which entitled them to attack their countries' enemies on the high seas in return for shares of the booty. By the Declaration of Paris of 1856 privateering was abolished between the signatory nations, in the event of war between them.

Privet, *Ligustrum*, a genus of shrubs in the Oleaceae from Asia and Europe. Some are cultivated for hedging and ornament. When not trimmed, the shrubs produce small white flowers, followed by blue-black berries.

Privilege. This term in English law has distinct meanings in different contexts. In legal proceedings certain documents and information are privileged from production in evidence at the trial. For instance, a party to an action cannot be compelled to produce documents containing advice from his legal advisers relating to the subject matter of the proceedings. The Crown can claim Crown privilege for the production of documentary or other evidence.

In defamation, certain statements although defamatory are, if made on certain occasions, privileged and therefore not actionable.

Privy Council. In Britain the Privy Council, like the Exchequer, the Treasury and Chancery, had its origins in the *Curia Regis* as part of the growth of executive and administrative organs of government between the 12th and 15th centuries in England.

The modern Privy Council consists of some three hundred persons who hold or have held high legal or political offices, together with the Archbishops of Canterbury and York, the Speaker of the House of Commons, a number of Commonwealth statesmen, and British ambassadors.

The full Privy Council now meets only to sign the proclamation of a new sovereign and when a sovereign announces his or her intention to marry. The political and administrative functions of the Council are exercised by the Queen as advised by those Cabinet ministers concerned with the business at hand. The lord president of the council is responsible for presenting the business to the Queen, who by convention gives her approval. Most of the business is in the form of proclamations (e.g. for proroguing, dissolving or summoning Parliament, or declaring war or peace) or orders in council, which may be legislative (e.g. statutory instruments implementing ministerial regulations), executive (e.g. setting up a new government department), or judicial (e.g. giving effect to a judgment of the Judicial Committee of the Privy Council). The lord president is also the member of the Cabinet in charge of the Privy Council Office and, since 1964, he has also been the leader of the House of Commons and therefore in charge of the government's business in the lower House.

Prix de l'Arc de Triomphe, horse race run at Longchamp, Paris. Established in 1920, it is for three-year-olds and upwards, colts and fillies, over 2·4 km of a testing right-hand grass course. Since the Second World War it has become one of the most important international races, often attracting the principal runners from half a dozen countries.

Prize-Fighting, the fore-runner to boxing, flourished in the 18th and 19th centuries. Participants fought bare-knuckled, and throwing an opponent, gouging, tripping, hair-pulling and scratching were all allowed. There were no weight divisions as we know them today and contests were in effect timeless. Rounds lasted for however long it took for one man to throw or knock down his opponent, following which there was a 30-second rest period. Both fighters were then required to 'come up to scratch'—a line drawn in the centre of the ring. A contest was decided when one or other figher was unable to come to the scratch line. Because fights were therefore in effect tests of endurance more than anything else, contests lasting many hours and over 100 rounds were not uncommon.

In the latter part of the 19th century, however, public opinion swung against the brutalities of bare-knuckle prize-fighting and with the drafting of the Marquess of Queensbury Rules in 1867, which made the use of gloves in contests compulsory, the modern sport of boxing was born. The last official bare-knuckle world championship fight was between John L. Sullivan and Jake Kilrain in 1889.

See also BOXING.

Probability, in logic, the presumption that some statement is likely to be true or that some event is likely to happen, when sufficient evidence to constitute absolute proof cannot be secured. The term is also applied in logic and mathematics to the amount of antecedent likelihood which exists for the occurrence of a certain event, as calculated from the relative frequency of the occurrence of similar events in the whole range of past experience. In this connection the investigation of probability has been performed chiefly in connection with games of chance.

Probability Theory, a branch of mathematics (first developed by Fermat and Pascal) for analysing randomness or unpredictability. There are many situations in which an action will have a known range of possible outcomes, but which outcome will result cannot be predicted exactly. For example, most people would say that each face of a die has a one-in-six chance of being uppermost. Probability theory enables guesses to be made with more confidence and much more complicated situations to be dealt with.

Calculation of Probabilities. If an action can lead to a definite number of equally likely outcome occurring is

$$\frac{\text{number of favourable outcomes}}{\text{number of possible outcomes}}$$

This is often called the 'classical definition' of probability. In practice, the more often an action is repeated, the closer the actual frequency of occurrence will approach the computed probability. Thus, only over several thousand throws of a die will the frequency of occurrence of any one number approach 1/6. Probability theory (and statistics, which is derived from it) describes the real world in the long-term.

From the classical definition: (1) a probability is a number between 0 and 1 inclusive (0 is for an impossible and 1 for a certain outcome); (2) if two types of outcome are mutually exclusive (i.e. cannot occur simultaneously) then the probability that either of them will occur is equal to the sum of their individual probabilities. These properties can be used to define probabilities in situations where the classical definition cannot be used. The complete collection of possible outcomes of an action is called the 'population' or the 'sample space' and the numerical probabilities describe the 'probability distribution' of the outcomes. These must be assigned to represent 'ideal' values of the frequency of occurrence of each outcome, either on the basis of previous observation of subjective estimate. Often it is assumed that a real-life probability distribution is of the same form as one of the standard distributions, such as the normal distribution, which have been extensively studied in probability theory.

Probate, of a will, is a document issued, in England, by the Family Division of the High Court of Justice, which certifies the validity of the will and the executor's title to administer the testator's estate.

See also REGISTRAR.

Probation, a form of punishment whereby an offender is treated in the community under the supervision of a probation officer rather than being required to serve a custodial sentence. The development of probation is perhaps the most characteristic feature of the British and US penal systems. In Europe it has not played the same rôle, owing primarily to the existence of the fixed sentence for a given offence. When probation is used it generally takes the form of a suspended sentence, a comparatively recent introduction into English law, and European countries support no institutions comparable to the British probation service.

Proboscidea, see ELEPHANT.

Proboscis Monkey, a large Borneo species of leaf-eating monkey (*Nasalis larvatus*). The male's bright red nose is prolonged to hang below the upper lip.

Process, in English law, the whole course of proceedings in a civil or criminal cause. In a more limited sense process denotes either: (1) the writ, e.g. of summons, by which the defendant is compelled to appear in court, or (2) the writs which issue at the instance of a party e.g. to compel some third person to do some act connected with the production of documentary evidence.

In Scots law 'process' means the proceedings in a cause and the documents relating to it.

Proclamation, constitutional mode of declaring the will of the chief executive of a state. All British proclamations are made by the Queen in Council and must pass under the Great Seal. They are principally used for declarations of war, peace or state of emergency, for proroguing, dissolving and summoning Parliament, and on ceremonial occasions such as the accession of the monarch.

See also PRIVY COUNCIL.

Proconsul. Under the early Roman republic a proconsul was a consul whose year of office was prolonged in order to allow him to complete a victorious campaign. Later the term was applied to one who, having served his term as consul, received the government of a province.

Procopius (fl.6th century), Byzantine historian, secretary to Belisarius on his North African, Italian and Persian campaigns. His works, written in Greek, are the *History of the Wars* and *Buildings of Justinian*.

Procyon, in astronomy, Alpha Canis Minoris, a first magnitude star in Canis Minor. Procyon and Sirius are similar in that both are relatively close to us and have white dwarf companions.

Producer Gas is a gas of low calorific value (about 15 per cent that of natural gas) formed by the action of air and/or steam on coke or coal at 1000–1200°C. The gas produced contains carbon monoxide (29 per cent), hydrogen (11 per cent), carbon dioxide (5 per cent) and nitrogen (55 per cent). It is generally used immediately, for example, in a blast furnace.

Production. Before the publication of Adam Smith's *The Wealth of Nations* in 1776, the term 'production' was used to mean the making of material commodities only. Since then it has been used to mean any economic activity which serves to satisfy human needs whether by creating material goods or by providing a service. In this sense production includes the creation of industrial or agricultural products as well as services such as water, electricity, gas or roads, or those provided by the professions.
See also COMPETITION; COST.

Productivity, term much used in economics, statistics, business, politics and the media, especially in connection with incomes policy and wage negotiations. Since the beginning of the 20th century productivity has been used to mean output per factor-unit, or factor requirements per unit of output. By factor unit is meant a unit of one of the factors of production. In developed industrial economics, especially where there is a shortage of skilled labour, great importance is attached to labour productivity in comparison with the productivity of land or with the output of machinery.

Professional Wrestling, see WRESTLING.

Professor. In Britain the university authorities appoint most professors, but the regius professors at the older universities are chosen by the Crown. In the USA the term is used more freely. There permanent university and college teaching posts carry the titles professor, associate professor and assistant professor. A full professor, who is also chairman of a department or division, would correspond to the holder of a chair in Britain.

Profits Tax, first called National Defence Contribution when introduced in Britain by Neville Chamberlain in 1937 as a temporary tax on the profits arising out of rearmament. In 1946 the decision was taken to retain the tax, and it was renamed 'profits tax'. In 1965 it was superseded by corporation tax as the basis for company taxation.

Profumo, John (Dennis) (1915–), former British politician. In 1963, while he was secretary of state for war, his involvement with Christine Keeler, who was also the mistress of a Soviet naval attaché, and the misinformation he gave to the House of Commons about the situation, erupted into a scandal that threatened to bring down Harold Macmillan's government. Profumo resigned and has since become warden of Toynbee Hall in the East End of London.

Progesterone, one of two female hormones secreted by the ovaries. It plays a major rôle in controlling the menstrual cycle, and maintaining the uterus in condition for possible conception. During pregnancy it helps to protect the embryo from expulsion, and to develop the mammary glands ready for lactation.

Programme Music, term applied to instrumental music based on a literary, pictorial, historical, biographical, autobiographical or other extra-musical subject, and not intended to appeal as music in an abstract sense only. The earliest composers of programme music attempted musical descriptions of actions and events; later, the musical portrait was especially cultivated. Another popular form has been battle music, from Jannequin's *The Battle* to Tchaikovsky's *1812* overture. The tradition of nature representation includes Beethoven's 'Pastoral' Symphony and Debussy's *La Mer*.
In the 19th century the romantic programme symphony and symphonic poem became fashionable and have remained popular.

Progressive Education, see EDUCATION.

Prohibition, in the sense of laws forbidding the sale of intoxicating liquors, originated in Maine, USA, in 1846. The entry of the USA into the First World War gave the dry movement enormous impetus because of the need to save cereals for food. In December 1917 Congress passed a proposed prohibition amendment (18th) to the constitution through both houses by the required two-thirds majority and it became operative on 16 January 1920. The law could not be adequately enforced in the large cities. The data of the US Department of Justice show that over 51 per cent of all cases heard in the federal courts in 1930 were for violations of the liquor laws. Prohibition became a major political issue, and finally, by the 21st amendment, 5 December 1933, prohibition was repealed.
Experiments in prohibition have been made and abandoned in Iceland, Finland, Norway and in certain provinces of Canada. The grant of dominion status to India and Pakistan was followed by the adoption of prohibition on a large scale. Prohibition is also in force in certain Arab countries, such as Saudi Arabia.
See also TEMPERANCE MOVEMENT.

Projection, see MAPS.

Prokofiev, Sergey Sergeyevich (1891–1953), Russian composer. He left Russia in 1918, but returned there in 1932. Like many other composers, Prokofiev was severely criticised by the Soviet authorities for his style. His efforts at more popular music can be seen in such works as *Peter and the Wolf*, and the film music for *Ivan the Terrible* and *Alexander Nevsky*. His operas include *The Love of Three Oranges*, *The Gambler* (after Dostoevski), and *War and Peace* (after Tolstoy). He also wrote ballet music, seven symphonies, two violin and five piano concertos and many piano works. His early music was distinguished by its hard brilliance, but his later works show a mellowing and maturity of style.

Prokop, Andreas (1380–1434), Hussite leader. He joined the army of Jan Žižka when the War of the Hussites began, and after Žižka's death in 1424 Prokop became the Taborite leader. He was a master of strategy, and won a number of victories over superior forces. Prokop's radical social beliefs turned the nobility against him, and in 1434 he was killed at the battle of Lipan by an army led by Bohemian nobles.

Prokopyevsk, city in Kemerovo *oblast* of the RSFSR, USSR, in south Siberia, north-west of Novokuznetsk. It is one of the biggest coking-coal mining centres of the Kuznetsk Basin and has engineering (mining equipment, ball-bearings), food and light industries. Founded in 1918 as a coal-mining settlement, it became a town in 1931. Population (1980) 266,000.

Proletariat, poorer classes of the community. The term *proletarius* was traditionally applied by Servius Tullius to the poorest class of Roman citizens, whose only wealth was their offspring (*proles*). In Marxist social theory the proletariat denotes those with no capital, forced to sell their labour to others. They will eventually form the revolutionary class that will overthrow capitalism.

Prologue (Greek *pro*, before; *logos*, speech), introduction to a play, poem or discourse. Aristotle applied the term to that part of a tragedy preceding the *parodos*, or first speech of the chorus. The word is also used for the person who speaks the prologue to a play.

Promenade Concerts, a type of popular orchestral concert, cultivated especially at the Queen's Hall, London, from 1895, under the direction of Sir Henry Wood, and continued at the Albert Hall. A special feature is that the floor of the hall is left bare for people to stand.

Prometheus (Greek, forethought), in Greek legend a Titan who stole fire from heaven for man, and warned Epimetheus against receiving Pandora as a gift from Zeus. The earliest teacher and benefactor of mankind, Zeus punished his presumption by chaining him on Mount Caucasus, where an eagle daily devoured his liver, but finally he was set free by Heracles.

Promethium, chemical element, symbol Pm, atomic number 61, one of the lanthanides. It does not occur in nature, as it is very unstable. It was isolated and identified in the course of US nuclear research at Oak Ridge during the Second World War.

Promissory Note, unconditional promise in writing, signed by the promiser, to pay on demand, or at a fixed or ascertainable future time, a definite sum of money to, or to the order of, a named person or to bearer. No form of words is essential, but an instrument promising to do anything in addition to the payment of money is not a promissory note. A bank-note is a promissory note issued by a banker and payable to bearer on demand.
See also NEGOTIABLE INSTRUMENT.

Pronghorn Antelope, *Antilocapra americana*, a North American ruminant, somewhat resembling the antelope, but differing from it in having branched horns that are shed each year. The animal stands about 1 m high and as it can reach speeds of about 100 kilometres per hour over short distances it is one of the fastest mammals.

Pronoun, part of speech which is used instead of a noun; that is, it indicates something specific without using its name. For example, in 'Where is the exit?' 'It's over there', 'it' is the pronoun for 'exit'.

Proof, in English law, means the establishment to the satisfaction of a judge or jury by oral or documentary evidence of the facts alleged. In legal slang it is the recognised term for the written or typed evidence of witnesses, prepared by the solicitor for the use of counsel so that the latter may know what a witness is going to be called to prove.

Proof, Burden of. In English law the general rule is that the burden of proving any fact alleged lies on him who pleads such fact, not on him who denies or 'traverses' it.

Proof Spirit, as defined by Act of Parliament, is such a spirit as shall at a temperature of 51°F (10·5°C) weigh exactly $\frac{12}{13}$ of an equal measure of distilled water, also at 51°F. It contains 57·06 per cent by volume or 49·24 per cent by weight of absolute alcohol. Spirits are termed 'under' or 'over' proof, according as they are stronger or weaker than proof spirit.

Propaganda, art of propagating and instilling a belief, particularly a religious or political belief. Propaganda is the modern equivalent of rhetoric which aims to persuade those incapable of understanding proofs. It is a potent weapon for evil if used without thought for the truth. Propaganda has been practised since earliest times, but the advent of modern mass-media has made it much easier to appeal to wide domestic and foreign audiences.

Since 1918 the word has acquired a normally derogatory and sinister sense owing to the propaganda methods of fascist and communist governments.

Propane, C_3H_8, a gaseous alkane hydrocarbon with boiling point −45°C, and a component of bottled heating gas.

Proper, heraldic term used to describe any charge depicted in its natural colours.

Proper Motion of a star, the rate at which its position on the celestial sphere is changing after all observational effects, precession, aberration, parallax, etc., have been eliminated. It results from a combination of the star's and Sun's motion in space, and is usually expressed in seconds of arc per year. The largest known one, that for Barnard's star, is 10·27″ of arc per year, or 1° in 350 years. A large proper motion indicates that a star is relatively close to the Sun, and that its transverse velocity is high.

Property is either the exclusive right of possessing, enjoying and disposing of a thing (i.e. ownership as opposed to possession) or the subjects of such exclusive right. The division of property (in the latter sense) in English law, is into: (1) things real consisting of (a) corporeal or immoveable property, e.g. lands, and (b) the rights and profits annexed to and issuing out of these, or incorporeal property, e.g. rents, common rights, etc. and (2) things personal, consisting of goods, money and other moveables and including leaseholds and choses in action.

See also Chattels; Personal Property.

Prophecy means 'forth-telling', and not 'foretelling' or 'future-telling', which in Greece was done by the *mantis*. The term 'prophet' thus means 'interpreter' or 'spokesman', one who speaks for God or for any deity, as the inspired revealer or interpreter of His Will. The common belief that a prophet is *primarily* one who forecasts future events is inaccurate.

Prophylaxis, or prophylactic treatment. Drug treatment used to prevent the onset of an infectious disease. The drugs should be relatively non-toxic since they may have to be given for prolonged periods. An example is antimalarials used to prevent infection after the bite of an infected mosquito.

See also Preventive Medicine.

Proportion, in the visual arts, the due relation of parts to a whole. The concern with proportion began with the Renaissance. Rules were adopted by architects and painters, e.g. by Alberti and Leonardo da Vinci who researched into the proportions of the human figure. Painters incorporated such geometrical ratios as 'root two' (5:7) and the Golden Section (5:8). It is noteworthy that a painter as recent as Constable should have made the proportions of his picture *The Cornfield* such that the canvas would enclose an equilateral triangle, and *The Cenotaph* a 45° isosceles triangle. In modern architecture, proportion depends mainly on intuitive judgment, although several architects, notably Le Corbusier, have designed according to their own theories of proportion.

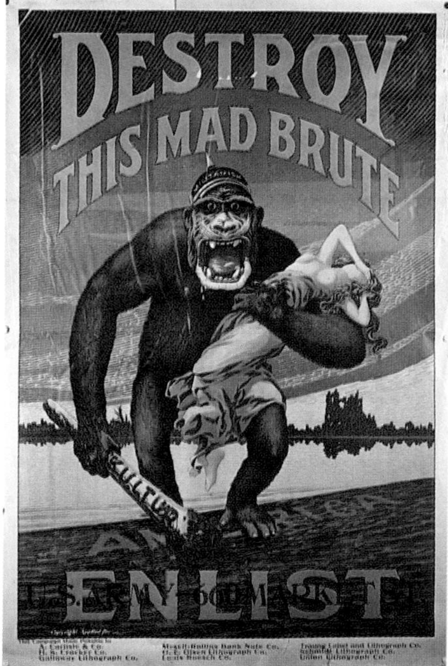

Propaganda. *American war poster, 1917–18.*

Proportional Representation, any system of voting which ensures that political parties or other groups shall secure seats in proportion to their voting strength. Proportional systems are either: (1) the single transferable vote, the proportional representation of the English-speaking world; or (2) party list systems, common in Europe. All forms necessitate constituencies, each electing several members.

In (1) the voter numbers the candidates in order of preference. In order to secure election a candidate must secure a quota usually calculated as follows:

$$\frac{\text{total valid votes cast}}{\text{number of seats} + 1} + 1$$

All first preferences are counted and any candidate securing the necessary quota is declared elected. 'Surplus' votes of elected candidates are then redistributed as necessary until the full number of candidates is elected. In (2), the party list system, the elector votes for a party, and each party is allotted seats in proportion to its total votes, sometimes (as in Israel or the Netherlands), over the whole country, more usually over a city or similar population area.

Proposition, in philosophy, a term for that which a statement expresses. It is propositions rather than statements that are true or false, although usage on this point varies.

Propranolol, a synthetic drug used to antagonise some of the effects of adrenaline in patients with angina to reduce the increased force and rate of the heart beat caused by exercise and stress. It is also an antihypertensive agent, and is used to treat cardiac arrhythmias.

Proprietary Medicines, medicines or drugs manufactured by pharmaceutical firms, offered to the medical profession for use in the treatment of disease under medical supervision and under prescription.

Propylaeum, in architecture, a monumental entrance gateway, especially to a sacred enclosure. The Propylaea to the Acropolis at Athens (437–433 BC), designed by Mnesicles, is unusually complex for the period, and is most ingeniously handled.

Prorogation, in Britain, terminates a session of Parliament and sets the date for a new session. The period between sessions is known as a recess. All business, including bills before Parliament, is terminated by prorogation and must, if desired, be reintroduced anew the following session.

See also Parliament.

Proscenium, in an ancient Greek or Roman theatre, a high stage; in a modern theatre, it is the architectural frontispiece of the stage, towards the auditorium.

See also Theatre.

Prose, written expression of thought without any attempt at metrical form. Prose and verse are the two principal divisions of literature.

Proselytes (from Greek), converts, originally to the Jewish faith. The term is now used to describe a convert to any faith or set of ideas.

Prosimian, any member of the suborder Prosimii, in the order Primates. The suborder includes the tree-shrews, lemurs, lorises, sifakas, indris, avahis and the aye-aye. They are primitive primates, which bear a strong resemblance to the insectivores, from which they may be descended.

Prosody (Greek *prosōdia*), science of versification; that part of the study of language which deals with the forms of metrical composition, including as its two divisions accent and quantities of syllables.

See also Metre; Rhyme; Rhythm; Verse.

Prostaglandins, derivatives of the long-chain fatty acid prostenoic acid. Prostaglandins were discovered in seminal fluid (and were therefore assumed to come from the prostate) in the 1930s but have since been found in many tissues (and also synthesised); they exhibit a variety of actions according to their chemical structure and the organ concerned. They cause contractions of the uterus and are used to induce abortion in the mid-trimester of pregnancy, to induce labour and also may have contraceptive action by dislodging the fertilised egg from the uterus. Prostaglandins may be involved in maintaining blood flow to metabolically active tissues. The analgesic (pain-relieving), antipyretic (fever-reducing) and anti-inflammatory actions of aspirin, paracetamol, indomethacin and phenylbutazone are due to the inhibition of prostaglandin synthesis.

Prostate, a gland and accessory male sexual organ, which surrounds the neck of the bladder and the first part of the urethra in man and other mammals. It secretes an important factor of the spermatic fluid. In older men, the prostate gland very commonly undergoes a benign form of enlargement, and obstructs the urethra, causing difficulty in passing urine. Obstruction to the outflow of urine by the prostate may also cause retention of a residual amount of urine after micturition, which becomes infected and causes a chronic cystitis. The treatment of an enlarged prostate is surgical removal, either through a low incision on the anterior abdominal wall, or, on occasion, via an operating cystoscope.

Prostatitis, or inflammation of the prostate gland, is frequently caused by gonorrhoea, and sterility may result. The prostate gland is also subject to cancer, and the fact that cancer of this organ can be successfully treated with the synthetic female sex hormone, stilboestrol, was one of the more important recent discoveries in cancer research.

Prosthetic Groups, see COENZYMES; PROTEINS.

Prostitution, offering of the human body commonly for the purpose of intercourse or sexual gratification in return for payment or reward. Prostitution may be either heterosexual or homosexual. In Britain acts of personal and private prostitution between mutually consenting adults of opposite sex are no longer a criminal offence; and the Sexual Offences Act 1967 legalised sexual acts in private between consenting males over the age of 21.

It is important to distinguish prostitution from other forms of sexual activity, such as promiscuity. The distinguishing mark of prostitution is payment for sexual acts.

Protactinium, metallic chemical element, symbol Pa, atomic number 91, atomic weight 231·0359; one of the actinides. It was discovered in 1917 by Soddy, who isolated it from pitchblende, in which it is present to the extent of about 1 part in 10^7.

Protagoras (c.486–c.415 BC), Greek sophist, born at Abdera in Thrace. He was the author of a famous saying, 'Man is the measure of all things', which fairly sums up his teaching; for he taught that there were no absolute standards of truth. This view denies the law of contradiction, and is the subject of an elaborate refutation by Aristotle (*Metaphysics*, III, 5, 6).

Proteaceae, a family of trees and shrubs, found chiefly in Australasia and southern Africa. The principal genera are *Protea*, *Grevillea*, *Banksia*, *Hakea*, *Lomatia* and *Embothrium*. Many of the inflorescences are beautiful and much used both fresh and dried by florists.

Protector, title formerly bestowed in England upon the person to whom was entrusted the care of the kingdom during a king's minority, e.g. Lord Protector Somerset during the minority of Edward VI. Cromwell assumed the title of 'Lord Protector' by way of analogy, though in reality he wielded the power of a monarch.

Protectorate, indefinite term denoting primarily and historically a state which has surrendered part of its rights to a protector, remaining in other respects independent. British protectorates were territories for which Britain assumed the responsibility for external affairs and defence.

Proteins, large complex macromolecules, forming some of the most important parts of living cells. They consist of chains of amino acids connected together by peptide bonds in a specific sequence, which can determine to some extent the properties of the molecule. A peptide bond is formed between the $-NH_2$ (or amino) group of one amino acid, and the $-COOH$ (or carboxyl) group of the acid preceding it in the chain.

Proteins can be classified in several ways. Structural classification divides them into simple proteins, which on hydrolysis yield only amino acids, and conjugated proteins, which yield either organic or inorganic compounds in addition to amino acids. These extra components are called prosthetic groups, and can be as simple as inorganic ions or as complicated as flavin nucleotides. Proteins can also be classified according to their conformation, the major groups being fibrous proteins, physically tough and generally insoluble, and globular proteins, compact and generally soluble. Proteins can also be classified according to function, and are classed as enzymes, storage proteins, toxins, hormones and structural proteins.

Proteins fulfil a vast range of the body's requirements, and the fact that there can be such diversity of structure allows for this. For example, structural proteins such as α-keratin in hair, skin and feathers, or collagen in connective tissue such as tendons and ligaments, must be tough, strong, fibrous and rope- or wire-like. On the other hand, albumin, a storage protein important in maintaining the blood's osmotic pressure, is small, compact and spherical, in order to travel in the bloodstream. Enzymes have to maintain rigidly a specific shape in order to function.

See also ENZYMES; NUTRITION.

Protestantism, term denoting a major branch of Christianity, commonly applied to all those parties who adhere to the principles of the Reformation, whatever may be the differences between them in order or doctrine.

At the second Diet of Speyer, in 1529, a decree was received from the Emperor Charles V forbidding all further action in the direction of reformation until a general council should have met. The decree received the sanction of the Diet, but a solemn protest against it was made by the princes and cities who favoured the Reformation; originally legal and political, the term came into general theological use. At first Protestantism denoted the position of the Lutherans as opposed to both Catholics and Reformed (Zwinglian or Calvinist); but it has come to be used more generally, with varying shades of meaning.

Proteus, typical genus of the family Proteidae, which contains tailed amphibians of the order Urodela; the three species are commonly known as olms. They are about 30 cm long and white with red gill-bunches in the dark, but in the light they become black. The eyes are completely covered with skin and they are blind, as their habitat is confined to the subterranean waters of parts of Yugoslavia. They have small, weak limbs. Spawning takes place in April, and the eggs are fastened singly to stones. *P. anguineus* is the best-known species.

Protista, a term introduced by Haeckel in 1866 to describe all unicellular organisms including single-celled algae, fungi, protozoa and bacteria. They are autonomous units which depend upon complex structures within the cell for their functional versatility. At this grade of organisation, certain forms exhibit both plant- and animal-like characteristics; amongst the flagellates, for example, there are intermediate types such as *Euglena* which have chlorophyll like a plant, yet move about like an animal.

See also TAXONOMY.

Protocol (Greek *protos*, first, and *kolla*, glue), a sheet glued to the front of a manuscript and bearing an abstract of the contents and purport. In diplomacy a protocol may be: (1) the minutes of a conference or negotiations; (2) a diplomatic instrument recording the details on which agreement has been reached; (3) an actual agreement, proclaiming views or aims, which is not binding on the signatories. Protocol is also the term used to describe the ceremonial rules governing relations between states.

Protocols of the Elders of Zion, falsified anti-Semitic document. The Protocols, to the number of 24 (in one version 27), were supposedly an authentic report of secret meetings of Jewish elders, who at the first Zionist congress, held in Basel in 1897, conceived a conspiracy to blow up the major capitals of Europe.

Proton, the nucleus of an atom of hydrogen, of mass $1{\cdot}673 \times 10^{-27}$ kg, about 1837 times the mass of the electron, and having a positive charge equal in magnitude to that of the electron, $1{\cdot}602 \times 10^{-19}$ Coulombs. Atomic nuclei consist of protons and neutrons in combination, the positive charge on the nucleus being due to the protons.

See also ATOM; ATOMIC NUMBER.

Protoplasm, term introduced by Purkinje in 1840 to describe the fundamental living substance of which all organisms are composed. It consists mainly of water, protein and lipids with some salts and carbohydrates, and is usually organised into units called cells.

Protozoa, the phylum in which are collected all single-celled microscopic living organisms. Well known non-pathogenic examples are *Euglena*, *Paramecium* and *Amoeba*, which are easily found in samples of pond water. Pathogenic members of the phylum Protozoa include *Plasmodium*, the malarial parasite, and *Entamoeba histolytica*, the cause of amoebic dysentery.

Protozoa is usually included as a phylum within the animal kingdom, but has been raised by some authors to subkingdom or even kingdom level because of the highly specialised nature of the organisms within the group. Far from being simple unicellular forerunners of all metazoan (many-celled) forms, Protozoa is a heterogeneous collection

of highly advanced and specialised organisms often with complicated life-histories. Protozoan cells have all normal metazoan cell structures in their cytoplasm and carry out the same basic intracellular processes.
The phylum is divided into four. (1) The Flagellata contains protozoa which possess a flagellum and reproduce by binary fission. Many members possess chlorophyll; some, such as *Euglena* and *Volvox*, live in fresh water, others are parasitic. (2) In the Sarcodina, typical members, such as *Amoeba*, have pseudopodia, extensions of the cytoplasm to form a 'false foot'. Many are contained in shells but the pseudopodia may be extended through openings to allow feeding and movement. This class contains some of the largest and most beautiful protozoa. (3) The Ciliata contains protozoa that possess cilia at some stage covering a part or the whole of the organism. They have two kinds of nuclei and sexual reproduction is by conjugation. Examples are *Paramecium* and *Vorticella*. (4) The Sporozoa is a group of parasitic forms and includes *Plasmodium*, the malarial parasite.

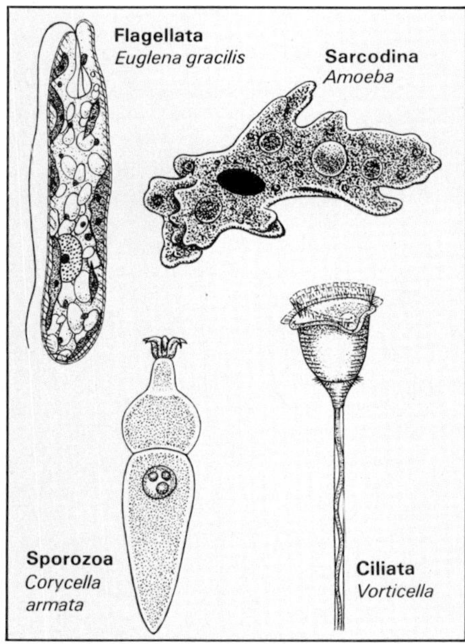

Protozoa. *A species from each of the four divisions of the phylum.*

Proudhon, Pierre Joseph (1809–65), French socialist. In 1840 his first important work, *Qu'est-ce que la propriété*, was published, which contained his famous maxim, 'Property is theft'—*La propriété c'est le vol.* He escaped to Brussels to avoid prosecution for his attack on the Church, *De la justice dans la révolution et dans l'Église*, and died at Passy on his return.
Proudhon in his socialism was an economist and not a politician; his ideal was perfect freedom, equality and justice. He ridiculed the idea of a revolutionary change of society but sought the abolition of property. To him property, like slavery, was the murder of individual freedom.
His fundamental conception was that all labour, mental and physical, of high or low class, should be remunerated at the same scale, on the principle that service pays service, and that time is the criterion of value.

Proust, Marcel (1871–1922), French author. Until forced by asthma to lead the life of an invalid, he was received into the stilted Paris society of the 1890s. Retiring to seclusion, he set out to portray, with immense creative genius, the society he had quitted.
The first part of *À la recherche du temps perdu* was published in 1913, but Proust's phenomenal reputation was largely posthumous. He recalls every detail of his childhood as if the past still existed, and as if events did not happen but exist, that is, men come to events, they do not occur. Proust denies the existence of the human soul and sees reason or intellect as merely an instrument which constructs simply errors and delusions.
Proust's importance rests not only on his philosophy; his precision of detail has also attracted much attention. He possesses brilliant psychological insight and shows great artistry in his creation of characters and incidents. His style is among the most original in literature, and has had a great influence on the 20th-century novel.

Provençal is one of the Romance languages. In its strict sense, the term Provençal refers only to the dialect of Provence proper, that is, of the south-eastern corner of France, but in a broader and frequently-used sense it covers the language of most of the south of France, including three other dialectal groups, a northern one (Limousin, Auvergnat, Dauphinois), Languedocien, and Gascon (which differs markedly from the other dialects in pronunciation and grammar). In the broad sense, the language is also known as the *langue d'oc* (*oc* being the word for 'yes'—French is likewise referred to as the *langue d'oïl*, *oïl* being an earlier form of *oui*) and as Occitan (a term derived from the medieval Latin rendering of *langue d'oc* as *lingua occitana*).

Provençal Literature. The 'golden age' of Occitan literature, that of the troubadours, opens with the 11 love songs of Guilhem IX, Duke of Aquitaine. Some of his poems show a realistic eroticism, but in others there are already the beginnings of a different conception of love, that of *amour courtois*, that was to be the characteristic of many later troubadours. The Albigensian Crusade, which from 1209 onwards ravaged the Midi, destroyed the influence of the southern noblemen, dealing an almost fatal blow to the literature they had encouraged.
Occitan literature declined rapidly in the later Middle Ages. There was a partial revival at the time of the Renaissance.
A further revival in the 19th century led in 1854 to the formation by a group of Provençal poets, chief among them Mistral, Roumanille and Aubanel, of the Félibrige, a society whose aims were to purify and codify the native tongue and restore it, by using it in their literary works, to a position of dignity.

Provence, former maritime province of France. It was bounded on the south by the Mediterranean, and derived its name from the Roman province of Gaul known simply as *Provincia* (The Province). It included the area covered by modern *départements* of Basses-Alpes and Bouches-du-Rhône, together with some parts of Drôme, Vaucluse and Alpes-Maritimes. Its boundaries were continually changing. Its capital moved from Aix to Arles, with Marseilles as another important city. On the death of Raymund-Bérenger IV (1245) the province passed to his daughter, Beatrice; by her marriage with Charles of Anjou it came under Angevin rule. It was during the preceding period, however, under the house of Barcelona, that Provence became the seat of that literature which has given the chief celebrity to its name and the chief interest to its history.

Proverb (Latin *pro*, forth to the world, and *verbum*, word), fragment of folk-literature or, as the Greeks phrased it, 'a wayside saying' (*Paroimia*), embodying a moral lesson or obvious truth.
To Aristotle 'a proverb is a remnant from old philosophy, preserved amid countless destructions, by reason of its brevity and fitness for use'. Cervantes speaks of proverbs as 'short sentences drawn from long experience'; Bertrand Russell described them as 'one man's wit and all men's wisdom'; and a profound truth is enshrined in the observation of the Abbé de Saint-Pierre that proverbs are the echoes of experience.
Adages are as old as the hills, and are common to all languages and people; the Spanish have as many as 30,000, whilst Wander estimated the Germans to have about 145,000. These concise expressions were especially popular in the Middle Ages and abound in the writings of Cervantes, Rabelais and Montaigne; they are more rarely used today, though fresh coinages are still made.

Proverbs, Book of (Latin *Proverbia*), the first and most famous of the wisdom books of the Bible. Tradition ascribes the Book of Proverbs to Solomon, whose name is attached to some chapters (i. 1; x. 1; xxv. 1). We possess collections of Egyptian and Sumerian proverbs from the 3rd millennium and this makes the antiquity of such collections certain; and there is a close likeness of some of the material in Proverbs with the Egyptian book of wisdom called the 'Teaching of Amenemope', c.1000 BC.

Providence, port of entry and capital of Rhode Island, USA, on Narragansett Bay, 65 km south-west of Boston, Massachusetts. Its industries were for long dominated before the First World War by textile manufacturing, but when, in the 1920s, this industry was captured by the southern states, Providence turned to its present specialisation, jewellery, and to diversified manufactures, e.g. machinery and rubber goods. Settled by Roger Williams (1636), it contains Roger Williams Park to the south. Population (1980) 156,304.

Provincias Vascongadas, see BASQUE PROVINCES.

Proxy (derivation apparently the same as that of proctor), agency of a substitute, or by extension the name for the agent himself. In company law a proxy is a writing authorising a person to vote in place of a shareholder at a certain meeting or a series of meetings. Proxies are also utilised in bankruptcy proceedings.

Prud'hon, Pierre Paul (1758–1823), French historical and portrait painter. He won the Prix de Rome (1784), where he resided till 1789, becoming a friend of Canova. His chief works include *Justice and Divine Vengeance Pursuing Crime*, 1808 (Louvre); *Rape of Psyche*, 1812; *Interview between Napoleon I and Francis*

II after Austerlitz; and *The Empress Josephine*. He also decorated the Louvre with ceiling paintings. His style was influenced by Correggio and Leonardo.

Prune, a dried plum, and also the name of varieties of plum trees which are cultivated as their fruits are specially suitable for drying on account of their firm texture. The art of plum drying is most highly developed in California and more than a third of the imports are derived from that state; but the finest quality comes from France, where the fruit is boiled immediately after gathering and when cool is exposed to the sun in trays until thoroughly desiccated.
See also FOOD PRESERVATION.

Prunella, or prunello, a smooth black or purplish woven woollen fabric, particularly popular in the 17th and 18th centuries, used for the uppers of gaiters and shoes and for many items of clerical, academic and legal wear. A coarse-weave textile, prunella is similar to a 'shalloon', a loosely woven material with twill on both sides.

Pruning, the art of regulating plant growth by cutting shoots and branches with the object of regulating the shape, and/or increasing the production of flowers or fruit. Pruning encourages vegetative growth; light pruning favours the initiation of flowers leading to heavier fruit yields. Therefore, where new vegetative growth is required, pruning should necessarily be severe. In later years pruning is less severe and is devoted to the removal of diseased or weak growth, to keeping the branch work open to air and sun, and to the renewal and formation of fruiting wood.
See also ESPALIER; FRUIT-FARMING; GARDENING.

Prunus, a genus of deciduous and evergreen trees and shrubs in family Rosaceae, bearing white or pink flowers. Almonds, peaches, apricots, plums and cherries belong to the genus. Other species include *P. padus*, the bird cherry; *P. laurocerasus*, the cherry laurel, and *P. lusitanica*, the Portugal laurel, both evergreen shrubs.

Prussia, former name of a region in northern Europe. Prussia has varied considerably in size and political construction at different times. It has been: (1) the land of the Borussi, tribes of Slav origin, covering regions on the east bank of the River Vistula, as well as the whole of the later province of East Prussia; (2) 1525–1866, a duchy, ruled by the Hohenzollern dynasty from Brandenburg, which in 1710 took the title of 'kings of Prussia'. From that time Prussia came to be applied, at first unofficially, as a description of all the Hohenzollern lands; (3) 1866–1918, the largest and most influential German state. The term was again expanded to cover all the conquests made while Bismarck was in power. This meant that it applied to almost all northern Germany; (4) 1918–45, the remnants of (3) left to Germany after the peace treaties following the First World War. This last Prussia was a republic.

Prussia, West, see POLISH CORRIDOR.

Prussian Blue, $K^+Fe^{2+}[Fe(CN)_6]^{3-}\cdot nH_2O$, a dark blue solid which is obtained from a ferrous salt and potassium ferricyanide (originally called Turnbull's blue), or from a ferric salt and potassium ferrocyanide. As a dye it has been superseded by aniline products, but is still used as a pigment in water-colour painting.

Prussic Acid, see HYDROCYANIC ACID.

Prynne, William (1600–69), English Puritan, antiquarian and pamphleteer. Prynne wrote some 200 pamphlets and books but is chiefly remembered for his *Histrio-Mastix* in 1632, a savage attack on the stage, which he published at a time when Queen Henrietta Maria was about to act in a play. For this supposed insult to the queen, he was committed to the Tower. He sat for Parliament for Newport in Cornwall and became parliamentary prosecutor. But he was soon in opposition again: he regarded the Commonwealth and Protectorate as illegal. After the return of the king he sat in Parliament for Bath. Charles II appointed him keeper of the records in the Tower and on these he did considerable research and published some important material.

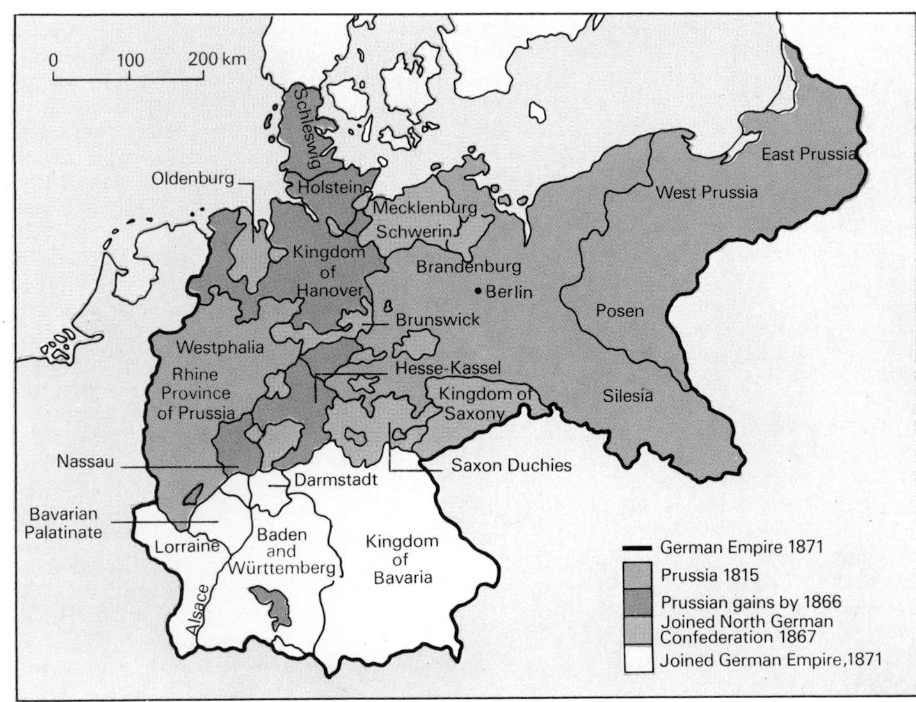

***Prussia** formed the nucleus around which Germany was unified in the 19th century.*

Przemyśl, town of Poland, in Rzeszów province, 64 km south of Rzeszów, on the River San. It is one of the oldest towns in Poland, and has been the seat of Russian Orthodox and Roman Catholic dioceses since medieval times. The economy of the town is broadly based including metallurgy, timber and tourism. Population (1974) 56,521.

Przewalski's Horse, see HORSE.

Przhevalsk (formerly *Karakol*), capital of the Issyk-Kul *oblast* of the Kirgiz SSR, USSR, 12 km east of Lake Issyk-Kul. There are food and light industries. The town was founded in 1869. Nearby, on the shore of Lake Issyk-Kul, is the grave of the Russian explorer Przhevalski, discoverer of the early type of horse now known as Przhevalski's horse. Population (1974) 48,000.

Przybyszewski, Stanislaw (1868–1927), Polish writer. Popularly known as one of the 'satanists' and 'visionaries' in the cosmopolitan circle of writers, painters and intellectuals of Berlin in the 1890s, he is today best known for his associations with Dehmel, Strindberg and particularly Munch, who painted his portrait, and about whom he was one of the first to write. His oblique and intense mind gave expression to the complex, if confused, ideas of his age and he was a precursor in literature of modern psychoanalytical trends and psychological thinking.

Psalms, Book of. The psalms, 150 in number, are poetic outpourings of devotion to God, deeply spiritual and showing every aspect of the religious character, and are a book of the Old Testament. They are used in the services not only of the Jewish but also of the Christian Church. They were the prayer book of Christ, and he apparently recited one of them on the cross (Matt. xxvii. 46). Originally they were all attributed to David but it is now thought that there were a number of authors.

Psaltery, plucked string instrument introduced into Europe in the 12th century from the Middle East. A shallow box, wider at one side than the other, with strings across the upper surface. The strings were plucked with quill plectra. A mechanised version became the harpsichord.

Pseudohalogens, volatile molecules consisting of more than two atoms, which in their reactions resemble halogens. Pseudohalogens form anions resembling halide ions. The most important are cyanogen $(CN)_2$, oxocyanogen $(OCN)_2$ and thiocyanogen $(SCN)_2$.

Pseudomorphism, assumption by a mineral of a form other than that which really belongs to it. Pseudomorphs may generally be recognised by the absence of sharpness in the crystal angles, while the faces usually present a granular, dull or earthy aspect. Pseudomorphs may be formed in several ways, such as: (1) by *infiltration*, when the cavity previously occupied by a crystal is refilled by the deposit of different mineral matter from the infiltration of a solution; (2) by *investment*, or a superficial encrustation of one mineral on the crystal of another; (3) by *replacement*, which is a slow and gradual substitution of particles of new and different mineral matter and (4) by *alteration* or the gradual chemical change which crystals sometimes undergo, their composition becoming so altered that they are no longer the same minerals, although they retain their old forms.

Pseudonym, term denoting a fictitious name used by an author, or other artist, who wishes to conceal his real identity. The secret is usually only a temporary one, but sometimes the anonymity is preserved for a long period. Sir Walter Scott's novels were published for years as 'by the author of *Waverley*'. The first works of Richardson, Fielding, Smollett, Jane Austen, Dickens, the Brownings and Matthew Arnold were anonymous. Pen-names are also often used by scholars or professional men who wish to keep their frivolous writings separate from their more important occupations. Charles Lutwidge Dodgson wrote his children's stories as Lewis Carroll and his works on mathematics under his real name.

Pseudoscorpions, members of the order Pseudoscorpiones of the class Arachnida. They are very small, usually less than 8 mm long, and resemble scorpions in having pincers (pedipalps); the rear end, however, is not narrowed and there is no sting. Book scorpions, genus *Chelifer*, are often found in old books, but most pseudoscorpions live as predators in decaying leaf-mould.

Psi, an alternative term for extrasensory perception.
See also EXTRASENSORY PERCEPTION.

Psilocybin, an indole alkaloid found in the sacred mushroom *Psilocybe mexicana*. Psilocybin is chemically related to lysergic acid diethylamide (LSD) and has hallucinogenic properties similar to, but weaker than, those of LSD. It has occasionally been used in psychotherapy.

Psittacidae, see PARROT.

Psittacosis (Greek *psittacos*, parrot) or ornithosis, a disease of parrots which acquired prominence in 1930 when some 800 human cases occurred in Europe, transmitted by South American parrots. Formerly believed to be a virus, the psittacosis agent (like that causing trachoma) is now considered to be a member of a distinct biological group, the Chlamydia. Symptoms resemble those of typhoid or of pulmonary disease: sudden onset of fever, sore throat, headache, and malaise followed by severe non-productive cough. An atypical form of pneumonia usually develops. Broad spectrum antibiotics are valuable in treatment. Other birds, particularly pigeons, doves, budgerigars and lovebirds, also act as hosts of psittacosis.

Pskov (Estonian *Pihkva*), capital city, economic and cultural centre of Pskov *oblast*, USSR, situated near the shore of Lake Pskov to the south-west of Leningrad. It has building, engineering (electrical, radio, textile machinery), and food industries. It is one of the oldest and historically most important Russian cities. It was known as an outpost of Novgorod from 903, was capital of the independent Pskov Republic (1348–1510), then became a Muscovite fortress, and until the building of St Petersburg was the foremost centre for trade with Western Europe. Population (1980) 177,000.

Psoriasis, a chronic, relapsing skin eruption, the cause of which is unknown, but affected persons are thought to have an inherited predisposition. It has a localised distribution, appearing especially on the elbows and knees, and adjacent parts of the limbs, the scalp and lumbar regions, and consists of very scaly patches which often become chronic. Psoriasis is not contagious. Because the cause is unknown, treatment is unsatisfactory in the long term, but intensive therapy with skin softeners, locally applied tar ointment and ultraviolet light will temporarily clear it up.

Psychagogue, a conjuror of the dead.
See also NECROMANCY.

Psyche, in Greek legend, princess whom Aphrodite, jealous of her beauty, ordered Cupid (Eros) to inspire with love for the vilest of men; but Cupid himself fell in love with her. Unseen and unknown, he visited her each night until finally Psyche lit her lamp to see him while he slept, and he woke and fled. Psyche wandered in search of him and they were reunited.

Psychiatry, the medical speciality concerned with the study, diagnosis and treatment of mental illness. Modern concepts about the causes of mental illness emphasise the interdependence of body and mind.

Psychiatric diseases are generally divided into the following main categories: organic psychoses (toxic delirium, dementia, encephalitis, etc.), which are caused by infection, poisoning or another external agent; functional psychoses (manic depression, schizophrenia) which have emotional, social or innate constitutional causes; epilepsies; psychoneuroses (anxiety states and phobias) in which the person is able to reason and work rationally although he may feel upset; psychopathies (such as abnormal personalities or drug addiction); and mental subnormality.

The borderlines between the different categories are not clearly demarcated, nor are the categories mutually exclusive.

Where the disturbance of behaviour is based on underlying physical illness, the treatment is largely that of the underlying physical cause, while using drugs to secure symptomatic relief from the anxiety and restlessness. Functional psychoses respond to major tranquillisers, with antidepressant drugs and electro-convulsive therapy for severe depression. For the psychoneuroses mild tranquillisers may be used.

Psychological treatment is used to modify a person's response to his environment, to enable him to deal better with his circumstances, and to help him achieve an increased understanding of himself and his symptoms. Psychotherapy ranges from discussion of the problems with support and reassurance given where called for, to a much deeper analysis which aims at the patient's gaining a thorough understanding of his own attitudes and unconscious hopes and fears.

Psychical Research, or parapsychology, scientific study of the facts and causes of mediumistic and other alleged supernormal phenomena beyond normal consciousness. Such phenomena, as yet unexplained by known laws, include telepathy, clairvoyance, psychokinesis (movement of objects without contact), precognition, divining, 'faith healing' and hauntings.

Organised psychical research originated with the foundation of the Society for Psychical Research in London in 1882. Other societies with similar aims include the American Society of Psychical Research, and the Institut Métapsychique in Paris. In 1927 a parapsychological laboratory was started in Duke University, North Carolina, under J. B. Rhine, which became an active centre for experimental research. In 1953, Professor Tenhaeff became the first European professor of parapsychology in the University of Utrecht. There are studentships in psychical research at Trinity College, Cambridge, and at New College, Oxford. In New York, the Parapsychology Foundation is a centre for publication and for the award of grants for research.

Psychoanalysis, a form of treatment developed by Freud, Breuer, Ferenczi and others in the 1890s, which has since developed into a body of knowledge and a method of enquiry into man's psychological functioning. As a theoretical system, psychoanalysis rests on three basic concepts. The central concept is that of the 'unconscious', a reservoir within one's mental state which contains elements and experiences of which one is unaware, but which may be to some extent brought into preconscious and conscious awareness, or inferred from aspects of behaviour. The second and related basic concept is that of 'resistance', a process by which unconscious elements are forcibly kept out of the conscious awareness by an active repressive force. Freud came to experience the third basic concept in his work with his earliest patients, in that they transferred to him aspects of their past relationships with others, and thus their previous feelings coloured their relationship with him. This feature has been called 'transference'. The analysis of the transference in all its manifestations has become a vital aspect of current psychoanalytic practice. Psychoanalysis recognises the significance of the defence mechanisms, the infantile roots of neurosis, and the crucial rôle of early experiences in forming the adult personality. The significance of early infantile experience has been further elaborated in the field of child analysis, particularly in the work of Melanie Klein and her students, who pay particular attention to the development of the infant in the first six to eight months of life.

A psychoanalyst normally sees his patients five times a week, for fifty minutes, and asks his patients to free associate, so far as this is possible. It is the task of the analyst to grasp the underlying meaning of the free associations and to interpret their probable significance to the patient, linking aspects of the patient's historical past with the way in which he is now experiencing the relationship to the analyst. The aims of psychoanalytic treatment include not only relief from specific symptoms, but also a freeing from irrational inhibitions and anxieties, so that the quality of the patient's life will be enhanced. Although psychoanalysis began as a form of treatment for psychoneurosis, more recent work has shown its applicability to psychosis in selected patients.

Psychodidae, a family in the order Diptera, class Insecta. These are the moth flies, sewage flies and sandflies. They are small delicate

flies belonging to the suborder Diptera. All have dense hairs covering the body and the pointed wings, with characteristic venation. The adults are small flies with biting mouthparts.
The family is divided into two subfamilies, Psychodinae and Phlebotominae. The subfamily Phlebotominae are the sandflies and are vectors of *Leishmania* which causes kala azar and oriental sore in the Old World and similar diseases in the New World (e.g. leishmaniasis). They also transmit sandfly fever, a viral disease. Oroya fever caused by *Bartonella bacilliformis* is transmitted by *Phlebotomus* in South America.

Psychokinesis, or PK, a term invented by the scientific researcher, Dr J. B. Rhine and used in parapsychology to describe the ability to control and move objects by means of the mind only, without any physical contact being involved.

Psychologism, in philosophy, is the doctrine that the principles of logic ultimately rest on psychology. This view is reflected in the old-fashioned expression 'laws of thought' for the principles of logic. The most powerful modern influence to undermine psychologism has been the development of mathematical logic since the later decades of the 19th century. Indeed logic applies to any field whatever, so that the principles of logic cannot themselves depend on any particular science. This argument against psychologism was originally used by Kant in the *Critique of Pure Reason.*

Psychology may be broadly defined as the scientific study of behaviour, although the word itself, which is derived from the Greek, means the science of the soul. Modern psychology is regarded as an experimental discipline with roots in both the biological and social sciences, applying the scientific method to the description, explanation and modification of every facet of human behaviour, including 'internal' events, such as thinking, which are regarded as suitable subjects for scientific study. There are several branches of study.
Biological psychology is concerned with the origins and relationships between physical structure, and function, and behaviour, and includes work on animals and humans.
Cognitive psychology refers to all the processes by which the sensory input is transferred, reduced, elaborated, stored, recovered and used, particularly the study of remembering and of thinking.
Developmental psychology is concerned with changes including the post-natal effects of the intra-uterine environment, through the preschool, school and young adult periods to middle and old age.
The measurement of psychological variables and the design and analysis of experiments make up a well-developed and highly specialised branch of psychology which requires a grasp both of basic mathematics and the complex body of test theory which has grown up.
The psychology of perception is an attempt to account for 'the appearance of things'.
The study of personality is concerned with individual differences in everyday personal behaviour, particularly in such emotionally important areas as sex, aggression and interpersonal behaviour generally.
Psycholinguistics is concerned with the experimental study of language, particularly of grammatical rôles.
Social psychology studies the behaviour between two or more persons.
Clinical psychology is not to be confused with clinical psychiatry. The latter is practised by medically qualified persons, with a special training in the diagnosis and treatment of psychological problems. The clinical psychologist's rôle is to apply the methods and findings of general experimental psychology to the solution of the clinically encountered problems of psychological functioning.
Educational psychology includes research and advice on matters relating to the educational guidance and personal adjustment of preschool and school children.
Engineering psychology is concerned with problems such as skilled performance under stress and man-machine systems.
Occupational psychology is concerned with more immediately practical problems such as those of selection, training, and the arrangement of working conditions.
See also CLINICAL PSYCHOLOGY; EDUCATIONAL PSYCHOLOGY; INDUSTRIAL PSYCHOLOGY; PSYCHIATRY.

Psychometry, the alleged psychic ability to 'read' the nature and history of animate and inanimate objects, purely through the sense of touch. There are numerous accounts of psychics able to tell the sex and various other facts about a person, either living or dead, by holding an object belonging to that person. However, not nearly enough is yet known or understood about psychometry to accord it scientific verification, although some interesting experiments concerning it are being conducted in various parts of the world.

Psychoneurosis is a state of conflict within a person that affects his behaviour in a way which distresses him. Psychoneuroses fall into three groups: anxiety states, obsessional states and hysteria. These states differ from psychosis in that the person is aware that he is ill.
Obsessional states. In these states a person suffers a continuous preoccupation with some set of ideas which interferes with or completely stops him from thinking about other issues. In obsessive ruminative states it is very difficult to stop the repetitive thoughts. In obsessive compulsive states a relentless compulsion to perform some activity makes it almost impossible for the person to proceed with any task in a smooth, natural way.
An obsessional person commonly feels powerless to do what he would like to accomplish smoothly and without inhibition. The condition can be treated successfully by psychotherapy and psychoanalysis.
Anxiety states are emotional reactions characterised by morbid or pathological anxiety. Although the patient may relate his condition to some event the anxiety which he experiences is out of proportion to this event. The real stress lies within the person.
Hysteria refers to the appearance of symptoms in a person who shows no physiological or objective evidence of illness when something is to be gained by the illness. Even though there is no physical evidence of actual damage, the person suffers in a very real way, and the symptoms set in unconsciously. This condition is distinct from malingering, which is conscious. 'An attack of the hysterics' is not related to the condition of hysteria.

Psychopathology, the study of abnormal mental functioning, leading to the description of the symptoms of psychiatric illness. It implies a knowledge of what might be regarded as normal functioning in various areas such as perception, memory and intellect as well as normal ways of making and sustaining relationships with others.
See also PSYCHIATRY; PSYCHOSIS.

Psychosis, a serious mental illness, more severe than psychoneurosis. Most psychoses satisfy the legal criteria of insanity. The most definite symptoms are persistent delusions or hallucinations; the malady may also show itself in extreme impulsiveness in action, leading sometimes to sudden attempts at suicide. Memory is often disturbed. Some psychotic sufferers are in a state of deep depression.
There is never a single cause for psychosis or psychoneurosis. Overwork, so often blamed for a nervous breakdown, is never a sufficient explanation. There are four groups of factors: constitutional, psychological, physical and social, which must be considered in every case. Some psychoses are organic reactions, and may be caused by infection, degenerative brain changes, and brain diseases or trauma. One form of degenerative disease of the brain, known as *general paralysis of the insane*, is due to advanced syphilis. Victims of *manic depressive psychosis* may be either elated (mania) or depressed (melancholia). In *schizophrenia* the sufferer is absorbed in fantasy to the exclusion of normal social activities. *Paranoia* is characterised by delusions which may be of grandeur and power, or of persecution or jealousy.
There are several methods of treatment. Psychotherapy, sometimes combined with the use of drugs (tranquillisers or antidepressants) may have some success. ECT (electroconvulsive therapy) is used for treating severe depression. When all other treatment has failed recourse may be had to prefrontal leucotomy, in which the association paths between the frontal lobes and the thalamus of the brain are severed; but this may induce serious and permanent damage to the mental functions.
Modern practice involves an attempt by the doctor to understand the patient, and to learn, through the discovery of the purposive character of the symptoms, obsessions and delusions, the real character of the inner conflict which they simultaneously express and conceal. There is still a difference of opinion about whether there is a distinct break between the neuroses and the psychoses, or whether the psychoses are merely developments of the neuroses.

Psychotherapy, the non-physical treatment of emotional problems by a professionally trained therapist, who establishes and uses a relationship with a person so as to change or eliminate disturbing symptoms or states of mind, and facilitate personality growth and development. In psychotherapy the person is helped to use his capacity to think and respond with feeling, in order to gain an understanding of the nature and origin of his difficulties in relating to others, and dealing effectively with anxiety and conflicts.
This task of expanding self-understanding may be carried out in an individual or group

setting. Therapeutic sessions may be held one to five times a week. Psychotherapy also varies in the level of the work, ranging from a superficial, supportive, reassuring nature to that which is conducted on a deeper, symbolic level, and which is concerned with the history and development of the problems. Psychoanalysis is regarded as being the most intensive and thorough form of psychotherapy.

Ptah, god of Memphis in ancient Egypt, always represented as a primitive human statue or mummy. He rose to importance when Memphis became the capital on the union of Egypt under the 1st Dynasty.

Ptarmigan, *Lagopus mutus*, small grouse frequenting the highest mountains in its more southern range, and extending throughout the arctic and sub-arctic regions of the northern hemisphere. It is an excellent instance of protective coloration, assimilating itself perfectly to its surroundings by the plumage changing through white, grey, red or brown, except for the wings, underparts and legs, which are always white.

Pteranodon, see PTERODACTYLS.

Pteridium, see BRACKEN.

Pteridophyta, a division of the plant kingdom comprising ferns, horsetails, clubmosses and a few fossil groups. Some biologists class the Pteridophyta as a subdivision of Tracheophyta. Pteridophytes are spore bearing, with true roots, stems and leaves, and those of the horsetails are so small that photosynthesis is a function largely of the outer layers of the stem. Bracken (*Pteridium aquilinum*) and horsetails spread partly by means of long underground stems, which send up shoots at intervals. They and the other pteridophytes show alternation of generations. Each plant produces asexual spores, which germinate in suitable, damp conditions, to form gametes. The gametes form male and female sexual organs, which join to form an embryo from which a new plant grows. In Carboniferous times the Pteridophyta were the dominant plants, and the origin of the coal measures. Many of them grew to tree size.

Pteridosperms, or 'seed-ferns', a group of fossil plants having fern-like foliage but possessing seeds. Their leaves are common fossils in the coal measures. *Lyginopteris, Neuropteris* and *Alethopteris* are typical genera.

Pteris, now *Pteridium*, see BRACKEN.

Pterodactyls, extinct Mesozoic flying reptiles of the order Pterosauria, whose limbs were highly adapted for flight. The bones were hollow and air-filled, while the fourth finger of the forelimb was enormously elongated to support a flying membrane which ran back along the body and thigh. They were probably fish-eaters. Early forms such as *Rhamphorhynchus* still had a long reptilian tail and numerous teeth. *Pterodactylus*, from the Jurassic period, was about the size of a sparrow, with a very short tail, and teeth only in the front part of the mouth. *Pteranodon*, from the Cretaceous period, was much larger, with a wingspan exceeding 8 m, a long crest extending back from the skull, and a long toothless beak. It is now doubted by most authorities that the pterodactyls were capable of flapping flight. Unlike the modern birds, their sternum (breastbone) was insufficiently developed to allow for the attachment of really large flight muscles, and from our knowledge of the physiology of modern animals it seems probable that they were mainly gliding animals.

Pterodactyls. Pteranodon, *was the largest of the Cretaceous pterodactyls.*

Pterophyta, the division of vascular plants comprising living and extinct ferns. Some classifications group ferns with all the lower non-seed-bearing plants in the Pteridophyta.

Pteropods, see SEA BUTTERFLIES.

Ptolemaic System, a name sometimes used to describe the geocentric idea of the universe generally held by the medieval schoolmen, ideas which owed far more to Aristotle than to the author of the *Almagest*. The Earth was regarded as a fixed sphere round which the heavens revolved. Earth, the stable element, occupied the lowest place and then above it in turn came the other elements, water, air and fire, beyond which was the quintessence, the transparent crystalline spheres that carried the celestial bodies. To account for the motion of the planets the outermost sphere to which the stars were attached carried within it a number of slowly moving spheres carrying, in order from the Earth, the Moon, Mercury, Venus, the Sun, Mars, Jupiter and Saturn. Matter beneath the sphere of the Moon was regarded as subject to decay whereas celestial matter was held to be everlasting and unchanging.

Ptolemy, or Ptolemaeus, family name of a dynasty of Macedonian kings who ruled in Egypt from 323 to 30 BC. The founder, *Ptolemy I*, who ruled 323–282 BC, assumed the title of king in 305 BC. It was Ptolemy I who commenced the great library and museum at Alexandria.

Ptolemy, also known as Claudius Ptolemaeus, (fl.2nd century AD), Egyptian astronomer and geographer, who lived in Alexandria. His astronomical writings, under their Arabic title of the *Almagest*, were the only authoritative work till the time of Copernicus.
See also ASTRONOMY.

Ptolemy II, posthumously called Philadelphus (309–246 BC), who ruled 285–246 BC, was chiefly famous for his splendid court and general delight in luxury, and his encouragement of commerce.

Ptolemy III (Euergetes I) (282–221 BC), reigned 246–221 BC. He left many monuments in Egypt, among them the unfinished temple of Edfu.

Ptolemy IV, called Philopator (244–203 BC), reigned 221–203 BC. He was a debauchee who started the gradual decline of his kingdom.

Ptolemy V, called Epiphanes (c.210–181 BC). The Rosetta Stone dates from his reign.

Ptolemy VI, called Philometor (180–145 BC) and *Ptolemy VIII* (Euergetes II), (d.116 BC). They ruled for a time jointly.

Ptolemy IX (nicknamed Lathyros or Chickpea) and *Ptolemy X* (Alexander I). During a long period of domestic strife, they ruled alternately in Egypt and Cyprus, until Ptolemy X was killed in a rising (88 BC). Ptolemy IX then ruled until 80 BC.

Ptolemy XI, Alexander II (d.80 BC), entered Alexandria with the support of Rome, married his step-mother, Berenice III, assassinated her, and was at once killed by the mob. He was the last of the legitimate line.

Ptolemy XII, known as Auletes (c.95–51 BC), the flute player, an illegitimate son of Ptolemy IX. Elected by the Alexandrians after the assassination of Ptolemy XI (80 BC), he left Egypt to his children, Cleopatra VII, aged 17, and her brother, Ptolemy XIII.

Ptolemy XIII, reigned 51–47 BC after the death of his father, Ptolemy XII. He assassinated Pompey in 48 BC, and died in the war with Caesar, after which his younger brother, *Ptolemy XIV*, became joint-ruler with Cleopatra VII and was soon poisoned.

Ptolemy XV (Caesarion) (b.47 BC), Cleopatra VII's son by Julius Caesar. He was murdered by Octavianus Caesar (30 BC).
See also EGYPT, ANCIENT.

Ptyalin, see SALIVA.

Pu Yi, Henry, see XUAN TONG.

Puberty, the years during which sexual maturation occurs. There is some evidence that the age of onset of puberty may be declining, and it is earlier in girls than in boys. The changes which occur are a spurt in growth, changes in hormone production, the appearance of the secondary sexual characteristics, enlargement of the sexual organs, and in girls the onset of menstruation (menarche). These changes are accompanied by increased sexual interest, which may be handicapped by considerable gaucheness and self-consciousness. The onset of puberty in girls may start as early as ten years with the beginning of breast development. One breast may develop before the other. Menstruation begins on the average at 13 years. Pubic hair appears at 11 years in girls and about 12 years in boys.

Public Debt. In a developed economy the government often borrows money from its citizens in order to finance its expenditure, particularly in times of war. It pays interest on this money and may either undertake to repay the borrowed money on or before a specified date or give no promise of a date of repayment. In Britain, the beginning of the national debt may be said to date from the reign of Charles II (1660–85), when the London goldsmiths began the practice of advancing money to the Exchequer on the security of an assignment of part of the public revenue. But it was not till 1694, when the Bank of England was incorporated, that it really became a permanent institution.

The public debt of Great Britain is classified into: (1) the Permanent or Funded Debt, which the government is under no obligation to redeem at any stated time; (2) the Unfunded Debt, made up of loans repayable at certain dates; and (3) Terminable annuities, by means of which the capital sum, at the expiration of the annuity, is written off the public debt.

Public Expenditure, in Britain, the amount spent each year by central and local government. Details of public expenditure are published annually in two accounts, the Consolidated Fund and the National Loan Fund, in the government's White Paper on Public Expenditure, and in the Estimates presented to Parliament. The annual estimates are prepared by departments in the autumn of each year and are vetted by the Treasury before being approved by the Cabinet. They are presented to Parliament in January and February and eventually authorised by the passing of the annual Appropriation Act in July or August.

Public expenditure increased considerably in the post-war period with the growth of the welfare state, but increased more sharply during the 1960s and 1970s.

Public Health. Public health differs from curative medicine in two ways; it is essentially concerned with the prevention of disease rather than its treatment, and its mode of action is directed less towards the individual person or patient than to the community as a whole.

In Britain, the period from the 1850s to the 1950s saw immense improvements in the 'state of the public health'. These were the result first of the measures of environmental control which brought a clean water supply, proper sanitation and drainage, improved housing conditions and better food standards. All these helped to eradicate the diseases due to filth, squalor and overcrowding, but their very success threw into even sharper relief the acute infectious diseases which were the killers of early life. It was the discoveries of the early bacteriologists which, by revealing the principles of immunity, provided the public health movement with its second main instrument of prevention, namely specific immunisation. By the use of vaccines and toxins, these diseases, which formerly took a heavy annual toll of child life, were brought under control. It was mainly through the application of these two preventive measures (environmental control and immunisation) combined with, and contributing to, a rising standard of living—itself bringing with it improved levels of nutrition—that the great advances in the health of the people during the past century came about.

In the period following the Second World War a noticeable change began to take place in the health problems of the community. These were no longer associated, as in the past, with dirt, deficiency and deprivation, but with excess. A relatively affluent society was producing the health problems associated with excess—excessive eating, smoking, drinking, speeding and licence—giving rise to such conditions as coronary disease, lung cancer, alcoholism, death and disablement on the road, drug addiction, and venereal diseases. These constituted the new challenge to the public health movement. But these problems could not be solved by the methods of environmental control and immunisation which had been so successful in the past. A new weapon was needed and found in health education; and it is mainly through the methods of health education that the public health services aim to combat the new threats to life and health in modern society.

Public Holidays, see BANK HOLIDAYS.

Public House, a shop whose main purpose is to serve alcoholic drinks for consumption on the premises, strictly controlled by legislation. Having some features in common with an inn, it is distinguished, strictly speaking, by not providing overnight accommodation for travellers, and so a publican like other shopkeepers has no obligation to serve everyone who calls. There is also some similarity with a tavern, which will usually have restaurant facilities.

See also LICENSING LAW.

Public Meeting. In English law any person may meet another person or an indefinite number of persons at any appointed place subject to the limits imposed by the common-law offence of 'unlawful assembly' and by certain statutes and local bylaws. An unlawful assembly consists of three or more persons assembled for a purpose forbidden by law or with intent to carry out any purpose lawful or unlawful in a manner likely to cause reasonable persons to fear a breach of the peace. Among acts by meetings forbidden in public places are the blocking up of public thoroughfares or interfering with the general convenience of other people, or the annoying thereby of tenants of adjacent houses.

See also PUBLIC ORDER ACTS.

Public Opinion Polls. From unscientific beginnings in the United States in the early 19th century, public opinion polls began using statistical sampling techniques in the early 20th century. Since the Second World War and particularly during the 1960s the popularity of the opinion polls grew. In Britain two methods of sampling opinion are practised by the polls; random and quota sampling. The former consists in selecting persons to be interviewed at random from lists of names that cover the whole of Britain, such as the Electoral Registers. Quota sampling involves selecting a sample of people which is representative of the population in terms of certain criteria such as age, occupational group, sex and region.

The techniques used in polling are most commonly used in the sphere of commercial market research and all polling companies do more market research than opinion polling.

Public Order Acts (1936 and 1963). The first act was passed at a time when various para-military organisations (particularly the British Union of Fascists), in imitation of the Fascists and Nazis, adopted black, brown, green or other distinctive shirts, marched in procession, and held political meetings which not infrequently led to disturbances of the peace. The Public Order Act 1936 prohibits both para-military organisations and the wearing of uniforms in connection with political objects. However, if the chief of police is satisfied that no risk of public disorder will be run, he may, with the consent of the secretary of state, permit the wearing of uniforms, absolutely or subject to conditions. The Public Order Act 1963 increased the penalties for offences under the 1936 Act.

Public Prosecutions, Director of. In England it is the duty of the director, under the superintendence of the attorney-general, to take criminal proceedings in cases of importance or difficulty.

Public Relations, a term defined by the Institute of Public Relations as 'the deliberate, planned and sustained effort to establish and maintain mutual understanding between an organisation and its public'.

In Britain the start of organised public relations is generally agreed to have been the establishment of the Empire Marketing Board in 1926 under Sir Stephen Tallents, with the object of 'bringing the Empire alive to the mind of people in Britain'. The success of the Empire Marketing Board, and the news of the spread of public relations in the USA, encouraged the expansion of public relations in government departments such as the Post Office, in local government, and in many branches of industry.

See also ADVERTISING.

Public Revenue, consists mainly of taxation, which reached very high levels during the Second World War and has remained high ever since.

Direct taxes such as income tax and capital transfer tax, are collected by the Board of Inland Revenue; while the collection of indirect taxes, which in recent years have increased more rapidly than direct taxes, is the province of the Board of Customs and Excise. The accountant and comptroller general transfers money daily from the general account of the Commissioners of Customs and Excise to the Consolidated Fund at the Bank of England, retaining a small amount for current expenses. The Board of Inland Revenue operates in a similar way.

See also PUBLIC EXPENDITURE; TAXATION.

Public School. This term has varied widely in meaning in different countries. In the USA it refers, logically enough, to a school which is not under private ownership and control. In Britain, it means precisely the opposite—namely, a school financially independent of the state, and charging fees for its education. In its narrower connotation it also signifies a boarding school, all or most of whose pupils are boarders. They may not be run at a profit: most, if not all, are registered as charities. Public schools in the UK were often founded for religious or philanthropic reasons, and most boarding schools have a denominational affiliation. Contrary to popular belief, they are not, generally, of great antiquity and the majority were founded in the mid-19th century. The British public school has, since 1850, been responsible for educating a very large proportion of the leading figures in British public life. Among the most famous public school masters are Thomas Arnold, headmaster of Rugby, Thring of Uppingham, and Henry Montagu Butler of Harrow. Critics complain that they encourage class isolation. The term 'Public School' is being superseded by the term 'Independent School'.

Public Utilities, corporations operated in the public interest for the supply of essential services, such as water, gas, electricity and transport.

Publicity, see PROPAGANDA.

Publishers Association, the representative trade organisation of British book publishers. Founded in 1896 to check (by means of the Net Book Agreement, upheld by the Restrictive Practices Court in 1962) the price-cutting then disastrously affecting booksellers, the Publishers Association's prime object soon became the co-operative promotion and protection of book publishers' interests and the widest possible spread of printed books throughout the world. There are some 390 members representing about 93 per cent of the UK book-publishing turnover.

Publishing refers specifically to the production and distribution of reading matter in printed form. It includes newspapers, periodicals, music, and, in particular, books.

The reproduction of manuscripts in Greece, Rome and Europe in the Middle Ages depended on copiers employed by booksellers, who thus became the producers, or publishers, of their own stock-in-trade. With the development of printing in Europe the scope for writers and publishers widened and soon the early printed books known as incunabula were being produced. The printer was both bookseller and publisher to begin with, but gradually separation of these activities began and in the 15th century the first independent publishers appeared. From about 1500, the important centre of book publishing was in the Netherlands where one of the earliest firms was founded by Christophe Plantin (1514–89).

In England the Copyright Act was passed in 1709 and led to the replacement of patronage (whereby an author's work was printed through the favour of a wealthy patron) by subscription. By the beginning of the 19th century publishing had come to be a profession in its own right as distinct from bookselling. Technical advances in papermaking, printing and bookbinding made production costs cheaper; distribution improved with better transport and communications, and many printing houses which exist today were then established.

In Britain the crisis caused by price-cutting was solved by the Net Book Agreement of 1899, which provided that no book published at a 'net price' might be sold for less than that price, and retailers were required to accept this condition before they obtained supplies.

Major developments which marked the progress of publishing during the post-war years included the development of book clubs; the mass-marketing of paperbacks; the growth of educational and textbook production; and the increase in the range and quality of children's books. Publication in paper covers has long been standard practice in France, but the era of the cheap mass-produced paperback really started in 1935 when Allen (later Sir Allen) Lane launched Penguin Books.

Today, publishing books consists of selecting an author's manuscript; planning and commissioning authors to write books; negotiating agreements with authors, artists and editors; planning and supervising the production; and copyrighting and selling the finished product. Normally the publisher finances the manufacture and selling of books and pays an author by royalties.

Pueblos. *A cliff palace in the Mesa Verde National Park, Colorado, built around* AD *1200.*

Puccini, Giacomo (1858–1924), Italian composer. His one-act opera *Le Villi* was entered for a competition which was won by Mascagni. *Le Villi* was produced in 1884, and drew Ricordi's attention to Puccini; he commissioned another opera, *Edgar*. Puccini had his first great success with *Manon Lescaut* in 1893. Three years later he wrote his most popular work, *La Bohème*. Puccini was the dominant figure in Italian music in his time. His operas combine the sensuous melody of Verdi with the richness of modern impressionist harmony. His other works include *Tosca*, *Madama Butterfly*, *La fanciulla del West*, *La rondine*, *Trittico* (*Il tabarro*, *Suor Angelica* and *Gianni Schicchi*), and *Turandot*, which was completed by Franco Alfano.

Puck, otherwise Robin Goodfellow, mischievous elf in folklore. He figures in Shakespeare's *A Midsummer Night's Dream*, as well as in Goethe's *Faust*, and is also used by Drayton, Burton and Ben Jonson.

Puddingstone, a term applied to some conglomerates with well-rounded pebbles within a fine-grained matrix of contrasting colour. One such example is the Hertfordshire puddingstone.

Pudovkin, Vsevolod Illarionovich (1893–1953), Soviet film director. His best known films include the silent *Mother* 1926, after Gorki's novel; *The End of St Petersburg*, 1927; and *Storm Over Asia*, 1928. *Deserter*, 1933, was the best of his sound films. Unlike Eisenstein, whose predilection for montage effects he shared, Pudovkin was interested in the individual rather than the mass. He was also a script-writer, and occasionally acted. His theories of film-making are outlined in the books *Film Technique* and *Film Acting*, 1929.

Puebla, capital of Puebla state in Mexico, its full name being Puebla de Zaragoza. Situated at an altitude of 2060 m on the south-west slope of La Malinche volcano in the valley of Puebla, the city is an important and growing commercial and industrial centre. Its principal industries are cotton and woollen textiles, glass, pottery, tiles, cement and food processing. Population (1978) 677,959.

Pueblo, city of Colorado, USA, 160 km south of Denver and on the Arkansas river. It grew as a route centre and service point for the irrigated farmlands of the Arkansas valley, but in 1881 a steelworks opened which uses local coal and brings in iron ore from Utah and Wyoming. Population (1980) 101,500.

Pueblo, term for a town or village in Spain or Spanish America, more especially a communal village or settlement of Indians. In US archaeology pueblo is applied to a tribal dwelling of the Amerindians of New Mexico and Arizona.

Pueblos, name given to those American Indian peoples who occupy the Pueblo area of Arizona and New Mexico, so called because of the Pueblo architecture of rock dwellings, cliff houses and stone houses in the open country; they make remarkable black-on-white decorated pottery. The culture seems to have originated in the Rio Grande valley. Most other American Indian peoples lived in more fragile non-stone shelters. The Pueblo peoples belong to several linguistic groups, but share similar cultures, of which a common feature is the Snake Dance. There are 30 peoples in all, of which the Hopi and the Zuñi are the best known.

Puerto Rico, Commonwealth of, formerly called Porto Rico, an island of the West Indies, one of the Greater Antilles, 97 km east of San Domingo. Puerto Rico is a self-governing commonwealth associated with the USA.

The island is about 161 km long, average width 63 km, with an area of 8897 km². A mountain range crosses from east to west. The highest point is Cerro de Punta (1338 m). From the mountains the land slopes gradually to the sea on the north and west, and more abruptly on the south and east. The mountain slopes facing north are deeply intersected by the many streams which have formed narrow valleys and sharp ridges. The higher slopes are forested, providing a source for timber such as sandalwood and ebony. In 1980 the island population was 3,187,566.

Sugar is the principal crop cultivated along with tobacco, pineapples, bananas and coffee for export; beans, maize and rice are grown for home markets. Manufacturing involves chemicals, domestic appliances, alcohol, food-processing and cigars.

Puerto Rico is administered by a governor, elected for a four-year term, and a 14-member cabinet. The bicameral legislative assembly consists of a 27-member Senate and 51-member House of Representatives. As US citizens, Puerto Ricans are represented in the US House of Representatives. There have been long-standing efforts to have the island made a state of the USA. Full independence has also been advocated.

Puerto Rico was discovered in 1493 by Columbus, and in 1508 was explored by Ponce de León. It remained a Spanish dependency for 400 years until it was ceded to the USA in 1898 by treaty after the Spanish-American War. US military rule was lifted in 1900 by the Foraker Act which provided for a governor. Full US citizenship was conferred in 1917 by the Jones Act which also established the constitution (amended in 1952).

Puff-adder, *Bitis arietans*, snake in the family Viperidae. It is a native of Africa and Arabia, and is very poisonous. It attains a length of 1·5 m, is yellowish-brown in colour, has a depressed head and small eyes. It is nocturnal and carnivorous, and when surprised hisses loudly: hence its name.

Puff-ball, common name given to the fruiting-body of fungi of the order Lycoperdales in subdivision Basidiomycotina.

See also BOVISTA; CALVATIA.

Puffer, or globe-fish, a marine fish of the family Tetraodontidae, order Tetraodontiformes. They are so named because of their power of distending a gullet sac with air, and thus assuming an almost globular form. Most of the species are found in tropical and subtropical seas, where they feed on corals, molluscs and crustaceans, for which their hard, beak-like snouts are peculiarly adapted. Some of them are highly poisonous owing to the chemical tetrodotoxin in the skin. This is extracted and used in medical research as it inhibits the conduction of nerve impulses. They are armed with small spines, and vary in size from a few cm to 50 cm. They are nearly always brilliantly coloured.

Puffin, a bird of the family Alcidae or auks, suborder Alcae, order Charadriiformes. The body is compact and the plumage close; the head is large, with a stout bill, with which the puffin catches fish. The common puffin, *Fratercula arctica*, lays its eggs in any crevice of the rocks or in a burrow which it makes. The complete range is in the north Atlantic and adjacent arctic areas. It is a little larger than a pigeon, and lays only a single egg at a time. The tufted puffin, *Lundae currata*, is another important member of the family.

Puffin Island, otherwise Priestholm or Ynys Seiriol, lies off the north-east coast of Anglesey. It is 0·8 km long and is noted as the home of puffins. In the 6th century Seiriol, a hermit, had a cell on the island.

Pug, smallest dog of the mastiff family, of Chinese origin. It has a short, square body, a massive, round, wrinkled head, and a curled tail. The weight is 6–8 kg.

Pugachev, Emelyan Ivanovich (1726–75), Cossack leader of a popular rebellion in Russia during the reign of Catherine II, the Great. He proclaimed himself Emperor Peter III in 1773 and issued a 'manifesto' promising liberation of the serfs. Many Cossacks, peasants and nomadic Bashkirs and Kazakhs took part in the rebellion, which continued until the end of 1774. Pugachev was himself betrayed after the destruction of his army and executed.

Puget, Pierre (1620–94), French painter and sculptor. The emotionalism of his sculptural style and his uncompromising character made Colbert averse to employing him at Versailles. He worked for some years in Genoa, Marseilles and Toulon, but was accorded belated recognition with his statue of Milo of Crotona, and a relief of Alexander and Diogenes, both now in the Louvre. He invented a specifically French version of the baroque idiom, which remained an inspiration to French sculptors for two centuries.

Puget Sound, inlet of the Pacific Ocean, in Washington, USA, extending from the eastern end of the strait of Juan de Fuca in a direct line for about 160 km south to Olympia. It has an area of about 5180 km^2 and a number of islands; Whidbey, Vashon and Bainbridge being the largest. The two main branches are Admiralty Inlet and Hood Canal. A government navy yard is situated at Bremerton.

Pugin, Augustus Welby Northmore (1812–52), British architect. He was the pioneer of the revival of Gothic architecture in the 19th century. In 1836–43 he was employed by Sir Charles Barry in providing the detailed drawings for the Houses of Parliament. He became a Roman Catholic, and designed many Roman Catholic churches, including the cathedral of St George at Southwark. His churches include St Giles, Cheadle, Staffordshire (1841–46) and St Augustine, Ramsgate (1846–51).

Puglia, see APULIA.

Pugwash Conferences, gatherings of scientists, named from their first meeting at Pugwash, Nova Scotia, in July 1957. The first meeting was convened after an appeal by Albert Einstein, Bertrand Russell and others, for distinguished scientists of different nations to meet and discuss the arms race. Successive meetings have considered the scientist's responsibility regarding armaments, economic developments, population trends and environmental issues.

Puisne Judge. In England and Wales the judges of the High Court of Justice, other than the lord chief justice of England, the master of the rolls, the president of the Family Division, and the vice-chancellor, are termed puisne judges.

Pula, seaport in Croatia, Yugoslavia, in the south of the peninsula of Istria. It is said to have been founded by the Thracians, was destroyed by Julius Caesar, and was rebuilt by Augustus at the request of his daughter Julia, for which reason it was called *Pietas Julia.* The town has remarkable Roman remains, including an arena, 137 m in diameter, a temple, and several gates. The harbour is very large and deep, there is a busy trade, and there are shipbuilding yards. Population (1971) 47,000.

Pulci, Luigi (1432–84), Italian poet. For many years he was a prominent member of the Medici circle but later became involved in religious controversies that led to his being accused of heresy. He is remembered for his narrative poem *Morgante*, a semi-burlesque re-working of a folk poem belonging to the Carolingian tradition. It prepared the way for the chivalric poems of Boiardo and Ariosto.

Pulcinella, see PUNCHINELLO.

Pulitzer, Joseph (1847–1911), US newspaper proprietor. He bought the *St Louis Despatch*, merged it with a German paper to form the *Post-Despatch*, and by 1880 had become its sole owner. In 1883 he bought the New York *World*; he brought to New York a journalism different from any it had previously known. It revelled in the sensational, but also made slashing attacks on the forces of corruption in business and politics.

Among Pulitzer's gifts was the endowment of a school of journalism at Columbia University and a fund for presenting annual cash prizes for the best newspaper work, drama and literature in the United States each year.

See also JOURNALISM; NEWSPAPERS.

Pullman, George Mortimer (1831–97), US inventor. He invented the Pullman sleeping-car. He built his first car in 1859, and in 1864 the 'Pioneer', at a cost of $18,000, the first of the cars to bear his name. He also founded a model township for his workmen, called Pullman, now absorbed in Chicago.

Pulmonary Collapse, or atelectasis, a condition in which part of a lung ceases to expand and contain air. It may be caused by: the blockage of a bronchus by a tumour or foreign body; by paralysis of the respiratory muscles, as in poliomyelitis; by inflammatory exudate as in the case of an effusion of fluid in pleurisy; or by air in the pleural space, as in pneumothorax, where pressure is exerted on the lung from the outside. When the collapse is extensive or involves the whole lung, respiratory embarrassment is severe. Total collapse of both lungs is fatal.

Pulp, in paper-making, see PAPER.

Pulpit (Latin *pulpitum*, a raised platform or stage from which actors recited), in Christian churches, a raised structure, approached by steps, from which a sermon is preached; usually placed at one side of the nave.

Pulpitum. A massive stone gallery or rood-screen separating the nave from the ritual choir in a large church.

Pulsars, or pulsating radio stars, were first identified in 1967 as compact radio sources that emitted very rapid, intense, but sharply defined, pulses of radiation with extreme regularity.

They are now known to be rapidly rotating neutron stars formed by the gravitational collapse of stars suffering supernovae explosions. At the end of 1982 some 330 had been discovered.

See also ASTRONOMY; RADIO ASTRONOMY.

Pulse, the periodic change in the volume of arteries brought about by the flow of blood through them from the pumping action of the heart. As the heart contracts, at each systole, blood leaves the left ventricle and is expelled under pressure into the aorta. The elastic walls of the aorta are suddenly distended and this distension is communicated to the other arteries, the movement becoming feebler and feebler as it travels away from the heart. Where an artery approaches very near the surface, the intermittent distension of its walls can be perceived visually, or if it can be compressed against a hard structure, such as bone, the throbbing can be discerned by touch. It is customary to gauge the action of the heart by feeling the throbbing of the radial artery at the wrist, as it can be conveniently compressed against the bone.

The normal pulse is regular in rate and volume. The frequency of pulse beats varies with age, sex and other conditions. In a newborn baby the rate is 130 to 140 times per minute; in an adult man about 72 per minute; in an adult woman 80 per minute. The rate is lower when the subject is sitting, and lower still when lying down. Eating, exertion, excitement and stimulants increase the rate. Certain abnormalities of the rhythm and rate of the pulse indicate cardiac disorders, but their interpretation is a matter for a practised observer.

Pulse, the edible seeds of leguminous crop plants such as beans, lentils and peas. The term may also be used for the entire plant.

Puma, *Felis concolor*, a large American species of the cat family, Felidae, in order Carnivora. Unlike its relation, the jaguar, it shows no trace of the feline markings when adult, the upper parts being a uniform yellowish-red and the undersurface a lighter colour. Puma is the Peruvian name for *F. concolor* and cougar the Brazilian. *F. concolor* is also known as the mountain lion; the name of panther was given to it by the early settlers. It is found in extremely varied environments: pampas, prairie, jungle, coniferous forest. It formerly occurred from Alaska south to Cape Horn, but in North America it has now been largely exterminated, except in national parks and reserves. It is a good climber, taking refuge in trees when hunted, and itself hunts chiefly at night; the diet is very varied. The puma is timid in the presence of man and shows great reluctance to attack, unlike the jaguar; it is easily tamed.

Pumice, a very light igneous rock formed when lava rich in volatiles degasses vigorously, causing a froth. The froth, when solidified, forms a glassy sponge-like rock often capable of floating on water. Pumice can be used as a household abrasive.

Pump, a machine for lifting fluids, or transferring them from one place to another. The work done by a pump is measured by the weight of fluid lifted and the total head in metres. The total head is equivalent to the distance through which the fluid is lifted and includes suction head, delivery head, and losses due to the friction of the fluid in the pipes, bends and valves calculated in metres of head. The suction head is due to atmospheric pressure on the surface of the fluid, and would raise a column of water 9·8 m in a complete vacuum. Owing to leaks and pipe friction it is only practical to attain a suction head of 7·5 m. For volatile fluids such as petrol there should be no suction head, and the pump should be below the level of the fluid, as the vacuum would otherwise cause the fluid to vaporise.

Punch and Judy. *A modern Punch glove-puppet. The puppet-show arrived in England in the 1660s.*

The principal types of pump are: (1) reciprocating, (2) rotary, (3) centrifugal. Other means of raising fluids include the hydraulic ram, air-lift pumps, Archimedes' screw, and chain pumps.

Reciprocating Pumps. The simplest form is the suction pump. The barrel is fitted with a piston worked by a handle pivoted in the pump casing. Valves are provided in the piston and at the lower end of the barrel, both opening in an upward direction. On the upward stroke of the piston the piston valve remains closed and the air in the chamber between the valves becomes attenuated and is therefore at reduced pressure. The atmosphere pressing on the water in which the pump is sunk thus forces the water into the chamber. On the downstroke of the piston, the barrel valve is immediately closed and the compression causes any air in the chamber to escape through the piston valve.

Rotary Pumps. These include a wide variety of designs, the object of which is the elimination of impulses obtained in reciprocating pumps by providing in effect a piston moving continuously in one direction. No valves are required, as the flow is always in one direction, and as the air is exhausted from the suction pipe the atmospheric pressure forces the fluid to the pump in the same manner as in reciprocating pumps. The suction head is usually limited to a few metres, as rotary pumps rely on fine running clearances instead of the more positive seal obtained with a plunger and valves. Viscous fluids such as thick oils can be handled with many types of rotary pump owing to the absence of valves.

Centrifugal Pumps have a spiral casing in which an impeller (a series of vanes) rotates at high speed, the fluid being thrown outwards by centrifugal force and then collected in the casing which directs the flow of fluid along the delivery pipe.

Other Types of Pump. The pulsometer steam pump is in a class by itself, using steam pressure directly on the surface of the water for forcing water up the rising main and using the vacuum created by condensation for filling the suction pipe with water.

See also AIR-PUMP; DIFFUSION PUMP.

Pumpkin, see CUCURBITACEAE.

Pun, form of word-play using words of the same sound but different meanings, as in 'Is life worth living? That depends on the liver'. The pun may also depend on different applications of the same word, as in Belloc's line 'His sins were scarlet, but his books were read'.

See also FIGURE OF SPEECH.

'Punch', notable British humorous magazine, founded in 1841. Since then its fame as a magazine of humour and political satire has become world-wide. It is noted for a high standard of literary and dramatic criticism.

Punch and Judy, best-known English puppet-play (for hand- or glove-puppets), traditionally given at the seaside or on city streets, but now mainly limited to indoor parties.

Punchinello (Pulcinella), traditional figure of the commedia dell'arte and ancestor of Punch, having something in common with Harlequin (Arlecchino). He wears a black mask and a large nose, has a humped back, and is a rogue and stupid braggart.

Punctuation, the insertion in written or printed matter of standard symbols to ensure quick and accurate reading, and to separate constituent elements. The stops and signs correspond to the necessary pauses and inflections in speech.

Punctuation was invented by the Greeks, but present symbols are derived from the 15th-century Venetian printer Aldus Manutius. In descending order the stops are: full stop; colon; semicolon; and comma (. : ; ,). Other points used are the question and exclamation marks (?!); hyphen -; dash —; brackets [ ];

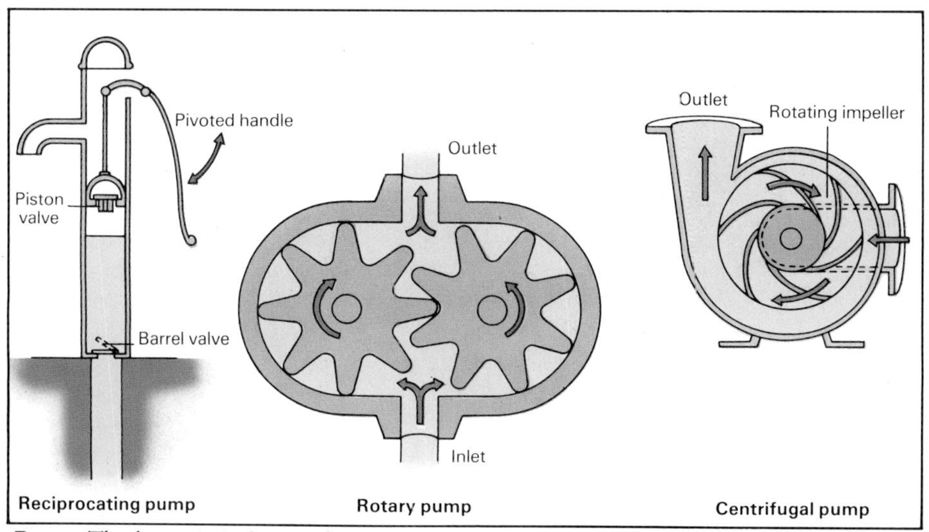

Pump. *The three principal types of equipment.*

parentheses (); apostrophe '; and quotation marks " ".

Punic Wars, name given to the conflict between Rome and Carthage, which ended in the latter's ruin after three periods of hostilities. The principal cause of the Punic Wars was the Roman alliance with Greek cities in southern Italy, who saw themselves threatened by the power of the Carthaginians in Sicily. The first (264–241 BC) was centred upon Sicily. It ended with the reduction of most of the island to the status of a Roman province, after the victory off the Aegates. The second war (218–201 BC) was almost entirely the work of Hannibal. It ended with his defeat at Zama by P. Cornelius Scipio Africanus Major the Elder and the acceptance by Carthage of a humiliating peace. The third war (149–146 BC) was decisive. Carthage had gradually rebuilt its fortifications, and Rome found a pretext for war when the Carthaginians attacked the Numidian king Masinissa. Carthage was taken by a Roman army under Scipio Africanus Minor and razed to the ground.

See also CATO, MARCUS PORCIUS; SCIPIO AEMILIANUS.

Punjab, or Panjab (Sanskrit, five rivers), geographical region of north-west India and Pakistan drained by the River Indus and its five tributaries, the Jhelum, Chenab, Ravi, Beas and Sutlej. These rivers have built up extensive plains from continual flooding and changes in course. To the north they are broken by the Salt Range between the Indus and Jhelum, and the Himalayan foothills, from which the rivers issue. Summers are hot with most rainfall lost by high evaporation, and cool, mostly dry and, occasionally, frosty winters. The semi-desert nature of the Punjab has been transformed by irrigation. Agriculture is based on wheat and pulses in the wet season and cotton as an irrigated dry-season cash crop together with wheat and grams. Maize, rice and sugarcane are also grown. In drier parts, millet, wheat and stock raising predominate. Most of Pakistan's major cities are located on the plains, indicating their rôle in that country's economy. Oil is found in the Salt Range.

Punjab, or Panjab, state of north-west India bordering Pakistan and covering 50,362 km^2; it had 16,669,755 people in 1981. State government is through a legislative assembly based at Chandigarh. Since 1966 the state has formed a more coherent unit with 60 per cent of the poulation being Punjabi-speaking Sikhs. Before then, the state was joined with present-day Haryana as Punjab state, together with a predominantly Hindu area now reorganised as Himachal Pradesh state.

Punjabi, an Indo-Aryan language; standard Punjabi, written in *gurmukhi* script, is the official language of the state of Punjab, India. Punjàbi (or Panjabi), in a wider sense is the mother tongue of 37,000,000 people throughout the world: some 10,000,000 people (1961) acknowledge standard Punjabi in India (including over 60 per cent of the population of Punjab State as it is now constituted, post-1966); the bulk of the remainder are in Pakistan, speaking related Punjabi, Lahnda and Siraiki dialects.

See also INDIA, *Language*.

Punkah, or punka (Hindi *pankha*, fan), device for ventilating apartments used in India and tropical climates. It was generally a movable fan-like frame of wood covered with canvas or calico and hung from the ceiling. A servant outside the room kept the fan in motion by pulling a cord passing over a pulley through the wall. It has now been superseded by an electrically operated fan called a punka fan. This consists of an electric motor suspended from the centre of the ceiling which operates a three- or four-bladed rotor (similar to an inverted helicopter rotor).

Punt, flat-bottomed shallow river boat, broad and square at both ends, and propelled by a pole. It has no stem, keel or sternpost, and the width at each end is at least one-half of the width at the widest part. Subject to these conditions, a punt may be any length or width.

Punta Arenas, capital of the province of Magallanes, Chile, and the most southerly city in the country. Situated on the Strait of Magellan, nearly equidistant from the Pacific and the Atlantic, it is the centre of the sheep-farming industry and a key port. Coal and oil are exported as well as sheep, mutton, wool, etc. Population (1975) 67,600.

Pupa, see CHRYSALIS.

***Purcell.** A portrait by John Closterman, 1695.*

Pupil, the circular central aperture in the iris curtain immediately in front of the crystalline lens of the eye, through which light may pass and be focused on the retina. Under the influence of intense light, and when one views near objects, the pupil contracts, but poor light or the viewing of distant objects causes it to dilate. This contraction and dilatation may also be caused by the action of various drugs. For instance, opium causes it to contract, while belladonna and cocaine cause it to dilate. This action affords a method of detecting whether a person is addicted to drugs.

Puppets, inanimate figures moved by human agency, usually in some form of theatrical show. There are many different forms and methods of manipulation: *marionettes* are moved from above by strings; *glove or hand* puppets are manipulated by the performer's fingers, *rod* puppets are operated by rods to the head and hands; *flat figures* are best known in the toy theatre; *shadow puppets* are held between a light and translucent screen.

Puppet theatre has featured in almost all developed civilisations. In Europe by the 16th century they seem to have been closely linked with the *commedia dell'arte*, though in England they played mainly familiar folk stories and popular incidents from the Old Testament. With the introduction of Punch into England in the 17th century these two traditions were brought together.

In the 18th century the puppet theatre became a fashionable form of entertainment and operas composed for puppets included works for Count Esterhazy's theatre in Hungary by Joseph Haydn.

In the latter part of the 19th century the puppet theatre was discovered by artists and writers as a medium worthy of serious attention. *Ubu Roi*, for example, was originally written for puppets by Alfred Jarry in 1888. This intellectual interest, however, has been confined to a minority. For the general public, puppets have increasingly come to be regarded as an entertainment for children.

Purbeck Beds, see JURASSIC SYSTEM.

Purbeck, Isle of, peninsula district of south-east Dorset, England, between Poole Harbour and the English Channel, terminating southwards in St Alban's Head. The northern ridge of the Purbeck Hills (chalk) traverse it from east to west.

Purcell, Henry (1659–95), English composer. Purcell was a chorister at the Chapel Royal and, from 1683, keeper of the instruments. He was made 'composer in ordinary' to the king in the same year. He succeeded his teacher Blow as organist of Westminster Abbey and became one of the Chapel Royal organists. These official duties required the composition of much church music. His many anthems include *My Heart is Inditing* for the coronation of James II in 1685. He wrote an opera, *Dido and Aeneas*; several semi-operas and masques, notably *King Arthur* (with Dryden) and *The Fairy Queen* (adapted from *A Midsummer Night's Dream*); music for plays; odes for the court; canticles; songs; and instrumental music.

Purdah, in India, a curtain, especially one serving to screen women from being seen by strangers; hence, figuratively, the Indian system of secluding women of rank.

Purgatives, see LAXATIVES.

Purgatory ('a place of cleansing', from Latin *purgare*), in Roman Catholic theology, place in which the souls of the departed who died in a state of grace but have not fully paid the temporal penalty for their sins are detained until they have done so. According to the Council of Florence (1438–45), the souls in purgatory can be helped by the prayers of the faithful on earth. It was denied by Luther, whom most protestants have followed, though a form of purgatory is believed in by some in the Anglican Church; and the Orthodox Church also rejects it, though prayers are said for the repose of the dead.

Puri, or Jagannath, town of Orissa state, India. It is famous for a temple built in honour of Jagannath, one of the titles of Vishnu-Krishna. Several festivals are celebrated each year, the chief one being that of the *rath* (car), on which the statue of the god is drawn to a nearby temple. This car of Jagannath is the origin of the term juggernaut. Population (1971) 72,750.

Purification of the Blessed Virgin Mary, feast on 2 February in the Christian Church, commemorating the purification of Mary 40 days after the birth of her son, according to Jewish law (Lev. xii. 2–5), and the presentation of Christ in the temple (Ex. xiii. 11–16; Numbers xviii. 15–16). In the East it is mainly a festival of Christ, but in the West it has been mainly dedicated to Mary, with the addition of the procession of candles in her honour first recorded under Sergius I (687–701); hence it is also known as Candlemas. But the earlier emphasis on the Presentation of Christ in the Temple is now commonly restored.

Purim, or the Feast of Lots, Jewish minor festival, commemorating the deliverance of the Jews of Persia from the plot of Haman. The book of Esther in which these events are recorded, is read aloud in the synagogue on Purim, which is celebrated on 14 Adar. This was the day Haman had planned to kill the Jews, having fixed the date by casting lots. A special banquet (*se'udah*) is held in the afternoon of the feast and is often accompanied by plays and masquerades. Purim carnivals have become an annual attraction of present-day Israel.

Puritanism, a term of varying usage, employed in England in the 16th and 17th centuries to describe the most extreme Protestants, both within and without the Church of England. An enduring feature of Puritanism, popularly defined, was a high sense of duty and morality, and rigorous private devotions. To this was added, but incorrectly, the parody of a strait-laced Puritan, opposed to most forms of art, the theatre and sports.

Extreme Protestant views had first penetrated into England under Edward VI, and during Mary's reign a number of clergy fled to Geneva and absorbed Calvin's ideas. The real trouble developed in the reign of Charles I when Archbishop Laud and his bishops began to enforce strict conformity on the 'high church' model. Throughout the Commonwealth and Protectorate periods extreme Puritanism developed as a large number of sects, ranging from the Quakers to the Diggers. With the Restoration of 1660 all attempts to establish a Puritan commonwealth came to an end; Anglicanism was restored. But the Puritans had a lasting effect on the established church and society as a whole, even though they failed in the end to capture it.

Purkinje, Johannes Evangelista (1787–1869), Czech pioneer histologist and physiologist. He observed the 'Purkinje phenomenon', that fields of different colour and equal brightness become unequally bright when illumination is decreased. A talented microscopist, he was the first to use a compound microscope, and by 1838 he had observed cell-division. He discovered the skin's sweat glands and excretory ducts, the neurons in the cortex of the cerebellum (Purkinje cells), and the fibre network in cardiac muscle (the Purkinje system). He demonstrated the importance of fingerprints, and produced a system of classification.

Purple Colours are obtained by an admixture of red and blue light, the colours varying from scarlet to violet according to the predominance of red or blue. In the case of paints, purple colours are obtained by mixing red and blue pigments in varying proportions. Tyrian purple, which was held in great repute in the ancient world, was obtained from the juice of a shellfish called *Murex* or *Conchylium*. Owing chiefly to the luxuriousness of the purple cloth made in those times, purple became a symbol of royalty.

See also DYE.

Purple Goatsbeard, see SALSIFY.

Purser, originated in the king's ships in the 14th century, under the name of 'clerk', later changed to 'burser' and eventually to purser. In the Merchant Navy, the purser is the officer in a ship's company who keeps the accounts and, usually, manages provisions.

***Pushkin.** An 1835 portrait by Frankenberg.*

Purslane, *Portulaca oleracea*, small succulent annual herb, native to tropical Asia. It is grown in gardens, the tops of the young shoots being cooked and eaten as a vegetable or pickle.

Pursuivant, lowest rank of herald.

See also HERALD.

Purus, group of nomadic, hunting and gathering Brazilian Indians, who live around the lower course of the River Purus, a tributary of the Upper Amazon. They live in temporary huts erected on swampy islands.

Pus, the liquid made up of the debris from a local bacterial infection. If, for example, a wound in the skin becomes infected, polymorphic white blood cells accumulate in the area in great numbers, phagocytosing the bacteria and releasing enzymes to break down cells killed by the infection. This cellular detritus, often with some living leucocytes and bacteria still to be dealt with, forms pus, which is sealed off from the body fluids by the formation of scar tissue.

Pusan (Japanese *Fusan*), chief port of South Korea, on the south-east coast. The chief exports are rice, beans, hides and silks, while cotton goods and Japanese consumer goods are imported. The fisheries are also of some importance. It has a good harbour. Population (1972) 1,900,000.

Pusey, Edward Bouverie (1800–82), British cleric. In 1828 he became regius professor of Hebrew at Oxford. It was with the object of stemming the rising tide of rationalism that he joined Newman in the issue of *Tracts for the Times* soon after their inception (1833) and became one of the leaders of the Oxford Movement.

Pushkin, Aleksandr Sergeevich (1799–1837), Russian poet. He was of noble birth and was brought up on the ideas of the Enlightenment and the French Revolution. For voicing his political and atheistic ideas he was twice banished. Too proud and independent for the court camarilla to tolerate him, he was constantly a target for intrigues, leading to a duel in which he was fatally wounded.

His early lyric poetry was influenced by Voltaire, Parny, Anacreon, and by the Russian Classicists, such as Derzhavin, and Romantics, for example Zhukovsky. In the early 1820s he was influenced by Byron; he discarded Romanticism and turned to a style distinguished by a completely natural manner and precision. His subject matter ranges from the lyrical to the political and the bawdy. His masterpiece is the 'novel in verse' *Evgeny Onegin* (1823–31), which is as much Pushkin's own commentary on literature and life as a story, told in brilliantly witty and varied verse. In his works Pushkin laid the foundations of modern Russian literature and language. He is recognised by Russians as the national genius whose work most truly reflects the essence of their country.

Pushkin (formerly *Tsarskoye Selo*; 1917–37, *Detskoye Selo*), town in Leningrad *oblast* of the RSFSR, USSR, 24 km south of Leningrad. It has famous 18th-century imperial palaces and parks and interesting 19th-century buildings. There is a Pushkin memorial museum (formerly the *lycée* where the poet was educated). Population (1970) 79,000.

Puskas, Ferenc (1926–), Hungarian footballer, who played in 84 internationals for his country, scoring 85 goals. He also made four appearances for Spain. His international début was against Austria in 1945; he developed into one of the finest inside-forwards of the post-war era.

Pustule, a small elevation of the epidermis filled with pus or lymph. A papule (a dry pimple) may, when infected, become a pustule.

See also RASH.

Putrefaction, degradation or decay of organic matter, brought about by saprophytic organisms, which include certain fungi and bacteria present in soil, water and the intestines of animals.

See also SAPROPHYTE.

Putrid Sea, see AZOV, SEA OF.

Putsch, German-Swiss word, meaning thrust or push. In the 20th century it has acquired an international meaning as an unexpected revolt of limited size and duration, aiming at an overthrow of the existing government by force. The most famous putsch was the 'Munich beer-cellar putsch' of Adolf Hitler and his followers in November 1923, but the coup was a failure and Hitler was arrested and imprisoned.

Putting the Shot or Weight, see THROWING.

Putty, see GLAZING.

Putumayo, river of South America rising in the Andes of southern Colombia and for most of its length forming the boundary between Colombia, Ecuador and Brazil. It generally flows south-east draining a vast area of rain forest. At São Antonio de Icá it joins the Amazon. In Brazil the river is known as the Icá. Its total length is about 1600 km, most of which is navigable by small craft.

Putumayo, intendency of southern Colombia, bordering on Ecuador to the south and occupying the drainage basin of the Putumayo river. The capital is Mocoa. It forms part of the eastern tropical lowlands, for the most part densely forested or covered in jungle. It is very sparsely populated and partly unexplored. Area 26,520 km². Population (1973) 29,137.

Puvis de Chavannes, Pierre Cécile (1824–1898), French painter. He recreated the monumentality of early Italian frescoes with his poetic, allegorical decorations in simple colour-areas with rhythmic linear ordering. In Paris he decorated the Panthéon, the Hôtel de Ville and the amphitheatre of the Sorbonne. He developed an entirely new style of wall-painting technically, oil paint on canvas which was cemented to the wall.

Pyelitis, inflammation of the renal pelvis, the expanded upper portion of the ureter where it is attached to the kidney. Infection may occur either from the bloodstream or ascend from the bladder: the infecting organism is often *Escherichia coli*, but it may be tuberculous, or caused by a streptococcal or staphylococcal organism. More commonly the kidney itself becomes involved, and the disease is known as pyelonephritis.

Pyelonephritis, inflammation of the kidney, usually caused by bacterial infection, also affecting the walls of the renal pelves, ureters and bladder. It can be acute or chronic. There may be an underlying cause that has allowed the infection to become established. This could be an obstruction to the flow of urine, leading to a rise in pressure within the kidneys and possibly slowing the flow of urine, which would give bacteria a chance to multiply. However, most infections occur in normal urinary tracts. The condition occurs 10 to 20 times more often in young women than in young men, but equally in both sexes after the age of 60. It may also occur as the result of a generalised body infection associated with conditions such as endocarditis (inflammation of the heart lining). Both acute and chronic forms are treated by antibiotics.

Pygmalion, in Greek legend, King of Cyprus. He fell in love with an ivory statue of a girl he had made, and Aphrodite breathed life into her.

Pygmies, a people of very small stature, living in tropical Africa as nomadic hunters and gatherers. A group well studied by anthropologists is the Mbuti of the Ituri forest of Zaire. They live in small fluid bands and have no organised political structure. Their technology is simple and their knowledge of flora and fauna very great. They believe in a benevolent forest deity and their rituals involve very harmonious songs. The Pygmies trade with the settled Bantu people who are their neighbours and most of them now speak Bantu languages.

Pylon, in ancient Egyptian architecture, the flanking towers to a temple; now refers to towers of lattice-steel construction carrying overhead electric transmission lines in open country.

Pyloric Stenosis, congenital hypertrophic pyloric stenosis is a relatively common disorder of young babies caused by an overgrowth of the muscle surrounding the *pylorus*, the opening of the stomach into the small intestine, which prevents the stomach from emptying. The condition is not truly congenital, since it only becomes apparent in the second or third week of life. The chief symptom is vomiting which occurs in a projectile manner immediately after feeds. The baby is very hungry and feeds ravenously, only to bring up the milk virtually unaltered by digestion. Most cases require surgery, the operation being minor and usually very successful. For reasons which are unknown the condition is commonest in first-born male infants.

Pylos (modern Navarino), ancient town on the west coast of Messenia, Greece. It was prominent during the Peloponnesian War, fortified by the Athenians in 425 BC, and retained by them till its recapture by the Spartans in 409 BC. There are important Mycenaean remains.

Pym, John (1584–1643), English parliamentarian. He entered Parliament in 1621, and in a few years became one of the leading speakers in the House of Commons. He gradually became one of the most effective leaders against the government's oppressive measures, and in 1640 was intimately associated with the impeachment of Strafford and Laud. He was one of the Five Members whom Charles I came in person to Westminster to arrest in 1642. Pym was subsequently concerned with organising for war. He secured the Scots alliance and kept Parliamentary forces in the field by raising taxes and maintaining supplies. His death in 1643 left a gap in the Parliamentary leadership which could not be adequately filled.

P'yŏngyang, capital of North Korea, on the Taedong river, 56 km from its mouth. It is said to date from 1122 BC, and was the scene of great battles between the Chinese and Japanese in 1592 and 1894. Under Japanese rule it was called *Heijo*. During the Korean War (1950–53) it was almost completely destroyed, but has since been rebuilt. The main centre for heavy industry in the country, it has iron and steel, chemical, cement, rubber, and textile plants and railway workshops. Population (1970) 1,500,000.

Pyorrhoea. Periodontal disease, which affects the tissues around the teeth, is now the commonest cause of tooth loss. It is most prevalent in adults of between 25 and 45 years, but can affect people of any age. It is an irreversible disease, but the effects can be limited by treatment. The disease is characterised by inflammation and destruction of the attachment of the tooth to the supporting bone and gums, leading to loosening and movement of the affected teeth and ultimately loss of the teeth.

Pyracantha, a genus of about seven thorny evergreen shrubs, in the family Rosaceae; *P. coccinea*, firethorn, of Asia Minor, and *P. rogersiana*, of China, are typical, and much grown in gardens for their red, orange or yellow berry-like fruits.

Pyramid, as a geometrical figure, has a polygonal or square base with triangular sides sloping to an apex. As a stone structure on a square base the pyramid belongs peculiarly to Egypt. There are also great earth pyramids to the sun and moon at Teotihuacán in Mexico, although weathering has eroded much of the pyramidal form.

In Egypt from the 3rd to the 12th Dynasties, royal tombs were usually in the form of pyramids. The Step Pyramid of Zoser is the oldest stone building in the world. Zoser was apparently buried in a granite chamber under the pyramid, and the pyramid formed a staircase to the sky by which the king ascended to the realm of the sun god. A few miles from Cairo to the west of the Nile are the three Pyramids of Giza. The greatest of these is that of Cheops which was 147 m high when built and covers 5 ha of ground. The most advanced tools used in the construction of the pyramids were copper saws and copper tubular drills with quartz sand abrasive; the raising of large stone blocks was done by sleds and earth ramps.

Pyramus and Thisbe. Legendary Babylonian lovers who were to meet and elope together. Thisbe arrived first, but fled from a lioness, dropping her veil, which the lioness tore to pieces with its blood-stained jaws. Pyramus found it, and thinking Thisbe was

Pyrenees. *The French Pyrenees near Lescun, the granite peaks contrasting with cultivated valleys.*

dead, killed himself. She returned and killed herself upon his corpse. The story has been immortalised in Shakespeare's *A Midsummer Night's Dream*.

Pyrenean Mountain Dog, large, extremely handsome dog of ancient origin which has been used for centuries to protect flocks on both sides of the Pyrenees from wolves and bears and as a guard and guide dog. Despite its great size it is gentle and docile so that the breed is valued as a companion. The height is 68–81 cm for dogs, 63–73 cm for bitches, and the weight is 45–55 kg.

Pyrenees, mountain system of Europe, stretching for some 400 km from the Bay of Biscay to Cape Creus in the east, forming a natural barrier between France and Spain. The highest peaks, which include Néthou, or Aneto (3405 m), Posets (3367 m), Mont Perdu (3353 m), and Viñamala (3298 m), are all in the central range. Precipitation is much greater at the western end, so that these slopes are wooded. In the east bare granitic masses tower above the olive groves and vineyards in the valleys. The Pyrenees were mined by the Romans and Carthaginians, and copper, silver, coal, lignite, lead and iron ore are still found. There are only a few passes. The Garonne is the only river of any size that rises in the Pyrenees, and there are a few small lakes. The semi-independent republic of Andorra lies within the chain.

Pyrenees, Peace of the, treaty signed in 1659 between France and Spain on the Île des Faisans, in the River Bidassoa, which separates France from Spain. By one of the terms a marriage was arranged between Louis XIV and the Infanta of Spain, Maria Theresa.

Pyrenoid, colourless, small, round, highly refractive plastids (organelles) in plants, such as those found in the brown or red algae. In green algae, they form starch.

Pyrenomycetes, the flask fungi, a group of Ascomycotina, characterised by flask-shaped fruiting-bodies, which either open at the top or else decay to liberate the spores. Some species are parasitic on plants, others on insect larvae, and some are saprophytes. *Claviceps purpurea* is the cause of the ergot disease of rye; *Cordyceps* attacks certain caterpillars. *Eurotium aspergillus* is the greenish mould which attacks jam. This is a very large group of some 640 genera and 6000 species, the largest group of ascomycete fungi.

Pyrethrum, *Chrysanthemum coccineum* (*Pyrethrum roseum*), of south-western Asia. Its many varieties are cultivated for their large flower heads in various colours and fine foliage.

Pyrethrum, insecticide, made from the powdered heads of *Chrysanthemum coccineum*.

Pyridine, C_5H_5N, heterocyclic tertiary amine found in coal-tar and bone-oil from which it is obtained by fractional distillation of the basic portion. It is a colourless liquid with boiling point 115 °C, and with a characteristic, unpleasant odour, and is a weak base. It is particularly stable to oxidation, being unattacked by boiling nitric or chromic acids. It is used as a solvent, a denaturant for alcohol, and in the synthesis of a wide variety of organic compounds. Electronically and structurally, pyridine is an analogue of benzene, and its properties are typical of aromatic compounds.

Pyrite, or iron pyrites, is the most widespread and commonly occurring sulphide mineral. It has a brassy yellow colour which accounts for its nickname, 'fool's gold'. It is rarely of economic importance itself but its presence may draw attention to vein or replacement deposits which might contain copper pyrites or gold. Its hardness is 6·6 and it crystallises in the cubic system. Striated cubes, octahedra and pyritohedra are common, but it may be massive, granular, radiated, reniform or globular. It is identical in chemical composition and hardness to marcasite.

Pyroclastic Rocks are rocks formed by the accumulation of fragmentary material ejected by a volcano during explosive activity. They are usually of acid or intermediate composition. Pyroclasts are primarily classified according to size; fragments greater than 32 mm in diameter are classed as blocks (if they are angular) or bombs (if they show aerodynamic rounding). Fragments between 32 and 4 mm are classed as lapilli, and particles less than 4 mm in diameter are classed as tuff or 'ash'. Pyroclastic rocks are characteristically unsorted rocks, i.e. they contain particles of various sizes and are therefore named according to the proportion of the various size fractions present. Thus a rock with 10 per cent bombs and 90 per cent tuff-size fragments will be called an agglomeratic tuff.

Pyrogallol, or pyrogallic acid, 1,2,3-trihydroxybenzene, or benzene-1,2,3,-triol, $C_6H_3(OH)_3$, formed from gallic acid, is a colourless crystalline substance with melting point 132 °C. It is readily soluble in water, the solution turning red with ferric chloride. Its alkaline solution rapidly absorbs oxygen, and becomes black, and for this reason is used in gas analysis. A powerful reducing agent, it was once used extensively in photography for developers.

Pyrometer, high temperature thermometer. One widely used type is the platinum resistance pyrometer, the readings of which can readily be calibrated to the absolute temperature scale. The platinum wire, in a silica case, is plunged into the furnace. The electrical resistance is measured by a Wheatstone bridge and the temperature of the furnace is deduced. This may be used up to 1200°C to an accuracy of $\pm$0·01°C. Thermoelectric pyrometers are made for direct-reading, continuous record work. It can be used to measure the temperature at a precise place, since the junction is so small that it can be inserted in any small aperture.

For temperatures between 1200 and 3000°C optical pyrometers must be used. The most common is the 'disappearing filament' type, in which a visual comparison is made between a standard electric lamp and the furnace viewed through absorption screens until an exact match is obtained.

Pyrope, see GARNET.

Pyrotechnics, art of making fireworks for amusement and for utilitarian purposes. 'Pyrotechnic' means 'explosive-actuated', and the term now includes many devices used in spacecraft, underwater vehicle systems and in production methods such as metal forming, cladding and riveting. Simple firework mixtures were known in China and the East from very early times, but it was not until the principle of the gun was devised, in 14th-century Europe, that a mixture suitable for use as a propellant came to be known as gunpowder.

Firework mixtures are of two types: those producing force and sparks and those providing flame. In England, 5 November, 'Guy Fawkes Day', is the occasion for general firework celebration; in the USA, 4 July, Independence Day, is similarly observed. Pyrotechnic signals, illuminating and incendiary devices, distress rockets and flares, and line-carrying rockets, are very important military and life-saving devices.

See also EXPLOSIVES.

Pyroxene, name given to a group of structurally, physically and chemically related minerals. Similar to the amphiboles, they differ in being single chain silicates without hydroxyl ions. They crystallise in the orthorhombic and monoclinic systems. Orthorhombic pyroxenes form a continuous series from enstatite ($MgSiO_3$) to hypersthene ($FeSiO_3$). They usually occur as irregular grains or masses in basic and ultrabasic rocks which are low in calcium, such as norites, peridotites and pyroxenites. Of the monoclinic pyroxenes, diopside ($CaMgSi_2O_6$) and hedenbergite ($CaFeSi_2O_6$) form another continuous series with augite (the commonest pyroxene) falling compositionally between the two. Augite shows substitution of aluminium for magnesium and silica. Augite is abundant in basic and ultrabasic rocks. Its dark green to black crystals impart the characteristic dark appearance to basalts and gabbros.

Pyrrhus (c.318–272 BC), King of Epirus. He claimed descent from Achilles' son Neoptolemus the reputed founder of the race of the Molossians. Driven from his kingdom at the instigation of Cassander in 302, he was present at Ipsus in the following year, and in 295 was assisted by Ptolemy I to regain his throne. Pyrrhus aimed at emulating Alexander the Great, and tried to win the throne of Macedon; but though he acquired considerable territory in Macedonia, his brother-in-law, Demetrius, was chosen king. War broke out between them (291); Demetrius was forced to flee (287), but Pyrrhus was soon ousted by the Macedonian Lysimachus (286).

His next famous exploit was aiding the people of Tarentum against Rome (280). His defeat of the consul Laevinus at Heraclea was marked by such heavy losses that the phrase 'a Pyrrhic victory' came to mean a victory almost counterbalanced by misfortune. Pyrrhus could not prevail on the Senate to make peace, and after defeating the Romans at Asculum (279) he went to Sicily to aid the Greeks against Carthage. On returning to Italy (275) he fought an indecisive battle at Beneventum against the consul M. Curius, and withdrew to Epirus. He made himself master of Macedonia again (273), but was killed the following year during a riot at Argos.

Pythagoras (fl.c.540–c.510 BC), Greek philospher, born at Samos. About 531 he emigrated to Croton, where he established a religious society whose aim was to liberate the soul from corruption of the body by study and the practice of asceticism. He wrote nothing, though various works, including the

Pythagoras theorem of Euclid, were attributed to him. From casual references in later writers it is learnt that his central belief was that of metempsychosis. He discovered the numerical ratios which determine the principal musical intervals, and his school was thus led to interpret the world in terms of number.

Pythagoras' Theorem states a relationship between the lengths of the sides of a right-angled triangle. In a triangle *ABC*, right-angled at A,

$$BC^2 = AC^2 + BA^2.$$

The square of the length of a line segment is equal to the area of a square with the line as one of its sides, which leads to the traditional verbal statement of the theorem: the square on the hypotenuse is equal to the sum of the squares on the other two sides.

Pythagorean triplets are sets of three positive integers x, y, z which satisfy the equation $x^2 + y^2 = z^2$ and so are the lengths of sides of right-angled triangles. If u and v are any positive integers and $u > v$ then

$$x = 2uv,\ y = u^2 - v^2,\ z = u^2 + v^2$$

is a Pythagorean triplet. The first five triplets are (3, 4, 5), (6, 8, 10), (5, 12, 13), (9, 12, 15), (8, 15, 17).

Pytheas (4th century BC), Greek navigator and astronomer, probably a contemporary of Alexander the Great. He sailed from Massilia (Marseilles) to northern Europe and apparently circumnavigated Britain. Accounts of his voyage are fragmentary and subject to many different interpretations. How far north he went is not clearly known; 'Thule' (his farthest north) has been identified with the Orkneys, the Shetlands, Iceland and Norway. He may also have visited Denmark and the Baltic Sea. For many centuries geographers dismissed accounts of his voyage as fantasy.

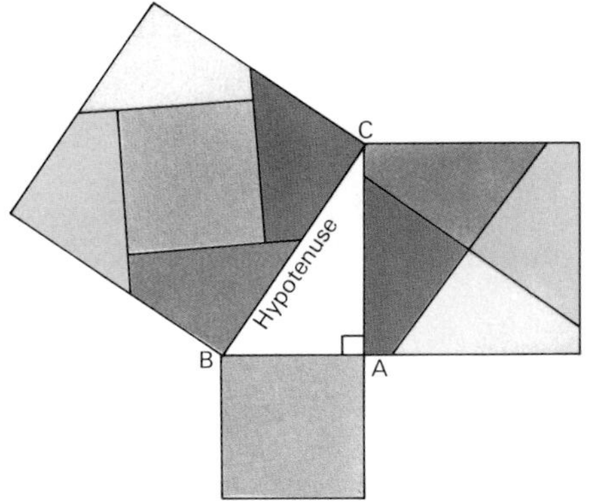

Pythagoras' Theorem. A practical model demonstrating the classical geometric theorem.

Python, a genus of large non-poisonous snakes, belonging to the family Boidae. They are found in most tropical parts of the Old World, and sometimes reach a length of 9 m. *P. reticulatus* is the commonest species in South-East Asia, while farther west *P. molurus* is more common. The pythons of Africa are smaller than those of Asia. The smaller ones feed on small mammals and birds; the larger on mammals as large as pigs.

Pyx, small box, generally of precious metal, in which the consecrated host used in the service of Holy Communion is reserved or carried to the sick.

Q

Q, seventeenth letter of the English alphabet. It represents the *koppa* of the earliest Greek alphabets, which survived only as a numerical symbol for 90. The Latin alphabet adopted from the Etruscan three signs having the phonetic value of *k*; *c*, *k* and *q*. In time it dropped the *k*, and used *c* for the sounds of *g* (the letter *g* was created at a later stage) and *k*, the letter *q* being retained for the sound *k* when followed by *u*. In the oldest form of the English alphabet there was no *q*; *cw* or *kw* were used for the sound of *qu*. In some words *qu* is pronounced as *k*, for example, pique, oblique, liquor.
See also ALPHABET.

'Q', see QUILLER-COUCH, SIR ARTHUR THOMAS.

Q-factor, in an oscillatory circuit, the ratio of inductive reactance, $2\pi fL$, to equivalent resistance.

Q Fever (synonym: coxiellosis), a disease found world-wide, due to the microbial pathogen *Coxiella burnetti* (once known as *Rickettsia burnetti*). The symptomatology is extremely variable and includes cough, chest pain, fever, chills, profound sweats, malaise and prostrating headache. Some patients develop heart infection (endocarditis). The disease cycle exists in the wild and is maintained by ticks, which feed upon cattle, goats, sheep, and some rodents, but the disease is transmitted to man by inhalation of dust containing the microbe. For this reason, all those working with animals or animal products show a higher incidence of the disease. The pathogen can also be passed on by cow's milk, and is one of the reasons for pasteurisation. Antibiotic therapy is usually effective in curing the disease.

Qadafi, Muammar (1942–), Libyan president. At Benghazi military academy he set up a Free Officers' Movement with the aim of overthrowing the ultra-traditionalist regime of King Idris; its first meeting was held in 1964. Finally, on 1 September 1969, Qadafi led the bloodless coup and became chairman of the 12-man Revolutionary Command Council which was to rule the country. He also promoted himself to colonel and commander-in-chief of the Libyan armed forces. His zeal and great personal charisma won popular support. Qadafi promoted a unique blend of Islamic fundamentalism and national socialism, rejecting capitalist materialism and communist atheism. This was the basis for an Islamic cultural revolution, xenophobia, and several abortive efforts at political union in the cause of pan-Arabism. He directed Libya's huge oil revenues into economic development through national enterprises and, allegedly, support for foreign guerrilla movements. His more grandiose schemes lost Qadafi sympathy outside Libya and within his own ruling council. His premier, Maj. Abdessalam Jalloud, gradually took over most of the affairs of state, while Qadafi has increasingly devoted more of his time to political theory.

Qairwan, see KAIROUAN.

Qandahar, see KANDAHAR.

Qasida, verse form used by Persian, Arab, Turkish and Urdu poets, which differs from the *ghazal* mainly in subject matter and length. It may be a panegyric or a satire, and didactic, philosophical or religious. The *qasida* is longer than the *ghazal*, and may exceed a hundred lines. The poet's name is not introduced into the final line as it is in the *ghazal*. This form was already highly developed in pre-Islamic Arabic poetry, and still exists in the 20th century.

Qatar, an independent sheikhdom in a peninsula of the same name on the south coast of the Persian Gulf, east of Bahrain. The total area is approximately 22,000 km². The physiography of Qatar comprises a low dry limestone plateau which reaches 75 m in altitude, and a coastal zone with a number of oases supplied by artesian water. Doha, the capital, is the only urban centre of importance, containing three-quarters of the state's total estimated population in 1978 of 200,000. The Qatar peninsula is mostly desert, and only 0·1 per cent of the area is cultivated. Crops include melons, potatoes, fruit and cereals. Fishing is of more significance.

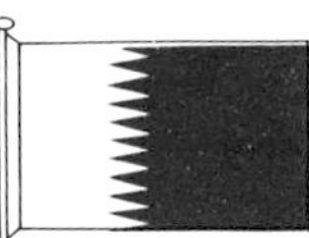
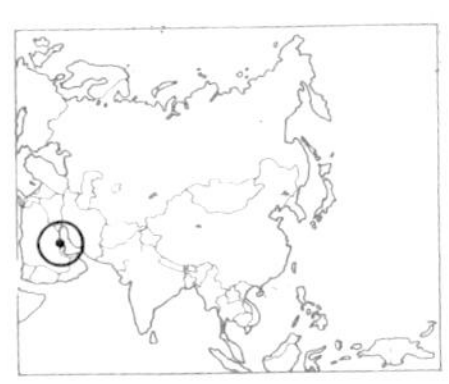

Qatar
Area: 22,000 km²
Population: 200,000
Capital: Doha

Oil accounts for over nine-tenths of Qatar's national income, and 96 per cent of its export proceeds. Reserves are sufficient to last until the turn of the century, and there are large reserves of natural gas. At Umm Said, south of Doha, a major industrial complex includes a £125 million fertiliser industry, an ammonia plant, and two seawater desalination plants.

Executive power resides in the cabinet of ministers headed by the Prime Minister. The cabinet appoints three members of the consultative assembly; the rest are elected. In April 1972 an advisory council with 20 nominated members was set up.

Arabic is the official language, but English is also widely used for government and business purposes.

History. The desert peninsula attracted no interest from foreign powers until 1916, when Britain signed a treaty extending earlier agreements with the sheikh to consolidate its control over the Gulf, then strategically important to the Indian empire. Oil was struck in Qatar in the 1930s, but production did not really start until 1949. After early enthusiasm for the Federation of Arab Emirates, which was to follow British withdrawal from the Gulf, Qatar elected for independence, achieved in 1971. The first emir was deposed by his cousin, Sheikh Khalifa bin Hamad al-Thani, in a bloodless coup in February 1972, and although the position of the royal house was retained, the new regime has taken a more active course in establishing social services and industry. National control over the exploitation of oil and gas was achieved in 1977.

Qattara Depression, area in the north of Egypt, about 210 km west of Cairo. It covers about 19,500 km^2, and lies 135 m below sea-level at its deepest point. There is a steep escarpment on its northern edge.

Qazvin, town of Iran in the Central province. Qazvin was a flourishing town throughout the Middle Ages, but was laid in ruins by the Mongols in the 13th century. It was the capital of Persia under the Safavid ruler Tahmasp. It is a route centre with connections north through the Elburz Mountains, east to Tehran, and west to Tabriz and Hamadan. Population (1974) 110,000.

Qingdao (Tsingtao), city on the south-east shore of Jiaozhou Bay (formerly Kiaochow Bay), a fine natural harbour in Shandong province of eastern China, almost equidistant between Peking and Shanghai. Qingdao has also become the best seaside resort in north China, whilst at the same time its heavy industry sector has also been growing, particularly in the fields of locomotive manufacture, tyre production, cement and chemicals. Population (1970) 1,900,000.

Qinghai (Tsinghai), a remote and sparsely populated province of western China. Mountainous in its eastern and southern parts, the north-western part of the province is occupied by the Chaidamupendi depression, a large area of interior drainage between 2500 and 3000 m above sea-level. The climate of the basin is harsh and arid with extremely cold winters. Much of it is desert and formerly almost unpopulated. However in more recent years important oil deposits have been discovered in this area. The capital of the province is Xining. The most widespread ethnic group are Tibetans. Area 721,000 km^2. Population (1972) about 2,000,000.

Qishm, or Qeshm, barren island in the Strait of Hormuz, Iran. It is about 110 km long and 7 km wide. The chief town is also called Qishm.

Qom, or Qum, town of Iran in Central province. It contains the shrine of Fatima (died 816), the sister of the 6th Imam, Ali-ar-Reza, and is a noted place of pilgrimage for Muslims of the Shiite sect. Pottery and textiles are the main industries. The town is a route centre. Population (1974) 169,000.

Quack, abbreviation of *quacksalver*; an unqualified medical practitioner, a seller of nostrums; one who pretends to medical knowledge, skill and healing powers he does not possess, usually for gain.

Quadragesima (Latin, fortieth), Latin name for the season of Lent which begins 40 days before Easter, without counting the Sundays. The name is derived from that given to the first Sunday in Lent by analogy with the Sundays that precede it, Septuagesima, Sexagesima and Quinquagesima. From it is derived the French word for Lent, *carême*.

Qatar. *Doha, the capital city, is the only important urban centre.*

Quadrant, one of the earliest astronomical instruments, suggested but probably not constructed by Ptolemy, to determine altitudes of stars. A quarter-circle of wood, brass or even stone is set up in a vertical plane; the arc of the quadrant is graduated in degrees, with the zero set vertically beneath the centre of the arc by means of a plumb-line. A sighting rod or tube, pivoted at the centre of the arc, is aimed at the star, whose altitude is read upon the graduated arc. The quadrant was developed by Arabic astronomers, reaching large sizes. Tycho Brahe used a 2-metre brass quadrant, attaining an accuracy better than 1 minute of an arc. Auzout and Picard used a telescope with cross-hairs, instead of a sighting-rod, thus greatly improving the accuracy. Mural quadrants, attached to a wall of the building, were standard equipment of observatories during the 18th century.

Quadraphony, using four loudspeakers as opposed to the two of stereophony. Quadraphony was introduced to give 'concert-hall' realism. In the pop-music and avant-garde fields, the back channels have been used equally with the front, and works have been designed to be played with loudspeakers surrounding the listener.

In Hafler Surround Sound stereophonic recordings are played back through four speakers: the back pair are wired across the positive terminals of the front pair, and play the difference between the stereophonic channels. Quadraphonic recordings are issued in one of three systems. CD-4 is discrete; the four channels are kept separate at all times. CD-4 tapes use separate tracks for each channel, while CD-4 discs are cut with a 4-channel groove. QS and SQ are matrix systems: the four channels are reduced to two by use of complex phase relationships.

Quadratic Equation, an equation in which the highest power of the unknown quantity is the second. The general form of a quadratic equation is

$$ax^2 + bx + c = 0,$$

the solution of which is

$$x = \frac{-b \pm \sqrt{(b^2 - 4ac)}}{2a}$$

If the quadratic expression can be factorised, this will simplify the solution, but many quadratic equations are not easily expressed as factors. When $b^2 = 4ac$ the equation has a single solution, $-b/2a$. If $b^2 < 4ac$ then its two solutions are both complex numbers.

In the British Museum (and elsewhere) there are Babylonian clay tablets (c.1600 BC) with mathematical texts in cuneiform giving numerical solutions to school problems involving quadratic equations.

See also EQUATION.

Quadrature. A celestial body is said to be 'in quadrature' when its longitude differs from that of the Sun by 90°.

Quadrilateral, a geometrical figure consisting of four distinct points (called vertices) joined by four distinct line segments which intersect only at the vertices. Quadrilaterals may be convex or nonconvex. The sum of the internal angles of a convex quadrilateral is 2π (360°).

The area of an irregular quadrilateral may be found by dividing it into two triangles. A quadrilateral is *cyclic* if its vertices all lie on a circle. Opposite pairs of angles of a cyclic quadrilateral add up to π (180°).

Quadrille, square dance of French origin derived from the cotillion in which an even number of couples take part. There are five separate figures, the whole forming a set of quadrilles. It was popular in early 19th-century France at the court of Napoleon I and in 1816 was introduced to England by Lady Jersey. Later the dance spread outside court circles and the style was adapted to suit the environment and character of different regions.

Quadruple Alliance, formed in 1718 between Britain, Austria, France and Holland, with the primary object of thwarting Cardinal Alberoni, the Spanish minister, who was bent on regaining for Spain some of the dominions it had lost by the Treaty of Utrecht. Spain was powerless against the

Quadruple Alliance. In 1834 another Quadruple Alliance of Britain, France, Portugal and Spain, was designed to exclude Dom Miguel from the Portuguese throne.

Quaestor, name common to two distinct classes of officers in ancient Rome: (1) The criminal *quaestores*, or Roman commissioners, were a body to whom the Comitia delegated its criminal jurisdiction. (2) The *quaestores classici* were officers charged with the superintendence of the public treasury. A special body, the military quaestors, accompanied the consuls to the field, took charge of the military chest, and exercised supervision over pay, provisions and booty.

Quagga, see ZEBRA.

Quaid-i-Azam, title of the Pakistani leader and leader of the Muslim League, Mohammed Ali Jinnah, the first governor-general of Pakistan.

Quail, *Coturnix*, small genus of gamebirds, in family Phasianidae, order Galliformes, with a remarkably extensive range. The common quail, *C. coturnix*, ranges over Europe, Asia and Africa, and has been introduced into the USA and New Zealand. Great numbers spend the winter in North Africa. The quail is about 18 cm long, reddish-brown in colour, throat white with a black patch at the bottom; the breast is pale chestnut, and the belly yellowish-white. The nest is a small hollow in the ground, and in it are laid about 10 yellowish-white eggs blotched with brown. The bird feeds upon grain seeds and insects. Other species of the genus *Coturnix* are found in Africa, India and Australia. These include the painted quail, *Coturnix chinensis*, of Australasia. This is the smallest gamebird and closely related to *Coturnix adamsoni* of Africa. The painted quail has a grey-blue breast, red underparts, black and white throat markings and brown streaked upperparts. The female is mainly brown. The bobwhite, *Colinus virginianis*, belongs to the New World quails, with a hooked tip to the bill.

Quakers, see FRIENDS, SOCIETY OF; FOX, GEORGE.

Quaking Grass, common name of some grasses of the genus *Briza*.

Qualities, Primary and Secondary, a distinction dating back to Democritus, but first stated and named by Robert Boyle. It received its classic statement in Locke's *Essay Concerning Human Understanding*, which holds that material objects possess five primary qualities—size, shape, motion or rest, number and solidity—and many secondary qualities such as colour, taste, smell and sound. The distinction derives from the theory of representative realism, in which the qualities actually inherent in objects are seen as distinct from, and as causes of, the 'ideas' or 'sensa' which are the objects of immediate awareness. Both Descartes and Locke emphasise the objective reality of matter as deduced from its primary qualities.

Quango, acronym formed from quasi-autonomous non-governmental organisation, being government-financed bodies in Britain, including the Monopolies Commission. Since 1979 the Conservative government has abolished the majority of them.

Quant, Mary (1934–), British dress designer who so invigorated London fashion in the early 1960s that it temporarily replaced Paris in world leadership. She also markets cosmetics and soft furnishings.

Quantity Surveying, compiling a 'bill of quantities', describing each article and the quantity required for the erection of a building. This 'bill' is prepared from a set of architects' plans. An estimate of cost and such information as will assist both the architect and building owner to arrive at their final decision are also necessary. The bills of quantities are sent to contractors, inviting tenders.

The quantity surveyor must have a technical training in building construction, with knowledge of materials and land surveying, and must be conversant with the building regulations and contract law, and with council and local authority by-laws.

Quantock Hills, range of hills in north-western Somerset, England, extending 13 km between Taunton and the coast at Quantock. They form a series of irregular ridges, chiefly of greywacke and limestone. The highest point is Willsneck (387 m).

Quantum Theory. This was first proposed by Max Planck in 1900 following his investigations of red-hot bodies. Laws of classical radiation failed to account for the distribution of energy between the various wavelengths in the electromagnetic spectrum of the radiation. Planck suggested that the vibrating charges in atoms emitted or absorbed radiation only in amounts E which were multiples of some fundamental unit or *quantum* of energy, hf or hc/λ, i.e. $E = nhf$, where f is the frequency and equals c/λ, λ is wavelength and c the velocity of light *in vacuo*, n is any integer, and h is Planck's constant $6{\cdot}63 \times 10^{-34}$ J s. E varies according to the number n of quanta.

The theory received strong confirmation in 1905 when Einstein used it to explain photoelectricity. Einstein considered light to be quanta of energy, particle-like, not wave-like, so that its energy was not absorbed gradually, but in a single event (photons, wave-particle duality).

In 1913 the theory was applied by Bohr to the calculation of the wavelengths (colours) emitted by atoms in the gaseous state. He found he could explain the spectrum emitted by hydrogen by postulating (1) that the allowed orbits were those in which the electron moved with angular momentum $nh/(2\pi)$ ($n = 1,2,3\ldots$), and (2) that radiation was emitted as photons of energy $E = hc/\lambda$. To radiate a photon, the electron jumps discontinuously from one orbit E_1 to another E_2, carrying off the energy difference $E_1 - E_2$. The Bohr theory was extended by Sommerfeld and others, to X-ray visible, ultraviolet and infrared regions. The quantum theory also proved successful in specific heat, electrical conduction, chemical combination, and the periodic table.

In 1924 de Broglie argued that since light behaves like waves and like particles (photoelectric effect), then perhaps electrons, protons and matter could be expected to show wave-like behaviour. Schrödinger, Heisenberg and others developed wave mechanics and treated electrons as a diffuse wave motion. Using ideas of standing waves, they were able to give reasons for Bohr's postulate (1) and to give a full explanation of spectra from atoms, solids and gamma-rays, and to explain radioactivity. Wave mechanics is the foundation of all modern physics, as well as much of chemistry.

Quarantine, the period during which a ship suspected of having cases of infectious disease on board is detained from communication with the shore. As originally instituted, quarantine was practised for the plague, and later for yellow fever and Asiatic cholera. The first Act of Parliament concerning quarantine in England was passed in 1710, but quarantine in the original sense is abolished now in England, America and several European states, though the name is still applied to the modern detention methods which have superseded it.

The importation into Britain of certain animals is subject to various quarantine regulations. The isolation of the animal for six months after landing is obligatory.

Quarks, see ELEMENTARY PARTICLES.

Quarry and Quarrying, place from which stone, sand, gravel or other minerals are excavated; the process of excavating. The term 'quarry' is usually but not always restricted to workings in the open air, as distinguished from mines. The suitability of a stone for quarrying depends on (1) its quality; (2) the possibility of cheap and ready conveyance to a large market; and (3) its inclination and depth below the surface. The principal deposits worked by quarrying are sandstones, limestones, marble, ironstones, slates and granite. The sandstones are classified as flagstones, freestones and tilestones. A thick deposit of sandstone may provide all three classes of stone at different levels or 'lifts'. Deposits that outcrop on the surface are best won by open-pit work or quarries, while thick or deep deposits are best worked by underground methods. In open-pit work it is sometimes necessary to remove the soil or waste rock over the valuable stone before excavation can start.

Since the early 1970s the concept of the 'super-quarry' has come into existence. Such quarries have an annual output of 10–15 million tonnes per year. In such quarries up to 250,000 t of rock are brought down with each blast, involving the use of up to 100 t of high explosive.

Quart, see METROLOGY.

Quarter, see METROLOGY.

Quarter Days, appointed for the payment of ground rents, and for the incoming and outgoing of tenants, occur in England on 25 March (Lady Day), 24 June (Midsummer Day), 29 September (Michaelmas Day), and 25 December (Christmas Day).

In Scotland the equivalent are Term Days which fall on Candlemas (2 February), Whitsunday (a fixed date), Lammas (1 August), and Martinmas (11 November).

Quarter-deck, originally a smaller deck placed above the half-deck and covering about a quarter of the vessel. The term formerly denoted that part of the spar deck extending between the poop and the mainmast, used by officers only. In modern men-of-war it is the name given to that part of the upper deck abaft the after superstructure.

Quarter Sessions, see CROWN COURT, THE.

Quartet, in music, usually refers to a string quartet consisting of two violins, viola and cello, but can refer to mixed forces, as with the flute quartets of Mozart where one violin

is replaced by a flute; it can also refer to vocal chamber music for four singers.
See also CHAMBER MUSIC.

Quarto, (4to) sheet of paper folded so as to make four leaves, or a book printed on paper so folded.

Quartz, see SILICA.

Quartz Crystal Oscillators, see OSCILLATORS.

Quartz Glass, see SILICA GLASS.

Quartzite, rock formed essentially of quartz grains which have been cemented together by percolating solutions, or which have been welded together by recrystallisation during metamorphism.

Quasar, an object that appears to be a star but has a spectrum showing a large red shift and containing broad emission lines. Assuming their red shifts to be cosmological, that is, due to their velocities of recession, quasars are the brightest and most distant objects known. In radio wavelengths they are as bright as the brightest peculiar radio galaxy; in the optical range they far outshine the brightest elliptical galaxies; and in the infrared they pour out even greater amounts of energy. Quasars are subject to rapid and irregular changes of brightness which indicate that the volumes from which the energy is emitted must be extremely small when compared with normal galactic dimensions. Moreover there are indications of smaller structure within these overall diameters. The much studied quasar 3C 273 was found in 1972 to consist of several components whose relative brightnesses change within a few weeks, making the quasar appear to grow or shrink in size.
The source of the vast energy of quasars is likely to be matter falling onto a very compact object, such as a black hole. A black hole 100 million times the mass of the Sun, but as small as the solar system, could easily fuel a quasar.
See also COSMOLOGY; GALAXY; RADIO ASTRONOMY.

Quasimodo, Salvatore (1901–68), Italian poet. He is the chief exponent of the literary movement known as Italian Hermeticism (which parallels French Symbolism in using language as a way of exploring the inner world of meaning through evocation and association). Much of his work is related to contemporary historical events. Quasimodo received the Nobel Prize for literature in 1959.

Quassia, certain Caribbean and South American trees of family Simaroubaceae, especially *Quassia amara* and *Picrasma excelsa.* The bark and roots have been used as drugs to reduce fever.

Quaternary System, the most recent geological period, between the Tertiary System, which ended two million years ago, and the present. It is divided into the Pleistocene and Holocene (or Recent) periods. The Pleistocene period spanned the last major glacial period in the Earth's history. The climatic deterioration leading to the advance of ice from the poles is known to have begun around five million years ago in the Antarctic, spreading relatively slowly towards the mid-latitudes, and as a result of these changes, ice sheets began to advance from the polar ice caps towards the equator. At least four periods of ice-advance occurred in Britain, separated by interglacial periods when temperatures rose and the land surface re-emerged in part from the ice cover.
The Holocene period began about 10,000 years ago and was a time of rising sea-level (the Flandrian transgression). This caused the final severing of England from the Continent by the formation of the English Channel. At the same time the 8-metre raised beach of Scotland was cut; this has since risen due to the isostatic uplift of the land surface after the retreat of the ice.

Quatrain, four rhymed lines which may be of any length, but linked by a unity of thought, as, for example, in an epigram, for which the quatrain is often used.

Quatrefoil, in architecture and heraldry, an ornament consisting of four cusps around an arch or circle.

Quatre-Bras, village in the province of Brabant, Belgium, situated about 16 km south of Waterloo. It was the scene of a battle on 16 June 1815 between the British under the Duke of Wellington and the French under General Ney, when the latter were repulsed.

Quaver, note in music equal in duration to an eighth of a semibreve or two semiquavers. American and German terminology uses 'eighth note' for quaver. Smaller divisions are called semiquavers, demisemiquavers, hemidemisemiquavers.

Que Que, see KWEKWE.

Quebec, province of Canada, the largest in the dominion and peculiar in its continued tradition of French language and culture. It is bounded on the north by Hudson Strait, on the west by Ontario, on the south by the USA and New Brunswick, and on the east by the Labrador coast of Newfoundland. Area 1,540,680 km².
The geology of Quebec falls into three distinct divisions: the Laurentian Shield, the St Lawrence basin, and the Appalachian Mountains. The shield reaches south to the St Lawrence and covers around 90 per cent of the province in a series of platform-like surfaces that rise eastwards to the mountain rim in Labrador which rises to some 3350 m. The main surface levels are between 300 and 450 m and between 900 and 1200 m.
The Appalachian Mountains form a triple barrier characterised by intensive folding and granitic intrusions. The surface takes the form of a rolling plateau into which short, swift-flowing rivers have cut a series of deep, steep-sided valleys. Eastwards these mountains rise to over 1200 m. Between these two upland blocks the St Lawrence river threads its way from the Great Lakes to the Atlantic. The valley of the river is made up of three basins—the St Lawrence estuary below Quebec, the middle St Lawrence plains, and the Ottawa valley. This low-lying area bounded to the north and south by steep mountain bluffs has emerged as the main agricultural area in the province and the area of major population concentration.
The population of Quebec province in 1981 was 6,438,403. The major cities are Montreal, Quebec (the capital) and Laval. The people of the province were assured security to retain their French language, customs and tenures, and religion under the Quebec Act, 1774. Eighty-seven per cent of the population are French-speaking.
Those farms on the estuarine terraces of the lower St Lawrence tend to be small dairy concerns producing milk and cream for sale to the cities and creameries. Potatoes and peas are the main cash crops, and hay and roots are grown as cattle fodder. Upstream from Quebec a greater range of farm specialisation has developed. In addition to dairying there are poultry (especially turkey farms), orchards, market gardening, small fruits, and fur ranching concerns. In the Montreal plain the clay lands of the central area are mainly under hay and oats and support a thriving dairy industry.
The Laurentian Shield and the Appalachian Mountains are of little agricultural importance, but are the main mineral producing regions. The Temiskaming-Abitibi basin has rich gold and copper deposits as well as smaller but important deposits of silver, lead, zinc and lithium. Chibougamaw is the centre of a more recently discovered copper-gold deposit. Zinc is also mined. The most important development of recent years has been the opening up of the vast iron-ore field in the Ungava trough. On the south side of the

Quebec. *Quebec city, overlooking the St Lawrence River. Chateau Frontenac is on the left.*

river rich deposits of asbestos are mined at Black Lake, Thetford and Robertsonville. The leading industry is pulp and paper which are manufactured at numerous places along the St Lawrence Valley. Newsprint is another major industry in Quebec city, Montreal and several other centres. Shipbuilding and repairing is carried on at Quebec city, Sorel and Montreal; consumer durables, textiles and clothing are manufactured at Quebec city and Montreal, and there is oil refining and petrochemicals processing at Montreal. Arvida on the Saguenay has grown up as the largest aluminium smelting centre in North America.

The Quebec legislative assembly has 108 members, elected for five years, under a lieutenant-governor. Quebec has its own educational system, based on the French model.

The area has been known by several names during the past centuries: New France or Canada (1535–1763); province of Quebec (until 1790); Lower Canada (until 1846); and in 1867 it was called the province of Quebec once more. The territory of Ungava was added to the province under the Quebec Boundaries Extension Act, 1912.

Quebec, capital of Quebec province, Canada, and former capital of Canada, situated on the left bank of the St Lawrence, at the mouth of the St Charles river, 290 km north-east of Montreal. It is picturesquely sited, on a promontory between two rivers, its citadel crowning the precipitous front of Cape Diamond. Before the arrival in Canada of any European explorers, the Indians had chosen this exceptional site for the construction of an entrenched camp, which was visited by Samuel de Champlain a few years before he founded Quebec in 1608. Quebec was captured by the English in 1609 and again in 1759, and finally ceded to England in 1763.

As the provincial capital Quebec is an important administrative centre and also acts as the retailing, wholesaling and service focus for the numerous dispersed communities in the north and east of the province. Tanneries, boot and shoe factories, textile plants, clothing, wooden articles, pulp and paper manufacturing, and printing and publishing have always been important activities. These have been joined by metal working plants, machinery factories, electronics, and a wide range of consumer durables. Quebec is particularly well located for pulp and paper production since it is able to draw on large forest reserves to the north. It also has ample supplies of electricity and is an ocean port. It is a noted centre for the export of lumber and wheat. The opening of the St Lawrence Seaway in 1959 retarded the growth of shipping at Quebec, but it still handles a considerable volume. Population (city) 186,000; (metropolitan area) 534,193.

Quécha, or Quicha, ancient people of Peru. Under the Inca kingdom of the 14th and 15th centuries they subjugated all the country from Ecuador to Bolivia and northern Chile. Their state was a theocratic tyranny. At the fall of the Incas they submitted to the Spaniards. Today they are small-scale farmers, often living in depressed circumstances, and number about 4 million.

Queen, Ellery, joint pseudonym of Frederic Dannay (1905–), and Manfred Lee (1905–71), both born in Brooklyn, who collaborated in writing detective stories. Both were successful in the advertising business when they entered together for a detective-story prize, and won it with *The Roman Hat Mystery*, 1929. For some time they took elaborate precautions to conceal their identity, even wearing masks at literary parties, but later this pretence was abandoned, though the pseudonym was retained.

Their novels are classics of their type. Queen is the fictitious detective as well as the pseudonymous author, and two volumes of *Adventures of Ellery Queen*, 1934, 1940, have appeared. There is also an Ellery Queen monthly magazine, containing detective stories by various authors.

Queen, see CROWN; SOVEREIGNTY.

Queen Charlotte Islands, archipelago in the north Pacific, off the north-west coast of British Columbia, Canada, from which it is separated by Hecate Strait on the east and Dixon Entrance on the north. It consists of about 150 islands, the main ones being Graham Island, Moresby Island and Kunghit Island. The people are chiefly engaged in lumbering, fishing and game hunting. Population (1971) 3000.

Queen Consort, see CONSORT.

'Queen Elizabeth 2', Cunard liner built for a dual role of cruising in the winter and a passenger service from Southampton to New York in the summer. She was launched in September 1967, entering service in January 1969. Gross tonnage 65,000, length 294 m, beam 32 m, speed $28\frac{1}{2}$ knots (53 km/h), she can carry 2025 passengers.

Queen Elizabeth Islands, group of islands in the Canadian Arctic archipelago lying north of Lancaster and Viscount Melville Sounds. They include Ellesmere, Devon, Melville, Axel, Heiberg, Bathurst, Cornwallis, Prince Patrick and the Ringnes Islands. They were named in 1954 in honour of Queen Elizabeth II. There are virtually no indigenous inhabitants, but meteorological stations and Royal Canadian Mounted Police posts have been established in the area.

Queen-of-the-Meadows, see MEADOW SWEET.

Queens, borough of New York city, covering an area of 280 km². It was constituted in 1898, and the population in 1980 was 1,891,325. It includes the former towns of Jamaica, Flushing and Long Island City. Queens is connected with Manhattan by a web of bridges and tunnels; it has New York's municipal airports, including La Guardia and Kennedy. Its industries are concentrated in Long Island City. It has huge railroad yards, express terminals and shipping facilities, as well as many residential areas (Jackson Heights and Forest Hills).

Queen's Award, a British award to individual firms for achievement in technology or exports. It was instituted in 1965.

Queen's Bench Division, one of the three divisions of the High Court of Justice in England and Wales, the other two being the Chancery Division and the Family Division. Theoretically all the divisions have jurisdiction in all matters both of common law and equity; but in practice the Queen's Bench Division deals principally with common law actions for damages for breach of contract or commission of a tort, actions for recovery of land or goods, applications for orders of *certiorari* and *mandamus*, election petitions, and cases relating to the registration of electors. The lord chief justice of England is the head of the Queen's Bench Division.

Queen's Counsel, or King's Counsel. QCs are those barristers of the English Bar who wear silk gowns and sit 'within the Bar'; hence colloquially called 'silks' or 'leaders'. They take precedence over and 'lead' juniors, i.e. all who wear stuff gowns and sit outside the Bar.

Queen's Country, see LAOIS.

Queen's Evidence, or King's Evidence. In English law, when one of several persons jointly charged with a crime gives evidence so as to secure the conviction of his accomplices, such evidence is called queen's evidence.

Queen's Printers are the holders of the patent for printing the Bible and the Book of Common Prayer. The first holder of an English Bible patent was Richard Grafton. Since 1769 the patent has been continuously held by the Eyre family, of Eyre & Spottiswoode. In England the University Presses of Oxford and Cambridge enjoy the privilege of freedom to print the Bible and the Book of Common Prayer. There is a separate patent for Scotland.

Queen's Proctor, in England and Wales, represents the Crown in admiralty and matrimonial causes. The Treasury solicitor holds the office at the present day, and is generally a barrister. He intervenes to stop decrees *nisi* in divorce being made absolute on the ground that all the material facts have not been before the court or where he detects collusion, or at any stage of divorce proceedings where it would be against morality to dissolve the marriage tie.

Queensberry, Earls and Marquesses of, Scottish titles, borne by the Douglas family. Sir William Douglas of Drumlanrig, Dumfriesshire, was created 1st Earl of Queensberry in 1633 by Charles I. The 3rd Earl, whose name also was William, was important in the history of Scotland during the latter half of the 17th century. In 1680 he was lord chief justice of Scotland. His son joined William of Orange, and ultimately became the keeper of the privy seal. After the Union he was practically the director of all Scottish affairs. His son married a daughter of the Earl of Clarendon; but with his decease the British title became extinct, and the dukedom of Queensberry passed to his cousin William, Earl of March. He became known as 'Old Q' and was a well-known character of the latter end of the 18th century. He died without legitimate issue, and Sir Charles Douglas became marquess of Queensberry.

Queensberry, John Sholto Douglas, 8th Marquess of (1844–1900), British patron of prize-fights, and famous for having given his name to the Marquess of Queensberry rules which were introduced in 1867 and had a direct effect on modern boxing.

Queensberry Rules, see BOXING.

Queensland, north-eastern state of the Commonwealth of Australia. It includes the adjacent islands in the Pacific Ocean and in the Gulf of Carpentaria. It is the second largest

***Queensland.** The Glasshouse Mountains, situated outside Brisbane.*

state of the Australian Commonwealth, with an area of 1,727,200 km². The coastline, which is about 2250 m in length, is bordered by the Barrier Reef.

The country is fairly flat to the west of the main Dividing Range, which is a coastal range of old rocks which runs from New South Wales to Cape Melville, a continuation of the Australian Alps of Victoria and the Blue Mountains of New South Wales; the highest peaks are Bartle Frere (1582 m) and Bellenden Ker (1591 m). To the north of Cape Melville the coastal range yields to a flat ridge capped with sandstone, which runs through Cape York peninsula and gradually declines in elevation until it reaches Cape York. The great western plain extends from the coastal range to the South Australian border, and from New South Wales to the Gulf of Carpentaria. The main drainage systems are the Brisbane, Burdekin, Mackenzie, Dawson, Isaac and Burnett rivers, and the intermittent Norman, Flinders, Mitchell, Leichhardt, Diamantina, Barcoo and Warrego rivers.

The capital is Brisbane, population (1980) 1,028,900. Other main cities are Toowoomba, Rockhampton, Townsville, Cairns, Bundaberg, Mackay, Ipswich and Maryborough. The population of Queensland in 1980 was 2,247,800.

The major cultivated areas are on the coastal plains and valleys of the east coast where there is high rainfall and temperatures. Some 95 per cent of the total Australian sugar-cane crop is grown in small fragmented areas of these coastal plains. About half the cultivated area of Queensland is under grains, the most important of which are wheat and grain sorghum. The major grain area is the Darling Downs. Other crops include oats, peanuts, sunflower, soyabeans, maize, hay crops and fruit (notably bananas and pineapples).

The coastal plains and valleys are grazed by dairy cattle, and beef cattle are raised in the drier inland areas and fattened on the rich coastal pastures. Sheep are mainly concentrated in the dry central regions of the state. The industries are mainly connected with the processing of primary produce, such as sugar-cane, wheat, fruit or milk, although general and electrical engineering and textile manufacture are increasing in importance. Shipbuilding is long-established at Brisbane and alumina refining at Gladstone.

In Queensland, as in all parts of Australia, the most spectacular economic development in the last 10 years has been in mining. Mount Isa is one of the older mining centres where lead, zinc, silver and copper are mined. Another old mining centre, Mount Morgan, produces copper and gold. Uranium has been mined at Mary Kathleen since 1954, but production has fluctuated considerably.

Newer mineral developments include bauxite, black coal, nickel, oil and natural gas. Legislation is vested in a parliament of one house, the Legislative Assembly, which comprises 82 members, returned for three years. There is a governor and lieutenant-governor, with an executive council of ministers.

Queensland was visited by Captain Cook in 1770, but little was known of the country until 1823, when Surveyor-General Oxley discovered the River Brisbane. The first settlement (penal) was at Moreton Bay in 1824, but in 1842 it was finally broken up, and from that year free settlers were admitted to the country, since when progress has been remarkably rapid. Pastoral occupation of the Darling Downs began in 1840. The progress made by settlers led to a separatist movement, and the north-eastern part of the colony of New South Wales (as it then was) was created a separate colony with the name of Queensland by letters patent of 8 June 1859.

Queenstown, see COBH.

Queirós, José Maria Eça de (1845–1900), Portuguese author. In 1875 he published his first important novel, *O Crime do Padre Amaro*, a scandalous story of the sexual exploits of a priest which was put on the Index by the Catholic Church. *O Primo Basílio*, 1878, which was similarly a tale of adultery by a middle-class lady, caused a sensation, and was followed by *Os Maias*, 1888, again a fine and detailed analysis of middle-class life, full of characteristically sharp satire of contemporary morals. Its author had by now won the designation the 'Portuguese Zola', but his other novels turn away from strictly contemporary affairs.

Queirós was of aristocratic and aloof temperament, disgusted by the backward manners and taste of his country. His polished style and sharp satire have won him a reputation as Portugal's greatest novelist.

Quenching, see CHILL HARDENING.

Queneau, Raymond (1903–76), French writer, born at Le Havre. His works include the poems *Chêne et chien* (described as a 'roman en vers'), 1937; *Les Ziaux*, 1943; and *L'Instant fatal*, 1946, three volumes which were gathered together with additional poems under the title *Si tu t'imagines* in 1952. A volume of 'nouvelles', *Une Trouille verte*, appeared in 1947, and a brilliant volume of pastiches, *Exercices de style* (the same episode recounted in 99 different styles), in 1947.

Among Queneau's novels are *Le Chien-dent*, 1933; *Les Derniers jours*, 1935; *Odile*, 1937; *Les Enfants du limon*, 1938; *Rude hiver*, 1939; *Pierrot mon ami*, 1942; *Loin de Rueil*, 1944; *Bucoliques*, 1947; *Saint Glinglin*, 1948; *Le Dimanche de la vie*, 1952; and *Zazie dans le métro*, 1959. He also wrote film scenarios and made translations from English.

Quercia, Jacopo della, see DELLA QUERCIA, JACOPO.

Quercus, see OAK.

Querétaro, capital of Querétaro state in Mexico. In 1810 the movement for Mexican independence was launched here, and it was here that the Emperor Maximilian was executed on the Cerro de las Campanas. Querétaro is important as an agricultural centre and as a centre of communications; its main industries are cotton textile manufacturing and potteries. Population (1975) 150,000.

Quern (Old English *cweorn*), hand-mill, used before the invention of water-mills or windmills for grinding corn. The usual kind consisted of two circular stones, the upper being pierced by a hole in the centre and revolving on a wooden or metal pin inserted in the lower. The grain was dropped into the opening, and the upper stone revolved by a stick in a hole near the edge.

Quesnay, François (1694–1774), French economist and physician. He devoted himself to economic studies, and founded the sect of the 'Économistes'. Quesnay is sometimes described as the first modern economist.

Quesnel, Pasquier (1634–1719), French Jansenist theologian; joined the French Oratory (1657). His edition of the works of Leo the Great (1675) was condemned for

Gallicanism, and placed on the Index (1676). Quesnel was banished from Paris for his Jansenist views (1681), and having refused to subscribe to a decree condemning Jansenism (1684), fled to Brussels, where Arnauld befriended him. The Jesuits, always hostile, had him imprisoned (1703), but he escaped to Amsterdam, to found the still-existing Jansenist congregation. His *Nouveau Testament avec les réflexions morales*, 1693–94, was condemned by the bull *Unigenitus*, 1713. His *Lettres* were edited by Le Courayer, 1721–23.

Quetta (Pashto *Kamatan*, fort), town of Pakistan, lying at a height of 1525 m, 35 km north-west of the Bolan Pass. It is the chief town of Baluchistan, and is the site of a staff college. The railway branches from here to Chaman on the Afghan frontier and from Sibi through Quetta to the Persian frontier at Bostan. Quetta is a great centre for fruit growing, and also trades in wood, carpets and leather. Population (1972) 159,000.

Quetzal, or resplendent trogon, a beautiful, long-tailed tropical American bird, *Pharomachrus mocinno*, of the order Trogoniformes. The colouring of the male is: belly bright red, head and breast golden green, back blue, and tail white underneath. It has a train of blue-green plumes (tail coverts) that hang far beyond the true tail feathers. There is a crest on the head and decorative drooping feathers on the wings. Including its tail, the male quetzal is about 1·3 m long. The female is much smaller and lacks the long tail and decorative plumes. Its diet is mostly fruit. It is the national emblem of Guatemala, and was considered sacred by the Aztecs and Mayas.

Quetzalcoatl (from *quetzalli*, green feather, and *cohuatl*, snake), hero-god of the ancient Mexicans. He is sometimes represented as one of the four chief Mexican gods, controller of the air and winds, who assisted in the creation of man; but more frequently as a man with supernatural attributes who tried to abolish human sacrifice. In a Toltec legend Quetzalcoatl was a fair-skinned man who disappeared across the sea, promising to return.

Queuille, Henri (1884–1970), French statesman. He held office several times from 1933 onwards, and in 1940 was minister of finance. After the collapse of France he crossed to England and joined de Gaulle. With the acute domestic crisis of mid-1948, when the political situation demanded a premier of middle-class liberal outlook, Queuille became premier; he remained in office until October 1949. Queuille was premier again in July 1950 and in March–August 1951.

Quezon, Manuel Luis (1878–1944), first president of the Philippines. Quezon went to the USA as resident commissioner in Washington to plead for independence. His efforts resulted, in 1916, in the passing of the Jones Act, providing for a measure of autonomy and eventual independence. He then returned to Manila, becoming a senator there. In 1934 he was instrumental in the passage of the Tydings-McDuffie Bill, which increased Filipino powers of self-government and gave a promise of freedom in 1946. In 1935 he was elected the first president of the commonwealth of the Philippines. His second term was inaugurated in an air-raid shelter in December 1941, and in 1942 he left the island for Australia.

Quezon City, city in Rizal province on Luzon. It replaced Manila as the capital of the Philippines in July 1948 and remained so until Manila again became the capital in May 1976. It is situated to the east of the metropolis. Population (1980) 1,165,865.

Quiberon, peninsula, fishing town and seaside resort of the *département* of Morbihan, Brittany, France, opposite Belle Île. The peninsula (an island before the Middle Ages) is united to the mainland by an isthmus defended by Fort Penthièvre. There are sardine and lobster fisheries.

Quicklime, see CALCIUM.

Quicksand, bed or mass of loose, moving sand, saturated with water to such an extent that it readily yields to pressure, cannot support the weight of people or animals, and so is able to engulf them.

Quicksilver, see MERCURY.

Quid Pro Quo, in English law, the giving of one thing for another; or the mutual consideration and performance of both parties to a contract.

Quietism, a form of mysticism which has shown itself at different times in the Christian Church. The fundamental tenet of Quietism is that the final state of union with God is reached when the soul is in a state of perfect inaction, and that in this union the soul is passive under the action of the Divine Light.

***Quetzalcoatl.** An effigy of the snake-headed god on the steps of the Temple of Warriors.*

Quiller-Couch, Sir Arthur Thomas (1863–1944), English writer and critic. While at university he published, in 1887, *Dead Man's Rock*, which was a considerable success, and enabled him to begin a literary career. This 'thriller' owed much to the influence of R. L. Stevenson, whose unfinished *St Ives* Quiller-Couch completed about this time. He left Oxford in 1887, having lectured in classics at Trinity for a year. After four years' literary work in London he settled in Cornwall.

His prominence as a critic dates from the publication of his *Oxford Book of English Verse*, 1900, which established him for many years as an arbiter of poetic taste and judgment. In his early days he wrote under the pseudonym of 'Q'. He was knighted in 1910, and in 1912 he was appointed King Edward VII Professor of English Literature at the University of Cambridge. He was general editor of the Kings Treasuries of Literature (258 volumes), begun in 1920, and edited with J. D. Wilson the comedies in the New Cambridge edition of Shakespeare.

Quilter, Roger (1877–1953), British composer. His works include a light opera, incidental music for Shakespeare's *As You Like It*, the *Children's Overture* on nursery tunes, the song-cycle *To Julia* (Herrick), and about 100 songs to words by Shakespeare, Herrick, Blake, Tennyson and others.

Quilting, see EMBROIDERY.

Quimper, French town, capital of the *département* of Finistère, situated about 58 km south-east of Brest on the River Odet. Its cathedral, dating from the 13th century, is a beautiful example of Gothic architecture. Quimper manufactures pottery, jams, biscuits, and electrical goods and is the commercial focus for south Finistère. Population (1975) 60,510.

Quince, *Cydonia oblonga*, in family Rosaceae; a small tree native to Central Asia and grown for its ornamental beauty and fruit, which is valued for the making of jellies and preserves. Quince is also valued as a dwarfing stock for pears. The Japanese quince belongs to the related genus *Chaenomeles*.

Quincey, Thomas de, see DE QUINCEY, THOMAS.

Quincy, city of Norfolk county, Massachusetts, USA, on Quincy Bay, 13 km south of Boston, noted for its granite quarries. It has historical interest and was the birthplace of John Hancock, John Adams and John Quincy Adams. The first (horse-drawn) railroad in the USA was built here to haul granite. Population (1980) 84,743.

Quine, Willard Van Orman (1908–), US philosopher, professor at Harvard, a leading figure in modern logic and a critic of Positivist epistemology. His work in logic is a refinement of the Russell-Whitehead attempt to reduce mathematics to logic. At the same time Quine holds that in adopting a given system of logic we have to assume that certain entities exist. His view is that the kinds of things that must be assumed will depend on the kinds of variables that occur in statements. He rejects the sharp distinction between analytic and synthetic statements, since no adequate criteria for the former being necessary seem to be discoverable.

Quinine, the chief alkaloid, found in the bark of various species of *Cinchona* from which it is obtained by mixing the bark with milk of lime, treating with boiling alcohol, and extracting the alkaloid in the form of the sulphate by adding dilute sulphuric acid. The sulphate, which is the form most generally met with, is soluble in large amounts of cold water, but is more readily soluble in hot water and in alcohol. It kills the malarial parasite in human blood and prevents development of the parasite in the red blood cells. However, its use in the prophylaxis and treatment of malaria has been superseded by the development of new, less toxic drugs and it is now reserved for chloroquine-resistant malarial cases. Dilute solutions are used, for their bitter taste, in tonic waters and aperitifs.

Quinones, a group of chemical compounds containing one or more six-carbon rings which include two C = O groups. The simplest member of this class of organic compounds, benzoquinone ($C_6H_4O_2$), is obtained by oxidising aniline with potassium dichromate and sulphuric acid. It is a yellow crystalline solid, melting at 116 °C, has an irritating smell, is volatile in steam, and dissolves sparingly in water but readily in alcohol and ether. Many other quinones can be obtained by the oxidation of certain hydroxy- and amino-compounds with chromic acid. Anthraquinone, $C_{14}H_8O_2$, is important as the source of many dyestuffs. Benzoquinone yields quinol when reduced. Quinones form many natural pigments in plants, and are used in dyes and indicators. Vitamin K is a quinone.

Quinquagesima (Latin, fiftieth), the Sunday before Ash Wednesday. Counting roughly, this Sunday is 50 days before Easter.

Quinsy, see TONSILITIS.

Quintet, a musical composition for varied forces, for example the clarinet quintet of Mozart (for clarinet and string quartet), the string quintet of Schubert (with a second cello added to the basic string quartet), the piano quintet of Schumann (with piano added to the basic strings), and the piano and wind quintet of Mozart (for piano, clarinet, oboe, horn and bassoon). It can also refer to a vocal piece, usually an ensemble in an opera such as the famous quintet in Wagner's *Meistersinger*.
See also CHAMBER MUSIC.

Quintilian, Marcus Fabius Quintilianus (c.AD 40–c.100), Latin critic and rhetorician, born at Calagurris, Spain; educated at Rome, which he left early in Nero's reign. Returning with Galba in 68, he quickly achieved fame and wealth as a teacher, and in 88, or soon afterwards, was entrusted with the education of Domitian's grand-nephew.
His principal and sole surviving work is the famous *Institutio Oratoria*, an exhaustive treatise on the education of an orator. His style is good, his taste impeccable, while his moral tone is in striking contrast with the general degradation of his age.

Quintuple Treaty (1839), celebrated 'scrap of paper', the breach of which was the immediate cause of the entry of Britain into the First World War. It was by this treaty that the neutrality of Belgium was guaranteed by the Great Powers. The king of the Netherlands agreed with the five powers (Austria, France, Britain, Prussia and Russia) to recognise the existence of Belgium as 'an independent and perpetually neutral state'. Its violation by Germany in 1914 was not seriously defended by the German government.
See also BELGIUM, *History*; NEUTRALITY.

Quirinal, one of the seven hills on which Rome was built, north of the Palatine, and one of the oldest quarters of the city. On it stands the former palace of the kings of Italy, known by the same name.

Quirinus, see ROMULUS.

Quirites, name which the citizens of Rome assumed in their civic capacity. It is connected with Quirinus, an ancient Sabine deity.
See also ROMULUS.

Quiroga, Horacio (1878–1937), Uruguayan writer of short stories. After an early bohemian life in the city, Quiroga attempted to live as a pioneer in Misiones, north Argentina, his work alternating between teaching and absurd business ventures. His perfectly worked stories concern incidents where the moral fibre of the protagonists is tested against superhuman manifestations and an aggressive, hostile tropical nature.
As he progressed out of purely literary themes, as in *Los arrecifes de coral*, 1901, he developed a hard, bony style aimed at revealing the 'softness' of urban culture in *Cuentos de amor, de locura y de muerte*, 1917; *El salvaje*, 1920; and *Los desterrados*, 1926. He was a writer of perfectly carved stories.

Quisling, Vidkun Abraham Lauritz (1887–1945), Norwegian politician. He entered politics in 1929, and maintained a strong anti-communist position. He became defence minister in 1931, later founding a fascist party, the Nasjonal Samling. His actions during the Second World War made his name a synonym for a traitor. He proclaimed himself prime minister after the German invasion in 1940, but the Germans dismissed him. However, in 1942 Quisling was appointed 'minister-president' of a puppet, German-controlled government. After the war Quisling was found guilty of treason and excuted.
See also NORWAY, *History*.

Quito, capital of the province of Pichincha, and of Ecuador, situated 270 km north-east of Guayaquil. At nearly 3000 m above sea-level, it has a temperate climate though close to the equator. The city was originally the capital of the Incas, established on the site of an old Indian village on the slopes of the volcano Pichincha. The volcano is no longer active, and on its lower slopes are small farms devoted chiefly to growing grain and potatoes. The manufactures include shoes, woollen and cotton materials, saddles, blankets, carpets and food products. Several light engineering works have been set up. Although it is the capital, Quito is neither so large nor so important as Guayaquil. Population (1974) 559,000.

Qum, see QOM.

'Quo Vadis?', see SIENKIEWICZ, HENRYK.

Quoin, external angle of a building. In Renaissance architecture, quoins are often emphasised by rustication.
See also MASONRY.

Quota, the quantities of permitted imports, or the quantity of output agreed by arrangement between firms, or the amount of each member's contribution to the International Monetary Fund, which determines its drawing rights.

Quotidian Fever, see MALARIA.

Quraish, name of the tribe to which the Prophet Mohammed belonged. Although it does not appear to be of great antiquity, it was very prominent in pre-Islamic Arabia as the guardian of the Kaaba at Mecca, which was a place of pilgrimage for all Arabs and consequently a source of wealth to the Quraish.

Quran, see KORAN, THE.

R

R, eighteenth letter of the English alphabet. The earliest form of *r* was the North Semitic 4; the Latin and English *r* is derived from the Greek. In the ancient languages *r* was rolled; in modern European languages pronunciation varies considerably. The typical English *r* is much weaker than the articulated French sound. In most American English and in many regional British accents, /r/ is pronounced wherever *r* is written; in other accents and in Received Pronunciation no /r/ is now pronounced where the following sound is not a vowel, for example, *farm, court*.
See also ALPHABET.

Ra, Egyptian sun god, worshipped at Heliopolis as the solar disc itself. Ra was believed to travel across the sky daily in a boat, returning nightly through the underworld to the east in another boat. By the 4th Dynasty the king, who had been identified with Horus, was declared to be 'son of Ra', which became one of the royal titles, Ra becoming the supreme deity. In Heliopolitan theology Ra was assimilated with Atum, and in the New Kingdom with Ammon, being eventually replaced completely by Osiris.

Raab, see GYÖR.

Raasay, island of Highland Region, Scotland. It is 20 km long by 3 km wide. Crofting, farming and forestry are the main occupations. Population 163.

Rab, Yugoslav island in the Adriatic Sea, off the north coast of Dalmatia. The capital, also called Rab, has a Venetian palace and a 15th-century cathedral. It has a growing tourist industry, and produces wine, fruit and silk. Area 155 km^2; population 8000.

Rabat, city and one of the four capitals of Morocco, on the west coast opposite Salé, which serves as the port of Fez, 280 km to the east. Most of Morocco's government buildings are in Rabat. Textiles, asbestos, carpets and pottery are manufactured; other exports include skins, wax, cork, slippers and beans. Population (1971) 367,620.

Rabat, town of west Malta, stretching along the spur from the fortified walls of Mdina. It covers much of the site of the Roman city and has various relics of the Roman period. There are extensive early Christian catacombs under the town in which the dead of all periods have been buried, and there are troglodyte dwellings and cave churches. Rabat is in a rich agricultural region producing pigs, goats, wheat and vines. Population 13,000.

Rabaul, chief port of the island of New Britain, Papua New Guinea. The harbour may once have been a great volcanic crater which became broken at one side, and consequently is connected with Blanche Bay. Rabaul was established in 1910 as the capital of German New Guinea. Commercial activities centre on the harbour which exports copra and cocoa. Population (1979) 32,000.

Rabbi (Hebrew, my master), title given to recognised teachers of the law among the Jews. After the destruction of the Temple, and the rise of the rabbinic schools, it finally became extended to all those authorised to decide legal and ritualistic problems. Rabbi is now the title of the Jewish spiritual leaders, generally given by established rabbinical seminaries.

Rabbit, herbivorous mammals of the family Leporidae of order Lagomorpha. The rabbit has, by its extreme fecundity, its great adaptability, and the decrease in its natural enemies, spread rapidly and widely in temperate zones of the world. The wild rabbit resembles the hare, but is smaller, with shorter head, ears, hind legs and feet, is greyer in colour, and lacks black tips to the ears. Both the rabbit and the hare belong to the family Leporidae, but to separate genera. The most common rabbits are in the genera *Oryctolagus* (the Old World rabbit) and *Sylvilagus* (the cottontails). They are gregarious and polygamous, burrowing extensively in the soil. They start to breed at about six months. There are 4–8 litters in the year with 3–9 young per litter.

The rabbit ranks second only to the rat as an agricultural pest. Destruction is a legal obligation. The spread of the virus disease myxomatosis caused severe reduction of the population for a while. Under domestication rabbits may be kept as pets or bred for exhibition, fur, or for meat. Domestic rabbits are larger than wild ones, more variable in colour and in features, such as pendent or lop ears, and length of coat.

Rabelais, François (c.1494–c.1553), French satirist and humorist, author of *Gargantua and Pantagruel*. He was trained for the religious life by the Franciscans but in 1524 was licensed to be transferred to the Benedictines, and in 1530 gave up the regular for the secular priesthood. In 1531 he studied medicine at Montpellier, and later at Lyons, where he edited works of Hippocrates and Galen.

In 1532 or 1533 there appeared, under the pseudonym Alcofribas Nasier (an anagram of François Rabelais), his *Pantagruel*, the second of the five books of his great work. The first book, *Gargantua*, appeared in 1534, the *Third Book* in 1546, and the *Fourth Book* partly in 1548 and in full in 1552. In 1562, nine years after Rabelais's death, came a *Fifth Book* (with additions in 1564); its authenticity has been questioned, though it is now generally regarded as in essence by Rabelais, but possibly edited and revised by another.

The exuberant humour and rich epic life of his tales have a deeper than surface meaning. But today, as in the past, the inner meaning is variously interpreted.

Rabies, or hydrophobia (fear of water), a fatal disease in animals caused by a virus. It is transmitted to humans by the bite of an infected animal, usually a dog, fox or wolf. In the USA skunks act as the principal host, in Africa and India it is the mongoose, while vampire bats are the main vectors in South America.

The incubation period is from two weeks to eight months. The virus lodges in the central nervous system, and the disease is characterised by violent muscular spasms, similar to the symptoms of tetanus and affecting mainly the neck muscles. The spasms are increased by drinking, or even the sight of, water, hence the name hydrophobia.

Development of a rabies vaccine by Pasteur has led to a marked reduction in the mortality of the disease. The vaccine, however, does not produce an antibody response in the patient's blood before 14 days. In recent years a powerful hyperimmune serum has been developed which has the advantage of producing an immediate passive type of immunity in the recipient and thus an immediate high level of resistance to the infection.

Rabin, Yitzhak (1922–), Israeli army officer and politician. He rose to be chief-of-staff during the overwhelming Israeli victory over the Arabs in 1967. He returned from being ambassador in Washington, 1968–72, to become, in 1974, Israel's first native-born prime minister. He began his ministry during the unsettled time after the 1973 war, and resigned in 1977, to be succeeded by Shimon Peres.

Raccoon, *Procyon*, a genus of animals in the family Mustelidae of order Carnivora. The common raccoon (*P. lotor*) ranges over the greater part of the USA. It spends the day in hollow trees, leaving them at nightfall to hunt for food, which consists largely of young birds, small animals and also molluscs and other aquatic creatures. It will also eat fruits and berries. It is an excellent swimmer. The fur is brown in colour, and is long and thick, and consequently valuable. The tail is long, bushy, and is ringed with black and white. The crab-eating raccoon (*P. cancrivorus*) ranges from Panama throughout a large part of the South American continent.

Race. All the many different kinds of living man belong to a single species, *Homo sapiens*. The races of man are less different from each other than are subspecies of many other animals. There is no universally recognised classification of the subdivisions of man. Human variants do not fall neatly into groups but grade into one another. Human races constitute localised gene pools which are interconnecting, and it is therefore impossible to draw sharp boundaries between them.

One very general classification of the races is given below. Mankind is divided into three main races:

Caucasoid. Consists of Mediterranean, Nordic, Alpine, Dinaric, Armenoid, and east Baltic races, all of Europe. The east Indians of India and the Polynesians of the Pacific are often included in this category. Within this division is the subdivision of the *Australoids*, *Archaics*, or *Proto-Caucasoids*, including four interesting and probably related groups: the Australian Aborigines, the Veddahs of Ceylon, the Pre-Dravidians of southern India, and the Ainu of northern Japan.

Negroid. Consists of the African Negroes (the True Negroes of West Africa, the Forest Negroes of West-Central Africa, the Nilotic Negroes and Half-Hamites of East Africa, the Bantu-speaking Negroes of Central and South Africa); the Oceanic Negroes of Papua and Melanesia; and the Pygmies (the Negrillos of Africa and the Negritos of the Andaman Islands, Malaya and the Philippines). Sometimes the Bushmen-Hottentots of the Kalahari Desert are included here, although they are not Negroes but representatives of an archaic stock.

Mongoloid. Consists of the Palaeoasiatics (the older populations of Siberia, the Eskimo, and the Indians of the Americas) and the Neoasiatics (Chinese, Koreans, Japanese, Tungus, the Samoyeds and Lapps, and the Indonesian-Malays of Indonesia, Malaysia and Madagascar).

Race Meetings, see GREYHOUND RACING; HORSE RACING.

Racehorse, see HORSE; HORSE RACING.

Rachel, younger daughter of Laban, sister of Leah, and favourite wife of Jacob. Jacob was tricked by Laban into marrying Leah to avoid the younger sister's marrying before the elder. Rachel was also given him on condition of service. Rachel for long remained childless, but at length bore Joseph. The two sisters stood by Jacob in his dispute with Laban and fled with him, Rachel carrying off her father's teraphim (images). On their way from Bethel to Hebron Rachel died giving birth to Benjamin.

Rachel, Elisa (1820–58), pseudonym adopted by Elizabeth Félix, French tragic actress of Jewish descent. At the age of nine she was singing in the streets of Paris, where she came to the notice of Choron, founder of the conservatoire, who took her as a pupil. In 1837 she made her début in *La Vendéenne*. Her two greatest triumphs were achieved in Racine's *Phèdre* and Scribe and Legouvé's *Adrienne Lecouvreur*.

Rachmaninov, Sergei Vassilievich (1873–1943), Russian composer, pianist and conductor. The failure of his first symphony in St Petersburg depressed him; but in London in 1899 he played and conducted his own music with success. He returned to Moscow and wrote his second piano concerto, the op. 23 preludes and some songs. He conducted at the Bolshoi (1904–06), and then spent two years in Dresden, where he composed his second symphony, the first piano sonata, the symphonic poem *The Isle of the Dead*, and the third piano concerto. After the Russian Revolution, 1917, he settled in the USA where he worked as a pianist and conductor. He also wrote a third symphony, a fourth piano concerto, the *Rhapsody on a Theme of Paganini*, two more operas, choral works, piano pieces and songs. As a pianist Rachmaninov stood in the very first rank.

Racine, Jean (1639–99), French dramatist. His first play, the tragedy of *La Thébaïde, ou les frères ennemis*, was acted by Molière's company at the Palais Royal in 1664 with some success. His second, *Alexandre le Grand*, 1665, was produced by the same company, but later given to the rival actors at the Hôtel de Bourgogne, thus leading to a rupture with Molière. His peculiar genius was revealed in *Andromaque*, 1667; this was followed by the successful comedy *Les Plaideurs*, 1668, and the tragedies *Britannicus*, 1669; *Bérénice*, 1670; *Bajazet*, 1672; *Mithridate*, 1673; *Iphigenie*, 1674; and *Phèdre*, 1677. He then abandoned the stage, but returned with two plays on Old Testament themes, *Esther*, 1689, and *Athalie*, 1691. Racine's art represents the supreme achievement of classical tragedy. The tragic situation is always based on a psychological crisis, and his insight into the human heart often foreshadows modern psychology. Although Racine portrays many passions, such as hate, ambition, pride, the tragedy generally revolves round a passionate love. His artistry was consummate; he was a master of the classical alexandrine, and he was unequalled in his dramatic effects and in the variety and purity of his language.

Rack, instrument of torture, consisting of an oblong frame of wood slightly raised from the ground. At one end was a fixed bar and at the other a movable one (sometimes both were movable). The bar was extended by a windlass until the victim's joints were dislocated, or he died, or answered the questions of his torturers.

Racket, woodwind instrument played with a double reed. Its appearance gave rise to the name sausage bassoon. The racket is used in early music groups.

Rackets a racket-and-ball game for two or four players played in a similar manner to its derivative, squash, but with a harder ball and on a court three times the size.
See also SQUASH RACKETS.

Rackham, Arthur (1867–1939), British water-colour painter and illustrator. In his twenties he drew illustrations for *Pall Mall Budget* and *Graphic*. He developed a delicate style, now appreciated as an aspect of Art Nouveau. He illustrated editions of many famous children's books and adult classics.

Racoon, see RACCOON.

Racquets, see RACKETS.

Rad, the unit of measurement of the absorbed dosage of radiation. It is an acronym for **R**adiation **A**bsorbed **D**ose. One rad is equal to 0.01 joule per kg of irradiated material (100 ergs per g).

Radach, Radak, or Ralik, see MARSHALL ISLANDS.

Radar, term derived from 'radio detection and ranging'. Techniques whereby distant objects are detected, and their directions and ranges measured, by means of radio waves sent out and reflected back by the object to the source.

Principles of Radar. A transmitter sends out a short pulse of waves, usually in a certain direction. If the pulse impinges on and is reflected from an object and the reflected pulse is received, say, 2 μs after emission, the object must be 300 m away, since the velocity of radio waves is 3×10^8 m/s, or 300 m in 1 μs. In practise, a continued series of pulses is emitted at intervals so timed that a reflected pulse can be recorded before the next pulse is sent out. To get sharp definition of an object, a narrow beam of high power is required. With an aerial of moderate size, this can be attained only at high frequency. Further, a short duration of pulse of well defined shape is desirable. The interval between pulses is determined by the maximum range. As seen in the above example, the minimum interval for 300 m range is 2 μs. The aerial must be directive, and is usually capable of being pointed in various directions. The paraboloid or parabolic-cylindrical type is often used, and scanning (pointing) is achieved by mechanical motion of the aerial. Spiral scanning covers a solid angle of space round a fixed direction; rotation round a vertical axis combined with a vertical rocking motion explores a cylinder round the aerial. Simple rotation round a vertical axis is used on aircraft and ships as an aid to navigation. Radars in military aircraft now have flat-plate aerials, some of which are scanned not by moving the aerial but by electronically phasing pulses from different parts of the aerial to bend the beam in different directions. For frequencies up to 600 MHz the transmitter is a valve or transistor oscillator with resonant transmission line as oscillatory circuit; for higher frequencies, the magnetron is used. The receiver is a super-heterodyne valve or transistor receiver. The signal is usually presented on the screen of a cathode-ray tube. A trigger switch automatically separates the transmitter from the aerial at the termination of a pulse and isolates the receiver during pulse times.

Radcliffe, Ann (1764–1823), English novelist. In 1787 she married William Radcliffe, editor and proprietor of a weekly newspaper. She published her first book, *The Castles of Athlin and Dunbayne*, in 1789, and it deservedly attracted little attention. Her next story, *A Sicilian Romance*, 1790, was much better. This was followed by *The Romance of the Forest*, 1791; the more celebrated *Mysteries of Udolpho*, 1794; and *The Italian*, 1797. She excelled in depicting scenes of mystery and terror, and is one of the most distinguished of the gothic novelists.

Radcliffe, John (1650–1714), English physician. He bequeathed funds which provided for the building of the Radcliffe Observatory and Infirmary, Oxford, for the enlarging of St Bartholomew's Hospital, London, and for travelling fellowships in medicine. The Radcliffe Camera, the reading-room of the Bodleian Library, bears his name.

Radcliffe-Brown, Alfred Reginald (1881–1955), British anthropologist. Influenced by Durkheim. He rejected evolutionist and diffusionist theories as 'conjectural history', viewing anthropology as a natural science, i.e. a comparative science. His works include *The Andaman Islanders*, 1922, and *Structure and Function in Primitive Society*, 1952.

Radcliffe Committee, set up under the chairmanship of Lord Radcliffe to inquire into the working of the British monetary system in 1957. Its report, *Committee on the Working of the Monetary System* (Cmnd 827) was published in 1959. It recommended changes in the financial control of the economy following on its main conclusion that monetary control by changes in bank-rate was only partially effective.
See also BANKS AND BANKING; INFLATION AND DEFLATION; MONETARY POLICY; MONEY.

Radetzky, Josef Wenzel, Count von (1766–1858), Austrian soldier. He served throughout the Turkish and revolutionary wars. From 1831 he commanded the Austrian army in Italy and his fame rests on his masterly defence of the Quadrilateral, and his subsequent crushing victories at Custozza and Novara over Charles Albert, King of Sardinia, during 1848–49. These successes, which saved Austria from collapse, were commemorated by the famous Radetzky march by Johann Strauss the Elder.

Radhakrishnan, Sir Sarvepalli (1888–1975), Indian philosopher and educationist, President of the Republic of India, 1962–67. Radhakrishnan was leader of the Indian delegation to UNESCO (1946–52) and chairman of the executive board (1948–49). He was elected Vice-President of India in 1950, and on the death in 1962 of Rajendra Pradad was elected President. In his writings he sought to explain Indian thought to the West.

Radial Artery, the artery felt on the thumb side of the wrist and used most often for examining the pulse. It runs into the palm of the hand and joins a branch of the ulnar artery, forming an anastomosis.

Radial Velocity, the line-of-sight velocity of a celestial object usually found by measuring the Doppler shift of its spectral lines. The first such measure was made on Sirius by Huggins in 1867. If a line of wavelength λ is shifted by $\Delta\lambda$ the radial velocity is $(\Delta\lambda/\lambda)c$, where c is the velocity of light, the shift being towards the blue if the object is approaching, to the red if receding. The velocity given in catalogues is this measured velocity 'corrected to the Sun' by removing the effect of the Earth's

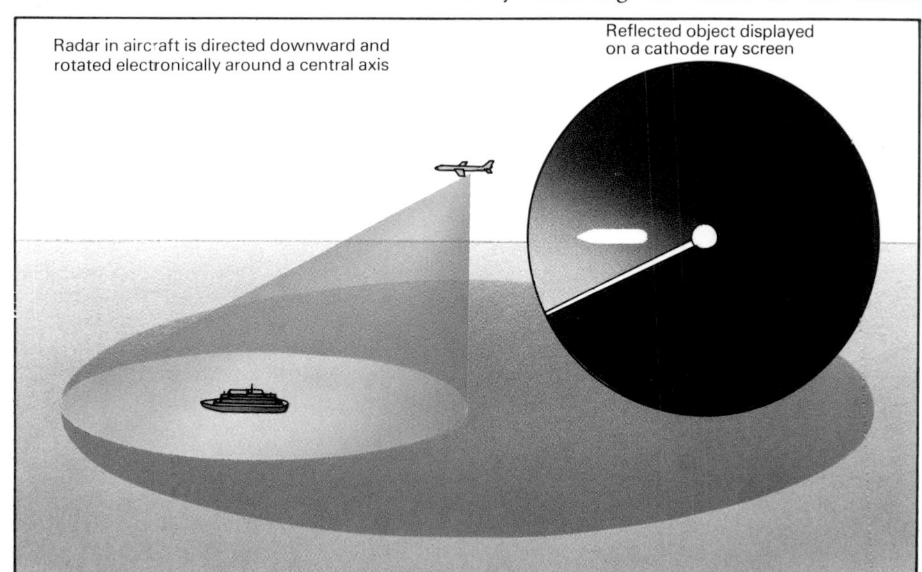

Radar. *Radio waves are reflected back by surface features to give an image on a cathode-ray tube.*

orbital motion. Radial velocities of nearby stars rarely exceed a few score $km\,s^{-1}$, but the apparent velocities of recession of distant galaxies are a considerable fraction of the velocity of light. Such very high velocities are referred to as *red shifts*, and measured by a parameter z which is the ratio of the increase of wavelength to the undisplaced value. According to relativity theory the relation between z and v, the velocity of recession producing it, is

$$(1 + z) = \sqrt{[(1 + v/c)/(1 - v/c)]}.$$

The largest quasar red shifts observed are typically $z = 3{\cdot}5$ corresponding to a velocity of recession 91 per cent that of light.
See also GALAXY; QUASAR; RADIO ASTRONOMY; STAR.

Radian, a unit of angle, one of the supplementary SI units. If two radii of a circle mark off on the circumference an arc equal in length to one radius, then the angle between them is 1 radian. One radian = 57.296°, or 57° 17′ 45″.

Radiation, term used principally of electromagnetic waves, i.e. radio, heat, light, ultraviolet, X-rays and gamma radiation. These transmit energy, and do not require a material medium. Their velocity of propagation in a vacuum is $c = 3 \times 10^8$ m/s. The shortest wavelength radiations are gamma rays, especially those occurring as part of cosmic radiation, with wavelengths of the order of 10^{-15} m. Waves from radioactive isotopes have wavelengths of about 10^{-11} to 10^{-10} m, ultraviolet (UV) about 10^{-8} m, and visible light from 4×10^{-7} (violet) to 8×10^{-7} m (red). Studies of radiation emitted by hot bodies led to the quantum theory. Prévost enunciated the Law of Exchanges that recognises that all bodies are continuously losing heat by radiation. Thus a cold object brought into a warm room loses heat by radiation to the room, but absorbs heat radiated from the room at a faster rate, and the net result is that its temperature is raised to that of the room. Even then the exchange still proceeds, but the body now radiates at the same rate as it receives from the room. A black body absorbs radiant heat more readily than a white body or a polished body under identical circumstances. It is black because it absorbs practically all wavelengths that fall on it, just as a white body reflects practically all wavelengths. But in an enclosure with walls impervious to heat, when all temperature differences have disappeared, the net radiations from all bodies are identical and include all wavelengths. Such radiation is known as 'black body' radiation. It is the radiation that would be emitted by a perfectly black body under the same circumstances. Stéfan discovered that the radiation from such an enclosure is directly proportional to the fourth power of its absolute temperature. Later Planck enunciated his quantum theory of radiation.
The term radiation is also sometimes applied to alpha-particles and beta-particles emitted by radioactive isotopes, and to cosmic radiation.
See also SPECTRUM AND SPECTROSCOPE; X-RAYS.

Radical, in politics, term which came into general use as a synonym for 'Liberal', but is capable of application to any politician or political supporter whose political creed involves some root-and-branch reform. The radical proper may be said to have been partly the product of the ideas germinating in Europe from the philosophy of Rousseau after the French Revolution, and partly an inevitable outcome of the growth of industrial society. In recent years the term has again come into use, since radical outlooks have emerged that are no longer identifiable with Liberal, Socialist or Communist policies—for example, the various 'New Left' trends and 'sexual radicals'.

Radical, in mathematics, a symbol $a^{1/n}$, where n is a positive integer, indicating the nth root of a. A radical is said to be in simplified form when a is an integer that has no factors which have integral nth roots. Thus $12^{1/2}$ in simplified form is $2 \times 3^{1/2}$ and $(2/3)^{1/3}$ in simplified form is $2^{1/3}/3^{1/3}$. Sometimes $a^{1/n}$ is represented by the symbol $\sqrt[n]{a}$. $\sqrt[n]{\ }$ is called a radical sign and n is called the index of the radical.
See also SURD.

Radical, in chemistry, a grouping of atoms which occurs as part of a molecule, and is transferred as a whole in a chemical reaction without disintegration, as, for example, the methyl radical (CH_3) in the conversion of methyl alcohol into methyl bromide, $CH_3OH + HBr \rightarrow CH_3Br + H_2O$.

Radiesthesia, the technique of using a pendulum as a dowsing instrument, to discover not only the location of an object, but also various other facts about it, such as its character. The pendulum usually consists of a thread, one end of which is held in the hand, the other ending in a weight, and moves in three ways: parallel backwards and forwards; clockwise in a circle; and anticlockwise in a circle.
The term radiesthesia was first coined by a French researcher, Bouly, following experiments which indicated that the pendulum reacted to radiation from the objects over which it was held.
Currently, radiesthesia is being used in many fields, including the sexing of chickens before they hatch, medical diagnosis, the tracing of missing persons and objects, and mineral prospecting.

Radiguet, Raymond (1903–23), French novelist. He is famous for two novels, *Le Diable au corps*, 1923, and *Le Bal du comte d'Orgel*, 1924, his style being remarkable for its classical restraint and lucidity. He died of typhoid.

Radio, telecommunication by electromagnetic waves travelling through space. In 1873 Clerk Maxwell established the identity of electromagnetic and light waves travelling at 3×10^8 m/s in empty space. In 1888 Hertz succeeded in the experimental demonstration of waves. Marconi invented a magnetic detector and established 'wireless telegraphy' between England and France (1899) and across the Atlantic (1901). Although any oscillating electric circuit emits waves, the radiation is inefficient unless the circuit is similar in size to the wavelength. The wavelength corresponding to a frequency of 50 Hz is 300,000/50 = 6000 km, and to obtain waves of appreciable intensity with circuits of reasonable size, high-frequency oscillations are needed. About 1900, W. O. Richardson was investigating the emission of electrons from hot bodies. This led to the invention by Fleming (1904) of the first thermionic valve to which Lee de Forest added the 'grid' (1907). As the potentialities of the valve as rectifier, detector, amplifier and oscillation generator were realised, the valve replaced earlier apparatus. Transmission of sound became possible by modulation. Sound waves are translated into alternating currents in the microphone, and the output is superimposed on the continuous 'carrier wave', producing a wave train of irregular shape or irregular frequency. This is passed to the aerial and radiated into space. Impinging on any aerial tuned to the correct frequency, the induced oscillations pass to the receiver, where the carrier wave is filtered off and the remainder translated back into sound in the loudspeaker.
Developments in transmitter and receiver design have greatly improved the quality of 'signals' transmitted and have made possible the use of a range of frequencies from 10 kHz to 30,000 MHz, corresponding to wavelengths of 30 km to 1 cm. The longer waves need larger transmitters and carry more power, while short waves are more easily directed, and transmitters are smaller and more efficient. The shortest waves are used in radar, aircraft communication, and short-distance transmission. The waves travel in almost straight lines from a directive aerial. Waves of 10 to 100 m (30 to 3 MHz) are used for long-distance communication.
The development of radiocommunication has stimulated the invention of apparatus that has found further applications in other branches of science. High-frequency generators of microwaves are used in cooking, communications, dielectric heating, localised heat-treatment of metals, and in electrotherapy; amplifiers and rectifiers are used in various instruments, and regulation and control apparatus; and the investigation of the ionosphere has yielded information of value in geophysics.
See also RADIO BEACONS; RADIO WAVES; TELEVISION.

Radio Altimeter, device for determining the height of an aircraft above ground. A transmitter on the aircraft sends out a frequency-modulated wave which is reflected from the ground back to a receiver on the aircraft which also receives the outgoing waves. The latter are at a different stage of modulation; superposition of the two frequencies produces a 'beat note'. The frequency of the beat depends on the time taken for the wave to reach the ground and return. Thus a beat-frequency meter can be graduated to read the height in metres. The frequency used is about 1200 to 1500 MHz, and heights can be measured to accuracies of about 1 m.

Radio Astronomy is the part of astronomy dependent on observations made through the atmospheric 'radio window', i.e. in wavelengths between a few millimetres and 20 m. In the 1940s attention was concentrated on the continuous radiation from the Milky Way, on the Sun, on meteors, and on obtaining echoes from the Moon and other members of the solar system, but interest shifted to the

Radio Astronomy. *The Effelsberg radio telescope near Bonn in West Germany.*

'radio stars' as the discrete sources which were being discovered in ever increasing numbers were then called. The first was found in Cygnus in 1946. Many were quite strong but for some time none could be identified with optical objects. Resolution could be improved by using shorter wavelengths or by building bigger telescopes but even with a wavelength of 10 cm a radio dish 22 km in diameter would be required to give a resolution of 1 arc second. The largest radio dish yet built is Cornell University's 1000-foot (305-metre) diameter reflector at Arecibo in Puerto Rico. A more usual size is about 25 m. Resolution is obtained by combining large arrays of tuned antennae spread over wide areas into an interferometer of which many ingenious forms have been developed.

Several hundred thousand sources are now observable of which some 12,000 had been individually catalogued by 1970. The usual identification for the brighter northern sources is the Third Cambridge Catalogue (3C) published in 1959 and revised in 1962. The first identifications of optical counterparts were made at Sydney by Bolton, Stanley and Slee in 1949. They identified Taurus A with the Crab Nebula, the remnants of the supernova of AD 1054. Though several of the stronger sources, including the strongest, Cassiopeia A, have been identified with former novae, the great majority seem to be galaxies in which the radio emission as compared with the optical is about 100,000 times stronger than in normal galaxies like our own. Not all extragalactic radio sources are extensive; in particular quasars, first recognised in 1963, are intrinsically extremely bright and very condensed. Some highly compact sources are not extragalactic. In 1967 Jocelyn Bell found the first of the pulsars, over 150 of which were known by 1975.

Radio Beacons consist of an aerial, receiver and pulse transmitter. If a ship or aircraft sends out a signal received by the radio beacons, the receiver output triggers the pulse transmitter, which then emits a pulse of known code pattern. The beacon is identified by the code, and the distance can be determined from the time delay of reception. Radio beacons are used for identifying landing fields, coastlines or other geographical features.

Radio Galaxy, see GALAXY; RADIO ASTRONOMY.

Radio Receiver. The simplest receiver consists of a tuned oscillatory circuit, a signal rectifier and a speaker. Modern receivers are of the superheterodyne type (superhets). A frequency changer is employed in which the wanted signal is mixed with a locally produced signal to give: (1) a signal of frequency equal to the sum of the frequencies of the wanted station and the local oscillation, and (2) a signal equal to the difference between them. One of these products is fed to a fixed tuned amplifier, the intermediate frequency (IF) amplifier. In modern transistor radios, these processes are all done by a single transistor in a 'self-oscillating mixer' stage. This IF is at about 465 kHz in the usual long, medium and short wave receiver, and at 10·7 MHz in a receiver for frequency-modulated waves at very high frequency.

Radio-sonde, an instrument now used by all the major meteorological services for measuring pressure, temperature and humidity of the atmosphere to great heights. Several different patterns are in use. The British radio-sonde consists essentially of a free balloon carrying instruments for measuring pressure, temperature and humidity. The instruments are made to cause changes in the electrical constants of a small radio, which transmits signals to a receiver on the ground. A more advanced instrument is the radar-sonde which measures not only pressure, temperature and humidity but also wind speed and direction at the same time.

See also METEOROLOGY.

Radio Telescope, see RADIO ASTRONOMY.

Radio Transmitting, see TRANSMITTER.

Radio Waves. Radio waves represent an electromagnetic field travelling with the velocity of light from the aerial into space. At any point, the field is defined by an electric and a magnetic force (vector) at right angles to one another, the direction of propagation being perpendicular to both. If the electric force is vertical, then the wave is 'vertically polarised'. A certain minimum field strength, expressed in microvolts per metre, is necessary for satisfactory reception. The field strength normally decreases with distance from the transmitter (attenuation) and is affected by any conducting surface present, such as the surface of the Earth or ionised regions in the atmosphere, and the waves are refracted and reflected by variation in the characteristics of the atmosphere. Waves emitted from a vertical aerial near the ground are vertically polarised and travel parallel to the surface. At low frequencies they suffer little attenuation. From elevated directive aerials, space waves are emitted at high frequency, travelling direct to the receiving aerial. The waves travelling upwards in the atmosphere are reflected from the ionosphere. The reflected wave is known as the sky wave. At frequencies of 20 to 100 kHz the sky wave is reflected near the lower boundary of the ionosphere, the ground wave is only very slightly attenuated, and transmission is not subject to diurnal or seasonal variation. As the frequency increases, attenuation becomes greater and signal strength at longer distance is more variable.

See also APPLETON LAYER.

Radioactivity is the spontaneous emission of particles or electromagnetic radiation by atomic nuclei which are unstable. The loss of a particle results in the transmutation of the nucleus to a different element. For example, nuclei of uranium decay with emission of an alpha-particle to yield thorium:

$$U \rightarrow Th + \alpha$$

The thorium is unstable, and will decay into palladium (also unstable) with the emission of a beta-particle (an electron):

$$Th \rightarrow Pa + \beta$$

The decay is terminated when the stable nucleus of lead is reached. The number of radioactive substances is large and can be divided into: the uranium series, the actinium series, and the thorium series.

Alpha-particles are the nuclei of helium atoms expelled from radioactive substances with a velocity about one-tenth of the velocity of light. The charge carried by an alpha-particle is twice the charge on an electron but is positive.

Beta-particles are fast electrons, expelled very near the velocity of light, 3×10^8 m/s.

Gamma-rays are electromagnetic waves of very high frequency.

Light waves in the visible spectrum have wavelengths of the order of 10^{-7} m; X-rays have wavelengths of the order of 10^{-10} m; the 'hardest' gamma-rays from radioactive substances have wavelengths of the order of 10^{-12} m.

Being charged, alpha- and beta-particles can be deflected by electric and magnetic fields, but gamma-rays are not.

Radioactive Half-life. The time taken for half the radioactive atoms in a substance to disintegrate is called the half-life. Thus after five half-lives, $^1/_{32}$ of the original radioactive atoms will still not have disintegrated, and after 10 half-lives, $^1/_{1024}$ will still remain. No known chemical or physical agency can alter the rate of this disintegration, apart from disrupting the nucleus by bombarding it with high-energy particles.

It is illuminating to follow the transformations in the uranium series. The disintegration of the original uranium is slow, the half-life being $4{\cdot}5 \times 10^9$ years, and it takes place, by alpha emission, to form uranium X_1, a radioactive isotope, $_{90}Th^{234}$, of thorium. This atom has a half-life of 24·1 days and emits a beta-particle to form uranium X_2, a radioactive isotope, $_{91}Pa^{234}$, of palladium. After three more stages the product nucleus is radium, which has a half-life of 1620 years, ultimately forming radon, or radium emanation, a chemically inert gas which is alpha-active with a half-life of 3·82 days. After eight more stages radium G is formed, which is a stable isotope, $_{82}Pb^{206}$, of lead, and does not disintegrate. Rutherford found that 1 g of radium suffered $3{\cdot}7 \times 10^{10}$ disintegrations per second and this led to the unit of radioactivity, the curie, $3{\cdot}700 \times 10^{10}$ disintegrations per second.

Nuclei and Isotopes. Useful quantities of radioactive isotopes can be obtained by bombarding materials by streams of neutrons.

It is possible to produce, for example, radioactive sodium and phosphorus and other elements that are found in the living body. Extremely minute quantities of radioactive materials can be detected by suitable electrical apparatus such as a geiger-mueller counter.
See also ATOM; DATING IN ARCHAEOLOGY (AND GEOLOGY); TRANSMUTATION OF THE ELEMENTS.

Radiocarbon Dating, see DATING IN ARCHAEOLOGY (AND GEOLOGY).

Radiogram, see RECORD PLAYER.

Radiography, see MASS RADIOGRAPHY; RADIOLOGY; X-RAYS.

Radioisotope, see ISOTOPE.

Radiolaria, see SARCODINA.

Radiolocation, see RADAR.

Radiology, principally the study of the production and use of X-rays. These rays have proved invaluable to doctors in aiding them to diagnose many internal conditions from radiographs of diseased or malformed regions of the body. Different tissues have different absorption coefficients for X-rays and hence 'shadows' are produced when the transmitted X-rays fall on a fluorescent screen or photographic plate. Radiological diagnosis, not only of diseases and deformities of bone, but also of certain affections of the circulatory, respiratory, digestive and urogenital systems may now be made after appropriate impregnation of the cavities or tissues with substances rendering them opaque, and so making it possible to obtain radiographs of them.

Radiometer, instrument for detecting and measuring radiation, consisting of four thin discs of glass, mica or metal carried on aluminium arms at right angles to each other, and pivoted so as to rotate with as little friction as possible in a glass globe partly exhausted. The discs are coated with lampblack on one side so that on rotation bright and black surfaces succeed each other alternately. On exposure to a source of light or heat the black surfaces absorb heat in greater quantity, and their temperature is raised; the molecules of air coming in contact rebound with greater energy, and the greater reaction between the molecules and the black surfaces causes the discs to rotate, their black surfaces receding from the source of radiant energy.

Radiometric Dating, see DATING IN ARCHAEOLOGY (AND GEOLOGY).

Radiometry, the measurement of rate of flow of electromagnetic radiation, mainly of infrared, visible and ultraviolet light. The total flux in a beam is measured either as the amount of energy flow per unit time, i.e. the power in watts, or as the number of photons per unit time. Radiometry is also concerned with measuring flux per unit area of surface.
See also PHOTOGRAPHY; PHOTOMETRY.

Radiotherapy, treatment of disease by means of X-rays and radioactive substances, e.g. radium. In addition to X-rays, radio waves have also been used, e.g. in diathermic therapy, which aims at heating the body, and athermic therapy using short waves and weak currents. The use of the latter is controversial. The chief use of radiotherapy is for malignant disease, i.e. cancer, but it is also used for skin diseases, e.g. ringworm. The different types of cancer vary in their susceptibility to radiotherapy, and, moreover, those which are highly susceptible may recur. Good results are obtained with cancers which are slow growing and moderately radio-sensitive, e.g. those of the face, lip, mouth, breast, bladder and uterus. Surgery and radiotherapy are frequently used in combination. Nuclear reactors now provide a ready source of artificially made radioactive isotopes which, compared with radium, are relatively cheap and easy to obtain.

Radish, *Raphanus sativus*, an annual plant in the family Cruciferae, the root of which is used in salads; it has been cultivated from ancient times.

Radium, metallic chemical element, symbol Ra, atomic number 88, atomic weight 226·0254, a member of the group of alkaline earths. It was discovered by Marie Curie in 1898 when working with her husband on the radioactivity of uranium compounds. It was identified as a result of their observation that the radioactivity of some samples of pitchblende (an impure uranium oxide ore) was much greater than would correspond to the uranium present. This extra activity was correctly ascribed to some unknown radioactive element of great activity, later named radium. Radium is similar in its properties (apart from its radioactivity) to the alkaline earths, calcium, strontium and barium. The most profitable source of the element is pitchblende, and this occurs in large quantities in Czechoslovakia. About 6000 kg of pitchblende produce 1 g of radium. The metal itself may be obtained by electrolytic separation from radium chloride. It is white and melts at 700°C. It is rapidly attacked on exposure to air, and it is generally sold in the form of radium chloride or bromide, both white salts. The half-life of radium is about 1620 years. The immediate product of its disintegration is radon, a chemically inert gas, which also disintegrates by the expulsion of an alpha-particle. Radium bromide ($RaBr_2$) is the most important radium compound, in that it has been used as a source of alpha-rays for the localised treatment of small cancers.
See also URANIUM; X-RAYS.

Radius, in geometry, see CIRCLE.

Radius, in anatomy, is the smaller companion bone to the ulna in the forearm. Its larger end is attached to the wrist, the smaller to the elbow. The biceps muscle is attached to it just below the crook of the arm. Colles's fracture occurs at the wrist end about 2 cm from the articulation.

Radius of Gyration. If a body of mass M has a moment of inertia I about an axis, then the length k defined by $I = Mk^2$ is the radius of gyration. If the mass were concentrated at a point distance k from the axis, the moment of inertia would be unchanged.

Radon, or niton, chemical element, symbol Rn, atomic number 86, atomic weight 222; one of the inert gases. It is a colourless gas, boiling at about -62°C, and rapidly disintegrates into helium and a radioactive solid (radium D). Radon is used in radiotherapy, and is obtained by dissolving a radium salt in water. Radon is spontaneously evolved by radium. Owing to its short half-life (4 days), it can only be obtained in trace quantities, but these are sufficient for its medical uses.

Raeburn, Sir Henry (1756–1823), self-taught Scottish portrait painter. Raeburn settled in 1787 at Edinburgh, and soon acquired fame. All the Scottish notabilities of the day, except Burns, sat for him. His work earned for him the title of 'the Scottish Reynolds'.

Raeder, Erich (1876–1960), German admiral. He was promoted commander-in-chief of the German navy 1935–43, being superseded by Doenitz, and was virtually in retirement after 1943. At the Nuremberg trial he was sentenced (1946) to imprisonment for life. He was released in 1955.

Raeto-Romance, see ROMANSH.

Raffia, see RAPHIA.

Raffles, Sir (Thomas) Stamford (1781–1826), British administrator, patron of science, and founder of Singapore. In 1810 he went to Calcutta and assisted Lord Minto in preparation for the conquest of Java from the Dutch (who had sided with the French). After the taking of Java, Raffles was appointed governor and proved a benevolent and enlightened ruler until 1816 when the island was returned to the Dutch. From 1818 to 1823 he was lieutenant-governor of Sumatra, the East India Company acquiring Singapore on his advice in 1819.

Rafflesia, genus of 12 species of stemless plants, family Rafflesiaceae, chiefly Malayan, and parasitic on the roots of members of the Vitidaceae. *R. arnoldii* carries the largest flowers known. Often they are nearly ½ metre across and weigh several kg; they smell of rotten meat and are pollinated by carrion flies.

Ragged Schools, institutions first begun by John Pounds, a Portsmouth shoemaker, in 1820, which supplied free education, and sometimes bodily necessities, for destitute children.

Raglan, Fitzroy James Henry Somerset, 1st Baron (1788–1855), British soldier. He was wounded at Waterloo, and had his right arm amputated. He was military secretary at the Horse Guards from 1827 until 1852, when he became master-general of the ordnance. He went in 1854 to command the British troops sent against Russia in the Crimean War, but died of dysentery before Sevastopol.

Ragnarök, the Norse doomsday, at which the gods would contend with the forces of evil and each side would destroy the other, after which a new heaven and earth would appear, cleansed and refreshed.
See also MYTHOLOGY.

Ragtime, a form of syncopated piano music popular in the USA from 1897 to 1917. Ragtime influenced popular songs and its syncopation and rhythm also influenced jazz, which it preceded. Ragtime enjoyed a revival in the 1970s. A well-known composition is Scott Joplin's *Maple Leaf Rag* (1899).

Ragusa, town in Sicily, capital of Ragusa province and 175 km south-east of Palermo. It has fine Baroque and medieval palaces and churches, including a cathedral. It has asphalt mines, and oil has been discovered in the district. Population (1974) 58,800.

Ragweed, *Ambrosia artemisiifolia*, a North American member of the Compositae which is wind-pollinated. Ragweed pollen is a major cause of hayfever (allergic rhinitis) in the USA.

Ragwort, *Senecio jacobaea* of the Compositae, an abundant weed in waste places, now almost cosmopolitan, bearing a flat cluster of bright yellow flower heads and strongly lobed leaves. There are also marsh ragwort, *S. aquaticus*; hoary ragwort, *S. erucifolius*; and Oxford ragwort, *S. squalidus*, from southern Italy, now widespread in Britain.

Rahman, Mujibur (1920–75), known as Shaikh Mujib, the first president of Bangladesh. From 1966, when he presented a six-point plan for the autonomy of East Pakistan, he spent three years as a political prisoner. In the 1970 elections he won an absolute majority in the Constituent Assembly. In the following year, when talks with West Pakistan failed, he declared East Pakistan independent, forces from the West invaded, and Shaikh Mujib was imprisoned and sentenced to death. After Pakistan's defeat by India in 1972 he was released and became president of the new state of Bangladesh. In 1975, after introducing a new constitution that made Bangladesh a one-party state, Shaikh Mujib lost much popular support and was assassinated in an army coup in August 1975. See also BANGLADESH, *History*; PAKISTAN, *History*.

Raikes, Robert (1735–1811), British philanthropist. In 1757 he succeeded his father as printer and proprietor of the *Gloucester Journal*. He continued this work until 1802. He had early been active in the agitation for prison reform, and in 1780 started a Sunday school at Gloucester, which developed into a national movement.

Rail, a bird of the family Rallidae (over 100 species), order Gruiformes, marsh birds with a long bill curved at the tip. European representatives include the land-rail or corncrake, coot, moorhen or waterhen, and the water-rail, *Rallus aquaticus*. The king, clapper and Virginia rails are North American species. The weka, *Gallirallus australis*, is a rail species native to New Zealand.

Railways. Mineral railways using wooden beams were in use in central Europe as early as the 14th and 15th centuries, and in the 18th century iron bars on sleepers became widely used for coal transport. The first powered railway was the Stockton to Darlington line, opened in 1825, using George Stephenson's steam locomotive *Locomotion*. This began the great era of British railway expansion, and by 1870 all the main lines of the modern UK system were operating. The Railways Act (1921) grouped these into four systems (London, Midland and Scottish; London and North Eastern; Great Western; and Southern), while the Transport Act (1947) established what is now British Rail. In 1981 British railways totalled 17,734 km in length.

Until the 19th century British railways continued to lead the world, but later developments came mainly from the USA and European countries who were not hampered by limitations of speed and weight imposed by old track. Railways were both commercially and politically important in the early development of the USA, and the first locomotives and iron rails were imported from Britain. The first transcontinental line, the Union Pacific, was completed in 1869 and began a period of vast expansion and invention, including the Westinghouse air-brake (1869), the automatic coupler (1871), the block-signal system (1874) and the refrigerator car (1875). In Canada, the transcontinental Canadian Pacific line was opened in 1885. European railways form an extensive system, all of the same gauge (1·43 m) except the USSR, Spain and Portugal.

Before block signalling and telegraphs were introduced, a time interval was the only means of keeping a proper distance between following trains. Today the former are being replaced by automatic installations in which trains themselves work the signals, and some of which can be controlled by computer.

The world's first functional electric railway was opened at Brighton, Sussex, in 1883, and the first electric underground railway, the City and South London, followed in 1890. The electricity supply can be carried by overhead contact wire or conductor rails. Underground systems are found in cities such as New York, Paris, Berlin and Tokyo, while famous tunnels include the Simplon (20 km) under the Alps and the New Cascade (12·5 km) under the Rockies. Mountain railways, which include the rack-and-pinion (first used in Britain in 1811) and the funicular systems, are now also worked by electric traction.

There have been many schemes for high-speed monorails and hovertrains but as yet none has been commercially successful, although a test hovertrain reached 500 km/h in Japan in 1979. Orthodox railways have also been developed or adapted for high speed passenger travel. British Rail runs a high-speed train (maximum speed 200 km/h) on existing track, while in 1981 the first section of a new line from Paris to Lyon (maximum speed 260 km/h) was opened, and Germany, Italy and Japan also have high-speed trains. The top speed reached by an orthodox railway locomotive is 380 km/h, in the 1981 trials for the Paris–Lyon line.

Rain, see PRECIPITATION.

Rain-gauge. Usually made of copper, the upper detachable cylinder containing a funnel. The measuring-glass is graduated to show the amount of rainfall.

Rate-of-rainfall gauges are also installed at some stations. Modern developments are towards rendering rainfall and rate-of-rainfall recording automatic with outputs which can be fed into a computer by paper or magnetic tape. As yet, rainfall records are still mainly obtained by a pen tracing on a chart attached to a revolving cylinder.

Rain-making. In many societies there is a belief that, by invoking extra-human sources, certain people can control rainfall. These rain-makers may be important men in the community and the authority of chiefs and kings may rest largely upon this power. Rain is usually made by the manipulation of rain-stones or other sacred objects or by prayer.

Rainbow, a curved, coloured spectrum seen in the sky. In 1637 Descartes found that of 10,000 rays of sunlight striking one side of a spherical raindrop, after refraction on entering, one internal reflection at the opposite side, and refraction again on leaving, those between 8500 and 8600Å all had an angle of deviation within a few minutes of the minimum angle of deviation. There is therefore a narrow concentrated beam of light emerging from the raindrop at the minimum angle of deviation, which, as the colours are dispersed, gives a spectrum, the red having an angle of deviation of about 137°, the violet 139·5°. Thus all drops on a cone centred about the shadow of the observer at an angle of about 42° will appear bright in the sunlight, the colour varying from violet at about 40½° to red at about 43°. The bow cannot be seen from the ground if the Sun is at a greater elevation than 40°; from an aircraft the bow sometimes is a complete circle. This is the primary bow. With two internal reflections the raindrops will reflect a secondary bow, at angles from about 50° for red to 54° for violet. See also HALO.

Raine, Kathleen Jessie (1908–), English poet. Her first volume of verse, *Stone and Flower*, 1943, drew upon her knowledge of biology for its realistic descriptions of the natural world. Her later verse includes *Collected Poems*, 1956, and *The Lost Country*, 1971. Kathleen Raine was strongly influenced by the visionary poets William Blake and William Butler Yeats, and her own work is notable for its symbolism and allusion to esoteric systems of learning and philosophy, as well as for its precision.

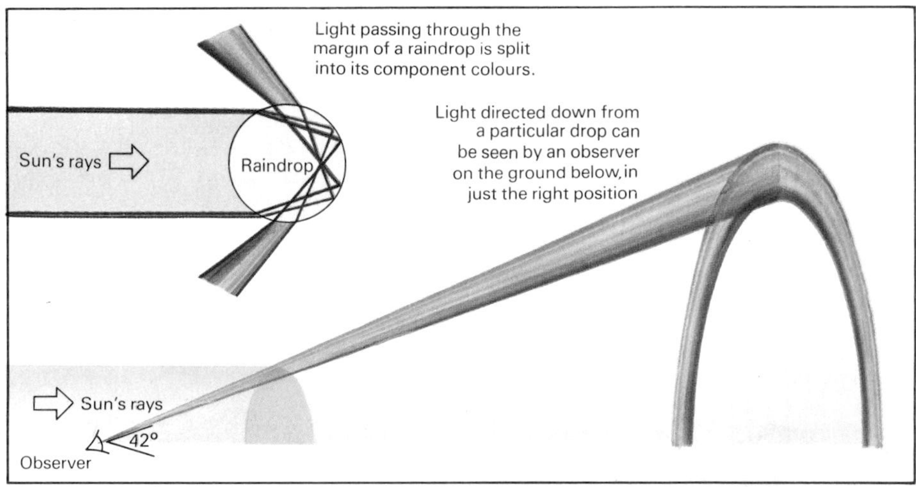

Rainbow. *On the ground a rainbow is seen as an arc, subtending an angle of 42° about an observer's shadow. The observer sees different colours reflected from different raindrops.*

Rainier III, Prince Louis Henri Maxence Bertrand (1923–), Prince of Monaco. He succeeded his grandfather in 1949, and married Grace Kelly, the American film actress, in 1956. She died in 1982.

Rainier, Mount, mountain in the state of Washington, USA, sometimes known also as Mount Tacoma. It is 4392 m high, the highest peak in the Cascade Range. It is volcanic in origin, and glaciers radiate out from the peak.

Raised Beach, see BEACH, RAISED.

Raisin, name given to certain species of grape when dried. Raisins are usually dark brown and larger than a currant. Quantities of raisins are exported from the Mediterranean shores, while others come from France and California. The variety known as muscatel is partly dried while attached to the vine, and is grown near Malaga, Spain. The process of drying takes place in the sun or in specially heated houses.

Sultanas are made by drying certain types of large white grapes. They are light golden brown, large raisins, and are eaten raw or cooked. Dried *currants* are made by drying small, dark grapes, and are used mostly in cooking. The fresh currant is an entirely unrelated fruit.

Raja, title borne by a Hindu prince. Rajas were in existence in India from very early times; the title was, as a rule, hereditary, although men of conspicuous valour and wisdom were also elected rajas. Chiefs of greater importance than the ordinary rajas were called *maharaja*, or 'great raja'.

Rāja Yoga, see YOGA.

Rajasthan, state of India made up of a union of the former princely states of the Rajputs known as Rajputana, covering 342,214 km^2. The Aravalli Hills form a dividing line within the state and separate parts of the basins of the Indus and Ganges rivers. The Thar Desert occupies the north-west section of the state and is less productive than the south-east, where projects such as the Rajasthan and Chambal canals have extended the irrigable crop area by one-third. Millet, wheat and barley are the main food crops with a surplus for sale to other states. Cotton and sugar cane are the industrial crops. In the drier areas, cattle, sheep and camels predominate as income earners. Manufacturing is based on cotton textiles, cement and mineral exploitation: brown coal at Bikaner, salt from Sambhar salt lake, copper, limestone, mica, zinc (smelted at Udaipur), gypsum and marble. Rajasthani is the main language, but Hindi is used increasingly. Most of the 34,102,912 population are Hindus but with a significant minority of Jains, who are frequently traders and moneylenders. The capital city is Jaipur.

Rajkot, town of Gujarat state, India, at the centre of rail and road routes with growing textile and chemical industries. It is the former capital of the princely state of Rajkot. Population (1981) 444,156.

Rajput (Thakurs), eleven-million strong peoples of north and central India whose dominance of the Punjab, Kashmir and Central Himalayas from the eighth century was destroyed by the Muslim conquest. Traditionally warriors, their class system, in which women may marry men of higher status, ranges from princes to agriculturalists. Today most of the mainly landowning Rajputs are Hindu; a minority are Muslim.

Rákóczy, noble Hungarian family, the principal members of which were:

George I (1593–1648), who became Prince of Transylvania in 1630 and conquered many towns in Hungary.

George II (1621–60), son of George I. He was deposed by the Porte in 1657, but was reinstated in 1658. Defeated by the Turks, he was wounded in battle and died.

Francis II (1676–1735), grandson of George II, leader of a famous Hungarian insurrection (1703–11). Francis II was elected Prince of Transylvania in 1704, and prince of the confederation of Hungarian nobles in 1705. After defeats inflicted on the insurgents by the armies of Emperor Joseph I of Austria, Francis fled abroad where he died.

Raleigh. *A portrait of the courtier, 1588.*

Raleigh, Sir Walter, also spelt Ralegh (c.1552–1618), English courtier, soldier, explorer, poet and historian. In 1578 he joined Sir Humphrey Gilbert in the latter's unsuccessful expedition under a royal patent to found settlements in North America, and in 1580 he served in Ireland. It was on his return from Ireland that Leicester, his patron, gave him a chance to appear at court. In the course of a few years he was knighted, made lord warden of the Stannaries, captain of the guard, and lieutenant-general of the County of Cornwall (1587).

In 1584 Raleigh drew up a plan for colonising what is now Virginia and Carolina (he named Virginia in honour of the Virgin Queen) and laid it before the queen and her council. On 7 April two vessels, fitted out at the cost of Raleigh and his associates, sailed round the West Indies and Carolina, and their report induced Raleigh vigorously to prosecute his design of planting a colony in Virginia. Raleigh also joined in the enterprise to find the North-West Passage, which resulted in the discovery of Davis Strait.

In 1595 he went in search of El Dorado or Manoa. The expedition was a failure but his account of it, *Discoverie of Guiana*, remains a fascinating and persuasive work.

From 1600 to 1603 he was governor of New Jersey.

The death of Elizabeth I totally changed Raleigh's fortunes. The new sovereign and his old enemies combined against him. Raleigh was tried for high treason, found guilty after a mockery of a trial, and sentenced to death. He was reprieved and spent the next 13 years in the Tower, occupying himself with writing and scientific experiments.

Raleigh was released in 1616 to undertake a second voyage to El Dorado. But, like the first, it was a failure and Raleigh was involved in a battle with the Spaniards at just the time when James was negotiating a Spanish marriage for his son and thus wanted peace at all costs. Raleigh returned to England in 1616, a broken and dying man. The Spanish ambassador demanded that he be punished for his outrage, James agreed without demur, and Raleigh was beheaded in Old Palace Yard, Westminster, on 29 October 1618.

Raleigh was primarily a courtier and a royal favourite, an intellectual giant, a gifted poet and historian. At the same time he was greedy, ambitious for power, and unscrupulous. His literary accomplishments were considerable. The *History of the World*, planned and begun during Raleigh's imprisonment in the Tower, is one of the finest specimens of Elizabethan prose. Raleigh's poems, the authenticity of some of which has been questioned, are largely of a philosophic type.

Raleigh, capital city of the state of North Carolina, USA. An old regional centre, it has developed industrially with the growth of the cotton and synthetic fibre textile industries, and also processes tobacco and forest products. Apart from the state government, it has North Carolina State University. Population (1980) 148,300.

Rally Driving, see MOTOR RACING.

Rallying, sporting event for motor cars driven over a set course, divided into a predetermined number of stages. In major events, rallies are run on both public and private roads, the latter being used for time trials. Cars are standard production models to which modification is allowed; they have two-man crews—a driver and a navigator. Points are won and lost both for going too fast (on public roads) and too slow (on time trials) and for rule infringements, particular to each individual event, which can be of several days' duration. The two major events in the world are the RAC Rally, held in Britain, and the East Africa Safari Rally. These, and other events, are part of the World Championships, which are competed for annually. Perhaps the best-known of all rallies—the Monte Carlo—is no longer the major event it once was.

See also MONTE CARLO RALLY.

Ram, The, see ARIES.

Rāma, in Hindu mythology, the hero of the great Sanskrit epic, the Rāmāyana, the Rāma-Chandra, or seventh incarnation of Vishnu.

Ramadan, ninth month of the Muslim year, during which falls the night of Destiny, when the fates of men for the coming year are fixed; popular opinion favours the 27th as the great night. It is the month of fasting: believers must abstain from food, drink, perfume, smoking and sexual intercourse from a little before sunrise till sunset; special services are held during the night. Those who are able rest during the day, and make the most of the night. Since the Muslims have a lunar calendar, i.e. 12 months of 29–30 days, the season of Ramadan varies from year to year.

Ramah, name of several places in Palestine, of which two (which may be identical) are important: (1) city of Benjamin, the traditional site of Rachel's tomb, just outside Bethlehem; (2) birthplace of Saul.

Rāmakrishna, originally Gadādhar Chattopadhyaya (1836–86), Hindu sage, whose teaching has influenced many westerners. Rāmakrishna had an experience of ecstasy as a child of six when he saw a flight of snow-white cranes pass across a dark thundercloud. As a young man he became a priest at a temple devoted to the goddess Kali in Dakshineśwar.

Raman Spectroscopy depends on the fact that energy can be made to interact with an induced dipole as well as a permanent dipole. In the case of infrared spectroscopy the absorption of energy depends on the permanent dipole of the molecule. In Raman spectroscopy the dipole is induced in an otherwise symmetrical molecule by an applied electric field. The induced dipole is dependent on the inherent polarisability of the molecule under investigation. A helium-neon laser beam is often used as the source. See also SPECTRUM AND SPECTROSCOPE.

Ramapithecus, see MAN.

Rāmāyana, one of the two great Sanskrit epics of ancient India, the other being the Mahabharata. The Rāmāyana is in seven books with about 24,000 couplets.

Rambert, Dame Marie (1888–1982), founder and director of the Ballet Rambert. From 1920 she was one of the principal architects of English ballet. Having studied under Cecchetti, she was one of the founders of the Cecchetti Society. In 1930 she launched the Ballet Club, later to become the Ballet Rambert.

Ramblers' Association, formed in Britain in 1935 by the coalition of regional federations of rambling clubs, the first of which was founded in 1905. The Association's objects are to protect rights of way and the countryside, and to encourage the enjoyment of the countryside on foot.

Rambouillet, French town in the *département* of Yvelines, at the southern end of the great forest of Rambouillet, 45 km south-west of Paris. There is a 14th-18th-century château, once a royal estate, now the summer residence of the President of the Republic. Population (1975) 20,056.

Rameau, Jean Philippe (1683–1764), French composer. He wrote nearly 40 operas, other stage works, motets, cantatas, concertos, and many harpsichord pieces. He was a famous theorist, publishing a *Traité* and *Nouvelles Réflexions* on harmony.

Ramée, Marie Louise de la, see OUIDA.

Ramée, Pierre de la, see RAMUS, PETER.

Rameses, name of several kings of ancient Egypt. *Rameses I*, the founder of the 19th Dynasty, lived about 1320 BC; he reigned only two years. *Rameses II* (Osymandyas), 1304–1237, one of the most famous of Egyptian kings, the third of the 19th Dynasty, was the son of Seti I. His greatest achievements in architecture were the excavation of the rock temples of Abu Simbel, the completion of the great hall of Karnak, the building of a temple at Abydos and the addition of the first court and pylon at Luxor. Early in his reign he provoked and fought a long war against the Hittites. This war ended by a treaty, copies of which are extant, leaving Egypt impoverished and suffering from an incurable decline. *Rameses III* (1198–66 BC), second king of the 20th Dynasty, was famous for his victory over the confederation of people from Crete, Cyprus, Philistia and the north Mediterranean, who combined with the Libyans and attacked Egypt by land and sea. Rameses won a great naval battle probably near Pelusium, and also defeated the land force. Eight other kings of the name of Rameses followed Rameses III; they were mainly ineffectual and increasingly overshadowed by the High Priests of Amun. See also EGYPT, ANCIENT.

***Rameses II.** A sculpture from 1250 BC.*

Ramón y Cajal, Santiago (1852–1934), Spanish neuro-histologist. He made fundamental discoveries about the origin and termination of olfactory nerve fibres, the cerebral cortex, the structure of sensory ganglia in man and animals, the retina, and the regeneration of nerves. In 1906 he shared (with C. Golgi) the Nobel Prize for medicine for his work on the histology of the nervous system.

Rampant, in heraldry, describes an animal standing on its sinister hind leg and usually facing to the dexter; for example, the lion rampant in the Scottish royal arms.

Rampion, *Campanula rapunculus*, a biennial plant in family Campanulaceae, with long white radish-like roots. The leaves are occasionally used as a winter salad. Like the round-headed rampion, *Phyteuma tenerum*, and the spiked rampion, *P. spicatum*, of the same family, they are found in Europe and Asia.

Ramsay, Allan (1686–1758), Scottish poet. *Fables and Tales* and *A Tale of Three Bonnets*, a political allegory, appeared in 1722; *The Tea-Table Miscellany*, an anthology of popular songs, including some of his own, 1724–27; and the pastoral drama, *The Gentle Shepherd*, in 1725. After 1730 Ramsay ceased to write. He edited *The Evergreen*, a collection of old Scots poems, in 1724, making the works of Dunbar, Henryson and others available to later writers, and he was chiefly responsible for the renaissance of Scottish literature in the 18th century.

Ramsay, Allan (1713–84), British painter. He practised as a portrait painter in Edinburgh until about 1736 when he went to study in Italy, returning to settle in London. He became a favourite of George III in preference to Reynolds, and one of Dr Johnson's circle. He excelled in portraits of women, e.g. *Margaret Lindsay, the Painter's Wife*, c.1755 (National Gallery of Scotland). Around 1768 he gave up painting and concentrated on literary interests.

Ramsay, Sir William (1852–1916), British chemist. He is chiefly remembered for the discovery of the inert gases. After the discovery by Lord Rayleigh of the minute difference in density between atmospheric nitrogen and that prepared chemically, Ramsay joined Rayleigh in research that resulted in the discovery of argon, announced in 1895. Ramsay then investigated the inert gas contained in certain minerals, and in one (uraninite) he found helium, already spectroscopically discovered in the Sun. Xenon, krypton and neon, similarly inactive gases and present as traces in the atmosphere, were in turn discovered. Ramsay was awarded the Nobel Prize for chemistry in 1904.

Ramsey, Sir Alf (1922–), an association footballer for Southampton, Tottenham Hotspur and England. He was capped 32 times for England and then joined Ipswich Town as manager in 1955. After raising Ipswich to be First Division champions in 1961–62 he took charge of England's international side, being appointed national team manager in 1962. Under him England won the World Cup in 1966.

Ramsey, Arthur Michael, Baron (1904–), English prelate, archbishop of Canterbury, 1961–74. He became bishop of Durham in 1952. In 1956 he was appointed archbishop of York, and in 1961 he succeeded Fisher as archbishop of Canterbury.

Ramsey's period as archbishop is remembered for the ecumenical dialogues he encouraged, most notably the talks on union between the Church of England and the Methodists, and for the 'Honest to God' controversy provoked by Bishop John Robinson. In 1966 he visited Pope Paul VI.

Ramsgate, port and resort in Kent, England. The harbour was completed in 1763, and after George IV spent a season here in 1827, it became a popular resort. The hoverport was opened in 1969 for passenger and vehicle transfer to Calais. Population (1981) 39,642.

Ramus, Peter, or Pierre de la Ramée (1515–72), French philosopher, humanist and mathematician. In 1543 he published his new system of logic, with strictures on the logic of Aristotle, which the king ordered to be suppressed. In 1551 he was appointed professor of philosophy and eloquence in the Collège de France. Ramus was driven from Paris several times, and in 1568 he went to Germany and gave lectures on mathematics at Heidelberg, where he made public profession of Protestantism. Shortly after his return to Paris he was killed in the massacre of St Bartholomew.

Ramuz, Charles Ferdinand (1878–1947), Swiss writer. Among his major novels are the semi-autobiographical *Vie de Samuel Belet*, 1913; *La Grande peur dans la montagne*, 1926; *Derborence*, 1935; and *Le Garçon savoyard*, 1937. He also published diaries and memoirs, including *Paris, notes d'un Vaudois*, 1939. He collaborated with Stravinsky on *The Soldier's Tale*, 1918.

Rana, see FROGS.

Rancagua, town of central Chile, capital of O'Higgins province, 80 km by train south from Santiago. It is primarily an agricultural centre but also serves the El Teniente copper mine. There is some industry including light engineering and vehicle assembly. Population (1976) 117,550.

Ranch, see RANGE.

Rand, usual name of the Witwatersrand, South Africa, a gold-mining district in Transvaal province. *Rand* in Afrikaans means ridge, in this case referring to the watershed between the Orange and Limpopo rivers.

Range, a vague term for the vast areas over which sheep and cattle are grazed in the USA. The North American ranches have their parallel in the *estancias* of South America, in Uruguay and the Argentine, and in the sheep 'stations' of Australia. A 'ranch' is a farm unit covering a large area within the dry grasslands, or 'range', of the western and mountain states of the USA.

'Free range' is used for chickens that are allowed to run free in the farmyard instead of being raised indoors in special houses.

Rangefinder, or telemeter, instrument for measuring or calculating the distance of an object.

The stadiametric method of rangefinding is based on the angle subtended by a known target dimension such as the span of an aircraft seen from directly astern or the height of an enemy tank.

In survey 'subtense techniques', an accurately known distance marked on a 'subtense bar' is held by the surveyor's assistant, and the angle it subtends is measured very accurately by a theodolite. The basic idea of the coincidence rangefinder was due to Adie in 1860. The object is viewed through widely spaced left and right reflective prisms whose angular settings, or whose output rays, are rotated to bring the two images (possibly the top and bottom halves of the target) into coincidence. Small rangefinders of this kind are used on cameras, and before radar was invented, ship and anti-aircraft gunnery depended on rangefinders with bases as long as 13 m.

Rangefinding by radar depends on the principle of measuring the time elapsing between sending out a pulse of radio waves travelling at a speed of 3×10^8 m/s and receiving the echo. Modern electronics can measure short time lapses accurately and even the earliest radars could boast an accuracy of 25 m up to 15 km. Using 10 cm or shorter waves modern radars can give an answer within a few cm.

The laser rangefinder works on the same principle as radar except that the pulse consists of light of a single wavelength. One pulse only is used for the measurement, with accuracy of 1 mm or better; interferometric methods can be much more accurate.

Rangoon. The Golden Pagoda at Shwe Dagon. It was the centre of the pre-colonial city.

Ranger, formerly in England a sworn officer of the forest appointed by the king to watch the deer and prevent theft. The term is now applied to a government official connected with public parks and forests. Irregular mounted troops were also called Rangers (for example, Connaught Rangers). In the US army commando troops are called rangers. The ranger is also a senior grade in the girl guide movement.

Rangoon, capital of Burma, situated on the left bank of the Rangoon river, 34 km from the sea, and linked to the Irrawaddy by the Twante Canal. The city itself is the country's main port and centre of communications. The trade of the port has declined since colonial days, but its main exports remain rice and timber. It is also the country's main industrial centre. The city is dominated by the magnificent golden Shwe Dagon pagoda. Population (1973) 3,662,312.

Ranjit Singh (1780–1839), 'the lion of the Punjab', Indian ruler and founder of the Sikh kingdom in the Punjab, who laid the foundation of his power when he obtained Lahore. His ideal was realised by 1820 when the Punjab, from the Sutlej to the Indus, was consolidated under his rule. The strength of his state did not last long after his death.

Rank, in the Armed Forces, the position of seniority occupied by an officer, non-commissioned officer, private, rating or aircraftman in the hierarchy of his Service.

Ranke, Leopold von (1795–1886), German historian. He edited the *Historisch-politische Zeitschrift*, and in 1841 was appointed historiographer of Prussia. His numerous works include *Die römischen Päpste im 16. und 17. Jahrhundert*, 1834–39; *Zwölf Bücher preussischer Geschichte*, 1874, 1878–79. He did much to found the tradition of modern historical criticism and research, stressing the power of ideas rather than individuals.

Ransom, John Crowe (1888–1974), US poet and critic. He founded the *Kenyon Review* in 1939 and was a member of The Fugitives, a group of writers connected by their faith in Southern agrarianism in the face of the forces of urbanisation and industrialisation. His works of criticism include *God without Thunder*, 1930; *The World's Body*, 1938; *New Criticism*, 1948; and *Studies in Modern Literature*, 1951.

Ransome, Arthur Mitchell (1884–1967), English writer, journalist and critic. As a journalist in Moscow for the *Daily News* and the *New York Times*, he observed the Russian Revolution. He was also a student of folklore, and the stories he collected in Russia were published as *Old Peter's Russian Tales*, 1916. He loved sailing and fishing, and his interest in these subjects is evident in the famous books he wrote for children, including *Swallows and Amazons* (1931).

Ranunculaceae, buttercup family, a family of about 40 genera and 700 species of dicotyledons, cosmopolitan but mainly in north temperate regions and consisting of herbaceous perennial plants (except in the genus *Clematis* which includes woody climbers), often with much divided leaves.

Most Ranunculaceae are poisonous plants containing alkaloids, sometimes of medicinal value. Apart from this, the main use of the family is horticultural, species of *Clematis*, *Delphinium*, *Ranunculus*, *Anemone*, *Helleborus* (including Christmas rose), *Eranthis* (winter aconite), *Aquilegia* (columbine), *Thalictrum* and other genera being grown for their decorative flowers.

Ranunculus, buttercup or crowfoot, a genus of 247 herbaceous species, including meadow, woodland, alpine, marsh and aquatic plants. The terrestrial and marsh species usually have flowers with five yellow petals but some have white, pink or red flowers. The lesser celandine (*R. ficaria*) is a yellow-flowered member of the genus. The water crowfoots (*R. aquatilis* and related species) have white flowers and are usually aquatic plants with much-divided submerged leaves and floating leaves.

Rapallo, Italian seaport and winter resort in Liguria. It is situated on a bay on the Italian Riviera 25 km east of Genoa. There are tunny fisheries, and lace and olive-oil are manufactured here. Population (1974) 22,300.

Rapanui, see EASTER ISLAND.

Rape, see BRASSICA.

Rape is the offence of having sexual intercourse with a woman without her consent; intention to commit the offence has to be proved. The prosecution must prove penetration, even the slightest, failing which there may still be a conviction for the attempt or, at least, for indecent assault. Rape is punishable in England with imprisonment for life.

Raphael Santi, also Rafaello Sanzio (1483–1520), Italian painter. Perugino's art influenced Raphael at an early age as the early *Crucifixion* in the National Gallery, London, demonstrates. Raphael's *Vision of a Knight* (National Gallery), *St Michael* and *St George* (Louvre), and *The Three Graces* (Chantilly) were all painted during his early days at Urbino. In 1504 he went to Florence, where he came under the influence of Michelangelo and Leonardo da Vinci. He lived there for four years, observing and making drawings from works of Florentine masters. Some of the chief paintings of this period are *La Madonna del Granduca* (Pitti), *Madonna del Giardino, Holy Family with the Lamb, Ansidei Madonna, The Entombment of Christ, St Catherine* (National Gallery), *La Belle Jardinière* (Louvre).

About 1508 Raphael went to Rome and by 1509 was working for Pope Julius II in the decoration of apartments in the Vatican, the whole of the fresco work soon being entrusted to him. His real fame rests on these large conceptions such as the *School of Athens* and *Mass of Bolsena* (Vatican). The famous Cartoons for tapestry (Victoria and Albert Museum, London) are splendid examples of his composition. During the last six years of his life in Rome he produced many celebrated works, including *St Cecilia*, the *Madonna di S. Sisto, Lo Spasimo, The Transfiguration* (unfinished at his death). His versatility and powers of assimilation are further proved by the impressive development of his portraiture, from the early Leonardesque *Doni* portraits, to the Roman style of *La Donna Velata* (Pitti, Florence) and *Beazzano and Navagero* (Doria Gallery, Rome). In 1514 he succeeded Bramante as the chief architect of St Peter's.

Raphael. St Catherine of Alexandria, *painted between 1504 and 1509.*

Raphia, genus of tropical palms with large pinnate leaves and huge fruit spikes sometimes 90 kg in weight. *R. rafinifera* is the raffia or roffia palm, but *R. pendunculata* yields the tying material used by gardeners. *R. vinifera* (the bamboo palm) is used for winemaking, as is *R. hookeri*, the wine palm.

Rapier, a sword with a long narrow blade, introduced in the 16th century into England from Italy, adapted for both cutting and thrusting, and later for the use of the point only. It was popular for civilian use, and employed in duelling in the 16th and 17th centuries. The hand was protected by elaborate guards.
See also ARMOUR; SWORD.

Rare Earths, see LANTHANIDES.

Rare Gases, see INERT GASES.

Rarefaction, process of reducing the density of a gas. This is usually accomplished by means of an air-pump.
See also AIR-PUMP.

Rarotonga, chief island of the Cook Islands. Its volcanic peaks rise to over 609 m clothed to their summits in rich vegetation. There are two breaks in the fringing reef, on the north shore, forming small harbours at Avarua, the main settlement, and at Avatiu. The island was discovered in 1820 and transferred to New Zealand in 1901. Area 67 km^2; population (1976) 9,811.

Ras al-Khaimah, see UNITED ARAB EMIRATES.

Ras Shamra, see UGARIT.

Ras Tafari Makonnen, see HAILE SELASSIE I.

Rash, a superficial eruption of the skin, generally consisting of minute papules (dry pimples) or pustules (pus-filled pimples) or a redness (erythema) due to congestion of the capillaries. It may be caused by external irritation, by the action of certain drugs or by gastric and intestinal disturbances, or it may be symptomatic of a specific fever, such as measles, scarlet fever or of an allergic reaction.

Rashi (c.1040–1105), name of the Rabbi Solomon Yitzhaki, one of the greatest of the rabbinical scholars; born in Troyes, France. He was the first to compose a commentary on the Talmud and the books of the Old Testament. His classically simple and incisive commentaries, indispensable in Talmudic and Biblical studies, are printed in all modern Jewish texts. Rashi had no sons, but his sons-in-law, the Tosaphists, became famous commentators of Talmudic law.

Rasht, or Resht, district and town of Gilan province, Iran; also its provincial capital. The Sefid Rud flows through the district. Rice, tobacco, tea, silk and jute are produced; it is a major silk manufacturing centre. The town is a trade centre, mainly through its port of Pahlevi, particularly for trade with the USSR. Population (1974) 187,000.

Rasmussen, Knud Johan Victor (1879–1933), Danish Arctic explorer. He visited Lapland in 1901, and accompanied the (1902–04) expedition to study the Eskimos of Kap York, Greenland. Between 1905 and 1918 he made several ethnographic expeditions. From 1921 till 1924 Rasmussen journeyed from Greenland across Arctic America to the north-east corner of Siberia.

The champion of the Eskimo people, Rasmussen established an Eskimo settlement at Thule (north-east Greenland) in 1910.

Raspberry, *Rubus idaeus*, a prickly shrub in the family Rosaceae, with pinnate leaves, white and hoary beneath, and drooping white flowers, followed by red, white or black fruits which are highly valued for dessert, preserves and other culinary uses.

Rasputin, Grigori Efimovich (1872–1916), Russian mystic. Born a Siberian peasant, Rasputin was ignorant and licentious, but was credited with powers of hypnotism and clairvoyance. Introduced to the imperial court in 1905, he apparently on several occasions saved the life of the heir to the throne (who suffered from haemophilia) and thus gained unlimited influence over the empress. During the First World War, Rasputin practically ruled Russia through ministers appointed on his recommendation after he had secured the dismissal of all the liberal ministers. This scandalised the public, and after all attempts to remove Rasputin had failed he was murdered at a dinner-party by two relatives of the emperor and the leading right-wing Duma member, Purishkevich.

Rastafarianism, a religious-political movement which originated among the blacks of Jamaica. The faith is biblical but not Christian and grew from the Back to Africa movement of the 1930s and the work of prophets such as Marcus Garvey. It took its name and was inspired by the coronation of Ras (Prince) Tafari as Haile Selassie, Emperor of Ethiopia. His titles for many Jamaicans confirmed biblical prophecy, and proved his divinity and messianic leadership of the black race which was looked on as being the true tribe of Israel.

Rat, a number of rodents, chiefly larger members of the genus *Rattus*, in family Muridae. The common brown, Norway or Hanoverian rat (*R. norvegicus*) is believed to have originated in central Asia, but is now distributed over a very large area of the world, nearly always occurring in close association with man. Almost as widely distributed is the black rat (*R. rattus*), which also was probably a native of Asia, having gradually spread westwards. Both species of rat may carry fleas which transmit bubonic plague to human beings.

Rata (*Metrosideros robusta*), a New Zealand tree, in family Myrtaceae, which in its native habitat attains a great height and bears red flowers. Its hard timber has many uses, in shipbuilding and the manufacture of Maori clubs and canoe-paddles.

Ratak, see MARSHALL ISLANDS.

Ratel, or honey badger, *Mellivora*, a genus of animals in the family Mustelidae of order Carnivora. The body is powerfully built, the legs are short, with long claws. The tail is short and the ears are rudimentary. Two species are sometimes recognised: the Indian ratel or badger (*M. ratel*) occurs throughout India, feeding on a variety of small animals and also on honey; the cape ratel (*M. capensis*) is widely distributed throughout southern Africa. Like the skunk, the ratel produces a foul-smelling secretion from its anal glands.

Rates, in the UK, taxes levied on property by local government. It is based on a notional rented value and accounts for just under half of all local-government income. Commercial property is normally rated more highly than domestic property; agricultural land is exempt.

Rathaus, German term (Dutch *radhuis*) for the seat of town government, usually translated by the English town hall. The *rathaus* became a symbol of medieval mercantile sovereignty, and in the Middle Ages its size and splendour were regarded as proof of the independence and wealth of its city. Many medieval *rathäuser* still exist.

Rathenau, Walther (1867–1922), German industrialist, statesman and writer. During the First World War he presented to Falkenhayn, then war minister, an economic plan for countering the Allied blockade, and was appointed minister of reconstruction. In 1920 he became foreign minister and negotiated the Rapallo Treaty but was assassinated in 1922. His *In Days to Come*, 1921, is a criticism of socialism and a protest against the domination of machinery in the widest sense of the word.

Rathlin Island, island 10 km off the north coast of County Antrim, Northern Ireland, opposite Ballycastle. It was the refuge of Robert Bruce, King of Scotland.

Rational Numbers, see FRACTIONS; NUMBERS.

Rationalism, primarily a philosophical movement but one whose results have been felt principally in theology. Rationalism is an attitude rather than a definite doctrine; it assumes the superiority of reason over sensation as a medium of cognition, and asserts reason to be an independent source of knowledge and the final standard of criticism in philosophy, aesthetics and religion alike. Philosophical rationalism was first formulated by Descartes in his *Discours de la méthode*, 1637; he contends that there are elementary *a priori* concepts from which the whole of knowledge can be deduced mathematically—as opposed to those who contend that the mind is blank until some sense-impression of an object is conveyed to it. The rationalistic process was accepted also by Spinoza, who constructed his *Ethics* on the mathematical lines of axioms and postulates, definitions and propositions; and by Leibniz, who advanced the idea of a logic and dialectic that should express philosophy by the same kind of rational method as that by which his calculus expressed truths in pure mathematics. Theological rationalism is opposed to supernaturalism and to rationally indefensible dogma, and refuses to accept Scripture as an infallible history of divine revelation.

Rattan, a type of palm with slender but very long climbing stems, usually having spines or hooks on the stems and leaves. Rattan genera include *Calamus* and *Daemonorops*; the stems yield various forms of cane.
See also PALMAE.

Rattan-Cane, see PALMAE.

Rattigan, Sir Terence Mervyn (1911–77), English dramatist. In 1936 he scored a success with his ingenious comedy *French Without Tears*. Others of his plays are *After the Dance*, 1939; *Flare Path*, 1942; *While the Sun Shines*, 1943; *Love in Idleness*, 1944; *The Winslow Boy*, 1946; *The Browning Version*, 1948; *The Deep Blue Sea*, 1952; *The Sleeping Prince*, 1953;

***Ravenna.** A 6th-century mosaic of the Empress Theodora and her court in the Church of San Vitale, famed for its superb mosaics.*

Separate Tables, 1954; *Ross*, 1960; *Man and Boy*, 1963.

Rattlesnakes, or pit vipers (Crotalidae), snakes found only in North and Central America. They have a number of horny flat rings on the end of the tail, which are loosely connected together, and make a loud rattle when vibrated. The head is large behind, and bears a characteristic depression or deep pit (organ sensing infrared radiation, hence temperature) on each side of the face between the eyes and the nostrils. The common rattlesnake (*C. confluentus*) grows to about 2·4 m long; the body is grey above, with irregular cross-bars and yellow flanks and a vertebral line. It is a sluggish reptile, living on rodents, and rarely attacks human beings unless molested. The bites of rattlesnakes are usually fatal, but not invariably.

Rauschenberg, Robert (1925–), American artist. He has been one of the major influences on the modern Pop Art movement, developing a type of collage, called 'combined painting', incorporating large three-dimensional objects, usually with technological associations.

Ravel, Maurice (1875–1937), French composer who studied under Fauré at the Paris Conservatory. His music shows the influence of Impressionism, neoclassicism and jazz. His most important works include the opera *L'Heure espagnole*; *Daphnis et Chloé*; the piano sonatina and *Gaspard de la nuit*; two piano concertos; and the popular *Bolero* as well as much chamber music. A characteristic work is the opera *L'Enfant et les sortilèges* which illustrates most of the styles that influenced him. *La Valse* and his orchestration of Mussorgski's *Pictures at an Exhibition* are widely performed today.

Raven, *Corvus corax*, one of the largest of the birds in order Passeriformes (family Corvidae), widely distributed in the northern hemisphere, but rare in some countries on account of its destruction by farmers and gamekeepers. It is about 60 cm long, and has a wingspan of nearly 1 m. The plumage is dense black, glossed with purple; the beak and mouth, tongue, legs and feet are also black. The bulky nest is built in cliffs or in the fork of a tall tree.

Ravenna, Italian city and capital of Ravenna province, situated some 65 km east of Bologna. It stands on the site of *Classis*, an Adriatic naval base in the time of Augustus, although it is now situated some 10 km from the coast, to which it is connected by canal. In AD 404 Honorius transferred the seat of the Western Empire to Ravenna, and after the barbarian invasions it remained the capital under Odoacer and Theodoric the Great. The beautiful 6th-century mausoleum of Galla Placidia (sister of Honorius) is decorated inside with some of the splendid mosaics for which Ravenna is famous; among other structures renowned for their mosaics are the churches of San Vitale (530), San Apollinare in Classe (549), and San Apollinare Nuovo (526). Since the discovery in the area of methane deposits in 1952 and the canal improvements, synthetic rubber, fertiliser, oil refining and petro-chemical plants have burgeoned around Ravenna. It is Italy's fifth-ranking port. Population (1979) 139,392.
See also ITALIAN ARCHITECTURE.

Ravi, river of the Punjab plains, rising in the Himalayas and joining the Chenab after 720 km. Since 1960 its waters have been controlled by India and are linked to the Beas by a canal at Madhapur.

Ravioli, see PASTA.

Rawalpindi, city of Pakistan. The city is one of Pakistan's largest military centres. It is situated on the north bank of the River Leh, 175 km south-east of Peshawar. An oil refinery is situated on the outskirts of the city, and it also has metalworking and locomotive industries. Population (1981) 928,000.

Rawlinson, Sir Henry Creswicke (1810–1895), British soldier and orientalist. In 1833 he was sent to reorganise the Shah's troops in Persia, where he studied and transcribed the undeciphered cuneiform texts and copied the trilingual Behistun rock inscriptions. His published works are the foundation of our knowledge of cuneiform inscriptions and the history of Babylonia and Assyria.

Rawsthorne, Alan (1905–71), British composer. His works include *Symphonic Studies*; overtures; three symphonies; concertos for clarinet, oboe, violin, cello, piano, and two pianos; a concerto for strings; chamber music; piano works and songs.

Ray, John, also Wray (1627–1705), English botanist. He enjoyed the friendship of Willoughby, the zoologist, whose works he edited. In his company he toured for three years in Europe, the scientific fruits of his travels being embodied in *Stirpium Europaearum extra Britannias nascentium Sylloge*, 1694. His other publications are *Synopsis methodica stirpium Britannicarum*, 1690; *Historia generalis Plantarum* (3 vols), 1686–1704; and his treatise on zoology, *Synopsis methodica Animalium quadrupedum et Serpentini Generis*, 1693.

Ray, Man (1890–1976), US photographer, painter and film maker, notable for his connection with the Dada and Surrealist movements in the USA. His most significant contribution to these fields were his objects, such as his metronome with an eye attached entitled *Object to be Destroyed*. Much of his best work was in photography, in which he employed sophisticated effects.

Ray, Nicholas (1911–), US film director. His first film, *They Live By Night* (1949), won him instant recognition, and suggested his major concerns: a compassionate romanticism struggling against the effects of social maladjustment and psychic disorientation. His best work remains emblematic of the 1950s, particularly *Rebel Without a Cause*, 1955, with James Dean; but all his films display a trenchant probing of human relationships: *In a Lonely Place*, 1950; *On Dangerous Ground*, 1951; *The Lusty Men*, 1952; *Johnny Guitar*, 1954; *Bigger Than Life*, 1956; *Bitter Victory*, 1958; *Wind Across the Everglades*, 1958; *The Savage Innocents*, 1961.

Ray, Satyajit (1921–), Indian (Bengali) film director. In 1947 he and a friend founded the Calcutta Film Society. Encouraged by the visit of Jean Renoir to India to film *The River*, Ray made *Pather Panchali*, 1955, with his own money. The success of this film in Europe awakened world interest in the Indian cinema, and enabled Ray to continue making a remarkable series of films notable for their gentle humour and affectionate humanity. He followed his first film with two sequels, *Aparajito*, 1957, and *The World of Apu*, 1959; and his subsequent films include *The Music Room*, 1958; *Goddess*, 1960; *Three Daughters*, 1961; *Charulata*, 1965; *Days and Nights in the Forest*, 1969; *Distant Thunder*, 1974; *Middleman*, 1975; and *The Chess Player*, 1977.

Ray, any fish of the order Batoidei in class Chondrichthyes, distinguished by their flattened bodies and enormously expanded pectoral fins. The gill-slits are on the undersurface of the head. In most species, on top of the head, just behind the eyes, is a pair of openings (spiracles), through which water is taken in for respiration.
See also STINGRAY; TORPEDO.

Rayleigh, John William Strutt, 3rd Baron (1842–1919), British physicist. He was professor of experimental physics at Cambridge, 1879–84, professor of natural philosophy at the Royal Institution, 1887–1905, secretary of the Royal Society, 1884–96, and president, 1905–08. He was chancellor of the University of Cambridge from 1908. His work included research in the fundamental electrical units, Boyle's Law at low pressures, optics and capillarity, the dynamical theory of gases, hydrodynamics, the mechanics of flight, photography, theory of the telephone, the distribution of alternating currents in conductors, and pure mathematics. In calculating atomic weights he discovered a discrepancy between atmospheric nitrogen and nitrogen obtained from mineral compounds, which led to his discovery, with Sir William Ramsay, of argon in 1894 for which he and Ramsay shared the 1904 Nobel Prize. He took considerable interest in psychical research.

Man Ray. Portrait of D. A. F. de Sade, *1940.*

Raynaud's Disease, a condition affecting the fingers and hands (less commonly also the feet, toes, nose and ears) in which there is abnormal spasm of the blood vessels on exposure to low temperatures. The affected part may go very pale and cold and after a while feel numb, as the blood supply to it is dramatically reduced. The condition usually affects women and is thought to be due to an overactive sympathetic nervous system (which is responsible, among other things, for controlling the tone of the blood vessels).

Rayon, synthetic fibre. In the UK the term is obsolete. However, in the USA and other countries it is still used to describe fibres known in the UK as cupro, modal or viscose.

Razin, Stepan Timofeevich, familiarly known as Stenka Razin (d.1671), leader of a peasant rebellion in Russia in 1670, a Don Cossack. He seized large tracts of land in the south-east of European Russia and all the towns on the Volga from Astrakhan to Samara. He was finally defeated and broken on the wheel in Moscow. Razin is a popular hero in Russian folklore.

Razor (Old French *rasor*; Latin *rasare*, to scrape), cutting instrument, used chiefly for shaving hair. The traditional 'cut-throat' razor, consisting of a single blade with a very keen edge attached to a handle, has been almost entirely superseded by 'safety' razors or electric razors.

Razor-Backs, see FIN-WHALES.

Razor-Shell, common name given to molluscs of the family Solenidae including the genera *Solen* and *Ensis*. They are widely distributed bivalve molluscs with very elongated shells, the valves of which are open at both ends, and are almost straight. The foot is highly developed; it can be pointed or contracted for boring rapidly into sand, and with it the razor-shell can retain so tight a hold that the foot often has to be torn off before the creature can be removed.

Razorbill, or black-billed auk, *Alca torda*, the only remaining species of a genus which included the now extinct great auk, *A. impennis*, in order Charadriiformes. It breeds on the sea rocks on various parts of the coasts of Greenland, Iceland, Scandinavia and the British Isles, and in the Bay of Fundy and Gulf of St Lawrence, making no nest, and laying only one egg, which is white with brown markings. The razorbill is about 40 cm long; the head, neck and upper surface are glossy black, and the breast and underparts pure

***Razorbill.** The black-billed auk,* Alca torda.

white. The black beak is large and much compressed, and the end is curved. The bird is a capable swimmer and diver.

Reactance. An electric circuit containing inductors (i.e. coils) or capacitors presents an opposition to the flow of alternating current (a.c.). This impedance differs from resistance because of the reactance of these components to a.c. A changing current through a coil produces a changing magnetic field which in cutting the coil gives an electromotive force opposing the original voltage. A capacitor stores energy during part of the cycle and releases it later in the cycle. The reactance is the component of impedance arising from electrostatic and electromagnetic inertia. It depends on the capacitance, inductance and frequency.

Read, Sir Herbert Edward (1893–1968), English poet, literary and art critic. A careful and conscientious craftsman of free verse, he published a succession of volumes from 1919 onwards, his *Collected Poems* appearing in 1946. As a critic he belonged to the school of Coleridge, his works including *Reason and Romanticism*, 1926; *English Prose Style*, 1928; *The Sense of Glory*, 1929; *Wordsworth*, 1930; *Form in Modern Poetry*, 1932; *In Defence of Shelley*, 1935; *Essays in Literary Criticism*, 1938; and *The True Voice of Feeling*, 1953. His reputation as an art critic rests mainly on his inter-war years, when he defended the work of new English artists such as Henry Moore, Barbara Hepworth and Ben Nicholson, as well as writing several influential works on the educational and social rôle of art.

Read, Herbert Harold (1889–1979), British geologist, who was acknowledged as an authority on igneous and metamorphic rocks, especially plutonic rocks and their origin. He was largely responsible for seven Geological Survey memoirs and several textbooks, including *The Granite Controversy*, a classic work on the origin of granite.

Reade, Charles (1814–84), English novelist and dramatist. In 1851 his tragedy, *Angelo*, was produced at the Olympic. He then wrote, in collaboration with Tom Taylor, the popular comedy *Masks and Faces*, which he turned into the novel *Peg Woffington*, 1853. Reade's next novel, *Christie Johnstone*, 1853, is one of his best, followed by *It is Never Too Late to Mend*, 1856, an exposure of the prison system. He wrote many other novels and plays but his masterpiece is *The Cloister and the Hearth: a Tale of the Middle Ages*, 1861. It is one of the liveliest of historical novels, surveying the customs of Holland, Germany, France and Italy in the 15th century. *Hard Cash*, 1863, is an exposure of the private asylum.

'Reader's Digest', US monthly periodical, founded in 1922, which initially condensed already published material and then began successfully to commission original work. With its many editions, it has the largest circulation of any magazine in the world.

Reading, Rufus Daniel Isaacs, 1st Marquess of (1860–1935), English judge and administrator. He was the first Jew to fill the offices of lord chief justice of England, viceroy of India and foreign secretary.

Reading, county town of Berkshire, England, 58 km by rail west of London, on the Kennet, at its confluence with the Thames. Traditionally a cloth town, Reading now has extensive office development, mixed manufacturing, boat-building yards and engineering works, being also an important railway junction. Population (1981) 123,731.

Reading, city and county seat of Berks county, Pennsylvania, USA, on the Schuylkill river, 72 km north-west of Philadelphia by rail. Reading grew as an iron and steel centre and still has steel plants, foundries and heavy engineering industries. Textiles are the chief light industry. Population (1980) 78,686.

Reagan, Ronald Wilson (1911–), 40th President of the United States. He was a sports announcer in Des Moines, Iowa (1932–37) and a motion picture actor in Hollywood (1937–54), becoming president of the Screen Actors Guild (1947–52 and 1959–60). Later he became a TV actor and producer, and in 1964 became active in Republican politics in California. In 1966 he was elected governor of California, serving until 1974. He defeated Carter in the 1980 presidential election.

His policies have been characterised economically by large cuts in non-defence government spending and severe reductions in the numbers of federal employees. Although this led to lower inflation, unemployment soared to reach 10 per cent by his second year. He has been responsible for the biggest peacetime build-up of American military forces and his foreign policy has hardened against Communist expansion, exemplified by the backing of Central-American right-wing governments and the sending of troops to counter a Marxist takeover in Grenada in 1983. In January 1984 he announced his decision to stand for a second term.

Real, Spanish silver coin first struck in the 14th century and the principal unit of currency in Spain until replaced by the peseta in 1869.

Real Numbers. Any number, positive or negative, which is either a whole number (or zero) or consists of a whole number (or zero) plus a decimal fraction, whether the decimal terminates or not, is a real number. The set of real numbers is denoted by **R**.

See also NUMBERS.

Real Presence, in Christian theology, the substantial presence of the body, blood, soul and divinity of Jesus under the species of the Eucharistic bread and wine after consecration. The doctrine of the real presence is held by the Roman Catholic and Orthodox churches, and also by many Anglican theologians. According to the Roman Catholic Church, the real presence is effected by transubstantiation, i.e. the 'substance' of the bread and wine is changed, while the 'accidents' (appearance, weight, etc.) remain the same. This, the scholastic explanation, is not admitted by the Orthodox and Anglican churches; but traditional Orthodox theologians use the Greek equivalent of the word (*metousiōsis*), and their teaching is accepted by the Roman Catholic Church.

Real Property, or realty. Real property comprises (1) corporeal hereditaments or immoveables such as lands, buildings, minerals, trees and all other things which are part of or affixed to land; (2) incorporeal hereditaments which are not things, but rights such as easements, profits, rent-charges, tithes, advowsons, reversions; and (3) personal property 'notionally' converted in equity into real property.

Real Tennis (old French *real*, royal), a racket-and-ball game for two or four people. It is one of the oldest court games in the world; the modern game closely resembles the version played in 1100. Most other court games, including lawn tennis, have evolved from it. The game is played in a four-walled court divided by a net. The ball may be played off the walls as in squash; scoring is similar to lawn tennis. The court built by Henry VIII at Hampton Court in 1529 is the oldest in the world where the game is still played.

See also TENNIS, LAWN.

***Ronald Reagan** spent 17 years in films before entering politics. This still is from* Cattle Queen of Montana, *1954.*

Realism, in philosophy, an interpretation of life as opposed to Idealism. It involves the beliefs that time, space and their attributes are real (transcendental Realism), that phenomena exist apart from our consciousness or conception (empirical Realism), and that our perception of them is governed by direct intuitive cognition. It has figured in philosophy from the beginning, e.g. in Socrates, Plato and Aristotle. During the Middle Ages the term Realism was used in scholastic philosophy to denote the teaching of the 'reality' of universal ideas; Realism in this sense was thus contrasted with Nominalism. St Thomas Aquinas and Duns Scotus were moderate Realists.

Realty, see REAL PROPERTY.

Reaping. In the beginning of the 19th century cereal crops were harvested, as in prehistoric times, by means of the reaping hook or sickle, or scythe. In some parts of the world these tools are still used. A reaping machine was first introduced by the Rev. Patrick Bell in 1826. It only cut the corn and laid it in a swathe at the side. About 1885, the binder, which gathers the bundle, ties it with string, and throws it off the machine, was introduced. This was a very complicated machine, but its employment, resulting in the dropping of the price of corn, was of great importance.

Separate threshing is eliminated by the combine harvester, which cuts and threshes in one operation. The combine can be one of three types: tractor drawn and powered; tractor drawn and self-powered; or self-propelled, of which the last is now nearly universal.

Reardon, Ray (1932–), Welsh snooker player. He won the World Professional title six times during the 1970s and was BBC 'Pot Black' champion in 1969, and again after a ten year gap in 1979. He captained Wales in the World Team Championships in 1979 and 1980. By 1983 he was ranked No. 1 in the world and was also runner-up in the Benson and Hedges Masters, which he last won in 1976.

Reason, as a philosophical term, refers to the faculty of rational thought. Sometimes the term is used in the sense of rationality, the principle of order constituting that faculty. See also LOGIC; PHILOSOPHY; RATIONALISM.

Réaumur, René Antoine Ferchault de (1683–1757), French scientist. An able natural historian, he left an exhaustive history of insects (1734–42). Besides discovering the white opaque glass and the thermometer which bears his name, he wrote monographs on subjects as different as turquoise mines, the silk of spiders, auriferous rivers, the chemistry of iron and steel, and the manufacture of tinplate. For his thermometer he used a mixture of $\frac{4}{5}$ alcohol and $\frac{1}{5}$ water, calling the freezing point 0° and the boiling point 80°.

Rebec, musical instrument of Arab origin, popular in the Middle Ages. It was made in the shape of an elongated half-pear, the body and neck being carved from a single block of wood. Normally with three strings, it was played with a bow. It was capable of greater agility than the fiddle, and was used for dance music until supplanted by the violin in the 18th century. It survives as a folk instrument in Eastern Europe.

Rebekah (Rebecca), wife of Isaac, and mother of Esau and Jacob (Gen. xxiv and xxvii).

Rebirth, as a Buddhist doctrine, is not to be confused with the Hindu belief in Reincarnation. Whereas the latter posits the continuation of a distinct entity or soul through a series of innumerable lives and deaths, the Rebirth doctrine of Buddhism denies the continuation of a fixed entity from one moment to the next, let alone one life to the next. From the subcellular level upwards, birth and death are occurring in every moment. There is continuity, but no thing that continues, and the only permanence is impermanence.

Rebus, riddle or puzzle which is set out *non verbis sed rebus*, not with words but with things, that is, with pictures representing words or syllables; for example, a cat sitting on a log might represent catalogue. In heraldry the term is applied to punning devices on a coat of arms, such as the broken spear on the shield of Nicholas Breakspear (Pope Adrian IV).

Récamier, Jeanne Françoise, Madame (1777–1849), French society leader. A record of the social triumphs of Mme Récamier would involve notice of nearly all that was distinguished in Paris during a space of about 50 years. To the famous Mme de Staël she was bound by ties of extreme affection, and the most distinguished *ami* of her later years was M. de Chateaubriand.

Receiver, Official, an officer of the High Court who, on the making of a receiving order against an individual, or a partnership, or of a compulsory winding-up order against a limited company, administers the property concerned. In bankruptcy matters where the creditors do not appoint a non-official trustee, the official receiver realises the assets and distributes the proceeds to creditors. Other administrative matters for which he is responsible include the conduct of public examinations of debtors, and reports to the Court on applications for discharge from bankruptcy.

In company liquidations, if the creditors and contributories do not wish for the appointment of a liquidator, the official receiver acts as such.

Receiving Order, order by a court for the protection of the estate of a debtor who has committed an act of bankruptcy by placing the estate under the court's custody and control through the official receiver (or officer of the court).

Recession, a downward movement in the trading cycle which may prove temporary or may develop into an economic depression. A recession is characterised by a decline in production and therefore in employment, producing a decline in household income and therefore in consumption. Manufacturers become caught in a downward spiral, and are unwilling to risk investment in new capacity or techniques.

Recessive Gene, see HEREDITY.

Recife (or Pernambuco), capital of the state of Pernambuco, north-east Brazil. It is the most important town and port in north Brazil, being much used as a port of call by ocean-going liners. The main exports are sugar and cotton, and the chief industries include sugar refining, spirit distilling, cotton textiles, cement and vegetable oils. Population (1980) 1,184,215.

Reciprocity. Shortly expressed, the theory of reciprocity of exchange in international trade means that one country declines to receive imports from another country except on condition that the latter accepts the commodities of the former in return.

Recitative, declaration in singing with fixed notes but often without definite metre or time. It is comparable to prose episodes in verse drama. Recitative serves to modulate to or near the key of the set musical number, usually an aria, that follows it, and also to give the singer an opportunity for dramatic declamation.

Recklinghausen, city in North Rhine-Westphalia, Federal Republic of Germany, in the Ruhr, 53 km north-east of Düsseldorf. Its present prosperity dates from the 19th-century development of the Ruhr coalfields. There are some coal-mines remaining and new industries such as chemicals, metallurgy and textiles. Population (1980) 119,600.

Recognisance, in English law, an obligation which a man enters into before a court or a magistrate, binding himself to do some particular act, e.g. to be of good behaviour for a specified period, or to pay a debt. If the condition of the recognisance is broken, the recognisance becomes forfeited, and if the recognisance was entered into with sureties, the sureties too become the absolute debtors of the Crown for the sums for which they bound themselves.

Record Player, formerly called gramophone, a device for reproducing sound stored on a record, or disc. In the ordinary player the record takes the form of a disc with a continuous spiral groove on each side. It is placed on a turntable, which rotates at a constant speed ($33\frac{1}{3}$, 45, or 78 revolutions per minute). The stylus of a pickup is placed in the groove and vibrates as the record spins. The vibrations are converted in the pickup head into electrical impulses, which are passed to an amplifier and thence to a loudspeaker, or in a stereo system to a pair of speakers.

All the electrical components add 'hum' and 'noise' to the signal; uneven speed of the turntable adds 'wow', uneven turntable bearings add rumble, and resonances in the speaker add 'coloration'. Modern 'hi-fi' equipment is designed to reduce these unwanted additions to the sound to a minimum.

In recent years an entirely different kind of record player has appeared on the market—the compact-disc player. The disc is rotated on a turntable like an ordinary disc, but is 'played' by means of a laser beam instead of a stylus and pickup.

See also SOUND RECORDING AND REPRODUCTION.

Recorder, musical instrument of the duct flute family, having a soft and sweet tone. The family also includes the flageolet, tin-whistle, pipe and galoubet. Instruments of the true recorder family have seven finger-holes and a thumb-hole, and a compass of about two octaves. It was a favourite instrument in Tudor times. It became known as the *flûte-à-bec* or English flute, and was subsequently superseded by the stronger-toned transverse or German flute, but is again in use. The English flageolet has six finger-holes and normally lacks the thumb-hole; it was designed as an easy version of the recorder for amateur use, but was later elaborated. The French flageolet, with four finger-holes and two thumb-holes, was more often a professional's instrument.

Recorder, in England and Wales, part-time judge of the Crown Court competent to hear the more trivial offences tried at the Crown Court.

Recording Machine, device used mainly for dictation (the 'dictaphone') and transcription of correspondence, but which may also record telephone conversations or conference proceedings.

Originally, the speech was recorded on wax

cylinders, but electromagnetic methods are now used employing magnetic disc or tape, usually cassettes. Research is also proceeding on techniques involving digitised speech held in the store of a computer. It is usually possible to erase the discs or tapes, and continually reuse them. Multi-channel tape, up to 50 mm in width, and using both analog and digital information, is used for some scientific records of simultaneous events. To a large extent, however, these have been superseded by recording computers using digitisation and tape-drives.
See also TAPE RECORDER; VIDEO RECORDING.

Recrystallisation, technique widely employed in organic chemistry for the purification of solid substances. It is necessary to select a suitable solvent which will dissolve the impure material readily when hot but only slightly when cold. The material is then dissolved in the minimum of boiling solvent and filtered if necessary to remove any insoluble impurities. On cooling, the pure substance crystallises out, leaving the impurities in solution. The process is repeated if necessary to ensure complete purity.

Rectification, in chemistry, process of purifying volatile spirits by fractional distillation; they are then known as rectified spirits.

Rectified Spirit, alcohol which has been purified and strengthened by fractional distillation. It is a constant boiling mixture of 95 per cent alcohol and 5 per cent water.

Rectifier, a device permitting current flow in one direction only. It is most often used to convert an oscillatory current to a unidirectional one, as in transforming a.c. mains current supply to a d.c. output.

Rector, in the Church of England, a clerk in holy orders who has the cure of a parish and also full possession of all rights and privileges attached to it. These originally included the greater and lesser tithes, whereas a vicar received only the lesser. After the abolition of tithes in 1936, the distinction between a rector and a vicar disappeared, but since 1968 the head of a 'team ministry' has been called a rector.

Rectum, the lower part of the large intestine. It commences at the end of the sigmoid flexure and extends to the anus.
The rectum receives by peristaltic motion the residue of food material from the large intestine. An accumulation takes place until the mass produces a desire to empty the rectum. This is accomplished by the relaxation of the interior and exterior sphincter muscles of the anus. The motion of defaecation is partly voluntary and partly involuntary; the exterior sphincter is relaxed by an effort of the will, but the inner muscles act involuntarily on receipt of the accustomed stimuli. If from any cause these stimuli evoke no response, the faeces are retained, producing constipation. Many of the disorders to which the rectum is liable are due to constipation.

Red, regarded, with blue and yellow, as a 'primary colour'.
See also COLOUR; PIGMENT.

Red Admiral Butterfly, *Vanessa atalanta*, a butterfly widely distributed in the northern hemisphere with black wings crossed by scarlet bands and marked with white and blue spots. The spiny black caterpillar feeds on nettles.

Red Army, name borne by the army of the Soviet Union since the revolution of 1917. During the inter-war years the Red Army improved steadily in equipment and general efficiency; but progress was hampered by overstrict political control at all levels, and periodical purges of senior officers on political grounds. At its peak, during the Second World War, it reached a strength approaching 20 million, and by the end of the hostilities in May 1945 the Red Army had played a major part in the defeat of Germany.
Since 1945 the Red Army's rôle has been seen as an offensive-defensive one, with the offensive rôle increasing since 1949 and the formation of the North Atlantic Treaty Organisation.
See also UNION OF SOVIET SOCIALIST REPUBLICS.

Red Admiral Butterfly, Vanessa atalanta.

Red Clay, see SEDIMENTARY ENVIRONMENTS.

Red Cross, The, international organisation for the relief of suffering, owes its inception to the Swiss banker Jean Henri Dunant (1828–1910), who, moved by the sufferings of the wounded at the battle of Solferino (June 1859), published *Un Souvenir de Solferino*, 1862, urging the formation of voluntary aid societies, with a permanent existence, to succour the wounded in time of war. As a result an international conference was held in Geneva in 1863, attended by delegates from 16 European countries, and followed in 1864 by a diplomatic conference which signed the first Geneva Convention. As an emblem of neutrality the convention adopted a red cross on a white ground (the colours of the Swiss flag reversed) and the motto 'inter arma caritas'. The International Red Cross Committee is composed of 25 Swiss citizens, and has its seat in Geneva.

Red Currant, see CURRANT.

Red Deer, *Cervus elaphus*, a large deer widely distributed throughout Europe, Asia and North Africa. A full-grown male (stag or hart) stands 1·2 m at the withers, and typical antlers measure about 80 cm in length and have a spread of 80 cm. They may have as many as 12 or even 14 tines or points. The antlers are shed in April or May, and a few days afterwards the new growth appears. While the new antlers are developing they are covered with a thick velvet. They are full-grown in about 12 weeks, and the 'velvet' is then rubbed off. Hornless stags sometimes occur. During the breeding season the colour is a rich brown, turning grey at the approach of winter. The young are spotted with white. The wapiti replaces the red deer in North America but is very similar.

Red-hot Poker, or flame-flower, the common name of the various species of *Kniphofia* from Africa, a genus of the Liliaceae. Some species and hybrids are cultivated for ornament.

Red Letter Days, greater festivals of the Christian Church's year, which in the old manuscripts or early printed ecclesiastical calendars were inscribed in red. Apart from Sundays, there are 29 red letter days in the Anglican Book of Common Prayer, described as 'all the Feasts that are to be observed in the Church of England'.

Red River, important western tributary of the Mississippi, which rises in Staked Plains, Texas, USA, passing through a canyon 160 km long and 300 m deep. It later forms the boundary between the states of Oklahoma and Texas, then flows through Arkansas and Louisiana, and enters the Mississippi about 500 km above the Gulf of Mexico. It has a length of about 2100 km.

Red River of the North. This river flows through the USA and Canada. It forms the boundary between Minnesota and North Dakota. At first it flows south-west, then makes a great curve, joining the Bois de Sioux river. It then joins the Assiniboine near Winnipeg, and empties itself into that lake. Length 1062 km (837 km in the USA).

Red Rum, bay gelding (foaled 1965). He won a record three Grand Nationals in 1973, 1974 and 1977 and finished runner-up in 1975 and 1976. He also became the first horse to win both the English and Scottish Nationals in the same year, 1974. Withdrawn on the eve of the 1978 National because of a bruised heel, he was retired and became the first racehorse to be made into a limited company.

Red Sea, a branch of the Indian Ocean, running north-west from the Gulf of Aden for 1932 km. The width varies from 145 to 306 km, separating Saudi Arabia and the Yemen on the east from Ethiopia, Sudan and Egypt on the west. Although narrow, it is very deep and reaches over 2300 m in parts. At the northern end it divides into two long narrow gulfs, those of Aqaba and Suez, which are separated by the Sinai Peninsula. The Gulf of Suez is linked with the Mediterranean Sea by the Suez Canal. There are no rivers flowing into the Red Sea, so the only exchange of water is with the Gulf of Aden through the narrow and shallow straits of Bab-el-Mandeb.
The principal harbours are Jiddah (the port for Mecca) on the Arabian coast, Eilat in Israel on the Gulf of Aqaba, and Suez, Sudan and Massawa on the African coast.

Red Shift, a shift of the lines in a spectrum towards the red usually caused by a velocity of recession or by a strong gravitational field.
See also COSMOLOGY; GALAXY; QUASAR; RADIAL VELOCITY.

Red Spider, *Tetranychus*, a tiny reddish suctorial mite, not a true spider, which causes much damage to plants, especially those in dry greenhouses, by sucking the sap from the leaves, causing them to become yellow and die. Infested leaves can be cleaned by sponging with soft soap and water.

Redditch, town in the county of Hereford and Worcester, England, 19 km south of Birmingham. Its chief manufactures are needles and fishing tackle, and motor cycles, bicycles and springs. Redditch was designated a New Town in 1974. Population (1981) 66,854.

Redgrave, Sir Michael Scudamore (1908–), British actor and producer. He made his first appearance at the Playhouse, Liverpool, in 1934, where he married Rachel Kempson. He soon became one of the leading actors of the day, his Hamlet, Antony and Lear being much admired. He also appeared in many modern plays, and in films, among them *Thunder Rock*, *The Browning Version*, *The Dam Busters*, *The Loneliness of the Long-Distance Runner* and *Goodbye Mr Chips*. In 1952 he was appointed director of the new Yvonne Arnaud Theatre at Guildford, where he made several appearances in leading parts. His three children, Vanessa (1937–), Corin (1939–) and Lynn (1943–) have also made successful careers on the stage and screen.

Redmond, John Edward (1856–1918), Irish politician. When the Nationalist party split in 1890 over the Parnell-O'Shea divorce scandal, Redmond became leader of the Parnellite minority, and when the party re-united in 1900 became leader of the whole. After the general elections of 1910 Redmond held considerable power in the House of Commons. However, his prestige and that of the Nationalist party gave way to the rising power of Sinn Féin.
See also HOME RULE.

Redon, Odilon (1840–1916), French painter and lithographer. He first became noted for lithographs of a fantastic and dream-like nature, inspired partly by the graphic work of Goya and partly by Poe, Baudelaire and Huysmans. His work was seen as a major contribution to Symbolism, especially by the literary symbolists, in particular Mallarmé. From 1890 onwards he produced oil paintings and pastels, brilliant in colour.

Redpoll, *Acanthis flammea*, a small finch, characterised by the deep crimson crown of the head and vermilion breast.

Redstart, *Phoenicurus*, genus of birds allied to the thrushes, in the family Muscicapidae, order Passeriformes. The common redstart, *P. phoenicurus*, is a summer visitor to Europe from Africa, nesting in hollow trees, where it lays about six greenish-blue eggs with red spots. Its upper parts are dark grey and the forehead pure white, the throat is black and the upper parts of the tail and tail coverts are rust red. The black redstart, *P. ochruros*, is a sooty black with rust upper tail coverts as in the common redstart. Redstarts of the New World are the wood warblers; they are unrelated to the Old World species.

Reductio ad Absurdum, see ABSURDUM, REDUCTIO AD.

Reduction, in chemistry, the complimentary process to oxidation.
See also OXIDATION.

Redwing, *Turdus iliacus*, a thrush in family Muscicapidae, order Passeriformes, somewhat smaller than the song thrush and with an inferior song. Its back is darker than that of the common thrush; the feathers beneath the wings are a bright rust colour, and there is a distinct white line over the eye. It breeds in Siberia and Scandinavia.

Redwood, see SEQUOIA.

Reed, Sir Carol (1906–76), British film director. He went into film production in 1930. His films have included *The Stars Look Down*, *Night Train to Munich*, *Kipps*, *The Young Mr. Pitt*, *The Way Ahead*, *Odd Man Out*, *The Fallen Idol*, *The Third Man*, *A Kid for Two Farthings*, *Our Man in Havana*, *The Running Man*. He was a director with the Army Cinematograph Service, 1942–45, and directed *The True Glory*, a picture of the war from D-Day to VE-Day.

Reed, John (1887–1920), US journalist. He covered the Mexican revolt of 1914 and the East European Front in the First World War. In 1919 he organised the Communist Labor party (USA) and founded and edited its organ, the *Voice of Labor*. Indicted for sedition, he took refuge in Russia, joining the Communist leaders. He died of typhus and was buried in the Kremlin. His publications include *Ten Days that Shook the World*, 1919.

Reed, name of various tall aquatic grasses. The common reed, *Phragmites australis* (*communis*), is a tall plant, with long leaves, a dense, drooping, purple-brown plume of florets and a perennial rootstock. It is found in swamps and shallow water, except in very poor and acid conditions, throughout the world, yielding an abundance of stout, durable grass of great value for thatching. *Arundo donax* is a reed-grass of southern Europe. *Glyceria maxima* is a reed-grass. *Cyperus papyrus* (technically a sedge) is the paper reed of North African swamps.

Reed-mace, see BULRUSH; TYPHA.

Reed Warbler, see WARBLERS.

Reedbuck, see ANTELOPE.

Reeds (music), the vibrating tongues generating the sound of woodwind instruments (except flutes) and some organ pipes. These are all beating reeds, normally made of cane; in the organ they are metal. Clarinets, saxophones, bagpipe drones and organs have single reeds beating against a mouthpiece or shallot; oboes, bassoons, shawms, crumhorns and most bagpipe chanters have double reeds, two blades of cane beating against each other. Free reeds, metal blades vibrating to and fro in a frame, are used in harmoniums, mouth-organs, concertinas, accordions, etc.

Reefing, the operation of reducing the sail area which a ship presents to the wind. Today roller reefing is popular; the boom is able to rotate and the sail is wrapped around the boom.

Reel (dance). The term was originally used in Scotland to refer to any communal dance, but it can also apply to a musical rhythm in 2-4 or 4-4 time and to an interweaving dance figure. Scottish dances performed in reel style usually have a figure of eight pattern, are performed either in longways or circular formation, and often include a progressive movement occurring when dancers change partners or couples change position in a set. Reels are also danced in other countries.

Rees, Merlyn (1920–), British politician. After war service he went to university and became a lecturer in economics. From 1972 to 1974 he was opposition spokesman on Northern Ireland affairs and was secretary of state for Northern Ireland 1974 to 1976 and later home secretary from 1976 to 1979. He became opposition spokesman for home affairs 1979 to 1980 and spokesman for energy from 1980.

Refectory, communal dining-hall of a monastery or college, usually furnished with long 'refectory tables' and benches.

Referendum, a device by which a proposal is submitted to the electorate for approval. In some cases the referendum precedes executive or legislative action and in others it is a ratification of an executive or legislative act, which may have no legal force until approved by a referendum. Referenda are used in many states of the United States and in a number of cases are combined with the initiative, by which measures may be proposed by a specified number of electors for enactment or enforce the submission to a referendum of proposals made by the state legislature.
British political tradition has normally rejected the referendum. In 1975, however, Britain used a national referendum to determine whether or not to remain a member of the European Economic Community.

Reflection and Refraction of Light. At a boundary between two media, e.g. an air-glass interface, some of the energy in a beam of light is reflected and some travels on into the new medium and is refracted (bent). The law of reflection states that the incident and reflected rays make equal angles with the normal (perpendicular) at the point of incidence of the ray, and also that the two rays and the normal all lie in a common plane. The law of refraction states that the sine of the angle of refraction (i.e. the angle between the refracted ray and the normal) divided by the sine of the angle of incidence is a constant, and that the incident and refracted rays and the normal lie in one plane. The ratio of the two sines is the refractive index of the medium, the refractive index of vacuum being taken as unity. The refractive index of a medium is equal to the speed of light in a vacuum divided by the speed of light in the medium. If the light falls on the boundary from the medium of higher refractive index, and if the angle of incidence on the boundary exceeds a limiting value (varying for different media) there is no refracted ray and all the light is reflected internally. This total internal reflection is the reason for the silvery appearance of bubbles of air in water. Certain crystals show double refraction or birefringence.
See also OPTICS; POLARISATION OF LIGHT; REFRACTIVE INDEX.

Reflex, see CONDITIONED REFLEX; SPINAL CORD.

Reformation, name given to a movement in the Western Church in the 16th century that led to the rejection of the jurisdiction of the pope by the 'Protestant' churches, and their separation from the Roman Catholic Church.
Causes. By the early 16th century the Roman Catholic Church was in need of reform. The papacy had become an Italian political power;

many of the higher clergy were concerned with worldly authority; and moral standards were low. The Reformation owed much to the Renaissance spirit. Humanists were able to demonstrate that documents establishing papal supremacy were spurious, and the printing press was an important factor in the dissemination of Protestant belief.

Course. The Reformation began in Germany with the career of Martin Luther who, in 1520, attacked the authority of the pope and called on Germans to unite against papal exploitation and to reform the Church. In 1521 Luther appeared at the Diet of Worms to defend his views before Charles V, and was excommunicated. But a number of princes supported him and neither Charles nor the pope was sufficiently strong to crush the movement. Lutheranism continued to spread until at the Diet of Augsburg in 1555 it was decided that it was for each German prince to choose the religion of his principality.

The Reformation in Switzerland began at Zurich in 1520 independently of Luther, and was led by the humanist priest Huldreich Zwingli. In 1525 the mass was abolished and in 1530 Geneva expelled its bishops and established its political freedom. In 1536 Jean Calvin, the French reformer, settled in Geneva.

In France the reformers found an ally in Marguerite of Navarre, sister to King Francis, and for a time enjoyed toleration. However, Henry II, Francis's successor, set himself to extirpate the movement. That the Huguenots survived is in large measure due to Calvin's exertions in providing literature and ministers. By 1559 there were 50 organised churches. It was not until 1598 that, by the Edict of Nantes, Huguenots were given liberty of conscience and worship.

In England, Tyndale's translation of the New Testament (1526), with Luther's own notes, spread the ideas of the Reformation to a wide audience. Reform was helped when Henry VIII made England independent of the pope in order to divorce Catherine of Aragon, and the new views became prominent when the reformer Thomas Cranmer was made Archbishop of Canterbury (1533). With the succession, in 1547, of Henry's Protestant-educated son, Edward, Cranmer was able to go further in reform. However, Edward was succeeded in 1553 by his Roman Catholic sister, Mary, who put to death over 300 Protestants, including Cranmer. But Mary's attempt to return papal supremacy failed, and when her sister, Elizabeth, succeeded her in 1558, the restoration of Protestantism was welcomed.

The Reformation was also effective in Scotland, Sweden and the Netherlands.

Reformed Churches, the religious societies which followed the teaching and ecclesiastical organisation of Calvin and Zwingli rather than those of Luther. In Germany the Reformed and Lutheran churches co-exist. Of the other Protestant churches, those of Scotland, Holland, France, Poland, Switzerland and most of those in the USA belong to the former group. The Reformed churches differ from the Lutheran in their total rejection of consubstantiation, in regarding the Lord's Supper as only a commemorative meal, and in rejecting ceremonial and ornaments retained by the Lutherans, such as the crucifix.

Refraction, see REFLECTION AND REFRACTION OF LIGHT.

Refraction, Errors of, in the case of vision, are due to constitutional or pathological abnormalities in the cornea, crystalline lens, or shape of the eye which cause abnormal refraction of light rays; or to muscular changes leading to deficient accommodation.

Presbyopia (old sight) is due chiefly to changes in the mechanical properties and shape of the lens and contractile power of the ciliary muscles, with advancing age; near objects are indistinct. In *hypermetropia* (long sight) the eyeball is short and the focus of the rays lies behind the retina, producing a condition similar to presbyopia, but applying to objects at all distances; both are corrected by convex lenses. When the eyeball is long, so that the focus lies in front of the retina, *myopia* or short-sightedness is found; distant objects are indistinct. Concave lenses produce correct vision.

Astigmatism is due to the abnormal shape of the cornea or lens, and the rays of light in different planes are not refracted to the same focus. Cylindrical glasses, correcting corneal curvature, are used to correct astigmatism.

Asthenopia is eye-fatigue, due to overstrain of the muscles of the eye, or to a neuropathic condition, consequent on the various defects of refraction. In *anisometropia* the two eyes have very different refractions.

Refractive Index, the ratio of the speed of light in a vacuum divided by the speed of light in the medium. As a physical constant of the medium, but dependent on the wavelength of the light, it determines the angles at which rays are refracted into and out of the medium, and also the proportions of light intensity reflected at the surface of the medium. Typical values range from 1·52 (spectacle glass) to 2·42 (diamond) for solids. See also REFLECTION AND REFRACTION OF LIGHT; REFRACTOMETER; REFRACTOMETRY.

Refractometer, instrument for measuring the refractive index of a liquid. The two most common types are the Abbé and the Pulfrich, both critical-angle refractometers.

Refractometry, the measurement of refractive indices of optical materials. The classical approach is to make a prism of glass with an angle of about 60° and use a spectrometer to measure the angle A of the prism and the angle D of minimum deviation. Refractive index $n = \sin\frac{1}{2}(A + D)/\sin\frac{1}{2}A$. This method is accurate to within a few parts in 10^6, and it can be used for liquids with a hollow prism. Refractive indices of gases are determined by interferometric methods.

Refractories, materials, usually non-metallic, which are used in the construction of furnaces, flues and crucibles on account of their resistance to heat. The chemical composition should correspond to the reactions which occur in a furnace. For instance, basic substances should not be heated in refractory articles of an acid or siliceous nature, and vice versa, since the two will react together to form a fresh compound (a salt), which is less heat-resisting than either the acid or the base taken separately.

See also METALLURGY.

Refrigeration, cooling of a substance. The term is popularly associated with the processing and preservation of foodstuffs, and in these fields it is of prime importance; it is, however, used widely in numerous other important fields. One of the more obvious examples is air conditioning; there are, however, many applications in industry, such as in the liquefaction of gases and the shrink-fitting together of metal parts; in building construction, where the setting of poured concrete is assisted by the removal of the heat generated in the mass; in mining, where mud is hardened by freezing so that it may be more easily excavated; in problems of diminishing the skin heat of high-speed aircraft and guided missiles, etc. There are even applications in the field of entertainment, e.g. ice rinks. The lowest possible temperature is known as an absolute zero. It is −273·15°C, or 0 K, and physicists have gradually reached to within a fraction of a degree of it. Refrigeration methods and techniques have played an important part in this and other research, including those experiments in which special climatic conditions have to be simulated.

Regal, small portable organ, said to have been invented about 1460, originally employing only reed pipes. It was particularly popular during the 16th and 17th centuries; Monteverdi used it for unearthly effect in his opera *Orfeo* (1607). The regal effect was also incorporated into the organ proper.

Regalia, in law, the attributes or privileges of or belonging by virtue of his prerogative to the sovereign, which, according to writers on civil law, comprise the power of life and death, war and peace, the administration of justice, monopoly of coinage, the power of assessment, and the ownership of waifs, estrays, royal fish, treasure trove, etc.

See also CROWN.

Regalia, the ensigns or visible marks of royalty, or, more accurately, the apparatus of a coronation. In England the chief regalia proper, kept in the Tower of London, are the three crowns, the queen consort's crowns or diadems, the king's royal and other sceptres, signifying kingly authority, the two orbs, representing the domination of Christianity, the jewelled sword of state and four other state swords, the ampulla and spoon, the golden spurs of chivalry and coronation ring, the state trumpets, and the bracelets or armills. The regalia of Scotland comprise the crown, sceptre, sword of state, and mace, and are kept in Edinburgh Castle.

In France, the crown, the sword (*La Joyeuse*), and the spurs of Charlemagne have survived. The French crown diamonds and gems were frequently reset for each succeeding monarch, but many famous jewels and stones were lost during the Revolution. The leading example of Italian regalia is the iron crown of Lombardy. The crown of the former German Empire, dating from the Franco-Prussian War of 1871, is modelled on that of Charlemagne. The imperial crown made for Catherine II of Russia was one of the sumptuous items of the regalia of the Romanovs, which were formerly kept at the Winter Palace.

See also CROWN.

Regeneration, the regrowth of lost or

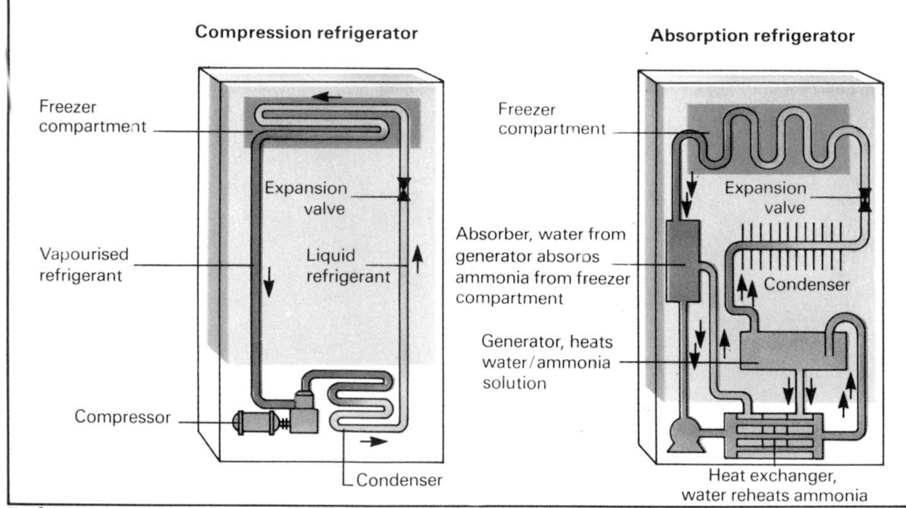

***Refrigeration.** There are two forms of domestic refrigerator in common use: the compression refrigerator, in which the refrigerant is compressed and allowed to expand in the freezer compartment, thus absorbing heat; and the absorption refrigerator in which ammonia vapour is released from solution in water, condensed, and then allowed to expand, again absorbing heat.*

injured parts. Most organisms have some capacity for regeneration; in general, however, regenerative powers are associated with primitiveness. The more specialised the cells of an organism have become, the less able they are to dedifferentiate (return to an unspecialised state with capacity for respecialisation in a new direction) and replace those cells which have been lost or damaged. Thus many lower invertebrate animals such as sponges, hydroids and planarian worms are able to regenerate whole new individuals from minute body fragments, whilst at higher levels of complexity powers of regeneration become limited to specific regions prone to damage, e.g. the legs of crabs and the tails of certain lizards. In mammals regeneration is restricted to the renewal of tissues such as skin and blood cells which die continually and are replaced by the proliferative activity of specialised tissue regions.

Regeneration, theological term derived from the words of Jesus to Nicodemus: 'Except a man be born again [*or* from above] he cannot see the kingdom of heaven'. In Roman Catholic theology regeneration is identified with receiving sanctifying grace in baptism and the term means initial justification; but Protestants think regeneration a sensible change of heart and life, not necessarily connected with any external rite.

Regensburg (formerly *Ratisbon*), city in Bavaria, Federal Republic of Germany, on the Danube at its confluence with the Regen, 104 km north-east of Munich. During the Middle Ages it was a prosperous mercantile town. The Reichstag met here from 1613 until 1806, and in 1810 the city became part of Bavaria. The palace of the Princes of Thurn and Taxis was formerly an abbey; its chapel is partly 8th-century. The Danube here is spanned by a 12th-century bridge. Regensburg has a university, and electrical and chemical industries, clothing and food manufacture have been established. Population (1980) 131,800.

Regent, one who exercises the power of the sovereign during the absence or incapacity of the sovereign.

Reger, Max (1873–1916), German composer. His music is characterised by rich harmonic effects and great dexterity of contrapuntal part-writing. His best and most frequently performed works are for the organ. Variations proved the best mode for his ideas, and he is among the best exponents of this form in the 19th century. His work includes chamber music, church music, orchestral works, piano music and songs.

Reggae, a form of rock music which originated in the West Indies and has become associated with the Jamaican cult of the Rastafarians. It is characterised by an insistent repetitive beat and often takes the form of protest songs. It has links both with calypso and with American rhythm and blues. It became widely popular in the 1970s, mainly due to the work of Jamaican singer and composer Bob Marley.

Reggio di Calabria (Greek *Rhegion*, Latin *Rhegium*), Italian seaport, capital of Reggio di Calabria province, and largest town of Calabria, on the Strait of Messina, 320 km south-east of Naples. It was destroyed by earthquakes in 1783 and 1908 (when 35,000 persons perished), and on each occasion was rebuilt. The main industries are fruit preserving and the manufacture of olive oil and furniture. Population (1979) 181,293.

Reggio nell'Emilia (ancient *Regium Lepidum*), Italian city and capital of Reggio nell'Emilia province, situated on the Crostolo some 55 km north-west of Bologna. It lies on the Aemilian Way and it has a 13th-century cathedral. The city is the centre of a rich agricultural district, and has textile, agricultural machinery and locomotive industries. Population (1979) 130,000.

Regicides, term applied to those who bring about the death of a king, more particularly in British history to the men who were appointed to the parliamentary committee to try King Charles I, and in French history to the members of the French Convention who voted for the death of Louis XVI.

Regiment (late Latin *regimentum*, from *rego*, I rule), largest permanent unit of the British army. The development of the regiment may be dated from the 16th century, when armies were permanently organised in companies and regiments.

Regina, capital of Saskatchewan, Canada, 575 km from Winnipeg. It was founded in 1882 and it became the capital of the new province of Saskatchewan in 1905. The town was named in honour of Queen Victoria. A singularly handsome town centre with many striking buildings, particularly those of the provincial and federal governments, it stands surrounded by a vast prairie. Industrial output includes agricultural products, petroleum products, and such manufactures as cement, cindercrete, paper and boxes, paints and varnishes, farm machinery, furniture, and storage tanks. It is connected by pipeline with the Alberta oil-fields. Population (1980) 153,848.

Registered Stock, or inscribed stock. Stock is said to be inscribed or registered when the name of the stockholder is inscribed in the stock register of the state or corporation issuing it. In contradistinction to registered stock is that stock which is issued in the form of bearer bonds with dividend coupons attached.

See also STOCK.

Registers, Parish. Registers of a kind appear to have been kept in every age. In the Roman provinces officials were appointed as public registrars to keep records of names for the settlement of disputes, proof of freedom, and certification of births and deaths. In France it appears that registers were kept with surprising regularity from about 1308. Public registers were not regularly kept in England before 1538. From that date, however, until 1837 they form a useful record of the manners, customs and events of three centuries of English social history. The national records of births, deaths and marriages have been compiled since 1837, and so less reference is made to public registers maintained since then.

See also REGISTRATION OF BIRTHS, MARRIAGES AND DEATHS.

Registrar. In England and Wales the registrars in bankruptcy in the High Court and the county courts are the officials who e.g. hear bankruptcy petitions, make receiving orders, and grant orders of discharge to bankrupts.

The registrar of a district registry, acting on behalf of the Family Division of the High Court, grants probate of wills or letters of administration. The registrar of the Principal Registry of the Family Division is an official invested with all the authority of a judge in chambers in matters of probate and divorce and other matters.

The registrar of companies registers companies formed under the Companies Act 1948. He is an officer of the Department of Trade.

The registrar of the county court may hear cases in which the amount involved is not over £75.

The duties of the registrars of the Chancery Division are e.g. to make up lists of the cases for trial and to assist the judges during the hearing of cases.

The solicitors' registrar is the official whose duty it is to issue certificates empowering solicitors to practise.

Registration of Births, Marriages and Deaths. In Britain, prior to 1837, the only official recognised records relating to births, marriages and deaths were the parish registers. Comprehensive civil registration of births, marriages and deaths was inaugurated by the Births and Deaths Registration Act 1836.

Registration of Title. The official Land Registry was established in England to simplify and lessen the cost of dealings in land by establishing a state register of landowners. The Land Transfer Act 1897 introduced the principle of compulsory registration. The Land Registration Act 1925 is the basis of the modern law and the machinery for the purchases and sale of land is similar to that for stocks and shares. Simple forms, analogous to those used on transfers of stocks and shares, are provided. The cost of buying, selling or mortgaging registered land is much less than the cost of dealing with unregistered land. Once registered, the title to land is guaranteed by the state except that no guarantee is given in respect of rights to which the particular title is subject.

Regnault, Henri Victor (1810–78), French chemist and physicist. His discoveries in organic chemistry won him election to the Académie des Sciences, and he became director of the imperial porcelain factory of Sèvres. Regnault is famed for his researches in connection with specific heat and expansion of gases. He also experimented on compounds of chlorine, and discovered carbon tetrachloride, dichloroethylene, trichloroethylene and vinyl chloride. He wrote largely on chemical and physical subjects, chiefly for scientific periodicals.

Régnier, Henri François Joseph de (1864–1936), French poet and novelist. In the 1880s Regnier appeared as a Symbolist poet, beginning with *Les Lendemains*, 1885, while among his other volumes were *Les Médailles d'argile*, 1900, and *Vestigia flammae*, 1921. His novels include *La Double maîtresse*, 1900; *Les Vacances d'un jeune homme sage*, 1903; and *Le Mariage de minuit*, 1903.

Reguardant, or regardant, in heraldry, used of an animal such as a lion which is depicted with its head turned to look back over its shoulder.

Regulus, in metallurgy, see MATTE.

Rehoboam ('the people is enlarged', 1 Kings xii, xiv), son of Solomon and Naamah, an Ammonite princess. Rehoboam ascended the throne c.930 BC at the age of 41, and reigned 17 years. Discontent had been excited by the high taxation and forced labour imposed during his father's reign. The northern tribes had probably resolved to break away whatever happened. They had already recalled Jeroboam from exile in Egypt, to lead a deputation to Rehoboam to demand relief. Rehoboam, however, gave a most insolent and tyrannical reply, whereupon the northern tribes drew off in resentment, stoned the officer, Adoram (Adonoram), sent to make terms with them, and made Jeroboam their king. Thus the national union was dissolved; only Judah and Benjamin remained loyal to the dynasty of David.

Reich, Wilhelm (1897–1957), Austrian psychoanalyst. He emphasised the sexual basis of emotional life even more strongly than Freud, arguing that repressive modern culture inhibited full experience of orgasm and thus brought about not only individual neurosis but also dictatorship and war. In view of his later theories—e.g. of the existence of 'orgone energy', a sort of all-pervasive sexual ether—Reich has often been dismissed as a crank, and he remains a controversial figure.

Reichenberg, see LIBEREC.

Reichstadt, Duke of, see NAPOLEON II.

Reichstag (German, Day of the Empire), former name for the German legislature. In 1919 the Reichstag gained supreme power. It was elected by universal suffrage under a system of proportional representation. The National-Socialist regime preserved the Reichstag in name, but Hitler eliminated opposition. By passing the Enabling Act (1933) the Reichstag voted its own virtual elimination. After this it was convened only to hear declarations of national policy made from time to time by Hitler.

In 1949 representative government was restored in the German Federal Republic, and elections were held. This legislature, however, was called the Bundestag.

See also GERMAN FEDERAL REPUBLIC, HISTORY.

Reid, Thomas (1710–96), Scottish philosopher. He published his *Inquiry into the Human Mind on the Principles of Commonsense*, 1762, as an answer to Hume, and in 1764 was appointed professor of moral philosophy at Glasgow, succeeding Adam Smith. His essays on the *Intellectual Powers of Man* appeared in 1785, and their ethical complement—the essays on the *Active Powers of the Human Mind*—in 1788. Reid is the leading representative of the school of common sense, by which phrase he meant the beliefs common to rational beings as such, and not vulgar opinion. His *Inquiry* expresses his doctrine that belief in an external world is intuitive or immediate.

Reigate, residential town in Surrey, England, 30 km from London. There was originally a castle here, built by de Warennes (Earls of Surrey) in the 12th century. Population (1981) 52,554.

Reims (English *Rheims*), French city in the *département* of Marne, 130 km north-east of Paris, on the right bank of the River Vesle, a tributary of the Aisne. Here Clovis I was baptised in 496 by St Remi or Remigius, which started the custom of crowning kings of France at Reims. The chief glory of the town is the magnificent Gothic cathedral of Notre Dame, begun in 1211, the western façade of which is one of the masterpieces of the Middle Ages. Reims, with Épernay, is a centre for the marketing of Champagne wines. It has chemical, mechanical, metallurgical, textile and foodstuff manufactures. Population (1975) 183,610.

Reincarnation, or metempsychosis, doctrine according to which the soul of a human being enters after death into another body, whether of man or animal. Belief in reincarnation is a doctrine of Hinduism, Jainism and Sikhism while a similar 'evolution of the soul' from mineral to human is a belief of the Sufis. Buddhist *rebirth* differs from reincarnation.

Reincarnation is the belief that an individual soul (*jiva:* Hindu) comes into the world and makes its way from a lowly condition to the very highest, that of liberation (*moksha:* Hindu).

Reincarnation is irreconcilable with the main body of Christian theology, although some scholars have detected its influence in the post-exile literature of the Jews.

Reindeer, *Rangifer tarandus*, a species of deer, the only one which has been domesticated for any significant length of time. In size reindeer are similar to the red deer but with shorter neck and legs. It is the only species in which the female bears antlers, these being shorter and more slender than those of the male. Antlers are cast annually. The hoofs are broad and rounded and the dew-claws are well developed and enable the animal to walk easily on snow and boggy ground. Lappish and other reindeer owners still sometimes use them for transport. A trained male reindeer can pull a loaded sled weighing 130 kg about 50 km a day on a good snow surface. Reindeer supply excellent meat, skins, milk after calving, and other products. They graze on grass and small plants as well as lichens in summer, but lichens of many species form their principal food for the rest of the year.

Reindeer are now found mainly in northern Europe and Asia. In some parts, for instance Norway, wild herds are stalked. Wild reindeer are called caribou in Alaska and Canada, where the barren-ground variety migrate over extensive areas in huge herds. Woodland caribou occur in some Canadian forests. Newfoundland caribou have been hunted nearly to extinction in the past, but are now protected.

See also LAPLAND.

Reinforced Concrete was invented in France c.1850. It is a combination of concrete, which has little resistance to tensile, shearing and twisting forces, and steel, which has a high resistance to tensile forces. Reinforced concrete is designed so that, generally, all the compressive forces are resisted by the concrete and all the other forces by the steel reinforcement. The reinforcement is generally in the form of mild or high-tensile steel bars up to 50 mm in diameter. The use of reinforcement has made possible the erection of large cantilevers, thin domes, long spans, and shapes that would be impossible or uneconomical in any other material. It has also made possible reinforced concrete beams, transmission-line poles, lamp and fence posts, and many other products which can be made in a factory away from the site.

Prestressed Concrete was conceived by Freyssinet and Magnel. If a beam is loaded at mid span, tensile stresses will be induced in its underside because when a beam is bent its underside is lengthened, and its top shortened. If, however, pressure is applied at both ends of the beam so that it is in compression it will have a greater resistance to bending.

Reinhardt, Max (1873–1943), Austrian-born actor and theatre director. Although an excellent actor, he ceased to act in 1903 to give all his time to production, in which he inaugurated a new era and influenced the theatres of Europe and America. He was one of the first to re-employ devices which are now common, like the apron stage, and he brought back to the theatre a sense of urgency and communication which was in danger of being lost. He was also an excellent producer of Shakespeare, but no less adroit in his productions of intimate modern plays in small theatres. When Hitler came into power in 1933, Reinhardt left Germany and continued his work in America where he died. See also THEATRE.

Reinsurance. When an insurer has accepted a risk which might involve the payment of an amount too large to be carried by the insurer alone, the risk is spread by reinsuring part of it with other insurers. These other insurers can be either those transacting direct business or companies formed for the sole purpose of underwriting reinsurances.

Reisz, Karel (1926–), British film director. After working as a critic and teacher, and publishing *The Technique of Film Editing*, 1953 (new edition, with section by G. Miller, 1968), he made two well-received documentaries, *Momma Don't Allow*, 1956, with Tony Richardson, and *We Are the Lambeth Boys*, 1958. Since then he has directed *Saturday Night and Sunday Morning*, 1960; *Night Must Fall*, 1963; *Morgan—A Suitable Case for Treatment*, 1965; *Isadora*, 1969; and *The French Lieutenant's Woman*, 1981.

Reith, John Charles Walsham, 1st Baron Reith of Stonehaven (1889–1971), British administrator. He became the first general manager of the BBC in 1922, and was its director-general, 1927–38. A Puritan by instinct and upbringing, Reith left a strong personal imprint on the BBC. The 'Reithean tradition' was based on a dedicated belief in the virtues of public service broadcasting, a desire to improve the taste of the audience and a paternal attitude towards it.

He left the BBC to become chairman of Imperial Airways, and was the first chairman of the British Overseas Airways Corporation. He became MP for Southampton in 1940 and was successively minister of information, minister of transport and minister of works and buildings.

Relapsing Fever, an acute infectious disease occurring among famine-stricken people. It is caused by species of spirochaetes of the genus *Borrelia* (or *Treponema*). The period of incubation is from 5 to 7 days; the fever starts with severe pains in the back and limbs, rigors and a high temperature. In untreated cases delirium, jaundice, enlargement of the spleen, profuse sweating and intense thirst are characteristic of the acute stage. These symptoms continue for about a week, when they cease by crisis. A week later another paroxysm commonly occurs. Recovery is the general ending, but in untreated epidemics mortality rates of 40 per cent have been recorded.

Relative Density, or specific gravity, of a substance is the ratio of the mass of any volume of that substance to the mass of an equal volume of water at 4°C. In the SI system it is numerically equal to one thousandth of the density.

Relative Humidity, see HYGROMETER.

Relativity is the theory of the physical world based on the hypothesis that the general laws of physics are the same for all observers, whether they are at rest, moving with uniform velocity, or moving with non-uniform (i.e. accelerated) motion. It attempts to establish whether laws discovered from experiments involving objects moving with everyday velocities also apply to objects (or for observers) moving at high velocities, as with atomic particles.

Relativity is divided into two theories: the *Special Theory of Relativity*, which applies to observers moving only with uniform motion; and the *General Theory*, which applies to all observers. The special theory is firmly established and corroborated by experiment; the general theory has had a number of its predictions confirmed, but not to the extent of conclusively eliminating alternative explanations. Current developments in astronomy and cosmology involve the theory of general relativity deeply and give it strong support.

Einstein in 1905 took the great conceptual step forward of rejecting the idea of an aether, relative to which bodies could be said to be at rest or in motion. He based the whole of the Special Theory of Relativity on two postulates: (1) the principle of relativity that the laws of nature appear the same to all unaccelerated observers, whatever their velocities relative to one another, and (2) the principle of the constancy of the velocity of light that to all unaccelerated observers the velocity of light in free space appears to have the same value, c, 3×10^8 m/s, regardless of the relative velocity of the observer and the light source. From these premises several intuitively familiar concepts must be modified: for example, an object moving rapidly past the observer will appear to him to be shorter and heavier than at rest relative to the observer, and a clock will appear to be running slower. These changes only become appreciable at speeds approaching the speed of light. (Length, mass and clock rates change by the factor $1/\sqrt{(1 - v^2/c^2)}$, where v is the velocity of the moving body or clock.)

In his General Theory of Relativity (1915), Einstein showed that the gravitational attraction exerted by heavy bodies could be described in terms of 'warping' of space and time in their vicinity. It accounts for a peculiarity in the behaviour of the motion of the perihelion of the orbit of the planet Mercury. It accounts for the observed bending of a light beam in its passage past a massive body such as the Sun. A third verification is found in the shift towards the red end in the spectra of the Sun, and in particular of stars of great density such as white dwarfs.

See also ANTIPARTICLE; ATOMIC BOMB; FISSION; FUSION; NUCLEAR POWER; POSITRON.

Relay, an electrical device used to control the operation of a circuit when required. For example, if an electric motor is overloaded and takes too much current, a relay can be used to disconnect the machine.

The relay is usually an electromagnetic device such that when the current flowing through a coil exceeds a certain pre-determined value, a piece of iron (called the armature) is pulled in towards the iron core of the coil, causing other circuits to come into operation by way of contacts 'made' or 'broken' by the movement of the armature.

Relics (Old French *relique*; Latin *reliquiae*, from *relinquere*, to leave behind), remains of the bodies of holy persons, or other objects connected with them, which are revered for their sake. The practice is both older and more widespread than Christianity, and is found, for example, among Buddhists. The miracles that are well attested in connection with certain relics are taken as divine approval of this veneration, as well as a sign of the power of the saint's prayers with God. The huge popularity of relics and the entirely uncritical attitude of the Middle Ages led to abuses, against which the reformers reacted to the extent of sweeping away the whole cultus. The Roman Catholic Church preserves both doctrine and practice; the public veneration of relics is strictly controlled by Canon Law.

Relief, feudal incident originating, in England, at a time when fiefs were not hereditary, being sums paid to the lord by the heir before he could enter upon possession of his lands. For relief from forfeiture of a lease, see LANDLORD AND TENANT.

Reliefs, see LOW-RELIEF; HIGH-RELIEF.

Religion, from Latin *relegere*, to gather together, or *religare*, to bind together, may broadly be defined as the acceptance of obligations towards powers higher than man himself. It also implies: (1) The belief that these higher powers are of a personal nature, not merely blind forces. In some (so-called higher) religions there is the recognition of one Divine Being. (2) The ascription to the Being or Beings of certain moral qualities. (3) The idea that the deity is to be obeyed, or at least placated, or retribution will follow. (4) In most religions the idea of reward and punishment after death. From this it will be seen that religion covers beliefs, i.e. 'faith', and actions, i.e. 'morals'. Acts of 'worship' embody the beliefs in ritual actions.

In antiquity and in the Middle Ages the universality of religion was taken for granted, though its forms were known to differ widely. Today whole countries, for example the USSR, are militantly atheistic, and appear to have succeeded in creating overwhelmingly secular societies; in others, e.g. Poland, religion retains its hold over the masses despite official disapproval.

Apart from the outright dismissive belief that religion originates in fear of the unknown, the origin of religion has been variously explained. (1) The Bible tells of an original divine revelation of Monotheism. (2) Some philosophers such as Plato, by the use of reason, have arrived at monotheistic belief. (3) Others hold that man's primitive conception of a personal force behind the powers of nature is an application, however crude, of the principle of causality. (4) Man may have an intuition of God, and of his dependence upon Him. (5) The animist theory supposes that the tremendous phenomena of nature were to be attributed to powerful spirits inhabiting the elements. (6) Another theory maintains that the oldest form of religion is the veneration of the totem or sacred animal or plant of the tribe. (7) Fetish worship supposes that it is possible to imprison a spirit or power inside a small object, carried for protection.

The principal religions in the world today are as follows (1) Polytheistic and primitive religions: central regions of South America; the native tribes of Canada, Siberia and Australia; central Africa. Animism is found among Negroes, Red Indians, Maoris, Javanese and the old Mexicans. (2) Judaism; the religion of the Jews which is the basis of Christianity and

Islam, and a strict ethical monotheism. (3) Hinduism, the ancient pantheistic religion of India, where it still holds the vast majority of the people. (4) Buddhism, an offshoot of pantheistic Hinduism. (5) Shinto, the native religion of Japan. (6) Confucianism, derived from the philosopher Confucius. It became the state religion of China, though many Chinese were followers of Taoism, a mystical religion that is essentially pantheistic. (7) Christianity, which is strictly monotheistic. (8) Islam, a strictly monotheistic religion inspired by Judaism and Christianity.

Religious Education remains one of the most controversial issues in education in many countries of the world. Early education was provided in India by the Brahmins (Hindu religious leaders), in Buddhist countries by the monks, in Islamic lands through the Koran by the *mullahs*, in Christian regions by priests. The rise of secularism created problems of control in education. In the Netherlands groups of parents wishing to set up denominational schools receive running costs. In France contracts between Church schools and the national government enable tax funds to be made to these schools. In the UK the only prescribed subject in the curriculum is religious instruction. Each Local Education Authority works out an 'agreed syllabus' on the advice of the various denominations, and parents have the right to withdraw children from the morning assembly and religious instruction lessons. In the USA interpretations of the Constitution have placed a wall of separation between Church and state. Parochial schools receive no public money.

See also EDUCATION.

Reluctance, in magnetism, is the ratio of the magneto-motive force acting on a circuit to the flux in it.

Remand, Remand Homes and Remand Centres. Under English law, a court of summary jurisdiction is empowered to remand an accused person either in custody or on bail, with or without sureties. An adult person remanded in custody is sent to prison. Prisoners on remand and those awaiting trial by the higher courts are kept separately from other prisoners.

Remand homes for offenders under the age of 17 were provided either by the local authorities or voluntary societies. They have been merged into the community homes system.

Remarque, Erich Maria, pseudonym of Erich Paul Remark (1898–1970), German novelist. He fought in the army in the First World War and made his name with the war novel *Im Westen Nichts Neues* (*All Quiet on the Western Front*), 1929. In Germany 500,000 copies were sold in less than three months from publication.

His later novels, though less outstanding, continued the theme of a world in which the individual was crushed by its irrationalism and blind cruelty. After living in Switzerland for 11 years he went to the USA and became an American citizen.

Rembrandt Harmensz van Rijn (1606–69), Dutch painter, etcher and draughtsman. His wide range of interests covered portraiture, landscape, mythological, religious and genre scenes. Rembrandt briefly attended Leiden University (1620) before entering the studio of a Leiden painter, Jacob van Swanenburgh, for three years. Much more important for his artistic development, however, was the period of about six months (probably in 1624) that he spent training under Pieter Lastman in Amsterdam. Rembrandt's early works have predominantly religious or allegorical themes which were to maintain a prominent place in his art throughout his career.

Rembrandt soon outstripped Lastman, especially in his brilliant handling of light and shade and in his ability to suggest states of mind through facial expression. His reputation was first made with his portraits when he had finally moved from Leiden to Amsterdam (1631 or 1632) where he remained for the rest of his life. He became Amsterdam's leading portraitist for a decade, acquired considerable wealth, and moved into a large house in 1639 with his wife Saskia (whom he had married in 1634), and spent lavishly on his art collection. His *Self-portrait with Saskia*, c.1635 (Dresden), shows him at the height of his prosperity. It is one of several hundred self-portraits, for Rembrandt portrayed himself more often and more revealingly than any other artist, through the whole range of human emotion. Saskia was his favourite model from their betrothal in 1633 to her death in 1642, as indeed Hendrijke Stoffels, with whom Rembrandt lived from about 1649 to her death in 1663, was later to become.

Rembrandt's work of the 1630s shows a Baroque dynamism particularly apparent in *The Night Watch*, 1642, possibly his most famous work. Rembrandt's worldly success declined at about this time, culminating in his bankruptcy in 1656. He still received important commissions, but began to paint more to please himself, becoming more interested in depicting inner life. He developed his broad, free brushwork and perfected his technique with light and shade, which he used to express tenderness rather than drama. His art continued to develop in profundity and subtlety to the end of his life. His very late portraits and religious works are his greatest achievements. *The Return of the Prodigal Son* shows his spiritual depth.

Rembrandt's range and output were vast. Apart from his greatness as a painter he was a powerful draughtsman and a great etcher. Over six hundred paintings are known by him, about three hundred etchings and almost

Rembrandt. Self-portrait, Aged 34, *1640. He painted over 40 self-portraits.*

two thousand drawings. Rembrandt was also a teacher and many of the important figures of 17th-century Dutch painting were trained in his studio. His subsequent influence on European art was enormous. After general misunderstanding and neglect, his reputation rose in the second half of the 19th century, and Rembrandt is probably now more loved and admired by both public and academic critic than any other Old Master.

Remington, Philo (1816–89), US inventor. He superintended the manufacturing department of his father's small-arms factory, and invented the breech-loading rifle (1873) which bears his name. He put the first (Sholes) typewriter on the market in 1874 which later bore the name E. Remington and Sons, the typewriter manufacturers.

Remittent Fever, see MALARIA.

Remonstrance, Grand, statement introduced into Parliament by John Pym in 1641, which narrated in a series of clauses the alleged unconstitutional acts and illegalities of Charles I, both in Church and state matters. The debate on the Grand Remonstrance was followed by a division in which it was carried by 11 votes.

Remora, see SUCKING FISH.

Remus, twin brother of Romulus.
See also ROMULUS.

Renaissance (or Revival of Learning), concept covering the whole development of Italian culture from the 14th to the early 16th century. Integral with this process was the rediscovery of classical antiquity and, as this was by definition pagan, its revival coloured the whole view of the Renaissance as both anti-medieval and anti-Christian. Petrarch gave the Renaissance its literary impulse by restoring a sense of classical latinity and initiating the recovery and revision of all the corpus of ancient texts which followed in the early 15th century. A century later another Florentine, Leon Battista Alberti, introduced to painting the illusion of the third dimension created by a mathematically based perspective. By this revolution in approach the flat religious art of the Gothic and Byzantine world, with its gold backgrounds and its primary unblended colours, was swept away. Alberti's approach to architecture was also epoch-making. Both as a theoretician and as a practising architect he proposed a rational architecture complete with columns (which seemed to Alberti the noblest ornament) and orders, capable of infinite modulation.
As in Florence, so in Mantua, Ferrara, Milan, Urbino and Naples, the new aspects of culture flourished in a courtly environment. The search for classical manuscripts was extended as far as Byzantium and, with the threat to and the fall of the Eastern Empire in 1453, scholars from the East added to the Greek influence in Renaissance learning. The 15th century in Italy saw a blaze of splendour: from Masaccio and Donatello to Botticelli, Piero della Francesca, Cosimo Tura and Andrea Mantegna. At the beginning of the 16th century the climax of the High Renaissance was reached in the work of Michelangelo, Raphael and Leonardo da Vinci. Although 1530 is often taken as something of a terminus of the Renaissance in Italy, in Venice the artistic splendour was carried through the whole century by painters such as Titian, Veronese and Tintoretto and by the most influential of all architects, Palladio.
The Renaissance made its impact on France after Charles VIII invaded Italy in 1494 in that Italian art and artists found their way into France. The impact of Humanism and the Italian Renaissance on the rest of Europe was a various one. A circle of scholars that centred on Sir Thomas More welcomed Erasmus to England and it was the latter who more than any other single figure embodied Humanist scholarship for northern Europe. But in political thought and historiography Italy did give the clearest lead. *The History of the Florentine People*, written in Latin by Leonardo Bruni, Chancellor of Florence, heralded at the distance of a century the work of Machiavelli, whose *Prince* (1513) is the foundation-stone of political discussion and whose *Florentine History*, with Guicciardini's *History of Italy*, is the fundamental document of modern historical writing.

Renaissance Architecture. The cultural centre of Florence was the birthplace of Renaissance architecture; Rome, which contained the classical ruins from which the Renaissance architects first drew their inspiration, was an unimportant city by comparison.
The stages by which the new Renaissance doctrines of architectural design gradually overcame the prevailing Gothic tradition were: (1) Italian craftsmen and architects working in other countries; (2) Italian books on architecture, mentioned above; (3) visits of architects and wealthy aristocrats to Italy in order to study the Roman ruins.
See also architecture articles under individual countries.

Renaissance Architecture. *The façade of Michelangelo's Basilica of St Peter's in Rome.*

Renascence, see RENAISSANCE.

Renault, Mary, pseudonym of Mary Challans (1905–83), English novelist. She emigrated to South Africa in 1948. She is best known for her historical novels, especially those set in the ancient Hellenic world, Greece and Minoan Crete. Among them are *The King Must Die*, 1958; *The Bull From the Sea*, 1962; *The Mask of Apollo*, 1966; *The Persian Boy*, 1972; and *Funeral Games*, 1981. Her novels with contemporary settings include *The Charioteer*, 1953, about the Second World War.

Rendzina and Terra Rossa Soils. The distribution and location of these soils is determined by the presence of limestone. Rendzinas are normally shallow soils as the weathering of limestone leaves only small quantities of impurities from which these soils develop. They are normally less than 50 cm thick, have a neutral to slightly alkaline pH value, and may carry a natural vegetation as they are often unsuitable for cultivation owing to their low water storage capacity. Terra Rossa soils are related to the rendzina and represent the end stage of soil formation on limestones. Hence they are very old and thicker than the rendzina and are characterised, as the name suggests, by red coloration.

Renfrew, royal burgh (since 1396) in Strathclyde Region, Scotland, on the Clyde, 10 km west of Glasgow. Once a great Clyde port, today it has shipbuilding and various engineering industries, and manufactures iron goods, furniture and chemicals. Population (1981) 21,396.

Reni, Guido, also simply known as Guido (1575–1642), Italian painter. Going to Rome in 1600, he was influenced by Caravaggio and more tellingly by Raphael and the Antique, but he developed a sophisticated classicism of his own. In 1613 he painted his most celebrated work, *Aurora*, a ceiling fresco in the Palazzo Rospigliosi. He returned to Bologna in 1614 and became the most important painter there. In the 1630s his style became broader in handling and cooler in colour.

Renner, Karl (1870–1950), Austrian lawyer, Socialist and statesman. He entered the Austrian parliament in 1907, and became leader of the Social-Democrats. On the dissolution of the Empire he led the Austrian delegation to St Germain-en-Laye, 1919, where the frontiers of the Austrian Republic were settled. From 1919 to 1920 he was chancellor. After the Second World War he headed the provisional government set up by the Allies, and at the end of 1945 he was elected president of the Austrian Republic.

Rennes, French town in the *département* of Ille-et-Vilaine, 80 km south-east of St-Malo. The town is an important railway junction and military headquarters. The *palais de justice*, built in the early 17th century, was the seat of the parlement of Brittany. The chief manufactures are textiles, leather, vehicles, electrical goods, clothing, pharmaceuticals and agricultural implements; there are also foundries and printing works. Rennes is the main commercial centre for western France. Population (1975) 205,733.

Rennet, preparation obtained from the fourth stomach of the calf, having the power of coagulating or clotting milk so that the fat is entangled in the curd.
See also RENNIN.

Rennie, John (1761–1821), British civil engineer. In 1790 he began constructing canals, and amongst his numerous works in England are the Avon and Kennet, Rochdale, and Lancaster canals; Waterloo and London bridges (since removed and replaced by new bridges); the London and East India docks on the Thames; Sheerness and Chatham dockyards; Holyhead and Kingstown harbours; and Plymouth breakwater.

Rennin, digestive enzyme found in the gastric juice of man and other mammals. It is responsible for the clotting of milk in the stomach by the conversion of the soluble caseinogen into insoluble casein. A commercial extract of rennin known as rennet is used for preparing junket from milk by the same process as occurs naturally in the stomach.

Reno, city of Nevada, USA, and county seat of Washoe county, on the Truckee river. It is a rail, air, commercial and tourist centre, and the second largest city in the state. Meat packing, dairying, forest products and flour milling are important industries. Reno is also famous as a gambling resort. It has achieved worldwide notoriety as the so-called capital of divorce. Population (1980) 82,220.

Renoir, Jean (1894–1979), French film director. Son of the painter, Pierre-Auguste Renoir, and trained as a painter and potter, Renoir began directing films in 1924, his films showing the same sensuous love of humanity as did his father's paintings. Among his finest films are *Nana*, 1926; *La Chienne*, 1931; *Boudu Sauvé des Eaux*, 1932; *Une Partie de Campagne*, 1936; *La Grande Illusion*, 1938; *La Règle du Jeu*, 1939; *The Golden Coach*, 1954; *French Can-Can*, 1956; *Le Déjeuner sur l'Herbe*, 1960; *Le Petit Théâtre par Jean Renoir*, 1969. The *nouvelle vague* directors were strongly influenced by Renoir's example, as were Italian director Luchino Visconti (in his neo-realist phase), and the Indian Satyajit Ray. Today Renoir's poetic realism is recognised as one of the most exquisite achievements in cinema history. See his self-study, *My Life and My Films*, 1974.

Renoir, Pierre-Auguste (1841–1919), French artist. He was apprenticed to a Paris porcelain-maker, and later painted fans and blinds. In 1861 he studied painting under Gleyre, and in his *atelier* he met Sisley, Monet and Bazille. He painted landscapes with his friends at the Salon in 1864. Ten years later he took part in the first Impressionist exhibition. His early work shows the influence of Courbet, but Monet guided him to open air effects, which he painted with much gaiety. Contemporary Paris life produced the masterpiece *Le Déjeuner des Canotiers* (Washington). The study of Ingres and a visit to Italy (1881) alienated him from Impressionism. In later life, settled at Cagnes, he entered a new period, in which he painted nude studies.

Pierre-Auguste Renoir. Near the Lake*, 1880. Renoir's style was influenced by Monet.*

Rent, in general usage, money or other periodic payment made for the use of land, buildings, the hire of capital goods, or the use of consumer durables. It may be regarded as a form of interest on capital.

In economics, the term 'economic rent' has a more specialised meaning—this being the surplus earned by a factor of production in a certain employ over what that factor could earn in the next best alternative employment. Alternatively the term 'economic rent' may be described as the surplus above the income necessary to keep the factor of production at work. Either way economic rents can arise only where the supply of the factor of production is, in the short term at least, fixed, or nearly so, and are due to an increase in demand for the factor.

See also LANDLORD AND TENANT.

Reparations, payments, in money or kind, by a defeated country in accordance with the demands of the victors. This expression was used initially for the payments to be made by Germany after the First World War. Reparations following the Second World War, as applied by the Potsdam Agreement, were paid to the war-devastated countries, not out of current production but by the transfer of technical productive capital equipment (industrial plant, installations, ships, etc.).

Repatriation, return to their countries of origin of persons displaced from there as refugees or prisoners of war.

Repeal, formal abrogation of an act of Parliament. Acts, however ancient, which remain unrepealed are still law, and cannot, in strict theory, lapse by desuetude, however incongruous their provisions may be in modern conditions.

Repertory Theatre, strictly speaking, a theatre with a permanent company and a nightly change of bill, like the Comédie Française and other European theatres. Certain companies in England, such as the Royal Shakespeare Company and the National Theatre, compromise by offering constantly changing programmes of several plays during the season.

Representatives, House of, see UNITED STATES OF AMERICA.

Repression, see FREE ASSOCIATION.

Reproduction. The simplest method of reproduction is found in unicellular organisms (bacteria, unicellular algae, fungi and protozoa) in which a cell divides to form two identical daughter cells. Even this apparently simple process is in reality a complex sequence of events for it is essential that each daughter cell receives a complete set of components, or organelles. The simplest multicellular animals, e.g. sponges or *Hydra*, reproduce by budding, in which a portion of the organism is constricted and grows into a new organism, which may either separate or remain attached to the parent. Many plants, from simple filamentous algae to flowering plants, can reproduce by fragmentation, in which a detached portion develops into a complete individual. In multicellular animals the body is more highly differentiated and individual parts lack the ability to regenerate the whole, although some flatworms can multiply by transverse fission; the separated posterior and anterior halves can regenerate new front and rear ends respectively. With these exceptions, reproduction in multicellular organisms involves specialised reproductive cells which have the capacity to form new individuals. In asexual reproduction a single parent gives rise to offspring which are identical to itself and to each other whilst sexual reproduction involves the fusion of cells or cell nuclei from two different individuals. The life cycles of plants generally include both sexual and asexual reproduction; fungi such as the mould *Mucor* produce asexual spores and are also capable of reproducing sexually; in the mosses, ferns and their allies there is a regular alternation of sexual and asexual phases in the life cycle. In flowering plants sexual reproduction is usual although asexual methods are widespread.

See also BIOLOGY; EMBRYOLOGY.

Reproductive Tract, Female, see CERVIX; FALLOPIAN TUBES; MAMMARY GLAND; OVARY; UTERUS; VAGINA.

Reproductive Tract, Male, the male organs involved in reproduction. Externally, the male genitals comprise the penis and the scrotum, which contains the testes and epididymis. The testes are structures analogous to the ovaries in the female, and like them have a dual function; first, the production of *gametes*, or sex cells (which in the male are known as sperm or spermatozoa), and second, the secretion of sex hormones, principally testosterone, which is responsible for the sexual characteristics of the male body.

Reptilia, a class of vertebrates which has much in common with birds, and was included with them by Huxley in the primary group, Sauropsida, reptile-like animals. Reptiles are cold-blooded, and have skin covered with scales or scutes to help keep moisture in the body. They are oviparous or ovoviviparous (they lay eggs or the young develop in eggs retained inside the mother), and are all air-breathers, which distinguishes them from the Amphibia. Unlike most amphibians, reptiles are born in the adult form: there is no metamorphosis from a tadpole stage and the young do not live in water. The four chief orders of existing reptiles are: Chelonia, tortoises and turtles; Squamata, lizards (suborder Sauria) and snakes (suborder Serpentes or Ophidia); Rhynchocephalia, represented by a single New Zealand lizard (*Sphenodon*); and the Crocodilia.

Reptiles reached their maximum development in the Mesozoic era, which has been called the Age of Reptiles, and displayed a remarkable adaptive relation to specialised habitats. In the sea there were Ichthyosaurs, Plesiosaurs, Mesosaurs and other forms; the Pterodactyls had adapted themselves to flight independently of the first birds (*Archaeopteryx*), which were themselves half reptilian; while on land lived the Therapsid mammal-like reptiles, Rhynchocephalians and the herbivorous and carnivorous groups of Dinosaurs. Apart from the groups that survive today, all other reptiles died out by the end of the Cretaceous period.

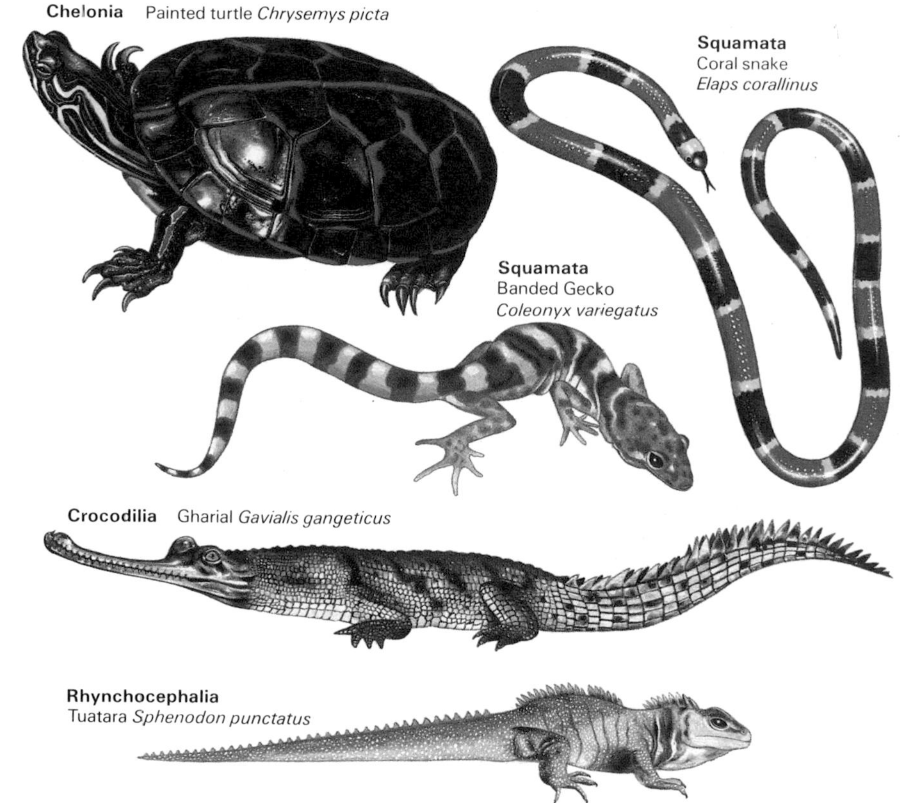

Reptilia. *Representative species from the four orders of living reptiles.*

Repton, Humphry (1752–1818), English landscape-gardener. He worked in partnership with J. Nash as his architect. He laid out Russell Square and Bloomsbury Square in London, c.1800 and some 200 landscape gardens. He wrote many books on landscape.

Republic (Latin *res publica*, the state; from *res*, affair, and *publica*, public), state in which the sovereignty does not reside in an hereditary ruler, but in the people themselves, or a section of them. Thus a republic may be aristocratic, oligarchic or democratic.

Republican Party, one of the two major political parties of the USA. The name was originally used for the Democratic Party founded by Thomas Jefferson. The modern Republican Party was founded in 1854 by a union of Northern Whigs, Democrats and Independents, all of whom were opposed to slavery. In 1860 the Republican Party succeeded in securing the election of Abraham Lincoln.

After the Civil War the Republican Party was the dominant party in the country until Cleveland's election in 1884. The Republican Party was again in power from 1888 to 1892. In 1896 it controlled Congress and the presidency once more until 1912. In 1920 the party regained the presidency and kept it until 1932. The Republican Party returned to power with Eisenhower as their leader in 1952; President Eisenhower was re-elected in 1956 but subsequently Richard Nixon narrowly failed to win the presidency in 1960. The party regained the presidency in 1968 with the election of Nixon. Upon his resignation in 1974, Gerald Ford became president, but was defeated when he stood for re-election in 1976. In 1980 Ronald Reagan regained the presidency for the party.

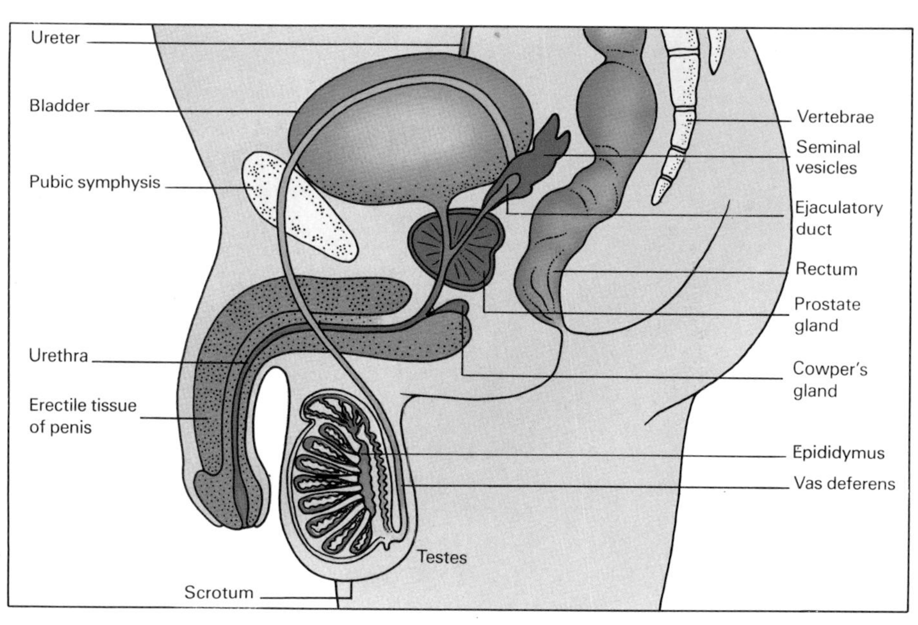

Male Reproductive Tract. *A lateral view of the male genital organs and hind part of the gut.*

Reredos, in churches, ornamented wall or screen at the back of the high altar.

Res Judicata, in English law, a question which, having been settled by a final judgment, is disposed of for all time. No question of fact that has once been finally determined in a legal tribunal can ever be reopened in a court of law. But a final judgment is only final as between the original parties to it or those claiming through them, and no stranger to the suit is barred from getting the same issue set down for trial.

Resale Price Maintenance, the practice by which manufacturers stipulate and attempt to enforce prices to be charged for the resale of their (usually) branded goods by wholesalers and/or retailers. It was first introduced in Britain in the 1890s following pressure by small traders in order to counter price cutting by large-scale retailers. It was finally made illegal in most cases by the 1964 act, which allowed RPM only in those instances where a manufacturer could demonstrate that its retention on his goods was in the public interest.

See also MONOPOLY; PRICE.

Reseda, a genus of the family Resedaceae, found in Europe to central Asia. It includes *R. luteola*, the dyer's rocket or weld, *R. lutea*, the wild mignonette, and *R. odorata*, the common garden mignonette, which is cultivated for its sweet-scented flowers.

Reserpine, an alkaloid obtained from the roots of some species of *Rauwolfia* (e.g. serpentia, *R. vomitoria*); it has also been synthesised. It is used as an antihypertensive, but, owing to its severe depressant and sedative actions and to its adverse effects, including gastro-intestinal troubles, lethargy and strange dreams, it has led to many suicides and is now less popular.

Reservoir. A reservoir for storage of water is classed as a 'storage or impounding' reservoir when it is intended to store up water during wet weather for use during drought, and as a 'service' reservoir in the case of a comparatively small covered reservoir supplying purified water by gravity to town mains.

Resht, see RASHT.

Resia, Passo di (German *Reschenenscheideck*), Alpine pass on the Austro-Italian border, just east of the Swiss frontier. It lies between the Rhaetian and Ötztaler Alps. It is crossed by a road which runs from Bolzano (Italy) to Nauders in the Inn valley. Altitude 1507 m.

Resin. There are two types, natural resins and synthetic resins. The natural resins are amorphous solids or, occasionally, semi-solid substances obtained chiefly as exudations from certain plants following injury to the tissues. The secretion exudes in globules or tears, which harden on exposure to the air. Some are also found as fossils, e.g. amber, copal and kauri. Resins are mostly yellow or brown; they have no tendency to crystallise and no definite melting-point. They are not pure chemicals but are mixtures of resinic acids and terpenes, usually disolved in ethereal oils. The hard resins are chiefly used in making varnishes and lacquers, and include copal, kauri, accroides, manila, dammar, sandarac, mastic, elemi, penak and benzoin. Other resins are: colophony, podophyllin, scammony, gamboge, yacca and pontianic. Oleo-resins are mixtures of plant resins and essential oils, and may be normal plant products or result from incisions made in the plant tissue. They are known as balsams, and include myrrh, frankincense (olibanum), opopanax and storax, and are used for the production of perfumes and medicinal ointments.

Synthetic resins are relatively low molecular weight polymeric materials with a highly cross-linked structure. They are frequently formed as precursors of the thermosetting plastics, polymers of much higher molecular weight into which the resins are converted by heat, pressure or catalysts. Important groups are the phenol-formaldehyde and related urea- and melamine-formaldehyde resins used in the production of surface laminates for household and kitchen furniture. The alkyd resins are much used in paints and varnishes. Polyurethane resins find widespread use as surface coatings, adhesives and solid foams. Epoxy resins and polyester resins are frequently used in conjunction with reinforcing agents such as glass fibre, asbestos or carbon fibres to produce composites suitable as structural materials in building car bodies, dinghy hulls and Earth satellites.

Resistance, in electricity, a measure of the opposition to flow of direct current, the ratio under steady conditions of the voltage across the circuit to the current. It is measured in ohms, $1\,\Omega = 1\,V/1\,A$. The resistance R of a wire of uniform cross-section S, length l, is $R = \rho l/S$, where ρ is the resistivity or specific resistance of the material, which varies slightly with temperature.
See OHM'S LAW; UNITS, ELECTRICAL.

Resistance Movements, term which came into use in the Second World War to denote the underground organised resistance of the peoples of countries occupied by the Germans, Italians and Japanese. Such resistance took the form of irregular fighting forces, such as the Maquis of France or the Partisans of Russia or Yugoslavia.
See also GUERRILLAS.

Resistor, electrical circuit element used to provide resistance.

Resnais, Alain (1922–), French film director. For some years he made short films—*Van Gogh*, 1948; *Guernica*, 1951; *Les Statues meurent aussi*, 1952; *Nuit et brouillard*, 1955—which showed his preoccupation with contemporary politics and the interaction of past and present. His full-length features are *Hiroshima mon amour*, 1959; *L'Année dernière à Marienbad*, 1961; *Muriel*, 1963; *La Guerre est finie*, 1966; *Je t'aime, je t'aime*, 1968; *Stavisky* 1974; and *Providence*, 1977.

Resolution, formal expression of opinion of a legislative or corporate body; or of a meeting or any association of individuals; or of a formal proposition brought before a public body or meeting for discussion and adoption.

Resolving Power, in optics, the fineness of detail which can be distinguished. For an astronomical telescope it means the smallest angle between two stars which can be seen as separate; for a microscope it is the smallest separation between two closely spaced points or lines which can be seen.

Resonance, in physics, the setting up of vibrations in a system by an applied periodic force having a frequency almost exactly equal to one of the natural frequencies of the system. If there is little damping of the vibrations their amplitude may become very large even if the inertia of the system is great and the applied force small. Resonance may occur as a result of the impact of sound waves. It is frequently troublesome because of the engineering problems it presents. Bridges and other structures may be endangered if they are subjected to periodic forces of frequency close to the natural frequency of some part of their structure. A related phenomenon occurs in some types of electrical circuits.

Resonance, Electric, occurs in oscillatory circuits when in series connection the reactive voltages, or in parallel circuits the reactive currents, are equal and opposite in phase and thus cancel out. For very high frequencies, transmission lines, two parallel wires of certain length, or two coaxial conductors, are used as resonant circuits. Such lines, like power transmission lines, have inductance and capacitance distributed along the length, the resistance is negligible, and the Q-factor is high. The length of the line is adjusted to half of the wavelength corresponding to the desired resonant frequency. This gives a current distribution with maximum at the middle and zero at the ends. For ultra-high frequencies the cavity resonator is used. See also CAVITY RESONATOR; HARMONICS; MODULATION; OSCILLATORY CIRCUIT; Q-FACTOR.

Resonator, Optical, an arrangement of mirrors in which light is reflected back and forth in a stable pattern. If there is a source of light inside the resonator the intensity will build up to an equilibrium determined by various losses. Optical resonators find their chief use as a component of most lasers. Amplification by stimulated emission takes place in the light bouncing about in the resonant cavity.

Respighi, Ottorino (1879–1936), Italian composer. He arranged music by Rossini for Diaghilev's ballet *La Boutique fantasque* and made his name especially with his symphonic poems, *Fontane di Roma*, *Pini di Roma*, *Vetrate di chiesa* and *Trittico botticelliano*, and orchestral arrangements of old airs and dances for the lute. He also wrote chamber music and songs.

Respiration, External, the process by which an animal takes in oxygen from the air or water and gives out carbon dioxide. The oxygen is used by the animal's cells for internal respiration, chemical reactions that create energy and give off carbon dioxide. Most animals, and most tissues in their bodies, get energy by aerobic respiration, but a few living organisms, and animal tissues under certain circumstances, are able to perform anaerobic respiration, which does not require oxygen, but is a less efficient way of producing energy.

The simplest method, which works for single-celled organisms and some multicellular animals where no cell is far from the surface, is to exchange gases by diffusion through the skin. Larger animals need a more efficient method, though in many, including amphibians, diffusion continues either through the outer skin or through special areas, such as through the membranes lining the mouth or excretory tube.

Insects have a system of tubes, the tracheae, running through the body, branching into smaller tubules with thin linings. The tracheae open to the outside through pores called spiracles, which can be closed when the insect is inactive. Gases move through the tracheae mostly by diffusion, helped sometimes by movements of the abdominal muscles and by other muscle movements (e.g. during flight).

Water-dwelling animals usually have elaborate gills through which blood flows for gaseous exchange. Some fish and most other vertebrates have a special organ, the lung, in which gas exchange occurs between the blood and the air. In lungfish this is a simple sac, but in large land vertebrates it is an elaborate system of air pockets in contact with blood vessels and is served by two pumps: the heart pumps the blood through and chest movements pump the air in and out.

Respirators, appliances for warming or purifying inhaled air, inhaling medicated vapours or supplying air when deficient. For industrial use the prevalence of dust or steel particles is countered by the use of a mask in which the air is filtered through a fine gauze, magnetised if necessary. In smoke-laden or gas-filled atmospheres an oxygen apparatus is used. When the respiratory muscles are inactive, for example, through poliomyelitis, use is made of a mechanical respirator or iron lung. Oxygen is supplied from a cylinder to the crews of high-altitude aircraft. The development of chemical warfare in the First World War led to the introduction of military respirators, and 'gas masks' were supplied to the civilian population, as well as to the armed forces, in the Second World War. In all types filters were devised containing materials to absorb the gases, and with the introduction of new gases new filters were required.

Respiratory Distress Syndrome, a common disorder of premature babies resulting from immature lungs. There is temporary widespread collapse of the small air spaces throughout the lungs, which leads to difficulty in transferring oxygen to the blood. Modern methods of care have altered the outlook in this disease and most infants now recover, although in some a period of artificial respiration may be necessary, using a mechanical breathing device.

Rest, in music, interval of silence between notes.
See also NOTATION.

Rest-harrow, small shrubby species of the genus *Ononis*, belonging to the Leguminosae, and having pink flowers. Rest-harrow is a much tougher plant than most low-growing vegetation, and the name derives from its being strong enough to stop a harrow from passing.

Restaurant, generally a place where meals are served for consumption on the premises. In its wider sense the restaurant business would include any cafés, tea-shops, refreshment rooms and canteens where meals are served at tables by waiting staff.

Restitution of Conjugal Rights, see DIVORCE.

Restoration, in England and Scotland, re-establishment of the monarchy in the person of Charles II, 29 May 1660. In France the term is sometimes used to describe the reinstatement of the Bourbons in 1814.
See also ENGLISH HISTORY.

Restoration (of easel paintings), term strictly defined as skilled treatment carried out on the surface of paintings to restore them to their original appearance; this includes removal of dirt, discoloured varnishes and other surface accretions such as retouching and overpaint. More generally, emphasis is placed on the *conservation* of paintings which covers all aspects of their preservation, consolidation, cleaning and restoration.

Restraint of Marriage. In English law, contracts and conditions in restraint of marriage in wills or settlements *inter vivos* are void as against public policy. But a settlement or will may give a limited interest determinable on marriage. A husband is entitled to direct that his widow's interest in his property shall go to someone else if she marries again.
See also MARRIAGE LAW.

Restrictive Practices, generally agreements between companies, trade unions and professional associations to restrict competition by fixing prices and restricting entry.
Agreements affecting the supply of goods or commercial services for the UK market are controlled by the Restrictive Trade Practices Acts 1956 and 1968, as amended by the Fair Trading Act 1973. Such agreements (including those relating to common prices, approved lists of dealers, and the limitation of production) have to be registered with the director-general of Fair Trading, who is responsible for bringing them before the Restrictive Practices Court set up under the 1956 Act. If the court finds the restriction contrary to the public interest, the agreement is void.
See also CONSUMER PROTECTION; MONOPOLY; PRICE; RESALE PRICE MAINTENANCE.

Resurrection, rising again of the body and its reunion with the soul. In its widest sense a belief in resurrection is not peculiar to Christianity; anticipations of it are found in Zoroastrianism and later Judaism. Christian belief in the resurrection is founded on the rising of Jesus and His subsequent appearances to the disciples. The preaching of the resurrection seems, indeed, to have formed a large part of the apostolic mission. The fullest New Testament expositions of the belief occur in 1 Cor. xv and 1 Thess. iv, where the Apostle explains the spiritual nature of the risen body. St Paul insisted that the resurrection of Jesus guaranteed the spiritual resurrection of Christian believers to eternal life.

Resurrection Plants. *Selaginella lepidophylla*, a club moss native to Texas and South America, curls up tight when dry, unrolling and resuming growth when placed in water. *Anastatica hierochuntica*, the rose of Jericho, a species of Cruciferae, is native to western Asia. The plant curls stems and seedpods in on itself in the dry season, and the dry ball so formed is blown and rolled by the wind. When moistened the plant develops into a fern-like plant up to 30 cm across.

Resuscitation, assistance given to a collapsed or unconscious person in cases of severe injuries and accidents, haemorrhage, drowning, electrocution, poisoning, or following arrhythmia or coronary thrombosis, when the heart-beat and breathing may suddenly cease, depriving the brain of oxygen and nutrition; if this lasts more than three or four minutes, there may be permanent brain damage. Thus it is vital that oxygen should be introduced into the lungs and blood made to circulate in the arteries immediately. The chief resuscitation procedures practised are of artificial respiration, usually mouth-to-mouth respiration, and external cardiac massage. Cardiac massage keeps the circulation going in cases where the heart has either stopped or is beating feebly.

Retainer. The object of a retainer is to secure the services of a particular barrister or solicitor, either for general legal work or for a specific matter; or, in general, to secure the services of any kind of consultant or specialist.

Reticulo-Endothelial System, various groups of cells present in the bone marrow, spleen, liver and lymph. Their main functions are: the destruction of red cells with the resultant production of bilirubin and iron-containing chemicals which are recirculated to the bone marrow; the formation of antibody; and the ingestion of bacteria by phagocytosis, and their destruction.

Retina, see EYE.

Retinoscopy, see VISION, DEFECTS OF.

Retort, in chemistry, apparatus in which an object is subject to distillation or decomposition by heat, a neck conducting off the volatile products. The retort of the laboratory is made of glass, porcelain or platinum, is flask-shaped, and has a long neck attached in which the products of distillation are condensed and from which they pass into the receiver.

Retreat, military operation, either forced or strategical, by which troops retire before an enemy. It differs from a flight in being orderly and under control. The word also denotes the playing or beating of retreat by a military band, or by a single bugle, at sunset, when traditionally the unit or garrison flags are lowered.

Retriever, valuable all-round gun dog. There are four varieties, all of which are of the same origin. The labrador is the most common. The flat-coated retriever, formerly known as the wavy-coated retriever, is believed to carry some collie blood as well as setter and labrador blood. The golden retriever is said to be derived from the wavy-coated retriever. It is a rich golden colour and is a very popular companion and gun dog. The curly-coated retriever is traceable to cross-breeding with the poodle and Irish water spaniel from which it derives its excellence as a water dog. In all varieties the height is about 58 cm and weight about 40 kg.

Reuben. Eldest son of Jacob and Leah. Reuben is represented as more merciful to Joseph than his brother. His descendants formed the Israelite tribe of that name.

Réunion, Île de la, formerly known as Île de Bourbon, island of the Mascarene group in the Indian Ocean, forming, until 1946, a French colony. It is 800 km east of Madagascar, of volcanic origin, and is divided into two portions, east and west, by a chain of mountains and a plateau. The highest point, Piton des Neiges, reaches an altitude of 3069 m and is surrounded by extinct craters. The chief products are sugar, rum, manioc, vanilla, tapioca, starch, vetiver and geranium (palmarosa) oil. St Denis is the capital, and St Louis, St Pierre, St Benoît and St Paul are other towns. Pointe-des-Galets on the north-west coast is the main port.
Réunion was discovered by Pedro de Mascarenhas in 1513. France annexed it in 1638. In 1946 the status of Réunion was changed to that of a *département* of France, and in 1974 it became a region. Area 2510 km^2; population (1979) 484,924.

Reuters, the leading international news organisation founded by Paul Julius Reuter in 1851; it supplies a world-wide service of general, political and sports news to newspapers and other media outlets, and information on finance, commodities, trade and industry to business world-wide.

Reval, or Revel, see TALLINN.

Revelation, in theology, the unveiling of some truth by God to man. The term is used in a more restricted sense for the truths revealed in Scripture and (by Roman Catholics) in the traditions of the Church.

Revelation, Book of, or Apocalypse, the last book of the Bible. Its author names himself John, and writes to seven churches of Asia Minor. He is identified as the apostle John by Justin Martyr (c.AD 140), and Polycarp, John's disciple, martyred at Smyrna in c.AD 155, quotes the work. By some it has been attributed, after Eusebius, to John the Presbyter, but the separate existence of this person has never been proved.

The meaning of the book has been a constant subject of dispute. It has repeatedly served as a foundation for millenarian views. The first part (chapters i-iii) consists of letters of encouragement or warning to the bishops, or 'angels', of the Asiatic churches. The body of the prophecy (chapter ix-xxii) undoubtedly deals with the end of the world, though there are allusions to contemporary events and to the Christian liturgy of the 1st century.

Revels, Master of the, name of an English official formerly attached to royal and noble families. He was also known as the 'Lord of Misrule', and his chief function was to preside over plays and performances of mountebanks, ballad singers, etc., and generally supervise and arrange the amusements of the court or great house as the case might be.

Revere, Paul (1735–1818), American patriot. He served as a soldier, became a gold- and silver-smith in Boston, took part in the 'Boston Tea Party' (1773), and became a member of the Boston 'Anti-British Society'. His midnight ride to Lexington and Concord (April 1775) to warn the people of the approach of the British troops was made famous by Longfellow's poem, *The Midnight Ride of Paul Revere*.

Revival, in religion, name given to various movements intended to cause a renewal of zeal and fervour in the cause of religion. The term is a modern one, and is perhaps best used only in its modern connection. In this case revivals are a feature of Protestant church life by which, under the influence of vigorous and fervid preaching, conversion is experienced by the unconverted and additional zeal is stimulated in church members.

Revival of Learning, see RENAISSANCE.

Revolution, a fundamental change in the internal constitution of a country brought about by the inhabitants. A revolution is thus to be distinguished both from conquest and from a mere coup. Originally 'revolution' had reactionary tendencies, as the etymology suggests, indicating a reversion to an original, usually better, state of affairs; or to a 'revolving' of the wheel of fortune upon which human fate was supposed to depend. However, since the French Revolution it has usually been understood to mean a radical and irreversible change in the sense of innovation, rather than restoration.

Revolution of 1905 in Russia, was the culmination of two movements—the constitutional movement of the Zemstvos and the liberal intelligentsia in general, and the revolutionary movement of the underground parties, chiefly the Russian Social Democratic Workers' party and the Socialist Revolutionaries. The revolution started with the 'Bloody Sunday' in January, when a workers' demonstration was fired on in St Petersburg. This was followed by country-wide open political agitation, the appearance of soviets, political strikes, including the general strike of October 1905, seizure by the peasants of landlords' estates, mutinies in the armed forces (e.g. the battleship *Potëmkin*), armed uprisings, including one in Moscow in December 1905, and the virtual breakdown of authority in parts of the country, in some cases for several weeks. General unrest lasted till the summer of 1907. The main results of the revolution were the establishment of a constitutional regime with a legislative Duma, the legitimation of political parties and trade unions, the impetus it gave to Stolypin's agrarian reform, and the disillusionment of the progressive section of the intelligentsia with revolutionism.

Revolver, a firearm in which a number of barrels, or a cylinder with several chambers, revolve on a central axis so that each barrel or chamber is presented to the firing mechanism in turn. Firearms with revolving barrels, known as pepper-boxes, are no longer in use and the term revolver currently refers to hand-guns with a revolving cylinder and a fixed barrel.

Reward, return for some voluntary act; but the corrupt taking or advertising of rewards may bring the offender within the English criminal law. Advertising a reward for the return of stolen or lost articles is lawful, but to add words to the effect that no questions will be asked or enquiries made renders the person so advertising liable to a penalty.

Reykjavík, capital of Iceland, situated on the south-west coast of Faxa Bay. Reykjavík is a Viking foundation, established by Ingolf in 874, but the present city is largely modern and has developed only since the late 19th century, when the commercial fisheries grew. In 1945 the heating of Reykjavík by piped water from the hot springs and geysers was completed. It is the main port of Iceland, occupied in fishing and allied industries, shipbuilding and other trades. Population (1979) 83,536.

Reymont, Wladyslaw Stanislaw (1867–1925), Polish novelist. He won the Nobel Prize in 1924 for his peasant epic *Chlopi*, 1902–09. Composed of four parts, corresponding to the four seasons, its epic conception of village life and sound psychological motivations make compelling reading.

Reynaud, Paul (1878–1966), French statesman. He was minister of finance under Daladier from 1938 to 1940. He was critical of the appeasement policy, and, after the Munich Pact, broke away from Flandin's pro-appeasement party. He won a considerable reputation by his speeches calling for a vigorous conduct of the war, becoming prime minister, 23 March 1940, in succession to Daladier, who had signed the Munich Pact. On the collapse of France, however, he was imprisoned by Pétain. In August 1948 he took office for the first time since 1940 as minister of finance. From 1953 to 1954 he was deputy premier under Laniel.

Reynolds, Sir Joshua (1723–92), British portrait painter. In 1740 his family sent him to study under Thomas Hudson in London. He visited Italy in 1749 and studied the Renaissance masters. He was soon acknowledged as the finest portrait painter in England. In 1768 he was appointed president of the newly-founded Royal Academy. He founded the Royal Academy Schools, giving his first lecture to students there in 1769. His 15 *Discourses*, 1769–82, present the theory of the Grand Manner, that art must be more ideal

Reykjavík. *The capital and main port of Iceland owes its development to the fishing industry.*

than realistic. Reynolds's literary interests were wide. He was the founder of the Literary Club, and a close friend of Dr Johnson.

Reynolds painted historical themes, but is remembered chiefly for his portraits. He was particularly influenced by classical antiquity, Michelangelo, Raphael and Titian. He followed da Vinci in experiments in colour combinations and effects and also 'imitated' Rembrandt's chiaroscuro.

Reza Shah Pahlavi, see Riza Shah Pahlavi.

Rha, see Volga.

Rhabdomancy, a method of divination involving the use of a divining rod. Its history can be traced fairly far back in time; ancient Egyptian records mention the use of a rod or stick for this purpose. In modern times, 'divining rod' normally refers to a forked branch or similar object held in the hands and used for discovering the presence of minerals, water or other substances underground.

Rhamnaceae, the buckthorn family, a family of about 50 genera and 800 species of shrubs and trees, usually with rather small whitish flowers having sepals, petals and stamens in fours or fives and producing berry-like fruits, occasionally edible. Some genera have thorny stems and reduced leaves, for example *Colletia*. The genus also includes *Rhamnus*, *Frangula*, *Ziziphus* and *Ceanothus*.

Rhapsody, originally a recited or chanted poem (especially an epic), the term became adapted to music; like capriccio, the term carries connotations of free, fanciful composition rather than music controlled by strict form.

Rhazes, or al-Razi (c.850–925), Persian physician. His most important medical works were the *Al-Hawi* or *Continens*, a great encyclopaedia of medicine in 25 books, first printed in Latin in 1486, and the *Liber Almansoris*, named after the prince Al Mansur, a compilation from various earlier writers, showing how completely Greek medicine was transmitted to the Arabs; it was first printed in 1476. Rhazes gave the first medical descriptions of smallpox and measles, and was the first to devote an entire treatise to the diseases of children.

Rhea, the south American ostrich in family Rheidae, order Rheiformes. It has three toes, a feathered head and neck, small well-feathered wings and a rudimentary tail. It looks rather like the ostrich, but is smaller, only about 1·2 m high. There are two species: *R. americana* has been slaughtered in enormous numbers in recent years, though attempts have been made with considerable success to domesticate it. Darwin's rhea, *Pterocnemia pennata*, is smaller, has shorter, feathered legs, and mottled plumage. It occurs in Patagonia.

Rhea Fibre, see Boehmeria.

Rhee, Syngman (1875–1965), Korean statesman. From 1919 he was named president by the Korean provisional government in Shanghai. In 1945 he returned to Korea and was president of the republic from 1948 until he resigned in the face of violent, student-led demonstrations against him in April 1960.

See also South Korea, *History*.

Rheims, see Reims.

Rhein, see Rhine.

Rhenium, metallic chemical element, symbol Re, atomic number 75, atomic weight 186·2. It was discovered by Noddack and Tacke in 1925, in certain platinum ores. Rhenium is a grey metal, relative density 20, with a very high melting point of 3165°C. Rhenium is used to make protective coatings for metals and to make alloys. Its compounds are useful catalysts.

Rheology, study of the deformation and flow of matter. If forces are applied to many kinds of solids in such a way as to change their shapes, and the changes are not too large, practically complete recovery occurs when the forces are removed. Other materials, such as putty, may be deformed by even small forces, and afterwards show incomplete recovery of shape.

See also Elasticity; Viscosity.

Rheostat, controllable electrical resistance. It may be a pile of carbon plates, the contact resistance between which can be varied by pressure exerted at the ends, or a length of wire wound on a ceramic core with a contact sliding along the coils. Liquid rheostats have two electrodes immersed in a liquid; at least one plate is movable horizontally so as to vary the volume of liquid between them.

Rhesus Factor, a substance (agglutinogen) first discovered in 1940 in the red blood cells of the rhesus monkey, whence its name is derived. It is present also in 85 per cent of humans, who are said to be Rh-positive, the remaining 15 per cent being Rh-negative. The rhesus factor is inherited, and the offspring of an Rh+ father and Rh− mother may itself be Rh+. The Rh− mother reacts to the presence of the Rh+ foetus by producing an agglutinin in her blood plasma. This agglutinin causes agglutination and destruction of Rh+ red cells in a subsequent foetus, with results which are frequently fatal for the child. A similar undesirable reaction occurs if an Rh− person, previously sensitised by a transfusion of Rh+ blood, is subsequently given a further transfusion of Rh+ blood.

See also Blood Transfusion.

Rhesus Monkey, *Macaca mulatta*, a macaque common in northern India, in some parts of which it is attached to temples and regarded as sacred. It is 46–60 cm long, with a tail of 18–20 cm. The hair is straight and fairly long, and is greyish or greenish brown. The face is flesh-coloured and the callosities bright red. This species is much used for research work.

See also Rhesus Factor.

Rhetoric (Greek *rhētorikē*), originally the art of speaking effectively in public, but the meaning was later extended to express the theory of eloquence, whether spoken or written.

The greatest work on the subject is a treatise by Aristotle. He defines rhetoric as the faculty of perceiving on any given subject what is best adapted to persuade. During the Middle Ages rhetoric was a key subject in university education.

Rhetorical Question, a question put, not in expectation of an answer, but as a more striking substitute for a statement, as in Gray's lines:

> What female heart can gold despise,
> What cat's averse to fish?

See also Figure of Speech; Rhetoric.

Rheumatic Fever, a diffuse inflammatory disorder involving many organs (but most prominently the joints and the heart) which follows throat infection with a type of streptococcus bacterium. The disease is thought to be a result of the formation of antibodies acting against the individual's own tissues in some way set off by the streptococcal infection. It was formerly common in childhood, but has become rare. The decline in incidence is attributed to improved living standards. The disease is self-limiting and the main hazard is damage to the heart valves. *Chorea* or St Vitus's dance is a form of rheumatic fever which attacks the nervous system.

Rheumatism, lay term for ill-defined aches and pains in various parts of the body, popularised because of its convenience in describing pains of which the true cause is not readily apparent.

See also Arthritis; Lumbago; Rheumatic Fever.

Rhine, Joseph Banks (1895–1980), US parapsychologist who has possibly contributed more than anyone else to the serious scientific study of psychic phenomena. His research, conducted over many years, as well as the numerous books he has written on the subject, have largely been responsible for making extrasensory perception (ESP) a term familiar to most people. In 1927 the Parapsychology Laboratory at Duke University, Ohio, was established under his direction, and he began a series of countless experiments involving different aspects of the phenomena to which he gave the general heading of extrasensory perception. Over a long period of time, he amassed sufficient statistical evidence to support belief in the existence of ESP, although his findings are still not accepted by all scientists.

Rhine (German *Rhein*; French *Rhin*; Dutch *Rijn*; Latin *Rhenus*), one of the major rivers of Europe, flowing through Switzerland, Federal Republic of Germany and Holland. Its length is 1320 km, of which some 719 km are in the Federal Republic of Germany. It drains an area of some 220,000 km^2 and it is navigable for 885 km. The Rhine rises in two headstreams called the *Vorderrhein* and the *Hinterrhein* (and other glacial streamlets), in the Swiss canton of Grisons. It runs north-west—forming for part of its course the border between Switzerland, Liechtenstein and Austria—to and through Lake Constance, and over the falls at Schaffhausen. In this part of its course it separates Germany (on the north) from Switzerland (on the south). After Basel, it turns north through a wide valley, to Mainz; flowing at first between Alsace-Lorraine in France and Baden-Württemberg in Germany, and later between the German *Länder* of Rhineland-Palatinate (on the left bank) and Baden-Württemberg and Hessen (on the right bank). From Mainz it flows west to Bingen and then generally north-west past Koblenz to Bonn. From Bonn the river flows past Köln, Düsseldorf and Duisburg, and enters Holland north-west of Emmerich. It is joined by the Moselle at Koblenz, and by the

Ruhr at Duisburg; other important confluents in this part of its course are the Nahe, which joins it at Bingen, and the Lahn. On entering Holland it begins to divide into several branches, forming a great delta.
The Rhine is the major navigable waterway of Western Europe. Over 110 million t of traffic cross the Dutch frontier annually. The main traffic today is iron ore being moved from Rotterdam to the Ruhr. Other major upstream cargoes are refined petrol, coal and grain. Downstream traffic at the frontier is dominated by sand and gravel, and steel products. Sea-going traffic is important as far as Köln. Tourist traffic is important in the picturesque gorge section between Bingen and Bonn.

Rhine and Marne Canal, system connecting the Rhine and Marne rivers, cut between 1838 and 1853. It is 360 km long and runs from the Ill at Strasbourg to Vitry-le-François, crossing the Meuse, Moselle and Meurthe rivers.

Rhine Province, Rhineland, or Rhenish Prussia (German *Rheinprovinz, Rheinlande*), former province of Prussia, bordered on the west by the Netherlands, Belgium and Luxembourg, and on the east by Westphalia and Hesse-Nassau. It lay on both banks of the Rhine, and was composed of five governmental districts: Cologne, Aachen, Düsseldorf, Trier and Koblenz. The capital was Koblenz. In the 1945 organisation of the new German *Länder*, Cologne, Aachen and Düsseldorf were incorporated in North Rhine-Westphalia, while Trier and Koblenz became part of the Rhineland-Palatinate.

Rhine-Rhône Canal unites the two rivers after which it is named. It was cut between 1783 and 1834, is nearly 350 km long, and runs from the Saône, a tributary of the Rhône, to the Ill, near Strasbourg.

Rhineland-Palatinate (German *Rheinland-Pfalz*), *Land* of the Federal Republic of Germany, bordered on the north by North Rhine-Westphalia, on the east by Hessen and Baden-Württemberg, on the south by France, on the south-west by the Saarland, and on the west by Luxembourg and Belgium.
The region is divided between the fertile river valleys and the poorer, forested upland regions. The Eifel lies to the north. Vines are grown over the greater part of the region and account for 75 per cent of the nation's wine output. In the river valleys, potatoes, cereals, sugar beet, fruit and tobacco are grown, whilst in the upland areas, stock rearing is more important. Industries include chemicals, engineering, leather, textiles, pottery and glass. The main cities are Mainz (the capital), Koblenz, Trier, Ludwigshafen, Kaiserslautern and Worms. Area 19,840 km²; population (1979) 3,633,200.
See also Rhine Province.

Rhine Wines, see German Wines.

Rhinitis, see Hay Fever; Nose.

Rhinoceros, a genus of family Rhinocerotidae in the order Perissodactyla (the horse order), of which five species still exist, three in Asia and two in Africa. Specimens of the extinct woolly rhinoceros have been found embedded in ice; the skin was without folds and covered with hair and wool. The anterior horn was of remarkable size. The living ones are, with the exception of the elephant, the largest and most powerful terrestrial mammal. The head is large and the skull elongated; the brain cavity is relatively very small. Rhinoceroses are of low intelligence; the senses of smell and hearing are highly developed. The limbs are moderately long and stout, with three toes on each foot. The hide is scantily covered with hair; the face bears one or two median conical and recurved horns, which are composed of a mass of epidermal hairs.
The two African rhinoceroses are the 'black' or prehensile-lipped species (*Diceros bicornis*), found mainly in the mountain forests and the arid bush, and the 'white' or square-mouthed species (*Ceratotherium simum*), which is a dull brown-black in colour, and, though once common in southern Africa, is now confined to southern parts of tropical Africa. The Asiatic species are *Rhinoceros unicornis* and *R. sondaicus*, both of which are one-horned, and *Didermocerus sumatrensis*, which is two-horned and has a smooth skin and ears fringed with long hairs.

Rhinoceros. *The white rhino of Africa is the largest species and grows to around 3000 kg. The Sumatran is the smallest and usually only reaches 1000 kg.*

Rhinoplasty, a cosmetic operation to correct congenital malformations of the nose.

Rhizoid, a unicellular or filamentous hair-like outgrowth. It is the characteristic organ for nutrient and water absorption in the lower land plants and some algae.

Rhizome, see Vegetative Reproduction.

Rhodanthe, *Helipterum manglesii*, has flowers of the dry and unfading kind called everlasting. It is found in western Australia and is about 30 cm high, with white or pink daisy-like flowers which are silvery beneath.

Rhode Island (Little Rhody State), smallest of the United States of America, and one of the six New England states that belonged to the original 13 states of the American Union. It lies between Massachusetts on the east and north and Connecticut on the west, and its southern shores are washed by the Atlantic Ocean. The northern and eastern parts of the state are hilly and the land slopes toward the south; the highest point is Jerimoth Hill (247 m). The three main rivers are the Blackstone, Pawtucket and Pawcatuck. Rhode Island has 75 km of Atlantic coast, and Narragansett Bay affords a further 560 km. Total area 3110 km².
In 1978 there were 75,791 acres of farmland, about 11 per cent of the total land area. The state's economy is basically industrial, and manufacturing employs one-third of the workforce. Before the First World War the cotton textile industry in this region dwarfed all others. New industries such as electronics occupy the old premises of textile firms. The population in 1980 was 947,154.
Rhode Island was first settled in 1636 by Roger Williams and others who were expelled from Massachusetts because of their religious opinions. Settlers of every creed were admitted. In 1790 the state accepted the federal constitution and entered the Union as the 13th state. The state capital is Providence.

Rhodes, Cecil John (1853–1902), Anglo-South African statesman. In Kimberley in 1874 he had a big holding in the diamond fields. In 1889 De Beers Consolidated Mines was established with Rhodes as chairman.
Rhodes entered public life in South Africa in 1881, when he took his seat in the Cape legislature. He was largely responsible for the annexation of Bechuanaland in 1884. In his efforts to secure northern expansion, Rhodes was favoured by the fact that he was virtual dictator, with large powers, of the South Africa Company, the chartered company in whose interest in 1890 Dr Jameson established himself at Salisbury. In the same year Rhodes became prime minister of the Cape. He held office until the 'Jameson Raid' (unauthorised and unsuccessful invasion of the Transvaal) of 1895 compelled his retirement. He died on 26 March 1902, and was buried according to his instructions, in the Matopo Hills.
Rhodes left a fortune of £6 million sterling. He instituted scholarships at Oxford for students of the USA and the colonies.

Rhodes, Zandra (1940–), British dress designer, noted for printing her own fabric designs and evolving garments from them.

Rhodes (Greek *Rodhos*), one of the Greek Dodecanese Islands, lying 19 km off the coast of Turkey. It is 75 km long with a maximum width of 38 km; area 1417 km². Its surface is mountainous, with fertile valleys producing fruit, especially fine grapes, olives, tobacco, vegetables and wine. Other products are oil, leather, sesame seed and sponges. There is an airport, and the tourist trade is of great economic value, with Rhodes a frequent port-of-call for cruise ships. Its capital is Rhodes, formerly a strong fortress, encircled by triple walls and moats. At the mouth of Rhodes harbour stood the celebrated Colossus of Rhodes, one of the 'seven wonders' of the world, an enormous statue of bronze, which was toppled by an earthquake in 224 BC. Population (1971) (island) 68,900; (town) 32,900.

At the outbreak of the Peloponnesian War (431 BC) Rhodes was a member of the Delian league, but in 412 BC it joined the Spartan alliance and became the principal base of the Spartans. In 408 BC the capital, Rhodes, was built on the designs of Hippodamus and enhanced the commercial importance of the island.

Rhodes was deprived of its independence by the Roman Emperor Claudius I, and its prosperity received a final blow from an earthquake in 155. During the Middle Ages Byzantine rule in Rhodes was challenged by Arab raiders. In 1310 the island was seized by the Knights of St John of Jerusalem, who lost it to the Turks after a famous siege in 1522. The Greeks took over the Dodecanese Islands, including Rhodes, in 1947.

Rhodesia, see ZIMBABWE.

Rhodesia and Nyasaland, Federation of, or Central African Federation, created on 1 August 1953, and dissolved with effect from 31 December 1963.

The federation consisted of the self-governing colony of Southern Rhodesia (now Zimbabwe) and the British protectorates of Northern Rhodesia and Nyasaland (now Zambia and Malawi respectively).

Rhodium (Greek *rhodon*, rose), chemical element, symbol Rh, atomic number 45, atomic weight 102·9055, a metal of the platinum group, in whose ores it is found. It is a very hard white metal, ductile and malleable (relative density 12·1; melting point 1907°C). It is insoluble in acids, but alloyed with platinum and some other metals it dissolves in aqua regia. It is used, alloyed with platinum, for thermoelectric functions of some pyrometers, and electrodeposited rhodium has a high reflective power. Rhodium and its compounds are also used as catalysts.

Rhododendron, genus belonging to the Ericaceae, of evergreen and deciduous shrubs and trees with leathery leaves and groups of colourful flowers, mostly from Asia but also in Europe and North America. The presence of lime in soils is usually harmful to rhododendrons.

Botanists include azalea in the genus *Rhododendron*: both plants have similar soil requirements.

Rhondda, an urban and industrial area of Mid Glamorgan, South Wales, situated on the major coalfield some 25 km from Cardiff. It consists of a series of linear industrial settlements following the two rivers, Rhondda Fawr and Rhondda Fach. It was a world-famous coal-mining area but there is now only one colliery in operation as against 40 in 1924. A variety of new light industries including clothing, electrical accessories and engineering have been attracted here.

Rhondda, two rivers of South Wales, uniting at Porth and entering the right bank of the Taff near Pontypridd.

Rhône, major river of Europe, rising at the Rhône Glacier (altitude 1825 m) in the canton of Valais, Switzerland. It is a turbulent mountain torrent until it reaches Brieg. At Martigny it changes course from south-west to north-west, and finally enters Lake Geneva at Villeneuve. So far the river falls 1426 m, over 170 km; from Geneva to Lyons (200 km) the fall is only 210 m. This second section is marked by numerous narrow gorges, as the waters wind about the southern spurs of the Jura Mountains. Above Lyons the chief tributary is the Ain, just below which is its confluence with the Saône, through which the Rhône is connected to the Rhine, Moselle, Seine and Loire. The third section is from Lyons to the Mediterranean Sea, near Marseilles; tributaries are the Isère, Drôme and Durance on the left, and the Ardèche on the right. Vienne, Avignon and Arles stand along the left bank. The river is navigable as far as Lyons. Length 800 km.

Rhodes. *The Castle of the Knights of St John overlooks the town of Lindos.*

Rhubarb, *Rheum rhaponticum*, a perennial herbaceous plant of the Polygonaceae, cultivated for its edible leaf stalks, which are utilised as a spring fruit. The rhubarb of pharmacy is derived from *R. palmatum*, and is a mild laxative.

Rhum or Rum, a bare, mountainous island in the Inner Hebridean group, lying off the west coast of Scotland, south-west of Skye. The land area is about 13 km by 14 km, and the highest point is Askival at 810 m. The National Conservancy acquired Rhum in 1957, since when it has been a base for geological, botanical and zoological research.

Rhus, commonly known as sumach, sumac or shumack, a genus of shrubs or trees, mostly poisonous, of temperate regions and belonging to the Anarcardiaceae. The leaves of *R. coriaria* provide a tanning and dyeing material; the bark of *R. verniciflua*, the lacquer tree, yields the Japanese lacquer; *R. succedanea* has fruits yielding wax. *R. toxicodendron*, the poison oak, *R. radicans*, the poison ivy, and *R. vernix*, the poison elder or sumach, are American species with highly poisonous sap and toxic to the touch. *R. cotinoides* and *R. typhina*, the staghorn sumach, are popular fast-growing garden shrubs for autumn foliage colour.

Rhyme, or rime, is the arrangement of word-endings—identical in vowel and following consonant or consonants but not having the same consonant before the vowel—at the conclusion of two or more lines. Rhymes in which the final syllable is accented are known as masculine rhymes, for example 'name', 'fame'; those in which the final syllable is unaccented are termed feminine rhymes, for example 'scattered', 'shattered'.

Rhyolite, an acid igneous rock essentially of quartz and feldspar in a microcrystalline form. It may be porphyritic in texture, and is usually vesicular; it may also show flow-banding.

Rhys, Ernest Percival (1859–1946), English poet and editor. He became associated with the publishing firm of J. M. Dent in 1894, and later was made editor of the *Everyman's Library* series of classics. The series (which produces inexpensive editions of the classics of literature) was planned at first for a thousand volumes, reaching this total ten years after Rhys's death.

Rhys also wrote stories, criticism and volumes of verse.

Rhythm, regular and measured beat or movement in language, music or action. Both verse and prose may be rhythmical, but the rhythm of the former is more regular and obvious. True poetical rhythm is modified by the emotion it conveys, while its nature varies with the subject of the verse. Rhythm in verse is marked by feet, analogous to bars in music, and the 'time' of these is indicated by various distinctive names, trochaic, dactylic, etc. Stress, accent, time-signature and duration of notes, or groups of notes, all play their part in creating musical rhythm.

Ribbentrop, Joachim von (1899–1946), German politician and diplomat. He joined the National Socialist party in 1932, becoming Hitler's plenipotentiary for foreign affairs. He was appointed German ambassador in London, where later his intense unpopularity provoked hostile demonstrations in Downing Street (1936–37). In 1937 Ribbentrop became foreign minister; he signed the German-Soviet Pact of 23 August 1939. He was tried at Nuremberg and sentenced to death in 1946.

Ribble, river in England, which flows through Yorkshire and Lancashire from the Pennines to the Irish Sea. The main town on its course is Preston. Length 120 km.

Ribbon-fish, any species of the family Trachypteridae, order Lampridiformes. They are pelagic fishes (that is, they live in the open sea, well above the ocean bed), and have elongated and compressed bodies which have a ribbon-like appearance. There is no anal fin, but the dorsal fin is as long as the body, and the ventral fins have from one long ray to nine smaller ones. They are seldom found alive, and are usually seen floating dead on the surface of the ocean. *Trachypterus arcticus*, the deal-fish, occurs in the north Atlantic. The oar-fish (*Regalecus*) also belongs to this family. The front end of the dorsal fin is crest-like and is coloured a brilliant red. *Regalecus* grows to a length of at least 6 m, and when seen at the sea surface with its crest erected has undoubtedly been mistaken for a 'sea-serpent'.

Ribeirão Prêto, town of Brazil, in São Paulo state, 400 km by rail from São Paulo city. It is the centre of a rich coffee- and sugar-growing area, and is also an important industrial centre. Its main industries include cotton weaving, meat processing, distilleries and light engineering. It is important as a distribution point for the western part of the state and for parts of the states of Minas Gerais, Mato Grosso and Goiás. Population (1975) 259,000.

Ribera, José (Jusepe) de (1591–1652), Spanish painter. In 1616 he settled in Naples after studying in Rome. In his realism, often rugged and extravagant, and in his leanings towards harrowing subjects, he owes much to Caravaggio. His later work became more classical in feeling, probably reflecting Bolognese influence. He was highly influential in Naples and Spain (where many of his works were exported), and he was also a fine etcher.

Ribes, see CURRANT; GOOSEBERRY.

Riboflavin, see VITAMINS.

Ribonucleic Acid (RNA), see NUCLEIC ACIDS.

Ribosome, particle composed of ribonucleic acids and proteins which is the site of protein synthesis in the cell. In most organisms it consists of two parts of different size and composition which can readily separate and rejoin as required. Many small cofactors are associated with ribosomes, and these carry out various roles in the process of protein synthesis.

Ribs, arched bones that form the wall of the thorax (chest). In man there are 24. The ribs, together with the sternum and backbone, form a bony framework. These bones protect the organs of the thoracic cavity, and are capable, due to their arched form, of resisting considerable pressure. The diaphragm and muscles between adjacent ribs are responsible for the respiratory movements which fill the lungs.

Ricardo, David (1772–1823), British political economist. He joined his father on the London Stock Exchange and pursued a very successful career as a broker, which enabled him to retire at the age of 42. Ricardo was one of the original promoters of the Geological Society of London and wrote on political economy from a mercantile standpoint, particularly on currency and taxation, and was the first to enunciate clearly the quantity theory of money. But he is chiefly remembered for his theory of rent.
See also CLASSICAL ECONOMISTS.

Ricci, Matteo (1552–1610), Italian missionary to China. He joined the Society of Jesus in 1571, and after four years' work in India (1578–82) undertook the evangelisation of China. In the years 1583–1601 he worked at Chao-K'ing, Shao-chow, and Nanking. In 1601 he established himself in Peking, where he was the first Catholic missionary and lived as a Chinese.

Ricci (Rizzi), Sebastiano (1659–1734), Italian painter. He travelled widely, but is best known for his work in England. Most of his decorative work has been destroyed (the main exception being the apse of Chelsea Hospital chapel), but there are about 30 of his religious paintings at Hampton Court.

Riccio, David, see RIZZIO, DAVID.

Rice, *Oryza sativa*, a marsh plant in the family Gramineae, cultivated in nearly all warm countries where artificial irrigation is possible. Rice in the husk is known as 'paddy' rice, and the irrigated fields as paddies. Rice is grown throughout the Far East, in Egypt and other Mediterranean countries, Brazil, the USA, and in some West Indian islands. The international Rice Research Institute near Manila in the Philippines was founded in 1960 to study and develop new breeds of rice.

Rice-paper, which is really a misused term, is made from the pith of *Fatsia papyrifera* (family Araliaceae), a tree which grows in the island of Taiwan.

Rich, Edmund, see EDMUND (RICH), SAINT.

Rich, John (c.1692–1761), British pantomimist and theatre manager, son of Christopher Rich, holder of the patent under which John, who inherited it, built and managed the first Covent Garden Theatre. He developed the ideas of Weaver, who introduced the Continental form of pantomime from France, and, as Lun, was a famous Harlequin. Under him the pantomime developed rapidly into a purely English entertainment which was eventually to culminate in the traditional Christmas show.

Richard I, Coeur-de-Lion (1157–99), King of England, third son of Henry II and Eleanor of Aquitaine. He succeeded to the English throne in 1189, and at once prepared to join the Third Crusade. He reached Acre in June 1191, within a month forced it to surrender, and shortly after took possession of Ascalon. He defeated Saladin near Arsuf in that year, and in the following year defeated him again at Jaffa. Because his brother, John, had usurped his authority at home, Richard was compelled to conclude a truce, and hastened to Europe. He was captured near Vienna by the Duke of Austria, who handed him over to the Emperor Henry VI. He had to pay a ransom of 150,000 marks for his freedom, which he obtained in March 1194. The return of Richard settled the fate of John's insurrection, but owing to the alliance between John and Philip Augustus, king of France, he was unable to return to the East. He went to Normandy in May 1194, defeated Philip, and two years later made peace with him. He was mortally wounded in besieging the castle of Châlus.
During Richard's reign important constitutional, financial and legal developments occurred. His long absences made necessary baronial co-operation to carry on the administration of the kingdom. The accounts of the chroniclers point to Richard as the most popular of all medieval kings; but his relations with the king of France illustrate his lack of diplomacy; and his reign really laid the foundations for the baronial revolt of 1214.

***Richard II,** a portrait in Westminster Abbey.*

Richard II (1367–1400), King of England, younger son of Edward, Prince of Wales (The Black Prince), succeeded Edward III in June 1377. During his minority there was a struggle for the control of affairs, and in 1382, attaining his majority, he attempted to wrest the government of the country from John of Gaunt, Duke of Lancaster. The struggle was continuous until 1397, when he summarily condemned the Earl of Arundel and the Duke of Gloucester to death. A rising in 1399, under Henry of Lancaster, Duke of Hereford, was successful, and Richard surrendered and was imprisoned at Pontefract, where he died on 14 February 1400.

Richard's position was from the start difficult; he succeeded to a kingdom weakened by expensive wars and disheartened by recent defeats, disorganised by the Black Death, and in the midst of a period of social transition. His reign was a conflict in which Richard appears as struggling for the trappings of power even more than for power itself: he has been called the last of the medieval English kings to rule by virtue of divine right. His actions, especially in his last years, suggest a progress from chronic instability to something closely allied to insanity.

Richard III (1452–85), King of England, younger brother of Edward IV. When Edward died in 1483, he left the young king, Edward V, and the kingdom in Richard's charge. Richard rapidly became dissatisfied with simply being regent. By the end of June 1483, he was king and Edward V and his brother were in the Tower. The offer of the crown to Richard by an incomplete parliament gave a legal cloak to his seizure of power. Richard had few supporters among the nobility and the common people were disturbed by ugly rumours about what had happened to the Princes in the Tower. Richard did his best to re-establish his reputation by ruling efficiently and energetically but nevertheless, when Henry of Richmond, the sole remaining Lancastrian claimant to the throne, invaded the country in 1485 he gained widespread support. Richard met him in battle at Bosworth, was defeated, and killed. See also ROSES, WARS OF THE.

Richards, Sir Gordon (1904–), British jockey. He first rode in 1920, becoming champion jockey five years later, a position he held from 1925 to 1953, with only short intervals in 1926, 1930 and 1941. In 1947 he broke all records by riding 269 winners. He was a trainer from 1955 to 1970 and has since acted as racing manager to a number of well-known owners of horses.

Richards, I(vor) A(rmstrong) (1893–1979), English critic. A leading authority on semantics, he collaborated with C. K. Ogden in *The Meaning of Meaning*, 1923, and with him was the founder of Basic English. Richards was an early advocate of the importance of the psychology of the reading experience, and his emphasis on the words on the page became the cornerstone of the 'new criticism'.

Richards, Viv (1952–), West Indian cricketer and outstanding batsman. He made his début in 1971–2 for the Leeward Islands and joined Somerset in 1974. By the end of the 1976 West Indies tour of Britain, he had scored more runs in a calendar year of test cricket than anyone else before him. In the same year he scored a personal best of 291 against England at the Oval; in 1977 he scored over 2000 runs.

Richardson, Henry Handel, pseudonym of Ethyl Florence Lindesay Richardson (1870–1946), Australian novelist. Leipzig supplies the background for her first novel, *Maurice Guest*, 1908. In 1910 appeared a semi-autobiographical novel of school life called *The Getting of Wisdom*. But with the publication of *Australia Felix*, 1917, the first volume of her Australian trilogy *The Fortunes of Richard Mahony*, she had begun her best work. The background of this volume is Ballarat in the gold rush, and its keynote is frustration and cultural barrenness. The second volume, *The Way Home*, 1925, reflects the contrast between 'colonial intelligence' and English social civilisation, and the concluding volume, *Ultima Thule*, 1929, shows the frustrated Mahony gripped by insanity. Her other books are *The End of a Childhood and Other Stories*, 1934, and *The Young Cosima*, 1939, in which Wagner and Liszt are interpreted with brilliant insight.

***Richard III** by an unknown artist.*

Richardson, Henry Hobson (1838–86), US architect. In Boston, where he lived, he designed Trinity Church, 1872; the Sever and Austin Halls at Harvard; the City Hall, Albany; several railway stations and houses; the town hall and library of North Easton; and the Marshall Field Warehouse at Chicago, 1885. His style is mainly derived from the Romanesque in its feeling for mass and its stable forms, but was not historically oriented.

Richardson, Sir Ralph David (1902–83), British actor. His first stage appearance, as Lorenzo in *The Merchant of Venice*, was in Brighton in 1921. In 1926 he appeared in *Yellow Sands* at the Haymarket Theatre, London. In 1944 Richardson rejoined the Old Vic as joint director. After the Second World War he played numerous leading classical rôles such as Macbeth, Volpone, Cyrano, Vershinin and Uncle Vanya. His most notable Shakespearean part was his superb rendering of Falstaff in *Henry IV*. Modern plays in which he appeared included *An Inspector Calls, A Day by the Sea, The Complaisant Lover, Home, No-Man's Land, West of Suez* and *Early Days*.

Richardson, Samuel (1689–1761), English novelist. An originator of the modern novel, he did not write seriously until he was past 50 when, in 1740, *Pamela* appeared. The story is told in the form of a correspondence. The heroine is a maid-servant and her story struck a true note of sentiment, exploded the prevalent idea that dukes and princesses were the only suitable heroes and heroines, and won immediate and phenomenal popularity.

In 1748 *Clarissa*, Richardson's masterpiece, was published, and in 1753 *Sir Charles Grandison*, in which the author embodies his ideal of a Christian gentleman.

Richardson has the distinction of having evoked the genius of Henry Fielding, whose first novel, *Joseph Andrews*, was begun as a parody of *Pamela*.

Richardson, Tony (1928–), British film and stage director. Richardson was artistic director of the Royal Court Theatre and a director of Woodfall Film Productions from 1958. He has directed plays and produced as well as directing films. His best-known films are *The Loneliness of the Long Distance Runner*, 1962; *Tom Jones*, 1962; *The Charge of the Light Brigade*, 1968; *Laughter in the Dark*, 1969; and *Hamlet*, 1969.

Richborough, port and harbour on the south-east coast of Kent, England. It was created in 1916 as a transport depot.

Nearby are the remains of the Roman castle and fortress of *Rutupiae*.

Richelieu, Armand Jean du Plessis, Cardinal, Duc de (1585–1642), French statesman. He was originally intended for the army, but when, in 1607, his elder brother resigned the bishopric of Luçon, in the family preferment, Richelieu was given the benefice. He soon showed a flair for politics. In 1614 he was a clerical deputy at the States-General. He then became almoner to Anne of Austria, wife of Louis XIII, and by gaining the favour of the Queen-Mother, Marie de Médicis, and her confidants he was made secretary of state. He was rewarded with a cardinal's hat (1622), and by 1624 was chief minister and the supreme power in the country.

During the period of his power he kept constantly before him the ideal of a state in which the power of the Crown would be absolute, and which should be supreme and unassailable in Europe, and he did much towards its realisation. Richelieu devoted all his energies to the subjugation of Huguenots and nobles. Abroad, France was still menaced on every frontier by the power of the Hapsburgs. Richelieu intervened in the Thirty Years' War with the skill of the master-intriguer, giving subsidies to the Hapsburgs' opponents, even to the king of Sweden, the champion of Protestantism. He saw the struggle as a war of territory, not of religion, and his efforts ensured that, at the Peace of Westphalia, France gained strengthened frontiers and enhanced prestige. As a patron of science and literature Richelieu rebuilt and endowed the Sorbonne, and founded the royal printing house at Paris, the botanic garden and the French Academy.

Richet, Charles Robert (1850–1935), French physiologist. He became famous through his discovery of anaphylaxis (1890), and was awarded the Nobel Prize in 1913 for his work on this subject. He also studied the treatment of nervous diseases, and his work on serum therapy was of great importance. He collaborated in the writing of a physiological dictionary, and edited the *Revue scientifique* from 1899 until 1902.

Richler, Mordecai (1931–), Canadian writer. Richler's mordant, witty novels include *The Acrobats*, 1954; *Son of a Smaller Hero*, 1955; *The Apprenticeship of Duddy Kravitz*, 1959; *The Incomparable Atuk*, 1963, and *Cocksure*, 1968, both extravagant satires; and *St Urbain's Horseman*, 1971, his most ambitious work. Richler's writing also includes short stories, essays, filmscripts and plays for radio and television.

Richmond, ancient market town, at the foot of Swaledale in North Yorkshire, England; the centre of farming districts and a garrison town serving nearby Catterick Camp. Of the castle, founded by Alan Rufus in 1071, there remains the Norman keep, on a natural eminence above the Swale. Population (1981) 7731.

Richmond, capital of Virginia, USA, 160 km south of Washington DC, standing on the James river (209 km from its mouth), whose falls originally supplied power for the mills. The state's second largest city, it is the financial, cultural, commercial, transport and distribution centre for a large part of the South, and also a port. A great tobacco market and tobacco-processing centre, it also manufactures synthetic and cotton textiles, fertilisers, metal goods, foundry products, food products, chemicals, agricultural equipment and furniture; printing and publishing are extensively carried on. The city became capital of Virginia in 1779. Population (1980) 219,214.

Richmond and Lennox, Frances Teresa Stewart, Duchess of (1647–1702), English courtier, mistress of Charles II. She was a noted beauty, and was the original model for Britannia on British coins.

Richmond-upon-Thames, a London borough created on 1 April 1965, comprising the former boroughs of Richmond, Twickenham and Barnes. The population of the borough in 1981 was 157,867.

Richmond is a royal borough and Edward I built a palace here in the 13th century. It was rebuilt and enlarged by Henry VII; an archway, Wardrobe Court, and the Gatehouse are the only remains. Richmond Park (999 ha with 11 gates) was enclosed as a hunting and pleasure ground by Charles I, and still shelters herds of wild deer.

Richter, Hans (1843–1916), Austrian conductor. In 1866 he met Wagner, with whose music he became pre-eminently associated, and from 1897 was associated chiefly with the Hallé Orchestra. He premièred several important works, including Wagner's *Ring* and some by Elgar.

Richter, Jean Paul Friedrich (1763–1825), German humorous and satirical writer. His first efforts, of a satirical nature, were not received very favourably, but in 1793 appeared *Die unsichtbare Loge*, which brought him immediate fame. In 1804 he finally settled in Bayreuth. During 1800–03 he wrote the great romance, *Titan*, which he himself thought his principal novel, and *Flegeljahre*, 1804–05. His satirical style appears again in *Reise des Feldpredigers Schmelzle nach Flätz*, translated into English by Carlyle. An idyll, *Leben Fibels*, appeared in 1812. He wrote on education in his work *Levana*, 1807, and propounded his theory of art in the *Vorschule der Aesthetik*, 1804.

His collected works were first published in 1826–38, and in a critical edition by E. Berend, 1927–42, who also edited his letters, 1922–26.

Richter, Sviatoslav (1915–), Soviet pianist, recognised internationally for his virtuoso technique, interpretative skill and wide repertoire. He studied at the Moscow and Odessa Conservatoires, winning the Stalin Prize in 1949 and the Lenin Prize in 1961.

Richter Scale, see EARTHQUAKE.

Rickets, a deficiency disease of infancy due to lack of the anti-rachitic vitamin D, and characterised by poor nutrition and improper development of the bones. The newborn infant has acquired sufficient vitamin D from its mother during intrauterine life to support it in normal health for the first few months of its separate existence. If after that time there is a deficiency of the vitamin in its diet or a lack of sunlight, due to climate or wearing too much clothing, the symptoms of rickets appear.

See also NUTRITION; NUTRITIONAL DEFICIENCY DISEASES.

Ricketts, Howard Taylor (1871–1910), US pathologist, after whom are named the *Rickettsia* bodies living in lice and other arthropods, which can be transmitted to man and animals. Ricketts discovered the insect vectors of Rocky Mountain spotted fever and of tabardillo. *Rickettsia prowazeki* causes typhus fever; *R. psittaci* is responsible for psittacosis in parrots and occasionally in man. He died of typhus contracted while studying the disease.

Ricochet, name given to the rebounding from a flat surface, as of a stone from water, or cannon ball or bullet from ground or water.

Riddle (Old English *raedan*), question, statement or verse, expressed with intentional obscurity in order to excite the reader or hearer to the discovery of the hidden meaning.

The most famous riddle is perhaps that propounded by the Sphinx, and answered by Oedipus; What is that which walks on four legs and two legs and three legs? The answer is Man (on all fours as a child, erect as a man, and in old age with a stick).

Ridgeway, prehistoric track along the English Berkshire Downs from Avebury across White Horse Hill to Streatley, south of and parallel to the Icknield Way. The Ridgeway Path for ramblers extends as far north as Ivinghoe Beacon, Hertfordshire.

Riding. The horse is believed to have been domesticated between 3000 and 2000 BC, and was probably a pack and draught animal before being ridden.

Present-day riding has its roots in the art of classical equitation, as practised at the court riding schools of Europe during the Renaissance, and also in the precepts of an Italian cavalry officer named Federico Caprilli (1868–1907), whose advocation of the forward seat revolutionised cross-country riding.

Modern riding equipment, known as 'tack' (harness refers to driving equipment), consists basically of bridle and saddle. The bridle consists of a metal bit placed in the horse's mouth and held in place by leather cheek pieces attached to a headpiece which rests behind the horse's ears. Reins, usually of leather, are attached to the metal rings of the bit. There are numerous types of bit, the snaffle being the most common.

The saddle is built on a framework, traditionally made of beechwood reinforced with steel and called a tree. Webs, serge and finally pigskin are stretched over the tree to form the seat. Attached to the tree are panels; flaps on which the rider's legs rest; and stirrup bars from which are suspended on adjustable leathers the stirrup irons for the feet. The saddle is kept in place by a girth of leather, webbing or nylon, passed round the horse's belly. In side-saddle riding, the rider sits with both legs on the near (left) side of the horse, the pommels which keep the legs in position giving great security.

The rider controls the horse by means of signals to which the horse, in the early stages of training, is taught to respond. The 'natural aids' are the hands, which act on the mouth via the reins; the legs, which exert pressure on the horse's sides; the seat, which exerts pressure on the back; and the voice. To these may be added the 'artificial aids' of whip and spur.

See also CAVALRY; HORSE RACING; SHOW JUMPING; THREE-DAY-EVENTING.

Ridley, Henry Nicholas (1855–1956), British botanist. In 1889 he was appointed director of the botanical gardens in Singapore. He was largely responsible for the establishment of the rubber industry in Malaya. His writings were numerous, the best known being *Flora of the Malay Peninsula* (5 vols), 1922–25, and *The Dispersal of Plants Throughout the World*, 1930.

Ridley, Nicholas (c.1500–55), English prelate. He became chaplain to Archbishop Cranmer (1537), chaplain to Henry VIII, canon of Canterbury (1541) and of Westminster (1545), and bishop of Rochester (1547). He quickly became one of the leaders of the Reformed Church, took part in the first revision of the Prayer Book (1548) and the establishment of Protestantism at Cambridge, and succeeded Bonner as bishop of London in 1550. On the death of Edward VI, Ridley supported Lady Jane Grey, but was arrested by Mary and sent to the Tower. In 1554 he was condemned for heresy, and burned at Oxford at the same time as Latimer (1555).

Riefenstahl, Leni (1902–), German film director, actress and photographer. She is best-known for her direction of *The Triumph of the Will*, 1934, the vast documentary commissioned by Hitler in praise of himself and Nazism. Her subsequent *The Olympiad*, 1936, was made with the total co-operation of the Nazi government, and constitutes another piece of epic fascist propaganda, although in 1952 she was cleared of charges of Nazi collaboration.

Riemann, Georg Friedrich Bernhard (1826–66), German mathematician. He made important contributions to analysis, especially complex analysis, in which he developed the theory of Riemann surfaces, which allows a one-many mapping to be represented as a collection of (single-valued) functions. In 1854 he gave an account of non-euclidean geometry in terms of differential geometry. Riemann became a professor at Göttingen in 1859.

Rienzi, Cola di (c.1313–54), Italian political reformer. In May 1347 he invited all the citizens to a meeting in the Capitol. The new laws he there proposed were at once adopted, and he was made tribune of the new republic. For a short time his rule was popular and successful, but the nobles, with the consent of the pope, drove him out of the city at the end of the year. He was restored by Innocent VI in August 1354, but was killed by the mob in October. Wagner's opera was based on Bulwer Lytton's *Rienzi.*

Rievaulx Abbey (also Rivaulx), ruined Cistercian foundation situated near Helmsley, North Yorkshire, England, dating from 1131, with a magnificent chancel of c.1230 and extensive remains among the monastic buildings. The word means 'valley of the Rye' from a small river that flows by the ruins. There is also a village of Rievaulx.

Rif, Er Rif, or Riff, mountainous strip of coast in northern Morocco, stretching for about 300 km from Ceuta to Algeria. There are some 1,500,000 people (called Riffs) in the Rif region.

Rifbjerg, Klaus (1931–), Danish novelist, poet and playwright. Among the most versatile and productive of 20th-century authors, his main success has been as a Modernist poet and novelist. The poems in *Konfrontation,* 1960, register a meeting between the self and the modern world, in which *things* predominate, and in both vocabulary and syntax he breaks new ground. His first novel, *Den kroniske uskyld,* 1958, is an illusionless portrayal of schoolboy love, written in the jargon of the 1950s. The later *Operaelskeren,* 1966, describes the adventures of a professor of mathematics who sees life in terms of calculations.

Rifle. All modern rifles are of the breechloading type, and fire a cartridge. The cartridge is supported in the breech of the barrel by a member known as the breech block, which usually contains the firing mechanism. Pressure on the trigger actuates a piece known as the sear, which releases the striker or hammer; this is then thrown forward to fire the cartridge by means of a powerful spring which hitherto has been kept in a state of compression. The most popular types of bolt actions employed are those based on the Mauser system, and are identical in essentials to the German military rifle (Model 1898) action.

Rifle-bird, or rifleman-bird, bird of paradise, *Ptiloris paradisea,* in the family Paradisaeidae, order Passeriformes. It occurs in Australia and New Guinea, and is purplish-black in colour with patches of green bronze. The English name is said to have been given by settlers in Australia from the resemblance of the colour of the plumage to that of the uniform of the Rifle Brigade.

Rifle Shooting is divided into three categories—bigbore, smallbore and air rifle—and three subdivisions—prone, kneeling and standing.

Smallbore events are held over both 50 m and 300 m distances. In the former, the target is of 162·4 mm diameter; in the latter 1000 mm diameter. Bigbore is only shot over 300 m with the 1000 mm target; air rifle shooting is generally over 10 m, with the target 46 mm wide.

Competitions are decided over a pre-determined number of shots, either 40, 60 or 120, an equal number of shots to be fired in each of the prone, kneeling and standing positions. Targets are divided into nine concentric circles, scoring between 1 and 10 points. The team, or individual, scoring the highest number of points is the winner.

See also CLAY-PIGEON SHOOTING; PISTOL SHOOTING.

Rift Valley, or graben, an elongated trough in the Earth's crust bounded on either side by normal faults. Rift valleys are also sites of volcanic activity. The East African Rift System is an outstanding example; it stretches over 4000 km from Syria and the Dead Sea Rift Valley in the north, through the lakes of East Africa to the Zambesi in the south. The mid-oceanic ridges found in all the major ocean basins are characterised by a central rift valley. Ocean ridges and rift valleys both mark regions of tension in the crust where blocks of crust are moving apart, and the continental rift valleys represent the sites of future opening ocean basins.

The volcanic activity associated with rifting in places gives rise to thick accumulations of lava, and large volcanoes such as Kilimanjaro and Mount Kenya may be built up.

See also LANDFORMS, STRUCTURAL.

Riga, capital and economic and cultural centre of the Latvian SSR, USSR, one of the principal Baltic ports of the USSR, situated on the Western Dvina near its mouth. There are varied engineering (electrical, transport, agricultural equipment), chemical, light, food and woodworking industries. It is an important transport centre. Founded in 1201 by Bishop Albert, the founder of the Order of Brothers of the Sword, Riga enjoyed far-reaching autonomy under the Livonian Order until the break-up of Livonia in 1561. It was conquered by Peter the Great in 1710 and ceded to Russia in the Treaty of Nystad (1721). It was capital of the province of Livonia (Livland) and capital of independent Latvia (1918–40). Population (1980) 803,000.

Riga, Gulf of, on the east coast of the Baltic Sea, south of the Gulf of Finland, separated from the Baltic by Saaremaa Island. It is 160 km long and 96 km at its widest. The greatest depth is 54 m; it is frozen from December to April. The Western Dvina flows into it past the port of Riga.

Rigel, Beta Orionis, a first magnitude star in Orion. It is a blue supergiant and intrinsically the brightest of the first magnitude stars, its luminosity being about 25,000 times that of the Sun.

Rigging, see SAILS AND RIGGING; YACHT.

Right, Petition of, see PETITION OF RIGHT.

Right Whale, Balaenidae, a family of large whales characterised by the absence of a dorsal fin or grooves on the throat, and the large head containing plates of baleen or whalebone. When feeding, the enormous lower jaw is dropped to act as a scoop and then raised and the water expelled through the plates of baleen hanging from the upper jaw. The small crustaceans or krill on which the animal feeds are trapped and swallowed. Their name stems from early days of whaling when they were the 'right' whales to catch. The most important species are the Greenland right whale, *Balaena mysticetus,* and the Atlantic or Biscayan right whale, *Eubalaena glacialis.*

Rights, Declaration and Bill of, see BILL OF RIGHTS.

Rights Issue, an offer of new shares in a company to existing shareholders. The new shares are offered at below the market price in a certain proportion to existing holdings, depending upon the amount of capital that the company wishes to raise. It is a relatively cheap method of raising capital for a company as it avoids the costs involved in launching a new issue.

Rigi, or Righi, mountain of Switzerland, rising between lakes Lucerne and Zug. Its popularity with tourists is due to the fine view it commands. Height 1800 m.

Rigidity, see ELASTICITY; MATERIALS, STRENGTH OF.

Rigor, a sensation of chill accompanied by shivering, which is characteristic of the initial stage of many feverish conditions. Notwithstanding the feeling of intense cold, the actual body temperature is higher than normal, and the sensation is due to a disturbance of the cutaneous heat-regulating mechanism, the surface capillaries being for the time constricted.

Rigor Mortis, the stiffening of the muscles that takes place after death. It usually starts in the face four to eight hours after death, reaching the distal parts of the body (hands and feet) after about twelve hours, and wearing off during the next twenty-four hours. The state of rigor mortis can be used to give a rough indication of the time of death.

Rigveda, see VEDA; VEDISM.

Rijeka (Italian *Fiume*), seaport in Croatia, Yugoslavia, on the River Riječina, at the head of the Bay of Kvarner. It is the largest Yugoslav port on the Adriatic, and is the cultural and economic centre of the Croatian coast.

In September 1919 a small irregular force under Gabriele d'Annunzio seized the town on behalf of Italy—a venture which influenced Mussolini and Farinacci in the march on Rome. In 1920 by the Treaty of Rapallo Rijeka was declared an independent free port. After continuing series of disorders, the town and a small surrounding district were eventually given to Italy in 1924, but the suburb of Sušak was left to Yugoslavia as a port. After the Second World War Rijeka was among the former Italian possessions ceded to Yugoslavia by the peace treaty of 1947.

Rijeka has an airport, railway connections with Italy, Trieste and Hungary, and a deep and busy harbour for commercial and naval ships. The principal manufactures are machinery, olive oil, tobacco and textiles; there are also shipbuilding yards, and a large trade in timber. Population (1971) 116,000.

Rijswijk (English *Ryswick*), town in the province of South Holland, 3 km south-east of The Hague. In the castle the treaty between Britain, the Netherlands, Spain, France and the Holy Roman Empire was signed in 1697. Population 52,605.

Rikyu, full name Sen-no-Sōeki (1521–91), greatest of the Japanese tea masters. Under the patronage of Taikō Hideyoshi, he consolidated earlier canons of architecture, pottery and etiquette connected with the tea ceremony, and brought the art of flower arrangement into the centre of Japanese aesthetics.

Riley, Bridget (1931–), British artist. Her

compositions in black and white and colour, contrived to create a powerful retinal impact, have made her the best-known British exponent of Op Art. An exhibition of her work was held by the Arts Council in 1971.
See also OP ART.

Riley, Terry (1935–), US composer. His music, involving the frequent repetition and overlapping of short modal fragments, has had a great influence on 'serious' and 'pop' musicians since the mid-1960s. Among his works are *In C, Keyboard Studies, A Rainbow in Curved Air* and *Persian Surgery Dervishes.*

Rilke, Rainer Maria (1875–1926), German poet. Rilke travelled a great deal in Europe, living for some time in Paris, where he was secretary to the sculptor Rodin. He spent the last years of his life in Switzerland.
His first collection of poems, *Leben und Lieder*, 1894, is generally conventional. In *Advent*, 1898, and *Mir zur Feier*, 1899, he moved further towards a depersonalised idiom in an attempt to arrive at a standpoint of complete objectivity and realism. When he fully achieves this, as in many of the *Neue Gedichte*, 1907–08, *Duineser Elegien*, 1922, and the *Sonette an Orpheus*, 1922, the intense, all-pervasive spirituality of his poetry has few rivals. Rilke's other notable publications include *Buch der Bilder*, 1902, and his greatest prose work, *Die Aufzeichnungen der Malte Laurids Brigge*, 1910.

Rimbaud, Jean Arthur (1854–91), French poet. In 1871 he wrote the famous poem *Le Bateau ivre*, and in 1873 published his prose work, *Une Saison en enfer*. Subsequently he lived an adventurous life as a tramp, soldier and merchant.
While he was living in Abyssinia, his friend Verlaine, believing him to be dead, published his poems under the title of *Les Illuminations*, 1886. These took Paris by storm and originated the decadent movement, and from Rimbaud stem also the Symbolists and the Surrealists. A further volume of his poems, *Reliquaire*, was published in 1891. His complete works were published by the *Mercure de France* in 1898.

Rime, see PRECIPITATION.

Rimet Jules, see WORLD CUP.

Rimini (ancient *Ariminum*), Italian city and seaside resort in Emilia-Romagna, 45 km south-east of Forli. It is on the Adriatic, at the mouth of the Marecchia river, which is here canalised. Under the Romans Rimini became an important port, and was the junction of the Flaminian Way, the Aemilian Way and the Popilian Way (to Venice). It was then possessed successively by the Byzantines, the Goths, the Longobards and the Franks. In 1239 it came under the rule of the Malatesta family, who held it for three centuries. The cathedral, or *Tempio Malatestiano*, is one of the greatest of Renaissance monuments.
Rimini today is best known as a seaside resort. It is the centre of a 50 km strip of coastline, from Cervia to Cattolica, that attracts about 10 million tourists a year. Population (1979) 127,714.

Rimsky-Korsakov, Nikolai Andreievich (1844–1908), Russian composer. He became a professor at St Petersburg Conservatoire, director of the Free School Concerts and conductor of the Russian Symphony Concerts. His first opera, *The Maid of Pskov*, was produced in 1873 and was followed by 15 others; one of the finest is *The Golden Cockerel*. Some of his most characteristic music is in the operas, where he exploited his talent for colourful, exotic harmony and orchestration. He left also three symphonies, a piano concerto, orchestral and instrumental music, songs and church music. The symphonic suite *Schéhérazade*, 1888, is probably his best known work.

Rímur (plural of *ríma*), a peculiarly Icelandic type of narrative poetry, generally a metrical version of a prose tale or saga.
It is uncertain at what date *rímur* were first composed (the oldest surviving specimen is preserved in Flateyjarbók and is dated to about 1350), but they soon became more popular than any other form of poetry. In the 19th century they fell into disfavour, although interest has been gradually reviving.

Rinehart, Mary Roberts (1876–1958), US novelist. Earliest and greatest of America's women detective-story writers, she made a reputation with her first novel, *The Circular Staircase*, 1908: others are *The Man in Lower Ten*, 1909; *The Amazing Adventures of Letitia Carberry*, 1911; *The Amazing Interlude*, 1917; and *The Red Lamp*, 1925.

Ring (Old English *hring*), circular ornament for the finger, ear, nose or lip. The ring is probably the most significant type of jewellery in existence, capable at various points in its history of being used as a badge of office, a token of freedom, a token of love and pledge of marriage, and a panacea against illness and evil.

Ring Dyke, an igneous intrusion which at the surface manifests itself as a circular or arcuate outcrop of 3–5 km radius and in thickness ranging from a few metres up to, in one extreme example, 1·6 km. Below the surface the dyke has a steep outward dip, giving the form of a truncated hollow cone. The mechanism of formation is thought to be the down-faulting of a conical mass of rock followed by the intrusion of magma from below into the resulting annular space.

Ring of the Nibelungs, The, see NIBELUNGS.

Ring Ouzel, mountain song-bird, *Turdus torquatus*, with brownish-black plumage, and a broad white patch on the throat. It nests in heather or on banks in moorland districts. It belongs to the thrush family, Muscicapidae, order Passeriformes.

Rings, Fairy, see FAIRY RINGS.

Ringworm, or tinea, a contagious skin disease due to infection with parasitic fungi of the group called dermatophytes, which includes *Microsporum audouini* and *Trichophyton*. They invade only the epidermis, the nails and the hair. They cause little disability, but because of their prevalence and their contagiousness they cause social problems.
Tinea pedis, 'athlete's foot', occurs either on the soles of the feet, where it appears as irritating, pinhead-size vesicles, or between the toes, where it appears as thick, white, sodden-looking scales. Secondary infection may occur. Tinea pedis is contracted and spread from walking barefoot on infected floors, for example in dressing-rooms or bathing-places. An essential part of treatment is to sterilise socks and slippers and to avoid foot perspiration.

Rio de Janeiro. *The city is dominated by a 38 m-high statue of Christ.*

Tinea tonsurans or favus is a type of ringworm of the scalp that nearly always affects children, especially boys, between the ages of 5 and 10. The easily seen, scaly patches are not truly bald, and when looked at closely the hairs are seen to be broken off, leaving the area covered with stumps. Griseofulvin taken by mouth is specific against ringworm and favus infections.
See also MYCOSIS.

Río Bravo, see RÍO GRANDE.

Rio de la Plata, see PLATA, RIO DE LA.

Rio de Janeiro, city of Brazil and one of the principal seaports of South America. For over 100 years to 21 April 1960 it was the federal capital of Brazil, and is now the capital of the state of Rio de Janeiro. It is situated on the south-west side of Guanabara Bay, one of the finest natural harbours in the world, which measures 24 km by from 3 to 11 km, and occupies a narrow strip of alluvial land between the mountains and the sea, being remarkable for the beauty of its position. The conical Sugar Loaf Mountain, 389 m high, ascended by an aerial cableway, stands at the harbour entrance; and Corcovado, 693 m high, rises from among the buildings of the city. Guanabara Bay, at the entrance (about 1·6 km wide) of which are the Fort Santa João and Fort Santa Cruz, provides anchorage of 130 km^2. Industries include iron and steel, shipbuilding, cement, textiles, sugar refining, tyres, pharmaceuticals, ceramics, sheet glass, and a wide range of foodstuff manufacturing. The port handles a substantial proportion of Brazil's exports and imports. The population of the city in 1980 was 5,093,232. It was discovered on 1 January 1502 by Gonçalo Coelho, the Portuguese navigator. Some French colonists were the first settlers in the neighbourhood (1555). The Portuguese took possession of it in 1567.

Rio Grande (Mexican name, Río Bravo), river of the USA and Mexico, rising in the Rocky Mountains, Colorado, and flowing as the US–Mexico border through New Mexico and Texas to the Gulf of Mexico. This river shared by the USA and Mexico carries insufficient water for the demands of both countries' users, and the flow is the subject of international agreements.

Rio Grande (do Sul), seaport of Brazil, in the state of Rio Grande do Sul on the strait leading to the Lagóa dos Patos. It has a large harbour and is among Brazil's six most important ports. It is the main distributing centre for the southern part of the state and exports dried meat, wool, hides and tobacco. There are cotton, wool and jute factories, an oil refinery, and fisheries. Population 117,000.

Rio Muni, mainland province of Equatorial Guinea, a coastal enclave between 1° and 2° north of the equator, lying between Cameroon and Gabon on the west coast of Central Africa. Its main town is Bata.

Río Tinto, river of Spain which rises in the Sierra de Aracena and flows south-westwards through the province of Huelva to the Atlantic Ocean at Huelva. Situated near the source of the Río Tinto is one of the greatest copper-pyrites producing centres in the world, called Minas de Río Tinto.

Rioja, see SPANISH WINES.

Riot, in English law, an assembly of at least three persons who, having a common purpose, execute or attempt that purpose with violence, displayed in such a manner as to alarm one person of reasonable firmness or courage.
Under the Riot Damages Act 1886, the local police authorities can be sued for damage done to private property during a riot.

Ripon, market town in North Yorkshire, England, on the Ure. Ripon grew up round the abbey, which was founded by missionaries in the 7th century. Paint and varnish are the main locally manufactured products, and there is also a trade in agricultural produce. Population (1981) 11,952.

Risorgimento, The Italian (Italian, Resurrection), name given to the period and process of Italy's national unification. Although this was achieved with the occupation of Rome in 1870, the term also implies the development of an awareness of cultural nationalism, and is therefore generally applied to the period from the Enlightenment to the late-19th century.
See also ITALY, *History*.

Rite (Latin *ritus*, religious custom), use or habit of worship. The Christian liturgy is divided into two main rites, the Eastern and the Western. The word rite is sometimes loosely used for the subdivisions of these: those made on the basis of language or of form.

Ritornello (Italian, little return), originally a refrain, and in the early 17th century a recurrent instrumental piece played in the course of a musical stage work; later, the instrumental passages between vocal portions of an anthem or aria, and the orchestral *tutti* in concertos, especially in rondo movements, where the same theme returns several times.

Ritual activity is found in some form or other in all human societies. Despite efforts to reduce religious belief and ritual activity to psychological or material determinants, it now seems that such phenomena are necessary components of social and psychological life. Rituals are carried out to improve crop fertility, to overcome enemies, to compete with rivals, to achieve enlightenment, to allay misfortune, to cure sickness of the mind and body, to legitimise important events such as marriage, to offset the effects of incest and other infringments of taboos and social rules, and to exorcise spirits.
From the study of ritual anthropologists have now extended the accepted meaning of the term to cover all behaviour which has to conform to certain rules, the infringement of which is thought to entail consequences of a supernatural kind. Thus present-giving at Christmas and Thanksgiving dinner are rituals, but so are all meals, a school classroom, the Opening of Parliament, the Investiture of the President of the United States, and even warfare.

Riukiu Islands, see RYUKYU ISLANDS.

Rivaulx Abbey, see RIEVAULX ABBEY.

River, a large body of flowing water restricted in its channel by adjacent banks and levées. Throughout history rivers have generated settlement, cultivation, transportation and water power.
Rivers are often classified by their stage of development. A youthful stream is typified by a narrow V-shaped valley with numerous waterfalls, lakes and rapids. When maturity is reached the river is said to be graded; erosion and deposition are delicately balanced as the river meanders across the extensive floodplain. At this stage the floodplain is characterised by extensive meanders, scrolls, ox-bow lakes and levées. River capture occurs when a stream is diverted by the encroachment of an adjacent stream actively eroding at a lower level.
The two dominant activities within a river are the erosion and transportation of material in the form of solutes, bedload and suspended load. Bedload rocks move by rolling along the bed or by saltation (jumping), and suspended-load particles are carried by the turbulent river flow. The soluble load is important in certain areas of the world (e.g. semi-arid and limestone regions). There most of the rivers' erosive work is performed by removing soluble salts. The velocity of water in rivers, which determines the amount of suspended load and bedload carried, varies greatly, reaching its maximum near the centre of the channel and being considerably reduced by friction near the banks. Over 95 per cent of the total energy within a river is spent on overcoming such frictional effects.
See also DESERT; FLOOD; HYDROLOGY; WATER SUPPLY.

River Horse, see HIPPOPOTAMUS.

Diego Rivera. Tarascan (Michoacan) Civilisation, *painted in 1942.*

Rivera, Diego (1886–1957), Mexican painter. His most outstanding work appears in his frescoes, where his portrayal of historical subjects shows a treatment owing much to ancient Mexican folk-art. His commitment to various shades of Marxist revolutionary ideas also looms large in his work.

Riverina, district of New South Wales, Australia, in the south-west of the state, lying between the Lachlan and Murray rivers. It has fine sheep-grazing and wheatlands. Pasture land covers the biggest area, but 109,000 ha irrigated by the Murrumbidgee is under rice. The main towns are Hay, Narrandera, Deniliquin and Lecton.

Rivers, A. H. L. Fox Pitt-, see PITT-RIVERS, AUGUSTUS HENRY.

Riverside, city in southern California, USA. It is situated some 90 km east of Los Angeles. Riverside has the state's Citrus Research Center and Agricultural Experiment Station. Population (1980) 169,677.

Rivet, fastener for clamping together two sheets, consisting of a cylinder with a preformed head at one end. The rivet is passed through the two pieces of material and the other end is flattened out into a second head by pressure or a series of hammer blows. Riveting is a simple method, dating back to very ancient times, for the cheap and easy fastening together of metal.

Rivette, Jacques (1928–), French film director and critic. One of the founders of the *Nouvelle Vague*, he began work on his first film, *Paris nous appartient*, in 1957, though it was not released till 1961. He has made only six feature films, yet he ranks as one of the most significant, aesthetically, of the *Nouvelle Vague* directors: his other films are *La Religieuse*, 1965; *L'Amour fou*, 1968; *Out One: Spectre*, 1973; *Céline et Julie vont en bateau*, 1974. He also made a film for televison on Jean Renoir, 1966.

Riviera, name given to a narrow strip of coast bordering the Ligurian Sea. Strictly speaking, it lies between La Spezia and Nice including Monaco, but in general usage the term includes the Italian coast as far as Leghorn (the Italian Riviera) and the French coast as far as Hyères (the French Riviera). Sheltered to the north and open on the south, the Riviera enjoys a delightful climate, marred only by an occasional bitter wind. The best-known towns on the Riviera are Hyères, St-Tropez, Cannes, Juan-les-Pins, Antibes, Nice, Monaco, Menton, Ventimiglia, Bordighera, San Remo, Savona, Genoa, Rapallo, La Spezia and Leghorn.

Riyadh, city of Saudi Arabia, of which it is jointly capital with Jidda, which lies 850 km to the south-west. The old walled city has been largely demolished as a result of the expansion and modernisation which followed in the wake of the discovery of oil and the subsequent wave of prosperity. The city is now a thriving commercial centre with modern buildings; it is the terminus of a railway to the port of Dammam, 450 km to the north-east. Population (1976) 667,000.

Riza Shah Pahlavi (1878–1944), Shah of Iran, the founder of the Pahlavi dynasty, the reigning house of Iran until 1979. Following a coup in 1921, he became commander-in-chief and minister for war. In 1923 he became prime minister. On 12 December 1925 the constitution was modified to exclude the Kajar dynasty, and Riza accepted the throne and was crowned the following year.

He carried out a vigorous policy of westernisation in every sphere of Iranian life. In 1941 Riza Shah abdicated in favour of his son, Mohammed Riza.

See also IRAN, *History*.

Rizzio, David, also spelt Riccio (1533–66), Italian musician. He travelled to Scotland in 1561 in the train of the ambassador of the Duke of Savoy, and became known to Mary Queen of Scots, who in 1564 appointed him her French secretary. He soon acquired great influence with Mary, and to some degree he directed her policy, which greatly angered her husband, Darnley, and several of the nobles. On suspicion of being the queen's lover, he was seized in her presence and murdered in an adjacent room.

RNA, see NUCLEIC ACIDS.

Roach, *Leuciscus rutilus*, a species of teleost fish in family Cyprinidae, order Cypriniformes, found in the fresh water of Europe generally. Its lower fins are tinged with red and it has rather large scales. It is related to the dace and chub, and swims in shoals in rivers and lakes. It is used as live-bait for fishing.

Roads, highways along which men, animals or wheeled vehicles travel. In antiquity, the Romans were great road-makers, and it is thought they acquired the art from the Carthaginians; relics of Roman roads still exist in Britain, with carriageways about 5 m wide: they are often marked by two parallel ditches, the causeway between which was excavated to a firm foundation. Around 1750 in England there began another important period of road-building which ended in the mid-19th century with the development of the railway. This phase of road-making in England is associated with the names of two famous civil engineers, Thomas Telford (from 1803) and James Loudon Macadam (from 1813). Telford used a hand-packed foundation of vertical stones 300 to 450 mm high, covered with 60-millimetre stone in a layer 100 to 150 mm thick above it, while Macadam used such broken stone ('macadam') in both foundation and surfacing. Telford's system proved the better, and is still used. The advent of the motor-car stimulated another bout of road building and the development of new surfaces and mechanised methods of road-making.

Roanoke (formerly Big Lick), city in Virginia, USA, on the Roanoke river in Great Valley, 65 km west of Lynchburg. Roanoke owed its prosperity to the Virginia railway. It is the industrial, trade and rail centre for a rich agricultural area; it is particularly known as a textile-manufacturing town. Population (1980) 100,427.

Roanoke, river of Virginia and North Carolina, USA, formed by the Dan and Staunton rivers. Rising in the Allegheny Mountains, it flows over 700 km across the Appalachian valley and then south-east out into the western end of Albemarle Sound.

Roanoke Island, an island 20 km long and 5 km wide, lying in Roanoke Sound, North Carolina, USA. It was first explored in 1584 and, in the three years succeeding, two attempts were made to found here the first English colony in the Atlantic coastal region. When a follow-up expedition arrived in 1590, however, no trace could be found of the colonists.

Roaring Forties, nautical expression for regions south of latitude 40 °S, in the Southern Ocean, where strong westerly winds prevail.

Rob Roy, alias Robert Macgregor (1671–1734), Highland freebooter. He derived his main income from cattle-lifting and exacting money for affording protection against thieves. He espoused the Jacobite cause in 1691, and in consequence of this and his plundering raids the penal laws were renewed against his clan in 1693. In 1712 he was accused of fraudulent bankruptcy, and in 1715 followed in the wake of the rebel army at Sheriffmuir and stood watching for the booty. He surrendered to the Duke of Atholl in 1717, but soon escaped, probably through the protection of the Duke of Argyll, to be again captured and imprisoned. He was, however, pardoned in 1727, and lived the rest of his life as a peaceful subject.

Robbe-Grillet, Alain (1922–), French writer. An outstanding exponent and theorist of the *nouveau roman*, his novels include *Les Gommes*, 1953; *Le Voyeur*, 1955; *La Jalousie*, 1957; *Dans le labyrinthe*, 1959; and *La Maison de rendez-vous*, 1965. His other writings include *Instantanés*, 1961; *Pour un nouveau roman*, 1963; and many more, such as *L'Immortelle*, 1963; and *L'Éden et après*, 1970. He also wrote the scenario for the film *L'Année dernière à Marienbad*, 1961.

Robbery, in English law, is defined by the Theft Act 1968 as committed by a person who commits theft and uses force on any person or puts any person in fear of being subjected to force at that time.

Robbia, Luca della (1399–1482), Italian sculptor. He early devoted himself to sculpture, though brought up as a goldsmith, and probably studied with Ghiberti. He is best known for his works in enamelled terracotta. He also executed a beautiful series of bas-reliefs for the Cantoria in the Cathedral of Florence; the tomb of the Bishop of Fiesole; and a bronze door for the sacristy of Florence Cathedral. His nephew Andrea continued the production of 'Robbia ware', and five of Andrea's seven sons after him.

Robbins, Jerome (1918–), US dancer and choreographer, associate artistic director of the New York City Ballet (NYCB). Robbins, an engaging character dancer, made his reputation overnight with the smash hit of his first ballet, *Fancy Free*, 1944, for the American Ballet Theatre. As well as working in ballet, he had choreographed and directed Broadway musicals, of which the most celebrated was *West Side Story*, 1957. In recent years he has returned to ballet, making such diverse works as a new version of *Les Noces*, 1965, and a pure dance work, *Dances at a Gathering*, to Chopin piano music.

Robbins, Lionel Charles Robbins, Baron (1898–), British economist. He was professor of economics from 1929 to 1961 at the London School of Economics. He was chairman of the committee that issued the Robbins Report on higher education and was president of the British Academy, 1962–67.

Robbins Report, 1963, named after the chairman, Lord Robbins, of a committee appointed by the Prime Minister to study higher education in Great Britain.

Its recommendations were that a modest expansion of universities was needed, that Colleges of Advanced Technology should be given the status of universities, that training colleges should be more closely associated with the universities and should be renamed Colleges of Education within the framework of university Schools of Education, and that at least some of their students should prepare for and receive special degrees in education.

Robens of Woldingham, Alfred Robens, Baron (1910–), British politician and administrator. He was a Labour MP from 1945 to 1960. In 1960 Robens became deputy chairman of the National Coal Board, and was chairman during 1961–71. He became chairman of Vickers Ltd in 1971.

Robert I (d.1035), Duke of Normandy, known also as Robert the Devil. He was the father of William the Conqueror. He governed his duchy with ability and ruthlessness.

When his only (illegitimate) son, William, was seven years old Robert died of fever.

Robert I of Scotland, see Bruce, Robert.

Robert II (c.1055–1134), surnamed 'Curthose', eldest son of William I (the Conqueror), whom he succeeded as Duke of Normandy in 1087. After the accession of William II to the English throne, the two brothers were soon at variance and William twice invaded Normandy. In 1096 peace was made and thus Robert was able to take part in the First Crusade. He returned home with a great reputation for valour. When Henry I became king of England, Robert contested his claim, unsuccessfully invading England in 1101. Henry invaded Normandy in turn in 1106 and at the battle of Tinchebray defeated and captured his brother. Robert remained in captivity until his death in 1134.

Robert II (1316–90), King of Scotland from 1371 to 1390. He acted as regent during the exile and captivity of his uncle, David II. In 1371 he succeeded David, and became the founder of the Stewart dynasty.

***Robespierre,** one of the most powerful leaders of the French Revolution.*

Robert III (1340–1406), King of Scotland. He succeeded in 1390. The war with England broke out again on the accession of Henry IV in 1399. Henry entered Scotland at the head of a powerful army, and later Henry Percy (Hotspur) made a more destructive inroad. Robert was only the nominal ruler of Scotland; real power was in the hands of his brother, the Duke of Albany.

Roberts, Sir Charles George Douglas (1860–1943), Canadian poet and nature writer. In Britain he was best known, along with E. Thompson Seton, for his animal stories. In Canada he was acclaimed the 'father of Canadian literature', mainly because of his poetry.

Roberts of Kandahar, Pretoria and Waterford, Frederick Sleigh Roberts, Ist Earl (1832–1914), British soldier. During the Indian Mutiny he won the Victoria Cross. He also served in Abyssinia; and on the outbreak of the Afghan War, 1878–80, he was appointed to command the Kuram division of the army. In 1880 he was put in command of the force sent to Kabul. From Kabul he proceeded on his victorious march to the relief of Kandahar. Roberts was commander-in-chief of the forces in India from 1885 to 1893. He was promoted lieutenant general in 1883, general in 1890, and field marshal in 1895.

In December 1899 he was sent to South Africa to take command of the British forces in the Boer War. In 1901 he followed Lord Wolseley as commander-in-chief. On the outbreak of the First World War he was appointed colonel-in-chief of the Indian contingent in France. He went there on 11 November 1914, caught a chill, and died at St Omer.

Roberts, William (1895–), British painter. From the Vorticist and Futurist movements he derived a personal and somewhat grotesque style, depicting a mechanised humanity. Examples of his work as a war artist are in the Imperial War Museum.

Robertson, J. Forbes-, see Forbes-Robertson, Sir Johnston.

Robeson, Paul (1898–1976), US actor and singer. He appeared in America in *Emperor Jones*, and several other plays by Eugene O'Neill, and then embarked upon a successful career as a concert singer, specialising in Negro spirituals. He came to London in 1928, appearing in the title roles of *Emperor Jones* and *Othello*, and in the musical play *Showboat*. He played several of his most successful roles on the screen and in 1942–45 appeared in *Othello* in the USA. This was considered by many to be the finest performance of his career. In later years he devoted himself increasingly to left-wing politics.

Robespierre, Maximilien Marie Isidore (1758–94). French revolutionary leader. In 1789 he was one of the deputies of the Third Estate at the States-General. His fanaticism, self-confidence and oratorical skill soon made him well known and he quickly established a secure position among the Jacobins, the extremist group.

In September 1792 he was elected to the National Convention, the organ which proclaimed the French republic. After the execution of Louis XVI and the downfall of the Girondists, Robespierre became a member of the newly formed Committee of Public Safety, the body which was the real ruler of France and in which he was supreme. His power was now unchallenged, but his tyranny soon caused a plot for his destruction. He absented himself from the meeting of the Convention on 27 July 1794, at which he was openly accused of despotism, and when, too late, he tried to obtain a hearing, his power had gone, and a decree of arrest was sent out against him. He fled, but was captured and guillotined on 28 July. His death marked the beginning of the reaction against the Revolution which he had characterised in its most extreme form.

See also France, *History*.

Robey, Sir George, real name George Edward Wade (1869–1954), British music-hall comedian. He made his first professional appearance on the stage in 1891. Soon afterwards he came to fame with 'The Simple Dimple', a very ordinary music-hall ditty rendered intensely comical by Robey enunciation, grimaces and gestures. His interrogative eyebrows became famous. He took part in many revues and films, and had some success as a serious actor, notably as Falstaff in *Henry IV* in 1935. His publications include *My Life up to Now*, 1908, and *Looking Back on Life*, 1933.

Robin, see Robin Redbreast.

Robin Hood, legendary English hero celebrated especially in ballads, the leader of a band of outlaws, expert archers dressed in Lincoln green, who lived in Sherwood Forest. With companions, Robin Hood lived a life of freedom and philanthropy, robbing the rich to give to the poor, and oppressing no righteous man. There may be some historical basis for his legend, but many of the customs and practices associated with his name suggest that he is a character of Mayday celebrations.

Robin Redbreast, *Erithacus rubecula*, a common species of the family Muscicapidae in the order Passeriformes. It has long been protected from human cruelty by an extraordinary amount of superstition and legend. Its song is continued through most of the year, and is especially noticeable in winter. The adults have an orange breast, with brown back and white underparts.

The American robin is a migratory thrush; numerous other thrushes and flycatchers worldwide are also known as robins.

Robinia, a genus of leguminous plants, growing wild only in America. *R. pseudacacia*, the false acacia or locust-tree, is often grown in parks and gardens. It is a tree with pinnate leaves and straight thorns on the young twigs. The shrubs *R. hispida*, rose acacia, and *R. kelseyi* are also cultivated.

Robinson, Edward G. (1893–1973), American film actor, born Emanuel Goldenberg in Romania. His best known part was as the gangster in *Little Caesar*, 1930. He played other similar rôles throughout the 1930s, but later extended his range to embrace such characters as the insurance agent in *Double Indemnity*, 1943, and the con-man in *The Outrage*, 1964, as well as parodying his own gangster rôle in *Key Largo*, 1948.

***Edward G. Robinson** is best remembered for his gangster rôles in the 1930s.*

Robinson, Edwin Arlington (1869–1935), US poet. Robinson's first volume, *The Torrent and the Night Before*, 1896, had been

followed by a revised version, *The Children of the Night*, 1897. *Town Down the River*, 1910, contains the well-known poem 'Miniver Cheevy', but it was not until he was middle-aged that he became famous with *The Man Against the Sky*, 1916. In 1922 his *Collected Poems* were awarded the Pulitzer Prize.
Later poems, mainly psychological studies, include *The Man Who Died Twice*, 1924 (another Pulitzer Prize winner). He also wrote several long poems on Arthurian legends—which brought him his third Pulitzer Prize. His *Selected Letters* were published in 1940.

Robinson, Joan Violet (1903–), British economist. She is the most important member of the post-Keynesian Cambridge school of economics, and her theoretical contributions to the subject are many and distinguished. Her books include: *Economics of Imperfect Competition*, 1933; *Essay on Marxian Economics*, 1942; *The Accumulation of Capital*, 1956; *Economic Heresies*, 1971; and (with John Eatwell) *An Introduction to Modern Economics*, 1973.

Robinson, John Arthur Thomas (1919–), British theologian. He was suffragan bishop of Woolwich, 1959–69. His popularisation of some current theological trends in *Honest to God*, 1963, and *The New Reformation*, 1965, caused widespread controversy. In 1969 he became assistant bishop of Southwark, and also lecturer in theology, fellow, and dean of chapel at Trinity College, Cambridge.

Robinson, Sugar Ray, real name Walker Smith (1920–), US boxer; he was welterweight champion of the world from 1946 to 1951, and defended this title five times, undefeated. He took the world middleweight title in 1951 by defeating Jake LaMotta in 13 rounds. In all he lost the title six times and won it seven times. He was rated by some as the best boxer of his era.

Robinson, William Heath (1872–1944), British artist. Robinson illustrated Hans Andersen's *Fairy Tales*, *Arabian Nights*, Poe's *Tales of Mystery and Imagination*, *Don Quixote*, and Rabelais. His best-known work, however, was his humorous drawings for periodicals, his speciality being grotesque and laborious mechanisms involving the most complicated operation in order to perform the simplest possible tasks.

Robot, a programmable machine capable of human-like activity. Robots are being increasingly used in industry to carry out repetitive tasks such as spot welding, loading and painting. Recent research is aimed at bringing robots into use in hostile environments such as nuclear reactors and developing an ability in them to 'see' and respond to complex shapes through the use of lasers. In 1982 there were estimated to be 1152 robots in industrial use in Britain, compared with 13,000 in Japan and 6250 in the United States.

Robson, Dame Flora (1902–84), British actress. She made her first professional stage appearance in 1921. In 1933 she joined the Old Vic Company. She established a reputation as a fine actress in such plays as *Romeo and Juliet*, *Captain Brassbound's Conversion* and *The Winter's Tale*. Modern plays include *Black Chiffon*, *The Innocents* and *The Aspern Papers*. She appeared in a number of films, including *Fire Over England*, *Caesar and Cleopatra* and *Black Narcissus*.

Roc, or rukh, fabulous bird, often identified with the Arabian *'anqa'* and the Persian *simurgh*. It was supposed to be of enormous size and capable of performing wonderful feats of strength, for example carrying off elephants to feed its young. The legend of the roc appears in the Arabian Nights.

Rocambole, *Allium scordoprasum*, a species of onion, known also as sand leek.

Rochdale, town of Greater Manchester Metropolitan County, situated in the Roch river valley at the southern end of the Rossendale upland. Traditionally associated with the wool trade, Rochdale became a prosperous cotton town. In recent times, the cotton industry has been partly replaced by engineering and clothing industries. Population (1981) 92,704.

Rochdale Canal, runs from Sowerby Bridge in Yorkshire, England, to the Bridgewater Canal in Manchester. Opened in 1804, it used the lowest pass through the Pennines, and many factories, of which a large number are now in ruins, line its banks. It is now closed to navigation.

Roche Abbey, ruined Cistercian abbey in South Yorkshire. Roche was founded in 1147, and was one of the earliest buildings in England constructed in the Gothic style.
See also CISTERCIANS.

Roche, Mazo de la, see DE LA ROCHE, MAZO.

Roche Moutonnée, rocky outcrops in glaciated landscapes, smoothed and striated on the upstream side by abrasion, but craggy and plucked on the downstream side. Roches moutonnées are distinguished from crag and tail by the absence of a streamlined tail.

Rochefort (-sur-Mer), French seaport in the *département* of Charente-Maritime, on the River Charente, 30 km south-east of La Rochelle. It has naval schools and manufactures aircraft parts. Population (1975) 32,884.

Rochester, John Wilmot, 2nd Earl of (1647–80), English poet and courtier. He became one of the profligate set at the court of Charles II. Rochester was, in effect, the last significant courtier-poet in England. Some of his poetry was inaccessible for many years because of its obscenity.

W. Heath Robinson. How to Dispense with Servants in the Dining Hall.

Rochester, city, commercial centre and port in Kent, England. Traces of the walls of Roman *Durobrivae* exist, standing where Watling Street crosses the tidal Medway. A Norman cathedral, a Benedictine priory and later a castle were built, all of which have important remains. The Medway Port Authority control the dockyard, one of the most important for cargo handling in Kent (with Grain and Sheerness). Population (1981) 52,505.

Rochester, city in New York state, USA. It is situated just south of the shore of Lake Ontario. Its industry is dominated by the Eastman Kodak photographic concern; Eastman's home here is now a museum, commemorating his pioneer work in photography. Population (1980) 241,509.

Rochester, town and county seat of Olmsted county, Minnesota, USA, 112 km south-east of St Paul. It is the seat of the famous Mayo Clinic (founded 1889), the Mayo Foundation for Medical Education and Research, and of numerous other hospitals. Population (1980) 54,287.

Rochet, linen garment, the lower part often of lace, worn as part of the choir dress by prelates. Anglican bishops wear a rochet, with full lawn sleeves (in the 18th century enormous 'balloon sleeves') bound at the wrists, under the chimere.

Rock. A rock is a naturally occurring accumulation of one or more different species of minerals. The study of rocks is termed geology.

Rock-climbing. Historically, rock-climbing began during the last century as a concomitant of fell walking or as practice for alpine climbing. Early climbs were mostly in narrow 'gullies', requiring ample use of knee, foot, backside and brute strength; later climbs were on ridges or inclined slabs where balance and agility were at a premium. Until about 1930 equipment was largely confined to nailed boots and hemp rope, though gym shoes facilitated the earlier slab climbs. Since then, much new gear has been developed; nylon rope, crash hats and the use of running belays have made it safer.
Although solo climbing has recently become fashionable, the usual and recommended procedure is for a competent leader to take a 'rope' of other climbers up a rock face, paying out the rope while he advances up each pitch (section) of the climb. En route the leader leaves his rope running through metal snaplinks attached by rope loops to spikes of rock or nuts jammed in suitable cracks, thus minimising the length of any fall by use of these 'running belays'. Some controversy surrounds the use of further aids to climbing such as pitons (pegs) which can be driven into cracks, stirrups for the feet where there are no foot-holds, and bolts which may be drilled into blank walls.

Rock Cress, see ARABIS.

Rock Drills, see PNEUMATIC TOOLS.

Rock-fish, see WRASSE.

Rock Garden, see GARDENING.

Rock Music form of popular music which first developed in the USA in the early 1950s, played on electric guitars and characterised by repetitive lyrics and driving rhythms. Rock grew out of the combined influence of black rhythm-and-blues and white folk music, and in the form of rock 'n' roll was exemplified in Bill Haley and the Comets' song *Rock around the Clock* (1955); Elvis Presley was rock 'n' roll's most famous exponent. In the early 1960s rock began to diversify; folk rock, for example, with a folksong element and more substantial lyrics, was developed by Bob Dylan and others. English rock music found its form only with the development of the Mersey Sound and groups such as the Beatles and the Rolling Stones. In the early 1970s an authentic black rhythm-and-blues element was introduced in the work of Jimi Hendrix and Eric Clapton, while groups such as Pink Floyd and The Who created lengthy symphonic works using electronic equipment. The end of the 1970s saw a return to the original aggressive rock style in the form of punk rock or 'new wave'.

Rock Oil, see PETROLEUM.

Rock-rabbit, see HYRAX.

Rock Salmon, see DOGFISH.

Rock Salt, see SODIUM.

Rock Temples, hewn out of solid rock, are found in many parts of the world, notably in India, Sri Lanka, Egypt, Arabia and China. There are also some interesting examples in the USA, one being in Missouri near Salt River. Examples are to be found in India at Ellora and Elephanta, in Sri Lanka at Dambulla, in Egypt at Abu-Simbel (Ipsambul), in Arabia at Petra.
See also INDIA, *Architecture*.

Rockall, uninhabited rocky island, part of a reef in the Atlantic, more than 450 km west of Ardnamurchan Point in Scotland, and 420 km from Bloody Foreland, Ireland. It lies in an area extremely dangerous to shipping, and gives its name to a weather forecast area of the meteorological service.

Rockefeller, John Davison, junior (1874–1960), US industrialist and philanthropist, only son of J. D. Rockefeller. He entered his father's business, and soon became his leading assistant in the oil and coal enterprises. When his father retired all his affairs were put into the hands of the son, who devoted much time to superintending the gifts made by the various Rockefeller foundations. Among his lavish gifts were a large sum towards the restoration of Reims cathedral; land worth about $8·5 million as a site for United Nations buildings in New York; and $5 million for the cultural complex, the Lincoln Center, New York.
See also FOUNDATIONS.

Rockefeller, John Davison (1839–1937), US businessman. In 1865 Rockefeller joined Samuel Andrews, inventor of a process for cleaning crude oil, in founding the firm of Rockefeller & Andrews, which soon became Rockefeller, Andrews & Flagler, the leading oil firm in Cleveland. In 1870, these three and associates incorporated the Standard Oil Company, with a capital of $1 million. By 1880 the corporation controlled about 90 per cent of US oil refineries. In 1881 Rockefeller founded the first of those gigantic combinations which were described as 'trusts'. The Standard Oil Trust was sued in the courts under many charges; the Standard Oil Company of New Jersey was reorganised in 1899 with a capitalisation of $110 million to take the place of the Standard Oil Company of Ohio as the core of the Trust. Finally, in 1911, the US Supreme Court ordered the dissolution of the Standard Oil Trust on the ground that it was a combination in restraint of trade under the Sherman Anti-Trust Law. Meanwhile Rockefeller had become the world's richest man.
The suits against all companies and the exposure of some of the business methods employed inflamed public anger. But his huge gifts to science, education and public health gained him popularity in his later years. To charities and education institutions he gave in his lifetime more than $500 million. These activities were carried on by his son, John Davison junior, and by his grandsons.

Rockefeller, Nelson Aldrich (1908–79), US politician, a member of the famous Rockefeller family. He was assistant secretary of state 1944–45, and special assistant to President Eisenhower 1954–55. He was elected Republican governor of New York state, 1959, and remained governor until 1974. A prominent member of the liberal wing of the Republican party, he sought the presidential nomination in 1960, 1964 and 1968. He was appointed vice-president by President Ford in 1974.

Rocket, term applied to several plants of different genera all belonging to the Cruciferae. *Cakile maritima*, the sea-rocket, is almost cosmopolitan on coasts; it has a long tap-root and fleshy leaves. Some species of *Barbarea* are known as yellow-rocket or wintercress, and *Hesperis matronalis* is also a rocket. London rocket is *Sisymbrium irio*, so called from its abundance in London after the Great Fire (1666).

Rocket, a vehicle propelled by a jet created from materials carried on board. The jet can be derived from stored gas, or the products of combustion of suitable chemicals, or from gas heated by nuclear or electrical power. The gases are accelerated to the speed of sound by necking down the efflux pipe, and then accelerated to supersonic speed in an expanding cone. The nozzle increases the speed of the jet at the expense of its temperature.
The total dry weight of a rocket can be as little as 5 to 10 per cent of its total weight when fuelled. Even so, orbital speed is not attained by a typical rocket, and a second stage must also be used. This is a smaller rocket carried up inert by the larger first stage rocket, and ignited after separation from the spent first stage (booster). By the use of multiple staging any desired speed may be built up, at the expense of decreasing the mass of the final payload.
See also SPACE TRAVEL.

'Rocket', The, steam locomotive built by George Stephenson which in October 1829 won the famous Rainhill competition, and so decided the use of locomotives on the Liverpool and Manchester Railway.

Rockfoil, see SAXIFRAGE.

Rockhampton, town of Queensland, Australia, on the River Fitzroy, 637 km north of Brisbane. It is the port for one of the largest and richest pastoral belts in Australia, for gold and copper of the famous Mount Morgan mines, and also pyrites, salt and limestone. Population (1980) 53,500.

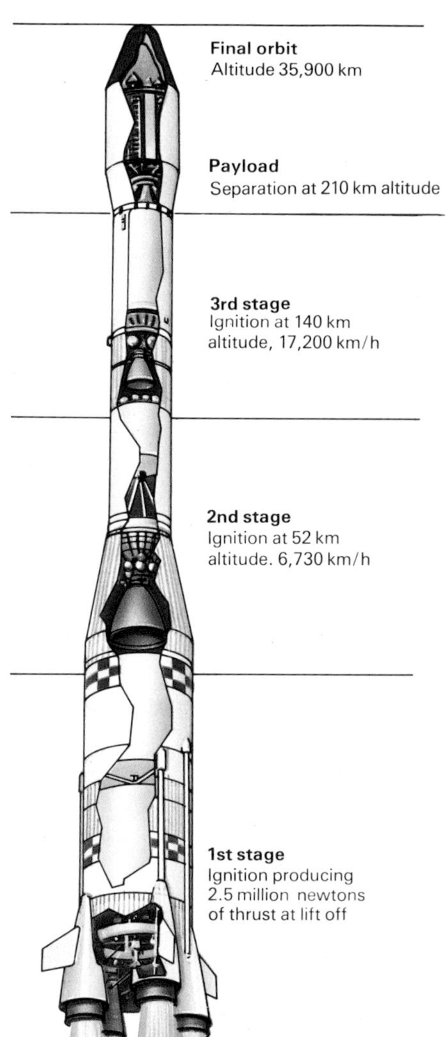

Rocket. *The three-stage launch vehicle Ariane stands 47.4 m high and weighs 207 tonnes.*

Rockingham, Charles Watson-Wentworth, 2nd Marquess of (1730–82), British statesman. He was a Whig, and held several minor offices from 1751 until 1762; but three years later became prime minister for a short time and repealed the Stamp Act. He led the opposition in the House of Lords until March 1782, when he again formed an administration, but he was an ineffectual leader.

Rocky Mountain Spotted Fever (tick-borne typhus), a disease caused by a small organism of the rickettsia group, *Rickettsia rickettsii*, transmitted to humans by the bite of an infected tick normally parasitic on dogs, foxes, rabbits and rodents. The disease takes the form of an abrupt fever, with prostrating headache, occasional rigors, rash, and flecks of haemorrhage into the skin. There is a high mortality rate in the untreated. Treatment by antibiotics is usually successful.

Rocky Mountains, the most important mountain system in North America, crossing New Mexico, Utah, Colorado, Idaho, Wyoming, Montana, Canada and Alaska. It is the main watershed of the American continent, a distance of 5150 km. The Rockies were first seen, apart from early Spanish explorers, when Verendrye sighted the Bighorn range

Rocky Mountains. In Canada, the Rocky Mountains extend 725 km; the highest peak is Mount Logan.

of Wyoming in 1738. For another hundred years their history was that of a barrier to trade and travel, but by 1870 the Union Pacific railroad had been built across them.

The highest peaks are in Alaska. In the St Elias range (Yukon frontier) are Mount Logan (6050 m), the highest peak in Canada, St Elias (5488 m), and Fairweather (4663 m). In the Wrangell range is Mount Blackburn (4919 m), and in the Alaskan range, Mount McKinley (6187 m), the highest peak of North America.

The resources of the Rockies are well-known, apart from hydroelectric power generation. Copper, iron ore, silver, gold, lead, zinc, molybdenum and uranium are the most important metallic resources, but non-metallic reserves are also most important. The intermontane basins of the Rockies yield oil and natural gas, and the region also has large coal reserves.

See also CANADA; UNITED STATES OF AMERICA.

Rockrose, a name given to the genera *Helianthemum* and *Cistus* in family Cistaceae. *Helianthemum* species are mainly small creeping plants, often with woody stems. *Cistus* species are upright shrubs, coming mainly from the Mediterranean region and having mostly pink or purple flowers, which resemble in general appearance those of the wild rose. A number of species and hybrids of both genera are grown in gardens.

Rococo (French *rocaille*, rock-work), a style in architecture and interior decoration popular in early 18th-century France. It succeeded the weighty splendour of the Louis XIV style with more delicate ornamental forms, based on asymmetrical curves and C-scrolls. This pretty, ornate style was echoed in furniture, porcelain and silverware. A similar decorative approach full of airiness and gaiety is found in the paintings of Tiepolo, Boucher and Fragonard. The Rococo style was superseded by Neo-classicism in the late 18th century.

Rodentia, mammals that include small, gnawing animals, such as rats and mice. They vary in size from the capybara, which is over 1 m long including its tail, to the dormouse, which may only be 8 cm long with the tail.

As a whole their diet is vegetarian, and the dentition is specialised. There are only two kinds of teeth, incisors and grinders (molars), two incisors being present in both upper and lower jaws. These have open roots and continue to grow throughout the animal's life. Many rodents are burrowers, some are aquatic and some are arboreal, and many hibernate. Among the rodents are the most destructive of man's enemies. They eat grain, the stalks of edible grasses and root crops, both in the field and in storage. They carry several diseases transmissible to man, including plague and scrub typhus. They are useful, however, as sources of fur, food, laboratory animals, and as pets. Rodents are found all over the world and Rodentia is the largest mammalian order.

The order Rodentia is divided into three suborders. Suborder Sciuromorpha includes squirrels, gophers, pouched mice and beavers. Suborder Myomorpha includes mice, rats, hamsters, lemmings, muskrats, voles and gerbils. Suborder Hystricomorpha includes porcupines, guinea-pigs, agoutis, chinchillas and others.

Rodeo (Spanish *rodear*, to go round), popular form of entertainment in countries with a heritage of stock raising, notably the USA, Canada, Australia. A rodeo is based on five principal contests: saddle and bareback bronco riding, bull riding, calf roping and steer wrestling. The rodeo developed from the 18th-century fiesta and came into being during the early days of the North American cattle industry.

Roderic (d.711), last Visigoth King of Spain. His short reign marks the beginning of Arab domination in Spain. He was defeated in 711 by the Arab or Saracenic forces under Tarik which had invaded Spain. He is the hero of Scott's *Vision of Don Roderick* and Southey's *Roderick the Goth*.

Rodgers, Richard Charles (1902–79), American composer of musical comedies for stage and film. He began his career in the 1920s with lyricist Lorenz Hart. After Hart's death in 1943 he collaborated with Oscar Hammerstein II until the latter's death in 1960. His greatest successes include *Pal Joey*, 1940; *Oklahoma*, 1943; *South Pacific*, 1958; and *The Sound of Music*, 1959.

Rodin, François Auguste (1840–1917), French sculptor. From 1871 to 1877 he worked in Brussels but subsequently he returned to Paris, where most of his finest work was accomplished. Here he became the best-known and most successful sculptor of his day. Casts of his statues were purchased for collections all over the world. His *Monument to Victor Hugo*, representing the poet nude, and his Balzac (in dressing-gown) caused a great sensation. Some of his finest pieces are *The Burghers of Calais, The Kiss, St John the Baptist, Danaïd, Eve, The Thinker, The Hand of God, The Prodigal Son* and *The Gate of Hell*, a colossal inspiration, after Dante's *Inferno*. He made many etchings, and his drawings have an individual beauty. His most important works are the Musée Rodin in Paris, a building which was made available to Rodin at the height of his career.

Rodney, George Brydges Rodney, 1st Baron (1719–92), British admiral. In 1759 he bombarded Le Havre and destroyed the flotilla designed for the invasion of England. At the end of 1779 he defeated the Spanish fleet off Cape St Vincent. His famous naval victory of the Battle of the Saints over the combined French and Spanish fleets secured to Britain its West Indian colonies. The battle was fought off Dominica on 12 April 1782.

Rodrigo, Joaquin (1902–), Spanish composer. Blind from the age of three, he studied with Dukas in Paris and travelled in Europe before settling in Madrid. A prolific composer, Rodrigo has written the best-loved guitar concerto, the *Concierto de Aranjuez*; his *Fantasia para una Gentilhombre* is also popular.

Roe Deer or roebuck, *Capreolus capreolus*, a small deer, native to central and southern Europe, and other races range as far east as China. The buck stands about 66 cm at the shoulder, and is 1·2 m in length from nose to tiny tail. The colour in summer is reddish-brown (in winter the redness disappears), and the underparts are yellowish-grey. The young at first are reddish-brown with white spots.

Roebuck, see ROE DEER.

Roehm, Ernst, see RÖHM, ERNST.

Rodentia. Representative species from the three suborders.

Roemer, Olaus, or Ole, (1644–1710), Danish astronomer and mathematician. His most celebrated discovery was the finite velocity of light. Observations in Paris of Jupiter's satellites had disagreed with Cassini's tables, and Roemer in 1675 demonstrated that the error was due to the time taken by light to traverse the changing distance between Jupiter and Earth. He announced that light took 11 minutes to travel the distance between the Earth and the Sun. He developed the transit instrument which was to become the fundamental instrument of positional astronomy.

Roeselare (French *Roulers*), town in the province of West Flanders, Belgium, 19 km north-west of Courtrai. A famous weaving centre in the Middle Ages, it now cultivates flax and manufactures lace, linen, gloves, carpets, pottery and tiles. Population (1981) 51,945.

Rogation Days (Latin *rogare*, to ask), until recently in the Roman Catholic Church 25 April (the Greater Litanies) and the three days preceding Ascension Day (the Lesser Litanies), so called because the litany was on these days chanted in procession, if possible outside the church, and often around the crops.

Both observances are now replaced among Roman Catholics by days of prayer locally appointed. The Anglican Book of Common Prayer retains the Lesser Rogations only, among the days of fasting and abstinence. A Rogation procession has in some places been revived among Anglicans.

Rogation Flower, see MILKWORT.

Roger de Coverley, Sir, dance said to have been invented by the great-grandfather of Roger de Coverley, or Roger of Cowley, near Oxford. It is a type of English country long dance which includes the figure of threading-the-needle. As a social dance, it achieved its greatest popularity during the 19th century.

A character called Sir Roger de Coverley was also used in *The Spectator* by Addison and Steele to represent a typical member of the country gentry.

Rogers, Ginger (1911–), American actress and dancer, real name Virginia McMath. She is known, above all, for her singing and dancing partnership with Fred Astaire in a series of films during the 1930s, including *Top Hat*, 1935, *Swing Time*, 1936, and *Follow the Fleet*, 1936. She is also noted for her comedy rôles in films such as *Bachelor Mother*, 1939, and *The Major and the Minor*, 1942.

Rogers, John (c.1500–55), English cleric. He abandoned the Catholic faith and became a pastor at Wittenberg (1537). Under Edward VI he was a prebendary of St Paul's. He was imprisoned for his views and outspoken preaching in Mary's reign, condemned by Gardiner and Bonner, and burned at Smithfield. Rogers prepared 'Matthew's' Bible from the version of Tyndale and Coverdale.

Roget, Peter Mark (1779–1869), British lexicographer and physician, chiefly remembered as the author of a *Thesaurus of English Words and Phrases*, 1852 (and many later editions), inspired by John Wilkins. This storehouse of words was organised by Roget in what seemed to him logical conceptual groups but, with an alphabetic index later added, it is used now more as a dictionary of synonyms and antonyms.

Rogier van der Weyden, also called Roger de la Pasture (1400–64), Flemish painter. In 1436 he became official painter to Brussels city. In this capacity he painted the altarpiece for the Chamber of Justice in the *hôtel de ville* (destroyed in the 17th century). Rogier's *Last Judgment* is in the museum of the hospital at Beaune. His work continues and extends the Flemish tradition begun by the two Van Eyck brothers, Hubert and Jan, in keeping the rich colour made possible by the oil technique and its capacity for minutely rendered detail, but deepening its humanism. His portraiture also shows a desire to describe the inner life of his subjects.

Rogue, see VAGRANTS.

Rohe, Ludwig Mies van der, see MIES VAN DER ROHE, LUDWIG.

Röhm, Ernst (1887–1934), German politician. Röhm was one of the original members of the National Socialist party and an intimate friend of Hitler. In 1931 he became Hitler's chief of staff and leader of the SA and SS. He was shot during the purge of 30 June 1934 on charges of plotting against Hitler.

Rohmer, Eric (1920–), French film director and critic. He worked on the editorial board of *Cahiers du cinéma* in the fifties, while making short films and teaching. In 1959 he made his first feature, *Le Signe du Lion*, after which he commenced the six *Moral Tales: La boulangère de Monceau*, 1962 (a 16 mm short); *La Carrière de Suzanne*, 1963 (also in 16 mm); *La Collectioneuse*, 1966; *Ma Nuit chez Maud*, 1969; *Le Genou de Claire*, 1970; *L'Amour, L'Après-midi*, 1972 and *La Femme de l'Aviateur*, 1981.

Rohmer, Sax, pseudonym of Arthur Ward (1886–1959), English novelist. He specialised in exotic thrillers featuring a sinister oriental villain whose name appears in many of his book-titles, from *Dr Fu Manchu*, 1913, to *The Drums of Fu Manchu*, 1939.

Roland, Chanson de, earliest and finest of the extant *chansons de geste*. Composed about 1100, it is the legendary account of an historical event of 778 when, as Charlemagne was returning from Spain, his rearguard was ambushed by Basques, or Gascons, in the Pyrenees. It tells how, prompted by the traitor Ganelon, the Saracens ambush and slay Roland (here Charlemagne's nephew), his companion Oliver, and the 12 Peers of France in the pass of Roncesvalles (Roncevaux). Charlemagne, summoned by Roland's horn, arrives too late to save them, but destroys the pagans and Ganelon.

Rolfe, Frederick William (1860–1913), English novelist, who called himself Baron Corvo. At the age of 26 he became a Roman Catholic and studied for the priesthood, but he was thought unsuited for the calling and was dismissed. He then followed a roving life. He published two collections of short stories, *Stories Toto Told Me*, 1898, and *In His Own Image*, 1901. *Hadrian VII*, 1904, and *Don Tarquinio*, 1905, are novels. *Chronicles of the House of Borgia* appeared in 1901. In 1908 he moved to Venice, where he remained for the rest of his life. Here he wrote his masterpiece, *The Desire and Pursuit of the Whole*, published posthumously in 1934.

Roll-on Roll-off Ship. The disadvantage of the container ship is that not all loads are suitable for loading into containers. Therefore on many trades a combination of ferry and container ship is employed. The large difficult loads are taken on road vehicles into the ferry portion, usually in the stern, while the containers are loaded into container cells forward. A typical ship of this type can carry 700 containers and 900 cars or other road vehicles.

Rolland, Romain (1866–1944), French author. In 1903 he became a professor of the history of music at the Sorbonne, and it was in musical history that he achieved his first great success, with his biography *Beethoven*, 1903. Then in 1906 came *Jean-Christophe*, the first of his studies of an imaginary musician, evolved from the ideals of the German cultural period represented by Beethoven and Goethe. Ten volumes were issued 1906–12, and for this remarkable work Rolland was awarded the Nobel Prize for literature in 1915.

During the First World War Rolland aroused much controversy; his articles and uncompromisingly pacifist efforts to judge the war objectively led to accusations that he was pro-German.

Later books on Indian thinkers and religious leaders, such as his *Mahatma Gandhi*, 1924, were widely read in the East, but are less well known in France.

Roller Skating, sport with basic technique and principles similar to those of ice skating. The main difference is the 'dry' surface and the roller skate itself, which has four composite wheels cushioned by ballbearings, with rubber toe-stops instead of the ice skate's toe-pick. Roller speed skating and five-a-side roller hockey, an adaptation of field hockey to roller skates, are usually staged outdoors. Men's speed titles are contested over distances of 500, 1500, 5000 and 10,000 m, women's over 500, 3000 and 5000 m.

Rollers, name given to any species of the family Coraciidae, order Coraciiformes, on account of the curious habit of both male and female birds rolling over when in flight. These birds occur exclusively in the Old World, and are found in the woods of hilly districts. They are usually brightly coloured and quite large, about 25 to 32 cm long.

Rollier, Auguste (1874–1954), Swiss physician. A pioneer in the treatment of tuberculosis by heliotherapy, his clinic in Leysin was world famous.

Rolling Mills. In early times malleable iron was generally hammered down into shape. Rolling mills were later used to replace the older water tilt-hammers and steam-hammers. Although modern rolling may be said to have originated with Henry Cort's invention of grooved rolls in 1784, rolling was practised for many years before this. In 1728 John Payne and Major Hanbury of Pontypool were granted a patent for rolling tin-plates, instead of the previous method of hammering.

Modern practice is based almost exclusively on the use of electrical power. These developments have probably constituted the outstanding features in steel and non-ferrous metal-rolling practice, but the improvements

Rolls-Royce. *A 1907 Silver Ghost. In total 6173 were built in the UK between 1906 and 1925.*

in mill design and gain in dimensional accuracy of the product, through automatic gauge control and the application of automation and on-line computer control, have all played a major role in achieving high mill efficiencies.

See also IRON AND STEEL.

Rolls, Charles Stewart, see ROLLS-ROYCE.

Rolls-Royce, British manufacturers of aero- and marine-engines and of luxury motor cars. Henry Royce (1863–1933) and the Hon. Charles Stewart Rolls (1877–1910) first met in 1904 when Royce Limited was producing Royce cars designed by their great engineer and C. S. Rolls and Company were dealers in high-grade continental cars.

The first Rolls-Royce factory was opened at Derby in July 1908, and Rolls-Royce cars rapidly established a reputation for quality. Production also occurred in the USA.

In 1914 Royce designed his first aero-engine, the Eagle. This became famous in the First World War, establishing aero-engine manufacture as an important activity of the company. During the Second World War the Merlin aero-engine powered many of Britain's leading military aircraft. Towards the end of the war the company entered the field of jet propulsion, and Rolls-Royce jet and propjet engines today power more aircraft in operation on the world's civil air routes than those of any other aero-engine manufacturer.

Rolls of Arms, medieval manuscript records of armorial bearings in the form of rolls or books, usually of vellum. The arms are sometimes recorded pictorially and sometimes verbally.

Romains, Jules, pseudonym of Louis Farigoule (1885–1972), French author. Romains was a founder of Unanimism, on which he wrote *La Vie unanime*, 1908, a volume of poems. He wrote successful plays, including *Knock*, 1923, *Volpone*, 1929, and *Donogoo*, 1930. But his outstanding achievement was as a novelist, with *Les Copains*, 1913, and especially *Les Hommes de bonne volonté*, 27 volumes, 1932–47, a 'continuous novel' attempting to survey realistically the whole panorama of contemporary life. Later novels include *Une Femme singulière*, 1957, and *Le Besoin de voir clair*, 1958.

Roman Army. The backbone of the Roman army was, and remained far into the 3rd century AD, the legion. Attached to the legion were units of horse and foot, recruited outside Italy. The cavalry was mainly from Gaul, Germany and Spain; the infantry were light-armed troops, e.g. Balearic slingers and Cretan archers. This organisation remained substantially the same until the time of Diocletian (AD 284).

In the later Empire barbarians began to serve Rome under their own leaders. After the reign of Diocletian such bodies came to preponderate in the Roman army.

Roman Catholic Church. For the doctrine, nature and history of the Catholic Church up to the Reformation see CHRISTIANITY; CHURCH HISTORY; PAPACY.

The Roman Catholic Church teaches that Christ is the invisible head of the church. He is represented on earth by the Bishop of Rome as successor to St Peter, to whom Christ gave the keys of the kingdom of heaven. The first Vatican Council (1870) declared the pope's authority to be everywhere *episcopal, ordinary* and *immediate*. Nevertheless, it is normally exercised through the partiarchs, metropolitans and other bishops who rule local churches by ordinary jurisdiction. The near-eastern churches are directly responsible to their patriarch, but Rome is always the final court of appeal. In the west, dioceses, governed by bishops, are grouped into provinces under archbishops called 'metropolitans'. They have little ordinary jurisdiction outside their own dioceses except the power to summon and preside over a provincial council. As a general rule, the sacraments are administered by bishops and priests. Only bishops can ordain, but priests and bishops can confirm, absolve from sins, offer Mass, and anoint the sick. Baptism is normally administered by a priest but, in an emergency, anyone can baptise. The sacrament of marriage is conferred by husband and wife on each other, but is usually witnessed by a priest as a representative of the church. The second Vatican Council (1961–65) led to a re-evaluation of all vocations within the church, especially the laity, and emphasised the need to reject exclusiveness and to be involved in all world-social activities.

There are five archiepiscopal and 15 episcopal sees in England and Wales, and two archiepiscopal and six episcopal sees in Scotland. In the 1970s the estimated number of Roman Catholics in England and Wales was around 4·1 million and in Scotland 816,000. In Europe the church has consolidated its position; conservatism marks its intellectual life, while politically its policy has been to seek a *modus vivendi* with national governments, whether Catholic or non-Catholic.

Missionary work among the heathens has characterised the church since St Paul's day and it was only in early medieval times that Europe ceased to be the main theatre of Roman Catholic missionary work and the western church was able to turn its attention to extra-European unbelievers, mainly the Muslims. The founding of mendicant orders in the 13th century provided the church with a body of men admirably adapted for missionary work. In the 16th century the Jesuits undertook to go as missionaries wherever the pope might send them. In the 19th century new religious orders devoted wholly to missionary work were founded. The development of the Catholic church in the USA, Australia, Canada, South America, and, indeed, in Britain has been greatly influenced through the centuries by both the forcible transportation and voluntary emigration of Irish Catholics.

Roman Catholic Emancipation, see CATHOLIC EMANCIPATION.

Roman Curia, see CURIA ROMANA.

'Roman de la Rose', French poem of 21,000 lines, written in octosyllabic couplets; one of the most popular and influential Romances of the later Middle Ages. The first section, written about 1235 by Guillaume de Lorris, is a dream allegory of the wooing of a lady (the Rose) in the Garden of Love, by the dreamer, the courtly lover. Left unfinished, the work was continued in 1280 by Jean de Meung, in a very different style and tone. The translation of part of the poem into English is attributed to Chaucer, whose own work was influenced by the poem's concept of idealised love.

Roman-Dutch Law, compound system of law, of which the basic principles are those of the Law Natural, made up of German customs modified by the principles of Roman law and developed by later Dutch customary law. The legal systems of South Africa and Sri Lanka are based on Roman-Dutch law.

Roman Empire, Holy, see HOLY ROMAN EMPIRE.

Roman History. The Latini were a branch of the Indo-European peoples who came into Italy from across the Alps towards the end of the second millennium BC. The numerous hill-top settlements gradually coalesced into larger city states, the greatest of which was Rome. The earliest period of Rome is shrouded in legend, although it is probable that government by kings was adopted about the end of the 7th century BC. At the end of the 6th century BC the last king, Tarquinius Superbus, was expelled, the monarchy abolished, and an aristocratic republican constitution set up. Two annually-elected magistrates, called consuls, were appointed, although in an emergency these might be superseded by a dictator.

In the first half of the 5th century BC the Romans and Latins conducted a successful defensive against a variety of hostile peoples and in the second half went over to the offensive and to final victory. In 390 Rome was sacked by invading Gauls and, although the Capitol never fell, the Romans never forgot this disaster. By 275 Rome had conquered the whole of Italy except Cisalpine Gaul. Its triumph had been achieved not only by force of arms, but also by its policy of colonisation and road building. Most importantly, a common culture superseded local languages, cults and customs.

The First Punic War ended with the acquisition of Rome's first overseas province, Sicily, in 241 BC. Corsica and Sardinia followed in 238, Spain in 206, and North Africa in 146. In the north Cisalpine Gaul was acquired, and Roman control extended along the coast to Marseilles in the west, and down the Dalmatian coast in the east. Between 146 BC and 31 BC Rome was subjected to a period of civil disorder sparked off by its failure to come to terms with the problems involved in governing overseas provinces. The final outcome was that Octavian emerged supreme and, seeing all sections of the Roman world exhausted by civil war, managed to find constitutional forms to disguise his autocratic powers, thus restoring peace to the Mediterranean.

For more than 200 years Rome and its Empire was governed monarchically, first by the Julio-Claudians, then, after an interval of civil war, by the Flavians. With the death of Domitian in AD 96 the Empire went, by election of the Senate, to Nerva. For the next 83 years it chanced that none of the emperors had a direct male heir and, therefore, selected the most suitable to rule. Between the reigns of Marcus Aurelius (161–80) and Diocletian (abdicated 305) a succession of soldier-emperors came and went, until Diocletian abandoned the last pretence of a diarchy of emperor and Senate. After his abdication there was intermittent civil war until Constantine the Great emerged as sole emperor. In his reign Christianity was granted toleration (312) and the Empire was divided into East and West by the foundation of a new capital at Byzantium. After the death of Theodosius (395), waves of Goths, Visigoths, Huns and Vandals ravaged the Western Empire. In 451 the Vandal Genseric sacked Rome and finally, in 476, the emperor Romulus Augustulus resigned the throne to Odoacer, who governed as patrician of Italy, under Zeno, the erstwhile Eastern emperor, who now ruled a reunited Empire.

Roman Law, the body of law, developed over many hundreds of years by the Romans, which forms the basis of much modern civil law. The first known codification was the Twelve Tables (450 BC). The period to 150 BC saw the development of the *jus civile*, i.e. law as administered between Roman citizens.

The magisterial edict then became the chief reforming factor in Roman law. It was also a time when the *jus gentium* began to assume importance: this was that part of Roman law which the Romans applied both to themselves and to foreigners, and came to mean the practical law which Roman courts administered to all free men, regardless of citizenship.

The peace established by the inauguration of the Empire did much to foster progress in the field of Roman law; there was also a large increase in the amount of legal literature. The 2nd century AD saw the development of the existing principles throughout the field of law.

The creation of the Eastern Empire by Constantine, and the spread of Christianity, resulted in the introduction of new ideas, while political changes in the collapsing Empire had a marked effect upon private law. But it was not until the era immediately preceding Justinian I that there was a true legal revival, which enabled Justinian to accomplish his grand design of a definitive codification of Roman law, the *Corpus Iuris Civilis* or Justinian Code, published in the 6th century AD.

See also ROMAN DUTCH LAW.

Roman Numerals, see NUMERALS.

Romance, literary form of French origin.

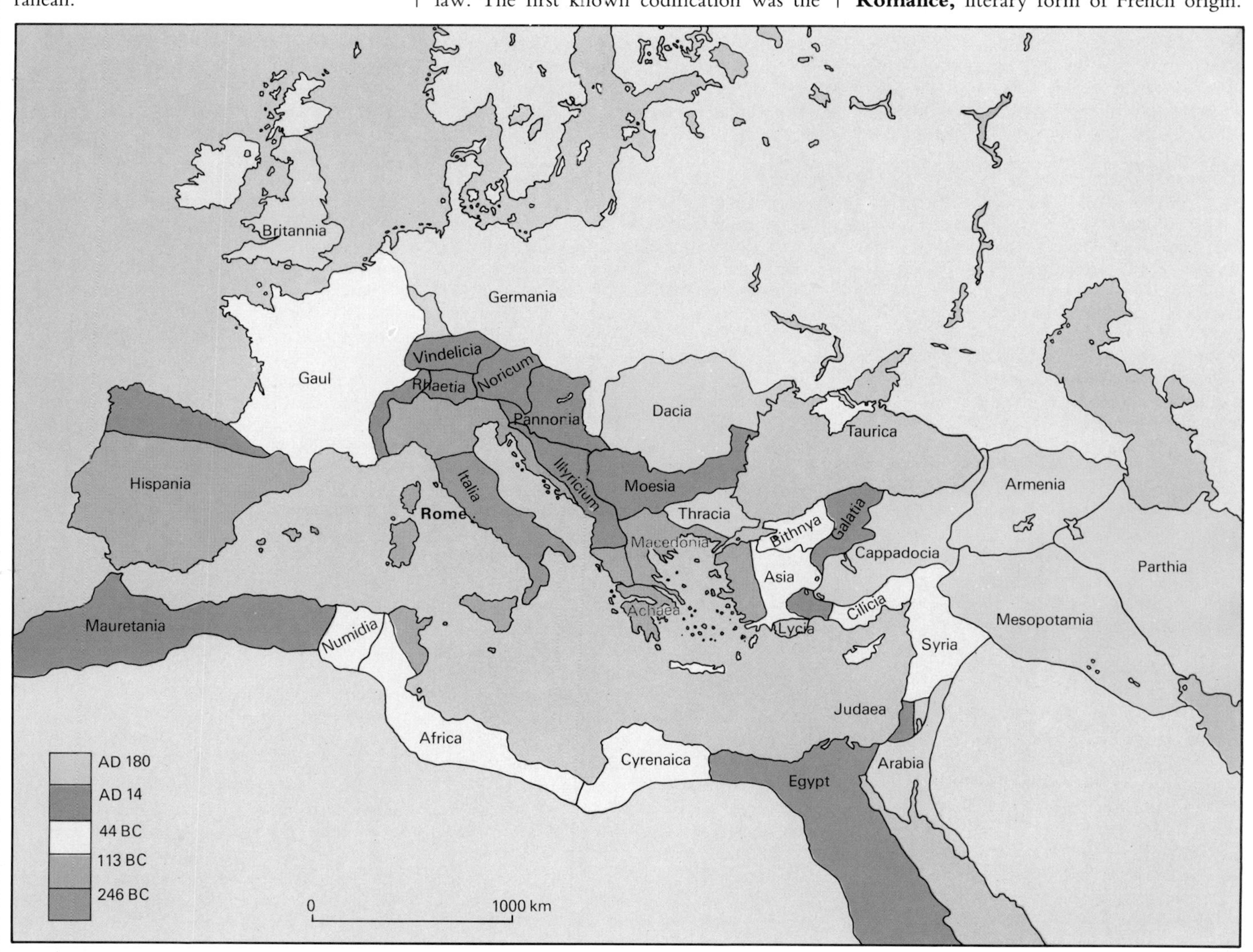

***Roman History.** The development and expansion of the Roman Empire from 246 BC to its greatest extent in AD 180.*

The word *roman* originally meant a translation from Latin, and then, by the mid-12th century, any vernacular narrative; the sense of fictitious narrative in verse or prose predominated from the 13th century.
From about 1150 the romance appears as a recognisable genre rivalling the epic *chansons de geste*. Various literary and social factors contributed to its emergence and popularity. In particular, the increased prestige of women, together with a contemporary enthusiasm for Ovid, is reflected in the love interest which the romance introduced into French narrative literature.
The medieval romance reflects the spiritual, moral and sentimental preoccupations of a chivalric age and presents the many facets of *courtoisie*, the ideal of social behaviour in aristocratic society.

Romance Languages, the languages derived from Latin, after a long process of continual change.
The Romance languages are: French; Italian; Portuguese; Romanian; Spanish; Occitan, more usually known as Provençal; Catalan; the group of Alpine dialects known collectively as Rhaeto-Romance; Sardinian, which is in many respects the most archaic of the Romance languages; Dalmatian, a language standing both geographically and linguistically between Italian and Romanian, which lingered on the Adriatic island of Veglia until the 19th century, the last known speaker dying in 1898.
The Romance languages developed not from classical Latin but from Vulgar Latin (popular spoken Latin). The Vulgar Latin period covers approximately the first five centuries of the Christian era; the next four centuries, before the emergence of the Romance languages as such, may be termed the Romance period.
The general trend in Vulgar Latin and the Romance languages was towards the reduction of inflections and the replacement of synthetic by analytic constructions.
See also ROMANSH.

Romanesque Architecture. The term 'Romanesque' is applied to the style of architecture which, in most European countries, followed the collapse of the ancient Roman Empire (the Christian architecture of which is known as Early Christian) and preceded the introduction of the Gothic style, c.1200. Generally Romanesque buildings occur in the countries of Europe where the Roman Catholic Church prevailed, while Byzantine was adopted in countries where the Orthodox or Greek Church was supreme.

***Romanesque Architecture.** The 11th-century abbey of Cerisy le Forêt in Normandy.*

Romania (Land of the Romans), name used by the Byzantines for their own Empire, and adopted from them by Westerners (especially the Venetians) who used it for the Aegean area, in particular the lands in their possession after the Fourth Crusade in 1204.

Romania
Area: 237,500 km²
Population: 22,050,000
Capital: Bucharest

Romania, or Rumania, republic of Eastern Europe (Socialist Republic of Romania), bounded on the north and north-east by the USSR (Ukraine), on the west by Hungary and Yugoslavia, on the south by Bulgaria, and on the east by the Black Sea. The River Danube forms the greater length of the southern frontier. Area 237,500 km².
The Carpathians curve from north to west through Romania, occupying the greater part of the country. They have here three main ranges: the eastern Carpathians, the Transylvanian Alps, and the Bihor Mountains. They enclose the Transylvanian plateau in the centre of the country. To the south and east of the Carpathians is the great plain of the River Danube. The river enters Romania by way of the Bazias–Turnu-Severin gorge (Iron Gate). The Danube flows into the Black Sea on the north-east coast of Romania, through a broad three-branched delta.
In 1979 the population was 22,050,000. The capital is Bucharest.
About three-fifths of the country is used for farming, but there are contrasts between the plains of Wallachia, Moldavia and Pannonia, where almost all land is cultivated, and the mountainous areas of the Carpathians where much of the steeply-sloping land is forested. The chief crops are maize and wheat on the plains. Vines and orchards are common on the lower slopes of the mountains. Most land is farmed by collectives and state farms. All major industry is owned by the state. The varied ferrous and non-ferrous ores in the mountain areas have been exploited, and the metallurgical industries have been expanded, especially those at Hunedoara and Resita which use local iron-ore and coal. Manganese is the most important of the non-ferrous minerals. Industries include engineering, food-processing and fertilisers.
Romania is a major producer of petroleum, and has reserves of natural gas and coal.
The unit of currency is the *leu*, of 100 *bani*.
The legislative body is the Grand National Assembly, which consists of one deputy for each 40,000 of the population, elected for a five-year term. The assembly elects a State Council, which acts for it between the brief assembly sessions. The executive body of government is the Council of Ministers, appointed by the Grand National Assembly. The president, elected by the assembly, presides over the two councils.
The official language is Romanian.
History. Romania was constituted in 1856 by the Treaty of Paris out of the principalities of Wallachia and Moldavia. This guaranteed their existing privileges although they remained under the suzerainty of Turkey. In 1858 it was decided that both Moldavia and Wallachia should have separate assemblies, but that a central commission should be established in Focsani for common justice. Both assemblies were to elect their own prince—they chose unanimously Prince Alexander John Cuza in 1859 and thus the union was satisfactorily accomplished. The Treaty of Berlin (1878) gave Romania its independence, and in 1881 Romania became a kingdom. Romania declared war on Austria-Hungary in 1916 and in 1917 Romania was included in the agreement between Germany and Russia to suspend hostilities. In the 1930s Romania was hard hit by the world economic crisis, and economic hardship and fear of Communism lent support to right-wing groups, the most important being Codreanu's Iron Guard. In 1940, following a coup by the Iron Guard, Antonescu, with German support, formed a government and crushed the Iron Guard. King Carol was forced to flee. Romania joined the German invasion of Russia in 1941; but in 1944 the Soviet counter-offensive was successful. In 1945 the National Democratic Front, with Soviet backing, assumed power. In 1947 Romania was declared a republic and in 1948 elections were held in which the Communists gained an overwhelming victory. The Socialist Democracy and Unity Front replaced the Popular Democratic Front as the only effective party in 1980. Romania has shown itself to be an awkward member of Comecon and the Warsaw Pact, challenging several spheres of Soviet policy.
Language. Romanian is one of the Romance languages. There are four dialectal groups of Romanian, separated from one another by Slavonic and Greek-speaking territory: (1) Daco-Romanian or Romanian proper, spoken not only in Romania but also in parts of neighbouring states including Soviet Moldavia, Yugoslavia and a few villages in Hungary and Bulgaria; (2) Macedoromanian or Aromanian, spoken by some scattered communities in Greece, Albania, Yugoslavia and Bulgaria (perhaps 350,000 speakers in all); (3) Meglenite or Meglenoromanian, spoken in an area on the Greek-Yugoslav border; (4) Istrian, spoken in a few villages in the Adriatic peninsula of Istria in the territory surrendered by Italy to Yugoslavia in 1945.
Romanian presents many grammatical features that differentiate it from all the other Romance languages, such as a postposed definite article. There is also a two-case system with one form for nominative-accusative and another for genitive-dative, and a conjugational system that is in many respects different from that of the other Romance languages. The earlier Romanian texts are all in the Cyrillic alphabet used for Church Slavonic, but in the course of the 18th century the Latin alphabet came into general use.

Romano, Giulio, see GIULIO ROMANO.

Romanov, House of, ruling house of Russia from 1613 to the February Revolution in 1917. The first tsar of the house of Romanov, Michael Fëdorovich, who came from an old boyar family, was elected at the end of the Time of Troubles in the early 17th century. From Peter the Great the Romanovs bore the title of emperor, which Peter first took in 1721.
See also NICHOLAS II.

Romans, Epistle to the, unanimously accepted as a genuine epistle of St Paul forming, indeed, part of the central group of his writings, with 1 and 2 Cor. and Gal. It is an orderly exposition of the principles of the Christian religion and salvation in Christ as opposed to Jewish legalism. It is the longest of the apostle's writings, and possibly the greatest, containing an epitome of his whole doctrine. The main theme of the epistle is the relationship between Jew and Gentile, and their common salvation through the death of Christ.

Romansh, Romaunsch, or Rhaeto-Romance, one of the Romance languages, or rather a group of related Romance dialects spoken in Switzerland and Italy. There are three dialectal groups of Romansh, which are spoken in geographically separated areas: Rumantsch; Ladin; and Friulan.
Rumantsch or *Bündnerromanisch* is spoken in the Grisons (Graubünden), the easternmost canton of Switzerland. Romansh-speakers in Switzerland now number about 50,000. *Ladin* is spoken by only a few thousand people in some Dolomite valleys in the Alto Adige province of northern Italy. *Friulan* is widely spoken—perhaps by as many as half a million people—in the Udine province of north-east Italy.

Romansh Literature. With the exception of one 12th-century fragment, literature in the Romansh dialect of the Grisons canton of Switzerland dates only from the time of the Reformation. Secular literature begins with the Romantic movement in the 19th century. Among the principal Romansh writers of the later period are A. Tuor, G. S. Muoth, Z. Pallioppi, G. F. Caderas, Gian Fontana, G. M. Nay and Peider Lansel. In recent times literature of every sort has been written in the language. In the Friulan dialect, a few poems dating from the 16th century are known. Friulan literature, however, does not compare in quantity with that of Romansh.

Romantic Movement, term applied to a general artistic upheaval, beginning at the end of the 18th century and culminating about 1830–40, whose effects in painting, sculpture, music and literature continued to be felt throughout the 19th century. Romanticism was a reaction against the accepted view of art and society and vigorously rejected the forms of 'Classical' art. 'Romanticism' and 'Classicism' are now generally regarded as the two major artistic philosophies of Western culture.
European Romanticism had its origins in the social changes of the 18th century, in a new awareness of nature as it was probed by science, in a reaction against industrialisation, and in intellectual support for radical political ideas. There was renewed interest in medievalism, in fantasy (expressed in the popularity of Gothic melodrama), in folklore, and keen inquiry into the part the artist should play in the changing world.
Although certain ideas were common to many Romantics, there was no formal school or 'movement'; individuality was the keynote of Romanticism, each artist seeking to express the truth in his own way.

Romanus I Lecapenus (c.870–948), Byzantine Emperor. A peasant by birth, he rose to become admiral and proclaimed himself emperor and regent for Constantine VII, Porphyrogenitus in 920. Romanus promulgated the first of a series of laws to protect the peasantry from exploitation and enserfment. He was deposed in 944.

Romany, see GYPSY.

Rome (Italian *Roma*), capital of both the province of Rome and the Republic of Italy, and formerly the capital of the Roman Republic which later on became the Roman Empire; even later it was the capital of the Papal States and, from 1871 to 1946, of the Kingdom of Italy. Until the Reformation it was the centre of the whole of Western Christendom. It stands on the Tiber, 24 km from its mouth, at the southern edge of the Etruscan hill country, overlooking the plain of the Campagna di Roma. The river flows through the city on a tortuous north–south course: on the right bank (west) is the Vatican City. The Seven Hills, all on the east side of the Tiber, are still recognisable. The active business life of the city is centred in the lower ground between the hills, the Pincio quarter and the river. This lower portion, within the vicinity of the Vatican and Trastevere, formed the medieval city, but few secular buildings of medieval date remain. Most of the great palaces and churches were erected or remodelled in the 16th and 17th centuries. Between 1870 and the First World War the city again underwent drastic reconstruction. St Peter's basilica, the largest church in the world, is in the Vatican City; before it is the beautiful piazza designed by Bernini. The Vatican Palace, which adjoins St Peter's, is the residence of the pope.
The rapid growth that Rome has experienced since 1871 (and which still continues), has been stimulated largely by tertiary sector employment—from its rôles as capital of Italy, headquarters of the Catholic church, and focus of tourism and pilgrimage. However, industries are also developing, chiefly on the south and east side of the city—engineering, printing, chemicals, electronics, plastics and clothes. Population (1979) 2,911,671.

Rome, King of, see NAPOLEON II.

Rome-Berlin Axis, the political and, later, military entente between Hitler and Mussolini, concluded, ostensibly, to present a common front against Bolshevism. The term 'Axis' became a common description for the countries allied to Germany in the Second World War.
See also WORLD WAR, SECOND.

Rommel, Erwin Johannes Eugen (1891–1944), German general of the Second World War. On the outbreak of the Second World War he was given command of the 7th Panzer Division, and on 12 June 1940 Rommel received the surrender of 12,000 Allied troops in Normandy.
After the defeat of Graziani in Libya Rommel was appointed to command German troops there. He advanced in the summer of 1942 from Gazala to Alamein. But he was not adequately supplied with ammunition and reserve tanks; and with the arrival of Montgomery, Rommel was defeated at Alamein (1942).
After the Allied victories in North Africa Rommel was given command in northern Italy, in Holland and in north and north-west France. On 17 July Rommel was severely injured when his car was shot up by the RAF. He was suspected of complicity in the plot against Hitler (July 1944) and forced to commit suicide.
See also WORLD WAR, SECOND.

Rome. *The Roman Forum seen from the Palatine Hill. The Arch of Severus is in the background.*

Romney, George (1734–1802), British artist. First appointed to Christopher Steele, portrait painter at Kendal, Romney came to London in 1762. His portraits rivalled those of Reynolds in popularity. Perhaps his most famous sitter was Lady Hamilton, whom he presented in such ideal rôles as *Contemplation* or *Ariadne*.

Romney Marsh, a former bay between Hythe in Kent and Fairlight in Sussex, England, of which degraded cliffs are still visible. Shingle spits grew outwards from the headlands to form a bar behind which sedimentation took place. There is an area of shingle, Dungeness Foreland, in which old shorelines can be found, and former marshland. The latter was virtually completely reclaimed by the 17th century to give a rich sheep-grazing area.

Romulus, mythical founder of Rome, son of Mars and twin brother of Remus. Their uncle Amulius ordered them to be drowned; but they were miraculously saved and reared by a she-wolf. On reaching manhood, they expelled the usurper, Amulius. They began to build a city on the Tiber, but quarrelled over its site and name. Romulus killed Remus for laughing at his walls on the Palatine. He made the Capitol an asylum for refugees and adventurers, and his citizens found themselves wives by carrying off the women of the Sabine race. Romulus was carried up to heaven, and worshipped as the god Quirinus by the Romans.

Romulus Augustulus (b.c.461), last of the Western Roman emperors, 475–76. His father, the patrician Orestes, proclaimed him when he was still a child, but in 476 the Herulian chief Odoacer raised a revolt, killed Orestes and deposed Romulus who retired to Campania.

Ronaldsay, North, most northerly of the Orkney Islands, Scotland, 4 km north-east of Sanday, from which it is separated by the North Ronaldsay Firth. Area 10 km². Population (1971) 134.

Ronaldsay, South, most southerly of the Orkney Islands, Scotland, 9 km north-east of Duncansby Head, containing the village of St Margaret's Hope. The surface is level and well cultivated; it is connected to Mainland, Orkney, by Churchill Barrier. Length 13 km. Area (including adjacent islands) 46 km². Population (1971) 776.

Rondeau, verse-form of French origin. The term occurs in the 13th century, applied to the music of the words accompanying a dance or 'round'.

Rondel, synonym of rondeau.

Rondo (French *rondeau*), musical form whose general principle is that of a return to an initial theme, as a refrain, with episodes between. The *rondeau* of the 17th century and the early 18th century had contrasting episodes. Later the episodes became linked to the principal theme by transformation and development, especially in the works of Haydn. Haydn and Mozart, and their successors, used sonata–rondos in symphonies, concertos, etc., in which sonata tonality governed the form. The rondo survived also as an independent piece.

Ronsard, Pierre de (1524–85), French poet. He was one of the *Brigade* or group of poets that later (about 1556) was known as the Pléiade, and he published in 1550 four books of *Odes* (a fifth book followed in 1522) in the manner of Pindar and Horace.
Throughout the reign of Charles IX (1560–74), Ronsard was court poet. He composed various *Discours* in verse and *Discours des misères de ce temps*, 1562. After the death of Charles IX, Ronsard lost his position at court. The major production of his later years is his *Sonnets pour Hélène*, 1578. Ronsard ranks among the greatest of all French poets.

Röntgen, Wilhelm Konrad (1845–1923), German physicist, who held chairs successively at the universities of Hohenheim, Strasbourg, Giessen and Würzburg. In 1895 he discovered Röntgen or X-rays. He became professor of experimental physics at Munich in 1899, and received the Nobel Prize in 1901. Röntgen researched the electromagnetic rotation of polarised light, the ratio of the specific heats of gases, conduction of heat through crystals, etc.

Rood (Old English *rōd*), cross or crucifix, generally with the figures of the Virgin and St John standing on either side, placed in English churches at the entrance to the chancel and over a screen known as the rood-screen. Modern roods are found in a number of churches, both Anglican and Roman Catholic; in the absence of a screen they hang from the chancel arch.

Rood, see METROLOGY.

Roodeport, town of the Transvaal, South Africa, 19 km north-west of Johannesburg. A municipality and centre of the Rand goldfields, it has increased greatly in size and importance since 1930. Population (1980) 165,315, including 83,217 whites.

Roof, covering for a structure to provide protection from the elements. Roofs are usually sloping but can be flat. The two most common types of roof are the 'pitched', sometimes called 'saddleback' roof, in which two sides slope outwards from the ridge, and the 'hipped' roof, in which the two ends are also sloping, leaving no gables. A third type is the 'gambrel' roof, a hipped roof in which triangular gables rise from halfway up the end roofs vertically to the ridge. A 'mansard' is a roof with a double pitch, at first steep and then gentle to accommodate a large attic (named after François Mansart, the French architect). A 'helm' roof is square with gables on all sides, its roofs rising to a point.
Large span roofs may be covered by space domes, such as the geodesic domes of Buckminster Fuller. Alternatively, thin shells can be constructed of reinforced concrete. A good example of the hyperbolic paraboloid roof can be seen in the roof of the Commonwealth Institute in London. The advantage of this shape lies in the fact that it is possible to lay straight lines along a doubly-curved surface, which thus considerably facilitates the fabrication of the form work. Another design used for large spans, as in the Munich Olympic Games Stadium, is the tension cable construction.
See also GABLE; HAMMER-BEAM ROOF.

Rook, *Corvus frugilegus*, a gregarious bird of the crow family which nests colonially in rookeries of up to hundreds of pairs. The adult male is about 46 cm long, and the plumage is black with a purple gloss. The legs, toes and claws are black. Rooks destroy vast numbers of noxious insects, and the mischief they do is probably more than compensated by this service.

Roon, Albrecht Theodor Emil, Count von (1803–79), German soldier. He was one of the military organisers in the war with Austria (1866) and the effectiveness of the Prussian army in the Franco-Prussian War (1870–71) was largely due to him. He became president of the Cabinet in 1873, but resigned in the same year.

Roosevelt, Anna Eleanor (1884–1962), US politician and writer, daughter of Elliott Roosevelt and niece of Theodore Roosevelt. In 1905 she married Franklin Delano Roosevelt, a distant cousin. After his election to the presidency she became well known as a writer on current topics and as a public speaker. As a journalist she became famous for her column 'My Day', begun in 1935. After her husband's death she remained an immensely popular figure in American public life, and continued to have some influence in the Democratic party.

Roosevelt, Franklin D(elano) (1882–1945), 32nd President of the USA. President Theodore Roosevelt was a distant cousin. He was elected as a Democrat to the New York Senate, 1910 and 1912; and served as assistant secretary to the navy, 1913–20. He was Democratic vice-presidential candidate in 1920; a year later he contracted poliomyelitis. In 1928 he was elected governor of New York State and was re-elected in 1930.
In 1932, in the midst of the economic depression, the Republicans again chose Herbert Hoover as their presidential candidate. At the Democratic national convention Roosevelt was finally nominated. His nomination pledge of 'a new deal for the American people' seized the popular imagination, and he won the election easily.
Roosevelt's inauguration speech pledged immediate and drastic action. With a Democratic majority in Congress, he was able to obtain reform legislation. By 1935 Roosevelt could claim some success, but he was also under political attack from both Left and Right. Nevertheless he was confident of winning re-election as president in 1936, and did so by a landslide margin.
In foreign affairs Roosevelt took what steps he could to reinforce the cause of peace. When the European war broke out Roosevelt declared America's neutrality. In 1940 he broke with tradition, and stood for a third presidential term. He won comfortably, and quickly introduced his lend-lease proposals, indicating that a better-armed Britain was essential to American liberty and plainly intimating that America would become the 'arsenal of democracy'. In early 1940 he defined the 'four freedoms' essential to world peace. Having sent troops to Iceland, he met Churchill and drew up the Atlantic Charter. On 7 December 1941 the Japanese attacked Pearl Harbor and the United States declared war. In 1943 Roosevelt met Churchill in Casablanca to consider every aspect of the war.
In November 1943 Roosevelt met with Churchill and Chiang Kai-shek to discuss future military operations against Japan, and later met with Stalin for the first time. At

Franklin D. Roosevelt, with Churchill and Stalin at the Yalta conference in 1945.

home, he succeeded in obtaining the Democratic presidential nomination for the fourth time, and was again elected president. In February 1945 he met with Churchill and Stalin at Yalta, where agreement was reached for joint military operations against Germany. Shortly afterwards, he died at Warm Springs, Georgia.

There is little doubt as to the exceptional qualities of Roosevelt as president and political leader in times both of serious economic depression and war. His greatness lay perhaps in his pragmatism in dealing with the problems of a complex nation, rescuing the economy and changing basic foreign policy attitudes.

Roosevelt, Theodore (1858–1919), 26th President of the USA. He was elected to the New York State Legislature in 1881. In 1897 President McKinley named him assistant secretary of the navy. Roosevelt was strongly in favour of war with Spain, and did much to put the navy in a state of preparedness. After war was declared, Roosevelt, with his friend Dr Leonard Wood, then a surgeon in the US army, raised the volunteer regiment which became famous as the Rough Riders. Roosevelt resigned his navy post to join his regiment. In 1898 he was elected governor of New York State. Nominated vice-president on the Republican national ticket (1900), Roosevelt succeeded President McKinley on the latter's assassination (6 September 1901). In 1904 he was re-elected, but did not seek a third term in 1908, when he was succeeded by W. H. Taft. Roosevelt disagreed with Taft's policy and founded the Progressive (Bull Moose) party. He stood as its presidential candidate in 1912, and though unsuccessful, split the Republican vote by so doing and ensured the election of Woodrow Wilson.

The biggest positive feature of Roosevelt's presidency was the Hay-Pauncefote Treaty, which made possible the Panama Canal scheme. In 1904 Roosevelt intervened in the Russo-Japanese War, and induced the warring countries to send delegates to Portsmouth, New Hampshire, where a peace was signed. For this he was awarded the Nobel Peace Prize in 1906.

Root, Elihu (1845–1937), US statesman. He was secretary of war in McKinley's Cabinet (1899–1904), and secretary of state under Theodore Roosevelt (1905–09). Root was elected as senator (Republican) for the term 1909–15, and was a peace advocate, and member of the Permanent Court of Arbitration at The Hague. He was a Nobel Peace Prize winner in 1912.

Root, the underground portion of nearly all club mosses, horsetails, ferns and higher plants. Usually the root penetrates into the soil, fixes the plant, and absorbs water and essential minerals. A primary root is that formed after germination of a seed by the growth of the radicle, and this may give off secondary roots from which a third series may arise, and so on. Adventitious roots are secondary roots growing from the stems and other parts of the plant. Aerial or sub-aerial roots are those, mostly of adventitious character, which do not grow down into the ground, but remain in the air.

Root, in algebra, synonym for the 'solution' of an equation. It is also a number which when multiplied by itself will equal a given number. Formally, the nth root of a is a number whose nth power is a. An nth root is denoted by $a^{1/n}$. Then $(a^{1/n})^n = a$. For example $27^{1/3} = 3$, because $3^3 = 27$. A second root of a is usually called a 'square root' of a and is sometimes denoted by $\sqrt{a}$. A third root of a is usually called a 'cube root' of a.

Root Nodules, rounded swellings on the roots of leguminous plants such as peas, containing symbiotic bacteria, species of the genus *Rhizobium*, which fix atmospheric nitrogen. The symbiosis is an important one in agriculture since pastures provided with legumes such as clover have a built-in system of biological nitrogen enrichment.

Plant groups other than legumes have root nodules often containing fungi. These are involved in the uptake of phosphate from the soil.

Root Pruning of fruit trees checks exuberant vegetative growth and encourages fruiting. Root pruning is useful on excessively vigorous trees, but not successful unless supported by pruning of the shoots.

Root Tuber, a swollen food-containing organ which may be formed from the whole or part of a root, as in the dahlia.

Rootstock, the horticultural term for the root system of a plant that is not of the same genetic material as the aerial portion. Rootstocks are essential for varieties of a range of plants, such as fruit trees, roses and rhododendrons which do not root readily from cuttings. Such varieties have to be grafted on to rootstocks, often of a wild source, which are produced from seeds or cuttings. Another use of the rootstock is to induce resistance in root systems to soil-borne pests and diseases. These have been bred for vines, tomatoes and cucumbers.

See also Grafting.

Rope and Rope-making. Rope is a term applied to the larger dimensions of twisted fibres or steel wires. Fibre rope of smaller diameters up to approximately 1 cm is usually regarded as cordage. Thread is composed of two or three twisted yarns and twine is made of a dozen yarns or so. Cord is made of three or more strands while string comes under the heading of cord or twine. The general method of manufacture is the same in all cases—the yarns are twisted together into strands and the strands twisted together to form the rope.

Wire rope is used for many industrial applications, on cranes, excavators, drilling rigs and suspension bridges.

Rope Trick, most discussed trick that Indian jugglers or 'magicians' are said to perform. It is supposed to be performed as follows: the magician tosses one end of a coil of rope high into the air, where it stays, and climbs up the rope and vanishes. While the onlookers are gazing upwards wondering what has become of him, the juggler unconcernedly reappears among them. It is said that when Houdini went to India he could find no one who would or could perform the Rope Trick. Indian magic, like all 'magic', is a combination of skill, illusion and showmanship, and sometimes hypnotism enters into it as well.

Rorke's Drift, 45 km from Dundee, Natal, South Africa. Here a handful of British soldiers made a stand against a Zulu army on 22 January 1879.

Rorqual (Norwegian *röyrkval*, red whale), whales of the family Balaenopteridae. The name is used most often for the five species of the genus *Balaenoptera*, which includes the blue, fin and sei whales. The humpback whale is also sometimes called a rorqual. These whales have a dorsal fin and a grooved belly, which distinguish them from the whale family Balaenidae, the right whales.

Rosa, Salvator (1615–73), Italian painter, who for the 18th and 19th centuries was the archetype of the Romantic artist on account of his rebellious attitude towards society and his extravagant lifestyle. Artistically, he is most important for the creation of a new type of landscape showing wild and savage scenery. He also painted battle-pieces, seascapes and bizarre scenes of witchcraft.

Rosa, Monte, the highest mountain in Switzerland; the chief peak, the Dufourspitze, being 4634 m and a second peak, the

Nordend, 4612 m in height. It is situated on the frontier between Switzerland and the Italian provinces of Novara and Turin.

Rosacea, see ACNE.

Rosaceae, a family of about 100 genera and 2000 species of dicotyledons, including herbs, shrubs and trees. There is a wide range of structure in the family. Most Rosaceae have flowers with five sepals, five petals (not jointed to each other), numerous stamens and numerous separate carpels (sections of the ovary). Rosaceae grown for their flowers include the very many forms of rose, also species of *Spiraea*, *Geum* and *Potentilla*, as well as forms of *Crataegus* (hawthorn) and the various fruit tree genera. The family is also of great economic value for fruit, including strawberry (*Fragaria*); blackberry, loganberry and raspberry (*Rubus*); apricot, cherry, peach and plum (*Prunus*); apple (*Malus*) and pear (*Pyrus*).

Rosaniline (4,4′,4″-triamino-3-methyl triphenyl carbinol, $C_{20}H_{21}N_3O$), organic base forming salts used in dyeing. The term rosaniline is, in commerce, applied to the chloride, fuchsine or magenta, which possesses a brilliant red colour, although the rosaniline base is colourless. Rosaniline dyes silk, wool and tannined cotton a brilliant red, but the colour is not very fast, so rosaniline is generally employed as an intermediate chemical in the manufacture of faster dyes, such as aniline blue.
See also DYE.

Rosario, city and river port on the right bank of the River Paraná in the province of Santa Fe, Argentina, 280 km by rail and 320 km by river north-west of Buenos Aires. Rosario is primarily a distribution centre and export outlet for the rich agricultural provinces of Entre Ríos, Santa Fe and Córdoba. The staple export is wheat, followed by cattle, flour, sugar and linseed. Rosario is now the second city of Argentina. Population (1975) 750,455.

Rosary, Christian practice of repeating prayers while counting on a string of beads. The prayers of the Roman Catholic rosary include the Lord's Prayer repeated 15 times, and the Hail Mary 150 times, the latter being divided into decades, or tens, each Lord's Prayer preceding a decade of Hail Marys. The beads most commonly used constitute a chaplet, or third of a rosary, in which the *Gloria Patri* (Glory be to the Father) is repeated after each decade of Hail Marys.

Roscelin (c.1050–c.1122), French philosopher and theologian. He did much to propagate Nominalism, but the application of his theories to the dogma of the Trinity led him into trouble with the Church.

Roscius Gallus, Quintus (c.126–62 BC), Roman comic actor. His great histrionic powers were acquired, or at least developed, by careful study of the leading forensic orators, particularly Hortensius. The name Roscius has been applied to many modern actors.

Roscoff, fishing village of Brittany, France, in the *département* of Finistère. It has a zoological laboratory, and is a seaside resort. There are ferry links to south-west England. Population (1975) 3800.

Roscommon, inland county of the Republic of Ireland in the province of Connaught. It was established as a county about 1580. It is 97 km long and 58 km broad. There are some extensive bogs and numerous lakes, Loughs Boderg, Allen and Ree being the largest. Agriculture, especially cattle grazing, is the leading occupation. Roscommon, the capital, is a market town, 150 km north-west of Dublin. Area 2564 km²; population (1979) 54,189.

Rose, *Rosa*, a large genus of flowering plants in the family Rosaceae, admired and cultivated for the beauty and fragrance of their blooms. They are natives of the northern hemisphere. The five-petalled flowers are followed by the usually red or black fruit or hips. These are a valuable source of vitamin C (ascorbic acid).

Rose, a popular charge in heraldry. Although often described as 'conventional', the heraldic rose is an exact reproduction of the wild rose.

Rose Apple, *Eugenia jambos*, Malayan evergreen tree of the Myrtaceae (myrtle family). It grows between 6 and 9 m high, has oval, leathery leaves, and clusters of small, four-petalled white flowers. The fruits are yellowish-white fragrant drupes, used in confectionery.

Rose Hips, see ROSE.

Rose-mallow, see HIBISCUS.

Rose of Jericho, see RESURRECTION PLANTS.

Rose of Sharon, *Hypericum calycinum*, a low shrub with large, handsome, solitary yellow flowers, sometimes grown as a cover plant for game and cultivated in gardens.

Rose-water, water scented with the distilled essence of roses. In the East rose-water is sprinkled over the hands after eating and the custom is occasionally followed in Europe.

Rose-water Ointment, see COLD CREAM.

Rose Window, in Gothic architecture, circular window usually filled with elaborate tracery, in early examples arranged like the spokes of a wheel.

Rosebay Willowherb, see WILLOWHERB.

Rosebery, Archibald Philip Primrose, 5th Earl of (1847–1929), British statesman. He succeeded his grandfather in the earldom in 1868. In 1885 he was in the Cabinet as lord privy seal and first commissioner of works. He was foreign secretary for six months in the brief Liberal administration of 1886. In 1889, when the London County Council came into existence, Rosebery became its first chairman. In 1892 he was invited by Gladstone to return to the Foreign Office. In March 1894, after Gladstone's resignation, he accepted the premiership as first lord of the Treasury and president of the Council; he resigned in June 1895, after defeat in the Commons. In 1896 Rosebery resigned his leadership of the Liberal party.
Among Rosebery's wide interests was the turf; he did much to raise the prestige of English horse-racing, and his horses won the Derby in 1894, 1895 and 1905.

Rosemary, *Rosmarinus officinalis*, a member of the Labiatae from southern Europe and Turkey. It is an evergreen shrub with dark green narrow leaves, cultivated for its flowers and leaves, from which oil of rosemary is distilled. *Ledum palustre*, sometimes called the marsh rosemary, and *Andromeda polifolia*, bog rosemary, are both species of Ericaceae, the heather family.

Rosenberg, Isaac (1890–1918), English poet and painter. He was strongly influenced by Blake, and the Hebrew scriptures, interests reflected in his mythical poetry. However, he is best known for his war poems, written between 1916 and 1918, which deal powerfully and imaginatively with the horrors of trench life. His *Collected Works* appeared in 1937, with an introduction by Siegfried Sassoon.

Rosenberg Case. In 1940 Julius Rosenberg and his wife Ethel, both members of the Communist party in the USA, began attempting to transmit to the USSR military secrets. When Mrs Rosenberg's brother, Sgt David Greenglass, was assigned to the atomic-bomb project at Los Alamos, Rosenberg obtained top-secret data on nuclear weapons from him. This he gave to Harry Gold, who delivered it to the Soviet vice-consul. Arrested by the FBI in 1950, Greenglass turned State's evidence, and received a 15 years' prison sentence; Gold was sentenced to 30 years in prison. The Rosenbergs were sentenced to death and executed.

Roses, Wars of the, English baronial wars of the 15th century during which the rival houses of York and Lancaster struggled for supremacy. The name, derived from the supposed selection of roses as badges, the adherents of York wearing white roses, those of Lancaster red, is probably a later romantic attribution. The wars began in the reign of Henry VI who was subject to recurring fits of insanity and was dominated by the Beauforts and his wife, Margaret of Anjou, who, together, formed the core of the Lancastrian party. Henry's claim to the throne was through the third son of Edward III, whereas Richard of York was a descendant of both the second and fifth sons and, until the birth of Prince Edward, in 1453, was the king's heir presumptive.
Richard of York served as protector during Henry's periods of insanity, but the Lancastrians regained control when the king recovered. The first episode of war in 1455 ended in Yorkist victory, but in 1459 the Yorkist leaders were forced to flee abroad. They returned in 1460; Richard was defeated and killed at Wakefield, but his son, Edward, Earl of March, won the battle of Mortimer's Cross and was proclaimed king as Edward IV. Edward reigned peacefully for a few years, until, in 1470, the earl of Warwick turned against him, and briefly restored Henry VI to the throne. After Warwick's defeat and death, peace reigned, with the Yorkists supreme. After Edward IV's death in 1483, his brother Richard, appointed regent to the young Edward V, declared him and his younger brother illegitimate and seized the throne as Richard III. The final struggle in the Wars of the Roses took place at the battle of Bosworth Field, 1485. Richard was killed and Henry Tudor, the Lancastrian claimant, became king as Henry VII, uniting the houses of York and Lancaster by his marriage with Elizabeth of York, eldest daughter of Edward IV.

Rosetta (Arabic *Rashid*), decayed native city on the 'Rosetta' branch of the Nile in Egypt. The famous 'Rosetta Stone' was found near here in 1799.

Rosetta Stone, a slab of black basalt, inscribed with three different scripts, which provided the key for the decipherment of hieroglyphic writing. It was discovered in 1799 near St Julien, 6 km north of Rosetta, by Boussard, a French officer. Napoleon had it deposited for study at the French Institute in Cairo. On the capitulation of Egypt to the British, the Rosetta Stone, shipped in 1801 to England, passed into the British Museum.

Rosewood, wood of various trees, so called on account either of a rose-like fragrance, or a rose colour. The best fragrant rosewood, often called palisander wood, is derived from *Dalbergia nigra* of the Leguminosae, a native of Brazil, whence it is exported in large, heavy slabs. The wood is chiefly used in veneer and cabinet work.
See also TIMBER.

Rosicrucians, members of a mystical brotherhood perpetuating the teachings of the Mystery Schools of ancient Egypt, who traditionally regard Amenhotep IV as their first Grand Master. Announcing itself publicly in the 17th century, the *Fama Fraternitatis* allegorically attributed its origin to Christian Rosenkreuz, a German nobleman of the 14th century. This tract, mistakenly credited to others, was prepared under the direction of Francis Bacon, the Fraternity's Imperator in that cycle of its activity. Its emblem was a golden cross with a single red rose at its centre. The men and women of the Rosy Cross dedicated themselves to the study of God and Nature's laws.

Rosin, see PAINT.

Roskilde, seaport and residential town on the Roskilde Fjord, on the island of Sjælland, Denmark, 32 km south-west of Copenhagen. Until 1443 this town was the capital of Denmark, and its cathedral, dating from the 12th century, contains the tombs of the Danish kings. Population (1975) 49,800.

Ross, Sir James Clark (1800–62), British rear-admiral and explorer. He made five voyages in search of the North-West Passage, and accompanied Parry in his effort to reach the North Pole (1827). Whilst with his uncle, Captain John Ross, he discovered the north magnetic pole (1831). In his *Voyage of Discovery and Research to South and Antarctic Seas*, 1847, he gives the results of his own experiences in the *Erebus* (1839–43). He named Mount Erebus and Victoria Land (Antarctica), and the Ross Sea bears his name.

Ross, Sir John (1777–1856), British rear-admiral and Arctic explorer, who made two important voyages of polar exploration in 1818 and 1829–33.

Ross, Man of, see KYRLE, JOHN.

Ross, Sir Ronald (1857–1932), British physician and malariologist. He entered the Indian Medical Service in 1881. While on leave in London in 1894 he met Patrick Manson, who explained his hypothesis that malaria was transmitted by the mosquito. Ross returned to India, and in 1897–98 discovered the life-cycle of the parasite of bird malaria, thus proving Manson's theory. For his work he received the Nobel Prize in 1902.

Ross Dependency, sector of the continent of Antarctica claimed by New Zealand. It lies between 160°E and 150°W and includes the islands lying between these degrees of longitude and south of 60°S. Victoria Land, Edward VII Land, Ross Sea and Balleny Isles are included.

Ross Sea, part of the Pacific Ocean extending deep into Antarctica between Victoria Land on the west and Marie Byrd Land on the east. The sea was named after Sir James Clark Ross who discovered it in 1841. The entire southern part is occupied by the Ross Ice Shelf.

Rosse, William Parsons, 3rd Earl of (1800–67), British astronomer. Wanting a powerful telescope, he quickly realised that it would have to be a reflector and that he would have to build it himself. By 1842 he had produced speculum metal mirrors 183 cm in diameter. He incorporated these into a telescope 17 m long which was used between 1845 and 1878 mainly for the observation of nebulae and clusters. Lord Rosse was the first to detect the spiral nature of many of the galaxies.

Rosselli, Cosimo (1439–1507), Italian painter, born in Florence; studied under Neri di Bicci. His *Last Supper* and two other frescoes were painted for the Sistine Chapel at the invitation of Sixtus IV. In S. Ambrogio, Florence, hangs his fine *Procession of the Miraculous Chalice*. His pictures are dignified, despite a hard and mannered style. Fra Bartolommeo and Piero di Cosimo were his pupils.

Rossellini, Roberto (1906–77), Italian film director. His great achievement was to pioneer cinematic Neo-Realism, along with De Sica. *Rome—Open City*, 1945, *Paisà*, 1946 and *Germany—Year Zero*, 1948, are harrowing descriptions of the struggle to survive in war-torn Europe. In the 1950s his liaison with Ingrid Bergman brought films such as *Europa 51*, 1951, and *Viaggio in Italia*, 1953, and at the end of the decade he became one of the first major directors to devote his attention to television, making fine historical studies such as *La Prise de Pouvoir par Louis XIV*, 1966, *Acts of the Apostles*, 1968, and *Socrates*, 1970.

Rossellino, Antonio (c.1427–c.1479), Italian sculptor. His masterpiece, a tomb for a Portuguese prince and cardinal who died in 1459, is in San Miniato, Florence, undamaged. The carving on this beautiful monument, like the marble medallion relief of the Virgin and Child now in the Bargello at Florence, suggests that Rossellino's style was a delicate, but less vigorous, adaptation of Donatello's. Of his four artist brothers, Bernardo (see below) is best known.

Rossellino, Bernardo (1409–c.1464), Italian architect and sculptor. As an architect he designed buildings, and strongholds at Orvieto, Civita Vecchia and Spoleto, and restored basilicas in Rome for Nicholas V and Pius II. The Victoria and Albert Museum, London, possesses his relief portrait of a doctor, and the church of Santa Croce, Florence, his splendid monument to Bruni the historian (1443). He had four artist brothers, the sculptor Antonio Rossellino (see above) being best known.

Rossetti, Christina Georgina (1830–94), English poet, sister of Dante Gabriel and William Michael Rossetti. In 1862 she published her best work, *Goblin Market and Other Poems*, which contains, as do her other volumes, many exquisite lyrical pieces. The sadness that pervades her writing may be due to an unhappy love affair in her youth, and to the ill health she constantly suffered. Her poetry has a unique simplicity and purity of tone; she responded with sensitivity to natural beauty, and in her devotional poetry lays stress on ultimate hopes and realities.

Rossetti, Dante Gabriel (1828–82), British painter and poet, son of Gabriele Rossetti and brother of Christina and William Michael Rossetti. Rossetti was as much attracted to literature as to art. He translated Dante, beginning his labours in 1845, and two years later wrote *The Blessed Damozel* and several of his best sonnets. *The Blessed Damozel* and his prose story, *Hand and Soul*, appeared in the *Germ*, 1850, which was edited by his brother William. He was briefly a pupil of Ford Madox Brown and then in 1848 formed the Pre-Raphaelite Brotherhood with Holman Hunt and Millais. Between 1850 and 1860 he produced many of his best pictures, mainly in water-colour, his subjects almost all from Dante or the 'Morte d'Arthur', and his chief model, Elizabeth Siddal. In 1857–58 he worked on the Arthurian frescoes for the Oxford Union with Burne-Jones and William Morris, and initiated a second phase of the Pre-Raphaelite movement. In 1860 he married Elizabeth Siddal, but she died within two years.

Dante Gabriel Rossetti. Monna Vanna, *1866. Rossetti was a founder of the Pre-Raphaelite Brotherhood.*

Rossetti, Gabriele (1783–1854), Italian poet, father of Dante Gabriel, Christina and William Michael Rossetti. In 1824, banished from his country because of his liberal ideas, he settled in London as professor of Italian at King's College. Besides poems, he wrote three critical studies of Dante.

Rossetti, William Michael (1829–1919), English author and art critic, brother of Christina and Dante Gabriel Rossetti. For a short time he was editor of the *Germ*, founded in 1850 as the official organ of the Pre-Raphaelite Brotherhood. His best-known works are a translation in blank verse of Dante's *Inferno*, 1865; *Lives of Famous Poets*, 1878; *Life of Keats*, 1887; *Memoir of Dante Gabriel Rossetti*, 1895; and *Reminiscences*, 1906.

Rossini, Gioacchino (1792–1868), Italian composer. When he was 18 his first opera was produced at Venice. For the next 18 years he went from success to success all over Europe. Among the best of his 38 operas were *La scala di seta*, *L'Italiana in Algeri*, *La Cenerentola*, *La gazza ladra*, *Semiramide*, *Le Comte Ory* and *Guillaume Tell*. His masterpiece is *Il barbiere di Siviglia*, 1816, which was at first unsuccessful. Rossini settled in Paris where he lived for the rest of his life, except for intermittent stays at Bologna, where he directed the Liceo Musicale (1839–48), and for the years 1848–55 which he spent at Florence. He ceased producing operas at the age of 37 and wrote only the *Stabat Mater*, the *Petite Messe solennelle* and small occasional works in his later years.

Rosslare, seaport of County Wexford, Republic of Ireland, and terminus of car ferry services from Fishguard and Le Havre. To the north is the seaside resort of River Strand. Population (1971) (of Rosslare Harbour) 725, (of Rosslare Strand) 588.

Rostand, Edmond (1868–1918), French dramatist and poet. *Les Musardises*, poems, was published in 1890. His farcical *Les Romanesques*, 1894, was followed in 1895 by *La Princesse lointaine*, *La Samaritaine*, 1897, and *L'Aiglon*, 1900. The heroic drama *Cyrano de Bergerac*, 1897, was an outstanding success; in 1910 this was followed by *Chantecler*. Rostand was a skilful and talented dramatist in the Romantic tradition.

Rostock, port of the German Democratic Republic, 190 km north of Berlin. It is on the Baltic Sea, at the head of the estuary of the River Warnow, 13 km from the river mouth. The city was founded in the 12th century on the site of a Wendish stronghold, and was once a member of the Hanseatic League. Rostock is East Germany's chief seaport, and has oil-refining, chemicals, engineering and milling industries. Its outport is at Warnemünde. Population (1979) 226,667.

Rostov (long known as Rostov the Great), town in southern Yaroslavl *oblast* of the RSFSR, USSR, on Lake Nero, 60 km south-west of Yaroslavl. The town has been known since 862; it was the capital of Central Russia in the 11th century. It was conquered by the Muscovites in 1474 and was an important commercial centre during the 16th–19th centuries. Population (1974) 31,000.

Rostov-on-Don, capital city, economic and cultural centre of Rostov *oblast*, USSR, on the Don, 46 km from its mouth. It is one of the largest engineering centres in the USSR (agricultural machinery, aircraft, shipbuilding); there are also tobacco and other food industries, shoe-making and textile industries. It is an important transport centre. Population (1980) 946,000.

Rostropovich, Mstislav (1927–), Russian cellist, conductor and pianist. He studied at the Moscow Conservatoire, where he became a professor in 1957, and has since appeared all over the world. Shostakovich, Britten, Lutoslawski and many others composed cello concertos for him. He is now also well known as a conductor.

Rotation of Crops, the system of growing crops in some particular order with the objects of utilising fully the plant foods in the upper and lower part of the soil; of checking insect and fungus pests by depriving them for a period of their essential food; of distributing labour economically; and of providing a variety of food for cattle and other livestock.

Roth, Philip (1933–), US writer. His first published book was a short novel, *Goodbye, Columbus*, and short stories, 1959, followed by the novels *Letting Go*, 1962, and *When She Was Good*, 1967, Roth became known outside America with the best-selling *Portnoy's Complaint*, 1969, a painfully funny account of the psychological burdens of a Jewish upbringing in the United States. Jewish dislocations and the problem of writing fiction have been themes of his more recent books, *The Great American Novel*, 1973, *My Life as a Man*, 1974, and *The Professor of Desire*, 1977.

Rothenburg ob der Tauber, commune in Bavaria, Federal Republic of Germany, standing high above the valley of the Tauber, 50 km south-east of Würzburg. It was once a free city of the empire and has still a wealth of medieval architecture. It is a major tourist centre on the Romantische Strasse and one of the most visited of German towns. Population (1970) 12,500.

Rothenstein, Sir John (Knewstub Maurice) (1901–), British art historian and museum director. From 1938 to 1964 he was director of the Tate Gallery. He was rector of St Andrews University 1964–67, and in recent years visiting professor at several American universities. His publications include *The Life and Death of Conder*, 1938; *Augustus John*, 1943; *Introduction to English Painting, One Hundred Modern Foreign Paintings in the Tate Gallery*, 1949; *Modern English Painters*, 1974; and an autobiography, *Summer's Lease*, 1965.

Rothenstein, Sir William (1872–1945), British artist. He was principal of the Royal College of Art from 1920 to 1925 and professor of Civic Art at Sheffield University from 1917 to 1926. His work includes lithographs and etchings, as well as landscapes, portraits and interiors in oils. His best-known painting is *A Doll's House* (Tate Gallery). He completed over 200 portraits of airmen during the Second World War, which he presented to the nation.

Rotherham, town of South Yorkshire, England, situated between Sheffield and Doncaster at the junction of the Rother with the Don, 10 km from Sheffield. The Chapel of Our Lady (c.1483) on the old Rotherham Bridge is one of only four extant chapels built on bridges in England.

There is coal-mining in the vicinity, and Rotherham is the railway clearing-house of a large colliery area. There are large steel and brass-works; iron and steel sheets, bars and rods are made as well as a range of manufactured articles. Population (1981) 81,988.

Rothermere, Harold Sidney Harmsworth, Viscount (1868–1940), British newspaper proprietor, the younger brother of Alfred Harmsworth, later Viscount Northcliffe. He became, at 21, a partner in the publishing business known as Harmsworth Brothers, later called Amalgamated Press. From 1914 he was proprietor of the *Daily Mirror*, supplemented by his founding of the *Sunday Pictorial* a year later. On the death of Lord Northcliffe in 1922, Rothermere gained control of the *Daily Mail*. His son, Esmond Cecil Harmsworth, the 2nd Viscount, became chairman of Associated Newspapers. See also JOURNALISM; NEWSPAPERS.

Rothesay, royal burgh in Argyll and Bute District, Strathclyde Region, Scotland, on the island of Bute, 48 km by rail and sea from Glasgow. There is a good harbour, some fishing is carried on, and it is a popular tourist centre and holiday resort in the Firth of Clyde. Population (1981) 5408.

Rothko, Mark (1903–70), US painter. During the mid-1940s he painted in a style influenced by Surrealism but by the end of the decade he had evolved his distinctive manner employing large flat areas of matt colour which would cover the large-scale canvas almost to its edges. These paintings strongly influenced younger painters in the USA and Great Britain by their exploitation of the power of pure colour.

Rothschild, Jewish family famous for their immense financial transactions. The founder of the family was Mayer Amschel Rothschild (1743–1813), of Frankfurt am Main. After the founder's death, his eldest son, Amschel Mayer (1773–1855), carried on the Frankfurt business, the other four sons having opened branches: Solomon (1774–1826) at Vienna; Nathan Mayer (1777–1836) in London; Karl (1780–1855) at Naples; and James (1792–1868) at Paris. In the London house Nathan was succeeded by Lionel (1808–79), who was returned to Parliament for the City of London in 1849 and 1852, but on account of his religion was unable to sit until 1858. He was MP until 1874, and at his death was succeeded in the business by his son, Nathan (1840–1915), who was raised to the peerage as Baron Rothschild in 1885. The Nathaniel Mayer Rothschild merchant bank is unique as the headquarters of the London bullion market, where the price of gold is fixed each day, and which handles as much as three-quarters of the world's dealings in gold.

Rotifera, a phylum of minute animals consisting of about 1800 species, mostly less than 1 cm long. They occur mostly in fresh water, but a number of species have been found in the sea and others in damp moss. Their distribution is very extensive, and the terrestrial forms in particular are remarkably tolerant to desiccation and low temperatures.

Rotorua, town of North Island, New Zealand, situated on the south-western fringe of a lake of the same name, in an area of geysers, hot springs and boiling mud pools. It is a Maori centre, and is state-managed as a health and tourist resort. Sawmilling and farming are basic industries. Population (1980) 47,600.

Rotten Borough, a constituency which retained its original representation in Parliament, although its population had become severely depleted. The 1832 Reform Act disenfranchised such boroughs (of which there were over 140 out of a parliamentary total of 658) in Britain, thereby putting an end to one of the worst excesses of electoral bribery and corruption.

Rotterdam, most important port and second largest city of the Netherlands, situated in the province of South Holland on the Rhine estuary, 90 km south-west of Amsterdam. Its name comes from the little river Rotte, which here joins the Nieuwe Maas. The Nieuwe Waterweg (New Waterway), which is 35 km long and navigable for the largest sea-going vessels, connects the town with the North Sea at the Hook of

Holland. The port owes much of its importance to the transit trade to Germany and Switzerland along the Rhine. Rotterdam suffered a devastating German air attack in May 1940, which erased the centre of the town. Since the war much of Rotterdam has been rebuilt. Progressive westward extension of port facilities now reaches the North Sea coast at Europoort. Rotterdam is the biggest and busiest Atlantic port in Europe. Its industries include shipbuilding, chemicals, oil refining, textiles, vehicles, engineering and margarine. Population (1980) 579,194.

Rotunda, a circular building, usually domed, e.g. the Pantheon at Rome.

Rouault, Georges (1871–1958), French painter. He exhibited in the Fauve show of 1905, but always remained independent of this group. Rouault belongs primarily to the Expressionist school, conveying, that is, a personal mood or emotional state, and his work possesses some element of mysticism. His impressively tragic religious paintings set him apart from contemporary artists.

Roubaix, French town in the *département* of Nord, on the Roubaix canal, 9 km north-east of Lille. It has been a prosperous cloth-making town since the 15th century, and together with Tourcoing is the centre of the French woollen industry. There are also other textile, chemical and machinery manufactures. Population (1975) 109,797.

Roubiliac, Louis François, also Roubillac (1702/5–62), French sculptor. Apart from a short visit to Rome in 1752, he spent all his working life in England. Dramatic and brilliantly executed funeral monuments by him are to be found in Westminster Abbey, Worcester Cathedral and Warkton Church, Northamptonshire. His statue of Shakespeare, carved for the actor Garrick (British Museum), typifies the lively realism of his full length portraits and busts.

Rouble (Russian *rubl'*), unit of the Russian monetary system. Originally the rouble was a silver ingot of fixed weight; it was first issued as a coin by Peter the Great in 1704. There are 100 kopeks in a rouble.

Rouen, French city, capital of the *département* of Seine-Maritime, situated on both banks of the River Seine, 120 km north-west of Paris. The river is tidal as far as the city, and Rouen is thus a port of importance; it is also a busy railway junction. It was the capital of Normandy, and here William the Conqueror died, Arthur of Brittany was murdered, and Joan of Arc was burned. The cathedral, on the site of a previous church, dates from the 13th to 16th centuries. The port of Rouen handles oil, coal, fruit, pulp and paper. The city has important textile, petrochemical, engineering, paper, clothing, electronic and nylon industries. Population (1975): conurbation 388,711; city 118,332.

Rouge, see COSMETICS.

Rouget de Lisle, Claude Joseph (1760–1836), French soldier and composer. He was the author and composer of the French national anthem, the *Marseillaise*.

Roulers, see ROESELARE.

Roulette, gambling game, played with a wheel (*roulette*) let into the centre of an oblong table covered with a green cloth. The table is divided into three columns of figures, marked from 1 to 36 alternately in red and black. The six spaces at the two sides of the columns of figures are called, respectively, *rouge*, to mark red numbers; *noir*, for black numbers; *impair*, for odd numbers; *manque*, numbers from 1 to 18; *pair*, even numbers; and *passe*, all numbers from 19 to 36. The wheel itself contains a brass cylinder within a narrow, inclined ivory ledge, and is made to revolve on a pin by means of a cross-head. The outer edge of this cylinder is partitioned into 37 small compartments numbered irregularly from 1 to 36, and coloured alternately red and black, the 37th space being the 0 or zero. The object of the game is to win money by placing stakes on a fancied number or other division. The players having put their stakes on that portion of the cloth which represents the chance selected, the *tourneur* or croupier throws a small ivory ball round the ledge of the wheel, at the same time revolving the cylinder in the opposite direction. When the wheel stops the ball drops into one of the little compartments, the number of which is the winning number. If, for example, it is 27, the croupier announces, 'Vingt sept, rouge, impair et passe', rakes the lost stakes into the bank and pays the winner.

***Henri Rousseau.** The Jungle: Tiger Attacking a Buffalo, 1908, typifies the artist's style.*

Round, or rota, kind of canon; its successive entries consist of complete melodies rather than phrases. Unlike canons, rounds are sung with the theme in its original position or in the octave, never at other intervals. An older name was rota. *Sumer is icumen in* is a typical early round. A later example is in the quartet in the first act of Beethoven's opera *Fidelio*. See also CATCH.

Round Table. The exact origin of the Round Table is uncertain. It is part of the tradition of the Arthurian romance, in which the knights of King Arthur's court quarrelled for precedence, and a table was devised, round in shape, where all could sit equally. According to one romance, Merlin made the table for Uther Pendragon, and another states that it first belonged to the father of Guinevere, King Leodegran of Cornwall. It had one vacant place, the 'Siege Perilous', awaiting the arrival of the Grail hero Galahad.

Roundels, or roundelays, country songs of the 14th century, so called from the French *rondelet*, because their words returned to the opening lines again and again; also round dances.

Roundels, in heraldry, general term for circular charges of various tinctures. Those coloured or (gold) are called bezants or besants; argent (silver) ones are plates; gules, torteaux; azure, hurts; sable, pellets. A roundel blazoned barry wavy argent and azure is a fountain.

Rounders, bat-and-ball game. It became popular in the 18th century, and at first had only a vague form, on which players grafted their own individual rules. Two teams of nine play two innings each, the bowler delivers the ball underarm to reach the batsman between head and knees, and the batsman scores a rounder by hitting the ball in front of him and running the diamond, outside posts one, two and three and touching post four. He can take sanctuary at any post, but cannot score unless he completes the course at one go.

Roundheads, nickname for the Parliamentarian party during the English Civil War. It appears to have been used first in 1641, and was, like 'Cavalier', originally a term of abuse, referring to the close-cropped hair style affected by some extreme Puritans. In actual fact there was little difference in the dress and hair style of most prominent Royalists and Parliamentarians.
See also ENGLISH HISTORY.

Roundworm, see NEMATODA.

Rous, Francis Peyton (1879–1970), US physiologist noted for his work in cancer research. Shortly after taking up an appointment at the Rockefeller Institute in New York he succeeded in transplanting a spontaneous tumour, which had appeared in a fowl, by means of cell grafts. He then repeated this operation, only by means of cell-free filtrates. These findings were inconsistent with current theories about the characteristics of cancerous growths, and were treated with scepticism; however Rous's later research (in the 1930s) consolidated his earlier findings and helped to explain how cancerous cells could fail to reveal themselves until a promoting agent operated. Rous received the Nobel Prize in 1966.

Rousseau, Henri Julien (1844–1910), French painter. His 'naïve' pictures were known to Gauguin and later much admired by Picasso and his circle, and between 1886 and 1910 he exhibited at the Salon des Indépendants. *The Sleeping Gypsy*, 1897 (New York), *The Muse Inspiring the Poet*, 1909 (Kunstmuseum, Basel), and *The Snake-Charmer*, 1907 (Louvre) are among his notable works, many of which are in the USA.

Rousseau, Jean Baptiste (1671–1741), French poet. He early gained fame by his poetry and epigrams. In 1688 he attended the French ambassador to Denmark, and later visited England with Marshal Tallard. On his return he devoted himself to poetry, and it was the point of his satiric epigrams that caused him to be driven from France. He spent the last 30 years of his life in exile. He wrote some comedies and operas, but it is on his lyric poetry that his fame chiefly rests.

Rousseau, Jean-Jacques (1712–78), French writer and philosopher. After a tempestuous youth and a variety of occupations, he was invited by Diderot to contribute to the *Encyclopédie*. His romantic novel *Julie, ou la nouvelle Héloïse* was published in 1759. This novel of frustrated and noble passion had a European vogue and is one of the landmarks of the developing Romantic Movement. *Émile*, which appeared in 1762, expounded a new system of education, based on natural development and the power of example; it was to have a tremendous impact on European educational theories. In 1762 he also published *Du Contrat social*, in which he expounded his theory of the surrender of the individual's natural rights to the whole society under the sovereign direction of the 'general will'. His writing equally offended the government, the clerics and contemporary philosophers. His *Confessions*, published posthumously in 1782, revealed his weaknesses with unprecedented frankness, and may be regarded as the founding work in the modern tradition of autobiographical novels and confessions.

Rousseau, Pierre Étienne Théodore (1812–67), French landscape painter. He led the movement against the then prevailing classical style. The Salon was hostile to his work so that he was known as 'le grand refusé', and in 1833 he retired to Barbizon, where he spent the latter part of his life. His work has breadth and harmony of colour and is dark in tone.

Roussel, Albert (1869–1937), French composer. His works include the opera *Padmâvati*; the ballets *Le Festin de l'araignée* and *Bacchus et Ariane*; *Psalm 80* and other choral works; four symphonies; chamber music; piano works and songs.

Rout, see RIOT.

Roux, Pierre Paul Émile (1853–1933), French bacteriologist. With Pasteur and C. E. Chamberland he studied anthrax, discovering vaccination with the attenuated virus.

From 1888 to 1890, Roux worked with Alexandre Yersin, confirming and extending Loeffler's discovery of the diphtheria bacillus and showing that the toxin released by it was responsible for the first signs of the disease. This was the first bacterial toxin to be discovered. With L. Vaillaud, Roux did important work on the prevention and treatment of tetanus by antitoxic serum. He also demonstrated the use of diphtheria antitoxin developed from horse serum. With I. Metchnikoff, Roux worked on the problem of syphilis, showing that it could be transmitted from man to the anthropoid apes.

Rove Beetle, any member of the family Staphylinidae in order Coleoptera. The characteristic feature of these beetles is the very short elytra (wing cases) which conceal large, well-developed wings that are intricately folded away. The family includes some 20,000 species. Most of these beetles are small and inconspicuous, except *Staphylinus olens* (the devil's coach-horse), which attains an unusual size (28 mm). They are omnivorous.

Rowan, see MOUNTAIN ASH.

Rowe, Nicholas (1674–1718), English dramatist and poet. Rowe's dramatic works were mainly tragedies and include *The Ambitious Stepmother*, 1701; *Tamerlane*, 1702; *The Fair Penitent*, 1703; *Jane Shore*, 1714; and *Lady Jane Grey*, 1715. From 1715 he was poet laureate in succession to Nahum Tate.

Rowing, art of propelling a boat through water by means of oars. Rowing was practised in ancient times both in small craft and galleys in which several hundred oarsmen plied oars mounted in banks. Competitive rowing as practised today began in the early years of the 19th century at Oxford and Cambridge Universities.

Henley Regatta was instituted in 1839 and before long every Thames-side town had its regatta, as did many provincial towns where suitable water was to be found.

The world governing body for amateur rowing is the Fédération Internationale des Sociétés d'Aviron (FISA), which is responsible for an international code of rules and also organises the Olympic Regatta, world championships for men and women, held every year apart from those in which the Olympic Games are held. For men's and junior championships (under 18), the former over a distance of 2000 m and the latter 1500 m, the events are for eights, coxed and coxless fours and pairs, quadruple, double and single sculls. For women's championships (1000 m) the events are for eights, coxed fours, coxless pairs, quadruple (coxed), double and single sculls. Lightweight championships, introduced in 1974, are restricted to eights, coxless fours and single sculls.

See also BOAT RACE; HENLEY ROYAL REGATTA.

Rowlandson, Thomas (1756–1827), British caricaturist and painter. In 1777 he settled in London as a portrait painter. After 1781, he specialised in caricature satirising contemporary society. He drew in pen and tinted his drawings. He contributed illustrations to Ackerman's *Poetical Magazine*, 1790, to accompany William Combe's *Tour of Dr Syntax* (published in book form, 1812–21), and illustrated many books. His masterpiece *Vauxhall Gardens* (well-known in the aquatint engraving from it) was rediscovered in 1945.

Rowntree, Joseph (1836–1925), British Quaker cocoa and chocolate manufacturer and philanthropist. The Joseph Rowntree Village Trust was formed in 1904 to put his ideas into practice, and considerable progress was made during his lifetime, after which the work was carried on by Seebohm Rowntree and others. Joseph was interested in all social problems, in adult education and the activities of the Society of Friends; and the village, New Earswick, acted as a focal point for these interests.

Rowse, A(lfred) L(eslie) (1903–), British historical writer. A prolific writer of history books, of books about Cornwall, and a Shakespearean scholar, Rowse's works include: *A Cornish Childhood*, 1942; *The Elizabethan Renaissance*, 1971; and *Shakespeare the Man*, 1973.

Royal Academy of Arts, London, founded 1768, the oldest established society in Great Britain solely devoted to the fine arts. It also appears to be unique in the world as a self-supporting, self-governing body of artists which, on its own premises, conducts art schools and holds open exhibitions of the arts of present and past periods.

The 50 Royal Academicians and 25 Associates are all painters, engravers, sculptors or architects resident in the UK and elect one of their number to be president.

It is through its exhibitions that the Academy has become best-known to the world at large.

Royal Academy of Dramatic Art, London, has provided a comprehensive training for the professional theatre ever since 1904,

Thomas Rowlandson. The Miseries of London, *an 18th-century traffic accident.*

when it was founded by the great actor-manager Beerbohm Tree. It moved to its present site in Gower Street in 1905 and was granted a royal charter in 1920.

Royal Air Force, see AIR FORCE, ROYAL.

Royal and Ancient Golf Club of St Andrews, spiritual home of world golf, in continuous operation since its inception in 1754. The rules of golf were formulated by the 'Royal and Ancient' and today the club is the game's ultimate world authority.

St Andrews itself is on the Fife coast, in Scotland, some 48 km north-east of Edinburgh. Records show that golf, or a form of it, was played here as early as 1552. The legendary Old Course, 6936 yards with a par 73, has come to be regarded as the supreme test of a player's skill and endurance. St Andrews is a regular venue for the Open Championship, and is unique in that although actual membership of the club is an honour bestowed on only a few, the course itself is public and can be played by anyone paying the necessary green fee.

See also GOLF; OPEN GOLF CHAMPIONSHIP.

Royal Antelope, *Neotragus pygmaeus*, the smallest of all antelopes, being no more than 30 cm high. It and its tiny relatives, such as Bates's dwarf antelope (*N. batesi*), are inhabitants of dense jungle and do not venture onto the plains with their larger relatives. They are slenderly built, with very thin legs, no thicker than a pencil, and are generally brown in colour. They are nocturnal and live in inaccessible areas, and very little is known of their habits.

Royal Assent, see ASSENT, ROYAL.

Royal Ballet, The, the national ballet company of Britain, now centred at the Royal Opera House, Covent Garden. Founded as the Vic-Wells Ballet by Ninette de Valois in 1931, the company first appeared at both the Sadler's Wells (where a school was also opened) and the Old Vic Theatres, and by the outbreak of war in 1939 was already established at the former theatre as the most important manifestation of English ballet. The status of the company, renamed the Sadler's Wells Ballet in 1941, increased enormously during the war, and in 1946 the company moved to Covent Garden, a second company, the Sadler's Wells Theatre Ballet, then being formed. In 1956 the organisations were incorporated by a Royal charter, and became the Royal Ballet.

Royal British Legion, membership organisation of British ex-Service men and women, founded in 1921 by the amalgamation of four ex-service societies, which united to form one national organisation under the leadership of F.-M. Earl Haig, its first president. The British Legion is democratic, non-political and non-sectarian, and membership is open to all British (or naturalised) men and women who served in the Forces. Its purpose is to assist all ex-service men and women, their widows and dependants, in pension matters, to relieve distress, to find employment, and re-establish them on their return to civilian life.

Royal Canadian Mounted Police, formerly the North-West Mounted Police. The force was given its present name in 1920 when it was made responsible for enforcing federal law throughout the whole of Canada.

***Royal Hospital, Chelsea,** founded in 1682. It was inspired by the Hôtel des Invalides in Paris.*

Among its many duties, it is specially empowered to deal with smuggling offences by land, sea and air, and is responsible for the suppression of the traffic in narcotics. It is the sole police force operating in the Northwest and Yukon Territories. The force is administered by the Canadian Minister of Justice. Its headquarters are at Ottawa.

Royal Commission. A royal commission, in Britain, is a body appointed to gain information about the operation of existing laws, as a preliminary to their amendment, or on various matters, social, educational or otherwise, to report to the government its recommendations on matters of broad policy. A royal commission has no power to compel disclosure of documents, nor even to administer an oath or compel persons to give evidence.

Royal Family, term used in Great Britain for the sovereign and members of his or her family. The sovereign and certain other members of the royal family have a sum awarded to them, called the Civil List, in consideration of the sovereign assigning to the nation life interest in the hereditary revenues of the Crown.

Royal Fern, see OSMUNDA.

Royal Flying Corps was formed in Britain on 13 May 1912, and developed out of the Air Battalion of the Royal Engineers formed on 1 April 1911, as the first step in creating a British Army air arm. In July 1914 the naval wing separated from the RFC, and became the Royal Naval Air Service, and on 1 April 1918 the RFC and the RNAS merged to become the Royal Air Force.

Royal Free Hospital, Hampstead, London, England, is an undergraduate teaching and district general hospital for all types of illness in association with the Royal Free Hospital School of Medicine, formerly the London School of Medicine for Women. The Hospital was originally founded in 1828 by Dr William Marsden and was incorporated by royal charter in 1892.

Royal Geographical Society, founded in 1830 to advance geographical knowledge by exploration and research. In the 19th century it contributed to opening up Africa by supporting Livingstone, Speke and Grant, Cameron and others, and revived British interest in the Antarctic, sharing in the organisation of many expeditions from Capt. Scott's to the Trans-Antarctic expedition sent out in 1956. The Society's Map Room contains some 600,000 sheets and 2000 atlases and is probably the largest private collection of maps in Europe. It is open to the public.

Royal Horticultural Society, founded as the Horticultural Society of London, in 1804, by John Wedgwood, son of the famous potter. From the time it was given its royal charter in 1809, the Society has had a practical interest in the discovery, introduction and propagation of new and rare flowering plants and vegetables, and through its numerous shows and competitions, culminating in the great annual Chelsea Flower Show, as well as through its publications, has stimulated the interest of gardeners to the extent that the Society is considered to be the world's premier body devoted to gardens, gardening and horticulture generally.

Royal Hospital, Chelsea, London, England, founded by King Charles II in 1682 as a retreat for veterans of the regular army who had become unfit for duty, either after 20 years' service or as a result of wounds. The Hospital accommodates between 400 and 500 men. It was built by Wren (1682–92), and is the most notable building in Chelsea. The Chelsea Flower Show is held annually in the grounds.

Royal Household, see HOUSEHOLD, ROYAL.

Royal Institute of International Affairs, organisation for the study and discussion of international problems, based at Chatham House, London. Like its American counterpart, the Council on Foreign Relations, it was founded as an independent organisation following discussions between the British and American delegations to the 1919 Peace Conference. The research programme is devoted to matters of immediate and longer-term interest concerned with significant aspects of world developments. Extensive work is undertaken on economic, financial and legal questions, as well as on political and diplomatic affairs.

Royal Institution of Great Britain, The, organisation for the 'promotion, diffusion and extension of science and useful knowledge', founded in London, 1799. In its laboratories Young, Davy, Faraday, Tyndall, Dewar, the Braggs and others conducted their researches. It has a fine library, a museum depicting the life and work of Faraday, and a famous lecture theatre.

Royal Jelly, a substance used to feed bee larvae. Royal jelly is produced by the lateral pharyngeal glands in the workers' heads; it is rich in proteins. All bee larvae get this jelly for the first three days; drone and worker larvae are then fed beebread, a mixture of pollen and honey. If the hive wishes to make a new queen, the workers construct a specially shaped cell and feed the larva in it on royal jelly exclusively.
See also BEE.

Royal Marines, see MARINES, THE ROYAL.

Royal Mint, see MINT.

Royal National Life-boat Institution (RNLI), which was founded in 1824, operates the 24-hour lifeboat service round Britain, Ireland and the Channel Islands, with 135 offshore lifeboats and 122 inshore lifeboats. Each offshore lifeboat has a full-time mechanic, but all other lifeboat men are volunteers, rewarded for services and exercises. The RNLI is a charity, obtaining its income from over 2000 fund-raising branches and special gifts made by individuals, trusts and companies.

Royal Navy, see NAVY.

Royal Opera House, Covent Garden (formerly Covent Garden Theatre), now the pre-eminent house of opera and ballet in London. The first theatre on this site was erected in 1732 by John Rich, opening on 7 December 1732 with a revival of Congreve's *The Way of the World.* At this time plays, pantomimes and operas were produced. The building was burnt down on 20 September 1808. A new theatre designed by Robert Smirke opened on 18 September 1809 with *Macbeth.* In 1846–47 the interior was reconstructed and the theatre opened as the Royal Italian Opera in 1847. It was destroyed by fire on 5 March 1856 and the present building, designed by Sir Edward M. Barry, arose in its place, opening on 15 May 1858 with Meyerbeer's *Les Huguenots.* During the latter half of the 19th century it housed many famous opera seasons, and in 1946 it also became the home of the Royal Ballet Company and of the Royal Opera.

Royal Photographic Society, learned society, founded in 1853 and the oldest society of its kind in the world. The main object of the society is the promotion of photography in all its aspects.

Royal Shakespeare Company, the company of the Shakespeare Memorial Theatre, Stratford. The theatre was built in 1932 and replaces an earlier structure built for the first Shakespeare festival in 1879. Although the germ of the company can be traced back to Garrick's drama productions at Stratford to celebrate the Shakespeare jubilee of 1769, the company has functioned under its present name only since 1961. Peter Hall was its first director. The Barbican is the company's London home for year-round performance.

Royal Society (Royal Society of London for Improving Natural Knowledge), oldest scientific society in Great Britain, and one of the oldest in Europe. The nucleus of the Society came into existence about 1645 and in 1662 Charles II, who had previously become a patron, granted the first charter. Subsequent charters in 1663 and 1669 conferred further privileges on the Society, which was in its early days essentially a group of enthusiasts for the new experimental philosophy and who from the start excluded political and religious topics from their weekly meetings. Wren was one of the Society's earliest presidents. Newton was elected a fellow in 1671, and served as president from 1703 until his death in 1727. In 1848 control of the Society passed wholly into the hands of men of science, and election to its fellowship became a recognition of their high achievement. The number of fellows of the Royal Society is about 800 and there are 80 foreign members.

Royal Society for the Prevention of Cruelty to Animals, organisation founded in England in 1824 to prevent cruelty and promote kindness to animals. Now a registered charity funded by voluntary contributions, it has over 200 inspectors in England and Wales, who investigate cases of cruelty and work to bring offenders to court. Recently its membership has been divided over whether or not the organisation should play a more active rôle in opposing blood sports and experiments with animals.

Royal Society for the Protection of Birds was founded in 1889 and incorporated under royal charter in 1904. It is the national body in the United Kingdom responsible for the protection and conservation of wild birds, and their place in nature.

Royal Society of Arts, The (Royal Society for the Encouragement of Arts, Manufacturers and Commerce), learned society, founded in London in 1754. Its scope includes all the fine and applied arts and the sciences, and the membership is 10,500 fellows.

Royal Society of Edinburgh was founded in 1731 as the Philosophical Society of Edinburgh. It was constituted 'for the promotion of science and literature', receiving charters in 1783 and 1811. The Society is today Scotland's major publisher of original research papers, especially in mathematics.

Royal Succession, see SUCCESSION, ROYAL.

Royal Ulster Constabulary, police force of Northern Ireland. In 1787 the first police force in Ireland was formed under warrant of the lord lieutenant. In 1822, under an act of the imperial Parliament, a permanent, trained police force was set up for the whole of Ireland, commanded by four inspectors-general, one for each province. In 1836 control of the four provincial forces was centralised under one inspector-general with headquarters in Dublin. In 1867 Queen Victoria granted to the force the title of the Royal Irish Constabulary. The RUC is commanded by the chief constable, who is assisted by a deputy chief constable and six assistant chief constables. The headquarters of the RUC is in Belfast.

Royalist, term frequently used of monarchist parties. In England it is applied especially to the party which supported Charles I and, after 1649, Charles II, during the civil wars and the Commonwealth.
See also ENGLISH HISTORY.

Royalty. Popularly royalty is synonymous with monarchy, and a king is styled monarch or sovereign although he may possess no more than a portion of the sovereign power in a state. Royalty properly denotes the status of a person of royal rank, such as a king, queen, reigning prince or grand duke, or any of their kindred.

Royce, Sir (Frederick) Henry, see ROLLS-ROYCE.

Royce, Josiah (1855–1916), US philosopher. He became a professor at Harvard in 1892 and established himself as one of the foremost American philosophers, influenced by Hegel in his Objective Idealism. His books include *Spirit of Modern Philosophy*, 1892; *The Conception of God*, 1895; and *The Conception of Immortality*, 1900.

RSFSR, see RUSSIAN SOVIET FEDERATED SOCIALIST REPUBLIC; UNION OF SOVIET SOCIALIST REPUBLICS.

Ruapehu, intermittently active volcano (2796 m) in North Island, New Zealand, near Ohakune.

Ruba'i (plural Ruba'iyyat), or quatrain, used by Persian, Arab and Turkish poets, consisting of four half-lines complete in themselves. Edward FitzGerald's translations of the quatrains of Omar Khayyam have made this verse form familiar to English readers.

Rubber, any material which, after vulcanisation, can be extended to several times its original length and rapidly recover that original length when the extending force is removed. The term covers both the natural product and synthetic materials.
Natural rubber is made from the latex, a milky, sticky fluid, that is found in the bark of more than 2000 plant species. The only commercially viable source is the tree *Hevea brasiliensis*, indigenous to the Amazon river basin. The world's leading rubber-producing countries are Malaysia, Indonesia, Thailand, Sri Lanka and India. The plantations there of *H. brasiliensis* come from seed taken from Brazil to Kew Gardens in London in 1876 and 1877, and raised as plants. The plants were then transported to the Far East.
The latex is carried in tubes which spiral up the tree in the inner bark; great skill is required to cut through enough bark to tap the latex without going too far and damaging the cambium layer underneath. The latex is shipped, either as a liquid, or coagulated by the addition of formic acid, and dried as sheets.
Synthetic rubber was developed in Europe and the USA during the Second World War, when Japanese invasions cut off supplies from the Far East. It is made from the products or by-products of oil-refineries (e.g. butadiene, styrene, isoprene, ethylene and propylene).
Natural rubber becomes hard in cold weather and soft and sticky in hot weather. The process of vulcanisation, discovered by the American Charles Goodyear in 1839, makes rubber consistent at all temperatures. In vulcanisation, a mixture of natural rubber and sulphur is heated for some time; the amount of sulphur added and the time and temperature affect the hardness of the final product.
In manufacture, dry rubber is generally

mixed with other ingredients, such as fillers, mineral oils and colouring matter; this process is called compounding. The rubber compound is processed by extrusion, calendering, spreading or moulding, followed by vulcanisation. In moulding the vulcanisation is often carried out simultaneously. Seamless goods are made by dipping a former of the desired shape in compounded latex; a thin film of latex adheres to the former, and can be built up in layers if desired.

Rubbra, Edmund (1901–), British composer. His most important works are the ten symphonies, the cello sonata and the viola concerto; he has also written much distinctive choral and church music, an opera, orchestral pieces, chamber music and songs.

Rubella, see MEASLES.

***Rubens,** A Portrait of his daughter, 1615. Rubens was one of the greatest baroque artists.*

Rubens, Sir Peter Paul (1577–1640), Flemish painter. In 1600 he visited Italy, where he finally took up his residence at the court of Mantua. His stay at Venice brought him under the influence of Titian and Paolo Veronese, and affected his later development, probably teaching him much of the art of colour in which he excelled. In 1605 he visited the Spanish court, where he executed many portraits. Three years later he returned to Antwerp, where he married Isabella Brant (1609). Many pupils came to his studio here and they helped Rubens execute the flood of orders he received; hence the difficulty in establishing a true Rubens work. In 1620 he received the commission for the series of paintings of the life of Marie de' Medici, now in the Louvre. In 1629 he visited England, where he was warmly received by Charles I, for whom he decorated the ceiling of the Banqueting Hall, Whitehall, being knighted in 1630. Having become a widower in 1626, he married Helena Fourment in 1630. She appears in many of his paintings. Rubens is a master of those parts of his art which act immediately on the senses, especially in the portrayal of the tumult and energy of human action in full power and emotion. He shows the early baroque period at its most human and richest. His influence on painters—Watteau, Delacroix, Manet and many others—has been enormous.

Rubiaceae, bedstraw family, a very large family of dicotyledons, having about 450 genera and 6000 species. Many tropical Rubiaceae have berries. The main use of the family is for coffee (*Coffea*) and quinine (*Cinchona*), but the flowers of some tropical species are also valued, for example the fragrant blooms of *Gardenia*.

Rubicon, small stream of ancient Italy, flowing into the Adriatic. Under the Roman republic it formed the boundary between Italia and Gallia Cisalpina. Caesar crossed it with his army in 49 BC and this constituted an act of war against the republic; hence the proverbial significance of 'crossing the Rubicon'. It has been identified with the modern Fiumicino, west of Rimini.

Rubidium, metallic chemical element, symbol Rb, atomic number 37, atomic weight 85·4678, one of the alkali metals. It is quite widely distributed, occurring in rare minerals, such as pollux and lepidolite, and in tea, coffee, cocoa and tobacco. The metal is obtained by heating a mixture of the carbonate with carbon and calcium carbonate, or alternatively by the electrolysis of fused rubidium hydroxide in a nickel crucible. It is a white, chemically active metal, melting at 39°C, and its properties are very similar to those of potassium.

Rubik's Cube, mathematically-based puzzle invented in 1975 by Professor Erno Rubik of Hungary. It consists of a large cube made up of 27 smaller cubes, fastened together in such a way that though they interlock each line can be rotated. Each side of the large cube is covered with a different colour, and the puzzle is to restore the cube to this conformation from any random arrangement. The number of possible configurations is said to be 43,252,003,274,489,856,000.

Rubinstein, Anton Grigoryevich (1829–1894), Russian pianist and composer. In 1862 he founded the St Petersburg Conservatoire of which he was director (1862–67, 1887–91). From 1854 he made successful concert tours in Europe and America. His compositions include five piano concertos, six symphonies, 18 operas, and oratorios. As a pianist, he was the only serious rival to Liszt.

Rubinstein, Artur (1886–1982), Polish-born American pianist. He gave his first recital at the age of 11. He studied in Berlin and toured North America in 1906 and South America in 1918. Best known for his playing of the classical repertory, Rubinstein was undoubtedly one of the greatest pianists of the century.

Rublyov, Andrey, also Rublev (c.1370–c.1430), Russian artist who worked in Moscow, and is the most famous of the Russian icon painters. His work is distinguished from that of the Cretan Byzantine School by its delicate colouring, rhythmic composition and more emotional feeling. What little of his work survives is to be seen in the Troitsa-Sergios-Lavra monastery, now a museum, near Moscow, which contains his masterpiece, the *Holy Trinity*.

Rubrics (Latin *ruber*, red), rules and directions for the conduct of divine service given in the service books of the Christian Church. They are so called because they were originally written or printed in red.

Rubus, a genus of shrubs and herbs of the family Rosaceae. *R. chamaemorus* is the herbaceous cloudberry, the remaining species being mostly woody plants with more or less spiny stems. The pink-flowered *R. spectabilis*, native to North America, is grown for its flowers; other species are grown mainly for their fruits. The raspberry (*R. idaeus*) and the Japanese wineberry (*R. phoenicolasius*) are closely related; the loganberry (*R. loganobaccus*) is derived from a hybrid between a type of raspberry and a form of blackberry. Blackberries are forms of *R. fruticosus*. The dewberry is *R. caesius*.

Ruby, precious stone of corundum, and thus of the same composition as sapphire, except for the substance, chromium, causing the red coloration. It crystallises in the hexagonal system, has a range of colour from pink to deep red or violet, has a specific gravity of 4, and a hardness of 9. Star rubies have a six-rayed star formed by internal reflection from sets of needle-like inclusions and are highly prized. True or oriental rubies are found in greatest quantity in Burma and Thailand, also in Sri Lanka and Afghanistan.

Rudaceous Rocks, coarse-grained sedimentary rocks, usually of restricted extent. Rudites are divided into breccia, where the component fragments are angular, and conglomerate, where they are rounded.

Rudbeckia, a genus of the Compositae from North America. *R. hirta*, black-eyed Susan, and *R. laciniata*, cone flower, are popular garden species.

Rudd, or red eye, a freshwater fish, *Scardinius erythrophthalmus*, allied to the roach and belonging to the order Cypriniformes. It is tinged with bronze, and has reddish fins, the dorsal being farther back than that of the roach. It is found in European lakes and sluggish streams. The largest are over 1 kg and may be as much as 45 cm long.

Rude, François (1784–1855), French sculptor. Between 1815 and 1827, he made himself a career as an architectural sculptor in Brussels. After returning to Paris, his Neapolitan *Fisherboy* won him acclaim, but his masterpiece is the colossal relief *Le Départ des Volontaires de 1792*, better known as *La Marseillaise*, on the Arc de Triomphe.

Rudolf I (1218–91), German king and Holy Roman Emperor. He succeeded his father as head of the family in 1239, and having become the most powerful prince in the country, was elected king of the Germans in 1273. He is chiefly memorable as the founder of the greatness of the house of Hapsburg.

Rudolf II (1552–1612), Holy Roman Emperor, King of Bohemia and of Hungary. Rudolf became emperor in 1576. Personally mild and withdrawn, Rudolf was unable to restrain the growing religious extremism of the period. There was a Turkish invasion in 1593, and a Hungarian rebellion in 1604. In 1606 the Archduke pronounced Rudolf unfit to rule, and in 1608 Rudolf ceded to his brother, Matthias, all his territories except Bohemia, Lusatia and Silesia. He was compelled to abdicate the throne of Bohemia in favour of Matthias in 1611. An enigmatic monarch, addicted to occult sciences such as alchemy and astrology, Rudolf amassed the finest art collection of his age.

Rudolf, Franz Karl Joseph (1858–89), Archduke and Crown Prince of Austria-

Hungary, only son of the Emperor Francis Joseph. He was a good linguist and keen traveller, and besides assisting in the publication of *Die Österreichische-Ungarische Monarchie in Wort und Bild*, 1886, he wrote *A Journey in the East*, 1884, and *Fifteen Days on the Danube*, 1885. He married Stephanie, daughter of the King of the Belgians, in 1881; the marriage was a failure, and Rudolf committed suicide with his mistress, a Baroness Vetsera, in circumstances which have never been fully clarified, at Mayerling near Vienna.

Rudolf, Lake, see TURKANA, LAKE.

Rue, or herb of grace, the hardy evergreen shrub, *Ruta graveolens*, of the Rutaceae, containing a volatile, acrid oil once used medicinally as a narcotic and stimulant. Goat's rue is *Galega officinalis*, a member of the Leguminosae; meadow rue is *Thalictrum flavum* (Ranunculaceae).

Ruff, frill made from linen or lawn and worn on top of the neckband, popular with both sexes in the 16th and 17th centuries.

Ruff, *Philomachus pugnax*, is a member of the bird family Scolopacidae that breeds in an area stretching from north-western Europe to the Bering Straits. The males (ruffs) vary considerably in plumage, but during the breeding season the neck is surrounded by a ruff or frill of purple-black feathers barred with chestnut, which falls at the end of June. The females (reeves) have no ruff; they lay four spotted green eggs in a nest of coarse grass made amongst reeds or rushes.

Ruffe, or pope, the perch-like fish *Acerina cernua*. It is a species of family Percidae in order Perciformes, is edible and inhabits the fresh water of Europe. The dorsal fin is continuous in the ruffe, whereas in the perch there are two separate fins.

Rufus, William, see WILLIAM III.

Rug, see CARPET.

Rugby, town in Warwickshire, England, situated on the River Avon 19 km south-east of Coventry and 132 km north-west of London. Rugby expanded with the advent of the London and Birmingham railway in 1838. It is an important railway centre and market town with electrical and engineering industries, though it is probably most famous for Rugby School. The manufacture of Portland cement is a considerable local industry. Population (1981) 59,564.

Rugby League, see FOOTBALL.

Rubgy Union Football, see FOOTBALL.

Rügen, island in the Baltic Sea, separated from the Mecklenburg coast of the German Democratic Republic by the Strela Sound (2 km wide). Since 1936 it has been connected with Stralsund on the mainland by a causeway. The soil is fertile, cattle are reared, and there are fisheries. The capital is Bergen. Area 966 km^2; population (1970) 90,000.

Ruggles, Carl (1876–1971), US composer and painter. Most of his music was produced between 1920 and the mid-1940s, after which he gave his attention to painting. His music is marked by atonal harmony, intense declamatory melodies and sinuous polyphony. His works include *Sun-treader* for orchestra, *Angels* for brass ensemble and four *Evocations* for piano.

Ruhr, river in the Federal Republic of Germany, which rises near Winterberg at the eastern boundary of North Rhine-Westphalia, and flows north and west to enter the Rhine at Duisburg. Length 239 km. The Ruhr basin (German *Ruhrgebiet*) is one of the most important areas of heavy industry in Europe, due mainly to its extremely rich coalfield. The chief cities in the basin are Essen, Bochum, Dortmund, Duisburg, Recklinghausen and Gelsenkirchen. The greater part of the country's production of coal, iron and steel is in the area.

Ruisdael, Jacob van, also Ruysdael (1628/9–82), greatest of Dutch landscape painters. He developed a style in which drama and intensity of mood take over from the tradition of atmospheric purity. Ruisdael expressed the power and majesty of nature against which man is powerless. His influence was enormous in Holland and elsewhere, and he had many imitators, the most distinguished being his pupil, Hobbema. Typical examples of his work are the *Jewish Cemetery*, c.1660 (Dresden) and *Landscape with a Castle and Church*, c.1668 (National Gallery).

Ruff, Philomachus pugnax.

Ruiz, Juan (c.1283–c.1351), Spanish poet, known as the Archpriest of Hita. Little is known of his life except that he was imprisoned between 1333 and 1347 by order of the Archbishop of Toledo for a breach of ecclesiastical regulations. The *Libro de buen amor*, a remarkable work by which Ruiz is remembered, consists of narrative poems of varying length, interspersed with lyrical songs, fables and stories. The poems, written in an autobiographical style, describe love affairs, successful and otherwise.

Rule of Faith (*Regula Fidei*), short statements of belief which the early Christian Church put into the mouth of those about to be baptised, and which formed the safeguard and expression of the orthodox faith. They are the basis of the Catholic creeds.

Rule of Law, historically a British tradition. The rule of law limited the coercive powers of government by tying them to previously announced general rules which applied to everyone in given circumstances so that each person knew his rights and obligations and could order his life accordingly.
In modern times every enactment of the legislature is misnamed a law. But this conception of a 'law' is compatible with tyranny. Many modern so-called laws are merely orders to state officials concerning their administration of the machinery of government. This administrative law is not law in the 'rule of law' sense, because it is not general but particular, not equal but discriminatory, not certain but unpredictable. In a free society the citizen is subject to the coercion only of previously accepted, general, impersonal rules, and this constitutes the rule of law.

Rule of the Road, in shipping. In order to regulate the flow of traffic, and prevent collisions, an internationally recognised set of rules, known as the International Regulations for Preventing Collisions at Sea, is published and their observance is mandatory for all ships on the high seas. The regulations presently in force date from an International Safety of Life at Sea conference held in London in 1960; they came into force in 1965. A new set of regulations published in 1972 came into force in 1977.

Rum, probably derived from *rumbullion*, a Devon word for 'a great tumult', once known as Barbados Waters, a spirit which is a by-product of the manufacture of sugar from the sugar cane. It comes white from the still with a very high degree of alcohol. In the past the heavier dark rums which owed their colour to caramel were regarded as the typical rum, but of late lighter white rums have been taking their place both in their home, the West Indies, and elsewhere.

Rum, island off the west coast of the Highland Region of Scotland. It is owned by the Nature Conservancy Council and is managed as a national nature reserve. Population (1971) 40.

Rumania, see ROMANIA.

Rumelia (The land of the Romans), name given by the Turks to a district in the Balkan Peninsula corresponding to Thrace and part of Macedonia. Eastern Rumelia was made an autonomous province of Turkey by the Congress and Treaty of Berlin in 1878. In 1885, however, it was incorporated in Bulgaria, where it is now included in the provinces of Plovdiv, Khaskovo, Stara Zagora and Burgas.

Rumex, family Polygonaceae, a genus of about 200 species of annual, biennial and perennial herbs of temperate regions, including sorrel, with sour-tasting leaves, and dock, usually characterised by a deep tap-root.

Rumination, chewing the cud, a step in the digestive process of cattle, sheep, goats, deer, antelopes and giraffes, all members of the suborder Ruminantia of order Artiodactyla. Camels are also ruminants but have evolved separately from the Ruminantia for millions of years. These animals eat grass or leaves, swallowing the bulky food quickly, as they are always ready to flee from predators. The food enters the first stomach, the rumen or paunch, which is very large. Here the cellulose in the plant cell walls is broken down by bacteria and protozoa (microscopic organisms). Later the animal brings it up again, as the cud, which it chews thoroughly, then swallows into the second stomach, the reticulum, from which it moves on through the third and fourth stomachs, the omasum and abomasum, being further digested at each stage.

Rummy, card game for several persons, and having a large number of variations. Each player attempts to obtain, from the hand dealt to him, and from the pack, certain scoring combinations, either of the same denomination (e.g. three or more kings) or in sequence of the same suit (e.g. five, six, seven of hearts). Sets and sequences are usually declared during play; first out wins. The game is descended from Mah Jong. The technique required to become a good player is very similar.
See also CARDS, PLAYING.

Rump Parliament, see LONG PARLIAMENT.

Runch, see CHARLOCK.

Runcorn, town in Cheshire, England, on the south bank of the Mersey on the Manchester Ship Canal. Here too, the Bridgewater Canal reaches the Mersey, but that is of more historic than current economic significance. The chemical industry is dominant though a wider range of manufacturing is desired, since Runcorn has been expanded in Runcorn New Town. Population (1981) 64,391.

Rundstedt, Karl Rudolph Gerd von (1875–1953), German soldier. He was recalled at the outbreak of war in 1939, and was made commander-in-chief East and military governor of Poland. Before the end of 1939 he took over the command of Army Group A in the West. In 1941 he resumed command in the East before retiring on grounds of ill health. In March 1942 he was recalled to become commander-in-chief West, an appointment he was still holding when the Allied landings took place in June 1944. He continued to serve until March 1945.

Runeberg, Johan Ludvig (1804–77), Finnish poet who wrote in Swedish. He founded the *Helsingfors Morgonblad* (1832), contributing to it many of his poems and tales. Among his finest works are the idylls *Elgskyttarne*, 1832; *Hanna*, 1836; *Julqvällen*, 1841; and romances *Nadeschda*, 1841; and *King Fjalar*, 1844 (*King Fialar*, 1912). His epic *Fänrik Ståls Sägner*, 1848, 1860 (*The Songs of Ensign Stål*, 1925), dealing with the Swedo-Russian War, is perhaps his most famous work, and the prefatory 'Vårt Land' was adopted as Finland's national hymn.

Runes (term connected with the old Germanic root *ru-* and the Gothic *runa*, meaning mystery, secret, secrecy), ancient script which may be considered as the 'national' writing of the pre-Christian Germanic tribes. Although in limited use, runes lingered for a long time after the introduction of Christianity, and their use for charms and memorial inscriptions lasted into the 16th century. The origin of the name is probably due to the fact that, like most primitive peoples, the Germanic peoples of northern Europe, Britain, Scandinavia and Iceland attributed magic powers to the mysterious written symbols.

Running events are generally divided into sprinting, middle-distance and long-distance running. Other running events include cross-country running and relay races.
Strictly speaking, sprinting means running at top speed, but scientifically this is possible only over a short distance, around 20 m. But for practical purposes, sprinting can be said to apply to all races up to 400 m. Middle-distance running applies from 800 up to 5000 m, though the enormous improvement in records up to 10,000 m has led many to classify this latter event as middle-distance. The most popular long-distance event is the Marathon, over 42,195 m (26 miles 385 yards), though world records are also accepted for various distances up to 30,000 m. In races up to 400 m, competitors have to keep to their own lanes which are 1·22 m wide. The first 100 m of an 800-m race is also run in separate lanes.
Sprinting. In sprint races (and hurdling) the start is all-important. Sprinters used to dig starting holes in the track for a crouch start, but in 1929 an American 'invented' starting blocks which were fixed to the track and gave a more rigid start. The winner is the runner whose 'torso' first reaches the edge of the finish line.
Middle-distance. In addition to the events included in the Olympic Games, races are held over 1000, 3000, 20,000, 25,000 and 30,000 m and also occasionally over 1, 2, 3, 6 and 15 miles. With the exception of the 1 mile, no world records are now recognised for imperial distances. In the Olympics, 800 m is the longest race run by women.
Marathon Race. It was included in the first modern Olympic meeting in 1896, when it was run from the plains of Marathon to the newly-constructed marble stadium in the heart of Athens. The race was to commemorate the mythical story that after the Battle of Marathon in 490 BC, a courier, Pheidippides, ran from the field of battle to Athens (a distance of about 40 km), announced that the Athenians had defeated the Persians and then dropped dead.
Cross-country. One of the oldest forms of running. British Cross-country Championships, a Senior Race of 9 miles (14·48 km), a Junior of 6 miles (9·6 km) and one for Youths of 4 miles (6·43 km) takes place, with over 2000 competitors in all participating. Similar races are held for women.
Relay Races. The most practised events are the two men's and two women's events included in the Olympic Games—4 × 100 and 4 × 400 m. The former is run in lanes, while in the latter the first 500 m are run in lanes. A tubular baton 30 cm long and weighing 50 g must be carried throughout the race and must be passed from one runner to the next within a 20-m take-over zone.
See also HURDLING; STEEPLECHASING.

Runnymede, or Runnimede, meadow of the Thames, near Egham, Surrey, England, where the barons forced King John to seal the Magna Carta on 15 June 1215.

Runyon, (Alfred) Damon (1884–1946), US author and humorist. He was a war correspondent and then a columnist, but made his name in short-story writing. He gave unique, grotesque portrayals of the types of New York's underworld, using all the resources of American slang to add humour and colour to his situations. His books include *Guys and Dolls*, 1932; *Blue Plate Special*, 1934; and *Money from Home*, 1935.

Rupert of Bavaria, Prince (1619–82), known as 'Rupert of the Rhine'. In 1642 he was appointed General of the Horse in the English Royalist army by his uncle, Charles I, and soon proved himself a brilliant, if impetuous and often impatient, cavalry leader. He served at Edgehill, Chalgrove Field, took Bristol, and raised the sieges of Newark and York. Then, in July 1644, he was utterly defeated at Marston Moor and in 1645 at Naseby. After the death of Charles I he gained command of a small squadron of English ships loyal to the new king, and from 1639 to 1652 acted as part admiral, part buccaneer.
He commanded at sea during the Second Dutch War of 1664–67 and was appointed to the Board of Admiralty during the Third Dutch War.

Rupture, see HERNIA.

Rural Dean, ecclesiastical officer whose duty it is to assist the bishop by supervising parts of the diocese. The office was revived in the Church of England and its duties considerably extended during the 19th century. The rural dean presides over a ruridecanal chapter of the clergy, and since 1970 over a Deanery Synod of clergy and lay delegates.

Rurik (Russian *Ryurik*) (d.879), semi-legendary founder of the Russian ruling house of Rurikidae. He was leader of a Varangian (Scandinavian) band of warriors, and from 862 sat as prince in Novgorod. Rurik's successor, Oleg, founded the great Kievan state.

Ruscus, see BUTCHER'S BROOM.

Ruse (Turkish *Rushchuk*), town of north-east Bulgaria, capital of Ruse province, on the right bank of the River Danube (opposite Giurgiu), 241 km north-east of Sofia. It dates from Roman times, and was destroyed by the barbarians in the 7th century. It was rebuilt on a site some 25 km to the south, but in the 17th century, under the Turks, again developed on its original site. Metal goods, textiles, foodstuffs, furniture, leather and chemicals are manufactured and there is an oil refinery. Population (1978) 168,700.

Rush, name generally given to members of the family Juncaceae, but sometimes also used for other narrow-leaved plants, especially members of the Cyperaceae. Rush basketry is usually made from *Scirpus lacustris*, flowering rush is *Butomus*. Rushes are cosmopolitan in distribution and frequent damp localities.

Rush Nut, see CYPERUS.

Rushmore, Mount, in the Black Hills of South Dakota, USA, 40 km south-west of Rapid City, out of which the heads of four US presidents, George Washington, Thomas Jefferson, Abraham Lincoln and Theodore Roosevelt, have been sculpted to a height of about 18 m. The project was first begun in 1927, but was not completed until 1941, after six and a half years' of work. The site is a national memorial and a popular tourist attraction.

Rusk, Dean (1909–), US politician and scholar. He joined the State Department in 1946. From 1952 to 1961 he was president of the Rockefeller Foundation, but returned to the state department to become secretary of state to Kennedy in 1961, retaining this post under Johnson.

Ruskin, John (1819–1900), English author, art critic and artist. He first became widely known in 1843, when he published the first volume of *Modern Painters*, in which he came forward with a defence and appreciation of Turner. The second volume, published in 1846, attracted even wider attention. The third and fourth volumes appeared in 1856, and the fifth and last in 1860. In 1848 he married Euphemia Chalmers Gray. In 1855 his wife obtained a decree of nullity in an undefended suit and married Millais. He wrote and illustrated *The Seven Lamps of Architecture* in 1849, and *The Stones of Venice*, 1851–53, which established him as the leading authority on architecture as well as art. During 1854–59 he taught drawing at the Working Men's College, Red Lion Square (and persuaded Rossetti to do likewise), and produced *The Elements of Drawing*, 1857. During 1858–69 he taught at Winnington, a girls' school in Cheshire, and produced his controversial essays on economics for the *Cornhill Magazine* (subsequently issued as *Unto This Last*, 1862). Under the headings of education and political economy he wrote *Sesame and Lilies*, 1865, *The Ethics of the Dust*, 1866, and *The Crown of Wild Olive*, 1866. He was first Slade professor of Fine Art at Oxford from 1870 to 1879 and he again occupied the chair from 1883 to 1885. From 1885 he published from time to time *Praeterita*, an autobiography which, however, was never completed.

Russelia, a small genus of evergreens, of the Scrophulariaceae, of which *R. juncea*, the coral plant, and *R.* × *lemoinei* are grown for their pendant scarlet, tubular flowers.

Russell, Bertrand Arthur William, 3rd Earl (1872–1970), British philosopher, second son of John, Viscount Amberley, and grandson of the first Earl, Lord John Russell, the Victorian prime minister. In 1895 he became a Fellow of Trinity College, and in 1903 he published *Principles of Mathematics*. Together with A. N. Whitehead he wrote *Principia Mathematica*, 1910–13, in which he tried to establish his view that mathematics can be reduced to a branch of logic and derived from a few basic axioms. When the First World War broke out, Russell, an outspoken pacifist, was deprived of the lectureship he had held at Trinity since 1910. He was eventually reinstated at Trinity in 1944. A Fellow of the Royal Society from 1908, in 1949 he became an honorary Fellow of the British Academy and was awarded the Order of Merit. In 1950 he won the Nobel Prize for literature. In his later years he campaigned for unilateral nuclear disarmament, supporting civil disobedience as a method of agitation (for which he went briefly to prison in 1961), and also against US involvement in Vietnam.

As a philosopher, Russell took up a whole series of positions but always retained the same general critical approach, inspired by mathematics: the method of building up knowledge from basic elements that are as reliable as possible, with the help of the smallest possible number of basic assumptions.

Russell's writings on education, ethics and politics had a great impact, particularly in the 1930s, but are not of the same calibre as his work in logic and epistemology.

Russell, George William, see 'Æ'.

John Ruskin. *A water-colour by von Herkomer, painted in 1879.*

Russell, Henry Norris (1877–1957), US astronomer. At Princeton, where he was the director of the university observatory from 1912 to 1947, Russell worked on many aspects of astronomy, including the photometry of eclipsing binaries, stellar evolution, and the interpretation of celestial and laboratory spectra. He first plotted the relationship between the absolute magnitude of a star and its spectral type, which clearly showed the existence of giant and dwarf stars, about 1913, confirming what Hertzsprung had already deduced. This plot or its variations, now known as the H-R, or Hertzsprung-Russell diagram, is still the cornerstone of theories of stellar evolution.

See also ASTRONOMY.

Russell, John Russell, 1st Earl (1792–1878), British statesman. He entered Parliament as a Whig, and was an ardent supporter of reform. When Melbourne came into power in 1835 he was home secretary. He led the Opposition against Peel, and when Peel retired in 1846 he formed an administration. In 1852 he was defeated and resigned, but accepted a seat in Aberdeen's Cabinet. He was created Earl Russell in 1861, and four years later, on the death of Palmerston, again became prime minister, but held office for only a few months, resigning when his reform bill failed.

Russell, Ken (1927–), British film director. He worked as a free-lance photographer, 1951–57, before becoming a television film director for the BBC, 1958–66. *Elgar*, *Debussy*, *Isadora Duncan* and other film biographies made his name, though their mannered, semi-fictionalised treatment gave rise to the criticism that they lacked real substance. Since leaving the BBC Russell has made films for the cinema which are also visual tours-de-force: *Women in Love*, after D. H. Lawrence; *The Music Lovers*, on the life of Tchaikovsky; *The Devils*, after Huxley's *Devils of Loudun*; the musical *The Boyfriend*; *Tommy*; *Mahler*; *Lisztomania*; and *Altered States*.

Russell, Lord William (1639–83), English politician. After the Restoration he entered Parliament and was soon regarded as one of the main opponents of court policy. Becoming entangled with the Rye House conspirators, he was, on very flimsy evidence, found guilty of treason and beheaded. The Whigs came to regard him as a martyr for religious and civil liberty.

Russell, Sir William Howard (1820–1907), British journalist. Having joined the staff of *The Times*, he was sent as war correspondent to the Crimea. His letters from there caused a profound sensation, and led to improvements in army conditions. In describing the battle of Balaklava he used the phrase 'thin red line', which has become a classic expression.

Russia, colloquial name of pre-1917 Russian Empire and present USSR.

See also RUSSIAN SOVIET FEDERATED SOCIALIST REPUBLIC; UNION OF SOVIET SOCIALIST REPUBLICS.

Russian Architecture. The story of Russian architecture begins in 988, when Vladimir I, Grand Duke of Kiev, was converted to Christianity. At first, architects and craftsmen had to be sent to Constantinople to be trained, and naturally they brought back the Byzantine style. At Kiev, their finest buildings were the Cathedral of St Sophia (1036, now much altered in appearance), the Lavra (1073), St Michael (1070) and the Monastery of the Caves. The chief examples from the next century were the cathedral of the Mizhorski Monastery at Pskov; and the churches of the Intercession at Nerl and of the Saviour at Nereditsa. Domes were largely used, often from 5 to 20 on a single church, and were of the characteristic Russian onion-shape.

There was no architecture of note in Moscow until 1477, when Italian architects and craftsmen were imported to rebuild the Cathedral of the Dormition. Other Italians designed the Palace of Facets, and rebuilt or remodelled the Kremlin in 1485–92, producing a picturesque medley. In most churches of the 16th century the Russian plan, with numerous domes, continued to be followed.

When the new city of St Petersburg (later Leningrad) was founded by Peter the Great in 1703, the architects chiefly employed were the Russian Zemtsov, the Italians Trezzini and Michetti, the German Schädel and the Frenchman Le Blond. The style of the lay-out and of the buildings followed Renaissance rather than Byzantine tradition; and under Elizabeth (1714–62) the leading architects in St Petersburg were Italians. Her successor, Catherine the Great, likewise employed an Italian, Quarenghi, as well as the Russians Bazhenov, Kazakof and Starov.

As in eastern Europe, there was a 'Greek Revival' during the first quarter of the 19th century, and revived classicism persisted up to the middle of that century. Zakharov's Admiralty in St Petersburg (1806) is the most distinguished surviving Neoclassical building.

At the time of the Revolution young architects were following the leaders of the 'Suprematist' and 'Constructivist' artistic movements, and the new 'Modern Architecture' was at first given official encouragement, with El Lissitzky, Tatlin and Vesnin producing the advanced architectural concepts of the twenties. In 1932 national classicism triumphed, a situation which lasted until the sixties. Recent buildings vary in style from the stark and advanced 'functional' architecture of western Europe to a vague striving after a new and distinctive national style.

Russian Art. *Icon painting.* The early 11th- and 12th-century icons were essentially Byzantine in inspiration and limited in colour, whereas in the next two centuries, brilliant colours are a quality of the icons of the Novgorod school, which gradually evolved an individual style. The art reached its zenith before the end of the 14th century in the work of Andrei Rublyov, and for a century or more his influence was predominant.

Painting. Despite the founding of an academy in 1754 by Catherine the Great, court patronage of painting continued to be given chiefly to foreign painters. In the 18th century Russian painting was devoted almost solely to portraiture. The leading Russian exponents were D. G. Levitski and his pupil Y. L. Borovikovski. Venetsianov evolved his own naturalistic style as a genre painter. His pupil Aleksiev, the first Russian landscape painter of any real note, is outstanding as a colourist. Italian art strongly influenced Russian art in the early 19th century, as is shown in the work of Brülov and Ivanov, especially in portraiture and in religious studies. It was not until Savva Mamontov, in the 1870s, assembled on his Moscow estates the group of artists later known as 'the Wanderers', that Russian artists attempted any union with their culture. Like the Pre-Raphaelites in England, they sought a closer link with their craft heritage, making furniture and household objects. The leading spirits were the sculptor Antokolsky and the painter Vassily Polenov. However, it was left to Mikhail Vrubel to indicate the future direction of Russian art.

Towards the end of the 19th century Russian art in most spheres was influenced by modernism and impressionism. In 1899 began the brilliant phase of Russian ballet design, in which the names of A. Benois, Léon Bakst and Serge Diaghilev are eminent. The period 1910–18 shows a constant shifting of groups, all dominated by a desire for entirely abstract, non-representational art. Major figures were El Lissitzky and Rodchenko. The artist most totally committed to abstract painting was Kasimir Malevich, founding the 'Suprematist' school.

Russian Architecture. *The Orthodox church in Yalta, with characteristic onion domes.*

For a brief period following the Revolution, these artists gained control of the art schools. Their ideas then travelled from Russia with Lissitzky and Naum Gabo when the communist party decreed a return to social realism in art. Some artists rejected painting entirely —Tatlin turning to architecture. The period (1922–27) was marked by the formation of groups of painters seeking a new style, such as the Association of Russian Revolutionary Artists (ARRA) whose members depicted themes from the revolution. Since then, however, Soviet art has been dominated by an academic and backward-looking approach to subjects from Revolutionary history.

Although working mainly in France and Germany, the work of Marc Chagall, a Russian Jew, must be mentioned, since his subjects were taken from Russian life and folklore, but with a fantasy far removed from the spirit of Soviet art.

Goldsmiths' and Silversmiths' Work. Russian goldsmiths' and silversmiths' work is remarkable for richness of colour through enamelling and liberal use of jewels. Peter Carl Fabergé (1846–1920) was the most renowned of Russian goldsmiths. The Imperial Easter Eggs and other pieces he produced for the Court are among the most exquisite of all goldsmith's work.

Sculpture. The art of sculpture was frowned upon in the Orthodox Church as savouring of idolatory. It was not until the importation of Western ideas in the 18th century that there came about a spirit of toleration. The earliest notable Russian sculptor was Count Carlo Rastrelli (d.1744). As representatives of the classic period may be mentioned Shchedrin (d.1825), a versatile sculptor of statues, monuments and bas-reliefs, whose dynamic statue of Marsyas is in the Academy of Fine Arts (Leningrad); and Gordiev and Prokofiev. Among sculptors of the 19th century whose works reveal a naturalistic vein are Kamenski, Antokolski and Troubetskoy.

The main direction of Soviet sculpture since the revolution has been towards the creation of monumental works depicting episodes arising from the conflict between the Bolsheviks and the 'White' Russians.

Russian Federal Republic, see RUSSIAN SOVIET FEDERATED SOCIALIST REPUBLIC.

Russian History. The first Russian states arose in Transcaucasia and Central Asia (Khorezm, Sogdiana) in the 9th–6th centuries BC. The northern shores of the Black Sea was another early scene of political developments, populated in succession by Kimmerians and Scythians and later colonised by the Greeks and Romans. In the first century AD the Black Sea steppes were invaded from the west by Goths and from the east by Huns. There were three early centres of political consolidation among the eastern Slavs. In the 9th century the northern centre fell to the Vikings, who founded a state with its capital at Kiev. This fell under Byzantine cultural influence and in 988 embraced Christianity. Less than a century later it began to split up. In 1236 the Mongol armies appeared on the Volga and one by one conquered the disunited Russian principalities, except Novgorod. The Russian princes became vassals of the 'Golden Horde', under Batu Khan. During the 14th century most western and southern principalities escaped Tatar domination and passed under a new power, the Grand Duchy of Lithuania, which had been founded in the mid-13th century. Within the territory still retained by the Horde, the principality retained by Moscow expanded and defeated the Tatars in 1380. It continued to absorb its neighbours and rivals and finally proclaimed the unification of all Russian lands as its official programe. Alongside the external growth of the Muscovite state went its internal consolidation. The feudal traditions and the power of the Boyars were stamped out by the new coalition of monarchy and the lower gentry. Ivan IV, the Terrible, who assumed the title of Tsar of all Russia, pursued this policy with cruelty.

There followed a 15-year period of near anarchy, civil war and foreign invasion, known as the Time of Troubles, which ceased with the establishment of the House of Romanov in 1613. The Romanovs continued the policies of their predecessors. In 1694 Zemsky Sobor passed a code of law that established peasant serfdom. A new epoch in Russian history begins with Peter the Great, who transformed the old Muscovite state into a westernised empire, which participated in European diplomacy and extended its territories in the west and south to include the Baltic Provinces and the Black Sea shores. In the 19th century, the quest for reform was strong and widespread. The Reign of Alexander II was the time of the Great Reform, which began with the emancipation of the serfs in 1861. The next two reigns were filled with efforts by the monarchy to reassert the principle of autocracy in the face of the growth in the working-class and the beginning of the labour movement. In this environment the first political parties were perforce semi-conspiratorial, illegal organisations.

The revolution of 1905 brought about a legislative Duma, elected by popular vote, with legal political parties and trade unions. But all these developments were cut short by the First World War, which exacerbated relations between the public, the court and the government. The bloodless February Revolution of 1917 was welcomed by almost everyone, but the democratically minded Provisional Government was unequal to the task of building a new state, particularly in the face of opposition from the Bolsheviks.

See further under UNION OF SOVIET SOCIALISTS REPUBLICS, *History*.

Russian Language. Russian is the most important language of the Slavonic branch of the Indo-European group of languages, and belongs, with Belorussian and Ukrainian, to the eastern group of the Slavonic subdivision of the Balto-Slavonic branch.

Russian is the chief language of the USSR, and is spoken by the most numerous of the Slavonic peoples, the Great Russians, numbering over 114,000,000.

The Russian alphabet, known as Cyrillic, consists of 33 letters.

See also UNION OF SOVIET SOCIALIST REPUBLICS.

Russian Literature. The conversion to Christianity marks the real beginnings of Russian literature, though there was a rich oral folklore tradition which continued to evolve until the 19th century. In spite of Church disapproval, it provided the main form of culture for most Russian people, who were illiterate. It is now considered to be in decline.

Early Russian literature was primarily ecclesiastical and didactic—literate people were usually clerics. From the middle of the 11th century the dominant theme is the call for political unity, as in the magnificent epic *Lay of the Host of Igor*, 1187. Historical literature revived as a result of the rise of Muscovy and defeat of the Tatars at Kulikovo Pole in 1380. Simultaneously, a religious revival sparked off developments in ecclesiastical prose.

The 16th century was marked by ecclesiastical and secular polemic. In the 17th century, the old system of literature broke down. Writers turned to folklore for inspiration and began to write primarily for entertainment.

In the late 17th century Muscovite intellectual life was greatly influenced by Ukrainian clerics from Kiev, who were acquainted with European Baroque and medieval Western literature through their contacts with Poland. They introduced the theatre and formal verse into Russia.

Modern Russian literature began in the 18th century when the Classicist school adopted French classical standards and began to regulate literary Russian. Successive Western influence brought to Russia two new literary trends which partly overlapped with the later Classicism. The Sentimental school was headed in Russia by Nikolai Karamzin; the Romantic by Vasili Zhukovski.

With Pushkin Russian literature emerged from its apprenticeship and achieved maturity. His highest achievements, both in verse and prose, offered later writers models of form, content (realistic treatment of everyday subjects) and language which was pruned of artificiality and cliché.

With the advent of Realism, prose replaced poetry as the main form of literary expression and literature was increasingly obliged to reflect social problems. The novel emerged as the principal genre. Turgenev and Goncharov both dealt with social problems in their novels, though each maintained his artistic independence.

Several prose writers of outstanding talent rebelled against the rather limited view of the need for social criticism in art. Tolstoi transcended the limits of social realism and, by facing his heroes not only with their environment but also with themselves, posed moral dilemmas and philosophical questions. Dostoevski went further in the development of the novel of ideas, confronting his characters and readers with spiritual problems, and rejecting conventional realism for a world that reflects the inner struggles of his characters.

On the eve of the new century the reaction against social demands on literature developed into a frontal attack by the Symbolists, who revived poetry, enriching its techniques and seeking in their verse an ultimate reality beyond everyday phenomena. The Symbolists were soon confronted by two new trends, the Acmeists, who rejected their vagueness and mysticism in favour of clarity and precision, and the Futurists, who rejected traditional poetic diction for a new expressive language of poetry.

During the Civil War that followed the Revolution, many writers emigrated. In Russia, most writers felt that they had a responsibility to create literary forms appropriate to the new age, though their degree of adherence to communism, and attitude to literary experimentation, varied. Purely proletarian writers were few and the organisations set up to promote them of little influence before 1929. Mayakovski and the Futurists fostered the avant-garde in literature since in their view it was appropriate to the revolutionary regime, and the Constructivist poets strove for techniques that would match their revolutionary and industrial subject matter. But many writers were less committed, some belonging to the group called the Serapion Brothers who believed in the independence of literature from politics.

During Stalin's 'revolution from above'—the first Five-Year Plan and the Collectivisation of Agriculture—the Association of Proletarian Writers assumed a quasi-dictatorial position in the field of letters, but in 1932 it was abolished by Party decree, together with all the other literary associations, and a single Union of Soviet Writers was established whose members were soon committed to the official conformity of Socialist Realism.

The atmosphere was somewhat relaxed during the Second World War: some poets, such as Pasternak and Akmatova, were permitted to publish. In 1946, however, Party control was re-established in an even more oppressive form, rendering the years 1946 to 1953 practically sterile. Only after Stalin's death did a 'thaw' occur. The works of proscribed authors, both living and dead, began to appear in print, though often after considerable delay, for the doctrine of Socialist Realism has never been revoked, and the cultural climate has fluctuated between relative liberalism and repression.

Criticism of Stalinism was initially discreet, but became increasingly overt and has extended to fundamental criticisms of the system, thanks to the illegal circulation of manuscripts (*samizdat*) and publication abroad (*tamizdat*). The authorities responded by forcing offending figures to emigrate. The effect of this on Soviet literature must inevitably be detrimental.

Russian Music. Apart from the traditional music of the Greek Church and a rich and varied folk-art, Russia made no significant contribution to music before the 19th century. Italian opera had been introduced by the court, and during the reign of Catherine II (1762–94), herself the author of librettos, Italian composers produced operas in Russia by invitation. The Napoleonic invasion of 1812 was followed by a great artistic revival, led by the poet and dramatist Pushkin; in Russia the connection between music and letters has always been close, and Russian music received a significant boost.

The first Russian composer of distinction was Glinka, whose operas *A Life for the Tsar*, 1836, and *Russlan and Ludmilla*, 1842, are landmarks. Glinka's conscious nationalism was extended by Dargomyzhski and by the St Petersburg group known as the Five: Balakirev, Cui, Borodin, Rimsky-Korsakov and Mussorgski. None of these was a professional composer by training. The leader and mentor of the group was Balakirev, who in 1862 founded the Free School of Music at St Petersburg in opposition to the conventional teaching of the official conservatories. Rimsky-Korsakov wrote the first Russian symphony while a midshipman on a naval cruise. Of the Five, Mussorgski had most genius and least training; his opera *Boris Godunov* has deeply influenced modern music.

The leading composer in Moscow was Tchaikovsky, whose style, though not without a national strain, was more influenced by the cosmopolitan Western tradition. His successors Taneyev, Arensky and Rachmaninov followed the cosmopolitan line. Glazunov wrote symphonies and chamber music in the traditional idiom. A more eccentric course was steered by Scriabin, who aimed at a synthesis of all the arts.

Early in the 20th century Russian national opera and ballet achieved world-wide fame and influence through the activities of the impresario Diaghilev; but the creative tradition was shattered by the revolution of 1917. Many composers took refuge in exile, including Rachmaninov, Glazunov, Medtner and Stravinsky. Stravinsky's early ballets have a strongly Russian flavour; his later work is cosmopolitan, neoclassical and anti-romantic. Prokofiev, a prolific composer of much vivacity, was for some years in exile, but returned to Russia in 1934. During the Soviet era valuable work has been done in the collection of folk-music; but the exercise of political pressure on composers led to a decline of artistic standards. Shostakovich, whose first Symphony (1925) showed originality, was more than once censured by the authorities for 'anti-people formalism', but his talent proved strong enough to mature independently. Similar strictures were passed on Prokofiev, Myaskovsky, the Armenian Khachaturian, and others. The succeeding generation included journeymen such as Karaev and political opportunists such as Khrennikov; but the rise of a still younger generation, coupled with cautious admission of modern Western developments, has established some promising figures, notably Alfred Schnittke (1934–).

Russian Orthodox Church, see EASTERN ORTHODOX CHURCH.

Russian Revolution, see UNION OF SOVIET SOCIALIST REPUBLICS, *History*.

Russian Soviet Federated Socialist Republic (abbreviated RSFSR), official name of the largest, most populous and economically most important constituent republic of the USSR. It comprises most of the territory with predominantly Great Russian population—the larger part of European USSR, Siberia and the Far East. Its 16 autonomous republics take up only about one-quarter of its territory, the rest consists of other administrative units: six *krai*, 49 *oblasti*, five autonomous *oblasti*, and ten national *okruga*. In many respects the RSFSR is less of a separate entity than the smaller constituent republics, its institutions being identical with those of the

USSR or overshadowed by the latter. Area 17,075,400 km² (three-quarters of the USSR total); population (1980) 138,400,000, 55 per cent of the USSR total. Great Russians comprise 83 per cent, Tatars 3·7 per cent, and Ukrainians 2·6 per cent of the population.

Russian Wolfhound, see Borzoi.

Russo-Japanese War (1904–05), The essential cause of this war lay in the conflicting interests of Russia and Japan on the mainland of Asia. Russia sought a port in the Far East which would be free from ice. In 1896 it secured a lease of Port Arthur from China. In 1900 Russia extended its power over the Chinese province of Amur. Japan withdrew its minister from St Petersburg (26 January 1904), and within two days had landed troops at Chemulpo, and a day after defeated the Russian fleet at Port Arthur. Port Arthur surrendered. In October 1904 the Russian Baltic fleet had sailed to the Far East. It was surrounded on 27 May by the Japanese fleet in the straits of Tsushima and practically annihilated. This was the decisive battle of the war. In August terms of peace were arranged at Portsmouth, USA. Russian rights in Port Arthur and Dalny passed to the Japanese; Korea became a Japanese sphere of influence; Manchuria was evacuated by both armies and restored to China.

Rust, see Corrosion of Metals.

Rust Fungi, the Uredinales, a large and important order of fungi, comprising about 4500 species, all of which are obligate parasites of seed plants and ferns. The name rust refers to the appearance of the summer spores (uredospores), which are formed in tremendous numbers on the leaves or stems of the host. It is said to cause a reduction in the wheatcrop of North America and Australia of up to 50 per cent.

Rustication, in Roman and Renaissance architecture, a method of working external blocks of stone to produce an effect of massive strength, especially at the base of buildings. The margins of each block are usually chiselled smooth, with the centre panel projecting more or less roughly.

Rustless Steel, see Nickel.

Rutaceae, the citrus family, a family of about 100 genera and 800 species of dicotyledonous shrubs and trees, from Europe and Asia. The leaves are commonly evergreen and leathery in texture, oily and aromatic when crushed. Some species have thorns. The flowers usually have five or four sepals and petals, with stamens double the number of the petals. The fused carpels vary in number, and the fruit is of variable type, sometimes dry as in *Ruta* (rue), or a berry as in *Skimmia.* The most valuable products of the family are citrus fruits.

Ruth, the second of five of the 'Megilloth' or Festal 'Rolls', an anonymous Old Testament work of great beauty, giving an exquisite picture of life in the time of the Judges. The central figure is Ruth, a Moabitess, who by a Levirate marriage became the great-grandmother of Kind David and an ancestress of Christ. In the Jewish canon it is placed between the Song of Songs and the Lamentations, and in the Jewish ritual it is read on the Feast of Weeks or Pentecost.

Ruth, George Herman ('Babe') (1895–1948). American baseball player renowned for his prodigious home-run hitting and exuberant personality. He began his career as a pitcher and later became a batter. In 1919 he set a home-run record of 29 and beat it with 54 the next season. In 1927 he established a home-run record of 60. On retirement in 1935 he had collected a record total of 714 home-runs—a record which stood until 1974 when it was beaten by Hank Aaron.

Ruthenia, latinised form of the name 'Russia', sometimes used to denote an ethnological region of Central Europe chiefly in the Transcarpathi *oblast* of the Ukrainian SSR, USSR. It belonged to Czechoslovakia during 1918–39, was occupied by Hungary in 1939, and ceded to the USSR in 1945.

Ruthenium, metallic chemical element, symbol Ru, atomic number 44, atomic weight 101·07. It is found in platinum ore, and is usually obtained from the residues left when osmium is separated from osmiridium. It is a grey metal resembling platinum, has a relative density of 12, fuses in an electric arc, and has the power of absorbing gases.

Rutherford, Dame Margaret (1892–1972), British actress. She did not appear on the stage until 1925, at the Old Vic. She first came into prominence as Bijou Furse in *Spring Meeting,* 1938, and Miss Prism in *The Importance of Being Earnest,* 1939, in which she later played Lady Bracknell. Among her later successes were Madame Arcati in *Blithe Spirit,* 1941; Miss Evelyn Whitechurch in *The Happiest Days of Your Life,* 1948, in which she was also filmed; Mme Desmortes in *Ring Round the Moon,* 1950; Lady Wishfort in *The Way of the World,* 1952 and 1956; and Mrs Malaprop in *The Rivals,* 1966. She was an accomplished comedienne and had a successful film career.

Ernest Rutherford. *He won the Nobel Prize for chemistry in 1908.*

Rutherford of Nelson, New Zealand, Ernest Rutherford, 1st Baron (1871–1937), New Zealand physicist. After studying Hertzian waves his work on the radioactivity of uranium was developing when he accepted in 1898 the professorship of physics at McGill. During his nine years there he carried out great work on radioactivity and showed the corpuscular nature of alpha radiation. In 1907 he was appointed professor of physics at Manchester, where he developed, with Hans Geiger, the electrical method for counting alpha particles. In collaboration with T. D. Royds, he showed that alpha particles in which the positive charge had been neutralised were helium atoms. He determined the number of alpha particles in unit volume of gas, and the result, $2{\cdot}75 \times 10^{19}$ atoms per cm³, conformed to Avogadro's Law and provided a direct proof of the discrete nature of matter. In 1911 he made perhaps his greatest contribution to science by proposing that an atom consists of a massive central nucleus with a positive charge around which negatively charged electrons move in orbits. In the First World War he organised research on underwater acoustics to combat submarines, but in 1917 resumed his work on nuclear physics, attacking by new methods the problem of alpha-particle scattering. In 1919 he was elected Cavendish professor of experimental physics at Cambridge, and great improvements were made by his colleagues in experimental technique. In 1932 the disintegration of nuclei was accomplished for the first time by means of charged particles, and the properties of the neutron which Rutherford had predicted some 12 years previously were studied.

Rutherfordium, Rf, or kurchatovum, Ku, the names and symbols proposed for the chemical element with atomic number 104; the discovery and name have been under dispute. In 1964 at the Joint Institute for Nuclear Research, Dubna, USSR, it was announced that the element had been synthesised; the name proposed was kurchatovum, after Soviet scientist Igor Kurchatov. It was announced in 1969 at the Lawrence Radiation Laboratory, University of California, that the element had been identified, and the name rutherfordium, after Lord Rutherford, was proposed. The name has yet to be settled.

Ruthwell, village in Dumfries and Galloway Region of Scotland, 16 km south-east of Dumfries, noted for its 7th-century runic cross, decorated with carvings of scenes from the life of Christ and verses in runic characters in Old English from the contemporary poem *The Dream of the Rood.* Population (parish), (1971) 475.

Rutile, mineral consisting of titanium dioxide (TiO_2). It crystallises in the tetragonal system, and twinning phenomena are frequent. The crystals are normally reddish-brown with a specific gravity from 4·2 to 5·2, according to the amount of ferric oxide present; hardness 6½. Rutile has a widespread occurrence in igneous rocks, gneisses and schists. It also occurs as tiny needles in quartz and micas. Together with ilmenite and sphene it is a source of titanium, and is used for white paint pigment.

Rutland, midland county of England until amalgamated with Leicestershire in 1974. With an area of 39,000 ha, Rutland was the smallest county in England.

Ruwenzori, range of mountains on the borders of Uganda and Zaire. It was discovered by Stanley (1887–89), and has a length of 105 km with a breadth of about 48 km. The highest point is Mount Margherita (5119 m), this and other peaks having a permanent snow-cap. The range has been identified as Ptolemy's 'Mountains of the Moon'.

Ruysdael, Salomon van (1600/3–70), Dutch landscape painter. From early works of winter landscapes in the manner of Esaias van de Velde, he painted river and dune scenes like Jan van Goyen. After 1645 his landscapes became more monumental with tree masses filling the canvas. He preferred to paint actual places, but sometimes used combination motifs. Among his late works are winter skating scenes and also still-lifes. He was the uncle of Jacob van Ruisdael.

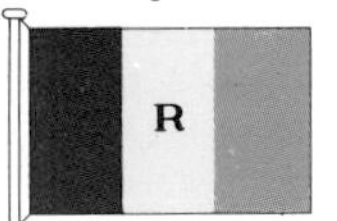

Rwanda
Area: 26,338km²
Population: 4,650,000
Capital: Kigali

Rwanda, small landlocked republic in Central Africa, bordered by Zaire, Uganda, Tanzania and Burundi. It was formed in 1962 on the break-up of the UN trust territory of Ruanda-Urundi administered by Belgium. Area 26,338 km^2.

The country lies astride the Zaire–Nile divide and is mainly mountainous. The highest peaks are volcanic, Karisimbi reaching 4507 m, but the rocks are mainly part of the old basement complex, tilted to form the eastern shoulder of the Great Rift Valley. Much of the valley floor is occupied by Lake Kivu which forms the western border of the country. The country is very densely settled, with an estimated population of 4,650,000 in 1978. The capital is at Kigali.

Agriculture is mainly at subsistence level with the major crops being sweet potatoes, cassava and sorghum. Coffee, tea and cotton are the main commercial crops. Livestock raising is widespread. 85 per cent of the population are dependent upon agriculture for their livelihood. Minerals found include tin ore, tungsten and gold. Natural gas reserves are beginning to be exploited. Manufacturing industry is mainly small scale, chiefly food processing.

The military coup, led by Major-General Juvénal Habyalimana in July 1973, meant constitutional revisions which included the dissolution of the Legislative Assembly with all power concentrated through a President (Habyalimana) no longer tied to a four-year term, and a military commission. The new constitutional direction was towards a more centralised form of government. After further constitutional revision in 1978 the President rules with a Council of Ministers.

French and the predominant native language, Kinyarwanda, are both in official use.

History. The pastoralist Batutsi moved into the area of present-day Rwanda over 400 years ago, and in the process established their dominance over the Bahutu people. The first European known to have reached Rwanda and Burundi was a German, Grad von Goetzen in 1894, the area subsequently being annexed as a German colony. During the First World War, Rwanda and Burundi passed into Belgian control, and after the war were administered jointly as a Belgian mandate under the League of Nations and later as a United Nations trusteeship. Only after 1957 did the current of nationalism and independence begin to influence Rwanda. After a brief but violent civil war in 1959 between the Batutsi and Bahutu factions, Rwanda achieved its independence in 1962. Since independence there has been continued tension and conflict between the dominant Bahutu and minority Batutsi communities, although the regime of Gen. Juvénal Habyalimana has attempted to remove the sources of conflict.

Ryazan (until 1778, *Pereyaslav-Ryazanski*), capital city, economic and cultural centre of Ryazan *oblast*, USSR, 2 km from the River Oka. There are engineering, oil-refining, food and light industries. It has been known since 1095 and was the capital of Ryazan principality from the early 14th century until 1521. Population (1980) 462,000.

Rybinsk (formerly *Shcherbakov*), city in Yaroslavl *oblast* of the RSFSR, USSR, on the Volga. It has engineering (printing machinery, road building equipment), shipbuilding, woodworking and food industries. The settlement has been known since the 12th century and its commercial development dates from the 16th. Before 1917 it was a centre of the grain and caviar trade of the Volga basin, visited during the summer by thousands of merchants. Population (1980) 241,000.

Rybinsk Reservoir, artificial lake in central USSR, created by a dam on the Volga above Rybinsk. Area 4550 km^2; average depth 5·6 m. It forms part of the Volga–Baltic Waterway.

Rydal Water, small lake in Cumbria, England, between Ambleside and Grasmere. From 1817 to his death in 1850, Wordsworth made his home at Rydal Mount.

Ryder, Albert Pinkham (1847–1905), US painter. He is esteemed for a poetic imaginative quality. Paintings such as *Flying Dutchman* and *Jonah and the Whale* have caused him to be compared with Herman Melville.

Ryder Cup, a trophy competed for during alternate years by two teams of professional male golfers representing the United States and Great Britain and Europe. At its inception in 1927 it was planned that the tournament—played in turn in America and Britain—should be for British and American golfers only, but such was the domination of the latter, that in 1979 the format was changed slightly to allow for the inclusion of European golfers in the British team. The playing format tends to alter slightly from meeting to meeting, but is generally a combination of foursome, better-ball and singles matches.

Rye, town in East Sussex, England. A major medieval port handling iron and timber and the cross-channel trade, Rye is now over 3 km from its harbour, which has silted up. Steep, cobbled streets are flanked by timbered and Georgian houses. Population (1981) 4293.

Rye, *Secale cereale*, a hardy grass, unknown in a wild state, extensively cultivated in the colder parts of Europe and Asia for its grain, which is somewhat similar to that of wheat, but which lacks the gluten-forming properties of that cereal. Its flour makes a dark-coloured, coarse-crumbed bread. Its grain is used in whisky and gin making.

Rye Grass, *Lolium perenne*, perennial rye grass and *L. multiflorum*, Italian rye grass, are fodder grasses. The seeds of *L. temulentum*, darnel, are poisonous.

Rye House Plot, The, name given to a conspiracy by Whig extremists to murder Charles II and the Duke of York in 1683. The plot was betrayed and the alleged conspirators, including the Earl of Essex, were arrested. Essex committed suicide and the others were executed.

Rykov, Aleksei Ivanovich (1881–1938), Soviet Communist. After the Bolshevik seizure of power he advocated a coalition government of all Socialist parties. He was chairman of the Supreme Council of National Economy, 1918–20 and 1923–24, deputy chairman of the council of People's Commissars, 1921–24, and succeeded Lenin as chairman, 1924–30. In the inner-party struggle after Lenin's death Rykov supported Stalin against Trotsky and Zinoviev, but joined the Right Opposition against the compulsory collectivisation of agriculture and was one of its principal leaders. After the defeat of the opposition Rykov was commissar for posts and telegraphs, 1931–37. At the last of the big show trials of the Great Purge in 1938 he was sentenced to death.

Ryle, Gilbert (1900–76), British philosopher. He was Waynflete professor of metaphysical philosophy at Oxford, 1945–68. One of the most influential of British philosophers, Ryle argued in his *The Concept of Mind*, 1949, that the mind-body dualism and similar philosophical problems were 'category mistakes'—in this case, the mistake of describing as a separate category (mind) what are in fact only certain aspects of behaviour in general. He also published *Dilemmas*, 1954, and *Plato's Progress*, 1956. His *Collected Papers: Vol. 1, Critical Essays*, and *Vol. 2, Collected Essays* were published in 1971.

Ryle, Sir Martin (1918–), British astronomer, the 12th Astronomer Royal. At the end of the Second World War Ryle moved to the Cavendish Laboratory, Cambridge, where he created a very strong radio astronomy research team which developed various powerful interferometric techniques, including that of aperture synthesis. Ryle himself became especially interested in isolated radio sources and their cosmological implications. In 1972 he was appointed astronomer royal and in 1974 he shared the Nobel Prize for physics with his colleague and former student, Antony Hewish.

Rysbrack, John Michael (c.1693–1770), Flemish sculptor, studied in Antwerp and went to England, 1720. He had an extensive practice in monumental sculpture, his work being found in many churches throughout the country. Perhaps his finest monument is that to Sir Isaac Newton, 1731, in Westminster Abbey. He rivalled Roubiliac in portrait busts.

Ryukyu Islands (also Riukiu, Nansei, Luchu or Loochoo), a chain of islands which stretch between Kyūshū, Japan, and Taiwan, and belong to Japan. There are about 60 large islands. The total area is 4595 km^2, inhabited by 1,200,000, making it one of the most densely populated areas in the world.

After the defeat of Japan in 1945, the United States occupied the entire archipelago. In 1953 the Tokara and Amami groups were returned to Japan, and became part of Kagoshima prefecture. The southern Ryukyus were returned to Japan in 1972, and are now administered as Okinawa prefecture.

S

S, nineteenth letter of the English alphabet and eighteenth of the Greek and Latin alphabets. Ancient Semitic had four sibilants, only one of which transferred directly to Greek; the Latin and English *s* has descended from the Greek *sigma*. Its normal sound in English is the *s* in *this*, for its sound in such a word as *these* would be more accurately denoted by *z*. In the words *sure* and *sugar* it has the sound of *sh*. S generally remains constant through the classical and Low German groups of languages, although High German *s* sometimes corresponds to *t* in English: as English *water*, High German *Wasser*; English *that*, High German *das*.
See also ALPHABET.

SA and SS (*Sturmabteilung, Schutzstaffel*), paramilitary organisations of the Nazi party. The SA or 'brown-shirts' (infantry and cavalry) was the storm troop, or army, of the early Nazi party. It was organised in 1922. Hitler organised a special detachment to be his own political executive. This was the origin of the SS (the protective squadron), or 'black-shirts', formally organised in 1928 as an élite by the side of the SA. Both organisations were notorious for their brutality, but after a purge of the SA in 1934 most of the real power remained with the SS, whose chief was Himmler.
See also GERMAN HISTORY.

Sá-Carneiro, Mário de (1890–1916), Portuguese poet. An outstanding writer, after a brief affiliation with Futurism he turned to a sincere and original mode of expression which conveys the agonising despair of his lost and high-flown ideals, and reveals an egotism undermined by a tragic sense of social inadequacy. Sá-Carneiro committed suicide in Paris.
Among his most important works are *A Confissão de Lucio*, 1914; *Céu em Fogo*, 1915; and *Indicios de Ouro*, 1937.

Saadi, or Muslih-ud-Din (c.1213–1291), Persian poet. From 1226 he spent some 30 years travelling. In the course of these journeys he was taken by the crusaders and put to work on the fortifications of Tripoli. He was saved from this slavery by a rich merchant who gave him his daughter in marriage.
Saadi's best-known works are the *Gulistan* (Rose-garden), a collection of anecdotes with ethical reflections and maxims, written mainly in prose but interspersed with verse, and the *Bustan* (Orchard), a long didactic poem. His ghazals, or odes, are considered to be of the highest order. These and many other poems appear in his *Kulliyyat* (Collected Works).

Saadia ben Joseph, Sa'id al-Fayyumi (892–942), Jewish philosopher. In 912 he completed his first great work, a Hebrew dictionary. He next published a work in defence of traditional Judaism and against Karaism and other heresies. He left Egypt at the age of 23 with the intention of settling in Palestine; but his contests against various innovators of the calendar brought him into such prominence that c.928, David ben Zakkai, head of the Jewish community of Babylonia, appointed Saadia as Gaon (president) of the School of Sura. He wrote in Arabic, into which language he translated most of the Bible. He dealt also with the Talmud and liturgies, and produced some works combining religion with philosophical reasoning, showing a thorough acquaintance with Aristotle.

Saale, river of the German Democratic Republic, which rises in the Fichtelgebirge and flows north past Jena and Halle to join the River Elbe 26 km south-east of Magdeburg. It is navigable for 160 km to Naumburg. Length 364 km.

Saar (French *Sarre*), river of France and southern Federal Republic of Germany, which rises in the Vosges mountains, and, flowing north-west through Lorraine and the Rhineland, joins the Moselle 8 km above Trier. Length 245 km.

Saarbrücken (French *Sarrebruck*), city of the Federal Republic of Germany, capital of the Saarland. It stands on the Saar, 64 km south-east of Trier. It is the centre of a coal-mining district and is an important industrial city with a steelworks and electrical and mechanical engineering industries. Population (1979) 194,452.

Saarinen, Eero (1910–61), Finnish-American architect. His personal style, with characteristic sweeping curves, is evident in the Yale Hockey Rink, 1958, and Kresge Auditorium, Massachusetts. He designed the United States Embassy, London, 1955–60, and the TWA terminal at Kennedy Airport, New York, 1962.

Saarland (French *Sarre*), *Land* of the Federal Republic of Germany, lying between the French *département* of Moselle and the German *Land* of Rhineland-Palatinate. The term was first used in 1918. Saarland was administered by the League of Nations after the First World War, in accordance with the provisions of the Treaty of Versailles. In 1935 the population decided by plebiscite to return to Germany, and in that year the territory reverted to the Reich. At the end of the Second World War, the area became a *Land* in the French zone of occupation. Early in 1947 the French detached an area containing over 200,000 inhabitants from Saarland proper. In November 1947 a new constitution making Saarland an autonomous state, politically separated from Germany but having economic union with France, was ratified. Saarland returned to Germany (the Federal Republic) on 1 January 1957, and its economic re-integration with Germany was completed on 31 December 1959.
Saarland's importance is derived from its rich coalfields, and its dependants, the iron and steel industries. Area 2570 km²; capital, Saarbrücken; population (1979) 1,068,600.

Sabadell, city in the province of Barcelona, Spain, 16 km north of Barcelona city. It has textiles and paper industries and a trade in agricultural produce and oil. Population 159,408.

Sabah, state of Malaysia, with a total area of 80,520 km², situated at the northern tip of the island of Borneo, roughly 1125 km east of Peninsular Malaysia. Sabah consists of a long belt of coastal lowlands, dissected by rivers, arcing from the south-western border with Sarawak round to the north-eastern tip of the state, and a largely rainforest-covered and mountainous interior dominated by the Crocker Range in the west (including Mount Kinabalu, at 4101 m the highest mountain in Malaysia). Sabah's western half is the most populated, with the smallest farm holdings and a local economy of shifting cultivation, subsistence rice farming, and fishing; but the eastern half, with most of the timber and oil-palm production, and a fast-growing cocoa industry, is less populated and accessible but by far the richer half of the territory. With 88 per cent of its area (about 64,750 km²) under forest, mainly of the valuable *Dipterocarpus* species, Sabah's major product is timber. Rice, rubber and oil-palm are the main commercial crops. Large-scale copper mining (in the Mount Kinabalu region) and offshore oil production (from the Samarang field) both began in 1975. The largest port is Sandakan, centre of the timber industry and said to be the world's most important timber port. Kota Kinabalu (population 41,000) is the state capital.
Sabah has a legislative assembly presided over by a chief minister, and an executive council to advise the appointed governor (or *Yang Di-Pertuan Negara*). Population (1980 1,002,608.
The territory of Sabah was, with the exception of Labuan and some minor western areas, bought from the sultan of Brunei by British traders in the 1870s. In 1881 the British North Borneo Company was incorporated by royal charter, and possession of the Borneo territories was formalised in 1888, when the British established a protectorate over the area under company jurisdiction. After the Second World War, North Borneo, with the addition of Labuan, became a Crown Colony. In 1963 it joined the Federation of Malaysia, and was renamed Sabah.

Sabatier, Paul (1854–1941), French chemist. Sabatier is noted for originating a method of hydrogenation of organic compounds using finely-divided nickel as a catalyst. He published *Le Catalyse en chimie organique* in 1912, and in the same year was awarded (with Victor Grignard) the Nobel Prize for chemistry.

Sabbatai Zevi, (1626–76), Jewish mystic, who proclaimed himself Messiah in 1666 and became the centre of a large messianic movement within the Jewish community, which even survived his apostasy to Islam. Nathan of Gaza, Sabbatai's 'prophet' and propagandist, guided this anguished charismatic personality who became the centre of messianic speculations and movements (the *Dormele* sect in Turkey survived up to the

20th century), which have affected Jewish thought profoundly.

Sabbath (from Hebrew *shabath*, to rest, to cease, to end), Jewish day of rest. The Hebrew Sabbath falls on Saturday, but it begins at sunset on Friday and lasts through Saturday until three stars are visible. The early Christians observed the Sabbath as Jews, and the Lord's Day as Christians. Luther, Zwingli, Calvin, Beza, Knox, etc., all favoured the lax observance, and the same is true of the English reformers. Strict Sabbatarianism began with the Puritans.

Sabbatical Year, institution of the ancient Hebrews, occurring every seventh year, based on Leviticus xxv. 2–7, and Deuteronomy xv. 1 ff. The land was to be left untilled, the vineyards were to be undressed, and the spontaneous produce of both was to be enjoyed by all the people in common. If a loan had not been repaid by the Sabbatical Year it could no longer be claimed. Yet, no person should for this reason refuse to lend to such as would borrow.

Sabians, a people mentioned in the Koran as 'people of the book' along with Christians and Jews, and therefore entitled to protection by Muslims, but no one knows who they were. In the 2nd Muslim century the star-worshippers of Harran in northern Mesopotamia claimed to be the Sabians of the Koran; their claim was allowed with the result that they survived till the 11th century. The name is also given to the Mandaeans, the so-called Christians of St John in southern Iraq, another survival from paganism. The name Sabian is probably a corruption of an Aramaic word meaning to dip, bathe.

Sabines, a people of Italy, of Umbro-Sabellian stock and allied to the Oscans. Their lands were bounded on the north by Picenum, on the west by Etruria and Umbria, on the south by Latium, and on the east by Samnium; the chief town was Reate (modern Rieti). In very early times elements of the Sabine race went to form part of the Roman people. This fact is reflected in a famous legend, according to which the Sabine women were carried off by the subjects of Romulus during a festival. Their menfolk marched against the ravishers, but as the two sides were about to join battle the Sabine women, holding their babies, rushed between them. Peace was made, and a portion of the Sabines united with the Romans to form one people under the general name 'Quirites'.

Sable, *Martes zibellina*, a valuable fur-bearing animal which, on account of excessive hunting, is now restricted to part of Siberia, where it is captured in its winter coat for the lustrous fur of commerce. It is about 50 cm long, exclusive of the tail, and the colouring is usually brown. Like other members of the marten family, Mustelidae, order Carnivora, it is nocturnal in habit, and feeds on rodents and birds.

Sabre-toothed Tigers, extinct Pleistocene carnivores with extraordinarily developed sabre-shaped upper canine teeth.

Saccharin is a white crystalline solid, melting point 220° C. It is about five hundred times as sweet as sugar, and is used as a sweetening agent, particularly by diabetics and others for whom sugar is contra-indicated.

Sabines. The Rape of the Sabine Women *by Nicolas Poussin.*

Saccharum, a genus of tall grasses, chiefly tropical, in family Gramineae, of which the most important species is *S. officinarum*, the sugar cane of the East Indies and the source of the cane sugar of commerce.
See also SUGAR.

Sacchi, Andrea (1599–1661), Italian painter. He upheld classical theories against the Baroque ideas of Pietro da Cortona in an important controversy (which Sacchi and his followers won) in the Academy of St Luke. Sacchi's ceiling fresco *Divine Wisdom* (c. 1629–33) is in the Palazzo Barberini, the same building that contains Cortona's *Divine Providence*, and makes possible close comparison of the practical application of the theories expounded by the two men. Sacchi's pupil, Maratta, continued the classical tradition.

Sachs, Hans (1494–1576), German shoemaker-poet. He flourished at the time of the Reformation, during which he was converted to Protestantism and which he helped to propagate by his ready pen. His production was voluminous, and more than six thousand different compositions, including *Schwänke*, dialogues, Shrovetide plays, tragedies and comedies, are ascribed to him. In his *Meisterlieder* he spread a knowledge of Luther's Bible among the poorer classes, and even made use of classical subjects. The best of his plays are folk-comedies. Sachs is the central figure in Wagner's opera *Die Meistersinger*.
See also MEISTERSINGER.

Sachs, Nellie (1891–1970), Jewish poet. She fled to Sweden in 1940, and in 1966 was awarded a Nobel Prize, sharing the honour with the Israeli writer, S. Y. Agnon. Her poetry and plays are filled with Kabbalistic and Hasidic symbolism, and deal mainly with the Nazi persecution of the Jews. *O The Chimneys: Selected Poems*, was published in 1967.

Sackbut, the Old English name for the trombone.

Sackville, Lord George (1716–85), British soldier, notorious for his seemingly cowardly behaviour on the battlefield of Minden, where he failed to execute a repeated order to charge. He was court-martialled, disgraced and adjudged incapable of serving thereafter in any military capacity. He attached himself to Lord North, was made secretary of state for the colonies in 1775, and had the direction of the American war, which ended in defeat for the British.

Sackville-West, Hon. Victoria (1892–1962), English poet, novelist, and biographer. In 1913 she married Harold Nicolson, and the story of their strange relationship is told in *Portrait of a Marriage*, 1973, by their son, Nigel Nicolson. With her husband she travelled to the Middle East, writing an account in *Passage to Teheran*, 1926. She won recognition with *Heritage*, 1919, a novel, and *The Heir*, 1922, short stories, but became more widely known after her long poem *The Land*, 1926, won the Hawthornden prize. Her novels include *The Edwardians*, 1930, and *All Passion Spent*, 1931.

Sacrament, originally the Roman soldiers' oath of fidelity (*sacramentum*), in Christian theology it came partly to mean a sacred mystery (e.g. the Incarnation), partly an outward sign or rite whereby spiritual grace is imparted. Later, this ritual use of the word prevailed, and in the Roman Catholic and Orthodox churches seven sacraments were held to be of divine origin, i.e. Baptism, Confirmation, the Eucharist, Penance, Extreme Unction (now called Anointing of the Sick), Holy Orders, and Matrimony.
In the Protestant churches, the term sacrament is reserved for Baptism and Holy Communion. The Anglican teaching declares that these two sacraments only are generally necessary for salvation.

Sacramento, capital of California, USA. The city is situated on the banks of the

Sacramento river, in what was, in the first few decades of the state's existence, the pivot of its affairs—midway between San Francisco and the goldfields of the Sierra Nevada slopes, at the point where the first transcontinental routes entered the Central Valley. Over 40 per cent of the workforce are classed as government employees. The city has food-processing industries serving the irrigated farmlands of the Central Valley. Population (1980) 274,488.

Sacrifice, the making of an offering to a deity by the representative of a social group, to propitiate the deity for an infringement of the moral code; to ensure its cooperation and that of the dead spirits in providing for the welfare of the living; or as a sign of respect for the deity. The object sacrificed consists of something believed to be valued by the deity and has included human beings. The most common object sacrificed is food, which is generally offered to the deity and then consumed by the participants in the ritual, who thereby enhance the links that bind them.

Sacrilege, in English law, comprises the following offences: (1) breaking into any church, chapel, meeting-house, or other place of divine worship, and committing a felony of any kind therein; (2) being already in any such place, committing a felony, and breaking out. The punishment may (in theory) extend to imprisonment for life. In common law sacrilege seems to have denoted only stealing goods out of a church or chapel.

In theology sacrilege is distinguished as *personal*, as when violence is done to a cleric; *local*, covering the legal offences mentioned above; and *real*, e.g. abuse of the sacraments and violation of a vow.

Sacristan, title given to the person in charge of the vestry and the sacred ornaments of a church.

See also SEXTON.

Sacristy, in any large church, a room for the storage of sacred vessels and vestments.

Sacrum, compound triangular bone at the base of the spine formed of five united vertebrae between the last lumbar vertebra above and the coccyx below, and forming the back of the pelvis.

Sadat, Anwar (1918–1981), Egyptian politician. A regular officer in the Egyptian army, he was one of the Free Officers who overthrew King Farouk in 1952. He was vice-president, 1969–70 and succeeded to the presidency after Nasser's death, setting Egypt on a course of greater economic and political liberalisation. He gained enormous prestige through Egyptian success in the 1973 war against Israel, and, with US mediation, negotiated interim withdrawal agreements with Israel in Sinai in 1974 and 1975. In 1977 he made a historic journey to Jerusalem in a new attempt to achieve a peaceful settlement in the Middle East. He was awarded the Nobel Peace Prize, jointly with Menachim Begin, for his part in the settlement between Israel and Egypt in 1979. He was assassinated by Muslim extremists.

See also EGYPT, *Modern History*.

Saddleback, or Blencathra, part of the Skiddaw mountain group in the Cumbrian Lake District, England. It provides a fine ridge walk above steep valleys descending to the surrounding lowland on the east side, and the gentler slopes of Mungrisdale Common and Skiddaw Forest, with Skiddaw itself to the west. Height 868 m.

Sadducees (origin and meaning of name uncertain), Jewish party of aristocratic priests at the time of Christ. They were materialistic in teaching, and denied the resurrection of the body, predestination, and, according to Acts xxiii. 8, the existence of angels and spirits. After the final destruction of the Temple in AD 70 the Sadducees died out.

Sade, Donatien Alphonse François, Comte, usually called Marquis de (1740–1814), French writer. He served as an army officer in the Seven Years' War, and afterwards led a life of such extreme sexual excess and debauchery that he was imprisoned in 1768, exiled in 1772, and again sent to prison in 1777, where he remained until 1790. In prison he wrote the novels and treatises published during the Revolutionary period: *Justine, ou les malheurs de la vertu*, 1791; *Aline et Valcour* and *La Philosophie dans le boudoir*, 1795; and *La Nouvelle Justine*, 1797. Others of his works, such as *Les 120 Journées de Sodome, ou l'école de libertinage* (3 vols), 1931–35, were not published until long after Sade's death.

In 1801 Sade was again arrested, and in 1803 he was pronounced insane and committed to the asylum at Charenton where he spent the rest of his life. There his plays were performed by the inmates. From his name comes the word 'sadism'.

Sadism, see SEXUALITY, HUMAN.

Sadleir, Michael Thomas Harvey (1888–1957), English biographer, novelist, and publisher. He is chiefly known for his commentaries on Trollope, which were largely responsible for a revival in his popularity. His novels include *Fanny by Gaslight*, 1940.

Sadler's Wells Ballet, see ROYAL BALLET, THE.

Sadowa, Czechoslovak village, 13 km north-west of Hradec Králové, the scene (1866) of the victory of the Prussians over the Austrians in the Seven Weeks' War.

Safety Lamp, see DAVY LAMP.

Safflower, *Carthamus tinctorius*, a species of the Compositae, common to Asia, Africa, and around the Mediterranean. It yields a light, edible oil that is used in cooking and for oil paints, and is cultivated for this purpose in warm areas including Australia and parts of North America. The flowers contain a red dye that was important before the invention of the synthetic dyes.

Safflower Oil, kardiseed or kurdee seed oil (iodine value 140 ± 10) is obtained from the seeds of *Carthamus tinctorius*, cultivated in India, the Middle East, Canada, the USA, and Australia. The oil, which is obtained from the seeds of the plant by pressing or by solvent extraction, does not yellow with age and is useful in the manufacture of paint and varnishes. It is also used in cooking oils and, after hardening by hydrogenation, in the manufacture of margarine.

Safi, seaport and fishing harbour of Morocco on the Atlantic coast, south-west of Casablanca. Safi is connected by rail to the phosphate deposits at Khouribga. It has a large chemical complex. Population (1971) 129,112.

Saga, a particular type of prose narrative written in Iceland between about 1200 and 1400. The best sagas distinguish themselves as masterpieces of medieval prose. Sagas are usually divided into six categories of which the *family sagas* are the most important group and are sometimes simply termed 'the sagas'. They describe events purported to have taken place in Iceland between 900 and 1030 and their theme is most frequently family feuds, although they also take the form of personal and family histories. For example, Egils saga Skalla-Grímssonar recounts the life story of the poet Egill Skala-Grímsson.

The *kings' sagas* relate the lives of Scandinavian, primarily Norwegian, monarchs. Of the greatest importance is Snorri Sturluson's *Heimskringla*. The *mythical-heroic sagas* (*fornaldarsögur*) tell of events, mostly fabulous, purporting to have taken place in Scandinavia, and to a lesser extent in Germany, before the settlement of Iceland. Most important is *Völsunga saga*, with its story of the greatest Norse hero, Sigurdr the Dragon-Slayer, counterpart of the German Siegfried. The *contemporary sagas* (or *Sturlunga saga*), recount events in Iceland in the 12th and 13th centuries. *Bishops' sagas* relate the lives of Icelandic bishops, while *knights sagas* are mostly adaptations of foreign romances.

Sagan, Françoise, pseudonym of Françoise Quoirez (1935–), French writer. Her first novel, *Bonjour tristesse*, 1954, was an immediate success and was followed by *Un Certain sourire*, 1956; *Dans un mois, dans un an*, 1957; *Aimez-vous Brahms*, 1959. She has also written plays, including *Château en Suède*, 1960; *Les Violons parfois*, 1962; *La Robe mauve de Valentine*, 1963; *Bonheur, impair et passe*, 1964; and *Zaphorie*, 1973.

Sage, *Salvia officinalis*, in family Labiatae, a dwarf evergreen shrub of southern Europe, is the garden sage, which provides the herb for cookery and essential oil for perfumery. Jerusalem sage is *Phlomis fruticosa*, and sage of Bethlehem is *Pulmonaria officinalis*.

Sage Grouse, *Centrocercus urophasianus*, a large grouse which inhabits the sagebrush districts of the western USA. It has soft, dense plumage, is mottled yellowish-brown in colour, with a long, 20-feathered tail. At each side of the male's neck is an inflatable air sac, distended during the mating season.

Sagebrush, low aromatic evergreen shrubs of genus *Artemisia* of the Compositae that cover the northern Rocky Mountain states of the USA. The name is given particularly to *A. tridentata*.

Sagittaria, a genus of water-side perennial herbs, in family Alismataceae. *S. sagittifolia*, arrowhead, is found in Europe, North America and Asia; *S. latifolia* is the North American wapato or duck potato.

Sagittarius, 'the Archer', a bright southern constellation and the ninth sign of the zodiac. It covers the central regions of the Galaxy and abounds with star clouds, clusters and nebulosities.

Sago, a starchy food obtained from the soft inner portion of the sago palm, *Metroxylon rumphii*, and other trees which are native to Indonesia. The trunks are cut into sections and split, the soft centre being removed and pounded in water till the starch separates.

Saguenay, river of Canada draining the shallow Lake St John, famous for its salmon, and running for 160 km south-east into the St Lawrence at a point 190 km north-east of Quebec. From Ha Ha Bay, a favourite summer resort, the river is open to craft of all sizes. The Jesuit, Father Dequen, was the first European to go up the Saguenay to Lake St John in 1647, and Tadoussac, a French-Canadian village at the river's mouth, has been the centre of Jesuit and Franciscan missions since the 17th century.

Sagunto, town in the province of Valencia, Spain, lying on the Palancia, 29 km north of Valencia city. Sagunto is overlooked by an Iberian, Roman, Moorish, and modern citadel, crowning a steep hill. It has a large trade in oranges, has steel works, and exports Teruel iron-ore from its port, which is 5 km away on the Mediterranean coast. Population (1971) 45,000.

Sahara (properly *Sahra*, wilderness), largest desert in the world, covering about 9 million km² of North Africa, from the Mediterranean southward to the Sudan, and from the Atlantic eastward to the Red Sea.

The Sahara is mostly an elevated plateau with a mean altitude of 600 m, the surface of which is diversified by lofty tablelands and mountains. The summits of the central Hoggar highlands and of the Tibesti Mountains, farther to the east, rise as high as 2600 m and are snow-capped for several months of the year, whilst to the north-east and north-west of the Hoggar peaks extends the ridge of the Muidir plateau (320 km), and that of the Tasili of the Asjer (480 km), which has a mean altitude of 1500 m. South of the Hoggar are the mountains of Air (2000 m). The Igidi, which with the West and East Erg stretches from Cape Blanco to the south of Tunisia (2000 km), is a vast belt of sand-hills. But these do not account for more than one-ninth of the area of the Sahara. The Hammada al-Homra and the *hammada* of Murzuk, etc., are vast, undulating granite-strewn surfaces; and there are also interminable tracts of stones and water-worn pebbles, called *serir*. Other areas, e.g. the Libyan Desert, are covered in soft sand, sometimes blown by the wind into high dunes, continually shifting and changing contour.

Ancient watercourses prove that rivers formerly flowed through the desert, and the presence of salt and of marine shells proves that parts of it were once under the sea. The process of drying up is still continuing.

The Sahara contains rich mineral resources, of which oil and natural gas are the most important. There is iron ore in Algeria and Mauritania, and phosphates in Morocco and the former Spanish Sahara.

The interior districts have the highest temperatures of Africa, as afternoon temperatures may exceed 44° C in summer, but in winter the mean in the interior is below 15° C and frosts are not unusual. Though more or less rainless, the Sahara is not without subterranean water, and the wells of the oases, e.g. those of the Tuat group in the north-central Sahara, are conducive to cultivation on a limited scale.

Sahel, Arabic name applied to the coastal range of hills in Algeria and to the eastern coastal plain of Tunisia, but mainly used to denote the region which lies between the Sahara desert and the tropical areas of West Africa. The Sahel extends across northern Senegal, southern Mauritania, Mali, Upper Volta, southern Niger, north-eastern Nigeria and southern Chad; it is mainly savanna with some deciduous trees. In good rainfall conditions the Sahel provides pasture for cattle, sheep and other livestock, but it is vulnerable to drought; during an exceptionally severe drought, 1968–74, the Sahara advanced southwards into it and greatly reduced its capacity to support pastoral life.

Saïda, town in north-western Algeria. The town is in a strategic location, and has been a stronghold of Algerian nationalism and the French Foreign Legion. It trades in sheep, wool, and textiles, and is noted for its leatherwork. Population 33,497.

Saiga, *Saiga tatarica*, a small antelope about 80 cm high. Fossils show that saigas formerly roamed over a wide area of Europe and Asia. By the early 1920s only about 1000 survived, mostly in Kazakhstan, in the USSR. A careful conservation programme saved the saiga, and now herds in Kazakhstan number more than 2,000,000, providing a useful source of meat and hides. Saigas have protuberant, rounded noses, which are particularly developed in adult males.

Saigon, see Ho Chi Minh City.

Sailfish, a bony, ray-finned fish of the genus *Istiophorus*, in the order Perciformes of class Actinopterygii. The snout is long and pointed and the dorsal fin unusually large. It is blue above, silver below, and over 3 m long.

Sailing, the use of a boat fitted with one or more sails for cruising or competitive racing. Apart from the large square-rigged vessels of the past, now used only for sail-training purposes, pleasure sailing craft range from dinghies of little more than 2 m long and ocean-going yachts which can be as much as 30 m in length. Yachts may be classified into sloops, cutters, schooners, ketches, etc. according to the number of masts they have and the configuration of the sails.

Sailing as a sport is organised by class of vessel, all boats of the same design competing against each other. The classes taking part in the Olympic Games are: Finn (4·5 m); 470 (4·7 m); Flying Dutchman (6·05 m); Star (6·91 m); Soling (8·16 m); Tornado, a catamaran (6·1 m). Yacht racing can be further divided into coastal and offshore racing. Dinghy races normally take place round short regatta-type courses. Because of its cheapness, dinghy sailing has grown markedly in popularity since the Second World War.

Sailplane, see Gliding.

Sails and Rigging, term applied to the masts and sails used to propel a sailing-ship, the derricks and cranes of any ship, and also the davits on which the lifeboats are carried. Today, with the demise of the sailing-ship, the term is mainly used to cover the derricks that are used to load and discharge a general cargo. It was by their rig that sailing-ships were recognised. Although there are many different types of rig they fall mainly into two classes: square rig, where the sails are carried at right angles to the line of the keel; and fore-and-aft rig, where the sails are carried in line with the keel.

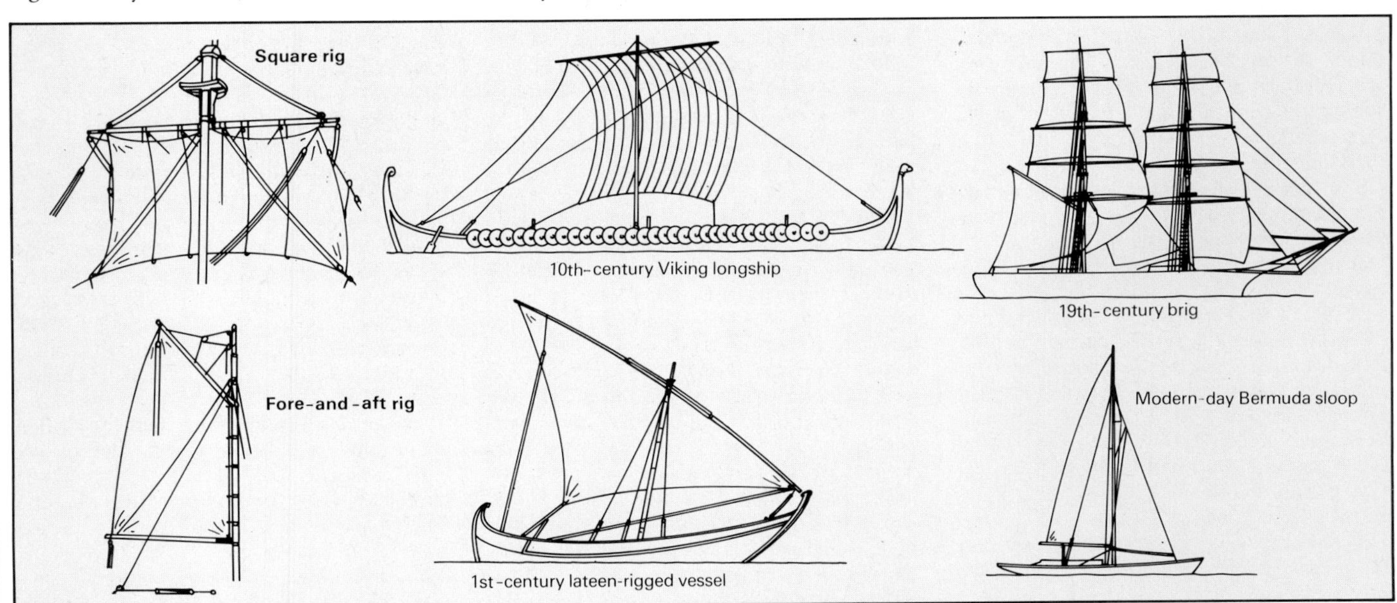

Sails and Rigging. *The square-sailed ship has its origins in vessels such as the Viking longship; fore-and-aft sails derive from the ancient lateen rig.*

Sainfoin, *Onobrychis sativa*, a handsome, perennial leguminous plant bearing rosy-red flowers in axillary spikes. It is sometimes grown as a fodder plant and makes excellent hay.

Saint (Latin *sanctus*, Old French *saint*). Though St Paul uses the word *hagioi*, saints, in addressing the Christian congregations to which he writes, the name is today used in a more restricted sense. A saint is thus a person remarkable for special holiness and piety. Such recognition of special holiness by the Church was not at first marked by judicial procedure. The holy man was famed in his own district. After his death, his memory was venerated, and perhaps miracles were worked at the place where his body rested. Sometimes his fame spread far and wide. There was thus a considerable possibility of error, and scandals led to a restriction of the right of 'canonisation' to the bishop of the diocese. For modern procedure, see CANONISATION.

Saint, in the case of geographical names, see ST. For individual saints see under the proper name of each.

St Albans, Viscount, see BACON, FRANCIS, BARON VERULAM, VISCOUNT ST ALBANS.

St Albans, since 1877 a city and the seat of a bishop, 32 km north-west of London, in Hertfordshire, England. The chief industries are printing, engineering, hosiery, clothing, and orchid culture. It is the successor to the important Romano-British town of Verulamium. There in 303 or earlier took place the martyrdom of St Alban, the Roman convert and first Christian martyr in England. The Benedictine abbey founded by Offa in honour of the saint, c.793, and the medieval town, arose on the opposite side of the valley from Verulamium, that being the spot to which, according to tradition, St Alban was led for execution. Population (1981) 50,888.

St Andrews, town on St Andrews Bay in Fife Region, Scotland, 18 km south-east of Dundee. Legend claims that the town was so called because it harboured the relics of St Andrew, which a certain bishop, named St Regulus or Rule, brought here from Patras in Achaea. St Andrews is an important tourist resort, but its fame today depends on its university, one of the oldest in Scotland (1411), and on its golf links. The golf club was instituted in 1754, and took the title 'Royal and Ancient' by the wish of King William IV. Population (1981) 11,302.

St Augustine, in St Johns county, Florida, USA, 60 km south-east of Jacksonville. It is the oldest town in the USA, having been settled by Spaniards in September 1565. It is a port of entry, and a shrimping and shipping centre. Population (1980) 11,985.

St Austell, market town in Cornwall, England, 21 km south-east of Truro. St Austell was formerly the centre of a tin- and copper-mining district. There are important china-clay works nearby. Population (1981) 36,639.

St Bartholomew, Massacre of, see BARTHOLOMEW, MASSACRE OF ST.

St Bernard, name of two passes across the Alps. The Great St Bernard pass (2467 m high and 85 km long) leads from Martigny in canton Valais, Switzerland, to Aosta in Italy, across the Pennine Alps; the Little St Bernard (2188 m high and 63 km long) leads from the Isère valley in French Savoy, to Aosta across the Graian Alps. The first pass, Alpis Poenina, seems to have been opened in 57 BC by Servius Galba, for Julius Caesar, and the road was in existence by AD 69. The famous hospice was founded, or as some say refounded, by St Bernard of Menthon, and has been served by Augustinian monks since the 12th century. The Little St Bernard, known to the Romans as Alpis Graia, was the chief pass until the opening of the pass at Mont Genèvre in 75 BC. The hospice here was also founded by St Bernard.

St Bernard Dog, huge and powerful dog which originated in the Augustinian hospice at the summit of the St Bernard Pass through the Alps, where it was used to act as a guide and to search for and aid travellers who had lost their way. The height of a dog at the shoulder averages about 70 cm, and the weight 90 kg.

St Bride's, church in the city of London. The earliest extant reference to a church on this site is dated 1222, and excavations in 1952 revealed the existence of two or possibly three earlier churches, as well as remains of a Roman dwelling. The church was destroyed in the Great Fire and the present structure, one of Wren's masterpieces, was built in 1670–84, and destroyed except for the steeple in the air raid of 29 December 1940, but has been restored.

St Christopher, see ST KITTS.

St-Cloud, a western suburb of Paris. The historic château associated with the names of Marie Antoinette and Napoleon among others, was demolished in 1871, but the beautiful park remains. The Sèvres porcelain factory is here.

St Croix, or Santa Cruz, largest of the Virgin Islands of the USA in the West Indies, with an area of 1210 km^2. Together with the other Virgin Islands it was purchased from Denmark in 1917. The highest peak is Mount Eagle, 355 m. Earthquakes and hurricanes are frequent. St Croix has rolling uplands and enjoys a soil better than the companion islands. The chief towns are Christiansted on the northern shore, and Frederiksted on the western side, commercially the more important place. The island was discovered by Columbus on his second voyage in 1493. Population (1980) 49,013.

St David's, cathedral town in Dyfed, south-west Wales, on the small River Alun just 2 km from the sea. David, the patron saint of Wales, settled here in the 6th century, and his relics are preserved in the cathedral. Population 1690.

St David's Head, promontory at the entrance to St George's Channel, in Whitesand Bay, Dyfed, south-west Wales.

St Denis, town and capital of the French Île de la Réunion in the Mascarene group in the Indian Ocean. Population (1974) 103,513.

St-Étienne, French town, capital of the *département* of Loire, on the River Furens south-west of Lyon. It has been a centre of iron and then steel industries since the 16th century, but the coalfield on which it was founded has now ceased production. Present-day manufactures include aero-engines, armaments, and textiles, and associated chemicals and dyes. Population (1975) 221,775; conurbation 334,846.

Saint-Évremond, Charles de Marguetel de Saint-Denis (c.1616–1703), French writer. He fought with distinction in the Thirty Years' War. He had to flee, however, in 1661, first to Holland and then to England, where he spent the rest of his life, and became the chief figure at the salon of the duchess of Mazarin in London.

His fame as a French writer lies in the often witty expression of the Pyrrhonian viewpoint and the Epicurean ideal, illustrated in his *Conversation avec le Père Canaye*.

Saint-Exupéry, Antoine de (1900–44), French writer and aviator. His most important books, based on the experience of himself and other aviators and expressing humanist values in the context of 20th-century civilisation, include *Courrier Sud*, 1928; *Vol de nuit*, 1931; *Terre des hommes*, 1939; and *Pilote de guerre*, 1942. However, his most famous work is *Le Petit prince*, 1943, a children's book which also has philosophical implications.

St Gallen, capital of St Gallen canton, Switzerland, and situated just south of Lake Constance. The town grew up around a Benedictine monastery founded in the 7th century by the Irish missionary St Gall. It is an industrial centre specialising in embroidered cotton textiles and nylon. Population (1980) 75,847.

St George's, capital and chief port of Grenada in the West Indies. The outer harbour is an open roadstead and the inner one is a well-sheltered natural harbour of great charm. The town is built around the submerged volcanic crater forming St George's Bay; it is remarkable for its steep streets, some of which are stepped. Population (1978) 30,813.

St George's Channel, sea passage extending 160 km northeast to southwest between the Irish Sea and the Atlantic Ocean, and separating County Wexford in south-eastern Ireland from south-west Dyfed in Wales. The narrowest point lies between St. David's Head in Wales and Carnsore Point in Ireland.

St Gotthard, a major Alpine pass in Switzerland between Altdorf in canton Uri and Bellinzona in Ticino. There has been a hospice on the summit (2114 m) since 1331. A good road was first constructed over the pass between 1820–24. The St Gotthard railway tunnel extends from Göschenen to Airolo (some 15 km). It was built between 1872 and 1980.

St Helena, British island and crown colony in the South Atlantic Ocean, 1125 km south-east of Ascension and 1930 km from Mossamedes, the nearest African port, in latitude 15°55′S and longitude 5°42′W. It is volcanic in origin, 16 km long and 10 km wide, its area being 121 km^2. The island is well watered by abundant, clear springs. The main crops are vegetables and flax; there are no exports.

St Helena was formerly an Admiralty coaling station. A cable station links the colony with the outside world through Cape Town and Ascension. Jamestown is the capital and only town; it is a free port. Population (estimated 31 December 1979) 5,223.

St Helena was discovered by the Portuguese commander João da Nova Castell in 1502, on his return voyage to Lisbon from

India. The island became a port of call for ships of various nations voyaging between the East Indies and Europe. In 1659 it was annexed and occupied by Captain John Dutton, on behalf of the East India Company. It remained in possession of the company, except for an interval between 1815 and 1821 when the British government took it over. Napoleon lived in exile at Longwood (5 km inland from Jamestown) from 1815 until his death in 1821. In 1834, it was brought under the direct government of the Crown. In 1922 the island of Ascension, till then under Admiralty control, was made a dependency of St Helena and in 1938 Tristan da Cunha with the neighbouring uninhabited islands of Gough, Nightingale, and Inaccessible, also became a dependency.

St Helens, town in Merseyside Metropolitan County, England, 16 km east of Liverpool, mainly known for its glass industry, dating back more than 200 years. Coal has been mined since the 16th century, and in 1757 the 'Sankey Canal' was constructed to carry it. Glass-working is by far the major industry though other manufactures include pharmaceutical products, tanning, metal-working, and brewing. Population (1981) 98,769.

St Helier, capital of Jersey, Channel Islands, lies on the south coast of the island at the eastern end of St Aubin's Bay. The harbour and much of the town are overshadowed by a large hill on which stands Fort Regent, which has been developed as a tourist attraction. The harbour is sheltered by a breakwater extending seawards from Elizabeth Castle. Population (1971) 26,460.

St Ives (so called from Ia, an Irish virgin and martyr), picturesque seaside resort, with magnificent beaches, on St Ives Bay, on the north coast of Cornwall, England, 30 km from Land's End. An artists' colony was founded by Sickert and Whistler and St Ives still attracts artists as well as holidaymakers. Population (1981) 10,985.

St James's Palace, London, was built by Henry VIII in 1530–36. Of Henry's palace only the imposing gateway survives, since much was destroyed by fire in 1809. It became the official residence of the sovereign from 1698, when Whitehall Palace was destroyed by fire, until 1837, when Queen Victoria made Buckingham Palace the official residence. The British Court is still officially styled 'the Court of St James'. Charles I spent his last night here. It is now used for apartments for court officials. Adjacent is the Queen's Chapel, 1623–27, by Inigo Jones. St James's Park (enlarged by Charles II) was the grounds of the palace.

St John, city of New Brunswick, Canada, at the mouth of the St John river, 105 km south of Fredericton. It was discovered by Samuel de Champlain on St John the Baptist's Day (24 June) in 1604. It is an important fishing, railway, and distributing centre for the surrounding districts. It has a thriving shipbuilding industry producing trawlers and small vessels. Other port industries include food processing, brewing, clothing, oil refining, and paint manufacture. It is one of the winter ports of Canada for ships from Europe. Population (1976) 85,956.

St John, river of New Brunswick, Canada, draining into the Bay of Fundy at St John. One branch rises in Quebec, the other, called the Walloostook, begins in the highlands north of Maine, USA, and for 130 km forms the international boundary between the USA and Canada. Fredericton is the limit of navigation for larger vessels. The river produces 80 per cent of New Brunswick's hydro-electric power. Length 645 km.

St John, Knights of, see HOSPITALLERS.

St John Lateran, see LATERAN CHURCH OF ST JOHN.

St John of Jerusalem, Order of, see HOSPITALLERS.

St John's, capital of Newfoundland, Canada, on the east coast of the island, in the peninsula of Avalon. The centre of seal- and cod- fisheries, it has excellent harbour, wharf, and dry-dock accommodation. The city is the administrative capital as well as the service and wholesale centre of the province. Industrial activity is limited to textiles, electronics, and woodworking. Population (1976) (city) 86,576; (metropolitan area) 143,390.

St Johns, capital and port of Antigua in the West Indies, situated on the north-west coast and forming the commercial centre of the island; its port handles all the island's agricultural produce. Population (1975) 24,000.

St John's Wort, *Hypericum*, a genus of plants of Hypericaceae having oval leaves in opposite pairs and yellow flowers. The stamens are numerous and grouped in three or five bundles. They are so called since they come into flower about the feast of St John Baptist (June 24). Rose of Sharon (*H. calycinum*) and other shrubby species are often grown in shrubberies.

St Joseph, county seat of Buchanan county, Missouri, USA, first established as a trading post in 1826. It is on the Missouri river, 80 km north-west of Kansas City. It has large stockyards, and is engaged in the industries of slaughtering, meat-packing, and grain-milling, and has an important grain market. Population (1980) 76,691.

Saint-Just, Louis Antoine Léon Florelle de Richebourg de (1767–94), French revolutionary leader. Having become friendly with Robespierre, he became deputy of the *département* of Aisne to the National Convention (1792). The following year he was appointed a member of the Committee of Public Safety. Having proposed that the Convention should control all military operations, he was sent to the armies of the Rhine and Moselle. He carried out his mission with such relentless vigour that on his return he was elected to the presidency of the Convention (February 1794). He was later guillotined with Robespierre.

St Kilda, most remote of the Outer Hebrides islands of Scotland, 220 km west of the mainland in the Atlantic Ocean. It is about 5 km long by 4 km broad, with precipitous, rock-bound shores. It is now a bird sanctuary and a tracking station for the South Uist rocket range.

St Kitts, or St Christopher. With Nevis it is one of the West Indies Associated States. The island has an area of 168 km². It is 37 km long and has a central range of rugged mountains culminating in Mount Misery (1131 m) overlooking a fertile plain at the south-east of which is Basseterre, the capital and port of the island. The island economy is based on sugar cane and Sea Island cotton. Tourism is the most rapidly developing industry.

Basseterre on St Kitts is the seat of government for St Kitts-Nevis. Discovered by Christopher Columbus in 1493 and named after his patron saint, the island was settled by the English in 1623. Population (1980) 35,104.

St Kitts-Nevis
Area 261 km²
Population: 44,400
Capital: Basseterre

St Kitts-Nevis, independent country situated in the Leeward Islands group, and consisting of the two islands of St Kitts (see above) and Nevis; until 1967 the island of Anguilla was also part of the state. The main industries are sugar and cotton. In Nevis there is a high percentage of small-scale farming. There is a governor, an eight-member cabinet, and an elected house of assembly. Area 261 km². Population (1980) 44,400.

History. St Kitts-Nevis, along with Anguilla, was a British colony from 1650 until 1967. St Christopher-Nevis-Anguilla became a state in association with the United Kingdom in 1967. Later in 1967 Anguilla broke off relations with St Kitts-Nevis which culminated in 1976 with its formal separation from St Kitts-Nevis. St Kitts-Nevis became fully independent in 1983.

Saint-Laurent, Yves (1936–), French fashion designer, who was employed as Dior's assistant at the age of 17, and succeeded him as head of the House of Dior on Dior's death in 1957. At Dior, Saint-Laurent introduced the A-line silhouette and fur-trimmed leather. In 1962 he opened his own fashion house and continues to be extremely influential in the world of fashion, popularising in turn minidresses, trousers for women and, more recently, a more formal, tailored look.

St Lawrence, river of North America, issues from Lake Ontario, and is fed by the Great Lakes, whose surplus waters are taken to the Atlantic after a north-easterly course of 1125 km. The St Louis river, which flows into Lake Superior near Duluth, is accounted as its headwaters: and the length from the source of this river to the Gulf of St Lawrence is 3060 km. Between Lakes Superior and Huron the river is known as the St Mary, between Lakes Huron and St Clair as the St Clair; it becomes the Detroit between St Clair and Erie, and the Niagara between Erie and Ontario. This great waterway is navigable to Fort William at the head of Lake Superior, a series of canals having been constructed to avoid cataracts and rapids. The total drainage area, including the Great Lakes system, is over 1·3 million km², and the basin contains one-half of the world's fresh water.

St Lawrence Seaway, a deep-water channel connecting the St Lawrence river with the Great Lakes, allowing the passage of ships with 7·6-m draught from Montreal to Lake Ontario. The seaway was opened for navigation in April 1959. Ocean-going freighters can sail over 4185 km from the Atlantic to Port Arthur and Fort William at the head of Lake Superior.

St Leger, traditionally the fifth and last of the classic horse races run annually in England. It takes place over a 2·92-km course at Doncaster, Yorkshire, and is contested by three-year-old colts (who carry 57 kg) and fillies (55·5 kg). It is the oldest classic, dating back to 1776, though it was not called the St Leger until 1778.

St Louis, city of Missouri, USA, standing on the west bank of the Mississippi river, 27 km below its confluence with the Missouri. It is an important market for livestock, grain, wool, and lumber. Among large industries are food processing, brewing, distilling and the manufacture of chemicals, drugs, clothes, shoes, machinery, aeroplanes, automobiles, and iron and steel products; petroleum, rubber, and tobacco are processed and there is a large printing and publishing industry. Roads and railways converge on the Mississippi bridges and a large number of long-distance truck lines have their base here. With the rapid increase in river traffic on the Mississippi, water transport is also important; the port of St Louis (30 km frontage) handles oil, coal, sulphur, grain, cement, sugar, farm products, and manufactured goods. The city was founded in 1764, as a fur-trading post, by the Frenchman Pierre Laclède, and was named after Louis IX of France. It passed into the possession of the USA in 1803, as part of the Louisiana Purchase. Population (1980) 448,640.

St Louis, town in Senegal, West Africa, on an island at the mouth of the River Senegal. Founded in 1659, it was the first French settlement on the mainland of West Africa, and was the capital of Senegal until 1958, when the seat of government was transferred to Dakar. St Louis is a commercial centre, and has an important fishing industry. Population (1980) 96,594.

St Lucia
Area: 616 km²
Population: 113,000
Capital: Castries

St Lucia, one of the Windward Islands, 39 km due south of Martinique and 48 km north-east of St Vincent. It has an area of 616 km^2 and a population (estimate 1979) of 113,000, mainly of African descent. Of volcanic formation, St Lucia is very mountainous with fertile valleys. The Pitons, two remarkable sugar-loaf mountains on the east side, have been for generations a landmark for sailors; Gros Piton is 798 m and Petit Piton 275 m. Near by is La Soufrière, a low-lying volcanic crater generally in a state of low-level activity. The capital is Castries.

Bananas, sugar cane, cocoa, coconuts, citrus fruits, and food crops are grown. Manufacturing includes rum, edible oils, cigarettes, and mineral waters. Castries has a good harbour and so has Vieux Fort. The East Caribbean dollar (EC$) is in use.

The island is administered by a governor-general acting on the advice of the Prime Minister. There is an assembly of 21 members, 17 of whom are elected by adult suffrage, and a Senate.

History. In 1718 the French king granted the island to the Marquis d'Estrées, but when the Marquis tried to colonise it the English objected. After a long period of dispute it was finally ceded to Britain in 1814. St Lucia, along with other Windward and Leeward Islands after agreements with the UK in 1966, became a West Indies Associated State on 1 March 1967 and gained full independence in 1979.

St Luke's Summer, see INDIAN SUMMER.

St-Malo, seaport in the *département* of Ille-en-Vilaine, France, 80 km north-west of Rennes. It stands on an island on the right bank of the estuary of the Rance. There are many fine 16th- and 17th-century stone houses grouped in winding, narrow streets around the cathedral. It is a busy fishing, trading, and passenger port, and has shipbuilding and electrical industries. Population 69,450.

Saint-Martin, Louis Claude de (1743–1803), French mystic and author. He became a prominent member of a group of masonic Rosicrucians called the Elect Cohens. His philosophy is based on the belief that human beings have a divine power which they have forgotten how to use. All that is required is that they realise this inner divinity, through self-awareness, and fulfil their function as the managers of universal harmony. Saint-Martin's mysticism attracted many followers who called themselves Martinists and exerted considerable influence in the last century.

St Martin (Dutch *Sint Maarten*), island in the West Indies, in the Leeward group with an area of 96 km^2, 62 km^2 of which is French and the rest Dutch. The French section, lying to the north, is a dependency of Guadeloupe. The Dutch section forms, with St Eustatius and Saba, a dependency of the Netherlands Antilles. The French capital is Marigot and the Dutch Philipsburg. The island was occupied by the French and the Spanish between 1640 and 1648, in which year it was divided between the French and Dutch. Population of the Dutch section in 1979 was 11,379 and the French part about 6000.

St Marylebone, part of the City of Westminster, London. It was originally the village of Tyburn, and later became St Marylebone from the dedication of the 15th-century church near the River Tyburn (St Mary-at-the-Bourne).

St Michael's Mount, precipitous mass of granite and slate rock, near St Mount's Bay, Cornwall, England, connected with Marazion by a causeway submerged at high tide. It was the seat of a chapel belonging to the abbey of Mont St Michel in Normandy, and was a place of pilgrimage.

St Moritz, commune in the canton of Graubünden, Switzerland, situated on the lake in the Upper Engadine. Its famous mineral springs and beautiful scenery have caused it to become an international tourist centre, renowned for its winter sports and luxury hotels. It lies at an altitude of over 1830 m. The population (1974) of 5770 is German- and Romansch-speaking.

St-Nazaire, French seaport in the *département* of Loire-Atlantique, situated at the mouth of the River Loire, on the Bay of Biscay. Shipbuilding and aircraft construction are important, and the town has iron foundries, and manufactures chemicals and foodstuffs. In the Second World War the Germans used it as a submarine base in the Battle of the Atlantic. There are now important oil refineries nearby. Population (1975) town: 69,769; conurbation: 119,418.

St Paul, city on the upper Mississippi river in Minnesota, USA. St Paul grew as a river port on a bend of the Mississippi just below its confluence with the Minnesota river. It became the state capital in 1858, but its main growth period began with the coming of the railways; it became, and remains, one of North America's greatest railway cities, and such rail-based activities as stockyards and meat-packing plants followed. Scandinavian cultural traits predominate in the (1980) population of 268,248.

***St Paul's Cathedral.** The choir and high altar.*

St Paul's Cathedral is the cathedral church of the City of London, the largest Protestant church in England. Its history begins with an early 7th-century cathedral built by Ethelbert, King of Kent, with Mellitus as the first bishop of London. This building was destroyed by fire in 1087, and a new one was begun and not completed until 1287, combining Norman, transitional and Early English styles. It had the tallest spire and was probably the largest church in Christendom. It was largely destroyed in the Great Fire of 1666. Sir Christopher Wren at first thought that St Paul's should be restored, but later agreed that a new edifice was required. Building began in 1675, the plan undergoing considerable alteration before completion in 1711. Wren achieved a magnificently successful union of Gothic plan and Classic detail, and the interior is of majestic proportions and beauty.

The dome is ingeniously constructed to give a more reposeful outline than that of St Peter's in Rome and its steeply curving ribs help support the lantern. Wren's lantern is supported on a brick cone, concealed between the inner dome and the outer, which is of wood and lead, and curves almost hemispherically. The furnishings include carved stalls by Grinling Gibbons.

St Peter Port, parish and only town of Guernsey, Channel Islands. The harbour is excellent and the town, of which steps are a marked feature, is very picturesque. The old covered market is known as the French Halles. Population (1971) 16,303.

St Peter's (San Pietro in Vaticano), the Patriarchal Basilica of St Peter, adjoining the Vatican in Rome. Although it is the scene of important public papal functions, it is not the papal cathedral, and in this sense it ranks second to the Lateran Church of St John. The Piazza S. Pietro in front of the basilica is enclosed by Bernini's magnificent elliptical colonnade (1655–67). The basilica itself stands on a historic site once occupied by a chapel built over the tomb of St Peter by Pope Anacletus at the beginning of the 2nd century. In the place of this chapel Constantine the Great erected a basilica in 330, and it was here that Charlemagne was crowned Emperor of the West on Christmas Eve, 800. Pope Nicholas V decided in 1452 to reconstruct the basilica, and in 1506 Pope Julius II entrusted the task to Bramante, who planned a church in the form of a Greek cross, with a central dome. Following several discarded plans, Michelangelo reverted to the basic design of Bramante, and his work was continued after his death by Vignola, Pirro Ligorio and Giacomo della Porta. Pope Paul V, however, later decided that the building should, after all, be in the form of a Latin cross, and the nave was accordingly extended by Maderno, by whom the façade also was built (1606–12). The basilica was consecrated by Pope Urban VIII in 1626.

St Peter's is the largest church in the world: it covers an area of 49,576 m²; its length is 185 m; the height of the ceiling is 43·5 m; and the height to the top of the cross on the dome is 132 m. The dome has a diameter of 42 m.

St Petersburg, city of Florida, USA, situated on the west side of Tampa Bay. Population (1980) 236,893.

See also TAMPA.

St Petersburg, see LENINGRAD.

St Pierre, seaport town of Martinique, French West Indies, on the west coast of the island at the foot of the volcano, Mont Pelée. Formerly the chief commercial centre of Martinique, it was entirely destroyed in 1902 by an eruption, every citizen but one being killed. Population (1974) 5434.

St-Pierre and Miquelon, French *département* comprising eight small islands off the south coast of Newfoundland, Canada; the territory is named after the two biggest. They are barren and rocky, with little vegetation. The capital is St-Pierre, on the island of the same name. The population is almost exclusively employed in fishing with some subsistence farming.

The islands were ceded to Britain under the Treaty of Utrecht (1713), returned to France in 1763, captured by the British again in 1794, but given back to France under the Treaty of Ghent (1814). Area 242 km²; population (1974) 5840.

St-Quentin, French town in the *département* of Aisne, on the Somme, 33 km south of Cambrai. It has a beautiful 12th-century Gothic church and 13th-century *hôtel de ville.* It has important textile, electrical and metal industries. Population 70,700.

Saint-Saëns, Camille (1835–1921), French composer. In 1871, with Romain Bussine, he founded the Société Nationale de Musique. His opera *Samson et Dalila* was produced at Weimar in 1877. As well as much choral, orchestral and instrumental music, his works include the symphonic poem *Danse macabre*, incidental music for the *Antigone* of Sophocles, and *Carnaval des animaux*.

Saint-Simon, Claude Henri de Rouvroy, Comte de (1760–1825), French writer and philosopher. His theories and projects for a reformation of society on socialistic lines were put forward in *L'Industrie*, 1817; *L'Organisateur*, 1819–20; *Du Système industriel*, 1821; *Catechisme des industriels*, 1823–24; and *Nouveau Christianisme*, 1825. Saint-Simon gathered a few ardent disciples, and influenced at various periods such men as Thierry and Comte; he lived a life of privation and died, after an attempt at suicide in 1823, in great poverty.

See also SOCIALISM.

Saint-Simon, Louis de Rouvroy, Duc de (1675–1755), French writer of memoirs, soldier, courtier, and politician. During his long connection with the court, he collected a mass of material, varying from the most important details from the highest authorities to mere servant gossip, which he wrote out during his retirement at La Ferté-Vidame from 1723 until his death.

His writings, partly his own memoirs and partly an amplification of Dangeau's *Journal*, are the greatest of their kind. After his death they were confiscated as state papers. The first full edition was published in 21 volumes in 1829.

Saint-Simonism, see SAINT-SIMON, CLAUDE HENRI DE ROUVROY, COMTE DE.

St Stephen's Crown (of Hungary) is a stemma type of royal diadem which had great political significance. Before 1918 no royal coronation was authentic in Hungary without this crown. Tradition claimed that it had been a gift from Pope Sylvester II to Stephen, for his inauguration in 1000, and invested it with sanctity as if royal power originated in it.

St Thomas, West Indian island purchased with the other Virgin Islands from Denmark by the USA for $25 million in January 1917. It is 61 km east of Puerto Rico, and has a fine harbour. St Thomas has mountainous terrain and poor soil. The development of marine research, game fishing, and tourism has increased lately. Bay rum from the bayberry-tree (*Pimenta acris*) is now almost the sole export. Rum is distilled. Area 73 km². Population (1980) 44,218.

St Thomas à Becket, see BECKET, THOMAS.

St Vincent
Area: 388 km²
Population: 117,646
Capital: Kingstown

St Vincent, one of the Windward Islands group lying at latitude 13°10′N and longitude 60°57′W; it is 29 km in length and 8 km wide, with an area (including dependencies) of 388 km² and a population in 1978 of 117,646. It includes the northern part of the Grenadines archipelago as a dependency. St Vincent's capital is Kingstown.

Like the other islands of the Windwards, St Vincent is volcanic in its origin. A ridge of well-wooded mountains extends from north to south; at the northern end is La Soufrière, a volcano 1234 m high which erupted in 1902 with the loss of 2000 lives. Mount St Andrew in the south dominates the Kingstown valley, and spurs diverge from the main range to make most picturesque valleys. The Grenadines are a cluster of considerable charm, the main islands being Bequia, Cannouan, and Mayreau, and Mustique which is being privately developed.

St Vincent is the world's leading producer of arrowroot, although bananas account for over half of the island's exports. Copra, cocoa, cassava, coconuts, nutmegs, and groundnuts are also produced. The East Caribbean dollar (EC$) is in use.

The St Vincent government is administered by a governor-general, advised by a cabinet and elected legislative assembly. There is also a Senate.

History. St Vincent was discovered by Columbus on 22 January 1498, St Vincent's Day in the Spanish calendar, but it remained in native Carib hands until the 17th century, when Charles II of England included it in a grant made to the Earl of Carlisle. In 1668 Francis, Lord Willoughby made a treaty by which the Caribs acknowledged themselves subjects of the English king. In 1762 General Monckton seized it and organised its colonisation. The island was captured by the French in 1779 but restored to Britain in 1783 by the Treaty of Versailles. After a revolt the Caribs were, in 1796, deported to Ruatan Islands in the Bay of Honduras. The island became a member of CARIFTA (Caribbean Free Trade Area) in 1968 and became independent in 1979.

St Vincent, John Jervis, 1st Earl (1735–1823), British admiral of the fleet. In 1797 he ventured to close with the Spanish fleet off Cape St Vincent in spite of tremendous odds; the result was a brilliant victory, in which Nelson participated. In the Addington ministry he served as first lord of the Admiralty. He was an exceedingly strict disciplinarian and averted a mutiny in the fleet at Spithead by his strong measures.

St Vincent, one of the Cape Verde Islands.

St Vincent, Cape (Portuguese *Cabo de São Vicente*), cape in Algarve province, Portugal, the extreme south-westerly point of continental Europe. Several notable naval battles have been fought off the cape: (1) in 1780, during the War of American Independence, after Spain had joined the French, Admiral Rodney defeated the Spanish fleet there and passed supplies into Gibraltar, which was under siege; (2) on 14 February 1797, in the Napoleonic Wars, Admiral Jervis and Commodore Nelson won a victory over the combined French and Spanish fleets, which removed the danger of a French invasion of Ireland; (3) the battle in which Sir Charles Napier defeated Dom Miguel in 1833.

St Vitus Dance, see CHOREA.

Sainte-Beuve, Charles Augustin (1804–1869), French literary critic. With the object of spreading the Romantic movement he published his *Tableau de la poésie française et du théâtre français au seizième siècle*, 1828. In 1834 he published *Volupté*, his only novel, and in 1837 delivered at Lausanne his famous lectures on Port-Royal.
His period of real greatness dates from his visit to Italy in 1840. During the next nine years he wrote almost entirely for the *Revue des deux mondes*. In 1844 he was elected to the Académie and in 1848 was made professor of French literature at Liège, where he delivered his famous course of lectures on *Chateaubriand et son groupe littéraire sous l'Empire*. From 1849 onwards his main works were the literary articles which appeared every Monday, and were later collected as *Causeries du lundi* and *Nouveaux lundis*.
Saintpaulia, a genus of tropical African perennial herbs in family Gesneriaceae. *S. ionantha*, the African violet, is a popular indoor plant in Europe and America, flowering almost continuously, with violet-blue or pink flowers.
Saints, Battle of the, name given to Adm. Rodney's victory over the French fleet under de Grasse near the Saints Island, off Dominica, on 12 April 1782.
Saints' Play, one of the main forms of vernacular religious drama of the Middle Ages, popular throughout western Europe. Originating in the *lectio* (reading), the saints' play dramatises incidents from the life and death of those individuals who successfully attempt to imitate Christ's perfect example of virtuous conduct. In spite of the few survivors, there is no doubt that the saints' play rivalled the other vernacular genres in popularity in the late Middle Ages, and there is ample evidence that a large number of saints' plays were regularly performed during this period.
Saipan, island of the Mariana Islands, having the seat of government at Garapan. The principal agricultural products are sugar, coffee, and copra. Manganese and phosphate deposits occur. Occupied by the Japanese in the Second World War, in 1947 it became part of the US Trust Territory of the Pacific and its administrative centre. Area 121 km^2; population (1971) 10,458.
Saithe, see Coal-Fish.
Sakai, an aboriginal people living in Sumatra and the central forest region of the Malay Peninsula. They are hunters and gatherers, and also practise a rudimentary form of agriculture. Their average height is just under 1·5 m and they have brown skins and wavy hair. Their numbers are declining today.
Sakai, city of Ōsaka-fu, Japan, it lies immediately to the south of Ōsaka, from which it is separated by the Yamato river. By the Muromachi period (1339–1573), Sakai had already emerged as the chief port of Ōsaka Bay, a role which it later lost to Ōsaka. Since the 19th century, however, Sakai has grown as an important manufacturing centre and its industries include iron and steel, shipbuilding, oil refining, petrochemicals, textiles, cutlery, and bicycles. Population (1979) 787,000.
Saké, national colourless beverage of Japan, fermented from rice.
Sakhalin (formerly Japanese *Karafuto*), island in the Soviet Far East between the Sea of Okhotsk and the Sea of Japan, separated from the mainland by the Tatar Strait and from Hokkaidō (Japan) by La Perouse Strait. The northern third is lowland; farther south, two mountain ranges (highest point 1609 m) are separated by the valley of the Poronai and Tym rivers. Sakhalin has coal, oil, and gold deposits, a cool monsoonal climate, and coniferous and mixed forest vegetation. There are fishing, lumbering, cellulose, and paper industries; vegetables are grown, and there is also dairy-farming. Oil is extracted and piped across the Tatar Strait to Komsomolsk-na-Amure. Japan held the southern half 1905–45. Area 76,400 km^2. Population (1970) 616,000.
Sakharov, Andrei Dimitrievich (1921–), Soviet physicist and dissident. His work on nuclear fusion was instrumental in the development of the Russian hydrogen bomb in the 1940s. In the 1960s he took a stand against nuclear weapons, and was awarded the Nobel Peace Prize in 1975. His defence of civil liberties in the USSR, particularly free speech, brought him into conflict with the Soviet authorities, and in 1980 he was sent into internal exile in the city of Gorki, despite international protest and growing concern for his health.
'Saki', see Munro, H(ector) H(ugh).
Saki, the popular name of *Pithecia* and *Chiropotes*, genera of New World monkeys in the family Cebidae, consisting of four species. These have a long, non-prehensile tail. They are found only in the Amazon valley and Guyana.
Sakkara, on the high ground west of the Nile, 23 km south-west of Cairo, the necropolis of Memphis containing important relics of all periods of ancient Egyptian history, particularly of the first six dynasties.
The step pyramid of Zoser at Sakkara is the oldest stone building in the world. The 5th Dynasty pyramid of Unas is the first to contain pyramid texts. Nearby is the recently discovered 'lost' tomb of King Horemheb and the 5th Dynasty tomb of Nefer, containing the oldest mummy. Here too are the catacombs in which the sacred Apis bulls of Memphis were buried in huge stone sarcophagi.
See also Pyramid; Serapis.

Sakkara. *The step pyramid of Zoser, built on the west bank of the Nile, c.2800 BC.*

Sal Ammoniac, see Ammonia.
Salad, a dish made from mixtures of herbs, leafy plants, nuts, fruits, vegetables, eggs, meat or fish. Salad may be served either as an hors d'oeuvres, or as an accompaniment to a main dish (either hot or cold), or as a main course.
Saladin (1138–93), Sultan of Egypt and Syria. In 1171 he suppressed the Fatimid dynasty and constituted himself sovereign of Egypt. On the death of Nureddin in 1174 he declared himself sultan, was recognised as sovereign by the princes of northern Syria, and in 1187 inflicted a crushing defeat on the Christians at Tiberias. His success caused great alarm to Europe, and led to the Third Crusade. In 1191 Acre fell into the hands of Philip II of France and Richard Coeur-de-Lion. But although Saladin was defeated, and Jaffa and Caesarea retaken, Richard was forced to leave Saladin in possession of Jerusalem and to agree to a truce. Saladin died at Damascus, and is remembered for his kindliness and chivalry. He was also an art patron and builder of schools and mosques.
See also Crusades.
Salado, Río, three rivers in Argentina: the first, in the north, rising in the Andes, flowing south-east to join the Paraná, 384 km north-west of Buenos Aires. Length 2030 km.
The second, in the eastern part of the province of Buenos Aires, is about 640 km long and of value for irrigation, flowing west into Samborombón Bay.
The third, in the west, is about 1368 km long and has an upper course, Desaguadero, and a course through La Pampa province known as Chadileo. It flows southwards, then south-east before emptying into the Colorado river.
Salamanca, capital of the province of Salamanca, Spain, on a height overlooking the River Tormes. It is one of the great cultural centres of Spain, and its university, founded in the early 13th century, was once one of the most renowned in Europe. Population (1981) 167,131.

Salamanca, Battle of, fought on 22 July 1812, was one of Wellington's most important victories in the Peninsular War. Wellington, having taken the border fortresses Badajoz and Ciudad Rodrigo for use as bases of operations, marched into Spain in June. On 22 July, forced by his French adversary Marmont, Wellington was retreating towards Ciudad Rodrigo. Marmont tried to cut the line of retreat by a move which extended the French line. In half an hour three French divisions were routed and scattered to the winds. The French lost 8000 killed and wounded, besides 7000 prisoners. Allied losses, out of an equal force of about 40,000 were just over 5000. The French were saved from even greater destruction by Wellington's failure to press the pursuit as strongly as might have been done.

Salamander, common name for members of the amphibian order Urodela. There are about 300 species, all with tails, most with four legs. They are usually about 10 to 15 cm long, but *Megalobatrachus japonicus*, the giant salamander of Japan, can reach 180 cm. Their colour may be muddy or they may have brightly coloured stripes and spots. They eat insects and worms, and live in water or in damp areas in northern temperate regions.

Fertilisation is either external or internal, often taking place in water. The larvae have external gills. Some remain in the larval form, although they become sexually mature and breed; this is called neoteny. The Mexican axolotl and the mud puppy, *Necturus maculosus*, of North America, are neotenic.

Salamis, island of Greece off the coast of Attica. It was the scene of the victory of the Greeks over the Persians in 480 BC. Now the island's chief town, Salamis, is a naval station. Area 93 km²; population (1971) 18,364.

Salazar, Antonio de Oliveira (1889–1970), Portuguese dictator. He entered politics in the 1920s, and after the military coup of May 1926 he became minister of finance, but soon resigned. In 1928 he was again finance minister, and was offered the premiership in 1932, which he organised into a virtual dictatorship of a Fascist type under the 1933 constitution, which was accepted by plebiscite in 1933. In the 1930s he carried out reforms in social conditions, developed the industries, and entered on schemes of public works and education. He kept Portugal neutral in the Second World War.

After 1945 Salazar's domestic policies brought a measure of improvement and industrialisation. All political organisations other than the régime-controlled National Union were banned, and the ban repressively enforced. After 1960 increasing demands were made on the national budget by the cost of maintaining Portugal's African colonies against the local liberation movements, at the expense of domestic development.

Sale, town of Victoria, Australia, centre of a grazing, agricultural, irrigation, and dairying district 206 km east of Melbourne. The town's development has now been boosted by the discovery of offshore oil and gas. Population (1976) 12,111.

Salé, also Sallee or Sali (Arabic *sla*, sacred), seaport on the west coast of Morocco, on the north side of the mouth of Bou Regreb, opposite Rabat, 175 km west of Fez; it is noted for its carpets. In the 16th century the town was the headquarters of the 'Sallee Rovers' (Barbary pirates). Population (1971) 155,557.

Salem, city of Tamil Nadu state, India, 320 km south-west of Madras, with handicraft and large-scale textile manufacturing, and modern chemical and electrically based industries. Population (1981) 361,177.

Salem, capital of Oregon, USA, on the Willamette river, 84 km south of Portland. Besides the organs of state government, the city has processing plants for the products of the fertile Willamette farmlands and of the Cascade forests to the east. Population (1980) 89,161.

Salep, a nutritious powder obtained from the tuberous roots of *Orchis mascula* (of family Orchidaieae) and allied species. In water it swells to a jelly, and a drink prepared from it was formerly much used to allay gastro-intestinal irritation. It has nutritive value and can be used as a mucilage, a medium in which medications can be suspended. It is still sometimes given to invalids and children.

Salerno (ancient *Salernum*), Italian city and seaport, capital of Salerno province in Campania, built on the narrow strip between the Apennines and the Gulf of Salerno, 45 km south-east of Naples. There are ceramic, cotton, and paper industries. Salerno is famous for the school of medicine which flourished there throughout the Middle Ages. In the Second World War it was the scene of major Allied troop landings in 1943. Population (1979) 162,000.

Salerno, Gulf of, inlet of the Tyrrhenian Sea, in Campania, Italy. It is about 60 km wide and the island of Capri marks the north-west corner. The chief towns on its shores are Salerno and Amalfi.

Sales Management. With general acceptance of the marketing concept, the overall responsibility in a company for ascertaining the needs of the market(s) it serves, designing the product range, and ensuring that demand is met adequately by an efficiently organised distribution system, is that of a marketing manager. Popularly used, however, the terms sales manager or sales director still loosely refer to this broad area of action. Sales management in its new or more narrowly defined sense relates solely to one or more of the following: (1) the management of a sales force; (2) organisation of physical distribution; (3) control of regional or product-based sales organisations; (4) administration of order-handling, invoicing, and collection of cash through sales offices.

Sales Promotion, a term used to refer to all types of promotion apart from advertising, personal selling, and public relations. Probably the most widely used form of sales promotion is a reduction in selling price for a limited period (a 'special offer'). Another common technique is to make available some valuable or useful object (a 'premium') at a special price to purchasers of a product, who must send in package labels with their money, or to give away something with each package of the product (an 'on-pack premium').

Salford, industrial city immediately west of Manchester, and part of Greater Manchester Metropolitan County, England. It is separated from Manchester only by the River Irwell, an inconspicuous stream hidden behind industrial buildings near the city centre. The docks of the Manchester Ship Canal are within Salford. Though cotton and other textile factories were the traditional industries, engineering also became significant when the Ship Canal was constructed. Population (1981) 98,024.

Salic Law, code of laws of the Salian Franks, or more particularly that Salian law which excluded females from inheriting lands. The so-called salic law of France of the 14th century was a fundamental pact, by virtue of which males only could inherit the throne.

Salicin, a bitter crystalline glucoside derived from the bark of young shoots of the poplar and willow trees. It has antipyretic and analgesic properties similar to those of aspirin but often produces skin rashes.

Salicylic Acid is a white crystalline solid, with a melting point of 155°C. It was discovered in 1838 by Piria, who prepared it from a substance present in willow bark (*Salix*). Nowadays it is manufactured from sodium phenate. Salicylic acid has bacteriostatic and fungicidal properties and is generally applied externally in dusting powders, lotions or ointments for the treatment of skin conditions such as eczema, psoriasis, and dandruff and to destroy warts and corns. It is also used as a food preservative in butter, fruit, meat and beer. The sodium salt is less toxic. Its derivative aspirin, or acetylsalicylic acid, is an important drug with pain relieving, fever reducing, and anti-inflammatory actions. *Methyl salicylate,* or oil of wintergreen, is applied in liniments and ointments for the relief of pain in lumbago, sciatica and rheumatism. Phenyl salicylate is a sunscreen agent in some creams and lotions.

Salieri, Antonio (1750–1825), Italian composer. He became conductor of the court opera in Vienna. He toured widely and was admired by Gluck. He wrote 43 operas, and oratorios, cantatas and symphonies, and was founder of the Vienna Conservatory.

Saline Plants, see HALOPHYTES.

Salinger, J(erome) D(avid) (1919–), US writer. From 1946 he contributed mainly to the *New Yorker*. His novel *The Catcher in the Rye*, 1951, about an intelligent and sensitive 16-year-old boy at odds with the world and himself, has become perhaps the most popular and widely-read novel among young people in the United States. Salinger writes often of people at breaking point, withdrawing from the prevailing insincerity and heartlessness of the world to find love and trust, often in children.

Salisbury, Countess of, wife of the Black Prince, see FAIR MAID OF KENT.

Salisbury, Robert Arthur Gascoyne-Cecil, 3rd Marquess of (1830–1903), British statesman. In the Derby administration of 1866 he was appointed secretary for India. When Disraeli came into power in 1874 Salisbury again went to the India Office; but in 1878 he went to the Foreign Office, where he soon acquired a reputation for knowledge and efficiency. Shortly after he became foreign secretary he went with Disraeli to the Berlin Congress, from which they returned according to the words of the Prime Minister, bringing 'peace with honour'. On Disraeli's death in 1881 Salisbury became the Conservative leader; and when, four years later, Gladstone was defeated, he formed his first administration. He was beaten at the general election of 1885, but was returned to power in the following year. He held office until 1892, and then again from 1895 until his resignation on 11 July 1902.

Salisbury, Robert Arthur James Gascoyne-Cecil, 5th Marquess of (1893–1972), British statesman. From 1935 until 1938 he was parliamentary under-secretary for foreign affairs, from which post he resigned in 1938 with Eden in protest against Chamberlain's appeasement policy towards Germany. In 1940 he entered Churchill's Cabinet. From 1945 to 1951 he was leader of the Opposition peers, in 1951 lord privy seal and leader of the House of Lords, and from 1952 to 1957 lord president of the council. Generally regarded in terms of political seniority as one of the Conservative 'elder statesmen', he resigned his government offices in March 1957.

Salisbury, Robert Cecil, Earl of (c.1563–1612), English statesman, succeeded his father, Lord Burghley, as secretary of state in 1596. In 1601 he began a secret correspondence with James VI and on the death of Elizabeth became James's chief adviser. He built Hatfield House.

Salisbury, cathedral city of Wiltshire, England, at the confluence of the Avon with three small rivers, 131 km south-west of London. It was moved from Old Sarum at the beginning of the 13th century, and built on a settled plan 3 km below the old citadel by Bishop Poore. Salisbury has developed into an important agricultural market and service centre; it also has breweries and several light industries. Population (1981) 35,355.

Salisbury, Zimbabwe, see HARARE.

Salisbury Cathedral. Bishop Richard Poore commenced the erection of the present cathedral in 1220. Except for its crowning tower and spire, it is a building of uniform Early English design, built to one plan, in the form of a double cross, unlike any other English cathedral except Exeter. Its designer is unknown, though he may have been a churchman, Elias de Derham. The cloisters and octagonal chapter-house were added c.1270–1300, and the upper part of the tower and the spire, 1334–60.

Extensive alterations were carried out in the 18th century. At the intersection of the nave with the principal transept rises the spire, which is 123 m in height from the pavement, the tallest spire in England. The cloisters, on the south side, are the finest example in England of the late 13th-century style.

Salisbury Plain, undulating tract of open chalk downs in Wiltshire, England, between Salisbury and Devizes, about 32 km by 25 km. It has been used as an army training area at least since the time of the Napoleonic Wars. The plain is the finest open-air museum of archaeology in Britain. It abounds in prehistoric burial mounds and earthworks, particularly of the Bronze and Early Iron Ages, and there are extensive remains of 'Celtic'-type field-systems and of Romano-British settlements. About 16 km north of Salisbury is Stonehenge.

Salish, North American Indian people, often called Flatheads, who belong to the Salishan linguistic group and live in Montana and westwards. They were friendly with the whites, and were converted to Christianity by the famous Jesuit missionary Father de Smet. They number about 5000.

See also FLATHEADS.

Earl of Salisbury. *A portrait of Robert Cecil painted in 1602 by John de Critz the Elder.*

Saliva, the fluid secreted into the mouth prior to a meal and during the process of eating. It is produced by three pairs of salivary glands situated around the mouth. These are called the parotid, the submandibular and the sublingual glands. Saliva is secreted in response to the stimulus produced by the sight, smell, thought or presence in the mouth of food. Its functions are mainly the formation of the bolus (mass) of food and its lubrication to facilitate its passage through the oesophagus. Saliva contains ptyalin, an enzyme which initiates the digestion of starch. Also, by its moistening action of the tongue, mouth and pharynx, saliva aids the mechanical process of speech.

Salix, a genus of trees and shrubs of the Salicaceae, mostly occurring in north temperate and arctic regions. Most of the tree species of the genus, the willows, have spear-shaped leaves. Possibly the most important economically is the cricket-bat willow, *S. alba* var *coerulea*; *S. fragilis* (crack willow), *S.* × *chrysocoma* (weeping willow) and other species are used as decorative trees, especially near water. *S. aurita*, *S. caprea* (goat or pussy willow) and *S. cinerea* are large shrubs with oval leaves; they are generally called sallow, and, like all species of *Salix*, they have male and female catkins on separate plants appearing in early spring before the leaves. *Salix* species grown to provide flexible twigs for basketry are called osier.

Salk, Jonas Edward (1914–), US physician and scientist. In 1954 he developed a vaccine for the prevention of poliomyelitis. The disease has almost been eradicated in the USA and Europe due to mass vaccination campaigns. He is the founding director of the Salk Institute for Biological Sciences, California.

Sallow, see SALIX.

Sallust, full name Gaius Sallustius Crispus (86–34 BC), Roman historian. In 49 Caesar appointed him quaestor. He accompanied Caesar on the African campaign (46), and was appointed by him governor of Numidia. He laid out the splendid gardens (*Horti Sallustiani*) on the Quirinal. On his return from Africa he retired into private life.

It was probably during those years of retirement that Sallust wrote his account of Catiline's conspiracy, *Bellum Catilinarium*, and of the war against Jugurtha, *Bellum Jugurthinum*. During the same period, no doubt, Sallust produced the five books of his *Histories*, which covered the years 78–67 BC, and of which only fragments survive.

Salmon, *Salmo* and *Oncorhynchus*, genera of important food and sporting fishes, zoologically of exceptional interest on account of their remarkable life-history and ready response to varying conditions of life. The Atlantic salmon (*S. salar*) occurs naturally only between latitudes 42° and 75°N; it swims up rivers to spawn, but its rapid growth is made entirely in the sea, where it feeds mostly upon herrings and other pelagic fish.

Salmon Fishing, see ANGLING.

Salmonella, see FOOD-POISONING.

Saló, republic set up in 1943 in German-occupied northern Italy by Mussolini, centred on the town of the same name. The true object of setting up the republic was supply of men for the German war effort. The republic collapsed in 1945.

Salome, in Matt. xiv. 6, the daughter of Herod Philip by his wife Herodias, who had deserted him for his brother Herod Antipas; Herodias instigated her as a young girl in her teens to ask for the head of John the Baptist as a reward for dancing (Mark vi. 22). Her name, not mentioned in the New Testament, is given by Josephus. She married (1) Philip the Tetrarch, and (2) Aristobulus, son of Herod of Chalcis.

Salome, one of the holy women who followed Jesus from Galilee, witnessed his crucifixion from afar (Mark xv. 40) and afterwards visited the sepulchre (Mark xvi. 1).

Salonika, see THESSALONIKI.

Salop, see SHROPSHIRE.

Salsify, *Tragopogon porrifolius*, a biennial purple plant in the family Compositae, related to the dandelion and cultivated for its thick white tap-root, which is used as a vegetable.

Salsola, saltwort, a genus of shrubs and herbs in family Chenopodiaceae, with fleshy awl-shaped leaves and small axillary flowers. *S. kali* is a much-branched plant, with leaves terminating in sharp spines, common on sandy seashores through the northern hemisphere. Its ash was formerly much used in soap and glass-making.

Salt, in chemistry, a name given to a whole class of compounds of which sodium chloride or 'common' salt is a typical example. Salts may be regarded as compounds derived from acids by the replacement of part or all of the hydrogen of the latter by metals. Thus sulphuric acid (H_2SO_4) forms *sulphates*, e.g. sodium sulphate, Na_2SO_4, and sodium bisulphate, $NaHSO_4$. Salts are made by neutralising the acid with the appropriate metallic oxide, hydroxide or carbonate, and in other ways. Sodium chloride, NaCl, is a compound of the metal sodium (Na) with the green poisonous gas chlorine (Cl). It is found in large deposits in many districts, e.g. Cheshire (England), Stassfurt (Germany), Wieliczka (Poland), and the USA. It is also present in the dissolved state in sea-water, where it has been carried by rivers. Synthetically it may be made by burning sodium in chlorine, or by neutralising hydrochloric acid with caustic soda.

The total annual world production of salt is about 200 million tonnes. It is used as a condiment, for preserving food, and in very many chemical industries.

Salt-glaze Ware, term for a Staffordshire 18th-century earthenware, made impervious by a thin glaze formed by the action of common salt being introduced to the kiln at its highest temperature.

See also STONEWARE.

Salt Lake City, capital of Utah, USA, and county seat of Salt Lake county, 605 km north-west of Denver, Colorado. It was laid out in 1847 by the Mormon Church, under Brigham Young, and became a city in 1851. Its chief industries are the manufacture of sugar, textiles, pottery, boots and shoes, confectionery, tobacco, and cutlery, and there are smelters and food preparation industries. Copper, lead, zinc, coal, and iron mines are worked nearby. Salt Lake City is the world headquarters of the Mormon Church. Population (1980) 162,960.

Salta, capital of Salta province in Argentina, about 1240 km north-west of Buenos Aires. The town, situated at an altitude of 1170 m, is on the River Arias in the Lerma valley. It does a considerable entrepôt trade with Bolivia and Chile. Population (1975) 176,216.

Saltillo, capital of Coahuila state, Mexico. Situated at an altitude of 1575 m in the extreme south-east corner of the state, its prime importance is as a rail and road communications centre. There is a university here. Population (1975) 211,000.

Salto, town of Uruguay, situated on the Uruguay river, facing Concordia (Argentina), 590 km by rail from Montevideo and 320 km by river from Buenos Aires. It is a livestock centre. Population (1975) 80,000.

Saltpetre, common name for potassium nitrate, see POTASSIUM.

Saltram, a house 5 km east of Plymouth, Devon, England. Classical façades were added to the original Tudor house c.1750, and Adam designed the saloon and dining-room in 1768 for the Parker family. It is set in a landscaped park and has a fine orangery and summer-house.

Saltykov, Mikhail Yevgrafovich (1826–89), Russian satirical writer who used the pseudonym N. Shchedrin, and is also often called Saltykov-Shchedrin. He was co-editor of *The Contemporary* and editor of its successor as the leading radical monthly, *Notes of the Fatherland*. In his *Provincial Sketches*, 1856, and many other sketches, tales, and longer works, he developed the art of social and political satire directed against traditional and contemporary Russian conditions. He gives a powerful if gloomy picture of the decay of the backward provincial gentry in his famous novel, *The Golovlev Family*, 1872–76.

Saluki, or gazelle hound, breed of dog. Resembling in general shape the English greyhound, it has large oval eyes and long ears covered with long silky hair. The colours are white, cream, golden-red, etc. There is also a short-coated variety. The height is 58–71 cm, bitches somewhat smaller.

Salute (Latin *salutare*, to salute), mark of respect for the rank or uniform of the person saluted. In Britain, a royal salute consists of 21 guns.

Salvador (full name São Salvador da Bahía de Todos os Santos), capital of the state of Bahía, Brazil, and the third largest city in the country. It stands on a peninsula which encloses Bahía de Todos os Santos (All Saints Bay). It contains many fine buildings dating from its golden era of 1549–1763 during which period it was the capital of Brazil. It has always been a leading port and also has food and tobacco processing, textiles, metallurgy, cement, shipbuilding and repairs, and a number of consumer industries. Population (1980) 1,496,276.

Salvador, El, see EL SALVADOR.

Salvage (marine), in law, means the compensation allowed to persons who save a ship, apparel, and cargo, or what formed part of these, or freight, from shipwreck, capture, or similar jeopardy. Salvors have a maritime lien over ship, freight, and cargo for their salvage, and their right takes priority over all other liens which may already have attached to the subject-matter of the claim. The salvage money is divided in certain proportions among the owners, captain, and other officers, and the crew of the salving vessel. The owner of an aircraft is entitled to a reasonable reward for salvage services rendered by the aircraft to any property or persons in any case where the owner of a ship would be so entitled.

Salvaging is the term used in connection with the refloating or saving of sunken or wrecked vessels.

See also TUG.

Salvation Army, international religious movement composed of men and women who, moved by the love of God, seek the spiritual and social betterment of their fellows. William Booth, the founder of the movement, had been a Methodist minister. In 1878 came the change of name to the Salvation Army. The general superintendent of the Christian mission became the general, a convenient shortening of a rather cumbrous title; military terminology inevitably followed, a uniform was designed, the bonnet appeared, a flag was employed to head street marches, and brass bands became a familiar feature. In 1880 a training college for officers was opened and the work was established in the USA. Within another 10 years Salvationists were at work in Australia, India, South Africa, Canada, New Zealand, the West Indies, and nine of the principal European countries. During the same decade the Salvation Army's influence on social conditions began to be felt, for example in the passing of the Criminal Law Amendment Act (1885).

In the early 20th century the Salvation Army's work continued to be expanded, and it now operates in over 80 countries and over 100 languages. It imposes a rigorous moral code on all who join the movement.

Salvia, in family Labiatae, a genus of annual or perennial herbs and shrubs found in temperate and warm regions. *S. officinalis* is the common sage used as a herb. *S. sclarea*, the biennial clary; *S. splendens*, scarlet sage, a Brazilian shrub grown as an annual in colder areas; *S.* × *superba* and *S. patens* and others are valued flowering plants for borders.

Salvinia, a genus of aquatic ferns in family Salviniaceae from the tropics and subtropics. *S. natans* is a pretty little floating plant with small fern-like leaves, and is sometimes cultivated.

Salween, or Salwin, river of South-East Asia, rising in Tibet (China) and flowing principally through Burma in a southerly direction, finally entering the Gulf of Martaban at the town of Moulmein. It has a total length of about 3000 km but is not navigable owing to rapids.

Salzburg (Roman *Juvavum*), city and capital of Salzburg province in Austria, situated on the Salzach. It has the great fortress of Hohensalzburg overlooking the city, and numerous fine Romanesque, Gothic, and Baroque churches. The birthplace of Mozart, it has had since 1920 a celebrated annual musical festival. An important transport focus, it is a tourist and conference centre. The city has large breweries, and traditionally manufactures musical instruments and textiles. Population (1981) 138,317.

Samādhi, in Hindu philosophy, a state of absorption of the ordinary mind into limitless awareness. The last stage of Rāja Yoga in which the ordinary mind is transcended and a new consciousness of existence arises.

Samara, see KUIBYSHEV.

Samaria, the central province or section of ancient Palestine, having Judaea on the south, and Galilee on the north.

Samaria, ancient city and capital, founded by Omri (c.887–876 BC), the fifth king of the Northern Kingdom or Israel. It is situated on a hill 91 km above the surrounding valley, and when fortified took even an Assyrian army three years to capture. Omri and his successor, Ahab (c.876–853), levelled the top of the hill, banked its sides, and built inner and outer walls around the summit. The city was provided with royal palaces, with a number of large cisterns, and a cemented water pool. In 722 BC Samaria was destroyed by the Assyrian king, Sargon II. Later it was rebuilt, and under Alexander the Great (who planted Macedonian colonists there, 331 BC) it became a Hellenistic city. Herod the Great rebuilt, fortified and enlarged it. Samaria was captured and burned during the Jewish revolt in AD 66, but later rebuilt, and c.180–230 it enjoyed a period of prosperity. Excavations were carried out at Samaria in 1908–10 and in 1931–35.

Samaritans, inhabitants of Samaria, whose origins are obscure. The Samaritans themselves derive their name from *shamerim*, 'keepers', i.e. of the Torah. The term in its usual modern sense first occurs in the New Testament and refers to an ultra-conservative religious group, based in Shechem, which apparently emerged from the matrix of Judaism sometime during the 300 years before the Christian era.

The Samaritans declared the Jerusalem Temple to be schismatic. They venerated only the Pentateuch as canonical and kept the law with exemplary strictness, but never de-

Samarkand. *The Registan, an old Mohammedan college, built in the 14th and 15th centuries.*

veloped a rabbinic system. It was held against them by the Jews that they pronounced the name of God, a practice they have now dropped. The hatred between them and the Jews is well attested.

The Samaritans suffered less than the Jews under Antiochus, but a great deal from the Jews themselves under the Hasmoneans. John Hyrcanus destroyed their temple in c.107 BC. It was rebuilt in AD 135, and finally destroyed in 484, for political rather than religious motives. The Samaritans continued to worship on Mount Gerizim, and still do so. They have maintained their separateness from the Jews. In 1960 the Samaritans numbered 214 at Nablus (Shechem) and 132 at Holon, near Tel-Aviv. The two groups were reunited as a result of the Six Day War in 1967.

Samaritans, The, an organisation which befriends the suicidal and despairing. It consists almost entirely of unqualified, but very carefully selected and supervised, volunteers and was started by the Rev. Chad Varah at his church of St Stephen Walbrook in the City of London in 1953. It has since spread all over the world.

Samarium, metallic chemical element, symbol Sm, atomic number 62, atomic weight 150·4. It is a member of the family of lanthanides. Samarium occurs in such minerals as monazite and gadolinite, and may be obtained in the metallic state (melting point 1350 °C) by the electrolysis of the fused chloride, $SmCl_3$.

Samarkand, capital city of Samarkand *oblast* USSR, south-west of Tashkent. It is one of the oldest cities in Central Asia, dating from the 3rd or 4th millennium BC. From the 6th century AD until 1220 (when it was destroyed by Genghis Khan), it was a centre of the Islamic culture, and an important city on the 'Silk Route'. In the 14th century, Timur (Tamerlane) made it his capital, and the city flourished once more. By the 18th century the city was in severe decline, and was for a while uninhabited. It was not until it became a provincial capital of the Russian Empire in 1887 that its recovery began. It is now an engineering, superphosphates, cotton, and silk-producing centre, and it also has a university. The city is nowadays being promoted as a tourist attraction, especially for foreigners. Population (1980) 481,000.

Samian Ware, or terra sigillata, red glazed pottery which was mass-produced in Gaul and Germany and used throughout and even beyond the Roman Empire.

See also EARTHENWARE.

Samizdat (Russian: self-publication), the dissemination in the USSR, by unofficial means, of political or literary work that has been banned by the authorities. The works of Sakharov and Solzhenitsyn among others have been circulated in this way.

Samoa, formerly Navigators' Islands, archipelago of volcanic islands in the Pacific, stretching from north-west to south-east, between 168° and 173°W and 13°30′ and 14°30′S. The forests are luxuriant and the vegetation rich. The natives are pure Polynesians. The larger group constitutes Western Samoa, formerly under New Zealand trusteeship, but now an independent state; the smaller group American or Eastern Samoa.

History. The earliest-known visit of Europeans was made by a Dutch expedition in 1721–22. In 1847 Britain appointed a consular agent, in 1853 the USA a commercial agent, and in 1861 Germany appointed a representative, and between them, these three controlled the destiny of the islands. Trouble arose frequently over rival claims by the Samoans to the chieftainship, and in 1869 the three foreign authorities undertook measures to ensure peace. Under the Anglo-German Agreement of December 1899 Britain renounced to Germany all rights over Western Samoa, and similarly to the USA all rights over Eastern Samoa. In 1914 a New Zealand expeditionary force took possession of Western Samoa and remained in occupation until the setting up of a civil government in 1920. Independence was granted in 1962. American (Eastern) Samoa came under the jurisdiction of the US Department of the Interior in 1951, with a civilian governor. In 1966 a new constitution was approved in which the authority of the governor was limited in favour of the legislature.

See also WESTERN SAMOA.

Samos (Greek *Samós*), island and department of Greece, in the Aegean Sea, separated from Turkey by the Mycale Channel. Samos is crossed by a mountain range, which reaches a height of 1440 m in the west. The capital, also called Samos, lies on the south-east side of the island. Samos's chief exports are wine, olive oil, leather, tobacco, and raisins.

Samos was the birthplace of Pythagoras and one of the chief centres of Ionian culture; its pottery was famous throughout the eastern Mediterranean in the 6th century BC. Area 466 km²; population (1971) 32,671.

Samothrace (Greek *Samothráki*), island of Greece in the Aegean Sea, rising to a height of over 1525 m, about 50 km from the coast of Thrace. The coasts are dangerous and there is no safe harbour. The soil is poor and olive oil is the only export. In antiquity Samothrace was the centre of worship of the Cabeiri. The island remained independent

Samoa. *American Samoa consists of a group of eight tropical islands in the South Pacific.*

throughout the ancient Greek and Roman periods. Area 181 km^2; population (1971) 3012.

Samoyed, dog which takes its name from the Samoyeds. In its native land it is used as a herd guard and bear-hunting animal, and it has been much employed by polar explorers. The modern Samoyed has a snowy-white, white and biscuit or cream coloured double coat; it is a powerful animal, weighing some 20–30 kg. Height for dogs is 53 cm, and for bitches 46 cm.

Samoyeds, group of peoples living on the shores of the Polar Ocean, who speak Finno-Ugrian related languages. They are semi-nomadic reindeer keepers in the north, sedentary fishers in the south (Tomsk Oblast), both now collectivised. They unsuccessfully resisted payment of tribute to Muscovy in the 16th and 17th centuries and in 1929–30 three Samoyed national districts were formed. The Samoyeds number about 29,000.

Sampan (Chinese *sanpan*), name given by Europeans to any small light boat of Far Eastern waters. The most common type is propelled by a single scull over the stern, and is partly covered by an awning. There are also larger craft with one or more masts and sails and diesel engines.

Samphire, the name of three distinct species of coastal succulent plants. Golden samphire, *Inula crithmoides*, of Europe and Asia is a member of the Compositae with fleshy stems and leaves, and bears golden yellow flower-heads.

Marsh samphire, *Salicornia*, of the Chenopodiaceae has several different species, both annual and perennial, which occur in salt-marshes throughout the world. They have fleshy jointed stems, with reduced leaves, and inconspicuous flowers and are eaten as a delicacy.

Rock samphire, *Crithmum maritimum*, belongs to the Umbelliferae; it has pinnately lobed succulent leaves and umbels of small white flowers. It occurs on cliffs and in rocky places.

Sampler (Latin *examplum*, French *essemplaire*), a sample piece of embroidery. It is thought that the concept of working test embroideries came from the East. Some of the earliest extant examples are Coptic fragments. One of the earliest European pieces is the Bayeux Tapestry. From the 16th to early 20th centuries, most samples were worked by young girls. Today the term 'sampler' usually implies a more compact square or rectangular embroidery, an exercise in stitching skill. Particularly popular as collectors' items are cross-stitched samplers, with a text or suitable inscription embroidered, and signed, in fine lettering.

Samson (Hebrew *Shimshôn*, meaning perhaps 'sunny'), last of the Judges before Samuel (c.1070 BC). He is represented as a life-long Nazarite. Samson possessed unusual physical strength, and his story relates his loss of power through the breaking of his Nazarite religious vow. He finally comes to grief through Delilah, a Philistine woman, who persuades him to reveal the source of his strength—his long Nazarite hair—and then cuts off his locks while he sleeps.

Samson, Saint (c.490–c.565), Welsh missionary; a disciple of St Illtyd, and later monk and abbot of the monastery on Caldey Island. After a visit to Ireland he lived in Cornwall, being consecrated bishop. About 525 he went to Brittany, built a monastery at Dol and spent the remainder of his life spreading Christianity throughout the region.

Samsun, seaport on the Black Sea coast of Turkey, and capital of Samsun province. The town is an important agricultural market, with tobacco-processing and light engineering industries. The port ships iron ore, brought by rail from Divriği, for the steel-works of Zonguldak. Population (1980) 198,749.

Samuel (Hebrew, meaning perhaps 'name of God'), the prophet and last and greatest of the Judges. He and Deborah were the only two judges to rule outside their own tribal group, and Samuel played the main part in the establishment of the kingdom. In his early years he was reared in the sanctuary of Shiloh. Samuel lived in the second half of the 11th century BC. Soon after Saul's accession (c.1050 BC), Samuel and he began to drift apart, and Samuel anointed the boy David to be Saul's eventual successor as king.

Sampler. *An 18th-century American example.*

Samuel, Books of. In the Septuagint, we find Samuel and Kings enumerated as 1, 2, 3, 4, 'Books of the Kingdoms'. From the Septuagint the partition passed into the *Vulgate*. The division of the Hebrew Samuel into two books appears for the first time in a Hebrew manuscript of 1448, and in Daniel Bromberg's edition, Venice, 1517. The title expresses Samuel's close connection with the institution of the monarchy. The two books centre on the monarchy and fall naturally into four divisions: (1) I. i–xv, the history of Samuel and the establishment of the monarchy; (2) I. xvi–II. viii, Saul's reign and his relations with David; (3) II. ix–xx, the period of David's rule; and (4) II. xxi–xxiv, various additional notes.

Samuel of Mount Carmel and Toxteth, Herbert Louis Samuel, Ist Viscount (1870–1963), British politician. Entering the Cabinet as chancellor of the Duchy of Lancaster in 1909, he became postmaster-general in 1910 and president of the Local Government Board in 1914. In 1915–16 he held, together, the offices of postmaster-general and chancellor of the Duchy of Lancaster. In 1916 he became home secretary but went into political exile with Asquith and lost his seat in 1918. From 1920 to 1925 he filled the difficult post of high commissioner to Palestine. In 1927 he returned to party politics as chairman of the Liberal party organisation. He was leader of the Liberal parliamentary party from 1931 to 1935. In 1938 he entered the Lords and led the Liberal party there from 1944 to 1955.

Samuelson, Paul Anthony (1915–), US economist, Professor of Economics, Massachusetts Institute of Technology, winner of the Nobel Prize in economics, 1970. He is best known for his elementary textbook, *Economics: an Introductory Analysis*, which first appeared in 1948. He was an adviser to Presidents Kennedy and Johnson.

Samurai, Bushi, or Buke, warrior caste of feudal Japan. It originated in the 9th century, when the central government became unstable. Powerful provincial clans, obliged to defend themselves, gradually rose to power, in which they were finally established in 1192. The samurai were notable for their dedication to duty and their martial skills, in particular their ability to shoot arrows while on horseback. The dominance of this class, to which some 6 per cent of the population belonged, lasted for eight centuries until the Meiji Restoration.

See also JAPAN, *History*.

San Andreas Fault, one of the Earth's major transform fault systems. It is named after a lake along its line, near San Francisco. It runs for about 970 km (600 miles) from Point Arena in north-west California to the Colorado Desert. It marks the boundary along which the Pacific and American tectonic plates slip past each other, at the rate of about 640 mm a year. Unfortunately the rocks do not move at a uniform rate: they stick and then move with a jerk, causing disastrous earthquakes such as that which devastated San Francisco in 1906, with the loss of 600 lives.

San Antonio, city of Texas, USA, properly San Antonio de Bejar, standing on the river of the same name. It was founded in 1718 and acquired the characteristic Spanish Colonial features—fort, mission, and township. The mission, later secularised, was the Alamo, to become famous for its defence in 1836 by Texans from the United States against a Mexican force under Santa Anna. In the second half of the 19th century San Antonio became a cattle town. It retains its connections with the range livestock industry and has developed others including services, agriculture and oil. It also possesses numerous military installations. Population (1980) 783,296.

San Bernardino, city and county seat of San Bernardino county, California, USA, 88 km north-east of Los Angeles, in a great fruit-growing district. There are foundries, canning plants, machine shops, and lumber mills. Mormons founded San Bernardino in 1851. Population (1980) 118,092.

San Cristóbal, city in Los Andes, Venezuela, capital of Tachira state, 56 km from the Colombian border and on the Pan-American Highway. There is cattle raising, a trade in coffee, and some modern industry. Population (1975) 151,700.

San Diego, city of southern California, USA, lying on San Diego Bay, 25 km north of the border with Mexico. The oldest Spanish settlement in California, it was founded in 1768, and provided a base for the expansion of the Spanish empire and missionary efforts northwards. Its splendid harbour made it both a fishing port and a US naval base. The Second World War also brought the aircraft and aerospace industries to the city. Population (1980) 870,000.

San Fernando, town and major port of Trinidad and Tobago in the West Indies, situated at the southern end of the Gulf of Paria 58 km south of Port of Spain. It is the administrative and trading centre for the southern half of the island. Population (1972) 33,800.

San Francisco, seaport of California, USA, and until the rise of Los Angeles, the chief commercial city of the Pacific coast. It is situated at the end of a peninsula with the Bay of San Francisco on one side and the Pacific Ocean on the other. Its site is unrivalled; the bay, which receives California's two great rivers, the Sacramento and San Joaquin, has over 500 km of shore-line and extends over an area of 1165 km². The entrance to the harbour lies through a strait called the Golden Gate, which is bridged to Marin county, and San Francisco Bay which is bridged to Oakland. The city is built on a series of hills.

As a city it is both colourful and distinctive; it stands out among American cities, as does New Orleans, because of a non-American quality which may be attributable to its Spanish origins but which is maintained by the cultural liveliness of its artists, poets, and writers and by the cosmopolitan character of its population; the most famous of its minority groups is the Chinese. Total population (1980) 674,073.

The bay side of the peninsula is still a port area (including the original Spanish *embarcadero*) and there is a naval shipyard at Hunters Point. But many industrial and freight handling activities are to be found across the bay in Oakland.

The original mission of San Francisco de Asis and a presidio, or fort (1776), was followed by a small trading settlement called Yerba Buena (1835). But these were quite eclipsed when gold was discovered 150 km inland in 1848, and the great rush to California began. San Francisco became the port of entry for those who arrived by sea. A boom town grew up, unrivalled on the Pacific coast, and then in 1906 the city was almost entirely destroyed by an earthquake, caused by movement along the San Andreas fault, followed by a fire which lasted three days and caused the loss of many lives.

San Francisco Conference was opened by President Truman on 25 April 1945. The representatives of 50 nations met to draw up the charter of the United Nations in conformity with the joint promise made on 12 January 1942 by the original United Nations to continue to act together after the end of the war for the organisation of peace. The chief result of the conference was the United Nations Charter, but besides producing an agreed charter, the delegates also drew up the statute of the International Court of Justice and arranged for a preparatory commission which would set going the machinery of the UNO.

San José, capital of Costa Rica and of the province of San José. Situated at an altitude of 1161 m in the broad fertile valley of the central plateau, it is the economic, political, and cultural centre of the country though it only became the capital in 1823, succeeding Cartago. It is important as a communications centre. Most of Costa Rica's somewhat limited industry is in the city. Population (1979) 250,079.

San Jose, city of central California, USA, at the head of the southern arm of San Francisco Bay. The first settlement in the area was made by the Spanish as early as 1777. Industries include electronics and branches of the aerospace industry. Population (1980) 625,763.

San Juan, capital of San Juan province, Argentina, on the banks of the Río San Juan. It is the commercial and industrial centre of the province handling the products of the area. Population (1975) 112,582.

San Juan, capital of Puerto Rico in the West Indies, and built on a small island connected with the north coast by bridges. It is one of the largest ports in the Caribbean. San Juan is the trading, shipping, processing, cultural, and banking centre of Puerto Rico. Among its industries are sugar milling and refining, alcohol and rum distilling, and cigar and cigarette making; it also manufactures buttons, needlework, pharmaceuticals, clothing, and cement. Population (1980) 432,973.

San Luis Potosí, capital of San Luis Potosí state in Mexico. Situated at an altitude of 1800 m, it is the centre of a rich agricultural and cattle-raising district, and is an important mining centre. It has a considerable industrial complex including metallurgical and refining plants, an arsenic plant, woollen textile spinning and weaving mills, railway workshops, tanneries, and a number of consumer goods industries. Population (1975) 281,500.

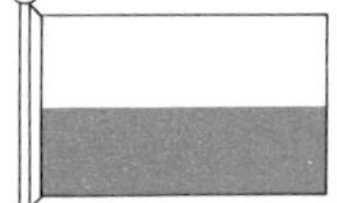

San Marino
Area: 61 km²
Population: 21,622
Capital: San Marino

San Marino, independent republic in the Italian peninsula, on the slopes of Mount Titano, about 16 km south-west of Rimini. It is one of the oldest states in Europe, its independence dating from the 13th century. A treaty of friendship with Italy was concluded in 1897, and last renewed in 1953.

Legislative power in San Marino is vested in a Great and General Council of 60 members, elected every five years, two of whom are appointed every six months to act as Captains-Regent (*Capitani reggenti*). The main products are cereals, wine, cattle, building stone, ceramics, and textiles. The *lira* is the currency and there is a customs union with Italy. The tourist industry is large (2½ million visitors a year). Its national flag consists of two equal horizontal stripes of white and light blue. Area 61 km². Population (1981) 21,622.

San Marino, capital city of San Marino republic, situated on Mount Titano (765 m), 30 km north-west of Urbino. It is accessible only by one modern highway, or funicular. Population (1971) 4500.

San Martín, José de (1778–1850), South American soldier, the liberator of Peru and Chile. He took part in the creation of the Argentine Republic, and was made a general of the Argentine army in 1816. San Martín invaded Chile with an Argentine force, and contributed to the independence of Chile from Spain. He pursued his anti-Spanish campaign in Peru, from where he succeeded in driving out the Spaniards in 1821. He was

***San Francisco** is built on a hilly peninsula. Its architecture reflects its cosmopolitan nature.*

made president of a governing council of five members. Soon after this he left South America for Europe. He spent the last 25 years of his life in Paris.

San Michele, small island in Veneto, Italy. It is the cemetery for Venice, and lies in the lagoon north of the city. It has a fine 15th-century Renaissance church.

San Pedro Sula, town of Honduras and capital of the department of Cortés. Founded in 1536 by the Spaniards, it is today Honduras's second most important city and the commercial centre for the banana and sugar cane industries. Population (1980) 342,800.

San Remo, Italian seaport in Liguria, 20 km west of Imperia. It is a fashionable bathing and sporting resort, the most important on the Italian Riviera. The town has a trade in fruit and flowers (the largest market in Italy). Population (1974) 47,700.

San Salvador, Bahamas, name given by Columbus to the first island he discovered in the New World on 12 October 1492. The modern name is Watling's Island. It has never been finally settled whether this was indeed Columbus's first landfall. Area 168 km². Population (1970) 700.

San Salvador, national capital of El Salvador. Founded by Pedro de Alvarado in 1525, it is situated at an altitude of 671 m at the foot of San Salvador volcano in the Valle de las Hamacas (Valley of Hammocks), a name derived from the frequency of earthquakes in the area. The city was virtually destroyed by earthquakes in 1854. San Salvador is the largest city in El Salvador and is the country's commercial, industrial, and cultural centre. Population (1979) 914,662.

San Sebastián, capital of the province of Guipúzcoa, Spain, on the Bay of Biscay at the mouth of the River Urumea. There is a palace, formerly a summer residence of the Spanish royal family, and the town is a fashionable resort. San Sebastián has a small fishing harbour, and a large trade in wine, fruit, textiles, cork, and minerals from the nearby port of Pasajes. Glass, paper, flour, soap, and beer are manufactured. Population (1981) 175,576.

San'a, or Sanaa, capital of the Yemen Arab Republic, on the central plateau 2210 m above sea-level. The land is fertile, and water is abundant. Length from east to west 5 km; width nearly 2 km; population (1975) 447,898. The trades are shoe-making, tailoring, weaving, handicrafts in general, and oil mills. The town lies on a north-south trade route which ends at Aden.

Sanatorium (from the Latin *sanare*, to cure), establishment for certain forms of medical treatment, or for the general treatment of convalescent patients.

Sanction, in jurisprudence, a term used to denote a penalty of any kind declared against a transgression of any law. It also denotes the measures intended to enforce the fulfilment of international treaty obligations, e.g. the sanctions imposed by Britain and the UN members against Rhodesia after its government's unilateral declaration of independence in November 1965.

Sanctuary, a place, including sacred or consecrated precincts, where criminals could not be apprehended. The custom existed among the Greeks and among the Jews. In England immunity was extended for 40 days, and applied to all crimes save sacrilege and high treason; the fugitive had to confess his guilt, clad in sackcloth, before the coroner, and swear to leave the kingdom. The right was abolished by law in 1624, so far as concerned felons, though debtors were able to take refuge in London and elsewhere until the end of the 17th century.

In a Christian church, the sanctuary is the presbytery or portion of the church reserved for the clergy or the part containing the altar.

Sand, George, pseudonym of Amandine Lucile Aurore Dudevant (1804–76), French novelist. In Paris, at first she devoted herself mainly to poets and musicians, especially Alfred de Musset and Chopin. With Musset she went to Italy, but the relationship ended when they discovered their incompatibility of temperament. Her liaison with Chopin began during the early stages of his fatal illness. Later she became interested in political and social schemes, under the influence of Lamennais, Leroux, and Michel de Bourges. The Revolution of 1848 brought disillusionment, and she retired to Nohant.

Her output was enormous and among her chief works are *La Mare au diable*, 1846; *La Petite Fadette*, 1848; and *François de Champi*, 1850.

Sand, one of the three elemental particles in soil, formed principally by the physical weathering of rocks, with sandstones (cemented sand particles) producing the greatest quantities. Sands are composed of resistant minerals which have not been destroyed in the weathering processes and may consist of between 90 and 95 per cent quartz grains. The remaining common minerals are feldspars, micas, tourmaline, garnet, and magnetite. The shape of sand particles may indicate its origin. Angular sand is often deposited from ice, rounded sand originates under desert conditions and is shaped by the wind, and sub-angular grains are produced by waves, streams, and ice meltwater.

See also CLAY; LOAM; SILT.

Sand-blasting, the use of sand, projected in a stream of compressed air, as an abrasive. A 'ground-glass' effect can be produced on plain glass, though acid etching is now more usual. Metal forgings and castings can be cleaned by this method, steel grit or shot often replacing sand; walls of buildings may also be cleaned by sand-blasting.

Sand-bug, name given in the USA to a crustacean of the family Hippidae (*Hippa talpoidea*) which burrows in the sand.

See also CRUSTACEA.

Sand-casting, an ancient method of casting metal for artistic or industrial purposes using a mould made from clay and fine sand.

See also CIRE-PERDUE.

Sand-eel, a species of the family Ammodytidae, belonging to the order Perciformes. They are all small, carnivorous fishes, and are found swimming near the coasts of temperate seas of the northern hemisphere. Their bodies are covered with small scales, the swim-bladder is absent, and they have long, sharply pointed snouts by means of which they bury themselves in the sand.

Sand-glass, an instrument for measuring time known to have been in use as early as AD 330. It consists essentially of a double bulb with a narrow intervening neck. This double bulb is mounted in a reversible wooden frame, and is charged with just sufficient dry sand to run through the neck from one bulb to the other in a given period of time. Today they are most used as egg-timers.

Sand-grouse, birds of the family Pteroclididae, in the pigeon order Columbiformes. They frequent for the most part the deserts of Asia and Arabia. The birds have compact bodies, short bills, long and pointed wings, a wedge-shaped tail, and short legs and toes. Their coloration is protective, resembling the sand on which they dwell, and their diet consists of both vegetable matter and insects.

Sand-lizard, *Lacerta agilis*, a lizard found on sandy heaths in western and central Europe, growing to nearly 20 cm in length. The male is brownish above, and in the spring a bright green on the flanks and belly. The female is brownish or greyish and mottled all over. They are active burrowers.

Sand-martin, *Riparia riparia*, a bird of the swallow family, Hirundinidae, order Passeriformes. It is an early summer visitor to Europe from North Africa and to the higher latitudes of North America from the south, nesting in burrows made on the vertical faces of cuttings, sandy river-banks or sandpits.

Sandal, earliest and simplest form of footwear, composed of a sole fastened on to the foot by means of straps or thongs. Sandals were worn by the Jews as well as by the ancient Greeks and Romans. They are still a common form of footwear.

See also BOOTS AND SHOES.

Sandalwood, fragrant wood of *Santalum album* (family Santalaceae), a small evergreen tree with panicles of red flowers. The heartwood is used for carving, incense, and perfume, and when distilled yields an oil used medicinally by Hindu doctors.

Sandarac, gum exuded by the arar tree, *Tetraclinis articulata* (family Cupressaceae), native of Morocco. It is used for making varnish; when powdered it is called 'pounce'.

Sandburg, Carl (1878–1967), US poet. His most notable books of verse are *Chicago Poems*, 1916; *Cornhuskers*, 1918; *Smoke and Steel*, 1920; and *Good Morning America*, 1928. His two books of *Rootabaga Stories*, 1922, tales for children, were also successful. Among his later works are *Mary Lincoln: Wife and Widow*, 1932; *The People: Yes*, 1936; *Abraham Lincoln: the War Years* (four volumes), 1939; *Storm over the Land*, 1942; and *Home Front Memo*, 1943. *Always the Young Strangers*, 1953, is autobiographical.

Sanderling, *Calidris alba*, a bird of the Scolopacidae, order Charadriiformes. It is a small wader, 20 cm long. Its summer plumage is a speckled chestnut on the upper parts, head and chest, and white underneath. In winter it is mainly white with light grey underparts. It only stays on its breeding grounds in arctic America, Siberia and Greenland for about six weeks, after which it migrates south to the coasts of all the continents.

Sandflea, see JIGGER.

Sandfly, see PSYCHODIDAE.

Sandfly fever, phlebotomus fever, or three days' fever, prevalent in Mediterranean regions, is caused by a virus which is transmitted by the sandfly *Phlebotomus papatasii*. The symptoms are sudden high fever, severe headache and general aching. The fever usually subsides on the third day, but pain and depression continue for some days.

Sandhopper, *Talitrus saltator*, a segmented arthropod of the order Amphipoda in class Crustacea. The animals are about 1 cm long. They are common along most sea-shores, where they burrow in the sand above high-water mark. They are closely akin to the shore-hopper, *Orchestia gammarellus*, found among rocks.

Sandpiper, various members of the snipe family, Scolopacidae, order Charadriiformes, characterised by long slender bill compressed and grooved at the tip. The common sandpiper, *Tringa hypoleucos*, has a rapid and easy flight, and is a skilful swimmer and diver, feeding on worms and small insects. The bird is about 18 cm long, the head and back are greenish-brown with irregular markings on the plumage. The underparts are white. The green sandpiper, *T. ochropus*, is a larger bird, and from a short distance appears to be black and white in colour. Its cry is extremely shrill. Other species are the wood sandpiper, *T. glareola*, and the redshank, *T. totanus*, a handsome, graceful bird often gathering in large flocks on the coast in winter. Most sandpipers breed in the Arctic and winter in temperate regions of Eurasia and North America.

Sandringham, parish of Norfolk, England, 13 km north-east of King's Lynn. In 1862 King Edward VII, then Prince of Wales, bought an estate here, and in 1867–70 built a house which is still a private country residence of the royal family.

Sandstone, a clastic sedimentary rock composed of rounded grains of sand cemented together by a matrix; the grains range in size from $\frac{1}{16}$ mm to 2 mm diameter. Most sandstones are composed largely of quartz grains, cemented together by a matrix which may be calcareous, siliceous, ferruginous, argillaceous, or composed of sulphide (especially pyrite), fluorite, or anhydrite. In addition to quartz, a sandstone may contain significant amounts of feldspar, mica, glauconite, shell remains, rock particles, iron oxides, and 'heavy minerals' such as tourmaline, hornblende, zircon, and sphene.

Sandstones may be accumulated by wind action (aeolian sandstones) or deposited by water, either in marine, brackish, or fresh-water environments.

The most important economic functions of sandstones are as oil and water reservoirs; this is made possible by their very permeable and porous nature. Heavy accessory minerals such as gold, platinum, diamonds, and cassiterite may become concentrated in 'placers' in stream sands, while beach sands may contain placers of ilmenite, magnetite, zircon, or monazite. Very pure quartz sandstones are quarried for use as glass sands.

Sanderling. Calidris alba.

Sandstorm, see STORM.

Sandwich, John Montagu, 4th Earl of (1718–92), British politician. At the age of 30 he was first lord of the Admiralty, and a few years later a principal secretary of state. As an administrator, however, he was a complete failure, allowing the navy to fall into neglect, and he is remembered chiefly for his association with the notorious Hell Fire Club. He is the 'Jemmy Twitcher' of the *Beggar's Opera*. Capt. Cook perpetuated his name by calling the Sandwich Isles, now the Hawaiian Islands, after him, and the familiar snack bears his name because he made use of this convenient form of meal in order not to have to leave the gaming-table.

Sandwich, now a resort but formerly one of the original Cinque Ports and a prosperous medieval wool port of Kent, England. Prosperity thereafter relied on the refugee Huguenot cloth workers and market gardeners. The latter is still an important occupation. Population (1981) 4227.

Sandwich Islands, see HAWAII.

Sangallo, family of Italian artists and architects. The most prominent members were Giuliano Giamberti (1445–1516), his brother Antonio Sangallo (1455–1534), and their nephew, also Antonio Sangallo (1483–1546). Giuliano Giamberti's numerous works include a palace at Savona for the Cardinal della Rovere (now converted into the convent of Santa Chiara) and the Gondi and Strozzi palaces at Florence. His masterpiece is S. Maria delle Carceri, Prato (1485–91), the first Renaissance church on a Greek cross plan.

His brother Antonio visited Rome where he ingratiated himself with Alexander VI. One of his schemes was the conversion of Hadrian's mausoleum into the castle of St Angelo.

The younger Antonio found an instructor and protector in Bramante. His masterpiece is the Farnese Palace (1534–46). Among other works he was responsible for a project for completing St Peter's.

Sanger, Frederick (1918–), British chemist. In 1951 he became head of the division of protein chemistry, at the Medical Research Council, Cambridge. During the period 1943–55 he determined the sequence of amino-acids in the insulin molecule, and so was the first person to elucidate the structure of a protein. For this work he was awarded the Nobel Prize for chemistry in 1958.

Sanger, George (1825–1911), British showman, known as 'Lord' George Sanger, born at Newbury, Berkshire, son of a showman who had fought at Trafalgar. He began as a conjuror with his brother John, with whom he leased the agricultural hall, and later, in 1871, Astley's amphitheatre. Subsequently he travelled over Europe with his circuses. He was murdered by an employee. Sanger wrote *Seventy Years a Showman* (new ed. 1952).

See also CIRCUS.

Sangha (Pāli, assembly), the Order of Buddhist monks, and one of the Three Refuges 'taken' by Buddhists. It is the oldest monastic order in the world. After his Enlightenment, the Buddha resolved to share the Truth he had discovered with the rest of humankind, and so he established the Sangha and exhorted his monks to go forth and proclaim the *Dhamma*. The earliest *bhikkhus* (monks) were wandering mendicants.

See also BUDDHISM.

Sanhedrin (from Greek *sunedrion*, council) was the supreme court of justice and legislative council among the Jews. It probably dated from the time of the exile, and consisted of 71 members, drawn from different classes among the people, with a predominance of scribes and men famous for their learning. It ceased to exist by AD 425.

Śankara (AD 789–820), one of the most renowned theologians of India. He was the great exponent of Advaita (non-dual) Vedanta, as well as being a religious reformer. He travelled widely in India and founded a number of monastic orders. He is chiefly known for his reinterpretation of the Upanishads and Bhagavad Gītā in the light of the supreme realisation of the self's identity with Brahman ('That art thou').

Sansculottes (i.e. 'without breeches'), name given in scorn, at the beginning of the French Revolution, by the court party to the Paris mob. The latter accepted the intended insult as a compliment, and the term soon became the distinctive appellation of a 'good patriot'.

Sanskrit, the main sacred and classical language of ancient India, is an early form of the Indo-Aryan language, cousin of the Greek, Latin, and Slavonic languages in the Indo-European group. It is one of the 14 languages officially recognised in the constitution of modern India, with some 200,000 people claiming fluency (1961). At the peak of its influence, Sanskrit religious and philosophical works were studied and translated by such peoples as the Arabs, Chinese, Javanese, and Thais.

See also INDIA, *Language;* INDIA, *Literature*.

Sansovino, Andrea, real name Contucci (1460–1529), Italian sculptor and architect. He executed the bronze group of the *Baptism of Christ* for the cathedral baptistery in Florence. Between 1491 and 1501 he made visits to Spain and Portugal, then worked in Rome, sculpting a *Madonna and Child with St Anne* for the church of St Augustine, and the Sforza and della Rovere tombs in the retro-choir of S. Maria del Popolo. In his later years he was working on the Holy House at Loreto.

Santa Ana, capital of Santa Ana department, and the second largest and second most important town in El Salvador. Situated at an altitude of 637 m on the slope of the volcano Santa Ana, it lies on the Pan-American Highway. In addition to being the 'coffee capital' of El Salvador, it also has a substantial proportion of the country's industry. Population (1970) 162,937.

Santa Barbara, city and county seat of Santa Barbara county, southern California, USA, on the site of an old Spanish mission settlement. It has fisheries and a canning industry, and there is fruit packing in association with nearby areas of intensive irrigation agriculture. Population 74,542.

Santa Clara, capital of Villa Clara province, Cuba, 249 km south-east of Havana by rail or road. It is the second largest inland city of Cuba, and the centre of a fertile agricultural region. A fine transport centre, it is linked by rail with its port, Cienfuegos, 64 km to the south. Population (1981) 525,402.

Santa Claus, see NICHOLAS, SAINT.

Santa Cruz, city of eastern-central Bolivia, capital of Santa Cruz department, on the Rio Piray. It lies in an area of tropical lowland. The city was founded in the 1560s by Spaniards from Paraguay, who established it at what is now San José de Chiquitos; it was moved to its present site in 1595 following persistent Indian attacks. Santa Cruz is a trade centre on the Cochabamba highway, with railway links to the Atlantic-coast ports of Brazil; it trades in sugar, rice, coffee and tobacco and manufactures refined sugar, cigarettes, leather goods and alcohol. Population (1976) 255,568.

Santa Cruz de Tenerife, capital of the island of Tenerife, Canary Islands, Spain. It is a port of call for ships on the African and South American routes. There are textile manufactures, oil refineries, and a tourist industry. Population (1981) 190,784.

Santa Fe, capital of Santa Fe province in Argentina, on the right bank of the River Paraná, 380 km by river and 480 km by rail north of Buenos Aires. It is an important distributing centre for the area and export outlet for its agricultural and processed products. It is the furthest point up the river accessible to ocean-going vessels. Population (1975) 244,655.

Santa Fe, capital of the state of New Mexico, USA. The city is situated at over 2000 m above sea-level, on the western slopes of the Sangre de Cristo Mountains, 25 km east of the Rio Grande. It was founded by the Spanish in 1609, and represented the northern base of their penetration up the Rio Grande valley. It was designated as state capital when, in 1912, New Mexico was admitted to the Union. Today, it is a museum city of relics of the Hispanic culture and of that of the Indians who lived in the area before the Europeans came. It has the oldest public building (the palace of the governors) and the oldest church (San Miguel) in the USA. Population (1980) 48,953.

Santa Isabel, see MALABO.

Santa Marta, Caribbean seaport and capital of Magdalena department, Colombia. Coffee, cocoa, bananas, and hides are among the principal exports. The town has a history of four centuries and close associations with Bolívar. Population (1973) 128,000.

Santalaceae, the sandalwood family, which includes about 30 genera and 400 species of dicotyledons; all members are partial parasites having chlorophyll but obtaining some nourishment from the roots or stems of host plants. Most Santalaceae are tropical or subtropical trees or shrubs, including *Santalum* (sandalwood); *Thesium humifusum* (bastard toadflax) occurs in western Europe. It is a small, narrow-leaved creeping plant.

Santals, or Sonthals, one of the largest groups of aboriginal peoples in India, numbering about 3·25 million. Their language is Santali and they live mainly in West Bengal, Bihar and Orissa states. Traditionally, they were shifting agriculturalists who also hunted and gathered. Today they use bullock and plough, work as share-croppers and agricultural labourers, or are employed in coal-mines and steel factories.

Santander, province of Spain in Castilla la Vieja, with a coastline on the Bay of Biscay. It is traversed by the Cantabrian Mountains, and contains the headwaters of the Ebro. There are forests and pasture land, and there are deposits of copper, iron, lead, and coal. Area 5460 km²; population 484,000.

Santayana, George (1863–1952), US philosopher. As a philosopher he was somewhat of an eclectic, but his writings are full of imaginative insights in the many fields in which his interests lay. His masterpiece was probably *The Life of Reason*, 1905–06. Published in five volumes, it treats of reason in society, religion, art, and science. His style has been widely admired for its graceful expression of urbane scepticism.

Santiago, capital of Chile, the fourth largest city of South America, standing 510 m above sea-level, 184 km by rail east of Valparaiso. It is the cultural, commercial, and manufacturing centre of Chile. It occupies an area of 21 km², and is traversed by the Mapocho river. Santiago was founded by Pedro de Valdivia in 1541, and was finally freed from Spanish control between 1810 and 1818. Population (1975) 3,186,000.

Santiago de Compostela, city in the province of La Coruña, Spain. It was once the capital of Galicia. Santiago has been famous since the 11th century for the great pilgrimage to the shrine of St James (Sant' Iago) the Apostle, the patron saint of Spain. Textiles, chocolate, and soap are made, and there is a trade in agricultural produce. Population (1981) 93,693.

Santiago de Cuba, third largest city of Cuba and capital of Oriente province. It has a magnificent but almost land-locked harbour, 8 km long and 3 km broad. There are manufacturers of iron goods and tobacco, and the chief exports are sugar, coffee, various fruits, tobacco, mahogany, cedar, hides, wax, manganese, iron ore, and copper. The city was founded in 1514 by Diego de Velásquez. Population (1981) 563,455.

Santiago del Estero, capital of Santiago del Estero province in Argentina, on the Rio Dulce, 140 km south-east of Tucumán. It is the commercial and industrial centre of the province and its economic activity is confined to handling the province's products: meat, wheat, maize, linseed and timber. Population (1975) 105,127.

Santo Domingo, capital of the Dominican Republic. Founded in 1496 by Bartholomew Columbus, it retained the name until 1936 when it was changed to Ciudad Trujillo by the dictator of the Dominican Republic, Rafael Leonidas Trujillo Molina. On his assassination and the overthrow of his régime in 1961, the original name was restored. It is the republic's leading city politically, economically, and culturally, and is also the chief port handling a substantial proportion of the country's exports and imports. Population (1975) 922,528.

Santo Domingo, the name by which the island of Hispaniola in the West Indies was known from about 1496 when Bartholomew Columbus (brother of Christopher) founded the town of Santo Domingo on the south coast of the island. The western part of the island was occupied by the French and called Saint-Domingue until 1804 when the Republic of Haiti was established.

Santos, seaport in the state of São Paulo, Brazil, 56 km south-east of the city of São Paulo. The volume of import-export trade handled by the port exceeds that of Rio de Janeiro, and it is also the leading coffee port of the world. Around the city there has been considerable industrial development including an oil refinery and a steelworks. Population (1980) 411,000.

São Miguel, largest island of the Azores, Portugal, in the Atlantic some 1450 km west of Lisbon. The island consists of two volcanic massifs either side of a broad valley. There are no natural anchorages, but the island is fertile, and pineapples, oranges, tea, grapes, and tobacco are among the crops. São Miguel is a tourist resort with a mild climate, and thermal springs are found. Ponta Delgada is the port and capital. Area 746 km²; population (1970) 149,878.

São Paulo, capital of São Paulo state, Brazil. The leading industrial city of Brazil, it is today probably the most populous of South America with 7 million inhabitants. Situated 64 km from the coast, 400 km from Rio, and 750 m above sea-level, it is the centre of a rich coffee-producing area. It is a cosmopolitan city not only of industry and commerce, but also of fine cultural and educational facilities.

Sao Tomé and Principe
Area: 964 km²
Population: 83,000
Capital: São Tomé

São Tomé and Príncipe, republic in the Gulf of Guinea, off the west coast of Africa, consisting of the two main islands that form the title plus the rocky islets of Pedras Tinhosas and Rolas. Area 964 km².

Both major islands are composed of narrow coastal lowlands and rugged central volcanic highlands rising to 2000 m. The capital is São Tomé and the population of the republic was estimated in 1977 at 83,000.

The economy is basically agricultural and reliant on the export crops of cocoa, copra, bananas, coffee, and coconut. Native dialects and Portuguese are spoken.

The constitution of 1975 provides for one legal political party (*Movimento de Libertação de São Tomé e Principe*) which nominates candidates for the Presidency and People's Assembly. The Assembly is elected for a four-year term and in turn elects the President, who appoints the cabinet.

History. In 1485 the Portuguese were the first Europeans to reach this archipelago off the coast of present-day Gabon. The Portuguese used the islands as administrative centres for the slave trade to the plantations of Brazil and the Caribbean and practised plantation agriculture in the islands themselves. The abolition of slavery in the Portuguese colonies by the decrees of 1869 and 1875 made little difference to the plantation workers, who were given the status of 'contract' workers but were effectively still slaves. The situation changed little until the 1960s when political resistance within the islands was inspired by the formation in Ghana of the Committee for the Liberation of São Tomé and Principe (CLSTP), which organised a strike of plantation workers in 1963. The CLSTP became the Movement for the Liberation of São Tomé and Principe (MLSTP) and received indirect encouragement in 1974 with the coup in Portugal. In 1975 São Tomé and Principe became an independent republic with the MLSTP being the sole legal party.

Saône, river of eastern France, rising in the Faucilles Mountains (Vosges) and flowing south past Gray, Châlon, and Mâcon, to join the Rhône at Lyons. The chief tributaries are the Doubs and the Ognon. It is connected by canal with the Loire, Seine, Meuse, Moselle, and Rhine. Length 480 km.

Sap, the watery fluid in living plants, that ascends from the roots, through the xylem vessels of the stem, to the leaves. It consists of water and minerals in very dilute solution absorbed from the soil by the roots. The descending sap contains sugars and other nutrients manufactured in the leaves. It travels through the sieve tubes of the phloem to the cells throughout the plant.

Sapir, Edward (1884–1939), US linguist. He did much valuable work on the American Indian languages (inspired by Franz Boas), especially their classification. He was also keenly interested in anthropology and psychology and their relation to linguistics. His *Language*, 1921, is one of the first general text books of linguistics, not only historical but also synchronic, and is highly readable, although lacking the rigour Bloomfield was to supply.

Sapodilla, *Achras sapota*, in the family Sapotaceae, a tropical evergreen tree bearing white flowers followed by edible fruits.

Saponification, in soap manufacture, the conversion (hydrolysis) of fats into soap by the use of ammonium, sodium, or potassium hydroxides; since different amounts of the alkali are needed for different oils and fats, the saponification value is used to determine the identity and purity of the latter. In organic chemistry saponification is the hydrolysis of esters to form acids and alcohols.

Sapotaceae, a family of about 35 genera and 600 species of tropical trees. Some species produce latex, the source of gutta-percha and chicle for chewing gum; others have edible fleshy fruits with nut-like seeds. The main genera are *Achras, Madhuca* and *Palaquium*.

Sappan Wood, wood of *Caesalpinia sappan*, a native of southern Asia, used as a dye.

Sapphire, variety of corundum, Al_2O_3. It includes all corundum gemstones other than red (named ruby). Sapphire without a colour adjective refers to blue sapphire, those found in Kashmir being famed for their colour.

Sappho (b. c.612 BC), Greek lyric poet of the Aeolian school, head of a female literary society on Lesbos. She married Cercylas, to whom she bore a daughter, Cleis, and was a friend of Alcaeus. Sappho's subjects are mostly personal, written for her friends, though some poems are based on folksong, and she wrote in the dialect of Lesbos. She used a great variety of metres, including the Sapphic, which is named after her.

Sapporo, capital of the island of Hokkaidō, Japan, on the Ishikari river. Sapporo was laid out as an entirely new settlement after 1869, and became the headquarters for the colonisation of Hokkaidō. Industries include brewing, flour milling, and butter and cheese manufacture. Population (1979) 1,319,000.

Saprophytes (Greek *sapros*, decaying; *phyton*, a plant), plants not confined to any one group, but most numerous among the Fungi, which, being wholly or partly devoid of chlorophyll, are unable to manufacture the organic carbon compounds from carbon dioxide and water, necessary for their nutrition. They derive their food from dead plants and animals, as distinct from parasites, which are dependent upon living hosts for their sustenance. Dry-rot of timber is caused by a saprophytic fungus (*Merulius lacrymans*); other saprophytes are the moulds of jam, cheese and other foods. On the whole, saprophytes are essential components of the global ecosystem, rapidly converting dead organisms into simple compounds which then become available for the nutrition of other organisms. Among higher plants the yellow bird's-nest (*Monotropa hypopitys*) and many other orchids, including the British bird's-nest orchid (*Neottia nidusavis*), are saprophytes.

Saraband, or zarabanda, Spanish dance first mentioned in the late 16th century, when it appears to have been a dance of much sexual suggestiveness. In the late 16th century, the music had a distinctive rhythm, using alternate bars of 6-8 and 3-4 time, and the dance was normally accompanied by castanets. In the late 17th and the 18th centuries it was favoured in French and English society, the French version being a stately dance in 3-2 time, for a single couple. Occasionally it was danced as a solo.

Sarajevo, the former capital of Bosnia; a view across the valley of the Miljacka.

Saracens, name (origin unknown) given by Greek writers from the 1st century AD to the Bedouin Arabs who lived in Mesopotamia and Arabia Petraea, that is, on the confines of the Roman and Persian empires. It was the customary name given by Christians of the Middle Ages to their Muslim enemies in eastern Europe, to the Moors in Spain, and in the *Chanson de Roland* to the Basques.
See also CRUSADES; MOHAMMED; SALADIN.

Saragat, Giuseppe (1898–), Italian politician. In 1947 Saragat led the wing of the Socialist party which in 1951 adopted the title of the Italian Social Democratic party. Saragat was foreign secretary from 1963 to 1964, and then president of the Republic from 1964 to 1971.

Saragossa, see ZARAGOZA.

Sarajevo (Turkish *Bosna-Serai*), capital of the republic of Bosnia-Hercegovina, Yugoslavia. The place did not become important until the 16th century, when it developed rapidly under Turkish domination. As the capital of Bosnia, it later became the centre of the revolutionary movements of Bosnia and Herzegovina against the domination of Austria. It was at Sarajevo that Archduke Francis Ferdinand was assassinated in 1914. The principal industries are tobacco, carpets, silk, pottery, and sugar, and there are breweries and timber yards. Population (1971) 292,263.

Saransk, town in the European RSFSR, USSR, and capital of the Mordovian ASSR, on the River Insar in the Volga basin. It has varied industries including electrical engineering, light engineering, and food, and is the cultural centre of the Mordovians. It was founded in 1641 as a fort. Population (1980) 271,000.

Saratov, capital city, economic and cultural centre of Saratov *oblast*, USSR, on the right bank of the Volga, north of Volgograd. It is an important industrial and transport centre—varied engineering, gas, and oil industries, flour mills, etc. It is here that Baku oil is transferred to the railway for Central USSR; it is also the starting-point of a natural gas pipeline to Moscow. From the mid-17th century it was an important centre of the fish and salt trade; from the mid-19th century till the 1920s it was the most populous city on the Volga, and the foremost centre of grain trade and flour-milling in Russia; heavy industry has developed since the 1930s. Population (1980) 864,000.

Sarawak, state of Malaysia, with a total area of 121,400 km² (76 per cent forest, 20 per cent arable), situated in northern Borneo. An alluvial and often swampy coastal plain (about 50 km wide) is succeeded by a well-wooded, undulating and mountainous interior—with few peaks higher than 1370 m. Rivers flow often steeply through gorges and over rapids to the plain, where they are mostly navigable.

The main agricultural exports are timber, palm oil, pepper and rubber. Sarawak is Malaysia's major source of pepper, and the world's third largest producer. It has an estimated 97,720 km² of forest and accounts for nearly all of Malaysia's oil production.

Population (1978 estimate): 1,173,906 (mainly Dayaks). The state capital is Kuching (population 63,535) with Sibu the next major town (50,635).

Sarawak has a legislative assembly (or Council Negri) of elected members, and an executive council to advise an appointed governor. The national language is Malay, the state religion is Islam.

Sarawak became a separate state in 1842, after Muda Hassim, Sultan of Brunei, gave the adventurer James Brooke feudal title of rajah over the territory around Kuching. Later accessions (between 1861 and 1905) brought most of present-day Sarawak under Brooke's control. While it was still being extended at the expense of Brunei, Sarawak became a British Protectorate in 1888. Sarawak's cession to the British Crown took place in 1946. In 1963 the Crown Colony of Sarawak joined the Federation of Malaysia.

See also SABAH.

Sarcasm (Greek *sarkazein*, to tear flesh), a cutting or satirical remark. It is frequently confused with irony, for which it has almost become a synonym. Strictly speaking, the two figures of speech are distinct, for irony involves saying the opposite of what is meant, whereas sarcasm involves saying what is meant in such a way as to convey contempt or ridicule. An example is the couplet on the Lake Poets:

> They lived in the Lakes—an appropriate quarter
> For poems diluted with plenty of water!

See also FIGURE OF SPEECH.

Sarcodina, class of Protozoa containing the amoebae. They are typified by the presence of one or more pseudopodia which are extended from the main part of the animal as organs of locomotion and feeding. The cytoplasm is differentiated into endoplasm and ectoplasm. There is no special mouth and food is simply enveloped by an advancing pseudopodium, then pushed into the cytoplasm within a vacuole. Reproduction is by binary fission. They are microscopic or just barely visible to the naked eye. There are five main orders.

Amoebida contains organisms that have no shell, form a protective covering, a cyst, to endure adverse conditions, and have the typical broad, blunt pseudopodia. Some live in marine or freshwater, e.g. *Amoeba proteus*, others may be parasitic, e.g. *Entamoeba histolytica*, which causes amoebic dysentery.

Testacida includes organisms that have similar pseudopodia to the amoebae, but the animal is contained in a single-chambered shell with one large opening.

Foraminifera includes mainly marine species. Some are planktonic but many live on the sea-bed. The many-chambered shell has vast numbers of small holes through which the pseudopodia extend. They are very fine and branch and rejoin to form a feeding network, and are also used in locomotion.

Heliozoida, the sun-animalcules, includes spherical, mainly freshwater forms with very fine pseudopodia radiating from the surface, each stiffened by a fine rod, and which are used for feeding.

Radiolaria includes only marine organisms, many of which are planktonic. They are spherical, and from the ectoplasm radiate very fine pseudopodia which may branch to form a network for feeding. Locomotion is limited to drifting with the plankton. A gelatinous, frothy layer, acting as a flotation device, may be retained by the siliceous skeleton. The latter may be extremely intricate with barbs, spines, and thin needles radiating from the capsule and extending beyond the surface of the animal.

Sarcophagus. *A Lycian sarcophagus of about 40 BC, from the Royal Cemetery at Sidon.*

Sarcophagus, stone receptacle for the dead. One of the earliest and most noteworthy sarcophagi is that of Seti, who reigned in Egypt in the 13th century BC, wrought out of a solid mass of aragonite and semi-translucent; it is now preserved in the Soane Museum, London. In the British Museum is an Etruscan sarcophagus dating from 500 BC; the Etruscans used terracotta, and carved their coffins either in the form of a couch with a recumbent figure of the dead, or of a diminutive shrine. The oldest-known Roman sarcophagus is that of Scipio in the Vatican, which dates from the 3rd century BC. Under the influence of Constantine the Great, when Christianity was granted toleration throughout the Roman Empire, stone sarcophagi were widely used, and a great impetus was given to figure sculpture in Europe. Lead sarcophagi, some of them decorated, were also used in Roman times.

Sardine, a term applied in Mediterranean countries to young pilchards (*Sardina pilchardus*), and especially to those prepared in Portugal or Brittany and tinned. It has also been applied to brislings or young sprats (*Clupea sprattus*) similarly preserved in Norway, where the pilchard is unknown. *Sardinops sagax* of South African waters and *S. coeruleus* of the Pacific coast of North America are also known as 'sardines'. But strictly speaking sardine is the trade name for one-year-old pilchards.

Sardinia (Italian *Sardegna*), island in the Mediterranean Sea, about 240 km south-west of the promontory of Orbetello in Tuscany, and 12 km south of Corsica, from which it is separated by the Strait of Bonifacio. It forms an administrative region of Italy, and consists of four provinces: Cagliari, Nuoro, Oristano, and Sassari. Sardinia is very mountainous, the highest point being Gennargentu (1834 m) near the centre. The main hilly mass of the north-eastern two-thirds of the island is separated from the hills of the south-west by the broad alluvial plain of Campidano, in which stands the city of Cagliari. The chief rivers are the Mannu, Flumendosa, and Tirso all flowing south out of the central mass of hills. The Campidano is mainly devoted to extensive cereal farming and is the major focus of present land reform and agricultural investment. Most of the rest of the island is hilly and used for raising sheep. Lead and zinc mining is declining and the extraction of lignite, kaolin, and barite is more important. There has been much industrial growth recently, mostly near Cagliari and Sassari. Tourism is of increasing importance, spear-headed by the luxurious Costa Smeralda development on the north-east coast near Olbia. The regional capital is Cagliari. Area 24,089 km². Population (1980) 1,601,586.

In the 11th century Sardinia became a kingdom, although in 1190 it had to recognise the supremacy of Pisa, which was then contested by Genoa. Aragon next captured it (1323–26). Ruled by a Spanish viceroy (1478–1713), it then passed to the emperor, and finally to the Duke of Savoy in 1718, who then took the title King of Sardinia. His descendant, Victor Emmanuel II, became King of Italy in 1861.

Sardis, capital of the former kingdom of Lydia and of the Byzantine province of Lydia. It fell successively a prey to the Cimmerians (7th century BC), the Persians under Cyrus (546 BC), the Athenians and Ionians (498 BC), and Antiochus the Great (215 BC). After being finally taken by the Turks in 1304, it entered a permanent decline.

Sardou, Victorien (1831–1908), French dramatist. The successor to Scribe, he produced all forms of drama at an outstanding rate and, becoming one of the most popular writers of his kind, he speedily amassed a considerable fortune. For Sarah Bernhardt, he wrote *Fédora*, 1882; *Théodora*, 1884; and *La Tosca*, 1887. His other plays include *Les Pattes de mouche*, 1860; *Nos Intimes* 1861; *La Famille Benoiton*, 1865; *Maison neuve*, 1866; *Rabagas*, 1872; and *L'Oncle Sam*, 1873.

Sargasso Sea, a calm region in the North Atlantic Ocean lying between 20° and 40° N and bounded on the west and north by the swift north-eastward flowing Gulf Stream, on the east by the Canary current, and on the south by the North Equatorial current. Under the influence of the earth's rotation, this clockwise (anti-cyclonic) gyre causes the water to pile up towards the centre of the Sargasso Sea, which is about 1 m higher than the sea-level on the eastern coast of the USA.

The Sargasso derives its name from a floating brown seaweed, *Sargassum natans*, which was first observed there by Christopher Columbus in 1492.

Sargassum, a genus of brown Algae, a seaweed with about 150 species. It is also called gulfweed or rockweed. It floats by means of many small air-bladders, but also grows attached to rocks. The Sargasso Sea in the Atlantic Ocean is named after the floating seaweed, mostly *S. natans*, that is brought to the area by the ocean currents.

S. muticum, a Japanese species, was found in 1973 growing in two localities in Britain, Pemberton on the Isle of Wight and in Portsmouth Harbour. The recent introduction of this fast-growing species worries ecologists and others since the species can grow at the rate of 3 cm per day, supplanting slower-growing indigenous species. It is a distinct threat to the establishment of oyster beds.

Sargent, John Singer (1856–1925), US portrait painter. He studied in Florence, and in Paris under Carolus Duran. He had a studio in Paris about 1880–84, after which he lived chiefly in England. For 25 years he held attention by his portraits. A famous full-length is *Lord Ribblesdale*, in the Tate Gallery. In his later years he gave up portraiture for landscape, mainly in water-colour. Among his most notable works are his mural decorations at Boston Public Library.

Sargent, Sir Malcolm (1895–1967), British conductor. From 1923 he taught at the Royal College of Music. In 1928 he became conductor of the Royal Choral Society and was later conductor of the London Symphony, Halle and Liverpool Philharmonic orchestras. He was chief conductor of the BBC Symphony Orchestra (1950–57), and of the Promenade Concerts from 1948 until his death.

Sargeson, Frank (1903–82), New Zealand novelist and short-story writer. He wrote short stories and novels in New Zealand when little prose of consequence had been produced there. He first came to prominence with his novels in the 1940s but his reputation was confirmed with the publication of *Memoirs of a Peon*, 1965, and the more popular *The Hangover*, 1967. Once his stories were considered grim, and his world 'sad and savage'; critics later emphasised the courage and affection he evokes.

Sargon I (the legitimate king), first king and founder of the Dynasty of Agade (Sumer), c.2400 BC. He is cited in later literature as the 'ideal king'.

Sargon II, King of Assyria, 721–705 BC. A general in the Assyrian army, he usurped the crown on the death of Shalmaneser V. His major enemy was Urartu in the north, and in 714 BC, he sacked a number of its cities. In the south, Merodach-baladan caused continuous trouble until Sargon crowned himself king of Babylon (709 BC).

Sark, fourth largest of the Channel Islands, and lies some 10 km east of Guernsey. It is 5·6 km long by 2·4 km wide and has an area of 510 ha. The island is divided into two parts, Great and Little Sark, joined by the Coupée, a razor-edged, natural causeway about 7 m in height. Colonised mainly from Jersey in the 16th century by Hélier de Carteret, Sark has its own constitution and laws. It is a self-governing, feudal state, and its head, if a man, is known as the Seigneur and if a woman as the Dame. The parliament or Court of Chief Pleas, meeting in his or her presence, consists of the Seigneur or Dame, the Seneschal, the 40 Tenants, and 12 Deputies. Motor cars are prohibited, horse-drawn vehicles or tractor-trailers being used instead. Income tax, estate duties, and divorce are non-existent. The people, known as Sarkese, are mainly engaged in farming, fishing, and the tourist trade. Population (1971) 584.

Saros, originally a Babylonian cycle of 3600 years now chiefly used for the cycle of 6585⅓ days (18 years 11⅓ days) which very nearly equals both 223 lunations and 19 eclipse years. If an eclipse of the Sun or Moon is recorded at one period of this cycle, which was discovered by the Chaldaeans, a similar eclipse at the same period in the next cycle can be safely predicted.

Saroyan, William (1908–81), US writer. His volume of short stories *The Daring Young Man on the Flying Trapeze*, 1934, showed the originality and force of his writing, and his plays aroused controversy by their realism. In 1942 he began a theatre of his own in New York. In 1939 Saroyan published *My Heart's in the Highlands* and *The Time of Your Life* (the latter awarded the Pulitzer Prize, which he rejected). *The Human Comedy*, 1943, was filmed.

Sarraute, Nathalie (1900–), French writer. A practitioner of the so-called *nouveau roman*, her works include *Tropismes*, 1939; *Portrait d'un inconnu*, 1948; *Martereau*, 1953; *L'Ere du soupçon*, 1956 (criticism); *Le Planétarium*, 1959; *Les Fruits d'or*, 1963; and *Vous les entendez?*, 1972, a play.

Sarsaparilla, roots of various species of the genus *Smilax* (family Liliaceae), especially *S. officinalis*, a native of Central America, from which the long spirally twisted rhizomes are imported in bundles. A drink, bright pink in colour, is made by boiling the dried roots. Among the numerous substitutes is the root of *Hemidesmus indicus* (Asclepiadaceae, the milkweed family).

Sartre, Jean-Paul (1905–80), French novelist, dramatist, and philosopher. His first two plays were *Les Mouches*, 1943, and *Huis clos*, 1944, and in 1945 he founded *Les Temps modernes*, which he also edited. In subsequent years his name was chiefly associated with the philosophy known as Existentialism.

Sartre's first major philosophical work was *L'Être et le néant*, 1943. His other philosophical publications include *Situations*, ten volumes, 1947–76.

His first novel was *La Nausée*, 1938. He was awarded the Nobel Prize for literature in 1964 but refused it.

Sartre belonged to the atheist wing of Existentialist philosophy. He saw man as basically making his own destiny and as forced to make his own decisions without relying on powers higher than himself. That is what human freedom amounts to.

Sarum, Old, situated on a spur of the chalk downs on the northern boundary of Salisbury, Wiltshire, England. It was occupied by the Romans and is listed as *Sorbiodunum* in the Antonine Itinerary. A motte with a wooden keep was probably built here after the Norman Conquest and the cathedral was started in 1078 after the see of Sherborne was translated to Old Sarum. This was demolished in 1331. The bishop's castle was built early in the 12th century. Remains of the Norman works and the ground plan of the cathedral and castle can be seen.

Sarum Use, or Rite, the manner of conducting the liturgy according to the books traditionally ascribed to St Osmund, Bishop of Salisbury (1078), but really compiled and consolidated in the 13th century, probably by Richard Poore (died 1237). It is a variant of the Roman rite, with some interesting older features such as the offertory procession at High Mass. Traces of it remain in the selection of Sunday gospels in the Anglican Book of Common Prayer and the Roman Catholic form of marriage service in England.

Sash-window (French *chassis*, a frame), strictly speaking a 'double-hung sash', in contradistinction to a 'casement'. The sash is in two pieces, sliding in vertical grooves, balanced by cords, pulleys, and counterweights or patent spring balances. This type of window was introduced into England in the late 17th century.

See also JOINERY.

Saskatchewan, province of Canada, bounded on the north by the North-West Territories, on the south by the USA, east by Manitoba, and west by Alberta. Area 651,900 km², of which 35,550 km² is water surface.

The north has a low-lying undulating surface pitted with innumerable lakes, bogs, and bare rock. Only in those areas where morainic deposits were left by the retreating ice sheet have stands of coniferous forest become established. The sedimentary rocks of the south were laid down by eastward-flowing rivers, which carried material eroded from the Rocky Mountains. These deposits, which infill the entire prairie area, have been subjected to repeated uplift which accounts for the three levels or prairie steps. Mainly because of the dryness of the climate, trees do not thrive in the southern part of the province and this accounts for the presence of the prairie, an extensive area of natural grassland.

The population totalled 968,313, in 1981 and includes many people of German, Scandinavian, and Slav origin. The capital is Regina and other major centres are Saskatoon, Moose Jaw, and Prince Albert.

The main area of arable land is the central

section of the prairie area (the zones of dark brown and black soils). Here the main crop is wheat, with oats, barley, rye, and flax all of much less importance.

Forests cover 45 per cent of the province, mainly in the north, but the stands of spruce, larch, jackpine, poplar, and birch are not great enough to attract a widespread lumber industry. Production is confined to the areas north of Prince Albert in the western part of the province.

Manufacturing is concerned mainly with the processing of local raw materials: flour milling, brewing, dairy produce, meat packing, and wood products. Newer industries include cement, oil refining, chemicals, and fertilisers. The provincial government is vested in a lieutenant-governor and the legislative assembly, elected for five-year terms. The seat of government is Regina.

The area comprising modern Saskatchewan was a valuable one in the era of the fur traders. The first European to reach the area was Henry Kelsey, an employee of the Hudson's Bay Company, who penetrated the Carrot river valley in 1690. Settlement generally did not begin until after 1870, when the Hudson's Bay Company Territory was acquired by Canada. A stream of settlers flowed into the area in the early 1880s, dwindled to a trickle in the next decade in the face of recurring drought and world-wide depression, then swelled to a flood after the turn of the century. Saskatchewan, like Alberta, was created a province under the 1905 acts and was admitted to the dominion of Canada on 1 September 1905.

Saskatchewan, river of Canada formed by two branches, north and south, both rising in western Alberta. It flows east to Lake Winnipeg and thence to Hudson Bay as the Nelson or Katchewan river. Length 1931 km.

Saskatoon, city of Saskatchewan, Canada, on the South Saskatchewan river. Founded in 1882, Saskatoon was named after the native berry found along the river. As the centre of a large agricultural area, the city produces flour, linseed oil, glycol, glucose, and mixed feeds; it also has meat packing and chemical plants, ironworks, machine shops, and oil refineries. Potash is mined nearby. Population (1981) 154,210.

Sassafras, a large deciduous tree, *S. albidum*, of the Lauraceae, native to North America, bearing racemes of greenish-yellow flowers. From the aromatic root-bark an essential oil, used by perfumers, is obtained. The dried root is used in pharmacy, and a type of beer is made from young shoots.

Sassari, city in Sardinia, capital of Sassari province, situated 175 km north-west of Cagliari. It is the market and service centre of northern Sardinia and also has a cotton factory. New industrial growth is taking place at Porto Torres 18 km to the north-west along the coast—chiefly in chemicals and oil. Population (1979) 119,600.

Sassetta, real name Stafano di Giovanni (c.1392–1450), Italian painter of the Sienese School. He represents the medieval tradition in which there is also evidence of the 15th century advance in pictorial science. Panels from altarpieces by him are now widely distributed, e.g. the *Apotheosis of St Francis* from Sansepolcro, 1437–44 (part in the National Gallery, London).

Sassoon, Siegfried Lorraine (1886–1967), English poet and novelist. In the First World War he served as second lieutenant, was twice wounded, and was awarded the Military Cross; his war experiences affected him deeply and made him a pacifist. While in a sanitorium he met Wilfred Owen, whose work he influenced, and whose poems, after Owen's death, he published. Sassoon's own poetry is among the best written at the time of the First World War. His *Collected Poems, 1908–1956*, appeared in 1961.

A trilogy of novels often taken as autobiographical are: *Memoirs of a Fox-Hunting Man*, 1928, which was awarded both the Hawthornden and the Tait Black Memorial prizes; *Memoirs of an Infantry Officer*, 1930, a classic description of his war experiences; and *Sherston's Progress*, 1938.

Satan, see DEVIL.

Satanism, the worship of the powers of evil (regarded as equally potent with those of good), in the person of Satan. It has always been closely allied with witchcraft and black magic. The worship of the devil takes the form of obscene rites and often includes the Black Mass, a parody and desecration of the Christian Mysteries.

Sateen, a shiny cotton cloth used for linings and dress goods.

Satellite, in astronomy, a smaller body accompanying a larger. Its most frequent use is to describe the moons that revolve round several of the planets.

Satellite, Artificial. Since the launching of the first artificial Earth satellite, *Sputnik I*, on 4 October 1957, thousands of satellites have been sent into orbit for military, scientific, and communications purposes. A very small proportion are manned. The majority are military, almost all being launched for surveillance and military research. Civilian satellites are used for communications (TV, radio, telephone), for meteorological surveillance, land use, geodetic measurement and mapping, navigation systems, oceanography and many scientific purposes including astronomy. Communications satellites are positioned 35,890 km above the Earth, at which point they appear motionless.

See also SPACE TRAVEL, SATELLITE COMMUNICATIONS.

Satellite Communications, the world-wide system of radio and television broadcasting using satellites. Two kinds of satellites are used: passive, which merely act as reflectors for signals; and active, which receive and amplify the signals before beaming them back to Earth; the active satellites use solar energy to provide their power. Most communications satellites are synchronous, that is, they orbit the Earth in such a way that they remain in one position in the sky. Three such satellites, properly placed, can provide complete communications cover. The International Telecommunications Satellite Corporation provides an international service. Developments planned for the 1980s include direct broadcasting services which can be picked up by small antennas in people's homes.

Satie, Erik (1866–1925), French composer. His work, although harmonically and melodically naïve, is frequently witty and satirical, an aspect which strongly influenced many younger composers, including Poulenc, Auric and Milhaud. His works include the symphonic drama *Socrate*, ballets, operettas, many sets of pianoforte pieces, and four sets of songs.

Satin, lustrous silk fabric woven so that the warp and weft cross each other only occasionally, the weft being brought uppermost, and thus giving a continuous soft, bright surface. The best satin has a dull silk or wool silk back. Cotton backed satin is generally called 'sateen'.

Satinwood, a beautiful decorative wood of lustrous yellow colour, with a satin sheen and a coconut oil scent from trees of family Rutaceae (the citrus family). West Indian satinwood, *Fagara flavum*, grows in the West Indies, Bermuda, the Bahamas, and southern Florida, but its finest growths are to be found in Jamaica. Many fine pieces of furniture were made by Sheraton, Hepplewhite, and the Adam brothers in satinwood. African satinwood is produced from *Fagara macrophylla*.

East African satinwood, *Chloroxylon swietenia*, a member of the Flindersiaceae, is found in southern India and Sri Lanka.

Satire, the mocking or censuring of men, manners, actions, or beliefs by means of irony, ridicule, or sarcasm. Primarily thought of as a literary production, through the media of allegory, parody, burlesque, epigram, and lampoon, satire can also be employed through a combination of verbal and visual effects in film, television, and theatre.

Saturday, seventh day of the week, *Saturni dies*, which was dedicated by the Romans to Saturn (Old English *Saeternesdaeg*). As the sabbath it is the weekly rest-day of the Jews, and is also kept as such by certain Christian bodies, including the Seventh-day Adventists.

Saturn, or Saturnus, an early Roman god of sowing or of seed-corn. He was taken to be the father of Jupiter, Neptune, Pluto, and Juno. His festival, the Saturnalia, lasting seven days from 19 December, probably originated in rites connected with winter sowing, but in historical times was a season of popular merry-making. Legend represented Saturn as a mythical king of Italy who introduced social order and the arts of civilisation; his reign was a golden age.

Saturn is the sixth planet in order of distance from the Sun, and is best known for its 'rings'. The details of its orbit are: mean distance from the Sun, 9·5388 astronomical units or 1,427,010,000 km; eccentricity 0·0556; inclination to the ecliptic 2°29′; sidereal period 29·54 years; mean synodic period 378·1 days. The planet's vital statistics are: equatorial diameter 119,300 km; polar diameter 107,700 km; period of axial rotation 10 h 14 min; mean density 0.706 g/cm^3. The difference between the polar and equatorial diameters is over 10 per cent, and the average density is much smaller than that of any other planet.

Apart from its rings, Saturn resembles Jupiter, though it is smaller and, being further from the Sun, cooler. The temperature of the visible surface is about 94 K (−179°C). The

Saturn, *with three of its moons, photographed by* Voyager II *at a distance of 13 million miles.*

spectograph reveals more methane and less ammonia than in Jupiter's atmosphere; there is also much molecular hydrogen. The atmosphere, and probably the bulk of the planet, must consist largely of hydrogen and helium, but the central condensation contains heavier elements.

Saturn's Rings. The Voyager spacecraft have shown the three major rings visible through telescopes on Earth to comprise thousands of narrow ringlets of ice rock particles in a plane about 10 km thick. The particles vary in size from less than 1 m, in the tenuous outer rings, to tens of metres in the brighter rings, which extend out to a diameter of 270,000 km.

Satellites. Saturn has at least 17 satellites. Titan, the largest, is about 5140 km in diameter. Its atmosphere is mainly nitrogen, with methane, argon and trace amounts of hydrocarbons which give the satellite its red colour. There are four other satellites of between 1000 and 1500 km in diameter. These are typically, heavily cratered; Dione, however, has a relatively young surface. One half of Iapetus has the darkest colouring seen in the Solar System. The other satellites vary from 500 km down to 30–40 km.

See PLANETS.

Satyriasis, an abnormal insatiable desire for sexual relationships in a man. Like nymphomania in women, this apparent hypersexuality may mask a form of impotence where there is incomplete satisfaction, or it may represent a repetitive and compulsive attempt to obtain and sustain a good sexual relationship.

See also SEXUALITY, HUMAN.

Satyrs, mythical creatures of the woods and mountains, closely connected with Dionysus. They represent the vital powers of nature. They had men's bodies but goats' ears, horns, hoofs, and tails.

Saudi Arabia, Kingdom of, Arabian kingdom, comprising the Hejaz and Nejd, and the principality of ASIR. The kingdom occupies the whole of the central plateau of the Arabian Peninsula, and is bounded in the north by Jordan, Iraq, and Kuwait, in the west by the Red Sea, in the south by the Yemen and Yemen People's Democratic Republic, in the south-east by Oman, and in the east by the United Arab Emirates, Qatar, and the Persian Gulf. The total area is about 2·2 million km². The physiography takes the form of a north–south range of mountains (the Hejaz) down the Red Sea coast, rising from a narrow coastal plain, the Tihama, to an average height of 1200 m. The eastern slopes of Hejaz descend gently to the central plateau, Nejd, and down to the low-lying eastern province of el Hasa. The kingdom's two main areas of sandy desert, the An Nafud (5220 km²) and the Rub 'al Khali, the Empty Quarter (780,000 km²), are connected by the Dahna, a ribbon of sand 1300 km long and 25–30 km wide. The results of the only population census to be held in Saudi Arabia (1962–63), were repudiated by the government. The total population was estimated at 8·63 million in 1981. It is estimated that about 20 per cent of the total population are nomads, 55 per cent live in rural settlements, and the rest (a rapidly growing proportion) in urban areas. The principal cities are Mecca and Medina, the premier holy cities in Islam; Riyadh, the capital and administration centre of the kingdom, and Jidda, the chief port. Livestock breeding constitutes the principal agricultural activity. Steps are being taken however to increase crop production, which at present includes dates, barley, millet, and coffee.

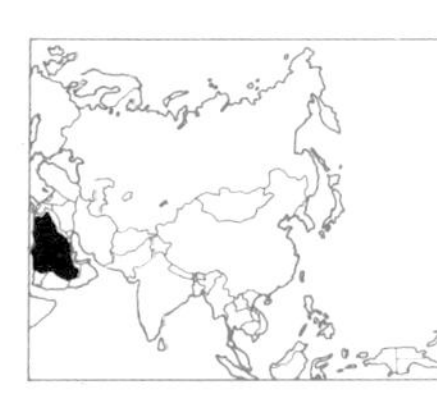

Saudi Arabia
Area: 2,200,000 km²
Population: 8,630,000
Capital: Riyadh

Oil was first discovered in 1938. The chief oil-fields are at Dhahran, Abqaiq, and Ain Dar. Other minerals, including gold, are worked in small quantities. Oil royalties are practically the only source of revenue apart from the tourist income derived from pilgrims to Mecca. These oil revenues have been used increasingly in recent years to finance industrial diversification.

The kingdom is ruled by the King in accordance with the Islamic holy law, the Shari'ah. The King appoints a council of ministers and decisions reached by the council, that have a council majority, are then passed to the King for royal sanction.

Saudi Arabia is the world centre of Islam; the vast majority of the population is Sunni Muslim. Arabic is the official language.

History. When the kingdom was formed in 1927, Ibn-Saud, Sultan of Nejd and King of Hejaz (c.1880–1953), set about unifying it. He organised the kingdom into two provinces, each under one of his sons as viceroy. Ibn-Saud granted to US concerns oil concessions which, on being exploited for the first time in commercial quantities in 1938, produced large sums in royalties and added greatly to the kingdom's revenue. In the Second World War Saudi Arabia remained nominally neutral until March 1945 when it came in on the side of the Allies. In the same year the Arab League was formed, with Saudi Arabia as a leading member. Ibn-Saud was succeeded, on his death in 1953, by the Crown Prince, ibn-Saud (1902–69). The new king was grossly corrupt and, in 1958, Crown Prince Faisal took charge of the government. Saud was finally deposed in favour of Faisal in 1964. In 1975 Faisal was assassinated and Crown Prince Khalid was proclaimed king.

See also ARABIAN HISTORY.

Sauerkraut, a form of pickled cabbage, much eaten in Germany and northern Europe. It is prepared from white or red cabbage, finely shredded and fermented in brine with juniper leaves. It is obtainable at delicatessen shops and also canned, and is served with sausages.

Saul, son of Kish, a Benjamite, first king of Israel, c.1050 BC. His first exploit was the deliverance of Jabesh-Gilead from its Ammonite oppressors. The rest of his reign was spent chiefly in border warfare against the Philistines. He was obstinate and violent and given to melancholia. He was a man of spiritual gifts (prophecy), but allowed them to decay, so that he quarrelled with Samuel and drove David from the kingdom. Yet his people remained faithful to him.

Sault Sainte Marie, town of Ontario, Canada, on the north side of the St Mary's river, and the short canal between Lakes Superior and Huron. It is a busy port with steamship connection to all five Great Lakes. The leading industry is steel. There are also oxygen and chemical works, railway car shops, dredging and construction companies, and fishing. Population (1976) 81,048.

Sault Sainte Marie, city in the USA, situated on the American, or southern, bank of the St Mary's river, in the state of Michigan. With its Canadian counterpart it serves the lake shipping; it has a number of chemical industries and plants processing forest products. Population (1980) 14,448.

Saumur, French town in the *département* of Maine-et-Loire, on the left bank of the Loire, 43 km south-east of Angers. It is the seat of a cavalry school, founded in 1768. It is the centre of a district producing both still and sparkling wines; the latter are known as *vins de Saumur.* Population (1975) 34,191.

Sauna, traditional Finnish bath-house heated by a stove filled with stones over which water is thrown to produce steam. The after-effect of a sauna is a general feeling of well-being and thus it is considered to have some therapeutic value. In recent years the sauna has become increasingly popular outside Finland.

Saury, or saury-pike (*Scomberesox saurus*), a member of the fish order Synentognathi, containing skippers and flying-fish. The saury is a long-bodied fish, closely related to the garfish.

Saussure, Ferdinand de (1857–1913), Swiss linguist. He studied with the neogrammarians, succeeded Bréal at the École des Hautes Études in 1881 and became professor of Indo-European (1901) and later of general linguistics (1907) at Geneva.

In 1916 his pupils Charles Bally and A. Sechehaye published the *Cours de linguistique générale* (English translation, 1959), based on notes of his lectures. This work, which earned de Saussure the title 'father of modern linguistics' first synthesised various areas of language study, such as phonetics, comparative-historical work, dialectology, and grammar into one discipline, introducing basic notions of early 20th-century linguistics, such as the 'langue'-'parole', 'synchronic'-'diachronic', and 'syntagmatic'-'associative' (later 'paradigmatic') distinctions, besides containing his famed analogy of language with a game of chess.

Savage, Michael Joseph (1872–1940), New Zealand statesman. He entered politics through trade unionism, and was elected member of parliament for Auckland West in 1919. Savage became the leader of the Labour party in 1933, and, in 1935, prime minister in New Zealand's first Labour government, as well as minister of external affairs, native affairs, and of a number of other departments. In 1938 he was returned to power with the loss of only one seat and held office until his death.

Savage, Richard (c.1697–1742), English poet; he claimed to be the illegitimate son of Richard Savage, fourth Earl Rivers, and Anne, wife of the second Earl of Macclesfield, but this was never substantiated. In 1730, when Eusden died, he applied for the poet-laureateship, but the office was given to Colley Cibber. Johnson, who knew him, had a high opinion of his powers, but it is difficult to see why from his writings. His works include several plays, and among his poems are *The Bastard*, 1728, and *The Wanderer*, 1729. He lived a bohemian existence and died in poverty.

Savannah, city in Georgia, USA, 400 km south-east of Atlanta. It is situated on the south bank of the Savannah river, which separates Georgia from South Carolina, and on Hutchinson Island, about 20 km from the open sea. Ocean-going vessels have an assured water depth of 11·5 m up to its harbour. The city was the principal port and settlement laid out by Oglethorpe when he founded the colony of Georgia in 1733. With a number of 18th-century buildings still intact, Savannah is a tourist attraction, particularly because of its subtropical climate and vegetation. The port grew with the cotton trade and, since that has fallen off, it has become a general outlet for Georgia produce. Most of the industries derive from the farm and forest produce of the hinterland, and include flour and cotton milling, sawmill products, and paper making. Population (1980) 133,672.

Savannah, river between Georgia and South Carolina, formed by the Tugaloo and Seneca rivers. Its course of 505 km is in a general south-east direction, and it flows into Tybee Sound, 29 km below Savannah. It is navigable for barge-tows to Augusta (340 km).

Savernake Forest, large area of woodland, mostly of beech trees, lying about 5 km to the south-east of Marlborough, Wiltshire, England. It covers 1620 ha and abounds in deer and game.

Savin, *Juniperus sabina*, a small tree or bush with scale-like leaves and light green fruit. It is sometimes cultivated for the tops and young leaves, which are used in medicine as a powerful diuretic.

Savings Banks are banks established for the receipt of small sums, and for the accumulation of compound interest. Probably the first instance in England was that set up in Tottenham by a Miss Priscilla Wakefield in 1804, but the genesis of the Trustee Savings Banks, as they are called today, was at Ruthwell in Dumfriesshire, where a savings bank was opened in 1810 by the Rev. Dr Henry Duncan. After this date they so increased in popularity that by 1817 they had become the subject of legislation.

The savings bank system in Britain underwent a great change in 1861 with the establishment of the Post Office Savings Bank and the acceptance by the state of direct responsibility to the citizen for the safe custody of his savings. There were thus in existence two classes of savings banks: Trustee and Post Office Savings Banks.

Under the Trustee Savings Bank Act 1964 Trustee Savings Banks are permitted to operate a current account service for depositors. Current accounts are non-interest bearing and depositors are supplied with cheque books with which to effect withdrawals, but they are not allowed overdraft facilities.

The National Savings Bank (formerly Post Office Savings Bank) which is the state savings bank of Britain, was set up to provide 'additional facilities for depositing small savings at interest with the security of the government for due repayment thereof'.

Savona, Italian seaport and capital of Savona province, situated 35 km south-west of Genoa. It is on the Riviera di Ponente, on the western shore of the Gulf of Genoa. The port is busy, and there are shipyards, and iron and steel, chemical, and textile industries. Population (1974) 76,300.

Savonarola, Girolamo (1452–98), Italian friar and reformer. He joined the Dominicans in 1474. Appointed prior of San Marco at Florence in 1491, he soon began to dominate the city through his fervid oratory, denouncing abuses in Church and State. In 1495 Pope Alexander VI summoned Savonarola to Rome and, after he had thrice disregarded this summons, excommunicated him (1497). Believing himself to be inspired directly by God and therefore entitled to disobey ecclesiastical authority, he disregarded the excommunication. By this time the Florentines themselves had begun to tire of Savonarola's lofty ideals. He was accused of heresy and cast into prison. In May 1498 he was hanged with two other Dominicans, and the bodies of all three were afterwards burnt.

Savory, *Satureia*, a genus of herbs in the family Labiatae. Summer savory, *S. hortensis*, is an annual used for flavouring and seasoning. Winter savory, *S. montana*, which is similarly used, is an evergreen perennial.

Savoy (French *Savoie*), historic name for a district in eastern France. Originally part of the kingdom of Burgundy, it was later part of Charlemagne's empire. When this empire broke up, Savoy reverted to Burgundy (933) and later became part of the Kingdom of Sardinia. It was finally ceded to France in 1860, and became a province. The capital was Chambery.

Saw-fly, an insect that, with the wood-wasps and other minor groups, belongs to the suborder Symphyta of order Hymenoptera. The term 'saw-fly' refers to the nature of the ovipositor, which is saw-like and serrated. The female lays her eggs in the leaves, stems or branches of plants. The larvae are plant feeders and resemble caterpillars.

The saw-flies and their allies are grouped into six superfamilies: Xyeloidea; Megalodontoidea; Silicoidea (wood-wasps or horn-tails); Orussoidea; Cephoidea (stem saw-flies); and Tenthredinoidea. Most saw-flies and wood-wasps are pests of forestry and agriculture.

Saw Shark, two genera of sharks, *Pliotrema* and *Pristiophorus*, in the family Pristiophoridae of order Selachii. They grow to 1 m long including the long, saw-like, toothed snout, which is used to attack prey. Although they resemble the sawfish, a ray, their gill-slits are on the sides of the head instead of underneath, and the front edge of the pectoral fins are free, not fused to the head and body. They are not dangerous to man.

Sawfish, any fish of the family Pristidae in the ray order Batoidei, distinguished by the prolongation of the rostrum of the skull with its double saw of lateral teeth. They occur chiefly in tropical seas, where they may grow 7 m long including the saw, which sometimes measures 2 m in length. They habitually grub about in the mud or sand for the small animals which are their food, or they may attack a shoal of fishes. Some species of sawfish invade rivers.

Saws may be divided into handsaws and machine saws. The carpenter's handsaw has a steel blade with a wooden, plastic, or metal handle, and may be a cross-cut saw for sawing across the grain of the wood or a rip saw for cutting along the grain; the difference lies in the shape of the teeth.

Machine saws are of three types. The first is simply a larger, more robust hacksaw operated by an electric motor through a crank and connecting rod. The second, the circular saw, has a rotating, disc-shaped blade with teeth on the circumference, and the third, the bandsaw, has the blade in the form of an endless flexible band which is tightly stretched over pulleys and has fine teeth along one edge.

Sax, Antoine Joseph, called also Adolphe (1814–94), was a maker and improver of all wind instruments. His inventions include the saxophone and the saxhorn.

Saxe, Maurice, Comte de (1696–1750), Marshal of France. He commanded a division in the Austrian Succession war, took Prague and Eger, and was promoted to be Marshal of France. After this he became one of the most important generals of his age. In 1745 he besieged Tournai and defeated the Duke of Cumberland at Fontenoy; in 1746 he gained the victory of Raucoux; and he was again successful at Lauffeld (1747) and at Maastricht.

Saxe-Gothaea conspicua, Prince Albert's yew, the only species of its genus in the family Podocarpaceae. It is a small evergeen, yew-like tree of Chile, of botanical interest as a possible link between the Araucariaceae and Podocarpaceae.

Saxhorn, family of brass wind instruments with a cup-shaped mouthpiece invented by Adolphe Sax. They consist of a conical tube which widens out into a bell at one end, and are furnished with valves. They are made in various keys from the soprano flügelhorn down to the tuba. They are used in military bands and in brass bands.

Saxifragaceae, a family of dicotyledons including about 30 genera and 600 species, mainly occurring in temperate regions. The family consists mainly of herbaceous plants but includes a few shrubs and trees. Some members of the Saxifragaceae are grown as decorative plants.

Saxifrage, *Saxifraga*, or rockfoil, of the Rosaceae, a large genus of annual and perennial plants with the leaves usually in basal rosettes but sometimes also arranged along the stems, and white, yellow, purple or red flowers. They grow mostly in mountainous areas. London pride is a garden hybrid *S x urbium*. Many species are of great value in the garden and some are grown as pot plants.

Saxo Grammaticus (c.1150–c.1220), Danish chronicler and historian. He became secretary to Absalon, Archbishop of Lund, who, in about 1185, encouraged him to begin his *Gesta Danorum* or *Historica Danica*. Written in Latin, its 16 volumes comprise the most vital information now surviving on ancient Denmark and the first phase of the Middle Ages. Using material from the Icelandic sagas, old customs, legal rulings, and ancient beliefs, appear beside authenticated history.

Saxon Language, see ANGLO-SAXON LANGUAGE.

Saxons, one element of a confederation of Germanic peoples who lived on the plains in the region of the Lower Elbe. The generic name is said to be derived from their national weapon, the *seax*, a short thrusting sword, in the same way that the Franks, the spearmen, took their name from the Old English *franca*, javelin. The confederacy was a loose one, characterised by its maritime outlook and by its insistent south-western spread in search of living space. Its migrations spread as far west along the Channel as Boulogne and the Bessin. The migration to Britain took place, according to belief, which is derived from Bede, in 449. The standard authority, Bede, states that the tribes who came to Britain at the invitation of the British chieftain, Vortigern, to help defend his country against Pictish and Irish invaders, were from three powerful Germanic peoples, the Saxons, Angles, and Jutes. The Saxons came from what Bede called Old Saxony, the Angles from Angulus (in Schleswig), and the Jutes from the area around the mouth of the Rhine; the people who settled in Kent, the Isle of Wight, and what is now southern Hampshire were descended from the Jutes, those in Essex, Sussex, and Wessex came from the homeland of the Saxons, while from the homeland of the Angles came the East Angles. By the end of the 6th century much of England was in Anglo-Saxon hands. Kent, East Anglia, Wessex, Bernicia, Deira, and finally Mercia had all developed into separate kingdoms.

Saxony (German *Sachsen*), former German electorate, then kingdom, and finally republic. Originally Saxony meant Germany between the North Sea, the Rhine and the Elbe; later it referred to only the south-eastern part of this area. The area of pre-1945 Saxony was 14,988 km².

History. After the final conquest of the Saxons by Charlemagne, they became one of the components of the Empire. Their country, in 850, was erected into a dukedom. Henry I obtained the throne in 919, and commenced the Saxon line of German sovereigns, which ended in 1024. After Lothair's accession to the Imperial throne in 1125, he handed over the Duchy (1127) to his son-in-law, Henry the Proud, the Guelphic Duke of Bavaria, who was thus the ruler of more than half Germany; but under his son, Henry the Lion, it was wrested (1180) from the house of Guelph. In 1260 the diminished Saxony was permanently divided into two portions, Saxe-Lauenburg and Saxe-Wittenberg, to the latter of which the electoral dignity remained.

By 1423 the Saxon elector was one of the most powerful princes of Germany. Frederick the Wise (1486–1525) favoured the Reformation, and firmly supported and protected Luther. Albert was the founder of the younger, ducal, or Albertine line, of whom the most celebrated was Maurice (1541–47). His brother, Augustus I (1553–86), considerably increased his territories. John George I (1611–56) allied himself with Gustavus Adolphus, and took part in the Thirty Years' War. The reign of Frederick Augustus I (1694–1733), who converted to the Catholic Church and gained the throne of Poland, well-nigh ruined the hitherto prosperous electorate.

King Frederick Augustus I (1763–1827), for his support of Napoleon, was deprived of the greater portion of Saxony, which was handed over to Prussia, but he retained the title of king, which had been conferred upon him in 1806. Anthony (1827–36) reformed the entire legislation of the country, and granted a liberal constitution, and the state's representatives first assembled on 27 January 1833. Saxony shared in the humiliation of Austria at Sadowa in 1866, thereafter becoming a member of the new German Empire in 1871. The republic was proclaimed on 9 November 1918, after a revolution, and the republican régime continued until 1933, when Hitler abolished the Diet.

See also GERMAN DEMOCRATIC REPUBLIC; GERMAN HISTORY.

Saxony, Lower, see LOWER SAXONY.

Saxophone, brass musical instrument invented by Adolphe Sax. It consists of a conical tube bent at both ends with a single-reed mouthpiece resembling that of the clarinet; it has elaborate keywork similar to that of the oboe. The saxophone was invented as a louder substitute for the oboe in military bands, where it is still used, and it has achieved prominence in jazz and dance bands. It is made in various pitches from soprano to bass and is a transposing instrument, usually in B flat or E flat.

Sayan Mountains, in Krasnoyarsk *krai* and Irkutsk *oblast*, and partly in Tuva ASSR, USSR, consisting of two ranges—the West Sayan, and the East Sayan, both running north-west to south-east, with the Minusinsk Basin between. The highest point (Munku-

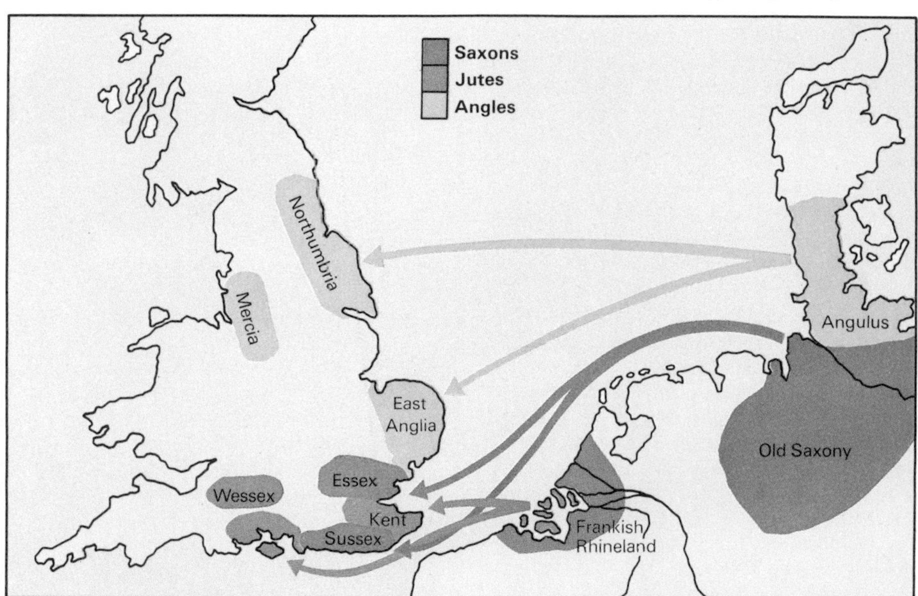

Saxons. *The homelands and routes of the Germanic invaders of England in the 5th century* AD.

Sardyk, in eastern Sayan) is 3491 m. The area contains iron and copper ores, gold, graphite, asbestos, and mica.

Sayers, Dorothy Leigh (1893–1957), English writer. Though she wished to be considered a serious writer, her detective novels, featuring Lord Peter Wimsey, were her most successful works. She produced her first play, *The Zeal of Thy House*, in 1937, and in 1942 she wrote a remarkable religious radio play, *The Man Born to be King*. She published a translation of Dante's *Inferno*, 1949, and of the *Purgatorio*, 1955.

Say's Law, a maxim of classical economics, according to which supply creates its own demand, and there can never be a general excess of commodities in the market. It was first enunciated by J. B. Say.

Scabbard, case or sheath which protects the blade of a sword, dagger, or bayonet when not in use.

Scabies, a parasitic disease of the skin caused by the presence of parasitic mites, much the most important to man being *Sarcoptes scabiei*, which burrows actively through the skin. Closely related mites produce the related condition known as mange in many domestic and wild animals.

Scabious, *Scabiosa*, a genus of annual and perennial plants. *S. columbaria*, small scabious, and *S. atropurpurea*, an annual, are European, while *S. caucasica* is the large scabious, much grown in gardens. Devil's-bit scabious is *Succisa pratensis*, and field scabious is *Knautia arvensis*. All are members of the Dipsacaceae.

Scafell Pike, in the Lake District, Cumbria, is the highest mountain (978 m) in England.

Scaffolding, term for the framework used by builders for supporting workmen and materials.

Scalar, in physics, adjective describing a quantity completely defined by a number and a unit, or scale in which it is measured, no reference being made to direction. Temperature, defined by the number of degrees Celsius or Fahrenheit; thermal energy, by the number of calories; and power, by the number of kilowatts, are examples.
See also VECTOR.

Scalds, see BURNS AND SCALDS.

Scale (Latin *scala*, ladder), in music, the succession of notes in an octave. In Western music the diatonic and chromatic are the most important. The diatonic scale of C major is C D E F G A B C. All the other diatonic major scales have the same arrangement of tones and semitones. The chromatic scale is made up of the twelve semitones. It gives no sense of key in itself, but can be arranged in different forms to provide the material of serial music.
See also SERIALISM.

Scale, Boiler, a hard, white deposit formed in boilers and kettles owing to precipitation on boiling of the calcium and magnesium bicarbonate present in most natural waters. Sclae is a bad conductor of heat, and the crust of scale formed on the inside of a boiler therefore wastes fuel. Water softening effectively prevents the formation of scale in domestic installations.

Scales, flat structures developed from the skin of many animals. The scales of most fish are derived from the dermis, or underskin. They are classified as *cycloid*, or circular; *ctenoid*, or tooth-edged; *ganoid*, or enamelled; and *placoid*, or tabular. Scales of reptiles are derived from the epidermis, or outer skin. Birds possess scales on their legs. Some mammals possess scales: pangolins and armadillos have them all over, and rats, beavers, and some marsupials on the tails. The patterns on the wings of the butterfly and similar insects are formed by scales, which fit so closely together that they appear to be a smooth surface.

Scallop, popular name of the family Pectinidae, of phylum Mollusca, with a characteristic finely sculptured shell that is often beautifully coloured. The scallop is classed in the subclass Bivalvia with the mussel and the pearl oyster. There are a number of edible species, including *Pecten maximus*, the great scallop or clam, and *Chlamys opercularis*, the queen scallop. The scallop has a distinct foot which spins threads (byssus) for attachment. The young are capable of rapid motion by opening and suddenly closing their shells. The shell of *P. jacobaeus*, called the St James's shell, was a badge of certain knightly orders, and was also worn by pilgrims to the shrine of Compostella.

Scalp, the soft tissue covering of the skull (excluding the face). It is arranged in five layers: (1) the skin; (2) the connective tissue binding the skin to the muscles beneath; (3) the epicranium, consisting of the two parts of the occipito-frontalis muscle and the aponeurosis or tendon between them; (4) a layer of loose areolar tissue or lymph space allowing free mobility of the surface layers; and (5) the pericranium or periosteum investing the skull bones. The second layer of connective tissue contains the abundant blood supply of the scalp, which is responsible for its remarkable capacity for healing.

Scalping. The cutting off of the forelock and part of the scalp of a dead enemy. It was practised by the Scythians, Celts, Teutons and North American Indians, for whom the scalp was as a victory trophy, and by American settlers, for whom the scalp was evidence enabling them to claim state bounties, e.g. Massachusetts offered £40 for adult male Indian scalps and £20 for those of women and children.

Scandinavia, term applied to the peninsula of northern Europe formed by Norway and Sweden. It also includes Denmark and Iceland as these countries are inhabited by similar races; it does not include Finland, which is racially and linguistically distinct.

Scandinavian Architecture. The earliest surviving buildings are churches in the Romanesque style of western Europe. In Denmark they include the cathedrals of Viborg (much restored), Ribe and Roskilde (c.1190), also the remarkable church at Kalundborg (1170); in Sweden, the heavily restored cathedral at Lund (12th century); and in Norway the diminutive timber or stave churches such as Borgund (12th century) which have a rather Oriental pagoda-like form. Of Gothic buildings, the chief examples are the cathedral of Odense in Denmark; the cathedrals of Uppsala and Linköping (13th century), and the monastic churches of Varnhem and Vadstena in Sweden; and the cathedrals of Trondheim and Stavanger in Norway.

The Renaissance reached Scandinavia in the 16th century mainly via Holland; and produced a crop of picturesque and imposing

Scandinavian Architecture. *The 12th-century stave church at Heddal, Norway.*

royal palaces. They included the so-called castles of Rosenberg (1620–24), Kronborg (1577–85) and Frederiksborg (1602–20) in Denmark; Gripsholm (1537) and Vadstena (1545) in Sweden; Akershus Castle (1624) at Oslo in Norway.

Dutch influence also prevailed in the next period, when the Baroque style, which had spread from Italy to other parts of Europe, reached Scandinavia. In Denmark it produced the palace of Charlottenborg (1672–83), the Vordingsborg (1671), as well as the curious twisted spire of St Saviour's church at Copenhagen (1682–96); in Sweden, the Riddarhuset at Stockholm (1652–55), the Karlberg Palace (1670), the huge palace of Drottningholm (begun 1662, by Nicodemus Tessin the Elder), and the Royal Palace at Stockholm (1697, by Tessin the Younger).

The Rococo style is seen at its best in the Amalienborg Palace (1760), the Prince's Palace, and the small Eremitagen Palace—all in Copenhagen; in the China Palace, at Drottningholm, Sweden; and also in many country-houses.

During the present century, in addition to a large number of admirably designed houses and public buildings, the most important architectural works in Scandinavia have been the remarkable Grundtvig Memorial Church near Copenhagen (1913–19), the City Hall at Stockholm (1911–23), by R. Östberg; Aarhus University, Denmark (1932–56); Stockholm Exhibition (1930) and Crematorium (1935–1940) by G. Asplund; the new Stockholm suburb of Vallingby (1949) by S. Markelius; Rødovre Town Hall (1955) by A. Jacobson; and various domestic projects by the designer of the Sydney Opera House (1956–73), Jørn Utzon.

Scandinavian Languages constitute one of three divisions of the Germanic branch of the Indo-European languages. The modern Scandinavian languages are represented by Icelandic, Norwegian, Swedish, and Danish, each of them having various dialects. While Swedish, Danish, and Norwegian differ from one another scarcely more than do some dialects within English, Icelandic is extremely archaic and differs relatively little from Old Norse.

See also DENMARK, *Language*; ICELAND, *Language*; NORSE LANGUAGES; NORWAY, *Language*; SWEDEN, *Language*.

Scandium, metallic chemical element, symbol Sc, atomic number 21, atomic weight 44·9559; it was predicted to exist by Mendeléev and was discovered by Nilson in 1879. It is one of the lanthanides and is a silvery-white, fairly soft metal. Melting point 1539°C. The metal itself is difficult to isolate, but it forms colourless salts and an oxide, Sc_2O_3. Scandium occurs in many minerals, e.g. gadolinite and wolframite, and is present in quantity in the Sun and stars.

Scantling, commercial term for a piece of square-sawn softwood 50–100 mm thick by 50–114 mm wide.

Scapa Flow, sea-basin in the Orkney Islands, Scotland, nearly enclosed by Mainland, Burray, South Ronaldsay, Walls, and Hoy. It was the main base of the British Fleet during the First World War. The surrendered German fleet scuttled itself here in 1919. Length 24 km; breadth 13 km.

Scapula, or shoulder-blade, the flat triangular bone which lies over the second to seventh ribs on the back. This spine continues laterally as a shelf of bone, the acromion, which forms the tip of the shoulder in man. The scapula is joined to the clavicle (collar-bone) at the acromion, and the humerus (armbone) fits into the glenoid cavity just below. The scapula is well protected by thick muscular coverings and is rarely fractured.

Scarab, Egyptian seal shaped to represent the scarabaeus beetle. The underside was engraved with the device or inscription which was to be impressed upon the sealing clay. A few scarabs were used as amulets and others were cut in commemoration of some event. Scarabs were made of pottery or paste, moulded in terra-cotta moulds, the underside flattened with a knife. In Roman times scarabs disappeared from use.

Scarabaeus, the scarab beetle, a member of the subfamily Coprinae in family scarabaeidae of order Coleoptera. Members of this subfamily generally feed on dung, mostly of herbivorous animals, and roll balls of dung into special underground chambers. Within these chambers they reshape these balls into a heap within which the female beetle lays a single egg. The best-known member of this genus is *Scarabaeus sacer*, revered by the ancient Egyptians.

Scarborough, seaside holiday resort on the North Yorkshire coast, England. The harbour serves fishing and cargo boats and yachts. The discovery of a medicinal water spring accounts for Scarborough's early popularity, and the spa remains its social centre. Population (1981) 43,103.

Scarfe, Gerald (1936–), British artist. Scarfe became nationally known in the 1960s as a cartoonist for *Private Eye*, *Punch*, and other magazines. The cruellest British cartoonist since Gillray, his victims are made to appear physically repulsive in the extreme.

Scarlatti, Alessandro (1660–1725), Italian composer. He produced his first opera in 1679. This was followed by many others until 1721, produced mainly in Rome and Naples. He did much to establish a type of opera which consisted almost entirely of *da capo* arias interspersed with recitatives. His melodic invention was matched by his skill as a writer for the orchestra. He also wrote masses and motets, vocal serenades, madrigals, chamber cantatas and sonatas.

Scarlatti, Domenico (1685–1757), Italian harpsichordist and composer, son and pupil of Alessandro. He was court musician to the Queen of Poland in Rome, for whom he wrote operas, and later at St Peter's, where he wrote mainly sacred music. In 1729 he was invited to Madrid where he wrote most of his harpsichord 'exercises', now called sonatas, which exhibit an original approach to harmony and frequently demand great virtuosity. Scarlatti was the most celebrated harpsichordist of his time, and his music provided the foundation for modern piano technique.

Scarlet Fever (scarlatina), an acute infectious disease caused by haemolytic streptococci, and characterised by fever and a scarlet rash on the trunk and limbs. It usually affects children. Infection of the throat is usual but other sites, such as wounds, may be the point of entry. The onset is sudden, and two to five days after infection, fever, malaise, and frequently vomiting develop. The rash appears soon afterwards and lasts for two or three days. Diagnostic appearances are seen on the tongue (strawberry tongue). Flaky peeling of the skin (desquamation) especially of the hands and feet, occurs after the rash. At present the disease is mild and very rarely complicated, but treatment with antibiotics is recommended to eradicate the organism and prevent its spread to others.

Scarron, Paul (1610–60), French comic poet, dramatist, and satirist. He chose an ecclesiastical life, for which his character and habits were ill suited. About 1637 he was crippled by disease. In 1652 he became acquainted with Mademoiselle d'Aubigné (afterwards Madame de Maintenon), whom he subsequently married. Under her influence, the society of his house, always a favourite resort of wits, became still more select and brilliant. Scarron's fame now rests on his realistic novel *Le Roman comique*, 1651–1657.

Scaup, *Aythya marila*, a duck species in the family Anatidae, order Anseriformes, which frequents northern Europe, Asia and America. The male duck is a greenish-black colour on the head, chest and tail coverts and it has a grey back and white flanks and underparts. The female is a dark brown colour but distinguished from the smaller tufted duck by white markings behind the bill. It is commonly seen in wintering flocks on estuaries or off the coast, rarely inland.

Scent, see PERFUMERY.

Scepticism, or the philosophy of doubting, has two main ideas: (1) that to arrive at truth one must believe everything to be false until it is proved to be true (Descartes' Method) and (2) that human knowledge can never arrive at truth—a denial of objective knowledge. The first school of Scepticism originated with Pyrrho of Elis (c.300 BC), whose teaching was largely influenced by the Protagorean denial of the possibility of real knowledge on the ground that individual and momentary cognition alone is possible. The adherents of this school extended Scepticism even to the principles of their own doubt. Other notable Sceptics include: Sextus Empiricus (2nd century AD) Montaigne (1533–92) and Hume (1711–76).

Sceptre, see REGALIA.

Schaffhausen, capital of the canton of the same name, Switzerland, situated 35 km north of Zürich on the Rhine above waterfalls. Its streets are narrow, its architecture medieval. Industries include aluminium at Neuhausen, silk and cotton goods, and machinery. Population (1980) 34,250.

Scheel, Walter (1919–), German politician. He joined the government in 1961 as minister for economic co-operation. Between 1967 and 1969 he was vice-president of the Bundestag, then in the latter year led his party into coalition with the SPD under Willy Brandt, becoming foreign minister and deputy premier. He was president of the German Federal Republic, 1974–79, succeeding Gustav Heinemann.

Scheele, Karl Wilhelm (1742–86), Swedish chemist. He was apprenticed to a chemist at Gothenburg, and subsequently made many important discoveries. In *A Chemical Treatise on Air and Fire*, 1777, he described his discovery (made some years earlier) of the existence of oxygen as the component of air which supports combustion. Among other substances, he discovered chlorine, glycerol, and tartaric, benzoic, oxalic, prussic and hydrofluoric acids, and he also described the pigment known as Scheele's green (copper arsenite).

Scheldt (Flemish *Schelde*, French *Escaut*), river of France, Belgium, and the Netherlands, rising in the *département* of Aisne, France, and flowing through Belgium into Holland, where it divides into two channels, north and south of the island of Beveland. The main channel reaches the North Sea near Flushing (Dutch *Vlissingen*). The total course of the Scheldt is 400 km, navigable as far as Cambrai, France, 320 km from the sea. The chief tributary is the Lys (Flemish *Leie*), and it is connected with the Somme, Seine, Sambre, Meuse, Rhine, and principal towns of Belgium by canals.

Schelling, Friedrich Wilhelm Joseph von (1775–1854), German Idealist philosopher. His system, known as Objective Idealism, regarded nature-philosophy and spirit-philosophy as co-ordinated and equal factors in the complete system of philosophy, instead of subordinating the objective (material, real) to the subjective (ideal, transcendental) as Fichte had done. To Schelling, artistic genius was the highest form of human consciousness.

Schenectady, city of New York state, USA. It is situated 20 km north-west of the state capital, Albany. Thomas Edison, the pioneer of electrical engineering, moved his workshops here. In due course (1892) the General Electric Corporation established itself in Schenectady and today the town is dominated by the industry. Population (1980) 67,972.

Scherzo (Italian, jest, sport), musical term for a movement usually of a light or humorous character. Generally one movement of a work, it may also be an independent work, as the scherzos of Chopin for piano. It was established mainly by Beethoven and Schubert, and developed from the minuet, which it replaced in sonata-form works. The term dates from the 17th century, when light Italian songs, and sometimes instrumental pieces, were called *scherzi musicali*.

Scheveningen, town and resort of the Netherlands, north-west of The Hague with which it is contiguous, on the west coast of South Holland. It has one of the finest beaches on the North Sea. There is an important fishing industry.

Schiaparelli, Giovanni Virginio (1835–1910), Italian astronomer. He was the first to show that certain meteor streams were the products of disintegrated comets. He detected on Mars the so-called *canali*, mistranslated 'canals', now known to be optical effects and not true lines.

Schick Test, see Diphtheria.

Schiedam, town in the province of South Holland, Netherlands, 6 km west of Rotterdam, the chief centre of the famous Holland gin. It also makes liqueurs and candles, and has a shipping trade and iron works. Population (1980) 74,895.

Schiele, Egon (1890–1918), Austrian artist associated with the Sezessionist movement and influenced by Klimt. He is most famous for his exaggerated and angular nudes, expressive of the nervous eroticism of the *fin de siècle* period. He was an influence on German Expressionism.

Egon Schiele. The Artist's Wife, *c.1912.*

Schiller, Johann Christoph Friedrich von (1759–1805), German poet. He began as a student of law, but disliking this subject, he changed to medicine. A chance glimpse of Goethe, however, determined him to become a poet.

After some early attempts at dramatic writing Schiller completed, in 1781, *Die Räuber* (The Robbers) which was first performed in Mannheim in 1782.

In 1783 Dalberg, director of the Mannheim Theatre, made him the 'theatre poet'. In 1785 he went to Leipzig at the invitation of his friend C. G. Körner, a man of letters and father of the German poet Karl Theodor Körner. Here he wrote powerfully dramatic psychological studies, *Der Verbrecher aus verlorener Ehre*, 1786, and *Der Geisterseher*, 1789. During this time he continued studying for further historical plays, constantly trying to perfect a metric form suitable for German drama. There was no example or model so he concentrated on the French classics, but was finally forced to evolve his own pattern. On a short visit to Weimar he met the poets Herder and Wieland, and their advice was of some help to him. In 1790 on Goethe's recommendation, he became professor of history at the University of Jena. Despite this gesture, Goethe was vaguely hostile to Schiller until 1794 when he collaborated in launching the literary magazine *Die Horen* and began their lifelong friendship.

Schiller's studies for *Fiesko, Don Carlos* (in which his blank verse was heard for the first time), and for later tragedies which he had already in mind, including his greatest drama, *Maria Stuart*, 1800, gave him an extensive knowledge of world history, and his marked interest in international relations found expression in the famous first lecture at Jena University, *Was ist und zu welchem Ende studieren wir Universalgeschichte*. His studies convinced him that history could be studied accurately only when related with philosophy. He therefore studied intensively Kant, the most important philosopher of his time.

As a philosopher Schiller did not evolve a new system, but he brought philosophy (especially Kant and the English philosophers Shaftesbury and Ferguson) nearer to the German public. In the later period of his life, at Weimar, his philosophy, certainly influenced by Goethe, became poetry again.

Schipperke, small black tailless dog, native of Belgium, where it was principally used on barges as a guard and vermin killer. Its weight is from 5 to 7 kg; its height is about 30 cm.

Schism (Greek *schisma*, a rent or division) is used both literally and figuratively in the New Testament of religious divisions, especially among Christians, and of those who separate from the main body of the Church. The greatest schism in church history was the division of Greek eastern and Latin western Christendom. The phrase 'Great Schism', however, is usually applied to the division inside western Christendom in the 14th century.

Schist, fine-grained foliated metamorphic rock, crystalline in nature, which easily divides into thin lenticular sheets.

Schistosomiasis, or bilharziasis, probably the second most important parasitic disease of Man. It is caused by flatworms of the genus *Schistosoma*, and is endemic in tropical Africa, the Middle and Far East, Central and South America, and the Caribbean area. Its range is increasing. It affects between 200 and 250 million people.

The worms live as adults in the small veins of the human body. In time their eggs penetrate the vein walls and enter the intestines or the bladder; they cause intestinal or bladder pain, with blood in the faeces or urine, and lead to bodily weakness. The eggs are voided with the motions and hatch in fresh water, releasing an active, swimming larva called a miracidium. This miricidium enters the body of a freshwater snail, and after a complicated cycle emerges from the snail as larvae known as cercariae. These larvae burrow into the skin of people who immerse themselves in the water.

Schizanthus, poor man's orchid, or butterfly flower, a genus of annual plants of the Solanaceae from South America, with daintily coloured flowers often borne in great profusion. A number of species and varieties are cultivated.

Schizophrenia, a mental illness, formerly called dementia praecox, that is the most common form of psychosis. The illness usually appears in adolescence and early adulthood, sometimes in an acute sudden breakdown.

The symptoms include a drying-up of interest in relationships, interests and activities, and an increasing preoccupation with strange and bizarre ideas. Language and speech become strange and disorganised and begin to appear to be nonsensical. Delusions about oneself, the body, sexual identity, and identity as a whole are likely to appear. The person may also suffer from extreme suspiciousness

and delusions of persecution, which may be very severe.
About half the people afflicted with this illness recover spontaneously and can resume a more or less normal life. About one quarter of people with the illness have recurrent attacks, while the remaining 25 per cent deteriorate despite treatment.
Childhood schizophrenia, which is different from and starts later than infantile autism, has a poor prognosis.
Various treatments are offered to these patients including drugs such as tranquillisers; social therapy, which aims at rehabilitating the person to a place in the community; and the various forms of psychotherapy, which are directed towards helping the individual with his emotional conflicts.
It is not fully understood why some people develop this illness. It appears there is a biochemical as well as a hereditary predisposition towards it. It is also apparent that the nature of the child's early relationship with the mother and the family enter into the aetiology of the condition.
Schizostylis, a small genus of South African herbs in family Iridaceae, of which *S. coccinea*, the Kaffir lily or crimson flag, is grown for its showy red flowers.
Schlegel, August Wilhelm von (1767–1845), German orientalist and critic, the brother of Friedrich Schlegel. In 1796 he went to Jena, where he collaborated with his brother in editing the *Athenäum*, and they were soon recognised as the leading spirits of Romanticism.
In 1818 he became professor of literature at Bonn, where he remained until his death, publishing several contributions to the study of Sanskrit and also his *Kritische Schriften*, 1828. His lectures on *Dramatic Art and Literature*, delivered at Vienna in 1808, were published in 1809–11. With his Shakespearean translations, they constitute his finest and most famous achievement.
Schlegel, Karl Wilhelm Friedrich von (1772–1829), German historian and literary critic. In 1809, having joined the Roman Catholic Church, he became court secretary at Vienna, where he edited *Concordia*, and delivered the lectures published subsequently as *Philosophie des Lebens*, 1828, and *Philosophie der Geschichte*, 1829. His *Über die Sprache und Weisheit der Indier*, 1808, formed the foundation of research on Indian philology.
Schlegel, who shared with his brother the critical leadership of literary Romanticism, has been called the originator of the Romantic Movement (as a creative artist he is insignificant). His early writings in the Jena *Athenäum* are the chief exposition of the aims of Romanticism.
Schlesinger, John (1926–), British film director, first won attention for his documentary *Terminus*, 1960. His early feature films, *A Kind of Loving*, 1962; *Billy Liar*, 1963; and *Darling*, 1964, were sharply observant about aspects of British social life. His version of Thomas Hardy's *Far from the Madding Crowd*, 1967 was less well received critically, but his first film in America, *Midnight Cowboy*, 1969, won the Academy Award as the best film of 1969 and Schlesinger won the best director award. Schlesinger's *Sunday Bloody Sunday*, 1971, also won international acclaim. He has also directed theatre and opera, notably *The Tales of Hoffmann*, 1980.
Schleswig (Danish *Slesvig*), seaport city in Schleswig-Holstein, Federal Republic of Germany, at the western end of the Schlei inlet of the Baltic, 50 km north-west of Kiel. It became a bishopric in the 10th century and until 1721 was a ducal residence. It has food preparation industries and is a tourist centre. Population (1970) 32,500.
Schleswig-Holstein, *Land* of North Germany, in the Federal Republic, bounded on the north by Denmark, on the east by the Baltic Sea and the German Democratic Republic, on the south by the *Länder* of Lower Saxony and Hamburg, and on the west by the North Sea and the Heligoland Bight. The northern half is Schleswig and the southern half is Holstein, the line of division lying along the River Eider. The Kiel Canal passes through the *Land*, connecting the Baltic with the Elbe estuary. The region is mainly agricultural. Cattle, sheep, pigs, and poultry are bred, and there is a large fishing industry. The main industries are shipbuilding, engineering, and textile manufacturing. The chief cities are Kiel (the capital), Lübeck, Flensburg, Neumünster, Rendsburg, and also Schleswig. Area 15,710 km²; population (1979) 2,599,000.
Holstein was originally an independent duchy, while the Margravate of Schleswig was annexed by Henry I, King of the Germans, in the 10th century. It was, however, ceded to the Danish king, Canute the Great, by Conrad II in 1032. Holstein also came under Danish rule, though, unlike Schleswig, it formed part of the Holy Roman Empire, and the two duchies remained annexed to the Danish crown until the 19th century.
After two outbreaks of war (1848–52 and 1863–64) Denmark ceded all claims to Schleswig-Holstein to the Emperor of Austria and the King of Prussia. Following the Seven Weeks' War between Austria and Prussia in 1866, Schleswig-Holstein became part of Prussia, and remained thus intact until after the First World War, when the frontier was redrawn more in accord with nationality. That part of northern Schleswig, some 3937 km², which was assigned to Denmark was renamed the South Jutland Provinces.
See DENMARK, *History*; GERMAN HISTORY.
Schlick, Moritz (1882–1936), German philosopher; he studied physics before turning to philosophy. In 1922 he became professor of the philosophy of the inductive sciences in Vienna, a chair previously occupied by Mach. He founded a Mach society, better known as the Vienna Circle, which was the matrix of Logical Positivism. In 1936 he was shot dead by a deranged student. Schlick, like other members of the Vienna Circle, was opposed to metaphysics. He accepted the verification theory of meaning but rejected Carnap's physicalism. He held that the test lay in the private sense experience of the individual.
Schlieffen, Count Alfred von (1833–1913), German field-marshal. Chief of the German general staff, 1891–1905, he greatly developed the German Army manoeuvres. His one dominating idea of encirclement persisted in the German leaders throughout the First and Second World Wars. The so-called Schlieffen Plan was, indeed, implicit in the whole conception of the German *Blitzkrieg*. His famous 'plan', founded on the hypothesis that Germany was surrounded by potential enemies, was to select one enemy for decisive defeat and destruction, and then to turn from the defensive to the offensive against the other enemy.
Schliemann, Heinrich (1822–90), German archaeologist. From his childhood it had been his life's ambition to excavate Homeric Troy, and by the end of 1863 he had amassed a sufficient fortune to fulfil his dreams. In four periods of excavation at Hissarlik he distinguished seven layers or cities, believing the second city from the bottom to be Homeric Troy. Since then Troy II and, more recently, Troy III have been identified with Homer's city. He began to work at Mycenae in 1876, and there excavated the five shaft graves, his most startling discovery; in 1884 he uncovered the ground plan of a Mycenaean palace at Tiryns.
See also AEGEAN CULTURE.
Schlumbergera of the family Cactaceae, formerly classified as *Epiphyllum*. A botanical genus chiefly from Mexico and South America including some popular indoor plants.
Schmidt, Bernhard Voldemar (1879–1935), Estonian optician and astronomer. From 1926 until his death Schmidt was a staff member of Hamburg Observatory, where he developed the radically new Schmidt camera.
Schmidt, Helmut (1918–), West German politician. He was a Socialist member of the Bundestag from 1953 to 1962 and again from 1965, becoming chairman of the parliamentary party in 1967. In 1969 he joined the Cabinet of Willy Brandt as minister of defence, switching in 1972 to the Ministry of Finance. In 1974 he succeeded Brandt as Chancellor and remained in the post until 1982.
Schnabel, Artur (1882–1951), Austrian pianist and composer. He studied at Vienna, where he made his début; he later travelled extensively. He excelled in the interpretation of Beethoven, Schubert and Brahms. In 1925–30 he taught at the State Academy, Berlin. His compositions include two symphonies, a piano concerto and chamber music.
Schnauzer, in structure a member of the terrier breed. It is a thick-set dog, with a broad head and a powerful blunt muzzle. The shoulders are flat and sloping, and the chest is broad and deep. The eyebrows are bushy, the ears small and the nose is black and full. It can be pepper and salt or black, and the height is from 45 to 48 cm at the shoulder. The miniature shnauzer stands from 30 to 33 cm at the shoulder.
Schneider Trophy, international trophy for aviation, presented in 1913 by Jacques Schneider, a French patron of aviation. It was open to seaplanes of all nations. Contests ended in 1931.
See also AERONAUTICS.
Schnitzler, Arthur (1862–1931), Austrian dramatist and novelist. His first plays were unsuccessful, but *Liebelei*, 1895, established his reputation. Schnitzler's romanticism in his depiction of Viennese life is mixed with a

morbid and cynical detachment, as in *Reigen*, 1900 (staged and filmed as *La Ronde*). Works of Schnitzler translated into English include (plays): *The Greek Cockatoo and other plays*, 1913; *Playing with Love*, 1914; *Gallant Cassian*, 1914; *Dr. Graesler*, 1924; *Professor Bernhardi*, 1927; (novels): *The Road to the Open*, 1913; *Casanova's Homecoming*, 1922.

Schockemohle, Alwin (1937–), West German show jumper, member of the gold-medal team at Rome in 1960, riding Ferdl. He achieved a remarkable list of Grand Prix successes with Donald Rex, who was his mount for the Mexico Olympics in 1968, where he won a team bronze medal. At Montreal in 1976 he won the Olympic Individual Event Gold medal on Warwick Rex and shared the team silver. He has been German Champion four times.

Paul Schockemohle (1945–), younger brother of Alwin, was European champion show-jumper in 1981.

Schoenberg, Arnold (1874–1951), Austrian composer. He showed early gifts and was mainly self taught. He was from the first a forward-looking artist, and in the early 20th century his first two string quartets, the *Chamber Symphony*, and other works caused concert-hall riots. He gradually approached, in works such as *Pierrot lunaire*, 12-note music, a form which he originated. From 1926 he taught at the Prussian Academy of Arts in Berlin. In 1933 he went to the USA; he held professorships in New York, Boston and Los Angeles, where he died. His three-act opera *Moses and Aaron* was left unfinished. The early *Gurrelieder* for solo voices, chorus and orchestra, and the symphonic poem *Pelleas and Melisande* are large-scale works. However, the 12-note system made him prefer smaller forms in his later music as a rule. His chamber music includes the early string sextet *Verklärte Nacht* and four string quartets. There are also choral works and many songs, including two sets with orchestra.

Scholasticism, term of wide meaning applied to the general theological and philosophical system of the Middle Ages. The early fathers of the church had left a vast 'occasional' literature of theology, apologetical and exegetical. It was the achievement of Scholasticism to produce an orderly synthesis of this traditional doctrine (scholastic theology) and to correlate it with a separate system of truths based on reason (scholastic philosophy). While the most prominent feature of Scholasticism was its function as a systematiser and rationaliser of religious dogma, its philosophic activity was marked by an almost entire reliance on the *a priori* or deductive method. St Albert the Great and St Thomas Aquinas were also masters of the physical sciences as they were understood in their day; but the spirit of the age was almost entirely absorbed in abstract thought, though there were exceptions, such as Roger Bacon. Hence Scholasticism as a movement developed almost entirely on logical and abstract lines, and the later schoolmen were denounced for spinning out distinctions of a more or less fruitless nature. See also ANSELM, SAINT; DUNS SCOTUS, JOHANNES; ERIGENA, JOHANNES SCOTUS; OCKAM, WILLIAM OF; ROSCELIN.

Schönbrunn, Baroque palace in south-west Vienna, Austria, formerly the Imperial summer residence. It was built in the 18th century during the reign of the Empress Maria Theresa and was modelled on the palace of Versailles, and has a famous park and zoo. A treaty between Austria and Napoleon was signed here on 14 October 1809.

Schools of Music. The earliest schools of music were ecclesiastical institutions for teaching the traditional plainsong of the Church. In the Baroque period the Italian *conservatori* were schools founded to maintain and educate illegitimate children. Music was part of the education and the *conservatori* became virtually music schools. One of the first was the Conservatorio di Santa Maria di Loreto in Naples (founded 1537).

In the modern sense schools of music are institutions where education leading to a career in music is available. Among the most important are the Royal Academy, Royal College and Guildhall School of Music in London, the Juilliard School in New York, the Paris Conservatoire and the Berlin Hochschule für Musik.

Schooner, name given to a fore-and-aft rigged vessel with two or more masts. There are two main varieties, the ordinary fore-and-aft schooner and the topsail schooner, which has a square topsail on the foremast.

Franz Schubert, *composer of over 600 songs.*

Schopenhauer, Arthur (1788–1860), German philosopher. Schopenhauer as a philosopher is a metaphysical thinker. His system belongs to the realm of Idealism though based on Kant's theory of perceptibility; but he is opposed to his predecessors in Idealism, i.e. Fichte, Hegel, and Schelling. It is a philosophy of pessimism, in which every man's life is at the mercy of the will—a blind driving force for which the reason is only a tool. Satisfaction of the will's desires merely causes greater desires to arise which must ultimately fail to be satisfied; and hence arise pain and sorrow. From these there is no escape, unless through the arts, ethics, and religion, all forms of idealism. His main work is *Die Welt als Wille und Vorstellung*, 1819 (The World as Will and Idea).

Schottische, term applied to a German dance step in 3-4 time. In the 19th century, Scott's Waverley novels became extremely popular in Europe and created a vogue for anything Scottish. Overtures and rhapsodies were written in a Scottish idiom. The step is found in many European folk-dances.

Schreiner, Olive Emilie Albertina (1855–1920), South African writer. Her works include *The Story of an African Farm*, 1883, written under the pseudonym of Ralph Iron. She was well known to her contemporaries as a publicist, and showed a remarkable perception of South African problems, in advance of her time. An early champion of women's rights, her writing, as her life, was distinguished by its energy, candour, and crusading vigour.

Schrödinger, Erwin (1887–1961), Austrian physicist, famous for interpreting atomic structure in terms of wave mechanics, for which he shared with P. A. M. Dirac the 1933 Nobel Prize for physics. He left Germany in 1933 and became a fellow of Magdalen College, Oxford, and in 1939 founded the School for Advanced Studies in Dublin, of which he became director and professor.

Schubert, Franz (Peter) (1797–1828), Austrian composer, the son of a schoolmaster. He began to learn the piano and violin at home and had lessons in singing, organ and counterpoint. In 1808 he became a chorister in the imperial chapel, where he also played the violin in the orchestra and sometimes conducted. At 13 he wrote a fantasy for piano duet and in 1811 composed his first song. He wrote chamber music for the family string quartet in which he played viola and in 1813 wrote his first symphony. At 17 he became assistant teacher in his father's school and wrote the song *Gretchen at the Spinning-Wheel* in the same year, and *Erlkönig* in 1815. The next year he left the school, and from then he lived a bohemian life among appreciative friends. They held private concerts ('Schubertiads') at which many of his works were first performed.

Among the many genres to which Schubert contributed, he regarded opera as his chief priority. But his operas are virtually forgotten and he is remembered above all for his songs, which number over 600. He was chiefly responsible for developing the *Lied*, which expressed, recreated and symbolised words by a variety of musical means, involving the piano as well as the vocal line in the expression of the text. Works such as the song-cycle *Die Winterreise* reveal the enigmatic, disturbing qualities of the poems. The same enigmatic, searching character is evident in the last string quartet in G. Schubert is also recognised as a careful, disciplined master of large-scale formal structures, which in spite of their length preserve a sense of unity and proportion. Examples are the string quintet and the 9th Symphony.

Schumacher, Kurt (1895–1952), German socialist politician. He was arrested in 1933, and spent 11 years in concentration camps. In 1945 he reorganised the German Social Democratic Party (SPD), and in 1949 became leader of the Opposition in the West German parliament.

Schuman, Maurice (1911–), French

politician. He began his career as a journalist and became well-known for his broadcasts on behalf of Gen. de Gaulle from London during the Second World War. He was a Social Catholic deputy and junior minister under the Fourth Republic. Pompidou made him minister for foreign affairs from 1969 to 1972.

Schuman, Robert (1886–1963), French politician. He became a prominent member of the centrist party after the Second World War, serving as finance minister (1946–47), and being premier (1947–48). From 1948 to 1953 Schuman was foreign minister and played a principal part in the creation of such organisations as NATO and the Council of Europe. His name is most prominently associated, however, with the European Coal and Steel Community, which owed its original inspiration to him in his 'Schuman Plan' of 1950.

Schuman, William (1910–), US composer. He studied at Columbia University and with Roy Harris, and held several teaching and administrative posts, notably that of president of the Juilliard School, 1945–62. In some respects he may be regarded as Harris's successor as an American symphonist, his works being notable for strong melodies, rhythmic vitality and vigorous block orchestration. He has composed ten symphonies, other orchestral pieces, chamber music and choral works.

Schuman Plan, see EUROPEAN COAL AND STEEL COMMUNITY.

Schumann, Clara (1819–96), German pianist, *née* Clara Wieck, wife of Robert Schumann. One of the most accomplished pianists of her day, she was largely responsible for the world's knowledge of her husband's compositions. She composed a piano concerto, piano music and songs. She taught at the Frankfurt Conservatorium, 1878–92.

Schumann, Elisabeth (1885–1952), German soprano. She joined the Hamburg Opera in 1909 and in 1919 the Vienna Opera, where she remained until 1938. She then settled in the USA and taught at the Curtis Institute, Philadelphia. She excelled in the lighter Mozartian parts, as Sophie in Richard Strauss's *Der Rosenkavalier*, and in songs of Schubert, Schumann, Brahms and Strauss.

Schumann, Robert (1810–56), German composer. He began to study the piano at the age of eight and made rapid progress; he also began to compose. He studied law at Leipzig University and at Heidelberg. By 1830, under the instruction of Friedrich Wieck at Leipzig, he had become an accomplished pianist and had composed songs and piano pieces. In 1831 he studied composition with Heinrich Dorn. In 1833, with others, he founded the *Neue Zeitschrift für Musik*. He married Friedrich Wieck's daughter Clara in 1840. In 1843 he was appointed professor of composition at the new Leipzig Conservatory, but left for Dresden in the following year, and in 1850 he became conductor of the Düsseldorf Orchestra. In 1854, after mental breakdowns, he moved to an asylum near Bonn, where he died.

He was an ardent apostle of romanticism and a champion of other composers, for example Chopin and Brahms. In his own work he was most successful in songs and piano music, where his gift for elliptical expression and his inclination for miniature structures were most fruitfully exploited, particularly in the song-cycle *Dichterliebe*. The larger-scale works, such as the symphonies and the string quartets, are influenced by Beethoven's structural innovations. Thematic cross-references between movements are an important unifying device. Schumann's music is unified also by literary and personal allusions, especially in the piano pieces. In *Carnaval*, two motifs based on the letters of his name and of the birthplace of his friend Ernestine von Fricken are threaded through a variety of pieces. In this work there also appear the carnival figures Pantalon and Columbine, as well as the *Davidsbündler* (Schumann's band of progressives), and Florestan and Eusebius (contrasting facets of his own personality).

With Mendelssohn and Brahms, Schumann forms a triad of composers who took up the new lyrical, subjective manner of the 19th century without abandoning classical forms and techniques.

Schuschnigg, Kurt von (1897–1977), Austrian statesman. In 1934 he became chancellor. Confronted with Hitler's demand for the annexation of Austria, he made a show of resistance, but was compelled, under threats, to sign an agreement to clear the way for Nazism in Austria. Schuschnigg tried to organise a plebiscite against Hitler, but he was forestalled by the sudden irruption of German troops on 12 March 1938. Austria was annexed and Schuschnigg was held as a prisoner throughout the war. He became professor of political science at St Louis University in the USA, in 1948, returning to Austria in 1967.

Schütz, Heinrich (1585–1672), German composer. He began to study law, then studied music at Venice under Giovanni Gabrieli. He later became attached to the electoral chapel at Dresden. In 1633, during the Thirty Years' War, he went to Copenhagen. He remained there and at other courts until 1641, when he returned to Dresden. Schütz was the leading composer of German sacred music of his time. He successfully transferred the vivid madrigal style of the Gabrielis and the newer recitative style of Monteverdi to Protestant sacred music. Yet he made little attempt to combine these with the Lutheran chorale tunes on which his contemporaries based their Italianate compositions. He is thus something of an isolated, though important, figure in the development of Protestant church music.

His works include madrigals; motets; psalms; sacred 'symphonies' and 'concertos', which use concerted vocal and instrumental forces; four settings of the Passion; and a Requiem.

Schwabe, Heinrich Samuel (1789–1875), German astronomer. In 1826 he began observations of the Sun with a small and inexpensive telescope; in 1843 he announced one of the most important discoveries in solar physics, the sunspot cycle, i.e., the 10- or 11-year periodicity in the number and activity of sunspots.

Schwarzenberg, Felix, Prince zu (1800–1852), Austrian statesman. Made head of government in December 1848, Schwarzenberg outmanoeuvred the constitutional opposition, repressed the Hungarian revolt, and inaugurated a decade of centralised absolutism. In foreign policy he set his face against German unification and forced Prussia to accept his leadership at the Convention of Olmütz.

Schwarzkopf, Elisabeth (1915–), German soprano. She studied in Berlin, where she made her operatic début in 1938, and was engaged at the Vienna State Opera from 1942. Subsequently she sang at Covent Garden, La Scala, Milan, and at Salzburg, San Francisco and Chicago. Best known as an interpreter of Mozart and of Richard Strauss, as a recitalist she excels in the songs of Hugo Wolf.

Schwarzschild, Karl (1873–1916), German astronomer. Schwarzschild made outstanding contributions to many branches of astronomy, to celestial mechanics, stellar dynamics, optical theory, the theory of radiative equilibrium, and photographic photometry, in which he developed the fundamental methods and published the first extensive reliable results. While at the Russian front he wrote two papers on the then very new theory of relativity, deriving the 'Schwarzschild radius', giving the minimum size a body can be without becoming a black hole.

Schwarzwald, see BLACK FOREST.

Schweitzer, Albert (1875–1965), French scholar and medical missionary. He was educated at the universities of Strasbourg, Paris, and Berlin, taking doctorates in philosophy, theology, music and, later, in medicine and surgery in order to qualify as a medical missionary in West Africa.

He went out to Lambaréné, in 1913, where he designed and founded a hospital defraying the costs and expenses by lecture tours and from the profits of his books. After the First World War he wrote various works indicative of his scepticism over the progress of civilisation and his feeling that the sacredness and freedom of human personality was being violated. These include *Philosophy of Civilisation*, 1923–25. He was awarded the Nobel Peace Prize in 1952.

Schwerin, town of the German Democratic Republic, capital of the district of Schwerin, and former capital of Mecklenburg and of the Grand Duchy of Mecklenburg-Schwerin. It manufactures machinery and chemicals. Population (1979) 117,400.

Schwitters, Kurt (1887–1948), German artist. His art went through a Cubist phase, then he became a Dadaist working in his native city, Hanover. He left Germany for Norway, then came to England in 1937. His most important works are constructions and collages made from scraps and bric-a-brac of all kinds, an art-form he called 'Merz'; some were so large that they filled a whole building, creating an 'environment'. One of these was made in a barn in Ambleside during the last years of his life and is now in Newcastle-on-Tyne.

Schwyz, capital of the canton of Schwyz, Switzerland, situated to the east of Lucerne. It lies at the foot of a massif 1899 m high. It mainly functions as a transhipment point for summer and winter tourists. Population (1974) 12,400.

Sciatica, neuralgia of the sciatic nerve. The condition may be due to a true neuritis (inflammation) of the sciatic nerve or to pressure on the nerve or its roots from bony or cartilaginous deformities of the lumbar spines, as in arthritis, a displaced spinal disc or from spinal growths. Pelvic growths or inflammatory conditions may also cause sciatica from pressure on the nerve trunk or from its involvement in the disease process. The pain distribution is that of the nerve, and is most marked in the back of the thigh, the calf, and the ankle. In severe cases there is weakness of the leg and muscle wasting, together with diminished or absent knee and ankle reflexes.

Science is the attempt to provide systematic, justifiable explanations of natural phenomena. Science is a continuing process in which explanatory systems (called 'theories') are built up and improved on over time by the work of numerous researchers. Theories that seem adequate at one period of time may be abandoned in favour of other theories at a later time. Science is a continual search for better answers to man's questions about the universe around him.

Three interrelated justifications can be offered for considering scientific statements to be particularly valuable descriptions of our universe: first, science attempts to be general and systematic; second, scientific statements are always capable of being tested; third, great effort is taken to ensure that science is objective.

A major feature of scientific statements is that it is possible to test their validity. If a statement cannot be tested then it is not scientific. The technique for testing is the 'experiment', which may be defined as a test of the validity of a statement (usually called a 'hypothesis') under controlled conditions. An experiment may be thought of as the application of a treatment, process, or procedure to specified materials followed by observation (usually measurement) of the effect—for example, spraying plants with an insecticide and later measuring insect damage to test whether the insecticide works. No experiment can be so tightly controlled that no errors are made and all external disturbing influences eliminated. It is usual to make several repetitions of an experiment and to use statistics to help in understanding the variation in the results produced. An experiment is always more convincing the more it is repeated or the more material is used.

Having settled the size of the experiment, the designer goes on to consider the experimental techniques to be used. The designer's objectives here are: (1) to secure uniformity in the application of treatments to each piece of material or in each repetition of the experiment; (2) to impose control over external influences so that each application of the experimental treatment produces its effect under comparable and desirable conditions; (3) to provide accurate measurements or records of the effects without requiring an observer to make subjective judgments.

Conclusions arrived at from theoretical principles using deductive logic are rarely controversial. The rules of logic are simple and the only area for dispute is normally the definition of terminology. However, few scientists (apart from mathematicians) spend much of their time on purely deductive arguments. The major activity of most scientists is to carry out experiments to test hypotheses. Scientific hypotheses are formulated by induction, by arguing general principles from particular instances. Induction is a fragile form of reasoning and any argument is capable of being disproved by a single counter-example. General acceptance of a scientist's conclusion that an experiment validated or invalidated a particular hypothesis depends primarily on acceptance that the experiment was designed correctly. For this reason the scientist must make available (usually in an article published in a specialist journal) a full description of his experiment. This detailed publication has a second important virtue: it enables others to repeat the experiment for themselves.

'Science', a weekly magazine published by the American Association for the Advancement of Science. It comprises mainly contemporary research papers in the fields of physics, chemistry and biology. It was first published in 1880, and its readership is international.

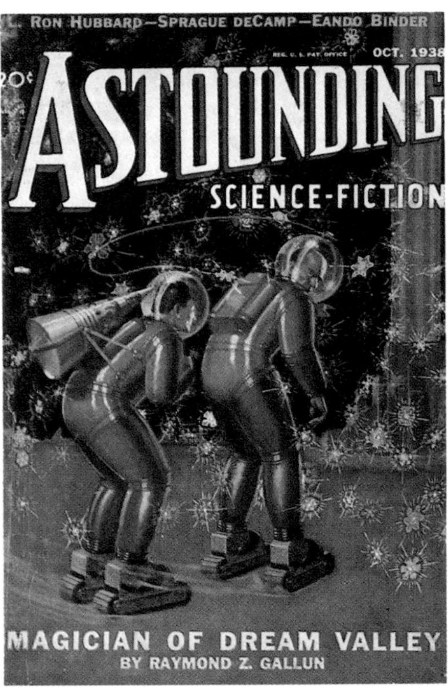

Science Fiction. *A vintage cover illustration from the US magazine, 1938.*

Science Fiction, a literary form which uses scientific possibilities as a basis for fantasy. Jules Verne and H. G. Wells were its first great practitioners, anticipating scientific development by many years in, for example, Verne's *Twenty Thousand Leagues Under the Sea*, 1869, and Wells's *The First Men in the Moon*, 1901. George Orwell in *1984*, 1949, and Aldous Huxley in *Brave New World*, 1932, confined their speculations to life on earth, but advances in space exploration, electronics and computing have inspired more recent writers. In the 1970s and 80s scientific fiction has grown increasingly popular, with a growing stress on a fantastic, other-world element. Leading writers include Isaac Asimov, Ray Bradbury and Brian Aldiss.

Science Museum, South Kensington, London. The collections illustrate the history and development of science, engineering and industry, often by items of prime historical importance. They include the physical and chemical sciences, astronomy, mathematics and computing, time measurement, motive power, textile machinery, machine tools, road and rail transport, aircraft and aero-engines, marine engineering and ship models, weights and measures, communications and domestic appliances.

Originally part of the South Kensington Museum (founded 1857), which became in 1899 the Victoria and Albert Museum, the science and engineering departments were administratively separated in 1909 and became known as the Science Museum.

'Scientific American', US monthly journal established in 1845 publishing review articles explaining scientific topics to the layman but also aimed at university science students.

Scientology, religio-scientific movement founded in the early 1950s in the USA by L. Ron Hubbard (1911–). The organisation moved its headquarters to East Grinstead, Sussex, in 1959. It originated as a theory of psychotherapy, which Hubbard called dianetics and which involved confronting painful experiences in order to exorcise them. Scientology itself requires a member to progress through many rigidly structured phases, shedding his physical and emotional bonds, until he has achieved his full spiritual potential. The counselling methods used by the movement have caused criticism and controversy.

Scilla, a genus of bulbous plants in family Liliaceae, bearing blue, pink or white flowers. *S. verna* is the vernal squill, and *S. autumnalis*, the autumnal squill. Several species, especially *S. bifolia* and *S. siberica*, are much valued in the garden. The squill of pharmacy is the dried scaly bulb of *Urginea maritima*, an Indian species of a related genus. The English bluebell was formerly placed in the genus *Scilla*.

Scilly Isles, island group lying 40 km southwest of Land's End, Cornwall, England. There are about 140 islands in all; many, however, are no more than clusters of rocks and only five (St Mary's, Tresco, St Martin's, St Agnes, and Bryher), are inhabited. The largest of these islands is St Mary's, with a population of 1958. The climate is a great factor in the island's main industry, the growing of spring flowers for market. Agriculture is important and the islands are a popular holiday resort. There is an air service between Penzance airport on the mainland and St Mary's, and a boat service between St Mary's and Penzance.

The islands are crowded with prehistoric features. Some, at least, of the villages belong to the Bronze Age. The total area of the isles is 1635 ha; population (1980) 2,000.

Scimitar (Persian *Shimshīr*), oriental curved sword once used in the East, especially by the Turks and Persians. The blade broadens from the handle, and has one cutting edge, which comes to a point, the back being shorter and thicker.

Scintillation Counter, a device for the detection and counting of charged atomic particles and ionising radiations, e.g, protons, cosmic rays, and gamma rays. Passage of the particle or radiation through certain substances (called scintillators) causes them to emit a brief flash of light which is detected by a photomultiplier. A variety of new phosphors or scintillators have been investigated, the more important ones now in use being sodium iodide activated with thallium, various plastics, and certain organic liquids. The great advantage of scintillation counters over some other counters (e.g. Geiger-Mueller counters) is that they can count at a rate of the order of a million particles per second, and are very useful for counting and measuring the energy of gamma rays, protons, alpha-particles, etc. The brightness of the light flash, and hence the strength of the pulse from the photomultiplier, is a function of the energy of the quantum or charged particle.

Scipio Aemilianus Africanus Numantinus, Publius Cornelius (c.185–123 BC), known as 'The Younger'. Roman general. He was adopted by P. Cornelius Scipio.

He served with great distinction in Spain (151 BC). On the outbreak of the third Punic War (149) he went to Africa, and won yet greater renown. Returning to Rome in 148 he was elected consul. Africa was assigned as his province (147). Carthage fell to his arms in the spring of 146. Consul a second time in 134, he was sent to Spain, and in the following year captured Numantia. On his return home and following the death of Tiberius Sempronius Gracchus, he took the lead in the anti-Gracchan party. His wife Sempronia, sister of the Gracchi, was implicated in his sudden death at the height of the crisis.

Scipio Africanus, Publius Cornelius (234–183 BC), Roman general, known as 'The Elder'. In 211 he was given command of the army in Spain where, in his first campaign (210), he took Carthago Nova, and during the next three years drove the Carthaginians from the peninsula.

Determined to carry the war into Hannibal's own homeland he crossed to Africa in 204. He defeated a Carthaginian army, and Hannibal was recalled from Italy. The second Punic War was brought to a close by Scipio's great victory over Hannibal at Zama, 19 October 202 BC. Carthage had no alternative but submission, and the final treaty was concluded in the following year. Scipio returned to Rome in 201, celebrated his triumph and received the surname Africanus.

Years later (184 BC) he was accused of having accepted bribes from Antiochus III, and he withdrew to his private estate at Liternum.

Scissors, cutting implement consisting of a pair of blades, made out of steel. Each blade is either forged by hand, or machine made, from one bar of steel, the 'bows' or finger holes being formed without welding.

Sclera, or sclerotic coat, the dense outer membrane of the eyeball. It serves as a protective coat, and is composed of fibrous tissue. It forms the 'white of the eye', and is pierced by the optic nerve at the rear. It is continuous with the cornea in front.

Sclerosis, a term used in pathology for the hardening of a tissue. When it occurs in an organ, the condition is called fibrosis. Arteriosclerosis is a common example.
See also ARTERIES, DISEASES OF.

Scofield, Paul (1922–), British actor. He made his first professional appearance in London in 1940 in *Desire Under the Elms.* He was with the Birmingham Repertory, and then went to the Shakespeare Memorial Theatre with Sir Barry Jackson. He played a wide variety of parts including the leading roles in *Timon of Athens* and *The Government Inspector*, 1965–66. Among his other parts were the twin brothers in *Ring Round the Moon*, the drunken priest in *The Power and the Glory*, Pierre in *Venice Preserved* and Sir Thomas More in *A Man for All Seasons.* His films include *A Man for All Seasons*, 1966, and *King Lear*, 1971. In 1971 he appeared in two National Theatre productions, *The Captain of Kopenick* and *The Rules of the Game*, and in 1977 played the title role in *Volpone* and Constantine Madras in *The Madras House* at the new National Theatre, where he also played the title role in *Othello* in 1980.

Scone, New and Old, villages in Tayside Region, Scotland. New Scone is situated on the Perth–Aberdeen road, 3 km north-east of Perth. Population (1981) 4102. Old Scone lies 2·5 km to the west, on the Perth–Braemar road. In its ancient palace (destroyed in the riots of 1559) the kings of Scotland were crowned. The coronation stone was removed to Westminster Abbey by Edward I in 1296.

Score, music written with separate parts on separate staves and with the coincident notes appearing vertically over each other so that the work can be read with comparative ease. Complete orchestral or choral scores are called full scores; arrangements of operas, oratorios, etc., for voices and piano are vocal scores; arrangements for piano only are piano scores; composers' sketches reduced to a few staves, to be elaborated and fully written out later, are known as short scores. The miniature or pocket score is intended for study or reference at home and for concert-goers to follow the music.

Score, see METROLOGY.

Scorel, Jan van (1494–1562), Dutch painter. He was profoundly influenced by Italian art, and was the first painter to bring Italian Renaissance ideals to what is now Holland. His work is characterised by clarity, precision and balance, and he is particularly admired for his incisive portraits. He was highly influential in Holland, Heemskerk and Mor being amongst his many pupils.

Scorpion Fly, common name for members of the insect order Mecoptera. Representative species include those of the genus *Panorpa*.

Among the male *Panorpa* the terminal abdominal segments are shaped in the form of a sting, similar to that of a scorpion, hence the name scorpion fly. The scorpion flies live in damp places close to water, and are regarded as useful insects because they destroy plant lice and other small pests. They are known to feed occasionally on plant and fruit juices.

Scorpions, animals of the order Scorpiones in class Arachnida (spiders and their allies). A few small species occur in temperate regions, but they are most abundant in tropical and subtropical regions, where some species attain a length of almost 25 cm. They feed on the juices of other arachnids and insects, seizing their prey with the powerful claws or palpi. They are nocturnal in habit, hiding during the day beneath stones and under the loose bark of trees. The females are viviparous, the eggs being hatched in the enlarged oviducts. Scorpions are notoriously pugnacious, but their sting, though painful, does not usually kill healthy adult human beings. The stinging organ is situated on the telson, at the hind end of the abdomen. There are about 600 different species of scorpion.

Scorpius 'the Scorpion', the eighth sign of the zodiac and a large bright southern constellation. The heart of the Scorpion, and the brightest star in it, is Antares (Alpha Scorpii), a red first magnitude star which is flanked by Sigma and Tau Scorpii in much the same way that Altair is by its two companions in Aquila. The Milky Way is particularly bright as it passes through Scorpius and the whole area is rich in clusters and nebulosities.

Scorzonera, a genus of perennial plants of the Compositae. The tap-roots of *S. hispanica* and *S. humilis* are used as a winter vegetable.

Scoter, the bird genus *Melanitta* in the family Anatidae of order Anseriformes. *M. nigra*, the common scoter or black duck, breeds in arctic regions and winters off the coasts of the temperate parts of the northern hemisphere. The female is entirely brown, while the male is black. *M. fusca*, the velvet scoter, is black with an orange bill and dark-red feet and has a white patch on the wing. The female is brown with a brownish bill, and has distinctive pale patches on its head.

Scotland, country forming the northern part of the British Isles, lying between 54°38′ and 60°51′30″N, and 1°45′32″ and 6°14′W. On the north and west it is bounded by the Atlantic Ocean and on the east by the North Sea. The boundary with England runs south-west to north-east from the Solway Firth to the mouth of the River Tweed. Almost 1000 islands lie offshore, about 150 of which are inhabited. There are four main groups: Shetland to the far north; Orkney Islands near the north coast; the Outer Hebrides in the far Atlantic west; and a loose group, the Inner Hebrides, off the west coast of the mainland. The area of Scotland is almost 77,171 km² and its maximum north-south length is almost twice its maximum mainland width of 243 km.

In 1975, Scotland was divided into 11 main administrative areas, namely the Highland, Grampian, Tayside, Fife, Lothian, Borders, Central, and Strathclyde Regions; and three islands areas: Shetland, Orkney, and Western Isles. These replaced the former 33 counties. Two great parallel faults have created the broad regional division of Scotland into the Central Lowlands with the Highlands to the north and the Southern Uplands to the south. Another major fault within the highlands creates the loch-filled trough of the Great Glen Fault between Inverness and Fort William. The coasts of the west are deeply indented by fiords (sea-lochs) and fragmented with peninsulas and islands. There are several great drowned inlets or firths on the east side. The Central and Western Highlands contain many high peaks of over 1000 m, culminating in the highest point in Britain, Ben Nevis, 1356 m, near Fort William. The mountains and plateaus of the Highlands are largely covered in heather moorland, but reafforestation is a notable landscape feature in many areas. Sheep-grazing, deer forests (which are not forests but moors), and grouse-shooting moors are the main land uses.

Much of the economic activity and the bulk of the population of Scotland is in the Central Lowlands between the Firths of Clyde and Forth. The grassy slopes of the Southern Uplands provide excellent sheep pasture and this is the principal economic activity of most of the area. Scotland at the time of the 1981 census contained a population of 5,117,146.

Despite their diverse origins, including Celts, Angles, and Normans, the Scots have fused in time into a fairly homogeneous population.

Agriculture is one of the largest and most important industries in Scotland. About two thirds of the total agricultural area is under rough grazing and one third under crops and grass. The most important crop is barley, closely followed by grass for silage and hay, then oats, turnips, and swedes.

Dairying occurs widely, but there is a concentration in south-west Scotland, where the wetter climate encourages the growth of good grass. Ayrshire cattle are one of the most important breeds of dairy cattle. Aberdeen-Angus and Shorthorns are the two most important breeds of beef cattle. Market gardening is concentrated in the Clyde valley and in the areas surrounding the cities of Glasgow, Edinburgh, and Dundee. Soft-fruit production is especially important in the Carse of Gowrie, Strathmore, and the Clyde valley. Sheep farms are mainly concentrated in the Southern Uplands and the Highlands.

The fishing industry falls into three main divisions, concerned respectively with white fish, herring, and shell-fish. The main fishing ports which dominate the industry are Aberdeen, Granton, Leith, Lossiemouth and Wick, with Fraserburgh, Peterhead, Lerwick, Stornoway, Ullapool, Mallaig, Tarbert, and Campbeltown.

Scotland's reputation as an industrial country formerly rested on shipbuilding and heavy engineering, but employment has declined in these sectors as well as in marine engineering, agriculture, coal and railways.

The electronics industry has expanded remarkably in recent years, especially in Fife, the Lothians, and Strathclyde. Manufacture of clocks, watches, cash registers, earth-moving equipment, precision instruments, and in the last few years equipment and instruments for the oil industry in the North Sea have helped to diversify the industrial structure. Old-established industries such as the textile industries of the Borders have retained their vitality.

The 120 distilleries in the Highland and Grampian Regions produce the whisky for which Scotland is internationally famous. Petrochemical industries are very important near Grangemouth. The official languages are English and Gaelic.

History. At the beginning of the 6th century the Scots, or Dalriads, from Ireland settled in that part of Scotland now known as Argyll. Scotland can at this time be described in the following divisions: in the north and east, the Picts; south of the Forth, the English in Lothian; in Argyll, the Scots; and in the south-west the Welsh in Strathclyde. Of these the Welsh and the Scots were Christian. In the 9th century the invasions of the Vikings so weakened the Picts that they were conquered with ease by Kenneth MacAlpine, King of the Scots of Dalriada. From this time the country began to be called Scotland.

Scotland. *Loch Torridon typifies the rugged beauty of Wester Ross.*

The Scottish kings admitted the vassalage for such English possessions as they held, whilst the English kings receiving that homage held that it was as suzerains of Scotland that they received it. The reign of Malcolm III (Malcolm Canmore) is of great importance in Scottish history. His marriage with Margaret, sister of Edgar Atheling, did much to bring Scotland into the general European stream of culture and ideas. David I was responsible for the feudalisation of the greater part of the country. David had been educated in England under the influence of Normans, and introduced Norman systems of land tenure, and Norman municipalities. In 1173 William the Lion attempted to seize Northumberland. He was defeated and captured at Alnwick, and signed later the Treaty of Falaise, by which he became the vassal of Henry II. However, in 1189 Richard I of England sold back the rights. William was succeeded in 1214 by his son, Alexander II, and the next two reigns were regarded as the golden age of Scottish history. Peace was maintained, and on the whole the country was prosperous. In 1249 Alexander III succeeded. In 1286 he was killed in a riding accident. His son and daughter had both died before him; his only heir was the Maid of Norway, his granddaughter, aged seven, and for the next few years Scotland was threatened with civil war between the followers of Robert Bruce and John de Baliol. The great ambition of Edward I, King of England, however, was to make a united Great Britain; he therefore exploited the situation to this end, appointing John Baliol King. Baliol was seen as a puppet and opposition under the leadership of William Wallace appeared in 1297. In that year, Wallace defeated the English at Stirling Bridge but was beaten at Falkirk in 1298.

By 1303 the English were able to overrun Scotland, but Edward I died in 1307 and under Robert Bruce the English army was routed by the Scots at Bannockburn in 1314. In 1328, the independence of Scotland was recognised by the Treaty of Northampton.

The policy of a Scottish alliance with France dates from the time of William the Lion. It had been prominent during the reign of Edward I, and during all the successive wars of England with France or Scotland it plays an important part. The next 200 years of Scottish history is the record of disaster and disorder. The curses of Scotland were its nobility, the frequent minorities and the inability of the central authority to quell disorder. The greatest catastrophe occurred in 1513 when an invading Scots army under James IV was beaten at Flodden in England.

In 1542 James V, in response to Henry VIII's anti-catholic actions, attempted to invade England, but was overwhelmed in the disaster of the rout of Solway. James left the field a dying man. Just before his death the news of the birth of his daughter, the future Mary Queen of Scots was announced. Mary was proclaimed queen, with her mother, Mary of Guise, a French princess, as regent.

Since the time of Edward I uniting England and Scotland had always been England's ambition. Henry VIII advocated the marriage of his son, Edward, to Mary Queen of Scots. After the death of Henry VIII the Protector, Somerset, attempted to carry out the same policy by the same means, but the young Queen was dispatched to France and there married to the French Dauphin, who died in 1560. In the meantime a great reform party had grown up which at first desired nothing more than the purifying of the Church (which, in Scotland, was notoriously corrupt). Scotland was by 1560 avowedly Presbyterian. The return of Mary from France brought with it no change from the Presbyterian settlement.

In 1567, Mary abdicated in favour of her son, James VI, by Darnley, in whose murder she was implicated. Mary lost support from the protestant nobility and was imprisoned in Loch Leven castle from which she escaped, fleeing to England after the battle of Langside.

Mary remained in England until her execution in 1587. James VI's policy toward the kirk was the introduction of an episcopacy, dependent on the Crown. James succeeded to the throne of England in 1603.

Charles I pressed the episcopacy question even farther than James. In 1633 Charles held a parliament in Edinburgh, and in 1637 attempted to introduce Archbishop Laud's liturgy. At St Giles's Church the famous riot broke out known as the 'Jenny Geddes riot'. The Church and the nobility petitioned against the liturgy, the Tables were formed, and finally the Covenant signed (February 1638). When Parliament was at war with the King it demanded help from the Scots. The Solemn League and Covenant was signed, which the Scots assumed would result in the establishment of Presbyterianism in England. Charles I surrendered to the Scots at Newark, and was by them finally handed over to the English. Disillusionment with the English parliamentarians subsequently set in, and finally, in 1648, the Scots marched into England to deliver the King. They were, however, defeated by Cromwell at Preston (1648). The execution of the King was regarded with horror by nearly all the Scots, and Charles II was recognised as king. Charles was approached and asked to sign the Covenants. He did so, but after his restoration episcopacy was restored to Scotland. This Church policy aroused the Covenanters to armed resistance, which was easily overcome, but which could quite easily have been prevented. The Catholic James II tried to exercise his power of dispensing with the laws in Scotland as he had in England, but finally came the revolution of 1688, when the throne was offered by the Scottish Convention to the Protestant William of Orange and his wife, Mary, daughter of James II. In 1690 the kirk was re-established on its Presbyterian basis.

The question of union between Scotland and England was debated until it seemed as though a rupture would take place between the two countries. In March 1707 the Act of Union, however, passed both Parliaments, and received the royal assent. It declared that Scotland was to have 45 members and 16 elected peers at Westminster, the kirk and laws of Scotland were safeguarded, and the trade privileges declared to be the same for both countries. See further under UNITED KINGDOM, *History*.

Art. As in Ireland, the earliest art form in Scotland is the Celtic style of ornament, pre-Christian in origin, but which attained a rich development with the introduction of Christianity. A special form of early Scottish art is found in Pictish carvings with vigorous representations of animals, a fine example being the Burghead Bull (British Museum).

Gothic art took no strong hold, and climate and conditions as in Ireland did not encourage wallpainting, but portraiture developed in the late 16th century and onwards.

In the 18th century Scottish and English painting became closely related, and English portraiture finds a handsome complement in the charming work of Allan Ramsay (1715–84), son of the poet, and in the masterly vigour of Sir Henry Raeburn. Another outstanding portrait-painter and etcher is Andrew Geddes (1783–1844); Alexander Nasmyth and his son Patrick are noted in the development of landscape, as also is the Rev. John Thompson (1778–1840). David Scott (1806–49) shows the influence of Romanticism. Sir David Wilkie, influenced by Dutch genre painting, gave an impetus to the sentimental story picture. William McTaggart (1835–1910) is celebrated for having arrived independently at a kind of Impressionism. The 'Glasgow School', formed about 1880, was a group influenced by French art and also by Whistler. Their leader was W. Y. Macgregor (1855–1923), and the group included Harrington Mann, Sir James Guthrie, Sir D. Y. Cameron, as well as the architect, designer and painter, pioneer of Art Nouveau, Charles Rennie Mackintosh. Scottish painters have since shown a decided leaning towards French art. In the 1940s 'modernism' had its interpreters in Robert Colquhoun and Robert MacBryde, but the 'Scottish school' is perpetuated in the work of William Gillies (1898–), Anne Redpath, Elizabeth Blackadder and Joan Eardley (1921–63).

Language. The language formerly spoken in Scotland derives from the Northern dialect of Old and Middle English which had already established itself in Lothian in the 7th century and which was considerably altered by the infusion of Norse elements from the Viking invasions. After the Normans arrived in Scotland in the 11th century, the language, now called *Inglis* from its English origin, spread rapidly all over the Lowlands at the expense of Gaelic which retreated to the sparsely populated Highlands, and gradually replaced it as the national language. It was later known as *Scottis*.

All the great literature of Scotland is written in this language from Barbour onwards during the Middle Scots period. With the Reformation in 1560, and the introduction of the English Bible in default of a Scots one, the Union of the Crowns and then of the Parliaments, English became the official speech of Scotland in the 18th century, but Scots staged a revival as a literary vehicle under Burns and Scott and their imitators.

Scottish Gaelic (*Gàidhlig*, or ancient *Goídelg*), with Irish and Manx, belongs to the Goidelic branch of the Celtic Languages. It was introduced into Scotland towards the end of the 5th century by immigrants from north-east Ireland. Gaelic is now spoken mainly in the Hebrides and on the northern and western seaboard of Scotland.

A considerable degree of dialect variation exists. Unlike the Irish dialects, those in Scotland form a continuous chain, thus making communication between speakers of different dialects easier. The dialects of the Hebrides are the most conservative in many respects and correspond most closely to the written norm.

Literature. Vernacular Literature. The earliest literature in the Scottish vernacular survives in fragments of minstrelsy dating from the 13th century. With John Barbour and his chronicle poem in romance form, *The Brus* (Bruce), 1375, Scottish poetry first takes shape. The 15th century was prolific in Scottish writers, beginning with King James I, whose poem *The King's Quair*, his own love story, frankly modelled on Chaucer, is of real poetic feeling. Most important of all, however, is William Dunbar, who has been described as 'the chief of the ancient Scottish poets' and whose works include *The Thrissil and the Rois* (The Thistle and the Rose), 1503, written to commemorate the marriage of James IV with Margaret of England. In the 17th century vernacular poetry was at a low ebb, but oral tradition was strong among the people and to it Scotland owes its splendid repertoire of ballad and folksong on which Allan Ramsay based his revival of the native literature in the 18th century. With Robert Burns the revived vernacular reached its greatest height. The modern Scottish renaissance movement began during the First World War. The outstanding genius of the revival is Hugh MacDiarmid (pseudonym of C. M. Grieve). He established an international reputation with such works as *Sangschaw*, *A Drunk Man Looks at the Thistle*, and *To Circumjack Cencrastus*.

Literature in English. When James VI of Scotland became King of England in 1603, the court poets who migrated with him all wrote in English. But not until the 18th century did Scottish writing, and especially philosophy, reach first-rate importance with David Hume, the philosopher and historian, and Adam Smith, the economist. Outside philosophy and science, 18th-century Scottish literature includes James Boswell as well as the two great authors Tobias Smollett, the novelist, and James Thomson, the poet. Sir Walter Scott, Scotland's greatest writer of imaginative prose, produced historical and romantic novels which were the finest of their kind ever written.

The importance of serious periodical literature throughout the 19th century is associated with Scottish writers. In 1802, for example, the first number of the *Edinburgh Review* appeared; founded by Sydney Smith and Francis Jeffrey, it became the outlet for other Scots men of letters. The Victorian literature of Scotland is represented by Mrs Oliphant, George MacDonald, and two poets of the 'Spasmodic School', Alexander Smith and R. W. Buchanan, but the great writer of the century was Thomas Carlyle. Other 19th century writers include Andrew Lang and J. M. Barrie. Scottish poetry after the First World War underwent important developments towards a more virile and distinguished national character and includes the work of Lewis Spence and Rachel Annand Taylor (1876–1960). Edwin Muir was a novelist, poet, and critic, Naomi Mitchison a novelist and poet. The latest of the writers in the old historical style were Neil Munro and John Buchan, Lord Tweedsmuir. More recent novelists include Eric Linklater (*Poet's Pub*, *Juan in America*), A. J. Cronin (*Hatter's Castle*, *The Citadel*) and Muriel Spark.

Gaelic Literature. The amount of literature written in the classical literary language which survives in Scotland is small as compared with Ireland.

The Gaelic poetic tradition was maintained by hereditary bardic families as in Ireland. Modern Gaelic poetry, in the vernacular and in stressed metres, is known chiefly from about 1600 onwards. The 18th century produced great changes in its themes and range and chiefly responsible for this was

Alexander MacDonald (c.1700–c.1770). The 19th century witnessed a decline in style and perhaps even in range, and the influence of Lowland song-measures, with their regular stress, was increasingly felt. The finest Gaelic poet of the 20th century is Somhairle Maclean (*Dàin do Eimhir*, 1943–). Apart from the short story, Gaelic prose is mainly represented by the folk-tale, and here the collection initiated by J. F. Campbell dominates the field.
See also CELTIC LANGUAGES; IRELAND, *Literature; WALES, Literature*.

Scotland, Church of, was founded by John Knox and Andrew Melville, basing themselves on the teachings of Calvin, and formed into a presbyterian hierarchy of courts as distinct from the episcopal hierarchy of men. On 20 December 1560 the first Assembly of the Church of Scotland was held, and the Confession of Faith, drawn up by John Knox, was ratified. In 1592 an Act guaranteeing the liberties of the Church of Scotland and sanctioning its presbyterian government was passed. Under the Stuarts, presbytery was discountenanced by law in favour of episcopacy, and not until 1690, in the reign of William III, was the Act of 1592, the charter of the Church of Scotland, fully restored. The government of the Church of Scotland is by kirk sessions, presbyteries, synods, and the General Assembly, the supreme court. The kirk session consists of the parish minister and ruling elders, elected by the congregation. The presbyteries consist of all parish ministers in a specified district with one ruling elder from every congregation. The provincial synods, of which there are 12, comprise three or more presbyteries. The presbyteries elect the two commissioners who sit in the General Assembly. By an Act of Union of 3 October 1929, the Church of Scotland was united with the former United Free Church of Scotland to form the United Church of Scotland.

Scotland Yard, off Whitehall in London, derived its name from a palace given by King Edgar (c.943–975) to King Kenneth of Scotland as his London quarters. It was the original headquarters of the Metropolitan Police, and the name was preserved when the headquarters moved to New Scotland Yard on the Victoria Embankment in 1890, and in 1966 to the Broadway, Westminster.

Scots Law. Scotland, at the time of the Union with England, retained its old legal system and its legal administration which, based as they were on Roman principles, were in marked contrast to those of England. Since the Union the criminal law of Scotland has been almost identical with that of England, although there are significant procedural differences. Although there are many points of contact between English and Scots law in the branches of the civil law, there are also many points wherein they differ fundamentally. In both countries the common law developed, through judicial decisions, on roughly similar lines; while the main principles of the law of evidence are identical and there is a tendency for Scots judges to make increasing use of English case-law. But in the field of substantive law Scots law and English law show a much more striking resemblance in modern than in old branches, for example in both countries the law of patents, trade marks, bills of exchange, and negotiable instruments is nearly identical. But the systems diverge radically in land laws and conveyancing, for the good reason that feudal holding is the foundation of the Scots law of heritage. Yet the Scots law of marriage, parent and child, prescription and succession, and the Scots procedure and arbitration, is quite dissimilar in spite of some analogies.

Scots Pine, see PINE.

Scott, C(harles) P(restwich) (1846–1932), British journalist. He joined the *Manchester Guardian* in 1871 and was its editor for 57 years (1872–1929), a record in journalism. He became proprietor of the *Guardian* in 1905, and governing director on his retirement from the editorship. His great work was to make a provincial newspaper a world force. Scott regarded his paper as a spiritual entity, not a commodity, and was determined to give accurate news and to be fair in controversy. He introduced and encouraged many brilliant writers in journalism, and by his precept formed what has been called the *Guardian* school of writers.
See also JOURNALISM; NEWSPAPERS.

Scott, Duncan Campbell (1862–1947), Canadian short-story writer and poet. Lifelong service in the department of Indian Affairs gave him a wide knowledge of Indian customs and traditions, and the landscape of the northern wilderness, which profoundly influenced his poetry and stories. Although his writings also include historical studies and plays, he is known chiefly as Canada's poet laureate. Such pieces as 'The Forsaken' and 'Half-breed Girl' are among the most famous in Canadian poetry.

Scott, Sir George Gilbert (1811–78), English architect, the most prominent of the mid-Victorian era. He practised with W. B. Moffat 1834–45, their commissions being mainly workhouses. In 1840 he won the competition for the Martyr's Memorial, Oxford, and also began his first church restorations. In 1844 he won the important competition for the church of St Nicholas at Hamburg. His first cathedral restoration, at Ely, came in 1847; it was followed by many others, in all some 40 cathedrals and 'minsters'. The enormous list of his new buildings includes St Giles, Camberwell (1844); the Albert Memorial (1863–72); Glasgow University; St Pancras Station and Hotel (designed 1865); the Great Hall of Bombay University; the India Office and Foreign Office, Whitehall (competition); and the chapels of Exeter College, Oxford (1856–1859), and St John's College, Cambridge (1863–69).

Scott, Sir Peter Markham (1909–), British naturalist writer, broadcaster and painter, son of Captain R. F. Scott. He is founder and director of the Wildfowl Trust, and chairman of the World Wildlife Fund. His publications include *A Thousand Geese*, 1953; *Wildfowl of the British Isles*, 1957. *The Eye of the Wind*, 1961, is an autobiography.

Scott, Robert Falcon (1868–1912), British explorer. He entered the navy in 1882, and became a commander in 1900. He led the national Antarctic expedition of 1901–04, which was the first to penetrate a significant distance into the interior of the continent. Appointed captain in 1904, he wrote an account of his first expedition, *The Voyage of the 'Discovery'*, in 1905. In 1910 he sailed again for the Antarctic in the *Terra Nova*, and reached the South Pole after Amundsen on 17 January 1912, with Captain Oates, Dr Wilson, Lieutenant Bowers, and P. O. Evans. The return journey was marked by ill-luck, illness, and bad weather. In November 1912, eight months after they had all died, a search-party discovered the tent and bodies of three of the explorers. All papers and instruments were recovered. Both expeditions published a series of scientific results.

Scott, Samuel (c.1702–72), British painter of marine and topographical views. He painted a number of sea fights (National Maritime Museum, Greenwich) and, with George Lambert, paintings of the East India company settlements, but is mainly known for views of the Thames at London, from 1735, comparable with those of Canaletto.

Scott, Sir Walter (1771–1832), Scottish novelist, historian, and poet. He became a lawyer and in 1799 published his first book, a metrical translation of Bürger's *Lenore*. When he issued the *Minstrelsy of the Scottish Border*, consisting of old ballads he had collected in the border country, popular interest in him began to grow rapidly. In 1805 he published a long narrative poem, *The Lay of the Last Minstrel*. In 1808 he followed this with a similar work, *Marmion*, succeeded in 1809 by *The Lady of the Lake*. These metrical stories had an instant and wide success, and made their author wealthy. With this money he supplied half the capital for starting the publishing house of Ballantyne, and in 1812 went to live at Abbotsford, near Melrose.

Scott's first novel was *Waverley*, issued anonymously in 1814. It was followed by *Guy Mannering*, 1815; *The Antiquary* and *Old Mortality*, 1816; *The Heart of Midlothian*, 1818; *Ivanhoe*, 1829; and *The Monastery* and *The Abbott*, 1820. For years the secret of the authorship was kept, since Scott considered novel-writing below the dignity of an eminent lawyer and country gentleman. In 1821 he published *Kenilworth*, and between 1821 and 1828 wrote many novels.

Misfortune then overtook him. In 1826 the firm of Ballantyne was made bankrupt. Scott felt himself under a moral obligation to satisfy the firm's creditors, and at the age of 55 set

Robert Falcon Scott, *Antarctic explorer.*

himself the task of paying off the enormous debt. Writing with his accustomed speed, he produced *The Fair Maid of Perth*, 1828, and *Anne of Geierstein*, 1829. He also compiled a life of Napoleon, 1827, and first series of his *Tales of a Grandfather*. The second series followed in 1828; but the author's powers were failing. Scott's health was giving way, and he went to the Continent to recuperate. He returned home to die, and was buried at Dryburgh Abbey.

Before his time Scottish history was virtually unknown to the public, but among the results of the Waverley novels was the founding of numerous learned societies, whose members found and published documents illustrating Scotland's past. Scott was the creator of the historical novel.

Scott, William (1913–), British painter. He is predominantly an abstract painter although he has also painted still-lifes and the nude, references to which can often be detected in his non-figurative painting.

Scottish National Party, a nationalist party in favour of Scotland being separated from and independent of the United Kingdom in order to safeguard the cultural and economic life of the country. The party was founded in 1928 and has fought parliamentary elections since 1929. By 1976 the party had a membership of some 80,000; no figures have been released since.

Scottish Terrier, formerly called the Aberdeen terrier, a keen sporting dog. The colour is steel grey, brindle, black or wheaten. The height is about 25–28 cm and the weight 8–10 kg.

Scotus, see DUNS SCOTUS; SCHOLASTICISM.

Scouts (originally Boy Scouts), organisation for boys, founded in 1908 by Lt-General Lord Baden-Powell as a world-wide movement which aims to encourage the physical, spiritual, and mental development of young people so that they may take a constructive place in society. They learn to be self-reliant, ready to help others, and work together. Great stress is laid on practical skills.

Total active UK membership was over 600,000 in 1980; in the Commonwealth nearly 2 million, whilst the aggregate World Membership is over 14 million in more than a hundred countries.

Scrabble, crossword board game with letter tiles which was invented by Alfred M. Butts in 1931 and was later developed, refined and trademarked as Scrabble Crossword Game by James Brunot in 1948. Letters have scoring values which can become doubled or trebled when occupying strategic positions on the board. Players have seven letters each and play them on to the board to build words, drawing replacements from the bag to keep their hand at seven. Two 'blanks' are available as 'jokers'. A 50 bonus is added for a complete word of seven letters put down from a hand. A word must adjoin another already on the table. Words can be extended and thus rescored.

Scranton, fourth largest city of Pennsylvania, USA, and county seat of Lackawanna county, on the Lackawanna river, 217 km from New York. It is the centre of a declining anthracite coalfield with mines beneath the city. It manufactures silk, cotton and woollen goods, and all kinds of machinery. Population (1980) 87,378.

Sir Walter Scott. Portrait by Landseer, 1824.

Scraper Board Drawing, see SGRAFFITO.

Scree, an accumulation of loose angular rock fragments formed on hill slopes and cliffs. The fragments are generally formed mechanically, either as a result of the breaking-up of the rock surfaces by the stresses due to frequent temperature changes or by the wedging action of frost in cracks in the rocks. The continued action of these processes may result in the piling up of thick scree slopes. They may be active if the material has not reached its natural angle of rest, but when this has occurred the scree is stabilised by vegetation growth.

Screen. In nearly all medieval and some Jacobean churches, two types of screen were erected: (1) the rood-screen, separating nave from chancel, and so called because it filled the space between the floor and the underside of the 'rood-beam', on which stood the 'rood', a crucifix; (2) a parclose screen, separating a chapel from the body of the church.

In the great hall of a medieval house, as in the halls of the Inns of Court in London and of the older colleges at Oxford and Cambridge, a panelled screen with doors between the hall itself and a lobby leading to the kitchens was called 'the screens'.

Screen Process Printing, or silk screen printing is a form of stencilling based upon an ancient art form.

In the modern technique, a stencil is attached to the underside of a screen made of fabric mesh and stretched over a frame. Ink is drawn across the mesh by a squeegee and forced on to paper, or other material, placed under the screen.

Stencils from simple designs are cut by hand from paper or special films, but for more complicated line or half-tone illustrations photographic stencils are prepared. The screens can be of silk or nylon, while metal meshes are used when long runs are anticipated.

The process is used for wallpaper and textiles, packaging, wrappers, labels, transfers, and for printing on glass, ceramics, and three-dimensional objects. It is also used for manufacturing such items as printed circuits in the electronics industry.

Screws, Bolts, and Nuts. Screws and bolts are fastening devices consisting of a straight or tapered cylinder round which a helical groove (called a thread) has been cut. Screws and bolts are used primarily to hold two pieces of material together and usually have a head which presses against the surface of one piece.

Scriabin, Alexander Nikolaevich (1872–1915), Russian pianist and composer. He was taught composition by Arensky at the Moscow Conservatoire. He toured western Europe as a pianist. Among his works are three symphonies, three tone-poems (including *The Poem of Ecstasy*), and many piano works.

His music at first showed the influence of Chopin, Liszt and Wagner, but his egotism and obsession for an esoteric mysticism turned him towards a highly individual creative path; carefully calculated harmonies held for him certain symbolic properties. He also attempted to expound his theories of key-colour relationships by including a part for 'colour-keyboard' in the symphonic poem *Prometheus*.

Scribe (Hebrew *sopher*), biblical word indicating a secretary or writer. Among the post-exilic Jews it was the peculiar office of the scribe to study the book of the Law, to read and explain it to the congregation, to transcribe it and multiply copies of it among the nation at large. The word scribe therefore signified one learned in the scriptures (Ezra vii. 6, 11). Scribes were given the title rabbi (master). The New Testament speaks of the Scribes and the Pharisees as a single group, because by then the Scribes were nothing more than the 'theologians' and casuists of the Pharisaic sect.

Scrip (abbreviation for 'subscription'), provisional document entitling the holder to a share or shares in a joint-stock company; exchangeable for a formal certificate when the necessary payments or subscriptions have been completed. Hence, loosely, share certificates in general, or certificate of stock subscribed to a bank or other company, or of a subscription to a loan. A scrip issue is an issue of new shares to shareholders in proportion to their existing holdings made, as distinct from a rights issue, without charge.

Scriptures, see BIBLE.

Scrofula, a form of tuberculosis, see KING'S EVIL.

Scrolls, Dead Sea, see DEAD SEA SCROLLS.

Scrolls of the Law, rolls of parchment containing the Torah or Five Books of Moses and used by the Jews in their synagogue services, of which the 'Reading of the Torah' is the central feature. Every synagogue must contain at least one set. The scrolls are kept in an ark (in the direction of Jerusalem), before which burns a perpetual light. The preparation of the scroll is a task requiring much care, erudition, and labour. It must be written by hand, in black, indelible ink, by accredited, professional scribes, on sheets of parchment especially prepared for the purpose, made from skins of animals permitted for food. The scrolls (sometimes 30–36 cm wide) are fastened at each end to wooden rods, so that they can be rolled from one end to the other. The scrolls contain only the consonantal text; it is unpointed and unpunctuated; no decorations or illuminations are permitted.

Scrotum, the pouch of skin behind the male penis that contains the testes and epididymis.

Sculpture is the art of representing form in three dimensions. The word itself implies carving, but it is generally accepted as covering (1) images cut out of hard materials such as marble, stone, wood, or ivory; (2) images modelled in soft materials, such as clay, plaster, or wax; and (3) assemblages of a predominantly non-utilitarian nature.

The earliest sculptures belong to the later or Upper Paleolithic phase of prehistory, and have been discovered mainly in south-west Europe. They are simplified representations in ivory, clay, or stone of animals and human figures, presumed to possess ritualistic significance. With the Sumerian civilisation of Mesopotamia and the Egyptian Old Kingdom in the middle of the 3rd millennium BC, sculpture begins to serve more ordered societies. Free-standing and relief sculptures, in which naturalism is constantly subjected to rigid representational formulae, express the hierarchic character of these societies. The Greek sculptors of the fifth century, inspired by the human body in motion, broke away from these rigid formulae. The most celebrated of these sculptors were Myron, Polyclitus of Argos, Praxiteles, and Phidias. Much Roman sculpture reflects Greek influence, but the Romans excelled in their own realistic portrait sculpture.

Elsewhere traditions of sculpture thrived notably in India, after the Greek invasion (Gandhara School) and during the Gupta period, AD 320–647; in China, during the Tang and Ming dynasties; and in Japan, during the 6th century AD. Other traditions exist in Africa and among the American Indians.

In Europe after the Roman dominance, sculpture was limited in scope, devoted largely to the ornamental detail of the capitals of columns, small ivory carvings, etc. The 11th century saw a revival of more ambitious undertakings, usually in an architectural context, as is demonstrated, for example, by the bronze doors of Hildesheim Cathedral. Between the 12th and 13th centuries the austere and vehement Romanesque style gave way to the more humane expression of religious feeling of the Gothic style. This evolution can best be seen in the sculpture of the French cathedrals and in particular Chartres. Both Germany and England produced architectural sculpture of a high order. In Italy, a long succession of sculptors, encouraged by understanding patrons, established a great tradition. It begins c.1260, with the Pisan sculptor Niccolo Pisano. Later Ghiberti, Donatello, Luca Della Robbia and Verrocchio gave figure sculpture a new dignity and power. The sculpture of the Italian Renaissance is comparable with that of ancient Greece, its greatest representative being Michelangelo. The achievement of the High Renaissance sculptors was followed by the sophistication and formal inventiveness in the work of the Mannerists Cellini and Giovanni da Bologna. The Baroque sculptors of the 17th century led by Bernini, were no less inventive. Their overt emotionalism and virtuoso handling were adopted throughout Europe.

Every country felt the effect of the Renaissance. In France it is notable in the work of Jean Goujon. In Germany the Vischer family of Nuremberg was notable, while in Spain Berruguete, a pupil of Michelangelo, introduced the Renaissance style.

***Sculpture.** Rodin's* The Kiss.

The Neoclassical movement, which grew up gradually during the 18th century, led to increasing respect for the example of the ancient Greeks. Imitation of the past, and a return to formal clarity prevailed. In the 20th century the insistence on formal relations resulted in a progressive departure from the ideal of realistic perfection in the human figure. It aroused in sculptors an interest in primitive or non-naturalistic sculpture of the past: Negro, archaic Greek, Aztec, Etruscan, early medieval. Works by Amadeo Modigliani, Gaudier-Brzeska, Jacob Epstein (as carver), Leon Underwood, and Henry Moore variously show this influence. It has tended to make modern sculpture an abstract art.

Pioneers of abstract or near-abstract sculpture were Alexander Archipenko, an adherent of Cubism; Constantin Brancusi, and Ossip Zadkine (1890–1967). Followers of the non-representational school who have developed experimental sculpture even further are Henri Laurens, Jacques Lipchitz, Jean Arp, A. Giacometti, Naum Gabo, Antoine Pevsner, Duchamp-Villon, Barbara Hepworth, Arthur Calder, and Reg Butler (1913–). They have frequently employed glass, metal, string, and wire combined with other sculptural materials in their constructions. Some think of sculpture not as a massive form but as a space to which outlines and sectional lines direct the eye. Later, welding techniques were added to the repertoire of the sculptor, pioneered by Gonzalez and Picasso.

SEE ALSO CHINA, *Art*; GIBBONS, GRINLING; GREEK ART, SCULPTURE; ITALIAN ART; JAPAN, *Art*; KINETIC ART; STONE CARVING.

Scunthorpe, town of Humberside, England, 40 km west of Grimsby. Its industry is dominated by the manufacture of iron and steel. The first ironworks (using local lean Frodingham ores) were opened in 1864. Steel making began in 1890. Population (1981) 66,353.

Scurvy, a dietary deficiency disease due to the absence of the anti-scorbutic vitamin C which is found in fruit juices, leaf vegetables, rhubarb, radishes, rose-hips and milk.

See also NUTRITION; NUTRITIONAL DEFICIENCY DISEASES; VITAMINS.

Scutage, or escuage (Latin *scutum*, shield), in feudal times a money tax frequently levied by the Crown as a substitute for the personal service of a knight or vassal. It was first exacted in England in 1159 and became much more valuable to the Crown than personal service as feudal armies declined. It was levied for the last time in 1327.

Scutari, see ÜSKÜDAR.

Scylla and Charybdis, in Greek legend, two sea-monsters who inhabited the northern end of the Straits of Messina. Scylla was a many-headed monster; Charybdis swallowed the sea and threw it up again three times a day. The legend represents the hazards to seamen of rocks and whirlpools in those waters.

Scyphozoa, see COELENTERATA; JELLYFISH.

Scythians, a nomadic people, originating from the Eurasian steppe-lands and comprising many tribes as far apart as China and Thrace, all of which display the cultural traits considered typical of Scythians. The earliest known phases of Scythian culture are represented by timber-graves in the Don basin, datable to c.900 BC or later. Around 700 BC there was a major migration movement into South Russia, thence across the Caucasus into Western Asia. Around 600 BC Scythians were located around Lake Urmia and in Armenia, as well as the Pontic steppes, where, because of their control of the Black Sea grain trade, they came into contact with the Greek colonies in the area. Eventually this western branch of the Scythians was absorbed by the Sarmatians. In Central Asia they were gradually displaced by the Achaemenidae, and further east by China.

Sea Anemone, polyps in class Anthozoa of phylum Coelenterata that do not form corals, and have tentacles that give them a resemblance to the flower anemones. Found attached to rocks and the shells of hermit crabs, they feed on small animals and can be seen at low tide on rocky shores, open in rock pools or when uncovered, closed up as a protection against dehydration. They can be spectacularly beautiful when submerged and opened, and show a great variety of colours.

Sea-Angling, see ANGLING.

Sea Bass, see BASS.

Sea-bream, fishes in the family Sparidae, order Perciformes. The fish of this family are often called porgies. They have an arched back, single dorsal fin, and a small mouth with good teeth. They are shallow-water, carnivorous fish of tropical and temperate waters, usually about 30 cm long. Many are valuable for sport or food.

See also BREAM.

Sea Buckthorn, or sallow thorn, *Hippophaë rhamnoides*, in family Elaeagnaceae, a deciduous shrub which grows on sand dunes in Europe and Asia. It has spiny branches, silvery leaves and small green flowers, followed by orange-yellow berries.

Sea Butterflies, or pteropods, a group of molluscs (class Gastropoda, subclass Opisthobranchia) comprising about 100 species, which are organised for swimming freely in the ocean, having a pair of fins developed from the sides of the mouth and neck, enabling the animal to progress by flapping. Once placed in a single taxonomic group, order Pteropoda, pteropods are now classified in two orders, Thecosomata and Gymnosomata. In some parts of the ocean the latter exist in immense numbers, colouring the water over vast tracts, and in high latitudes they, especially *Clione borealis*, constitute the food of the baleen or whalebone whales.

Sea Cow, Northern, *Hydrodamalis stelleri*, a sirenian once abundant in the North Pacific, exterminated in 1768 by sailors on account of its value as food. It was about 10 m long, with a small head and hard, naked, bark-like epidermis. The forelimbs were short and truncated, and the tail ended in a half-moon-shaped blade. The substitution of horny plates for teeth corresponds to the gum pads of the manatee. The males had large tusks. It fed on seaweeds.

Sea Cucumbers, animals in class Holothuroidea of phylum Echinodermata, characterised by an elongated appearance. The skeleton is reduced to microscopic ossicles. Sea cucumbers lie on their sides on the sea bottom. The mouth is surrounded by tentacles representing modified buccal tube feet. These vary greatly in form and are highly retractile. Some species feed on detritus adhering to the tentacles, which are inserted in the mouth in turn. Others are sediment feeders. Sea cucumbers show an unusual defence mechanism in which sticky threads are expelled from the anus entwining the attacker, so that the sea cucumber may crawl away. Most are dioecious (the animal is either male or female) and some species show brooding behaviour.

Sea Eagle, see ERNE.

Sea-elephant, see ELEPHANT SEAL.

Sea-Floor Spreading is the concept that the ocean floors are produced by a continuous process of volcanic activity along mid-ocean ridges; this new crust then slowly spreads away from the ridge axes. The principal evidence for this hypothesis is the existence of magnetic strips on the ocean floor.

All the major ocean basins contain a mid-ocean ridge – a submarine mountain range containing a central rift valley – which is volcanically and seismically active. The central rift is continually being intruded by basaltic material which has its source in the underlying mantle of the Earth. As this basalt solidifies it is magnetised in the direction of the Earth's magnetic field. Because at intervals the Earth's magnetic field reverses, reversely magnetised strips of rock are formed on either side of the rift. All the oceans show the same pattern of reversals. The only variable feature is the rate of spreading, which may vary in different oceans from less than 1 cm per year to 8 cm per year on each side of the mid-ocean ridge. It has been estimated that if spreading continued at this rate unchanged, the whole of the present Pacific could have been produced in 100 million years. The oldest parts of the ocean basins are in fact thought to be of Mesozoic age, that is between 225 and 65 million years old.

Sea Hare, a marine mollusc (class Gastropoda, subclass Opisthobranchia) of the genus *Aplysia*. *A. punctata* is widely distributed around Europe and occurs offshore amongst kelps. It comes on shore during the summer to spawn. The shell is greatly reduced and internal and the animal relies for protection on its cryptic coloration (matching the background) which it acquires from the algae upon which it feeds. When disturbed, it releases a purple fluid which acts as a smoke screen and allows it to escape either by crawling or by swimming by means of wing-like projections developed from the mantle. Similar species are found in coastal waters of most temperate and tropical areas.

Sea-holly, see ERYNGIUM.

Sea Horse, see HIPPOCAMPUS.

Sea Islands, group of islands along the coast of Georgia and South Carolina, USA, forming an offshore chain. Sea island cotton used to be the chief crop, but it was almost wiped out by the boll weevil. Rice and market garden crops are grown on the low marshy surface.

Sea-kale, *Crambe*, a genus of perennial herbs in the Cruciferae. *C. maritima* is the sea-kale of northern Europe cultivated for its delicious shoots. The vegetable is produced by forcing small sections of the roots to produce blanched shoots, which are eaten cooked. *C. cordifolia* and *C. orientalis* are grown for their handsome foliage, and small flowers.

Sea Lavender, see LIMONIUM.

Sea Laws, compendious name given by legal historians and other commentators of the 17th century to various medieval collections of maritime laws or customs.

The English law merchant (*lex mercatoria*), for example, adopted the judgments of Oléron, which were founded on the laws of the commune of that name, and these laws were incorporated in the *Black Book of the Admiralty*, which dates from the earlier part of the 14th century. The laws of Oléron were also adopted by the ports of northern France, Bruges, and other North Sea ports. The equitableness and general repute of these laws were so high that merchants repaired to London from all parts to obtain judgments in the English Court of Admiralty.

See also ADMIRALTY COURT.

Sea Lemon, a genus of molluscs (class Gastropoda, subclass Opisthobranchia, order Nudibranchia), typical of the family Dorididae. The species are usually white, brown or yellow, whence they are called sea lemons, but they often take the colour of their surroundings. *Archidoris pseudoargus* is the best known member of the genus, and feeds on the bread-crumb sponge, *Halichondria panicea*.

Sea Lettuce, any of several species of green algae. These seaweeds have wide lettuce-like fronds, translucent and varying in shade from light to dark green according to age. Sea lettuce is common on most rocky shores, especially where there is fresh or polluted water. The most common species is *Ulva lactuca*.

Sea Lily, see FEATHER STAR.

Sea-lion, a pinniped belonging to certain genera of the family Otariidae, which also includes the fur seals. Steller's sea-lion, *Eumetopias jubatus*, is the largest species.

See also FUR SEALS.

Sea-otter, *Enhydra lutris*, a carnivorous mammal of the family Mustelidae in order Carnivora. It resembles the common otter, but has smaller forefeet and its hind feet are fin-like. Its diet is shell-fish and sea-urchins, and its habitat the shores of the northern Pacific Ocean, being chiefly found near the Aleutian islands and Alaska. It is unusual in that it uses a tool, a rock, which it rests on its stomach while floating on the sea surface, and on which it breaks mollusc shells.

Sea-pike, *Centropomus undecimalis*, an American species of the family Serranidae, order Perciformes, closely related to the perches, and considered edible. In America any species of *Centropomus* is called robalo or snook. The name sea-pike is also given to several other unrelated fish, such as garpike and barracuda.

Sea Porcupine, or porcupine-fish, any fish in the family Diodontidae of the order Tetraodontiformes. They are characterised by the movable spines on their skin, and are able to puff themselves up in order to erect these spines. All the species occur in tropical seas. They have powerful beak-like tooth-plates and feed on corals and molluscs.

Sea-slater, common name for a group of intertidal arthropods of order Isopoda in class Crustacea. They have flat, segmented bodies, and resemble wood-lice. There are several species, of which *Ligia oceanica* is the most common.

Sea-snakes, snakes of family Hydrophiidae, are venomous reptiles, all of which are aquatic, and all but one species marine. Their

***Sea Anemones** are found in a variety of seashore habitats:* Tealia *lives among weed,* Anemonia *embedded in rock crevices, whereas* Metridium *is found in shallow water and rock pools.*

tails are compressed laterally, and form powerful swimming organs. The eyes are extremely small, have round pupils, and the snakes are practically blind when out of water. The poison secreted by the animals is very virulent, and is used by them to kill the fish on which they feed.

Sea-squirt, see TUNICATA.

Sea Swallow, see TERN.

Sea Urchins, animals of phylum Echinodermata, class Echinoidea. They have a spherical, heart-shaped or disc-shaped skeleton called a test, covered with spines.

Special seizing organs, pedicellariae, have grasping pieces on the ends which are moved by tiny muscles. Pedicellariae are used to clean the animal, to hold on to a rock, and for defence. Some sea urchins carry poison pedicellariae, which have poison sacs opening at the tip of the largest tooth. The venom paralyses small animals and may scare off larger ones.

Sea urchins eat all types of food, from organic detritus to small living animals, though each species has a preferred diet.

Sea urchins walk on their spines or on delicate hollow tube feet. These are extensions of the water vascular system, a fluid-filled system of canals and tubes running throughout the body. This system is unique to echinoderms. Sea urchins have separate male and female animals, and reproduce by fertilisation of eggs shed into the water.

Sea Waves and Swell, the generation of sea waves by the wind. When a light wind blows above still water it quickly generates ripples or capillary waves. They are short-lived if the wind ceases to blow. If a stronger wind blows for a longer time then these small waves grow into longer gravity waves. The exact mechanism by which the wind imparts energy to the wave is not yet fully understood, but it must, in general terms, be caused by the pressure differences induced between the forward and backward wave faces. The height of the generated waves increases with the velocity of the wind, the length of time for which it blows, and the distance of water over which it blows, known as the fetch.

The growth of waves is limited when the energy input from the wind is balanced by energy dissipation due to white-capping, breaking, and the production of mean currents. In the mid-ocean, storm waves of between 10 and 15 m are reasonably common. Higher waves over 20 m are often recorded, and in 1933 the USS *Ramapo* observed a wave 34 m high.

Long storm waves, once formed, are almost indestructible in the open sea. They travel thousands of kilometres and are destroyed only by running into shallow water, where they form breakers and surf on a beach.

Seagull, see GULL.

Seal, members of two families of marine Carnivora, Otariidae, which include the fur seals (as well as the sea-lions), and Phocidae, the true or earless seals They are sometimes placed with walruses in a separate order, Pinnipedia. The true seal has an elongate and somewhat fish-like body covered with a short, thick fur, and terminating in a short conical tail. The limbs are flippers adapted for swimming and are almost useless on land, the animal moving itself laboriously by wriggling. They are most abundant in Arctic and Antarctic regions, and though they resort to the shore for the breeding season, they spend most of the year in the sea, often travelling immense distances. They are hunted for their oil and skin.

The common seal (*Phoca vitulina*), a species of northern oceans, is yellowish-grey in colour and almost 2 m long. It is an animal of high intelligence, and is readily tamed and taught to perform tricks. Other seal species include the Greenland seal (*Pagophilus groenlandicus*), abundant off the coast of Newfoundland, *Pusa siberica* of Lake Baikal and *P. caspica* of the Caspian Sea. Peculiar to the southern hemisphere are Weddell's seal (*Leptonychotes weddelli*); the leopard seal (*Hydrurga leptonyx*); the crab-eating seal (*Lobodon carcinophagus*); and Ross's seal (*Ommatophoca rossi*).

See also FUR SEAL; SEA-LION.

Seal. The law, in the United Kingdom, recognises three royal seals, the Great Seal, the Privy Seal, and the Signet, or Privy Signet Seal. Since the union with Scotland (1707) there has been but one Great Seal of the UK; but a seal must be kept in Scotland and used to validate all grants which before 1707 used to pass under the Great Seal.

Seal, Lord Privy, one of the great officers of state in Britain. He was appointed originally to keep the privy seal of the king, so that no independent grants might be made without the knowledge of the king's council. His duties were abolished in 1884, but the office, now purely honorary, still exists and is generally held by a member of the Cabinet.

Sealing Wax, a mixture of resins and colouring matter used for taking the impressions of seals on documents and also for fastening packages.

See also WAX.

Sealyham Terrier, a dog that originated in Wales. It first came into prominence in 1910. The breed has short strong legs, and a very flexible body with a deep chest. The coat is white. Though intended as a sporting terrier, it is now popular as a house dog.

Séance, see SPIRITUALISM.

Search Coil, a coil of a few turns of wire, usually connected to a galvanometer, used in measurement of magnetic flux.

Search Warrant. In English law, the most usual occasion for the issue by magistrates of a search warrant is for the recovery of stolen goods. When a constable enters a house by virtue of a search warrant for stolen goods, he can seize not only the goods which he reasonably believes to be covered by the warrant but also any other goods which he honestly believes on reasonable grounds to have been stolen and to be material evidence on a charge of stealing or handling.

Searchlight, apparatus for projecting an intense beam of light for military and other purposes. It comprises an intense light source, in modern systems a xenon high-pressure arc-lamp of several kilowatts power or a similar lamp, at the focus of a paraboloidal mirror. The mirror may be a metre or so in diameter.

Searle, Humphrey (1915–82), British composer. He studied at the Royal College of Music and in Vienna, where he came under the influence of Webern, who introduced him to 12-note music. Various other influences went to form his style, which remains distinctive even when subjected to the 12-note system. His compositions include three large-scale works for speakers and orchestra: *The Riverrun* (James Joyce), *Gold Customs* and *The Shadow of Cain* (Edith Sitwell), both with chorus; two suites; five symphonies and other works for orchestra; two piano concertos; three operas, including *Hamlet* (1968); three ballets; chamber and piano music and songs. In 1965 he was appointed professor of composition at the Royal College of Music.

Seashore, the region covered part of the time by the sea, and partly exposed to the air; it is often called the littoral zone. It is of great biological interest, since it provides a home for species not found elsewhere. There are three basic kinds of seashore: rocky shores, where the action of the waves is generally at its most violent; shingle beaches; and sand and mud. Because of the constant grinding action of the stones of a shingle beach, no life is possible there.

Plants and animals living on the seashore must be capable of resistance to exposure and dessication for several hours of the day, except in landlocked seas such as the Mediterranean where there are virtually no tides. Seaweeds are found on rocks, to which they cling by holdfasts. On rocky shores the fauna is generally of the kind which can anchor itself to the rock such as limpets or molluscs. In sand and mud the predominant fauna is of the burrowing kind, which seeks shelter below ground when the tide is out.

Seashore, or foreshore, in English law is that land which 'lies within the ordinary flux and reflux of the tides'. The soil which is subject to high spring tides is rather to be considered as part of the adjoining *terra firma* and belonging to the same title. The ownership of the seashore or foreshore is in the Crown, unless the subject can prove it to be part of a manor or to have been granted to his predecessors in title either expressly by the Crown or implied before the time of legal memory. Private ownership in the foreshore is subject to the right of adjoining landowners freely to pass to and from the sea to their land, and to beach their boats.

Seasickness, nausea produced by the motion of a boat on the sea. Many explanations have been put forward as to its cause, the most generally held being that it is due to the unusual stimulation of the balancing mechanisms in the ears, and the discrepancy between the motion expected, seen, and felt. The pitching motion of the ship and the unexpected movements of the horizon are the primary factors. Overeating before sailing, tiredness, or emotional upset may make one more sensitive to the symptoms. Lying down on one's back at full length amidships will often ease the attack. Certain drugs, notably antihistamines, may be useful in preventing or easing the condition. Sedative drugs such as prochlorperazine are also helpful.

Seasoning, see CONDIMENT.

Seasons, the annual cycle in the changing periods of light and dark and consequently in the weather and growth patterns that result from the Earth's motion round the Sun. The seasons may be divided in various ways according to the geographical location, e.g.

wet and dry, hot and cold, but the most usual division is the astronomical one into spring, summer, autumn, and winter. The differences between summer and winter are due partly to the greater altitude of the Sun at noon in summer and partly to the greater number of hours it is above the horizon, both of which effects are more marked at higher latitudes than near the equator.

SEATO, see SOUTH-EAST ASIA COLLECTIVE DEFENCE TREATY.

Seattle, city in the state of Washington, USA, situated on the eastern shore of Puget Sound. It grew up as a port of entry to the goldfields of British Columbia and, more particularly, of the Klondike, and serves today as the chief supply port for Alaska. Shipbuilding and ship repair are industries common to all the ports of the Sound; so, too, are forest-based industries. The other main employer in the city is the aircraft industry. Population (1980) 491,900.

Seaweed, the larger marine algae. They are grouped by their colour into three divisions: Chlorophyta, green algae; Phaeophyta, brown algae; and Rhodophyta, red algae.

Although some seaweeds look superficially like higher plants, they do not have a stem, leaves, roots or flowers. Those that attach to rocks have a holdfast by which they grip, and the plant may have a stalk and fronds, but these do not have the organised interior structure that is found in higher plants.

Some seaweeds are flat, with broad lettuce-like leaves, others branch profusely, and many have air-bladders to keep them afloat. In general, green seaweeds are found highest on the shore, brown seaweeds grow near and below the low tide line, and the reds grow where they are rarely or never exposed.

Seaweeds contain many minerals, iodine, and vitamins. Many are a valuable source of food, others are used for animals, fertilisers, and for several chemical and pharmaceutical purposes. Agar, a jelly extracted from species of the red algae *Gelidium*, *Gracilaria* and others, is used for growing cultures in bacteriology. Other colloidal extracts, especially the alginates, are widely used in industry.

Sebastian, Saint (d.288), early Christian martyr. According to his Acts, which are not trustworthy, he was a Roman army officer who stood high in the esteem of the Emperor Diocletian. Having proclaimed himself a Christian, he was tied to a tree, used as a target by some archers, and finally dispatched with clubs.

Sebastiano del Piombo (1485–1547), Italian painter. The *Pieta* in Viterbo and the *Flagellation* in San Pietro, Montorio, were painted from drawings which Michelangelo provided for Sebastiano. From 1531 Sebastiano was keeper of the papal leaden seal, hence his name. His works include *Lazarus* (National Gallery, London)—painted in competition with Raphael's *Transfiguration* —*The Visitation* (Louvre), *Clement VII* (Naples Museum) and *Andrea Doria* (Doria Gallery, Rome).

Sebastopol, see SEVASTOPOL.

Seborrhoeic Dermatitis, see CRADLE CAP.

Second Empire, period in French history from December 1852, the overthrow of the Second Republic by Louis Napoleon (Napoleon III), to 4 September 1871, the proclamation of the Third Republic after the Emperor's surrender at Sedan. The period was one of industrial confidence and business prosperity, with the construction of railways, the extension of industry, and the development of Paris. Another characteristic of the Second Empire was its active and enterprising foreign policies.

Second Republic, period of French history from 24 February 1848, the abdication of Louis Philippe, to December 1852, when the Second Empire was established. The revolution of 1848 was romantic, utopian, and socialist. But when government was organised it was seen to be repressive.

Second Sight, form of premonition or divination which was at one time largely credited in the Highlands of Scotland, and is still believed to some extent today. The warning may take the form of a visual or auditory hallucination, a dream, or merely a feeling of impending calamity, while the events thus foretold are of varying importance, ranging from the death of a near relative to the most trivial circumstance. Second sight is regarded as a natural gift, which cannot be acquired.

Second World War, see WORLD WAR, SECOND.

Secret Societies. In Britain societies the names of whose members and officers are kept secret from the community at large, and societies whose members are required to take an oath binding them to engage in any mutinous or seditious purpose, or to disturb the peace, are by acts passed in 1799, 1817, and 1846 unlawful. Great Britain has not been a frequent seat of agitation in the form of secret societies, though Ireland was long notorious for them.

One influential secret society was that of the Camorra in southern Italy and Sicily, a society which continued to flourish up to the First World War. This society in its objects and effect on Italian social life was closely analogous to the Mafia, which has survived in Sicily and southern Italy and has offshoots in the USA.

In the USA the Ku Klux Klan remains a terrorising influence in some of the southern states, being anti-Negro, anti-Catholic, and anti-Semitic. Secret societies in Africa, such as the Title societies of the Ibo, the Poro society of the Mende, and many Leopard societies in West Africa, have ritual and governmental functions.

Secret Societies, Chinese, played an extremely important part in the life of the Chinese before 1949, and were probably originally formed as benevolent associations. The earliest claim to date from the 3rd century Han dynasty.

The laws of a society superseded the ordinary laws of the land, and all secret organisations were banned in China by imperial edict in 1662. Their most vigorous period however was undoubtedly the Ch'ing dynasty (1644–1912), when they partly constituted an underground revolutionary movement aimed at the overthrow of the Manchu government. They played a significant part in the Boxer Rebellion of 1900, and in the 1911 revolution.

Secretary Bird, *Sagittarius serpentarius*, an aberrant bird of prey placed in a separate family in the order Falconiformes. It is native to southern Africa. Its name comes from the apparent resemblance of the erectile crest of feathers, tipped with black, to a pen behind a clerk's ear. It is about 1·2 m high, and exceptionally long-legged. The upper surface is grey, shaded on the wing coverts with reddish-brown; the throat is white, and the long tail-feathers black and white. It is much valued, and officially protected on account of the readiness with which it kills poisonous snakes and other noxious animals with its powerful feet.

Secretary of State is the designation of the heads of most major government departments in the United Kingdom. Historically they are the constitutional channel of communication between Crown and subjects.

In the USA the secretary of state is a member of the Cabinet and third in line of succession after the president and vice-president. The secretary of state is responsible to the president for the conduct of US foreign policy and for relations with individual states. He is head of the State Department, is in formal charge of diplomatic negotiations, and has charge of all state papers; he publishes the statutes and resolutions of Congress and proclamations of the president, and is the custodian of the Great Seal. The first secretary of state was Thomas Jefferson, who was appointed in 1789.

Secretion, a substance formed by specialised cells or glands from material furnished by the fluid substances of the organism, and discharged by those cells to serve some special function. The salivary glands secrete saliva; the mammary glands secrete milk; the lachrymal glands secrete tears. The largest gland in the body is the liver, which secretes bile. The act of secretion is often influenced by distant nervous phenomena; thus, the sight of food stimulates the salivary glands to activity.

Secularism, materialistic and rationalistic movement started in England by George Holyoake in 1846. He defined secularism as a 'system of ethical principles', and said that 'it aims to substitute the piety of usefulness for the usefulness of piety'. Though Holyoake himself had in 1842 been imprisoned for blasphemy, the movement was not professedly anti-theistic or even anti-Christian; but its tendency was agnostic, and speedily became atheistic.

Securities, documents representing the holder's ownership of some property, not in his possession. Securities may take two forms. *Bonds* represent an obligation to pay the holder specific amounts at set times, and may be issued by governments or private corporations. *Stocks* represent ownership of an equity interest in the operations of a corporation.

Security Council, see UNITED NATIONS.

Sedan, French town in the *département* of Ardennes, on the River Meuse. Here Napoleon III surrendered to the Germans on 1 September 1871. It has textile and metallurgical manufactures and breweries. Population (1975) 25,430.

Sedan Chair, mode of conveyance especially fashionable in the 18th century and first used in the French city of Sedan. It was carried on poles, had a hinged door in front, windows at the sides, and a top which lifted so as to enable the occupant to stand up if he chose, and to allow the wearing of high head-dresses.

Sedatives, drugs used to calm an anxious patient without sending him to sleep, although it probably makes him sleepy. Many drugs used as hypnotics or tranquillisers act as sedatives when given in small doses and the actions of sedative drugs are very similar to those of the hypnotics. The benzodiazepine derivatives (diazepam, nitrazepam, chlordiazepoxide) are the safest drugs to use since in excess they are less dangerous than, for example, the barbiturates and they are less likely to produce dependence.
See also DRUG DEPENDENDENCE.
Seddon, Richard John (1845–1906), British-born New Zealand statesman. He arrived in New Zealand in 1866 after working in the Australian goldfields. As a miners' spokesman he entered Parliament in 1879, becoming premier in 1893, retaining this office till his death. His major achievements were the introduction of old age pensions, votes for women, and the nationalisation of the coalmines.
Sedge, see CAREX.
Sedgemoor, marshy tract of land in Somerset, England, to the east of Bridgwater and south of the Polden Hills. It was here that the Royalist forces defeated the Duke of Monmouth in 1685.
Sedgwick, Adam (1785–1873), British geologist. His most important work was on the Cambrian series in the Lake District and North Wales, where he elucidated the geological structure of the rocks and established a three-fold division of the Cambrian.
Sedilia, in church architecture, a row of seats, usually three in number, on the south side of the chancel, for the officiating clergy.
Sedimentary Environments, the conditions under which sedimentary rocks are formed; each rock type is attributable to a particular environment. Sedimentary environments are divided into non-marine and marine as follows:
Non-marine: (1) piedmont deposits, alluvial fans of coarse unsorted material brought down from young mountain ranges by river torrents into a desert environment. (2) Desert deposits, which include wind-blown sand and deposits of mud and chemical evaporites in enclosed desert basins or playas. (3) Lake deposits, which are usually rather varied sands, gravels, silts, muds, carbonates and organic deposits. (4) Glacial deposits, such as boulder clay, tillite and outwash gravels.
Marine: (1) Littoral deposits, which are deposited in the zone between extreme high and low tide. They include beach conglomerates, tidal flats of fine laminated silts and sand interdigitating with salt-marsh sediments, estuarine deposits and marine deltas. (2) Neritic deposits, between the low tide mark and the edge of the continental shelf. They are largely mud, sand and gravel. (3) Bathyl and abyssal deposits on the continental-shelf slope and in the abyssal zone. The areas close to the continental margins are covered by grey terrigenous muds. With the exception of turbidite flows, no coarse-grained material reaches these areas. In the abyssal zone the most common sediment is red clay, formed largely of meteoric, volcanic and wind-blown dust. The ocean floor contains various deep-sea oozes, the most common being globigerina ooze, which is composed of the shells of formanifera. Other oozes found consist of pterapods and radiolaria as well as diatoms.
Sedimentary Rocks are rocks composed of material deposited by water or air. They are classified primarily on the type of material forming the rock.
(1) *Clastic rocks* are composed of fragments of pre-existing rock or minerals, bound together by a cementing material, often quartz or calcite, which formed after the grains had been deposited. Clastic rocks form the vast majority of sedimentary rocks.
(2) *Organic rocks* are composed almost entirely of the remains of once living plants or animals. Such rocks are few in type; coal is common; diatomite, bone beds, tar sands, and oil shale are other organic sediments of restricted occurrence. Some limestones (reefs, etc.) should be considered as organic sediments.
(3) *Chemical rocks* are formed by the precipitation of chemical compounds and their deposition onto the sea bed, or by the evaporation of water in a land-locked basin causing the deposition of dissolved solids onto the drying bed of the basin. The most common rocks formed by this process are the limestones, rock salt and gypsum or anhydrite.
(4) *Pyroclastic rocks* are rocks formed from volcanic rock fragments. Strictly speaking these rocks are formed by sedimentary processes but are usually classified with the igneous rocks.
Sedimentary rocks are identifiable *in situ* and often in hand specimen by the presence of 'sedimentary structures', features caused by the manner of deposition of the clastic grains. By study of these structures with regard to orientation and distribution a sedimentologist can build up a picture of the environment in which the sediment was formed. Such features are: (1) bedding planes; (2) cross bedding; and (3) graded bedding.
Sedition is, in Britain, a common law offence, falling short of treason, which consists of acts done, words spoken and published, or writings capable of being a libel published with an intention e.g. to bring into hatred or contempt the Crown or the government and constitution of the UK, or to raise discontent or disaffection among the Crown's subjects. Prosecutions for sedition were frequent in the 18th and 19th centuries, but are almost unheard of today.
Sedum, stonecrop, a genus of annual or perennial succulent herbs or sub-shrubs in the family Crassulaceae, with star-like flowers. They are succulent and many species are cultivated.
Seed, the reproductive body of a flowering plant, the fertilised and matured ovule. Separation of the seed from the fruit leaves a scar, the hilum, at one end of which is a small hole or slit, the micropyle, by which air and moisture can enter. The embryo is usually made up of a plumule, the future stem, bearing one or more cotyledons or seed leaves at the base, and a radicle or first root. Seeds of angiosperms are enclosed in a fruit case. Those of monocotyledons have one seed leaf, those of dicotyledons have two seed leaves. Endosperm may or may not be present in either type. Seeds of gymnosperms (e.g. conifers) are naked and not enclosed in a fruit case, and have several cotyledons.
Seferis, Giorgios, or Giorgios Stylianou Seferiades (1900–71), Greek writer and diplomat. He spent the war years in Africa with the Greek government in exile, and his last appointment was as ambassador to Great Britain (1957–62). In 1963 he was awarded the Nobel Prize for literature.
The poems in the collection *Turning Point*, 1931, heralded a new spirit and style in Greek letters, which came to maturity with *Mythistorima*, 1935, in which the poet's intense and tragic feeling for Greece mixes with his personal search for universal truth.
Seghers, Hercules (1589–1638), Dutch painter and etcher. He was a pioneer of Dutch landscape painting, being one of the first painters to break away from the Flemish Mannerist tradition and paint flat panoramas. He was a great influence on Rembrandt, who admired him and owned some of his works, and on Philips Koninck. Only about fifteen paintings by Seghers are known, and his works have been confused with Rembrandt's. His etchings are also very rare, and are as original and mysterious as his paintings; he coloured them by hand, often using a different colour for each impression.
Segovia, Andrés (1894–), Spanish guitarist. He has performed throughout the world and established the guitar as a serious instrument by his virtuosity, artistry and his arrangements of the works of composers such as Bach and Handel.
Segovia, capital of the province of Segovia, Spain, standing on a high rock between the Eresma and the Clamores. The rivers join together below a fine *alcázar* (citadel). A Roman aqueduct dating from the reign of Trajan is still in use, bringing water to the city from a distance of 19 km. Wool and pottery are produced. Population (1971) 41,480.
Segre, Emilio (1905–), Italian-US physicist. In 1936 he was appointed director of the physics laboratory at the University of Palermo and there he identified a quantity of the previously unknown element technetium. The Fascist government deprived him of his post while he was visiting the USA in 1938 and he stayed there, working on the atom bomb and becoming a US citizen in 1944. At the University of California he collaborated in synthesising the unstable element astatine. He then sought to prove the existence of the antiproton. With O. Chamberlain he formed antiprotons from the impact of high-energy protons on copper in 1955, sharing with Chamberlain the 1959 Nobel Prize for physics.
Sei Whale, *Balaenoptera borealis*, a baleen whale of the rorqual or finback family Balaenopteridae that grows up to 20 metres in length. It is found from the north polar to the south polar seas, living in large groups and feeding on plankton. Mating takes place in summer in warm water far from the pack ice and a single young is born the following summer. The sei whale is related to the fin, minke and Bryde's whales.
Seif Dune, a compound longitudinal dune which forms when a strong wind operates from more than one direction. Seif dunes sometimes develop from barchans by the action of two prevailing winds.
Seine, river of France; the third longest, but economically the most important, in the

country. It rises on the plateau of Langres, 30 km north-west of Dijon, then flows north-west past Troyes across Champagne. It turns west and then south through the rich lands of Brie, past Nogent, the forest of Fontainebleau and Melun, through the north-eastern boundary of Beauce and then in a north-westerly winding course to Paris. It continues past Elbeuf and Rouen, through Normandy to its estuary (on which stands Le Havre) south of Cap de la Hève, on the English Channel. Throughout the lower half of its course the river meanders very considerably. The Seine and its tributaries, including the Yonne, Aube, Marne, and Oise, carry more than half of the inland water traffic of France. Length 775 km.

Seismology, see EARTHQUAKE.

Sejanus, Aelius (d. AD 31), Roman praetorian prefect. He gained great influence over Tiberius and became chief administrator of the Roman Empire. He set about undermining the position of various members of the Emperor's family in order to secure the succession for himself. Tiberius at last began to suspect Sejanus's designs on his own imperial power. The Senate decreed his death: he was strangled and thrown into the Tiber.

Sekondi-Takoradi, conurbation of two ports in south-west Ghana. Sekondi, much the older settlement, grew up from a trading fort on the coast and was connected by rail to Kumasi between 1898 and 1903. Because Sekondi lacked any natural harbour facilities, Takoradi harbour was built in the 1920s as a deep-water port. With rail links to the cocoa belt and also to the bauxite mines at Awaso, Takoradi handles just under half of Ghana's overseas trade. Population (combined, 1970) 254,543.

Selassie, Haile, see HAILE SELASSIE I.

Selborne, village in Hampshire, England, 7 km south-east of Alton. Selborne was the birthplace of Gilbert White (d.1793); the Hanger, between Selborne and Newton Valence is where White made many of the observations recorded in *The Natural History of Selborne*. Population (1971) 949.

Selby, market town in North Yorkshire, England, on the Ouse, 22 km south of York. The chief industries are the manufacture of oilcake, flour milling, shipbuilding, paper-making, and sugar-refining. To the west lies the rich Selby coalfield. Population (1981) 10,726.

Selden, John (1584–1654), English jurist and author. He was active in the drawing up of the Petition of Right of 1628.

Selden Roll, Aztec paper pictograph, in colours, lodged in the Bodleian Library in Oxford. It was made in the early 15th century and describes the history of the Toltec empire.

Selene, Greek goddess of the Moon, later identified with Artemis. She was a daughter of Hyperion, and sister of Helios (the Sun) and Eos (the Dawn). The Romans called her Luna, identified her with Diana and built her temple between the Aventine and the Circus Maximus.

Selenium, non-metallic chemical element, symbol Se, atomic number 34, atomic weight 78·96, closely related to sulphur and tellurium. It is an uncommon substance, though traces are found in association with sulphur and iron and copper sulphides (pyrites). It was discovered by Berzelius in 1817 and it was found in the 'flue dust' of iron pyrites burners, and in deposits in the lead chambers of old sulphuric acid works. Nowadays the main source is from anode mud deposited in the electrolytic extraction of copper. Selenium and its compounds are used in glass-making for removing the green tint due to iron impurities, but its most interesting use is in the manufacture of photoelectric cells used in various optical and electrical devices. Selenium exists in several allotropic forms, e.g., amorphous, monoclinic, and metallic; the last is the form used in selenium cells.

Seleucidae, the Seleucids, a Syrian dynasty founded in 312 BC by Seleucus I Nicator, which continued until 65 BC.

See also ANTIOCHUS III; ANTIOCHUS IV; DIADOCHI, WARS OF THE; SELEUCUS I NICATOR.

Seleucus I Nicator (c.358–280 BC), King of Syria and founder of the dynasty of the Seleucidae. Six kings of Syria were named Seleucus.

The son of Antiochus, a Macedonian who served with distinction under Philip II, he accompanied Alexander the Great on his expedition to Asia. After Alexander's death, Seleucus assumed power over all the eastern provinces which had formed part of Alexander's empire, from the Euphrates to the banks of the Oxus and the Indus. Having leagued himself with Ptolemy, Lysimachus, and Cassander against Antigonus, he obtained, by the latter's death, Syria and a large part of Asia Minor.

In 293 Seleucus consigned the government of all provinces beyond the Euphrates to his son Antiochus, granting him the title of king. In 285, with the help of Ptolemy and Lysimachus, he defeated and captured the Macedonian king Demetrius Poliorcetes, who had invaded Asia Minor. He was assassinated by Ptolemy Ceraunos, a younger son of his old friend and ally Lysimachus, when attempting to take the throne of Macedonia.

Self, Infinite, in Hindu philosophy, term applied to the awareness of God as the undifferentiated and timeless Ground. This awareness gives the Hindu a feeling of true identity, of having come home to his real self at last. Hence God is often spoken of as the Self, the knowledge of one's own being. Hindus believe that the eternal Self underlies the conscious personality and the changing, perishable body. The greatest goal of the spiritually inclined Hindu is to identify self with the Self; to melt away the barrier which seems to stand between the human mind and That from which it springs.

***Peter Sellers,** comic genius of radio and films.*

Self-denying Ordinance was passed in 1645 during a critical period of the English Civil War. It enacted that all members of Parliament, Lords or Commons, should resign their civil and military offices conferred by either or both of the houses of Parliament, or by authority derived from them. Thus Essex and other Presbyterians were removed and replaced by Cromwell's nominees, and since reappointment was allowed, Cromwell became commander of the cavalry.

Self-pollination, see POLLINATION.

Seljuks, name of several Turkish dynasties, descended from the Ghuzz chieftain, Seljuk, which reigned over large parts of Asia in the 11th, 12th, and 13th centuries. Seljuk migrated from the Kirghiz steppes to Jand, where he embraced Islam. His grandsons, Togrul Beg and Chaghri Beg Dand, became the leaders of the Ghuzz Turks, who invaded Persia at the beginning of the 11th century. In 1055 Togrul entered Baghdad and was proclaimed sultan. He was succeeded in 1063 by his nephew, Alp Arslan, who took Syria and Palestine from the Fatimite caliph of Egypt, and in 1071 defeated and captured the Byzantine Emperor Romanus Diogenes, who thereupon ceded a large part of Asia Minor. Alp Arslan was succeeded by his son, Malik Shah, in 1072. On his death civil war broke out between his sons, Barkyaruq and Mohammad. Under the latter (1104–17) the power and extent of the empire was restored; but his successor, Sanjar, the last of the Great Seljuk (1117–57), was largely occupied in defending the eastern frontier against fresh inroads of Ghuzz, who defeated and captured him in 1153, and eventually brought his reign to an end in 1157.

Selkirk, Alexander (1676–1721), Scottish sailor. He sailed in 1704 with Thomas Stradling, who, after a quarrel, landed him on the uninhabited island of Juan Fernández, from which he was rescued after five years by Capt. Woodes Rogers, who was afterwards governor of the Bahamas. Selkirk's adventures inspired Daniel Defoe's *Robinson Crusoe* and William Cowper's poem, *Alexander Selkirk*.

Selkirk, royal burgh, in the Borders Region of Scotland, on the banks of the Ettrick, 61 km south-east of Edinburgh. The manufacture of tweeds is the main occupation. Population (1981) 5417.

Sellafield, atomic plant in Cumbria, England, adjoining Calder Hall. At Sellafield plutonium is produced on a commercial scale from uranium.

See also NUCLEAR POWER.

Sellers, Peter Richard Henry (1925–80), British actor who became nationally famous in the radio programme *The Goon Show*. In recent years he made many successful films, which demonstrated his vivid powers of characterisation. They include: *I'm Alright, Jack*; *The Millionairess*; *Lolita*; *Dr Strangelove*; *What's New, Pussycat?* and the 'Pink Panther' series. His last film was *Being There* (1980).

Selwyn Lloyd, John, Baron, (1904–78), British Conservative politician. He served as foreign secretary under Anthony Eden (1955–60) during the Suez Crisis and supported Eden's policies. He was also chancellor of the exchequer (1960–2) but the unpopularity of his wage restraint policies led him to resign. He was subsequently Speaker of the House of Commons. (1971–6).

Semang, a 3000-strong Austro-asiatic-speaking group of south-east Malaysian aboriginal hunters and gatherers. The nomadic Semang bands, 20-30 strong, hunt with blowpipes and poisoned darts, and exchange forest products for salt with Malay neighbours, using 'silent trade', i.e. barter not involving direct contact. Today most practise some agriculture. They are Shamanists and have numerous deities.

Semantics is the generally accepted term for the study of meaning, and as such was first defined in 1883 by Michel Bréal. In its widest sense (for which *semiotics* is a more accurate term) semantics covers meaning conveyed by anything which can be termed symbolic, even an involuntary facial gesture. Applied to natural languages, however, semantics describes the meaning of: (1) grammatical items and constructions; (2) phonetic effects; and (3) vocabulary words and their meaningful elements or 'morphemes', which are the field of dictionaries and lexicology. It is to this last area that semantics is often restricted.

'Meaning' can be interpreted in different ways. Cognitive or conceptual meaning is seen in the 'logical' relationships between words in the same language; for example, *sameness of meaning* (synonyms and paraphrases); *oppositeness* (antonymy) of various kinds; *hyponymy* (the relationship between, for example, *roseflower*, or *pig-animal*). The second type of meaning is the relationship between words ('linguistic items') and real objects, for example, between the word *cat* and actual cats. This relationship has long been a source of philosophical debate. The third level of meaning is connotation, in the sense of additional overtones of meaning in which synonyms often differ from each other.

Semaphore, term originally meaning an instrument for signalling messages with discs and shutters in a framework, but now applied to all methods of communicating by the code which grew out of it. Invented by Edgeworth in 1767, semaphore was adapted by Chappe in 1794 for use between Paris and the frontier armies. In 1795 a further adaptation, introduced by Sir G. Murray, was accepted by the British Admiralty for communications between London and Portsmouth. In 1816 the British Admiralty adopted Sir H. Popham's semaphore for sea service. This was replaced by Pasley's in 1827. In 1890 the method was extended to the actual spelling of words, and the present system evolved whereby the relative position of two arms, human or mechanical, indicates different letters or numerals. Semaphore is no longer used as a means of communication between ships at sea.

Semarang, port in northern Java, Indonesia, and chief trade centre for central Java. It is linked by rail to Jakarta and Surabaya, 260 km to the east. Manufacturing includes textiles, rubber products, and footwear, and rubber, tobacco, and textiles are exported. Population (1975) 775,000.

Semibreve, largest musical note-value in current use, called the 'whole note' in Germany and America. It is half the value of the breve.
See also NOTATION.

Semiconductors are neither good electrical conductors nor insulators. The term usually refers to the crystalline form of silicon or germanium, or gallium arsenide, to which extremely carefully controlled small quantities of other substances have been added. The atoms of both silicon and germanium have four electrons in their outermost shell, and in a pure crystal all are linked with adjacent atoms, so none is free for conduction. Adding an element with five electrons in its outer shell, such as phosphorus or arsenic, makes 'free' electrons available. Such a material is called 'negative' or '*n* type'. Conversely the addition of atoms such as boron, aluminium, or gallium, with only three outer electrons, will result in vacancies in the lattice. This deficiency is called a 'hole' and behaves like a positive charge: this material is called '*p* type'. The conductivity can therefore be controlled by the addition of impurities.

Crystals can be made in which a '*p* type' region is adjacent to an '*n* type' region: this gives a *pn* junction. A 'sandwich' of three regions, either *pnp* or *npn*, is the basis of the transistor.

Seminal Vesicles, two small organs situated behind the bladder and above the prostate gland in the male mammal, which secrete a component of the seminal fluid.

Seminoles, North American Indian people, belonging to the Muskogean linguistic group. They are remembered for the fierce wars that they fought with the whites, the last in 1835–42 in the Everglades swamps of Florida, the losses and expenses of these wars being out of all proportion to the number of Indians concerned. After they surrendered, most of the Seminoles went to Oklahoma.

Semiotics, see SEMANTICS.

Semipalatinsk, capital city of Semipalatinsk *oblast*, USSR, south-east of Omsk. It is a communication centre at the junction of the Irtysh river and the Turksib railway. It has an important food industry (meat packing, flour milling, wines, and vodka). Population (1980) 286,000.

Semiquaver, note in music equivalent in value to half a quaver and a sixteenth of a semibreve. In America and Germany it is called 'sixteenth note'.
See also NOTATION.

Semiramis and Ninus, wife and husband who were, according to Diodorus, Justin and other classical authors, the legendary founders of Nineveh (Ninua). Semiramis was also confused with the goddess of war and love, Ishtar or Astarte. The legends probably originated in the deeds of two vigorous Assyrian queen-mothers: Sammuramat, who ruled for her son Adad-nirari III in 810–806 BC, and Naqi'a, wife of Sennacherib and mother of Esarhaddon, who administered Babylonia.

Semites, speakers of Semitic languages including Jews, Arabs, the Amharas of Ethiopia, and other peoples of North Africa.
See also ISRAEL; SEMITIC-HAMITIC LANGUAGES.

Semitic-Hamitic Languages. The Hamitic branch of this linguistic group includes ancient Egyptian and its descendant, the Coptic language, the Berber or Libyan dialects of North Africa, and the various Cushitic tongues of modern Ethiopia and the adjacent regions. The Semitic languages consist of north-east Semitic or Akkadian (consisting of Assyrian and Babylonian) now extinct; west Semitic or north-west Semitic, comprising Early Canaanite, Hebrew and the extinct allied languages, Phoenician (including Punic which was spoken by the ancient Carthaginians),

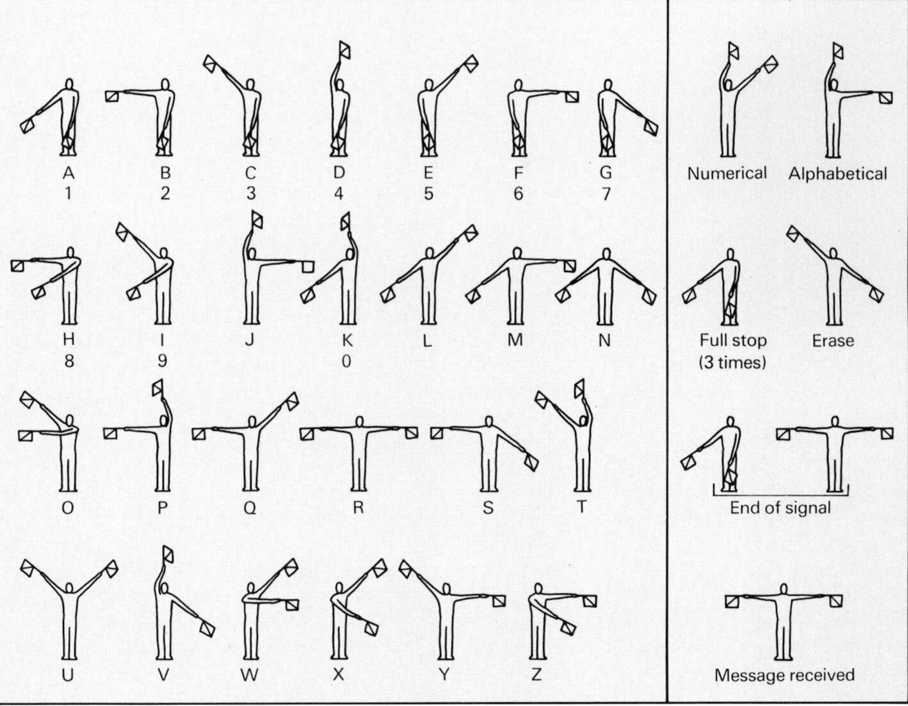

Semaphore. *The alphabet, developed in the 1890s, is still used on some railway systems.*

both extinct, and Aramaic, with its descendant the Syriac language; and south Semitic, subdivided into north Arabic or Arabic proper, spoken by about 100,000,000 people, and south Arabic, comprising the extinct languages spoken in south Arabia: Minaean, Sabaean, Himyaritic, and Hadhramautic, as well as Old Ethiopic, Amharic, Tigré, and Tigriña.
See also ARABIC LANGUAGE.

Semolina, an intermediate product in flour-milling, consisting of wheat endosperm in the form of particles of approximately 0·25–1 mm in diameter. The semolina from durum wheat is used industrially as the raw material in the manufacture of pasta. Domestically, semolina is used in making milk puddings.

Sempill, Robert (c.1595–1665), Scottish poet. A Royalist, he has left a picture of his times in the ballad, *Life and Death of Habbie Simson, Piper of Kibarchan*, 1640.

Senanayake, Dudley Shelton (1911–73), Prime Minister of Sri Lanka, 1960, 1962–63, and 1965–70; son of the Rt Hon. D. S. Senanayake. He was appointed Minister of Agriculture to Ceylon in the first parliament of 1947, and was ultimately responsible for several multi-purpose irrigation and colonisation schemes in the country. He led the United National Party to victory in 1965 but was severely defeated by Mrs Bandaranaike in the election of May 1970.

Senanayake, Dudley Stephen (1882–1952), Sinhalese politician. He entered the legislative council in 1922, became Minister for Agriculture and Lands, 1931, and was responsible for large agricultural and irrigation schemes designed to benefit the cultivator. In 1942 he was elected leader of the last State Council under British rule, and in 1947, when Sri Lanka (or, as it was then called, Ceylon) became an independent dominion, he became the first prime minister. Senanayake was a convinced nationalist, but also a sincere believer in the value of the Commonwealth connection. He was a supporter of the Ceylon National Congress until, thinking it infiltrated by Communists, he left to found the United National Party, which held office from 1947 to 1956.

Senate, chief governing body of the Roman republic for a period of 400 years. Originally it was the advisory council of the kings, and on the expulsion of the kings in 510 BC it continued to act, in theory, as adviser to the magistrates. In practice, however, although its decisions were only recommendations, they came to have the force of law. In time this caused difficulty, since after 287 BC the popular assembly was officially the sovereign body of Rome. The Senate originally numbered 300, later 600. From the time of Sulla election to the quaestorship carried automatic entry to the Senate, so that the composition of the Senate was indirectly subject to popular election. Membership was for life, though the censors could remove those guilty of misconduct. Under the Empire the Senate remained important until the 3rd century AD when the emperor Gallienus ruled that senators could not hold military appointments. The Senate retained some prestige and privileges, but its political influence went into a continuous decline.

Sendai, city of Miyagi-ken, Japan, 250 km north of Tokyo; it is the largest city of northern Japan, and a major administrative centre. Industries include brewing, confectionery, dairy and fish products. Special steels, cutlery, and electricity transmission lines are also manufactured. The Tanabata festival, held annually in early August, is a famous tourist attraction. Population (1980) 665,000.

Seneca, Lucius Annaeus (c.4 BC–AD 65), Latin Stoic philosopher, son of Marcus Annaeus Seneca. He was brought to Rome when still a child, and early devoted himself to the study of rhetoric. In 49 he was appointed tutor to the future emperor Nero. On the accession of Nero (54) Seneca's authority increased, and he shared the administration of affairs with Burrhus, the praetorian prefect. But his restraining hand soon made him irksome to Nero. He withdrew from public life, but was eventually implicated in the conspiracy of Piso, and committed suicide, together with his wife Pompeia Paulina.
Seneca's fame rests upon his writings. They have been variously estimated by critics, but all agree as to their clear and forcible style. They consist of ten *Dialogues*; 124 *Moral Letters* to Lucilius; the *Apocolocyntosis* (Pumpkinification) *of Claudius*; a group of *Moral Essays* which include the 'De Beneficiis' and 'Naturales Quaestiones'; and nine *Tragedies*.

Seneca, Marcus Annaeus (Lucius Annaeus) (c.55 BC–AD 41), Latin rhetorician. He visited Rome in the early years of Augustus, but returned to Spain and married Helvia, by whom he had three sons: the philosopher L. Annaeus Seneca, L. Annaeus Mela (father of the poet Lucan), and M. Annaeus Novatus. His extant writing consists of a book of *Suasoriae* (extracts from celebrated rhetoricians on standard school themes), and five of ten books of *Controversiae* (imaginary legal cases).

Senecas, North American Indian people, belonging to the Iroquois. There are estimated to be about 3000 Senecas in the USA and 300 in Canada.

Senecio, a genus of annual and perennial herbs, shrubs and trees of much diversity, belonging to the Compositae, and cosmopolitan. *S. jacobaea*, ragwort, and *S. vulgaris*, groundsel, are widespread weeds; *S. cruentus* is a parent of the gardener's cinerarias; *S. greyii, S. laxifolius* are grey-leaved, yellow-flowering shrubs; and *S. macroglossus* is the Cape ivy of South Africa. A number of succulent species occur in Africa.

Senefelder, Aloys (1771–1834), Austrian born in Prague, who was for a time an actor and playwright and who took up printing, inventing almost by chance the process of lithography, c.1796.

Senegal, a republic on the west coast of Africa. It lies south of the Senegal river, which forms the boundary with Mauritania, and west of the Falémé river, which divides it from Mali Republic, and north of Guinea-Bissau and Guinea. Gambia forms a narrow intrusion along the Gambia river almost cutting off the southern portion of the country known as Casamance. Area 196,722 km^2.
In the north the coast is bordered by sand dunes, while inland, monotonous plains are

Senegal
Area: 196,722 km^2
Population: 5,660,000
Capital: Dakar

dominated by ancient river valleys and deltas. Farther south the coastlands are deltaic and swampy with ria estuaries on the Casamance (and Gambia) rivers. The south-east of the country is much higher, forming a dissected plateau around 400 m high terminating at the Guinea border, where the land rises abruptly towards the Fouta Djallon Mountains.
The great majority of the 1980 population of 5,660,000 is rural in character. Population density decreases from Dakar (the capital) eastwards. All the major towns are of colonial origin and usually owe their foundation to the groundnut trade.
Agriculture is the chief activity of 70 per cent of the working population. The staple food crops are millet, sorghum, maize, rice, and cassava, but almost half the cropped land is occupied by groundnuts grown mainly for export. Livestock rearing is important, and is more closely integrated with cultivation than in most African countries.
Mining is confined to the working of two phosphate deposits. An iron-ore deposit has been found at Falémé. Manufacturing is better developed than in most West African countries, several factories dating from the late colonial period when they had all French West Africa as a market. It is heavily concentrated in and around Dakar, and includes groundnut milling, oil refining and various food, textile, chemical, and engineering industries. The currency unit is the CFA franc.
The amended constitution, adopted by a referendum on 22 February 1970 by 99·9 per cent of voters, confirms Senegal as a presidential republic. The president rules through a prime minister, and except in the spheres of justice, foreign policy, and defence, he requires the approval of the ministers. The 1970 amendment limited presidential tenure to a maximum of two five-year terms.
Legislative power is exercised by the elected National Assembly, which has 100 deputies and a five-year term.
The official language is French; among the numerous native tongues the most widespread are Wolof and Tokolor.
History. The Portuguese set up trading posts in the area in the 15th century, but their influence declined, and by the end of the 16th century the French had acquired rights in the small island of Gorée. The Senegal Company was chartered by Richelieu in 1633. In the mid-19th century a programme of internal development was carried out by the French administrator, founded on the principle of 'assimilation' to French institutions, laws, and customs. In 1958 Senegal was granted internal self-government and, after a short-lived partnership with Sudan as the Federation of Mali, achieved full independence in 1960. In 1970 a referendum was held which over-

Senegal. *The island of Gorée. This former French colony attained independence in 1960.*

whelmingly approved an amendment to the constitution, providing for the creation of the post of prime minister, and increasing the powers of the president. Abdou Diouf became president in 1981. In 1982 Senegal joined Gambia in the Confederation of Senegambia.

Senegal, major river of West Africa, formed by the confluence of the Falémé and the Bafing rivers which rise in the Fouta Djallon mountains of Guinea, and flow first north-west, joining to become the Senegal river near Bakel, and then flowing in an arc west and then southwards to its outfall near St Louis at 16° N. The river forms the northern border of Senegal with Mauritania, and is vital to both countries because of the agricultural potential of its seasonally flooded clay plains. Length 1600 km.

Senegambia, Confederation of, see GAMBIA, THE; SENEGAL.

Senghor, Leopold (1906–), President of Senegal (1960–80). In 1928 Senghor went to Paris to study at the Lycée Louis-le-Grand and later at the Sorbonne. In 1946 Senghor entered the political arena as one of Senegal's two deputies to the French National Assembly. Senghor founded the Senegalese Democratic Bloc (BDS) in 1948 and later created the Senegalese Progressive Union (UPS), which became the ruling party.

Senility, a condition of diminished power and functional efficiency characteristic of extreme old age. The most potent cause of the decrease in functional activity is the diminished elasticity of the coats of the arteries. The blood moves more sluggishly and the capillaries are insufficiently supplied, so that the tissues are not properly nourished. Fatty and calcareous degeneration of certain parts sets in and the effect is loss of muscular power, diminished nervous control, slow reaction to stimuli, and general feebleness. The brain is apt to suffer with other organs, and there is likely to be loss of mental activity, loss of memory, and, occasionally, senile dementia.

Senna, a drug obtained from the leaves or fruits of various species of *Cassia*, a genus of leguminous plants. The extracts from the fruits (pods) are less griping and therefore preferable to those from the leaf but both senna leaves and senna pods act as anthraquinone purgatives on the large intestine.

Sennar, town of the south-east Sudan, on the left bank of the Blue Nile. The Makwar dam was built here (1914–21), at a cost of £11,000,000 as part of the Gezira irrigation scheme. Sennar became a centre of African civilisation under the Fung dynasty which endured until the time of Mehemet Ali, whose son, Ismail, sent to deal with the Fung kingdom, soon reduced Sennar (1822). Population (1973) 10,000.

Sens, French town in the *département* of Yonne, 50 km north-west of Auxerre, on the River Yonne. It was known to the Romans, and has the earliest of the French Gothic cathedrals. There is a trade in agricultural produce, wine, and wood. Agricultural implements and chemicals are manufactured. Population (1975) 27,930.

Sensation, in metaphysics, means variously: (1) mental consciousness of the processes of physiological sensation; (2) subjective experience, as of pleasure or pain, arising from objective experience; (3) in Positivist philosophy, that form of sensibility which belongs to the organs of sense. Sensation is to be differentiated from perception, which means the reception of knowledge (as distinct from ideas or images) through the senses, but was used by some philosophers, e.g. Descartes, Locke, and Leibniz, with a very extended significance. Reid was the first to use the word perception in the special or limited sense, namely of the faculty acquisitive of knowledge of the external world.

Sense Datum, in philosophy, the elementary information supplied by the senses. According to sense datum theories of knowledge, it is out of sense data that the mind constructs its total perceptions.

Sensory Deprivation, that state in which proprioceptive stimuli arising from tendons, joints, muscles, and the vestibular canals, and sight and sound, are interfered with, resulting in a change in one's body image which in turn may alter one's sense of personal identity. Changes in body awareness can also be affected by spatial and temporal disorientation and as a result of infectious diseases and psychotomimetic drugs.

Seoul (Japanese *Keijo*), capital and cultural, commercial, and industrial centre of South Korea, on the Han river over 110 km from its mouth. The core is a walled city, with a royal palace. Its port is Inchŏn, 40 km away, with which it is connected by rail. Population (1975) 6,879,464.

Sepal, see FLOWER.

Separate Development, see APARTHEID.

Separation, see DIVORCE.

Sephardim, the Spanish and Portuguese branch of the Jewish community, descended from the Jews expelled from Spain (1492) and Portugal (1497), together with the descendants of those (the majority) forcibly converted at that time (the Marranos), and the descendants of earlier forced converts. The refugees of 1492 from Spain fled to Italy, North Africa, and the Levant. Many of these exiles and Marranos found their way to Britain in the guise of foreign Protestants. The most famous was Dr Rodrigo Lopez, Elizabeth I's physician. More of them settled in England in 1630, and were among those who secured toleration from Cromwell in 1656. Disraeli, Pinero, Sutro, Guedalla, Montefiore and Sassoon were all of Sephardic extraction. From 1656 to 1700 the Jewish community in England was almost entirely Sephardic. Then a number of Jews arrived from central Europe and established their synagogue, that of the Ashkenazim.

Sepia, brown pigment used as a water-colour. It is prepared from the colouring matter released from the ink bags of some species of cuttlefish to obscure their movements by clouding the water. The pigment is prepared by dissolving the dried contents of the bags in dilute aqueous alkali and precipitating with hydrochloric acid. Because of the evenness with which it can be easily spread on paper with a brush, it has been much used (from the 19th century onwards) in painting monochromes.

Sepoy (Persian *sepahi*), Hindustani word for an Indian soldier of the old Indian army (prior to partition in 1947). The term was used loosely for men of all Indian units. More correctly it was applied to distinguish the infantry soldier from the trooper (or *sowar*).

Sept, term commonly used in the past in Ireland and Scotland to denote a clan, or a branch of a clan.

September, the ninth month of the modern calendar year. Its name reflects its former position of seventh month in the ancient Roman calendar.

Septembrists, perpetrators of the massacres which took place in September 1792 in Paris. The victims were royalists and constitutionalists confined in prison, and the massacres were carried out by the commune of Paris in consternation at the approach of the Prussians, whose avowed object was to restore the King.

Septic Tank, a tank for settlement of suspended solids from sewage prior to secondary treatment by oxidation, and of such capacity as to be able to store the settled sludge for several months. The design is favoured for private sewage-disposal works for isolated buildings, or groups with a maximum population of about 300 persons, when used in conjunction with percolating filters or other acceptable aeration methods. The term should not be confused with cesspool.

Septicaemia (blood poisoning), any acute infection in which bacteria multiply in the blood stream, causing severe illness characterised by fever, shivering and sweating, headache and general malaise. Energetic treatment with antibiotics is required to prevent complications, especially localisation of bacteria within the tissues and septic shock due to liberation of toxins by bacteria.

Septuagint (Latin *septuaginta*, seventy), also known as LXX, the most ancient translation of the Hebrew scriptures, so called from the account of its origin first given in a spurious Greek work of the 2nd century BC known as *The Letter of Aristeas*, and repeated by Josephus and Eusebius. According to this, when Ptolemy II Philadelphus (285–286 BC), founded his great library at Alexandria, he was anxious to have a copy of the Hebrew scriptures. He sent a delegation to the high priest Eleazar in Jerusalem asking for a copy of the Law of Moses and for men able to translate it. Seventy-two elders, six out of each tribe, were sent to Alexandria for this work, and the translation of the Law into Greek was supposedly completed by them in 72 days. It is uncertain why out of 72 arose the term Septuagint. There may have been a popular association with the Hebrew *seventy elders* (Exod. xxiv. 1.9), or the number was simply rounded off.

Sepulchre, Church of the Holy, stands in the north-west corner of the Old City of Jerusalem, and is traditionally said to contain the tomb of Jesus.

Sequence. If f is a function whose domain is the set of positive integers and whose codomain is any set A, then f is called a sequence in A (or a sequence of elements of A). Sequences of real and of complex numbers have been studied extensively in mathematics. The main point of interest about a sequence is whether it has a limit as $n \rightarrow \infty$. In a real or complex sequence, called a 'Cauchy sequence' the values become clustered together as n increases and the sequence is said to be 'convergent'. A real sequence that tends to infinity or to minus infinity is called a divergent sequence.
See also SERIES.

Sequence, in music, device whereby a melodic figure is repeated rising or falling by a degree of the scale, at least twice in succession. It is called sequence only in cases where the composition retains the same key at that point, regardless of changes in the interval.

Sequestration. In English law a writ of sequestration is a process of execution under the Rules of the Supreme Court. Where any person has been ordered to pay money into court or do any other act within a limited time, and fails to obey, the aggrieved party may issue a writ of sequestration against the property of the disobedient party. This writ is directed to four sequestrators and gives them authority to enter the lands of the disobedient person and get into their hands not only the rents and profits of the real estate, but also all goods, chattels, and personal estate, and to detain these under sequestration until the person in default has cleared the aggrieved party; but they must get the leave of the court before they sell any of the goods and chattels sequestered, and the proceeds of such sale will be dealt with only as the court may direct.
In Scots law sequestration is the process by which a person or firm is declared bankrupt and their assets distributed among the creditors. The process may be initiated by creditors or by the debtor himself.

Sequin (Italian *zecchino*), popular name for the Venetian ducat, now applied to small discs of celluloid etc., used as trimming on clothing.

Sequoia, a genus of evergreen coniferous trees in family Taxodiaceae. They are the redwoods of California. They attain a height upwards of 100 m, and the trunk reaches a diameter of almost 8 m. They may live for 2500 to 3000 years. *S. sempervirens*, the coast redwood, is a very valuable timber tree.

Seraing, town in Belgium, an industrial suburb of Liège, situated on the River Meuse, 6 km south-west of the city. It has coal-mines and is the seat of the important Cockerill works, founded in 1817, comprising blast furnaces, smelting-houses, foundries, steelworks, and engineering shops. The famous crystal works of Val-Saint-Lambert is also situated in Seraing. Population (1980) 65,370.

Seraphim, order of angelic beings mentioned in Isaiah vi. 2-6 as guarding God's throne in heaven and continually proclaiming his glory.

Serapis, or Sarapis, late Egyptian divinity, chosen by Ptolemy I to be the deity of both his Greek and Egyptian subjects. Serapis became the official deity of the kingdom, replacing Osiris. After the Roman conquest, the cult of Serapis spread all over the Roman empire.

Serbia (Serbo-Croat, *Srbija*), constituent republic of Yugoslavia, incorporating the autonomous provinces of Vojvodina and Kosovo. It is bounded on the north by Hungary and Romania, east by Bulgaria, south by Macedonia, west by Croatia and Bosnia-Hercegovina, and south-west by Albania and Montenegro.
Serbia is a country of mountains and valleys, where the four great mountain systems of the Balkan peninsula—the Dinaric Alps, Balkan Mountains, Carpathians, and Rhodope Mountains—meet. Its northern part is in the basin of the Danube; other important rivers are the Sava, Morava, and Tisza, all tributaries of the Danube. The country is heavily forested, and is rich in minerals, including copper, antimony, coal, chrome, lead, and silver. Serbia is predominantly pastoral and agricultural. Wheat, maize, barley, flax, hemp, tobacco, sugar beet, fruit, and vines are grown, and there is much stock raising. There are textile, metallurgical, leather and brewing industries. The majority of the inhabitants belong to the Orthodox church. The principal towns are Belgrade (the capital), Niš, Kragujevac, and Leskovac. Area 88,360 km²; population (1981) 9,313,677.
The Serbs, a branch of the Slav race, settled in the Balkan Peninsula in the 7th century. After 1169 all the Serb countries except Bosnia were united into one kingdom under the Nemanya dynasty. The power of the Serbs was crushed by the Turks at the battle of Kosovo in 1389, and henceforward Serbia came first under Turkish overlordship, then, after 1459, under direct Turkish rule. In 1804 the Serbs revolted under a peasant leader, Karageorge, and a rudimentary Serb state was set up. But the Treaty of Bucharest in 1812 between the Russians and the Turks recognised Turkish suzerainty in Serbia. In the Russo-Turkish War of 1877, Serbia co-operated with Russia, and its troops advanced on Constantinople. At the Peace of San Stefano in 1878, Serbia did not, however, gain all that it felt entitled to, but at the Congress of Berlin in the same year the independence of Serbia was at last formally recognised, though Bosnia and Hercegovina were ceded to Austria.
On 28 June 1914 the Austrian Archduke Francis Ferdinand was assassinated in Sarajevo. Austria accused Serbia of being privy to this plot, issued an ultimatum unacceptable to Serbia, then declared war on 28 July. Eventually, on 21 December 1918, a united kingdom of the Serbs, Croats, and Slovenes was established under the Serbian king, Alexander Karageorge, and with a Serbian Radical, Protić, as premier. See further under YUGOSLAVIA, *History*.

Serbo Croat Language, see YUGOSLAVIA, *Language*.

Serenade, title of a musical composition, often with more than four movements. This light form of ensemble music is particularly associated with Haydn and Mozart but has been employed up to the present day. Originally the term meant a love-song played beneath a lady's window at night.

Seretse Khama, see KHAMA, SIR SERETSE.

Serf, unfree peasant whose relationship with his lord entailed varying privileges and rights on both sides, but necessarily included a total lack of freedom of movement on the part of the peasant; he could not leave his holding without his lord's permission. The serf held land from his lord, providing his means of subsistence from it. In return he might be obliged to work on his lord's demesne—and these works might be exceedingly onerous—and/or his lord might be entitled to any surplus produce of the serf's plot. Serfdom gradually died out in England with the growth of the cash economy and the drastic population decline after the Black Death. In many parts of the world serfdom was formerly the general condition of the peasant. In China it persisted from at least 2000 BC to modern times. In western Europe serfdom had died out by c.1550, but in Austro-Hungary it was not officially abolished till c.1800 and in Russia till 1816. It still persists in, e.g. parts of Asia.
See also FEUDALISM.

Serge, a loose-weave twilled worsted fabric with a rough surface. It was in common use from the 17th century on. Serge from Chalon was known as Shalloon. Serge today is usually dyed black, navy blue or other dark colours. Once used for coverlets and curtains it is now fashioned into coats and other items of clothing. Coat linings are made from rayon or silk serge, a twilled silk variety.

Sergius of Radonezh, Saint (1314–92), saint of the Russian Orthodox Church, founder of the famous monastery of the Holy Trinity near Moscow. In 1380, before the battle of Kulikovo against the Tatars, he blessed Prince Dmitriy Donskoy and predicted his victory. He is the most popular saint in Russia, and is considered the country's patron.

Serialism, in music, a means of organisation in which the melodic and harmonic elements of a composition are determined by reference to a fixed order of succession for the pitches (called a 'series' or 'note-row'). The series may contain any number of notes, but the most common form is one containing all 12 notes of the chromatic scale. Though various forms of serialism emerged during the period 1910–25 in the works of Schoenberg, Webern and J. M. Hauer (1883–1959), among others, the most common variety is the 12-note method developed by Schoenberg.

Sericulture, see SILK AND SILKWORMS.

Seriema, South American birds, resembling the secretary bird, but classified in the order Gruiformes. There are two species: *Cariama cristata*, the seriema, or crested screamer, is a common species of grasslands, with long legs, short wings, short and slightly hooked beak, a well-developed crest and long tail. *Chunga burmeisteri*, the black-legged seriema, is darker and has shorter legs, and lives in woodland.

Series (or progression), in mathematics, a sequence of associated numbers (terms) added together. A series may be finite, or infinite (never terminate). If $s(i)$ denotes the ith term of a sequence, then the sum of n terms (Sn), or the partial sum of terms from i equal to 1 to i equal to n inclusive can be expressed as

$$S(n) = \sum_{i=1}^{n} s(i)$$

If, as i increases, the numerical value of $s(i)$ increases, the series is said to be divergent. If $s(i)$ approaches 0, it is convergent, and the sum of the series is the limit as $i \to \infty$, or

$$\sum_{i=1}^{\infty} s(i)$$

For some series there are simple formulae for the partial sums. Examples for divergent series are:

Sum of the first n integers:
$s(i) = i \qquad S(n) = \frac{1}{2}n(n+1)$
Sum of the first n squares:
$s(i) = i^2 \qquad S(n) = \frac{1}{6}n(n+1)(2n+1)$
Sum of the first n cubes:
$s(i) = i^3 \qquad S(n) = \frac{1}{4}n^2(n+1)$
Arithmetic progression:
$s(i) = s(i-1) + d \quad S(n) = \frac{1}{2}n[s(1) + s(n)]$
Geometric progression:
$s(i) = ar^i \qquad S(n) = a\dfrac{1-r^{n+1}}{1-r}$

In the last case the series is convergent if $-1 < r < 1$; then $r^{n+1} \to 0$ as n increases and so $S(\infty) = \dfrac{a}{1-r}$.

See also SEQUENCE.

Serigraphy is the term given to screen process printing when used in fine art. The technique involves a stencilling process in which the stencil is affixed to a fine mesh of silk or man made fibre, known as the 'screen'. The screen is stretched over an open frame similar to the support of a canvas. The ink is pushed across its surface by a flexible blade and forced through the holes in the unmasked areas of the mesh on to the printing surface.

The medium was first used for original artistic expression in America in the 1830s.

See also PRINTMAKING.

Serjeants at Arms, are, in Britain, officers of the Crown and (with the exceptions below) attend the sovereign upon certain ceremonial occasions only, though once they possessed broad executive functions. Serjeants may attend other dignitaries on formal occasions, for example the lord mayor of London and the lord high steward. A serjeant at arms was first assigned to the Commons in the 15th century, and his successor is still appointed by the sovereign to attend on the Speaker while Parliament is sitting.

Serous Membranes, layers of tissue lining the closed cavities of the body, and characterised by the secretion of a serous fluid; they allow the organ to slide within its cavity. Such membranes are the pericardium, investing the heart; the two pleurae, investing the lungs (pleurisy is an inflammation of these); the peritoneum, investing the abdominal viscera; and the two tunicae vaginales, investing the testes.

Serowe, town in Botswana and centre of the Bamangwato tribe, founded in 1903 by Khama III. The Bamangwato tribe still has a *khama* as its chief. Population (1971) 15,723.

Serpent, bass wind instrument, so called from the shape of its wooden, leather-covered tapering tube. Like the cornett, it combines a cup mouthpiece with finger-holes. A French canon of Auxerre is the accredited inventor (1590), and it was used both in bands and in churches. It fell out of use in the 19th century but is now being revived.

See also OPHICLEIDE.

Serpent, see SNAKE.

Serpentine, general name covering minerals of the serpentine group, composed of hydrous magnesium silicate, $Mg_3[SiO_5](OH)_4$. The three main polymorphic forms are chrysotile, antigorite, and lizardite. Serpentine usually occurs as fine-grained, structureless or asbestiform masses, varying in colour from green to black and often mottled with red. It is found in ultrabasic rocks which have undergone low- to medium-grade metamorphism and often occurs as large rock masses. It is soft (hardness 4–6) and easily worked, and has been used extensively as an ornamental stone for carving and facing.

Serpula, the typical genus of the Serpulidae, a family of polychaete worms. The species are marine worms, which secrete a trumpet-shaped calcareous tube. This is fixed to rocks or shells, and itself often forms reddish coloured rocks when in masses, or assists in the formation of a substratum for coral reefs.

Serum, the liquid left after the blood corpuscles and fibrin of the blood have clotted. It is a straw-coloured liquid, rich in albumin. The term is employed in a general way to denote any body-liquid resembling the serum of the blood, especially animal fluids prepared to resist certain toxic agents.

See also IMMUNOLOGY.

Serval, *Felis serval*, a species of family Felidae in order Carnivora, found in Africa. It is a tawny-coloured tiger-cat bearing black spots, and is about 1 m long.

Servetus, Michael, or Miguel Serveto (1511–53), Spanish physician and theologian who described the pulmonary circulation. In 1553 his work, *Christianismi Restitutio*, was published anonymously: this includes the first printed description of the pulmonary circulation. Servetus was suspected to be the author and was arrested and imprisoned mainly through Calvin's influence. He escaped, and fled to Geneva, but was arrested on Calvin's orders, and was burnt at the stake.

Service Tree, *Sorbus domestica*, a small tree with pinnate leaves and small pear-shaped fruit. The wild service tree of Britain, *S. torminalis*, is a larger tree with lobed leaves and cymes of white flowers followed by small green mottled fruit known as 'chequers'.

Servius Tullius, sixth legendary king of Rome said to have reigned 578–534 BC.

Three important events are assigned to his reign by tradition. First he gave a new constitution to the Roman state. This constitution gave the plebs political independence. Secondly, he extended the *pomoerium*, or hallowed boundary of the city, incorporating the Quirinal, Viminal, and Esquiline hills. Thirdly, he established an alliance with the Latins by which Rome and the cities of Latium became the members of one league. By his constitution Servius Tullius incurred the hostility of the patricians, who conspired with his son-in-law, L. Tarquinius Superbus, to assassinate him. According to the legend, his daughter Tullia was one of the prime movers in this conspiracy.

Servomotors mean literally 'slave motors'; these are electrical, hydraulic, or pneumatic motors used in control systems to give an output that closely follows the input to the system. Servomotors must have suitable characteristics such as linear torque-speed relationship, high sensitivity (sensitivity means response to small signals), and high ratio of maximum torque to inertia. The ratings may range from a few watts to hundreds of kilowatts.

Sesame, *Sesamum*, a genus of annual plants in family Pedaliaceae, with axillary flowers like those of the foxglove. *S. indicum*, a common Indian plant, is cultivated for the oil obtained from the seeds. The seeds are also used on bread. The sesame grass of Central America is *Tripsacum*, in family Gramineae.

Sesame Oil, gingelly, beni, or benne oil (iodine value 110 ± 6) is derived from the seeds of the annual plant *Sesamum indicum*, widely grown in tropical, subtropical, and warm temperate regions. The main producing countries are North and South America, Egypt, India, and Thailand. The oil, which is stable and resists oxidation, is obtained by being pressed out in hydraulic and continuous-screw presses and by extraction with a solvent. It is pale yellow in colour, liquid at ordinary temperatures, and has a nut-like taste and odour. When refined it has neither taste nor odour and is used as a salad oil, for frying, in the manufacture of compound cooking fats, margarine, and mayonnaise.